The United States of America

W9-AOC-548

Land Elevation

Feet	Meters
10,000	3,000
5,000	1,500
2,000	600
1,000	300
500	150
0	0
Below Sea Level	Below Sea Level

Albers Equal-Area Projection

ATLANTIC OCEAN

GULF OF MEXICO

VIRGIN ISLANDS

PUERTO RICO

San Juan

BAHAMAS

CUBA

DOMINICAN REPUBLIC

HAITI

Key West

0   50   100 Miles
0   50   100 Kilometers

0   200   400 Miles
0   200   400 Kilometers

A PEOPLE AND A NATION

A PEOPLE AND A NATION

A History of the United States

Seventh Edition

Mary Beth Norton
Cornell University

David M. Katzman
University of Kansas

David W. Blight
Yale University

Howard P. Chudacoff
Brown University

Fredrik Logevall
University of California, Santa Barbara

Beth Bailey
University of New Mexico

Thomas G. Paterson
University of Connecticut

William M. Tuttle, Jr.
University of Kansas

Houghton Mifflin Company   Boston New York

Publisher: Charles Hartford
Editor-in-Chief: Jean Woy
Senior Sponsoring Editor: Sally Constable
Development Editor: Anne Hofstra Grogg
Editorial Assistant: Kisha Mitchell
Senior Project Editor: Bob Greiner
Editorial Assistant: Trinity Peacock-Broyles
Senior Production/Design Coordinator: Carol Merrigan
Senior Designer: Henry Rachlin
Senior Manufacturing Coordinator: Marie Barnes
Senior Marketing Manager: Sandra McGuire

Picture research by Pembroke Herbert and Sandi Rygiel, Picture Research Consultants & Archives.

Cover painting: *The Lei Maker* by Theodore Wores, 1901. Courtesy of the Honolulu Academy of Arts, Gift of Drs. Ben and A. Jess Shenson, 1986.

Printed in the U.S.A.

Library of Congress Catalog Number: 2003110158

ISBN: 0-618-37589-9

1 2 3 4 5 6 7 8 9-DOW-08 07 06 05 04

Brief Contents

CONTENTS

Special Features

Maps

Figures

Tables

◼ Links to the World

Legacy for a People and a Nation

PREFACE

Some readers might think that a book entering its seventh edition would be little changed from the previous version. Nothing could be further from the truth. In this seventh edition, *A People and a Nation* has undergone major revisions, while still retaining the narrative strength and focus that characterized its earlier editions and made it so popular with students and teachers alike. In the years since the publication of the sixth edition, new documents have been uncovered, new interpretations advanced, and new themes (especially globalization) have come to the forefront of American historical scholarship. The authors—including two new members of our team—have worked diligently to incorporate those findings into this text.

Like other teachers and students, we are always re-creating our past, restructuring our memory, rediscovering the personalities and events that have influenced us, injured us, and bedeviled us. This book represents our continuing rediscovery of America's history—its diverse people and the nation they created and have nurtured. As this book demonstrates, there are many different Americans and many different memories. We have sought to present all of them, in both triumph and tragedy, in both division and unity.

About *A People and A Nation*

A People and a Nation, first published in 1982, was the first major textbook in the United States to fully integrate social and political history. Since the outset, the authors have been determined to tell the story of *all* the people of the United States. This book's hallmark has been its melding of social and political history, its movement beyond history's common focus on public figures and events to examine the daily life of America's people. All editions of the book have stressed the interaction of public policy and personal experience, the relationship between domestic concerns and foreign affairs, the various manifestations of popular culture, and the multiple origins of America and Americans. We have consistently built our narrative on a firm foundation in primary sources—on both well-known and obscure letters, diaries, public documents, oral histories, and artifacts of material culture. We have long challenged readers to think about the meaning of American history, not just to memorize facts. Both students and instructors have repeatedly told us how much they appreciate and enjoy our approach to the past.

As has been true since the first edition, each chapter

opens with a dramatic vignette focusing on an individual or a group of people. These vignettes develop key questions, which then frame the chapters in succinct introductions and summaries. Numerous maps, tables, graphs, and charts provide readers with the necessary geographical and statistical context for observations in the text. Carefully selected illustrations—many of them unique to this book—offer readers visual insight into the topics under discussion, especially because the authors have written the captions. In this edition, as in all previous ones, we have sought to incorporate up-to-date scholarship, readability, a clear structure, critical thinking, and instructive illustrative material on every page.

What's New in This Edition

Planning for the seventh edition began at a two-day authors' meeting at the Houghton Mifflin headquarters in Boston. There we discussed the most recent scholarship in the field, the reviews of the sixth edition solicited from instructors, and the findings of our own continuing research. For this edition, we added two new colleagues, who experienced the intellectual exhilaration and rigor of such an authors' meeting for the first time. Beth Bailey, who has written acclaimed works on sexuality and popular culture in modern America, now writes the chapters and sections dealing with domestic matters after the 1920s. Fredrik Logevall, whose scholarship on the Vietnam War has won international recognition, now writes all the chapters and sections on foreign policy since the Civil War. These new authors have substantially reworked and reorganized the post-1945 chapters, in ways outlined below.

This seventh edition enhances the global perspective on American history that has characterized the book since its first edition. From the "Atlantic world" context of European colonies in North and South America to the discussion of international terrorism, the authors have incorporated the most recent globally oriented scholarship throughout the volume. We have worked to strengthen our treatment of the diversity of America's people by examining differences within the broad ethnic categories commonly employed and by paying greater attention to immigration, cultural and intellectual infusions from around the world, and America's growing religious diversity. At the same time, we have more fully integrated the discussion of such diversity into our narrative, so as not to artificially isolate any group from the mainstream. Treatments of environmental history and the history of technology have both been expanded. Finally, we have streamlined the useful chronologies that appear near the beginning of each chapter.

As always, the authors reexamined every sentence, interpretation, map, chart, illustration, and caption, refining the narrative, presenting new examples, and bringing to the text the latest findings of scholars in many areas of history, anthropology, sociology, and political science. More than a quarter of the chapter-opening vignettes are new, as is also true of the popular "Legacy" features introduced in the sixth edition.

To students who question the relevance of historical study, the legacies offer compelling and timely answers. Those brief essays, which follow the chapter summaries, explore the historical roots of contemporary topics. New subjects of legacies include the "self-made man" ideal, states' rights, reparations for slavery, Planned Parenthood, the Social Security system, the concern for human rights, and the Americans with Disabilities Act.

New "Links to the World"

In keeping with the emphasis on globalization in this edition, and building on the long-standing strength of this text in the history of American foreign relations, we have introduced a new feature in each chapter: "Links to the World." Examining both inward and outward ties between America (and Americans) and the rest of the world, the "Links" appear at appropriate places in each chapter to explore specific topics at considerable length. Tightly constructed essays detail the often little-known connections between developments here and abroad. The topics range broadly over economic, political, social, technological, medical, and cultural history, vividly demonstrating that the geographical region that is now the United States has never lived in isolation from other peoples and countries. Examples include the impact of American maize (corn) on the rest of the world, the introduction of coffee and tea into the American colonies, the discovery of gold in California, proposals to annex Cuba, baseball in Japan, Pan American Airways, the influenza pandemic of 1918, the 1936 Olympics, Barbie dolls, CNN, and the AIDS epidemic. Each "Link" highlights global interconnections with unusual and lively examples that will both intrigue and inform students.

Themes in This Book

Several themes and questions stand out in our continuing effort to integrate political, social, and cultural history. We study the many ways Americans have defined themselves—gender, race, class, region, ethnicity, religion, sexual orientation—and the many subjects that have reflected their multidimensional experiences. We highlight the remarkably diverse everyday lives of the American people—in cities and on farms and ranches, in factories and in corporate headquarters, in neighborhoods and in legislatures, in love relationships and in hate groups, in recreation and in work, in the classroom and in military uniform, in secret national security conferences and in public foreign relations debates, in church and in voluntary associations, in polluted environments and in conservation areas. We pay particular attention to lifestyles, diet and dress, family life and structure, labor conditions, gender roles, migration and mobility, childbearing, and child rearing. We explore how Americans have entertained and informed themselves by discussing their music, sports, theater, print media, film, radio, television, graphic arts, and literature, in both "high" culture and popular culture. We study how technology has influenced Americans' lives, such as through the internal combustion engine and the computer.

Americans' personal lives have always interacted with the public realm of politics and government. To understand how Americans have sought to protect their different ways of life and to work out solutions to thorny problems, we emphasize their expectations of governments at the local, state, and federal levels; governments' role in providing answers; the lobbying of interest groups; the campaigns and outcomes of elections; and the hierarchy of power in any period. Because the United States has long been a major participant in world affairs, we explore America's participation in wars, interventions in other nations, empire-building, immigration patterns, images of foreign peoples, cross-national cultural ties, and international economic trends.

Section-by-Section Changes in This Edition

Mary Beth Norton, who had primary responsibility for Chapters 1 through 8 and served as coordinating author, expanded coverage of ancient North America (the Anasazi and Mississippians); Brazil, the Caribbean islands, and Nova Scotia; witchcraft, especially the 1692 Salem crisis; migration to the colonies from England, Ireland, and Germany; the trade in African and Indian slaves and the impact of that trade on African and Native American societies; the trans-Appalachian west in peace and war; and slavery and gradual emancipation after the Revolution. She also reorganized Chapter 3 to consolidate related materials on politics and the imperial context, and extensively revised and expanded Chapter 6 to reflect recent scholarship. There are new sections on the West during the revolutionary era and on the experiences of ordinary Americans in wartime, both in and out of the military.

David M. Katzman, with responsibility for Chapters 9 through 12, has continued (as in the sixth edition) to sharpen the chronological flow in these chapters. He has broadened the discussion of political culture and emerging partisanship in the young republic, reflecting the current rethinking of politics at that time. He has expanded coverage of religious life and the links between religion and social and political reform. The discussions of families, immigrant lives (especially the Irish), and African American identity, culture, and communities have all been completely revised. Throughout, there is greater attention paid to technology, global ties, and popular culture.

David W. Blight, who had primary responsibility for Chapters 13 through 16, enhanced the discussion of women and gender throughout these chapters. He also added material on the lives of freed people, before, during, and after the Civil War; the impact of the Fugitive Slave Law; the West in the Civil War and Reconstruction eras; and the home front during wartime. He revised the interpretation of the Denmark Vesey slave rebellion and increased coverage of the Underground Railroad, and of the role of the Mormons and westward expansion in the slavery crisis. In Chapter 15, he developed new sections on how the Civil War shaped the future of Indians in the far West, as well as the conflict's significance abroad, especially in England.

Howard P. Chudacoff, responsible for Chapters 17 through 21 and 24, has increased the coverage of technology throughout his chapters, adding discussions of farming technology, the machine tool industry, technological education in universities, birth control devices, and the automobile. He has included new material on the environment as well, expanding his discussion of such topics as water supply and sewage disposal, the unanticipated effects of national parks, and the conservation movement. Topics related to ethnicity—including anti-Chinese violence and exclusion laws, Mexican immigration, and holiday celebrations by ethnic groups—also receive increased attention. He has reconfigured portions of Chapters 18, 19, and 21 to clarify the narrative.

Fredrik Logevall, with primary responsibility for Chapters 22, 23, 26, and 28, worked to internationalize the treatment of America's foreign relations by giving greater attention to the perspectives of nations with which we interacted, and by examining the foreign policy aims of such leaders as Joseph Stalin, especially in Chapters 23 and 26. He significantly expanded the coverage of

U.S. relations with the Middle East, showing the increasing importance of America's dealings with that region during the past four decades. He has also brought a sense of contingency to the narrative of American foreign relations, suggesting that matters might have turned out quite differently at various key junctures had policymakers reached different decisions. He made major changes in Chapter 28 (formerly Chapter 29), creating greater thematic unity and incorporating much new scholarship on the Cold War and relations with China and the Soviet Union.

Beth Bailey, primarily responsible for Chapters 25, 27, and 29, integrated the experiences and actions of various groups into the main narrative while still focusing on the diversity of the American people in the modern era. In general, she enhanced coverage of the South and West (especially Latinos and Mexican immigrants in the Southwest) and added material on gender, sexuality, and popular culture. Throughout these chapters she placed Americans' fears about their nation's future in an international context. In Chapter 25, she strengthened the discussion of New Deal policies, showing how assumptions about race and gender structured these important social programs. Chapter 27 has a stronger chronological framework, as well as new treatments of culture and daily life during WWII, in combat and on the home front. Chapter 29 (formerly Chapter 28) has been extensively revised, assessing the myriad transformations of American society and culture in the 1950s, with particular attention to race, labor, masculinity, McCarthyism, and the impact of new federal policies.

Post-1960 Chapters

Bailey and Logevall shared responsibility for the new Chapters 30 through 33. In these completely revamped chapters, domestic and foreign topics are discussed in tandem rather than separately, demonstrating the extensive linkages between them. The two authors collaborated closely to create a fresh and lively comprehensive, chronologically based narrative that places events in the United States in their appropriate international setting. The coverage of foreign relations includes increased attention to the Middle East and to the motivations of America's allies and opponents alike. The treatment of the Vietnam War now draws on Logevall's own scholarship, just as the discussion of recent popular culture and sexuality is based on Bailey's original research. Increased attention is given to the civil rights movement, the rise of second- and third-wave feminism, new patterns of immigration, and the growth of grassroots conservatism.

Teaching and Learning Aids

The supplements listed here accompany this Seventh Edition of *A People and a Nation*. They have been created with the diverse needs of today's students and instructors in mind, with extensive print and non-print resources available.

We are proud to announce the *History Companion*, your new primary source for history technology solutions. The *History Companion* has three components: the *Instructor Companion, the Student Study Companion,* and the *Student Research Companion.* Each of these components is described below: the *Instructor Companion* under instructor resources, and the *Student Research Companion* and *Student Study Companion* under student resources.

For the Instructor:

■ *The Instructor Companion* is an easily searchable CD-ROM that makes hundreds of historical images and maps instantly accessible in PowerPoint format. Each image is accompanied by notes that place it in its proper historical context and tips for ways it can be presented in the classroom. With this edition of *A People and a Nation*, this CD also includes a wealth of additional resources, including testing, lecture, and course planning tools. A computerized test bank is included complete with search functions, which allows instructors to design tests thematically by entering keywords to bring up particular questions. An Instructor's Resource Guide is also included that can aid in encouraging classroom discussions or constructively enhance a class presentation. This CD is free to instructors with the adoption of this Houghton Mifflin textbook.

■ A print **Test Bank,** prepared by George Warren of Central Piedmont Community College, also accompanies the text and contains many multiple choice, identification, geography, and essay questions for use in creating exams.

■ In addition, a series of **PowerPoint** slides, created by Barney Rickman of Valdosta State University, are included to assist in instruction and discussion of key topics and material.

■ The **Blackboard/WebCT Basic CD** provides instructors who want to offer all or part of their entire course online with much of the fundamental material for their course. From this base, instructors can customize the course to meet their needs.

■ **The Houghton Mifflin U.S. History Transparency Set, Volumes I and II,** is a set of standard U.S. history transparencies, taken from illustrations and maps in the Houghton Mifflin survey texts. Includes 150 full-color maps.

■ **BiblioBase for U.S. History** is a database of hundreds of primary source documents—including speeches, essays, travel accounts, government documents, and memoirs—covering U.S. history from the fifteenth century to the present. This comprehensive database enables you to create a customized course pack of primary sources to complement any U.S. history text. You can search for documents by period, region, approach, theme, and type and then view the documents in their entirety before choosing your course pack selections.

■ The **Rand McNally Atlas of American History** is offered for packaging with the textbook. Please contact your sales representative for additional information.

For the Student:

The **Houghton Mifflin History Companion** for *A People and a Nation*, Seventh Edition, has two student components.

■ The *Student Study Companion* is a free online study guide that contains ACE self-tests, flashcards, timelines, chronology exercises, graphic organizer exercises, map exercises, text feature exercises, web links, and Internet exercises. These study tools will help your students to be more successful.

■ The *Student Research Companion* is a free Internet-based tool with 100 interactive maps and 500 primary sources. The primary sources include headnotes that provide pertinent background information, and both the maps and the primary sources include questions that students can answer and email to their instructors.

■ **Study Guide Volumes I and II**, by George Warren, offers students learning objectives, vocabulary exercises, identification suggestions, skill-building activities, multiple choice questions, essay questions, and map exercises in two volumes.

■ **American Ethnic Identities: Online Activities**
By using examples throughout American history, these informative and lively activities will broaden your understanding of the different ethnic groups that make up the United States.

Acknowledgments

The authors would like to thank the following persons for their assistance with the preparation of this edition: Shawn Alexander, David Anthony Tyeeme Clark, Mike Ezra, David Farber, Max Bailey/Farber, Steve Jacobson, Andrea Katzman, Eric Katzman, Julee Katzman, Theo Katzman, Ariela Katzman-Jacobson, Elieza Katzman-Jacobson, Iris Jane Katzman, Sharyn Brooks Katzman, Danyel Logevall, Chester Pach, Cheryl Ragar, Ann Schofield, Daniel Williams, and Norman Yetman.

At each stage of this revision, a sizable panel of historian reviewers read drafts of our chapters. Their suggestions, corrections, and pleas helped guide us through this momentous revision. We could not include all of their recommendations, but the book is better for our having heeded most of their advice. We heartily thank:

Marynita Anderson, *Nassau Community College*
Erica R. Armstrong, *University of Delaware*
Jim Barrett, *University of Illinois at Urbana-Champaign*
Virginia R. Boynton, *Western Illinois University*
Robert Cottrell, *California State University, Chico*
Bruce Dierenfield, *Canisius College*
Lisa Lindquist Dorr, *University of Alabama*
Latricia E. Gill-Brown, *Pensacola Junior College*
Melanie Gustafson, *University of Vermont*
Jorge Iber, *Texas Tech University*
Anthony E. Kaye, *Pennsylvania State University, University Park*

Carol A. Keller, *San Antonio College*
Kathleen Kennedy, *Western Washington University*
Anne Klejment, *University of St. Thomas*
Carolyn J. Lawes, *Old Dominion University*
Patrick K. Moore, *University of West Florida*
Jared Orsi, *Colorado State University*
Chester Pach, *Ohio University*
Marie Jenkins Schwartz, *University of Rhode Island*
Erik R. Seeman, *SUNY-Buffalo*
Sayuri G. Shimizu, *Michigan State University*
Manisha Sinha, *University of Massachusetts, Amherst*
Evelyn Sterne, *University of Rhode Island*
Benson Tong, *Wichita State University*
Michael M. Topp, *University of Texas, El Paso*

The authors once again thank the extraordinary Houghton Mifflin people who designed, edited, produced, and nourished this book. Their high standards and acute attention to both general structure and fine detail are cherished in the publishing industry. Many thanks, then, to Jean Woy, editor-in-chief; Sally Constable, sponsoring editor; Ann Hofstra Grogg, freelance development editor; Bob Greiner, senior project editor; Sandra McGuire, senior marketing manager; Henry Rachlin, senior designer; Carol Merrigan, senior production/design coordinator; Marie Barnes, senior manufacturing coordinator; Pembroke Herbert, photo researcher; Charlotte Miller, art editor; and Kisha Mitchell and Trinity Peacock-Broyles, editorial assistants.

THE AUTHORS

Mary Beth Norton

Born in Ann Arbor, Michigan, Mary Beth Norton received her B.A. from the University of Michigan (1964) and her Ph.D. from Harvard University (1969). She is the Mary Donlon Alger Professor of American History at Cornell University. Her dissertation won the Allan Nevins Prize. She has written *The British-Americans* (1972), *Liberty's Daughters* (1980, 1996), *Founding Mothers & Fathers* (1996), which was one of three finalists for the 1997 Pulitzer Prize in History, and *In the Devil's Snare* (2002), which was one of five finalists for the 2003 *LA Times* Book Prize in History and which won the English-Speaking Union's Ambassador Book Award in American Studies for 2003. She has coedited *Women of America* (with Carol Berkin, 1979), *To Toil The Livelong Day* (with Carol Groneman, 1987), and *Major Problems in American Women's History* (with Ruth Alexander, 2003). She was general editor of the *American Historical Association's Guide to Historical Literature* (1995). Her articles have appeared in such journals as the *American Historical Review, William and Mary Quarterly*, and *Journal of Women's History*. Mary Beth has served as president of the Berkshire Conference of Women Historians, as vice president for research of the American Historical Association, and as a presidential appointee to the National Council on the Humanities. She has received four honorary degrees and in 1999 was elected a fellow of the American Academy of Arts and Sciences. She has held fellowships from the National Endowment for the Humanities, the Guggenheim, Rockefeller, and Starr Foundations, and the Henry E. Huntington Library.

David M. Katzman

Born in New York City and a graduate of Queens College (B.A., 1963) and the University of Michigan (Ph.D., 1969), David M. Katzman is professor of American studies and courtesy professor of history and African American studies at the University of Kansas. He has written *Before the Ghetto* (1973) and *Seven Days a Week* (1978), which won the Philip Taft Labor History Prize. He has coedited *Plain Folk* (1982) and *Technical Knowledge in American Culture* (1996). He has also coauthored *Three Generations in Twentieth-Century America* (1982). David has been a visiting professor at University College, Dublin, Ireland, the University of Birmingham, England, Hong Kong University, and the University of Tokushima, Japan. He was recently a Fulbright lecturer at Kobe University, Japan. He has also directed National Endowment for the Humanities Summer Seminars for College Teachers. He has sat on the Board of Directors of the National Commission on Social Studies and is coeditor of *American Studies*. At the University of Kansas, he has directed the Honors Program and chaired the American Studies Program, and in 2002 he received the Ned Fleming Trust Award for Excellence in Teaching. The Guggenheim Foundation, National Endowment for the Humanities, Ford Foundation, and Rockefeller Foundation have supported his research.

David W. Blight

Born in Flint, Michigan, David W. Blight received his B.A. from Michigan State University (1971) and his Ph.D. from the University of Wisconsin (1985). He is now a professor of history at Yale University. For the first seven years of his career, David was a public high school teacher in Flint. He has written *Frederick Douglass's Civil War* (1989) and *Race and Reunion: The Civil War in American Memory, 1863–1915* (2000). His edited works include *When This Cruel War Is Over: The Civil War Letters of Charles Harvey Brewster* (1992), *Narrative of the Life of Frederick Douglass* (1993), W. E. B. Du Bois, *The Souls of Black Folk* (with Robert Gooding Williams, 1997), *Union and Emancipation* (with Brooks Simpson, 1997), and *Caleb Bingham, The Columbian Orator* (1997). David's essays have appeared in the *Journal of American History*, *Civil War History*, and Gabor Boritt, ed., *Why the Civil War Came* (1996), among others. In 1992-1993 he was senior Fulbright Professor in American Studies at the University of Munich, Germany. A consultant to several documentary films, David appeared in the 1998 PBS series, *Africans in America*. In 1999 he was elected to the Council of the American Historical Association. David also teaches summer seminars for secondary school teachers, as well as for park rangers and historians of the National Park Service. His book, *Race and Reunion: The Civil War in American Memory* (2000), received many honors in 2002, including The Bancroft Prize, Abraham Lincoln Prize, and the Frederick Douglass Prize. From the Organization of American Historians, he has received the Merle Curti Prize in Social History, the Merle Curti Prize in Intellectual History, the Ellis Hawley Prize in Political History, and the James Rawley Prize in Race Relations.

Howard P. Chudacoff

Howard P. Chudacoff, the George L. Littlefield Professor of American History at Brown University, was born in Omaha, Nebraska. He earned his A.B. (1965) and Ph.D. (1969) from the University of Chicago. He has written *Mobile Americans* (1972), *How Old Are You?* (1989), *The Age of the Bachelor* (1999), and *The Evolution of American Urban Society* (with Judith Smith, 2004). He has also coedited with Peter Baldwin *Major Problems in American Urban History* (2004). His articles have appeared in such journals as the *Journal of Family History, Reviews in American History,* and *Journal of American History.* At Brown University, Howard has cochaired the American Civilization Program, chaired the Department of History, and serves as Brown's faculty representative to the NCAA. He has also served on the board of directors of the Urban History Association. The National Endowment for the Humanities, Ford Foundation, and Rockefeller Foundation have given him awards to advance his scholarship.

Fredrik Logevall

A native of Stockholm, Sweden, Fredrik Logevall received his B.A. from Simon Fraser University (1986) and his Ph.D. from Yale University (1993). He is associate professor of history and codirector of the Center for Cold War Studies at the University of California at Santa Barbara. He is the author of *Choosing War: The Lost Chance for Peace and the Escalation of War in Vietnam* (1999), which won three prizes, including the Warren F. Kuehl Book Prize from the Society for Historians of American Foreign Relations (SHAFR). His other publications include *The Origins of the Vietnam War* (2001), *Terrorism and 9/11: A Reader* (2002), and, as coeditor, the *Encyclopedia of American Foreign Policy* (2002). In 2003 Fred was awarded the Stuart L. Bernath Lecture Prize from SHAFR, and he is a past recipient of the UCSB Academic Senate Distinguished Teaching Award. He is on the editorial advisory board of the Presidential Recordings Project at the Miller Center of Public Affairs at the University of Virginia, and of the journal *Diplomatic History*, and he is chair of the steering committee of the University of California's Institute for Global Conflict and Cooperation.

Beth Bailey

Born in Atlanta, Georgia, Beth Bailey received her B.A. from Northwestern University (1979) and her Ph.D. from the University of Chicago (1986). She is now a professor of American studies and Regents Lecturer at the University of New Mexico. Her research and teaching fields include American cultural history (ninteenth and twentieth centuries), popular culture, and gender and sexuality. She is the author of *From Front Porch to Back Seat: Courtship in 20th Century America* (1988), a historical analysis of conventions governing the courtship of heterosexual youth; *The First Strange Place: The Alchemy of Race and Sex in WWII Hawaii* (with David Farber, 1992), which analyzes cultural contact among Americans in wartime Hawaii; *Sex in the Heartland* (1999), a social and cultural history of the post-WWII "sexual revolution"; *The Columbia Companion to America in the 1960's* (with David Farber, 2001); and is co-editor of *A History of Our Time* (with William Chafe and Harvard Sitkoff, 6th ed., 2002). Beth has served as a consultant and/or on-screen expert for numerous television documentaries developed for PBS and the History Channel. She has received grants from the ACLS and NEH, was the Ann Whitney Olin scholar at Barnard College, Columbia University, from 1991 through 1994, where she was the director of the American Studies Program, and held a senior Fulbright lectureship in Indonesia in 1996. She teaches courses on sexuality and gender, war and American culture, research methods, and popular culture.

A PEOPLE AND A NATION

Prom. Lupi

Portus Regalis sive E S

THREE OLD WORLDS CREATE A NEW 1492–1600

*a*s they neared the village called Cofitachequi on May 1, 1540, the band of Spanish explorers led by Hernán de Soto beheld a surprising scene. Villagers came to meet them, carrying their female chief, or *cacica*, "with much prestige on a litter covered in white (with thin linen)." The Lady of Cofitachequi, a Spanish chronicler recorded, was "young and of fine appearance." Speaking to Soto "with much grace and self-assurance," she welcomed the weary Spaniards to her domain in today's western South Carolina, giving de Soto a string of pearls from her neck. Her people offered gifts of "well tanned hides and blankets, all very good, and a large amount of jerked venison and dry wafers, and much and very good salt." Later, she gave the hungry men huge quantities of corn and, seeing that they especially valued pearls, suggested they take the ones they would find in nearby burial chambers.

The Spanish explorers had landed at Tampa Bay, Florida, about a year earlier. They would wander through what is now the southeastern United States for three more years, encountering many different peoples, whom they often treated with great cruelty. Always they futilely sought the greatest riches of all—gold and silver. The people of Cofitachequi told the Spaniards they might find these treasures in another ruler's domain, about twelve days' travel away. When de Soto left, he took the Lady with him as a captive. But the chronicler reported that she, "going one day with her slave women who were carrying her, stepped aside from the road and went into a wood saying that she had to attend to her necessities. Thus she deceived them and hid herself in the woods." Presumably, she then returned home.

Why had the Lady greeted de Soto's band so kindly? Perhaps she did not have enough men to resist the Spaniards. Her people had been devastated by an unknown "pestilence" two years earlier, the Spaniards learned, and they saw uninhabited settlements. Or possibly messengers had informed the Lady about de Soto's vicious treatment of villages he had previously encountered. Whatever her reasoning, the strategy worked: de Soto and his men moved on, and although they destroyed other villages and peoples, Cofitachequi survived to be recorded

◀ A 1591 print depicted what French adventurers saw in 1562 when they sailed into Port Royal River near today's Beaufort, South Carolina. From Theodor de Bry's *America,* the first book illustrating American scenes for a European audience. (John Carter Brown Library at Brown University)

3

by Spanish, French, and finally English visitors in the course of the next 130 years.

For thousands of years before 1492, human societies in the Americas had developed in isolation from the rest of the world. The era that began in the Christian fifteenth century brought that long-standing isolation to an end. As Europeans sought treasure and trade, peoples from different cultures came into regular contact for the first time. All were profoundly changed. The brief encounter of de Soto and the Lady of Cofitachequi illustrates many elements of those contacts and changes: cruelty and kindness, greed and deception, trade and theft, surprise and sickness, captivity and enslavement. By the time de Soto and his men landed in Florida in 1539, the age of European expansion and colonization was already well under way. Over the next 350 years, Europeans would spread their influence across the globe. The history of the tiny colonies that would become the United States must be seen in this broad context of European exploration and exploitation.

The continents that European sailors reached in the late fifteenth century had their own histories, which the intruders largely ignored. The residents of the Americas were the world's most skillful plant breeders; they had developed vegetable crops more nutritious and productive than those grown in Europe, Asia, or Africa. They had invented systems of writing and mathematics and created calendars as accurate as those used on the other side of the Atlantic. In the Americas, as in Europe, states rose and fell as leaders succeeded or failed in expanding their political and economic power. But the arrival of Europeans immeasurably altered the Americans' struggles with one another.

After 1400, European nations not only warred on their own continent but also tried to acquire valuable colonies and trading posts elsewhere in the world. Initially interested primarily in Asia and Africa, Europeans eventually focused mostly on the Americas. Their contests for trade and conquest changed the course of history on four continents. Even as Europeans slowly achieved dominance, their fates were shaped by the strategies of Americans and Africans, such as that of the Lady of Cofitachequi. In the Americas of the fifteenth and sixteenth centuries, three old worlds came together to produce a new. ■

American Societies

*H*uman beings originated on the continent of Africa, where humanlike remains about 3 million years old have been found in what is now Ethiopia. Over many millennia, the growing population slowly dispersed to the other continents. Because the climate was then far colder than it is now, much of the earth's water was concentrated in huge rivers of ice called glaciers. Sea levels were accordingly lower, and land masses covered a larger proportion of the earth's surface than they do today. Scholars have long believed that all the earliest inhabitants of the Americas crossed a land bridge known as Beringia (at the site of the Bering Strait) approximately 12,000 to 14,000 years ago. Yet striking new archaeological discoveries in both North and South America suggest that some parts of the Americas may have been settled much earlier, perhaps by seafarers crossing from northern Europe by island-hopping from Iceland to Greenland to Baffin Island, much as Norse explorers did many millennia later (see Map 1.1). When approximately 12,000 years ago the climate warmed and sea levels rose, Americans were separated from the peoples living on the connected continents of Asia, Africa, and Europe.

The first Americans are called Paleo-Indians. Nomadic hunters of game and gatherers of wild plants, they

ANCIENT AMERICA

spread throughout North and South America, probably moving as bands composed of extended families. By about 11,500 years ago the Paleo-Indians were making fine stone projectile points, which they attached to wooden spears and used to kill and butcher bison (buffalo), woolly mammoths, and other large mammals then living in the Americas. But as the Ice Age ended and the human population increased, all the large American mammals except the bison disappeared. Scholars cannot agree whether overhunting or the change in climate caused their demise. In either case, deprived of their primary source of meat, the Paleo-Indians found new ways to survive.

By approximately 9,000 years ago, the residents of what is now central Mexico began to cultivate food crops, especially maize (corn), squash, beans, and peppers. In the Andes Mountains of South America, people started to grow potatoes. As knowledge of agricultural techniques improved and spread through the Americas, vegetables and maize proved a more reliable source of food than hunting and gathering. Except for those living in the harshest climates, most Americans started to adopt a more sedentary style of life so they could tend fields

regularly. Some established permanent settlements; others moved several times a year among fixed sites. They became adept at clearing forests through the use of controlled burning. The fires not only created cultivable lands by killing trees and fertilizing the soil with ashes but also opened meadows that attracted deer and other wildlife. All the American cultures emphasized producing sufficient food to support themselves. Although they traded such items as shells, flint, salt, and copper, no society ever became dependent on another group for items vital to its survival.

Wherever agriculture dominated the economy, complex civilizations flourished. Such societies, assured of steady supplies of grains and vegetables, no longer had to devote all their energies to subsistence. Instead, they were able to accumulate wealth, produce ornamental objects, trade with other groups, and create elaborate rituals and ceremonies. In North America, the successful cultivation of nutritious crops such as maize, beans, and squash seems to have led to the growth and development of all the major civilizations: first the large city-states of Mesoamerica (modern Mexico and Guatemala), and then the urban clusters known collectively as the Mississippian culture and located in the present-day United States. Each of these societies, many historians and archaeologists now believe, reached its height of population and influence only after achieving success in agriculture. Each later declined and collapsed after reaching the limits of its food supply, with dire political and military consequences.

Archaeologists and historians still know little about the first major Mesoamerican civilization, that of the

MESOAMERICAN CIVILIZATIONS

Olmecs, who about 3,000 years ago lived near the Gulf of Mexico in cities dominated by temple pyramids. Two societies that developed approximately 1,000 years later, those of the Mayas and of Teotihuacán, are better recorded. Teotihuacán, founded in the Valley of Mexico about 300 B.C.E. (Before the Common Era), eventually became one of the largest urban areas in the world, housing perhaps 100,000 people in the fifth century C.E. (Common Era). Teotihuacán's commercial network extended hundreds of miles in all directions; many peoples prized its obsidian (a green glass), used to make fine knives and mirrors. Pilgrims must also have traveled long distances to visit Teotihuacán's impressive pyramids and the great temple of Quetzalcoatl—the feathered serpent, primary god of central Mexico.

On the Yucatán Peninsula, in today's eastern Mexico, the Mayas built urban centers containing tall pyramids and temples. They studied astronomy and created the first writing system in the Americas. Their city-states, though, engaged in near-constant warfare with one another. Warfare and an inadequate food supply caused the collapse of the most powerful cities by 900 C.E., thus ending the classic era of Mayan civilization. By the time Spaniards arrived five hundred years later, only a few remnants of the once-mighty society remained.

Ancient native societies in what is now the United States learned to grow maize, squash, and beans from

ANASAZI AND MISSISSIPPIANS

Mesoamericans, but the exact nature of the relationship of the various cultures is unknown. (No Mesoamerican artifacts have been found north of the Rio Grande, but some items resembling Mississippian objects have been excavated in northern Mexico.) The Hohokam, Mogollon, and Anasazi peoples of the modern states of Arizona and New Mexico subsisted by combining hunting and gathering with agriculture in an arid region of unpredictable rainfall. Hohokam villagers constructed extensive irrigation systems, but even so they occasionally had to relocate their settlements when water supplies failed. Between 900 and 1150 C.E. the Anasazi built fourteen "Great Houses" in Chaco Canyon, each a massive multistoried stone structure averaging two hundred rooms in size. The canyon, at the juncture of perhaps 400 miles of roads, served as a major regional trading and processing center for tur-

quoise, used then as now to create beautiful ornamental objects. Scholars have not determined why the Anasazi disappeared or where they went, but a major drought could well have forced them to move elsewhere.

At almost the same time, the unrelated Mississippian culture, which included the village of Cofitachequi, flourished in what is now the midwestern and southeastern United States. Relying largely on maize, squash, nuts, pumpkins, and venison for food, the Mississippians lived in substantial settlements. The largest of their urban centers was the City of the Sun (now called Cahokia), near modern St. Louis. Located on rich farmland close to the confluence of the Illinois, Missouri, and Mississippi Rivers, Cahokia, like Teotihuacán and Chaco Canyon, served as a focal point for both religion and trade. At its peak (in the eleventh and twelfth centuries C.E.), the City of the Sun covered more than 5 square miles and had a population of about twenty thousand—small by Mesoamerican standards but larger than any other northern community, and larger even than London in the same era.

Although the Cahokians never seem to have invented a writing system, these sun-worshippers developed an accurate calendar, evidenced by their creation of a woodhenge—a large circle of tall timber posts aligned with the solstices and the equinox. The city's main pyramid (one of 120 of varying sizes), today called Monks Mound, was at the time of its construction the third largest structure of any description in the Western Hemi-

■ Pueblo Bonito in Chaco Canyon in what is now the state of New Mexico. More than six hundred buildings were present on the well-defended site. The circular structures were kivas, used for food storage and for religious rituals. (David Muench photography)

sphere; it remains the largest earthwork ever built anywhere in the Americas. It sat at the northern end of the Grand Plaza, surrounded by seventeen other mounds, some used for burials. Yet after 1250 C.E. the city was abandoned. Archaeologists believe that climate change and the degradation of the environment, caused by overpopulation and the destruction of nearby forests, brought about the city's collapse.

The Aztecs' histories tell of the long migration of their people (who called themselves Mexica) into the

AZTECS

Valley of Mexico during the twelfth century. The uninhabited ruins of Teotihuacán, which by then had been deserted for at least two hundred years, awed and mystified the migrants. Their chronicles record that their primary deity Huitzilopochtli—a war god represented by an eagle—directed them to establish their capital on an island where they saw an eagle eating a serpent, the symbol of Quetzalcoatl. That island city became Tenochtitlán, the center of a rigidly stratified society composed of hereditary classes of warriors, merchants, priests, common folk, and slaves.

The Aztecs conquered their neighbors, forcing them to pay tribute in textiles, gold, foodstuffs, and human beings who could be sacrificed to Huitzilopochtli. They also engaged in ritual combat, known as flowery wars, to obtain further sacrificial victims. The war god's taste for blood was not easily quenched. In the Aztec year Ten Rabbit (1502) at the coronation of Motecuhzoma II (the Spaniards could not pronounce his name correctly, so they called him Montezuma), five thousand people are thought to have been sacrificed by having their still-beating hearts torn from their bodies.

The Aztecs believed that they lived in the age of the Fifth Sun. Four times previously, they wrote, the earth and all the people who lived on it had been destroyed. They predicted that their own world would end in earthquakes and hunger. In the Aztec year Thirteen Flint, volcanoes erupted, sickness and hunger spread, wild beasts attacked children, and an eclipse of the sun darkened the sky. Did some priest wonder whether the Fifth Sun was approaching its end? In time, the Aztecs learned that Thirteen Flint was called, by Europeans, 1492.

North America in 1492

*O*ver the centuries, the Americans who lived north of Mexico adapted their once-similar ways of life to very different climates and terrains, thus creating the diverse cultures that the Europeans encountered when they first arrived (see Map 1.1). Scholars often refer to such cultures by language group (such as Algonquian or Iroquoian), since neighboring Indian nations commonly spoke related languages. Bands that lived in environments not well suited to agriculture—because of inadequate rainfall or poor soil, for example—followed a nomadic lifestyle similar to that of the Paleo-Indians. Within the area of the present-day United States, these groups included the Paiutes and Shoshones, who inhabited the Great Basin (now Nevada and Utah). Because of the difficulty of finding sufficient food for more than a few people, such hunter-gatherer bands were small, usually composed of one or more related families. The men hunted small animals, and women gathered seeds and berries. Where large game was more plentiful and food supplies therefore more certain, as in present-day central and western Canada and the Great Plains, bands of hunters were somewhat larger.

In more favorable environments, larger groups combined agriculture with gathering, hunting, and fishing. Those who lived near the seacoasts, like the Chinooks of present-day Washington and Oregon, consumed fish and shellfish in addition to growing crops and gathering seeds and berries. Residents of the interior (for example, the Arikaras of the Missouri River valley) hunted large animals while also cultivating maize, squash, and beans. The peoples of what is now eastern Canada and the northeastern United States also combined hunting and agriculture. They regularly used controlled fires both to open land for cultivation and to assist in hunting.

Societies that relied primarily on hunting large animals like deer and buffalo assigned that task to men,

SEXUAL DIVISION OF LABOR IN NORTH AMERICA

allotting food preparation and clothing production to women. Before such nomadic bands acquired horses from the Spaniards, women—occasionally assisted by dogs—also carried the family's belongings whenever the band relocated. Such a sexual division of labor was universal among hunting peoples, regardless of their location. Agricultural societies, by contrast, differed in their assignments of work to the sexes. The Pueblo peoples (descendants of the Anasazi), who lived in sixty or seventy autonomous villages and spoke five different languages, defined agricultural labor as men's work. In the east, large clusters of peoples speaking Algonquian, Iroquoian, and Muskogean languages allocated most agricultural chores to women, although men cleared the land. In all the farming societies, women gathered wild foods and prepared food for consumption or storage, while men were responsible for hunting.

Everywhere in North America, women cared for young children, while older youths learned adult skills

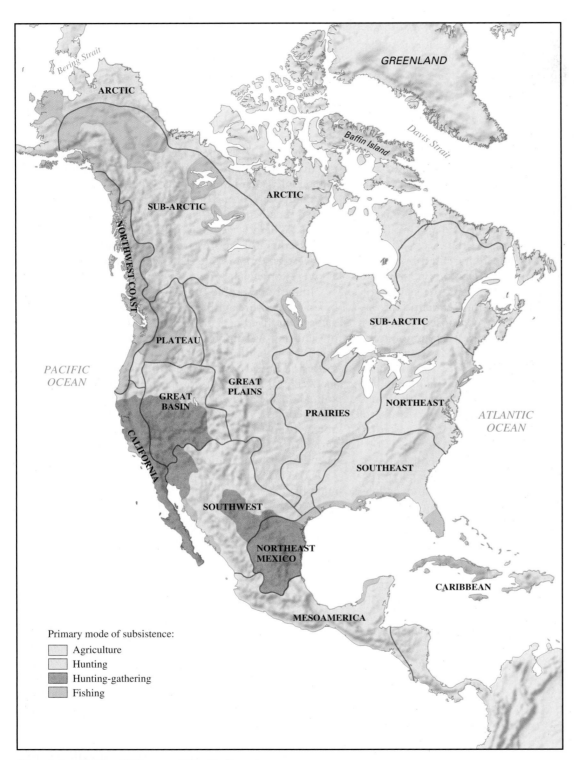

Map 1.1   Native Cultures of North America

The natives of the North American continent effectively used the resources of the regions in which they lived. As this map shows, coastal groups relied on fishing, residents of fertile areas engaged in agriculture, and other peoples employed hunting (often combined with gathering) as a primary mode of subsistence.

from the parent of the same sex. Young people usually chose their own marital partners, and in most societies couples could easily divorce if they no longer wished to live together. In contrast to the earlier Mississippian cultures, populations in these societies remained at a level sustainable by existing food supplies, largely because of low birth rates. Infants and toddlers were nursed until the age of two or even longer, and taboos prevented couples from having sexual intercourse during that period.

The southwestern and eastern agricultural peoples had similar social organizations. They lived in villages, sometimes with a thousand or more inhabitants. The Pueblos resided in multistory buildings constructed on terraces along the sides of cliffs or other easily defended sites. Northern Iroquois villages (in modern New York State) were composed of large, rectangular, bark-covered structures, or long houses; the name Haudenosaunee, which the Iroquois called themselves, means "People of the Long House." In the present-day southeastern United States, Muskogeans and southern Algonquians lived in large houses made of thatch. Most of the eastern villages were surrounded by wood palisades and ditches to aid in fending off attackers.

SOCIAL ORGANIZATION

In all the agricultural societies, each dwelling housed an extended family defined matrilineally (through a female line of descent). Mothers, their married daughters, and their daughters' husbands and children all lived together. Matrilineal descent did not imply matriarchy, or the wielding of power by women, but rather served as a means of reckoning kinship. Extended families were linked into clans defined by matrilineal ties. The nomadic bands of the Great Plains, by contrast, were most often related patrilineally (through the male line). They lacked settled villages and defended themselves from attack primarily through their ability to move to safer locations when necessary.

The defensive design of eastern and western villages discloses the significance of warfare in pre-Columbian America. Long before Europeans arrived, residents of the continent fought one another for control of the best hunting and fishing territories, the most fertile agricultural lands, or the sources of essential items like salt (for preserving meat) and flint (for making knives and arrowheads). Bands of Americans protected by wooden armor battled while standing in ranks facing each other, the better to employ their clubs and throwing spears, which were effective only at close quarters. They began to shoot arrows from behind trees only when they confronted the more accu-

WAR AND POLITICS

rate and longer-range European guns, which also rendered their armor useless. People captured by the enemy in such wars were sometimes enslaved and dishonored by losing their previous names and identities, but slavery was never an important source of labor in pre-Columbian America.

American political structures varied considerably. Among Pueblo and Muskogean peoples, the village council, composed of ten to thirty men, was the highest political authority; no government structure connected the villages. Nomadic hunters also lacked formal links among separate bands. The Iroquois, by contrast, had an elaborate political hierarchy incorporating villages into nations and nations into a confederation; a council comprising representatives from each nation made crucial decisions of war and peace for the entire confederacy. In all the North American cultures, political power was divided between civil and war leaders, who wielded authority only so long as they retained the confidence of the people. Autocratic rule of the sort common in Europe (see page 13) was unusual in these political systems. Women more often assumed leadership roles among agricultural peoples, especially those in which females were the primary cultivators, than among nomadic hunters. Female sachems (rulers) led Algonquian villages in what is now Massachusetts, but women never became heads of Great Plains hunting bands. Iroquois women did not become chiefs, yet clan matrons exercised political power. The older women of each village chose its chief and could both start wars (by calling for the capture of prisoners to replace dead relatives) and stop them (by refusing to supply warriors with necessary foodstuffs).

Americans' religious beliefs varied even more than did their political systems, but all the peoples were polytheistic, worshiping a multitude of gods. Each group's most important beliefs and rituals were closely tied to its means of subsistence. The major deities of agricultural peoples like the Pueblos and Muskogeans were associated with cultivation, and their chief festivals centered on planting and harvest. The most important gods of hunters, such as those living on the Great Plains, were associated with animals, and their major festivals were related to hunting. A band's economy and women's role in it helped to determine women's potential as religious leaders. Women held the most prominent positions in those agricultural societies in which they were also the chief food producers, whereas in hunting societies men took the lead in religious as well as political affairs.

RELIGION

A wide variety of cultures, comprising more than 5 million people, thus inhabited mainland North America when Europeans arrived. The hierarchical kingdoms of

■ Jacques Le Moyne, an artist accompanying the French settlement in Florida in the 1560s (see page 35), produced some of the first European images of North American peoples. His depiction of native agricultural practices shows the sexual division of labor: men breaking up the ground with fish-bone hoes before women drop seeds into the holes. But Le Moyne's version of the scene cannot be accepted uncritically: unable to abandon a European view of proper farming methods, he erroneously drew plowed furrows in the soil.   (John Carter Brown Library at Brown University)

Mesoamerica bore little resemblance to the nomadic hunting societies of the Great Plains or to the agricultural societies that dominated a significant share of the continent. The diverse inhabitants of North America spoke well over one thousand different languages. For obvious reasons, they did not consider themselves one people, nor did they—for the most part—think of uniting to repel the European invaders.

African Societies

Fifteenth-century Africa, like fifteenth-century America, housed a variety of cultures adapted to different terrains and climates (see Map 1.2). Many of these cultures were of great antiquity. In the north, along the Mediterranean Sea, lived the Berbers,

who were Muslims, or followers of the Islamic religion founded by the prophet Mohammed in the seventh century C.E. On the east coast of Africa, Muslim city-states engaged in extensive trade with India, the Moluccas (part of modern Indonesia), and China. In these ports, sustained contact and intermarriage among Arabs and Africans created the Swahili language and culture. Through the East African city-states passed waterborne commerce between the eastern Mediterranean and East Asia; the rest followed the long land route across Central Asia known as the Silk Road.

South of the Mediterranean coast in the African interior lie the great Saharan and Libyan Deserts, vast expanses of nearly waterless terrain crisscrossed by trade routes passing through oases. The introduction of the camel in the fifth century C.E. made long-distance travel possible, and as Islam expanded after the ninth century,

Venice
Constantinople
Azores
Tunis
Madeira
Islands
Ceuta
BERBERS
Tripoli
Canary
Islands
Alexandria
Cairo
*LIBYAN
DESERT*
EGYPT
SAHARA   DESERT
Red Sea
Nile R.
Cape Verde
Islands
GHANA
Cape Verde
MALI
Timbuktu
Gambia R.
RICE
COAST
UPPER GUINEA
GUINEA
ETHIOPIA
GRAIN
COAST
LOWER GUINEA
Benin
IVORY
COAST
GOLD
COAST
SLAVE
COAST
Cape Palmas
Gulf of Guinea
São Tomé
KONGO
River
BANTU PEOPLES
MUSLIM CITY STATES
Congo
*INDIAN
OCEAN*
*ATLANTIC

OCEAN*
PYGMIES
ZANZIBAR
ANGOLA
Zambezi River
Zimbabwe
MADAGASCAR
*KALAHARI
DESERT*
SAN

— Major trade routes

0   500   1000 Km.

0   500   1000 Mi.

Map 1.2   Africa and Its Peoples, c. 1400

On the African continent resided many different peoples in a variety of ecological settings and
political units. Even before Europeans began to explore Africa's coastlines, its northern regions
were linked to the Mediterranean (and thus to Europe) by a network of trade routes.

commerce controlled by Muslim merchants helped to spread similar religious and cultural ideas throughout the region. Below the deserts, much of the continent is divided between tropical rain forests (along the coasts) and grassy plains (in the interior). People speaking a variety of languages and pursuing different subsistence strategies lived in a wide belt south of the deserts. South of the Gulf of Guinea, the grassy landscape came to be dominated by Bantu-speaking peoples, who left their homeland in modern Nigeria about two thousand years ago and slowly migrated south and east across the continent.

WEST AFRICA (GUINEA)

West Africa was a land of tropical forests and savanna grasslands where fishing, cattle herding, and agriculture had supported the inhabitants for at least ten thousand years before Europeans set foot there in the fifteenth century. The northern region of West Africa, or Upper Guinea, was heavily influenced by the Islamic culture of the Mediterranean. As early as the eleventh century C.E., many of the region's

■ This decorative brass weight, created by the Asante peoples of Lower Guinea, was used for measuring gold dust. It depicts a family pounding fu-fu, a food made by mashing together plantains (a kind of banana), yams, and cassava. The paste was then shaped into balls to be eaten with soup. This weight, probably used in trading with Europeans, shows a scene combining foods of African origin (plantains and yams) with an import from the Americas (cassava), thus bringing the three continents together in ways both symbolic and real.
(Trustees of the British Museum. Photo by Michael Holford)

inhabitants had become Muslims. Trade via camel caravans between Upper Guinea and the Muslim Mediterranean was sub-Saharan Africa's major connection to Europe and West Asia. In return for salt, dates, silk, and cotton cloth, Africans exchanged ivory, gold, and slaves with northern merchants.

Upper Guinea runs northeast-southwest from Cape Verde to Cape Palmas. The people of its northernmost region, the so-called Rice Coast (present-day Gambia, Senegal, and Guinea), fished and cultivated rice in coastal swamplands. The Grain Coast, the next region to the south, was thinly populated and not readily accessible from the sea because it had only one good harbor (modern Freetown, Sierra Leone). Its people concentrated on farming and raising livestock.

In the fifteenth century, most Africans in Lower Guinea were farmers who practiced traditional religions, not the precepts of Islam. Believing that spirits inhabited particular places, they invested those places with special significance. As did the agricultural peoples of the Americas, they developed rituals intended to ensure good harvests. Throughout the region, individual villages composed of kin groups were linked into hierarchical kingdoms. At the time of initial European contact, decentralized political and social authority characterized the region's polities.

COMPLEMENTARY GENDER ROLES

The societies of West Africa, like those of the Americas, assigned different tasks to men and women. In general, the sexes shared agricultural duties. Men also hunted, managed livestock, and did most of the fishing. Women were responsible for childcare, food preparation, and cloth manufacture. Everywhere in West Africa women were the primary local traders. They managed the extensive local and regional networks through which goods were exchanged among the various families, villages, and small kingdoms.

Despite their different economies and the rivalries among states, the peoples of Lower Guinea had similar social systems organized on the basis of what anthropologists have called the dual-sex principle. In Lower Guinea, each sex handled its own affairs: just as male political and religious leaders governed men, so females ruled women. In the Dahomean kingdom, for example, every male official had his female counterpart; in the thirty little Akan states on the Gold Coast, chiefs inherited their status through the female line, and each male chief had a female assistant who supervised other women. Many West African societies practiced polygyny (one man having several wives, each of whom lived separately with her children). Thus few adults lived permanently in marital households, but the dual-sex system ensured that their actions were subject to scrutiny by members of their own sex.

Throughout Upper Guinea religious beliefs stressed complementary male and female roles. Both women and men served as heads of the cults and secret societies that directed the spiritual life of the villages. Young women were initiated into the Sandé cult, young men into Poro. Neither cult was allowed to reveal its secrets to the opposite sex. Although West African women (unlike some of their Native American contemporaries) rarely held formal power over men, female religious leaders did govern other members of their sex within the Sandé cult, enforcing conformity to accepted norms of behavior and overseeing their spiritual well-being.

West African law recognized both individual and communal land ownership, but men seeking to accumu-

SLAVERY IN GUINEA

late wealth needed access to labor—wives, children, or slaves—who could work the land. West Africans held in slavery on their own continent therefore composed essential elements of the economy. Africans could be enslaved for life as punishment for crimes, but more often such slaves were enemy captives or people who voluntarily enslaved themselves or their children in payment for debts. An African who possessed bondspeople had a right to the products of their labor, although the degree to which slaves were exploited varied greatly. Some slaves were held as chattel; others could engage in trade, retaining a portion of their profits; and still others achieved prominent political or military positions. All, however, found it difficult to overcome the social stigma of enslavement, and they could be traded or sold at the will of their owners.

West Africans, then, were agricultural peoples, skilled at tending livestock, hunting, fishing, and manufacturing cloth from plant fibers and animal skins. Both men and women were accustomed to working communally, alongside other members of their own sex or in family groups. They were also accustomed to a relatively egalitarian relationship between the sexes, especially within the context of religion. In the Americas, they entered societies that used their labor but had little respect for their cultural traditions.

European Societies

*I*n the fifteenth century, Europeans, too, were agricultural peoples. The daily lives of Europe's rural people had changed little for several hundred years. Split into numerous small, warring countries, Europe was divided linguistically, politically, and economi-

cally, yet in social terms Europeans' lives were more similar than different. European societies were hierarchical: a few families wielded autocratic power over the majority of the people. English society in particular was organized as a series of interlocking hierarchies; that is, each person (except those at the very top or bottom) was superior to some, inferior to others. At the base of such hierarchies were people held in a variety of forms of bondage. Although Europeans were not subjected to perpetual slavery, Christian doctrine permitted the enslavement of "heathens" (non-Christians), and some Europeans' freedom was restricted by such conditions as serfdom, which tied them to the land if not to specific owners. In short, Europe's kingdoms resembled those of Africa or Mesoamerica but differed greatly from the more egalitarian societies found in America north of Mexico (see Map 1.3).

Most Europeans, like most Africans and Americans, lived in small villages. Only a few cities dotted the landscape, most of them political capitals.

SEXUAL DIVISION OF LABOR IN EUROPE

European farmers, who were called peasants, owned or leased separate landholdings, but they worked the fields communally. Because fields had to lie fallow (unplanted) every second or third year to regain fertility, a family could not ensure itself a regular food supply unless the work and the crops were shared annually by all the villagers. Men did most of the fieldwork; women helped out chiefly at planting and harvest. In some areas men concentrated on herding livestock. Women's duties consisted primarily of childcare and household tasks, including preserving food, milking cows, and caring for poultry. If a woman's husband was a city artisan or storekeeper, she might assist him in business. Since Europeans kept domesticated animals (pigs, goats, sheep, and cattle) for meat, hunting had little economic importance in their cultures. Instead, hunting was primarily a sport for male aristocrats.

Unlike in African and American societies, in which women often played prominent roles in politics and religion, men dominated all areas of life in Europe. A few women—notably Queen Elizabeth I of England—achieved status or power by right of birth, but the vast majority were excluded from positions of political authority. Husbands and fathers likewise expected to control their families. European women generally held inferior social, economic, and political positions, yet within their own families they wielded power over children and servants.

Christianity was the dominant religion in Europe. In the West, authority rested in the Catholic Church, based in Rome and led by the pope, who directed a wholly

Map 1.3   Europe in 1490

The Europeans who ventured out into the Atlantic came from countries on the north-western edge of the continent, which was divided into numerous competing nations.

CHRISTIANITY male clergy. The Catholic Church had an uneasy relationship with both secular rulers and the populace at large. Although European peoples were nominally Catholic, many adhered to local belief systems the church deemed heretical and proved unable to extinguish. Kings would ally themselves with the church when it suited their needs, but often acted independently. Yet even so the Christian nations of Europe from the twelfth century on publicly united in a goal of driving nonbelievers (especially Muslims) not only from their own domains but also from the holy city of Jerusalem, which caused the series of wars known as the Crusades.

When the fifteenth century began, European nations were slowly recovering from the devastating epidemic of *EFFECTS OF PLAGUE AND WARFARE* plague known as the Black Death, which first struck them in 1346. The Black Death seems to have arrived in Europe from China, traveling with long-distance traders along the Silk Road to the eastern Mediterranean. The disease then recurred with particular severity in the 1360s and 1370s.

■ Daily life in early 16th-century Portugal, as illustrated in a manuscript prayer book. At top a prosperous family shares a meal being served by an African slave. Other scenes show male laborers clearing land and hunting birds (left) and chopping wood (right), while at bottom a woman plants seeds in a prepared bed and in the top background female servants work in the kitchen.   (Museu Nacional de Arte Antiga, Lisbon, Portugal)

Although no precise figures are available and the impact of the Black Death varied from region to region, the best estimate is that fully one-third of Europe's people died during those terrible years. A precipitous economic decline followed—in some regions more than half of the workers had died—as did severe social, political, and religious disruption because of the deaths of clergymen and other leading figures.

As plague ravaged the population, England and France waged the Hundred Years' War (1337–1453), initiated because the English monarchy claimed the French throne. The war interrupted overland trade routes through France connecting England and the Netherlands to the Italian city-states and thence to Central Asia. Merchants in the eastern Mediterranean found a new way of reaching their northern markets by forging a regular maritime link with the Netherlands that replaced the overland route. The use of a triangular, or lateen, sail (rather than the then-standard square rigging) improved the maneuverability of ships, enabling them to sail out of the Mediterranean and north around the European coast. Also of key importance was the perfection of navigational instruments like the astrolabe and the quadrant, which allowed oceangoing sailors to estimate their position (latitude) by measuring the relationship of the sun, moon, or certain stars to the horizon.

In the aftermath of the Hundred Years' War, European monarchs forcefully consolidated their previously diffuse political power and raised new revenues through increased taxation of an already hard-pressed peasantry. The long military struggle led to new pride in national identity, which eclipsed the prevailing regional and dynastic loyalties, and to heightened hostility to foreigners. In England, Henry VII in 1485 founded the Tudor dynasty and began uniting a previously divided land. In France, the successors of Charles VII unified the kingdom and levied new taxes. Most successful of all were Ferdinand of Aragón and Isabella of Castile, who married in 1469, founding a strongly Catholic Spain. In 1492 they defeated the Muslims, who had lived in Spain and Portugal for centuries, thereafter expelling all Jews and Muslims from their domain.

POLITICAL AND TECHNOLOGICAL CHANGE

The fifteenth century also brought technological change to Europe. Movable type and the printing press, invented in Germany in the 1450s, made information more accessible than ever before. Printing stimulated the Europeans' curiosity about fabled lands across the seas, lands they could now read about in books. The most important such work was Marco Polo's *Travels*, first published in 1477, which recounted a Venetian merchant's adventures in thirteenth-century China and, most intriguing, described that nation as bordered on the east by an ocean. Polo's account circulated widely among Europe's educated elites, first in manuscript and later in print. The book led many Europeans to believe that they could trade directly with China in oceangoing vessels instead of relying on the Silk Road or the route through East Africa. A transoceanic route, if it existed, would allow northern Europeans to circumvent the Muslim and Mediterranean merchants who hitherto had controlled their access to Asian goods.

Technological advances and the growing strength of newly powerful national rulers made possible the European explorations of the fifteenth and sixteenth centuries.

MOTIVES FOR EXPLORATION

Each country craved easy access to African and Asian goods—spices like pepper, cloves, cinnamon, and nutmeg (to season the bland European diet), silk, dyes, perfumes, jewels, sugar, and gold. Avoiding Muslim and Venetian middlemen and acquiring such valuable products directly would improve a nation's income and its standing relative to other countries, in addition to supplying its wealthy leaders with coveted luxury items.

A concern for spreading Christianity around the world supplemented the economic motive. The linking of materialist and spiritual goals perhaps seems contradictory today, but fifteenth-century Europeans saw no necessary conflict between the two. Explorers and colonizers—especially Roman Catholics—honestly sought to convert "heathen" peoples to Christianity. At the same time they hoped to increase their nation's wealth by establishing direct trade with Africa, China, India, and the Moluccas (also known as the Spice Islands).

Early European Explorations

Before European mariners could discover new lands, they had to explore the oceans. To reach Asia, seafarers needed not just the maneuverable vessels and navigational aids increasingly used in the fourteenth century but also knowledge of the sea, its currents, and especially its winds. Wind would power their ships. But how did the winds run? Where would Atlantic breezes carry their square-rigged ships, which, even with the addition of a triangular sail, needed to run before the wind (that is, to have the wind directly behind the vessel)?

Europeans learned the answers to these questions in the region that has been called the Mediterranean Atlantic, the expanse of the Atlantic Ocean that is south and west of Spain and is bounded by the island groups of the Azores (on the west) and the Canaries (on the south), with the Madeiras in their midst (see Map 1.4). Europeans reached all three sets of islands during the fourteenth century—first the Canaries in the 1330s, then the Madeiras and the Azores. The Canaries proved a popular destination for mariners from Iberia, the peninsula that includes Spain and Portugal. Sailing to the Canaries from Europe was easy because strong winds known as the Northeast Trades blow southward along the Iberian and African coastlines. The voyage took about a week, and the volcanic peaks on the islands

SAILING IN THE MEDITERRANEAN ATLANTIC

made them difficult to miss even with navigational instruments that were less than precise.

The problem was getting back. The Iberian sailor attempting to return home faced a major obstacle: the very winds that had brought him so quickly to the Canaries now blew directly at him. Early travelers to the islands sometimes used galleys powered by oarsmen as well as by sails, but even oarsmen had a difficult time fighting the contrary winds and currents. Another alternative was similarly tedious: tacking back and forth to the east and west, attempting each time to make more headway north. The problem seemed intractable, and in earlier eras European sailors had been unable to solve it. When confronted with contrary winds, they simply waited for the wind to change. But for the most part, the Northeast Trades did not change. They blew steadily, shifting slightly with the seasons but never reversing course.

What could be done? Some unknown seafarer figured out the answer: sailing "around the wind." If a mariner could not sail against the trade winds, he had to sail as close as possible to the direction from which the wind was coming without being forced to tack. In the Mediterranean Atlantic, that meant pointing his vessel northwest into the open ocean, away from land, until—weeks later—he reached the winds that would carry him home, the so-called Westerlies. Those winds blow (we now know, though the mariners at first did not) northward along the coast of North America before heading east toward Europe.

This solution must at first have seemed to defy common sense, but it became the key to successful exploration of both the Atlantic and the Pacific Oceans. Once a sailor understood the winds and their allied currents, he no longer feared leaving Europe without being able to return. Faced with a contrary wind, all he had to do was sail around it until he found a wind to carry him in the proper direction. This strategy might seem to take him hundreds of miles out of the way, but in the long run it was safer and surer than attempting the monumental task of tacking against the wind.

During the fifteenth century, armed with knowledge of the winds and currents of the Mediterranean Atlantic, Iberian seamen regularly visited the three island groups, all of which they could reach in two weeks or less. The uninhabited Azores were soon settled by Portuguese migrants who raised wheat for sale in Europe and sold livestock to passing sailors. The Madeiras also had no native peoples, and by the 1450s Portuguese colonists were em-

ISLANDS OF THE MEDITERRANEAN ATLANTIC

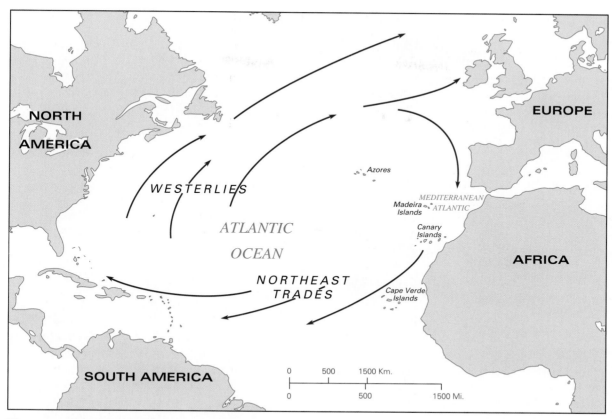

Map 1.4   Atlantic Winds and Islands

European mariners had to explore the oceans before they could find new lands.
The first realm they discovered was that of Atlantic winds and islands.

ploying slaves (probably Jews and Muslims brought from Iberia) to grow large quantities of sugar for export to the mainland. By the 1470s, Madeira had developed into a colonial plantation economy. For the first time in world history, a region had been settled explicitly to cultivate a valuable crop—sugar—to be sold elsewhere. Moreover, because the work involved in large-scale plantation agriculture was so backbreaking, only a supply of enslaved laborers (who could not opt to quit) could ensure the system's continued success.

The Canaries did have indigenous residents—the Guanche people, who began trading animal skins and dyes with their European visitors. In 1402 the French attacked one of the islands; thereafter, Portuguese and Spanish expeditions continued the sporadic assaults. The Guanches resisted vigorously, even though they were weakened by their susceptibility to alien European diseases. One by one the seven islands fell to Europeans,

who then carried off Guanches as slaves to the Madeiras or the Iberian Peninsula. Spain conquered the last island in 1496 and subsequently devoted the land to sugar plantations. Collectively, the Canaries and Madeira became known as the Wine Islands because much of their sugar production was directed to making sweet wines.

While some Europeans concentrated on exploiting the islands of the Mediterranean Atlantic, others used them as steppingstones to Africa. In 1415 Portugal seized control of Ceuta, a Muslim city in North Africa (see Map 1.2). Prince Henry the Navigator, son of King John I of Portugal, knew that vast wealth awaited the first European nation to tap the riches of Africa and Asia directly. Each year he dispatched ships southward along the African coast, attempting to discover an oceanic route to Asia. But not until after Prince Henry's death did

PORTUGUESE TRADING POSTS IN AFRICA

In the fifteenth and sixteenth centuries, caravels ventured into the open oceans, thereby changing the contours of the known world. This illustration from a manuscript account of William Barents's 1594 expedition into the Arctic Ocean shows the combination of square rigging and lateen sails that gave ships greater maneuverability and allowed them to navigate along unfamiliar coastlines far from their home ports.   (Bridgeman Art Library)

Bartholomew Dias round the southern tip of Africa (1488) and Vasco da Gama finally reach India (1498).

Long before that, Portugal reaped the benefits of its seafarers' voyages. Although West African states successfully resisted European penetration of the interior, they allowed the Portuguese to establish trading posts along their coasts. Charging the traders rent and levying duties on goods they imported, the African kingdoms set the terms of exchange and benefited considerably from their new, easier access to European manufactures. The Portuguese gained too, for they no longer had to rely on trans-Saharan camel caravans. Their vessels earned immense profits by swiftly transporting African gold, ivory, and slaves to Europe. By bargaining with African masters to purchase their slaves and then carrying those

bondspeople to Iberia, the Portuguese introduced black slavery into Europe.

An island off the African coast, previously uninhabited, proved critical to Portuguese success. São Tomé, located in the Gulf of Guinea (see Map 1.2), was colonized by the Portuguese in the 1480s. By that time Madeira had already reached the limit of its capacity to produce sugar. The soil of São Tomé proved ideal for raising that valuable crop, and plantation agriculture there expanded rapidly. Planters imported large numbers of slaves from the mainland to work in the cane fields, thus creating the first economy based primarily on the bondage of black Africans.

By the 1490s, even before Christopher Columbus set sail to the west, Europeans had learned three key lessons of colonization in the Mediterranean Atlantic. First, they had learned how to transplant their crops and livestock successfully to exotic locations. Second, they had discovered that the native peoples of those lands could be either conquered (like the Guanches) or exploited (like the Africans). Third, they had developed a viable model of plantation slavery and a system for supplying nearly unlimited quantities of such workers. The stage was set for a pivotal moment in world history.

The Voyages of Columbus, Cabot, and Their Successors

Christopher Columbus was well schooled in the lessons of the Mediterranean Atlantic. Born in 1451 in the Italian city-state of Genoa, Columbus, the largely self-educated son of a wool merchant, was by the 1490s an experienced sailor and mapmaker. Like many mariners of the day, he was drawn to Portugal and its islands, especially Madeira, where he commanded a merchant vessel. At least once he voyaged to the Portuguese outpost on the Gold Coast. There he acquired an obsession with gold, and there he came to understand the economic potential of the slave trade.

Like all accomplished seafarers, Columbus knew the world was round. (So, indeed, did most educated people: the idea that his contemporaries believed the world to be flat is a myth dating from the nineteenth century.) But he differed from other cartographers in his estimate of the earth's size: he thought that China lay only 3,000 miles from the southern European coast. Thus, he argued, it would be easier to reach Asia by sailing west than by making the difficult voyage around the southern tip of Africa. Experts scoffed at this crackpot notion, accurately predicting that the two continents lay 12,000 miles apart. When Columbus in 1484 asked the Portuguese authorities to back his plan to sail west to Asia, they rejected the proposal. After all, why should they adopt such a crazy scheme just as their efforts to round the Cape of Good Hope promised success?

Ferdinand and Isabella of Spain, jealous of Portugal's successes in Africa, were more receptive to Columbus's ideas. Urged on by some Spanish noblemen and a group of Italian merchants residing in Castile, the monarchs agreed to finance the risky voyage, in part because they hoped the profits would pay for a new expedition to conquer Muslim-held Jerusalem.

And so, on August 3, 1492, in command of three ships—the *Pinta,* the *Niña,* and the *Santa Maria*—Columbus set sail from the Spanish port of Palos.

The first part of the journey must have been very familiar, for the ships steered down the Northeast Trades to the Canary Islands. There Columbus refitted his square-rigged ships, adding triangular sails to make them more maneuverable. On September 6, the ships weighed anchor and headed out into the unknown ocean.

Just over a month later, pushed by favorable trade winds, the vessels found land approximately where Columbus had predicted (see Map 1.5). On October 12, he and his men landed on an island in the Bahamas, which its inhabitants called Guanahaní but which he renamed San Salvador. (Because Columbus's description of his landfall can be variously interpreted, three different places—Samana Cay, Plana Cays, and Mayaguana Cay—are today proposed as the most likely locations for his landing site.) Later he went on to explore the islands now known as Cuba and Hispaniola, which their residents, the Taíno people, called Colba and Bohío. Because he thought he had reached the Indies, Columbus referred to the inhabitants of the region as Indians.

Three themes predominate in Columbus's log, the major source of information on this first encounter. First,

he insistently asked the Taínos where he could find gold, pearls, and valuable spices. Each time, his informants replied (largely via signs) that such products could be obtained on other islands, on the mainland, or in cities in the interior. Eventually he came to mistrust such answers, noting, "I am beginning to believe . . . they will tell me anything I want to hear."

Second, Columbus wrote repeatedly of the strange and beautiful plants and animals. "Here the fishes are so unlike ours that it is amazing. . . . The colors are so bright that anyone would marvel," he noted, and again, "The song of the little birds might make a man wish never to leave here. I never tire from looking at such luxurious vegetation." Yet Columbus's interest was not only aesthetic. "I believe that there are many plants and trees here that could be worth a lot in Spain for use as dyes, spices, and medicines," he observed, adding that he was carrying home to Europe "a sample of everything I can," so that experts could examine them.

Third, Columbus also described the islands' human residents, and he seized some to take back to Spain. The Taínos were, he said, very handsome, gentle, and friendly, though they told him of fierce people who lived on other nearby islands and raided their villages. The

Map 1.5   European Explorations in America

In the century following Columbus's voyages, European adventurers explored the coasts and parts of the interior of North and South America.

Caniba (today called Caribs), from whose name the word *cannibal* is derived, were reported to eat their captives, but today scholars disagree about whether the tales were true. Columbus believed the Taínos to be likely converts to Catholicism, remarking that "if devout religious persons knew the Indian language well, all these people would soon become Christians." But he had more in mind than conversion. The islanders "ought to make good and skilled servants," Columbus declared. It would be easy to "subject everyone and make them do what you wished."

Thus the records of the first encounter between Europeans and America and its residents revealed the themes that would be of enormous significance for centuries to come, motivating such later explorers as Hernán de Soto as well. Above all, Europeans wanted to extract profits from North and South America by exploiting their natural resources, including plants, animals, and peoples alike. Christopher

EUROPEANS AND "AMERICA"

Columbus made three more voyages to the west, exploring most of the major Caribbean islands and sailing along the coasts of Central and South America. Until the day he died in 1506 at the age of fifty-five, Columbus believed that he had reached Asia. Even before his death, others knew better. Because the Florentine Amerigo Vespucci, who explored the South American coast in 1499, was the first to publish the idea that a new continent had been discovered, Martin Waldseemüller in 1507 labeled the land "America," as is evident in his map (reproduced on page 21). By then, Spain, Portugal, and Pope Alexander VI had signed the Treaty of Tordesillas (1494), confirming Portugal's dominance in Africa—and later Brazil—in exchange for Spanish preeminence in the rest of the Americas.

Five hundred years before Columbus, about the year 1001, the Norseman Leif Ericsson and other Norse had sailed to North America across the Davis Strait, which separated their villages in Greenland from Baffin Island (located northeast of Hudson Bay; see Map 1.1) by just

This map, produced in 1489 by Henricus Marcellus, represents the world as Christopher Columbus knew it, for it incorporates information obtained after Bartholomew Dias, a Portuguese sailor, rounded the Cape of Good Hope at the southern tip of Africa in 1488. Marcellus did not try to estimate the extent of the ocean separating the west coast of Europe from the east coast of Asia. (Trustees of the British Library)

In 1507 Martin Waldseemüller, a German mapmaker, was the first person to designate the newly discovered southern continent as "America." He named the continent after Amerigo Vespucci, the Italian explorer who realized that he had reached a "new world" rather than islands off the coast of Asia. (John Carter Brown Library at Brown University)

NORSE AND OTHER NORTHERN VOYAGERS

200 nautical miles, settling at a site they named Vinland. Attacks by local residents forced them to depart hurriedly from Vinland after just a few years. In the 1960s, archaeologists determined that the Norse had established an outpost at what is now L'Anse aux Meadows, Newfoundland, but Vinland itself was probably located farther south.

Later Europeans did not know of the Norse explorers, but some historians argue that in the 1480s sailors may have located the rich fishing grounds off the coast of Newfoundland but kept the information to themselves so they alone could fish there. Whether or not fishermen crossed the entire width of the Atlantic, they thoroughly explored its northern reaches. In the same way the Portuguese traveled regularly in the Mediterranean Atlantic, fifteenth-century seafarers voyaged between the European continent, England, Ireland, and Iceland. The mariners who explored the region of North America that was to become the United States and Canada built on their knowledge.

The winds the northern sailors confronted posed problems on their outbound rather than homeward journeys. The same Westerlies that carried Columbus and other southern voyagers back to Europe blew in the faces of northerners looking west. But mariners soon learned that the strongest winds shifted southward during the winter and that, by departing from northern ports in the spring, they could make adequate headway if they steered northward to catch sporadic easterly breezes. Thus, whereas the first landfall of most sailors to the south was somewhere in the Caribbean, those taking the northern route usually reached America along the coast of what is now Maine or the Canadian maritime provinces.

The European generally credited with "discovering" North America is John Cabot. More precisely, Cabot brought to Europe the first formal knowledge of the northern coastline of the continent and claimed the land for England. Like Columbus, Cabot was a master mariner from the Italian city-state of Genoa. He is known to have been in Spain when Columbus returned from his first trip to America. Calculating that England—which traded with Asia only through a long series of middlemen stretching from Belgium to Venice to the Muslim world—would be eager to sponsor exploratory voyages, Cabot sought and won the support of King Henry VII. He set sail from Bristol in late May 1497 in the *Mathew*, reaching his destination on June 24. Scholars disagree about the location of his landfall (some say it was Cape Breton Island, others Newfoundland), but all recognize the importance of his month-long exploration of the coast. Having achieved his goal, Cabot rode the Westerlies back to England, arriving just fifteen days after he left North America.

JOHN CABOT'S EXPLORATIONS

The voyages of Columbus, Cabot, and their successors finally brought the Eastern and Western Hemispheres together. The Portuguese explorer Pedro Álvares Cabral reached Brazil in 1500; John Cabot's son Sebastian followed his father to North America in 1507; France financed Giovanni da Verrazzano in 1524 and Jacques Cartier in 1534; and in 1609 and 1610 Henry Hudson explored the North American coast for the Dutch West India Company (see Map 1.5). All these men were primarily searching for the legendary, nonexistent "Northwest Passage" through the Americas, hoping to find an easy route to the riches of Asia. Although they did not attempt to plant colonies in the Western Hemisphere, their discoveries interested European nations in exploring North and South America.

Spanish Exploration and Conquest

*O*nly in the areas that Spain explored and claimed did colonization begin immediately. On his second voyage in 1493, Columbus brought to Hispaniola seventeen ships loaded with twelve hundred men, seeds, plants, livestock, chickens, and dogs—along

■ Artifacts from L'Anse aux Meadows, Newfoundland, a site the Norse called Straumond. These inconspicuous items reveal a great deal to archaeologists investigating the Norse settlements in North America. The small circular object, a spindle whorl for use in spinning yarn, discloses women's presence at Straumond; the nut comes from a tree that grows only south of the St. Lawrence River, thus indicating the extent of Norse travel along the coast. (L'Anse aux Meadows, Canada)

with microbes, rats, and weeds. The settlement named Isabela (in the modern Dominican Republic) and its successors became the staging area for the Spanish invasion of America. On the islands of Cuba and Hispaniola the Europeans learned to adapt to the new environment, as did the horses, cattle, and hogs they imported. When the Spaniards moved on to explore the mainland, they rode island-bred horses and ate island-bred cattle and hogs.

At first, Spanish explorers fanned out around the Caribbean basin. In 1513 Juan Ponce de León reached Florida and Vasco Núñez de Balboa crossed the Isthmus of Panama to the Pacific Ocean. In the 1530s and 1540s, conquistadors traveled farther, exploring many regions claimed by the Spanish monarchs: Francisco Vásquez de Coronado journeyed through the southwestern portion of what is now the United States at approximately the same time as Hernán de Soto explored the southeast and encountered the Lady of Cofitachequi. Juan Rodríguez Cabrillo sailed along the California coast; and Francisco Pizarro, who ventured into western South America, acquired the richest silver mines in the world by conquering the Incas. But the most important conquistador was Hernán Cortés, who in 1521 seized control of the Aztec Empire.

Cortés, an adventurer who first arrived in the West Indies in 1504, embarked for the mainland in 1519 in search of wealthy cities rumored to exist there. As he moved his force inland from the Gulf of Mexico, local Mayas presented him with a gift of twenty young female

CORTÉS AND MALINCHE

slaves. One of them, Malinche (soon baptized as a Christian and renamed Doña Marina by the Spaniards), who had been sold into slavery by the Aztecs and raised by the Mayas, became Cortés's translator. Although some modern-day Mexicans regard her as a traitor, others question why she would owe loyalty to those who had enslaved her. No one at the time of the conquest made such a suggestion; instead, both Europeans and Indians accorded her great respect. Malinche bore Cortés a son, Martín—one of the first *mestizos,* or mixed-blood children—and eventually married one of his officers. When the Aztec capital Tenochtitlán fell to the Spaniards in 1521, Cortés and his men seized a fabulous treasure of gold and silver. Thus not long after Columbus's first voyage, the Spanish monarchs—who treated the American territories as their personal possessions—controlled the richest, most extensive empire Europe had known since ancient Rome.

Spain established the model of colonization that other countries later attempted to imitate, a model with

SPANISH COLONIZATION

three major elements. First, the Crown maintained tight control over the colonies, imposing a hierarchical government that allowed little autonomy to New World jurisdictions. That control included, for example, limiting the number of people permitted to emigrate to America and insisting that the colonies import all their manufactured goods from

■ An early illustration of a Carib lean-to shelter, with baskets, a pot, a loom (hanging at left), and a hammock—a novel place to sleep that fascinated European observers. The man at center has coated his skin with annatto, a plant extract that served as both insect repellent and sunscreen. (1996 MAPes MONDe Ltd.)

Spain. Roman Catholic priests ensured the colonists' conformity with orthodox religious views. Second, most of the colonists sent from Spain were male. They took Indian—and later African—women as their sexual partners, thereby creating the racially mixed population that characterizes much of Latin America to the present day.

Third, the colonies' wealth was based on the exploitation of both the native population and slaves imported from Africa. The Mesoamerican peoples, many of whom lived in urban areas, were accustomed to autocratic rule. Spaniards simply took over roles once assumed by native leaders, who had also exacted labor and tribute from their subjects. The *encomienda* system, which granted tribute from Indian villages to individual conquistadors as a reward for their services to the Crown, in effect legalized Indian slavery. Yet in 1542 a new code of laws reformed the system, forbidding Spaniards from enslaving Indians while still allowing them to collect money and goods from their tributary villages. In response, the conquerors, familiar with slavery in Spain, began to import Africans in order to increase the labor force under their direct control. They employed Indians and Africans primarily in gold and silver mines, on sugar plantations, and on huge horse, cattle, and sheep ranches. Yet African slavery was far more common in the Greater Antilles (the major Caribbean islands) than on the mainland.

The New World's gold and silver, initially a boon, ultimately brought about the decline of Spain as a major

GOLD, SILVER, AND SPAIN'S DECLINE

power. The influx of unprecedented wealth led to rapid inflation, which (among other adverse effects) caused Spanish products to be overpriced in international markets and imported goods to become cheaper in Spain. The once-profitable Spanish textile-manufacturing industry collapsed, as did scores of other businesses. The seemingly endless income from American colonies emboldened successive Spanish monarchs to spend lavishly on wars against the Dutch and the English. Several times in the late sixteenth and early seventeenth centuries the monarchs repudiated the state debt, wreaking havoc on the nation's finances. When the South American gold and silver mines started to give out in the mid-seventeenth century, Spain's economy crumbled and the nation lost its international importance.

Spanish wealth derived from American suffering. The Spaniards deliberately leveled American cities, building cathedrals and monasteries on sites once occupied by Aztec, Incan, and Mayan temples. Some conquistadors sought to erase all vestiges of the great Indian cultures by burning the written records they found. With traditional ways of life in disarray, devastated by disease, and compelled to labor for their conquerors, many demoralized residents of Mesoamerica accepted the Christian religion brought to New Spain by friars of the Franciscan and Dominican orders.

The friars devoted their energies to persuading Mesoamerican people to move into new towns and to build

CHRISTIANITY IN NEW SPAIN

Roman Catholic churches. In such towns, Indians were exposed to European customs and religious rituals designed to assimilate Catholic and pagan beliefs. Friars deliberately juxtaposed the cult of the Virgin Mary with that of the corn goddess, and the Indians adeptly melded aspects of their traditional world-view with Christianity, in a process called syncretism. Thousands of Indians residing in Spanish territory embraced Catholicism, at least partly because it was the religion of their new rulers and they were accustomed to obedience.

The Columbian Exchange

a broad mutual transfer of diseases, plants, and animals (called the Columbian Exchange by the historian Alfred Crosby; see Figure 1.1) resulted directly from the European voyages of the fifteenth and sixteenth centuries and from Spanish colonization. The Eastern and Western Hemispheres had evolved separately for thousands of years, developing widely different forms of life. Many large mammals like cattle and horses were native to the connected continents of Europe, Asia, and Africa, but the Americas contained no domesticated beasts larger than dogs and llamas. The vegetable crops of the Americas—particularly maize, beans, squash, cassava, and potatoes—were more nutritious and produced higher yields than those of Europe and Africa, such as wheat, millet, and rye. In time, native peoples learned to raise and consume European livestock, and Europeans and Africans became accustomed to planting and eating American crops. The diets of all three peoples were consequently vastly enriched. Partly as a result, the world's population doubled over the next three hundred years.

Diseases carried from Europe and Africa, though, had a devastating impact on the Americas. Indians fell

SMALLPOX AND OTHER DISEASES

victim to microbes that had long infested the other continents and had repeatedly killed hundreds of thousands but had also left survivors with some measure of immunity. The statistics are staggering. When Columbus landed on

Maize

Maize, to Mesoamericans, was a gift from Quetzalcoatl, the plumed serpent god. Cherokees told of an old woman whose blood produced the prized stalks after her grandson buried her body in a cleared, sunny field. For the Abenakis, the crop began when a beautiful maiden ordered a youth to drag her by the hair through a burned-over field. The long hair of the Cherokee grandmother and the Abenaki maiden turned into silk, the flower on the stalks that Europeans called Indian corn.

Sacred to all the Indian peoples who grew it, maize was a cereal crop, a main part of their diet. They dried the kernels; ground into meal, maize was cooked as a mush or shaped into flat cakes and baked, the forerunners of modern tortillas. Indians also heated the dried kernels until they popped open, just as is done today. Although the European invaders of North and South America initially disdained maize, they soon learned that it could be cultivated in a wide variety of conditions—from sea level to twelve thousand feet, from regions with abundant rainfall to dry lands with as little as twelve inches of rain a year. Corn was also highly productive, yielding almost twice as many calories per acre as wheat. So Europeans, too, came to rely on corn, growing it not only in their American settlements but also in their homelands.

Maize cultivation spread to Asia and Africa. Today, China is second only to the United States in total corn production, and corn is more widely grown in Africa than any other crop. Still, the United States produces 45 percent of the world's corn—almost half of it in the three states of Illinois, Iowa, and Nebraska—and corn is the nation's single largest crop. More than half of American corn is consumed by livestock. Much of the rest is processed into syrup, which sweetens carbonated beverages and candies, or into ethanol, a gasoline additive that reduces both pollution and dependence on fossil fuels. Corn is an ingredient in light beer and toothpaste. It is used in the manufacture of tires, wallpaper, cat litter, and aspirin. Remarkably, of the ten thousand products in a modern American grocery store, about one-fourth rely to some extent on corn.

Today this crop bequeathed to the world by ancient American plant breeders provides one-fifth of all the calories consumed by the earth's peoples. The gift of Quetzalcoatl has linked the globe.

The earliest known European drawing of maize, the American plant that was to have such an extraordinary impact on the entire world. (Houghton Library, Harvard University)

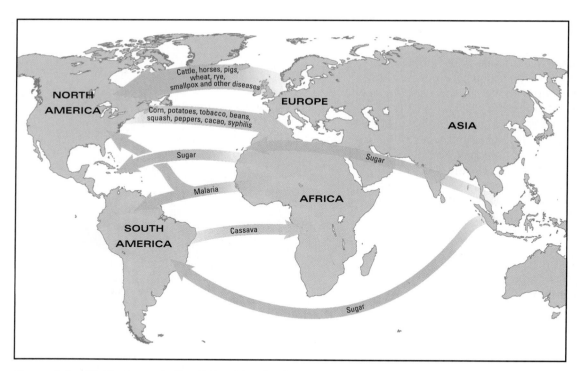

Figure 1.1 Major Items in the Columbian Exchange

As European adventurers traversed the world in the fifteenth and sixteenth centuries, they initiated the "Columbian Exchange" of plants, animals, and diseases. These events changed the lives of the peoples of the world forever, bringing new foods and new pestilence to both sides of the Atlantic.

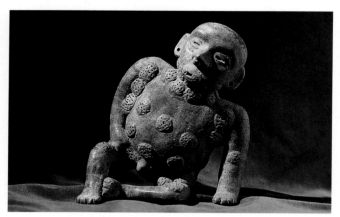

■ A male effigy dating from 200–800 C.E., found in a burial site in Nayarit, Mexico. The lesions covering the figurine suggest that the person it represents is suffering from syphilis, which, untreated, produces these characteristic markings on the body in its later stages. Such evidence as this pre-Columbian effigy has now convinced most scholars that syphilis originated in the Americas—a hypothesis in dispute for many years.   (Private Collection)

Hispaniola in 1492, approximately half a million people resided there. Fifty years later, fewer than two thousand native inhabitants were still alive. Within thirty years of the first landfall at Guanahaní, not one Taíno survived in the Bahamas. Overall, historians estimate that the arrival of the alien microorganisms could have reduced the precontact American population by as much as 90 percent, especially because the epidemics continued to recur at twenty- to thirty-year intervals.

Although measles, typhus, influenza, malaria, and other illnesses severely afflicted the native peoples, the greatest killer was smallpox, spread primarily by direct human contact. A Spanish priest recorded the vivid words of an old Aztec man who survived the first smallpox epidemic in Tenochtitlán. That epidemic, which began on Hispaniola in December 1518, was carried to the mainland by Spaniards in the spring of 1520. The epidemic peaked about six months later, fatally weakening Tenochtitlán's defenders. "It spread over the people as great destruction," the elderly Aztec remembered. "Some it quite covered [with pustules] on all parts—their faces,

■ A Spanish map from 1519 showing the coast of Hispaniola, focusing on what is now the modern nation of Haiti. The decorative figures, shown with tools for hunting and cultivation, appear to be African slaves imported as laborers to replace the Indian population, already being rapidly depleted by disease and mistreatment.   (Bibliothèque Nationale)

their heads, their breasts. . . . There was great havoc. Very many died of it." Largely as a consequence, Tenochtitlán surrendered, and the Spaniards built Mexico City on its site.

Far to the north, where smaller American populations encountered only a few Europeans, disease also ravaged the countryside. A great epidemic, probably smallpox coupled with measles, swept through the villages along the coast north of Cape Cod from 1616 to 1618. Again the mortality rate may have been as high as 90 percent. An English traveler several years later commented that the people had "died on heapes, as they lay in their houses," and that bones and skulls covered the ruins of villages. Because of this dramatic

depopulation of the area, just a few years later English colonists were able to establish settlements virtually unopposed.

The Americans, though, took a revenge of sorts. They gave the Europeans syphilis, a virulent venereal disease. The first recorded European case of the new ailment occurred in Barcelona, Spain, in 1493, shortly after Columbus's return from the Caribbean. Although less likely than smallpox to cause immediate death, syphilis was dangerous and debilitating. Carried by soldiers, sailors, and prostitutes, it spread quickly through Europe and Asia, reaching as far as China by 1505.

The exchange of three commodities had significant impacts on Europe and the Americas. Sugar, which was

SUGAR, HORSES, AND TOBACCO first domesticated in the East Indies, was being grown on the islands of the Mediterranean Atlantic by 1450 (see page 17). The insatiable European demand for sugar, which after initially being regarded as a medicine became a desirable luxury foodstuff, led Columbus to take Canary Island sugar canes to Hispaniola on his 1493 voyage. By the 1520s, plantations in the Greater Antilles worked by African slaves regularly shipped cargoes of sugar to Spain. Half a century later, the Portuguese colony in Brazil (founded 1532) was producing sugar on an even larger scale for the European market, and after 1640 (see pages 40–41), sugar cultivation became the crucial component of English and French colonization in the Caribbean.

Horses, which like sugar were brought to America by Columbus in 1493, fell into the hands of North American Indians during the seventeenth century. Through trade and theft, horses spread among the peoples of the Great Plains, reaching most areas by 1750. Lakota, Comanches, and Crows, among others, came to use horses for transportation and hunting, calculated their wealth in the number of horses owned, and waged wars primarily from horseback. Women no longer had to carry the band's belongings on their backs. Some groups that previously had cultivated crops abandoned agriculture altogether. Because of the acquisition of horses, a mode of subsistence that had been based on hunting several different animals, in combination with gathering and agriculture, became one focused almost wholly on hunting buffalo.

In America, Europeans encountered tobacco, which at first they believed to have beneficial medicinal effects. Smoking and chewing the "Indian weed" became a fad in Europe after it was planted in Turkey in the sixteenth century. Despite the efforts of such skeptics as King James I of England, who in 1604 pronounced smoking "loathsome to the eye, hatefull to the Nose, harmfull to the brain, [and] dangerous to the Lungs," tobacco's popularity climbed. Its connection to lung cancer was discovered only in the twentieth century.

The European and African invasion of the Americas therefore had a significant biological component, for the invaders carried plants and animals with them. Some creatures, such as livestock, they brought deliberately. Others, including rats (which infested their ships), weeds, and diseases, arrived unexpectedly. And the same process occurred in reverse. When the Europeans returned home, they deliberately took back such crops as maize, potatoes, and tobacco, along with that unanticipated stowaway, syphilis.

Europeans in North America

Northern Europeans, denied access to the wealth of Mesoamerica by the Spanish and beaten to South America by the Portuguese, were initially more interested in exploiting North America's abundant natural resources than in the difficult task of establishing colonies on the mainland. John Cabot reported that fish were so plentiful along the North American coast that they could be caught merely by lowering baskets over the side of a vessel. Europeans rushed to take advantage of the abundance of fish, a product in great demand in their homelands as an inexpensive source of nourishment. By the 1570s, more than 350 ships, primarily from France and England, were capitalizing on the bounty of the Newfoundland Banks each year.

European fishermen soon learned that they could augment their profits by exchanging cloth and metal *TRADE AMONG INDIANS AND EUROPEANS* goods like pots and knives for the native trappers' beaver pelts, which Europeans used to make fashionable hats. At first the Europeans conducted their trading from ships sailing along the coast, but later they established permanent outposts on the mainland to centralize and control the traffic in furs. All were inhabited chiefly by male adventurers, whose major aim was to send as many pelts as possible home to Europe.

The Europeans' demand for furs, especially beaver, was matched by the Indians' desire for European goods that could make their lives easier and establish their superiority over their neighbors. Some bands began to concentrate so completely on trapping for the European market that they abandoned their traditional economies. The Abenakis of Maine, for example, became partially dependent on food supplied by their neighbors to the south, the Massachusett tribe, because they devoted most of their energies to catching beaver to sell to French traders. The Massachusetts, in turn, intensified their production of foodstuffs, which they traded to the Abenakis in exchange for the European metal tools they preferred to their own handmade stone implements. The intensive trade in pelts also had serious ecological consequences. In some regions, beavers were completely wiped out. The disappearance of their dams led to soil erosion, especially when combined with the extensive clearing of forests by later European settlers.

Although their nation reaped handsome profits from fishing, English merchants and political leaders watched enviously as Spain's American possessions enriched Spain immeasurably. In the mid-sixteenth century,

English "sea dogs" like John Hawkins and Sir Francis Drake began to raid Spanish treasure fleets sailing home from the West Indies. Their actions caused friction between the two countries and helped to foment a war that in 1588 culminated in the defeat of a huge invasion force—the Spanish Armada—off the English coast. As a part of the contest with Spain, English leaders started to think about planting colonies in the Western Hemisphere, thereby gaining better access to valuable trade goods and simultaneously preventing their enemy from dominating the Americas.

The first English colonial planners saw Spain's possessions as both a model and a challenge. They hoped to reproduce Spanish successes by dispatching to America men who would similarly exploit the native peoples for their own and their nation's benefit. In the mid-1570s, a group that included Sir Humphrey Gilbert and his younger half-brother Sir Walter Raleigh began to promote a scheme to establish outposts that could trade with the Indians and provide bases for attacks on New Spain. Approving the idea, Queen Elizabeth I authorized first Gilbert, then Raleigh, to colonize North America.

Gilbert failed to plant a colony in Newfoundland, dying in the attempt, and Raleigh was only briefly more successful. After two preliminary expeditions, in 1587 he sent 117 colonists to the territory he named Virginia, after Elizabeth, the "Virgin Queen." They established a settlement on Roanoke Island, in what is now North Carolina, but in 1590 a resupply ship—delayed in leaving England because of the Spanish Armada—could not find them. The colonists had vanished, leaving only the word Croatoan (the name of a nearby island) carved on a tree. Recent tree-ring studies have shown that the North Carolina coast experienced a severe drought between 1587 and 1589, which would have created a subsistence crisis for the settlers and which could well have led them to abandon the Roanoke site.

Thus England's first attempt to plant a permanent settlement on the North American coast failed, as had similar efforts by Portugal on Cape Breton Island (early 1520s) and France in northern Florida (mid-1560s). All three enterprises collapsed because of their inability to be self-sustaining in foodstuffs and the hostility of neighboring peoples. Spanish soldiers wiped out the French colony in 1565 (see page 35), and neither the Portuguese nor the English were able to maintain friendly relations with local Indians.

The explanation for such failings becomes clear in Thomas Harriot's *A Briefe and True Report of the New*

■ John White, an artist with Raleigh's 1585 expedition (and later the governor of the ill-fated 1587 colony), illustrated three different fishing techniques used by Carolina Indians: to the left, the construction of weirs and traps; in the background, spearfishing in shallow water; in the foreground, fishing from dugout canoes. The fish are accurately drawn and can be identified today.   (Trustees of the British Museum)

Found Land of Virginia, published in 1588 to publicize Raleigh's colony. Harriot, a noted scientist who sailed with the second of the preliminary voyages to Roanoke, described the animals, plants, and people of the region for an English readership. His account revealed that although the explorers depended on nearby villagers for most of their food, they needlessly antagonized their neighbors by killing some of them for what Harriot himself admitted were unjustifiable reasons.

The scientist advised later colonizers to deal with the native peoples of America more humanely than his comrades had. But the content of his book suggested why that advice would rarely be followed. *A Briefe and True Report* examined the possibilities for economic development in America. Harriot stressed three points: the availability of commodities familiar to Europeans, like grapes, iron, copper, and fur-bearing animals; the potential profitability of exotic American products such as maize, cassava, and tobacco; and the relative ease of manipulating the native population to the Europeans' advantage. Should the Americans attempt to resist the English by force, Harriot asserted, the latter's advantages of disciplined soldiers and superior weaponry would quickly deliver victory.

Harriot's *Briefe and True Report* depicted for his English readers a bountiful land full of opportunities for quick profit. The people already residing there would, he thought, "in a short time be brought to civilitie" through conversion to Christianity, admiration for European superiority, or conquest—if they did not die from disease, the ravages of which he witnessed. Thomas Harriot understood the key elements of the story, but his prediction was far off the mark. European dominance of North America would be difficult to achieve. Indeed, some historians today argue that it never was fully achieved, in the sense Harriot and his compatriots intended, and that the societies that subsequently developed in North America owed as much to their native origins as to their immigrant ones.

Summary

The process of initial contact between Europeans and Americans that ended with Thomas Harriot near the close of the sixteenth century began approximately 250 years earlier when Portuguese sailors first set out to explore the Mediterranean Atlantic and to settle on its islands. That region of the Atlantic so close to European and African shores nurtured the mariners who, like Christopher Columbus, ventured into previously unknown waters—those who sailed to India and Brazil as well as to the Caribbean and the North American coast. When Columbus first reached the Americas, he thought he had found Asia, his intended destination. Later explorers knew better but, except for the Spanish, regarded the Americas primarily as a barrier that prevented them from reaching their long-sought goal of an oceanic route to the riches of China and the Moluccas. Ordinary European fishermen were the first to realize that the northern coasts had valuable products to offer: fish and furs, both much in demand in their homelands.

The wealth of the north could not compare to that of Mesoamerica. The Aztec Empire, heir to the trading networks of Teotihuacán as well as to the intellectual sophistication of the Mayas, dazzled the conquistadors with the magnificence of its buildings and its seemingly unlimited wealth. As an old man, Cortés's aide Bernal Díaz del Castillo recalled his first sight of Tenochtitlán, situated in the midst of Lake Texcoco: "We were amazed and said that it was like the enchantments . . . on account of the great towers and cues [temples] and buildings rising from the water, and all built of masonry." Some soldiers asked, he remembered, "whether the things that we saw were not a dream."

The Aztecs had predicted that their Fifth Sun would end in earthquakes and hunger. Hunger they surely experienced after Cortés's invasion; and, if there were no earthquakes, the great temples tumbled to the ground nevertheless, as the Spaniards used their stones (and Indian laborers) to construct cathedrals honoring their God and his son Jesus rather than Huitzilopochtli. The conquerors employed first American and later enslaved African workers to till the fields, mine the precious metals, and herd the livestock that earned immense profits for themselves and their mother country.

The initial impact of Europeans on the Americas proved devastating. Flourishing civilizations were, if not entirely destroyed, markedly altered in just a few short decades. The Europeans' diseases and livestock, along with a wide range of other imported animals and plants, irrevocably changed the American environment, affecting the lives of the Western Hemisphere's inhabitants. By the end of the sixteenth century, fewer people resided in North America than had lived there before Columbus's arrival, even taking into account the arrival of many Europeans and Africans. And the people who did live there—Indian, African, and European—resided in a world that was indeed new—a world engaged in the unprecedented process of combining foods, religions, economies, styles of life, and political systems that had developed separately for millennia. Understandably, conflict and dissension permeated that process.

LEGACY FOR A PEOPLE AND A NATION
Columbus Day

Each year, the United States celebrates the second Monday in October as a tribute to Christopher Columbus's landing in the Bahamas in 1492. When viewed in the context of other holidays that mark the birthdays of great Americans or key events in the nation's past, Columbus Day is an anomaly. After all, the Genoese mariner never set foot on North American soil.

The first known U.S. celebration of Columbus's voyage occurred in New York City on October 12, 1792, when a men's social club gave a dinner to mark its three hundredth anniversary. In the late 1860s, Italian American communities in New York City and San Francisco began to celebrate October 12, but not until the four hundredth anniversary in 1892 did a congressional resolution order a one-time national commemoration. Columbus Day was first observed as a national holiday in 1971, although a majority of the states already celebrated it (Colorado was the first, in 1907).

More than thirty years ago Congress proclaimed Columbus Day as a national holiday with little opposition, except from Americans of Scandinavian descent who would have preferred to honor the Norse explorers of 1001. Today, though, the annual observances can arouse strong emotions. The American Indian Movement (AIM), founded in 1968, has declared that "from an indigenous vantage point, Columbus' arrival was a disaster." Terming Columbus a "murderer," the AIM contends that he "deserves no recognition or accolades"—certainly not a holiday. At the same time, as immigration has increased the Latino presence in the United States, people of Hispanic descent have claimed Columbus as their own, insisting that his voyage was "a thoroughly Spanish event." In some cities—most notably New York—their celebrations rival those long organized by Italian Americans; in others, such as Miami, Hispanics control the official commemorations. Still other Latinos, especially those of Mexican descent living in Los Angeles, call October 12 Dia de la Raza and use it as an occasion to protest current U.S. immigration policy.

As ethnic diversity has increased in the nation, and as peoples of different origins have sought to claim a share of the American heritage, holidays have unsurprisingly become the occasion for heated contests. Each fall, the American people and nation therefore continue to confront the controversial legacy of Columbus's 1492 voyage.

The **history companion** *powered by Eduspace*
Your primary source for interactive quizzes, exercises, and more to help you learn efficiently.
http://history.college.hmco.com/students

THE BAHAMA OR LUCAYO ISLE

O C E

R:
Mosauites
C. del Anclote
of S.Espit.
Pijos P.
Matanzas
Canaveral
Bahama Bank
OtcHaqua
Mimbres
FLORIDA
Serrop. I.
Bahama I.
Carlos B.
Lucaye I.
Carlos
THE GULF OF FLORIDA
Muspa
Aleblaster or Zigatos I.
Guanahani or Catt I.
Caico Marquet
Bimini
Martirs
Providence I.
Yumaor Xuma
Triangulo
Tortuga
The Great
Bahama Bank
Yumeta or Long I.
Samana
B. of Matances
Old Bahama Streights
Mayaguana
Cape St
Anthony
Havana
CUBA ISLE
Porellicacos
Cuncepcion
de Pizarro
Mucoras
Verde I.
Miniporas
Caicos
Abrochos Here St W. fish'd for if Spanish
Comtoy
la Trinite
Pinos I.
los Hermanas
S Spiritu
Jardins
Inagua
Petite Paix
Tortuga I.
Mayze
Baiha
Mancenille
M.te Christo
Isabella ruind
P. Plata
Caico de P.
C. Francois
B. C. of Sam
Mugeres
P. Zagua
Cosumel I.
little Cayman
S.Iago
Nich Mo
Guanabe I.
French
S.John
I.
S. DOMINGO
Spaniards
Quita Sueno
Great Cayman
C Cruz
Seville
S.Ann
Caimites
Little Gouave
Leogane
Grocoua
S Domingo
Altavela
Beata
Mona
C. Raxo
of HONDURAS
Santanilla
P. Negrilla
S. Mary
Tiburon
C.
P.Moran
Abacou
Vachel
I.S. Catherine
Saona I.
I. JAMAICA
Carlile
Port Royal
Old Harbour
Misteriosa
Bivoras
Guanaja I.
B.2 Nuevo
C. Camaron
Viciosa
Serranilla
Parcel
Mountains of Ocha
HONDURAS
George del Olancho
C. Grattos a Dios
Quinta Suenos
Serrana or I. of Perls
C. S.to Romain
AIN
Carthago
Yare
Village of Indians
C. Coquibacoa
C. Kela
Rio de la Hacha
Nova segovia
CARAGUA
R. Vairopa
Mesquitos
R. Grande or Maddalena
la Ranche ria
Tagusalpa Jean
I. of Perles
I. St Catharine or Providence
Roncador
Luke Nicaragua
el Desaguader
Rio Barranca St Ramada
S. Martha
Vulcano of Bombaco
Rio de Lesovi
Escudo de Veragua
Madre de Popa
Maracaibo
COSTARICA
Carthagena
I. of Poios
Tolu
Teneriffe
los Reyes
VERAGUA
PANAMA
S.Sebastian de Buenavista
Tamalameque
SOUTH A
PART

EUROPEANS COLONIZE NORTH AMERICA 1600–1640

Captain William Rudyerd seemed like the sort of man any Puritan colony in the Americas would prize, so when his older brother urged the planners of the new settlement to appoint him muster master general, they readily agreed. Rudyerd, a veteran of wars on the European continent, followed the new dissenting English faith, as did the planners and many of the settlers. In the first years of the colony, Rudyerd proved to be a vigorous soldier who worked hard to train the settlers to defend themselves from attack. But he also proved to be a vigorous defender of his own status, and his actions wreaked havoc in the fragile community. The captain beat to death a servant suffering from scurvy (Rudyerd thought the servant was merely lazy), and he also quarreled continually with other settlers, whom he believed failed to show the proper respect to a gentleman of noble birth.

One of Rudyerd's antagonists was the Reverend Lewis Morgan, with whom the captain argued about religious books and the conduct of church services. Rudyerd, traditional minded despite his Puritan beliefs, found Morgan's encouragement of congregational psalm singing scandalously radical. The disagreements quickly escalated into exchanges of insults. "Your foul mouthed answer deserves rather sharp retribution than any equal respect from A gentleman," the captain once haughtily told the clergyman; "I have given you too Much respect; which has begot so much incivility."

Similar conflicts occurred in all the Anglo-American settlements, as gentlemen accustomed to unquestioning deference from their inferiors learned to their dismay that in a colonial setting their inherited social standing could be challenged by upstarts of various descriptions. But in Rudyerd and Morgan's colony the disputes were especially dangerous, because the two lived on Providence Island, an isolated Puritan outpost off the coast of modern Nicaragua.

◀ This early eighteenth-century British map of the Caribbean and Central America vividly illustrates the precarious position of the seventeenth-century Providence Island settlers, on their tiny island surrounded by Spanish territory on the mainland to the east, south, and west, and the Spanish-dominated Greater Antilles to the north.
(Colonial Williamsburg Foundation)

Providence Island, founded by a company of Puritan adventurers in 1630—the same year as the Massachusetts Bay colony—sought to establish an English beachhead in the fertile tropics that could lead to successful colonization of the Central American mainland. Yet the outpost's perilous location amid Spanish settlements, its failure to establish a viable local economy, and, ultimately, its desperate attempts to stay afloat financially by serving as a base for English privateers caused its downfall. That decision led the Spaniards to conclude that the Puritans *had* to be removed. Twice, in 1635 and 1640, Providence Island fended off Spanish attacks. But in May 1641 a large Spanish fleet of seven ships carrying two thousand soldiers and sailors captured the island, and the English survivors scattered to other Caribbean settlements or returned to England.

By this time, though, Spain no longer predominated in the Americas. France, the Netherlands, and England all had permanent colonies in North America by the 1640s. The French and Dutch colonies, like the Spanish outposts, were settled largely by European men who interacted regularly with indigenous peoples, using their labor or seeking to convert them to Christianity. Like the conquistadors, French and Dutch merchants (on the mainland) and planters (in the Caribbean) hoped to make a quick profit and then perhaps return to their homelands. The English, as Thomas Harriot made clear in the 1580s, were just as interested in profiting from North America. But they pursued those profits in a different way.

In contrast to other Europeans, most of the English settlers—including those of the failed Providence Island colony—came to America intending to stay. Especially along the northeast Atlantic coast of the continent, in the area that came to be known as New England, they arrived in family groups, sometimes along with friends and relatives from neighboring villages back home. They recreated European society and family life to an extent not possible in the other colonies, where migrant men found their sexual partners within the Indian or African populations. Among the English colonies, those in the Chesapeake region and on the Caribbean islands most closely resembled colonies founded by other nations. Their economies, like those of Hispaniola or Brazil, soon came to be based on large-scale agricultural production for the international market by a labor force composed of bonded servants and slaves.

Wherever they settled, the English, like other Europeans, prospered only after they learned to adapt to the alien environment, something the Providence Islanders never achieved. The first permanent English colonies survived because nearby Indians assisted the newcomers. The settlers had to learn to grow unfamiliar American crops such as maize and tobacco. They also had to develop extensive trading relationships with native peoples and with colonies established by other European countries. Needing laborers for their fields, they first used English indentured servants, then later began to import African slaves, copying the example of the Spanish in the Atlantic and Caribbean islands, and the Portuguese in São Tomé and Brazil. Thus the early history of the region that became the United States and the English Caribbean is best understood not as an isolated story of English colonization but rather as a series of complex interactions among a variety of European, African, and American peoples and environments. ■

■ The women of Acoma pueblo have long been accomplished potters. Before the arrival of Europeans with iron utensils, residents of the pueblo stored food and water in pots like this. The unusual shape derived from its function: the low center of gravity allowed a woman to balance the pot easily on her head as she carried water from a cistern to the top of the mesa.   (The Field Museum, #A109998c)

New Spain, New France, and New Netherland

Spaniards established the first permanent European settlement within the boundaries of the modern United States, but others initially attempted that feat. Twice in the 1560s groups of French Protestants (Huguenots) sought to escape persecution in their homeland by planting colonies on the south Atlantic coast. A passing ship rescued the starving survivors of the first, located in present-day South Carolina. The second, near modern Jacksonville, Florida, was destroyed in 1565 by a Spanish expedition under the command of Pedro Menéndez de Avilés. To ensure Spanish domination of the strategically important region (located near sea-lanes used by Spanish treasure ships bound for Europe), Menéndez set up a small fortified outpost, which he named St. Augustine—now the oldest continuously inhabited European settlement in the United States. Franciscan missionaries soon followed, but nearby Indians fiercely resisted the friars' efforts to Christianize them. Only after the native peoples were forcibly moved to mission towns did many assent to baptism. Even so, by the end of the sixteenth century a chain of Franciscan missions stretched westward across Florida and northward into the islands along the Atlantic coast.

More than thirty years passed after the founding of St. Augustine before conquistadors ventured anew into

NEW MEXICO

the present-day United States. In 1598, drawn northward by rumors of rich cities, Juan de Oñate, a Mexican-born adventurer, led a group of about five hundred soldiers and settlers to New Mexico. At first, the Pueblos greeted the newcomers cordially. When the Spaniards began to use torture, murder, and rape to extort food and clothing from the villagers, however, the residents of Acoma killed several soldiers. The invaders responded ferociously, killing more than eight hundred people and capturing the remainder. All the captives above the age of twelve were ordered enslaved for twenty years, and men older than twenty-five had one foot amputated. Not surprisingly, the other Pueblo villages surrendered.

Yet Oñate's bloody victory proved illusory, for New Mexico held little wealth. It also was too far from the Pacific coast to assist in protecting Spanish sea-lanes, which had been one of Oñate's aims (he, like others, initially believed the continent to be much narrower than it actually is). Many of the Spaniards returned to Mexico, and officials considered abandoning the isolated colony, which lay 800 miles north of the nearest Spanish settlement. Instead, in 1609, the authorities decided to maintain a small military outpost and a few Christian missions in the area, with the capital at Santa Fe (founded in 1610) (see Map 3.3). As in regions to the south, Spanish leaders were granted *encomiendas* guaranteeing them control over the labor of Pueblo villagers. But in the absence of mines or fertile agricultural lands, such grants yielded small profit.

QUEBEC AND MONTREAL

On the Atlantic coast, the French turned their attention northward, to the area that Jacques Cartier had explored in the 1530s. Several times they tried to establish permanent bases along the Canadian coast but did not succeed until 1605, with the founding of Port Royal. Then in 1608 Samuel de Champlain set up a trading post at an interior site the local Iroquois had called Stadacona when Cartier spent the winter there seventy-five years earlier. Champlain renamed it Quebec. He had chosen well: Quebec was the most easily defended spot in the entire St. Lawrence River valley, a stronghold that controlled access to the heartland of the continent. In 1642 the French established a second post, Montreal, at the falls of the St. Lawrence (and thus at the end of navigation by oceangoing vessels), a place the Indians called Hochelaga.

Before the founding of these settlements, fishermen served as the major transporters of North American beaver pelts to France, but the new posts quickly took over control of the lucrative trade in furs (see Table 2.1). Only a few Europeans resided in New France; most were men, some of whom married Indian women. The colony's leaders gave land grants along the river to wealthy seigneurs (nobles), who then imported tenants to work their farms. A small number of Frenchmen brought their wives and took up agriculture; even so, more than twenty-five years after Quebec's founding, it had just sixty-four resident families, along with traders and soldiers. With respect to territory occupied and farmed, northern New France never grew much beyond the confines of the river valley between Quebec and Montreal (see Map 2.1). Thus it differed significantly from New Spain, where Europeans resided in widely scattered locations and Spanish men sometimes directly supervised Indian laborers.

JESUIT MISSIONS IN NEW FRANCE

Missionaries of the Society of Jesus (Jesuits), a Roman Catholic order dedicated to converting nonbelievers to Christianity, also came to New France. First arriving in Quebec in 1625, the Jesuits, whom the Indians called Black Robes, tried to persuade indigenous peoples to live near French settlements and to adopt European agricultural methods. When that effort failed, the Jesuits concluded that they could introduce Catholicism to their new charges without insisting that they fundamentally alter their traditional ways of life. Accordingly, the Black Robes learned Indian languages and traveled to remote regions of the interior, where they lived in twos and threes among hundreds of potential converts.

TABLE 2.1

The Founding of Permanent European Colonies in North America, 1565–1640

Colony	Founder(s)	Date	Basis of Economy
Florida	Pedro Menéndez de Avilés	1565	Farming
New Mexico	Juan de Oñate	1598	Livestock
Virginia	Virginia Company	1607	Tobacco
New France	France	1608	Fur trading
New Netherland	Dutch West India Co.	1614	Fur trading
Plymouth	Separatists	1620	Farming, fishing
Maine	Sir Ferdinando Gorges	1622	Fishing
St. Kitts, Barbados, et al.	European immigrants	1624	Sugar
Massachusetts Bay	Massachusetts Bay Company	1630	Farming, fishing, fur trading
Maryland	Cecilius Calvert	1634	Tobacco
Rhode Island	Roger Williams	1636	Farming
Connecticut	Thomas Hooker	1636	Farming, fur trading
New Haven	Massachusetts migrants	1638	Farming
New Hampshire	Massachusetts migrants	1638	Farming, fishing

Map 2.1   European Settlements and Indian Tribes in Eastern North America, 1650

The few European settlements established in the east before 1650 were widely scattered, hugging the shores of the Atlantic Ocean and the banks of its major rivers. By contrast, America's native inhabitants controlled the vast interior expanse of the continent and Spaniards had begun to move into the West.

Using a variety of strategies, Jesuits sought to undermine the authority of village shamans (the traditional religious leaders) and to gain the confidence of leaders who could influence others. Trained in rhetoric, they won admirers by their eloquence. Immune to smallpox (for all had survived the disease already), they explained epidemics among the Indians as God's punishment for sin, their arguments aided by the ineffectiveness of the shamans' traditional remedies against the new pestilence. Drawing on European science, Jesuits predicted solar and lunar eclipses. Perhaps most important, they amazed the villagers by communicating with each other over long distances through marks on paper. The Indians' desire to learn how to harness the extraordinary power of literacy was one of the critical factors making them receptive to the missionaries' spiritual message.

Although the process took many years, the Jesuits slowly gained thousands of converts, some of whom moved to reserves set aside for Christian Indians. In those communities they followed Catholic teachings with fervor and piety. The converts replaced their own culture's traditional equal treatment of men and women with notions more congenial to the Europeans' insistence on male dominance and female subordination. Further, they altered their practice of allowing premarital sexual relationships and easy divorce because Catholic doctrine prohibited both customs.

Jesuit missionaries faced little competition from other Europeans for native peoples' souls, but French fur traders had to confront a direct challenge. In 1614, only five years after Henry Hudson explored the river that now bears his name, his sponsor, the Dutch West India Company, established an outpost (Fort Orange) on that river at the site of present-day Albany, New York. Like the French, the Dutch sought beaver pelts, and their presence so close to Quebec posed a threat to French domination of the region. The Netherlands, at the time the world's dominant commercial power, aimed primarily at trade rather than colonization. Thus New Netherland, like New France, remained small, largely confined to a river valley that offered easy access to its settlements. The colony's southern anchor was New Amsterdam, a town founded in 1624 on Manhattan Island, at the mouth of the Hudson River.

NEW NETHERLAND

As the Dutch West India Company's colony in North America, New Netherland was an unimportant part of a vast commercial empire that included posts in Africa, Brazil, the West Indies, and modern-day Indonesia. Autocratic directors-general ruled the colony for the company; with no elected assembly, settlers felt little loyalty to their nominal leaders. Few migrants arrived. Even a company policy of 1629 offering a large land grant, or patroonship, to anyone who would bring fifty settlers to the province failed to attract takers. (Only one such tract—Rensselaerswyck, near Albany—was ever fully developed.) As late as the mid-1660s, New Netherland had only about five thousand inhabitants. Some were Swedes and Finns who resided in the former colony of New Sweden (founded in 1638 on the Delaware River; see Map 2.1), which was taken over by the Dutch in 1655.

The American Indian allies of New France and New Netherland clashed with each other in part because of fur-trade rivalries. In the 1640s, the Iroquois, who traded chiefly with the Dutch and lived in modern upstate New York, went to war against the Hurons, who traded primarily with the French and lived in present-day Ontario. The Iroquois wanted to become the major supplier of pelts to Europeans and to ensure the security of their hunting territories. They achieved both goals by using guns supplied by the Dutch to virtually exterminate the Hurons, whose population had already been decimated by a smallpox epidemic. The Iroquois thus established themselves as a major force in the region, one that Europeans could ignore only at their peril. And the European demand for beaver pelts had proved to have a disastrous effect on native communities and their interactions.

The Caribbean

In the Caribbean, France, the Netherlands, and England fought openly in the first half of the seventeenth century. The Spanish concentrated their colonization efforts on the Greater Antilles—Cuba, Hispaniola, Jamaica, and Puerto Rico. They left many smaller islands alone, partly because of resistance by their Carib inhabitants, partly because the mainland offered greater wealth for less effort. But the tiny islands attracted other European powers: they could provide bases from which to attack Spanish vessels loaded with American gold and silver, and they could serve as sources of valuable tropical products such as spices, dyes, and fruits.

England was the first northern European nation to establish a permanent foothold in the smaller West Indian islands (the Lesser Antilles). English people settled on St. Christopher (St. Kitts) in 1624, then later on other islands such as Barbados (1627) and Providence (1630). France was able to colonize Guadeloupe and Martinique only by defeating the Caribs, whereas the Dutch more easily gained control of tiny St. Eustatius (strategically located near St. Kitts). In addition to indigenous inhabitants, Europeans had to worry about conflicts with

Wampum

When Europeans first came to North America, they quickly learned that native peoples highly valued small cylindrical beads made from whelk and quahog shells, known collectively as wampum. The white and purple beads had been strung on fibers for centuries to make necklaces and ornamental belts, but with the Europeans' arrival wampum changed its character, becoming a currency widely employed by both groups.

The transformation of wampum occurred not only because the Indians prized it and would trade deerskins and beaver pelts to acquire the beads, but also because Dutch and English settlers lacked an equally handy medium of exchange. These settlers had limited access to coins and currency from their homelands, yet they needed to do business with each other and with their native neighbors. Wampum filled a key need, especially in the first decades of settlement.

Whelk (white) and quahog (purple) shells were found primarily along the shores of Long Island Sound. Narragansetts, Montauks, Niantics, and other local peoples had long gathered the shells during the summers; women then fashioned the beads during the long northeastern winters. The shells were hard and brittle, so shaping them into hollow beads was a time-consuming task involving considerable skill. But Europeans' metal tools, including fine drills, allowed a rapid increase in the quantity and quality of wampum. Some villages gave up their hunter-gatherer modes of subsistence and settled permanently in shell-rich areas where they focused almost exclusively on the manufacture of wampum. What had been a seasonal task for women became their year-round work.

Wampum played a key role in the early economy of both New Netherland and New England. Dutch settlers in Manhattan traded such manufactured goods as guns and kettles, axes, or knives with the wampum makers, then transported wampum up the Hudson River to Fort Orange, where they used it to purchase furs and skins from the Iroquois. In 1627, Isaac de Rasière, a Dutch trader, introduced wampum to the English colonists at Plymouth when he offered it in exchange for corn. Ten years later, the Massachusetts Bay colony made wampum legal tender for the payment of debts under 12 pennies, at a rate of six white beads or three purple beads (which were rarer) to 1 penny. Wampum beads could be traded in loose handfuls but more often were strung on thin cords in set amounts worth English

equivalents ranging from 1 penny to 5 shillings (60 pennies) in white beads, or 2 pennies to 10 shillings (120 pennies) in purple beads. People trading larger sums measured in wampum always feared being short-changed. In 1660, one resident of New Netherland agreed to accept payment of a substantial debt in wampum only if his wife *personally* counted all the beads.

Wampum—originally with purely ornamental significance for its Indian makers—became an initial, indispensable link in the commerce between Europe and North America.

Before Europeans arrived in North America, wampum—requiring great skill to make—served primarily ceremonial purposes for native peoples, as in the "Four Huron Nations" wampum belt presented to Samuel de Champlain in 1611 to signify the alliance of France and the Hurons. But several decades later, after Dutch and English colonists came to rely on it as a medium of exchange and European tools made it easier to manufacture, wampum became far more utilitarian in design and appearance.
(Left: American Museum of Natural History, photographed by Craig Chesek; right: Musee de L'Homme)

Spaniards and with one another. Like Providence Island, many colonies changed hands during the seventeenth century. For example, the English drove the Spanish out of Jamaica in 1655, and the French soon thereafter took over half of Hispaniola, creating the colony of St. Domingue (modern Haiti).

Why did other Europeans devote so much energy to gaining control of the small volcanic islands neglected by Spain? The primary answer to that question is sugar. Europeans loved sugar, which provided its users with both a sweet taste and a quick energy boost. Entering the European market in substantial quantities at approximately the same time as coffee and tea—the stimulating, addictive, and bitter Asian drinks improved by the addition of a sweetener—sugar quickly became a crucial element of the European diet.

SUGAR CULTIVATION

Early in the 1640s, English residents of Barbados, who had already experimented unsuccessfully with growing tobacco, cotton, and indigo, discovered that the island's soil and climate were ideally suited for cultivat-ing sugar cane. At the time, the world's supply of sugar came primarily from the Wine Islands, São Tomé, and especially Brazil, where numerous farmers, each with a few servants or slaves, grew much of the crop. Small Brazilian producers took their cane to central mills, where it was refined into brown and white sugars in the most technologically sophisticated enterprise of the day. To pay for processing, they turned a large proportion of their crop over to the mill owners, themselves wealthier planters who lacked the ability to coordinate the actions of the independent farmers. This production method was highly inefficient.

That changed in Barbados. Between 1630 and 1654 the Dutch took control of northeastern Brazil, where they learned Portuguese techniques for growing the canes and, more important, for processing the crop. Dutch merchants taught those skills to Barbadians, expecting to sell them African slaves and to transport barrels of sugar products to Europe. The results must have exceeded their wildest dreams. The Barbados sugar boom that began in the 1640s was both explosive and

■ In the 1660s, a French book illustrated the various phases of sugar processing for curious European readers. Teams of oxen (A) turned the mill, the rollers of which crushed the canes (C), producing the sap (D), which was collected in a vat (E), then boiled down into molasses (K). African slaves, with minimal supervision by a few Europeans (foreground), managed all phases of the process.   (Library Company of Philadelphia)

lucrative, as planters there increased the size of their landholdings, adopted large-scale gang labor by bondspeople, and built their own sugar mills that could operate with great efficiency. Planters, slave traders, and Dutch shipping interests alike earned immense profits from introducing economies of scale into the production of sugar.

As other Caribbean planters embraced sugar-cane cultivation, Barbadians' profit margins were reduced. Even so, sugar remained the most valuable American commodity for more than one hundred years. In the eighteenth century, sugar grown by large gangs of slaves in British Jamaica and French St. Domingue dominated the world market. Yet, in the long run, the future economic importance of the Europeans' American colonies lay on the mainland rather than in the Caribbean.

English Interest in Colonization

The failure of Raleigh's Roanoke colony ended English efforts to settle in North America for nearly two decades. When the English decided in 1606 to try once more, they again planned colonies that imitated the Spanish model. Yet greater success came when they abandoned that model and founded settlements very different from those of other European powers. Unlike Spain, France, or the Netherlands, England eventually sent large numbers of men and women to set up agriculturally based colonies on the mainland. Two major developments prompted approximately 200,000 ordinary English men and women to move to North America in the seventeenth century and led their government to encourage their emigration.

The onset of dramatic social and economic change stimulated many English folk to move to North America. In the 150-year period after 1530, largely as a result of the introduction of nutritious American crops, England's population doubled. All those additional people needed food, clothing, and other goods. The competition for goods led to high inflation, coupled with a fall in real wages as the number of workers increased. In these new economic and demographic circumstances, some English people—especially those with sizable landholdings that could produce food and clothing fibers for the growing population—substantially improved their lot. Others, particularly landless laborers and those with very small amounts of land, fell into unremitting poverty. When landowners raised rents, took over common lands previously open to use by peasants, or decided to combine small holdings into large units,

SOCIAL CHANGE IN ENGLAND

they forced tenants off the land. Consequently, geographical as well as social mobility increased, and the population of the cities swelled. London, for example, more than tripled in size by 1650, when 375,000 residents lived in its crowded buildings.

Wealthy English people reacted with alarm to what they saw as the disappearance of traditional ways of life. Steady streams of the landless and homeless filled the streets and highways. Obsessed with the problem of maintaining order, officials came to believe that England was overcrowded. They concluded that colonies established in North America could siphon off England's "surplus population," thus easing social strains at home. For similar reasons, many English people decided that they could improve their circumstances by migrating from a small, land-scarce, apparently overpopulated island to a large, land-rich, apparently empty continent and its nearby islands. Among those attracted by prospects for emigration were such younger sons of gentlemen as William Rudyerd, who were excluded from inheriting land by wealthy families' practice of primogeniture, which reserved all real estate for the eldest son. Such economic considerations were rendered even more significant in light of the second development, a major change in English religious practice.

The sixteenth century witnessed a religious transformation that eventually led large numbers of English dissenters to leave their homeland. In 1533 Henry VIII, wanting a male heir and infatuated with Anne Boleyn, sought to annul his marriage to his Spanish-born queen, Catherine of Aragón, despite nearly twenty years of marriage and the birth of a daughter. When the pope refused to approve the annulment, Henry left the Roman Catholic Church. He founded the Church of England and—with Parliament's concurrence—proclaimed himself its head. In general, English people welcomed the schism, for many had little respect for the English Catholic Church. At first the reformed Church of England differed little from Catholicism in its practices, but under Henry's daughter Elizabeth I (child of his later marriage to Anne Boleyn), new currents of religious belief that had originated on the European continent early in the sixteenth century dramatically affected the English church.

ENGLISH REFORMATION

These currents were the Protestant Reformation, led by Martin Luther, a German monk, and John Calvin, a French cleric and lawyer. Challenging the Catholic doctrine that priests were intermediaries between laypeople and God, Luther and Calvin insisted that people could interpret the Bible for themselves. That notion stimulated the spread of literacy: to understand and interpret

■ London in 1616, with London Bridge at center right. Overcrowding in the city led many observers to conclude that American colonization could remove "excess" population and provide new employment for poverty-stricken persons. The rapidly growing community of London merchants also sought to develop new sources of overseas profits. (Trustees of the British Library)

the Bible, people had to learn how to read. Both Luther and Calvin rejected Catholic rituals, denying the need for an elaborate church hierarchy. They also asserted that faith in God was the key to salvation, rather than—as Catholic teaching had it—a combination of faith and good works. Calvin went further than Luther, stressing God's omnipotence and emphasizing the need for people to submit totally to God's will.

Elizabeth I tolerated diverse forms of Christianity as long as her subjects acknowledged her authority as head of the Church of England. During her long reign (1558–1603) Calvin's ideas gained influence within the English church, and some Catholics continued to practice their faith in private. By the late sixteenth century, many English Calvinists—those who came to be called Puritans because they wanted to purify the Church of England or Separatists because they wanted to leave it entirely—believed that the English Reformation had not gone far enough. Henry had simplified the church hierarchy; they wanted to abolish it altogether. Henry had subordinated the church to the interests of the state; they wanted a church free from political interference. And the

PURITANS AND SEPARATISTS

Church of England, like the Catholic Church, continued to include all English people in its membership. Puritans and Separatists preferred a more restricted definition; they wanted to confine church membership to persons they believed to be "saved"—those God had selected for salvation before birth.

Paradoxically, though, a key article of their faith insisted that people could not know for certain if they were "saved" because mere mortals could not comprehend or affect their predestination to heaven or hell. Thus pious Puritans and Separatists daily confronted serious dilemmas: If the saved (or "elect") could not be identified with certainty, how could proper churches be constituted? If one was predestined and could not alter one's fate, why should one attend church or do good works? Puritans and Separatists dealt with the first dilemma by admitting that their judgments as to eligibility for church membership only approximated God's unknowable decisions. And they resolved the second by reasoning that God gave the elect the ability to accept salvation and to lead a good life. Therefore, even though one could not earn a place in heaven by piety and good works, such practices could indicate one's place in the ranks of the saved.

TABLE 2.2

Tudor and Stuart Monarchs of England, 1509–1649

Monarch	Reign	Relation to Predecessor
Henry VIII	1509–1547	Son
Edward VI	1547–1553	Son
Mary I	1553–1558	Half-sister
Elizabeth I	1558–1603	Half-sister
James I	1603–1625	Cousin
Charles I	1625–1649	Son

Elizabeth I's Stuart successors, her cousin James I (1603–1625) and his son Charles I (1625–1649), exhibited less tolerance for Puritans and Separatists. As Scots, they also had little respect for the traditions of representative government that had developed in England under the Tudors and their predecessors (see Table 2.2). The wealthy landowners who sat in Parliament had grown accustomed to having considerable influence on government policies, especially taxation. But James I, taking a position later endorsed by his son, publicly declared his belief in the divine right of kings. The Stuarts insisted that a monarch's power came directly from God and that his subjects had a duty to obey him. They likened the king's absolute authority to a father's authority over his children.

THE STUART MONARCHS

Both James I and Charles I believed that their authority included the power to enforce religious conformity. Because Puritans and Separatists—and the remaining English Catholics—challenged many of the most important precepts of the English church, the Stuart monarchs authorized the removal of dissenting clergymen from their pulpits. In the 1620s and 1630s some English Puritans, Separatists, and Catholics decided to move to America, where they hoped to put their religious beliefs into practice unhindered by the Stuarts or the church hierarchy. Some fled hurriedly to avoid arrest and imprisonment.

In contrast to the migrations to New Spain and New France, which were largely funded by their governments, many of the dissenters and other English people who migrated to North America and the Caribbean were financed by joint-stock companies. Stock sales funded these forerunners of modern corporations, which had been developed decades earlier as a mechanism for pooling the resources of many small investors in trading voyages. They worked well for that purpose: no one risked too much money, and investors usually received quick returns. But joint-stock companies turned out to be a poor way to finance colonies because the early settlements required enormous amounts of capital and, with rare exceptions, failed to return much immediate profit. Colonies founded by such companies consequently suffered from a chronic lack of capital and from constant tension between stockholders and colonists, who claimed they were not being adequately supported by the investors.

JOINT-STOCK COMPANIES

The Founding of Virginia

The initial impulse that led to England's first permanent colony in the Western Hemisphere came from a group of merchants and wealthy gentry. In 1606, envisioning the possibility of earning great profits by finding precious metals and opening new trade routes, the men established the Virginia Company and obtained a charter from King James I. A settlement they financed in present-day Maine soon collapsed, but a second enterprise was more successful.

In 1607 the company dispatched 104 men and boys to a region near Chesapeake Bay called Tsenacomoco by its native inhabitants. There they established the palisaded settlement called Jamestown on a swampy peninsula in a river they also named for their monarch. They quickly constructed small houses and a Church of England chapel. Ill equipped for survival in the unfamiliar environment, the colonists were afflicted by dissension and disease. Moreover, through sheer bad luck they arrived in the midst of a severe drought (now known to be the worst in the region for 1,700 years), which persisted until 1612. The lack of rainfall not only made it difficult to cultivate crops but also polluted their drinking water.

JAMESTOWN

By January 1608, only thirty-eight of the original colonists remained alive. Many of the first immigrants were gentlemen unaccustomed to working with their hands and soldiers who had fought against Spain in the Netherlands. They resisted hard labor, attempted to maintain traditional social hierarchies, and retained elaborate English dress and casual work habits despite their desperate circumstances. Such attitudes, combined with the effects of chronic malnutrition and epidemic disease, took a terrible toll. Only when Captain John Smith, one of the colony's lower-status founders, imposed military discipline on the still-resistant colonists in 1608 was Jamestown saved from collapse. But after Smith's departure the settlement experienced a severe "starving time" (the winter of 1609–1610), during which at least one colonist resorted to cannibalism. Although more settlers (including a few women and children) arrived in 1608 and 1609 and living conditions slowly improved, as late as 1624 only 1,300 of approximately 8,000 English immigrants to Virginia remained alive.

Jamestown owed its survival to the Indians of Tsenacomoco, a group of six Algonquian villages known as the Powhatan Confederacy (see Map 2.1).

POWHATAN CONFEDERACY A shrewd and powerful leader, Powhatan was aggressively consolidating his authority over some twenty-five smaller bands when the Europeans arrived. Fortunately for the colonists, Powhatan at first viewed them as potential allies. He found the English colony a reliable source of useful items such as knives and guns, which gave him a technological advantage over his Indian neighbors. In return, Powhatan's people traded their excess corn and other foodstuffs to the starving settlers. But the initially cordial relationship soon deteriorated. The Indians' crops failed during the drought, and they no longer had surpluses to exchange, though the English suspected duplicity. English colonists kidnapped Powhatan's daughter, Pocahontas, holding her as a hostage. In captivity, she agreed in 1614 to marry a colonist, John Rolfe, perhaps as a form of diplomatic alliance. She sailed with him to England, where she died in 1616 after bearing a son.

The Jamestown colony and the coastal Indians had an uneasy relationship. English and Algonquian peoples had much in common: deep religious beliefs, a lifestyle oriented around agriculture, clear political and social hierarchies, and sharply defined gender roles. Yet the English and the Powhatans themselves focused on their cultural differences, not their similarities. English men regarded Indian men as lazy because they did not cultivate crops and spent much of their time hunting (a sport, not work, in English eyes). Indian men thought English men effeminate because they did "women's work" of cultivation. In the same vein, the English believed that Algonquian women were oppressed because they did heavy field labor.

ALGONQUIAN AND ENGLISH CULTURAL DIFFERENCES

Other differences between the two cultures caused serious misunderstandings. Although both societies were hierarchical, the nature of the hierarchies differed considerably. Among East Coast Algonquians, political power and social status were not necessarily passed down through the male line. Members of the English gentry inherited their position from their fathers, and English political and military leaders tended to rule autocratically. By contrast, the authority of Algonquian leaders rested on consensus. Accustomed to the European concept of powerful kings, the English sought such figures in native villages. Often (for example, when negotiating treaties) they willfully overestimated the ability of chiefs to make independent decisions for their people.

Furthermore, Algonquians and English had very different notions of property ownership. Most Algonquian villages held their land communally. It could not be bought or sold absolutely, although certain rights to use the land (for example, for hunting or fishing) could be transferred. Many English people, in contrast, were accustomed to individual farms and to buying and selling land. The English also refused to accept the validity of Indians' claims to traditional hunting territories, insisting that only land intensively cultivated could be regarded as owned or occupied. As one colonist put it, "salvadge peoples" who "rambled" over a region without farming it could claim no "title or propertye" in the land. Ownership of such "unclaimed" property, the English believed, lay with the English monarchy, in whose name John Cabot had laid claim to North America in 1497.

Above all, the English settlers believed unwaveringly in the superiority of their civilization. Although in the early years of colonization they often anticipated living peacefully alongside Native Americans, they always assumed that they would dictate the terms of such coexistence. Like Thomas Harriot at Roanoke, they expected native peoples to adopt English customs and to convert to Christianity. They showed little respect for traditional Indian ways of life, especially when they believed their own interests were at stake. The Virginia colony's treatment of the Powhatan Confederacy in subsequent years clearly revealed that attitude.

The spread of tobacco cultivation upset the balance of power in early Virginia. In tobacco—the American crop previously introduced to Europe by the Spanish—the settlers and the Virginia Company found the salable commodity for which they had been searching. John Rolfe planted the first crop in 1611. Nine years later Virginians exported 40,000 pounds of cured leaves, and by the late 1620s shipments had jumped dramatically to 1.5 million pounds. The great tobacco boom had begun, fueled by high prices and substantial profits for planters as they responded to escalating demand from Europe and Africa. The price later fell almost as sharply as it had risen, fluctuating wildly from year to year in response to increasing supply and international competition. Nevertheless, tobacco made Virginia prosper, and the colony developed from a small outpost peopled exclusively by males into an agricultural settlement inhabited by both men and women.

TOBACCO CULTIVATION

A comparison of the portrait of Sir Walter Raleigh and his son (left), with that of an Algonquian Indian drawn by John White, from Raleigh's Roanoke expedition (right), shows a dramatic difference in standard dress styles that, for many, must have symbolized the apparent cultural gap between Europeans and Americans. Yet the fact that both men (and the young boy) were portrayed in similar stances, with "arms akimbo," demonstrated that all were high status individuals. In Europe, only aristocrats were represented in such an aggressive pose. ([Left] National Portrait Gallery, London; [right] Trustees of the British Museum)

Successful tobacco cultivation required abundant land, since the crop quickly drained soil of nutrients. Farmers soon learned that a field could produce only about three satisfactory crops before it had to lie fallow for several years to regain its fertility. Thus the once-small English settlements began to expand rapidly: eager applicants asked the Virginia Company for large land grants on both sides of the James River and its tributary streams. Lulled into a false sense of security by years of peace, Virginians established farms at some distance from one another along the riverbanks—a settlement pattern convenient for tobacco cultivation but dangerous for defense.

To attract more settlers to the colony, the Virginia Company in 1617 developed the "headright" system.

VIRGINIA COMPANY POLICIES Every new arrival paying his or her own way was promised a land grant of 50 acres; those who financed the passage of others received similar headrights for each person. To ordinary English farmers, many of whom owned little or no land, the headright system offered a powerful incentive to move to Virginia. To wealthy gentry, it promised even

more: the possibility of establishing vast agricultural enterprises worked by large numbers of laborers. Two years later, the company introduced a second reform, authorizing the landowning men of the major Virginia settlements to elect representatives to an assembly called the House of Burgesses. English landholders had long been accustomed to electing members of Parliament and controlling their own local governments; therefore, they expected the same privilege in the nation's colonies.

Opechancanough, Powhatan's brother and successor, watched the English colonists steadily encroaching

INDIAN UPRISINGS on the confederacy's lands and attempting to convert its members to Christianity. Recognizing the danger his brother had overlooked, the war leader launched coordinated attacks all along the James River on March 22, 1622. By the end of the day, 347 colonists (about one-quarter of the total) lay dead, and only a timely warning from two Christian converts saved Jamestown itself from destruction.

Virginia reeled from the blow but did not collapse. Reinforced by new shipments of men and arms from

England, the settlers attacked Opechancanough's villages. For some years an uneasy peace prevailed, but then in April 1644 Opechancanough tried one last time to repel the invaders. He failed, losing his life in the war that ensued. In 1646, survivors of the Powhatan Confederacy accepted a treaty formally subordinating them to English authority. Although they continued to live in the region, their alliance crumbled and their efforts to resist the spread of European settlement ended.

The 1622 Powhatan uprising that failed to destroy the colony succeeded in killing its parent. The Virginia Company never made any profits from the enterprise, for internal corruption and the heavy cost of supporting the settlers offset all its earnings. In 1624 James I revoked the charter, transforming Virginia into a royal colony ruled by officials he appointed. James continued the headright policy the company had adopted. Because he distrusted legislative bodies, though, James at first abolished the assembly. But Virginians protested so vigorously that by 1629 the House of Burgesses was functioning once again. Only two decades after the first permanent English settlement was planted in North America, the colonists successfully insisted on governing themselves at the local level. Thus the political structure of England's American possessions came to differ from that of New Spain, New France, and New Netherland, all of which were ruled autocratically.

Life in the Chesapeake

By the 1630s, tobacco was firmly established as the staple crop and chief source of revenue in Virginia. It quickly became just as important in the second English colony planted on Chesapeake Bay: Maryland, given by Charles I to George Calvert, first Lord Baltimore, as a personal possession (proprietorship), which was settled in 1634. (Because Virginia and Maryland both border Chesapeake Bay—see Map 2.1—they are often referred to collectively as "the Chesapeake.") Members of the Calvert family intended the colony to serve as a haven for their persecuted fellow Catholics. Cecilius Calvert, second Lord Baltimore, became the first colonizer to offer freedom of religion to all Christian settlers; he understood that protecting the Protestant majority could also ensure Catholics' rights. (The policy was codified in Maryland's Act of Religious Toleration in 1649.)

In everything but religion the two Chesapeake colonies resembled each other. In Maryland as in Virginia, tobacco planters spread out along the riverbanks, establishing isolated farms instead of towns. The region's deep, wide rivers offered dependable water transportation in an age of few and inadequate roads. Each farm or group of farms had its own wharf, where oceangoing vessels could take on or discharge cargo. Consequently, Virginia and Maryland had few towns, for their residents did not need commercial centers in order to buy and sell goods.

The planting, cultivation, and harvesting of tobacco were repetitive, time-consuming, and labor-intensive tasks. Clearing land for new fields, necessary every few years, demanded heavy labor, and undesirable shoots had to be regularly removed by hand from tobacco stalks. Above all else, then, successful Chesapeake farms required workers. But where and how could they be obtained? Nearby Indians, their numbers reduced by war and disease, could not supply these needs. Nor were enslaved Africans available: merchants could more easily and profitably sell slaves to Caribbean sugar planters. Thus only a few people of African descent, some of them free, initially trickled into the Chesapeake. By 1650 about three hundred blacks lived in Virginia—a tiny fraction of the population.

DEMAND FOR LABORERS

Chesapeake tobacco farmers thus looked primarily to England to supply their labor needs. Because of the headright system (which Maryland also adopted in 1640), a tobacco farmer anywhere in the Chesapeake could simultaneously obtain both land and labor by importing workers from England. Good management would make the process self-perpetuating: a farmer could use his profits to pay for the passage of more workers and thereby gain title to more land. Success could even bring movement into the ranks of the planter gentry that began to develop in the region.

Because men did the agricultural work in European societies, colonists assumed that field laborers should be men. Such male laborers, along with a few women, immigrated to America as indentured servants—that is, in return for their passage they contracted to work for periods ranging from four to seven years. Indentured servants accounted for 75 to 85 percent of the approximately 130,000 English immigrants to Virginia and Maryland during the seventeenth century. The rest tended to be young couples with one or two children.

Males between the ages of fifteen and twenty-four composed roughly three-quarters of the servants; only one immigrant in five or six was female. Most of these young men came from farming or laboring families, and many originated in regions of England experiencing severe social disruption. Some had already moved several times within England before relocating to America. Often they came from the middling ranks of society—what their contemporaries called the "common sort." Their youth indicated that most probably had not yet established themselves in their homeland.

For such people the Chesapeake appeared to offer good prospects. Servants who fulfilled the terms of their indentures earned "freedom dues" consisting of clothes, tools, livestock, casks of corn and tobacco, and sometimes even land. From a distance at least, America seemed to offer chances for advancement unavailable in England. Yet immigrants' lives were difficult. Servants typically worked six days a week, ten to fourteen hours a day, in a climate much warmer than England's. Their masters could discipline or sell them, and they faced severe penalties for running away. Even so, the laws did give them some protection. For example, their masters were supposed to supply them with sufficient food, clothing, and shelter, and they were not to be beaten excessively. Cruelly treated servants could turn to the courts for assistance, sometimes winning verdicts directing that they be transferred to more humane masters or released from their indentures.

CONDITIONS OF SERVITUDE

Servants and their owners alike contended with epidemic disease. Immigrants first had to survive the process the colonists called "seasoning," a bout with disease (probably malaria) that usually occurred during their first Chesapeake summer. They then often endured recurrences of malaria, along with dysentery, typhoid fever, and other illnesses. Consequently, about 40 percent of male servants did not survive long enough to become freedmen. Even young men of twenty-two who successfully weathered their seasoning could expect to live only another twenty years at best.

For those who survived the term of their indentures, though, the opportunities for advancement were real. Until the last decades of the seventeenth century, former servants often became independent farmers ("freeholders"), thereafter living a modest but comfortable existence. Some even assumed positions of political prominence such as justice of the peace or militia officer. But in the 1670s tobacco prices entered a fifty-year period of stagnation and decline. Simultaneously, good land grew increasingly scarce and expensive. In 1681 Maryland dropped its legal requirement that servants receive land as part of their freedom dues, forcing large numbers of freed servants to live for years as wage laborers or tenant farmers. By 1700 the Chesapeake was no longer the land of opportunity it once had been.

Life in the early Chesapeake was hard for everyone, regardless of sex or status. Farmers (and sometimes their wives) toiled in the fields alongside servants, laboriously clearing land, then planting and harvesting tobacco and corn. Because hogs could forage for themselves in the forests and needed little tending, Chesapeake households subsisted mainly on pork and corn, a filling diet but not sufficiently nutritious. Families supplemented this monotonous fare by eating fish, shellfish, and wildfowl, in addition to vegetables such as lettuce and peas, which they grew in small gardens. The near impossibility of preserving food for safe winter consumption magnified the health problems caused by epidemic disease. Salting, drying, and smoking, the only methods the colonists knew, did not always prevent spoilage.

STANDARD OF LIVING

Few households had many material possessions other than farm implements, bedding, and basic cooking and eating utensils. Chairs, tables, candles, and knives and forks were luxury items. Most people rose and went to bed with the sun, sat on crude benches or storage chests, and held plates or bowls in their hands while eating meat and vegetable stews with spoons. The ramshackle houses commonly had just one or two rooms. Colonists devoted their income to improving their farms, buying livestock, and purchasing more laborers instead of improving their standard of living. Rather than making items such as clothing and tools, tobacco-growing families imported necessary manufactured goods from England.

The predominance of males (see Figure 2.1), the incidence of servitude, and the high mortality rates combined to produce unusual patterns of family life. Female servants normally could not marry during their terms of indenture because masters did not want pregnancies to deprive them of workers. Many male ex-servants could not marry at all because of the scarcity of women; such men lived alone, in pairs, or as the third member of a household containing a married couple. In contrast, nearly every adult free woman in the Chesapeake married, and widows usually remarried within a few months of a husband's death. Yet because of high infant mortality and because almost all marriages were delayed by servitude or broken by death, Chesapeake women commonly reared only one to three healthy children, in contrast to English women, who normally had at least five.

CHESAPEAKE FAMILIES

Thus Chesapeake families were few, small, and short-lived. Youthful immigrants came to America as individuals free of familial control; they commonly died while their children were still young. In one Virginia county, for example, more than three-quarters of the children had lost at least one parent by the time they either married or reached age twenty-one. For the most part, then, Chesapeake men (unlike their English fathers) could not establish long-term control over their

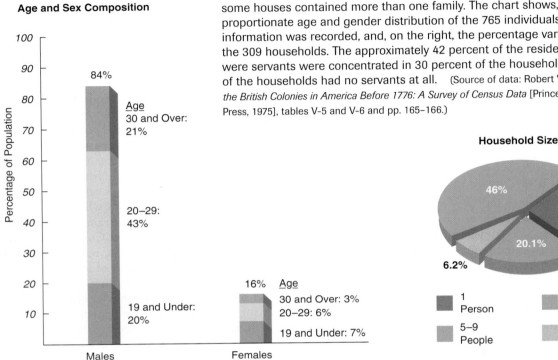

Figure 2.1 Population of Virginia, 1625

The only detailed census taken in the English mainland North American colonies during the seventeenth century was prepared in Virginia in 1625. It listed a total of 1,218 people, constituting 309 "households" and living in 278 dwellings—so some houses contained more than one family. The chart shows, on the left, the proportionate age and gender distribution of the 765 individuals for whom full information was recorded, and, on the right, the percentage variation in the sizes of the 309 households. The approximately 42 percent of the residents of the colony who were servants were concentrated in 30 percent of the households. Nearly 70 percent of the households had no servants at all. (Source of data: Robert V. Wells, *The Population of the British Colonies in America Before 1776: A Survey of Census Data* [Princeton: Princeton University Press, 1975], tables V-5 and V-6 and pp. 165–166.)

spouses or offspring. And the large number of orphaned children prompted a legal innovation: the establishment of orphans' courts to oversee the management of orphans' property and to ensure that such young people received the appropriate inheritance when they reached adulthood.

Because of the low rate of natural increase, throughout the seventeenth century immigrants composed a majority of the Chesapeake population, with important implications for regional political patterns. Most of the members of Virginia's House of Burgesses and Maryland's House of Delegates (established in 1635) were immigrants; they also dominated the governor's council, which simultaneously served as each colony's highest court, part of the legislature, and executive adviser to the governor. A cohesive, native-born ruling elite emerged only in the early eighteenth century.

Representative institutions based on the consent of the governed usually function as a major source of political stability. In the seventeenth-century Chesapeake,

CHESAPEAKE POLITICS

most property-owning white males could vote, and such freeholders chose as their legislators the local elites who seemed to be the natural leaders of their respective areas. But because most such men were immigrants lacking strong ties to one another or to the colonies, the assemblies' existence did not create political stability. Unusual demographic patterns thus contributed to the region's contentious politics.

The Founding of New England

The economic motives that prompted English people to move to the Chesapeake and Caribbean colonies also drew men and women to New England (see Map 2.2). But because Puritans organized the New England colonies, and also because of environmental factors, the northern settlements turned out very differently from their counterparts to the south. The differences became apparent even as the would-be colonists left England.

Hoping to exert control over a migration that appeared disorderly (and which included dissenters seeking

CONTRASTING
REGIONAL
DEMOGRAPHIC
PATTERNS

to flee the authority of the Church of England), royal bureaucrats in late 1634 ordered port officials in London to collect information on all travelers departing for the colonies. The resulting records for the year 1635 are a treasure trove for historians. They document the departure of 53 vessels in that year alone—20 to Virginia, 17 to New England, 8 to Barbados, 5 to St. Kitts, 2 to Bermuda, and 1 to Providence Island. On those ships sailed almost 5,000 people, with 2,000 departing for Virginia, about 1,200 for New England, and the rest for island destinations. Nearly three-fifths of all the passengers were between 15 and 24 years old, reflecting the predominance of young male servants among migrants to America.

But among those bound for New England, such youths constituted less than one-third of the total; nearly 40 percent were between ages 25 and 50, and another third were aged 14 and below. Whereas women made up just 14 percent of those going to Virginia, they composed almost 40 percent of the passengers to New England. Even from such composite figures, it is therefore evident that New Englanders often traveled in family groups. Moreover, they also brought more goods and livestock with them; ships bound for New England carried fewer passengers and considerably larger cargoes than those going elsewhere. Finally, the northern migrants also tended to travel with other people from the same regions: for example, aboard one vessel, more than half came from York; on another, nearly half came from Buckinghamshire. In short, although migrants to the Chesapeake and the islands most commonly left friends and families behind, those who moved to New England came in concert with their close associates. Their lives in North America accordingly must have been more comfortable and less lonely than that of their southern counterparts.

Among Chesapeake migrants, only the Catholics who moved to Maryland seem to have been motivated

CONTRASTING
REGIONAL
RELIGIOUS
PATTERNS

by religious concerns. Yet religion inspired many, although certainly not all, of the people who colonized New England. Puritan congregations quickly became key institutions in colonial New England, whereas neither the Church of England nor Roman Catholicism had much impact on the settlers or the early development of the Chesapeake colonies. Catholic and Anglican bishops in England paid little attention to their coreligionists in America, and Chesapeake congregations languished in the absence of

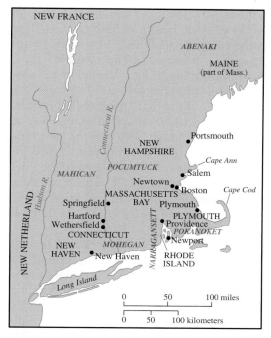

Map 2.2   New England Colonies, 1650
The most densely settled region of the mainland was New England, where English settlements and Indian villages existed side by side.

sufficient numbers of properly ordained clergymen. (For example, in 1665 an observer noted that only ten of the fifty Virginia parishes had resident clerics.) Not until the 1690s did the Church of England begin to take firmer root in Virginia; by then it had also replaced Catholicism as the established church in Maryland.

By contrast, religion constantly affected the lives of pious Puritans, who regularly reassessed the state of their souls. Many devoted themselves to self-examination and Bible study, and families prayed together each day under the guidance of the husband and father. Yet because even the most pious could never be certain that they were numbered among the elect, anxiety about their spiritual state troubled devout Puritans. That anxiety lent a special intensity to their religious beliefs and to their concern with proper behavior—their own and that of others.

Separatists who thought the Church of England too corrupt to be salvaged became the first to move to New

SEPARATISTS

England. In 1609 a Separatist congregation relocated to Leiden, in the Netherlands, where they found the freedom of worship denied them in Stuart England. But eventually the Netherlands worried them, for the nation that tolerated them also tolerated religions and behaviors they abhorred. Hoping to isolate themselves and their children from the corrupting influence of worldly temptations, these people, who came to be known as Pilgrims, received permission from the Virginia Company to colonize the northern part of its territory.

In September 1620, more than one hundred people, only thirty of them Separatists, set sail from England on the old and crowded *Mayflower*. Two months later they landed in America, but farther north than they had intended. Still, given the lateness of the season, they decided to stay where they were. Establishing their settlement on a fine harbor—the site of an Indian village wiped out by the epidemic of 1616–1618—the English people named it Plymouth.

Even before they landed, the Pilgrims had to surmount their first challenge—from the "strangers," or non-Separatists, who sailed with them to America. Because they landed outside the jurisdiction of the Virginia Company, some of the strangers questioned the authority of the colony's leaders. In response, the Mayflower Compact, signed in November 1620 on shipboard, established a "Civil Body Politic" as a temporary substitute for a charter. The male settlers elected a governor and initially made all decisions for the colony at town meetings. Later, after more towns had been founded and the population increased, Plymouth, like Virginia and Maryland, created an assembly to which the landowning male settlers elected representatives.

Mere survival also challenged the Pilgrims. Like the Jamestown settlers before them, they were poorly prepared to subsist in the new environment. Winter quickly descended, compounding their difficulties. Only half the *Mayflower*'s passengers lived to see the spring. But, again like the Virginians, the Pilgrims benefited from the political circumstances of nearby Indians.

INDIAN RELATIONS

The Pokanokets (a branch of the Wampanoags) controlled the area in which the Pilgrims settled. Their villages had suffered terrible losses in the recent epidemic, so to protect themselves from the powerful Narragansetts of the southern New England coast (who had been spared the ravages of the disease), the Pokanokets decided to ally themselves with the newcomers. In the spring of 1621, their leader, Massasoit, signed a treaty with the Pilgrims, and during the colony's first difficult years the Pokanokets supplied the English with essential

■ Some scholars now believe that this 1638 painting by the Dutch artist Adam Willaerts depicts the Plymouth colony about fifteen years after its founding. The shape of the harbor, the wooden gate, and the houses straggling up the hill all coincide with contemporary accounts of the settlement. No one believes that Willaerts himself visited Plymouth, but people returning from the colony to Holland, where the Pilgrims had lived for years before emigrating, could well have described Plymouth to him. (© J. D. Bangs, Courtesy of Leiden American Pilgrim Museum, The Netherlands)

foodstuffs. The settlers were also assisted by Squanto, an Indian who, like Malinche, served as a conduit between native peoples and Europeans. Captured by fishermen in the early 1610s and taken to Europe, Squanto had learned to speak English. Upon returning to North America, he discovered that his village had been wiped out by the great epidemic. Squanto became the Pilgrims' interpreter and a major source of information about the unfamiliar environment.

Before the 1620s ended, a group of Puritan Congregationalists (who hoped to reform the Church of England from within) launched the colonial enterprise that would come to dominate New England and would absorb Plymouth in 1691. Charles I, who became king in 1625, was more hostile to Puritans than his father had been. Under his leadership, the Church of England attempted to suppress Puritan practices, driving clergymen from their pulpits and forcing congregations to hold clandestine meetings for worship. Some Congregationalist merchants, concerned about their long-term prospects in England, sent out a body of colonists to Cape Ann (north of Cape Cod) in 1628. The following year the merchants obtained a royal charter, constituting themselves as the Massachusetts Bay Company.

MASSACHUSETTS BAY COMPANY

The new joint-stock company quickly attracted the attention of Puritans of the "middling sort" who were becoming increasingly convinced that they no longer would be able to practice their religion freely in their homeland. They remained committed to the goal of reforming the Church of England but concluded that they should pursue that aim in America. In a dramatic move, the Congregationalist merchants boldly decided to transfer the Massachusetts Bay Company's headquarters to New England. The settlers would then be answerable to no one in the mother country and would be able to handle their affairs, secular and religious, as they pleased.

The most important recruit to the new venture was John Winthrop, a member of the lesser English gentry. In October 1629, the Massachusetts Bay Company elected Winthrop as its governor. (Until his death twenty years later, he served the colony continuously in one leadership post or another.) Winthrop organized the initial segment of the great Puritan migration to America. In 1630 more than one thousand English men and women moved to Massachusetts—most of them to Boston, which soon became the largest town in English North America. By 1643 nearly twenty thousand compatriots had followed them.

GOVERNOR JOHN WINTHROP

On board the *Arbella,* en route to New England in 1630, John Winthrop preached a sermon, "A Model of Christian Charity," laying out his expectations for the new colony. Above all, he stressed the communal nature of the endeavor on which he and his fellow settlers had embarked. God, he explained, "hath so disposed of the condition of mankind as in all times some must be rich, some poor, some high and eminent in power and dignity, others mean and in subjection." But differences in status did not imply differences in worth. On the contrary: God had planned the world so that "every man might have need of other, and from hence they might be all knit more nearly together in the bond of brotherly affection." In America, Winthrop asserted, "we shall be as a city upon a hill, the eyes of all people are upon us." If the Puritans failed to carry out their "special commission" from God, "the Lord will surely break out in wrath against us."

Winthrop's was a transcendent vision. He foresaw in Puritan America a true commonwealth, a community in which each person put the good of the whole ahead of his or her private concerns. Although, as in seventeenth-century England, that society would be characterized by social inequality and clear hierarchies of status and power, Winthrop hoped that its members would live according to the precepts of Christian love. Of course, such an ideal was beyond human reach. Early New England had its share of bitter quarrels and unchristian behavior. Remarkably, though, the ideal persisted well into the third and fourth generations of the immigrants' descendants.

The Puritans expressed their communal ideal chiefly in the doctrine of the covenant. They believed God had made a covenant—that is, an agreement or contract—with them when they were chosen for the special mission

■ An English beaver felt hat, made by combining American beaver fur with wool and other fibers. Men and women in England and on the European continent wore such fashionable items, thus creating the insatiable demand for pelts that fueled the fur trade for many years.
(The Pilgrim Society, Plymouth, Massachusetts)

COVENANT
IDEAL

to America. In turn they covenanted with one another, promising to work together toward their goals. The founders of churches, towns, and even colonies in Anglo-America often drafted formal documents setting forth the principles on which their institutions would be based. The Pilgrims' Mayflower Compact was a covenant; so too was the Fundamental Orders of Connecticut (1639), which laid down the basic law for the settlements established along the Connecticut River valley in 1636 and thereafter.

The leaders of Massachusetts Bay likewise transformed their original joint-stock company charter into the basis for a covenanted community based on mutual consent. Under strong and persistent pressure from landowning male settlers, they gradually changed the General Court—officially the company's small governing body—into a colonial legislature. They also granted the status of freeman, or voting member of the company, to all property-owning adult male church members. Like the Virginia men who won the reestablishment of the House of Burgesses after the king had abolished it, the male residents of Massachusetts insisted that their reluctant leaders allow them a greater voice in their government. Less than two decades after the first large group of Puritans arrived in Massachusetts Bay, the colony had a functioning system of self-government composed of a governor and a two-house legislature. The General Court also established a judicial system modeled on England's, although the laws they adopted differed from those of their homeland (see page 55).

The colony's method of distributing land helped to further the communal ideal. Unlike Virginia and Maryland, where individual applicants acquired headrights and sited their farms separately, in Massachusetts groups of men—often from the same region of England—applied together to the General Court for grants of land on which to establish towns (novel governance units that did not exist in England). The men receiving such a grant determined how the land would be distributed. Understandably, the grantees copied the villages whence they had come. First they laid out lots for houses and a church. Then they gave each family parcels of land scattered around the town center: a pasture here, a woodlot there, an arable field elsewhere. They reserved the best and largest plots for the most distinguished among them (including the minister). People who had been low on the social scale in England received much smaller and less desirable allotments. Still, every man and even a few single women obtained land, thus sharply differentiating these villages from their English counterparts.

NEW ENGLAND
TOWNS

Thus New England settlements initially tended to be more compact than those of the Chesapeake. Town centers developed quickly, evolving in three distinctly different ways. Some, chiefly isolated agricultural settlements in the interior, tried to sustain Winthrop's vision of harmonious community life based on diversified family farms. A second group, the coastal towns like Boston and Salem, became bustling seaports, serving as focal points for trade and places of entry for thousands of new immigrants. The third category, commercialized agricultural towns, grew up in the Connecticut River valley, where easy water transportation made it possible for farmers to sell surplus goods readily. In Springfield, Massachusetts, for example, the merchant-entrepreneur William Pynchon and his son John began as fur traders and ended as large landowners with thousands of acres. Even in New England, then, the entrepreneurial spirit characteristic of the Chesapeake found some room for expression.

When migrants began to move beyond the territorial limits of the Massachusetts Bay colony into Connecticut (1636), New Haven (1638), and New Hampshire (1638), the same pattern of land grants persisted. (Only Maine, with coastal regions thinly populated by fishermen and their families, deviated from the standard practice.) The migration to the Connecticut valley ended the Puritans' relative freedom from clashes with nearby Indians. The first English people in the valley moved there from Massachusetts Bay under the direction of their minister, Thomas Hooker. Although their new settlements were remote from other English towns, the wide river promised ready access to the ocean. The site had just one problem: it fell within the territory controlled by the powerful Pequots.

INTERNAL
MIGRATION

The Pequots' dominance stemmed from their role as primary middlemen in the trade between New England Indians and the Dutch in New Netherland. The arrival of English settlers signaled the end of the Pequots' power over such regional trading networks, for previously subordinate bands could now trade directly with Europeans. Clashes between Pequots and English colonists began even before the establishment of settlements in the Connecticut valley, but their founding tipped the balance toward war. The Pequots tried without success to enlist other Indians in resisting English expansion. After two English traders were killed (not by Pequots), the English raided a Pequot village. In return, the Pequots attacked the new town of Wethersfield in April 1637, killing nine and capturing two. To retaliate, a Massachusetts Bay ex-

PEQUOT WAR

pedition the following month attacked and burned the main Pequot town on the Mystic River. The Englishmen and their Narragansett allies slaughtered at least four hundred Pequots, mostly women and children, capturing and enslaving many of the survivors.

For the next thirty years, New England Indians accommodated themselves to the spread of European settlement. They traded with the newcomers and sometimes worked for them, but for the most part they resisted acculturation or incorporation into English society. Native Americans persisted in using traditional farming methods, which did not employ plows or fences, and women rather than men continued to be the chief cultivators. When Indian men learned "European" trades in order to survive, they chose those—like broom making, basket weaving, and shingle splitting—that most nearly accorded with their customary occupations and ensured both independence and income. The one European practice they adopted was keeping livestock, for domesticated animals provided excellent sources of meat once earlier hunting territories had been turned into English farms and wild game had consequently disappeared.

Although the official seal of the Massachusetts Bay colony showed an Indian crying "Come over and help

JOHN ELIOT'S PRAYING TOWNS

us," most colonists showed little interest in converting the Algonquians to Christianity. Only a few Massachusetts clerics, most notably John Eliot, seriously undertook missionary activities. Eliot insisted that converts reside in towns, farm the land in English fashion, assume English names, wear European-style clothing and shoes, cut their hair, and stop observing a wide range of their own customs. Since Eliot demanded a total cultural transformation from his adherents—on the theory that Indians could not be properly Christianized unless they were also "civilized"—he understandably met with little success. At the peak of Eliot's efforts, only eleven hundred Indians (out of many thousands) lived in the fourteen "Praying Towns" he established, and just 10 percent of those town residents had been formally baptized.

The Jesuits' successful missions in New France contrasted sharply with the Puritans' failure to win many

MISSIONARY ACTIVITIES COMPARED

converts and the Franciscans' mixed results in New Mexico and Florida. Catholicism had several advantages, more fully exploited by Jesuits than Franciscans. The Catholic Church employed beautiful ceremonies, instructed converts that through good works they could help to earn their own

■ Among John Eliot's principal converts to Christianity was a young Native American named Daniel Takawampbartis. Ordained as a minister, he served at the head of the Indian congregation at Natick, Massachusetts, a "Praying Town," until his death in 1716. Members of his congregation made this desk for him in about 1677, incorporating elements of English design (brass pulls), Native American motifs (incised lines), and uniquely American hooved feet. The top, a hinged box, is intended to hold a Bible.   (The Morse Institute, Natick, Massachusetts. Photo by Mark Sexton of the Peabody Essex Museum, Salem)

salvation, and offered Indian women an inspiring role model—the Virgin Mary. In Montreal and Quebec but not in New Mexico, communities of nuns taught Indian women and children and ministered to their needs. Furthermore, the few French colonists on the St. Lawrence did not alienate potential converts by encroaching steadily on their lands (as did New Englanders) or by demanding labor tribute (as did New Mexicans). Perhaps most important, Jesuits recognized that Christian beliefs could be compatible with Native American culture. Unlike Puritans and Franciscans, Jesuits accepted converts who did not wholly adopt European styles of life.

What attracted Indians to these religious ideas? Conversion often alienated new Christians (both Catholic and Puritan) from their relatives and traditions—a likely outcome that must have caused many potential converts great mortality among the Indians," he noted in his diary in 1633. "Divers of them, in their sickness, confessed that the Englishmen's God was a good God; and that if they recovered, they would serve him." But most did not recover: in January 1634 an English scout reported that smallpox had spread "as far as any Indian plantation was known to the west." By July, Winthrop observed that most of the Indians within a 300-mile radius of Boston had died of the disease. Therefore, he declared with satisfaction, "the Lord hath cleared our title to what we possess."

Life in New England

New England's colonizers adopted lifestyles that differed considerably from those of both their Indian neighbors and their counterparts in the Chesapeake. Algonquian bands usually moved four or five times each year to take full advantage of their environment. In spring, women planted the fields, but once crops were established, they did not need regular attention for several months. Villages then divided into small groups, women gathering wild foods and men hunting and fishing. The villagers returned to their fields for harvest, then separated again for fall hunting. Finally, the people wintered together in a sheltered spot before returning to the fields to start the cycle anew the following spring.

Unlike the mobile Algonquians, English people lived year-round in the same location. And unlike residents of the Chesapeake, New Englanders constructed sturdy dwellings intended to last. (Many still survive to this day.) They used the same fields again and again, believing it was less arduous to employ manure as fertilizer than to clear new fields every few years. Furthermore, they fenced their croplands to prevent them from being overrun by the cattle, sheep, and hogs that were their chief sources of meat. Animal crowding rather than human crowding caused New Englanders to spread out across the countryside; all their livestock constantly needed more pasturage.

Because Puritans commonly moved to America in family groups, the age range in early New England was wide; and because many more women *NEW ENGLAND* migrated to New England than to the *FAMILIES* tobacco colonies, the population could immediately begin to reproduce itself. Lacking such tropical diseases as malaria, New England was also much healthier than the Chesapeake. Once Puritan settlements had survived the difficult first few years

■ In 1664 an eight-year-old girl, Elizabeth Eggington, became the subject of the earliest known dated New England painting. Her mother died shortly after her birth, perhaps because of childbirth complications; the girl's rich clothing, elaborate jewelry, and feather fan not only reveal her family's wealth but also suggest that she was much loved by her father, a merchant and ship captain. Unfortunately, Elizabeth died about the time this portrait was painted; perhaps it—like some other colonial portraits of young children—was actually painted after her death to memorialize her. (Wadsworth Atheneum, Hartford. Gift of Mrs. Walter H. Clark. Endowed by her daughter, Mrs. Thomas L. Archibald)

to think twice about making such a commitment. But surely many hoped to use the Europeans' religion as a means of coping with the dramatic changes the intruders had wrought. The combination of disease, alcohol, new trading patterns, and loss of territory disrupted customary ways of life to an unprecedented extent. Shamans had little success in restoring traditional ways. Many Indians must have concluded that the Europeans' own ideas could provide the key to survival in the new circumstances.

John Winthrop's description of a great smallpox epidemic that swept through southern New England in the early 1630s reveals the relationship among smallpox, conversion to Christianity, and English land claims. "A and established self-sufficiency in foodstuffs, New England proved to be even healthier than the mother country. Adult male migrants to the Chesapeake lost about ten years from their English life expectancy of fifty to fifty-five years; their Massachusetts counterparts gained five or more years.

Consequently, while Chesapeake population patterns gave rise to families that were few in number, small in size, and transitory, the demographic characteristics of New England made families there numerous, large, and long-lived. In New England most men married; immigrant women married young (at age twenty, on the average); and marriages lasted longer and produced more children, who were more likely to live to maturity. If seventeenth-century Chesapeake women could expect to rear one to three healthy children, New England women could anticipate raising five to seven.

The nature of the population had other major implications for family life. New England in effect created grandparents, since in England people rarely lived long enough to know their children's children. And whereas early Chesapeake parents commonly died before their children married, New England parents exercised a good deal of control over their adult offspring. Young men could not marry without acreage to cultivate, and because of the communal land-grant system they had to depend on their fathers to give them that land. Daughters, too, needed a dowry of household goods supplied by their parents. Yet parents relied on their children's labor and often seemed reluctant to see them marry and start their own households. These needs at times led to conflict between the generations. On the whole, though, children seem to have obeyed their parents' wishes, for they had few alternatives.

Another important difference lay in the influence of religion on New Englanders' lives. Puritans controlled the governments of Massachusetts Bay, Plymouth, Connecticut, and the other early northern colonies. Congregationalism was the only officially recognized religion; except in Rhode Island, founded by dissenters from Massachusetts, members of other sects had no freedom of worship. Some non-Puritans voted in town meetings, but in Massachusetts Bay and New Haven, church membership was a prerequisite for voting in colony elections. All the early colonies taxed residents to build meetinghouses and pay ministers' salaries, but only in New England were provisions of criminal codes based on the Old Testament. Massachusetts's first bodies of law (1641 and 1648) incorporated regulations drawn from scriptures; New Haven, Plymouth, New Hampshire, and

IMPACT OF RELIGION

Connecticut later copied those codes. All colonists were required to attend religious services, whether or not they were church members, and people who expressed contempt for ministers or their preaching could be punished with fines or whippings.

The Puritan colonies attempted to enforce strict codes of moral conduct. Colonists there were frequently tried for drunkenness, card playing, even idleness. Couples who had sex during their engagement—as revealed by the birth of a baby less than nine months after their wedding—were fined and publicly humiliated. (Maryland, by contrast, did not penalize premarital pregnancy, only bastardy.) More harshly treated were men—and a handful of women—who engaged in behaviors that today would be called homosexual. (The term did not then exist, nor were some people thought to be more likely than others to perform such acts.) Several men who had consenting same-sex relationships were hanged, as were other men suspected of bestiality (sex with animals). Executions for such offenses were far more common in New England than in the Chesapeake, even though men in the two regions probably behaved similarly.

In New England, church and state were thus intertwined to a greater extent than in the Chesapeake. Puritans objected to secular interference in religious affairs but at the same time expected the church to influence the conduct of politics and the affairs of society. They also believed that the state was obliged to support and protect the one true church—theirs. As a result, although they came to America seeking freedom to worship as they pleased, they saw no contradiction in refusing to grant that freedom to others.

Roger Williams, a Separatist who immigrated to Massachusetts Bay in 1631, quickly ran afoul of that Puritan orthodoxy. He told his fellow settlers that the king of England had no right to grant them land already occupied by Indians, that church and state should be kept entirely separate, and that Puritans should not impose their religious beliefs on others. Because Puritan leaders placed a heavy emphasis on achieving consensus in both religion and politics, they could not long tolerate significant dissent. In October 1635, the Massachusetts General Court tried Williams for challenging the validity of the colony's charter and for maintaining that New England Congregationalists had not separated themselves, their churches, or their polity sufficiently from England's corrupt institutions and practices.

ROGER WILLIAMS

Convicted and banished, Williams journeyed in early 1636 to the head of Narragansett Bay, where he founded the town of Providence on land he obtained from the

Narragansetts and Wampanoags. Because Williams believed that government should not interfere with religion in any way, Providence and other towns in what became Rhode Island adopted a policy of tolerating all religions, including Judaism. Along with Maryland the tiny colony founded by Williams thus presaged the religious freedom that eventually became one of the hallmarks of the United States.

A dissenter who presented a more sustained challenge to Bay Colony leaders was Mistress Anne Marbury Hutchinson. (The title *Mistress* re-

ANNE
HUTCHINSON

vealed her high status.) A skilled medical practitioner popular with the women of Boston, she greatly admired John Cotton, a minister who stressed the covenant of grace, or God's free gift of salvation to unworthy human beings. By contrast, most Massachusetts clerics emphasized the need for Puritans to engage in good works, study, and reflection in preparation for receiving God's grace. (In its most extreme form, such a doctrine could verge on the covenant of works, or the idea that people could earn their salvation.) After spreading her ideas for months in the context of gatherings at childbirths—when no men were present—Mistress Hutchinson began holding women's meetings in her home to discuss Cotton's sermons. She emphasized the covenant of grace more than did Cotton himself, and she even adopted the belief that the elect could be assured of salvation and communicate directly with God. Such ideas had an immense appeal for Puritans. Anne Hutchinson offered them certainty of salvation instead of a state of constant anxiety. Her approach also lessened the importance of the institutional church and its ministers.

Thus Hutchinson's ideas posed a dangerous threat to Puritan orthodoxy. So in November 1637, officials charged her with having maligned the colony's ministers by accusing them of preaching the covenant of works. For two days she defended herself cleverly, matching scriptural references and wits with John Winthrop himself. But then Anne Hutchinson triumphantly and boldly declared that God had spoken to her directly, explaining that he would curse the Puritans' descendants for generations if they harmed her. That assertion assured her banishment, for what member of the court could acknowledge the legitimacy of such a revelation? After she had also been excommunicated from the church, she and her family, along with some faithful followers, were exiled to Rhode Island in 1638. Several years later, after she moved to New Netherland, she and most of her children were killed by Indians.

The authorities in Massachusetts Bay perceived Anne Hutchinson as doubly dangerous to the existing order: she threatened not only religious orthodoxy but also traditional gender roles. Puritans believed in the equality before God of all souls, including those of women, but they considered actual women (as distinct from their spiritual selves) inferior to men. Christians had long followed Saint Paul's dictum that women should keep silent in church and submit to their husbands. Mistress Hutchinson did neither. The magistrates' comments during her trial reveal that they were almost as outraged by her "masculine" behavior as by her religious beliefs. Winthrop charged her with having set wife against husband, since so many of her followers were women. A minister at her church trial told her bluntly: "You have stept out of your place, you have rather bine a Husband than a Wife and a preacher than a Hearer; and a Magistrate than a Subject."

The New England authorities' reaction to Anne Hutchinson reveals the depth of their adherence to European gender-role concepts. To them, an orderly society required the submission of wives to husbands as well as the obedience of subjects to rulers and ordinary folk to gentry. English people intended to change many aspects of their lives by colonizing North America, but not the sexual division of labor, the assumption of male superiority, or the maintenance of social hierarchies.

Summary

By the middle of the seventeenth century, Europeans had come to North America and the Caribbean to stay, a fact that signaled major changes for the peoples of both hemispheres. Europeans had indelibly altered not only their own lives but also those of native peoples. Europeans killed Indians with their weapons and diseases and had but limited success in converting them to Christian sects. Contacts with indigenous peoples taught Europeans to eat new foods, speak new languages, and recognize—however reluctantly—the persistence of other cultural patterns. The prosperity and even survival of many of the European colonies depended heavily on the cultivation of American crops (maize and tobacco) and an Asian crop (sugar), thus attesting to the importance of post-Columbian ecological change.

Political rivalries once confined to Europe spread around the globe, as England, Spain, Portugal, France, and the Netherlands vied for control of the peoples and resources of Asia, Africa, and the Americas. In America, Spaniards reaped the benefits of their South and Central American gold and silver mines, while French people earned their primary profits from Indian trade (in

Canada) and cultivating sugar (in the Caribbean). Sugar also enriched the Portuguese. The Dutch, by contrast, concentrated on commerce—trading in furs and sugar as well as carrying human cargoes of enslaved Africans to South America and the Caribbean.

Although the English colonies, too, at first sought to rely on trade, they quickly took another form altogether when so many English people of the "middling sort" decided to migrate to North America. To a greater extent than their European counterparts, the English transferred the society and politics of their homeland to a new environment. Their sheer numbers, coupled with their need for vast quantities of land on which to grow their crops and raise their livestock, inevitably brought them into conflict with their Indian neighbors. New England and the Chesapeake differed in the sex ratio and age range of their immigrant populations, in the nature of their developing economies, in their settlement patterns, and in the impact of religious beliefs on their settlers' lives. Yet they resembled each other in the conflicts their expansion engendered. In the years to come, both regions would become embroiled in increasingly fierce rivalries besetting the European powers. Those rivalries would continue to affect Americans of all races until after the mid-eighteenth century, when France and England fought the greatest war yet known, and the Anglo-American colonies won their independence.

LEGACY FOR A PEOPLE AND A NATION
The Foxwoods Casino and the Mashantucket Pequot Museum

In 1992 the Mashantucket Pequots opened the enormously successful Foxwoods Resort Casino on their small reservation in southeastern Connecticut. Just six years later, in August 1998, the Pequots proudly inaugurated a new museum (built with some of their substantial profits) presenting their people's story, meticulously researched by historians and archaeologists. Both developments surprised many Americans, who associated Indians only with territories west of the Mississippi and did not realize that American Indians still lived in New England. The existence of the Pequots was particularly startling, because histories

had long recorded that the nation was destroyed in the Pequot War of 1637.

Survivors of the Mystic River massacre had regrouped in the Mashantucket swamps, building lives as farmers, laborers, and craftspeople. Some left the area, finding work on whaling vessels or eventually migrating to Wisconsin. But a few Pequots remained— the 1910 census, the source today for determining Pequot tribal membership, counted sixty-six residents of a reservation just 213 acres in size. By the 1970s, the residents had been reduced to two, and the state of Connecticut threatened to turn the reservation into a park. But an elder, Elizabeth George, persuaded several hundred people tracing descent from those listed in 1910 to return to live on the reservation. In 1983 the determined Pequots won formal federal recognition, and in turn that allowed them to build the profitable casino, a hotel, and several restaurants, and to begin purchasing more land.

Now the museum introduces the history of the Pequots and of eastern Algonquian peoples to hundreds of thousands of visitors each year. At its heart is a recreation of a Pequot village as it would have looked shortly before Europeans first arrived on Connecticut's shores, complete with sounds and smells controlled by state-of-the-art computers. Exhibits detail the origins of the Pequot War, and a film narrates the tale of the massacre. Furthermore, excavations nearby continue to uncover new evidence about the overlooked history of these indomitable descendants of America's early residents.

The Pequots' success has helped to embolden other eastern Algonquian nations—for example, Wampanoags and Mashpees—to reassert publicly their long-suppressed Indian identities. The Pequot people's dedication to preserving their culture and reaffirming their history has created a remarkable legacy for the nation.

The **history companion** powered by Eduspace®

Your primary source for interactive quizzes, exercises, and more to help you learn efficiently.

http://history.college.hmco.com/students

Why why should the world be minding
Therein a World of Evils Finding. Farewell thy James
Then Farewell World: Farewell thy Wars
thy foes, thy Tales, thy Wiles, thy Snares.
Truly Sounds Retreat: I am not sorye.
The Eternall Drawes to him my heart
By faith (which can my Foes Subvert)
Crowne me (after grace) with Glory. ʃ

NORTH AMERICA IN THE ATLANTIC WORLD 1640–1720

The *Seaflower*, Captain Thomas Smith, master, lay at anchor in Boston harbor in early September 1676, awaiting official documents signed by Governor John Leverett of Massachusetts and his Plymouth counterpart, Josiah Winslow. Like other mariners of the period, Smith expected to sell the cargo in his hold in the West Indies. But that cargo differed from most: it comprised human beings, nearly two hundred "heathen Malefactors—men, women, and Children."

The certificates from the governors, dated September 12, explained "To all People" the origins of Captain Smith's human cargo: "Philip an heathen Sachem . . . with others his wicked complices and abettors have treacherously and perfidiously rebelled against" these colonies. "By due and legall procedure" the captives on board the *Seaflower* were "Sentenced & condemned to perpetuall Servitude" as punishment for their "inhumane and barbarous crueltys murder, outrages and vilainies." The Pokanoket leader King Philip (called Metacom at birth and later renamed "Philip" by New Englanders) had been killed a month earlier in the war that bore his name. His captured wife and young son subsequently languished for months in a Boston jail; her fate is unknown, but the boy seems to have been sold into slavery, along with many shiploads of Philip's followers.

Only one prominent New Englander objected on moral grounds to the policy of selling the vanquished Algonquians into West Indian slavery. The Reverend John Eliot (see page 53) reminded the authorities that the Bay colony's charter called for the conversion of Indians, "not theire exstirpation." The colonists had a solemn duty, he contended, to "inlarge the kingdom of Jesus Christ"; "to sell them away for slaves, is to hinder the inlargement of his kingdom." If the Indians deserved to die, then "godly governors" should ensure that

◀ Captain Thomas Smith, a Boston mariner, painted this remarkable self-portrait in the late seventeenth century. It links his sailing career—illustrated in the background battle scene, which is thought to represent a combined Anglo-Dutch assault on a North African fort in 1670—with his pious Puritan faith. The skull under his hand serves to remind viewers of the brevity of life, which the poem underscores. "Why, why should I the World be minding?" the poet asks, looking forward to a future in which "The Eternall" would "Crowne me (after Grace) with Glory." (Worcester Art Museum, Worcester, Massachusetts, Museum purchase)

CHRONOLOGY

1642–46 • English Civil War

1649 • Charles I executed

1651 • First Navigation Act passed to regulate colonial trade

1660 • Stuarts restored to throne
• Charles II becomes king

1663 • Carolina chartered

1664 • English conquer New Netherland
• New York founded
• New Jersey established

1670s • Marquette, Jolliet, and La Salle explore the Great Lakes and Mississippi valley for France

1675–78 • King Philip's War devastates New England

1676 • Bacon's Rebellion disrupts Virginia government
• Jamestown destroyed

1680–1700 • Pueblo revolt temporarily drives Spaniards from New Mexico

1681 • Pennsylvania chartered

1685 • James II becomes king

1686–89 • Dominion of New England established, superseding all charters of colonies from Maine to New Jersey

1688–89 • James II deposed in Glorious Revolution
• William and Mary ascend throne

1688–99 • King William's War fought on northern New England frontier

1692 • Witchcraft crisis in Salem; nineteen executions result

1696 • Board of Trade and Plantations established to coordinate English colonial administration

1701 • Iroquois adopt neutrality policy toward France and England

1702–13 • Queen Anne's War fought by French and English

1711–13 • Tuscarora War (North Carolina) leads to capture or migration of most Tuscaroras

1715 • Yamasee War nearly destroys South Carolina

1718 • New Orleans founded in French Louisiana

they died "penitently," rather than depriving them of "all meanes of grace" by selling them as slaves. Not even Eliot, then, argued against enslavement itself, nor did he deny that the captured Algonquians deserved punishment. Rather, he believed that the chosen penalty would subvert God's plan for Massachusetts.

What the pious Captain Thomas Smith (whose self-portrait is reproduced on page 58) thought about his human cargo is unknown. The *Seaflower* arrived in Jamaica in November, and perhaps he disposed of some of the captives there. Eliot learned from a correspondent seven years later that a few enslaved Algonquians had ended up in Tangier (in modern Morocco) because so many countries had turned away the vessels carrying them. Some, it is now known, were carried to the tiny island of St. David's, part of Bermuda. Derided by other Bermudans as "Mohawks" (a generic term for "Indian" in the seventeenth century), they lived almost wholly isolated from other island residents until World War II. But they preserved in their oral histories the tale of New England Indian ancestry, and in the summer of 2002 were happily reunited with Wampanoags visiting from Massachusetts.

The tale of Thomas Smith and the *Seaflower*'s human cargo illustrates not only the English colonists' willingness to enslave "heathen" peoples and their increasingly contentious relationship with Native Americans, but also the participation of the mainland colonies in a growing international network. North America, like England itself, was becoming embedded in a worldwide matrix of trade and warfare. The web woven by oceangoing vessels—once composed of only a few strands spun by Columbus and his successors—now crisscrossed the globe, carrying European goods to America and Africa, West Indian sugar to New England and Europe, Africans to the Americas, and New England fish and wood products—and occasionally Indian slaves—to the Caribbean. Formerly tiny outposts, the North American colonies expanded their territorial claims and diversified their economies after the mid-seventeenth century.

Three developments shaped life in the mainland English colonies between 1640 and 1720: the expansion of slavery, especially in the southern coastal regions; changes in the colonies' political and economic relationships with England; and escalating conflicts with Indians and other European colonies in North America.

The explosive growth of the slave trade significantly altered the Anglo-American economy. Carrying human cargoes paid off handsomely, as many mariners and ship owners learned. Planters who could afford to buy slaves also reaped huge profits. At first primarily encompassing Indians and already enslaved Africans from the Caribbean, the trade soon came to focus on cargoes brought to the Americas directly from Africa. The arrival of large numbers of West African peoples dramatically reshaped colonial society and fueled the international trading system.

The burgeoning North American economy, invigorated by the arrival of so many laborers, attracted new attention from colonial administrators. Especially after the Stuarts had been restored to the throne in 1660 (having lost it for a time because of the English Civil War), London bureaucrats attempted to supervise the American settlements more effectively and to ensure that the mother country benefited from their economic growth. By the early eighteenth century, following three decades of upheaval, a new stability characterized colonial political institutions.

Neither English colonists nor London administrators could ignore other peoples living on the North American continent. As English settlements expanded, they came into violent conflict not only with powerful Indian nations but also with the Dutch, the Spanish, and especially the French. Moreover, all the European colonies confronted significant crises during the decade of the 1670s. By 1720, war—between Europeans and Indians, among Europeans, and among Indians allied with different colonial powers—had become an all-too-familiar feature of American life. No longer isolated from each other or from Europe, the people and products of the North American colonies had become integral to the world trading system and inextricably enmeshed in its conflicts. ∎

The Growth
of Anglo-American Settlements

etween 1642 and 1646 civil war between supporters of King Charles I and the Puritan-dominated Parliament engulfed the colonists' English homeland. Parliament triumphed, leading to the execution of the king in 1649 and interim rule by the parliamentary army's leader, Oliver Cromwell, during the so-called

TABLE 3.1		
Restored Stuart Monarchs of England, 1660–1714		
Monarch	**Reign**	**Relation to Predecessor**
Charles II	1660–1685	Son
James II	1685–1688	Brother
Mary	1688–1694	Daughter
William	1688–1702	Son-in-law
Anne	1702–1714	Sister, sister-in-law

Commonwealth period. But after Cromwell's death Parliament decided to restore the monarchy if Charles I's son and heir agreed to restrictions on his authority. Charles II did so, and the Stuarts were returned to the throne in 1660 (see Table 3.1). The new king subsequently rewarded nobles and others who had supported him during the Civil War with huge tracts of land on the North American mainland. The colonies thereby established made up six of the thirteen polities that eventually would form the American nation: New York, New Jersey, Pennsylvania (including Delaware), and North and South Carolina (see Map 3.1). Collectively, these became known as the Restoration colonies because they were created by the restored Stuart monarchy. All were proprietorships; in each of them, as in Maryland, one man or several men held title to the soil and controlled the government.

Charles's younger brother James, the duke of York, quickly benefited from his brother's generosity. In 1664,

NEW YORK acting as though the Dutch colony of New Netherland did not exist, Charles II gave James the region between the Connecticut and Delaware Rivers, including the Hudson valley and Long Island. James immediately organized an invasion fleet. In August James's warships anchored off Manhattan Island and demanded New Netherland's surrender. The colony complied without resistance. Although in 1672 the Netherlands briefly retook the colony during a later Anglo-Dutch war, the Dutch permanently ceded the province in 1674.

Thus James acquired a heterogeneous possession, which he renamed New York (see Table 3.2). In 1664 a significant minority of English people (mostly Puritan New Englanders who had moved to Long Island) already lived there, along with the Dutch and sizable numbers of Indians, Africans, Germans, French-speaking Walloons (from the southern part of modern Belgium), Scandinavians, and a smattering of other European peoples. The Dutch West India Company, the world's greatest

Map 3.1   The Anglo-American Colonies in the Early Eighteenth Century

By the early eighteenth century, the English colonies nominally dominated the Atlantic coastline of North America. But the colonies' formal boundary lines are deceiving because the western reaches of each colony were still largely unfamiliar to Europeans and because much of the land was still inhabited by Native Americans.

TABLE 3.2

The Founding of English Colonies in North America, 1664–1681

Colony	Founder(s)	Date	Basis of Economy
New York (formerly New Netherland)	James, duke of York	1664	Farming, fur trading
New Jersey	Sir George Carteret, John Lord Berkeley	1664	Farming
North Carolina	Carolina proprietors	1665	Tobacco, forest products
South Carolina	Carolina proprietors	1670	Rice, indigo
Pennsylvania (incl. Delaware)	William Penn	1681	Farming

slave-trading power at midcentury (see page 77), had actively imported slaves into the colony, intending some for resale in the Chesapeake. Many, though, remained in New Netherland as laborers; at the time of the English conquest, almost one-fifth of Manhattan's approximately fifteen hundred free and enslaved inhabitants were of African descent. Slaves then made up a higher proportion of New York's urban population than of the Chesapeake's rural people.

Recognizing the population's diversity, James's representatives moved cautiously in their efforts to establish English authority. The Duke's Laws, a legal code proclaimed in 1665, applied solely to the English settlements on Long Island, only later being extended to the rest of the colony. James's policies initially maintained Dutch forms of local government, confirmed Dutch land titles, and allowed Dutch residents to maintain customary legal practices. Each town was permitted to decide which church (Dutch Reformed, Congregational, or Church of England) to support with its tax revenues. Much to the dismay of English residents, the Duke's Laws made no provision for a representative assembly. Like other Stu-

arts, James distrusted legislative bodies, and not until 1683 did he agree to the colonists' requests for an elected legislature. Before then, an autocratic governor ruled New York.

The English takeover thus had little immediate effect on the colony. Its population grew slowly, barely reaching eighteen thousand by the time of the first English census in 1698. Until the second decade of the eighteenth century, New York City remained a commercial backwater within the orbit of Boston.

The English conquest brought so little change to New York primarily because the duke of York in 1664 regranted the land between the Hudson

NEW JERSEY and Delaware Rivers—East and West Jersey—to his friends Sir George Carteret and John Lord Berkeley. That grant left the duke's own colony hemmed in between Connecticut to the east and the Jerseys to the west and south, depriving it of much fertile land and hindering its economic growth. He also failed to promote migration. Meanwhile, the Jersey proprietors acted rapidly to attract settlers, promising generous land grants, limited freedom of

■ About 1650 a Dutch artist produced this copper engraving of New Amsterdam. Dominated by a prominent windmill, tall government buildings, and European-style row houses, the small community closely resembled towns in the Netherlands. Note the many contrasts to the view of Plymouth on page 50.   (Museum of the City of New York. Gift of Dr. N. Sulzberber)

religion, and—without authorization from the Crown—a representative assembly. In response, large numbers of Puritan New Englanders migrated southward to the Jerseys, along with some Barbadians and Dutch New Yorkers. New Jersey grew quickly; in 1726, at the time of its first census as a united colony, it had 32,500 inhabitants, only 8,000 fewer than New York.

Within twenty years, Berkeley and Carteret sold their interests in the Jerseys to separate groups of investors. The purchasers of all of Carteret's share (West Jersey) and portions of Berkeley's (East Jersey) were members of the Society of Friends, also called Quakers. That new, small sect rejected earthly and religious hierarchies. Quakers believed that anyone could be saved by directly receiving God's "inner light" and that all people were equal in God's sight. With no formally trained clergy, Quakers allowed anyone, male or female, to speak in meetings or become a "public Friend" and travel to spread God's word. The Quaker message of radical egalitarianism was not welcome in the hierarchical society of seventeenth-century England or the colonies, and Quakers encountered persecution every-where. Mary Dyer—who had followed Anne Hutchinson into exile—became a Quaker, returned to Boston as a missionary, and was hanged in 1660 (along with several men) for preaching Quaker doctrines.

The Quakers obtained their own colony in 1681, when Charles II granted the region between Maryland and New York to his close friend William Penn, a prominent member of the sect. Penn was then thirty-seven years old; he held the colony as a personal proprietorship, one that earned profits for his descendants until the American Revolution. Even so, Penn, like the Roman Catholic Calverts of Maryland before him, saw his province not merely as a source of revenue but also as a haven for persecuted coreligionists. Penn offered land to all comers on liberal terms, promised toleration of all religions (although only Christians were given the vote), guaranteed English liberties such as the right to bail and trial by jury, and pledged to establish a representative assembly. He also publicized the ready availability of land in Pennsylvania through widely distributed promotional tracts printed in German, French, and Dutch.

PENNSYLVANIA

■ William Penn, later the proprietor of Pennsylvania, as he looked during his youth in Ireland. In such pamphlets as the one shown here, Penn spread the word about his new colony to thousands of readers in England and its other colonial possessions.   (Historical Society of Pennsylvania)

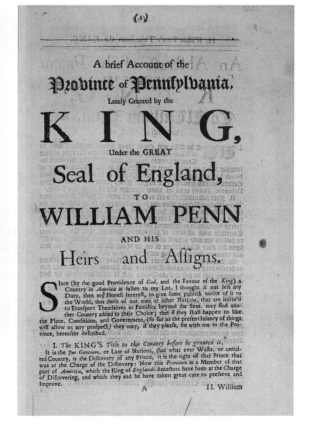

Penn's activities and the Quakers' attraction to his lands gave rise to a migration whose magnitude equaled the Puritan exodus to New England in the 1630s. By mid-1683, more than three thousand people—among them Welsh, Irish, Dutch, and Germans—had already moved to Pennsylvania, and within five years the population reached twelve thousand. (By contrast, it had taken Virginia more than thirty years to achieve a comparable population.) Philadelphia, carefully sited on the easily navigable Delaware River and planned to be the major city in the province, drew merchants and artisans from throughout the English-speaking world. From mainland and Caribbean colonies alike came Quakers seeking religious freedom; they brought with them years of experience on American soil and well-established trading connections. Pennsylvania's plentiful and fertile lands soon enabled its residents to begin exporting surplus flour and other foodstuffs to the West Indies. Practically overnight Philadelphia acquired more than two thousand citizens and started to challenge Boston's commercial dominance.

A pacifist with egalitarian principles, Penn attempted to treat native peoples fairly. He learned to speak the language of the Delawares (or Lenapes), from whom he purchased tracts of land to sell to European settlers. Penn also established strict regulations for trade and forbade the sale of alcohol to Indians. His policies attracted native peoples who moved to Pennsylvania near the end of the seventeenth century to escape repeated clashes with English colonists in Maryland, Virginia, and North Carolina. Most important were the Tuscaroras, whose experiences are described later in this chapter. Likewise, Shawnees and Miamis chose to move eastward from the Ohio valley. By a supreme irony, however, the same toleration that attracted Native Americans also brought non-Quaker Europeans who showed little respect for Indian claims to the soil. In effect, Penn's policy was so successful that it caused its own downfall. The Scots-Irish, Germans, and Swiss who settled in Pennsylvania in the first half of the eighteenth century clashed repeatedly over land with Indians who had also recently migrated to the colony.

CAROLINA The southernmost proprietary colony, granted by Charles II in 1663, encompassed a huge tract stretching from the southern boundary of Virginia to Spanish Florida. The area had great strategic importance: a successful English settlement there would prevent Spaniards from pushing farther north. The fertile semitropical land also held forth the promise of producing exotic and valuable commodities such as figs, olives, wines, and silk. The proprietors named their new province Carolina in honor of Charles, whose Latin name was Carolus. The "Fundamental Constitutions of Carolina," which they asked the political philosopher John Locke to draft for them, set forth an elaborate plan for a colony governed by a hierarchy of landholding aristocrats and characterized by a carefully structured distribution of political and economic power.

But Carolina failed to follow the course the proprietors laid out. Instead, it quickly developed two distinct population centers, which in 1729 split into separate colonies. Virginia planters settled the Albemarle region that became North Carolina. They established a society much like their own, with an economy based on cultivating tobacco and exporting such forest products as pitch, tar, and timber. Because North Carolina lacked a satisfactory harbor, its planters relied on Virginia's ports and merchants to conduct their trade, and the colonies remained tightly linked. The other population center, which eventually formed the core of South Carolina, developed at Charles Town, founded in 1670 near the juncture of the Ashley and Cooper Rivers. Many of its early residents migrated from Barbados, which was already overcrowded. These sugar planters expected to reestablish plantation agriculture in their new homeland.

But the Carolinians soon learned that tropical plants (including sugar) would not grow successfully on the mainland, and so they instead began to raise corn and herds of cattle, which they sold to Caribbean planters hungry for foodstuffs. Like other colonists before them, they also depended on trade with nearby Indians to supply commodities they could sell elsewhere. In Carolina, those items were deerskins (almost as valuable as beaver pelts in Europe) and Indian slaves, which were shipped to the West Indies and the northern colonies. Nearby Indian nations hunted deer with increasing intensity and readily sold captured enemies to the English settlers. During the first decade of the eighteenth century, South Carolina exported an average of 54,000 skins annually, and overseas shipments later peaked at 160,000 a year. Before 1715, Carolinians additionally exported an estimated 30,000 to 50,000 Indian slaves.

THE CHESAPEAKE AND NEW ENGLAND The English Civil War also affected the earlier English settlements, retarding their development. In the Chesapeake, struggles between supporters of the king and Parliament caused military clashes in Maryland and political upheavals in Virginia. But once the war ended and immigration resumed, the colonies expanded once again. Wealthy Chesapeake tobacco growers imported increasing numbers

■ Map from *A New Description of Carolina,* by John Ogilby, 1671 (with south at the top). Ogilby's tract, illustrated by a map drawn from information supplied by John Lederer, a German Indian trader, was intended to attract settlers to the new Carolina colony. He filled his text with information supplied by the Lords Proprietors, stressing the colony's pleasant climate, abundant resources, and friendly Native peoples, a message underscored by the peaceful scenes in the corner cartouches.   (Colonial Williamsburg Foundation)

of English indentured servants to work on their farms, which had by then begun to develop into large plantations. Freed from concerns about Indian attack by the final defeat of the Powhatan Confederacy in 1646 they—especially recent immigrants—eagerly sought to enlarge their landholdings.

In New England, migration essentially ceased after the Civil War began in 1642. While Puritans were first challenging the king and then governing England as a commonwealth, they had little incentive to leave their homeland, and few migrated after the Restoration. Yet the Puritan colonies' population continued to grow dramatically because of natural increase. By the 1670s, New England's population had more than tripled to reach approximately seventy thousand. Such a rapid expansion placed great pressure on available land. Colonial settlement spread far into the interior of Massachusetts and Connecticut, and many members of the third and fourth

generations had to migrate—north to New Hampshire or Maine, south to New York or New Jersey, west beyond the Connecticut River—to find sufficient farmland for themselves and their children. Others abandoned agriculture and learned such skills as blacksmithing or carpentry to support themselves in the growing towns.

The people who remained behind in the small yet densely populated New England communities experienced a new phenomenon after approximately 1650: burgeoning witchcraft accusations and trials. The rural Chesapeake, urban Philadelphia or Charles Town, and newer settlements largely escaped such incidents, even though most seventeenth-century people believed that witches existed. These allies of the Devil were thought to harness invisible spirits for good or evil purposes. For example, a witch might engage in fortunetelling, prepare healing potions or charms, or harm others by causing the death

WITCHCRAFT

of a child or valuable animals. Yet only New England witnessed many trials of accused witches (about one hundred in all before 1690). Most, though not all, of the accused were middle-aged women who had angered their neighbors. Historians have accordingly concluded that the dynamics of daily interactions in the close-knit communities, where the same families lived nearby for decades, fostered longstanding quarrels that led some colonists to believe that others had diabolically caused certain misfortunes. Even so, only a few of the accused were convicted, and fewer still were executed, because judges and juries remained skeptical of such charges.

That New England courts thus halted questionable prosecutions suggests the maturity of colonial institutions.

COLONIAL POLITICAL STRUCTURES By the last quarter of the seventeenth century, almost all the Anglo-American colonies had well-established political and judicial structures. In New England, property-holding men or the legislature elected the governors; in other regions, the king or the proprietor appointed such leaders. A council, either elected or appointed, advised the governor on matters of policy and served as the upper house of the legislature. Each colony had a judiciary with local justices of the peace, county courts, and, usually, an appeals court composed of the councilors.

Local political institutions also developed. In New England, elected selectmen initially governed the towns, but by the end of the seventeenth century, town meetings—held at least annually and attended by most free adult male residents—handled matters of local concern. In the Chesapeake colonies and both of the Carolinas, appointed magistrates ran local governments. At first the same was true in Pennsylvania, but by the early eighteenth century elected county officials began to take over some government functions. And in New York, local elections were the rule even before the establishment of the colonial assembly in 1683.

A Decade of Imperial Crises: The 1670s

*A*s the Restoration colonies were extending the range of English settlement on the North American landscape, the first English colonies and French and Spanish settlements in North America faced new crises caused primarily by their changing relationships with America's indigenous peoples. Between 1670 and 1680, New England, Virginia, New France, and New Mexico experienced bitter conflicts as their inter-

ests collided with those of America's original inhabitants. All the early colonies changed irrevocably as a result.

In the mid-1670s, Louis de Buade de Frontenac, the governor-general of Canada, decided to expand New France's reach into the south and west, hoping to establish a trade route to Mexico and to gain direct control of the valuable fur trade on which the prosperity of the colony rested. Accordingly, he encouraged the explorations of Father Jacques Marquette, Louis Jolliet, and René-Robert Cavelier de La Salle in the Great Lakes and Mississippi valley regions. His goal, however, brought him into conflict

NEW FRANCE AND THE IROQUOIS

■ Contemporary engraving of John Verelst's 1710 portrait of the Mohawk chief known as Hendrick to Europeans (his Indian name was rendered as "Dyionoagon" or "Tee Yee Neen Ho Ga Row"). Hendrick and three other Iroquois leaders visited London in 1710, symbolically cementing the Covenant Chain negotiated in 1677. His primarily European dress and the wampum belt in his hand accentuate his identity as a cross-cultural diplomatic emissary.   (John Carter Brown Library at Brown University)

with the powerful Iroquois Confederacy, composed of five Indian nations—the Mohawks, Oneidas, Onondagas, Cayugas, and Senecas. (In 1722 the Tuscaroras became the sixth.)

Under the terms of a unique defensive alliance forged early in the sixteenth century, a representative council made decisions of war and peace for the entire Iroquois Confederacy, although each nation still retained some autonomy and could not be forced to comply with a

Map 3.2 Louisiana, c. 1720

By 1720 French forts and settlements dotted the Mississippi River and its tributaries in the interior of North America. Two isolated Spanish outposts were situated near the Gulf of Mexico. (Source: Adapted from *France in America,* by William J. Eccles. Copyright © 1972 by William J. Eccles. Reprinted by permission of HarperCollins Publishers, Inc.)

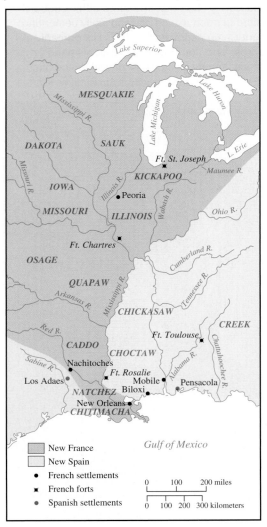

council directive against its will. Before the arrival of Europeans, the Iroquois waged wars primarily to acquire captives to replenish their population. Contact with foreign traders brought ravaging disease as early as 1633, intensifying the need for captives. Simultaneously, the Europeans' presence created an economic motive for warfare: the desire to dominate the fur trade and to gain unimpeded access to European goods. The war with the Hurons in the 1640s initiated a series of conflicts with other Indians known as the Beaver Wars, in which the Iroquois fought to achieve control of the lucrative peltry trade. Iroquois warriors did not themselves trap beaver; instead, they raided other villages in search of caches of pelts or attacked Indians from the interior as they carried furs to European outposts. Then the Iroquois traded that booty for European-made blankets, knives, guns, alcohol, and other desirable items.

In the mid-1670s, as Iroquois dominance grew, the French intervened, for an Iroquois triumph would have destroyed France's plans to trade directly with western Indians. Over the next twenty years the French launched repeated attacks on Iroquois villages. The English offered little assistance other than weapons to their trading partners, even though in 1677 New Yorkers and the Iroquois established a formal alliance known as the Covenant Chain. Its people and resources depleted by constant warfare, the confederacy in 1701 finally negotiated a neutrality treaty with France and other Indians. For the next half-century the Iroquois nations maintained their power through trade and skillful diplomacy rather than warfare.

The wars against the Iroquois initiated in the 1670s were crucial components of French Canada's plan to penetrate the heartland of North America. Unlike Spaniards, French adventurers did not attempt to subjugate the Indians they encountered. Nor, at first, did they even formally claim large territories for France. Still, when France decided to strengthen its presence near the Gulf of Mexico by founding New Orleans in 1718—to counter both westward thrusts of the English colonies and eastward moves of the Spanish—the Mississippi posts became the glue of empire. *Coureurs de bois* (literally, "forest runners") used the rivers and lakes of the American interior to travel regularly between Quebec and Louisiana, carrying French goods to outposts such as Michilimackinac (at the junction of Lakes Michigan and Huron), Kaskaskia (in present-day Illinois), and Fort Rosalie (Natchez), on the lower Mississippi River (see Map 3.2).

FRENCH EXPANSION

At most such sites lived a small military garrison and a priest, surrounded by powerful nations such as the Choctaws, Chickasaws, and Osages. Indians gained easy access to valuable trade goods by tolerating the minimal European presence, and France's primarily political and economic aims did not include systematic missionary work. The largest French settlements in the region, known collectively as *le pays de Illinois* ("the Illinois country"), never totaled much above three thousand in population. Located along the Mississippi south of modern St. Louis and north of Fort Chartres, the settlements produced wheat for export to New Orleans. In all the French outposts, the shortage of European women led to interracial unions between French men and Indian women and to the creation of mixed-race people known as *metís*.

In New Mexico, too, events of the 1670s led to a crisis with long-term consequences. Over the years under Spanish domination, the Pueblo peoples had added Christianity to their religious beliefs while still retaining traditional rituals, engaging in syncretic practices as had Mesoamericans. But as decades passed Franciscans adopted increasingly brutal and violent tactics in order to erase all traces of the native religion. Priests and secular colonists who held *encomiendas* also

POPÉ AND THE PUEBLO REVOLT

placed heavy labor demands on the population. In 1680 the Pueblos revolted under the leadership of Popé, a respected shaman, successfully driving the Spaniards out of New Mexico (see Map 3.3). Even though Spain managed to restore its authority by 1700, imperial officials had learned their lesson. Afterward, Spanish governors stressed cooperation with the Pueblos, no longer attempting to reduce them to bondage or to violate their cultural integrity. The Pueblo revolt constituted the most successful and longest-sustained Indian resistance movement in colonial North America.

When Spaniards expanded their territorial claims to the east and north, they followed the same strategy they adopted in New Mexico, establishing their presence through military outposts and Franciscan missions. The army maintained order among the subject Indians—to protect them from attack and ensure the availability of their labor—and guarded the boundaries of New Spain from possible incursions, especially by the French. The friars concentrated on conversions and allowed religious syncretism. By the late eighteenth century, Spain claimed a vast

SPAIN'S NORTH AMERICAN POSSESSIONS

Map 3.3

New Mexico, c. 1680
In 1680, the lone Spanish settlement at Santa Fe was surrounded and vastly outnumbered by the many Pueblo villages nearby.
(Source: Adapted from *Apache, Navaho, and Spaniard,* by Jack D. Forbes. Copyright © 1960 by the University of Oklahoma Press. Used by permission.)

Pueblo population c. 1680
■ 5,000
● 2,000–3,000
○ Less than 1,000
● Spanish settlement

■ In September 1671 a large number of Wampanoags renewed their long-standing alliance with the Plymouth colony by signing this document. Yet less than four years later the peace collapsed as King Philip launched devastating attacks on settlements in southern New England.   (Boston Athenaeum)

territory that stretched from California (first colonized in 1769 to prevent Russian sea-otter trappers from taking over the region) through Texas (settled after 1700) to the Gulf Coast. Throughout that region, the Spanish presence consisted of a mixture of missions and forts dotting the countryside, sometimes at considerable distances from one another.

In the more densely settled English colonies, hostilities developed in the decade of the 1670s not over religion (as in New Mexico) or trade (as in New France) but rather over land. Put simply, the rapidly expanding Anglo-American population wanted more of it. In both New England and Virginia—though for different reasons—settlers began to encroach on territories that until then had remained in the hands of Native Americans.

By the early 1670s the growing settlements in southern New England surrounded Wampanoag ancestral lands on Narragansett Bay. The local

KING PHILIP'S WAR

chief, King Philip (son of Massasoit, who had welcomed the Pilgrims in 1621), was troubled by the loss of territory and concerned about the impact of European culture and Christianity on his people. Philip led his warriors in attacks on nearby communities in June 1675. Other Algonquian peoples, among them Nipmucks and Narragansetts, soon joined King Philip's forces. In the fall, the Indian nations jointly attacked settlements in the northern Connecticut River valley, and the war spread to Maine, too, when the Abenakis entered the conflict. In early 1676, the Indian allies devastated well-established villages and even attacked Plymouth and Providence; later that year, Abenaki assaults forced the abandonment of most settlements in Maine. Altogether, the alliance wholly or partially destroyed twenty-seven of ninety-two northern towns and attacked forty others, pushing the line of English settlement back toward the east and south.

The tide turned in the south in the summer of 1676. The Indian coalition ran short of food and ammunition, and colonists began to use Christian Indians as guides and scouts. On June 12, the Mohawks—ancient Iroquois enemies of New England Algonquians—devastated a major Wampanoag encampment while most of the warriors were away attacking an English town. After King Philip was killed that August, the southern alliance crumbled. Fighting, though, continued on the Maine frontier for another two years. There the English colonists never defeated the Abenakis; both sides, their resources depleted, simply agreed to end the conflict in 1678.

As the chapter-opening vignette reveals, many surviving Wampanoags, Nipmucks, Narragansetts, and Abenakis were captured and sold into slavery, and still more died of starvation and disease. New Englanders had broken the power of the southern coastal tribes. Thereafter the southern Indians lived in small clusters, subordinated to the colonists and often working as servants or sailors. Only on the isolated island of Martha's Vineyard did some Wampanoags preserve their cultural identity intact.

But the settlers paid a terrible price for their victory in King Philip's War: an estimated one-tenth of the able-bodied adult male population was killed or wounded. Proportional to population, it was the most costly conflict in American history. New Englanders did not fully rebuild abandoned interior towns for another three decades, and not until the American Revolution did the region's per capita income again reach pre-1675 levels.

Not coincidentally, conflict with Indians simultaneously wracked Virginia. In the early 1670s, land-hungry Virginians avidly eyed rich lands north

BACON'S REBELLION

of the York River reserved for Native peoples by early treaties. Using as a pretext the July 1675 killing of an English servant by some Doeg Indians, settlers attacked not only the Doegs but also the Susquehannocks, a powerful nation that had recently occupied the area. In retaliation, Susquehannock bands raided outlying farms early in 1676. Governor William Berkeley, the leader of an entrenched coterie of large landowners, resisted starting a major war to further the aims of disgruntled men who overtly challenged his hold on power. Dissatisfied colonists, including former indentured servants unable to establish their own tobacco farms, rallied behind the leadership of a recent immigrant, the wealthy Nathaniel Bacon, who like other new arrivals had found that all the desirable land in settled areas was already claimed by earlier residents.

Berkeley and Bacon soon clashed. After Bacon held members of the House of Burgesses hostage until they authorized him to attack the Indians, Berkeley declared Bacon and his men to be in rebellion. As the chaotic summer of 1676 wore on, Bacon alternately pursued Indians and battled the governor's supporters. In September Bacon marched on Jamestown itself, burning the capital to the ground. But when Bacon died of dysentery the following month, the rebellion began to collapse. Even so, the rebels had made their point, and a new treaty signed in 1677 opened much of the disputed territory to English settlement.

The war, a turning point in Virginia's relationship with nearby Indians, also marked a turning point in the colony's internal race relations. After Bacon's Rebellion, Virginia landowners for the first time began to purchase large numbers of imported African slaves. Historians disagree about whether they did so in part because they feared dealing with successive waves of the discontented ex-servants who had followed Bacon's lead. But regardless of their motives, in the last two decades of the seventeenth century Anglo-Americans in the Chesapeake irrevocably altered the racial composition of their labor force.

African Slavery on the Mainland

In the 1670s and 1680s, the prosperity of the Chesapeake rested on tobacco, and successful tobacco cultivation depended, as it always had, on an ample labor supply. But fewer and fewer English men and women proved willing to indenture themselves for long terms of service in Maryland and Virginia. Population pressures had eased in England, and the founding of the Restoration colonies meant that migrants could choose other American destinations. Furthermore, fluctuating tobacco prices in Europe and the growing scarcity of land made the Chesapeake less appealing to potential settlers. That posed a problem for wealthy Chesapeake tobacco

■ European traders hoped to avoid purchasing sick slaves who would carry diseases on board their vessels, thereby causing high mortality rates among other bondspeople and destroying the profitability of the voyages. Some mistakenly believed that by tasting the slaves' sweat they could determine their captives' health. An artist sketched just such a scene in 1725. (*Traite général du commerce de l'Amérique*, by Chambon. Bibliothèque Municipale, Nantes, France)

growers. Where could they obtain the workers they needed? They found the answer in the Caribbean sugar islands, where since the 1640s Dutch, French, English, and Spanish planters had eagerly purchased African slaves.

Slavery had been practiced in Europe (although not in England) for centuries. European Christians—both Catholics and Protestants—believed

WHY AFRICAN SLAVERY?

that enslaving heathen peoples, especially those of exotic origin, was justifiable in religious terms. Some argued, piously, that holding heathens in bondage would lead to their conversion. Others believed that any heathen taken prisoner in wartime could legitimately be enslaved. Consequently, when Portuguese mariners reached the sub-Saharan African coast and encountered non-Christian societies holding slaves (see page 18), they purchased bondspeople as one component of the exchange of many items, especially gold. Starting in the 1440s, Portugal imported large numbers of these slaves into the Iberian Peninsula and the Wine Islands; one historian has estimated that by 1500, enslaved Africans composed about one-tenth of the population of Lisbon and Seville, the chief cities of Portugal and Spain.

Iberians then exported African slavery to their American possessions, New Spain and Brazil. Because the Catholic Church prevented the formal enslavement of Indians in those domains (see page 24) and free laborers saw no reason to work voluntarily in mines or on sugar plantations when they could earn better wages under easier conditions elsewhere, African bondspeople (who had no choice) became mainstays of the Caribbean and Brazilian economies. Sugar planters on English islands, who had the same problems of labor supply as did their French, Dutch, and Spanish counterparts, also purchased slaves.

Yet that slave system—well-established in the Caribbean by the mid-1650s—did not immediately take root in the English mainland colonies,

ATLANTIC CREOLES IN SOCIETIES WITH SLAVES

largely because they were then well supplied with English laborers. Before the 1660s, the few residents of African descent on the mainland varied in status: some were free, some indentured, some enslaved. All came from a population that the historian Ira Berlin has termed Atlantic creoles. Often of mixed race, many came to the English colonies from elsewhere in the Americas. Already familiar with Europeans, the Atlantic creoles fitted easily into established niches in the many-faceted hierarchical social structures of the early colonies. Berlin has characterized all the early mainland colonies as "societies with slaves"—that is, societies in which some people were held in perpetual

bondage but that did not rely wholly on slave labor. He usefully contrasts such communities with "slave societies," or societies in which slavery served as the fundamental basis of the economy.

The many ambiguities of status in societies with slaves are evident in early laws in which Virginians and Marylanders revealed the initial difficulty of developing all-encompassing definitions of enslavement. Several Virginia statutes employed the term *Christian* to mean "free person"; when at least one slave therefore claimed freedom as a consequence of conversion to Christianity, the House of Burgesses legislated (in 1667) that "the blessed sacrament of baptism" would not liberate bondspeople from perpetual servitude. The two colonies did not concur on how slave status would be transmitted to the next generation: Virginia in 1662 linked the condition of children to that of their mother, whereas Maryland two years later tied it to the status of their father. And when in 1670 the House of Burgesses sought for the first time to define who was enslaveable and who was not, it declared that "all servants not being christians imported into this colony by shipping shalbe slaves for their lives," but similar servants that "shall come by land" would serve only for a term of years. The awkward phrases attempted to differentiate Africans from Indians; Virginians saw both groups as distinguishable from English people but expressed those distinctions in terms of religion and geography rather than race.

Yet just a few years later, Chesapeake legislators started to employ racial terminology. As increasing numbers of

MAINLAND SLAVE SOCIETIES

slaves arrived each year, first from the Caribbean and then directly from Africa, the majority of the enslaved population changed from acculturated creole to newly imported African. Virginia in 1682 altered its definition of who could be enslaved, declaring bluntly that "Negroes, Moors, Mollatoes or Indians" arriving "by sea or land" could all be held in bondage for life if their "parentage and native country are not christian." Most of the English colonies, even those without many bondspeople, adopted detailed codes to govern slaves' behavior. By 1700 African slavery was firmly established as the basis of the economy in the Chesapeake and South Carolina as well as in the Caribbean. Under Berlin's definition, those colonies had become "slave societies."

English enslavers evidently had few moral qualms about these actions. Few at the time questioned the decision to hold Africans and their descendants—or captive Indians from New England or Carolina—in perpetual bondage. The convoluted and contradictory early attempts to define slave status and how it would descend to the next generation suggest, however, that seventeenth-century English colonists nevertheless initially lacked clear conceptual categories defining both "race" and "slave." They developed such categories and their meanings over time, through their experience with the institution of African and Indian slavery, originally adopted for economic reasons.

Between 1492 and 1770 more Africans than Europeans came to the Americas, the overwhelming majority of them as slaves. Most went to Brazil or the Caribbean: of at least 10 million enslaved people brought to the Americas during the existence of slavery, only about 260,000 were imported by 1775 into the region that became the United States. This massive trade in human beings is best understood within the context of the Atlantic trading system that developed during the middle years of the seventeenth century.

The Web of Empire and the Atlantic Slave Trade

*T*he elaborate Atlantic economic system is commonly called the triangular trade. In that context, the traffic in slaves from Africa to the Americas has become known as the middle passage because it constituted the middle leg of such a theoretical triangle. But both *triangular trade* and *middle passage* fail to convey the complexities of the commercial relationships that by the late seventeenth century linked the various elements of the Atlantic trading system in Europe, Africa, North and South America, and the Caribbean. People and products did not move across the ocean in easily diagrammed patterns. Instead, their movements created a complicated web of exchange that inextricably tied the peoples of the Atlantic world together (see Map 3.4).

The traffic in enslaved human beings served as the linchpin of the system. Although slavery had long been practiced, the oceanic slave *trade* was entirely new. The expanding network of commerce between Europe and its colonies was fueled by the sale and transport of slaves, the exchange of commodities produced by slave labor, and the need to feed and clothe so many bound laborers. Yet the various elements had different relationships within the system and with the wider web of exchange. Chesapeake tobacco and Caribbean and Brazilian sugar were in great demand in Europe, so planters shipped their products directly to their home countries. The profits paid for both the African laborers who grew their crops and European manufactured goods. The African coastal rulers who ran the entrepôts

ATLANTIC TRADING SYSTEM

where European slavers acquired their human cargoes received their payment in European manufactures and East Indian textiles; they had little need for most American products. Europeans purchased slaves from Africa for resale in their colonies and acquired sugar and tobacco from America, in exchange dispatching their manufactures everywhere.

New England had the most complex relationship to the trading system. The region produced only one item England wanted: tall trees to serve as masts for sailing vessels. To buy English manufactures, New Englanders therefore needed profits earned elsewhere—the Wine Islands and the Caribbean. Those islands lacked precisely the items that New England could produce in abundance: cheap food (primarily corn and salt fish) to feed the burgeoning slave population and wood for barrels to hold wine, sugar, and molasses. By the late 1640s, decades before the Chesapeake

NEW ENGLAND AND THE CARIBBEAN

■ By the middle of the eighteenth century, American tobacco had become closely associated with African slavery. An English woodcut advertising tobacco from the York River in Virginia accordingly depicted not a Chesapeake planter but rather an African, shown with a hoe in one hand and a pipe in the other. Usually, of course, slaves would not have smoked the high-quality tobacco produced for export, although they were allowed to cultivate small crops for their own use. (Colonial Williamsburg Foundation)

York Tobacco
LONDON

Map 3.4

Atlantic Trade Routes

By the late seventeenth century, an elaborate trade network linked the countries and colonies bordering the Atlantic Ocean. The most valuable commodities exchanged were enslaved people and the products of slave labor.

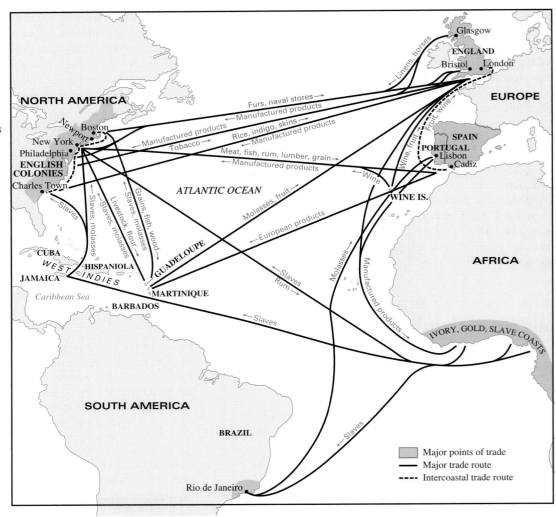

economy became dependent on *production* by slaves, New England's already rested on *consumption* by slaves and their owners. The sale of foodstuffs and wood products to Caribbean sugar planters provided New England farmers and merchants with a major source of income. After the founding of Pennsylvania, New York, and New Jersey, those colonies too participated in the lucrative West Indian trade.

Shopkeepers in the interior of New England and the middle colonies bartered with local farmers for grains, livestock, and barrel staves, then traded those items to merchants located in port towns. Such merchants dispatched ships to the Caribbean, where they sailed from island to island, exchanging their cargoes for molasses, sugar, fruit, spices, and slaves. The system's sole constant was uncertainty, due to the weather, rapid shifts in supply and demand in the small island markets, and the del-

icate system of credit on which the entire structure depended. Once they had a full load, the ships returned to Boston, Newport, New York, or Philadelphia to dispose of their cargoes, trading the items they did not use to other nearby colonies. Americans began to distill molasses into rum, a crucial aspect of the only part of the trade that could accurately be termed triangular. Rhode Islanders took rum to Africa and traded it for slaves, whom they carried to the West Indies to exchange for more molasses to produce still more rum.

Tying the system together was the voyage that brought Africans to the Americas, where they cultivated the profitable crops and—in the Caribbean—consumed foods produced in North America. That voyage, always traumatic, was sometimes fatal for the people who composed a ship's cargo. An average of 10 to 20 percent of the newly enslaved died en route. On unusually long or

The web of commerce across the Atlantic drove trade—and theft—to new levels. The last decades of the seventeenth century were the heyday of pirates, who, from bases in North America and the Caribbean, ranged the world. In New York and Charles Town, merchants asked few questions about the origins of valuable goods, and the solitary ocean voyages of merchant and slaving vessels were easy prey for resourceful marauders. The cargoes of precious metals, slaves, and luxury goods such as fine wines and silks made the return worth the risk.

As early as the sixteenth century, European kingdoms encouraged attacks on the commerce of rivals. Queen Elizabeth knighted Francis Drake for the treasure he stole from Spain. Though in wartime letters of marque could transform law-breaking pirates into legal privateers, authorized to prey on the enemy, the line between pirates and privateers was easily breached. Privateers could keep most of their booty, and the crews, with sailors of many nations, were loyal primarily to themselves.

The infamous Captain William Kidd (c. 1645–1701) was both pirate and privateer. Probably Scots by birth, he plundered in the Caribbean before settling in New York, where he married a rich widow and cultivated local politi-cians. In 1696 he returned to sea with new privateering credentials, issued in London. With a crew recruited in England and New York, he sailed to the Indian Ocean, picking up other mariners along the way. Kidd encountered no vessels he could legally capture, and his crew—composed largely of pirates—became restive, so he resumed marauding. Over the next months Kidd and his men seized Dutch and Portuguese ships and eventually a freighter sailing from India to the Moluccas. In late 1698, they headed for the Americas with a booty of valuable textiles. But in Boston, Kidd was arrested for piracy and murder. The English and colonial governments, he discovered, were newly committed to stamping out piracy. Sent to London for trial, he was convicted and hanged in May 1701.

Captain Kidd's exploits were a product of his time and place. In the 1690s international crews of buccaneers sailed from the Americas to wherever in the world they thought they would find rich prizes. The rapidly developing web of international commerce that linked the Western Hemisphere to Africa, Asia, and Europe also spawned the legendary thieves who preyed on it.

The sorts of valuable, exotic items pictured here were among the cargoes pirates sought. Fine ceramics and textiles from Asia commanded high prices from American and European purchasers who did not concern themselves with the origins of these desirable consumer goods. (Left: V&A Images, The Victoria and Albert Museum, London; right: The Metropolitan Museum of Art, purchased by subscription, 1879)

disease-ridden voyages, mortality rates could be much higher. In addition, another 20 percent or so of slaves died either before the ships left Africa or shortly after their arrival in the Americas. Their European captors also died at high rates, chiefly through exposure to such diseases as yellow fever and malaria, which were endemic to Africa. Just 10 percent of the men sent to run the Royal African Company's forts in Lower Guinea lived to return home to England, and one in every four or five European sailors died on slaving voyages. Once again, the exchange of diseases caused unanticipated death and destruction.

Most of the enslaved people carried to North America originated in West Africa. Some came from the Rice and Grain Coasts, especially the former, but even more had resided in the Gold and Slave Coasts and the Bight of

WEST AFRICA AND THE SLAVE TRADE

Biafra (modern Nigeria) and Angola (see Map 1.2). Certain coastal rulers—for instance, the Adja kings of the Slave Coast—served as middlemen, allowing the establishment of permanent slave-trading posts in their territories and supplying resident Europeans with slaves to fill ships that stopped regularly at coastal forts. Such rulers controlled European traders' access to slaves and simultaneously controlled inland peoples' access to desirable European goods such as cloth, alcohol, tobacco, and guns.

The slave trade had varying political and economic consequences for the nations of West Africa. The trade's centralizing tendencies helped to create such powerful eighteenth-century kingdoms as Dahomey and Asante (formed from the Akan States). Traffic in slaves thus destroyed smaller polities and disrupted traditional economic patterns, as goods once sent north toward the Mediterranean were redirected to the coast, and as local manufactures declined in the face of European competition. Further, the extent of nations' participation in the trade varied according to their involvement in warfare. Because prisoners of war constituted the bulk of the slaves shipped to the Americas, the most active traders were also the most successful in battle. Some nations even initiated conflicts specifically to acquire valuable captives.

The trade in human beings did not uniformly depopulate West Africa, a fertile and densely inhabited region. Instead, the slave trade affected African societies unevenly. For example, the growing state of Benin actively sold captive enemies to the Portuguese in the late fifteenth century; did not do so at the height of its power in the sixteenth and seventeenth centuries; and renewed the sale of prisoners in the eighteenth century when its waning power led to conflicts with neighboring states. Rulers in parts of Upper Guinea, especially modern Gambia and Senegal, largely resisted involvement with the trade; the

■ A Procession in Benin, 1668. A contemporary European engraving shows a royal procession leaving the city of Benin, capital of the prosperous West African kingdom. During the seventeenth century, the power of Benin's rulers scared off would-be challengers, and so the kingdom did not engage in frequent warfare. In the fifteenth and eighteenth centuries, by contrast, when the kingdom was weaker, it did capture and sell its enemies.   (Library of Congress)

few slave vessels that departed from that area were much more likely than others to experience onboard rebellions. Despite planters' preference for male slaves, women predominated in cargoes originating in the Bight of Biafra. And in such regions as the Gold Coast, the trade had a significant impact on the sex ratio of the remaining population. There a relative shortage of men increased work demands on women, encouraged polygyny, and opened new opportunities to women and their children.

This traffic in slaves chiefly benefited Europeans, despite its importance to some African kings. The European

EUROPEAN RIVALRIES AND THE SLAVE TRADE

economy, previously oriented toward the Mediterranean and Asia, shifted its emphasis to the Atlantic. Whereas European merchants' profits had once come primarily from trade with North Africa, the eastern Mediterranean, and China, by the late seventeenth century commerce in slaves and the products of slave labor constituted the basis of the European economic system. The irony of Columbus's discoveries thus became complete: seeking the wealth of Asia, Columbus instead found the lands that—along with Africa—ultimately replaced Asia as the source of European prosperity.

European nations fought bitterly to control the slave trade. The Portuguese, who at first dominated the trade, were supplanted by the Dutch in the 1630s. The Dutch in turn lost out to the English, who controlled the trade through the Royal African Company, a joint-stock company chartered by Charles II in 1672. Holding a monopoly on all English trade with sub-Saharan Africa, the company built and maintained seventeen forts and trading posts, dispatched to West Africa hundreds of ships carrying English manufactured goods, and transported about 100,000 slaves to England's Caribbean colonies. It paid regular dividends averaging 10 percent yearly, and some of its agents made fortunes. Yet even before the company's monopoly expired in 1712, many individual English traders had illegally entered the market for slaves. By the early eighteenth century, such independent traders carried most of the Africans imported into the colonies, earning huge profits from successful voyages.

English officials seeking a new source of revenue after the disruptions of the Civil War decided to tap into the profits produced by the expanding Atlantic trading system. Chesapeake tobacco and Caribbean sugar had obvious value, but other colonial products also had considerable potential. Additional tax revenues could put England back on a sound financial footing, and English merchants wanted to ensure that they—not their Dutch rivals—reaped the benefits of trading with English colonies. Parliament and the restored Stuart monarchs

accordingly began to draft laws designed to confine the proceeds of the English imperial web of trade primarily to the mother country.

Like other European nations, England based its commercial policy on a series of assumptions about the operations of the world's economic system.

MERCANTILISM

Collectively, these assumptions are usually called *mercantilism*, although neither the term itself nor a unified mercantilist theory was formulated until a century later. The theory viewed the economic world as a collection of national states, whose governments actively competed for shares of a finite amount of wealth. What one nation gained, another nation automatically lost. Each nation sought to become as economically self-sufficient as possible while maintaining a favorable balance of trade with other countries by exporting more than it imported. Colonies had an important role to play in such a scheme. They could supply the mother country with valuable raw materials to be consumed at home or sent abroad, and they could serve as a market for the mother country's manufactured goods.

Parliament applied mercantilist thinking to the American colonies in laws known as the Navigation

NAVIGATION ACTS

Acts. The major acts—passed between 1651 and 1673—established three main principles. First, only English or colonial merchants and ships could engage in trade in the colonies. Second, certain valuable American products could be sold only in the mother country or in other English colonies. At first, these "enumerated" goods included wool, sugar, tobacco, indigo, ginger, and dyes; later acts added rice, naval stores (masts, spars, pitch, tar, and turpentine), copper, and furs to the list. Third, all foreign goods destined for sale in the colonies had to be shipped by way of England, paying English import duties. Some years later, a new series of laws established a fourth principle: the colonies could not export items (such as wool clothing, hats, or iron) that competed with English products.

The Navigation Acts aimed at forcing American trade to center on England. The mother country would benefit from colonial imports and exports both. England had first claim on the most valuable colonial exports, and all foreign imports into the colonies had to pass through England first, enriching its customs revenues in the process. The laws adversely affected some colonies, like those in the Caribbean and the Chesapeake, because planters there could not seek new markets for their staple crops. In others, the impact was minimal or even positive. Builders and owners of ships benefited from the monopoly on American trade given to English and colonial merchants; the laws stimulated the creation of a lucrative

■ The harbor of Christiansted, St. Croix, in the Danish West Indies. Although this view was painted over one hundred years after the events discussed in this chapter, the town had not changed much in the interim. Scenes like this would have been very familiar to seventeenth- and eighteenth-century colonial mariners, for such ports existed all over the Caribbean. Anchored merchant vessels await the hogsheads of molasses being prepared for shipment at the wharf.   (1996 MAPes MONDe Ltd.)

colonial shipbuilding industry, especially in New England. And the northern and middle colonies produced many unenumerated goods—for example, fish, flour, meat and livestock, and barrel staves. Such products could be traded directly to the French and Dutch Caribbean islands as long as they were carried in English or American ships.

The English authorities soon learned that writing mercantilist legislation was far easier than enforcing it. The many harbors of the American coast provided ready havens for smugglers, and colonial officials often looked the other way when illegally imported goods were offered for sale. In ports such as St. Eustatius in the Dutch West Indies, American merchants could easily dispose of enumerated goods and purchase foreign items on which duty had not been paid. Consequently, Parliament in 1696 enacted another Navigation Act. This law established in America a number of vice-admiralty courts, which operated without juries. In England such courts

dealt only with cases involving piracy, vessels taken as wartime prizes, and the like. But since American juries had already demonstrated a tendency to favor local smugglers over customs officers (a colonial customs service was instituted in 1671), Parliament decided to remove Navigation Act cases from the regular colonial courts.

Enslavement of Africans and Indians

*F*ollowing Bacon's Rebellion, so many Africans were imported into Virginia and Maryland so rapidly that as early as 1690 those colonies contained more slaves than English indentured servants. By 1710 people of African descent composed one-fifth of the region's population. Even so, and despite sizable continuing imports, a decade later American-born slaves already outnumbered their African-born counterparts in the Chesapeake, and the native-born proportion of the slave population continued to increase thereafter.

Slaves brought from Africa tended to be assigned to outlying parts of Chesapeake plantations (called quarters),

AFRICAN ENSLAVEMENT IN THE CHESAPEAKE

at least until they learned some English and the routines of tobacco cultivation. Those from Upper Guinea might have grown the crop in Africa; one historian has speculated that slaves from that region, whence tobacco was exported by the 1680s, could have offered expert advice to Chesapeake planters, who at the time were still experimenting with curing and processing techniques. Such Africans—the vast majority of them men—lived in quarters composed of ten to fifteen workers housed together in one or two buildings and supervised by an Anglo-American overseer. Each man was expected to cultivate about two acres of tobacco a year. Their lives must have been filled with toil and loneliness, for few spoke the same language and all were expected to work for their owners six days a week. On Sundays, planters allowed them a day off. Many used that time to cultivate their own gardens or to hunt or fish to supplement their meager diets. Only rarely could they form families because of the scarcity of women among newly imported Africans.

Slaves usually cost about two and a half times as much as indentured servants, but they repaid the greater investment with a lifetime of service, assuming they survived—which large numbers, weakened by the voyage and sickened by exposure to new diseases, did not. Many planters could not afford to purchase such expensive workers. Thus the transition from indentured to enslaved labor increased the social and economic distance between richer and poorer planters. Those with enough money could acquire slaves, accumulate greater wealth, and establish large plantations worked by tens, if not hundreds, of bondspeople, whereas the less affluent could not even buy indentured servants, whose price rose because of scarcity. As time passed, Anglo-American society in the Chesapeake became more and more stratified—that is, the gap between rich and poor steadily widened. The introduction of large numbers of Africans into the Chesapeake thus had a significant impact on the shape of Anglo-American society, in addition to reshaping the population as a whole.

Africans who had lived in the Caribbean came with their masters to South Carolina from Barbados in 1670, composing one-quarter to one-third of the early population. The Barbadian slaveowners quickly discovered that African-born slaves had a variety of skills well suited to the semitropical environment of South Carolina.

AFRICAN ENSLAVEMENT IN SOUTH CAROLINA

African-style dugout canoes became the chief means of transportation in the colony, which was crossed by rivers and included large islands just offshore. Fishing nets copied from African models proved more efficient than those of English origin. Baskets that enslaved laborers wove and gourds that they hollowed out came into general use as containers for food and drink. Africans' skill at killing crocodiles equipped them to handle alligators. And, finally, Africans adapted their traditional techniques of cattle herding for use in America. Since meat and hides numbered among the colony's chief exports in its earliest years, Africans contributed significantly to South Carolina's prosperity.

Not until after 1700 did South Carolinians begin to import slaves directly from Africa. Nevertheless, by 1710 African-born slaves already outnumbered those born in the Americas, and they constituted a majority of the slave population in South Carolina until about midcentury. The similarity of the South Carolinian and West African environments, coupled with the large proportion of Africans in the population, ensured that more aspects of West African culture survived in that colony than elsewhere on the North American mainland. Only in South Carolina did enslaved parents continue to give their children African names; only there did a dialect develop that combined English words with African terms. (Known as Gullah, it has survived to the present day in isolated areas.) African skills remained useful, so techniques lost in other regions when the migrant generation died were instead passed down to the migrants' children. And in South Carolina African women became the primary petty traders, dominating the markets of Charles Town as they did those of Guinea.

The importation of large numbers of Africans coincided with the successful introduction of rice in South

RICE AND INDIGO

Carolina. English people knew little about the techniques of growing and processing rice. Unsurprisingly, they failed at their first attempts to raise the crop, for which there was strong demand in Europe. But people from Africa's Rice Coast had spent their lives working with rice. Although the evidence is circumstantial, the Africans' expertise almost certainly assisted their English masters in cultivating the crop profitably. Slaves on rice plantations, which were far larger than Chesapeake tobacco quarters, were each expected to cultivate three to four acres of rice a year. To cut expenses, planters also expected slaves to grow part of their own food. A universally adopted task system of predefined work assignments provided that after bondspeople had finished their set "tasks" for the day, they could then rest or work in their own garden plots or on other projects. Experienced slaves could often complete their tasks by early afternoon; after that, as on Sundays, their masters had no legitimate claim on their time.

Developers of South Carolina's second cash crop also used the task system and drew on slaves' specialized skills. Indigo, the only source of blue dye for the growing English textile industry, was much prized. Eliza Lucas, a young woman managing her father's plantations, accordingly began to experiment with indigo cultivation during the early 1740s. Drawing on the knowledge of slaves and overseers from the Caribbean, she developed the planting and processing techniques later adopted throughout the colony. Indigo grew on high ground, and rice was planted in low-lying swamps; rice and indigo also had different growing seasons. Thus the two crops complemented each other. South Carolina indigo never matched the quality of that from the Caribbean, but indigo plantations flourished because the crop was so valuable that Parliament offered Carolinians a bounty on every pound exported to Great Britain.

Among the people held in slavery in both Carolinas were Indian captives who had been retained rather than exported, many of them Catholic converts captured in raids that destroyed nearby Spanish missions early in the eighteenth century. In 1708, enslaved Indians composed as much as 14 percent of the South Carolina population.

INDIAN ENSLAVEMENT IN NORTH AND SOUTH CAROLINA

The widespread and lucrative traffic in Indian slaves significantly affected South Carolina's relationship with its indigenous neighbors. Native Americans knew they could always find a ready market for captive enemies in Charles Town, so they took that means of ridding themselves of real or potential rivals. Yet native groups soon learned that Carolinians could not be trusted. As settlers and traders shifted their priorities, first one set of former allies, then another, found themselves the enslaved rather than the enslavers.

At first the Carolinians themselves did not engage directly in conflicts with neighboring tribes. But in 1711 the Tuscaroras, an Iroquoian people, attacked a Swiss-German settlement at New Bern, North Carolina, which had expropriated their lands. South Carolinians and their Indian allies then combined to defeat the Tuscaroras in a bloody war. Afterward, more than a thousand Tuscaroras were enslaved, and the remnants of the group drifted northward, where they joined the Iroquois Confederacy.

Four years later, the Yamasees, who had helped to overcome the Tuscaroras, themselves turned on their

In 1726, William Smith, an employee of the Royal African Company, sketched this musician playing a traditional marimba-like instrument called a *balafo*. Later in the eighteenth century Virginians described slaves playing the same instrument, thus showing that African music came to North America with the enslaved multitudes.   (Joseph Regenstein Library)

onetime English allies. In what seems to have been long-planned retaliation for multiple abuses by traders as well as threats to their own lands, the Yamasees enlisted the Creeks and other Muskogean peoples in coordinated attacks on outlying English settlements. In the spring and summer of 1715, English and African refugees by the hundreds streamed into Charles Town. The Creek-Yamasee offensive was eventually thwarted when reinforcements arrived from the north, colonists hastily armed their African slaves, and Cherokees joined the fight against the Creeks, their ancient foes. After the war, Carolinian involvement in the Indian slave trade essentially ceased, for all their native neighbors moved away for self-protection: Creeks migrated west, Yamasees went south, and other groups moved north. The abuses of the Carolina slave trade thus in effect caused its own destruction.

Indian or African slavery was not of great importance to Spain's North American territories, which had no plantations or cash crops. Moreover, as slavery took deeper root in South Carolina, Florida officials in 1693 offered freedom to fugitives who would convert to Catholicism. Hun-

SLAVES IN SPANISH AND FRENCH NORTH AMERICA

dreds of South Carolina runaways took advantage of the offer, although not all won their liberty. Many settled in a town founded for them near St. Augustine, Gracia Real de Santa Teresa de Mose, headed by a former slave and militia captain, Francisco Menéndez.

In early Louisiana, too, slaves—some Indians, some Atlantic creoles—at first composed only a tiny proportion of the residents. But a growing European population demanded that the French government supply them with slaves, and in 1719 officials finally acquiesced, dispatching more than six thousand Africans, mostly from Senegal, over the next decade. The residents failed to develop a successful plantation economy, although they experimented with both tobacco and indigo. They did succeed in angering the Natchez Indians, whose lands they had usurped. In 1729 the Natchez, assisted by newly arrived slaves, attacked northern reaches of the colony, killing more than 10 percent of its European people. The French struck back, slaughtering the Natchez and their enslaved allies, but throughout much of the century Louisiana remained a society with slaves rather than a slave society.

Atlantic creoles from the Caribbean and Indians from the Carolinas and Florida composed almost all the bondspeople in the northern mainland colonies. Yet the intricate involvement of northerners in the web of commerce surrounding the slave trade ensured that many people of African descent lived in America north of Virginia, and that "Spanish Indians" became an identifiable component of the New England population. Some bondspeople resided in urban areas, especially New York, which in 1700 had a larger black population than any other mainland city. Women tended to work as domestic servants, men as unskilled laborers. At the end of the seventeenth century, three-quarters of wealthy Philadelphia households included one or two slaves.

ENSLAVEMENT IN THE NORTH

Yet even in the North most bondspeople worked in the countryside, the majority at agricultural tasks. Dutch farmers in the Hudson Valley and northern New Jersey were especially likely to rely on enslaved Africans, as were the owners of large landholdings in the Narragansett region of Rhode Island. Some bondsmen toiled in new rural enterprises such as ironworks, working alongside hired laborers and indentured servants at forges and foundries. Although relatively few northern colonists owned slaves, those who did relied extensively on their labor. Therefore, even though slavery overall did not make a substantial contribution to the northern economy, certain individual slaveholders benefited greatly from the institution and had good reason to want to preserve it.

Imperial Reorganization and the Witchcraft Crisis

*T*he crises of the 1670s in Virginia and New England focused the attention of reform-minded English officials on the mainland colonies. In the early 1680s, London administrators confronted a bewildering array of colonial governments. Massachusetts Bay (including Maine) functioned under its original charter. Neighboring Connecticut (having absorbed New Haven) and Rhode Island were granted charters by Charles II in 1662 and 1663, respectively, but Plymouth remained autonomous. Virginia, a royal colony, was joined in that status by New Hampshire in 1679 and New York in 1685 when its proprietor ascended the throne as James II. All the other mainland settlements were proprietorships.

By the 1670s, these colonial governments and their residents had become accustomed to a considerable degree of local political autonomy. The tradition of consent was especially firmly established in New England. Massachusetts, Plymouth, Connecticut, and Rhode Island operated essentially as independent entities, subject neither to the direct authority of the king nor to a proprietor. Everywhere in the English colonies, free adult men who owned more than a minimum amount of property (which varied from place to place) expected to have an influential voice in their governments, especially in decisions concerning taxation.

COLONIAL AUTONOMY CHALLENGED

After James II became king in 1685, such expectations clashed with those of the monarch. The new king and his successors sought to bring order to the apparently chaotic state of colonial administration by tightening the reins of government and by reducing the colonies' political autonomy. Simultaneously, officials used the Navigation Acts to reduce the colonies' economic autonomy. Administrators began to chip away at the privileges granted in colonial charters and to reclaim proprietorships for the Crown. Massachusetts (1691), New Jersey (1702), and the Carolinas (1729) all became royal colonies. The charters of Rhode Island, Connecticut, Maryland, and Pennsylvania were temporarily suspended but ultimately were restored to their original status.

The most drastic reordering of colonial administration targeted Puritan New England. Reports from America convinced English officials that New England was a hotbed of smuggling. Moreover, Puritans refused to allow freedom of religion to non-Congregationalists and

DOMINION OF NEW ENGLAND

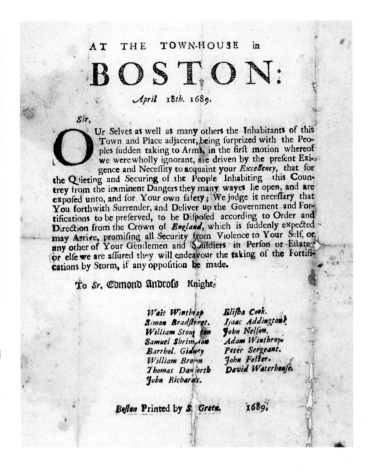

■ Sir Edmund Andros (1637–1714), the much-detested autocratic governor of the Dominion of New England, and a broadside issued at the height of the crisis caused by the Glorious Revolution, calling on Andros to surrender control of the government. The signers were the foremost leaders of the Massachusetts Bay colony, among them a son and grandson of John Winthrop.   (Portrait: Massachusetts State Archives; Broadside: Massachusetts Historical Society)

insisted on maintaining laws incompatible with English practice. New England thus seemed an appropriate place to exert English authority with greater vigor. The charters of all the colonies from New Jersey to Maine were revoked, and a Dominion of New England established in 1686. (For the boundaries of the Dominion, see Map 3.1.) Sir Edmund Andros, the governor, had immense power: Parliament dissolved all the assemblies, and Andros needed only the consent of an appointed council to make laws and levy taxes.

New Englanders endured Andros's autocratic rule for more than two years. Then they learned that James II's hold on power was crumbling. James had angered his subjects by levying taxes without parliamentary approval and by announcing his conversion to Catholicism. In April 1689, Boston's leaders jailed Andros and his associates. The following month they received definite news of the bloodless coup known as the Glorious Revolution, in which James was replaced on the throne in late 1688 by his daughter Mary and her husband, the Dutch prince

GLORIOUS REVOLUTION IN AMERICA

William of Orange. When Parliament offered the throne to the Protestants William and Mary, the Glorious Revolution affirmed the supremacy of both Parliament and Protestantism.

Thus the Bostonians quickly proclaimed their loyalty to William and Mary, writing to England for instructions about the form of government they should now adopt. Most of Massachusetts's political leaders hoped that the new monarchs would renew their original charter. In other colonies, too, the Glorious Revolution emboldened people for revolt. In Maryland the Protestant Association overturned the government of the Catholic proprietor, and in New York a militia officer of German origin, Jacob Leisler, assumed control of the government. Like New Englanders, the Maryland and New York rebels allied themselves with the supporters of William and Mary. They saw themselves as carrying out the colonial phase of the English revolt against Stuart absolutism.

But, like James II, William and Mary believed that England should exercise tighter control over its unruly American possessions. Consequently, only the Maryland rebellion received royal sanction, primarily because of its anti-Catholic thrust. In New York, Leisler was hanged for treason, and Massachusetts (including the formerly independent jurisdiction of Plymouth) became a royal colony with an appointed governor. The province retained its town meeting system of local government and continued to elect its council, but the new 1691 charter eliminated the traditional religious test for voting and office holding. A parish of the Church of England appeared in the heart of Boston. The "city upon a hill," as John Winthrop had envisioned it, had ended.

A war with the French and their Algonquian allies compounded New England's difficulties. King Louis XIV

KING WILLIAM'S WAR

of France allied himself with the deposed James II, and England declared war on France in 1689. (In Europe, this conflict was known as the War of the League of Augsburg, but the colonists called it King William's War.) Even before war broke out in Europe, Anglo-Americans and Abenakis clashed over the English settlements in Maine that had been reoccupied after the 1678 truce and were once again expanding (see page 70). Indian attacks wholly or partially destroyed a number of towns, including Schenectady, New York, and such Maine communities as Falmouth (now Portland), Salmon Falls (now Berwick), and York. Expeditions organized by the colonies against Montreal and Quebec in 1690 failed miserably, and throughout the rest of the conflict New England found itself on the defensive. Even the Peace of Ryswick (1697), which formally ended the war in Europe, failed to bring much respite from warfare to the northern frontiers. Maine could not be fully resettled for several decades because of the continuing conflict.

During the hostilities, New Englanders understandably feared a repetition of the devastation of King Philip's War. For eight months in 1692,

THE 1692 WITCHCRAFT CRISIS

witchcraft accusations spread like wildfire through the rural communities of Essex County, Massachusetts—precisely the area most threatened by the Indian attacks in southern Maine and New Hampshire. Earlier incidents in which personal disputes occasionally led to isolated witchcraft charges (see pages 66–67) bore little relationship to the witch fears that convulsed the region in 1692 while the war raged just to the north. Before the crisis ended, 14 women and 5 men were hanged, 1 man was pressed to death with heavy stones, 54 people confessed to being witches, and more than 140 people were jailed, some for many months.

The crisis began in late February when several young women in Salem Village (an outlying precinct of the bustling port of Salem) formally charged some older female neighbors with having tortured them in spectral

The Wonders of the Invisible World.

OBSERVATIONS

As well *Historical* as *Theological*, upon the NATURE, the NUMBER, and the OPERATIONS of the

DEVILS.

Accompany'd with,

I. Some Accounts of the Grievous Molestations, by DÆMONS and WITCHCRAFTS, which have lately annoy'd the Countrey; and the Trials of some eminent *Malefactors* Executed upon occasion thereof: with several Remarkable *Curiosities* therein occurring.

II. Some Counsils, Directing a due Improvement of the terrible things, lately done, by the Unusual & Amazing Range of EVIL SPIRITS, in Our Neighbourhood: & the methods to prevent the *Wrongs* which those *Evil Angels* may intend against all sorts of people among us; especially in Accusations of the Innocent.

III. Some Conjectures upon the great EVENTS, likely to befall, the WORLD in General, and NEW-ENGLAND in Particular; as also upon the Advances of the TIME, when we shall see BETTER DAYES.

IV. A short Narrative of a late Outrage committed by a knot of WITCHES in *Swedeland*, very much Resembling, and so far Explaining, That under which our parts of *America* have laboured!

V. THE DEVIL DISCOVERED: In a Brief Discourse upon those TEMPTATIONS, which are the more Ordinary *Devices* of the Wicked One.

By **Cotton Mather.**

Boston Printed by *Benj. Harris* for *Sam. Phillips.* **1693.**

■ The Reverend Cotton Mather of Boston, twenty-nine years old in 1692 at the time of the Salem witchcraft crisis, rushed this book—*The Wonders of the Invisible World*—into print shortly after the trials ended. He tried to explain to his fellow New Englanders the "Grievous Molestations by Daemons and Witchcrafts which have lately annoy'd the Countrey" by providing both brief trial narratives and examples of similar recent occurrences elsewhere, most notably in Mohra, Sweden.   (Massachusetts Historical Society)

form. Soon other accusers and confessors chimed in, some of them female domestic servants who had been orphaned in the Indian attacks on Maine. One had lost her grandparents in King Philip's War and other relatives in King William's War. These young women, perhaps the most powerless people in a region apparently powerless to affect its fate, offered their fellow New Englanders a compelling explanation for the seemingly endless chain of troubles afflicting them: their province was under direct assault not only by the Indians but also by the Devil and his allied witches.

The so-called afflicted girls accused not just the older women commonly suspected of such offenses but also prominent men from the Maine frontier who had traded with or failed to defeat the Indians. The leader of the witch conspiracy, accusers and confessors alike declared, was the Reverend George Burroughs, a Harvard graduate who had ministered in both Maine and Salem Village and was suspected of bewitching the soldiers sent to combat the Abenakis. The colony's magistrates, who were also its political and military leaders, were all too willing to believe such accusations, because if the Devil had caused New England's current troubles, they personally bore no responsibility for the terrible losses on the frontier.

In October, the worst phase of the crisis ended when the governor dissolved the special court established to try the suspects. He and several prominent clergymen began to regard the girls' descriptions of spectral torturers as "the Devil's testimony"—and everyone knew the Devil could not be trusted to tell the truth. Most critics of the trials did not think the girls were faking, nor did they conclude that witches did not exist or that confessions were false. Rather, they questioned whether the guilt of the accused could be *legally* established by the evidence presented in court. Accordingly, during the final trials (ending in May 1693) in regular courts, almost all the defendants were acquitted, and the governor quickly reprieved the few found guilty.

In 1696, England took a major step in colonial administration by creating the fifteen-member Board of Trade and Plantations, which thereafter served as the chief organ of government concerned with the American colonies. Previously, no single body in London had that responsibility. The board gathered information, reviewed Crown appointments in America, scrutinized legislation passed by colonial assemblies, supervised trade policies, and advised successive ministries on colonial issues. Still, the Board of Trade did not have any direct powers of enforcement. It also shared jurisdiction over American affairs not only with the customs service and the navy but also with a member of the ministry. Although this reform improved the quality of colonial administration, supervision of the American provinces remained decentralized and haphazard.

NEW IMPERIAL MEASURES

That surely made it easier for Massachusetts and the rest of the English colonies in America to accommodate themselves to the new imperial order. Most colonists resented alien officials who arrived in America determined to implement the policies of king and Parliament, but they adjusted to their demands and to the trade restrictions imposed by the Navigation Acts. They fought another of Europe's wars—the War of the Spanish Suc-

cession, called Queen Anne's War in the colonies—from 1702 to 1713, without enduring the stresses of the first, despite the heavy economic burdens the conflict imposed. Colonists who allied themselves with royal government received patronage in the form of offices and land grants and composed "court parties" that supported English officials. Others, who were either less fortunate in their friends or more principled in defense of colonial autonomy, made up the opposition, or "country" interest. By the end of the first quarter of the eighteenth century, most men in both groups had been born in America. They were members of elite families whose wealth derived in the South from staple-crop production and in the North from commerce.

Summary

The eighty years from 1640 to 1720 established the basic economic and political patterns that were to structure subsequent changes in mainland colonial society. In 1640 just two isolated centers of English population, New England and the Chesapeake, existed along the seaboard, along with the tiny Dutch colony of New Netherland. In 1720 nearly the entire east coast of North America was in English hands, and Indian control east of the Appalachian Mountains had largely been broken by the outcomes of King Philip's War, Bacon's Rebellion, the Carolina wars, and Queen Anne's War. To the west of the mountains, though, Iroquois power reigned supreme. What had been an immigrant population was now mostly American-born, except for the many African-born people in South Carolina; economies originally based on trade in fur and skins had become far more complex and more closely linked with the mother country; and a wide variety of political structures had been reshaped into a more uniform pattern. Yet at the same time the adoption of large-scale slavery in the Chesapeake and the Carolinas differentiated their societies from those of the colonies to the north. The production of tobacco, rice, and indigo for international markets distinguished the southern regional economies. They had become true slave societies, heavily reliant on a system of perpetual servitude, not societies with slaves, in which a few bondspeople mingled with larger numbers of indentured servants and laborers of other descriptions.

Even the economies of the northern colonies, though, rested on profits derived from the Atlantic trading system, the key element of which was traffic in enslaved humans, primarily Africans but also including Indians. New England sold corn, salt fish, and wood products to the West Indies, where slaves consumed the foodstuffs and whence planters shipped sugar and molasses in barrels made from staves crafted by northern farmers. Pennsylvania and New York too found in the Caribbean islands a ready market for their livestock, grains, and wheat flour. The rapid growth of enslavement drove all the English colonial economies in these years.

Meanwhile, from a small outpost in Santa Fe, New Mexico, and missions in Florida, the Spanish had expanded their influence throughout the Gulf Coast region and, by just after midcentury, as far north as California. The French had moved from a few settlements along the St. Lawrence to dominate the length of the Mississippi River and the entire Great Lakes region. Both groups of colonists lived near Indian nations and depended on the indigenous people's labor and goodwill. The Spanish could not fully control their Indian allies, and the French did not even try. The extensive Spanish and French presence to the south and west of the English settlements meant that future conflicts among the European powers in North America were nearly inevitable.

By 1720, the essential elements of the imperial administrative structure that would govern the English colonies until 1775 had been put firmly in place. The regional economic systems originating in the late seventeenth and early eighteenth centuries also continued to dominate North American life for another century—until after independence had been won. And Anglo-Americans had developed the commitment to autonomous local government that later would lead them into conflict with Parliament and the king.

LEGACY FOR A PEOPLE AND A NATION
Americans of African Descent

Before 1640, people of African descent composed only a tiny proportion of the population of the mainland North American colonies. After the 1670s, the rise of southern economies based largely on the enslavement of Africans, coupled with the widespread employment of enslaved Africans in northern colonies, dramatically altered the composition of the American population. By 1775, more than a quarter million Africans had been imported into the territory that later became the United States, constituting about 20 percent of the population at the time of the Revolution.

According to the 2000 census, 12.5 percent of the American people now claim descent from African ancestors. Because the legal importation of African slaves ended in 1808, and because the United States attracted relatively few voluntary migrants of African descent until late in the twentieth century, most of today's African Americans have colonial ancestors—a claim few Americans of European descent can make. Most European Americans are descended at least in part from the massive European migrations of the nineteenth and early twentieth centuries.

The modern African American population includes people with many different skin colors, reflecting the large number of interracial sexual relationships (both coerced and voluntary) that have developed during the long African residence in mainland North America. African Americans, both free and enslaved, have had children with both Europeans and Indians since the colonial period; more recently, they have intermarried with Asian immigrants. In large part the mingling of different peoples of color resulted from state miscegenation laws, which from the early years of the American republic until 1967—when they were struck down by the Supreme Court—forbade legal marriages between people of European descent and those of other races. That forced the non-European groups to seek partners only among themselves. And other state and federal laws then defined people with any appreciable African ancestry as "black."

Recently, increasing numbers of interracial unions have produced multiracial children. The 2000 census for the first time allowed Americans to define themselves simultaneously as members of more than one race. Opposition to this change came largely from leaders of the African American community, and on census forms people of African descent proved less willing to define themselves as multiracial than did people with other origins. The racial self-definition of this large component of the American people thus continues to be influenced by a legacy of discrimination.

The **history Companion** powered by Eduspace®
Your primary source for interactive quizzes, exercises, and more to help you learn efficiently.
http://history.college.hmco.com/students

AMERICAN SOCIETY TRANSFORMED 1720–1770

*W*as I in that Country I would not Stay one day longer in it," Alexander McAllister told his cousin in late 1770. "If god Spers [spares] you in this Cuntrie but a few years you will blis the day you left." McAllister, who as a youth had moved to North Carolina with his parents, clearly did bless the day he had left the Scottish Highlands. In many letters to friends and family back in Argyleshire, McAllister elaborated on the attractions of his adopted home at Cross Creek (near modern Fayetteville, North Carolina). Anyone could easily grow corn, wheat, barley, rye, oats, potatoes, and tobacco; "in truth it is the Best poor mans Cuntry I Ever heard of and I have had the opertunity of hearing from South & north." Lest his Scots correspondents think he exaggerated, McAllister assured them that other immigrants too were doing well. They had harvested "plenty of Corn for them Selves and famile and seemes to be very well Satisfied." Underscoring his point, he insisted that "ther is non but what is in a good way."

One historian has estimated that Alexander McAllister's letters were central to a network of correspondents that brought about five thousand of his fellow countrymen to North America in the two decades after the mid-1750s. His connections in the Highlands recognized that he was a ready source of advice, encouragement, and accurate information for potential emigrants. When Scots arrived in North Carolina with letters of introduction from people McAllister knew, he helped them find land and supplies. Although he understood that, as he told one correspondent, "the best [land] is taken up many years ago," and that newcomers' first two or three years would be hard, he never altered his recommendations. People should "take currage" and move to North America, McAllister asserted; "it will be of Benefitt to ther riseing generation." Certainly McAllister himself thrived in his new homeland; by the late 1780s, having fathered numerous children by two wives, he owned forty slaves and more than 2,500 acres of land. He served as an elder of the Presbyterian church, as a

◄ A farmer, probably an immigrant like Alexander McAllister, plows his field outside the town of Salem, North Carolina, in this 1787 painting by Ludwig G. von Redeken. (Collection of the Wachovia Historical Society)

CHRONOLOGY

1690 • Locke's *Essay Concerning Human Understanding* published, a key example of Enlightenment thought

1732 • Founding of Georgia

1739 • Stono Rebellion (South Carolina) leads to increased white fears of slave revolts

• George Whitefield arrives in America; Great Awakening broadens

1739-48 • King George's War disrupts American economy

1740s • Black population of the Chesapeake begins to grow by natural increase, contributing to rise of large plantations

1741 • New York City "conspiracy" reflects whites' continuing fears of slave revolts

1760s • Baptist congregations take root in Virginia

1760-75 • Peak of eighteenth-century European and African migration to English colonies

1765-66 • Hudson River land riots pit tenants and squatters against large landlords

1767-69 • Regulator movement (South Carolina) tries to establish order in backcountry

1771 • North Carolina Regulators defeated by eastern militia at Battle of Alamance

member of the colonial assembly, and as a state senator after independence was won. Although he was more successful than most migrants, his prosperity showed what some could achieve.

Alexander McAllister and other Highland Scots took part in a massive eighteenth-century migration of European and African peoples that by 1770 had changed the nature of the American population and the look of the American landscape. Ethnic diversity was especially pronounced in the small colonial cities, but the countryside too attracted settlers from many nations. Near McAllister's Cross Creek, for example, also resided large numbers of people from England, Germany, France, Wales,

and the Scottish lowlands. The British colonies south of New England drew by far the largest number of newcomers. Their arrival not only swelled the population but also altered political balances and affected the religious climate by introducing new sects. Unwilling immigrants too (slaves and transported convicts) clustered primarily in the middle and southern colonies.

Several key themes marked colonial development in the mid-eighteenth century: not only population growth (through natural increase as well as immigration) and the new ethnic diversity, but also the increasing importance of colonial urban centers, the creation of a prosperous urban elite, rising levels of consumption for all social ranks, and the new significance of internal markets. In the French and British mainland colonies, exports continued to dominate the economy. Settlers along the Atlantic and Gulf of Mexico coasts were tied to an international commercial system that fluctuated wildly for reasons having little to do with the colonies but inescapable in their effects. Yet expanding local populations demanded greater quantities and types of goods, and Europe could not supply all those needs. Therefore, in English and French America, as well as in the northern portions of New Spain known as the Borderlands (where exports were never an important element of the economy), colonists came increasingly to depend on exploiting and consuming their own resources (see Map 5.2).

Intermarried networks of wealthy families developed in each of Europe's American possessions by the 1760s. These well-off, educated colonists participated in transatlantic intellectual life, such as the movement known as the Enlightenment, whereas many colonists of the "lesser sort" could neither read nor write. The elites lived in comfortable houses and enjoyed leisure-time activities. Most colonists, whether free or enslaved, worked with their hands daily from dawn to dark. Such divisions were most pronounced in British America, the largest and most prosperous settlements on the continent. By the last half of the century, the social and economic distance among different ranks of Anglo-Americans had widened noticeably. As such stratification increased, so did conflicts—political, economic, and even religious—among people of diverse origins and social ranks.

In 1720 much of North America was still under Indian control. By 1770, in sharp contrast, settlements of Europeans and Africans ruled by Great Britain filled almost all of the region between the Appalachian Mountains and the Atlantic Ocean; and the British, following their victory over France in the Seven Years War (see pages 120–123), dominated the extensive system of rivers and lakes running through the heart of the continent. Spanish missions extended in a great arc from present-day northern California to the Gulf Coast. Such geographical, economic, and social changes transformed the character of Europe's North American possessions. ∎

Population Growth and Ethnic Diversity

*D*ramatic population growth characterized the British mainland colonies in the eighteenth century. Only about 250,000 European and African Americans resided in the colonies in 1700. Thirty years later, that number had more than doubled, and by 1775 it had become 2.5 million. Such rapid expansion appears even more remarkable when it is compared with the modest changes that occurred in French and Spanish North America. At the end of the eighteenth century, Texas had only about 2,500 Spanish residents and California even fewer; the largest Spanish colony, New Mexico, included just 20,000 or so. The total European population of New France expanded from approximately 15,000 in 1700 to about 70,000 in the 1760s, but only along the St. Lawrence River between Quebec and Montreal and in New Orleans were there significant concentrations of French settlers.

Although migration accounted for a considerable share of the growth in Anglo America, most of the gain resulted from natural increase. Once the difficult early decades of settlement had passed and the sex ratio evened out in the South (after 1700), the American population doubled approximately every twenty-five years. Such a rate of growth, unparalleled in human history until very recent times, had a variety of causes, chief among them women's youthful age at the onset of childbearing (early twenties for European Americans, late teens for African Americans). Since married women became pregnant every two or three years, women normally bore five to ten children. Because the colonies, especially those north of Virginia, were relatively healthful places to live,

a large proportion of children who survived infancy reached maturity and began families of their own. Consequently, about half of the American population was under sixteen years old in 1775. (By contrast, only about one-quarter of the American population was under sixteen in 2000.)

Even though Spaniards first brought enslaved Africans to the Americas in the sixteenth century, the height of the slave trade occurred in the eighteenth century, when about two-thirds of all slaves were carried across the Atlantic. Rice, indigo, tobacco, and sugar plantations expanded rapidly, thus steadily increasing the demand for bonded laborers. Furthermore, in the slaveholding societies of South America and the Caribbean, a surplus of males over females and appallingly high mortality rates meant that only a large, continuing influx of slaves could maintain the work force at constant levels. South Carolina, where rice cultivation was difficult and unhealthful (chiefly because malaria-carrying mosquitoes bred in the rice swamps), and where planters preferred to purchase men, resembled such colonies because it too required an inflow of Africans to sustain as well as expand its labor force. But in the Chesapeake the number of bondspeople grew especially rapidly because the new imports were added to an enslaved population that after 1740 began to sustain itself through natural increase. The work routines involved in cultivating tobacco, coupled with a roughly equal sex ratio, reduced slave mortality and increased fertility.

The involuntary migrants came from many different ethnic groups and regions of Africa (see Map 4.1). Standard slave-trading practice, in which a vessel loaded an entire cargo at one port, meant that people from the same area (enemies as well as allies) tended to be taken to the Americas together. That tendency was heightened by planter partiality for slaves of particular ethnic groups. Virginians, for example, evidently preferred to purchase Igbos from the Bight of Biafra (modern Cameroon, Gabon, and southeastern Nigeria), whereas South Carolinians and Georgians selected Senegambians and people from West Central Africa (modern Congo and Angola). Louisiana planters first chose slaves from the Bight of Benin (modern Togo, Benin, and southwestern Nigeria) but later bought many from West Central Africa. Rice planters' desire to purchase Senegambians, who had cultivated rice in their homeland, is easily explained, but historians disagree about the reasons for the other preferences. (Some contend, for example, that Chesapeake planters did not care about the ethnicity of

INVOLUNTARY MIGRANTS FROM AFRICA

Map 4.1 Major Origins and Destinations of Africans Enslaved in the Americas

As this schematic map shows, enslaved Africans were drawn from many regions of western Africa (with some coming from the interior of the continent) and were shipped to areas throughout the Americas.

their slaves, taking Igbos only because Carolinians and Georgians explicitly rejected them and so made them available for sale elsewhere.)

Thousands, possibly tens of thousands, of these enslaved Africans were Muslims. Some were literate in Arabic, and several came from aristocratic families. The discovery of noble birth could lead to slaves being freed to return home. Job Ben Solomon, for example, arrived in Maryland in 1732. Himself a slave trader from Senegal, he had been captured by raiders while selling bondspeople in Gambia. A letter he wrote in Arabic so impressed his owners that he was liberated the next year. Abd al-Rahman, brought to Louisiana in 1788, was less fortunate. Known to his master as "Prince" because of his aristocratic origins, he was not freed until 1829, through the assistance of a European he had befriended in West Africa.

Despite the approximately 280,000 slaves brought to the mainland, American-born people of African descent soon numerically dominated the enslaved population because of high levels of natural increase. A planter who owned adult female slaves could watch the size of his labor force expand steadily—through the births of their children, by then designated as slaves in all the

colonies—without making additional major purchases of workers. Not coincidentally, the first truly large Chesapeake plantations appeared in the 1740s. Even in South Carolina, where substantial imports continued, African-born slaves were outnumbered by American-born slaves as early as 1750. Some years later, the slaveholder Thomas Jefferson indicated that he fully understood the connections when he observed, "I consider a woman who brings a child every two years more profitable than the best man of the farm. What she produces is an addition to the capital, while his labors disappear in mere consumption."

In addition to the new group of Africans, about 585,000 Europeans moved to North America during the eighteenth century, most of them after 1730. Late in the seventeenth century, English officials decided to recruit German and French Protestants in order to prevent further large-scale emigration from England itself. Influenced by mercantilist thought, they had come to regard a large, industrious population at home as an asset rather than a liability. Thus they ordered the deportation to the colonies of "undesirables"—convicts and Jacobite rebels (supporters of the deposed Stuart monarchs)—but otherwise discouraged emigration. They offered foreign Protestants free lands and religious toleration, even financing the passage of some groups (for example, Germans sent to New York in the 1710s). After 1740 they relaxed citizenship (naturalization) requirements, insisting on only the payment of a small fee, seven years' colonial residence, evidence of adherence to Protestant beliefs, and an oath of allegiance to the king.

The patterns evident in the chapter-opening vignette applied generally to all the voluntary eighteenth-century European migrants. Early arrivals wrote home, urging others to come; those contacts created chains of migration from particular regions. The most successful migrants came well prepared, having learned from their American correspondents that land and resources were abundant, especially in the inland areas known as the backcountry, but that they would need capital to take full advantage of the new opportunities. People who arrived penniless did less well. Thus, for instance, the poverty-stricken folk (generally of English or German origin) who emigrated as indentured servants often struggled to survive after their terms of service had been completed.

One of the largest groups of immigrants—nearly 150,000—came from Ireland or Scotland. About 66,000 Scots-Irish descendants of Presbyterian Scots

NEWCOMERS FROM EUROPE

SCOTS-IRISH, GERMANS, AND SCOTS
who had settled in the north of Ireland during the seventeenth century joined some 35,000 people who, like Alexander McAllister, came directly to America from Scotland (see Table 4.1). Another 43,000, both Protestants and Catholics, migrated from southern Ireland. High rents, poor harvests, and religious discrimination (in Ireland) combined to push people from lands their families had long occupied. Many of the Irish migrants had supported themselves in Ireland by weaving linen cloth, but linen prices declined significantly in the late 1710s. Because the flax used in the weaving was imported from Pennsylvania and the less bulky cloth was largely exported back to the same place, vessels with plenty of room for passengers regularly sailed from Ireland to Pennsylvania. By the 1720s, the migration route was well established, fueled by positive reports of prospects for advancement in North America.

TABLE 4.1

Who Moved to America from England and Scotland in the Early 1770s, and Why?

	English Emigrants	Scottish Emigrants	Free American Population
Destination			
13 British colonies	81.1%	92.7%	—
Canada	12.1	4.2	—
West Indies	6.8	3.1	—
Age Distribution			
Under 21	26.8	45.3	56.8%
21–25	37.1	19.9	9.7
26–44	33.3	29.5	20.4
45 and over	2.7	5.3	13.1
Sex Distribution			
Male	83.8	59.9	—
Female	16.2	40.1	—
Unknown	4.2	13.5	—
Traveling Alone or with Families			
In families	20.0	48.0	—
Alone	80.0	52.0	—
Known Occupation or Status			
Gentry	2.5	1.2	—
Merchandising	5.2	5.2	—
Agriculture	17.8	24.0	—
Artisanry	54.2	37.7	—
Laborer	20.3	31.9	—
Why They Left			
Positive reasons (e.g., desire to better one's position)	90.0	36.0	—
Negative reasons (e.g., poverty, unemployment)	10.0	64.0	—

Note: Between December 1773 and March 1776, the British government questioned individuals and families leaving ports in Scotland and England for the American colonies to learn who they were, where they were going, and why they were leaving. This table summarizes just a few of the findings of the official inquiries, which revealed a number of significant differences between the Scottish and English emigrants.

Source of data: Bernard Bailyn, *Voyagers to the West* (New York: Knopf, 1986), Tables 4.1, 5.2, 5.4, 5.7, 5.23, and 6.1.

Such immigrants usually landed in Philadelphia or New Castle, Delaware. They moved into the backcountry of western Pennsylvania along the Susquehanna River, where the colonial government created a county named Donegal for them. Later migrants moved farther west and south, to the backcountry of Maryland, Virginia, and the Carolinas. Frequently unable to afford any acreage, they lived illegally on land belonging to Indians, land speculators, or colonial governments. In the frontier setting, they gained a reputation for lawlessness, hard drinking, and ferocious fighting, both among themselves and with neighboring Indians.

Migrants from Germany and German-speaking areas of Switzerland numbered about 85,000, most of them emigrating from the Rhineland between 1730 and 1755. They too usually arrived in Philadelphia, becoming known locally as Pennsylvania Dutch (a corruption of *Deutsch,* as the Germans called themselves). Late in the century they and their descendants accounted for one-third of Pennsylvania's residents. More important, they—like other ethnic groups—tended to settle together, and so they composed up to half of the population of some counties. Many Germans moved west and then south into the backcountry of Maryland and Virginia. Others landed in Charles Town and settled in the southern interior. The Germans belonged to a wide variety of Protestant sects—primarily Lutheran, German Reformed, and Moravian—and therefore added to the already substantial religious diversity of Pennsylvania. So many Germans had arrived by 1751 that Benjamin Franklin, for one, feared they would "Germanize" Pennsylvania. They "will never adopt our Language or Customs," he predicted (inaccurately).

The most concentrated period of immigration to the colonies fell between 1760 and 1775. Tough economic times in Germany and the British Isles led many to decide to seek a better life in America; simultaneously, the slave trade burgeoned. In those fifteen years alone more than 220,000 persons arrived—nearly 10 percent of the entire population of British North America in 1775. Late-arriving free immigrants had little choice but to remain in the cities or move to the edges of settlement; land elsewhere was fully occupied (see Map 4.2). In the peripheries they became the tenants of, or bought property from, land speculators who had purchased giant tracts in the (usually vain) hope of making a fortune.

Because of these migration patterns and the concentration of slaveholding in the South, half the colonial population south of New England had non-English origins by 1775. Whether the migrants assimilated readily into Anglo-American culture depended on patterns of

■ In December 1729, probably in New York's Hudson Valley, an unknown artist portrayed J. M. Stolle, son of a Palatine immigrant who came to North America from Germany in 1709. The young man's fancy clothing and the column and balustrade in the background suggest that the artist wanted to convey an image of the family's economic success, though whether that image was accurate is unknown.   (National Gallery of Art, Washington, D.C. Gift of Edgar William and Bernice Chrysler Garbisch)

MAINTAINING ETHNIC AND RELIGIOUS IDENTITIES settlement, the size of the group, and the strength of the migrants' ties to their common culture. For example, the Huguenots—French Protestants who fled religious persecution in their homeland after 1685—settled in tiny enclaves in American cities like Charles Town and New York. Unable to sustain either their language or their religious practices, they largely assimilated into the dominant culture within two generations. By contrast, the equally small group of colonial Jews maintained a distinct identity. Most were Sephardic, descended from persecuted Spanish and Portuguese Jews who had first fled to the Netherlands or its American colonies, then later migrated into English territory. In places like New York and Newport, Rhode Island, they established synagogues and worked actively to preserve their religion (for instance, by observing dietary

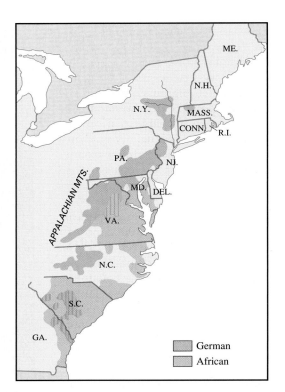

Map 4.2 Non-English Ethnic Groups in the British Colonies, c. 1775

Non-African immigrants arriving in the years after 1720 were pushed to the peripheries of settlement, as is shown by these maps. Scottish, Scots-Irish, French, and German newcomers had to move to the frontiers. The Dutch remained where they had originally settled in the seventeenth century. Africans were concentrated in coastal plantation regions.

laws and by trying to prevent their children from marrying Christians).

Members of the larger groups of migrants (Germans, Irish, and Scots) found it easier to sustain European ways. Some ethnic groups dominated certain localities. Near Frederick, Maryland, a visitor would have heard more German than English; in Anson and Cumberland Counties, North Carolina, the same visitor might have thought she was in Scotland. Where migrants from different countries settled in the same region, ethnic antagonisms often surfaced. One German clergyman in Pennsylvania, for example, explained his efforts to prevent German youths from marrying people of different ethnic origins by asserting that Scots-Irish migrants were "lazy, dissipated and poor" and that "it is very seldom that German and English blood is happily united in wedlock." Anglo-American elites fostered such antagonisms in order to maintain their political and economic power, and they frequently subverted the colonies' generous naturalization laws, thus depriving even long-resident immigrants of a voice in government.

The elites probably would have preferred to ignore the English colonies' growing racial and ethnic diversity, but ultimately they could not do so. When they moved toward revolution in the 1770s, they recognized that they needed the support of non-English Americans. Quite deliberately, they began to speak of "the rights of man," rather than "English liberties," when they sought recruits for their cause.

Economic Growth and Development

*T*he dramatic increase in the population of Anglo America served as one of the few sources of stability for the colonial economy, which was driven primarily by the vagaries of international markets. A comparison with French and Spanish America reveals significant differences. The population and economy of New Spain's northern Borderlands stagnated. The isolated settlements produced few items for export (notably,

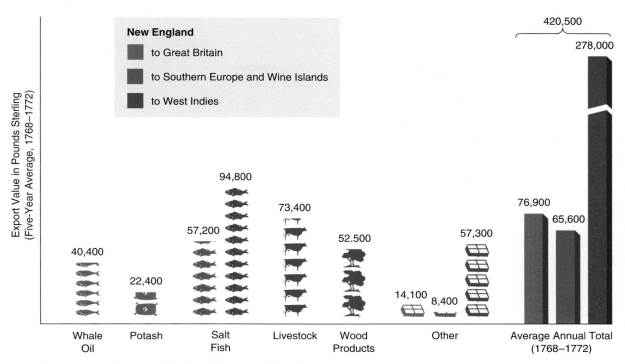

Figure 4.1   Regional Trading Patterns: New England

New England's major exports—salt fish, livestock, and wood products—were sold primarily in the West Indies.

(Source: James F. Shepherd and Gary M. Walton, *Shipping, Maritime Trade, and the Economic Development of Colonial North America* [Cambridge: Cambridge University Press, 1972]. Copyright 1972. Used by permission of Cambridge University Press.)

hides obtained from nearby Indians); residents more often exchanged goods illegally with their French and English neighbors than with Spanish Mexico or the Caribbean. French Canada exported large quantities of furs and fish, but monopolistic trade practices ensured that most of the profits ended up in the home country. The Louisiana colony required substantial government subsidies to survive, despite its active internal trade and some agricultural exports. Of France's American possessions, only the Caribbean islands flourished economically.

In British North America, by contrast, each year the rising population generated ever-greater demands for goods and services, leading to the development of small-scale colonial manufacturing and a complex network of internal trade. Roads, bridges, mills, and stores were built to serve the many new settlements. A lively coastal trade developed; by the late 1760s, more than half the vessels leaving Boston harbor sailed to other mainland colonies. Such ships not only collected goods for export and dis-

OVERVIEW OF
THE ANGLO-
AMERICAN
ECONOMY

tributed imports but also sold items made in America. The colonies thus began to move away from their earlier pattern of dependence on European manufactured goods. For the first time, the American population generated sufficient demand to encourage manufacturing enterprises. Iron making became the largest indigenous industry; by 1775, Anglo America's iron production—most of it for domestic consumption—surpassed England's.

The major energizing, yet destabilizing, influence on the colonial economy nevertheless remained foreign trade. Colonial prosperity still depended heavily on overseas demand for American products like tobacco, rice, indigo, fish, and barrel staves. The sale of such items earned the colonists the credit they needed to purchase English and European imports. If demand for American exports slowed, the colonists' income dropped, as did their ability to buy imported goods. Merchants were particularly vulnerable to economic downswings, and bankruptcies were common.

Despite fluctuations, the American economy slowly grew during the eighteenth century. That growth, which resulted partly from higher earnings from exports, in

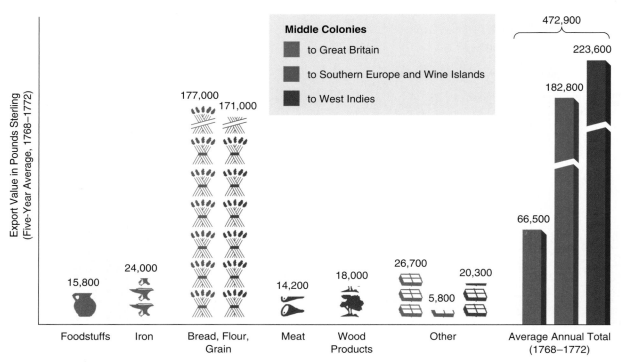

Figure 4.2 **Regional Trading Patterns: Middle Colonies**

The middle colonies' major trading partners were the West Indies, the Wine Islands, and southern Europe. Bread, flour, and grains were the region's most valuable exports. (Source: James F. Shepherd and Gary M. Walton, *Shipping, Maritime Trade, and the Economic Development of Colonial North America* [Cambridge: Cambridge University Press, 1972]. Copyright 1972. Used by permission of Cambridge University Press.)

WEALTH AND POVERTY

turn produced better standards of living for all property-owning Americans. Early in the century, as the price of British manufactures fell in relation to Americans' incomes, households began to acquire amenities such as chairs and earthenware dishes. Diet also improved as trading networks brought access to more varied foodstuffs. After 1750, luxury items like silver plate could be found in the homes of the wealthy, and the "middling sort" started to purchase imported English ceramics and teapots. Even the poorest property owners had more and better household possessions. Thus the colonists became consumers, in the sense that for the first time they could make choices among a variety of products and also could afford to buy items not essential for subsistence.

Yet the benefits of economic growth were unevenly distributed: wealthy Americans improved their position relative to other colonists. The native-born elite families who dominated American political, economic, and social life by 1750 had begun the century with sufficient capital to take advantage of the changes caused by population growth. They were the urban merchants who exported raw materials and imported luxury goods, the large landowners who rented small farms to immigrant tenants, the slave traders who supplied wealthy planters with their bondspeople, and the owners of rum distilleries. The rise of this group of moneyed families helped to make the social and economic structure of mid-eighteenth-century America more stratified than before.

New arrivals did not have the opportunities for advancement that had greeted their predecessors. Even so, few free settlers in rural areas (where about 95 percent of the colonists lived) appear to have been truly poor. But in the cities, families of urban laborers lived on the edge of destitution. In Philadelphia, for instance, a male laborer's average annual earnings fell short of the amount needed to supply his family with the bare necessities. Even in a good year, his wife or children had to do wage work; in a bad year, the family could be reduced to beggary. By the 1760s applicants for assistance overwhelmed public urban poor-relief systems, and some cities began to build workhouses or almshouses to shelter the growing number of poor people. Among them were recent immi-

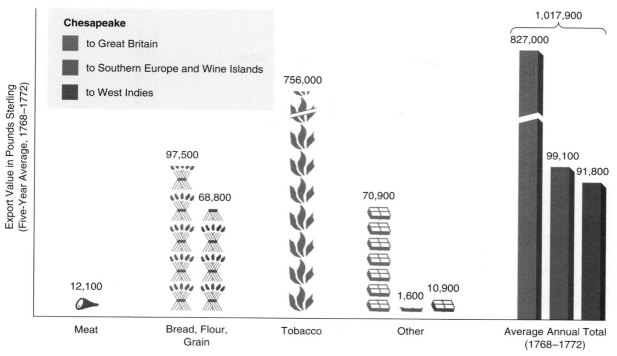

Figure 4.3   Regional Trading Patterns: The Chesapeake

Tobacco—legally exported only to Great Britain under the terms of the Navigation Acts—was the Chesapeake's dominant product. Grain made up an increasing proportion of the crops this region sold to other destinations.
(Source: James F. Shepherd and Gary M. Walton, *Shipping, Maritime Trade, and the Economic Development of Colonial North America* [Cambridge: Cambridge University Press, 1972]. Copyright 1972. Used by permission of Cambridge University Press.)

grants, the elderly and infirm, and widows, especially those with small children.

Within this overall picture, different regional patterns can be identified. New England, the middle colonies (Pennsylvania, New York, and New Jersey), the Chesapeake (including North Carolina), and the Lower South (South Carolina and Georgia) each had its own economic rhythm derived from the nature of its export trade.

In New England, three elements combined to influence economic development: the nature of the landscape, New England's leadership in shipping, and the impact of imperial wars. New England's poor soil failed to produce surpluses other than livestock, so wood products constituted important salable commodities. Farms were worked primarily by family members; the region had relatively few hired laborers. It also had the lowest average wealth per freeholder in the colonies. But New England had many wealthy merchants and professionals who profited substantially from trade with the Caribbean in items such as salt fish, livestock, and molasses (see Figure 4.1).

NEW ENGLAND AND KING GEORGE'S WAR

Boston, by the 1730s a major shipbuilding center, soon felt the impact when warfare between European powers resumed in 1739. British vessels clashed with Spanish ships in the Caribbean, sparking a conflict that became known in America as King George's War (Europeans called it the War of the Austrian Succession). The war initially energized Boston's economy, for ships—and sailors—were in great demand to serve as privateers. Wealthy merchants profited from contracts to supply military expeditions. But then New Englanders suffered major losses in Caribbean battles and forays against Canada. In 1745 a New England expedition captured the French fortress of Louisbourg (in modern Nova Scotia), which guarded the sea-lanes leading to New France. The expensive victory, though, led to heavy taxation of Massachusetts residents, and after the war unprecedented numbers of widows and children crowded Boston's relief rolls. The shipbuilding boom ended when the war did, the economy stagnated, and taxes remained high. Britain even returned Louisbourg to France in the Treaty of Aix-la-Chapelle (1748).

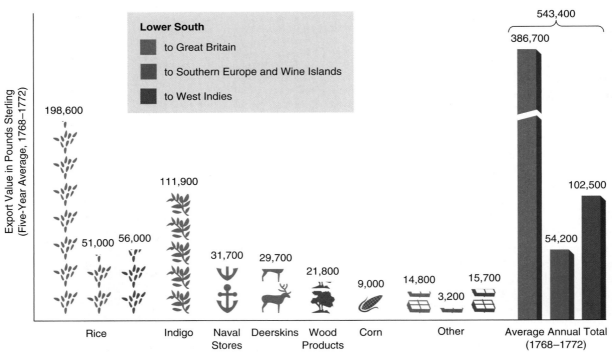

Figure 4.4   Regional Trading Patterns: The Lower South

Rice and indigo, sold primarily in the mother country, dominated the exports of the Lower South.

(Source: James F. Shepherd and Gary M. Walton, *Shipping, Maritime Trade, and the Economic Development of Colonial North America* [Cambridge: Cambridge University Press, 1972]. Copyright 1972. Used by permission of Cambridge University Press.)

King George's War and its aftermath affected the middle colonies and the Chesapeake more positively because of the greater fertility of the soil in those regions, where commercial farming prevailed. An average Pennsylvania farm family consumed only 40 percent of what it produced, selling the rest. New York and New Jersey both had many tenant farmers who leased acreage from large landowners, often paying their rent by sharing crops with their landlords. Prosperous landlords and farmers thus occupied an ideal position to profit from the wartime demand for grain and flour, especially in the Caribbean (see Figure 4.2). After the war a series of poor grain harvests in Europe caused flour prices to rise rapidly. Philadelphia and New York, which could draw on large fertile grain- and live-stock-producing areas, took the lead in the foodstuffs trade.

MIDDLE COLONIES AND THE CHESAPEAKE

Increased European demand for grain had a significant impact on the Chesapeake as well. After 1745, when the price of grain began rising faster than that of tobacco, some Chesapeake planters began to convert to-bacco fields to wheat and corn. By diversifying their crops, they could avoid dependency on one product for their income (see Figure 4.3). Tobacco still ruled the region and remained the largest single export from the mainland colonies. The value of tobacco exports was nearly double that of grain products, the next contender. Yet the conversion to grain cultivation brought about the first significant change in Chesapeake settlement patterns by encouraging the development of port towns (like Baltimore) to house the merchants who marketed the new products.

The Lower South too depended on staple crops and an enslaved labor force but had a distinctive pattern of economic growth. After Parliament in 1730 removed rice from the list of enumerated products (see page 77), South Carolinians could trade directly with continental Europe. Rice prices thereafter climbed steeply, doubling by the late 1730s (see Figure 4.4). But dependence on European sales had its drawbacks, as rice growers discovered when the outbreak of King George's War in 1739 disrupted trade with the continent. Rice prices plummeted,

LOWER SOUTH

and South Carolina entered a depression from which it did not emerge for a decade. Still, prosperity returned by the 1760s because of rapidly rising European demand for South Carolina's exports. Indeed, the Lower South experienced more rapid economic growth in that period than did the other colonial regions. Partly as a result, it had the highest average wealth per freeholder in mainland Anglo America by the time of the American Revolution.

Closely linked to South Carolina geographically, demographically, and economically was the newest
GEORGIA
settlement on the mainland, Georgia, chartered in 1732 as a haven for English debtors, who would be released from confinement if they agreed to relocate to the colony. Its founder, James Oglethorpe, envisioned Georgia as a garrison province peopled by sturdy farmers who would defend the southern flank of English settlement against Spanish Florida. Accordingly, its charter prohibited slavery. But Carolina rice planters successfully won the removal of the restriction in 1751. Thereafter, they essentially invaded Georgia, which—despite remaining politically independent and becoming a royal colony in 1752—developed into a rice-planting slave society resembling South Carolina.

King George's War initially helped New England and hurt the Lower South, but in the long run those effects were reversed. In the Chesapeake and the middle colonies, the war ushered in a long period of prosperity. These variations in economic experience highlight a crucial fact about the British mainland colonies: they did not compose a unified whole. Although linked economically into regions, they had few political or social ties beyond or even within those regions. Despite increasing coastal trade, the individual colonies' economic fortunes depended not on their neighbors in North America but rather on the shifting markets of Europe and the Caribbean. Had it not been for an unprecedented crisis in the British imperial system (discussed in Chapter 5), it is hard to see how they could have been persuaded to join in a common endeavor. Even with that impetus, they found unity difficult to maintain.

Colonial Cultures

a seventeenth-century resident of England's American possessions transported through time to 1750 would have been surprised not only by the denser and more diverse population but also by the new extremes of wealth and poverty visible in the growing cities. Native-born colonial elites sought to distinguish themselves from ordinary folk in a variety of ways as they consolidated their hold on the local economy and political power.

One historian has termed these processes "the refinement of America." Colonists who acquired wealth
GENTEEL CULTURE
through trade, agriculture, or manufacturing spent their money ostentatiously, dressing fashionably, traveling in horse-drawn carriages driven by uniformed servants, and entertaining one another at lavish parties. Most notably, they built large houses containing rooms designed for such forms of socializing as dancing, cardplaying, or drinking tea. Sufficiently well-off to enjoy "leisure" time (a first for North America), they

■ Elizabeth Murray, the subject of this 1769 painting by John Singleton Copley, was the wife of James Smith, a wealthy rum distiller. Her fashionable dress and pose would seem to mark her as a lady of leisure, yet both before and during her marriage this Scottish immigrant ran a successful dry goods shop in Boston. She thus simultaneously catered to and participated in the new culture of consumption. (Gift of Joseph W. R. Rogers and Mary C. Rogers. Museum of Fine Arts, Boston. Reproduced with permission. © Museum of Fine Arts, Boston)

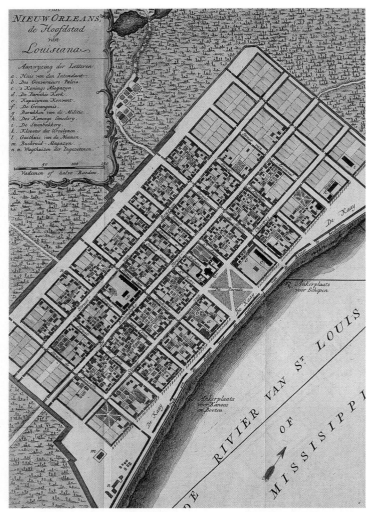

■ One of the very few institutions of higher learning open to females in eighteenth-century North America is clearly marked on this 1769 map from a Dutch atlas: the Ursuline convent in New Orleans. There young women studied religion and other subjects. As indicated in the label to the left, the convent is located at letter *k,* in the lower right corner of the map (which shows the area of the modern city known as the French Quarter). (Private Collection)

attended concerts and the theater, gambled at horseraces, and played billiards and other games. They also cultivated polite manners, adopting stylized forms of address and paying attention to "proper" ways of behaving. Although the effects of accumulated wealth were most pronounced in Anglo America, elite families in New Mexico, Louisiana, and Quebec as well set themselves off from the "lesser sort." Together these wealthy families deliber-

ately constructed a genteel culture quite different from that of ordinary colonists.

Men from such families prided themselves not only on their possessions and on their positions in the colonial political, social, and economic hierarchy, but also on their level of education and their intellectual connections to Europe. Many had been tutored by private teachers hired by their families; some even attended college in Europe or America. (Harvard, the first colonial college, founded in 1636, was joined by William and Mary in 1693, Yale in 1701, and later by several others—for example, Princeton, established in 1747.) In the seventeenth century, only aspiring clergymen attended college, studying a curriculum focused heavily on ancient languages and theology. But by the mid-eighteenth century, colleges broadened their curricula to include mathematics, the natural sciences, law, and medicine. Accordingly, a minuscule number of young men from elite or upwardly mobile families enrolled in college to study for careers other than the ministry. American women were mostly excluded from advanced education, with the exception of some who joined nunneries in Canada or Louisiana, and who could engage in sustained study within convent walls.

The intellectual current known as the Enlightenment deeply affected the learned clergymen who headed colonial colleges and their students. Around 1650, some European thinkers began to analyze nature in order to determine the laws governing the universe. They employed experimentation and abstract reasoning to discover general principles behind phenomena such as the motions of planets and stars, the behavior of falling objects, and the characteristics of light and sound. Above all, Enlightenment philosophers emphasized acquiring knowledge through reason, taking particular delight in challenging previously unquestioned assumptions. John Locke's *Essay Concerning Human Understanding* (1690), for example, disputed the notion that human beings are born already imprinted with innate ideas. All knowledge, Locke asserted, derives from one's observations of the external world. Belief in witchcraft and astrology, among other similar phenomena, thus came under attack.

The Enlightenment had an enormous impact on educated, well-to-do people in Europe and America. It supplied them with a common vocabulary and a unified view of the world, one that insisted that the enlightened eighteenth century was better, and wiser, than all previous ages. It joined them in a common endeavor, the effort to make sense of God's orderly creation. Thus American

THE ENLIGHTENMENT

naturalists like John and William Bartram supplied European scientists with information about New World plants and animals so that they could be included in newly formulated universal classification systems. So, too, Americans interested in astronomy took part in an international effort to learn about the solar system by studying a rare occurrence, the transit of Venus across the face of the sun in 1769. A prime example of America's participation in the Enlightenment was Benjamin Franklin, who retired from a successful printing business in 1748 when he was just forty-two, thereafter devoting himself to scientific experimentation and public service. His *Experiments and Observations on Electricity* (1751) established the terminology and basic theory of electricity still used today.

The experimentation encouraged by the Enlightenment affected the lives of ordinary Americans most dramatically through advances in medicine—specifically, the control of smallpox. The Reverend Cotton Mather, the prominent Puritan cleric, learned from his African-born slave about the benefits of inoculation (deliberately infecting a person with a mild case of a disease) as a protection against smallpox. When Boston in 1720–1721 suffered a major smallpox epidemic, Mather urged the adoption of inoculation despite fierce opposition from the city's leading physician. Mortality rates eventually supported Mather—of those inoculated, just 3 percent died; of others, 15 percent. Although inoculation was not widely accepted until midcentury, science provided colonial Americans with a means of preventing the greatest killer disease of all.

Enlightenment rationalism affected politics as well as science. Locke's *Two Treatises of Government* (1691) and other works by French and Scottish philosophers challenged previous concepts of a divinely sanctioned, hierarchical political order originating in the power of fathers over families. Men created governments and so could alter them, Locke declared. A ruler who broke his contract with the people and failed to protect their rights could legitimately be ousted from power by peaceful—or even violent—means. Government should aim at the good of the people, Enlightenment theorists proclaimed. A proper political order could prevent the rise of tyrants; God's natural laws governed even the power of monarchs.

The world in which such ideas were discussed was that of the few, not the many. Most residents of North America did not know how to read or write. Even those with basic literacy skills—a small proportion in French or Spanish America, about half of the people in British America—knew only the rudiments. Books were scarce

ORAL CULTURES

and expensive, and ordinary folk rarely had occasion to write a letter. No colony required children to attend school; European American youngsters who learned to read usually did so in their own homes, taught by their parents or older siblings. A few months at a private "dame school" run by a literate local widow might complete their education by teaching them the basics of writing and simple arithmetic. Few Americans other than some Church of England missionaries in the South tried to instruct enslaved children. And only the most zealous Indian converts learned Europeans' literacy skills.

Thus the cultures of colonial North America were primarily oral, communal, and—at least through the first half of the eighteenth century—intensely local. In the absence of literacy, face-to-face conversation served as the major means of communication. Information tended to travel slowly and within relatively confined regions. Different locales developed divergent cultural traditions, and racial and ethnic variations heightened those differences. Public rituals served as the chief means through which the colonists forged their cultural identities.

Attendance at church was perhaps the most important such ritual. In Congregational (Puritan) churches, church leaders assigned seating to reflect standing in the community. In early New England, men and women sat on opposite sides of a central aisle, arranged in ranks according to age, wealth, and church membership. By the mid-eighteenth century, wealthy men and their wives sat in privately owned pews; their children, servants, and the less fortunate still sat in sex-segregated fashion at the rear or sides of the church. In eighteenth-century Virginia, seating in Church of England parishes also conformed to the local status hierarchy. Planter families purchased their own pews, and in some parishes landed gentlemen customarily strode into church as a group just before the service, deliberately drawing attention to their exalted position. In Quebec City, formal processions of men into the parish church celebrated Catholic feast days; each participant's rank determined his placement in the procession. By contrast, Quaker meetinghouses in Pennsylvania and elsewhere used an egalitarian but sex-segregated seating system. The varying rituals surrounding people's entrance into and seating in colonial churches thus symbolized their place in society and the values of the local community.

Communal culture also centered on the civic sphere. In New England, governments proclaimed official days of thanksgiving (for good harvests, victories in war, and so forth) and days of fasting and prayer (when the colony

RELIGIOUS AND CIVIC RITUALS

■ Convicted criminals were publicly punished and shamed in front of their friends, relatives, and neighbors. A man might be put in the stocks for offenses such as contempt of authority, drunken and disorderly conduct, or theft. The intent was not simply to deter him from future misbehavior but to let his fate serve as a warning to all who saw his humiliating posture. (Library of Congress)

was experiencing difficulties such as droughts or epidemics). Everyone was expected to participate in the public rituals held in churches on such occasions. Monthly militia musters (known as training days) also brought the community together, since all able-bodied men between the ages of sixteen and sixty participated in the militia.

In the Chesapeake, important cultural rituals occurred on court and election days. When the county court met, men came from miles around to file suits, appear as witnesses, or serve as jurors. Attendance at court functioned as a method of civic education; from watching the proceedings men learned what behavior their neighbors expected of them. Elections served the same purpose, for property-holding men voted in public. An election official, often flanked by the candidates for the office in question, would call each man forward to declare his preference. The voter would then be thanked politely by the gentleman for whom he had cast his oral ballot. Traditionally, the candidates afterward treated their supporters to rum at nearby taverns.

Everywhere in colonial North America, the public punishment of criminals served not just to humiliate the offender but also to remind the community of proper behavioral standards. Public hangings and whippings, along with orders to sit in the stocks, expressed the community's outrage about crimes and restored harmony to its ranks. Judges often assigned penalties that shamed miscreants in especially appropriate ways. In San Antonio, Texas, for example, one cattle thief was sentenced to be led through the town's streets "with the entrails hanging from his neck"; and when a New Mexico man as-

saulted his father-in-law, he was directed not merely to pay medical expenses but also to kneel before him and to beg his forgiveness publicly. New Englanders reprieved after being convicted of capital offenses did not thereby escape public humiliation: frequently they were ordered to wear nooses around their necks for years as a constant reminder to themselves, their families, and their neighbors of their heinous violation of community norms.

The wide availability of consumer goods after the early years of the eighteenth century fostered new rituals centered on consumption, establishing novel links among the various residents of North America and creating what historians have termed "an empire of goods." First came the acquisition of desirable items. In the seventeenth century, settlers acquired necessities by bartering with neighbors or by ordering products from a home-country merchant. By the middle of the eighteenth century, specialized shops selling nonessentials had proliferated in cities such as New York, Philadelphia, and New Orleans. In 1770 Boston alone had more than five hundred stores, which offered consumers a vast selection of millinery, sewing supplies, tobacco, gloves, tableware, and the like. Even small and medium-size towns had one or two retail establishments. A colonist with money to spend would set aside time to "go shopping," a novel and pleasurable activity. The purchase of a desired object—for example, a ceramic bowl, a mirror, or a length of beautiful fabric—marked just the beginning of consumption rituals.

Consumers would then deploy their purchases in an appropriate manner: hanging the mirror prominently on

RITUALS OF CONSUMPTION

Exotic Beverages

As colonists became consumers, they developed a taste not only for tea (from China) but for coffee (from Arabia), chocolate (from Mesoamerica), and rum (distilled from sugar, which also sweetened the bitter taste of the other three). The demand for these once-exotic beverages in America and Europe helped reshape the world economy after the mid-seventeenth century. Indeed, one historian has estimated that approximately two-thirds of the people who migrated across the Atlantic before 1776 were involved in one way or another, primarily as slaves, in the production of tobacco, calico, and these four drinks for the world market. The exotic beverages had a profound impact, too, on custom and culture, as they moved swiftly from luxury to necessity.

Each beverage had its own pattern of consumption. Chocolate, brought to Spain from Mexico and enjoyed there for a century before spreading more widely throughout Europe, became the preferred drink of aristocrats, consumed hot at intimate gatherings in palaces and mansions. Coffee, by contrast, became the preeminent morning beverage of English and colonial businessmen, who praised its caffeine for keeping drinkers sober and focused. Coffee was served in new public coffeehouses, patronized only by men, where politics and business were the topics of conversation. The first coffeehouse opened in London in the late 1660s; Boston had several by the 1690s. By the mid-eighteenth century, though, tea had supplanted coffee as the preferred hot, caffeinated beverage in England and America. It was consumed in the afternoons, in private homes at tea tables presided over by women. Tea embodied genteel status and polite conversation. In contrast, rum was the drink of the masses. This inexpensive, potent distilled spirit, made possible by new technology and the increasing production of sugar, was devoured by free working people everywhere in the Atlantic world.

The American colonies played a vital role in the production, distribution, and consumption of each of these beverages. Chocolate, most obviously, originated in America, and cacao plantations in the South American tropics multiplied in size and number to meet the rising demand. Coffee and tea (particularly the latter) were as avidly consumed in the colonies as in England. And rum involved Americans in every phase of its production and consumption. The sugar grown on French and English Caribbean plantations was transported to the mainland in barrels and ships made from North American wood. There the syrup was turned into rum at 140 distilleries. The Americans themselves drank a substantial share of the distilleries' output—an estimated four gallons per person annually—but exported much of it to Africa. There the rum purchased more slaves to produce more sugar to make still more rum, and the cycle began again.

Thus new tastes and customs connected to four different beverages linked the colonies to the rest of the world and altered their economic and social development.

The frontispiece of Peter Muguet, *Tractatus De Poto Caphe, Chinesium The et de Chocolata,* 1685. Muguet's treatise visually linked the three hot, exotic beverages recently introduced to Europeans. The drinks are being consumed by representatives of the cultures in which they originated: a turbaned Turk (with coffeepot in the foreground), a Chinese man (with teapot on the table), and an Indian drinking from a hollowed, handled gourd (with a chocolate pot and ladle on the floor in front of him).   (Library of Congress)

This trade card (advertisement) issued by a Philadelphia tobacco dealer in 1770 shows a convivial group of wealthy men at a tavern. Both the leisurely activity depicted here and the advertisement itself were signs of the new rituals of consumption. Merchants began to advertise only when their customers could choose among different ways of spending money. (Library Company of Philadelphia)

a wall of the house, displaying the bowl on a table or sideboard, turning the fabric into a special piece of clothing. Individual colonists took pleasure in owning lovely objects, but they also proudly displayed their acquisitions (and thus their wealth and good taste) publicly to kin and neighbors. A rich man might even hire a portraitist to paint his family using the objects and wearing the clothing, thereby creating a pictorial record that also would be displayed for admiration.

Tea drinking, a consumption ritual dominated and controlled by women, played an especially important role in Anglo America. From early in the eighteenth century, households with aspirations to genteel status sought to acquire the items necessary for the proper consumption of tea: not just pots and cups but also strainers, sugar tongs, bowls, and even special tables. Tea provided a focal point for socializing and, because of its cost, served as a crucial marker of status. Wealthy women regularly entertained their male and female friends at afternoon tea parties. A hot and mildly stimulating drink, tea also appeared healthful. Thus even poor households consumed tea, although they could not afford the fancy equipment used by their better-off neighbors. Some Mohawk Indians adopted the custom, much to the surprise of a traveler from Sweden, who observed them drinking tea in the late 1740s.

Other sorts of rituals allowed the disparate cultures of colonial North America to interact with one another. Particularly important rituals developed on what the

RITUALS ON THE "MIDDLE GROUND"

historian Richard White has termed the "middle ground"—that is, the psychological and geographical space in which Indians and Europeans encountered each other. Most of those cultural encounters occurred in the context of trade or warfare.

When Europeans sought to trade with Indians, they encountered an indigenous system of exchange that stressed gift giving rather than formalized buying and selling. Although French and English traders complained constantly about the need to present Indians with gifts prior to negotiating with them for pelts and skins, successful bargaining required such a step. Over time, an appropriate ritual developed. A European trader arriving at a village would give gifts (cloth, rum, gunpowder, and other items) to Indian hunters. Eventually, those gifts would be reciprocated, and formal trading could then take place. To the detriment of Indian societies, rum became a crucial component of these intercultural trading rituals. Traders soon concluded that drunken Indians would sell their furs more cheaply; and some Indians refused to hunt or trade unless they first received rum. Alcohol abuse hastened the deterioration of villages already devastated by disease and dislocation.

Intercultural rituals also developed to deal with murders. Indians and Europeans both believed that murders required a compensatory act but differed in their notions of what that act should be. Europeans sought primarily to identify and punish the murderer. To Indians, such "eye for an eye" revenge was just one of many possible responses to murder. Compensation could also be accomplished by capturing another Indian or a colonist who could take the dead person's place, or by "covering the dead"—that is, by providing the family of the deceased with compensatory goods, a crucial strategy for maintaining peace on the frontiers. Eventually, the French and the Algonquians evolved an elaborate ritual for handling frontier murders that encompassed elements of both societies' traditions: murders were investigated and murderers identified, but by mutual agreement deaths were usually "covered" by trade goods rather than by blood revenge.

Colonial Families

Families (rather than individuals) constituted the basic units of colonial society; never-married adults were extremely rare. People living together as families, commonly under the direction of a marital pair, everywhere constituted the chief mechanisms for both production and consumption. Yet family forms and structures varied widely in the mainland colonies, and not all were headed by couples.

As Europeans consolidated their hold on North America during the first three-quarters of the eighteenth century, Native Americans had to adapt to novel circumstances. Bands reduced in numbers by disease and warfare recombined into new units; for example, the group later known as the Catawbas emerged in the 1730s in the western Carolinas from the fragmentary remains of several earlier Indian nations, including the Yamasees. Likewise, European secular and religious authorities reshaped Indian family forms. Whereas many Indian societies had permitted easy divorce, English, French, and Spanish missionaries frowned on such practices; and those societies that had allowed polygynous marriages (including New England Algonquians) redefined such relationships, designating one wife as "legitimate" and others as "concubines."

INDIAN FAMILIES

Continued high mortality rates created Indian societies in which extended kin took on new importance, for when parents died, aunts, uncles, and other relatives—even occasionally nonkin—assumed child-rearing responsibilities. Furthermore, once Europeans established dominance in any region, Indians there could no longer pursue traditional modes of subsistence. That led to unusual family structures as well as to a variety of economic strategies. In New England, for instance, Algonquian husbands and wives often could not live together, for adults supported themselves by working separately (perhaps wives as domestic servants, husbands as sailors). And in New Mexico, detribalized Navajos, Pueblos, and Apaches employed as servants by Spanish settlers clustered in the small towns of the Borderlands. Known collectively as *genizaros,* they lost contact with Indian cultures, instead living on the fringes of Latino society.

Wherever the population contained relatively few European women, sexual liaisons (both inside and outside marriage) occurred among European men and Indian women. The resulting mixed-race population of *mestizos* and *métis* worked as a familial "middle ground" to ease other cultural interactions. In New France and the Anglo-American backcountry, such families frequently resided in Indian villages and were enmeshed in trading networks. Often, children of these unions became prominent leaders of Native American societies. (For example, Peter Chartier, son of a Shawnee mother and a French father, led a pro-French Shawnee band in western Pennsylvania in the 1740s.) By contrast, in the Spanish Borderlands the offspring of Europeans and *genizaros* were treated as degraded individuals. Largely denied the privilege of legal marriage, they bore generations of "illegitimate" children of various racial mixtures, giving rise in Latino society to a wide range of labels describing degrees of skin color with a precision unknown in English or French America.

MIXED-RACE FAMILIES

Eighteenth-century Anglo-Americans used the word *family* to mean all the people who occupied one household (including any resident servants or slaves). The many European migrants to North America had more stable family lives than did Indian and *mestizo* peoples. European men or their widows headed households considerably larger than American families today. In 1790 the average home in the United States contained 5.7 free people; few such households included extended kin like grandparents. Family members—bound by ties of blood or servitude—worked together to produce goods for consumption or sale. The head of the household represented it to the outside world, managing the finances and holding legal authority over the rest of the family—his wife, his children, and his servants or slaves.

EUROPEAN AMERICAN FAMILIES

In English, French, and Spanish America alike, the vast majority of European families supported themselves through agriculture, by cultivating crops and raising livestock. The scale and nature of the work varied: the production of indigo in Louisiana or tobacco in the

One of the few extant depictions of a mixed-race family in eighteenth-century North America, by the Mexican artist Miguel Cabrera, 1763. The Spanish father and Indian mother have produced a *mestiza* daughter. Families such as this would have been frequently seen in New Mexico as well. (Private Collection)

Chesapeake required different sorts of labor from subsistence farming in New England or cattle ranching in New Mexico and Texas. Still, just as in the European, African, and Native American societies discussed in Chapter 1, household tasks were allocated by sex. The master, his sons, and his male servants or slaves performed one set of chores; the mistress, her daughters, and her female servants or slaves, a different set.

The mistress took responsibility for what Anglo-Americans called "indoor affairs." She and her female helpers prepared food, cleaned the house, did laundry, and often made clothing. Preparing food alone involved planting and cultivating a garden, harvesting and preserving vegetables, salting and smoking meat, drying apples and pressing cider, milking cows and making butter and cheese, not to mention cooking and baking. The head of the household and his male helpers, responsible for "outdoor affairs," also had heavy workloads. They planted and cultivated the fields, built fences, chopped wood for the fireplace, harvested and marketed crops, cared for livestock, and butchered cattle and hogs to provide the household with meat. So extensive was the work involved in maintaining a farm household that a married couple could not do it alone. If they had no children to help them, they turned to servants or slaves.

Most African American families lived as components of European American households—sometimes on plantations that masters perceived as one large family. More than 95 percent of colonial African Americans were held in perpetual bondage. Although many African Americans lived on farms with only one or two other slaves, others had the experience of living and working in a largely black setting. In South Carolina, a majority of the population was of African origin; in Georgia, about half; and in the Chesapeake, 40 percent. Portions of the Carolina low country were nearly 90 percent African American by 1790.

AFRICAN AMERICAN FAMILIES

The setting in which African Americans lived determined the shape of their families, yet wherever possible slaves established strong family structures in which youngsters carried relatives' names. In the North, the scarcity of other blacks often made it difficult for bondspeople to form stable households. In the Chesapeake, men and women who regarded themselves as married (slaves could not legally wed) frequently lived on different quarters or even on different plantations. Children generally resided with their mothers, seeing their fathers only on Sundays. Simultaneously, the natural increase of the population created wide American-born kinship networks among Chesapeake slaves. On large Carolina and Georgia rice plantations, enslaved couples not only usually lived together with their children but also accumulated property through working for themselves after they had completed their daily "tasks" (see pages 79–80). Some Georgia slaves sold their surplus produce at the market in Savannah, thereby earning money to buy nice clothing or such luxuries as tobacco or jewelry, but rarely enough to purchase themselves.

FORMS OF RESISTANCE

Because all the British colonies legally permitted slavery, bondspeople had few options for escaping servitude other than fleeing to Florida (see pages 80–81). Some recently arrived Africans stole boats to try to return home or ran off in groups to frontier regions to join the Indians or establish independent communities. Among American-born slaves, family ties strongly affected such decisions. South Carolina planters soon learned, as one wrote, that slaves "love their families

■ William L. Breton's watercolor of "The Old London Coffee House" in eighteenth-century Philadelphia shows a slave auction taking place on its porch. That such a scene could have occurred in front of such a prominent and popular meeting place serves as a reminder of the ubiquity of slavery in the colonies, north as well as south.   (Historical Society of Pennsylvania)

dearly and none runs away from the other," so many owners sought to keep families together for purely practical reasons. In the Chesapeake, where family members often lived separately, affectionate ties could by contrast cause slaves to run away, especially if a family member had been sold or moved to a distant quarter.

Although colonial slaves rarely rebelled collectively, they often resisted enslavement in other ways. Bondspeople uniformly rejected attempts by their owners to commandeer their labor on Sundays without compensation. Extended-kin groups protested excessive punishment of relatives and sought to live near each other. The links that developed among African American families who had lived on the same plantation for several generations served as insurance against the uncertainties of existence under slavery. If parents and children were separated by sale, other relatives could help with child rearing and similar tasks. Among African Americans, just as among Indians, the extended family thus served a more important function than it did among European Americans.

Most slave families managed to carve out a small measure of autonomy, especially in their working and spiritual lives and particularly in the Lower South. Enslaved Muslims often clung to their Islamic faith, a pattern especially evident in Louisiana and Georgia. Some

African Americans preserved traditional beliefs and others converted to Christianity (often retaining some African elements), finding comfort in the assurances of their new religion that all people would be free and equal in heaven. South Carolina and Georgia slaves jealously guarded their customary ability to control their own time after the completion of their "tasks." Even on Chesapeake tobacco plantations, slaves planted their own gardens, hunted, or fished to supplement the minimal diet their masters supplied. Late in the century, some Chesapeake planters with a surplus of laborers began to hire out slaves to others, often allowing the workers to keep a small part of their earnings. Such accumulated property could buy desired goods or serve as a legacy for children.

Just as African and European Americans resided together on plantations, so too they lived in unsegregated urban neighborhoods. (In 1760s Phil-

*LIFE IN
THE CITIES*

adelphia one-fifth of the work force was enslaved, and by 1775 blacks composed nearly 15 percent of the population of New York City.) Such cities were nothing but medium-sized towns by today's standards. In 1750 the largest, Boston and Philadelphia, had just seventeen thousand and thirteen thousand inhabitants, respectively. Life in the cities nonetheless differed considerably from that on northern farms, southern plantations, or southwestern ranches. City dwellers everywhere purchased food and wood in the markets. Urban residents lived by the clock rather than the sun, and men's jobs frequently took them away from their households. City people also had much more contact with the world beyond their own homes than did their rural counterparts.

By the 1750s, most major cities had at least one weekly newspaper, and some had two or three. Anglo-American newspapers printed the latest "advices from London" (usually two to three months old) and news from other English colonies, as well as local reports. Newspapers were available at taverns, coffeehouses, and inns, so people who could not afford to buy them could catch up on the news. Even illiterates could do so, since literate customers often read the papers aloud. Contact with the outside world, however, had its drawbacks. Sailors sometimes brought deadly diseases into port. Boston, New York, Philadelphia, and New Orleans endured terrible epidemics of smallpox and yellow fever, which Europeans and Africans in the countryside largely escaped.

Politics: Stability and Crisis in British America

*E*arly in the eighteenth century, Anglo-American political life exhibited a new stability. Despite substantial migration from overseas, most residents of the mainland had been born in America. Men from genteel families dominated the political structures in each province, for voters (free male property holders) tended to defer to their well-educated "betters" on election days.

Throughout the Anglo-American colonies, political leaders sought to increase the powers of elected assemblies relative to the powers of the governors and other appointed officials. Assemblies began to claim privileges associated with the British House of Commons, such as the rights to initiate all tax legislation and to control the militia. The assemblies also developed effective ways of influencing British appointees, especially by threatening to withhold their salaries. In some colonies (Virginia and South Carolina, for example), elite members of the assemblies usually presented a united front to royal officials, but in others (such as New York), they fought among themselves long and bitterly. To win hotly contested elections, New York's genteel leaders began to appeal to "the people," competing openly for the votes

RISE OF THE ASSEMBLIES

of ordinary voters. Yet in 1733 that same New York government imprisoned a newspaper editor, John Peter Zenger, who had too vigorously criticized its actions. Defending Zenger against the charge of "seditious libel," his lawyer argued that the truth could not be defamatory, thus helping to establish a free-press principle now found in American law.

Much of the business of colonial assemblies would today be termed administrative; only on rare occasions did they formulate new policies or pass significant laws. Assemblymen saw themselves as acting defensively to prevent encroachments on the colonists' liberties—for example, by preventing governors from imposing oppressive taxes. By midcentury, they were comparing the structure of their governments to Britain's balanced polity, a combination of monarchy, aristocracy, and democracy that had been thought to produce a stable polity since the days of ancient Greece and Rome. Drawing rough analogies, political leaders equated their governors with the monarch, their councils with the aristocracy, and their assemblies with the House of Commons. All three were believed essential to good government, but Anglo-Americans did not regard them with the same degree of approval. They viewed governors and appointed councils as potential threats to customary colonial ways of life, since such people primarily represented Britain. Many colonists saw the assemblies, however, as the people's protectors. And in turn the assemblies regarded themselves as representatives of the people.

Yet such beliefs should not be equated with modern practice. The assemblies, firmly controlled by dominant families whose members were reelected year after year, rarely responded to the concerns of their poorer constituents. Although settlements continually expanded, assemblies failed to reapportion themselves to provide adequate representation for newer communities—a lack of action that led to serious grievances among frontier dwellers, especially those from non-English ethnic groups. The colonial ideal of the assembly as the defender of the people's liberties must therefore be distinguished from the colonial reality: the most dearly defended were the wealthy colonists, particularly the assembly members themselves.

At midcentury, the political structures that had stabilized in a period of relative calm confronted a series of crises. None affected all the mainland colonies, but no colony escaped wholly untouched. The crises of various descriptions—ethnic, racial, economic, regional—exposed the internal tensions building in the pluralistic American society, foreshadowing the greater disorder of the revolutionary era. Most important, they demon-

■ In 1713 the colony of Massachusetts constructed its impressive State House in Boston. Here met the assembly and the council. The solidity and imposing nature of the building must have symbolized for its users the increasing consolidation of power in the hands of the Massachusetts legislature.   (The Bostonian Society)

strated that the political accommodations arrived at in the aftermath of the Glorious Revolution were no longer adequate to govern Britain's American empire. Once again, changes appeared necessary, and imminent.

One of the first and greatest crises occurred in South Carolina. Early one morning in September 1739, about

STONO REBELLION

twenty South Carolina slaves, most from Angola, gathered near the Stono River south of Charles Town. Seizing guns and ammunition from a store, they killed the storekeepers and some nearby planter families. Then, joined by other local slaves, they headed toward Florida in hopes of finding refuge at Gracia Real de Santa Teresa de Mose. By midday, however, the alarm had been sounded among slaveowners in the district. That afternoon a troop of militia attacked the fugitives, who then numbered about a hundred, killing some and dispersing the rest. More than a week later, most of the remaining conspirators were captured. The colony quickly executed those not killed on the spot, but for over two years rumors about escaped renegades haunted the colony.

The Stono Rebellion shocked slaveholding South Carolinians as well as residents of other colonies.

NEW YORK CONSPIRACY

Throughout British America, laws governing the behavior of African Americans were stiffened. The most striking response came in New York City, which had suffered a slave revolt in 1712. There the news from the South, coupled with fears of Spain generated by the outbreak of King George's War, set off a reign of terror in the summer of 1741. Hysterical whites suspected a biracial gang of thieves and arsonists of conspiring to foment a slave uprising under the guidance of a white schoolteacher thought to be a priest in the pay of Spain. By summer's end, thirty-one blacks and four whites had been executed for participating in the alleged plot. The Stono Rebellion and the New York conspiracy not only exposed and confirmed Anglo-Americans' deepest fears about the dangers of slaveholding but also revealed the assemblies' inability to prevent serious internal disorder. Events of the next two decades confirmed that pattern.

By midcentury most of the fertile land east of the Appalachians had been purchased or occupied. Consequently,

LAND RIOTS conflicts over land titles and conditions of landholding grew in number and frequency. In 1746, for example, some New Jersey farmers clashed violently with agents of the East Jersey proprietors. The proprietors claimed the farmers' land as theirs and demanded annual payments, called quit-rents, for the use of the property. Similar violence occurred in the 1760s in the region that later became Vermont. There, farmers holding land grants issued by New Hampshire battled with speculators claiming title to the area through grants from New York authorities.

The most serious land riots took place along the Hudson River in 1765–1766. Late in the seventeenth century, the governor of New York had granted huge tracts in the lower Hudson valley to prominent colonial families. The proprietors in turn divided these estates into small farms, which they rented chiefly to poor Dutch and German migrants who regarded tenancy as a step on the road to independent freeholder status. By the 1750s some proprietors earned large sums annually from quit-rents and other fees.

After 1740, though, increasing migration from New England brought conflict to the great New York estates. The New Englanders resisted the tenancy system. Many squatted on vacant portions of the manors, rejecting all attempts at eviction. In the mid-1760s the Philipse family sued New Englanders who had lived on Philipse land for two decades or more. New York courts upheld the Philipse claim, ordering squatters to make way for tenants with valid leases. Instead of complying, the farmers rebelled, terrorizing proprietors and loyal tenants, freeing their friends from jail, and on one occasion battling a county sheriff and his posse. The rebellion lasted nearly a year, ending only when British troops finally captured its leaders.

Violent conflicts of a different sort erupted just a few years later in the Carolinas. The Regulator movements of the late 1760s (South Carolina) and early 1770s (North Carolina) pitted backcountry farmers against wealthy eastern planters who controlled the provincial governments. Frontier dwellers, most of Scots-Irish origin, protested their lack of an adequate voice in colonial political affairs. South Carolinians for months policed the countryside in vigilante bands known as Regulators, complaining of lax and biased law enforcement. North Carolina Regulators, who primarily objected to heavy taxation, fought and lost a battle with eastern militiamen at Alamance in 1771. Regional, ethnic, and economic tensions thus combined to create these distur-

REGULATORS IN THE CAROLINAS

bances, which ultimately arose from frontier people's dissatisfaction with the Carolina governments.

A Crisis in Religion

The most widespread crisis, though, was religious. From the mid-1730s through the 1760s, waves of religious revivalism—today known collectively as the First Great Awakening—swept over various colonies, primarily New England (1735–1745) and Virginia (1750s and 1760s). Orthodox Calvinists sought to combat Enlightenment rationalism, which denied innate human depravity. Simultaneously, the economic and political uncertainty accompanying King George's War made colonists receptive to evangelists' spiritual messages. Moreover, many recent immigrants and residents of the backcountry had no prior religious affiliation, thus presenting evangelists with many potential converts.

The Great Awakening began in New England, where descendants of the Puritan founding generation still composed the membership of Congregational churches. Whether in full or "halfway" communion—the latter, a category established in 1662 to ensure that people who had not experienced saving faith would still be subject to church discipline—such members were predominantly female. From the beginnings of the Awakening, though, men and women responded with equal fervor. During 1734 and 1735, the Reverend Jonathan Edwards, a noted preacher and theologian, noticed a remarkable reaction among the youthful members of his church in Northampton, Massachusetts, to a message based squarely on Calvinist principles. Individuals could attain salvation, Edwards contended, only through recognition of their own depraved natures and the need to surrender completely to God's will. Such surrender brought to Congregationalists of both sexes an intensely emotional release from sin, coming to be seen as a single identifiable moment of conversion.

The effects of such conversions remained isolated until 1739, when George Whitefield, a Church of England clergyman already celebrated for leading revivals in England, arrived in America. For fifteen months he toured the British colonies, preaching to large audiences from Georgia to New England and concentrating his efforts in the major cities: Boston, New York, Philadelphia, Charles Town, and Savannah. A gripping orator, Whitefield in effect generated the Great Awakening. The historian Harry Stout has termed him "the first

GEORGE WHITEFIELD

Reverend George Whitefield, the charismatic evangelist who sparked the First Great Awakening in the mainland British colonies, attracted harsh critics as well as avid admirers. Here an English cartoonist satirizes him as a money-grubbing charlatan who hoodwinks his gullible followers into believing that he is a "Pious Churchman" motivated by "Holy Zeal." Whitefield's crossed eyes, obvious in this image as in others, played a prominent role in contemporary depictions of him.   (Trustees of the British Museum)

modern celebrity" because of his skillful self-promotion and clever manipulation of both his listeners and the newspapers. Everywhere he traveled, his fame preceded him. Thousands of free and enslaved folk turned out to listen—and to experience conversion. Whitefield's journey, the first such ever undertaken, created new interconnections among the previously distinct colonies.

Regular clerics initially welcomed Whitefield and the American-born itinerant evangelist preachers who quickly imitated him. Soon, however, many clergymen began to realize that although "revived" religion filled their churches, it ran counter to their own approach to doc-

trine and matters of faith. They disliked the emotional style of the revivalists, whose itinerancy also disrupted normal patterns of church attendance because it took churchgoers away from the services they usually attended. Particularly troublesome to the orthodox were the dozens of female exhorters who took to streets and pulpits, proclaiming their right (even duty) to expound God's word.

Opposition to the Awakening heightened rapidly, causing congregations to splinter. "Old Lights"—traditional clerics and their followers—engaged in bitter disputes with the "New Light" evangelicals. Already characterized by numerous sects, American Protestantism fragmented even further as the major denominations split into Old Light and New Light factions and as new evangelical sects—Methodists and Baptists—gained adherents. Paradoxically, the angry fights and the rapid rise in the number of distinct denominations eventually led to an American willingness to tolerate religious diversity. No single sect could make an unequivocal claim to orthodoxy, so they had to coexist if they were to exist at all.

IMPACT OF THE AWAKENING

Most significantly, the Awakening challenged traditional modes of thought, for the revivalists' message directly contested the colonial tradition of deference. Itinerant preachers, only a few of whom were ordained clergymen, claimed they understood the will of God better than did elite college-educated clerics. Moreover, they and their followers divided the world into two groups—the saved and the damned—without respect to gender, age, or status, the previously dominant social categories. The Awakening's emphasis on emotion rather than learning undermined the validity of received wisdom, and New Lights questioned not only religious but also social and political orthodoxy. For example, New Lights began to defend the rights of groups and individuals to dissent from a community consensus, thereby challenging one of the fundamental tenets of colonial political life. The egalitarian themes of the Awakening simultaneously attracted ordinary folk and repelled the elite.

Nowhere was this trend more evident than in Virginia, where tax money supported the established Church of England, and the plantation gentry and their ostentatious lifestyle dominated society. By the 1760s Baptists had gained a secure foothold in Virginia; inevitably, their beliefs and behavior clashed with the way most genteel families lived. They rejected as sinful the horseracing, gambling, and dancing that occupied much of the gentry's leisure time. They dressed plainly, in

VIRGINIA BAPTISTS

contrast to the gentry's fashionable opulence. They addressed one another as "Brother" and "Sister" regardless of social status, and they elected the leaders of their congregations—more than ninety of them by 1776. Their monthly "great meetings," which attracted hundreds of people, introduced new public rituals that rivaled the weekly Anglican services.

Strikingly, almost all the Virginia Baptist congregations included both free and slave members. At the founding of the Dan River Baptist Church in 1760, for example, eleven of seventy-four members were African Americans, and some congregations had African American majorities. Church rules applied equally to all members; interracial sexual relationships, divorce, and adultery were forbidden to all. In addition, congregations forbade masters from breaking up slave couples through sale. Biracial committees investigated complaints about church members' misbehavior. Churches excommunicated slaves for stealing from their masters, but they also excommunicated masters for physically abusing their slaves. One such slaveowner so dismissed in 1772 experienced a true conversion. Penalized for "burning" one of his slaves, Charles Cook apologized to the congregation and became a preacher in a largely African American church. Other Baptists decided that owning slaves was "unrighteous" and freed their bondspeople; the immensely wealthy Robert Carter, for one, manumitted hundreds of slaves in the 1790s.

Summary

*T*he Great Awakening thus injected an egalitarian strain into Anglo-American life at midcentury. Although primarily a religious movement, the Awakening had important social and political consequences, calling into question habitual modes of behavior in the secular as well as the religious realm. In short, the Great Awakening helped to break Anglo-Americans' ties to their seventeenth-century origins. So, too, did the newcomers from Germany, Scotland, Ireland, and Africa, who brought their languages, customs, and religions to British North America. The European immigrants settled throughout the English colonies but were concentrated in the growing cities and in the backcountry. By contrast, enslaved migrants from Africa lived and worked primarily within 100 miles of the Atlantic coast. In many areas of the colonial South, 50 to 90 percent of the population was of African origin.

The economic life of all Europe's North American colonies proceeded simultaneously on two levels. On the farms, plantations, and ranches on which most colonists resided, the daily, weekly, monthly, and yearly rounds of chores for men, women, and children alike dominated people's lives while providing the goods consumed by households and sold in the markets. Simultaneously, an intricate international trade network affected the economies of the British, French, and Spanish colonies. The bitter wars fought by European nations during the eighteenth century inevitably involved the colonists by creating new opportunities for overseas sales or by disrupting their traditional markets. The volatile colonial economy fluctuated for reasons beyond Americans' control. Those fortunate few who—through skill, control of essential resources, or luck—reaped the profits of international commerce made up the wealthy class of merchants and landowners who dominated colonial political and social life.

A century and a half after European peoples first settled in North America, the colonies mixed diverse European, American, and African traditions into a novel cultural blend that owed much to Europe but just as much, if not more, to North America itself. Europeans who interacted regularly with peoples of African and American origin—and with Europeans who came from nations other than their own—had to develop new identities and new methods of accommodating intercultural differences in addition to creating ties within their own potentially fragmenting communities. Yet at the same time the dominant colonists continued to identify themselves as French, Spanish, or British rather than as Americans. That did not change in Canada, Louisiana, or the Spanish Borderlands, but in the 1760s some Anglo-Americans began to realize that their interests did not necessarily coincide with those of Great Britain or its monarch. For the first time, they offered a direct challenge to British authority.

LEGACY FOR A PEOPLE AND A NATION
"Self-Made Men"

One of the most common American themes celebrates the "self-made man" (always someone explicitly *male*) of humble origins who gains wealth and/or prominence through his own extraordinary effort and talent. Most commonly, those cited as examples are such successful nineteenth-century businessmen as Andrew Carnegie (once a poor immigrant from Scotland) or John D. Rockefeller (born on a hardscrabble farm in a little town in upstate New York).

The initial exemplars of this tradition, though, lived in eighteenth-century America and the wider Atlantic world. Benjamin Franklin's *Autobiography* chronicled his method for achieving success as a printer after beginning life as the seventeenth child of a Boston candlemaker. From such humble origins Franklin became a wealthy, influential man active in science, politics, education, and diplomacy. Yet Franklin's tale is rivaled by that of a man apparently born a slave in South Carolina who subsequently worked for years as a sailor. He purchased his freedom, learned to read and write, held an important administrative post, married a wealthy young English woman, became an influential abolitionist, and eventually—like Franklin—published a popular autobiography. His first master called him Gustavus Vassa, the name he primarily used. But when publishing his *Interesting Narrative* in 1789, he called himself Olaudah Equiano.

In that *Narrative*, Equiano claimed to have been born in Africa in 1745, kidnapped at the age of eleven, and carried first to Barbados, then to Virginia, where he was purchased by the British naval officer who introduced him to a maritime life. For years scholars and students have relied on that account for its insights into the experience of the middle passage. But evidence recently uncovered by Vincent Carretta, while confirming the accuracy of much of Equiano's autobiography, shows that Equiano twice publicly identified his birthplace as Carolina and was three to five years younger than he claimed. Why would Equiano conceal his origins and alter his age? Carretta speculates that the *Narrative* gained part of its credibility from Equiano's African birth and that admitting his real age would have raised questions about the account of his early life by revealing his youth at the time of the reputed kidnapping.

Equiano, or Vassa, thus truly "made himself," just as Benjamin Franklin and many others have done. (Franklin tended to omit, rather than alter, inconvenient parts of his personal history—for example, his having fathered an illegitimate son.) Equiano used information undoubtedly gleaned from acquaintances who *had* experienced the middle passage to craft an accurate depiction of the horrors of the slave trade. In the process he became one of the first Americans to explicitly reinvent himself.

SEVERING THE BONDS OF EMPIRE 1754–1774

The two men must have found the occasion remarkable. The artist customarily painted portraits of the wealthy and high born, not of artisans, even well-connected, affluent ones. The subject himself was an artist—a maker of beautiful silver and gold objects, an engraver of cartoons and townscapes. The political sympathies of the painter, John Singleton Copley, lay primarily with Boston's conservatives, whereas the sitter, Paul Revere, was a noted leader of resistance to British policies. Yet sometime in 1768 Revere commissioned Copley to paint his portrait, and the result (opposite page) is one of the greatest works of American art.

Copley was thirty, Revere thirty-four. Each man had learned his trade from a parent. Revere's father, Apollos, who had arrived in Boston as a teenage Huguenot refugee early in the century, was an accomplished gold- and silversmith; Paul served as his father's apprentice and took over the family business when Apollos died in 1754. Copley, whose Irish parents had immigrated to Boston in the 1730s, was taught to paint by his stepfather, Peter Pelham, an English artist. The two young tradesmen had undoubtedly known each other for years. In 1763 and thereafter, Copley hired Revere to make silver and gold frames for the miniature portraits that were among his earliest works.

But their finest collaboration was the painting reproduced here. Copley portrayed Revere surrounded by the tools of his trade and contemplating a teapot he was crafting. The silversmith wears a loose-fitting linen shirt and an open vest rather than the formal dress usually worn by colonial artists' subjects. Even so, Revere is not actually at work: his clothes are too clean, and the table is too polished to be a work surface. The silversmith's pose and apparel convey an impression of thoughtfulness, virtuous labor, and solidity. The teapot too carries a message, especially in the year 1768. Simultaneously a reflection of a craftsman's skills and a prominent emblem of the new "empire of goods" in British America, it resonated with symbolism because, as shall be seen later in this chapter,

◀ John Singleton Copley's portrait of Paul Revere is generally regarded as one of his masterpieces. Copley captured Revere's character as a hard-working, respectable artisan—a man unafraid of displaying his humble origins to the world.   (Museum of Fine Arts, Boston. Gift of Joseph W., William B., and Edward H. R. Revere)

CHRONOLOGY

1754 • Albany Congress meets to try to forge colonial unity
• Fighting breaks out with Washington's defeat at Fort Necessity

1756 • Britain declares war on France; Seven Years War officially begins

1759 • British forces take Quebec

1760 • American phase of war ends with fall of Montreal to British troops
• George III becomes king

1763 • Treaty of Paris ends Seven Years War
• Pontiac's allies attack British forts in West
• Proclamation of 1763 attempts to close land west of Appalachians to English settlement

1764 • Sugar Act lays new duties on molasses, tightens customs regulations
• Currency Act outlaws paper money issued by the colonies

1765 • Stamp Act requires stamps on all printed materials in colonies
• Sons of Liberty formed

1766 • Stamp Act repealed
• Declaratory Act insists that Parliament can tax the colonies

1767 • Townshend Acts lay duties on trade within the empire, send new officials to America

1768–70 • Townshend duties resisted; boycotts and public demonstrations divide merchants and urban artisans

1770 • Lord North becomes prime minister
• Townshend duties repealed, except for tea tax
• Boston Massacre kills five colonial rioters

1772 • Boston Committee of Correspondence formed

1773 • Tea Act aids East India Company
• Boston Tea Party protests the Tea Act

1774 • Coercive Acts punish Boston and Massachusetts as a whole
• Quebec Act reforms government of Quebec
• First Continental Congress called

tea boycotts were an important component of colonial resistance to Great Britain. Both artist and subject, indeed, were to be active participants (though in very different ways) in the 1773 event known to history as the Boston Tea Party.

In retrospect, John Adams identified the years between 1760 and 1775 as the era of the true American Revolution. The Revolution, Adams declared, ended before the fighting started, for it was "in the Minds of the people," involving not the actual winning of independence but a fundamental shift of allegiance from Britain to America. Today, not all historians would concur with Adams that the shift he identified constituted the Revolution. But none would deny the importance of the events of those crucial years, which divided the American population along political lines and set the colonies on the road to independence.

The story of the 1760s and early 1770s describes an ever-widening split between Great Britain and Anglo America and among their respective supporters in the colonies. In the long history of British settlement in the Western Hemisphere, considerable tension had occasionally marred the relationship between individual provinces and the mother country. Still, that tension had rarely persisted for long, nor had it been widespread, except during the crisis following the Glorious Revolution in 1689. The primary divisions affecting the colonies had been internal rather than external. In the 1750s, however, a series of events began to draw the colonists' attention from domestic matters to their relations with Great Britain. It all started with the Seven Years War.

Britain's overwhelming victory in that war, confirmed by treaty in 1763, forever altered the balance of power in North America. France was ousted from the continent and Spain from Florida, events with major consequences for both the indigenous peoples of the interior and the residents of the British colonies. Indians could no longer play off European powers against one another and so lost one of their major diplomatic tools. Anglo-Americans no longer had to fear the French threat on their northern and western borders or the Spanish in the Southeast. The British colonies along the coast would never have dared to break with their mother country, some historians contend, had France still controlled the Mississippi River and the Great Lakes.

The British victory in 1763, then, dramatically affected all the residents of North America. That victory also had a significant impact on Great Britain, one that soon involved the colonies. Britain's massive war-related debt needed to be paid, and so Parliament for the first time imposed revenue-raising taxes on the colonies in addition to the customs duties that had long regulated trade. That decision exposed differences in the political thinking of Americans and Britons—differences that until then had been obscured by a shared political vocabulary.

During the 1760s and early 1770s a broad coalition of the residents of Anglo America, men and women alike, resisted new tax levies and attempts by British officials to tighten controls over provincial governments. The colonies' elected leaders became ever more suspicious of Britain's motives as the years passed. They laid aside old antagonisms to coordinate their responses to the new measures, and they slowly began to reorient their political thinking. As late as the summer of 1774, though, most were still seeking a solution within the framework of the empire; few harbored thoughts of independence. ■

Renewed Warfare Among Europeans and Indians

*I*n the mid-eighteenth century, the British colonies along the Atlantic seaboard were surrounded by hostile, or potentially hostile, neighbors: Indians everywhere, the Spanish in Florida and along the coast of the Gulf of Mexico, the French along the great inland system of rivers and lakes that stretched from the St. Lawrence to the Mississippi. The Spanish outposts posed little direct threat, for Spain's days as a major power had passed. The French were another matter. Their long chain of forts and settlements dominated the North American interior, facilitating trading partnerships and alliances with the Indians. In none of the three wars fought between 1689 and 1748 was England able to shake France's hold on the American frontier. Under the Peace of Utrecht, which ended Queen Anne's War in 1713, the English won control of such peripheral northern areas as Newfoundland, Hudson's Bay, and Acadia (Nova Scotia). But Britain made no territorial gains in King George's War (see Table 5.1 and Map 5.2).

During both Queen Anne's War and King George's War, the Iroquois Confederacy maintained the policy of neutrality it first developed in 1701. While British and French forces fought for nominal control of the North American continent, the confederacy skillfully manipulated the Europeans, refusing to commit warriors fully to either side despite being showered with

IROQUOIS NEUTRALITY

TABLE 5.1

The Colonial Wars, 1689–1763

American Name	European Name	Dates	Participants	American Sites	Dispute
King William's War	War of the League of Augsburg	1689–97	England, Holland versus France, Spain	New England, New York, Canada	French power
Queen Anne's War	War of Spanish Succession	1702–13	England, Holland, Austria versus France, Spain	Florida, New England	Throne of Spain
King George's War	War of Austrian Succession	1739–48	England, Holland, Austria versus France, Spain, Prussia	West Indies, New England, Canada	Throne of Austria
French and Indian War	Seven Years' War	1756–63	England versus France, Spain	Ohio country, Canada	Possession of Ohio country

■ An eighteenth-century Iroquois warrior as depicted by a European artist. Such men of the Six Nations confederacy dominated the North American interior before the Seven Years War. Lines drawn on maps by colonizing powers and the incursions of traders made little impact on their power.   (Library of Congress, Rare Book and Special Collections Division)

previous patterns, that conflict spread from America to Europe, decisively resolving the contest for North America. Trouble began in the mid-1740s, when at two treaty conferences Iroquois negotiators, claiming to speak for Delawares and Shawnees, ceded large tracts of the subordinate tribes' land to English colonists. Disgruntled Delawares and Shawnees migrated west, and Virginia land speculators (soon organized as the Ohio Company) began pressing to develop the ceded territory, focusing first on the crucial area where the Allegheny and Monongahela Rivers join to form the Ohio (see Map 5.1).

Yet not only was that region claimed by Pennsylvania as well, it was also vital to the French, for the Ohio River offered direct access by water to French posts on the Mississippi. A permanent British presence in the Ohio country would challenge France's control of the western fur trade and threaten its prominence in the Mississippi valley. Thus in the early 1750s Pennsylvania fur traders, Ohio Company representatives, and the French military all jostled for position in the region. A devastating 1752 raid by the French and Indians on a trading outpost at the site of modern Cleveland rid the region of Pennsylvanians, but the Virginians posed a more serious challenge. Accordingly, in 1753 the French pushed southward from Lake Erie, building fortified outposts at strategic points.

In response to the French threat, delegates from seven northern and middle colonies gathered in Albany,

ALBANY CONGRESS

New York, in June 1754. With the backing of London officials, they sought two goals: to persuade the Iroquois to abandon their traditional neutrality and to coordinate the defenses of the colonies. They succeeded in neither. The Iroquois listened politely to the colonists' arguments but saw no reason to change a policy that had served them well for half a century. And although the Albany Congress delegates adopted a Plan of Union (which would have established an elected intercolonial legislature with the power to tax), their provincial governments uniformly rejected the plan—primarily because those governments feared a loss of autonomy.

While the Albany Congress delegates deliberated, the war they sought to prepare for was already beginning. Governor Robert Dinwiddie of Virginia sent a small militia troop to build a palisade at the forks of the Ohio, then later dispatched reinforcements. When a substantial French force arrived at the forks, the first contingent of Virginia militia surrendered, peacefully abandoning the strategic site. The French then began to construct the larger and more elaborate Fort Duquesne. Upon learning of the confrontation, the inexperienced young officer who commanded the Virginia reinforcements pressed on—

gifts by both. The Iroquois continued a longstanding conflict with Cherokees and Catawbas in the South, thus giving their young warriors combat experience and allowing the replacement of population losses by acquiring new captives. They also cultivated peaceful relationships with Pennsylvania and Virginia, in part to obtain the colonists' imprimatur for their domination of the Shawnees and Delawares. And they forged friendly ties with Algonquians of the Great Lakes region, thereby thwarting potential assaults from those allies of the French and simultaneously making themselves indispensable middlemen for commerce and communication between the Atlantic coast and the West. Thus the Iroquois consolidated their control over the entire American interior north of Virginia and south of the Great Lakes.

But even the Iroquois could not prevent the region inhabited by the Shawnees and Delawares (now western Pennsylvania and eastern Ohio) from providing the spark that set off a major war. In a significant reversal of

Map 5.1   European Settlements and Indians, 1754

By 1754, Europeans had expanded the limits of the English colonies to the eastern slopes of the Appalachian Mountains. Few independent Indian nations still existed in the East, but beyond the mountains they controlled the countryside. Only a few widely scattered English and French forts maintained the Europeans' presence there.

ward instead of awaiting further instructions. He attacked a French detachment and then allowed himself to be trapped in his crudely built Fort Necessity at Great Meadows, Pennsylvania. After a day-long battle (on July 3, 1754), during which more than one-third of his men were killed or wounded, twenty-two-year-old George Washington surrendered. He and his men were allowed to return to Virginia.

Washington's grievous blunder helped ignite a war that eventually would encompass nearly the entire world. He also ensured that the Ohio Indians, angry with the Iroquois and trading partners of the French, would support France in that conflict. In July 1755, a few miles south of Fort Duquesne, a combined force of French and Indians ambushed British and colonial troops readying a renewed assault on the fort. In the devastating defeat, General Edward Braddock was killed

SEVEN YEARS WAR

and his surviving soldiers were demoralized. The Pennsylvania frontier then bore the brunt of repeated attacks by Ohio Indians for two more years. After news of the debacle reached London, Britain—already poised for renewed conflict with old enemies—declared war on France in 1756, thus formally beginning the Seven Years War.

For three years one disaster followed another. British officers tried without much success to coerce the colonies into supplying men and materiel to the army. The war went so badly that Britain began to fear that France would try to retake Newfoundland and Nova Scotia. Afraid that the approximately twelve thousand French residents of Nova Scotia would abandon their pledges of neutrality, British commanders forced about seven thousand of them from their homeland—the first large-scale modern deportation. Ships crammed with Acadians sailed to each of the mainland colonies, where the dispirited exiles encountered hostility and discrimination as they

■ A 1769 Dutch atlas charted the successful British attack on Quebec ten years earlier. Ships of the British fleet fill the St. Lawrence River. Cannon on the southern shore bombard the fortified town (indicated by the lines across the river). And to the left of the city, on the Plains of Abraham, the string of small red blocks represents the British troops who had stealthily climbed the heights at night to confront Quebec's French defenders (the blue blocks).   (Private Collection)

The First Worldwide War

Today we call two twentieth-century conflicts "world wars," but the first worldwide war predated them by more than a century. The contest began in the backwoods of southwestern Pennsylvania, in the spring of 1754, over a seemingly local quarrel—whether Britain or France would build a fort at the forks of the Ohio. That it eventually involved combatants around the world attests not only to the growing importance of European nations' overseas empires but also to the increasing centrality of North America in their struggles for dominance.

Previous wars among Europeans had taken place mostly in Europe, though overseas colonies occasionally got involved. But the contest at the forks of the Ohio helped to reinvigorate a conflict between Austria and Prussia that sent the nations of Europe scrambling for allies. Eventually England, Hanover, and Prussia lined up against France, Austria, and Russia, joined by Sweden, Saxony, and, later, Spain. The war in Europe would last seven years. In 1763 these nations signed a peace treaty that returned the continent to the status quo before the war, but elsewhere, in the rest of the world, Britain had decisively vanquished both France and Spain.

"Elsewhere" included a mind-boggling list of battles. In the Caribbean, Britain seized the French islands of Guade-loupe and Martinique and took Havana from Spain. In North America, the British recaptured the French fortress of Louisbourg and conquered the capital of New France, Quebec. In Africa, the British overwhelmed France's slave-trading posts in Senegambia. In India, British forces won control of Bengal by defeating both a local ruler and French soldiers stationed there. Three years later the British beat a French army at Pondicherry. So four months after France lost Canada, its influence in India was also extinguished. At the very end of the war, a British expedition took Manila in the Philippines from Spain. The commander there had not yet learned that his nation had declared war on Britain, so the assault caught him unawares.

Thus the war that started in the American backcountry revealed the steadily growing links between North America and the rest of the world. And the aftermath exposed an unexpected further link. Both winners and losers had to pay for this first worldwide war. Financial struggles in Britain and France, though separate, ultimately produced similar outcomes: revolutions abroad (for Britain, in America) and at home (for France).

In 1771 the artist Dominic Serres, the Elder, depicted British naval vessels attacking the French fortress at Chandernagore in India in 1757 (at left in background). Cannon fire from the warships was critical to the British victory, one of the keys to the conquest of India during the Seven Years War. (National Maritime Museum, London)

were dispersed into widely scattered communities. After 1763 the survivors relocated: some returned to Canada, others traveled to France or its West Indian islands, and many eventually settled in Louisiana, where they became known as Cajuns.

Led by William Pitt, the civilian official placed in charge of the war effort in 1757, Britain finally pursued a successful military strategy. Pitt agreed to reimburse the colonies for their wartime expenditures and placed recruitment in local hands, thereby gaining greater American support for the war. Colonial militiamen thereafter primarily served as support troops for the large numbers of red-coated regulars sent to North America from Britain. In July 1758, British forces recaptured the fortress at Louisbourg, winning control of the entrance to the St. Lawrence River and cutting the major French supply route. In the fall, the Ohio Indians accepted British peace overtures and the French abandoned Fort Duquesne. Then, in a stunning attack in September 1759, General James Wolfe's regulars defeated the French on the Plains of Abraham and took Quebec. Sens-

ing a British victory, the Iroquois abandoned their traditional neutrality, hoping to gain a postwar advantage by allying themselves with Britain. A year later the British captured Montreal, the last French stronghold on the continent, and the American phase of the war ended.

In the Treaty of Paris (1763), France ceded its major North American holdings to Britain. Spain, an ally of France toward the end of the war, gave Florida to the victors. France, meanwhile, ceded Louisiana west of the Mississippi to Spain, in partial compensation for its ally's losses elsewhere. The British thus gained control of the continent's fur trade. No longer would the English seacoast colonies have to worry about the threat to their existence posed by France's extensive North American territories (see Map 5.2).

The overwhelming British triumph stimulated some Americans to think expansively. People like the Philadelphia printer Benjamin Franklin, who had long touted the colonies' wealth and potential, predicted a glorious new future for British North America—a future that included not just geographical expansion but also economic de-

Map 5.2   European Claims in North America

The dramatic results of the British victory in the Seven Years (French and Indian) War are vividly demonstrated in these maps, which depict the abandonment of French claims to the mainland after the Treaty of Paris in 1763.

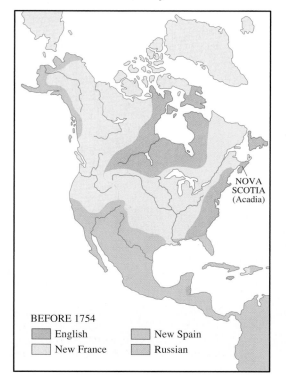

BEFORE 1754

▢ English   ▢ New Spain
▢ New France   ▢ Russian

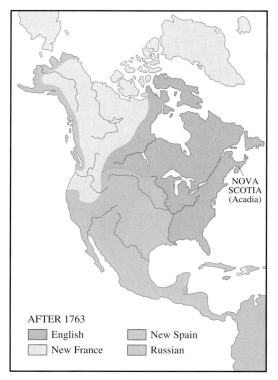

AFTER 1763

▢ English   ▢ New Spain
▢ New France   ▢ Russian

velopment and population growth. Such men were to lead the resistance to British measures in the years after 1763. They uniformly opposed any laws that would retard America's growth and persistently supported steps to increase Americans' control over their own destiny. Many of them also invested heavily in western land speculations.

1763: A Turning Point

*T*he great victory over France had an irreversible impact on North America, felt first by the indigenous peoples of the interior. With France excluded from the continent altogether and Spanish territory now confined to west of the Mississippi, the diplomatic strategy that had served the Indians well for so long was now obsolete. The consequences were immediate and devastating.

Even before the Treaty of Paris, southern Indians had to adjust to the new circumstances. After Britain gained the upper hand in the American war in 1758, Creeks and Cherokees lost their ability to force concessions by threatening to turn instead to France or Spain. In desperation, and in retaliation for British atrocities, Cherokees attacked the Carolina and Virginia frontiers in 1760. Though initially victorious, the Indians were defeated the following year by a force of British regulars and colonial militia. Late in 1761 the two sides concluded a treaty under which the Cherokees allowed the construction of British forts in their territories and opened a large tract of land to European settlement.

The fate of the Cherokees in the South portended events in the Ohio country. There, the Ottawas, Chippewas, and Potawatomis reacted angrily when Great Britain, no longer facing French competition, raised the price of trade goods and ended traditional gift-giving practices. Settlers rapidly moved into the Monongahela and Susquehanna valleys. A shaman named Neolin (also known as the Delaware Prophet) urged Indians to oppose British incursion on their lands and European influence on their culture. For the first time since King Philip in 1675, an influential native leader called for the unity of all tribes in the face of an Anglo-American threat. Contending that Indian peoples were destroying themselves by becoming dependent on European goods (especially alcohol), Neolin advocated resistance, both peaceful and armed. If all Indians west of the mountains united to reject the invaders, Neolin declared, the Master of Life would replenish the depleted deer herds and once again look kindly upon his people.

NEOLIN AND PONTIAC

Benjamin West, the first well-known American artist, engraved this picture of a prisoner exchange at the end of Pontiac's Uprising, with Colonel Henry Bouquet supervising the return of settlers abducted during the war. In the foreground, a child resists leaving the Indian parents he had grown to love. Many colonists were fascinated by the phenomenon West depicted—the reluctance of captives to abandon their adoptive Indian families. (Ohio Historical Society)

Yet, ironically, Neolin's call for a return to native traditions itself revealed European origins; his reference to a single Master of Life showed the influence of a syncretic Christianity on his thinking.

Pontiac, the war chief of an Ottawa village near Detroit, became the leader of a movement based on Neolin's precepts. In the spring of 1763, Pontiac forged an unprecedented alliance among Hurons, Chippewas, Potawatomis, Delawares, Shawnees, and Mingoes (Pennsylvania Iroquois). Pontiac then laid siege to Fort Detroit while war parties attacked other British outposts in the Great Lakes. Detroit withstood the siege, but by late June all the other forts west of Niagara and north of Fort Pitt (formerly Fort Duquesne) had fallen to the alliance. Indians then raided the Virginia and

Pennsylvania frontiers at will throughout the summer, slaying at least two thousand settlers. Still, they failed to take the strongholds of Niagara, Fort Pitt, or Detroit. In early August, colonial militiamen soundly defeated a combined Indian force at Bushy Run, Pennsylvania. Conflict ceased when Pontiac broke off the siege of Detroit in late October. A treaty ending the war was finally negotiated three years later.

The uprising demonstrated that the huge territory Britain had acquired from France would be difficult to govern. Officials in London had no experience managing such a vast area, particularly one inhabited by restive peoples—the remaining French settlers along the St. Lawrence and the many Indian communities. In October, the ministry issued the Proclamation of 1763, which designated the headwaters of rivers flowing into the Atlantic from the Appalachians as the temporary western boundary for colonial settlement (see Map 5.1). Its promulgators expected the proclamation to prevent clashes by forbidding colonists to move onto Indian lands until tribes had given up their territory by treaty. But it infuriated two distinct groups of colonists: those who had already squatted on lands west of the line (among them many recent Scots-Irish immigrants) and land-speculation companies from Pennsylvania and Virginia.

PROCLAMATION OF 1763

In the years after 1763, the latter groups (which included such men as George Washington, Thomas Jefferson, Patrick Henry, and Benjamin Franklin) lobbied vigorously to have their claims validated by colonial governments and London administrators. At a treaty conference at Fort Stanwix, New York, in 1768, they negotiated with Iroquois representatives to push the boundary line farther west and south, opening Kentucky to their speculations. The Iroquois, still claiming to speak for the Delawares and the Shawnees—who used Kentucky as their hunting grounds—agreed to the deal, which brought them valuable trade goods and did not affect their own territories. Yet even though the Virginia land companies eventually gained the support of the House of Burgesses for their claims, they never made any headway where it really mattered—in London—because administrators there realized that significant western expansion would require the expenditure of funds they did not have.

The hard-won victory in the Seven Years War had cost Britain millions of pounds and created an immense war debt. The problem of paying it, and of finding the money to defend the newly acquired territories, bedeviled King George III, who in 1760 suc-

GEORGE III

ceeded his grandfather, George II. The twenty-two-year-old monarch, an intelligent, passionate man with a mediocre education, was unfortunately an erratic judge of character. During the crucial years between 1763 and 1770, when the rift with the colonies grew ever wider and a series of political crises beset England, the king replaced ministries with bewildering rapidity. Although determined to assert the power of the monarchy, George III was immature and unsure of himself. He often substituted stubbornness for cleverness, and he regarded adherence to the status quo as the hallmark of patriotism.

The man he selected as prime minister in 1763, George Grenville, believed that the American colonies should be more tightly administered than previously. Grenville confronted a financial crisis: England's burden of indebtedness had nearly doubled since 1754, from £73 million to £137 million. Annual expenditures before the war had amounted to no more than £8 million; now the yearly interest on the debt alone came to £5 million. Grenville's ministry had to find new sources of funds, and the British people themselves were already heavily taxed. Since the colonists had benefited greatly from wartime expenditures, Grenville concluded that Anglo-Americans should be asked to pay a larger share of the cost of running the empire.

Grenville did not question Great Britain's right to levy taxes on the colonies. Like all his countrymen, he believed that the government's legitimacy derived ultimately from the consent of the people, but he defined consent differently from the colonists. Americans had come to believe that they could be represented only by men who lived nearby and for whom they or their property-holding neighbors actually voted; otherwise, they could not count on legislators to represent their interests properly. Grenville and his English contemporaries, however, believed that Parliament—king, lords, and commons acting together—by definition represented all British subjects, wherever they resided (even overseas) and whether or not they could vote.

THEORIES OF REPRESENTATION

Parliament saw itself as collectively representing the entire nation; the particular constituency that chose a member of the House of Commons had no special claim on that member's vote, nor did he have to live near his constituents. According to this theory of government, called *virtual representation,* the colonists were seen as virtually, if not actually, represented in Parliament. Thus their consent to acts of Parliament could be presumed. In the colonies, by contrast, members of the lower houses of the assemblies were viewed as specifically representing the regions that had elected them. Before Grenville proposed to tax the colonists, the two notions coexisted because no conflict exposed the central contradiction. But events of the 1760s revealed the incompatibility of the two definitions of representation.

The same events threw into sharp relief Americans' attitudes toward political power. The colonists had

REAL WHIGS

become accustomed to a central government that wielded limited authority over them, affecting their daily lives very little. Consequently, they believed that a good government was one that largely left them alone, a view in keeping with the theories of a group of British writers known as the Real Whigs. Drawing on a tradition of dissenting thought that reached back to John Locke and even to the English Civil War, the Real Whigs stressed the dangers inherent in a powerful government, particularly one headed by a monarch. Some of them even favored republicanism, which proposed to eliminate monarchs altogether and rest political power more directly on the people. Real Whigs warned the people to guard constantly against government's attempts to encroach on their liberty and seize their property. Political power was always to be feared, wrote John Trenchard and Thomas Gordon in their essay series *Cato's Letters* (originally published in London in 1720–1723 and reprinted many times thereafter in the colonies). Rulers would try to corrupt and oppress the people. Only perpetual vigilance could preserve the people's precious yet fragile liberty, which was closely tied to their right to private property.

Britain's attempts to tighten the reins of government and to raise revenues from the colonies in the 1760s and early 1770s convinced many Americans that the Real Whigs' reasoning applied to their circumstances, especially because of the link between liberty and property rights. Excessive and unjust taxation, they believed, could destroy their freedoms. They began to interpret British measures in light of the Real Whigs' warnings and to see oppressive designs behind the actions of Grenville and his successors. Historians disagree over the extent to which those perceptions were correct, but by 1775 a large number of colonists believed they were. In the mid-1760s, however, colonial leaders did not immediately accuse Grenville of conspiring to oppress them. They at first merely questioned the wisdom of the laws he proposed.

Parliament passed the first such measures, the Sugar and Currency Acts, in 1764. The Sugar Act (also known as the Revenue Act) revised existing customs regulations

SUGAR AND CURRENCY ACTS

and laid new duties on some foreign imports into the colonies. Its most important provisions, strongly advocated in London by the influential planters of

the British Caribbean, aimed at discouraging American rum distillers from smuggling French West Indian molasses, thereby increasing demand for sugar from British islands. It also established a vice-admiralty court at Halifax, Nova Scotia, to adjudicate violations of the law, along with other maritime offenses. Although the Sugar Act appeared to resemble the Navigation Acts, which the colonies had long accepted as legitimate, it broke with tradition in being explicitly designed to raise revenue, not to channel American trade through Britain. The Currency Act effectively outlawed most colonial issues of paper money, because British merchants had long complained that Americans were paying their debts in inflated local currencies. Americans could accumulate little sterling, since they imported more than they exported; thus the act seemed to the colonists to deprive them of a useful medium of exchange.

The Sugar and Currency Acts were imposed on an economy already in the midst of depression. A business boom accompanied the Seven Years War, but the brief spell of prosperity ended abruptly in 1760 when the war shifted overseas. Urban merchants could not sell all their imported goods to colonial customers alone, and without the military's demand for foodstuffs, American farmers found fewer buyers for their products. The bottom dropped out of the European tobacco market, threatening the livelihood of Chesapeake planters. Sailors were thrown out of work, and artisans found few customers. In such circumstances, the prospect of increased import duties and inadequate supplies of currency aroused merchants' hostility.

Individual American essayists and incensed colonial governments protested the new policies. But, lacking any precedent for a united campaign against acts of Parliament, Americans in 1764 took only hesitant and uncoordinated steps. Eight colonial legislatures sent separate petitions to Parliament requesting the Sugar Act's repeal. They argued that its commercial restrictions would hurt Britain as well as the colonies and that they had not consented to its passage. The protests had no effect. The law remained in force, and Grenville proceeded with another revenue plan.

The Stamp Act Crisis

*T*he Stamp Act (1765), Grenville's most important proposal, was modeled on a law that had been in effect in Britain for almost a century. It touched nearly every colonist by requiring tax stamps on most printed materials, but it placed the heaviest burden on merchants and other members of the colonial elite, who used printed matter more frequently than did ordinary folk. Anyone who purchased a newspaper or pamphlet, made a will, transferred land, bought dice or playing cards, applied for a liquor license, accepted a government appointment, or borrowed money would have to pay the tax. Never before had a revenue measure of such scope been proposed for the colonies. The act also required that tax stamps be purchased with sterling, which was scarce, and that violators be tried by vice-admiralty courts, in which judges alone rendered decisions. Americans feared the loss of their right to trial by a jury of their peers. Finally, such a law would break decisively with the colonial tradition of self-imposed taxation.

The most important colonial pamphlet protesting the Sugar Act and the proposed Stamp Act was *The*

■ In 1765 a clerk in the offices of British tax officials prepared this register to contain examples of the tax stamps intended for use in the American colonies. But because the law was never enforced and soon repealed, the register is largely empty, and the other volumes the clerk anticipated were never readied at all.   (The British Library Philatelic Section, Inland Revenue Archives)

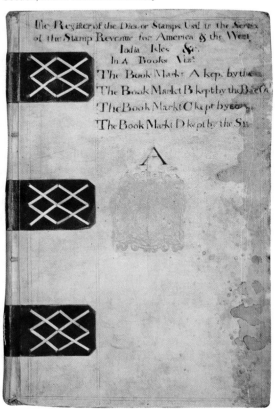

JAMES OTIS'S RIGHTS OF THE BRITISH COLONIES

Rights of the British Colonies Asserted and Proved, by James Otis Jr., a brilliant young Massachusetts attorney. Otis starkly exposed the ideological dilemma that confounded the colonists for the next decade. How could they justify their opposition to certain acts of Parliament without questioning Parliament's authority over them? On the one hand, Otis asserted, Americans were "entitled to all the natural, essential, inherent, and inseparable rights" of Britons, including the right not to be taxed without their consent. "No man or body of men, not excepting the parliament . . . can take [those rights] away," he declared. On the other hand, Otis admitted that under the British system established after the Glorious Revolution, "the power of parliament is uncontrollable but by themselves, and we must obey. . . . Let the parliament lay what burthens they please on us, we must, it is our duty to submit and patiently bear them, till they will be pleased to relieve us."

Otis's first contention, drawing on colonial notions of representation, implied that Parliament could not constitutionally tax the colonies because Americans were not represented in its ranks. Yet his second point both acknowledged political reality and accepted the prevailing theory of British government: that Parliament was the sole, supreme authority in the empire. Even unconstitutional laws enacted by Parliament had to be obeyed until Parliament decided to repeal them.

According to orthodox British political theory, there could be no middle ground between absolute submission to Parliament and a frontal challenge to its authority. Otis tried to find such a middle ground by proposing colonial representation in Parliament, but his idea was never taken seriously on either side of the Atlantic. The British believed that colonists were already virtually represented in Parliament, and Anglo-Americans quickly realized that a handful of colonial delegates to London would simply be outvoted.

Otis published his pamphlet before the Stamp Act was passed. When Americans first learned of the act's adoption in the spring of 1765, they reacted indecisively. Few colonists—even appointed government officials—publicly favored the law. But colonial petitions had already failed to prevent its adoption, and further lobbying appeared futile. Perhaps Otis was correct: the only course open to Americans was to pay the stamp tax, reluctantly but loyally. Acting on that assumption, colonial agents in London sought the appointment of their American friends as stamp distributors so that the law would at least be enforced equitably.

Not all the colonists resigned themselves to paying the new tax. A twenty-nine-year-old lawyer serving his

PATRICK HENRY AND THE VIRGINIA STAMP ACT RESOLVES

first term in the Virginia House of Burgesses was appalled by his fellow legislators' unwillingness to oppose the Stamp Act. Patrick Henry later recalled that he was "young, inexperienced, unacquainted with the forms of the house and the members that composed it"—but he decided to act. "Alone, unadvised, and unassisted, on a blank leaf of an old law book," he wrote the Virginia Stamp Act Resolves.

Little in Henry's earlier life foreshadowed his success in the political arena he entered so dramatically. The son of a prosperous Scottish immigrant to western Virginia, Henry had little formal education. After marrying at eighteen, he failed at both farming and storekeeping before turning to the law as a means of supporting his wife and their six children. Henry lacked legal training, but his oratorical skills made him an effective advocate, first for his clients and later for his political beliefs. A prominent Virginia lawyer observed, "He is by far the most powerful speaker I ever heard. Every word he says not only engages, but commands the attention; and your passions are no longer your own when he addresses them."

Patrick Henry introduced his seven proposals near the end of the legislative session, when many burgesses had already departed for home. Henry's fiery speech led the Speaker of the House to accuse him of treason. (Henry denied the charge, contrary to the nineteenth-century myth that he exclaimed, "If this be treason, make the most of it!") The few burgesses remaining in Williamsburg adopted five of Henry's resolutions by a bare majority. Although they repealed the most radical of the five the next day, their action had far-reaching effects. Some colonial newspapers printed Henry's seven original resolutions as if they had been uniformly passed by the House, even though one was rescinded and two others were never debated or voted on at all.

The four propositions adopted by the burgesses repeated Otis's arguments, asserting that the colonists had never forfeited the rights of British subjects, among which was consent to taxation. The other three resolutions went much further. The one that was repealed claimed for the burgesses "the only exclusive right" to tax Virginians, and the final two (those never considered) asserted that residents of Virginia need not obey tax laws passed by other legislative bodies (namely Parliament), terming any opponent of that opinion "an Enemy to this his Majesty's Colony."

■ In 1795 the artist Lawrence Sully painted the only known life portrait of Patrick Henry. The old man's fierce gaze reflects the same intensity that marked his actions thirty years earlier, when he introduced the Virginia Stamp Act Resolves in the House of Burgesses. (Mead Art Museum, Amherst College. Bequest of Herbert L. Pratt, Class of 1985)

The burgesses' decision to accept only the first four of Henry's resolutions anticipated the position most

CONTINUING LOYALTY TO BRITAIN

Americans would adopt throughout the following decade. Though willing to contend for their rights, the colonists did not seek independence. They rather wanted some measure of self-government. Accordingly, they backed away from the assertions that they owed Parliament no obedience and that only their own assemblies could tax them. Indeed, declared the Maryland lawyer Daniel Dulany, whose *Considerations on the Propriety of Imposing Taxes on the British Colonies* was the most widely read pamphlet of 1765, "The colonies are dependent upon Great Britain, and the supreme authority vested in the king, lords, and commons, may justly be exercised to secure, or preserve their dependence." But, warned Dulany, a superior did not have the right "to seize the property of his inferior when he pleases"; there was a crucial distinction between a condition of "dependence and inferiority" and one of "absolute vassalage and slavery."

Over the next ten years, America's political leaders searched for a formula that would enable them to control their internal affairs, especially taxation, but remain under British rule. The chief difficulty lay in British officials' inability to compromise on the issue of parliamentary power. The notion that Parliament could exercise absolute authority over all colonial possessions inhered in the British theory of government. Even the harshest British critics of the ministries of the 1760s and 1770s questioned only the wisdom of specific policies, not the principles on which they rested. In effect, the Americans wanted British leaders to revise their fundamental understanding of the workings of their government. But that was simply too much to expect.

The ultimate effectiveness of Americans' opposition to the Stamp Act rested on more than ideological arguments over parliamentary power. The decisive and inventive actions of some colonists during the late summer and fall of 1765 gave the resistance its primary force.

In August the Loyal Nine, a Boston social club of printers, distillers, and other artisans, organized a demonstration against the Stamp Act. Hoping to show

ANTI–STAMP ACT DEMONSTRATIONS

that people of all ranks opposed the act, they approached the leaders of the city's rival laborers' associations, based in Boston's North End and South End neighborhoods. The two gangs, composed of unskilled workers and poor tradesmen, often battled each other, but the Loyal Nine convinced them to lay aside their differences to participate in the demonstration. All colonists, not just affluent ones, would have to pay the stamp taxes.

Early on August 14, the demonstrators hung an effigy of Andrew Oliver, the province's stamp distributor, from a tree on Boston Common. That night a large crowd led by a group of about fifty well-dressed tradesmen paraded the effigy around the city. The crowd tore down a small building they thought was intended as the stamp office, making a bonfire near Oliver's house with wood from the structure. Beheading the effigy, they added it to the flames. Demonstrators broke most of Oliver's windows and threw stones at officials who tried to disperse them. In the midst of the melee, the North End and South End leaders drank a toast to their successful union. The Loyal Nine achieved success when Oliver publicly promised not to fulfill the duties of his office. One Bostonian jubilantly wrote to a relative, "I believe people never was more Universally pleased not so much one could I hear say he was sorry, but a smile sat on almost every ones countinance."

But another crowd action twelve days later, aimed this time at Oliver's brother-in-law, Lieutenant Governor Thomas Hutchinson, drew no praise from Boston's respectable citizens. On the night of August 26, a mob reportedly led by the South End leader Ebenezer MacIntosh attacked the homes of several customs officers. The crowd then completely destroyed Hutchinson's elaborately furnished townhouse in one of Boston's most fashionable districts. The lieutenant governor reported that by the next morning "one of the best finished houses in the Province had nothing remaining but the bare walls and floors." His trees and garden were ruined, his valuable library was lost, and the mob "emptied the house of every thing whatsoever except a part of the kitchen furniture." But Hutchinson took some comfort in the fact that "the encouragers of the first mob never intended matters should go this length and the people in general express the utmost detestation of this unparalleled outrage." (A portrait of Hutchinson is on page 130.)

The differences between the two Boston mobs of August 1765 exposed divisions that would continue to

AMERICANS' DIVERGENT INTERESTS

characterize subsequent colonial protests. Few residents of the colonies sided with Great Britain during the 1760s, but various colonial groups had divergent goals. The skilled craftsmen who composed the Loyal Nine, and merchants, lawyers, and other members of the educated elite preferred orderly demonstrations confined to political issues. For the city's laborers, by contrast, economic grievances may have been paramount. Certainly, their "hellish Fury" as they wrecked Hutchinson's house suggests a resentment against his ostentatious display of wealth.

Colonists, like Britons, had a long tradition of crowd action in which disfranchised people took to the streets to redress deeply felt local grievances. But the Stamp Act controversy drew ordinary urban folk into the vortex of transatlantic politics for the first time. Matters that previously had been of concern only to the gentry or to members of colonial legislatures were now discussed on every street corner and in every tavern. Benjamin Franklin's daughter observed as much when she informed her father, then serving as a colonial agent in London, that "nothing else is talked of, the Dutch [Germans] talk of the stompt act the Negroes of the tamp, in short every body has something to say."

The entry of unskilled workers, slaves, and women into the realm of imperial politics both threatened and aided the elite men who wanted to mount effective opposition to British measures. On the one hand, crowd ac-

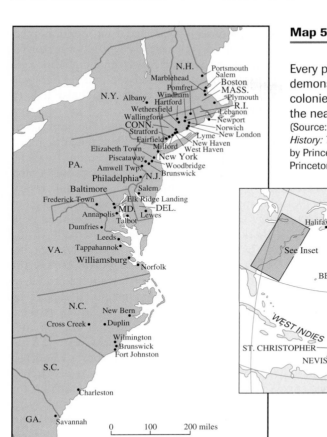

Map 5.3   Sites of Major Demonstrations Against the Stamp Act

Every place named on these maps was the site of a demonstration against the Stamp Act of 1765; British colonies outside the eventual United States joined in the nearly universal opposition to the hated measure. (Source: From Lester J. Cappon et al., eds., *Atlas of Early American History: The Revolutionary Era, 1760–1790.* Copyright © 1976 by Princeton University Press. Reprinted by permission of Princeton University Press.)

tion could have a stunning impact. Anti–Stamp Act demonstrations occurred in cities and towns stretching from Halifax in the north to the Caribbean island of Antigua in the south (see Map 5.3). They were so successful that by November 1, when the law was scheduled to take effect, not one stamp distributor was willing to carry out his official duties. Thus the act could not be enforced. But on the other hand, wealthy men recognized that mobs composed of the formerly powerless—whose goals were not always identical to theirs (as the Boston experience showed)—could endanger their own dominance of the society. What would happen, they wondered, if the "hellish Fury" of the crowd turned against them?

They therefore attempted to channel resistance into acceptable forms by creating an intercolonial association, the Sons of Liberty. New Yorkers organized the first such group in early November, and branches

SONS OF LIBERTY spread rapidly through the coastal cities. Composed of merchants, law-

yers, and prosperous tradesmen like Paul Revere, the Sons of Liberty by early 1766 linked protest leaders from Charleston, South Carolina, to Portsmouth, New Hampshire. Not surprisingly, in light of the central role of taverns as settings for the exchange of news and opinions, a considerable number of members were tavern owners.

The Sons of Liberty could influence events but not control them. In Charleston in October 1765, an informally organized crowd shouting "Liberty Liberty and stamp'd paper" forced the resignation of the South Carolina stamp distributor. The victory celebration a few days later—the largest demonstration the city had ever known—featured a British flag with the word "Liberty" emblazoned on it. But the new Charleston chapter of the Sons of Liberty was horrified when in January 1766 local slaves paraded through the streets similarly crying "Liberty!" Freedom from slavery was not the sort of liberty elite slaveowners had in mind.

In Philadelphia, too, resistance leaders were dismayed when an angry mob threatened to attack Benjamin Franklin's house. The city's laborers believed Franklin to be partly responsible for the Stamp Act, since he had obtained the post of stamp distributor for a close friend. But Philadelphia's artisans—the backbone of the opposition movement there and elsewhere—were fiercely

■ The haughty and powerful Thomas Hutchinson, lieutenant governor of Massachusetts, whose townhouse in Boston's North End was torn apart by a mob on August 26, 1765. (Massachusetts Historical Society)

loyal to Franklin, one of their own who had made good. They gathered to protect his home and family from the crowd. The house was saved, but the resulting split between the better-off tradesmen and the common laborers prevented the establishment of a successful working-men's alliance like that of Boston.

During the fall and winter of 1765–1766, opposition to the Stamp Act proceeded on three separate fronts.

OPPOSITION AND REPEAL Colonial legislatures petitioned Parliament to repeal the hated law, and courts closed because they could not obtain the stamps now required for all legal documents. In October nine colonies sent delegates to a general congress, the first since the 1754 Albany Congress. The Stamp Act Congress met in New York to draft a unified but conservative statement of protest that stressed the law's adverse economic effects rather than its perceived violations of Americans' rights. At the same time, the Sons of Liberty held mass meetings, attempting to rally public support for the resistance movement. Finally, American merchants organized nonimportation associations to pressure British exporters. By the 1760s, one-quarter of all British exports went to the colonies,

and American merchants reasoned that London merchants whose sales suffered severely would lobby for repeal. Since times were bad and American merchants were finding few customers for imported goods anyway, a general moratorium on future purchases would also help to reduce their bloated inventories.

In March 1766, Parliament repealed the Stamp Act. The nonimportation agreements had had the anticipated effect, creating allies for the colonies among wealthy London merchants. But boycotts, formal protests, and crowd actions were less important in winning repeal than was the appointment of a new prime minister, chosen by George III for reasons unrelated to colonial politics. Lord Rockingham, who replaced Grenville in the summer of 1765, had opposed the Stamp Act, not because he believed Parliament lacked power to tax the colonies but because he thought the law unwise and divisive. Thus although Rockingham proposed repeal, he linked it to passage of a Declaratory Act, which asserted Parliament's authority to tax and legislate for Britain's American possessions "in all cases whatsoever."

News of the repeal arrived in Newport, Rhode Island, in May, and the Sons of Liberty quickly dispatched messengers to carry the welcome tidings throughout the colonies. They organized celebrations commemorating the glorious event, all of which stressed the Americans' unwavering loyalty to Great Britain. Their goal achieved, the Sons of Liberty dissolved. Few colonists saw the ominous implications of the Declaratory Act.

Resistance to the Townshend Acts

*T*he colonists had accomplished their immediate aim, but the long-term prospects were unclear. In the summer of 1766, another change in the ministry in London revealed how fragile their victory had been. The new prime minister, William Pitt, had fostered cooperation between the colonies and Great Britain during the Seven Years War. Now, however, Pitt was ill much of the time, and another man, Charles Townshend, became the dominant force in the ministry. An ally of Grenville and a supporter of colonial taxation, Townshend decided to renew the attempt to obtain additional funds from Britain's American possessions (see Table 5.2).

The duties Townshend proposed in 1767 were to be levied on trade goods like paper, glass, and tea, and thus seemed to be nothing more than extensions of the existing Navigation Acts. But the Townshend duties differed from previous customs levies in two ways. First, they applied to items imported into the colonies from Britain, not from foreign countries. Thus they violated mercantilist theory (see page 77). Second, the revenues were designed to fund the salaries of some royal officials in the colonies. Those men, previously paid from local taxation, would therefore be freed from what had been a powerful weapon to ensure their cooperation, for assemblies would no longer be able to threaten to withhold their salaries, as had been done regularly in the past. Additionally, Townshend's scheme provided for establishing an American Board of Customs Commissioners and vice-admiralty courts at Boston, Philadelphia, and Charleston. Both moves angered merchants, whose profits would be threatened by more vigorous enforcement of the Navigation Acts.

In 1765, months had passed before the colonists protested the Stamp Act. The passage of the Townshend Acts, however, drew a quick response. One series of essays in particular, *Letters from a Farmer in Pennsylvania*, by the prominent lawyer John Dickinson, expressed a broad consensus. Eventually all but four colonial newspapers printed Dickinson's essays; in pamphlet form they went through seven American editions. Dickinson contended that Parliament could regulate colonial trade but could not exercise that power to raise revenue. By distinguishing between trade regulation and unacceptable commercial taxation, Dickinson avoided the sticky issue of consent and how it affected colonial subordination to Parliament. But his argument created a different, and equally knotty, problem. In effect it obligated the colonies

JOHN DICKINSON'S FARMER'S LETTERS

to assess Parliament's motives in passing any law pertaining to trade before deciding whether to obey it. That was unworkable in the long run.

The Massachusetts assembly responded to the Townshend Acts by drafting a letter to circulate among the other colonial legislatures, calling for unity and suggesting a joint petition of protest. Not the letter itself but the ministry's reaction to it united the colonies. When Lord Hillsborough, recently named to the new post of secretary of state for America, learned of the circular letter, he ordered Governor Francis Bernard of Massachusetts to insist that the assembly recall it. He also directed other governors to prevent their assemblies from discussing the letter. Hillsborough's order gave colonial assemblies the incentive they needed to join forces to oppose this new threat to their prerogatives. In late 1768 the Massachusetts legislature met, debated, and resoundingly rejected recall by a vote of 92 to 17. Bernard immediately dissolved the assembly, and other governors followed suit when their legislatures debated the circular letter.

The number of votes cast against recalling the circular letter—92—assumed ritual significance for the supporters of resistance. The figure 45 already had symbolic meaning because John Wilkes, a radical Londoner sympathetic to the American cause, had been jailed for libel in Britain for publishing an essay entitled *The North Briton*, No. 45. In Boston, Paul Revere made a punch-bowl weighing 45 ounces that held 45 gills (half-cups) and was engraved with the names of opposition legislators; James Otis, John Adams, and others publicly drank 45 toasts from it. In Charleston the city's tradesmen decorated a tree with 45 lights and set off 45 rockets. Carrying 45 candles, they adjourned to a tavern, where 45 tables were set with 45 bowls of wine, 45 bowls of punch, and 92 glasses.

RITUALS OF RESISTANCE

Such public rituals served important unifying and educational functions. Just as the pamphlets by Otis, Dulany, Dickinson, and others acquainted literate colonists with the issues raised by British actions, so public rituals taught illiterate Americans about the reasons for resistance and familiarized them with the terms of the argument. When Boston's revived Sons of Liberty invited hundreds of city residents to dine with them each August 14 to commemorate the first Stamp Act uprising, and the Charleston Sons of Liberty held their meetings in public, crowds gathered to watch and listen. Likewise, the public singing of songs supporting the American cause helped to spread the word. The participants in such events openly expressed their commitment to the cause of resistance and encouraged others to join them.

TABLE 5.2	
British Ministries and Their American Policies	
Head of Ministry	**Major Acts**
George Grenville	Sugar Act (1764)
	Currency Act (1764)
	Stamp Act (1765)
Lord Rockingham	Stamp Act repealed (1766)
	Declaratory Act (1766)
William Pitt/ Charles Townshend	Townshend Acts (1767)
Lord North	Townshend duties (except for the tea tax) repealed (1770)
	Coercive Acts (1774)
	Quebec Act (1774)

■ Paul Revere crafted a punchbowl to commemorate the 92 members of the Massachusetts Assembly who in 1768 voted against rescinding the circular letter. The bowl was also linked symbolically to John Wilkes by its size and weight, and through its use in rituals incorporating the number 45. (Courtesy, Museum of Fine Arts, Boston. Gift by Subscription and Francis Bartlett Fund. Reproduced with permission. © 1999 Museum of Fine Arts, Boston. All rights reserved.)

During the campaign against the Townshend duties, the Sons of Liberty and other American leaders made a deliberate effort to involve ordinary folk in the resistance movement. Most important, they urged colonists of all ranks and both sexes to sign agreements not to purchase or consume British products. The new consumerism that previously had linked colonists economically now linked them politically as well, supplying them with a ready method of displaying their allegiance. As "A Tradesman" wrote in a Philadelphia paper in 1770, it was essential "for the Good of the Whole, to strengthen the Hands of the Patriotic Majority, by agreeing not to purchase British Goods."

As the primary purchasers of textiles and household goods, women played a central role in the nonconsumption

DAUGHTERS OF LIBERTY

movement. In Boston more than three hundred matrons publicly promised not to buy or drink tea, "Sickness excepted." The women of Wilmington, North Carolina, burned their tea after walking through town in a solemn procession. Women throughout the colonies exchanged recipes for tea substitutes or drank coffee instead. The best known of the protests, the so-called Edenton Ladies Tea Party, actually had little to do with tea. It was a meeting of prominent North Carolina women who pledged formally to work for the public good and to support resistance to British measures.

Women also encouraged home manufacturing. In many towns, young women calling themselves Daughters of Liberty met to spin in public in an effort to persuade other women to make homespun, thereby ending the colonies' dependence on British cloth. These symbolic displays of patriotism—publicized by newspapers and broadsides—served the same purpose as the male rituals involving the numbers 45 and 92. When young ladies from well-to-do families sat publicly at spinning wheels all day, eating only American food and drinking local herbal tea, and later listening to patriotic sermons, they were serving as political instructors. Many women took great satisfaction in their newfound role. When a New England satirist hinted that women discussed only "such triffling subjects as Dress, Scandal and Detraction" during their spinning bees, three Boston women replied angrily: "Inferior in abusive sarcasm, in personal invective, in low wit, we glory to be, but inferior in veracity, sincerity, love of virtue, of liberty and of our country, we would not willingly be to any."

But the colonists were by no means united in support of nonimportation and nonconsumption. If the Stamp

DIVIDED OPINION OVER BOYCOTTS

Act protests had occasionally (as in Boston and Philadelphia) revealed a division between artisans and merchants on the one side and common laborers on the other, resistance to the Townshend Acts exposed new splits in American ranks. The most significant—which arose from a change in economic circumstances—divided urban artisans and merchants, allies in 1765.

The Stamp Act boycotts had helped to revive a depressed economy by creating a demand for local products and reducing merchants' inventories. But in 1768 and 1769, merchants were enjoying boom times and had no financial incentive to support a boycott. As a result, merchants signed the agreements only reluctantly, sometimes violating them secretly. In contrast, artisans supported nonimportation enthusiastically, recognizing that the absence of British goods would create a ready market for their own manufactures. Thus tradesmen formed the core of the crowds that coerced both importers and their customers by picketing stores, publicizing offenders' names, and sometimes destroying property.

Such tactics were effective: colonial imports from England dropped dramatically in 1769, especially in New York, New England, and Pennsylvania. But they also aroused heated opposition, creating a second major division among the colonists. Some Americans who supported resistance to British measures began to question the use of violence to force others to join the boycott. In addition, wealthier and more conservative colonists were frightened by the threat to private property inherent in the campaign. Political activism by ordinary colonists challenged the ruling elite's domination, just as its members had feared in 1765.

Disclosures that leading merchants had violated the nonimportation agreement caused dissension in the ranks of the boycotters, so Americans were relieved when news arrived in April 1770 that the Townshend duties had been repealed, with the exception of the tea tax. A new prime minister, Lord North, persuaded Parliament that duties on trade within the empire were ill-advised. Although some colonial leaders argued that nonimportation should continue until the tea tax was repealed, merchants quickly resumed importing. The rest of the Townshend Acts remained in force, but repealing the duties made the other provisions (establishing vice-admiralty courts and the American Board of Customs Commissioners, and promising to pay officials' salaries from customs revenues at some future time) appear less objectionable.

TOWNSHEND DUTIES REPEALED

Confrontations in Boston

*a*t first the new ministry in London did nothing to antagonize the colonists. Yet on the very day Lord North proposed repeal of the Townshend duties, a confrontation between civilians and soldiers in Boston led to the death of five Americans. The origins of the event that patriots called the Boston Massacre lay in repeated clashes between customs officers and the people

A

VERSE,

Occasioned by seeing the North-Spinning, in *BOSTON*.

BOSTON, behold the pretty Spinners here,
  And see how gay the pretty Sparks appear:
See Rich and Poor all turn the Spinning Wheel,
All who Compassion for their Country feel,
All who do love to see Industry live,
And see Frugality in *Boston* thrive.

Britain, behold thy Trade stole from thy Hand,
And carried on in *Boston's* distant Land:
See now thy Trade and Trades men, all expire,
And see them all cut short of their Desire,
Th' Desire they had that *Boston's* Trade should spoil,
That they might reap the Fruit of all our Toil;
          they might   what we've been striving for,
And rule us by the Parliamental Law:
But thanks to GOD, their ill Designs are cropt,
And their Tirannical Designs are stopt.

Now they have run their Chain's extended Length,
And exhausted all their once encourag'd Strength:
Now have their ill Designs all found an end,
Now they have made a Foe of every Friend:
Now let them starve and die the Death of those
Who do the Interest of their King oppose.

BOSTON: Printed and Sold 1769.

■ A 1769 Boston broadside commended the spinners, "Rich and Poor," who had "Compassion for their Country" and promoted "Frugality" during the Townshend Act crisis. The poet put into verse precisely the message the spinners intended to convey. (Massachusetts Historical Society)

of Massachusetts. The decision to base the American Board of Customs Commissioners in Boston was the source of the problem.

Mobs targeted the customs commissioners from the day they arrived in November 1767. In June 1768 their seizure of the patriot leader John Hancock's sloop *Liberty* on suspicion of smuggling caused a riot in which prominent customs officers' property was destroyed. The riot in turn helped to convince the ministry in London that troops were needed to maintain order in the unruly port. The assignment of two regiments of regulars to their city confirmed Bostonians' worst fears; the redcoats constantly reminded city dwellers of the oppressive potential of British power. Guards on Boston Neck, the entrance to the city, checked all travelers and their goods. Redcoat patrols roamed the city day and night, questioning and sometimes harassing passersby. Military parades were held on Boston Common, accompanied by martial music and often the public whipping of deserters and other violators of army rules. Parents began to fear for the safety of their daughters, who were subjected to soldiers' coarse sexual insults. But the greatest potential for violence lay in the uneasy relationship between the soldiers and Boston laborers. Many redcoats sought employment in their off-duty hours, competing for unskilled jobs with the city's ordinary workingmen. Members of the two groups brawled repeatedly in taverns and on the streets.

Early on the evening of March 5, 1770, a crowd of laborers began throwing hard-packed snowballs at soldiers

BOSTON MASSACRE

guarding the Customs House. Goaded beyond endurance, the sentries acted against express orders and fired on the crowd, killing four and wounding eight, one of whom died a few days later. Resistance leaders idealized the dead rioters as martyrs for the cause of liberty, holding a solemn funeral and later commemorating March 5 annually with patriotic orations. Paul Revere's engraving of the massacre (based on a drawing by John Singleton Copley's half-brother Henry Pelham and reproduced on page 135) was part of the propaganda campaign.

Leading patriots wanted to ensure that the soldiers did not become martyrs as well. Despite the political benefits the patriots derived from the massacre, they probably did not approve the crowd action that provoked it. Ever since the destruction of Hutchinson's house in August 1765, men allied with the Sons of Liberty had supported orderly demonstrations and expressed distaste at such uncontrolled riots as the one that provoked the Boston Massacre. Thus when the soldiers were tried for the killings in November, John Adams and Josiah Quincy Jr., both unwavering patriots, acted as their defense attorneys. Almost all the accused were acquitted, and the two men convicted were released after being branded on the thumb. Undoubtedly the favorable outcome of the trials persuaded London officials not to retaliate against the city.

For more than two years after the Boston Massacre and the repeal of the Townshend duties, a superficial

A BRITISH PLOT?

calm descended on the colonies. The most outspoken colonial newspapers, such as the *Boston Gazette,* the *Penn-*

sylvania Journal, and the *South Carolina Gazette,* published essays drawing on Real Whig ideology and accusing Great Britain of deliberately scheming to oppress the colonies. After the Stamp Act's repeal, the patriots had praised Parliament; following repeal of the Townshend duties, they warned of impending tyranny. What had seemed to be an isolated mistake, a single ill-chosen stamp tax, now appeared to be part of a plot against American liberties. Essayists pointed to Parliament's persecution of the British radical John Wilkes, the stationing of troops in Boston, and the growing number of vice-admiralty courts as evidence of plans to enslave the colonists. Indeed, patriot writers played repeatedly on the word *enslavement.* Most free colonists had direct knowledge of slavery (either as slaveholders themselves or as neighbors of slaveowners), and the threat of enslavement by Britain must have hit them with peculiar force.

Still, no one yet advocated complete independence from the mother country. Although the patriots were becoming increasingly convinced that they should seek freedom from parliamentary authority, they continued to acknowledge their British identity and their allegiance to George III. They began, therefore, to envision a system that would enable them to be ruled by their own elected legislatures while remaining subordinate to the king. But any such scheme violated Britons' conception of the nature of their government, which posited that Parliament wielded sole, undivided sovereignty over the empire. Furthermore, in the British mind, Parliament encompassed the king as well as lords and commons, so separating the monarch from the legislature was impossible.

Then, in the fall of 1772, the North ministry began to implement the Townshend Act that provided for governors and judges to be paid directly from customs revenues. In early November, voters at a Boston town meeting established a Committee of Correspondence to publicize the decision by exchanging letters with other Massachusetts towns. Heading the committee was the man who had proposed its formation, Samuel Adams.

Fifty-one in 1772, Samuel Adams was thirteen years older than his distant cousin John and by a decade the

SAMUEL ADAMS AND COMMITTEES OF CORRESPONDENCE

senior of most other leaders of American resistance. He had been a Boston tax collector, a member and clerk of the Massachusetts assembly, an ally of the Loyal Nine, and a member of the Sons of Liberty. Unswerving in his devotion to the American cause, Adams drew a sharp contrast between a corrupt, vice-ridden Britain and the colonies, peopled by simple, liberty-loving folk. An experienced

■ Shortly after the Boston Massacre, Paul Revere printed this illustration of the confrontation near the customs house on March 5, 1770. Offering visual support for the patriots' version of events, it showed the British soldiers firing on an unresisting crowd (instead of the aggressive mob described at the soldiers' trial) and—even worse—a gun firing from the building itself, which has been labeled "Butchers Hall." (Courtesy of the John Carter Brown Library at Brown University)

political organizer, Adams continually stressed the necessity of prudent collective action in speeches in the Boston town meeting. His Committee of Correspondence thus undertook the task of creating an informed consensus among all the residents of Massachusetts.

Such committees, which were eventually established throughout the colonies, represented the next logical step in the organization of American resistance. Until 1772, the protest movement was largely confined to the seacoast and primarily to major cities and towns (see Map 5.3). Adams realized that the time had come to widen the movement's geographic scope, to attempt to involve more colonists in the struggle. Accordingly, the Boston town meeting directed the Committee of Correspondence "to state the Rights of the Colonists and of this Province in particular," to list "the Infringements and Violations thereof that have been, or from time to time may be made," and to send copies to the other towns in the province. In return, Boston requested "a free communication of their Sentiments on this Subject."

The statement of colonial rights prepared by the Bostonians declared that Americans had absolute rights to life, liberty, and property. The idea that "a British house of commons, should have a right, at pleasure, to give and grant the property of the colonists" was "irreconcileable" with "the first principles of natural law and Justice . . . and of the British Constitution in particular." The list of grievances complained of taxation without representation, the presence of unnecessary troops and customs officers on American soil, the use of imperial revenues to pay colonial officials, the expanded jurisdiction of vice-admiralty courts, and even the nature of the instructions given to American governors by their superiors in London.

The entire document, which was printed as a pamphlet for distribution to the towns, exhibited none of the hesitation that had characterized colonial claims against Parliament in the 1760s. No longer were patriots—at least in Boston—preoccupied with defining the precise limits of parliamentary authority. No longer did they mention the necessity of obedience to Parliament. They were committed to a course that placed American rights first, loyalty to Great Britain a distant second.

The response of the Massachusetts towns to the committee's pamphlet must have caused Samuel Adams to rejoice. Some towns disagreed with Boston's assessment of the state of affairs, but most aligned themselves with the city. From Braintree came the assertion that "all civil officers are or ought to be Servants to the people and dependent upon them for their official Support, and every instance to the Contrary from the Governor downwards tends to crush and destroy civil liberty." The town of Holden declared that "the People of New England have never given the People of Britain any Right of Jurisdiction over us." The citizens of Petersham commented that resistance to tyranny was "the first and highest social Duty of this people." And Pownallborough warned, "Allegiance is a relative Term and like Kingdoms and commonwealths is local and has its bounds." Beliefs like these made the next crisis in Anglo-American affairs the final one.

Tea and Turmoil

The tea tax was the only Townshend duty still in effect by 1773. In the years after 1770, some Americans continued to boycott English tea, while others resumed drinking it either openly or in secret. As was explained in Chapter 4, tea figured prominently in both the colonists' diet and their social lives, so observing the boycott required them not only to forgo a favorite beverage but also to alter habitual forms of socializing. Tea thus retained an explosively symbolic character even though the boycott began to fall apart after 1770.

In May 1773, Parliament passed an act designed to save the East India Company from bankruptcy. The

TEA ACT

company, which held a monopoly on British trade with the East Indies, was critically important to the British economy (and to the financial well-being of many prominent British politicians who had invested in its stock). According to the Tea Act, legal tea would henceforth be sold in America only by the East India Company's designated agents, which would enable the company to avoid middlemen in both England and the colonies and to price its tea competitively with that offered by smugglers. The net result would be cheaper tea for American consumers. Resistance leaders, however, interpreted the new measure as a pernicious device to make them admit Parlia-

ment's right to tax them, for the less expensive tea would still be taxed under the Townshend law. Others saw the Tea Act as the first step in the establishment of an East India Company monopoly of all colonial trade. Residents of the four cities designated to receive the first shipments of tea accordingly prepared to respond to what they perceived as a new threat to their freedom.

In New York City, tea ships never arrived. In Philadelphia, Pennsylvania's governor persuaded the captain to sail back to Britain. In Charleston, the tea was unloaded and stored; some was destroyed, the rest sold in 1776 by the new state government. The only confrontation occurred in Boston, where both sides—the town meeting, joined by participants from nearby towns, and Governor Thomas Hutchinson, two of whose sons were tea agents—rejected compromise.

The first of three tea ships, the *Dartmouth*, entered Boston harbor on November 28. The customs laws

THE BOSTON TEA PARTY

required cargo to be landed and the appropriate duty paid by its owners within twenty days of a ship's arrival; otherwise, the cargo had to be seized by customs officers and sold at auction. After a series of mass meetings, Bostonians voted to post guards on the wharf to prevent the tea from being unloaded. Hutchinson refused to permit the vessels to leave the harbor. John Singleton Copley, whose father-in-law was a tea agent, tried to mediate the dispute.

On December 16, one day before the cargo would have been confiscated, more than five thousand people (nearly a third of the city's population) crowded into Old South Church. The meeting, chaired by Samuel Adams, made a final attempt to convince Hutchinson to send the tea back to England. But the governor remained adamant. In the early evening Adams reportedly announced "that he could think of nothing further to be done—that they had now done all they could for the Salvation of their Country." Cries then rang out from the back of the crowd: "Boston harbor a tea-pot tonight! The Mohawks are come!" Small groups pushed their way out of the meeting. Within a few minutes, about sixty men crudely disguised as Indians assembled at the wharf, boarded the three ships, and dumped the cargo into the harbor. By 9 P.M. their work was done: 342 chests of tea worth approximately £10,000 floated in splinters on the water.

Among the "Indians" were many representatives of Boston's artisans, including the silversmith Paul Revere. Five masons, eleven carpenters and builders, three leatherworkers, a blacksmith, two barbers, a coachmaker, a shoemaker, and twelve apprentices have been identified as participants. That their ranks also included

■ The planners of the Boston Tea Party met here, at the Green Dragon Tavern, sketched later by one of their number, the portrait painter John Johnson. (Courtesy, American Antiquarian Society)

GREEN DRAGON TAVERN

four farmers from outside Boston, ten merchants, two doctors, a teacher, and a bookseller illustrated the widespread support for the resistance movement. The next day John Adams exulted in his diary that the Tea Party was "so bold, so daring, so firm, intrepid and inflexible" that "I cant but consider it as an Epocha in history."

The North administration reacted with considerably less enthusiasm when it learned of the Tea Party. In

COERCIVE AND QUEBEC ACTS

March 1774, Parliament adopted the first of four laws that became known as the Coercive, or Intolerable, Acts. It ordered the port of Boston closed until the tea was paid for, prohibiting all but coastal trade in food and firewood. Later in the spring, Parliament passed three other punitive measures. The Massachusetts Government Act altered the province's charter, substituting an appointed council for the elected one, increasing the governor's powers, and forbidding most town meetings. The Justice Act provided that a person accused of committing murder in the course of suppressing a riot or enforcing the laws could be tried outside the colony where the incident had occurred. Finally, the Quartering Act allowed military officers to commandeer privately owned buildings to house their troops. Thus the Coercive Acts punished not only Boston but also Massachusetts as a whole, alerting other colonies to the possibility

that their residents, too, could be subject to retaliation if they opposed British authority.

After passing the last of the Coercive Acts, Parliament turned its attention to much-needed reforms in the government of Quebec. The Quebec Act thereby became linked with the Coercive Acts in the minds of the patriots. Intended to ease strains that had arisen since the British conquest of the formerly French colony, the Quebec Act granted greater religious freedom to Catholics—alarming Protestant colonists, who equated Roman Catholicism with religious and political despotism. It also reinstated French civil law, which had been replaced by British procedures in 1763, and it established an appointed council (rather than an elected legislature) as the governing body of the colony. Finally, in an attempt to provide northern Indians with some protection against Anglo-American settlement, the act annexed to Quebec the area east of the Mississippi River and north of the Ohio River. That region, parts of which were claimed by individual seacoast colonies, was thus removed from their jurisdiction—and the task of wealthy colonists who hoped to develop the Ohio Country became much more difficult.

Members of Parliament who voted for the punitive legislation believed that the acts would be obeyed and that at long last they had solved the problem posed by the troublesome Americans. But the patriots showed little inclination to bow to the wishes of Parliament. In their eyes, the Coercive Acts and the Quebec Act proved what they had feared since 1768: that Great Britain had embarked on a deliberate plan to oppress them. If the port of Boston could be closed, why not the ports of Philadelphia or New York? If the royal charter of Massachusetts could be changed, why not the charter of South Carolina? If certain people could be transferred to distant colonies for trial, why not any violator of any law? If troops could be forcibly quartered in private houses, did not that action pave the way for the occupation of all of America? If the Roman Catholic Church could receive favored status in Quebec, why not everywhere? It seemed as though the full dimensions of the plot against American rights and liberties had at last been revealed.

The Boston Committee of Correspondence urged all the colonies to join in an immediate boycott of British goods. But the other provinces hesitated to take such a drastic step. Rhode Island, Virginia, and Pennsylvania each suggested that another intercolonial congress be convened to consider an appropriate response, and in mid-June 1774 Massachusetts acquiesced. Few people wanted to take hasty action; even the most ardent patriots remained loyal to Britain and hoped for reconciliation with its leaders. Despite their objections to British policy, they continued to see themselves as part of the empire. Americans were approaching the brink of confrontation, but they had not committed themselves to an irrevocable break. So the colonies agreed to send delegates to Philadelphia in September to attend a Continental Congress.

Summary

Just twenty years earlier, at the outbreak of the Seven Years War in the wilderness of western Pennsylvania, no one could have predicted that the future would bring such swift and dramatic change to Britain's mainland colonies. Yet that conflict—which simultaneously removed France from North America and created a huge war debt Britain had to find ways to pay—set in motion the process leading to the convening of the First Continental Congress.

In the years after the war ended in 1763, momentous changes occurred in the ways colonists thought about themselves and their allegiances. The number of colonists who defined themselves as political actors increased substantially. Once linked unquestioningly to Great Britain,

they began to develop a sense of their own identity as Americans, including a recognition of the cultural and social gulf that separated them from Britons. They started to realize that their concept of the political process differed from that held by people in the mother country. They also came to understand that their economic interests did not necessarily coincide with those of Great Britain. Colonial political leaders reached such conclusions only after a long train of events, some of them violent, altered their understanding of their relationship with the mother country. Parliamentary acts such as the Stamp Act and the Townshend Acts elicited colonial responses—both ideological and practical—that produced further responses from Britain. Tensions escalated until they climaxed in the Tea Party. From that point on, there was to be no turning back.

In the late summer of 1774, the Americans were committed to resistance but not to independence. Even so, they had started to sever the bonds of empire. During the next decade, they would forge the bonds of a new American nationality to replace those rejected Anglo-American ties.

LEGACY FOR A PEOPLE AND A NATION
The Census and Reapportionment

When in the prerevolutionary years American colonists argued that "they were not represented in" Parliament, they developed a definition of representation very different from the understanding traditionally accepted in Great Britain. There, numbers did not matter: the entire British population was seen as being "virtually" represented in Parliament, regardless of how many men had the vote or how many electors lived in each district. In eighteenth-century Britain, some districts had few or no voters, some had many, and some heavily populated areas could vote for no one, because Parliament had not been reapportioned for centuries.

Americans, by contrast, placed great emphasis on the importance of being represented in government by someone for whom they—or at least their better-off male neighbors—had actually voted. And that carried with it the related desire for election districts that were regularly reapportioned in accordance with the movements and increase of the population; otherwise the goal of actual representation could not be ensured. Article 1, Section 2, of the U.S. Constitution thus provides for an "actual enumeration" of the nation's residents every ten years so that "representatives . . . shall be apportioned among the several States . . . according to their respective numbers." Each decade, from 1790 to 2000, the government has tried to count the nation's residents accurately—although, according to historians and demographers, it has often failed to achieve that goal. Even Thomas Jefferson, who as secretary of state oversaw the first census in 1790, recognized that it undercounted the population and should be adjusted upward.

The 2000 census, the planning for which Congress debated heatedly, turned out to be the most accurate in recent decades. It also led to two Supreme Court decisions: one outlining appropriate techniques for conducting the mandated "actual enumeration" of the American population, and another rejecting Utah's challenge to the final count. (Utah, which has only one member of the House and hoped to obtain a second, charged that the Census Bureau had improperly awarded a seat to North Carolina.) In other years too—especially 1920, near the close of an era of dramatic demographic change—planning and conducting the census proved highly contentious. The commonly unacknowledged origin of such contests lies in Americans' prerevolutionary experience.

Every ten years, in short, the nation must still wrestle with an enduring legacy of the colonial period: the need to enumerate the American people and to alter the boundaries of electoral districts according to the results.

The **history companion** powered by Eduspace®

Your primary source for interactive quizzes, exercises, and more to help you learn efficiently.
http://history.college.hmco.com/students

a REVOLUTION, INDEED 1774–1783

*T*he Shawnee chief Blackfish named his new captive Sheltowee, or Big Turtle, and adopted him as his son. Blackfish's warriors had easily caught the lone hunter, who was returning with a slaughtered buffalo to an encampment of men making salt at the briny spring known as Blue Licks. The captive then persuaded his fellow frontiersmen to surrender to the Shawnees (allies of the British) without a fight. It was February 1778. The hunter was Daniel Boone, who less than three years earlier had moved his family from North Carolina to the western region of Virginia known as Kentucky. Both his contemporaries and some historians have wondered about Boone's allegiance during the American Revolution, for he moved to the frontier just as the war began. His encounter with the Shawnees in 1778, which can be interpreted in several ways, highlights many ambiguities of revolutionary-era loyalties.

The Shawnees were seeking captives to cover the death (see pages 104–105) of their chief Cornstalk, who had been killed several months earlier while a prisoner of American militiamen in the Ohio country. Of the twenty-six men taken at the spring, about half were adopted into Shawnee families; the others—less willing to conform to Indian ways—were dispatched as prisoners to the British fort at Detroit. Boone, who assured Blackfish that in the spring he would negotiate the surrender of the women and children remaining at his home settlement of Boonesborough, watched and waited, outwardly content with his new life. In June 1778 he escaped, hurrying home to warn the Kentuckians of impending attack.

When Blackfish's Shawnees and their British allies appeared outside the Boonesborough stockade in mid-September, Boone proved amenable to negotiations. Although the settlers adamantly refused to move back across the mountains, fragmentary evidence suggests that they agreed to swear allegiance to the British in order to avert a bloody battle. But the discussions dissolved into a melee and the Indians then futilely besieged the fort for a week before withdrawing.

◀ A statue of George III standing in the Bowling Green in New York City was one of the first casualties of the American Revolution, as colonists marked the adoption of the Declaration of Independence by pulling it down. Much of the metal was melted to make bullets, but in the twentieth century the head—largely intact—was unearthed in Connecticut. (Lafayette College Art Collection, Easton, Pennsylvania)

CHRONOLOGY

1774 • First Continental Congress meets in Philadelphia, adopts Declaration of Rights and Grievances
• Continental Association implements economic boycott of Britain; committees of observation established to oversee boycott

1774–75 • Provincial conventions replace collapsing colonial governments

1775 • Battles of Lexington and Concord; first shots of war fired
• Second Continental Congress begins
• Washington named commander-in-chief
• Dunmore's proclamation offers freedom to patriots' slaves who join British forces

1776 • Paine publishes *Common Sense,* advocating independence
• British evacuate Boston
• Declaration of Independence adopted
• New York City falls to British

1777 • British take Philadelphia
• Burgoyne surrenders at Saratoga

1778 • French alliance brings vital assistance to the United States
• British evacuate Philadelphia

1779 • Sullivan expedition destroys Iroquois villages

1780 • British take Charleston

1781 • Cornwallis surrenders at Yorktown

1782 • Peace negotiations begin

1783 • Treaty of Paris signed, granting independence to the United States

With that threat gone, Boone was charged with treason and court-martialed by Kentucky militia. Although he was cleared, questions about the incident at Blue Licks and its aftermath haunted him for the rest of his life.

Where did Daniel Boone's loyalties lie? To the British? to the Americans? to other Kentuckians? His actions could be viewed in all three lights. Had he betrayed the settlers to Shawnees and sought to establish British authority in Kentucky? Had he—as he later claimed—twice deceived the Shawnees? Or had he rather made the survival of the fragile settlements his highest priority? Kentucky was a borderland—a region where British, Indians, and various groups of American settlers all vied for control. Boone and other residents of the Appalachian backcountry did not always face clear-cut choices as they struggled to establish themselves securely under such precarious circumstances.

Daniel Boone was not the only American of uncertain or shifting allegiance in the 1770s. As a civil war that affected much of North America east of the Mississippi River, the American Revolution uprooted thousands of families, disrupted the economy, reshaped society by forcing many colonists into permanent exile, led Americans to develop new conceptions of politics, and created a nation from thirteen separate colonies. Much more than a series of clashes between the British and patriot armies, it marked a significant turning point in Americans' collective history.

The struggle for independence required revolutionary leaders to accomplish three separate but closely related tasks. The first was political and ideological: transforming a consensus favoring loyal resistance into a coalition supporting independence. Pursuing a variety of measures (ranging from persuasion to coercion) to enlist all European Americans in the patriot cause, the colonies' elected leaders also tried to ensure the neutrality of Indians and slaves in the impending conflict.

The second task involved foreign relations. To win independence, patriot leaders knew they needed international recognition and aid, particularly from France. Thus they dispatched to Paris the most experienced American diplomat, Benjamin Franklin, who had served for years as a colonial agent in London. Franklin skillfully negotiated the Franco-American alliance of 1778, which was to prove crucial to winning independence.

Only the third task directly involved the British. George Washington, commander-in-chief of the American army, soon recognized that his primary goal should be not to win battles but to avoid losing them decisively. The outcome of any one battle was less important than ensuring that his army survived to fight another day. Consequently, the story of the Revolutionary War reveals British action and American reaction, British attacks and

American defenses and withdrawals. The American war effort was aided by the failure of British military planners to analyze accurately the problem confronting them. Until it was too late, they treated the war against the colonists as they treated wars against other Europeans: they concentrated on winning battles and did not consider the difficulties of achieving their main goal, retaining the colonies' allegiance. In the end, the Americans' triumph owed more to their own endurance and to Britain's mistakes than to their military prowess. ■

Government by Congress and Committee

*W*hen the fifty-five delegates to the First Continental Congress convened in Philadelphia in September 1774, they knew that any measures they adopted were likely to enjoy widespread support. That summer, open meetings held throughout the colonies had endorsed the idea of another nonimportation pact. Participants in such meetings promised (in the words of the freeholders of Johnston County, North Carolina) to "strictly adhere to, and abide by, such Regulations and Restrictions as the Members of the said General Congress shall agree to and judge most convenient." Committees of correspondence publicized these meetings so effectively that Americans everywhere knew about them. Most of the congressional delegates were selected by extralegal provincial conventions whose members were chosen at local gatherings, since governors had forbidden regular assemblies to conduct formal elections. Thus the very act of designating delegates to attend the Congress involved Americans in open defiance of British authority.

The colonies' leading political figures—most of them lawyers, merchants, and planters representing every

FIRST CONTINENTAL CONGRESS

colony but Georgia—attended the Philadelphia Congress. The Massachusetts delegation included both Samuel Adams, the experienced organizer of Boston resistance, and his younger cousin John, an ambitious lawyer. Among others, New York sent John Jay, a talented young attorney. From Pennsylvania came the conservative Joseph Galloway and his long-time rival, John Dickinson. Virginia elected Richard Henry Lee and Patrick Henry, both noted for their patriotic zeal, as well as George Washington. Most of these men had never met, but in the weeks, months,

and years that followed they became the chief architects of the new nation.

The congressmen faced three tasks when they convened at Carpenters Hall on September 5. The first two were explicit: defining American grievances and developing a plan for resistance. The third—articulating their constitutional relationship with Great Britain—was less clear-cut and proved troublesome. The most radical congressmen, like Lee of Virginia, argued that colonists owed allegiance only to George III and that Parliament was nothing more than a legislature for Britain, with no authority over the colonies. The conservatives—Joseph Galloway and his allies—proposed a formal plan of union that would have required Parliament and a new American legislature to consent jointly to all laws pertaining to the colonies. After heated debate, delegates narrowly rejected Galloway's proposal, but they were not prepared to embrace the radicals' position either.

Finally, they accepted a compromise position worked out by John Adams. The crucial clauses in the Congress's Declaration of Rights and Grievances declared that Americans would obey Parliament, but only because that action was in everyone's best interest, and asserted that colonists would resist all taxes in disguise, like the Townshend duties. Remarkably, such a position—which only a few years before would have been regarded as extreme—represented a compromise in the fall of 1774. The Americans had come a long way since their first hesitant protests against the Sugar Act ten years earlier.

With the constitutional issue resolved, the delegates readily agreed on the laws they wanted repealed (notably

CONTINENTAL ASSOCIATION

the Coercive Acts) and decided to implement an economic boycott while petitioning the king for relief. They adopted the Continental Association, which called for nonimportation of British goods (effective December 1, 1774), nonconsumption of British products (effective March 1, 1775), and nonexportation of American goods to Britain and the British West Indies (effective September 10, 1775).

The provisions of the Association—far more comprehensive than any previous economic measure adopted by the colonies—were carefully designed to appeal to different groups and regions. For example, the inclusive language of the nonimportation agreement banned the traffic in slaves as well as manufactures, which accorded with a longstanding desire of the Virginia gentry to halt, or at least to slow, the arrival of enslaved Africans on their shores. (Leading Virginians believed that continuing slave importations had discouraged the immigration to their colony of free Europeans with useful skills.) The

■ In 1775 a British cartoonist demonstrated his contempt for the pronouncements of the Continental Congress by setting his satire in a privy, or "necessary house," and showing a politician who has used a torn congressional resolution as toilet paper. The person at right is poring over a political pamphlet while portraits of John Wilkes and a man who has been tarred and feathered decorate the walls.   (Library of Congress)

delay of the nonconsumption agreement until three months after nonimportation took effect would allow northern urban merchants to sell items they had acquired legally before December 1. And both the novel tactic of nonexportation and its postponement for nearly a year served other interests. In 1773 small farmers in Virginia had already vowed to stop exporting tobacco to raise prices in a then-glutted market. The next year, they enthusiastically welcomed an Association that accomplished the same end, while permitting them to profit from higher prices for their 1774 crop, which had to be dried and cured before shipment. The delay of the nonexportation agreement also benefited the northern exporters of wood products and foodstuffs to the Caribbean, giving them a final season of sales before the embargo began.

To enforce the Continental Association, Congress recommended the election of committees of observation and inspection in every American local-

COMMITTEES OF
OBSERVATION

ity. By specifying that committee members be chosen by all men qualified to vote for members of the lower houses of colonial legislatures, Congress guaranteed the committees a broad popular base. In some places the committeemen were former local officeholders; in other towns they were men who had never before held office. Everywhere, these committeemen—perhaps seven to eight thousand in the colonies as a whole—became the local leaders of American resistance.

Such committees were officially charged only with overseeing implementation of the boycott, but in the course of the next six months they became de facto governments. They examined merchants' records and published the names of those who continued to import British goods. They promoted home manufactures, encouraging Americans to adopt simple modes of dress and behavior to symbolize their commitment to liberty and virtuous conduct. Since expensive leisure-time activities were believed to reflect vice and corruption, Congress urged Americans to forgo dancing, gambling, horseracing, cockfighting, and other forms of "extravagance and dissipation." Some committees extracted apologies from people caught gambling, partying, or racing. Thus private activities acquired public significance.

The committees gradually extended their authority over many aspects of American life. They attempted to identify opponents of American resistance, developing elaborate spy networks, circulating copies of the Continental Association for signatures, and investigating reports of questionable remarks and activities. Suspected dissenters were urged to support the colonial cause publicly; if they refused, the committees had them watched, restricted their movements, or tried to force them to leave the area. People engaging in casual political exchanges with friends one day could find themselves charged with "treasonable conversation" the next. One Massachusetts man, for example, was called before his local committee for maligning the Congress as "a Pack or Parcell of Fools" that was "as tyrannical as Lord North and ought to be opposed & resisted." When he refused to recant, the committee put him under surveillance.

While the committees of observation were expanding their power during the winter and early spring of

PROVINCIAL
CONVENTIONS

1775, the regular colonial governments were collapsing. Only a few legislatures continued to meet without encountering patriot challenges to their authority. In most colonies, popularly elected provincial conventions took over the task of running the government, sometimes entirely replacing the legislatures and at other times holding concurrent sessions. In late 1774 and early 1775, these conventions approved the Continental Association, elected delegates to the Second Continental Congress (scheduled for May), organized militia units, and gathered arms and ammunition. Unable to stem the tide of resistance, the British-appointed governors and councils watched helplessly as their authority crumbled.

Royal officials suffered humiliation after humiliation. Courts were prevented from holding sessions; taxes were paid to the conventions' agents rather than to provincial tax collectors; sheriffs' powers were challenged; and militiamen would muster only when committees ordered. In short, during the six months preceding the battles at Lexington and Concord, independence was being won at the local level, but without formal acknowledgment and for the most part without bloodshed. Not many Americans fully realized what was happening. The vast majority still proclaimed their loyalty to Great Britain, denying that they sought to leave the empire.

Contest in the Backcountry

*W*hile the committees of observation were consolidating their authority in the East, some colonists were heading west. Ignoring the Proclamation of 1763, pronouncements by colonial governors, and the threat of Indian attacks alike, land-hungry folk—many of them recent immigrants from Ireland and soldiers who demobilized in North America after the Seven Years War—swarmed onto lands along the Ohio River and its tributaries after the mid-1760s. Sometimes they purchased property from opportunists with grants of dubious origin; often, they simply surveyed and claimed land, squatting on it in hopes that their titles would eventually be honored. Britain's 1771 decision to abandon (and raze) Fort Pitt removed the final restraints on settlement in the region, for the withdrawal rendered the Proclamation of 1763 wholly unenforceable. By late 1775, thousands of new homesteads dotted the landscape of the backcountry from western Pennsylvania south through Virginia and eastern Kentucky into western North Carolina.

Few of the backcountry folk saw the region's native peoples in a positive light. (Rare exceptions were the

DISTRUST AND WARFARE

Moravian missionaries who settled with their Indian converts in three small frontier communities in the upper Ohio valley.) The frontier dwellers had little interest in the small-scale trade that had once helped to sustain an uneasy peace in the region; they only wanted land on which to grow crops and pasture their livestock. They interpreted Pontiac's uprising as a sign that no Indian—regardless of religion or tribal affiliation—could be trusted. That adamant and widely held opinion, first publicly exhibited when a group of fifty Scots-Irish men

from Paxton Township, Pennsylvania, massacred twenty peaceful Christian Conestoga Indians in two separate incidents in December 1763, reflected the thinking of many frontier dwellers.

In 1774 Virginia, headed by a new governor, Lord Dunmore, moved vigorously to assert its title to the rapidly developing backcountry. During the spring and early summer, tensions mounted as Virginians surveyed land in Kentucky, on the south side of the Ohio River—territory still claimed by the Shawnees, who rejected the Fort Stanwix treaty of 1768 (see page 124). "Lord Dunmore's war" consisted of one large-scale confrontation between Virginia militia and some Shawnee warriors. Neither side won a clear-cut victory, but in the immediate aftermath thousands of settlers—including Daniel Boone and his associates—flooded across the mountains.

When the Revolutionary War began just as large numbers of people were migrating into Kentucky, the loyalties of all Indians and settlers in the backcountry remained, like Boone's, fluid and uncertain. They were more or less at war with each other, but which side should either take in the imperial struggle? The answer might well depend on which could better serve their interests. Understanding that, the Continental Congress moved to reoccupy the site of Fort Pitt and to establish other garrisons in the Ohio country. Relying on such protection, as many as twenty thousand settlers poured into Kentucky by 1780. Yet frontier affiliations were not clear: the growing town of Pittsburgh, for example, harbored many active loyalists.

The native peoples' grievances against the European American newcomers predisposed many toward an alliance

INDIANS' CHOICES

with Great Britain. Yet some chiefs urged caution: after all, the British abandonment of Fort Pitt (and them) suggested that Britain lacked the will and ability to protect them in the future. Furthermore, Britain hesitated to make full and immediate use of its potential native allies. Officials on the scene recognized that neither the Indians' style of fighting nor their war aims necessarily coincided with British goals and methods. Accordingly, they at first sought from Indians only a promise of neutrality.

Recognizing that their standing with native peoples was poor, the patriots also sought the Indians' neutrality. In 1775 the Second Continental Congress sent a general message to Indian communities describing the war as "a family quarrel between us and Old England" and requesting that they "not join on either side" since "you Indians are not concerned in it." A group of Cherokees led by Chief Dragging Canoe nevertheless decided to

■ An eighteenth-century watercolor, by an unknown artist, showing the village and fort at
Detroit. Once a French stronghold, it had been taken over by the British after the Seven
Years War. American forces tried but failed to capture the fort during the Revolutionary
War.   (William L. Clements Library)

take advantage of the "family quarrel" to regain some
land. In the summer of 1776, they attacked settlements
along the western borders of the Carolinas and Virginia.
But a militia campaign destroyed many Cherokee towns,
along with crops and supplies. Dragging Canoe and his
die-hard followers fled to the west, establishing new villages; the rest of the Cherokees agreed to a treaty that
ceded still more of their land.

Bands of Shawnees and Cherokees continued to attack frontier settlements in the backcountry throughout
the war, but dissent in their own ranks
crippled their efforts. The British victory over France had destroyed the Indian nations' most effective means of
maintaining their independence: play-
ing European powers off against one another. Successful
strategies were difficult to envision under these new circumstances, and Indian leaders could no longer concur
on a unified course of action. Communities split asunder
as older and younger men, or civil and war leaders, disagreed vehemently over what policy to adopt. Only a few
communities (among them the Stockbridge Indians of
New England and the Oneidas in New York) unwaveringly supported the American revolt; most other native
villages either tried to remain neutral or hesitatingly
aligned themselves with the British. And the settlers

*INDIANS
DURING THE
REVOLUTION*

fought back: in 1778 and early 1779 a frontier militia
force under George Rogers Clark captured British posts
in modern Illinois (Kaskaskia) and Indiana (Vincennes),
but the Anglo-Americans could never mount an effective
attack against the redcoats' major stronghold at Detroit.

Warfare between settlers and Indian bands persisted
in the backcountry long after fighting between the patriot and redcoat armies had ceased. Indeed, the Revolutionary War itself essentially constituted a brief chapter
in the ongoing struggle for control of the region west of
the Appalachians that began in 1763 and continued into
the next century.

Choosing Sides

I n 1765, protests against the Stamp Act had won
the support of most colonists in the Caribbean
and Nova Scotia as well as in the future United
States. Demonstrations occurred in Halifax (the major
Nova Scotian port, founded 1748) as well as in Boston,
New York, and Charleston. Although provisions of the
1764 Sugar Act benefited Britain's Caribbean possessions, the Stamp Act levied higher duties on them than
on the mainland colonies; the residents of St. Christopher and Nevis in particular joined mainlanders in

demonstrating against the law (see Map 5.3). When the act went into effect, though, islanders loyally paid the stamp duties until repeal. And eventually a significant number of colonists in North America and the West Indies began to question both the aims and the tactics of the resistance movement. Doubts arose with particular urgency in Nova Scotia and the Caribbean.

Both the northern mainland and southern island colonies depended heavily on Great Britain militarily and

NOVA SCOTIA AND THE CARIBBEAN

economically. Despite the overwhelming British victory in the Seven Years War, they believed themselves vulnerable to French counterattack and were eager to have regular troops and naval vessels stationed within their borders. Additionally, sugar planters—on some islands outnumbered by their bondspeople 25 to 1—feared the potential for slave revolts in the absence of British troops. Neither region had a large population of European descent, nor were local political structures very strong. Fewer people lived in Halifax in 1775 than in the late 1750s, and the sugar islands had only a few resident planters to provide leadership, because successful men headed to England to buy great manors, leaving supervision of their property to hired managers.

Both Nova Scotians and West Indians had major economic reasons for ultimately choosing to support the mother country. In the mid-1770s the northerners finally broke into the Caribbean market with their cargoes of dried and salted fish. They also began to reduce New England's domination of the northern coastal trade, and once the shooting started they benefited greatly from Britain's retaliatory measures against the rebels' commerce. British sugar producers relied for their profits primarily on their monopoly of trade within the empire, for more efficient French planters were able to sell their sugar for one-third less. Further, the West Indian planters' effective lobbyists in London won the islands' exclusion from some provisions of the Townshend Acts. Accordingly, they could well have concluded that their interests could be adequately protected within the empire. Neither islanders nor Nova Scotians had reason to believe that they would be better off independent.

Many residents of the thirteen colonies—especially members of the groups that dominated colonial society

PATRIOTS

numerically or politically—reached different conclusions, choosing to support resistance, then independence. Active revolutionaries accounted for about two-fifths of the European American population. Among them were small and middling farmers, members of dominant Protestant sects (both Old and New Lights), Chesapeake gentry,

merchants dealing mainly in American commodities, city artisans, elected officeholders, and people of English descent. Wives usually but not always adopted their husbands' political beliefs. Although all these patriots supported the Revolution, they pursued divergent goals within the broader coalition, as they had in the 1760s. Some sought limited political reform, others extensive political change, and still others social and economic reforms. (The ways in which their concerns interacted are discussed in Chapter 7.)

Some colonists, though, found that they could not in good conscience endorse independence. Like their more radical counterparts, most objected to parliamentary policies, but they preferred the remedy of imperial constitutional reform. The events of the crucial year between the passage of the Coercive Acts and the outbreak of fighting in Massachusetts crystallized their thinking. Their objections to violent protest, their desire to uphold legally constituted government, and their fears of anarchy combined to make them sensitive to the dangers of resistance.

About one-fifth of the European American population remained loyal to Great Britain, firmly rejecting

LOYALISTS

independence. Most loyalists had long opposed the men who became patriot leaders, though for varying reasons. British-appointed government officials; Anglican clergy everywhere and lay Anglicans in the North, where their denomination was in the minority; tenant farmers, particularly those whose landlords sided with the patriots; members of persecuted religious sects; many of the back-country southerners who had rebelled against eastern rule in the late 1760s and early 1770s; and non-English ethnic minorities, especially Scots: all these groups feared the power wielded by those who controlled the colonial assemblies and who had shown little concern for their welfare in the past. Joined by merchants whose trade depended on imperial connections and by former officers and enlisted men from the British army who had settled in America after 1763, they formed a loyalist core that remained true to a self-conception that revolutionaries proved willing to abandon.

During the war, loyalists congregated in cities held by the British army. When those posts were evacuated at war's end, loyalists scattered to different parts of the British Empire—Britain, the Bahamas, and especially Canada. In the provinces of Nova Scotia, New Brunswick, and Ontario they re-created their lives as colonists, laying the foundations of British Canada. All told, perhaps as many as 100,000 Americans preferred exile to life in a nation independent of British rule.

Between the patriots and the loyalists, there remained in the middle perhaps two-fifths of the European

NEUTRALS American population. Some who tried to avoid taking sides were sincere pacifists, such as Quakers. Others opportunistically shifted their allegiance to whatever side happened to be winning currently. Still others simply wanted to be left alone; they cared little about politics and usually obeyed whoever was in power. Such colonists also resisted British and Americans alike when the demands on them seemed too heavy—when taxes became too high, or when calls for militia service came too often. Their attitude might best be summed up as "a plague on both your houses." Such people made up an especially large proportion of the population in the backcountry (including Boone's Kentucky), where Scots-Irish settlers had little love for either the patriot gentry or the English authorities.

To patriots, apathy or neutrality was as heinous as loyalism: those who were not for them were surely against them. By the winter of 1775–1776, the Second Continental Congress was recommending that all "disaffected" persons be disarmed and arrested. State legislatures passed laws prescribing severe penalties for suspected loyalists or neutrals. Many began to require all voters (or, in some cases, all free adult men) to take oaths of allegiance; the penalty for refusal was usually banishment to England or extra taxes. After 1777 many states confiscated the property of banished persons, using the proceeds for the war effort.

The patriots' policies helped to ensure that their scattered and persecuted opponents could not band together to threaten the revolutionary cause. *SLAVERY AND REVOLUTIONARY FERVOR* But loyalists and neutrals were not the patriots' only worry, for revolutionaries could not assume that their slaves would support them.

In New England, with few resident bondspeople, revolutionary fervor was widespread, and free African Americans enlisted in local patriot militias. The middle colonies, where slaves constituted a small but substantial proportion of the population, were more divided but still largely revolutionary. In Virginia and Maryland, where free people constituted a slender majority, the potential for slave revolts raised occasional but not disabling fears. By contrast, South Carolina and Georgia, where slaves composed more than half of the population, were noticeably less enthusiastic about resistance to Britain. Georgia sent no delegates to the First Continental Congress and reminded its representatives at the second one to consider its circumstances, "with our blacks and tories [loyalists] within us," when voting on the question of independence. On the mainland as well as in the Caribbean islands, therefore, colonists feared the potential enemy in their midst.

Bondspeople faced a dilemma during the Revolution. Above all, their goal was *personal* independence. *SLAVES' DILEMMA* But how best could they escape from slavery? Should they fight with or against their masters? African Americans made different decisions, but to most slaves, supporting the British appeared more promising. In late 1774 and early 1775, groups of slaves began to offer to assist the British army in return for freedom. Some bondspeople futilely petitioned General Thomas Gage, the commander-in-chief of British forces in Boston, promising to fight for the redcoats if he would liberate them. The most serious incident occurred in 1775 in Charleston, where Thomas Jeremiah, a free black harbor pilot, was brutally executed after being convicted of attempting to foment a slave revolt.

The slaveowners' worst fears were realized in November 1775, when Virginia's royal governor, Lord Dunmore, offered to free any slaves and indentured servants who would leave their patriot masters to join the British forces. Dunmore hoped to use African Americans in his fight against the revolutionaries and to disrupt the economy by depriving planters of their labor force. But only about one thousand African Americans initially rallied to the British standard, and many of them perished in a smallpox epidemic. Even so, Dunmore's proclamation led Congress in January 1776 to modify an earlier policy that had prohibited the enlistment of African Americans in the regular American army.

Although slaves did not pose a serious threat to the revolutionary cause in its early years, the patriots turned rumors of slave uprisings to their own advantage. In South Carolina, resistance leaders argued that unity under the Continental Association would protect masters from their slaves at a time when royal government was unable to muster adequate defense forces. Undoubtedly many wavering Carolinians were drawn into the revolutionary camp by fear that an overt division among the colony's free people would encourage rebellion by the bondspeople.

Patriots could never completely ignore the threats posed by loyalists, neutrals, slaves, and Indians as well, but only rarely did fear of these groups seriously hamper the revolutionary movement. Occasionally backcountry militiamen refused to turn out for duty on the seacoast because they feared Indians would attack at home in their absence. Sometimes southern troops refused to serve in the North because they (and their political leaders) were unwilling to leave their regions unprotected against a slave insurrection. But the practical impossibility of a large-scale slave revolt, coupled with dissension

New Nations

The American Revolution not only created the United States but led directly to the formation of three other nations: English-dominated Canada, Sierra Leone, and Australia.

In northern North America before the Revolution, only Nova Scotia had a sizable number of English-speaking settlers. Those people, largely New Englanders, had been recruited after 1758 to repopulate the region forcibly taken from the exiled Acadians. During and after the Revolution, however, many loyalist families, especially those from the northern and middle colonies, moved to the region that is now Canada, which remained under British rule. The provinces of New Brunswick and Upper Canada (later Ontario) were established to accommodate them, and some exiles settled in Quebec as well. In just a few years, the loyalist refugees transformed the sparsely populated former French colony, laying the foundation of the modern bilingual (but majority English-speaking) Canadian nation.

Sierra Leone, too, was founded by colonial exiles—African Americans who had fled to the British army during the war, many of whom ended up in London. Seeing the refugees' poverty, a group of charitable merchants—calling themselves the Committee to Aid the Black Poor—developed a plan to resettle the African Americans elsewhere. After the refugees refused to be sent to the Bahamas, fearing that in the West Indies they would be reenslaved, they concurred in a scheme to return them to the land of their ancestors. In early 1787, vessels carrying about four hundred settlers reached Sierra Leone in West Africa, where representatives of the Black Poor Committee acquired land from local rulers. The first years of the new colony were difficult, and many of the newcomers died of disease and deprivation. But in 1792 they were joined by several thousand other loyalist African Americans who had originally moved to Nova Scotia. The influx ensured the colony's survival; it remained a part of the British Empire until achieving its independence in 1961.

While the Sierra Leone migrants were preparing to sail from London in late 1786, the first prison ships were simultaneously being readied for Australia. At the Paris peace negotiations in 1782, American diplomats adamantly rejected British suggestions that the United States continue to serve as a dumping ground for convicts, as had been true throughout the eighteenth century. Britain thus needed another destination for the convicts sentenced in its courts to transportation for crimes such as theft, assault, and manslaughter. It decided to send them halfway round the world, to the continent Captain James Cook had explored and claimed in 1770. Britain continued to dispatch convicts to some parts of Australia until 1868, but, long before then, voluntary migrants had also begun to arrive. The modern nation was created from a federation of separate colonial governments on January 1, 1901.

Thus the founding event in the history of the United States links the nation to the formation of its northern neighbor and to new nations in West Africa and the Asian Pacific.

An early view of the settlement of black loyalists in West Africa, the foundation of the modern nation of Sierra Leone. (Miriam and Ira D. Wallach Division of Art, Prints and Photographs, The New York Public Library. Astor, Lenox, and Tilden)

Thomas Rowlandson, an English artist, sketched the boatloads of male and female convicts as they were being ferried to the ships that would take them to their new lives in the prison colony of Australia. Note the gibbet on the shore with two hanging bodies—symbolizing the fate these people were escaping. (National Library of Australia)

149

in Indian communities and the patriots' successful campaign to disarm and neutralize loyalists, ensured that the revolutionaries would by and large remain firmly in control of the countryside as they fought for independence.

War and Independence

*O*n January 27, 1775, Lord Dartmouth, secretary of state for America, addressed a fateful letter to General Thomas Gage in Boston, urging him to take a decisive step. Opposition could not be "very formidable," Dartmouth wrote, and even if it were, "it will surely be better that the Conflict should be brought on, upon such ground, than in a riper state of Rebellion."

After Gage received Dartmouth's letter on April 14, he sent an expedition to confiscate colonial military supplies stockpiled at Concord. Bostonians dispatched two messengers, William Dawes and Paul Revere (later joined by Dr. Samuel Prescott), to rouse the countryside. So when the British vanguard of several hundred men approached Lexington at dawn on April 19, they found a ragtag group of seventy militiamen—about half of the adult male population of the town—mustered on the common. The Americans' commander ordered his men to withdraw, realizing they could not halt the redcoats' advance. But as they began to disperse, a shot rang out; the British soldiers then fired several volleys. When they stopped, eight Americans lay dead and another ten had been wounded. The British moved on to Concord, 5 miles away.

BATTLES OF LEXINGTON AND CONCORD

There the contingents of militia were larger, Concord residents having been joined by groups of men from nearby towns. An exchange of gunfire at the North Bridge spilled the first British blood of the Revolution: three men were killed and nine wounded. Thousands of militiamen then fired from houses and from behind trees and bushes at the British forces as they retreated to Boston. By the end of the day, the redcoats had suffered 272 casualties, including 70 deaths. Only the arrival of reinforcements and the American militia's lack of coordination prevented much heavier British losses. The patriots suffered just 93 casualties.

By the evening of April 20, perhaps as many as twenty thousand American militiamen had gathered around Boston, summoned by local committees that spread the alarm across the countryside. Many did not stay long (they were needed at home for spring planting), but those who remained dug in along

FIRST YEAR OF WAR

siege lines encircling the city. For nearly a year the two armies sat and stared at each other across those lines. The redcoats attacked their besiegers only once, on June 17, when they drove the Americans from trenches atop Breed's Hill in Charlestown. In that misnamed Battle of Bunker Hill, the British incurred their greatest losses of the entire war: over 800 wounded and 228 killed. The Americans, though forced to abandon their position, lost less than half that number.

During the same eleven-month period, patriots captured Fort Ticonderoga, a British fort on Lake Champlain, acquiring much-needed cannon. Trying to bring Canada into the war on the American side, they also mounted a northern campaign that ended in disaster at Quebec in early 1776 after their troops were ravaged by smallpox. But the chief significance of the war's first year lay in the long lull in fighting between the main armies at Boston. The delay gave both sides a chance to regroup, organize, and plan their strategies.

Lord North and his new American secretary, Lord George Germain, made three central assumptions about the war they faced. First, they concluded that patriot forces could not withstand the assaults of trained British regulars. They and their generals were convinced that the 1776 campaign would be the first and last of the war. Accordingly, they dispatched to America the largest force Great Britain had ever assembled anywhere: 370 transport ships carrying 32,000 troops and tons of supplies, accompanied by 73 naval vessels and 13,000 sailors. Such an extraordinary effort, they thought, would ensure a quick victory. Among the troops were thousands of German mercenaries (many from the state of Hesse); eighteenth-century armies were often composed of such professional soldiers who hired out to the highest bidder.

BRITISH STRATEGY

Second, British officials and army officers treated this war as comparable to conflicts in Europe. They adopted a conventional strategy of capturing major American cities and defeating the rebel army decisively without suffering serious casualties themselves. Third, they assumed that a clear-cut military victory would achieve their goal of retaining the colonies' allegiance.

All three assumptions proved false. North and Germain vastly underestimated Americans' commitment to armed resistance. Battlefield defeats did not lead patriots to abandon their political aims and sue for peace. London officials also failed to recognize the significance of the American population's dispersal over an area 1,500 miles long and more than 100 miles wide. Although Britain would control each of the largest American ports

■ In 1775 an unknown artist painted the redcoats entering Concord. The fighting at North Bridge, which occurred just a few hours after this triumphal entry, signaled the start of open warfare between Britain and the colonies.   (Photography Courtesy of Concord Museum, Concord, Mass.)

at some time during the war, less than 5 percent of the population lived in those cities. Furthermore, the coast offered so many excellent harbors that essential commerce was easily rerouted. In other words, the loss of cities did little to damage the American cause, while British generals repeatedly squandered their resources to capture such ports.

Most of all, London officials did not initially understand that military triumph would not necessarily lead to political victory. Securing the colonies permanently would require hundreds of thousands of Americans to return to their original allegiance. After 1778 the ministry adopted a strategy designed to achieve that goal through the expanded use of loyalist forces and the restoration of civilian authority in occupied areas. But the new policy came too late. Britain's leaders never fully realized that they were fighting not a conventional European war but rather an entirely new kind of conflict: the first modern war of national liberation.

At least Great Britain had a bureaucracy ready to supervise the war effort. The Americans had only the Second Continental Congress, originally intended simply to consider the ministry's response to the Continental Association. Instead, the delegates who convened in Philadelphia on May 10, 1775, had to assume the mantle of intercolonial government. "Such a vast Multitude of objects, civil, political, commercial and military, press and crowd upon us so fast, that we know not what to do first," John Adams wrote a close friend early in the session. Yet as the summer passed, Congress slowly organized the colonies for war. It authorized the printing of money with which to purchase necessary goods, established a committee to supervise relations with foreign countries, and took steps to strengthen the militia. Most important, it created the Continental Army and appointed its generals.

SECOND CONTINENTAL CONGRESS

■ The plight of the redcoat soldiers besieged in Boston during the fall and winter of 1775–1776 attracted the sympathies of a British cartoonist. For "Six-Pence a Day," he noted, soldiers were exposed to "Yankees, Fire and Water, Sword and Famine," while their wives and children begged for assistance at home. The artist hoped to persuade men not to enlist in the British army.   (Courtesy of the British Museum, Department of Prints and Drawings, Satires)

Until Congress met, the Massachusetts provincial congress had taken responsibility for organizing the militiamen encamped at Boston. But that army, composed of men from all over New England, constituted a heavy drain on limited local resources. Consequently, Massachusetts asked the Continental Congress to assume the task of directing the army. As a first step, Congress had to choose a commander-in-chief, and many delegates recognized the importance of naming someone who was not a New Englander. John Adams later recalled that in mid-June he proposed the appointment of a Virginian "whose Skill and Experience as an Officer, whose independent fortune, great Talents and excellent universal Character, would command the Approbation of all America": George Washington. The Congress unanimously concurred.

Neither fiery radical nor a reflective political thinker, Washington had not played a prominent role in the prerevolutionary agitation. Devoted to the American cause, he was dignified, conservative, and respectable—a man of unimpeachable integrity. The younger son of a Virginia planter, Washington did not expect to inherit substantial property, planning to make his living

WASHINGTON AS LEADER

as a surveyor. But the early death of his older brother and his marriage to the wealthy widow Martha Custis made George Washington one of the largest slaveholders in Virginia. Though unmistakably an aristocrat, he was unswervingly committed to representative government and—thanks to his service in the Seven Years War—he had military experience. He also had remarkable stamina. In more than eight years of war, Washington never had a serious illness and took only one brief leave of absence. Moreover, he both looked and acted like a leader. More than six feet tall in an era when most men were five inches shorter, he displayed a stately and commanding presence. Other patriots praised his judgment, steadiness, and discretion, and even a loyalist admitted that Washington could "atone for many demerits by the extraordinary coolness and caution which distinguish his character."

Washington needed all the coolness and caution he could muster when he took command of the army outside Boston in July 1775. It took him months to impose hierarchy and discipline on the unruly troops and to bring order to the supply system. But by

BRITISH EVACUATION OF BOSTON

March 1776, when the arrival of cannon from Ticonderoga finally enabled him to put direct pressure on the redcoats in the city, the army was prepared to act. Yet an assault on Boston proved unnecessary. Sir William Howe, the new commander, had been considering an evacuation; he wanted to transfer his troops to New York City. The patriots' cannon decided the matter. On March 17, the British and more than a thousand of their loyalist allies abandoned Boston forever.

That spring of 1776, as the British fleet left Boston for the temporary haven of Halifax, the colonies were moving inexorably toward a declaration of independence. Though they had been engaged in combat for months, American leaders denied seeking a break with Great Britain until a pamphlet published in January 1776 advocated such a step.

Thomas Paine's *Common Sense* exploded on the American scene, quickly selling tens of thousands of copies. The author, a radical English printer who had lived in America only since 1774, called stridently for independence. Paine also challenged many common American assumptions about government and the colonies' relationship to Britain. Rejecting the notion that only a balance of monarchy, aristocracy, and democracy could preserve freedom, he advocated the establishment of a republic, a government by the people with no king or nobility. Instead of acknowledging the benefits of links to the mother country, Paine insisted that Britain had exploited the colonies unmercifully. And for the frequently heard assertion that an independent America would be weak and divided, he substituted an unlimited confidence in America's strength once freed from European control.

COMMON SENSE

He expressed these striking sentiments in equally striking prose. Scorning the rational style of most other pamphleteers, Paine adopted an enraged tone, describing the king as a "royal brute," a "wretch" who only pretended concern for the colonists' welfare. His pamphlet reflected the oral culture of ordinary folk. Couched in everyday language, it relied heavily on the Bible—the only book familiar to most Americans—as a primary source of authority. No wonder the pamphlet had a wider distribution than any other political publication of its day.

It is unclear how many people were converted to the cause of independence by reading *Common Sense*. But by the late spring independence had become inevitable. On May 10, the Second Continental Congress formally recommended that individual colonies form new governments, replacing their colonial charters with state constitutions. Perceiving the trend, the few loyalists still connected with Congress severed their ties to that body.

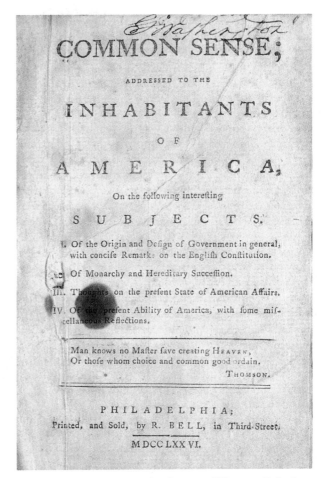

■ That America's patriot leaders read Thomas Paine's inflammatory *Common Sense* soon after it was published in early 1776 is indicated by this first edition, owned by George Washington himself.   (Boston Athenaeum)

Then on June 7 came confirmation of the movement toward independence. Richard Henry Lee of Virginia, seconded by John Adams of Massachusetts, introduced the crucial resolution: "that these United Colonies are, and of right ought to be, free and independent States, that they are absolved of all allegiance to the British Crown, and that all political connection between them and the State of Great Britain is, and ought to be, totally dissolved." Congress debated but did not immediately adopt Lee's resolution. Instead, it postponed a vote until early July, to allow time for consultation and public reaction. In the meantime, a five-man committee—including Thomas Jefferson, John Adams, and Benjamin Franklin—was directed to draft a declaration of independence.

The committee assigned primary responsibility for writing the declaration to Jefferson, who was well known for his eloquent style. Years later John Adams recalled that Jefferson had modestly protested his selection, suggesting that Adams prepare the initial draft. The Massachusetts revolutionary recorded his frank response: "You can write ten times better than I can."

The thirty-four-year-old Thomas Jefferson, a Virginia lawyer, had been educated at the College of

JEFFERSON AND THE DECLARATION OF INDEPENDENCE

William and Mary and in the law offices of a prominent attorney. A member of the House of Burgesses, he had read widely in history and political theory. That broad knowledge was evident not only in the declaration but also in his draft of the Virginia state constitution, completed just a few days before his appointment to the committee. Jefferson, an intensely private man, loved his home and family deeply. This early stage of his political career was marked by his beloved wife Martha's repeated difficulties in childbearing. While he wrote and debated in Philadelphia, she suffered a miscarriage at their home, Monticello. Not until after her death in 1782, from complications following the birth of their sixth (but only third surviving) child in ten years of marriage, did Jefferson fully commit himself to public service.

The draft of the declaration was laid before Congress on June 28, 1776. The delegates officially voted for independence four days later, then debated the wording of the declaration for two more days, adopting it with some changes on July 4. Since Americans had long ago ceased to see themselves as legitimate subjects of Parliament, the Declaration of Independence concentrated on George III (see the appendix). That focus also provided an identifiable villain. The document accused the king of attempting to destroy representative government in the colonies and of oppressing Americans through the unjustified use of excessive force.

The declaration's chief long-term importance, however, did not lie in its lengthy catalogue of grievances against George III (including, in a section deleted by Congress, Jefferson's charge that the British monarchy had forced slavery on America). It lay instead in the ringing statements of principle that have served ever since as the ideal to which Americans aspire: "We hold these truths to be self-evident: That all men are created equal; that they are endowed by their Creator with certain unalienable rights; that among these are life, liberty and the pursuit of happiness; that, to secure these rights, governments are instituted among men, deriving their just powers from the consent of the governed; that whenever any form of government becomes destructive of these ends, it is the right of the people to alter or to abolish it, and to institute new government." These phrases have echoed down through American history like no others.

The delegates in Philadelphia who voted to accept the Declaration of Independence could not predict the consequences of their audacious act. When they adopted the declaration, they were committing treason. Therefore, when they concluded with the assertion that they "mutually pledge[d] to each other our lives, our fortunes, and our sacred honor," they spoke no less than the truth. The real struggle still lay before them, and few had Thomas Paine's boundless confidence in success.

The Struggle in the North

In late June 1776, the first ships carrying Sir William Howe's troops from Halifax appeared off the coast of New York (see Map 6.1). On July 2, the day Congress voted for independence, redcoats landed on Staten Island. Washington marched his army of seventeen thousand south from Boston to defend Manhattan. Because Howe waited until more troops arrived from England before attacking, Americans could prepare to defend the city.

But Washington and his men, still inexperienced in fighting and maneuvering, made major mistakes, losing

Map 6.1   The War in the North, 1775–1777

The early phase of the Revolutionary War was dominated by British troop movements in the Boston area, the redcoats' evacuation to Nova Scotia in the spring of 1776, and the subsequent British invasion of New York and New Jersey.

NEW YORK AND NEW JERSEY battles at Brooklyn Heights and on Manhattan Island. The city fell to the British, who captured nearly three thousand American soldiers. (Those men spent most of the rest of the war on British prison ships anchored in New York harbor, where many died of smallpox and other diseases.) Washington then slowly retreated across New Jersey into Pennsylvania, and British forces took control of most of New Jersey. Occupying troops met little opposition; the revolutionary cause appeared to be in disarray. "These are the times that try men's souls," wrote Thomas Paine in his pamphlet *The Crisis.* "The summer soldier and the sunshine patriot will, in this crisis, shrink from the service of his country; . . . yet we have this consolation with us, that the harder the conflict, the more glorious the triumph."

The British then forfeited their advantage as redcoats stationed in New Jersey went on a rampage of rape and plunder. Washington determined to strike back. Moving quickly, he crossed the Delaware River at night to attack a Hessian encampment at Trenton early in the morning of December 26, while the redcoats were still recuperating from their Christmas celebration. The patriots captured more than nine hundred Hessians and killed another thirty; only three Americans were wounded. A few days later, Washington attacked again at Princeton. Having gained command of the field and buoyed American spirits with the two swift victories, Washington set up winter quarters at Morristown, New Jersey.

British strategy for 1777, sketched in London over the winter, aimed to cut New England off from the other colonies. General John Burgoyne, a subordinate of Howe and one of the planners, would lead an invading force of redcoats and Indians down the Hudson River from Canada to rendezvous near Albany with a similar force that would move east along the Mohawk River valley. The combined forces would then presumably link up with Sir William Howe's troops in New York City. But in New York Howe simultaneously prepared his own plan to capture Philadelphia. Consequently, in 1777 the British armies in America would operate independently; the result would be disaster (see Map 6.2).

Howe took Philadelphia, but he did so in inexplicable fashion, delaying for months before beginning the campaign, then taking six weeks to transport his troops by sea instead of marching them overland. Incredibly, at the end of the lengthy voyage, he ended up only 40 miles closer to Philadelphia than when he started. By the time Howe advanced on Philadelphia, Washington had had time to prepare its defenses. Twice, at Brandywine Creek

and again at Germantown, the two armies clashed near the patriot capital. Although the British won both engagements, the Americans handled themselves well. The redcoats captured Philadelphia in late September, but to little effect. The campaign season was nearly over; the revolutionary army had gained confidence in itself and its leaders; and, far to the north, Burgoyne was going down to defeat.

Burgoyne and his men had set out from Montreal in mid-June, traveling first by boat on Lake Champlain, then later marching slowly overland toward the Hudson, forced as they went to clear giant trees felled across their path by patriot militiamen. An easy triumph at Fort Ticonderoga in July was followed in August by two setbacks—the redcoats and Indians marching east along the

Map 6.2   Campaign of 1777

The crucial campaign of 1777 was fought on two fronts: along the upper Hudson and Mohawk River valleys, and in the vicinity of Philadelphia. The rebels won in the north; the British triumphed—at least nominally—in the south. The capture of Philadelphia, however, did the redcoats little good, and they abandoned the city the following year.

■ George Washington at the Battle of Princeton, 1779, by Charles Willson Peale. Two years after the battle, Peale created this heroic image of the Continental Army's commander, intended (as were all his portraits of revolutionary leaders) to instill patriotic sentiments and pride in its viewers.   (Courtesy of the Pennsylvania Academy of Fine Arts, Philadelphia. Gift of Maria McKean Allen and Phoebe Warren)

Mohawk River turned back after a battle at Oriskany, New York; and in a clash near Bennington, Vermont, American militiamen nearly wiped out eight hundred of Burgoyne's German mercenaries. The general's dawdling gave American troops time to prepare for his arrival. After several skirmishes with an American army commanded by General Horatio Gates, Burgoyne was surrounded near Saratoga, New York. On October 17, 1777, he surrendered his entire force of more than six thousand men.

The August 1777 battle at Oriskany divided the Iroquois Confederacy. The Six Nations had formally

IROQUOIS CONFEDERACY SPLINTERS

pledged to remain neutral in the war. But two influential Mohawk leaders, the siblings Mary and Joseph Brant, believed that the Iroquois should ally themselves with the British to protect their territory from land-hungry colonists. The Brants won over the Senecas, Cayugas, and Mohawks, all of whom contributed warriors to the 1777 expedition. But the Oneidas—who had been converted to Christianity by Protestant missionaries—preferred the American side and brought the Tuscaroras with them. The Onondagas split into three factions, one on each side and one supporting neutrality. At Oriskany, some Oneidas and Tuscaroras joined patriot militiamen in fighting their Iroquois brethren, shattering a league of friendship that had survived for over three hundred years.

The collapse of Iroquois unity and the confederacy's abandonment of neutrality had significant consequences. In 1778 Iroquois warriors allied with the British raided frontier villages in Pennsylvania and New York. To retaliate, the Americans the following summer dispatched an expedition under General John Sullivan to burn Iroquois crops, orchards, and settlements. The resulting devastation led many bands to seek food and shelter north of the Great Lakes during the winter of 1779–1780. A large number of Iroquois people never returned to New York but settled permanently in Canada.

Burgoyne's surrender at Saratoga brought joy to patriots, discouragement to loyalists and Britons. In exile in London, Thomas Hutchinson wrote of "universal dejection" among loyalists there. "Everybody in a gloom," he commented; "most of us expect to lay our bones here." The disaster prompted Lord North to authorize a peace commission to offer the Americans what they had requested in 1774—in effect, a return to the imperial system of 1763. That proposal came far too late: the patriots rejected the overture, and the peace commission sailed back to England empty-handed in mid-1778.

Most important, the American victory at Saratoga drew France formally into the conflict. Ever since 1763, the French had sought to avenge their defeat in the Seven Years War, and the American Revolution gave them that opportunity. Even before Benjamin Franklin arrived in Paris in late 1776, France covertly supplied the revolutionaries with military necessities. Indeed, 90 percent of the gunpowder used by the Americans during the war's first two years came from France, transported via the French Caribbean island of Martinique.

Benjamin Franklin worked tirelessly to strengthen ties between the two nations. He adopted a plain style of dress that made him conspicuous amid the luxury of the

■ Joseph Brant, the Iroquois leader who helped to persuade the Mohawks, Senecas, and Cayugas to support the British in the latter stages of the Revolution, as painted by Charles Willson Peale in 1797.
(Independence National Historic Park Collection)

arms, ammunition, clothing, and blankets. Second, Britain could no longer focus solely on the American mainland, for it had to fight France in the Caribbean and elsewhere. Spain's entry into the war in 1779 as an ally of France (but not of the United States) magnified Britain's problems, for the Revolution then became a global war. The French aided the Americans throughout the conflict, but in its last years that assistance proved vital.

Life in the Army and on the Home Front

*O*nly in the first months of the war was the revolutionaries' army manned primarily by the semi-mythical "citizen soldier," the militiaman who exchanged his plow for a gun to defend his homeland. After a few months or at most a year, the early arrivals went home. They reenlisted, if at all, only briefly and only if the contending armies came close to their farms and towns. Even then, such men could avoid service if they hired replacements.

After 1776 the ranks of the Continental Army— those who enlisted for long periods or for the war's duration—were filled primarily by young, single, or propertyless men who signed up to earn monetary bonuses or allotments of land after the war. As the fighting dragged on, those bonuses and land grants grew larger. To meet their quotas of enlistees, towns and states eagerly signed up everyone they could, including slaves and indentured servants (who were promised freedom after the war) and recent immigrants. Regiments from the middle states contained an especially large proportion of foreign-born troops; about 45 percent of Pennsylvania soldiers were of Irish origin and about 13 percent were German, some serving in German-speaking regiments.

DIVERSITY IN THE RANKS

Recruiters in northern states turned increasingly to African Americans, both slave and free. Southern states initially resisted the trend, but later all but Georgia and South Carolina also enlisted black soldiers. Approximately five thousand African Americans eventually served in the Continental Army, most winning their freedom as a result. They commonly served in racially integrated units but were assigned tasks that others shunned, such as cooking, foraging for food, and driving wagons. Overall, it appears that at any given time they composed about 10 percent of the regular army, though they seldom served in militia units.

Also attached to the American forces were a number of women, the wives and widows of poor soldiers, who

FRANCO-AMERICAN ALLIANCE OF 1778

court of King Louis XVI. Presenting himself as a representative of American simplicity, Franklin played on the French image of Americans as virtuous farmers. His efforts culminated in 1778 when the countries signed two treaties. In the Treaty of Amity and Commerce, France recognized American independence, establishing trade ties with the new nation. In the Treaty of Alliance, France and the United States promised—assuming that France would declare war on Britain, which it soon did—that neither would negotiate peace with the enemy without consulting the other. France also formally abandoned any claim to Canada and to North American territory east of the Mississippi River. In the years that followed, the most visible symbol of Franco-American cooperation was the Marquis de Lafayette, a young nobleman who volunteered for service with George Washington in 1777 and fought with American forces until the conflict ended.

The French alliance had two major benefits for the patriot cause. First, France began to aid the Americans openly, sending troops and naval vessels in addition to

■ Barzillai Lew, a free African American born in Groton, Massachusetts, in 1743, served in the Seven Years War before enlisting with patriot troops in the American Revolution. An accomplished fifer, Lew fought at the Battle of Bunker Hill. Like other freemen in the north, he cast his lot with the revolutionaries, in contrast to southern bondspeople, who tended to favor the British.   (Courtesy of Mae Theresa Bonitto)

overcame all helped to forge an esprit de corps that outlasted the war. The realities of warfare were often dirty, messy, and corrupt, but the officers drew strength from a developing image of themselves as professionals who sacrificed personal gain for the good of the entire nation. When Benedict Arnold, an officer who fought heroically for the patriot cause early in the war, defected to the British, they made his name a metaphor for villainy. "How black, how despised, loved by none, and hated by all," wrote one officer.

The officers' wives, too, prided themselves on their and their husbands' service to the nation. Unlike poor women, they did not travel with the army but instead came for extended visits while the troops were in camp (usually during the winters). Martha Washington and other officers' wives, for example, lived at Valley Forge in the winter of 1777–1778. They brought with them food, clothing, and household furnishings to make their stay more comfortable, and they entertained each other and their menfolk at teas, dinners, and dances. Socializing and discussing current events created friendships later renewed in civilian life when some of their husbands became the new nation's leaders.

Life in the American army was difficult for everyone, although ordinary soldiers endured more hardships than their officers. Wages, even when paid, were small, and often the army could not meet the payroll. Rations (a daily standard allotment of bread, meat, vegetables, milk, and beer) did not always appear, and men had to forage for their own food. Clothing and shoes the army supplied were often of poor quality; soldiers had to make do, or find their own. While in camp, soldiers occasionally hired themselves out as laborers to nearby farmers to augment their meager rations or earnings. When conditions deteriorated, troops threatened mutiny (though only a few carried out that threat) or, more often, simply deserted. One study shows that more than 80 percent of the wartime courts-martial charged soldiers with desertion.

HARDSHIP AND DISEASE

Endemic disease in the camps—especially dysentery, various fevers, and, early in the war, smallpox—made matters worse, sometimes discouraging recruiting. Most native-born colonists had neither been exposed to smallpox nor been inoculated against the disease, and so soldiers and civilians were vulnerable when smallpox spread through the northern countryside after the early months of 1774. The disease ravaged residents of Boston during the British occupation, the troops attacking Quebec in 1775–1776, and the African Americans who fled to join Lord Dunmore (1775) or Lord Cornwallis

came to the army with their menfolk because they were too impoverished to survive alone. Such camp followers—estimated overall to be about 3 percent of the number of troops—worked as cooks, nurses, and launderers in return for rations and low wages. The women, as well as civilian commissaries and militiamen who floated in and out of camp at irregular intervals, made up an unwieldy assemblage that officers found difficult to manage. Yet the army's shapelessness also reflected its greatest strength: an almost unlimited reservoir of manpower and womanpower.

The officers of the Continental Army developed an intense sense of pride and commitment to the revolutionary cause. The hardships they endured, the battles they fought, the difficulties they

OFFICER CORPS

■ Measles, typhus, diphtheria, dysentery, and other diseases ravaged military encampments, so medicine chests like the one shown here were essential equipment for the army. Doctors used crude remedies that often did more harm than good, for little was known about the causes of such afflictions. Smallpox was one of the few epidemics that eighteenth-century doctors could combat: inoculation was known to be an effective preventive measure as early as the 1720s.   (The West Point Museum Collection, U.S. Military Academy, West Point, N.Y. Photo by Josh Nefsky)

(1781). Because most British soldiers had already survived smallpox (which was endemic in Europe), it did not pose a significant threat to redcoat troops.

Washington recognized that smallpox could potentially decimate the revolutionaries' ranks, especially after it helped cause the failure of the 1775 Quebec expedition. Thus in Morristown in early 1777 he ordered that entire regular army and all new recruits be inoculated, although some would die from the risky procedure and survivors would be incapacitated for weeks. Those dramatic measures, coupled with the increasing numbers of foreign-born (and thus already immune) men who enlisted, helped to protect Continental soldiers later in the war, contributing significantly to the eventual American victory.

Men who enlisted in the army or served in Congress were away from home for long periods of time. In their absence their womenfolk, who previously had handled only the "indoor affairs" of the household, shouldered the responsibility for "outdoor affairs" as well. As the wife of

HOME FRONT

a Connecticut soldier later recalled, her husband "was out more or less during the remainder of the war [after 1777], so much so as to be unable to do anything on our farm. What was done, was done by myself." Similarly, John and Abigail Adams took great pride in Abigail's developing skills as a "farmeress." Like other female contemporaries, Abigail Adams stopped calling the farm "yours" in letters to her husband and began referring to it as "ours"—a revealing change of pronoun. Most women did not work in the fields themselves, but they supervised field workers and managed their families' resources.

Wartime disruptions affected the lives of all Americans. Even far from the battlefields, people suffered from shortages of necessities like salt, soap, and flour. Small luxuries like new clothing or even ribbons or gloves were essentially unavailable. Severe inflation added to the country's woes, eroding the value of any income. For those who lived near the armies' camps or lines of march, difficulties were compounded. Soldiers of both sides plundered farms and houses, looking for food or salable items; they burned fence rails in their fires and took horses and oxen to transport their wagons. Moreover, they carried smallpox and other diseases with them wherever they went. In such circumstances and in the absence of their husbands, women had to make the momentous decision whether to deliberately risk their children's lives by inoculating them with smallpox or to take the chance of the youngsters' contracting the disease "in the natural way," with its even greater risk of death. Many, including Abigail Adams, chose the former course of action and were relieved when their children survived.

Victory in the South

In early 1778, in the wake of the Saratoga disaster, Lord George Germain and British military leaders reassessed their strategy. The loyalist exiles in London persuaded them to shift the field of battle southward, contending that loyal southerners would welcome the redcoat army as liberators. Once the South had been pacified and returned to friendly civilian control, it could then serve as a base for once again attacking the middle and northern states.

Sir Henry Clinton, who replaced Sir William Howe, oversaw the regrouping of British forces in America. He ordered the evacuation of Philadelphia in June 1778 and sent a convoy that successfully captured the French Caribbean island of St. Lucia, which thereafter served as a key base for Britain.

SOUTH CAROLINA AND THE CARIBBEAN

He also dispatched a small expedition to Georgia at the end of the year. When Savannah and then Augusta fell easily into British hands, Clinton became convinced that a southern strategy would succeed. In late 1779 he sailed down the coast from New York to besiege Charleston, the most important city in the South (see Map 6.3). Although afflicted by smallpox, the Americans trapped in the city held out for months. Still, on May 12, 1780, General Benjamin Lincoln was forced to surrender the entire southern army—5,500 men—to the invaders. In the following weeks, the redcoats spread through South Carolina, establishing garrisons at key points in the interior. Hundreds of South Carolinians renounced allegiance to the United States, proclaiming their renewed loyalty to the Crown. Clinton organized loyalist regiments, and the process of pacification began.

Map 6.3   The War in the South

The southern war–after the British invasion of Georgia in late 1778–was characterized by a series of British thrusts into the interior, leading to battles with American defenders in both North and South Carolina. Finally, after promising beginnings, Cornwallis's foray into Virginia ended with disaster at Yorktown in October 1781.

Yet the triumph was less complete than it appeared. The success of the southern campaign depended on control of the seas, for the British armies were so widely dispersed and travel by land was so difficult that only through British naval vessels could the armies coordinate their efforts. For the moment, the Royal Navy safely dominated the American coastline, but French naval power posed a threat to the entire southern enterprise. American privateers infested Caribbean waters, seizing valuable cargoes bound to and from the British West Indies. Furthermore, after late 1778 France picked off British islands one by one, including Grenada—second only to Jamaica in sugar production—and, in 1781, St. Christopher as well. Even though in early 1781 the British captured and plundered St. Eustatius (the Dutch island that after French entry into the war served as the main conduit for the movement of military supplies from Europe to America), the victory did them little good. Indeed, it might well have cost them the war, for Admiral Sir George Rodney, occupied with securing the victory (and his personal profits from the plunder), failed to pursue the French fleet under Admiral François de Grasse when it subsequently sailed from the Caribbean to Virginia, where it played a major role in the battle at Yorktown (see page 161).

Then, too, the redcoats never managed to establish full control of the areas they seized in South Carolina. Patriot bands operated freely, and loyalists could not be adequately protected. The fall of Charleston failed to dishearten the patriots; instead, it spurred them to greater exertions. As one Marylander declared confidently, "The Fate of America is not to be decided by the Loss of a Town or Two." Patriot women in four states formed the Ladies Association, which collected money to purchase shirts for needy soldiers. Recruiting efforts were stepped up.

Nevertheless, the war in South Carolina went badly for the patriots throughout most of 1780. At Camden in August, forces under Lord Cornwallis, the new British commander in the South, crushingly defeated a reorganized southern army led by Horatio Gates. Thousands of enslaved African Americans joined the redcoats, seeking the freedom promised by Lord Dunmore and later by Sir Henry Clinton. Running away from their patriot masters individually and as families, they seriously disrupted planting and harvesting in the Carolinas in 1780 and 1781. More than fifty-five thousand slaves were lost to their owners as a result of the war. Not all of them joined the British or won their freedom if they did, but their flight had exactly the effect the British sought. Many served the redcoats well as scouts, guides, and laborers.

■ "A View from the Two-Gun Battery," St. Lucia, 1780, by Charles Forrest. Forrest, a British officer stationed in the West Indies during the Revolution, sketched this scene showing some of the island's defenses against a possible attack by the American or French Navy. (William L. Clements Library)

After the Camden defeat, Washington (who had to remain in the North to contain the British army occupying New York) appointed General Nathanael Greene to command the southern campaign. Appalled by conditions in South Carolina, Greene told a friend that "the word difficulty when applied to the state of things here . . . is almost without meaning, it falls so far short" of reality. His troops needed clothing, blankets, and food, but "a great part of this country is already laid waste and in the utmost danger of becoming a desert." Incessant guerrilla warfare had, he commented, "so corrupted the principles of the people that they think of nothing but plundering one another."

GREENE AND THE SOUTHERN CAMPAIGN

In such dire circumstances, Greene had to move cautiously. He adopted a conciliatory policy toward loyalists and neutrals, persuading South Carolina to pardon those who had fought for the British if they would now join patriot militias. He also ordered his troops to treat captives fairly and not to loot loyalist property. Recognizing that the patriots needed to convince a war-weary populace that they could bring stability to the region, he helped the shattered provincial congresses of Georgia and South Carolina to reestablish civilian authority in the interior—a goal the British were never able to accomplish. Since he had so few regulars (only sixteen hundred when he took command), Greene had to rely on western volunteers and could not afford to have frontier militia companies occupied in defending their homes from Indian attack. He accordingly pursued diplomacy aimed at keeping the Indians out of the war. Although royal officials cooperating with the redcoat invaders initially won some Indian allies, Greene's careful maneuvers eventually proved successful. By war's end, only the Creeks remained allied with Great Britain.

Even before Greene took command of the southern army in December 1780, the tide had begun to turn. In October, at King's Mountain, a force from the backcountry defeated a large party of redcoats and loyalists. Then in January 1781 Greene's trusted aide Daniel Morgan brilliantly routed the crack British regiment Tarleton's Legion at Cowpens. Greene himself confronted the main body of British troops under Lord Cornwallis at Guilford Court House, North Carolina, in March. Although Cornwallis controlled the field at the end of the day, most of his army had been destroyed. He had to retreat to Wilmington, on the coast, to receive supplies and fresh troops from New York by sea. Meanwhile, Greene returned to South Carolina, where, in a series of swift strikes, he forced the redcoats to abandon their interior posts and retire to Charleston.

Cornwallis headed north into Virginia, where he joined forces with a detachment of redcoats commanded by the American traitor Benedict Arnold. Instead of acting decisively with his new army of 7,200 men, Cornwallis withdrew to the peninsula between the York and James Rivers, where he fortified Yorktown and awaited supplies and reinforcements. Seizing the opportunity, Washington quickly moved more than 7,000 French and American troops south from New York City. When De Grasse's fleet arrived from the Caribbean just in time to defeat the Royal Navy vessels sent to relieve Cornwallis, the British general was trapped (see Map 6.3). On October 19, 1781, Cornwallis surrendered.

SURRENDER AT YORKTOWN

When news of the defeat reached London, Lord North's ministry fell. Parliament voted to cease offensive operations in America, authorizing peace negotiations. Washington returned with the main army to the environs of New York, where his underpaid—and, they thought, underappreciated—officers grew restive. In March 1783 they threatened to mutiny unless Congress guaranteed them adequate compensation for their services. Washington, warned in advance of the so-called Newburgh Conspiracy, met the challenge brilliantly. Summoning his officers, he defused the crisis with a well-reasoned but emotional speech drawing on their patriotism. How could they, he asked, "open the flood Gates of Civil discord, and deluge our rising Empire in Blood"? When at one point he fumbled for glasses, remarking in passing that "I have grown gray in your service and now find myself growing blind," eyewitnesses reported that many of the rebellious officers began to cry. At the end of the year, he stood before Congress and formally resigned his commission as commander-in-chief. Through such actions at the end of the conflict, Washington established an enduring precedent: civilian control of the American military.

The war had been won, but at terrible cost. More than twenty-five thousand American men died in the war, only about one-quarter of them from wounds suffered in battle. The rest were declared missing in action or died of disease or as prisoners of war. In the South, years of guerrilla warfare and the loss of thousands of runaway slaves shattered the economy. Indebtedness soared, and local governments were crippled for lack of funds, since few people could afford to pay their taxes. In the 1780s in Charles County, Maryland, for example, men commonly refused to serve in elective or appointive office because their personal estates would become liable for any taxes or fines they were unable to collect. Many of the county's formerly wealthy planters descended into insolvency, and in the 1790s a traveler observed that "the country . . . wears a most dreary aspect," remarking on the "old dilapidated mansions" that had once housed well-to-do slaveowners.

Yet Charles County residents and Americans in general "all rejoiced" when they learned of the signing of the preliminary peace treaty at Paris in November 1782. The American dip-

TREATY OF PARIS

lomats—Benjamin Franklin, John Jay, and John Adams—ignored their instructions from Congress to be guided by France and instead negotiated directly with Great Britain. Their instincts were sound: the French government was more an enemy to Britain than a friend to the United States. In fact, French ministers worked secretly behind the scenes to try to prevent the establishment of a strong, unified government in America. Spain's desire to lay claim to the region between the Appalachian Mountains and the Mississippi River further complicated the negotiations. But the American del-

egates proved adept at power politics, achieving their main goal: independence as a united nation. Weary of war, the new British ministry, headed by Lord Shelburne (formerly an outspoken critic of Lord North's American policies), made numerous concessions—so many, in fact, that Parliament ousted the ministry shortly after peace terms were approved.

The treaty, signed formally on September 3, 1783, granted the Americans unconditional independence. Generous boundaries delineated the new nation: to the north, approximately the present-day boundary with Canada; to the south, the 31st parallel (about the modern northern border of Florida); to the west, the Mississippi River. Florida, which Britain had acquired in 1763, reverted to Spain. The Americans also gained unlimited fishing rights off Newfoundland. In ceding so much land to the United States, Great Britain ignored the territorial rights of its Indian allies, sacrificing their interests to the demands of European politics. British diplomats also poorly served loyalists and British merchants. The treaty's ambiguously worded clauses pertaining to the payment of prewar debts and the postwar treatment of loyalists caused trouble for years to come, proving impossible to enforce.

Summary

The long war finally over, the victorious Americans could look back on their achievement with satisfaction and awe. Having unified the disparate mainland colonies, they had claimed their place in the family of nations and forged a successful alliance with France. With an inexperienced ragtag army, they had taken on the greatest military power in the world—and eight years later they had won. They accomplished their goal more through persistence and commitment than through brilliance on the battlefield. Actual victories were few, but their army always survived defeats and standoffs to fight again. Ultimately, the Americans simply wore their enemy down.

In winning the war, the Americans reshaped the physical and mental landscapes in which they lived. They abandoned the British identity once so important to them, excluding from their new nation all those unwilling to make a break with the mother country. In the families of Continental Army soldiers in particular they began the process of creating loyalty to an entity that had no prior existence—a nation they named "the United States of America." They also laid claim to most of the territory east of the Mississippi River and south of the

Great Lakes, thereby greatly expanding the land potentially open to their settlements and threatening the traditional Indian dominance of the continent's interior.

In achieving independence, Americans surmounted formidable challenges. But in the future they faced perhaps even greater ones: establishing stable republican governments at the state and national levels to replace the monarchy they had rejected, and ensuring their government's continued existence in a world of bitter rivalries among the major powers—Britain, France, and Spain. Those European rivalries worked to the Americans' advantage during the war, but in the decades to come they would pose significant threats to the survival of the new nation.

LEGACY FOR A PEOPLE AND A NATION
Revolutionary Origins

The United States was created in an event universally termed the "American Revolution." Yet many historians would contend today that it was not truly "revolutionary," if a revolution means overturning an earlier power structure. The nation won its independence and established a republic, both radical events in the context of the eighteenth century, but essentially the same men who had led the colonies also led the new country (with the exception of British officials and appointees). In sharp contrast, the nearly contemporary French Revolution witnessed the execution of the monarch and many aristocrats, and consequently a significant redistribution of authority. So the legacy of the "American Revolution" appears ambiguous, at once radical and conservative.

Throughout the more than two hundred years since the "revolution," groups of widely varying political views have claimed to represent its true meaning. From far left to far right, Americans frequently declare that they are acting in the spirit of the Revolution. People protesting discriminatory policies against women and minorities (usually "liberals") invoke the "created equal" language of the Declaration of Independence. Left-wing organizations rail against concentrations of wealth and power in the hands of a few, again citing the Revolution's egalitarian thrust. Those protesting higher taxes (usually "conservatives" wanting a reduced role for government) often adopt the symbolism of the Boston Tea Party. Right-wing militias arm themselves, preparing to defend their homes and families against a malevolent government, just as they believe the minutemen did in 1775. The message of the Revolution can be evoked to support extralegal demonstrations of any description, from invasions of military bases by antiwar protestors to demonstrations outside abortion clinics, all of which may be analogized to the demonstrations against British policies in the 1760s. But the Revolution can also be evoked to oppose such street protests, because—some would argue—in a republic change should come peacefully, via the ballot box, not the streets.

Just as Americans in the eighteenth century disagreed over the meaning of their struggle against the mother country, so the legacy of revolution remains contested in the first decade of the twenty-first century, both for the nation thus created and for today's American people.

The **history companion** powered by Eduspace®
Your primary source for interactive quizzes, exercises, and more to help you learn efficiently.
http://history.college.hmco.com/students

Forging a National Republic 1776–1789

*O*n December 26, 1787, a group of Federalists—supporters of the proposed Constitution—gathered in Carlisle, a town on the Pennsylvania frontier. The men planned to fire a cannon to celebrate their state convention's ratification vote two weeks earlier, but a large crowd of Antifederalists prevented them from doing so. First the Antis stood in front of the cannon, refusing to budge even though the Federalists threatened to fire the gun anyway. Then, moving from passive to active resistance, they attacked the Federalists, who eventually fled the scene as the angry Antis publicly burned a copy of the Constitution.

The next day, the Federalists returned in force to fire their cannon and to read the convention's ratification proclamation. Choosing not to create another violent confrontation, Antifederalists instead paraded around the town effigies of two supporters of the Constitution, then burned them. When Federalist officials later arrested several Antifederalists on riot charges, the Antifederalist-dominated militia mustered to break the men out of jail. Only a flaw in the warrant—which freed the arrestees legally—prevented another bloody brawl.

For several weeks thereafter, the participants in these events argued back and forth in the Carlisle newspaper about the meaning of the demonstrations. Pro-Federalist authors proclaimed that the respectable initial celebrants acted with "good order and coolness"; their Antifederalist opponents, by contrast, were "obscure" men, nothing but "a few worthless ragamuffins." In response, "One of the People" pronounced the Federalists "an unhallowed riotous mob." Although the Constitution's supporters had declared themselves to be "friends of government," he wrote, in fact they were not: through their support of a form of government that aimed to suppress the people's liberties, they had revealed their true identity as secret aristocrats.

The Carlisle riots presaged violent disputes over the new Constitution in Albany (New York), Providence (Rhode Island), and other cities. In late 1787,

◀ Women of the Ramsay-Polk family of Maryland, painted by James Peale about 1793. The sumptuous dresses and elaborate hats and hairdos mark these republican women as ladies of leisure. On the river wharf in the background, ready for shipping, are the hogsheads of tobacco (produced by slave labor) that made their leisure possible. (Courtesy, Hirschl & Adler Galleries)

Carlisle witnessed one incident in an ongoing struggle that began in 1775 and continued until the end of the eighteenth century. In that contest, Americans argued continually—in print and in person—over how to implement republican principles and over who represented the people's will. Easterners debated with westerners; in both regions, elites contended with ordinary folk. Public celebrations, like those in the small Pennsylvania town, played an important part in the struggle. After all, in a world in which only relatively few property-holding men had the right to vote, other people (and even voters themselves) expressed their political opinions in the streets rather than at the ballot box.

Republicanism—the idea that governments should be based wholly on the consent of the people—originated with political theorists in ancient Greece and Rome. Republics, theorists declared, were desirable yet fragile forms of government. Unless their citizens were especially virtuous—that is, sober, moral, and industrious—and largely in agreement on key issues, republics were doomed to failure. When Americans left the British Empire, they abandoned the idea that the best system of government balanced monarchy, aristocracy, and democracy—or, to put it another way, that a stable polity required participation by a king, the nobility, and the people. They substituted a belief in the superiority of republicanism, in which the people, not Parliament, were sovereign. During and after the war, Americans had to deal with the potentially unwelcome consequences of that decision, such as those evident in the Carlisle demonstrations. How could they ensure political stability? How could they foster consensus among the populace? How could they create and sustain a virtuous republic?

America's political and intellectual leaders worked hard to inculcate virtue in their fellow countrymen and countrywomen. After 1776, American literature, theater, art, architecture, and education all pursued explicitly moral goals. The education of women was considered particularly important, for as the mothers of the republic's children, they were primarily responsible for ensuring the nation's future. On such matters Americans could agree, but they disagreed on many other critical issues. Almost all white men assumed that women, Indians, and African Americans should have no formal role in politics, but they found it difficult to reach a consensus on how many of their own number should be included, how often elections should be held, or how their new governments should be structured.

Republican citizens had to make many other decisions as well. Should a republic's diplomacy differ from that of other nations? (For example, should the United States work to advance the cause of republicanism elsewhere?) And then there were Thomas Jefferson's words in the Declaration of Independence: "all men are created equal." Given that bold statement of principle, how could white republicans justify holding African Americans in perpetual bondage? Some answered that question by freeing their slaves or by voting for state laws that abolished slavery. Others responded by denying that blacks were "men" in the same sense as whites.

The most important task facing Americans in these years was the construction of a genuinely national government. Before 1765 the British mainland colonies had rarely cooperated on common endeavors. Many circumstances separated them: their diverse economies, varying religious traditions and ethnic compositions, competing land claims (especially in the West), and different political systems. But fighting the Revolutionary War brought them together and created a new nationalistic spirit, especially among those who served in the Continental Army or the diplomatic corps. Wartime experiences broke down at least some of the boundaries that previously had divided Americans, replacing loyalties to state and region with loyalties to the nation.

Still, forging a national republic (as opposed to a set of loosely connected state republics) was neither easy nor simple. America's first such government, under the Articles of Confederation, proved too weak and decentralized. But some of the nation's political leaders learned from their experiences and tried another approach when they drafted the Constitution in 1787. Some historians have argued that the Articles of Confederation and the Constitution reflect opposing political philosophies, the Constitution representing an "aristocratic" counterrevolution against the "democratic" Articles. The two documents are more accurately viewed as successive attempts to solve the same problems—for instance, the relationship of states and nation and the extent to which authority should be centralized. Both applied theories of republicanism to practical problems of governance; neither was entirely successful in resolving those difficulties. ■

Creating a Virtuous Republic

*W*hen the colonies declared their independence from Great Britain, John Dickinson recalled many years later, "there was no question concerning forms of Government, no enquiry whether a Republic or a limited Monarchy was best. . . . We knew that the people of this country must unite themselves under some form of Government and that this could be no other than the republican form"—in short, self-government by the people. But how should that goal be implemented?

Three different definitions of republicanism emerged in the new United States. Ancient history and political theory informed the first, held chiefly by members of the

VARIETIES OF REPUBLICANISM educated elite (such as the Adamses of Massachusetts). The histories of popular governments in Greece and Rome suggested that republics could succeed only if they were small in size and homogeneous in population. Unless a republic's citizens were willing to sacrifice their own private interests for the good of the whole, the government would collapse. A truly virtuous man, classical republican theory insisted, had to forgo personal profit and work solely for the best interests of the nation. In return for sacrifices, though, a republic offered its citizens equality of opportunity. Under such a government, rank would be based on merit rather than on inherited wealth and status. Society would be governed by members of a "natural aristocracy," men whose talent had elevated them from what might have been humble beginnings to positions of power and privilege. Rank would not be abolished but instead would be founded on merit.

A second definition, advanced by other members of the elite but also by some skilled craftsmen, drew more on economic theory than on political thought. Instead of perceiving the nation as an organic whole composed of people nobly sacrificing for the common good, this version of republicanism followed the Scottish theorist Adam Smith in emphasizing individuals' pursuit of rational self-interest. The huge profits some men reaped from patriotism by selling supplies to the army underscored such an approach. The nation could only benefit from aggressive economic expansion, argued men such as Alexander Hamilton. When republican men sought to improve their own economic and social circumstances, the entire nation would benefit. Republican virtue would be achieved through the pursuit of private interests, rather than through subordination to some communal ideal. Such thinking decisively abandoned the old notion of the Puritan covenant, which the first definition perpetuated in its emphasis on consensus though not in its stress on an aristocracy of talent rather than birth (see pages 51–52).

The third notion of republicanism was less influential but more egalitarian than the other two, which both contained considerable potential for inequality. Many of its illiterate or barely literate proponents could write little to promote their beliefs. Men who advanced the third version of republicanism, the most prominent of whom was Thomas Paine, called for widening men's participation in the political process. They also wanted government to respond directly to the needs of ordinary folk, rejecting any notion that the "lesser sort" should automatically defer to their "betters." They were, indeed, democrats in more or less the modern sense. For them,

When the great French sculptor Jean-Antoine Houdon prepared this bust of George Washington in 1785, he chose to show the revolutionary leader in classical garb rather than in contemporary clothing. Such images linked the aspirations of the new nation to the ancient republics American thinkers revered. (Collection of Dr. Gary Milan)

As citizens of the United States set out to construct their republic, they believed they were embarking on an unprecedented enterprise. With great pride in their new nation, they expected to replace the vices of monarchical Europe—immorality, selfishness, and lack of public spirit—with the sober virtues of republican America. They wanted to embody republican principles not only in their governments but also in their society and culture. They looked to painting, literature, drama, and architecture to convey messages of nationalism and virtue to the public, focusing on such themes until after the turn of the century.

VIRTUE AND THE ARTS

Americans faced a crucial contradiction at the very outset of their efforts. To some republicans, the fine arts themselves were manifestations of vice. Their existence in a virtuous society, many contended, signaled the arrival of luxury and corruption. What need did a frugal yeoman have for a painting—or, worse yet, a novel? Why should anyone spend hard-earned wages to see a play in a lavishly decorated theater? The first American artists, playwrights, and authors thus confronted an impossible dilemma. They wanted to produce works embodying virtue, but those very works, regardless of their content, were viewed by many as corrupting.

Still, they tried. William Hill Brown's *The Power of Sympathy* (1789), the first novel written in the United States, was a lurid tale of seduction intended as a warning to young women. In Royall Tyler's *The Contrast* (1787), the first successful American play, the virtuous conduct of Colonel Manly was contrasted (hence the title) with the reprehensible behavior of the fop Billy Dimple. The most popular book of the era, Mason Locke Weems's *Life of Washington*, published in 1800 shortly after George Washington's death, was intended by its author to "hold up his great Virtues . . . to the imitation of Our Youth." Weems could hardly be accused of subtlety. The famous tale he invented—six-year-old George bravely admitting cutting down his father's favorite cherry tree—ended with George's father exclaiming, "Run to my arms, you dearest boy. . . . Such an act of heroism in my son, is worth more than a thousand trees, though blossomed with silver, and their fruit of purest gold."

Painting and architecture, too, were expected to embody high moral standards. Two of the most prominent artists of the period, Gilbert Stuart and Charles Willson Peale, painted innumerable portraits of upstanding republican citizens. John Trumbull's vast canvases depicted milestones of American history such as the Battle of Bunker Hill, Burgoyne's surrender at Saratoga, and Cornwallis's capitulation at Yorktown. Such portraits

republican virtue was embodied in the untutored wisdom of the people as a whole, rather than in the special insights of a natural aristocracy or the pronouncements of wealthy individuals.

Despite the differences, the three strands of republicanism shared many of the same assumptions. For example, all three contrasted the industrious virtue of America to the corruption of Britain and Europe. In the first version, that virtue manifested itself in frugality and self-sacrifice; in the second, it would prevent self-interest from becoming vice; in the third, it was the justification for including even propertyless free men in the ranks of voters. "Virtue, Virtue alone . . . is the basis of a republic," asserted Dr. Benjamin Rush of Philadelphia, an ardent patriot, in 1778. His fellow Americans concurred, even if they defined virtue differently. Most agreed that a virtuous country would be composed of hard-working citizens who would dress simply and live plainly, elect wise leaders to public office, and forgo the conspicuous consumption of luxury goods.

Novels

The citizens of the United States, fiercely patriotic and proud of achieving political independence from Great Britain, also sought intellectual and cultural independence. In novels, poems, paintings, plays, and histories they explored aspects of their new national identity. Ironically, though, the standards against which they measured themselves and the models they followed were European, primarily British.

That was especially true of the most widely read form of literature in the new United States, the novel. Susanna Haswell Rowson's *Charlotte: A Tale of Truth,* the most popular early "American" novel, was actually composed in England, where the novel, as a literary form, originated. In the mid-eighteenth century Samuel Richardson had composed the first works of fiction that today are called novels, the very name revealing their "newness," or novelty. Written in epistolary style (that is, through letters drafted by the various characters) Richardson's novels—*Pamela* (1740), *Clarissa* (1748), and *Sir Charles Grandison* (1753)—all revolved around the courtship and sexual relationships of young adults. The same themes permeated *Charlotte* and Richardson's other American imitators, and for good reason. Changing social mores in the late eighteenth century largely freed English and American young people from parental supervision of their marital decisions. While giving them greater individual choice, that freedom also rendered girls particularly vulnerable to new dangers of deception and seduction by unscrupulous suitors. And these same young women, as a group, were the most avid readers of novels, especially as expanded women's education increased female literacy rates.

William Hill Brown's *Power of Sympathy* (1789) and Hannah Foster's *Coquette* (1797), fictional versions of true "seduction and abandonment" tales, had avid readerships, but neither matched the sales of *Charlotte,* which despite its subtitle, *A Tale of Truth,* had no known factual basis. Rowson, born in England but raised in Massachusetts as the daughter of a customs officer in the British service, lived with her family in England during the Revolution but permanently returned to the United States in 1793. Her popular novel, first published in London in 1791, was reprinted in Philadelphia three years later and eventually went through more than 160 editions. *Charlotte* (later titled *Charlotte Temple*) narrates the story of a naive young woman who elopes, pregnant and unmarried, with her seducer, only to be deserted when a beautiful, rich, and virtuous rival appears on the scene. After giving birth to her baby, Charlotte dies in her father's arms, with her last breath directing him to care for the child. "Oh my dear girls," Rowson cautions her readers, "pray for fortitude to resist the impulses of inclination, when it runs counter to the precepts of religion and virtue."

Generations of young American women sobbed over Charlotte's fate, visiting Trinity churchyard in lower Manhattan, where a real-life counterpart of the fictional heroine was reputed to be buried. Their tears and women's preference on both sides of the Atlantic for such sentimental novels linked the young readers and their nation to the former mother country from which they were nominally so eager to separate.

This "Eighth American Edition" (such statements on the title pages of early novels can rarely be trusted because some printings were pirated) of Susanna Rowson's *Charlotte Temple* included a "portrait" of its entirely fictional heroine. That engraving thus reinforced the subtitle, *A Tale of Truth.* (Courtesy, American Antiquarian Society)

and historical scenes were intended to instill patriotic sentiments in their viewers. Architects likewise hoped to convey in their buildings a sense of the young republic's ideals. When the Virginia government asked Thomas Jefferson, then minister to France, for advice on the design of the state capitol in Richmond, Jefferson unhesitatingly recommended copying a Roman building, the Maison Carrée at Nîmes. "It is very simple," he explained, "but it is noble beyond expression." Jefferson set forth ideals that would guide American architecture for a generation to come: simplicity of line, harmonious proportions, a feeling of grandeur.

Despite the artists' efforts (or, some would have said, because of them), some Americans began to detect signs of luxury and corruption by the mid-1780s. The resumption of European trade after the war brought a return to fashionable clothing for both men and women and abandonment of the simpler homespun garments patriots had once worn with pride. Elite families again attended balls and concerts. Parties no longer seemed complete without gambling and cardplaying. Social clubs for young people multiplied; Samuel Adams worried in print about the opportunities for corruption lurking behind plans for tea drinking and genteel conversation among Boston youths. Especially alarming to fervent republicans was the establishment in 1783 of the Society of the Cincinnati, a hereditary association for Revolutionary War officers and their male descendants. Although the organizers hoped to advance the notion of the citizen-soldier, opponents feared that the group would become the nucleus of a native-born aristocracy. All these developments directly challenged the United States's self-image as a virtuous republic.

Americans' deep-seated concern for the future of the infant republic focused their attention on their children, the "rising generation." Education had previously been seen as a private means to personal advancement, a concern only for individual families. Now schooling would serve a public purpose. If young people were to resist the temptations of vice and become useful citizens prepared for self-government, they would need a good education. In fact, the very survival of the nation depended on it. The 1780s and 1790s thus witnessed two major changes in educational practice.

EDUCATIONAL REFORM

First, some northern states began to use tax money to support public elementary schools. In 1789 Massachusetts became one of the first states to require towns to offer their citizens free public elementary education. Second, schooling for girls was improved. Americans' recognition of the importance of the rising generation led to the realization that mothers would have to be properly educated if they were to instruct their children adequately. Therefore, Massachusetts insisted in its 1789 law that town elementary schools be open to girls as well as boys. Throughout the United States, private academies were founded to give teenage girls from well-to-do families an opportunity for advanced schooling. No one yet proposed opening colleges to women, but a few fortunate girls could study history, geography, rhetoric, and mathematics. The academies also trained female students in fancy needlework—the only artistic endeavor considered appropriate for genteel women.

The chief theorist of women's education in the early republic was Judith Sargent Murray of Gloucester, Massachusetts. In a series of essays published in the 1780s and 1790s, Murray argued that women and men had equal intellectual capacities, although women's inadequate education might make them seem less intelligent. "We can only reason from what we know," she declared, "and if an opportunity of acquiring knowledge hath been denied us, the inferiority of our sex cannot fairly be deduced from thence." Therefore, concluded Murray, boys and girls should be offered equivalent scholastic training. She further contended that girls should be taught to support themselves by their own efforts: "Independence should be placed within their grasp."

JUDITH SARGENT MURRAY

Murray's direct challenge to the traditional colonial belief that, as one man put it, girls "knew quite enough if they could make a shirt and a pudding" was part of a general rethinking of women's position that occurred as a result of the Revolution. Both men and women realized that female patriots had made vital and important contributions to winning the war through their work at home and that their notions of proper gender roles had to be rethought. Americans began to develop new ideas about the role women should play in a republican society.

The best-known expression of those new ideas appears in a letter Abigail Adams addressed to her husband in March 1776. "In the new Code of Laws which I suppose it will be necessary for you to make I desire you would Remember the Ladies," she wrote. "Remember all Men would be tyrants if they could. . . . If perticuliar care and attention is not paid to the Laidies [sic] we are determined to foment a Rebelion, and will not hold ourselves bound by any Laws in which we have no voice, or Representation." With these words, Abigail Adams took a step that was soon to be duplicated by other disfranchised Americans. She deliberately applied the ideology developed to combat parliamentary supremacy to purposes revolutionary leaders had never

WOMEN AND THE REPUBLIC

■ Judith Sargent Stevens (later Murray), by John Singleton Copley, c. 1770-1772. The eventual author of tracts advocating improvements in women's education sat for this portrait two decades earlier, during her first marriage. Her clear-eyed gaze suggests both her intelligence and her seriousness of purpose.   (Terra Museum of American Art, Chicago, Illinois. Daniel J. Terra Collection)

intended. Since men were "Naturally Tyrannical," she argued, the United States should reform colonial marriage laws, which made wives subordinate to their husbands.

Abigail Adams did not ask that women be allowed to vote, but others claimed that right. The men who drafted the New Jersey state constitution in 1776 defined voters carelessly as "all free inhabitants" who met certain property qualifications. They thereby unintentionally gave the vote to property-holding white spinsters and widows, as well as to free black landowners. Qualified women and African Americans regularly voted in New Jersey's local and congressional elections until 1807, when they were disfranchised by the state legislature, which falsely alleged that they had engaged in widespread vote fraud. Yet the fact that women voted at all

was evidence of their altered perception of their place in the political life of the country.

Such dramatic episodes were unusual. After the war, European Americans still viewed women in traditional terms, continuing to believe that women's primary function was to be good wives, mothers, and mistresses of households. They perceived significant differences between the male and female characters. That distinction eventually enabled Americans to resolve the conflict between the two most influential strands of republican thought and led to new roles for some women. Because wives could not own property or participate directly in economic life, women in general came to be seen as the embodiment of self-sacrificing, disinterested republicanism. Through new female-run charitable associations founded after the war, better-off women assumed public responsibilities, in particular through caring for poor widows and orphaned children. Thus men were freed from the naggings of conscience as they pursued their economic self-interest (that other republican virtue), secure in the knowledge that their wives and daughters were fulfilling the family's obligation to the common good. The ideal republican man, therefore, was an individualist, seeking advancement for himself and his family. The ideal republican woman, by contrast, always put the well-being of others ahead of her own.

Together European American men and women established the context for the creation of a virtuous republic. But nearly 20 percent of the American population was of African descent. How did approximately 700,000 African Americans fit into the developing national plan?

The First Emancipation and the Growth of Racism

*R*evolutionary ideology exposed one of the primary contradictions in American society. Both European and African Americans saw the irony in slaveholders' claims that they sought to prevent Britain from "enslaving" them. Many revolutionary leaders voiced the theme. In 1773 Dr. Benjamin Rush called slavery "a vice which degrades human nature," warning ominously that "the plant of liberty is of so tender a nature that it cannot thrive long in the neighborhood of slavery." Common folk also pointed out the contradiction. When Josiah Atkins, a Connecticut soldier, saw Washington's plantation, he observed in his journal: "Alas! That persons who pretend to stand for the rights of mankind for the liberties of society, can delight in oppression, & that even of the worst kind!"

African Americans did not need revolutionary ideology to tell them that slavery was wrong, but they quickly took advantage of that ideology. In 1779 a group of slaves from Portsmouth, New Hampshire, asked the state legislature "from what authority [our masters] assume to dispose of our lives, freedom and property," pleading "that the name of slave may not more be heard in a land gloriously contending for the sweets of freedom." The same year several bondspeople in Fairfield, Connecticut, petitioned the legislature for their freedom, characterizing slavery as a "dreadful Evil" and "flagrant Injustice." How could men who were "nobly contending in the Cause of Liberty," they asked, continue "this detestable Practice"?

Both legislatures responded negatively, but the postwar years witnessed the gradual abolition of slavery in the North, a process that has become known as "the first emancipation." Vermont banned slavery in its 1777 constitution. Massachusetts courts decided in the 1780s that a clause in the state constitution prohibited slavery. Most of the other states north of Maryland adopted gradual emancipation laws between 1780 (Pennsylvania) and 1804 (New Jersey). Although New Hampshire did not formally abolish slavery, only eight slaves were reported on the 1800 census, and none remained a decade later. No southern state adopted similar general emancipation laws, but the legislatures of Virginia (1782), Delaware (1787), and Maryland (1790 and 1796) altered laws that earlier had restricted slaveowners' ability to free their bondspeople. South Carolina and Georgia never considered adopting such acts, and North Carolina insisted that all manumissions (emancipations of individual slaves) be approved by county courts.

EMANCIPATION AND MANUMISSION

Revolutionary ideology thus had limited impact on the well-entrenched economic interests of large slaveholders. Only in the North, where slaves were relatively few, could state legislatures vote to abolish slavery. Even there, legislators' concern for the property rights of owners of human chattel—the Revolution, after all, was fought for *property* as well as life and liberty—led them to favor gradual emancipation over immediate abolition. For example, New York's law freed children born into slavery after July 4, 1799, but only after they had reached their mid-twenties (by then having through their labor more than paid back the cost of their upbringing). The laws failed to emancipate the existing slave population, thereby leaving the owners' current human property largely intact. For decades, then, African Americans in the North lived in an intermediate stage between slavery and freedom. Although the emancipation laws forbade the sale of slaves to jurisdictions in which the institution remained legal, slaveowners regularly circumvented such provisions. The 1840 census still recorded the presence of slaves in several northern states; not until later that decade did Rhode Island and Connecticut, for instance, abolish all vestiges of slavery.

Despite the slow progress of abolition, the number of free people of African descent in the United States grew dramatically in the first years after the Revolution. Before the war they had been few in number; in 1755, for example, only 4 percent of African Americans in Maryland were free. Most slaves emancipated before the war were mulattos, born of unions between bondswomen and their masters, who then manumitted the children. But wartime disruptions radically augmented the freed population. Slaves who had escaped from plantations during the war, others who had served in the American army, and still others who had been emancipated by their owners or by state laws were now free. By 1790 nearly 60,000 free people of color lived in the United States; ten years later they numbered more than 108,000, nearly 11 percent of the total African American population.

GROWTH OF FREE BLACK POPULATION

In the Chesapeake, manumissions were speeded by economic changes such as declining soil fertility and the shift from tobacco to grain production, as well as by the rising influence of antislavery Baptists and Methodists. Since grain cultivation was less labor-intensive than tobacco growing, planters began to complain about "excess" slaves. They occasionally solved that problem by freeing some of their less productive or more favored bondspeople. The enslaved also seized the opportunity to negotiate agreements with their owners allowing them to live and work independently until they could purchase themselves with their accumulated earnings. The free black population of Virginia more than doubled between 1790 and 1810, and by the latter year nearly one-quarter of Maryland's African American population was no longer in legal bondage.

In the 1780s and thereafter, freed people from rural areas often made their way to northern port cities. Boston and Philadelphia, where slavery was abolished sooner than in New York City, were popular destinations. Women outnumbered men among the migrants by a margin of three to two, for they had better employment opportunities in the cities, especially in domestic service. Some freedmen also worked in domestic service, but larger numbers were em-

MIGRATION TO NORTHERN CITIES

ployed as unskilled laborers and sailors. A few of the women and a sizable proportion of men (nearly one-third of those in Philadelphia in 1795) were skilled workers or retailers. These people chose new names for themselves, exchanging the surnames of former masters for names like Newman or Brown, and as soon as possible they established independent two-parent nuclear families instead of continuing to live in their employers' households. They also began to occupy distinct neighborhoods, probably as a result of discrimination.

Emancipation did not bring equality. Even whites who recognized African Americans' right to freedom were unwilling to accept them as equals. Laws discriminated against freed people as they had against slaves. South Carolina, for example, did not permit free blacks to testify against whites in court. New Englanders attempted through indenture contracts to maintain control of freed youths. Public schools often refused to educate children of color. Freedmen found it difficult to purchase property and find good jobs. And though in many areas African Americans were accepted as members—even ministers—of evangelical churches, they were rarely allowed an equal voice in church affairs.

Gradually, freed people developed their own institutions, often based in their own neighborhoods. In Charleston mulattos formed the Brown Fellowship Society, which provided insurance coverage for its members, financed a school, and helped to support orphans. In 1794 former slaves in Philadelphia and Baltimore founded societies that eventually became the African Methodist Episcopal (AME) denomination. AME churches later sponsored schools in a number of cities and, along with African Baptist, African Episcopal, and African Presbyterian churches, became cultural centers of the free black community. Freed people quickly learned that, to survive and prosper, they had to rely on their own collective efforts rather than on the benevolence or goodwill of their white compatriots.

FREED PEOPLE'S INSTITUTIONS

Their endeavors were all the more important because the postrevolutionary years witnessed the development of a formal racist theory in the United States. European Americans had long regarded their slaves as inferior, but the most influential writers attributed that inferiority to environmental factors. They argued that African slaves' seemingly debased character derived from their enslavement, rather than enslavement being the consequence of inherited inferiority. In the Revolution's aftermath, though, slaveown-

DEVELOPMENT OF RACIST THEORY

■ A sailor of African descent posed proudly for this portrait around 1790. Unfortunately, neither the name of the sailor nor the name of the artist is known today.   (Private collection, photograph courtesy of Hirschl & Adler Galleries, New York)

ers needed to defend holding other human beings in bondage against the notion that "all men are created equal." Consequently, they began to argue that people of African descent were less than fully human and that the principles of republican equality applied only to European Americans. In other words, to avoid having to confront the contradiction between their practice and the egalitarian implications of revolutionary theory, they redefined the theory so that it would not apply to African Americans.

Simultaneously, the very notion of "race" appeared in coherent form, applied to groups defined by skin color as "whites" and "blacks." The rise of egalitarian thinking among European Americans both downplayed status distinctions within their own group and differentiated all "whites" from people of color—Indians and African Americans. (That differentiation soon manifested itself in new miscegenation laws adopted in both northern and southern states to forbid intermarriage between whites and blacks or Indians.) Meanwhile, a generation or two of experience as slaves on American soil forged the identity "African" or "black" from the various ethnic and national affiliations of people who had survived the transatlantic crossing. Strikingly, among the first to term themselves "Africans" were oceanic sailors—men whose wide-ranging contacts with Europeans caused them to construct a unified (and separate) identity for themselves. Thus in the revolutionary era "whiteness" and "blackness"—along with the superiority of the former, the inferiority of the latter—developed as contrasting terms in tandem with each other.

Such racism had several intertwined elements. First came the assertion that, as Thomas Jefferson insisted in 1781, blacks were "inferior to the whites in the endowments both of body and mind." There followed the belief that blacks were congenitally lazy and disorderly, even though owners had often argued, conversely, that slaves were "natural" workers. (No one seemed to notice the inherent contradiction.) Third was the notion that all blacks were sexually promiscuous and that African American men lusted after European American women. The specter of interracial sexual intercourse involving black men and white women haunted early American racist thought. Significantly, the more common reverse circumstance—the sexual exploitation of enslaved women by their masters—aroused little comment or concern.

African Americans did not allow these developing racist notions to go unchallenged. Benjamin Banneker, a free black surveyor, astronomer, and mathematical genius, directly disputed Thomas Jefferson's belief in Africans' intellectual inferiority. In 1791 Banneker sent Jefferson a copy of his latest almanac (which included his astronomical calculations) as an example of blacks' mental powers. Jefferson's response admitted Banneker's intelligence but indicated that he regarded Banneker as exceptional; Jefferson insisted that he needed more evidence before he would change his mind.

At its birth, then, the republic was defined by its leaders as an exclusively white male enterprise. Indeed, some historians have argued that the *A REPUBLIC FOR WHITE MEN ONLY* subjugation of blacks and women was a necessary precondition for theoretical equality among white men. They have pointed out that identifying a common racial antagonist helped to create white solidarity and to lessen the threat to gentry power posed by the enfranchisement of poorer white men. Moreover, excluding women from the political realm preserved all power for men, specifically those of the "better sort." Some schol-

ars have pointed out that it was less dangerous to allow white men with little property to participate formally in politics than to open the possibility that they might join with former slaves to question the rule of elites. That was perhaps one reason why after the Revolution the division of American society between slave and free was transformed into a division between blacks—some of whom were free—and whites. The white male wielders of power ensured their continued dominance in part by substituting race for enslavement as the primary determinant of African Americans' status.

Designing Republican Governments

In May 1776, even before adoption of the Declaration of Independence, the Second Continental Congress directed states to devise new republican governments to replace the provincial congresses and committees that had met since 1774. Thus American men initially concentrated on drafting state constitutions and devoted little attention to their national government—an oversight they later had to remedy.

At the state level, political leaders immediately faced the problem of defining a "constitution." Americans wanted to create tangible documents *STATE CONSTITUTIONS* specifying the fundamental structures of government, but at first legislators could not decide how to accomplish that goal. States eventually concluded that their constitutions should not be drafted by regular legislative bodies. Following the lead established by Vermont in 1777 and Massachusetts in 1780, they began to elect conventions for the sole purpose of drafting constitutions. Thus states sought direct authorization from the people—the theoretical sovereigns in a republic—before establishing new governments. After preparing new constitutions, delegates submitted them to voters for ratification.

The framers of state constitutions concerned themselves primarily with outlining the distribution of and limitations on government power—both crucial to the survival of republics. If authority was not confined within reasonable limits, the states might become tyrannical, as Britain had. Americans' experience with British rule permeated every provision of their new constitutions. States experimented with different solutions to the problems the framers perceived, and the early constitutions varied considerably in specifics while remaining broadly comparable in outline.

Under their colonial charters, Americans had learned to fear the power of the governor—usually, the appointed agent of the king or proprietor—and to see the legislature as their defender. Accordingly, the first state constitutions typically provided for the governor to be elected annually (commonly by the legislature), limited the number of terms he could serve, and gave him little independent authority. Simultaneously, the constitutions expanded the legislature's powers. Every state except Pennsylvania and Vermont retained a two-house structure, with members of the upper house having longer terms and being required to meet higher property-holding standards than members of the lower house. But they also redrew electoral districts to reflect population patterns more accurately, and they increased the number of members in both houses. Finally, most states lowered property qualifications for voting. As a result the legislatures came to include some members who before the war would not have been eligible to vote. Thus the revolutionary era witnessed the first deliberate attempt to broaden the base of American government, a process that has continued to the present day.

But the state constitutions' authors knew that governments designed to be responsive to the people would not necessarily provide sufficient protection if tyrants were elected to office. They consequently included explicit limitations on government authority in the documents they composed, attempting to protect what they regarded as the inalienable rights of individual citizens. Seven of the constitutions contained formal bills of rights, and the others had similar clauses. Most guaranteed citizens freedom of the press, the right to a fair trial, the right of consent to taxation, and protection against general search warrants. An independent judiciary was charged with upholding such rights. Most states also guaranteed freedom of religion, but with restrictions. For example, seven states required that all officeholders be Christians, and some continued to support churches with tax money. (Not until 1833 did Massachusetts become the last state to remove all vestiges of a religious establishment.)

LIMITING STATE GOVERNMENTS

In general, the constitution makers put greater emphasis on preventing state governments from becoming tyrannical than on making them effective wielders of political authority. Their approach to shaping governments was understandable, given the American experience with Great Britain. But establishing such weak political units, especially in wartime, practically ensured that the constitutions soon would need revision. Soon some states began to rewrite constitutions they had drafted in 1776 and 1777.

Invariably, the revised versions increased the powers of the governor and reduced the scope of the legislature's

REVISING STATE CONSTITUTIONS

authority. In the mid-1780s, some American political leaders started to develop a theory of checks and balances as the primary means of controlling government power. (In the mid-1770s, constitutions prescribed powerful legislatures to ensure good government, but wartime experiences led many to conclude that such arrangements often failed.) Americans sought to balance the powers of the legislative, executive, and judicial branches against one another. The national constitution they drafted in 1787 also embodied that principle.

Yet the constitutional theories that Americans applied at the state level did not at first influence their conception of national government. Since American officials initially focused on organizing the military struggle against Britain, the powers and structure of the Continental Congress evolved by default early in the war. Not until late 1777 did Congress send the Articles of Confederation to the states for ratification, and those Articles simply wrote into law the unplanned arrangements of the Continental Congress.

The chief organ of national government was a unicameral (one-house) legislature in which each state had one vote. Its powers included conducting foreign relations, mediating disputes between states, controlling maritime affairs, regulating Indian trade, and valuing state and national coinage. The Articles did not give the national government the ability to raise revenue effectively or to enforce a uniform commercial policy. The United States of America was described as "a firm league of friendship" in which each state "retains its sovereignty, freedom and independence, and every Power, Jurisdiction and right, which is not by this confederation expressly delegated to the United States, in Congress assembled."

ARTICLES OF CONFEDERATION

The Articles required unanimous consent of state legislatures for ratification or amendment, and a clause concerning western lands proved troublesome. The draft accepted by Congress allowed states to retain all land claims derived from their original charters. But states with definite western boundaries in their charters (such as Maryland and New Jersey) wanted other states to cede to the national government their landholdings west of the Appalachian Mountains. Otherwise, they feared, states with large claims could expand and overpower their smaller neighbors. Maryland refused to accept the Articles until 1781, when Virginia finally promised to surrender its western holdings to national jurisdiction (see Map 7.1). Other states followed suit, establishing the principle that unorganized lands would be held by the nation as a whole.

Map content and legend:

- Area of thirteen colonies after cessions, 1802
- N.Y. cedes to Congress, 1782
- Va. cedes to Congress, 1784
- N.C. cedes to Congress, 1790
- S.C. relinquishes claims to Ga., 1787 (Beaufort Convention)
- Ga. cedes to Congress, 1802

Massachusetts Cessions
- Mass. cedes to Congress, 1785
- Mass. relinquishes sovereignty and jurisdiction to N.Y., 1786 (Hartford Agreement); Mass. retains title to land
- Mass. relinquishes all claims to N.Y., 1786 (Hartford Agreement)

Connecticut Cessions
- Conn. relinquishes claims to Pa., 1782 (Congressional arbitration)
- Conn. cedes to Congress, 1786
- Conn. cedes Western Reserve to Congress, 1800

Map labels: BRITISH NORTH AMERICA, Lake Superior, Lake Michigan, Lake Huron, Lake Ontario, Lake Erie, NORTHWEST TERRITORY, Ohio R., Mississippi R., Tennessee R., SPANISH LOUISIANA, SPANISH FLORIDA, ME. (part of Mass.), N.H., MASS., CONN., R.I., N.Y., PA., N.J., MD., DEL., VA., N.C., S.C., GA.

Map 7.1   Western Land Claims and Cessions, 1782–1802

After the United States achieved independence, states competed with each other for control of valuable lands to which they had possible claims under their original charters. That competition led to a series of compromises among the states or between individual states and the new nation, which are indicated on this map.

The capacity of a single state to delay ratification for three years portended the fate of American government under the Articles of Confederation. The unicameral legislature, whether it was called the Second Continental Congress (until 1781) or the Confederation Congress (thereafter), was too inefficient and unwieldy to govern effectively. The Articles' authors had not given adequate thought to the distribution of power within the national government or to the relationship between the Confederation and the states. The Congress they created was simultaneously a legislative body and a collective executive (there was no judiciary), but it had no independent income and no authority to compel the states to accept its rulings. Under the Articles, national government lurched from crisis to crisis. (See the Appendix for the text of the *Articles of Confederation.*)

Trials of the Confederation

Finance posed the most persistent problem faced by both state and national governments. Because legislators at all levels levied taxes only reluctantly, both Congress and the states at first tried to finance the war simply by printing currency. Even though the money was backed only by good faith, it circulated freely and without excessive depreciation during 1775 and most of 1776. Demand for military supplies and civilian goods was high, stimulating trade (especially with France) and local production. Indeed, the amount of money issued in those years was probably no more than what a healthy economy required as a medium of exchange.

But in late 1776, as the American army suffered reverses in New York and New Jersey, prices began to rise

FINANCIAL
AFFAIRS

and inflation set in. The currency's value rested on Americans' faith in their government, a faith that was sorely tested in the years that followed, especially during the dark days of British triumphs in the South (1779 and 1780). State governments fought inflation by controlling wages and prices and requiring acceptance of paper currency on an equal footing with hard money. States also borrowed funds, established lotteries, and even levied taxes. Their efforts were futile. So too was Congress's attempt to stop printing currency altogether and to rely solely on money contributed by the states. By early 1780 it took forty paper dollars to purchase one silver dollar. Soon, Continental currency was worthless (see Figure 7.1).

In 1781, faced with total collapse of the monetary system, the congressmen undertook ambitious reforms. After establishing a department of finance under the

Figure 7.1   Depreciation of Continental Currency, 1777–1780

The depreciation of Continental currency accelerated in 1778, as is shown in this graph measuring its value against one hundred silver dollars. Thereafter, its value dropped almost daily.   (Source: Data from John J. McCusker, "How Much Is That in Real Money? A Historical Price Index for Use as a Deflator of Money Values in the Economy of the United States," *Proceedings of the American Antiquarian Society,* Vol. 101, Pt. 2 [1991], Table C-1.)

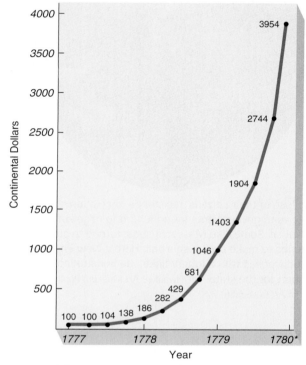

* Currency abandoned in April 1780

wealthy Philadelphia merchant Robert Morris, they asked the states to amend the Articles of Confederation to allow Congress to levy a duty of 5 percent on imported goods. Morris put national finances on a solid footing, but the customs duty was never adopted. First Rhode Island and then New York refused to agree to the tax. The states' resistance reflected fear of a too-powerful central government. As one worried citizen wrote in 1783, "If permanent Funds are given to Congress, the aristocratical Influence, which predominates in more than a major part of the United States, will fully establish an arbitrary Government." But states too needed revenue, and found it just as hard to come by. When they enacted new, heavy taxes after the war, farmers resisted their authority.

■ Because of their citizens' resistance to taxation, the early state governments found it hard to raise sufficient revenues. Some, like Massachusetts, turned to state-run lotteries to make up the shortfall. Here a New Englander proudly poses with a lottery ticket, demonstrating his support for the state. (Milwaukee Art Museum Purchase, Layton Art Collection)

Because the Articles denied Congress the power to establish a national commercial policy, the realm of foreign trade also exposed the new government's weaknesses. Immediately after the war, Britain, France, and Spain restricted American trade with their colonies. Americans, who had hoped independence would bring about trade with all nations, were outraged but could do little to change matters. Members of Congress watched helplessly as British manufactured goods flooded the United States while American produce could no longer be sold in the British West Indies, once its prime market. Although Americans reopened commerce with other European countries and started a profitable trade with China in 1784, neither substituted for access to closer and larger markets.

FOREIGN AFFAIRS

Congress furthermore had difficulty dealing with the Spanish presence on the nation's southern and western borders. Determined to prevent the republic's expansion, Spain in 1784 closed the Mississippi River to American navigation, thereby depriving the growing settlements west of the Appalachians of their access to the Gulf of Mexico. Congress, through its Department of Foreign Affairs, opened negotiations with Spain in 1785, but even John Jay, one of the nation's most experienced diplomats, could not win the necessary concessions. The talks collapsed the following year after Congress divided sharply: southerners and westerners insisted on navigation rights on the Mississippi, whereas northerners were willing to abandon that claim in order to win commercial concessions in the West Indies. The impasse made some congressmen question the possibility of a national consensus on foreign affairs.

Provisions of the 1783 Treaty of Paris too caused serious problems. Article Four, which promised the repayment of prewar debts (most of them owed by Americans to British merchants), and Article Five, which recommended that states allow loyalists to recover their confiscated property, aroused considerable opposition. States passed laws denying British subjects the right to sue for recovery of debts or property in American courts, and town meetings decried the loyalists' return. As residents of Norwalk, Connecticut, put it, few Americans wanted to permit the "Tory Villains" to return "while filial Tears are fresh upon our Cheeks and our Murdered Brethren scarcely cold in their Graves." State governments also had reason to oppose enforcement of the treaty. Sales of loyalists' land, houses, and other possessions had helped finance the war. Since most of the purchasers were prominent patriots, states had no desire to raise questions about the legitimacy of their property titles.

PEACE TREATY PROVISIONS

The refusal of state and local governments to comply with Articles Four and Five gave Britain an excuse to maintain military posts on the Great Lakes long after its troops were supposed to have withdrawn. Furthermore, Congress's inability to convince states to implement the treaty disclosed its lack of power, even in an area—foreign affairs—in which it had authority under the Articles of Confederation. Concerned nationalists argued publicly that enforcement of the treaty, however unpopular, was a crucial test of the republic's credibility in foreign affairs. "Will foreign nations be willing to undertake anything with us or for us," asked Alexander Hamilton, "when they find that the nature of our governments will allow no dependence to be placed on our engagements?"

Order and Disorder in the West

Congressmen also confronted knotty problems when they considered the status of land beyond the Appalachians. Although British and American diplomats did not discuss tribal claims, the United States assumed that the Treaty of Paris cleared its title to all land east of the Mississippi except the area still held by Spain. Still, recognizing that land cessions should be obtained from the most powerful tribes, Congress initiated negotiations with both northern and southern Indians (see Map 7.2).

At Fort Stanwix, New York, in 1784, American diplomats negotiated a treaty with chiefs who said they
represented the Iroquois; and at Hopewell, South Carolina, in late 1785 and early 1786, they did the same with emissaries from the Choctaw, Chickasaw, and Cherokee nations. In 1786 the Iroquois formally repudiated the Fort Stanwix treaty, denying that the men who attended the negotiations had been authorized to speak for the Six Nations. The confederacy threatened new attacks on frontier settlements, but everyone knew the threat was empty; the flawed treaty stood by default. At intervals until the end of the decade New York State purchased large tracts of land from individual Iroquois nations. By 1790 the once-dominant confederacy was confined to a few scattered reservations. In the South too the United States took the treaties as confirmation of its sovereignty, authorizing settlers to move onto the territories in question. European Americans poured over the southern Appalachians, provoking the Creeks—who had not agreed to the Hopewell treaties—to defend their territory by declaring war. Only in 1790 did they come to terms with the United States.

INDIAN RELATIONS

Western nations such as the Shawnees, Chippewas, Ottawas, and Potawatomis had already started to reject Iroquois hegemony as early as the 1750s (see page 118). After the collapse of Iroquois power, they formed their own confederacy and demanded direct negotiations with the United States. They intended to present a united front so as to avoid the piecemeal surrender of land by individual bands and villages. But they faced a difficult task. In the postwar world, Indian nations could no longer pursue the diplomatic strategy that had worked so well for so long: playing off European and American powers against one another. France was gone; Spanish territory lay far to the west and south; and British power was confined to Canada, north of the Great Lakes. Only the United States remained.

Map 7.2   Cession of Tribal Lands to the United States, 1775–1790

The land claims of the United States meant little as long as Indian nations still controlled vast territories within the new country's formal boundaries. A series of treaties in the 1780s and 1790s opened some lands to white settlement. (Source: From Lester J. Cappon et al., eds., *Atlas of Early American History: The Revolutionary Era, 1760–1790.* Copyright © 1976 by Princeton University Press. Reprinted by permission of Princeton University Press.)

At first the national government ignored the western confederacy. Shortly after state land cessions were completed, Congress began to organize the Northwest Territory, bounded by the Mississippi River, the Great Lakes, and the Ohio River (see Map 7.1). Ordinances passed in 1784, 1785, and 1787 outlined the process through which the land could be sold to settlers and formal governments could be organized.

ORDINANCES OF 1784 AND 1785

■ In 1784 Thomas Jefferson proposed a scheme for organizing the new nation's western lands. His plan would have divided the region on a grid pattern, yielding fourteen new states (with names such as "Metropotamia" and "Pelisipia") composed of 10-mile-square "hundreds." After a year of debate, Jefferson's plan was replaced by the one adopted in the Land Ordinance of 1785, which is described in the text. (Clements Library, University of Michigan)

To ensure orderly development, Congress in 1785 directed that the land be surveyed into townships 6 miles square, each divided into thirty-six sections of 640 acres (1 square mile). Revenue from the sale of the sixteenth section of each township was to be reserved for the support of public schools—the first instance of federal aid to education in American history. One dollar was the minimum price per acre; the minimum sale was one section. Thus Congress showed little concern for the small farmer: the resulting minimum outlay, $640, lay beyond the reach of ordinary Americans, except those veterans who received part of their army pay in land warrants. Proceeds from western land sales constituted the first independent revenues available to the national government.

The most important of the three land policies—the Northwest Ordinance of 1787—contained a bill of rights guaranteeing settlers freedom of religion and the right

NORTHWEST ORDINANCE

to a jury trial, forbidding cruel and unusual punishments, and nominally prohibiting slavery. Eventually, that prohibition became an important symbol for antislavery northerners, but at the time it had little effect. Some residents of the territory already held slaves, and Congress did not intend to deprive them of their property. Moreover, the ordinance also contained a provision allowing slaveowners to "lawfully reclaim" runaway bondspeople who took refuge in the territory—the first national fugitive slave law. The ordinance prevented slavery from taking deep root by discouraging slaveholders from moving into the territory with their human chattel, but not until 1848 was enslavement abolished throughout the region, now known as the Old Northwest. And by omission Congress implied that slavery would be legal in the territories south of the Ohio River.

■ The two chief antagonists at the Battle of Fallen Timbers and negotiators of the Treaty of Greenville (1795). On the left, Little Turtle, the leader of the Miami Confederacy; on the right, General Anthony Wayne. Little Turtle, in a copy of a portrait painted two years later, appears to be wearing a miniature of Wayne on a bear-claw necklace. (Left: Courtesy, Chicago Historical Society. Right: Independence National Historic Park)

The ordinance of 1787 also specified the process by which residents of the territory could organize state governments and seek admission to the Union "on an equal footing with the original States." Early in the nation's history, therefore, Congress laid down a policy of admitting new states on the same basis as the old and assuring residents of the territories the same rights held by citizens of the original states. Having suffered under the rule of a colonial power, congressmen understood the importance of preparing the new nation's first "colony" for eventual self-government. Nineteenth- and twentieth-century Americans were to be less generous in their attitudes toward residents of later territories, many of whom were non-European or non-Protestant. But the nation never fully lost sight of the egalitarian principles of the Northwest Ordinance.

In a sense, though, in 1787 the ordinance was purely theoretical. Miamis, Shawnees, and Delawares in the region refused to acknowledge American sovereignty. They opposed settlement violently, attacking unwary pioneers who ventured too far north of the Ohio River. In 1788 the Ohio Company, to which Congress had sold a large tract of land at reduced rates, established the town of Marietta at the juncture of the Ohio and Muskingum Rivers. But Indians prevented the company from extending settlement very far into the interior. After General Arthur St. Clair, the Northwest Territory's first governor, failed to negotiate a meaningful treaty with the Indians in early 1789, the United States could not avoid clashing with the western confederacy, composed of eight nations and led by the Miamis.

Little Turtle, the able war chief of the Miami Confederacy, defeated first General Josiah Harmar (1790) and then St. Clair himself (1791) in major battles near the present border between Indiana and Ohio. More than six hundred of St. Clair's men died, and scores more were wounded, in the United States's worst defeat in the entire history of the American frontier. In 1793 the Miami Confederacy declared that peace could

WAR IN THE OLD NORTHWEST

be achieved only if the United States recognized the Ohio River as its northwestern boundary. But the national government refused to relinquish its claims in the region. A new army under the command of General Anthony Wayne, a Revolutionary War hero, attacked and defeated the confederacy in August 1794 at the Battle of Fallen Timbers (near present-day Toledo, Ohio; see Map 7.2). Peace negotiations began after the victory.

By the summer of 1795, Wayne reached agreement with the Miami Confederacy. The Treaty of Greenville gave each side a portion of what it wanted. The United States gained the right to settle much of what was to become Ohio, the indigenous peoples retaining only the northwest corner of the region. Indians, though, received the acknowledgment they had long sought: American recognition of their rights to the soil. At Greenville, the United States formally accepted the principle of Indian sovereignty, by virtue of residence, over all lands the native peoples had not ceded. Never again would the United States government claim that it had acquired Indian territory solely through negotiation with a European or North American country.

The problems the United States encountered in ensuring safe settlement of the Northwest Territory revealed the basic weakness of the Confederation government. Not until after the Articles of Confederation were replaced with a new constitution could the United States muster sufficient force to implement the Northwest Ordinance. Thus, although the ordinance is often viewed as one of the few lasting accomplishments of the Confederation Congress, it must be seen within a context of political impotence.

From Crisis to the Constitution

*a*mericans involved in finance, overseas trade, and foreign affairs became acutely aware of the inadequacies of the Articles of Confederation. In those areas the Articles had obvious deficiencies: Congress could not levy taxes, nor could it impose its will on the states to establish a uniform commercial policy or to ensure the enforcement of treaties. Partly as a result, the American economy slid into a depression less than a year after war's end. Exporters of staple crops (especially tobacco and rice) and importers of manufactured goods suffered from the postwar restrictions European powers imposed on American commerce. Although recovery began by 1786, the war's effects proved impossible to erase, particularly in the Lower South. Some estimates suggest that between 1775 and 1790 America's per capita gross national product declined by nearly 50 percent.

The war, indeed, wrought permanent change in the American economy. The near-total cessation of foreign commerce in nonmilitary items during the war stimulated domestic manufacturing. Consequently, despite the influx of European goods after 1783, the postwar period witnessed the stirrings of American industrial development. For example, the first American textile mill began production in Pawtucket, Rhode Island, in 1793. Because of continuing population growth, the domestic market assumed greater relative importance in the overall economy. Moreover, foreign trade patterns shifted from Europe and toward the West Indies, continuing a trend that had begun before the war. Foodstuffs shipped to the French and Dutch Caribbean islands became America's largest single export, replacing tobacco (and thus accelerating the Chesapeake's conversion from tobacco to grain production). South Carolina resumed importing slaves on a large scale, as planters sought to replace workers lost to wartime disruptions. Yet without British subsidies American indigo could not compete with that produced in the Caribbean, and even rice planters struggled to find new markets.

ECONOMIC CHANGE AND COMMERCIAL REFORM

Recognizing the Confederation Congress's inability to deal with commercial matters, representatives of Virginia and Maryland met at Mt. Vernon (George Washington's plantation) in March 1785 to negotiate an agreement about trade on the Potomac River, which divided the two states for much of its length. The successful meeting led to an invitation to other states to discuss trade policy generally at a convention in Annapolis, Maryland. Although nine states named representatives to the meeting in September 1786, only five delegations attended. Those present realized that so few people could not have any significant impact on the political system. They issued a call for another convention, to be held in Philadelphia nine months later, "to devise such further provisions as shall . . . appear necessary to render the constitution of the federal government adequate to the exigencies of the Union."

The other states did not respond immediately. But then an armed rebellion in Massachusetts did what a polite invitation could not: convince doubters that reform was needed. Farmers from the western part of the state, many of them veterans, violently opposed the high taxes that had been levied by the east-

SHAYS'S REBELLION

ern-dominated legislature to pay off war debts. Courts had also begun to foreclose on the lands of tax defaulters. Daniel Shays, a former officer in the Continental Army, assumed the nominal leadership of the disgruntled western farmers. On January 25, 1787, he led about fifteen hundred men in an assault on the federal armory at Springfield, attempting to capture the military stores housed there. The militiamen mustered to defend the armory fired on their former comrades in arms, who then withdrew after suffering twenty-four casualties.

The westerners did not confine to the battlefield their challenge to the legitimacy of a government controlled by eastern merchants. Terming Massachusetts "tyranni-

cal," they insisted that "whenever any encroachments are made either upon the liberties or properties of the people, if redress cannot be had without, it is virtue in them to disturb government." They thereby explicitly linked their rebellion to the earlier independence struggle.

Such explosive assertions convinced many political leaders that the nation's problems extended far beyond trade policy. To some, the rebellion confirmed the need for a much stronger federal government. After most of the states had already appointed delegates, the Confederation Congress belatedly endorsed the proposed convention, "for the sole and express purpose

CONSTITUTIONAL
CONVENTION

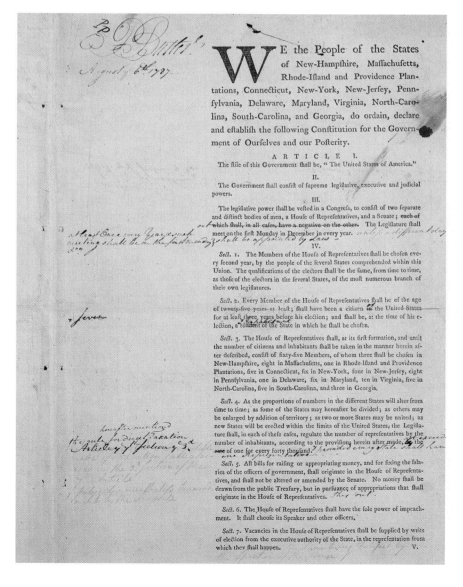

■ In August 1787 a first draft of the Constitution was secretly printed in Philadelphia for the use of convention members. Wide margins left room for additions and amendments, such as those made on this copy by the South Carolina delegate Pierce Butler. Note that in this early version the preamble does not yet read "We the people of the United States," but instead begins by listing the individual states. (The Gilder Lehrman Collection, © Collection of the New York Historical Society)

of revising the Articles of Confederation." In mid-May 1787, fifty-five men, representing all the states but Rhode Island, assembled in Philadelphia to begin their deliberations.

The vast majority of delegates to the Constitutional Convention were men of property and substance. They all favored reform; otherwise, they would not have come to Philadelphia. Most wanted to invigorate the national government and to give it new authority over taxation and foreign commerce. Many had been members of state legislatures, and some had helped to draft state constitutions. All were influenced in their Philadelphia deliberations by their understanding of the success or failure of those constitutions' provisions. Their ranks included merchants, planters, physicians, generals, governors, and especially lawyers—twenty-three had studied the law. Most had been born in America, and many came from families that had arrived in the seventeenth century. Most were Congregationalists, Presbyterians, or Angli-

■ James Madison (1751–1836), the youthful scholar and skilled politician who earned the title "Father of the Constitution." (Library of Congress)

cans. In an era when only a tiny proportion of the population had any advanced education, more than half of the delegates had attended college. A few had been educated in Britain, but most had graduated from American institutions: Princeton, with ten, counted the most alumni participants. The youngest delegate was twenty-six, the oldest—Benjamin Franklin—eighty-one. Like George Washington, whom they elected their presiding officer, most were in their vigorous middle years. A dozen men did the bulk of the convention's work. Of these, James Madison of Virginia was by far the most important; he deserves the title "Father of the Constitution."

The frail, shy James Madison was thirty-six years old in 1787. A Princeton graduate raised in western Virginia,

MADISON AND THE CONSTITUTION

he served on the local Committee of Safety and was elected successively to the provincial convention, the state's lower and upper houses, and the Continental Congress (1780–1783). Although Madison returned to Virginia to serve in the state legislature in 1784, he remained in touch with national politics, partly through his continuing correspondence with his close friend Thomas Jefferson. A promoter of the Annapolis Convention, he strongly supported its call for further reform.

Madison stood out among the delegates for his systematic preparation for the Philadelphia meeting. Through Jefferson in Paris he bought more than two hundred books on history and government, carefully analyzing their accounts of past confederacies and republics. A month before the Constitutional Convention began, he summed up the results of his research in a lengthy paper entitled "Vices of the Political System of the United States." After listing the flaws he perceived in the current structure of the government (among them "encroachments by the states on the federal authority" and lack of unity "in matters where common interest requires it"), Madison revealed the conclusion that would guide his actions over the next few months. What the government most needed, he declared, was "such a modification of the sovereignty as will render it sufficiently neutral between the different interests and factions, to controul one part of the society from invading the rights of another, and at the same time sufficiently controuled itself, from setting up an interest adverse to that of the whole Society."

Thus Madison set forth the principle of checks and balances. The government, he believed, had to be constructed in such a way that it could not become tyrannical or fall wholly under the influence of a particular faction. He regarded the large size of a potential national republic as an advantage in that respect. Rejecting the common assertion that republics had to be small to survive, Madison asserted that a large, diverse republic should be preferred. Because the nation would include many different factions, no one of them would be able to control the government. Political stability would result from compromises among the contending parties.

The so-called Virginia Plan, introduced on May 29 by Edmund Randolph, embodied Madison's conception

VIRGINIA AND NEW JERSEY PLANS of national government. The plan provided for a two-house legislature, the lower house elected directly by the people and the upper house selected by the lower; representation in both houses proportional to property or population; an executive elected by Congress; a national judiciary; and congressional veto over state laws. The Virginia Plan gave Congress the broad power to legislate "in all cases to which the separate states are incompetent." Had it been adopted intact, it would have created a government in which national authority reigned unchallenged and state power was greatly diminished. Proportional representation in both houses (however reckoned) would also have given large states a dominant voice in the national government.

The convention included many delegates who recognized the need for change but believed the Virginia Plan went too far in the direction of national consolidation. After two weeks of debate on Randolph's proposal, disaffected delegates—particularly those from small states—united under the leadership of William Paterson of New Jersey. On June 15 Paterson presented an alternative scheme, the New Jersey Plan, calling for strengthening the Articles rather than completely overhauling the government. Paterson proposed retaining a unicameral congress in which each state had an equal vote, but giving Congress new powers of taxation and trade regulation. Earlier Paterson had made his position clear in debate. Asserting that the Articles were "the proper basis of all the proceedings of the convention," he contended that the delegates' proper task was "to mark the orbits of the states with due precision and provide for the use of coercion" by the national government. Although the convention initially rejected Paterson's position, he and his allies won a number of victories in the months that followed.

The delegates began their work by discussing the structure and functions of Congress. They readily agreed that the new national government should have a two-

DEBATES OVER CONGRESS house (bicameral) legislature. In addition, they concurred, in accordance with Americans' long-standing opposition to virtual representation (see pages 124–125), that "the people" (however that term was defined) should be directly represented in at least one house of Congress. But they discovered that they differed widely in their answers to three key questions: Should representation in both houses of Congress be proportional to population? How was representation in either or both houses to be apportioned among the states? And, finally, how were the members of the two houses to be elected?

The last issue proved the easiest to resolve. To quote John Dickinson, the delegates thought it "essential" that members of the lower branch of Congress be elected directly by the people and "expedient" that members of the upper house be chosen by state legislatures. Since legislatures had selected delegates to the Confederation Congress, they would expect a similar privilege in the new government. If the convention had not agreed to allow state legislatures to elect senators, the Constitution would have run into significant opposition among state political leaders. The plan also had the virtue of placing the election of one house of Congress one step removed from the "lesser sort," whose judgment the wealthy convention delegates did not wholly trust.

The possibility of representation proportional to population in the Senate caused considerably greater disagreement. The delegates accepted without much debate the principle of proportional representation in the House of Representatives. But small states, through their spokesman Luther Martin of Maryland, argued for equal representation in the Senate. Such a scheme, they rightly supposed, would give them relatively more power at the national level. Large states, on the other hand, supported a proportional plan, for they would then be allotted more votes in the upper house. For weeks the convention deadlocked, neither side able to obtain a majority. A committee appointed to work out a compromise recommended equal representation in the Senate, coupled with a proviso that all appropriation bills originate in the lower house. But not until the convention accepted a suggestion that a state's two senators vote as individuals rather than as a unit was a breakdown averted.

The remaining critical question divided the nation along sectional lines rather than by size of state: how was

SLAVERY AND THE CONSTITUTION representation in the lower house to be apportioned among states? Delegates concurred that a census should be conducted every ten years to determine the nation's actual population, and they agreed that Indians who paid no taxes should be excluded for purposes of representation. Delegates from states with large numbers of slaves wanted African and European inhabitants to be counted equally; delegates from states with few slaves wanted only free people counted. Slavery thus became inextricably linked to the foundation of the new government. Delegates resolved the dispute by using a formula developed by the Confederation Congress in 1783 to allocate financial assessments among states: three-fifths of slaves would be included in population totals. (The formula reflected delegates' judgment that slaves were less efficient producers of wealth than free people, not that they were 60 percent human and 40 percent property.) The three-fifths compromise on representation won unanimous approval. Only two delegates, Gouverneur Morris of New York and George Mason of Virginia, later spoke out against the institution of slavery.

Although the words *slave* and *slavery* do not appear in the Constitution (the framers used euphemisms such as "other persons"), the document contained both direct and indirect protections for slavery. The three-fifths clause, for example, assured white southern male voters not only congressional representation out of proportion to their numbers but also a disproportionate influence on the selection of the president, since the number of each state's votes in the electoral college (see below) was determined by the size of its congressional delegation. In return for southerners' agreement that commercial regulations could be adopted by a simple majority vote in Congress (rather than two-thirds), New Englanders agreed that Congress could not end the importation of slaves for at least twenty years. Further, the fugitive slave clause required all states to return runaways to their masters. By guaranteeing that the national government would aid any states threatened with "domestic violence," the Constitution promised aid in putting down future slave revolts, as well as incidents like Shays's Rebellion.

Once delegates agreed on the knotty, conjoined problems of slavery and representation, they readily achieved consensus on the other issues confronting them. All concurred that the national government needed the authority to tax and to regulate commerce. But instead of giving Congress the nearly unlimited scope proposed in the Virginia Plan, delegates enumerated congressional powers and then provided for flexibility by granting it all authority "necessary and proper" to carry out those

CONGRESSIONAL AND PRESIDENTIAL POWERS

powers. Discarding the congressional veto contained in the Virginia Plan, the convention implied but did not explicitly authorize a national judicial veto of state laws. The Constitution plus national laws and treaties would constitute "the supreme law of the land; and the judges in every state shall be bound thereby," Article VI declared ambiguously. As another means of circumscribing state powers, delegates drafted a long list of actions forbidden to states. And—contrary to many state constitutions—they provided that religious tests could never be required of U.S. officeholders.

The convention placed primary responsibility for conducting foreign affairs in the hands of the president, who was also designated commander-in-chief of the armed forces. That decision raised the question, left unspecified in the Constitution's text, of whether the president (or Congress, for that matter) acquired special powers in times of war. With the consent of the Senate, the president could appoint judges and other federal officers. To select the president, delegates established an elaborate mechanism, the electoral college, whose members would be chosen in each state by legislatures or qualified voters. This system, they hoped, would ensure that the executive would be independent of the national legislature—and of the people. They also agreed that the chief executive should serve a four-year term but be eligible for reelection.

The final document still showed signs of its origins in the Virginia Plan, but compromises created a system of government less powerful at the national level than Madison and Randolph had envisioned. The key to the Constitution was the distribution of political authority— that is, separation of powers among executive, legislative, and judicial branches of the national government, and division of powers between states and nation. Two-thirds of Congress and three-fourths of the states, for example, had to concur on amendments. The branches balanced one another, their powers deliberately entwined to prevent each from acting independently. The president could veto congressional legislation, but that veto could be overridden by two-thirds majorities in both houses, and his treaties and major appointments required the Senate's consent. Congress could impeach the president and federal judges, but courts appeared to have the final say on interpreting the Constitution. These checks and balances would make it difficult for the government to become tyrannical. At the same time, though, the elaborate system would sometimes prevent the government from acting quickly and decisively. Furthermore, the Constitution drew such a vague line between state and national powers that the United States fought a civil war in the next century over that very issue.

The convention held its last session on September 17, 1787. Of the forty-two delegates present (others had returned home weeks earlier), only three refused to sign the Constitution, two of them in part because of the lack of a bill of rights. Benjamin Franklin had written a speech calling for unity; because his weak voice could not be heard, another delegate read it for him. "I confess that there are several parts of this constitution which I do not at present approve," Franklin admitted. Yet he urged its acceptance "because I expect no better, and because I am not sure, that it is not the best." Only then was the Constitution made public. The convention's proceedings had been entirely secret—and remained so until the delegates' private notes were published in the nineteenth century. (See the Appendix for the full text of the Constitution.)

Opposition and Ratification

Later the same month, the Confederation Congress submitted the Constitution to the states but did not formally recommend approval. The ratification clause provided for the new system to take effect once it was approved by special conventions in at least nine states, with delegates being elected by qualified voters. Thus the national Constitution, unlike the Articles of Confederation, would rest directly on popular authority (and the presumably hostile state legislatures would be circumvented).

As states began to elect delegates to the special conventions, discussion of the proposed government grew more heated. Newspaper essays and pamphlets vigorously defended or attacked the Philadelphia convention's decisions. The extent of the debate was unprecedented. Every newspaper in the country printed the full text of the Constitution, and most supported its adoption. It quickly became apparent, though, that disputes within the Constitutional Convention had been mild compared to divisions of opinion within the populace as a whole. Although most citizens concurred that the national government should have more power over taxation and foreign commerce, some believed that the proposed government held the potential for tyranny. As happened in Carlisle, Pennsylvania, the vigorous debate between the two sides frequently spilled out into the streets.

Those supporting the proposed Constitution called themselves Federalists. They built on the notions of

■ *The Federal Almanack* for 1789 trumpeted the virtues of the new Constitution. Not all Americans were so certain that the national government, here symbolized as an edifice supported by thirteen pillars, was as "solid, strong as time" as the printer proclaimed.   (American Antiquarian Society)

FEDERALISTS AND ANTIFEDERALISTS classical republicanism, holding forth a vision of a virtuous, collectivist, self-sacrificing republic vigorously led by a manly aristocracy of talent. Claiming that the nation did not need to fear centralized authority when good men drawn from the elite were in charge, they argued that the carefully structured government would preclude the possibility of tyranny. A republic could be large, they declared, if the government's design prevented any one group from controlling it. The separation of powers among legislative, executive, and judicial branches, and the division of powers between states and nation, would accomplish that goal. Thus people did not need to be protected from the powers of the new government in a formal way. Instead, their liberties would be guarded by "distinguished worthies"—men of the "better sort" whose only goal (said George Washington) was "to merit the approbation of good and virtuous men."

The Federalists termed those who opposed the Constitution Antifederalists, thus casting them with a negative tag. Antifederalists, while recognizing the need for a national source of revenue, feared a too-powerful central government. They saw the states as the chief protectors of individual rights; consequently, weakening the states could bring the onset of arbitrary power. Antifederalist arguments against the Constitution often consisted of lists of potential abuses of government authority.

Heirs of the Real Whig ideology of the late 1760s and early 1770s, Antifederalists stressed the need for constant popular vigilance to avert oppression. Indeed, some of the Antifederalists had originally promulgated those ideas—Samuel Adams, Patrick Henry, and Richard Henry Lee led the opposition to the Constitution. Such older Americans, whose political opinions had been shaped prior to the centralizing, nationalistic Revolution, peopled the Antifederalist ranks. Joining them were small farmers preoccupied with guarding their property against excessive taxation, backcountry Baptists and Presbyterians, and ambitious, upwardly mobile men who would benefit from an economic and political system less tightly controlled than that the Constitution envisioned. Federalists denigrated such men as disorderly, licentious, and even "unmanly" and "boyish" because they would not follow the elites' lead in supporting the Constitution.

As public debate continued, Antifederalists focused on the Constitution's lack of a bill of rights. Even if the new system weakened the states, critics

BILL OF RIGHTS   believed, people could still be protected from tyranny by specific guarantees of rights. The Constitution did contain some prohibitions on congressional power. For example, the writ of habeas corpus, which prevented arbitrary imprisonment, could not be suspended except in dire emergencies. But Antifederalists found such constitutional provisions to be few and inadequate. Nor were they reassured by Federalist assertions that the new government could not violate

people's rights because it had only limited powers. Opponents wanted the national governing document to incorporate a bill of rights, as had most state constitutions.

Letters of a Federal Farmer, perhaps the most widely read Antifederalist pamphlet, listed the rights that should be protected: freedom of the press and religion, trial by jury, and guarantees against unreasonable searches. From Paris, Thomas Jefferson added his voice to the chorus. Replying to Madison's letter conveying a copy of the Constitution, Jefferson declared, "I like much the general idea" but not "the omission of a bill of rights. . . . A bill of rights is what the people are entitled to against every government on earth, general or particular, and what no just government should refuse, or rest on inference."

As state conventions considered ratification, the lack of a bill of rights loomed ever larger as a flaw in the

RATIFICATION   proposed government. Four of the first five states to ratify did so unanimously, but serious disagreements then surfaced. Massachusetts, in which Antifederalist forces had been bolstered by a backlash against the state government's heavy-handed treatment of the Shays rebels, ratified by a majority of only 19 votes out of 355 cast. In June 1788, when New Hampshire ratified, the requirement of nine states was satisfied. But New York and Virginia had not yet voted, and everyone realized the new Constitution could not succeed unless those key states accepted it.

Despite a valiant effort by the Antifederalist Patrick Henry, pro-Constitution forces won by 10 votes in the Virginia convention. In New York, James Madison, John Jay, and Alexander Hamilton campaigned for ratification by publishing *The Federalist,* a political tract that explained the theory behind the Constitution and masterfully answered its critics. Their reasoned arguments, coupled with Federalists' promise to add a bill of rights to the Constitution, helped win the battle. On July 26, 1788, New York ratified the Constitution by the slim margin of 3 votes. Although the last states—North Carolina and Rhode Island—did not join the Union until November 1789 and May 1790, respectively, the new government was a reality.

Americans in many cities celebrated ratification (somewhat prematurely) with a series of parades on July 4, 1788. The carefully planned proces-

CELEBRATING
RATIFICATION   sions dramatized the history and symbolized the unity of the new nation, seeking to counteract memories of the dissent that had so recently engulfed such towns as Carlisle, Pennsylvania. Like pre-Revolution protest

■ The Philadelphia State House (the building now known as Independence Hall, but without its familiar tower), on the left; and, to its right, Congress Hall, where Congress met when Philadelphia served as the U.S. capital. Portrayed in front of the state house in this 1792 watercolor is the 33-foot-long vessel *Union,* an elaborately constructed ship carried through the city streets in the grand ratification parade of July 4, 1788.   (Philadelphia Museum of Art, Lent by the Dietrich American Foundation)

meetings, the parades served as political lessons for literate and illiterate Americans alike. The processions aimed to educate men and women about the significance of the new Constitution and to instruct them about political leaders' hopes for industry and frugality on the part of a virtuous American public.

Symbols expressing those goals filled the Philadelphia parade, planned by the artist Charles Willson Peale. About five thousand people participated in the procession, which featured floats portraying such themes as "The Grand Federal Edifice" and stretched for a mile and a half. Marchers representing the first pioneers and Revolutionary War troops paraded with groups of farmers and artisans dramatizing their work. More than forty groups of tradesmen, including barbers, hatters, printers, cloth manufacturers, and clockmakers, sponsored floats. Lawyers, doctors, clergymen of all denominations, and

congressmen followed the artisans. A final group of marchers symbolized the nation's future: students from the University of Pennsylvania and other city schools bore a flag labeled "The Rising Generation."

Summary

During the 1770s and 1780s the nation took shape as a political union. It began to develop an economy independent of the British Empire and attempted to chart its own course in the world in order to protect the national interest, defend the country's borders, and promote beneficial trade. Some Americans prescribed rules for the cultural and intellectual life they thought appropriate for a republic, outlining artistic and educational goals for a properly virtuous people. An integral part of the formation of the Union was the systematic formulation of American racist thought. Emphasizing race (rather than status as slave or free) as a determinant of African Americans' standing in the nation, and defining women as nonpolitical, allowed men who now termed themselves "white" to define republicanism to exclude all people but themselves and to ensure that they would dominate the country for the foreseeable future.

The experience of fighting a war and of struggling for survival as an independent nation altered the political context of American life in the 1780s. At the outset of the war, most Americans believed that "that government which governs best governs least," but by the late 1780s many had changed their minds. They were the drafters and supporters of the Constitution, who concluded from the republic's vicissitudes under the Articles of Confederation that a more powerful central government was needed. During ratification debates they contended that their proposals were just as "republican" in conception (if not more so) as the Articles.

Both sides concurred in a general adherence to republican principles, but they emphasized different views of republicanism. Federalists advanced a position based on the principles of classical republicanism, stressing the community over the individual. Antifederalists, fearing that elected leaders would not subordinate personal gain to the good of the whole, wanted a weak central government, formal protection of individual rights, and a loosely regulated economy. The Federalists won their point when the Constitution was adopted, however narrowly. The process of consolidating the states into a national whole was thereby formalized. The 1790s, the first decade of government under the Constitution, would witness hesitant steps toward the creation of a true nation, the United States of America.

LEGACY FOR A PEOPLE AND A NATION
Women's Education

Women today constitute a majority of the students enrolled in U.S. colleges and universities. Because women were denied all access to collegiate education in this country until the middle of the nineteenth century, that is a remarkable development. Moreover, it differentiates the United States from other nations, where the majority of university students are male. The origins of women's higher education lie deep, in the republican ideology of the 1770s and 1780s.

Once the United States had established republican forms of government at both state and national levels, its citizens began to worry about sustaining those governments—thought to be fragile and easily disrupted—for the decades and centuries to come. The future, everyone knew, lay in the hands of the nation's children, especially its sons. And theorists concluded that those sons could successfully perpetuate the republic only if they learned the lessons of patriotism from their mothers. Male and female reformers therefore began to contend that women in the United States should be better educated than those who lived under other forms of government. If American women were ignorant of the nation's history or principles of government, or if they did not know enough basic reading or arithmetic to assist their husbands in running farms or businesses, the republic was doomed to collapse. Mary Wollstonecraft made a similar argument on behalf of women's education in England, but without the rationale of republicanism, her words had little impact.

Some American reformers founded private academies (roughly equivalent to modern high schools) to teach young women from leading families such subjects as history, geography, mathematics, and languages. Some of the women who attended those academies later started educational establishments of their own—including Mary Lyon, who in 1837 founded Mt. Holyoke College in western Massachusetts, the first institution of higher education for women in the

United States. A few years later, some colleges for men (such as Oberlin, in Ohio) and state universities (for example, Michigan) admitted women as students, and a number of women's colleges were established. Not until the second half of the twentieth century, however, did American women gain truly equal access to higher education. In the 1970s such Ivy League universities as Yale and Princeton finally opened their doors to women students, and others (such as Cornell) that had restricted women's enrollment through quotas removed all constraints.

Along with the existence of the nation itself, increased educational opportunity for women is therefore one of the most important legacies of the revolutionary era for the American people.

The **history companion** *powered by Eduspace®*

Your primary source for interactive quizzes, exercises, and more to help you learn efficiently.
http://history.college.hmco.com/students

THE EARLY REPUBLIC: CONFLICTS AT HOME AND ABROAD 1789–1800

*I*n the last months of 1798, the wealthy Philadelphia matron Deborah Norris Logan became the target of widespread public criticism. Her husband, the Jefferson supporter Dr. George Logan, had undertaken a personal peace mission to France, fearing the looming prospect of war between the United States and its former ally. In his absence his wife loyally defended her husband's actions, and she in turn had to endure a campaign unlike any an American woman had ever previously experienced. That such an episode could occur at all suggested simultaneously the political symbolism now embodied by women, the growing division between the factions known as Federalists and Democratic-Republicans, and the significance of foreign affairs in the early republic.

First to attack was "Peter Porcupine," the Federalist newspaper editor William Cobbett, who observed with sly sexual innuendo in his *Porcupine's Gazette* in July that "it is said that JEFFERSON went to his friend Doctor Logan's farm and spent three days there, soon after the Doctor's departure for France. *Query: What did he do there? Was it to arrange the Doctor's valuable manuscripts?*" Later Cobbett suggested that both George and Deborah Logan should be placed in a pillory and publicly shamed for their actions—him, presumably, for treason (for that was the crime of which Federalists accused him) and her, Cobbett implied, for adultery. Understanding the symbolic significance of women's virtuous conduct in the fragile young republic, Democratic-Republican newspapers leaped to Deborah's defense. They attacked the vulgarity of the suggestions about her and Vice President Jefferson and insisted that not even a corrupt Londoner could have written "a greater libel upon public virtue or national morals."

Deborah Logan remained resolute in the face of such publicity. Although at first she secluded herself at her country estate, on Jefferson's advice she returned

◀ George and Deborah Logan, whose activities caused so much political controversy in 1798. Their elegant house, Stenton, where Jefferson visited her in her husband's absence, is still preserved as a historic site. (Left: Historical Society of Pennsylvania. Collection Atwater Kent Museum of Philadelphia. Right: Courtesy of the National Society of Colonial Dames of America in the Commonwealth of Pennsylvania at Stenton, Philadelphia)

CHRONOLOGY

1789 • Washington inaugurated as first president
• Judiciary Act of 1789 organizes federal court system
• French Revolution begins

1790 • Hamilton's *Report on Public Credit* proposes assumption of state debts

1791 • First ten amendments (Bill of Rights) ratified
• First national bank chartered

1793 • France declares war on Britain, Spain, and the Netherlands
• Washington's neutrality proclamation keeps the United States out of war
• Democratic-Republican societies founded, the first grassroots political organizations

1794 • Whiskey Rebellion in western Pennsylvania protests taxation

1795 • Jay Treaty with England
• Pinckney's Treaty with Spain

1796 • First contested presidential election: Adams elected president, Jefferson vice president

1798 • XYZ affair arouses American opinion against France
• Sedition Act penalizes dissent
• Virginia and Kentucky Resolutions protest suppression of dissent

1798–99 • Quasi-War with France

1800 • Franco-American Convention ends Quasi-War
• Gabriel's Rebellion threatens Virginia slaveowners

to Philadelphia to prove to the world George's "innocence and honor" and to show that she was "not afraid nor ashamed to meet the public eye." As reports emerged that her husband had been cordially received by French leaders, and that he had had some success in quelling hostilities, she reveled in the praise subsequently showered on him, later recalling that "almost every day, wishes for his safety and speedy return greeted my ears." George Logan was indeed enthusiastically welcomed home, at least by Jeffersonian partisans. Congress, controlled by Federalists, was less impressed. In January 1799 it adopted the so-called Logan Act, still in effect, which forbids private citizens from undertaking diplomatic missions.

The controversy caused by the Logans' actions was but one of many such battles in the 1790s. The fight over ratifying the Constitution turned out to presage an even wider division over the major political, economic, and diplomatic questions confronting the young republic: the extent to which authority (especially fiscal authority) should be centralized in the national government; the relationship of national power and states' rights; the formulation of foreign policy in an era of continual warfare in Europe; and the limits of dissent. Americans did not anticipate the acrimonious disagreements that rocked the 1790s. Believing that the Constitution would resolve the problems that had arisen under the Confederation, they mistakenly expected the new government to rule largely by consensus. And no one predicted the difficulties that would develop as the United States attempted to deal with Indian nations now wholly encompassed within its borders.

Most important of all, perhaps, Americans could not understand or fully accept the division of the nation's political leaders into two factions (not yet political parties), believing that only monarchies should experience such factional disputes. In republics, they believed, the rise of factions signified decay and corruption. As the decade closed, Americans still had not come to terms with the implications of partisan politics. ■

Building a Workable Government

*a*t first consensus appeared possible, as the nationalistic spirit expressed in the processions celebrating ratification of the Constitution carried over to the first session of Congress. Only a few Antifederalists ran for office in the congressional elections held late in 1788, and even fewer were elected. Thus the First Congress consisted chiefly of men who supported a strong national government. The drafters of the Constitution had deliberately left many key issues undecided, so the nationalists' domination of Congress meant that their views on those points quickly prevailed.

Congress faced four immediate tasks when it convened in April 1789: raising revenue to support the new government, responding to states' calls for a bill of rights, setting up executive departments, and organizing the federal judiciary. The last task was especially important. The Constitution established a Supreme Court but left it to Congress to decide whether to have other federal courts as well.

FIRST CONGRESS

James Madison, who had been elected to the House of Representatives, soon became as influential in Congress as he had been at the Constitutional Convention. A few months into the first session, he persuaded Congress to adopt the Revenue Act of 1789, imposing a 5 percent tariff on certain imports. Thus the First Congress quickly achieved what the Confederation Congress never had: an effective national tax law. The new government would have problems in its first years, but lack of revenue was not one of them.

Madison also took the lead with respect to constitutional amendments. At the convention and thereafter, he had consistently opposed additional limitations on the national government. He believed it unnecessary to guarantee people's rights explicitly when the government was one of limited powers. But Madison recognized that Congress should respond to public opinion as expressed in state ratifying conventions. Accordingly, he placed nineteen proposed amendments before the House. The states soon ratified ten, which officially became part of the Constitution on December 15, 1791 (see the Appendix for the Constitution and all amendments, including the Twenty-seventh, which was one of Madison's nineteen). Their adoption defused Antifederalist opposition and rallied support for the new government.

BILL OF RIGHTS

The First Amendment specifically prohibited Congress from passing any law restricting the right to freedom of religion, speech, press, peaceable assembly, or petition. The next two amendments arose directly from the former colonists' fear of standing armies as a threat to freedom. The Second Amendment guaranteed the right "to keep and bear arms" because of the need for a "well-regulated Militia." Thus the constitutional right to bear arms was based on the expectation that most able-bodied men would serve the nation as citizen-soldiers, and there would be little need for a standing army. The Third Amendment limited the conditions under which troops could be quartered in private homes. The next five pertained to judicial procedures. The Fourth Amendment prohibited "unreasonable searches and seizures"; the Fifth and Sixth established the rights of accused persons; the Seventh specified the conditions for jury trials in civil (as opposed to criminal) cases; and the Eighth forbade "cruel and unusual punishments." The Ninth and Tenth Amendments reserved to the people and the states other unspecified rights and powers. In short, the amendments' authors made clear that, in listing some rights, they did not mean to preclude the exercise of others.

While debating proposed amendments, Congress also considered the organization of the executive branch. It readily agreed to continue the three administrative departments established under the Articles of Confederation: War, Foreign Affairs (renamed State), and Treasury. Congress instituted two lesser posts: the attorney general—the nation's official lawyer—and the postmaster general. Controversy arose over whether the president alone could dismiss officials whom he originally had appointed with the Senate's consent. After some debate, the House and Senate agreed that he had such authority. Thus was established the important principle that the heads of executive departments are accountable solely to the president.

EXECUTIVE AND JUDICIARY

Aside from constitutional amendments, the most far-reaching piece of legislation enacted by the First Congress was the Judiciary Act of 1789, which defined the jurisdiction of the federal judiciary and established a six-member Supreme Court, thirteen district courts, and three circuit courts of appeal. Its most important provision, Section 25, allowed appeals from state courts to federal courts when cases raised certain types of constitutional issues. Section 25 thus implemented Article VI of the Constitution, which stated that federal laws and treaties were to be considered "the supreme Law of the Land." For Article VI to be enforced uniformly, the national judiciary had to be able to overturn state court decisions in cases involving the Constitution, federal laws, or treaties. Yet nowhere did the Constitution explicitly permit such action by federal courts. The Judiciary Act of 1789 presumed that the wording of Article VI implied the right of appeal from state to federal courts. In the nineteenth century, however, judges and legislators committed to states' rights challenged that interpretation.

During its first decade, the Supreme Court handled few cases of any importance, and several members resigned. (John Jay, the first chief justice, served only six years.) But in a significant 1796 decision, *Ware v. Hylton*, the Court for the first time declared a state law unconstitutional. That same year it also reviewed the constitutionality of an act of Congress, upholding its validity in the case of *Hylton v. U.S.* The most important case of the decade, *Chisholm v. Georgia* (1793), established that states could be sued in federal courts by citizens of other states. This decision, unpopular with state governments, was overturned five years later by the Eleventh Amendment to the Constitution.

Despite the constitutional provisions forbidding Congress from prohibiting the importation of slaves for twenty years, in early 1790 three groups of Quakers submitted petitions to Congress calling for an end to the foreign slave trade and favoring abolition in general. In the ensuing debates, the nation's first political leaders directly addressed the questions they had suppressed in euphemisms in the Constitution itself. Southerners vigorously asserted that not only should Congress reject the petitions, it should not even *discuss* them seriously. Had southern states thought that the federal government would consider interfering with the institution of slavery, their congressmen argued, they would never have ratified the Constitution. The legislators went on to develop a positive defense of slavery that presaged almost all the arguments offered on the subject during the next seven decades, insisting that slavery formed an integral part of the Union and that abolition would cause more problems than it solved, primarily by confronting the nation with the question of how to deal with a sizable population of freed people.

DEBATE OVER SLAVERY

Some northern congressmen—and, in his last published essay, Benjamin Franklin—contested the southerners' position, but a consensus soon emerged to quash such discussions in the future. Congress accepted a committee report denying it the power either to halt the slave trade before 1808 or to effect the emancipation of any slaves at any time, that authority "remaining with the

several States alone." The precedent thereby established held until the Civil War.

Domestic Policy Under Washington and Hamilton

George Washington did not seek the presidency. In 1783 he returned to Mount Vernon eager for the peaceful life of a Virginia planter. But his fellow countrymen never regarded Washington as just another private citizen. Unanimously elected to preside at the Constitutional Convention, he did not participate in debates but consistently voted for a strong national government. After the adoption of the new governmental structure, Americans concurred that only George Washington had sufficient stature to serve as the republic's first president, an office designed largely with him in mind. The unanimous vote of the electoral college merely formalized that consensus.

Reluctant to return to public life, George Washington nevertheless knew he could not ignore his country's call. Awaiting the summons to New York City, the nation's capital, he wrote to an old friend, "My movements to the chair of Government will be accompanied by feelings not unlike those of a culprit who is going to the place of his execution. . . . I am sensible, that I am embarking the voice of my Countrymen and a good name of my own, on this voyage, but what returns will be made for them, Heaven alone can foretell."

Washington acted cautiously during his first months in office in 1789, knowing that whatever he did would set precedents for the future. When the title by which he should be addressed aroused controversy (Vice President John Adams favored "His Highness, the President of the United States of America, and Protector of their Liberties"), Washington said nothing. The accepted title soon became a plain "Mr. President." By using the heads of the executive departments collectively as his chief advisers, he created the cabinet. As the Constitution required, he sent Congress an annual State of the Union message. Washington also concluded that he should exercise his veto power over congressional legislation very sparingly—only, indeed, if he became convinced a bill was unconstitutional.

WASHINGTON'S FIRST STEPS

Early in his term, Washington undertook elaborately organized journeys to all the states. At each stop, he was ritually welcomed by uniformed militia units, young women strewing flowers in his path, local leaders, groups of Revolutionary War veterans, and respectable

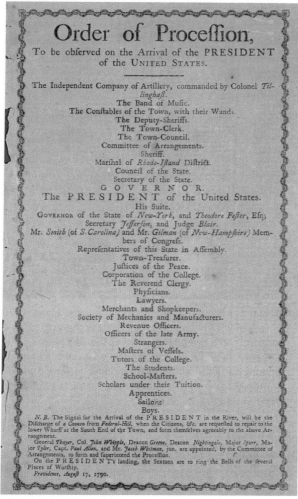

Order of Proceſſion,

To be obſerved on the Arrival of the PRESIDENT of the UNITED STATES.

The Independent Company of Artillery, commanded by Colonel *Til-linghaſt.*
The Band of Muſic.
The Conſtables of the Town, with their Wands.
The Deputy-Sheriffs.
The Town-Clerk.
The Town-Council.
Committee of Arrangements.
Sheriff.
Marſhal of *Rhode-Iſland Diſtrict.*
Council of the State.
Secretary of the State.
GOVERNOR.
The PRESIDENT of the United States.
His Suite.
GOVERNOR of the State of *New-York,* and *Theodore Foſter,* Eſq;
Secretary *Jefferſon,* and Judge *Blair.*
Mr. *Smith* (of *S. Carolina*) and Mr. *Gilman* (of *New-Hampſhire*) Members of Congreſs.
Repreſentatives of this State in Aſſembly.
Town-Treaſurer.
Juſtices of the Peace.
Corporation of the College.
The Reverend Clergy.
Phyſicians.
Lawyers.
Merchants and Shopkeepers.
Society of Mechanics and Manufacturers.
Revenue Officers.
Officers of the late Army.
Strangers.
Maſters of Veſſels.
Tutors of the College.
The Students.
School-Maſters.
Scholars under their Tuition.
Apprentices.
Sailors.
Boys.

N. B. The Signal for the Arrival of the P R E S I D E N T in the River, will be the Diſcharge of a *Cannon* from *Federal-Hill,* when the Citizens, &c. are requeſted to repair to the lower Wharff at the South End of the Town, and form themſelves agreeably to the above Arrangement.
General *Thayer,* Col. *John Whipple,* Deacon *Greene,* Deacon *Nightingale,* Major *Spurr,* Major *Tyler,* Capt. *Paul Allen,* and Mr. *Jacob Whitman,* jun. are appointed, by the Committee of Arrangements, to form and ſuperintend the Proceſſion.
On the P R E S I D E N T's landing, the Sextons are to ring the Bells of the ſeveral Places of Worſhip.
Providence, Auguſt 17, 1790.

■ When George Washington toured the nation during his first term in office, he was greeted by local leaders in elaborately orchestrated rituals. The organizers of the ceremony at Providence, Rhode Island, on August 17, 1790, issued this broadside to inform participants of their plans for a formal procession. While some Americans gloried in such displays of pomp, others feared they presaged the return of monarchy.   (The Huntington Library & Art Collections, San Marino, California)

citizens who presented him with formal addresses reaffirming their loyalty to the United States. The president thus personally came to embody national unity, simultaneously drawing ordinary folk into the sphere of national politics.

Washington's first major task as president was to choose the heads of the executive departments. For the

War Department he selected an old comrade-in-arms, Henry Knox of Massachusetts, who had been his reliable general of artillery during much of the Revolution. His choice for the State Department was his fellow Virginian Thomas Jefferson, who had just returned to the United States from his post as minister to France. And for the crucial position of secretary of the treasury, the president chose the brilliant, intensely ambitious Alexander Hamilton.

The illegitimate son of a Scottish aristocrat and a woman whose husband had divorced her for adultery and desertion, Hamilton was born in the British West Indies in 1757. His early years were spent in poverty; after his mother's death when he was eleven, he worked as a clerk for a mercantile firm. In 1773 Hamilton enrolled in King's College (later Columbia University) in New York City. Only eighteen months later, in late 1774, the precocious seventeen-year-old contributed a pamphlet to the prerevolutionary publication wars. Devoted to the patriot cause, Hamilton volunteered for service in the American army, where he came to Washington's attention. In 1777 Washington appointed the young man as one of his aides, and the two developed great mutual affection.

ALEXANDER HAMILTON

The general's patronage helped the poor youth of dubious background to marry well. At twenty-three he took as his wife Elizabeth Schuyler, daughter of a wealthy New York family. After the war, Hamilton practiced law in New York City and served as a delegate first to the Annapolis Convention and then to the Constitutional Convention. Although he exerted little influence at either gathering, his contributions to *The Federalist* in 1788 revealed him as one of the chief political thinkers in the republic.

In his dual role as secretary of the treasury and one of Washington's major advisers, Hamilton exhibited two traits that distinguished him from most of his contemporaries. First, he displayed an undivided loyalty to the nation as a whole. As a West Indian who had lived on the mainland only briefly before the war, Hamilton had no ties to a particular state. He showed little sympathy for, or understanding of, demands for local autonomy. Thus the aim of his fiscal policies was always to consolidate power at the national level. Further, he never feared the exercise of centralized executive authority, as did older counterparts who had clashed repeatedly with colonial governors, nor was he afraid of maintaining close political and economic ties with Britain.

Second, Hamilton regarded his fellow human beings with unvarnished cynicism. Perhaps because of his

■ John Trumbull, known primarily for his larger-than-life portraits of patriot leaders, painted this miniature (c. 1792–1794) of George Washington, who posed for it during his presidency. (Division of Political History, Smithsonian Institution, Washington, D.C.)

■ Alexander Hamilton, by James Sharpless, about 1796. This profile of Hamilton, painted near the end of Washington's presidency, shows the secretary of the treasury as he looked during the years of his first heated partisan battles with Thomas Jefferson and James Madison.   (National Portrait Gallery, Smithsonian Institution/Art Resource, N.Y.)

difficult early life and his own overriding ambition, Hamilton believed people to be motivated primarily by self-interest—particularly economic self-interest. He placed no reliance on people's capacity for virtuous and self-sacrificing behavior. This outlook set him apart from those Americans who foresaw a rosy future in which public-spirited citizens would pursue the common good rather than their own private advantage. Although other Americans (for example, Madison) also stressed the role of private interests in a republic, Hamilton went beyond them in his emphasis on self-interest as the major motivator of human behavior. And his beliefs significantly influenced the way in which he tackled the monumental task before him: straightening out the new nation's tangled finances.

In 1789, Congress ordered the new secretary of the treasury to assess the public debt and to submit recommendations for supporting the government's credit. Hamilton found that the country's remaining war debts fell into three categories: those owed by the nation to foreign governments and investors,

NATIONAL AND STATE DEBTS

mostly to France (about $11 million); those owed by the national government to merchants, former soldiers, holders of revolutionary bonds, and the like (about $27 million); and, finally, similar debts owed by state governments (roughly $25 million). With respect to the national debt, few disagreed: Americans recognized that if their new government was to succeed, it would have to repay at full face value those financial obligations incurred by the nation while winning independence.

The state debts were another matter. Some states—notably Virginia, Maryland, North Carolina, and Georgia—already had paid off most of their war debts by levying taxes and handing out land grants in lieu of monetary payments. They would oppose the national government's assumption of responsibility for other states' debts because their citizens would be taxed to pay such obligations. Massachusetts, Connecticut, and South Carolina, by contrast, still had sizable unpaid debts and would welcome a system of national assumption. The possible assumption of state debts also had political implications. Consolidating the debt in the hands of the national government would help to concentrate economic and political power at the national level. A contrary policy would reserve greater independence of action for the states.

Hamilton's first *Report on Public Credit*, sent to Congress in January 1790, stimulated lively debate. The

HAMILTON'S FINANCIAL PLAN

treasury secretary proposed that Congress assume outstanding state debts, combine them with national obligations, and issue new securities covering both principal and accumulated unpaid interest. Hamilton thereby hoped to ensure that holders of the public debt—many of them wealthy merchants and speculators—had a significant financial stake in the new government's survival. The opposition coalesced around James Madison, who opposed the assumption of state debts for two reasons. Not only had his state of Virginia already paid off most of its obligations, but he also wanted to avoid rewarding wealthy speculators who had purchased state and national debt certificates at a small fraction of their face value from needy veterans and farmers.

Prompted in part by Madison, the House initially rejected the assumption of state debts. The Senate, however, adopted Hamilton's plan largely intact. A series of compromises followed, in which the assumption bill became linked to the other major controversial issue of that congressional session: the location of the permanent national capital. Several related political deals were struck. A southern site—on the Potomac River—was selected for the capital, and the first part of Hamilton's financial program became law in August 1790.

Four months later Hamilton submitted to Congress a second report on public credit, recommending the

FIRST BANK OF THE UNITED STATES

chartering of a national bank modeled on the Bank of England. This proposal too aroused much opposition, primarily after Congress had already voted to establish the bank.

The Bank of the United States, to be chartered for twenty years, was to be capitalized at $10 million. Just $2 million would come from public funds, while private investors supplied the rest. The bank would act as collecting and disbursing agent for the Treasury and its notes would circulate as the nation's currency. Most political leaders recognized that such an institution would be beneficial, especially because it would solve the problem of America's perpetual shortage of an acceptable medium of exchange. But another issue loomed large: did the Constitution give Congress the power to establish such a bank?

James Madison answered that question with a resounding no. He pointed out that Constitutional

INTERPRETING THE CONSTITUTION

Convention delegates had specifically rejected a clause authorizing Congress to issue corporate charters. Consequently, he argued, that power could not be inferred from other parts of the Constitution. Madison's contention disturbed President Washington, who decided to request other opinions before signing the bill into law. Edmund Randolph, the attorney general, and Thomas Jefferson, the secretary of state, agreed with Madison that the bank was unconstitutional. Jefferson referred to Article I, Section 8, of the Constitution, which gave Congress the power "to make all Laws which shall be necessary and proper for carrying into Execution the foregoing Powers." The key word, Jefferson argued, was *necessary:* Congress could do what was needed but without specific constitutional authorization could not do what was merely desirable. Thus Jefferson formulated the strict-constructionist interpretation of the Constitution.

Washington asked Hamilton to reply to the negative assessments of his proposal. Hamilton's *Defense of the Constitutionality of the Bank*, presented to the president in February 1791, brilliantly expounded a broad-constructionist view of the Constitution. Hamilton argued forcefully that Congress could choose any means not specifically prohibited by the Constitution to achieve a constitutional end. He reasoned thus: if the end was constitutional and the means was not *un*constitutional, then the means was constitutional.

Washington concurred, and the bill became law. The bank proved successful, as did the scheme for funding the national debt and assuming the states' debts. The new nation's securities became desirable investments for its own citizens and for wealthy foreigners, especially those in the Netherlands, who rushed to purchase American debt certificates. The influx of new capital, coupled with the high prices American produce now commanded in European markets, eased farmers' debt burdens and contributed to a new prosperity. But two other aspects of Alexander Hamilton's wide-ranging financial scheme did not fare so well.

In December 1791, Hamilton presented to Congress his *Report on Manufactures*, the third and last of his

REPORT ON MANUFACTURES

prescriptions for the American economy. In it he outlined an ambitious plan for encouraging and protecting the United States's infant industries, such as shoemaking and textile manufacturing. Hamilton argued that the nation could never be truly independent as long as it relied heavily on Europe for manufactured goods. He thus urged Congress to promote the

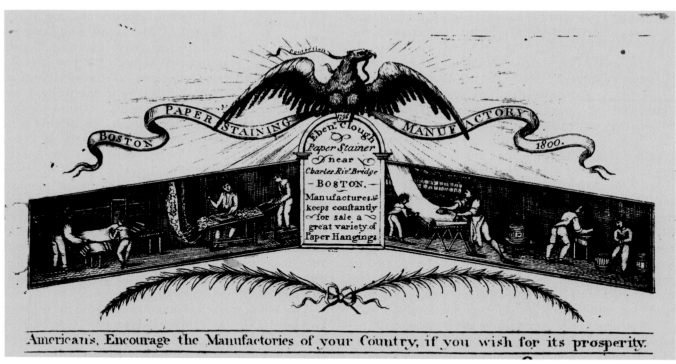

PAPER STAINING MANUFACTORY

BOSTON 1800.

Eben: Clough Paper Stainer near Charles Riv'r Bridge — BOSTON. — Manufactures & keeps constantly for sale a great variety of Paper Hangings

Americans, Encourage the Manufactories of your Country, if you wish for its prosperity.

■ Although Congress did not react positively to the arguments in Hamilton's *Report on Manufactures*, the owners of America's burgeoning industries recognized the importance of the policy Hamilton advocated. Ebenezer Clough, a Boston maker of wallpaper, incorporated into his letterhead the exhortation "Americans, Encourage the Manufactories of your Country, if you wish for its prosperity." (American Antiquarian Society)

immigration of technicians and laborers and to support industrial development through a limited use of protective tariffs. Many of Hamilton's ideas were implemented in later decades, especially after the United States greatly increased its cultivation of cotton and could therefore amply supply its textile mills, but few congressmen in 1791 could see much merit in his proposals. They firmly believed that America's future lay in agriculture and the carrying trade and that the mainstay of the republic was the virtuous small farmer. Therefore, Congress rejected the report.

That same year Congress accepted another feature of Hamilton's financial program, levying a tax on whiskey produced within the United States. Although proceeds from the Revenue Act of 1789 covered the interest on the national debt, the decision to fund state debts meant that the national government required additional income. A tax on whiskey affected relatively few farmers—those west of the mountains who sold their grain in the form of distilled spirits as a means of avoiding the high cost of transportation—and might also reduce the consumption of whiskey. (Eighteenth-century Americans, notorious for their heavy drinking, consumed about twice as much alcohol per capita as today's rate.) Moreover, Hamilton knew that those western farmers were Jefferson's supporters, and he saw the benefits of taxing them rather than the merchants who supported his own policies.

News of the tax set off protests in frontier areas of Pennsylvania, where residents were already dissatisfied with the army's as yet unsuccessful attempts to defeat the Miami Confederacy (see pages 181–182). To their minds, the same government that protected them inadequately was now proposing to tax them disproportionately. Unrest continued for two years on the frontiers of Pennsylvania, Maryland, and Virginia. Large groups of men drafted petitions protesting the tax, deliberately imitated crowd actions of the 1760s, and occasionally harassed tax collectors.

WHISKEY REBELLION

President Washington responded with restraint until violence erupted in July 1794, when western Pennsylvania farmers resisted a federal marshal and a tax collector trying to enforce the law. Three rioters were killed and several militiamen wounded. About seven thousand rebels convened on August 1 to plot the destruction of Pittsburgh but decided not to face the heavy guns of the fort guarding the town. Washington then took decisive action to prevent a crisis reminiscent of Shays's Rebellion. On August 7, he called on the insurgents to disperse and summoned nearly thirteen thousand militia from Pennsylvania and neighboring states. By the time federal forces marched westward in October and November (led at times by Washington himself), the disturbances had ceased. The troops met no resistance and arrested only twenty suspects. Two, neither of them prominent leaders of the rioters, were convicted of treason, but—continuing his policy of restraint—Washington pardoned both. The leaderless and unorganized rebellion ended with little bloodshed.

The chief importance of the Whiskey Rebellion lay not in military victory over the rebels—for there was none—but in the forceful message it conveyed to the American people. The national government, Washington had demonstrated, would not allow violent resistance to its laws. In the republic, change would be effected peacefully, by legal means. People dissatisfied with the law should try to amend or repeal it, not take extralegal action as they had during the colonial era.

The French Revolution and the Development of Partisan Politics

B y 1794, some Americans were already beginning to seek change systematically through electoral politics, even though traditional political theory regarded organized opposition—especially in a republic—as illegitimate. In a monarchy, formal opposition groups were to be expected. In a government of the people, by contrast, serious and sustained disagreement was taken as a sign of corruption and subversion. Such negative judgments, while widely held, still did not halt the growth of partisan sentiment.

Jefferson and Madison became convinced as early as 1792 that Hamilton's policies of favoring wealthy commercial interests at the expense of agriculture aimed

DEMOCRATIC- REPUBLICANS AND FEDERALISTS

at imposing a corrupt, aristocratic government on the United States. Characterizing themselves as the true heirs of the Revolution, they charged that Hamilton was plotting to subvert re-

■ A Federalist political cartoon from the 1790s shows "Mad Tom" Paine "in a rage," trying to destroy the federal government as carefully constructed (in classical style) by President Washington and Vice President Adams. That Paine is being aided by the Devil underscores the hostility to partisanship common in the era.   (The Huntington Library & Art Collections, San Marino, California)

publican principles. To dramatize their point, Jefferson, Madison, and their followers in Congress began calling themselves Democratic-Republicans. Hamilton in turn accused Jefferson and Madison of the same crime: attempting to destroy the republic. Hamilton and his supporters began calling themselves Federalists, to legitimize their claims and link themselves with the Constitution. Each group accused the other of being an illicit faction working to sabotage the republican principles of the Revolution. (In the traditional sense of the term, a faction was by definition dangerous and opposed to the public good.) Newspapers aligned with the two sides fanned the flames of partisanship, publishing virulent attacks on their political opponents.

At first, President Washington tried to remain aloof from the political dispute that divided Hamilton and

Jefferson, his chief advisers. Yet the growing controversy helped persuade him to seek a second term of office in 1792 in hopes of promoting political unity. But in 1793 and thereafter, developments in foreign affairs magnified the disagreements, for France—America's wartime ally—and Great Britain—America's most important trading partner—resumed the periodic hostilities that had originated a century earlier (see page 83).

In 1789 Americans welcomed the news of the French Revolution. The French people's success in limiting, and

FRENCH
REVOLUTION

then overthrowing, an oppressive monarchy seemed to vindicate the United States's own revolution. Americans saw themselves as the vanguard of an inevitable historical trend that would reshape the world in a republican mold. But by the early 1790s the reports from France were disquieting. Outbreaks of violence continued, and ministries succeeded each other with bewildering rapidity. Executions mounted; the king himself was beheaded in early 1793. Although many Americans,

■ Citizen Edmond Genêt's visit caused the first major diplomatic crisis in the new nation. His attempts to enlist Americans in support of the French Revolution raised troubling questions about the international role of the United States. (Collection of the Albany Institute of History and Art. Bequest of George Genêt)

including Jefferson and Madison, retained a sympathetic view of the revolution, others began to cite France as a prime example of the perversion of republicanism. As might be expected, Alexander Hamilton spoke for the latter group.

Debates within the United States intensified when the newly republican France became enmeshed in conflict with other European nations. Both because French leaders feared that neighboring monarchies would intervene to crush the revolution and because they sought to spread the republican gospel throughout the continent, they declared war first on Austria and then, in 1793, on Britain, Spain, and Holland. That confronted the Americans with a dilemma. The 1778 Treaty of Alliance with France bound them to that nation "forever," and a mutual commitment to republicanism created ideological bonds. Yet the United States was connected to Great Britain as well. In addition to their shared history and language, America and Britain had again become important economic partners. Americans still purchased most of their manufactured goods from Great Britain. Indeed, since the financial system of the United States depended heavily on import tariffs as a source of revenue, the nation's economic health in effect required uninterrupted trade with the former mother country.

The political and diplomatic climate grew even more complicated in April 1793, when Citizen Edmond Genêt,

CITIZEN GENÊT

a representative of the French government, landed in Charleston, South Carolina. As Genêt made his way north to New York City, he recruited Americans for expeditions against British and Spanish colonies in the Western Hemisphere, freely distributing privateering commissions. Genêt's arrival raised troubling questions for President Washington. Should he receive Genêt, thus officially recognizing the French revolutionary government? Should he acknowledge an obligation to aid France against Britain under the terms of the 1778 Treaty of Alliance? Or should he proclaim American neutrality?

For once, Hamilton and Jefferson saw eye to eye. Both told Washington that the United States could not afford to ally itself with either side. Washington concurred. He received Genêt but also issued a proclamation informing the world that the United States would adopt "a conduct friendly and impartial toward the belligerent powers." In deference to Jefferson's continued support for France, though, the word neutrality did not appear in the declaration.

Genêt himself was removed from politics when his faction fell from power in Paris; he subsequently sought political asylum in the United States. But his disappearance from the diplomatic scene did not diminish the impact of the French Revolution in America. The domestic divisions Genêt helped to widen were perpetuated by clubs called Democratic-Republican societies, formed by Americans sympathetic to the French Revolution and worried about the policies of the Washington administration. Such societies reflected a growing grassroots concern about the same developments that troubled Jefferson and Madison.

More than forty Democratic-Republican societies organized between 1793 and 1800. Their members saw
DEMOCRATIC-REPUBLICAN SOCIETIES
themselves as heirs of the Sons of Liberty, seeking the same goal as their predecessors: protection of people's liberties against encroachments by corrupt and self-serving rulers. To that end, they publicly protested government fiscal and foreign policy and repeatedly proclaimed their belief in "the equal rights of man," particularly the rights to free speech, free press, and assembly. Like the Sons of Liberty, the Democratic-Republican societies chiefly comprised artisans and craftsmen, although professionals, farmers, and merchants also joined.

The rapid growth of such groups, outspoken in their criticism of the Washington administration for its failure to come to the aid of France and for its domestic economic policies, deeply disturbed Hamilton and eventually Washington himself. Some newspapers charged that the societies were subversive agents of a foreign power. Their "real design," one asserted, was "to involve the country in war, to assume the reins of government and tyrannize over the people." The counterattack climaxed in the fall of 1794, when Washington accused the societies of having fomented the Whiskey Rebellion.

In retrospect, Washington and Hamilton's reaction to the Democratic-Republican societies seems disproportionately hostile. But it must be recalled that factional disputes were believed to endanger the survival of republics. As the first organized political dissenters in the United States, the Democratic-Republican societies alarmed elected officials, who had not yet accepted the idea that one component of a free government was an organized loyal opposition.

Partisan Politics and Relations with Great Britain

In 1794 George Washington dispatched Chief Justice John Jay to London to negotiate four unresolved questions in Anglo-American relations. The first point at issue was recent British seizures of American merchant ships trading in the French West In-

dies. The United States wanted to establish the principle of freedom of the seas and to assert its right, as a neutral nation, to trade freely with both combatants. Second, in violation of the 1783 peace treaty, Great Britain had not yet evacuated its posts in the American Northwest. Settlers there believed that the British were responsible for the renewed warfare in the region (see pages 181–182), and they wanted that threat removed. The Americans also hoped for a commercial treaty and sought compensation for the slaves who left with the British army at the end of the war.

The negotiations in London proved difficult, since Jay had little to offer in exchange for the concessions he
JAY TREATY
sought. Britain did agree to evacuate the western forts and ease restrictions on American trade to England and the West Indies. (Some limitations were retained, however, violating the Americans' desire for open commerce.) The treaty established two arbitration commissions—one to deal with prewar debts Americans owed to British creditors and the other to hear claims for captured American merchant ships—but Britain adamantly refused slaveowners compensation for their lost bondspeople. Under the circumstances, Jay did remarkably well: the treaty averted war with England at a time when the United States, which lacked an effective navy, could not have won such a conflict. Nevertheless, most Americans, including the president, expressed dissatisfaction with at least some parts of the treaty.

The Senate debated the Jay Treaty in secret, so members of the public did not learn its provisions until after Senate ratification (by the exact two-thirds vote needed, 20 to 10) in June 1795. The Democratic-Republican societies led protests against the treaty. Especially vehement opposition arose in the South, as planters criticized the failure to obtain compensation for runaway slaves and objected to the commission on prewar debts, which might make them pay off obligations to British merchants dating back to the 1760s. Once President Washington had signed the treaty, though, there seemed little the Democratic-Republicans could do to prevent it from taking effect. Just one opportunity remained: Congress had to appropriate funds to carry out the treaty provisions and, according to the Constitution, appropriation bills had to originate in the House of Representatives.

When the House debated the issue in March 1796, members opposing the treaty tried to prevent approval of the appropriations. To that end, they asked Washington to submit to the House all documents pertinent to the negotiations. In successfully resisting the House's request, Washington established the doctrine of executive privilege—the power of the president to withhold information from Congress if he believes circumstances warrant doing so.

The treaty's opponents initially appeared to be in the majority, but pressure for appropriating the necessary funds built as time passed. Frontier residents eagerly sought Britain's evacuation of its remaining outposts, for they feared a new outbreak of Indian war despite the signing of the Treaty of Greenville. Merchants wanted to reap benefits from expanded trade. Furthermore, in 1795 Thomas Pinckney of South Carolina had negotiated a treaty with Spain giving the United States navigation privileges on the Mississippi River, which would be an economic boost to the West and South. The popularity of Pinckney's Treaty (the Senate ratified it unanimously) helped to overcome opposition to the Jay Treaty. For all these reasons, the House appropriated the money by the narrow margin of 51 to 48.

Analysis of the vote reveals both the regional nature of the division and the growing cohesion of the Democratic-Republican and Federalist factions in

PARTISAN DIVISIONS IN CONGRESS

Congress. Voting for the appropriations were 44 Federalists and 7 Democratic-Republicans; voting against were 45 Democratic-Republicans and 3 Federalists. The final tally also divided by region. Southerners (including those three Federalists, who were Virginians) cast the vast majority of votes against the bill. Except for two South Carolina Federalists, no one representing a state south of Maryland voted "yes."

The small number of defectors on both sides reveals a new force at work in American politics: partisanship. Voting statistics from the first four Congresses show the ever-increasing tendency of members of the House of Representatives to vote as cohesive groups, rather than as individuals. If factional loyalty is defined as voting together at least two-thirds of the time on national issues, the percentage of nonaligned congressmen dropped from 42 percent in 1790 to just 7 percent in 1796. Significantly, this trend toward party cohesion occurred even though Congress experienced heavy turnover. Most congressmen served only one or two terms in office, and fewer than 10 percent were reelected more than three times. During the 1790s the majority slowly shifted from Federalist to Democratic-Republican. Federalists controlled the first three Congresses, through the spring of 1795. Democratic-Republicans gained ascendancy in the Fourth Congress. Federalists returned to power with slight majorities in the Fifth and Sixth Congresses, but the Democratic-Republicans took over—more or less for good—in the Seventh Congress in 1801.

To describe these shifts is easier than to explain them. The terms used by Jefferson and Madison (aristocrats

BASES OF PARTISANSHIP

versus the people) or by Hamilton and Washington (true patriots versus subversive rabble) do not adequately explain the growing divisions. Simple economic differences between agrarian and commercial interests do not provide the answer either, since more than 90 percent of Americans still lived in rural areas. Moreover, Jefferson's vision of a prosperous agrarian America rested on commercial farming, not rural self-sufficiency. Nor did the divisions in the 1790s simply repeat the Federalist-Antifederalist debate of 1787–1788. Even though most Antifederalists became Democratic-Republicans, the party's leaders, Madison and Jefferson, had supported the Constitution.

Yet certain distinctions can be made. Democratic-Republicans, especially prominent in the southern and middle states, tended to be self-assured, confident, and optimistic about both politics and the economy. Southern planters, firmly in control of their region and of a class of enslaved laborers, did not fear instability, at least among the European American population. They foresaw a prosperous future based partly on continued westward expansion, a movement they expected to dominate. Democratic-Republicans employed democratic rhetoric to win the allegiance of small farmers south of New England. Members of non-English ethnic groups—especially Irish, Scots, and Germans—found Democratic-Republicans' words attractive. Artisans also joined the coalition; they saw themselves as the urban equivalent of small farmers and valued their independence from domineering bosses. Democratic-Republicans of all descriptions emphasized developing America's own resources, worrying less than Federalists did about the nation's place in the world. Democratic-Republicans also remained sympathetic to France in international affairs.

By contrast, Federalists, concentrated among the commercial interests of New England, came mostly from English stock. Insecure and uncertain of the future, they stressed the need for order, authority, and regularity in the political world. Federalists had no grassroots political organization and put little emphasis on involving ordinary people in government. Wealthy New England merchants aligned themselves with the Federalists, but so too did the region's farmers who, prevented from expanding agricultural production because of New England's poor soil, gravitated toward the more conservative party. Federalists, like Democratic-Republicans, assumed that southern and middle-state interests would dominate the land west of the mountains, so they had little incentive to work actively to develop that potentially rich territory. In Federalist eyes, potential enemies—both internal and external—perpetually threatened the nation, which required a continuing alliance with Great Britain for its own protection. Their vision of international affairs may have been more accurate than that of the Democratic-Republicans, given the warfare in Europe, but it was also narrow and unattractive. Since the Federalist view held out little hope of a better future to the voters of any region, it is not surprising that the Democratic-Republicans prevailed in the end.

The presence of the two organized groups actively contending for office made the presidential election of

WASHINGTON'S FAREWELL ADDRESS

1796 the first serious contest for the position. Wearied by the criticism to which he had been subjected, George Washington decided to retire. (Presidents had not yet been limited to two terms, as they have been since the adoption of the Twenty-second Amendment in 1951.) In September Washington published his Farewell Address, most of which had been written by Hamilton. In it Washington outlined two principles that guided American foreign policy at least until the late 1940s: to maintain commercial but not political ties to other nations and to enter no permanent alliances. He also drew sharp distinctions between the United States and Europe, stressing America's uniqueness—its exceptionalism—and the need for independent action in foreign affairs, today called unilateralism.

Washington lamented the existence of factional divisions among his countrymen. Historians have often interpreted his call for an end to partisan strife as the statement of a man who could see beyond political affiliations to the good of the whole. But in the context of the impending presidential election, the Farewell Address appears rather as an attack on the legitimacy of the Democratic-Republican opposition. Washington advocated unity behind the Federalist banner, which he viewed as the only proper political stance. The Federalists (like the Democratic-Republicans) continued to see themselves as the sole guardians of the truth and the only true heirs of the Revolution. Both sides perceived their opponents as misguided, unpatriotic troublemakers who sought to undermine revolutionary ideals.

To succeed Washington, the Federalists in Congress put forward Vice President John Adams, with the diplomat

ELECTION OF 1796

Thomas Pinckney as his running mate. Congressional Democratic-Republicans chose Thomas Jefferson as their presidential candidate; the lawyer, Revolu-

tionary War veteran, and active Democratic-Republican politician Aaron Burr of New York agreed to run for vice president.

That the election was contested does not mean that the people decided its outcome. Voters could cast their ballots only for electors, not for the candidates themselves, and not all electors publicly declared their preferences. State legislatures, not a popular vote, selected more than 40 percent of the members of the electoral college; some electors had been picked even before Federalists and Democratic-Republicans named their presidential candidates. Moreover, the method of voting in the electoral college did not take into account the possibility of party slates. The Constitution's drafters had not foreseen the development of competing national political organizations, so the Constitution provided no way to express support for one person for president and another for vice president. The electors simply voted for two

■ John Adams, painted in 1798 by the English artist William Winstanley. Adams wears the same suit and sword he donned for his inauguration as the second president in March 1797. The open books and quill pen on the table suggest his lifelong love of reading and writing.
(U.S. Department of the Interior, National Park Service, Adams National Historic Site)

people. The man with the highest total became president; the second highest, vice president.

This procedure proved to be the Federalists' undoing. Adams won the presidency with 71 votes, but a number of Federalist electors (especially those from New England) failed to cast ballots for Pinckney. Thomas Jefferson won 68 votes, 9 more than Pinckney, to become vice president. The incoming administration was thus politically divided. During the next four years the new president and vice president, once allies and close friends, became bitter enemies.

John Adams and Political Dissent

John Adams took over the presidency peculiarly blind to the partisan developments of the previous four years. As president he never abandoned an outdated notion discarded by George Washington as early as 1794: that the president should be above politics, an independent and dignified figure who did not seek petty factional advantage. Thus Adams kept Washington's cabinet intact, despite its key members' allegiance to his chief rival, Alexander Hamilton. Adams often adopted a passive posture, letting others (usually Hamilton) take the lead when the president should have acted decisively. As a result, his administration gained a reputation for inconsistency. When Adams's term ended, the Federalists were severely divided, and the Democratic-Republicans had won the presidency. But Adams's detachment from Hamilton's maneuverings did enable him to weather the greatest international crisis the republic had yet faced: the Quasi-War with France.

The Jay Treaty improved America's relationship with Great Britain, but it provoked the French government to

XYZ Affair

retaliate by ordering its ships to seize American vessels carrying British goods. In response, Congress increased military spending, authorizing the building of ships and the stockpiling of weapons and ammunition. President Adams also sent three commissioners to Paris to negotiate a settlement. For months, the American commissioners sought talks with Talleyrand, the French foreign minister, but Talleyrand's agents demanded a bribe of $250,000 before negotiations could begin. The Americans retorted, "No, no; not a sixpence," and reported the incident in dispatches that the president received in early March 1798. Adams informed Congress of the impasse and recommended further increases in defense appropriations.

Convinced that Adams had deliberately sabotaged the negotiations, congressional Democratic-Republicans insisted that the dispatches be turned over to Congress. Adams complied, aware that releasing the reports would work to his advantage. He withheld only the names of the French agents, referring to them as X, Y, and Z. The revelation that the Americans had been treated with contempt stimulated a wave of anti-French sentiment in the United States. A journalist's version of the commissioners' reply, "Millions for defense, but not a cent for tribute," became the national slogan. Cries for war filled the air. Congress formally abrogated the Treaty of Alliance and authorized American ships to seize French vessels.

Thus began an undeclared war with France. Warships of the U.S. Navy and French privateers seeking to

Quasi-War with France

capture American merchant vessels fought the Quasi-War in Caribbean waters. Although Americans initially suffered heavy losses of merchant shipping, by early 1799 the U.S. Navy had established its superiority in the West Indies. Its ships captured eight French privateers and naval vessels, easing the threat to America's vital Caribbean trade.

The Democratic-Republicans, who opposed war and continued to sympathize with France, could do little to stem the tide of anti-French feelings. Since Agent Y had boasted of the existence of a "French party in America," Federalists flatly accused Democratic-Republicans (including the eccentric envoy George Logan) of traitorous designs. A New York newspaper declared that anyone who remained "lukewarm" after reading the XYZ dispatches was a "criminal—and the man who does not warmly reprobate the conduct of the French must have a soul black enough to be fit for treason Strategems and spoils." John Adams wavered between calling the Democratic-Republicans traitors and acknowledging their right to oppose administration measures. His wife was less tolerant. "Those whom the French boast of as their Partizans," Abigail Adams declared, should be "adjudged traitors to their country." If Jefferson had been president, she added, "we should all have been sold to the French."

Federalists saw this climate of opinion as an opportunity to deal a death blow to their Democratic-

Alien and Sedition Acts

Republican opponents. Now that the country seemed to see the truth of what they had been saying ever since the Whiskey Rebellion in 1794—that Democratic-Republicans were subversive foreign agents—Federalists sought to codify that belief into law. In 1798

■ This cartoon drawn during the XYZ affair depicts the United States as a maiden being victimized by the five leaders of the French government's directorate. In the background, John Bull (England) watches from on high, while other European nations discuss the situation.
(The Lilly Library, Indiana University, Bloomington, Indiana)

the Federalist-controlled Congress adopted a set of four laws known as the Alien and Sedition Acts, intended to suppress dissent and to prevent further growth of the Democratic-Republican faction.

Three of the acts targeted recently arrived immigrants, whom Federalists accurately suspected of being Democratic-Republican in their sympathies. The Naturalization Act lengthened the residency period required for citizenship and ordered all resident aliens to register with the federal government. The two Alien Acts, though not immediately implemented, provided for the detention of enemy aliens in time of war and gave the president authority to deport any alien he deemed dangerous to the nation's security.

The fourth statute, the Sedition Act, sought to control both citizens and aliens. It outlawed conspiracies to prevent the enforcement of federal laws, setting the maximum punishment for such offenses at five years in prison and a $5,000 fine. The act also tried to control speech. Writing, printing, or uttering "false, scandalous and malicious" statements against the government or the

president "with intent to defame . . . or to bring them or either of them, into contempt or disrepute" became a crime punishable by as much as two years' imprisonment and a fine of $2,000. Today any such law punishing speech alone would be considered unconstitutional. But in the eighteenth century, when organized political opposition was by definition suspect, many Americans supported the Sedition Act's restrictions on free speech.

The Sedition Act led to fifteen indictments and ten convictions. Outspoken Democratic-Republican newspaper editors who failed to mute their criticism of the administration composed most of the accused. But the first person found guilty—whose story exemplifies the others—was a Democratic-Republican congressman from Vermont, Matthew Lyon. The Irish-born Lyon, a former indentured servant who had purchased his freedom and fought in the Revolution, was indicted for declaring in print that John Adams had displayed "a continual grasp for power" and "an unbounded thirst for ridiculous pomp, foolish adulation, and selfish avarice." Though convicted, fined $1,000, and sent to prison for four months, Lyon did not lapse into silence. He conducted his reelection campaign from jail, winning an overwhelming majority. Leading Democratic-Republicans from around the country contributed to pay his fine.

Faced with prosecutions of their supporters, Jefferson and Madison sought an effective means of combating the acts. Petitioning the Federalist-controlled

VIRGINIA AND KENTUCKY RESOLUTIONS

Congress to repeal the laws would clearly fail. Furthermore, Federalist judges refused to allow accused individuals to question the Sedition Act's constitutionality. Accordingly, the Democratic-Republican leaders turned to the only other forum available for protest: state legislatures. Carefully concealing their own role—the vice president and congressman wanted to avoid being indicted for sedition—Jefferson and Madison drafted somewhat different sets of resolutions that were introduced into the Kentucky and Virginia legislatures, respectively, in the fall of 1798. Since a compact among the states created the Constitution, the resolutions contended, people speaking through their states had a legitimate right to judge the constitutionality of actions taken by the federal government. Both sets of resolutions pronounced the Alien and Sedition Acts unconstitutional, asking other states to join in a concerted protest against them.

Although no other state endorsed them, the Virginia and Kentucky Resolutions nevertheless had considerable influence. First, they constituted superb political propaganda, rallying Democratic-Republican opinion throughout the country. They placed the opposition party squarely in the revolutionary tradition of resistance to tyrannical authority. Second, the theory of union they proposed inspired southern states' rights advocates in the 1830s and thereafter. Jefferson and Madison had identified a key constitutional issue: How far could states go in opposing the national government? How could a conflict between the two be resolved? These questions would not be definitively answered until the Civil War.

Just as the Sedition Act was being implemented and northern state legislatures were rejecting the Virginia and Kentucky Resolutions, Federalists split

CONVENTION OF 1800

over the course of action the United States should take toward France. Hamilton and his supporters called for a declaration legitimizing the undeclared naval war. But Adams received a number of private signals—among them George Logan's report—that the French government regretted its treatment of the American commissioners. Acting on such assurances, Adams dispatched the envoy William Vans Murray to Paris to negotiate

with Napoleon Bonaparte, France's new leader, who was consolidating his hold on the country and eager to end messy foreign conflicts. The United States sought two goals: compensation for ships the French had seized since 1793 and abrogation of the treaty of 1778. The Convention of 1800, which ended the Quasi-War, provided for the latter but not the former. Still, it freed the United States from its only permanent alliance, thus allowing it to follow the independent diplomatic course George Washington had urged in his Farewell Address.

The results of the negotiations did not become known in the United States until after the presidential election of 1800. Even so, since Hamilton and many of his followers wanted to widen the Quasi-War, Adams's decision to seek a peaceful settlement probably cost him reelection because of the divisions it caused in Federalist ranks.

Indians and African Americans at the End of the Century

By the end of the eighteenth century, the nation had added three states (Vermont, Kentucky, and Tennessee) to the original thirteen and more than 1 million people to the nearly 4 million counted by the 1790 census. Nine-tenths of the approximately 1 million resident African Americans—most still enslaved—lived in the Chesapeake or the Lower South. After the signing of the Treaty of Greenville in 1795 (see page 182), all the Indian nations residing in U.S. territory east of the Mississippi River had made peace with the republic. Even though many Indian peoples still lived independently of federal authority, they came increasingly within the orbit of U.S. influence.

The new nation's policymakers, all of European American descent, could not ignore such large proportions of the population. How should the republic deal with eastern Indians, who no longer posed a military threat to the country? Did the growing population of bondspeople (augmented by more than ninety thousand imports directly from Africa before Congress ended the slave trade in 1808) present new hazards? The second question took on added significance after 1793, when in the French colony of St. Domingue (Haiti), mulattos and blacks under the leadership of Toussaint L'Ouverture overthrew European rule in a bloody revolt characterized by numerous atrocities on both sides.

In 1789 Henry Knox, Washington's secretary of war, proposed that the new national government assume the task of "civilizing" America's indigenous population.

Haitian Refugees

Although many European Americans initially welcomed the news of the French Revolution in 1789, few expressed similar sentiments about the slave rebellion that broke out soon thereafter in the French colony of St. Domingue (later Haiti), which shared the island of Hispaniola with Spanish Santo Domingo. The large number of refugees who soon flowed into the new United States from that nearby revolt brought with them consequences deemed undesirable by most political leaders. Less than a decade after winning independence, the new nation confronted its first immigration crisis.

Among the approximately 600,000 residents of St. Domingue in the early 1790s were about 100,000 free people, almost all of them slaveowners; half were whites, the rest mulattos. When in the wake of the French Revolution those free mulattos split the slaveholding population by seeking greater social and political equality, the slaves seized the opportunity to revolt. By 1793, they had triumphed under the leadership of a former slave, Toussaint L'Ouverture, and in 1804 they finally ousted the French, thereafter establishing the republic of Haiti. Thousands of whites and mulattos, accompanied by as many slaves as they could readily transport, sought asylum in the United States during those turbulent years.

Although willing to offer shelter to refugees from the violence, American political leaders nonetheless feared the consequences of their arrival. Southern plantation owners shuddered at the thought that slaves so familiar with ideas of freedom and equality would mingle with their own bondspeople. Many were uncomfortable with the immigration of numerous free people of color, even though the immigrants were part of the slaveholding class. Most of the southern states adopted laws forbidding the entry of Haitian slaves and free mulattos, but the laws were difficult if not impossible to enforce, as was a later congressional act to the same effect. And so more than 15,000 refugees—white, black, and of mixed race origins—flooded into the United States and Spanish Louisiana. Many ended up in Virginia (which did not pass an exclusion law) or the cities of Charleston, Savannah, and New Orleans.

There they had a considerable impact on the existing population. In both New Orleans and Charleston the influx of mulattos gave rise to heightened color consciousness that placed light-skinned people at the top of a hierarchy of people of color. Not coincidentally, the Charleston Brown Fellowship Society, composed exclusively of free mulattos, was founded in 1793. After the United States purchased Louisiana in 1803, the number of free people of color in the territory almost doubled in three years, largely because of a final surge of immigration from the new Haitian republic. And in Virginia, stories of the successful revolt helped to inspire local slaves in 1800 when they planned the action that has become known as Gabriel's Rebellion.

The Haitian refugees thus linked both European and African Americans to current events in the West Indies, indelibly affecting both groups of people.

A free woman of color in Louisiana early in the nineteenth century, possibly one of the refugees from Haiti. Esteban Rodriguez Miró, named governor of Spanish Louisiana in 1782, ordered all slave and free black women to wear head wraps rather than hats—which were reserved for whites—but this woman and many others subverted his order by nominally complying, but nevertheless creating elaborate headdresses. (Louisiana State Museum)

■ In 1805, an unidentified artist painted Benjamin Hawkins, a trader and U.S. agent to the Indians of the Southeast, at the Creek agency near Macon, Georgia. Hawkins introduced European-style agriculture to the Creeks, who are shown here with vegetables from their fields. Throughout the eastern United States, Indian nations had to make similar adaptations of their traditional lifestyles in order to maintain their group identity.   (Collection of the Greenville County Art Museum, South Carolina)

"CIVILIZING" THE INDIANS

"Instead of exterminating a part of the human race," he contended, the government should "impart our knowledge of cultivation and the arts to the aboriginals of the country." The first step in such a project, Knox suggested, should be to introduce to Indian peoples "a love for exclusive property"; to that end, he proposed that the government give livestock to individual Indians. Four years later, the Indian Trade and Intercourse Act of 1793 codified Knox's plan, promising that the federal government would supply Indians with animals and agricultural implements and would also provide appropriate instructors.

The well-intentioned plan reflected federal officials' blindness to the realities of native peoples' lives. Not only did it incorrectly posit that the Indians' traditional commitment to communal notions of landowning (see page 44) could easily be overcome, it also ignored the centuries-long agricultural experience of eastern Indian peoples. The policymakers focused only on Indian men:

since they hunted, male Indians were "savages" who had to be "civilized" by being taught to farm. That in these societies women traditionally did the farming was irrelevant because in the eyes of the officials, Indian women—like those of European descent—should properly confine themselves to child rearing, household chores, and home manufacturing.

Indian nations at first responded cautiously to the "civilizing" plan. The Iroquois Confederacy had been

IROQUOIS AND CHEROKEES

devastated by the war; its people in the 1790s lived in what one historian has called "slums in the wilderness." Restricted to small reservations increasingly surrounded by Anglo-American farmlands, men could no longer hunt and often spent their days in idle carousing. Quaker missionaries started a demonstration farm among the Senecas, intending to teach men to plow, but they quickly learned that women showed greater interest in their message. The same was true among the Cherokees of Georgia, where Indian agents found that women eagerly sought to learn both new farming methods and textile-manufacturing skills. As their southern hunting territories were reduced, Cherokee men did begin to raise cattle and hogs, but they startled the reformers by treating livestock like wild game, allowing the animals to run free in the woods and simply shooting them when needed, in the same way they had once killed deer. Men also started to plow the fields, although Cherokee women continued to bear primary responsibility for cultivation and harvest.

Iroquois men became more receptive to the Quakers' lessons after the spring of 1799, when a Seneca named Handsome Lake experienced a remarkable series of visions. Like other prophets stretching back to Neolin (see page 123), Handsome Lake preached that Indian peoples should renounce alcohol, gambling, and other destructive European customs. Even though he directed his followers to reorient men's and women's work assignments as the Quakers advocated, Handsome Lake aimed above all to preserve Iroquois culture by doing so. He recognized that, since men could no longer obtain meat through hunting, only by adopting a sexual division of labor that had originated in Europe could the Iroquois retain an autonomous existence.

African Americans had long been forced to conform to European American notions of proper gender roles and, unlike Indians, they had embraced Christianity as well during the Great Awakening. Yet, just as Cherokees and Iroquois adapted the reformers' plans to their own purposes, so too enslaved blacks found new meanings in the dominant society's ideas. Like their white compatriots, African Americans (both slave and free) became familiar with concepts of liberty and equality during the Revolution. They also witnessed the benefits of fighting collectively for freedom, rather than resisting individually or running away—a message reinforced by the dramatic news of the successful slave revolt in St. Domingue in 1793. And, as white evangelicals by the end of the century began to back away from the earlier racial egalitarianism of their movement, African Americans increasingly formed their own separate Baptist and Methodist congregations in the Chesapeake, as they did in Philadelphia and other urban centers (see page 173).

Such congregations near Richmond became the seedbeds of revolt. Gabriel, an enslaved blacksmith who argued that African Americans should fight for their freedom, carefully planned a large-scale revolt. Often accompanied by his brother Martin, a preacher, he visited Sunday church services, where blacks gathered outside of the watchful eyes of their owners. Gabriel first recruited to his cause other skilled African

GABRIEL'S
REBELLION

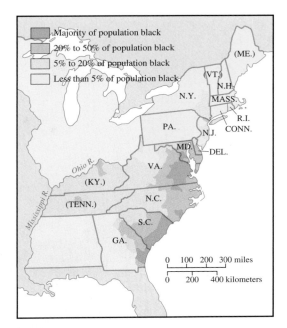

Map 8.1

African American Population, 1790: Proportion of Total Population   The first census clearly indicated that the African American population was heavily concentrated in just a few areas of the United States, most notably in coastal regions of South Carolina, Georgia, and Virginia. Although there were growing numbers of blacks in the backcountry—presumably taken there by migrating slaveowners—most parts of the North and East, with the exception of the immediate vicinity of New York City, had few African American residents.   (Source: From Lester J. Cappon et al., eds. *Atlas of Early American History: The Revolutionary Era, 1760–1790.* Copyright © 1976 by Princeton University Press. Reprinted by permission of Princeton University Press.)

Americans who like himself lived in semifreedom under minimal supervision. Next he enlisted rural slaves (see Map 8.1). The conspirators planned to attack Richmond on the night of August 30, 1800, set fire to the city, seize the state capitol, and capture the governor, James Monroe. At that point, Gabriel believed, other slaves and possibly sympathetic poor whites would join in.

The plan showed considerable political sophistication, but heavy rain forced a postponement. Several planters then learned of the plan from slave informers and spread the alarm. Gabriel avoided arrest for some weeks, but militia troops quickly apprehended and interrogated most of the other leaders of the rebellion. Twenty-six conspirators, including Gabriel himself, were hanged. Ironically, only those slaves who betrayed their fellows won their freedom as a consequence of the conspiracy.

■ Richmond, Virginia, at the time of Gabriel's Rebellion. This was the city as Gabriel knew it. The state capitol, the rebels' intended target, dominates the city's skyline as it dominated Gabriel's thinking.   (Maryland Historical Society)

That disastrous outcome did not end the unrest among Virginia's slaves. In 1802 a waterman named Sancho—a peripheral participant in Gabriel's plot—revived the plans for a revolt. This time word spread along Virginia and North Carolina rivers, carried by slaves who, like Sancho, worked on the boats that plied the two states' interconnected waterways. The incomplete plans disintegrated when the plots were revealed prematurely. Again, trials and executions followed, and twenty-five more African Americans lost their lives on the gallows.

At his trial two years earlier, one of Gabriel's followers had made explicit the links that so frightened Chesapeake slaveholders. He told his judges that, like George Washington, "I have adventured my life in endeavouring to obtain the liberty of my countrymen, and am a willing sacrifice in their cause." Southern state legislatures responded to such claims by increasing the severity of the laws regulating slavery. Before long, all talk of emancipation ceased in the South, and slavery became even more firmly entrenched as an economic institution and way of life.

Summary

*a*s the nineteenth century began, inhabitants of the United States faced changed lives in the new republic. Indian peoples east of the Mississippi River found that they had to give up some parts of their traditional culture to preserve others. Some African Americans struggled unsuccessfully to free themselves from the inhuman bonds of slavery, then subsequently confronted more constraints than ever because of increasingly restrictive laws.

European Americans too adjusted to changed circumstances. The first eleven years of government under the Constitution established many enduring precedents for congressional, presidential, and judicial action—among them establishment of the cabinet, interpretations of key clauses of the Constitution, and stirrings of judicial review of state and federal legislation. Building on successful negotiations with Spain (Pinckney's Treaty), Britain (the Jay Treaty), and France (the Convention of 1800), the United States developed its diplomatic independence, striving to avoid entanglement with European countries and their continental wars. Yet especially after 1793 internal political consensus proved elusive. The 1790s spawned vigorous debates over foreign and domestic policy and saw the beginnings of a system of organized political factionalism, if not yet formal parties. The Whiskey Rebellion, instigated by westerners outraged at tax policies formulated by eastern elites, showed that regional conflicts continued even under the new government. And the waging of an undeclared war against France proved extremely contentious, splitting one faction and energizing another.

At the end of the 1790s, after more than a decade of struggle, the Jeffersonian view of the future of republicanism prevailed over Alexander Hamilton's vision of a powerful centralized economy and a strong national government. As a result, for decades to come the country would be characterized by a decentralized economy, minimal government (especially at the national level), and maximum freedom of action and mobility for individual white men. Jeffersonian Democratic-Republicans, like other white men before them, failed to extend to white women, Indian peoples, and African Americans the freedom and individuality they recognized as essential for themselves.

LEGACY FOR A PEOPLE AND A NATION
Dissent During Wartime

The Quasi-War with France in 1798 and 1799, the nation's first overseas conflict, brought the first attempt to suppress dissent. By criminalizing dissenting speech, the Sedition Act of 1798 tried to quiet the Democratic-Republicans' criticism of the war in general and President John Adams in particular. Fifteen men (including a member of Congress) were fined and jailed after being convicted under the statute's provisions.

Although Americans might assume that their right to free speech under the First Amendment, more fully accepted now than it was two hundred years ago, today protects dissenters during a war, the history of the nation suggests otherwise. Each major conflict fought under the Constitution—the Civil War, World War I,

World War II, and Vietnam—has stimulated efforts by both government and individual citizens to suppress dissenting voices. For example, during the Civil War, the Union jailed civilian Confederate sympathizers, holding them under martial law for long periods. During the First World War, a Sedition Act allowed the government to deport immigrant aliens who too vocally criticized the war effort, among them several outspoken Socialists and anarchists. Moreover, citizens who objected to government policies were subjected to a variety of formal and informal sanctions by their neighbors. World War II brought the silencing of isolationists' voices, as those who had opposed American entry into the war were denied public outlets for their ideas. The consequences of antiwar protests in the Vietnam era still affect the nation today, for the American people remain divided over whether the proper course of action in the 1960s and 1970s was dissent from, or acquiescence in, government policy. Although during the first Persian Gulf war (1991) and the Afghanistan campaign (2001), military officials restricted reporters' access to the battlefront, during the war against Iraq (2003) that policy was reversed, with mixed results.

Freedom of speech is never easy to maintain, and wartime conditions make it much more difficult. When the nation comes under attack, whether from a foreign country or from terrorists, many patriotic Americans argue that the time for dissent has ceased and that all citizens should support the government. Others contend that, if freedom in the nation is to mean anything, people must have the right to speak their minds freely at all times. Events in the United States since the attacks of September 11, 2001, suggest that this legacy remains extremely contentious for the American people.

The **history companion** *powered by Eduspace®*

Your primary source for interactive quizzes, exercises, and more to help you learn efficiently.
http://history.college.hmco.com/students

HISTOIRE
DE
BARBARIE, ET DE SES
CORSAIRES.

Par R. P. F. PIERRE DAN, Bachelier en Theologie de la
Faculté de Paris, Mtre et Superieur du Conuent de l'ordre de la S.
Trinité et Redemption des Captifs fondé au Chasteau de Fontaine-bleau.

SECONDE EDITION.

Reueuë et augmenteé.

PARTISAN POLITICS AND WAR: THE DEMOCRATIC-REPUBLICANS IN POWER 1801–1815

*J*ohn Foss, captured by "pirates" off the Barbary Coast of North Africa in the 1790s, wrote of the "hellish tortures and punishments" inflicted "on the unfortunate Christians." Marched through Algiers, the party of nine ragged sailors heard shouts from the Islamic crowds praising the victories over "Christian dogs," and in prison they learned of ten other American vessels recently captured. In Algiers they became white slaves under African masters. Eventually the United States ransomed the captives, and four of the nine made it back to America; the others died of plague.

In the early nineteenth century, the Barbary captivity stories had the drama of modern gothic novels. "Pirates" took American men and women hostage from ships, held them in confinement, stripped and beat them as Christians, and humiliated them as Americans. In telling of white slaves with black masters, the tales turned American assumptions on their heads. Firsthand descriptions of Africa projected negative images of a despotic, depraved people, so very different from Americans. In the end, the Americans—at least those who survived to tell their stories—prevailed, and so the stories became epic affirmations of Western culture over "barbarians."

Americans loved to read these harrowing stories. John Foss's account of his captivity was reprinted twice in 1798. The fictional account of a woman held a slave in Algiers from 1800 to 1806, *History of the Captivity and Sufferings of Mrs. Maria Martin*, titillated Americans and went through twelve editions following its 1807 printing. Chained in prison, Martin described how "the enormous iron round my neck pained me," and how "her mind sunk under this accumulation of miserable sufferings." Finally, she wrote, "my liberty had been purchased by my country," and she heard the door of the dungeon slam shut

CHAPTER OUTLINE

The Jefferson Presidency and Marshall Court

Louisiana and Lewis and Clark

A New Political Culture

Indian Resistance

American Shipping Imperiled

LINKS TO THE WORLD
Industrial Piracy

"Mr. Madison's War"

Peace and Consequences

Summary

LEGACY FOR A PEOPLE AND A NATION
States' Rights and Nullification

◄ Christian monks purchase the freedom of Barbary Coast captives, held in chains, from their Muslim captors. (Photograph courtesy of the James Ford Bell Library, University of Minnesota)

CHRONOLOGY

1800 • Jefferson elected president, Burr vice president

1801 • Marshall becomes chief justice of the United States
     • Jefferson inaugurated as first Democratic-Republican president

1801–05 • United States defeats Barbary pirates in Tripoli War

1803 • *Marbury v. Madison* establishes judicial review
     • United States purchases Louisiana Territory from France

1804 • Burr kills Hamilton in a duel
     • Jefferson reelected president, Clinton vice president

1804–06 • Lewis and Clark explore Louisiana Territory

1805 • Prophet emerges as Shawnee leader

1807 • *Chesapeake* affair almost leads to war with Great Britain
     • Embargo Act halts foreign trade

1808 • Congress bans importation of slaves to the United States
     • Madison elected president, Clinton vice president

1808–13 • Prophet and Tecumseh organize Native American tribal resistance

1808–15 • Embargoes and war stimulate domestic manufacturing

1812 • Madison reelected president, Gerry vice president

1812–15 • United States and Great Britain fight the War of 1812

1813 • Death of Tecumseh ends effective pan-Indian resistance

1814 • Jackson's defeat of Creeks at Battle of Horseshoe Bend begins Indian removal from the South
     • Treaty of Ghent ends the War of 1812

1814–15 • Hartford Convention undermines Federalists

1815 • Battle of New Orleans makes Jackson a national hero

behind her. As a Christian, in chains and afterward, she felt morally superior to her captors.

In reality the "pirates"—from what Europeans called the Barbary states and Africans the Maghreb—had challenged the United States in a most fundamental way: was this new nation an independent, sovereign state that could protect its citizens and commerce abroad?

The issue was money. In 1801 the *bashaw* of Tripoli, angry over the United States's refusal to pay tribute for safe passage of its ships, sailors, and passengers through the Mediterranean, declared war on the United States. President Thomas Jefferson responded by sending a naval squadron to protect American ships in the area. The only other alternative was to abandon the Mediterranean Sea, which would have damaged American trade. After two years of stalemate, Jefferson ordered a blockade of Tripoli, but the American frigate *Philadelphia* ran aground in its harbor and three hundred American officers and sailors were captured. Jefferson refused to ransom them. With the blockade still in place, seven marines and four hundred soldiers of fortune marched overland from Egypt to seize the port of Derne, on the shores of Tripoli. Finally, by treaty with Tripoli in 1805, the United States paid $60,000 to free the *Philadelphia* prisoners, and the war was over. But the United States continued to pay tribute to the other three Barbary states (Algiers, Morocco, and Tunis) until 1815. Was the United States an independent sovereign nation? The question rankled, especially as Great Britain seemed to think not, and continued to treat the new nation as a colony.

In replacing John Adams as president, Thomas Jefferson piloted the young nation in new directions at home as well as abroad. In the tradition of the Revolution, Jefferson and his Democratic-Republican successor presidents soon sought to restrain the national government, believing that limited government would foster republican virtue. The Federalists, in contrast, advocated a strong national government with centralized authority to promote economic development. As factions competed for popular support, they laid the basis for a national political culture. Factionalism did not spring only from politics, however. Americans also divided along other lines: by class, race, ethnicity, gender, religion, and region.

Events abroad and in the West both encouraged and threatened Americans. Seizing one opportunity, the

United States purchased the Louisiana Territory, adding a vast land from which new states would soon be carved. But even as American interests turned westward, events in Europe and on the high seas of the Atlantic wrenched an about-face. Caught between the warring British and French, the United States found its ships seized, its foreign commerce interrupted, its sailors forcibly drafted, and its rights as a neutral and independent nation violated. In what some have called the second war for independence, the United States fought Great Britain to a standoff, while on another front routing Indian resistance and shattering Native American unity. A peace treaty restored the prewar status quo, but the war and the treaty affirmed U.S. sovereignty and strengthened America's determination to steer clear of further European conflicts. The war also stimulated industry and nationalism. In 1815 a secure, independent, and self-confident nation looked to the future with optimism. ■

■ This portrait of President Thomas Jefferson was painted by Rembrandt Peale in 1805. Charles Willson Peale (Rembrandt's father) and his five sons helped establish the reputation of American art in the new nation. Rembrandt Peale achieved fame for his presidential portraits; here he has captured Jefferson in a noble pose without the usual symbols of office or power, befitting the Republican age. (© Collection of The New-York Historical Society)

The Jefferson Presidency and Marshall Court

*I*n later years Thomas Jefferson would always refer to his winning the presidency as the "Revolution of 1800." The Democratic-Republicans, he believed, would restore government to its limited role, restrained and frugal. He stressed the republican virtues of independence, self-reliance, and equality, in contrast to the monarchical ambitions of the Federalists. To counter Federalist formality, Jefferson and his fellow Democratic-Republicans promoted simplicity, even in dress. They wore plain trousers instead of the wigs and knee breeches that George Washington and John Adams had favored.

Yet in his inaugural address in March 1801, Jefferson reached out to his opponents. Standing in the Senate

JEFFERSON INAUGURAL

chamber, the only part of the Capitol that had been completed, he appealed to the electorate not as party members but as citizens who shared common beliefs: "We are all republicans, we are all federalists." Nearly a thousand people strained to hear him lay out his vision of a restored republicanism: "A wise and frugal government, which shall restrain men from injuring one another, which shall leave them free to regulate their pursuits of industry and improvement, and shall not take from the mouth of labor the bread it has earned. This is the sum of good government," he concluded.

But outgoing president John Adams was not there to hear Jefferson's call for unity. He had left Washington before dawn to avoid the Democratic-Republican takeover. He and Jefferson had once been close friends but now disliked each other intensely. Both were thin-skinned, quick to take offense and quick to give it. Despite the spirit of Jefferson's inaugural address, the Democratic-Republicans and Federalists remained bitter opponents. Nonetheless presidential succession in 1801 took place by ballot rather than by arms, which some had feared.

To implement the restoration of republican values, Jefferson aggressively extended the Democratic-Republicans'

DEMOCRATIC-REPUBLICANS IN OFFICE

grasp on the national government. It was indeed a takeover. Virtually all of the 600 or so officials appointed during the administrations of Washington and Adams had been loyal Federalists; only 6 were known Democratic-Republicans. To bring into his administration men who shared his vision of an agrarian republic and individual liberty, Jefferson refused to recognize appointments that Adams had made in the last days of his presidency and dismissed Federalist customs collectors from New England ports. He awarded vacant treasury and judicial offices to Democratic-Republicans. By July 1803, Federalists held only 130 of 316 presidentially controlled offices. They accused Jefferson of "hunting the Federalists like wild beasts" and abandoning the olive leaf extended in his inaugural address.

The Democratic-Republican Congress, swept into office in the election of 1800, also proceeded to affirm its belief in limited government. Albert Gallatin, secretary of the treasury, and John Randolph of Virginia, Jefferson's ally in the House of Representatives, translated ideology into policy, putting the federal government on a diet. Congress repealed all internal taxes, including the whiskey tax. Gallatin cut the army budget in half and reduced the 1802 navy budget by two-thirds. He then moved to reduce the national debt from $83 million to $57 million, as part of a plan to retire it altogether by 1817. If Alexander Hamilton had viewed the national debt as the engine of economic growth, Jefferson saw it as the source of government corruption. Jefferson even closed two of the nation's five diplomatic missions abroad—at The Hague and Berlin—to save money.

More than frugality, however, distinguished Democratic-Republicans from Federalists. Before Jefferson's election, opposition to the Alien and Sedition Acts of 1798 had helped unite Democratic-Republicans (see pages 206–207). Jefferson now declined to use the acts against his opponents (as President Adams had done in suppressing Democratic-Republican editors) and pardoned those who had been convicted under the provisions. Congress let expire the Sedition Act in 1801 and the Alien Act in 1802. Congress also repealed the Naturalization Act of 1798, which had required fourteen years of residency for citizenship. The 1802 act that replaced it, while stipulating the registration of aliens, required of would-be citizens only five years of residency, loyalty to the Constitution, and the forsaking of foreign allegiance and titles. The new act would remain the basis of naturalized American citizenship into the twentieth century.

The Democratic-Republicans turned next to the judiciary, the last stronghold of Federalist power. To many

WAR ON THE JUDICIARY

Democratic-Republicans, the judiciary represented a centralizing force, one undemocratic by virtue of unelected judges appointed for life. Especially galling to Jefferson, John Marshall had become chief justice of the United States, appointed after Adams's defeat. During the 1790s not a single Democratic-Republican had occupied the federal bench; thus the judiciary became a battlefield following the revolution of 1800.

The first skirmish erupted over repeal of the Judiciary Act of 1801, which had been passed in the final days of the Adams administration. The act, designed to maintain Federalist control over the courts, created fifteen new judgeships, which Adams filled by signing "midnight" appointments until his term was just hours away from expiring. The act also reduced by attrition the number of justices on the Supreme Court from six to five. Since that reduction would have denied Jefferson a Supreme Court appointment until two vacancies occurred, the new Democratic-Republican–dominated Congress repealed the 1801 act.

Partisan Democratic-Republicans created another front in the war for control of the judiciary by targeting opposition judges for removal. Democratic-Republicans were especially infuriated with the Federalist judges who had refused to review the Sedition Act under which Federalists had prosecuted critics of the Adams administration. At Jefferson's prompting, the House impeached (indicted) Federal District Judge John Pickering of New Hampshire, an elderly, emotionally disturbed alcoholic. He was an easy target, and in 1805 the Senate convicted him, removing him from office.

The day Pickering was ousted, the House impeached Supreme Court Justice Samuel Chase for judicial misconduct. A staunch Federalist, Chase had pushed for prosecutions under the Sedition Act, had actively campaigned for Adams in 1800, and repeatedly had denounced Jefferson's administration from the bench. The Democratic-Republicans, however, failed to muster the two-thirds majority of senators necessary to convict him. Chase's acquittal preserved the Court's independence at a critical time before the role of the judiciary as an equal branch of government had been established. In failing to remove Chase, the Senate established the precedent that criminal actions, not political disagreements, were the only proper grounds for impeachment. In his tenure as president, Jefferson appointed three new Supreme Court justices. Nonetheless, under Chief Justice John Marshall, the Court remained a Federalist stronghold.

Jefferson and Marshall shared much in common. They were fellow Virginians, even distant cousins, and

JOHN MARSHALL

Marshall was of the generation of Madison and Monroe, the bright young men who formed Jefferson's intellectual entourage. Jefferson, however, viewed Marshall as a traitor to republicanism after Marshall became a Federalist in the 1790s. President Adams had appointed him secretary of state and then, in his last weeks as a lame-duck president, named Marshall chief justice. Though an autocrat by nature, Marshall possessed a grace and openness of manner that comple-

■ John Marshall (1755-1835) was chief justice of the United States from 1801 to 1835. This painting by John B. Martin captures Marshall's aristocratic bearing and strong will that would allow him to dominate the Court.   (Collection of the Supreme Court of the United States)

mented the new Republican political style. As a justice he adopted republican dress, wearing a plain black gown rather than the British robes of scarlet and ermine or the colorful academic garb worn by other justices. John B. Martin's portrait of Marshall in 1801 captures both his aristocratic bearing and his strong will. Under Marshall's domination, however, the Supreme Court retained a Federalist outlook even after Democratic-Republican justices achieved a majority in 1811. Throughout his tenure (1801–1835), the Court consistently upheld federal supremacy over the states and protected the interests of commerce and capital.

Marshall made the Court an equal branch of government in practice as well as theory. Judicial service became a coveted honor for ambitious and talented men. Previously people regarded it lightly, and justices had served only short terms. No judicial building was constructed in Washington; Congress considered it unessential, and the Court continued to meet in a chamber of the Capitol. Marshall unified the Court, influencing the justices to issue joint majority opinions rather than a host of individual concurring judgments. Marshall himself became the voice of the majority: from 1801 through 1805 he wrote twenty-four of the Court's twenty-six decisions; through 1810 he wrote 85 percent of the opinions, including every important one.

Marshall significantly increased the Supreme Court's power in the landmark case of *Marbury v. Madison* (1803), another skirmish in war over the judiciary. William Marbury, one of Adams's midnight appointees, had been named a justice of the peace in the District of Columbia. James Madison, Jefferson's new secretary of state, declined to certify Marbury's appointment so that the president could instead appoint a Democratic-Republican. Marbury sued, requesting a writ of mandamus (a court order forcing the president to appoint him). The case presented a political dilemma. If the Supreme Court ruled in favor of Marbury and issued a writ of mandamus, the president probably would not comply with it, and the Court had no way to force him to do so. But if the Federalist-dominated bench refused to issue the writ, it would be handing the Democratic-Republicans a victory.

MARBURY V. MADISON

Marshall brilliantly recast the issue to avoid both pitfalls. Speaking for the Court, he ruled that Marbury had a right to his appointment but that the Supreme Court could not compel Madison to honor the appointment because the Constitution did not grant the Court power to issue a writ of mandamus. In the absence of any specific mention in the Constitution, Marshall ruled, the section of the Judiciary Act of 1789 that authorized the Court to issue such writs was unconstitutional. In *Marbury v. Madison,* the Supreme Court denied itself the power to issue writs of mandamus but established its far greater power to judge the constitutionality of laws passed by Congress.

In succeeding years Marshall fashioned the theory of judicial review, the power of the Supreme Court to decide the constitutionality of legislation and presidential acts. Since the Constitution was "the supreme law of the land," he reasoned in *Marbury v. Madison,* any federal or state act contrary to the Constitution must be null and void. The Supreme Court, whose duty it was to uphold the law, would decide whether or not a legislative act contradicted the Constitution. "It is emphatically the province and duty of the judicial department," Marshall ruled, "to say what the law is." The power of judicial review established in *Marbury v. Madison* permanently enhanced the independence of the judiciary and breathed life into the Constitution. "Marshall found the Constitution paper and made it power," President James A. Garfield later observed.

Louisiana and Lewis and Clark

*D*emocratic-Republicans and Federalists divided sharply over more than just the Court; Jefferson's acquisition of the Louisiana Territory in 1803 was another point of contention. Jefferson shared with many other Americans the belief that the United States was destined to expand its "empire of liberty," and his presidency made western expansion a national goal.

Since American independence, Louisiana had held a special place in the nation's expansionist dreams. Louisiana defined the western border of the United States, which stretched along the Mississippi River from the Gulf of Mexico to present-day Minnesota. Spain had acquired the Louisiana Territory from France in 1763, at the end of the Seven Years War (see page 122). By 1800 hundreds of thousands of Americans in search of land had settled in the rich Mississippi and Ohio River valleys, intruding on Indian lands. These settlers floated their farm goods down the Mississippi and Ohio Rivers to New Orleans for export. Whoever controlled the port of New Orleans had a hand on the throat of the American economy. Americans preferred Spanish control of Louisiana to control by France, a much stronger power.

In secret pacts with Spain in 1800 and 1801, however, France had acquired the territory once again. The United States learned of the transfer only in 1802, when Napoleon seemed poised to rebuild a French empire in the New World. "Every eye in the United States is now focused on the affairs of Louisiana," Jefferson wrote to Robert R. Livingston, the American minister in Paris. American concerns intensified in October of that year when Spanish officials, on the eve of ceding control to the French, violated Pinckney's Treaty (see page 204) by denying Americans the privilege of storing their products at New Orleans prior to transshipment to foreign markets. "The Mississippi," Secretary of State James Madison wrote, "is to them [western settlers] everything. It is the Hudson, the Delaware, the Potomac and all navigable rivers of the Atlantic States formed into one stream." Western farmers and eastern merchants thought a devious Napoleon had closed the port; they grumbled and talked war.

Jefferson personally took charge. To relieve the pressure for war and to win western farm support, Jefferson prepared for war while sending Virginia governor James Monroe as his personal envoy to join Robert Livingston in France. Their mission: to buy the port of New Orleans and as much of the Mississippi valley as possible. Meanwhile, Congress authorized the call-up of eighty thousand militiamen in case war be-

LOUISIANA PURCHASE

came necessary. Arriving in Paris in April 1803, Monroe was astonished to learn that France already had offered to sell all 827,000 square miles of Louisiana to the United States for a mere $15 million. Napoleon had lost interest in the New World. Once he failed to recapture independent Haiti, the idea of a New World empire dissolved and Louisiana became superfluous. At the same time he needed money for renewed warfare against Britain. On April 30 Monroe and Livingston signed a treaty buying the vast territory whose exact borders and land were uncharted (see Map 9.1).

At one stroke of a pen, the Louisiana Purchase doubled the size of the nation and opened the way for continental expansion. It was the most popular achievement of Jefferson's presidency. But for Jefferson, the purchase presented a dilemma. For one thing, it conflicted with his commitment to debt reduction. And some questioned Jefferson's power to make such a move. To be sure, the purchase promised fulfillment of his dream of an agrarian republic "with room enough for our descendants to the hundredth and thousandth generation." It also facilitated the removal of eastern Indians by providing land for their exile. But was it constitutional? The Constitution nowhere authorized the president to acquire new territory and incorporate it into the nation.

Jefferson considered proposing a constitutional amendment to allow the purchase but decided against it. He believed that the president's implied powers to protect the nation justified the purchase. His long-standing interest in Louisiana and the West also allayed his constitutional concerns. As early as 1782, as an American envoy in France, Jefferson had suggested sending an exploratory mission across the continent to California. A naturalist and scientist, Jefferson seemed obsessed with the West—its geography, people, plants, and animals; he had long wanted to acquire, subdue, and exploit it. As secretary of state in the 1790s, he had been active in promoting a search for "the shortest & most convenient route of communications between the U.S. & the Pacific Ocean."

In 1803 Jefferson sent an expedition headed by Meriwether Lewis and William Clark to the Pacific coast via the Missouri and Columbia Rivers. The twenty-nine-year-old Lewis, a regular army officer in the 1790s, had exchanged rugged military life to be Jefferson's private secretary in 1801. As friend, teacher, role model, and father figure, Jefferson gave Lewis a "crash course" on the botany and the environment of the West, and he proved an exceptional student. The thirty-year-old Clark was an explorer and former soldier who had fought against and negotiated with native peoples. Aware of the risks as well as the scientific importance of

LEWIS AND CLARK

Map 9.1

Louisiana Purchase

The Louisiana Purchase (1803) doubled the area of the United States and opened the trans-Mississippi West for American settlement.

their mission, both were eager for the commission. The expedition also had political import, for the 1801 publication of Alexander MacKenzie's *Voyages from Montreal,* which described the first crossing of the continent in Canada in 1793, had raised fears that the British would dominate the West.

Lewis and Clark officially started their journey in May 1804. They traveled up the Missouri River and wintered at Fort Mandan in present-day North Dakota. There they selected their twenty-nine-member corps and were joined by Indian guides. In April 1805 they resumed their journey, traveling through present-day Montana. In August, having reached the navigable limits of the Missouri, they continued the journey with horses. Helped by a local Shoshone guide, they crossed the Bitterroot Mountains. Traversing the Rockies, "the most terrible mountains I ever beheld," wrote Sergeant Patrick Gass in his diary, proved their most dangerous and treacherous venture. At times they lost their way, tumbled down steep mountain trails, and slept in the snow, bone cold. Short of food, they had to kill a horse for meat. In November 1805 they reached the Pacific Ocean in present-day Oregon, where they wintered, and the following March began the return trek. Lewis and Clark split up to explore alternate routes and reunited in August 1806. They arrived back in St. Louis on September 23, 1806.

The original Corps of Discovery reflected American diversity. It included army regulars and young adventurers

■ This Charles M. Russell painting of the Lewis and Clark expedition depicts Sacagawea talking with Chinook Indians. A Shoshone, Sacagawea knew the land and the languages of the mountain Indians, and helped guide the Corps of Discovery.   (Courtesy, Montana Historical Society, Gift of the artist)

CORPS OF
DISCOVERY

from Kentucky. Among them were two half-French and half-Omaha men and another who was son of a French Canadian father and a Shawnee mother. Clark brought his slave York, whom he inherited in 1799 from his father. Immigrants included an Irishman and a German. Later at the Mandan villages the French Canadian trader Toussaint Charbonneau and his pregnant, fifteen-year-old Shoshone wife, Sacagawea, joined the expedition. Lewis and Clark took Charbonneau because they wanted Sacagawea, who knew the languages of the mountain Indians. She proved invaluable as a guide and translator, and she knew the land and the people better than anyone else. The youngest member of the group was Jean Baptiste Charbonneau, son of Sacagawea, born on February 11, 1805.

Headed by army officers, the expedition followed military rules. At times, however, it was more informal and democratic than army regulations or even civilian society allowed. When trouble arose, Lewis and Clark held courts-martial to discipline corps members for such infractions as drunkenness. Contrary to army rules, enlisted men sat on the court. When Sergeant Charles Floyd died of a ruptured appendix at the beginning of the journey, the soldiers elected Private Patrick Gass as his successor, a most unusual move. In November 1805, to determine where to locate winter quarters on the Pacific coast, all voted, including the slave York and the Indian woman Sacagawea. Yet issues of race and gender were present. Along the way Indians were astonished at York; many had not seen a black man before. They were curious about his skin color, his "short, curling hair," and his strength. At the end of the journey the names of York and Sacagawea did not appear on the roster Lewis submitted to the War Department. Neither received pay for their work though their assistance had been indispensable.

Although some Americans still believed that the West was uninhabited, Lewis and Clark knew better. They anticipated a crowded wilderness and hoped to cement U.S. relations with Indians. The explorers carried with them twenty-one bags of gifts for Native American leaders, both to establish goodwill and to stimulate interest in trading for American manufactured goods. They brought back stories not only of various peoples, but also of fauna and flora unknown to the western scientific community; they encountered the grizzly bear, bighorn sheep, and mountain goats. Lewis sent boxes of natural-history specimens to Jefferson, including plant and tree cuttings.

In time, the expedition became legendary and Lewis and Clark fabled American explorers. They mapped the West and, with their reports, promoted dreams of a continental empire. The corps members were well rewarded and basked in their renown. But one among them reaped few rewards: the slave York. In 1808 York demanded his freedom from Clark as a reward for his service to the expedition. York's wife, a slave, lived in Louisville, Kentucky, and he wished to join her. Clark let him visit her, and York proposed that he stay there, hiring himself out and sending money to Clark. Clark refused and in May 1809 York returned to Clark in St. Louis. Clark found

York "insolent and sulky. I gave him a severe trouncing the other Day, and he has much mended" his ways.

Other explorations followed Lewis and Clark's, further publicizing the land west of the Mississippi. In 1805 and 1806 Lieutenant Zebulon Pike sought the source of the continent-cutting river and a navigable water route west. When Pike and his men wandered into Spanish territory to the south, the Spanish held them captive for several months in Mexico. After his release, Pike wrote an account of his experiences that set commercial minds spinning. He described a potential commercial market in southwestern Spanish cities as well as bountiful furs and precious minerals. Over the next few decades, Americans avidly read accounts of western exploration. The vision of a road to the Southwest became a reality with the opening of the Santa Fe Trail in the 1820s, and settlement followed the trail.

EXPLORATION OF THE WEST

New Spain's Tejas (Texas) province bordered the Louisiana Territory. Provincial officials welcomed Americans interested in the land south of the territory, and American immigrants began to drift in. Some fought as volunteers with Indians and Mexican rebels in a twelve-year war with Spain that ended with Mexican independence in 1821. The establishment of an independent Mexico inspired these Americans to dream of an independent Texas nation—a place for white American settlers. Since they envisioned the West an uninhabited area, they did not imagine a place for Mexicans or indigenous peoples in the "empire of liberty."

A New Political Culture

*W*riting to English scientist Joseph Priestly in 1801, Jefferson described his presidency as the beginning of a new era. "The great extent of our republic is new. Its sparse habitation is new. The mighty wave of public opinion which has rolled over is new." Although the electorate was limited mostly to white males over twenty-one who held property, the Democratic-Republicans had taken their appeals to the people in the elections of 1800. While Federalists might think that for candidates to debate their own merits in front of voters was demeaning, a subversion of the natural political order, the Democratic-Republicans did not. Now in office they worked hard to keep public opinion on their side.

One way to control that "wave" of public opinion was through the press. The new president persuaded the *National Intelligencer* to move from Philadelphia to Washington, and during the ensuing Democratic-Republican ad-

THE PARTISAN PRESS

■ The German immigrant John Lewis Kimmell conveys the growing popular interest in elections in his 1815 painting, *Election Day in Philadelphia.* Elections combined civic duty with a party atmosphere, and even the disfranchised free blacks and women turned out to join the festivities.   (Courtesy, Winterthur Museum)

ministrations it served as the official voice. In 1801 Alexander Hamilton launched the *New-York Evening Post* as the Federalist vehicle to retake power. It boosted Federalists while often calling Jefferson a liar and depicting him as head of a slave harem. Newspapers circulated widely, linking parties, voters, and the government. Sold by subscription, the papers were readily available in taverns, coffeehouses, and hotels, where they were often read aloud. They not only helped build the party system but, like the parties, they also contributed to building a national political culture. In 1800 the nation had 260 newspapers; by 1810 it had 396. Editors were outrageously partisan.

After the Federalist defeat in 1800, a younger generation of Federalists began to imitate the popular appeals of the Democratic-Republicans. Led by such men as Josiah Quincy, a Massachusetts congressman, the Younger Federalists campaigned for popular support. Quincy cleverly presented the Federalists as the people's party, attacking Democratic-Republicans as autocratic planters. "Jeffersonian Democracy," Quincy gibed in

1804, was "an Indian word, signifying 'a great tobacco planter who had herds of black slaves.'" In attacking frugal government, the Younger Federalists played on fears of a weakened army and navy. Eastern merchants depended on a strong navy to protect ocean trade; westerners looked to the army to defend them as they encroached on the territory of Native Americans.

For Democratic-Republicans, distinctive regional interests inspired a new style of campaigning, symbolized by the political barbecue. In New York campaigners roasted oxen; on the New England coast they baked clams; in Maryland they served oysters; in Virginia they planked shad. Guests washed down their meals with beer and punch and sometimes competed in corn-shucking or horse-pulling contests. Voters demonstrated their allegiance by attending these events and displaying images of Democratic-Republican party leaders. Oratory became a popular form of entertainment, and candidates delivered lengthy and uninhibited speeches wherever crowds gathered. They attacked the character

GRASSROOTS CAMPAIGNING

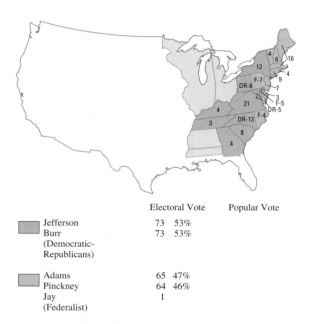

Electoral Vote   Popular Vote

Jefferson   73   53%
Burr   73   53%
(Democratic-
Republicans)

Adams   65   47%
Pinckney   64   46%
Jay   1
(Federalist)

Map 9.2   Presidential Election, 1800

The Democratic-Republicans, with their candidates Thomas Jefferson and Aaron Burr, won the electoral votes of the southern states, while the Federalists, the party of John Adams and Charles Cotesworth Pinckney, received votes primarily in New England. The parties split the votes of the middle states, but the Democratic-Republicans dominated the electoral-vote count there and won the election.

of their opponents, often making wild accusations that—given the slow speed of communications—might go unanswered until after the election. Slander and gossip were the rule of the day. Some historians have speculated that these developing party rituals helped contain more violent expression.

The opposition Federalists never mastered the art of campaigning. Older Federalists remained opposed to popular appeals. And though strong in Connecticut, Delaware, and a few other states, the Federalists were weak at the national level and could not manage sustained competition. Divisions among Federalists often undermined their success, and the extremism of some Older Federalists discredited most of the rest. A case in point was Timothy Pickering, a Massachusetts congressman and former secretary of state. Pickering opposed the Louisiana Purchase, feared Jefferson's reelection, and urged the secession of New England in 1803 and 1804. He won some support, but most Federalists balked at his plan for secession. Ever the opportunist, Vice President Aaron Burr, intrigued with Pickering's idea of northeastern independence, fantasized about leading New York

into secession, with other states following. But when Burr lost his bid to become governor of New York in 1804, dreams of a northern confederacy evaporated.

The controversies surrounding Burr illustrate the convergence of the political and the personal. In the election of 1800, he understood he was the vice-presidential candidate, but when all 73 of the Democratic-Republican electors cast ballots for both Jefferson and Burr (see Map 9.2), Burr challenged Jefferson for the presidency. The Constitution required that because neither had a plurality, the contest be decided in the House of Representatives, with each state's congressmen voting as a unit. It had taken thirty-five ballots for the House, still with a Federalist majority, to decide that Jefferson would be a lesser evil than Burr. In response to the tangle, the Twelfth Amendment to the Constitution (1804) changed the method of voting in the electoral college to allow for a party ticket.

BURR AND PERSONAL ANIMOSITY

For Burr, ever the opportunist, it was a short step from personal animosity into violence. He and the hothead Alexander Hamilton had long despised each other. Hamilton relentlessly blocked Burr's path. He thwarted Burr's attempt to steal the election of 1800 from Jefferson, and in the 1804 mudslinging New York gubernatorial race, he backed Burr's Democratic-Republican rival. Both Burr and Hamilton held grudges, and when Hamilton accused Burr of being a liar, Burr challenged him to a duel. With his honor at stake, Hamilton accepted even though his son Philip had died in 1801 from dueling wounds. Because New York had outlawed dueling, the two men met across the Hudson River at Weehawken, New Jersey, in July 1804. Hamilton did not fire, and he paid for that decision with his life. Burr was indicted for murder in New York and New Jersey and faced immediate arrest if he returned to either state.

Rather than preserving his honor, Burr's killing of Hamilton made him an outcast. His political career in ruins, Burr fled to start life anew in the West. He schemed to create in the Southwest a new empire carved out of the Louisiana Territory. With the collusion of General James Wilkinson, the U.S. commander in the Mississippi valley, Burr planned to raise a private army to grab land from the United States or from Spain (his exact plans remain unknown). Wilkinson switched sides and informed President Jefferson of Burr's devious intention. Jefferson personally assisted the prosecution in Burr's 1807 trial for treason, over which Chief Justice Marshall presided. Marshall construed treason narrowly, and the jury acquitted Burr, who fled to Europe.

Campaigning for reelection in 1804, Jefferson took credit for the restoration of republican values and the acquisition of the Louisiana Territory. The Democratic-Republicans claimed they ended the Federalist threat to liberty by repealing the Alien and Sedition and Judiciary Acts. They also boasted that they had reduced the size of government by cutting spending. American trade with Europe was flourishing, allowing Jefferson to demonstrate support for commerce too. Federalists had little to go on, though they did attack the president for paying too much for Louisiana and for exceeding his powers in buying it.

Jefferson's opponent in 1804 was Charles Cotesworth Pinckney, a wealthy South Carolina lawyer and former Revolutionary War aide to George Washington. As Adams's vice-presidential running mate in 1800, Pinckney had inherited the Federalist leadership. Jefferson dumped the disloyal Aaron Burr from the 1804 ticket, and he and his running mate, George Clinton of New York, swamped Pinckney and New Yorker Rufus King in the electoral college by 162 votes to 14, carrying fifteen of the seventeen states.

Indian Resistance

Lewis and Clark's account testified to the Indian presence in the West, and most Americans viewed Native Americans, no matter where they lived, as obstacles to American settlement. Violations of treaties and coerced new ones, forcing Indians to cede ever more land to the United States, continually shrunk Indian territory. With less land, Indians found hunting and agriculture more difficult. Not only their traditional ways but also their independence and existence were threatened. Encroachment by whites and the periodic ravages of disease—smallpox, measles, and influenza—brought further misery.

In the early 1800s two Shawnee brothers, Prophet (1775–1837) and Tecumseh (1768–1813), led a revolt against further American encroachment by fostering a pan-Indian federation that stretched from the Old Northwest to the South. Prophet's early life typified the experiences of the Indians of the Old Northwest. Born in 1775 a few months after his father's death in battle, Prophet, called Lalawethika ("Noisemaker"), as a young man was expelled to Ohio along with other Shawnees under the 1795 Treaty of Greenville (see page 182), and he later moved to Indiana. Within Prophet and Tecumseh's own lifetimes the Shawnees had lost most of their Ohio land; by the 1800s they occupied scattered sites in Ohio and in the Michigan and Louisiana territories. Dis-

THE PROPHET

placement left Lalawethika forlorn, and like many other Native Americans he turned to whiskey for escape. He also turned to traditional folk knowledge and remedies and in 1804 became a tribal medicine man. His medicine, however, could not stop the white man's diseases from ravaging his village.

Lalawethika emerged from his own battle with illness in 1805 as a new man, called Tenskwatawa ("the Open Door"), or "the Prophet." Claiming to have died and been resurrected, he traveled widely in the Ohio River valley as a religious leader, attacking the decline of moral values among Native Americans, warning of damnation for those who drank whiskey, condemning intertribal battles, and stressing harmony and respect for elders. He urged Indians to return to the old ways and abandon white customs: to hunt with bows and arrows, not guns; to stop wearing hats; and to refrain from eating bread and instead cultivate corn and beans. Whiskey, he preached, was made for whites; the forest had been created for Indians.

Prophet was building a religious movement that offered reassurance to the Shawnees, Potawatomis, and other displaced western Indians. As a leader his power came from his eloquence, conviction, and performance of miracles. By timing his invocations to coincide with a solar eclipse, he even seemed to darken the sun. His outspoken opposition to federal Indian policy drew others into his camp, and as his message spread to southern tribes, the federal government and white settlers became alarmed.

By 1808 Prophet and his older brother Tecumseh talked less about spiritual renewal and more about resisting American aggression. Together they invited Indians from all nations to settle in pan-Indian towns in Indiana, first at Greenville (1806–1808) on the Wabash, called Prophetstown by whites, and then at Tippecanoe (1808–1812). The new towns challenged the treaty-making process. The pan-Indian settlements denied the claims of Indians like Little Turtle and the Miamis, who had been guaranteed the land in exchange for enormous cessions. And the Americans viewed the new towns as places promoting Indian resistance. In effect Tecumseh was turning Prophet's religious movement into a political one. The British, who looked for alliances with Native Americans after renewed Anglo-American hostilities (see pages 232–233), encouraged Indians to defy the U.S. government. In repudiating land cessions to the government under the Treaty of Fort Wayne (1809), Tecumseh told Indiana's governor William Henry Harrison at Vincennes in 1810 that "the only way to check and stop this evil is, for all the red men to unite in claiming a

TECUMSEH

■ The Shawnee chiefs Tecumseh (*left*) and Prophet (*right*). The two brothers led a revival of traditional Shawnee culture and preached Native American federation against white encroachment. In the War of 1812 they allied themselves with the British, but Tecumseh's death at the Battle of the Thames (1813) and British indifference thereafter caused Native Americans' resistance and unity to collapse.　(Tecumseh: Field Museum of Natural History, Chicago, FMNH Neg. #A93851; Prophet: Chicago Historical Society)

common and equal right in the land, as it was at first, and should be yet; for it . . . belongs to all, for the use of each. . . . No part has a right to sell, even to each other, much less to strangers."

Tecumseh, a towering six-foot warrior and charismatic orator, soon overshadowed his brother as Shawnee leader. He dressed as a chief from a century before, exchanging his European shirts and cloth trousers for soft deerskin suits with fringes. He replaced the bright beads and ribbons sold by whites with dyed porcupine quills. He returned to traditional diet as well, refusing foreign food. Younger Indians flocked to him. Warriors found his political visions more relevant than Prophet's spirituality in protecting themselves against the United States. Convinced that only an Indian federation could stop the advance of white settlement, Tecumseh sought to unify northern and southern Indians by traveling widely, from Canada to Georgia, preaching Indian resistance. And he warned Harrison that Indians would resist white occu-

pation of the 2.5 million acres on the Wabash River that they had ceded in the Treaty of Fort Wayne.

But the Indians could not match the armed might of the United States. In November 1811, while Tecumseh was recruiting support in the South, Harrison moved against the Prophet and his followers. In the battle of Tippecanoe, the army burned the town and dispersed Prophet's and Tecumseh's supporters. The spiritual and political movement initiated by the brothers began to unravel. Tecumseh's death two years later (see page 234) would end their movement for Indian unity.

American Shipping Imperiled

"Peace, commerce, and honest friendship with all nations, entangling alliance with none," President Jefferson had proclaimed in his first inaugural address. Jefferson's efforts to stand aloof from

European conflict were successful until 1805. Thereafter the United States could not escape the web of European hostilities, and protection of American commerce and foreign relations occupied nearly all of Jefferson's second administration. The easy victory over the Barbary states would not be repeated against the British.

After the Senate ratified the Jay Treaty in 1795 (see pages 203–204), the United States and Great Britain appeared to reconcile their differences. Britain withdrew from its western forts and interfered less in American trade with France. Since the United States was Britain's best customer, and the British Empire in turn bought the bulk of American exports, both sides worked hard for good relations.

The economy of the early republic relied heavily on shipping, and the commercial fleet played a significant role in extending American trade not only to Britain but around the world.

U.S. Commerce

American fishermen explored the Atlantic, while whalers hunted for prey in the Atlantic and Pacific Oceans. Americans exported cotton, lumber, sugar, and other commodities to Europe, and brought back manufactured goods. The slave trade lured American sailing ships to Africa. Boston, Salem, and Philadelphia merchants opened trade with China, sending cloth and metal to swap for furs with Chinook Indians on the Oregon coast, then sailing to China to trade for porcelain, tea, and silk. Importing manufactured goods was more profitable than producing them at home.

Then in May 1803, two weeks after Napoleon sold Louisiana to the United States, renewal of the Napoleonic wars between France and Britain (and later Britain's continental allies, Prussia, Austria, and Russia) again trapped the United States between Britain and France on the high seas. For two years American commerce benefited from the conflict. As the world's largest neutral carrier, the United States became the chief supplier of grain to Europe. American merchants also gained control of most of the West Indian trade. But after defeating the French and Spanish fleets at the Battle of Trafalgar in October 1805, Britain's Royal Navy tightened its control of the oceans. Two months later Napoleon crushed the Russian and Austrian armies at Austerlitz. Stalemated, France and Britain launched a commercial war, blockading each other's trade. As a trading partner of both countries, the United States paid a high price.

All tension focused on the high seas, where Britain, commanding the world's largest navy, suffered a severe shortage of sailors. Too few men enlisted, and those in service frequently deserted, demoralized by harsh treatment. Some British sailors joined U.S.

Impressment of American Sailors

merchant ships, where conditions were better. The Royal Navy resorted to stopping American vessels and impressing, or forcibly detaining, British deserters, British-born naturalized American seamen, and other unlucky sailors suspected of being British. Perhaps six to eight thousand Americans were impressed in this way between 1803 and 1812. Moreover, alleged deserters—many of them American citizens—faced British courts-martial. Americans saw impressment as a direct assault on the independence of their new republic. The principle of "once a British subject, always a British subject" mocked U.S. citizenship and sovereignty.

The British violated other American rights as well. They interfered with U.S. trade with the West Indies by blocking goods the United States believed were part of neutral trade. They also searched and seized U.S. vessels within American territory offshore.

Neutral Rights

In February 1806 Americans denounced British impressment as aggression and a violation of America's neutral rights. In protest, Congress passed the Non-Importation Act, barring British manufactured goods from entering American ports. Since the act exempted most cloth or metal articles, it had little impact on British trade; instead, it warned the British what to expect if they continued to violate American rights. In November Jefferson suspended the act temporarily while William Pinckney, a Baltimore lawyer, joined James Monroe in London to negotiate a settlement. But the treaty Monroe and Pinckney carried home violated their instructions— it did not so much as mention impressment—and Jefferson never submitted it to the Senate for ratification.

Anglo-American relations steadily deteriorated. Then in June 1807, the forty-gun frigate U.S.S. *Chesapeake* left Norfolk, Virginia, headed to protect American ships in the Mediterranean. About 10 miles from shore, still inside American territorial waters, it met the fifty-gun British frigate *Leopard*. When the *Chesapeake* refused to be searched for deserters, the *Leopard* repeatedly fired its cannon broadside into the American ship. Three Americans were killed and eighteen wounded, including the ship's captain. The British seized four deserters from the Royal Navy—three of them American citizens; one of the deserters, British subject Jenkin Ratford, was hanged. Damaged and humiliated, the *Chesapeake* returned to port. Americans were outraged and united. "But one feeling pervades the nation," said a leading Democratic-Republican, former congressman Joseph Nicholson. "All distinctions of Federalism and Democracy are banished." The *Chesapeake* affair not only intensified the emotional impact

Chesapeake Affair

■ *Boarding and Taking of the American Ship* Chesapeake (1816) portrays crew from the British frigate *Leopard* fighting to search the *U.S.S. Chesapeake* for British navy deserters. The sailors of the *Chesapeake* resisted but the British overpowered them and seized four deserters, three of them American citizens. Americans were humiliated and angered by the British violation of American rights. (William L. Clements Library)

of impressment but also exposed American military weakness.

Had the United States been better prepared militarily, the ensuing howl of public indignation might have brought about a declaration of war. But the still-fledgling country was ill equipped to defend its neutral rights with force; it was certainly no match for the British navy. With Congress in recess, Jefferson was able to avoid hostilities, choosing instead what he called "peaceable coercion." In July the president closed American waters to British warships to prevent similar incidents, and soon thereafter he increased military and naval expenditures. In December 1807 Jefferson again put economic pressure on Great Britain by invoking the Non-Importation Act, followed eight days later by a new restriction, the Embargo Act.

The Embargo Act was intended to avoid war. Jefferson thought of it as a short-term measure to prevent confrontation between American merchant vessels and British and French warships and to put pressure on France and England by denying them American products. The embargo forbade all exports from the United States to any country. Foreign ships delivering goods left American ports with empty holds. U.S. exports dropped some 80 percent in 1808, but smuggling blossomed overnight.

Few American policies were as well intentioned and as unpopular and unsuccessful as Jefferson's embargo.

EMBARGO ACT

Although "peaceable coercion" had been an enlightened concept in international affairs, some Democratic-Republicans felt uneasy about interfering with trade. Federalists opposed the embargo vociferously. Some feared its impact abroad. "If England [were to] sink," Federalist vice-presidential candidate Rufus King said in 1808, expressing Federalist pro-British sympathies, "her fall will prove the grave of our liberties." Mercantile New England, the heart of Federalist opposition to Jefferson, took the brunt of the resulting economic depression. In the winter of 1808–1809, talk of secession spread through New England port cities.

Although general unemployment soared, some individuals benefited from the embargo. Merchants with ships abroad (those not idled by the embargo) and merchants willing to risk the lax enforcement to trade illegally could garner enormous profits. U.S. manufacturers received a boost, since the domestic market became theirs exclusively, and merchants began to shift their capital from shipping to manufacturing.

DOMESTIC MANUFACTURING

Factories were still new in America. English immigrant Samuel Slater set up the first American textile mill in Rhode Island in the 1790s. It used water-powered spinning machines that he had built from memorized British models. Though Federalists like Alexander Hamilton, through his *Report on Manufactures* (see

Industrial Piracy

Though Americans pride themselves on inventiveness and hard work, their start in industrial development depended on importing technology, sometimes by stealth. Great Britain, which in the late eighteenth century had pioneered the invention of mechanical weaving and power looms, knew the value of its head start in the industrial revolution and prohibited the export of textile technology. But the British-born brothers Samuel and John Slater, their Scottish-born power-loom-builder William Gilmore, and Bostonians Francis Cabot Lowell and Nathan Appleton evaded British restrictions and patents to establish America's first textile factories.

As an apprentice and then a supervisor in a British cotton-spinning factory, Samuel Slater had mastered the machinery and the process. Britain forbade the export of textile technology, so Slater emigrated to the United States disguised as a farmer. In 1790 in Pawtucket, Rhode Island, on the Blackstone River, he opened the first water-powered spinning mill in America, rebuilding the complex machines from memory. With his brother John and their Rhode Island partners—Moses and Obadiah Brown and William Almy—Slater later built and oversaw mills in Rhode Island and Massachusetts. In 1815 he hired a recent immigrant, William Gilmore, to build a water-powered loom like those used in Britain. Later in the 1820s the Slaters introduced British steam-powered looms. Spinning and weaving would now be done in New England factories organized on British models.

In 1810, Francis Cabot Lowell had the same idea as the Slaters: to build modern mills with mechanical, water-powered looms. Lowell took a family vacation to Britain, and, in Edinburgh, Scotland, he met fellow Bostonian Nathan Appleton. Impressed by the textile mills they had seen in Britain, they laid plans to introduce water-powered mechanical weaving into the United States. They knew they had to acquire the "improved manufactures" from Britain that had made Manchester famous as a textile center. Lowell went to Manchester, during the day visiting and observing the factories and meeting the factory managers. At night, he returned to his hotel to sketch from memory the power looms and processes he saw. Back in the United States, he and others formed the Boston Associates, which created the Waltham-Lowell Mills based on Lowell's industrial piracy. The Lowell boarding houses, however, were intended as an alternative to the tenements and slums of Manchester. Within a few years, textiles would be a major American industry, and the Associates would dominate it.

Thus the modern American industrial revolution began with international links, not homegrown American inventions. Ingenuity and industrial piracy put the United States on the road to industrial advancement.

This contemporary painting shows the Boston Manufacturing Company's 1814 textile factory at Waltham, Massachusetts. All manufacturing processes were brought together under one roof, and the company built its first factories in rural New England to tap roaring rivers as a power source. (Courtesy of Gore Place Society, Waltham, Mass.)

page 199), had pushed the United States to promote manufacturing, Jefferson envisioned an "empire of liberty" that was agricultural and commercial, not industrial. Holding fast to frugal, limited government, the Democratic-Republican policy did not promote industry. Still, disruption in commerce made domestic manufactures profitable. In 1807 there were twenty cotton and woolen mills in New England; by 1813 there were more than two hundred. The embargo actually had little impact on Britain. The British most severely hurt—West Indians and factory workers in England—had no voice in policy. English merchants actually gained because they took over the Atlantic carrying trade from the stalled American ships. And because of a successful British blockade of Europe, the embargo had little practical effect on the French. Indeed, it gave France an excuse to set privateers against American ships that had evaded the embargo and were, possibly, heading to British ports. The French cynically claimed that such ships were British ships in disguise because the embargo prevented American vessels from sailing.

As the election of 1808 approached, the Democratic-Republicans were weakened by factional dissent and

ELECTION OF 1808

dissatisfaction in seaboard states hobbled by the embargo. Although nine state legislatures passed resolutions urging Jefferson to run again, the president followed Washington's lead in renouncing a third term. He supported James Madison, his secretary of state, as the Democratic-Republican standard-bearer. For the first time, however, the Democratic-Republican nomination was contested. Madison won the endorsement of the party's congressional caucus, but Virginia Democratic-Republicans put forth James Monroe, who later withdrew, and some easterners supported Vice President George Clinton. Madison and Clinton headed the ticket.

Charles Cotesworth Pinckney and Rufus King again headed the Federalist ticket, but with new vigor. The Younger Federalists, led by Harrison Gray Otis and other Bostonians, made the most of the widespread disaffection with Republican policy, especially the embargo. Although Pinckney received only 47 electoral votes to Madison's 122, the Federalists offered genuine competition. Pinckney carried all of New England except Vermont, and he won Delaware and some electoral votes in two other states. Federalists also gained seats in Congress and captured the New York State legislature. The Federalist future looked promising.

Under the pressure of domestic opposition, the embargo eventually collapsed. In its place, the Non-Intercourse Act of 1809 reopened trade with all nations except Britain and France, and it authorized the president to

NON-INTERCOURSE ACT

resume trade with Britain or France if either of them ceased to violate neutral rights. On leaving office in March, Jefferson expressed the weight of his failure: "Never did a prisoner, released from his chains," he wrote, "feel such relief as I in shaking off the shackles of power."

The new act solved only the problems created by the embargo; it did not prevent further British and French interference with American commerce. For one brief moment it appeared to work. In June 1809 President Madison reopened trade with England after the British minister to the United States assured him that Britain would repeal restrictions on American trade. His Majesty's government in London, however, repudiated the minister's assurances, and Madison reverted to nonintercourse.

When the Non-Intercourse Act expired in 1810, Congress substituted a variant, Macon's Bill Number 2, that exchanged the proverbial stick for a carrot. The bill reopened trade with both Great Britain and France but provided that when either nation stopped violating American commercial rights, the president could suspend American commerce with the other. Madison, eager to avoid war, fell victim to French duplicity. When Napoleon accepted the offer, Madison declared nonintercourse with Great Britain in 1811. Napoleon, however, tricked him. The French continued to seize American ships, and nonintercourse failed a second time. But because the Royal Navy dominated the seas, Britain, not France, became the main focus of American hostility.

"Mr. Madison's War"

*T*hough unprepared for war in 1812, the United States under President Madison seemed unable to avoid it. Economic pressure had failed to protect American ships and sailors. In truth, the United States had limited influence over British policy because the conflict was part of the ongoing wars between Britain with its continental allies, and France. Having exhausted all efforts to alter British policy, and fearing for the survival of American independence, the United States drifted toward war. The Democratic-Republican "War Hawks," elected to Congress in 1810, cried loudest for war. Pro-war newspapers, like the *National Intelligencer*, declared, "Our cause is just, and if we are decided and firm, success is inevitable." Britain's response was too little, too late. In spring 1812, the admiralty ordered British ships not to stop, search, or seize American warships.

Then in June 1812, Britain reopened the seas to American shipping. Hard times had hit the British Isles: the Anglo-French conflict had blocked much British commerce to the European continent, and exports to the United States had fallen 80 percent. But two days after the change in British policy, before word of it had crossed the Atlantic, Congress declared war.

In his message to Congress on June 1, 1812, President Madison enumerated familiar grievances: impressment, interference with neutral trading rights, and British alliances with western Indians. More generally, the Democratic-Republicans resolved to defend American independence and honor, but some Americans saw in the war an opportunity to conquer and annex British Canada. In Congress partisanship, regional loyalties, and personal bitterness dominated debate. Most militant were the War Hawks, land-hungry southerners and westerners, all Democratic-Republicans, led by John C. Calhoun of South Carolina and first-term congressman and House Speaker Henry Clay of Kentucky. John Randolph of Roanoke, an opponent of war, charged angrily, "Agrarian cupidity, not maritime rights, urges war." He heard "but one word" in Congress: "Canada! Canada! Canada!" Most representatives from the coastal states, and especially the Northeast, opposed war because armed conflict with the Royal Navy would interrupt American shipping. On June 4, the House voted 79 to 49 for war; two weeks later the Senate followed suit, 19 to 13. Republicans favored war by a vote of 98 to 23; Federalists opposed it 39 to 0. On June 19, President Madison signed the bill. Critics instantly called it "Mr. Madison's War."

DEBATE ON THE WAR

During these years politics and personal animosities were often so intense that civility dissolved. Political compromise and cooperation, essential to politics, seemed almost impossible. But social events at the Executive Mansion, dominated by the magnetic Dolley Madison, provided the site for political compromises. She had, said one observer, "the magic power of converting enemies into friends." Jefferson had used small dinners to guide domestic politics and relations with Great Britain, but Dolley Madison made hosting an art. At state dinners, she sat at the head of the table, and made socializing a state craft. Under Dolley Madison, the White House took on its modern role as the focus of presidential politics. She introduced the inaugural ball. Her Wednesday evening socials in the oval drawing room brought all political factions together, the only place where political enemies talked cordially. James Madison lacked the intellect of Jefferson, but with his

DOLLEY MADISON AND FEMALE POLITICAL WORK

wife in the lead, he was far more successful a politician than had been Jefferson.

The war unfolded as a series of scuffles and skirmishes, for which the U.S. Army and Navy and the state militias were unprepared. Officers executed campaigns poorly, and full-scale battles happened rarely (see Map 9.3). But the Americans had the advantage of fighting close to home.

RECRUITMENT

Jefferson's warning that "our constitution is a peace establishment—it is not calculated for war" proved true. Though the U.S. Navy had a corps of experienced officers who had proved their mettle in the Barbary War, it was no match for the Royal Navy. The U.S. Army had neither an able staff nor an adequate force of enlisted men. By 1812 the U.S. Military Academy at West Point, founded in 1802, had produced only eighty-nine regular officers. Senior army officers were aged Revolutionary War veterans or political hacks. The army depended on state militias to recruit volunteers, but not all states cooperated. The government offered enlistees a sign-up bonus of $16, monthly pay of $5, a full set of clothes, and a promise of three months' pay and rights to purchase 160 acres of western land upon discharge. Forty-two percent of the enlistees were illiterate.

At first, recruitment in the West went well. Civic spirit, desire for land, strong anti-Indian sentiment, and fear of Tecumseh's pan-Indian appeals and resistance stimulated thousands of frontiersmen to enlist. The army made itself more acceptable to new recruits by abolishing flogging as punishment in 1812. Within a year, however, frontier enlistments declined. Word spread that the War Department was six to twelve months behind in paying soldiers. Supplies were inadequate; troops often lacked shoes, uniforms, or blankets, and the rations they received were sometimes spoiled.

Raising an army proved even more difficult in New England, where many viewed the conflict as a Democratic-Republican affair—"Mr. Madison's War"—and Federalists discouraged enlistments. Even some New England Democratic-Republicans declined to raise volunteer companies. Those who accepted promised their men that they would serve only in a defensive role, as in Maine where they guarded the coastline. Indeed, the inability of the United States to mount a successful invasion of Canada was due in part to the army's failure to assemble an effective force. Militias in New England and New York often refused to fight outside their states.

Nonetheless, Canada was tempting, and Americans expected to take it quickly. The mighty Royal Navy could not reach the Great Lakes separating the United States and Canada because there was no direct access to

Map 9.3   Major Campaigns of the War of 1812

The land war centered on the U.S.-Canadian border, the Chesapeake Bay, and the Louisiana and Mississippi Territories.

INVASION
OF CANADA

them from the Atlantic. Canada's population of just 0.5 million was a fraction of the United States's 7.5 million. Canada had 7,000 regulars in uniform; the United States, 12,000. And Americans hoped that the French in Canada might welcome U.S. forces.

Begun with high hopes, the invasion of Canada ended in disaster. The American strategy concentrated on the West, aiming to split Canadian forces and isolate the

pro-British Indians. At the outset of the war, Tecumseh joined the British, who promised him in return an Indian nation in the Great Lakes region. U.S. general William Hull, territorial governor of Michigan, marched his troops into Upper Canada, with the goal of conquering Montreal. More experienced as a politician than as a soldier, Hull had surrounded himself with newly minted colonels as politically astute and militarily ignorant as he was. Although his forces in the area outnumbered the

■ Michael Felice Corne depicts the U.S.S. *Constitution* engaging H.M.S. *Guerrière* in the Atlantic. The *Constitution*'s victories emboldened the U.S. Navy and earned the ship the nickname "Old Ironsides." (New Haven Colony Historical Society)

British and their Indian allies, Hull waged a timid campaign, retreating more than he attacked. His abandonment of Mackinac Island and Fort Dearborn in Chicago and his surrender of Fort Detroit left the entire Midwest exposed to the enemy. The only bright spot was the September 1812 defense of Fort Harrison in Indiana Territory by Captain Zachary Taylor, who provided the Americans with their first land victory. By the winter of 1812–1813, the British controlled about half of the Old Northwest.

The United States had no greater success on the Niagara front, where New York borders Canada. At the Battle of Queenstown, Canada, north of Niagara, the U.S. Army met defeat because the New York militia refused to leave New York. This frustrating scenario was repeated near Lake Champlain, when the New York militia's refusal to cross the border into Canada foiled American plans to attack Montreal. And the opposition proved tenacious; British regulars, their Indian allies, and Canadians, many who were loyalists who had fled to Canada at the time of the American Revolution, defeated the American invaders.

The navy provided the only good news in the first year of the war. The U.S.S. *Constitution,* the U.S.S. *Wasp,* and the U.S.S. *United States* all

NAVAL BATTLES

bested British warships on the Atlantic Ocean. The *Constitution*'s 1812 rout of H.M.S. *Guerrière* in the Atlantic emboldened the U.S. Navy and earned the American ship the nickname "Old

Ironsides." In the first year of war the Americans lost 20 percent of their ships, while in defeat the British lost just 1 percent of their vessels. The United States, however, could ill afford to lose *any* ships. Democratic-Republican frugality had left the navy with only seventeen ships in 1812. It could not fight the British in a general naval war, and thus Britannia ruled the waves.

The Royal Navy blockaded the Chesapeake and Delaware Bays in December 1812, and by 1814 the blockade covered nearly all American ports along the Atlantic and Gulf coasts. After 1811, American trade overseas had declined nearly 90 percent, and the decline in revenues from customs duties threatened to bankrupt the federal government and prostrate New England.

The contest for control of the Great Lakes, the key to the war in the Northwest, evolved as a shipbuilding race.

GREAT LAKES CAMPAIGN

Under Master Commandant Oliver Hazard Perry and shipbuilder Noah Brown, the United States outbuilt the British on Lake Erie and defeated them at the bloody Battle of Put-in-Bay on September 10, 1813. With this costly victory, the Americans gained control of Lake Erie.

General William Henry Harrison then began what proved to be among the United States's most successful land campaigns in the war. A ragged group of Kentucky militia volunteers who had been drafted into the regular army marched 20 to 30 miles a day to join Harrison's forces in Ohio. They were armed only with swords and

■ *Ballou's Pictorial Drawing-Room Companion* depicts the Battle of New Orleans, the last campaign of the War of 1812. Andrew Jackson's troops—army regulars, Tennessee and Kentucky volunteers, and two companies of African American volunteers from New Orleans—held off the better-trained British troops in January 1815. The battle made Andrew Jackson a national hero.   (Historic New Orleans Collection)

knives. Now 4,500 strong, Harrison's force attacked and took Detroit. Then they crossed to Canada, pursuing and defeating the British, Shawnee, and Chippewa forces on October 5 at the Battle of the Thames. In victory the United States captured 600 British troops and great amounts of war materiel; the United States regained control of the Old Northwest. Tecumseh died in the battle, and with his death expired Native American unity. Following the loss of their leader, some Indians joined the United States against Britain. After the Battle of the Thames, the Americans razed the Canadian capital of York (now Toronto). Though they did not have enough troops to hold the city, they looted and burned the Parliament building before withdrawing. The stunning land victory had the added effect of stopping the British on Lake Ontario and occupying British operations on Lake Erie.

After defeating Napoleon in Europe in April 1814, the British launched a land counteroffensive against the United States, concentrating on the Chesapeake Bay region. In retaliation for the burning of York—and to divert American troops from Lake Champlain, where the British planned a new offensive—royal troops occupied Washington, D.C., in August and set it ablaze, leaving the presidential mansion and parts of the city burning all night. Chaos ruled. The president and cabinet had planned to rendezvous in Frederick, Maryland, but Madison and his advisers fled to Virginia. Dolley Madison stayed in town long enough to oversee the removal of cabinet documents and—famously—save Gilbert Stuart's portrait of George Washington.

The British intended the attack on the capital only as a diversion. The major battle occurred in September 1814 at Baltimore, where the Americans held firm. Francis Scott Key, detained on a British ship, watched the bombardment of Fort McHenry from Baltimore harbor and the next morning wrote the verses of "The Star-Spangled Banner" (which became the national anthem in 1931). Although the British inflicted heavy damage both materially and psychologically, they achieved little militarily. Their offensive at Lake Champlain proved equally unsuccessful when American ships turned back a British flotilla at Plattsburgh. The British halted their offense; the war was stalemated.

The last campaigns of the war took place in the South, against the Creeks along the Gulf of Mexico and

Burning of Washington

CAMPAIGN AGAINST THE CREEKS

against the British around New Orleans (see Map 9.3). The Creeks had responded to the call of Tecumseh, whose mother was a Creek, to resist U.S. expansion. Some had died in Indiana Territory, at Prophetstown on Tippecanoe Creek, when General Harrison's troops routed Shawnee forces there in 1811. In December 1812 General Andrew Jackson raised his Tennessee militia to fight the Creeks. By late 1813 his anti-Creek campaign stalled for lack of supplies. His men, who had signed up for a year, muttered about going home. Jackson refused to discharge them; they could not, he said, abandon their posts on enemy ground. Officers repeatedly threatened to shoot any man who left. Indeed, in March 1814 Jackson executed John Woods, a militiaman, for disobedience and mutiny. This act broke the opposition within the ranks, and Jackson's men defeated the Creek nation at the Battle of Horseshoe Bend in Mississippi Territory in March 1814.

The victory began Jackson's rise to political prominence. In the 1814 Treaty of Fort Jackson, the Creeks ceded two-thirds of their land and withdrew to the southern and western part of Mississippi Territory (what is now Alabama); the removal of Indians from the South had begun. Jackson became a major general in the regular army and continued south toward the Gulf of Mexico. To forestall a British invasion at Pensacola Bay, which guarded an overland route to New Orleans, Jackson seized Pensacola—in Spanish Florida—in November 1814. Then, after securing Mobile, he marched on to New Orleans to defend it against the British.

The Battle of New Orleans was the last campaign of the war. Early in December the British fleet landed 1,500

BATTLE OF NEW ORLEANS

men east of the city, hoping to seize the mouth of the Mississippi River and thus strangle the lifeline of the American West. They faced American regulars, Tennessee and Kentucky volunteers, and two companies of free African American volunteers from New Orleans. For three weeks the British under Sir Edward Pakenham and the Americans led by Jackson played cat-and-mouse. Finally, on January 8, 1815, the two forces met head-on. In fortified positions, Jackson's poorly trained army held its ground against two frontal assaults from a British contingent of 6,000. At day's end, more than 2,000 British soldiers lay dead or wounded; the Americans suffered only 21 casualties. Andrew Jackson emerged a national hero, and Americans memorialized the battle in song and paintings. The Battle of New Orleans actually took place two weeks after the end of the war. Unknown to the participants, a treaty had been signed in Ghent, Belgium, on December 24, 1814.

Peace and Consequences

The U.S. government had gone to war reluctantly and throughout the conflict probed for a diplomatic end to hostilities. In 1813 President Madison eagerly accepted a Russian offer to mediate, but Great Britain balked. Three months later, British foreign minister Lord Castlereagh suggested opening peace talks. It took more than ten months to arrange meetings, but in August 1814 a team of American negotiators, including Henry Clay and John Quincy Adams, son of John and Abigail, began talks with the British in Ghent.

The Ghent treaty made no mention of the issues that had led to war. The United States received no satisfaction on impressment, blockades, or other maritime rights for neutrals. British demands for an independent Indian nation in the Northwest and territorial cessions from Maine to Minnesota likewise went unsatisfied. The Treaty of Ghent essentially restored the prewar status quo. It provided for an end to hostilities with the British and with Native Americans, release of prisoners, restoration of conquered territory, and arbitration of boundary disputes. Ironically, the treaty was concluded on December 24, 1814, but the news took 7 weeks to reach the United States and the war officially ended when the Senate ratified the treaty on February 17, 1815.

Why did the negotiators settle for so little? Events in Europe had made peace and the status quo acceptable at the end of 1814, as they had not been in 1812. Napoleon's defeat allowed the United States to abandon its demands, since peace in Europe made impressment and interference with American commerce moot issues. Similarly, war-weary Britain—its treasury nearly depleted—stopped pressing for a military victory.

The War of 1812 affirmed the independence of the American republic and ensured Canada's independence

CONSEQUENCES

from the United States. Nearly 300,000 troops had taken up arms to maintain independence; almost 2,000 died for the cause, and 4,000 were wounded. Although conflict with Great Britain over trade and territory continued, it never again led to war. The experience strengthened America's resolve to steer clear of European politics because the Anglo-French conflagration had drawn the United States into war. At the same time, with Indian resistance broken, U.S. expansion would spread south and west, not north to Canada.

Conflict carried disastrous results for most Native Americans. Although they were not a party to the Treaty of Ghent, the ninth article of the pact pledged the United States to end hostilities and to restore "all the possessions, rights, and privileges" that Indians had enjoyed before the war. Midwestern Indians signed more than a dozen treaties with the United States in 1815, but they had little meaning. With the death of Tecumseh, the Indians had lost their most powerful political and military leader; with the withdrawal of the British, they had lost their strongest ally. The Shawnees, Potawatomis, Chippewas, and others had lost the means to resist American expansion.

The war exposed contradictions and American fears about its growing African American population. In the Deep South, fear of arming slaves kept them out of the military except in New Orleans, where a free black militia dated back to Spanish control of Louisiana. In the border states, in the Chesapeake area, and in the Midwest, the British army recruited slaves, offering them freedom in return for joining their side. Thus the British assault on Washington and Baltimore included former slaves. Ironically, the United States made the same offer to slaves in Canada, and both sides gave freedom to slaves in the Old Northwest who joined the military. New York State offered freedom to slaves who enlisted, and compensated their masters. In Philadelphia black leaders formed a "Black Brigade" to defend the city.

The war also exposed weaknesses in defense and transportation at home. American generals had found U.S. roads inadequate to move troops and supplies. In the Northwest, General Harrison's troops had depended on homemade cartridges and gifts of clothing from Ohio residents; in Maine, troops had melted down spoons to make bullets. Improved transportation and a well-equipped army became national priorities; both were vital for westward expansion. In 1815 President Madison responded by centralizing control of the military and building a line of forts for coastal defense, and Congress voted a standing army of ten thousand men—one-third of the army's wartime strength but three times the size of the army during Jefferson's administration. In 1818 the National Road reached Wheeling, Virginia (now West Virginia), from its Cumberland, Maryland, beginning and carried settlers westward (see page 249).

Perhaps most important of all, the war stimulated economic growth. The embargo, the Non-Importation and Non-Intercourse Acts, and the war itself spurred the production of manufactured goods because New England capitalists began to invest in home manufactures and factories. The effects of these changes were far-reaching (see Chapter 10).

Finally, the conflict sealed the fate of the Federalists. Realizing that they could not win a presidential election in wartime, the Federalists joined renegade Democratic-Republicans in supporting New York City mayor DeWitt Clinton for president in the election of 1812. Federalist organization peaked at the state level as the Younger Federalists campaigned hard. The Federalists nevertheless lost to President Madison and vice-presidential candidate Elbridge Gerry of Massachusetts by 128 to 89 electoral votes; areas that favored the war (the South and West) remained solidly Democratic-Republican. The Federalists gained some congressional seats and carried many local elections, but their star was waning.

With the war stalemated and the New England economy shattered by embargo and war, delegates from New England met in Hartford, Connecticut, for three weeks in the winter of 1814–1815 to discuss revising the national compact or pulling out of the republic. Moderates prevented a resolution of secession, but the twenty-six convention delegates condemned the war and the embargo and endorsed radical changes in the Constitution, such as restricting the presidency to one term and requiring a two-thirds congressional vote to admit new states to the Union. The delegates plotted preserving New England Federalist political power as electoral strength was shifting to the South and West.

HARTFORD CONVENTION

The timing of the Hartford Convention proved lethal to the Federalists. The victory at New Orleans and news of the peace treaty made the convention look ridiculous, if not treasonous. Rather than harassing a beleaguered wartime administration, the Federalists found themselves in retreat before a rising tide of nationalism. Though the Federalists survived in a handful of states until the 1820s, the faction dissolved. The War of 1812, at first a source of revival as opponents of war flocked to the Federalist banner, helped speed its demise.

Summary

The 1800 election marked the peaceful transition in power from the Federalists to the opposition Democratic-Republicans. Thomas Jefferson replaced John Adams as president and sought both to unify the nation and to solidify Democratic-Republican control of the government. Jeffersonians favored frugal government, and they cut the budget, military forces, and diplomatic missions.

The Supreme Court under Chief Justice John Marshall remained a Federalist bastion. Both parties fought over the judiciary, and Marshall would ensure, until 1835, the dominance of Federalist principle: federal supremacy over the states and the protection of commerce and capital. In *Marbury v. Madison* (1803), the Supreme Court established its great power of judicial review.

Jefferson considered the acquisition of Louisiana Territory and the commissioning of Lewis and Clark's expedition among his significant presidential accomplishments. In a single act the United States doubled its size. Increasingly Americans looked westward, and Lewis and Clark's Corps of Discovery practiced "buckskin diplomacy" while exploring the land, flora, fauna, and people west of the Mississippi. Americans quickly moved to settle Louisiana.

With Jefferson and his successor James Madison, the Democratic-Republicans won every presidential election in this period. Though the electorate was limited only to males and mostly to whites, both the Federalists and the Democratic-Republicans competed at the grassroots level for popular support. Political conflict was bitter, and divisions were real. Sometimes they could prove fatal as in the Burr-Hamilton duel. Assisted by the partisan press and the social-politicking women, political intensity began to build a national political culture.

Despite internal divisions, the greatest threats came from abroad. In the war with the Barbary states, the United States sought to guard its commerce and ships on the high seas. The second war with Britain—the War of 1812—was fought for similar reasons but against a much more formidable power. The peace treaty reaffirmed American independence; thereafter the nation was able to settle disputes with Great Britain at the bargaining table. The war also dealt a serious blow to Indian resistance in the West and South. At the same time, embargoes and war forced Americans to look toward building domestic markets and jump-started American manufacturing. Military and diplomatic assertiveness brought Americans a sense of national identity and self-confidence.

LEGACY FOR A PEOPLE AND A NATION
States' Rights and Nullification

When the Constitution replaced the Articles of Confederation, the United States had a much stronger central government, but the exact nature of the relationship between the states and the central government was ambiguous, because Constitutional Convention delegates could not agree on whether states or nation should prevail in the event of irreconcilable conflict. The Tenth Amendment to the Constitution offered only a slight clarification: powers not delegated to the central government, it said, were reserved to the states or to the people. The exact nature of the federal system's shared power, and in fact who would determine which powers had been delegated to which authority, remained to be defined.

When New England Federalists met in Hartford at the end of 1814 to prepare a list of grievances against "Mr. Madison's War," they drew on the doctrine of nullification, first announced sixteen years earlier in the Kentucky and Virginia Resolutions, written by Thomas Jefferson and James Madison, respectively. Opposing the Alien and Sedition Acts, these "founding fathers" had asserted that if the national government assumed powers not delegated to it by the Constitution, states could nullify federal actions—that is, declare them inoperative within state borders. At Hartford, Federalist representatives of New England states discussed taking nullification a step further by actually seceding, or withdrawing from the Union. They backed away from this extreme step, but their formulation of the rights of states to evaluate and nullify federal authority left a legacy for dissent that would be played out in crises to the present day.

In the following decade, South Carolina nullified federal tariffs that it opposed, and in 1861 southern states threatened by Abraham Lincoln's election to the presidency claimed the right of secession. Although the Civil War supposedly settled the issue—states could neither nullify federal law nor secede—southern states opposing the Supreme Court's 1954 ruling in favor of school integration again claimed the right to nullify "unauthorized" federal policy within their borders. In the 1990s, some western states sought to nullify federal environmental laws. The Hartford Convention's legacy for a people and a nation provides Americans who dissent from national policy a model for using state governments as vehicles for their protests.

The **history companion** powered by Eduspace®

Your primary source for interactive quizzes, exercises, and more to help you learn efficiently.
http://history.college.hmco.com/students

THE OLD GRANITE STATE,

Judson.   Abby.   John.   Asa

A SONG,   Price 50 Cts Nett.

COMPOSED, ARRANGED AND SUNG BY

THE HUTCHINSON FAMILY.

CHAPTER **10**

1816–1845

NATIONALISM, EXPANSION, AND THE MARKET ECONOMY 1816–1845

*T*he Hutchinson Family, also known as the Tribe of Jesse, was the most popular singing group in nineteenth-century America. Abby, Asa, Jesse, John, and Judson Hutchinson—five of a family of sixteen children from rural New Hampshire—performed the patriotic, religious, and sentimental songs that had dominated popular music since the Revolution. They initiated new musical styles, wrote lyrics full of social commentary, and made entertainment a commodity, promoted and performed in the market economy.

Unlike most musical groups, the Tribe of Jesse not only sang but also presented well-rehearsed and elaborately produced performances. They used folk tunes that the audiences found familiar and enjoyed, but their lyrics explored controversial topics such as abolition and temperance. Their 1844 "Get Off the Track!" used imagery from railroads, the newest form of transportation, to hail the unstoppable power of the antislavery movement.

The Hutchinson Family traveled by rail, too, performing across the expanding United States but drawing their largest audiences in the growing cities of the North. The family's fee for a single night in the 1840s reached $1,000, about four hundred times a worker's daily wage. They had an entourage of managers, agents, and publishers. Hawkers sold sheet music, portraits, and songbooks at the Hutchinsons' concerts. The Hutchinson Family made a business of music and entertainment, selling nostalgia and reform.

The Hutchinsons' off-stage lives, too, bridged the old and the new. They had come from the farms of New Hampshire, as they sang in "The 'Old Granite State.'" They left home, they explained in song, with the blessing of their "aged parents," to sing of liberty, traveling "round the World." Besides their musical talent, the Hutchinson Family offered their audiences reassurance in a time of rapid change. By setting their lyrics to familiar hymns (we are "good old fashioned singers"), they connected their advocacy of reform with the comfortable

◀ The Hutchinson Family celebrated their native rural New Hampshire in "The 'Old Granite State,'" their most popular song. They made a business of performing, and hawkers sold their sheet music at concerts. (Courtesy of Lynn Historical Society, hand-colored by Sandi Rygiel, Picture Research Consultants, Inc.)

CHRONOLOGY

1815 • Madison proposes internal improvements

1816 • Second Bank of the United States chartered
• Tariff of 1816 imposes first substantial duties
• Monroe elected president, Tompkins vice president

1817 • Rush-Bagot Treaty limits British and American naval forces on Lake Champlain and Great Lakes

1819 • *McCulloch v. Maryland* establishes supremacy of federal over state law
• Adams-Onís Treaty with Spain gives Florida to the U.S. and defines Louisiana territorial border

1819–23 • Hard times bring unemployment

1820 • Missouri Compromise creates formula for admitting slave and free states
• Monroe reelected president, Tompkins vice president

1820s • New England textile mills expand

1823 • Monroe Doctrine closes Western Hemisphere to European intervention

1824 • *Gibbons v. Ogden* affirms federal over state authority in interstate commerce
• Monroe proposes Indian removal

1825 • Erie Canal completed

1830 • Railroad era begins
• Congress passes Indian Removal Act

1830s • McCormick reaper, Deere steel plow patented

1830s–40s • Cotton production shifts to Mississippi valley

1831 • Trail of Tears begins with the forced removal of the Choctaws
• Cherokees turn to courts to defend treaty rights in *Cherokee Nation v. Georgia*

1832 • Marshall declares Cherokee nation a distinct political community in *Worcester v. Georgia*

1834 • Women workers strike at Lowell textile mills

1835–42 • Seminoles successfully resist removal in Second Seminole War

1836 • Second Bank of the United States closes

1837 • *Charles River Bridge v. Warren Bridge* encourages new enterprises
• Panic of 1837 begins economic downturn

1839–43 • Hard times strike again

1842 • *Commonwealth v. Hunt* declares strikes lawful

1844 • Government grant sponsors first telegraph line

past. And by describing a bucolic future, they reassured their audiences that the present, with all its turmoil, would turn out well.

The Hutchinsons' concert tours exemplified the market economy, in which goods and services sold in cash or credit transactions created a network of exchange that bound distant enterprises together. The family performed in western areas in the 1840s that had had no American settlements twenty years before. The canals and railroads that carried them also increasingly linked the nation's regions after the War of 1812. People moved inland from the seaboard, farmed the rich lands across the Appalachians, and sold their crops at home and abroad. Grain went east to coastal cities, slave-grown cotton went to Europe, and ready-made men's garments from New York and Cincinnati sold across the nation. Increasingly, farmers turned to staple-crop agriculture and city people worked not for themselves but for others, for wages. These large-scale enterprises needed capital, and new financial institutions amassed and loaned it. Mechanization took hold; factories and precision-made machinery put home workshops and handcrafters out of business; on farms, horse-drawn reapers replaced farmhands. In turn, the increased specialization in plantation and commercial agriculture, manufacturing, transportation, and finance further fired the engines of the new nationwide, capitalist, market-oriented economy.

The end of the War of 1812 unleashed this growth. A new nationalist spirit encouraged the economy and promoted western expansion at home, trade abroad, and assertiveness throughout the Western Hemisphere. Economic growth and territorial expansion, however, generated new problems. Sectional conflicts over slavery and economic development created divisions. Migration and changes in the ways people worked created new tensions. Not everyone profited in wealth and opportunity as the Hutchinson Family did. Journeyman tailors, displaced by retailers and cheaper labor, found their trades disappearing. New England farm daughters who became wage workers found their world changing no less radically. Moreover, boom-and-bust cycles, now on a national scale, wrenched livelihoods and lives. Mills, factories, roads, canals, and railroads altered or destroyed the landscape.

Everywhere Americans were on the move. Settlement, North and South, moved to the interior, and farms and cities, linked by rivers, then roads, canals, and railroads, stretched to the Ohio and Mississippi River valleys and beyond. The Indian inhabitants attempted to hold their ground but were in the end removed to the West, pushed off their lands by the same drive for profit—a nationalist spirit reshaping national politics and the dynamic American economy.   ■

Postwar Nationalism

*N*ationalism surged after the War of 1812. Self-confident, Americans asserted themselves at home and abroad as Democratic-Republicans borrowed a page from the Federalists' agenda and encouraged economic growth. Though James Monroe would follow James Madison as the last of the presidents who had attended the Constitutional Convention, political power began to shift away from the founders of the republic. Congressional leaders Henry Clay and John C. Calhoun, and those who vied for the presidency in the 1820s—John Quincy Adams and Andrew Jackson—formed a new generation of political leaders with a national outlook.

James Madison inspired the postwar wave of nationalism. In his December 1815 message to Congress, he recommended economic development

NATIONALIST PROGRAM

and military expansion. His agenda included a national bank (the charter of the first bank had expired in 1811) and improved transportation. To raise government revenues and foster manufacturing, Madison called for a protective tariff—a tax on imported goods designed to protect American manufactures. Yet his program acknowledged Jeffersonian republicanism; only a constitutional amendment, Madison argued, could authorize the federal government to build local roads and canals.

Congressional leaders saw Madison's program as a way of unifying the country. Democratic-Republican John C. Calhoun of South Carolina and House Speaker Henry Clay of Kentucky believed that the tariff would stimulate industry. The agricultural slave South and West would sell cotton to the churning mills of New England and food to its mill workers. Goods would move on roads and canals, and tariff revenues would provide money to build them. A national bank would handle the transactions.

In the last year of Madison's administration, the Democratic-Republican Congress enacted much of the nationalist program. In 1816 it chartered the Second Bank of the United States to assist the government and to issue currency. Like its predecessor, the bank mixed public and private ownership; the government provided one-fifth of the bank's capital and appointed one-fifth of its directors.

Congress also passed a protective tariff to aid industries that had flourished during the War of 1812 but were now threatened by the resumption of overseas trade. The Tariff of 1816 levied taxes on imported woolens and cottons, and on iron, leather, hats, paper, and sugar, in effect raising their prices in the United States. Foreshadowing a growing trend, support for the tariff divided along sectional lines: New England and the western and Middle Atlantic states stood to benefit and applauded it, but the South did not.

The South did press for better transportation. It was Congressman Calhoun of South Carolina, not the president, who promoted roads and canals to "bind the republic together." However, on March 3, 1817, the day before he left office, Madison vetoed Calhoun's internal improvements (public works) bill as unconstitutional, though he did approve funds for extending the National Road to Ohio, deeming it a military necessity.

James Monroe, Madison's successor, continued Madison's domestic program, supporting tariffs and vetoing internal improvements. Monroe was

JAMES MONROE

the third Virginian elected president since 1801. A former senator and twice governor of Virginia, he had served under Madison as secretary of state and of war and used his close association with Jefferson and Madison to attain the presidency.

Among the nation's founders, Monroe was a most ordinary and colorless man who rarely had an original idea. But in 1816 he and his running mate, Daniel Tompkins, easily tromped the last Federalist presidential nominee, Rufus King, garnering all the electoral votes except those of the Federalist strongholds of Massachusetts, Connecticut, and Delaware. A Boston newspaper dubbed this one-party period the "Era of Good Feelings."

Led by Federalist chief justice John Marshall, the Supreme Court became the bulwark of a nationalist

McCULLOCH V. MARYLAND

point of view. In *McCulloch v. Maryland* (1819), the Court struck down a Maryland law taxing banks within the state that were not chartered by the Maryland legislature—a law aimed at hindering the Baltimore branch of the federally chartered Second Bank of the United States. The Bank of the United States had refused to pay the tax and sued. At issue was state versus federal jurisdiction. Speaking for a unanimous Court, Marshall asserted the supremacy of the federal government over the states. "The Constitution and the laws thereof are supreme," he declared. "They control the constitution and laws of the respective states and cannot be controlled by them."

In his opinion Marshall went on to consider whether Congress could issue a bank charter. The Constitution did not spell out such power, but Marshall noted that Congress had the authority to pass "all laws which shall be necessary and proper for carrying into execution" the enumerated powers of government. Marshall ruled that Congress could legally exercise "those great powers on which the welfare of the nation essentially depends." If the ends were legitimate and the means not prohibited, Marshall ruled, a law was constitutional. The Constitution was, in Marshall's words, "intended to endure for ages

■ John Quincy Adams (1767–1848), architect of the Monroe Doctrine, was secretary of state from 1817 to 1825. Thomas Sully's portrait, painted in 1825, captured Adams's determination and stubbornness. (New York State Office of Parks, Recreation, and Historic Preservation, Philipse Manor Hall State Historic Site)

to come, and consequently, to be adapted to the various causes of human affairs." The Supreme Court declared the bank charter legal. *McCulloch v. Maryland* thus joined nationalism and economics. By asserting federal supremacy, Marshall protected the commercial and industrial interests that favored a national bank; this was federalism in the tradition of Alexander Hamilton (see page 199). The decision was only one in a series of rulings that cemented the federalist view.

Monroe's secretary of state, John Quincy Adams, matched the self-confident Marshall Court in assertiveness and nationalism. A small, austere man once described by a British official as a "bulldog among spaniels," Adams, the son of John and Abigail Adams, was a superb diplomat who spoke six languages. From 1817 to 1825 he brilliantly managed the nation's foreign policy, stubbornly pushing for expansion, fishing rights for Americans in Atlantic waters, political distance from the Old World, and peace. An ardent expansionist, he nonetheless believed that expansion must come through negotiations, not war, and that newly acquired territories must bar slavery. The United States, Adams said in an 1821 Fourth of July speech, "goes not abroad, in search of monsters to destroy. She is the well-wisher to the freedom and independence of all."

JOHN QUINCY ADAMS

But in navigating international waters, Adams faced major challenges. U.S. northern and southern borders were not clearly defined and were a potential source of conflict with Great Britain and Spain. Both war and peace had left many issues with Great Britain unresolved; continued hostility could necessitate an armed U.S.-Canadian border, something neither side could afford. Moreover Great Britain was the largest buyer of American exports, and British textile mills depended on American cotton; both sides looked to commerce to cement better relations. The United States also sought to prevent European conflicts from spilling over into the New World, both to ensure peace in the Western Hemisphere and to build closer commercial relations with the emerging Latin American states.

Though an Anglophobe, Adams worked to strengthen the peace with Great Britain negotiated at Ghent (1814). He found a willing partner in Lord Castlereagh of the British Foreign Office. Though Castlereagh opposed the spread of republicanism and was oriented toward Europe, he recognized the importance of peaceful relations with the United States. In 1817 the two nations agreed in the Rush-Bagot Treaty to limit their naval forces to one ship each on Lake Champlain and Lake Ontario and to two ships each on the four other Great Lakes. This first disarmament treaty of modern times led to the demilita-

Map 10.1

Missouri Compromise and the State of the Union, 1820

The compromise worked out by House Speaker Henry Clay established a formula that avoided debate over whether new states would allow or prohibit slavery. In the process, it divided the United States into northern and southern regions.

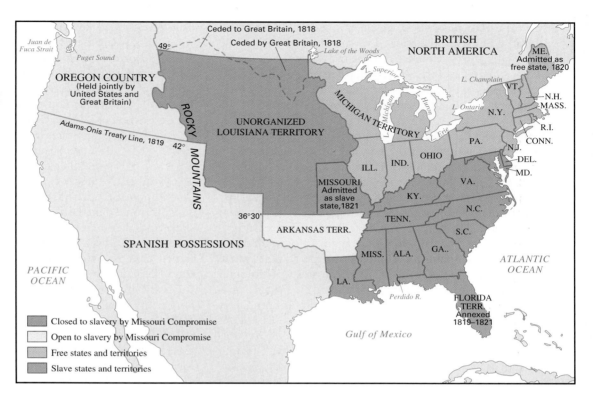

rization of the border between the United States and Canada. Adams then pushed for the Convention of 1818, which fixed the United States–Canadian border from Lake of the Woods in Minnesota westward to the Rockies along the 49th parallel (see Map 10.1). When they could not agree on the boundary west of the Rockies, Britain and the United States settled on joint occupation of Oregon for ten years (renewed indefinitely in 1827).

Adams next moved to settle long-term disputes with Spain. Although the 1803 Louisiana Purchase had omitted reference to Spanish-ruled West Florida, the United States claimed the territory as far east as the Perdido River (the present-day Florida-Alabama border) but occupied only a small finger of the area. During the War of 1812 the United States had seized Mobile and the remainder of West Florida. After the war Adams took advantage of Spain's preoccupation with domestic and colonial troubles to buy East Florida. During the 1818 talks, General Andrew Jackson occupied much of present-day Florida on the pretext of suppressing Seminole raids against American settlements across the border. Adams was furious with Jackson but defended his brazen act.

The following year, Don Luís de Onís, the Spanish minister to the United States, agreed to cede Florida to the United States without payment, while the United

States agreed to renounce its dubious claims to northern Mexico (Texas) and to assume $5 million of claims by American citizens against Spain. The Adams-Onís, or Transcontinental, Treaty also defined the southwestern boundary of the Louisiana Purchase and set the southern border of Oregon at the 42nd parallel (see Map 10.1). Expansion was achieved at little cost and without war.

When the Spanish flag was last lowered over St. Augustine on July 10, 1821, and at Pensacola on July 17, Florida residents differed in how they greeted the United States and its colonial governor, General Andrew Jackson. Some planter-slaveholders and traders welcomed the American flag, but Creeks and Seminoles, free blacks, runaway slaves, and Spanish-speaking town dwellers did not. Many feared Jackson, who had led raids against the Seminoles in Florida in 1814 and 1818. The Spanish encouraged residents to resettle in Mexico, Cuba, or Texas, but most stayed put though wary of the United States.

Conflict between the United States and European nations was temporarily resolved by the Rush-Bagot Treaty, the Convention of 1818, and the Adams-Onís Treaty, but events to the south still threatened American interests. John Quincy Adams's desire to insulate the United States and the Western Hemisphere from European conflict brought about his greatest achievement: the Monroe Doctrine.

The immediate issue was the recognition of new governments in Latin America. Between 1808 and 1822, the

INDEPENDENT STATES IN LATIN AMERICA

United Provinces of the Río de la Plata (present-day northern Argentina, Paraguay, and Uruguay), Chile, Peru, Colombia, and Mexico all broke free from Spain. Monroe and Adams moved cautiously, seeking to avoid conflict with Spain and to be sure of the stability of the new regimes. Then in 1822, shortly after the Adams-Onís Treaty was signed and ratified, the United States became the first nation outside Latin America to recognize the new states, including Mexico.

To the United States, Europe again offered potential threats to the stability of the New World. France, to bolster the weak Spanish monarchy against domestic rebellion, occupied Spain. The United States feared that France would return the new Latin American states to colonial rule. Great Britain, similarly distrustful of France, proposed a joint United States–British declaration against European intervention in the Western Hemisphere and a joint disavowal of territorial ambitions in the region. Adams rejected the British overture. Following George Washington's admonition to avoid foreign entanglements, he insisted that the United States act independently.

Despite clamors to take joint action with Great Britain, Adams refused to budge. Those who favored a multilateral move believed the United States needed British naval power to prevent French or Russian expansion in the New World. But Adams won. "It would be more candid, as well as more dignified," he argued, "to avow our principles explicitly to Russia and France, than to come in as a cockboat in the wake of the British man-of-war." Adams interpreted the British disavowal of territorial ambitions as an attempt to thwart American expansion.

President Monroe presented the American position—the Monroe Doctrine—to Congress in December 1823.

MONROE DOCTRINE

His message called for noncolonization of the Western Hemisphere by European nations, a principle that addressed American anxiety not only about Latin America but also about Russian expansion beyond Alaska and its settlements in California. He also demanded nonintervention by Europe in the affairs of independent New World nations, and he pledged noninterference by the United States in European affairs, including those of Europe's existing New World colonies.

The Monroe Doctrine proved popular at home. It tapped American nationalism and anti-British and anti-European feelings, and it eventually became the foundation of American policy in the Western Hemisphere. Monroe's words, however, carried no force. Indeed, the policy depended on the support of the British, who wanted to keep other European nations out of the hemisphere to protect their dominance in the Atlantic trade. Europeans ignored the Monroe Doctrine; it was the Royal Navy they respected, not American policy.

While nationalism brought Americans together, slavery divided them. Since the drafting of the Constitution,

"FIRE BELL IN THE NIGHT"

political leaders had tried to avoid the issue. The one exception was an act ending the foreign slave trade after January 1, 1808, which passed without much opposition. The act followed the expiration of the constitutional ban (Article I, Section 9) on ending the slave trade before 1808. In 1819, however, slavery crept onto the political agenda when Missouri residents petitioned Congress for admission to the Union as a slave state. Though slavery was dying out in the North, as ensured by gradual emancipation laws (see Chapter 13), border and southern states protected slavery, and Missouri wanted to enter the Union under those terms. For two and a half years the issue dominated Congress. "This momentous question," wrote Thomas Jefferson, fearful for the life of the Union, "like a fire bell in the night, awakened and filled me with terror" (see Map 10.1).

The debate transcended slavery in Missouri. The compromises that had kept the issue under wraps since the Constitutional Convention could collapse. Five new states had joined the Union since 1812: Louisiana (1812), Indiana (1816), Mississippi (1817), Illinois (1818), and Alabama (1819). Of these, Louisiana, Mississippi, and Alabama permitted slavery. Because Missouri was on the same latitude as free Illinois, Indiana, and Ohio (a state since 1803), its admission as a slave state would thrust slavery farther northward. It would also tilt the uneasy political balance in the Senate toward the slave states. In 1819 the Union consisted of eleven slave and eleven free states. If Missouri joined, slave states would have a two-vote edge in the Senate.

Moral issues made slavery an explosive question. Settlers from slave states—Kentuckians and Tennesseans—made up most of the new Missourians. But in the North slavery was slowly dying out, and many northerners had concluded that it was evil. When Representative James Tallmadge Jr. of New York proposed gradual emancipation in Missouri, a passionate and sometimes violent debate ensued. Southerners accused the North of threatening to destroy the Union. "If you persist, the Union will be dissolved," Thomas W. Cobb of Georgia shouted at Tallmadge. "Seas of blood can only extinguish" the fire Tallmadge was igniting, Cobb warned. "Let it come," retorted Tallmadge. The House, which had a northern majority, passed the Tallmadge Amendment, but the Senate rejected it. The two sides were deadlocked.

House Speaker Henry Clay promoted a compromise in 1820. Maine, carved out of Massachusetts, would become a free state balancing Missouri. In the rest of the Louisiana Territory north of latitude 36°30' (Missouri's southern boundary), slavery would be prohibited forever (see Map 10.1). The compromise carried, but the agreement almost unraveled in November when Missouri submitted a constitution that barred free blacks from entering the state. Opponents contended that Missouri would violate the federal constitutional provision that "the citizens of each State shall be entitled to all privileges and immunities of citizens in the several States." Proponents argued that many states, North and South, barred free blacks from entering. But, as historian Ira Berlin has noted, the United States was a slave society, and free people of color would not be equal to whites. In 1821 Clay produced a second compromise: Missouri guaranteed that none of its laws would discriminate against citizens of other states. (Once admitted to the Union, however, Missouri twice adopted laws barring free blacks.)

The Market Economy and Government's Role

Before canals and railroads, farmers had geared production to their own needs and to local and foreign, not national, markets. They lived in interdependent communities and exchanged labor and goods with their neighbors. Farm families produced much of what they needed—food, clothing, candles, soap, and the like—and traded for or purchased items they could not produce, such as cooking pots, horseshoes, coffee, tea, and sugar. The market for staple products—cotton, lumber, and sugar—was international, not domestic.

Increasingly in the years after the War of 1812, Americans became involved in the market economy—growing crops and producing goods specifically for cash and buying items produced by other people. Farms and slave plantations produced crops for market sales. Plantations raised rice, tobacco, sugar, or cotton; farmers grew only one or two crops or raised animals for market. Farm women gave up spinning and weaving and purchased cloth made by wage-earning farm girls in Massachusetts textile mills. Nonfarm men and women sold not goods but their labor for cash, working for wages. By buying goods at market, free farmers and workers increased the demand for manufactured things. Such a system encouraged specialization. It also energized transportation, as both goods and entertainment, like the Hutchinsons, circulated nationally.

Mechanization, the division of labor, new methods of financing, and improvements in transportation all fueled the expansion of the economy. Goods and services multiplied. This growth, in turn, prompted new improvements and greater opportunities for wage labor. The effect was cumulative; by the 1840s the economy was growing faster than in the previous four decades. While per capita income increased 50 percent between 1800 and 1840, the price of manufactured goods and food fell.

The pace of economic growth, however, was uneven. Prosperity reigned during two long periods, from 1823 to 1835 and from 1843 to 1857. But there were long stretches of economic contraction as well. Contraction and deflation (decline in the general price level) occurred again during the hard times of 1819–1823 and 1839–1843. During these periods banks closed, businesses went under, wages and prices declined, and jobs were hard to find or to keep. Yet even during boom periods major industries like construction offered only cyclical employment. In the 1820s and 1830s, laborers in Baltimore, for example, typically found steady work only from March through October.

EFFECTS OF BOOM AND BUST

In 1819 the postwar boom collapsed. Expansion had been built on easy credit; state banks had printed notes freely, fueling speculative buying of western land. Speculators had bought acreage to sell at a profit rather than to farm. Foreign investment in the United States had soared. When manufacturing fell in 1818, prices spiraled downward. The Second Bank of the United States cut back on loans, thus further shrinking the economy. The United States had a net outflow of capital for the first time since 1813. With urban workers, farmers, and southern planters having less money to spend, the economy declined.

The contraction devastated workers and their families. As a Baltimore physician noted in 1819, working people felt hard times "a thousand fold more than the merchants." They could not build up savings during boom times to get them through the hard times; often they could not make it through the winter without drawing on charity for food, clothing, and firewood.

The 1820s and 1830s were boom times. Internal improvement projects—streets, turnpikes, canals, and railroads—made regular work plentiful, as did building construction. In the 1830s foreign investment soared; from 1832 through 1839, the United States had a net capital inflow of $189 million, or $12 for every man, woman, and child.

■ E. Didier painted *Auction in Chatham Street* in 1834. Auction houses in New York and other cities boomed during hard times.   (Museum of the City of New York)

The Panic of 1837 and sustained contraction from 1839 through 1843 led to a bust cycle as workers were helpless to forces beyond their control. Money became tight. Internal savings and foreign investment, which had fueled economic expansion, declined sharply. In the Panic of 1837 many banks could not repay depositors, and states, facing deficits because of the decline in the economy, defaulted on their bonds. European, especially British, investors were furious, became suspicious of all U.S. loans, and withdrew money from the United States.

Hard times had come. New York countinghouses closed their doors. Hungry workers looted a flour merchant. Crowds of laborers gathered at closed banks demanding their deposits. Then, Philip Hone noted in his diary, "a deadly calm pervades this lately flourishing city. No goods are selling, no businesses stirring." In New York, the hungry formed bread lines in front of soup societies, and beggars crowded the sidewalks. In Baltimore in 1839, when hundreds of small manufacturers closed their doors, tailors, milliners, and shipyard and construction workers lost their jobs. Ninety miles to the north, Philadelphia took on an eerie aura. "The streets seemed deserted," Sidney George Fisher observed in 1842. "The largest [merchant] houses are shut up and to rent, there is no business . . . no money, no confidence." Only auctions boomed, as sheriffs sold off seized property at a quarter of pre-hard-times prices, a dismal scene as portrayed by artist E. Didier in *Auction in Chatham Street* in nearby New York (see the painting above). In smaller cities like Lynn, Massachusetts, shoemakers weathered the hard times by fishing and tending gardens while laborers became scavengers, digging for clams and harvesting dandelions.

What caused the boom-and-bust cycles that brought about such suffering? Generally speaking, they were a direct result of the market economy. As with the expansion following the War of 1812, prosperity stimulated demand for finished goods such as clothing and furniture. Increased demand in turn led not only to higher prices and still higher production but also, because of business optimism and expectation of higher prices, to speculation in land. Investment money was plentiful as Americans saved regularly, and foreign, mostly British,

CAUSES OF BOOM AND BUST

investors, bought U.S. bonds and securities. Then, as with the hard times of 1819, production surpassed demand, causing prices and wages to fall; in response, land and stock values collapsed. Investment money then flowed out of the United States.

In the economic thinking of the time, some considered this process beneficial—a self-adjusting cycle that eliminated unprofitable economic ventures. In theory, people concentrated on the activities they did best, and the economy as a whole became more efficient. Believers in the self-adjusting system also argued that it enhanced individual freedom, since theoretically each seller, whether of goods or labor, determined the price. But in fact the system tied workers to a perpetual roller coaster; they became dependent on wages—and on the availability of jobs—for their very survival. The cycles that governed the market economy influenced every corner of the country as even small localities became tied, or handcuffed, to regional and national markets.

The market economy also ushered in another type of boom-and-bust cycle: harvest and destruction. Canals and railroads spurred demand for distant resources, then accelerated the destruction of forests, natural waterways, and any landscape features that represented obstacles. Railroads made possible large-scale lumbering of pinewood forests in Michigan and Wisconsin. During the 1840s, lumber companies deforested millions of acres, leaving most of that land unfit even for agriculture. The process of harvest and destruction would eventually change the ecology of the United States.

The idea of a market economy drew on eighteenth-century republicanism. Advanced by members of the elite as well as by craftsmen, it emphasized economic liberty and individualism (see page 166). Limited, not active, government, adherents argued, fostered economic expansion because individuals pursuing their own private interests benefited the nation as a whole.

GOVERNMENT ECONOMIC ROLE

Nonetheless, the federal government played an active role in technological and industrial growth. Federal arsenals pioneered new manufacturing techniques that helped to develop the machine-tool industry. The United States Post Office fostered the circulation of information, a critical element in a market economy. The number of post offices grew from three thousand in 1815 to fourteen thousand in 1845. The post office also played a brief but crucial role in the development of the telegraph, financing the first telegraph line, from Washington to Baltimore, in 1844. Invented by artist Samuel F. B. Morse, the telegraph allowed information to travel faster, almost instantaneously, over long distances. To create an atmo-

sphere conducive to economic growth and individual creativity, the government protected inventions and domestic industries. Patent laws gave inventors a seventeen-year monopoly on their inventions, and tariffs protected American industry from foreign competition.

Government policy also fostered farm life. Republicanism associated farming with virtue, independence, and productivity, essential values in the new republic, and the federal government surveyed public land and opened it to settlement. Internal improvements such as harbors, roads, and canals—some underwritten by government—linked new farms in the West to markets in the East. When Indians got in the way of expansion, the federal government moved them across the Mississippi River (see pages 263–268).

The federal judiciary validated government promotion of the economy and encouraged business enterprise and risk taking. In *Gibbons v. Ogden* (1824), the Supreme Court overturned the New York State law that gave Robert Fulton and Robert Livingston a monopoly on the New York–New Jersey steamboat trade. Aaron Ogden, a successor, lost the monopoly when Chief Justice John Marshall ruled that the federal power to license new enterprises took precedence over New York's grant of monopoly rights. Marshall declared that Congress's power under the commerce clause of the Constitution extended to "every species of commercial intercourse," including transportation. Within a year, forty-three steamboats were plying Ogden's route.

LEGAL FOUNDATIONS OF COMMERCE

In defining interstate commerce broadly, the Marshall Court expanded federal powers over the economy while restricting the ability of states to control economic activity within their borders. Its action was consistent with *Dartmouth College v. Woodward* (1819), which protected the sanctity of contracts against interference by the states, and with *Fletcher v. Peck* (1810), which voided a Georgia law that violated individuals' rights to make contracts. "If business is to prosper," Marshall wrote, "men must have assurance that contracts will be enforced."

Federal and state courts, in conjunction with state legislatures, also encouraged the proliferation of corporations—organizations entitled to hold property and transact business as if they were individuals. Corporation owners, called shareholders, were granted *limited liability*, or freedom from responsibility for the company's debts beyond their original investments. Limited liability encouraged investors to back new business ventures. Shareholders elected managers who ran the corporation, though often managers controlled a majority of the voting stock.

CORPORATIONS

■ The Marshall Court encouraged business competition by ending state-licensed monopolies on inland waterways. *Gibbons v. Ogden* (1824) opened up the New York–New Jersey trade to new lines, and within a short time dozens of steamboats were ferrying passengers and freight across the Hudson River.   (© Collection of The New York Historical Society)

By 1817 the number of corporations in the United States had grown to two thousand, from three hundred in 1800. By 1830 the New England states alone had issued nineteen hundred charters, one-third to manufacturing and mining firms. At first each firm needed a special legislative act to incorporate, but after the 1830s applications became so numerous that states established routine procedures allowing businesses to incorporate easily.

Though legislative action created corporations, the courts played a critical role in extending their powers and

CHARLES RIVER BRIDGE V. WARREN BRIDGE

protecting them. Two Massachusetts cases in 1819, for instance, upheld the limited liability of stockholders. And the U.S. Supreme Court in *Charles River Bridge v. Warren Bridge* (1837) paved the way for new enterprises and technologies, favoring competition over monopoly and the public interest over implied privileges in old contracts.

The Massachusetts legislature had chartered the Charles River Bridge Company in 1785 and seven years later extended its charter for seventy years. In return for building a bridge between Charlestown and Boston, the owners received the right to collect tolls. In 1828 the legislature chartered another company to build the Warren

Bridge across the Charles nearby; the new bridge could collect tolls for six years, after which the bridge would be turned over to the state and be free of tolls. The Charles River Bridge Company sued in 1829, claiming that the new bridge breached the earlier charter, which was an exclusive contract, protected under *Dartmouth College v. Woodward.*

Speaking for a narrow 4-to-3 majority, Marshall's successor Roger Taney declared that the original charter did not confer the privilege of monopoly and that exclusivity could not therefore be implied. Taney ruled that charter grants should be interpreted narrowly and that ambiguities would be decided in favor of the public interest. New enterprises should not be restricted by old charters, and economic growth would best be served by narrowing the application of the *Dartmouth College* decision. In this way the judiciary promoted new technologies over old ones.

In promoting the economy, state governments far surpassed the federal government. From 1815 through the

STATES' SUPPORT FOR THE ECONOMY

1840s, for example, government money, mostly from the states, financed three-fourths of the nearly $200 million invested in canals. In the 1830s the states started to invest in rail construction.

Though the federal government played a larger role in constructing railroads than in building canals, state and local governments provided more than half of the capital for southern rail lines. State governments also invested in corporate and bank stocks, providing corporations and banks with much-needed capital. In fact, states actually equaled or exceeded private enterprise in their investments.

Pennsylvania, encompassing a vast area from the Delaware River to beyond the Appalachians, developed the nation's most extensive program of internal improvements to stimulate settlement and economic growth. The state invested $100 million in canals, railroads, banks, and manufacturing firms; its appointees sat on more than 150 corporate boards of directors. But Pennsylvania and other states did more than invest resources in industry. Through special acts and incorporation laws, they regulated the nature and activities of corporations and banks and used licensing to control industrial operations. Georgia, for example, regulated the grading and marketing of tobacco.

Largely as a result of these government efforts, the United States experienced uneven but sustained economic growth from the end of the War of 1812 until midcentury. Political controversy raged over questions of state versus federal activity—especially with regard to internal improvements and banking—but all parties agreed on the general goal of economic expansion. Indeed, during these years the major restraint on government action was not philosophical but financial: the public purse was small. As the private sector grew more vigorous, entrepreneurs looked less to government for financial support, and the states played less of a role in investment.

Transportation Links

Improved transportation facilitated economic growth. Outside the South, state governments invested heavily in roads, canals, and railroads, with much of the financing borrowed from Europe. With regional and national financial institutions increasingly concentrated in New York, Boston, and Philadelphia, northeastern seaboard cities became the center of American commerce. New York financial and commercial houses dominated the American export trade, not only of New England textiles but also, through affiliates in southern port cities, of southern cotton. The South's staple crop was marketed to, and through, the North. The Deep South, with most of its capital invested in slave labor and land, built fewer canals, railroads, and factories and remained mostly rural.

Water routes provided the cheapest and most available transportation. Before the War of 1812 nearly all commerce moved on navigable rivers, and bulk shipments—cotton in the South and grain in the West—continued to move to ocean port cities by water. Increasingly, however, settlement extended beyond the river links, and the federal and state governments, followed by private corporations, invested heavily in alternative transportation.

EAST-WEST LINKS In the 1820s new arteries opened up east-west travel. The National Road—a stone-based, gravel-topped highway originating in Cumberland, Maryland—reached Columbus, Ohio, in 1833. More important, the Erie Canal, completed in 1825, linked the Great Lakes with New York City and the Atlantic Ocean. The canal carried easterners and then immigrants to settle the Old Northwest and the frontier beyond; in the opposite direction, it transported western grain to the large and growing eastern markets. Railroads and later the telegraph would strengthen these east-west links. Other than the coastal cotton trade, links between the Deep South and the North were rare.

CANALS The 363-mile-long Erie Canal was a visionary enterprise. When the state of New York authorized its construction in 1817, the longest American canal was only 28 miles long. Vigorously promoted by Governor DeWitt Clinton, the Erie cost $7 million, much of it borrowed from British investors. The canal shortened the journey between Buffalo and New York City from twenty to six days and reduced freight charges from $100 to $5 a ton. By 1835 traffic was so heavy that the canal had to be widened from 40 to 70 feet and deepened from 4 to 7 feet. Skeptics who had called the canal "Clinton's big ditch" had long since fallen silent.

The success of the Erie Canal triggered an explosion of canal building. By 1840 canals crisscrossed the Northeast and Midwest, and total canal mileage reached 3,300—most of it built in the 1820s (see Map 10.2). None of the new canals enjoyed the financial success achieved by the Erie, however. As the high cost of construction combined with an economic contraction, investment in canals began to slump in the 1830s. By midcentury more miles were being abandoned than built; the canal era had ended.

RAILROADS Meanwhile, railroads boomed. The railroad era in the United States began in 1830 when Peter Cooper's locomotive, "Tom Thumb," first steamed along 13 miles of Baltimore and Ohio Railroad track. In 1833 the nation's second railroad ran 136 miles from Charleston to

LINKS TO THE WORLD

The United States as a Developing Nation

In the early nineteenth century, the United States was a "developing nation" as its economy slowly shifted from dependence on agriculture and raw materials to producing manufactured goods. In order to develop economically, the United States imported capital to finance international trade, internal improvements, and early factories.

American political and economic leaders in the early part of the nineteenth century talked as if they were masters of their own fate. In many ways, however, the United States remained economically dependent on its former mother country, Great Britain. The political independence that the United States won in the Revolutionary War and affirmed in the War of 1812 was not matched in the economic sphere.

Following the War of 1812, Americans depended on Britain for capital investment. Ninety percent of all U.S. foreign capital came from Britain, and around 60 percent of all British capital exports flowed to the United States. Americans used British capital to develop first the canals, then the railroads that facilitated American industrial development. For instance, from 1817 to 1825 the British invested $7 million in New York State bonds to finance the Erie Canal. Altogether, European investors provided 80 percent of the money to build the Erie, and the United States depended on mostly British capital to finance America's internal improvements.

As a developing nation, the United States imported more goods than it exported. In other words, Americans consumed more than they produced. It was able to do so because imported capital balanced the trade deficit. As in most developing countries, exports were concentrated in agricultural commodities; 50 percent of the value of all exports was in cotton. And British credit financed cotton sales.

As a developing nation, U.S. dependency on international capital was highlighted when imported capital was interrupted, as in the Panics of 1819 and 1837. Though the financial crises began in the United States, the hard times were made worse in both cases when British investors and creditors squeezed Americans. Economic crises in England led investors to pull out capital from the United States while merchants demanded that Americans pay what they owed to British creditors. Money became tight, and the economy declined.

Thus both economic development and hard times revealed the significance of international capital links to the United States, a developing nation.

In the 1820s canals like the Erie linked the West with eastern cities and the Atlantic Ocean, and thus world trade. U.S. exports were concentrated in agriculture, and the Erie and other canals carried grain to the world market. Charles Klackner published this view of a canal boat and its passengers, based on a contemporary painting by Edward Lamson Henry. Canal boats carried gentlemen and ladies as well as more modest citizens, many of them immigrants on their way to settling western lands. (Chicago Historical Society)

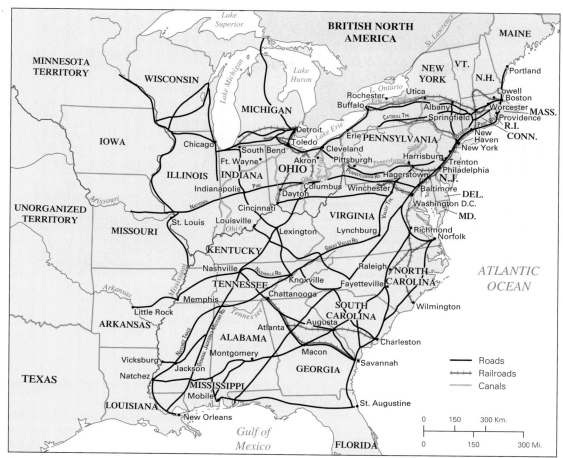

Map 10.2   Major Roads, Canals, and Railroads, 1850

A transportation network linked the seaboard to the interior. Settlers followed those routes westward, and they sent back grain, grain products, and cotton to the port cities.

Hamburg in South Carolina. By 1850 the United States had nearly 9,000 miles of railroad track.

The earliest railroads connected nearby cities, such as Philadelphia and Baltimore; not until the 1850s did railroads offer long-distance service at reasonable rates. The early lines had to overcome technical problems. Locomotives heavy enough to climb steep grades and pull long trains required strong rails and resilient track beds. Engineers met those needs by replacing wooden tracks with iron rails and by supporting the rails with ties embedded in gravel. A new wheel alignment—the swivel truck—permitted heavy engines to hold the track on sharp curves. Other problems persisted: the lack of a common standard for the width of track thwarted development of a national system. Pennsylvania and Ohio railroads, for instance, had no fewer than seven different track widths. A journey from Philadelphia to Charleston, South Carolina, involved eight different gauges, which meant that passengers and freight had to change trains seven times. Only at Bowling Green, Kentucky, did northern and southern railroads connect directly with one another.

Technology and investments in transportation dramatically reduced travel time and shipping. Before 1815, river transportation was the only feasible route for long-distance journeys. In 1815 a traveler took four days to go by stagecoach from New York City to Baltimore and nearly four weeks to reach Detroit. By 1830 the New York–Baltimore journey took a day and a half, while the Erie Canal reduced the New York–Detroit journey to two weeks. Before the War of

REDUCTION IN TRAVEL TIME AND COST

■ Railroads, introduced in the 1830s, soon surpassed canals. Easier, quicker, and cheaper to build than canals, they moved goods and people faster. David Matthews, the engineer of the Mohawk & Hudson's *John Bull,* drew this picture of his early locomotive. The Mohawk and Hudson offered competition to the slower Erie Canal boats. (© Collection of the New York Historical Society)

1812, wagon transportation cost 30 to 70 cents per ton per mile. By midcentury railroads brought the cost of land transportation down 95 percent and reduced the journey to one-fifth the time.

Commercial Farming

*a*lthough manufacturing increased steadily, agriculture remained the backbone of the economy and American exports. But increasingly the market economy altered farming. Though the plantation system had always been market oriented, self-sufficient farm households were becoming market oriented too. Equally important, the center of commercial farming moved westward. In the 1830s and after, the plantation South shifted toward the Mississippi River valley, while commercial farming came to dominate the Old Northwest and the Ohio River valley, then moved even farther westward to the prairies.

After the 1820s, northeastern agriculture began to decline. Eastern farmers had cultivated all the land available to them; expansion was impossible. Moreover, small New England farms with their uneven terrains did not lend themselves to the new labor-saving farm implements introduced in the 1830s—mechanical sowers, reapers, and threshers. As a result, many north-

NEW ENGLAND
AGRICULTURE

ern farmers either moved west or gave up farming for jobs in the merchant houses and factories.

But neither the countinghouse nor the factory depleted New England agriculture. The farmers who remained proved as adaptable on the farm as were their children working at copy desks and water-powered looms. By the 1850s many New England and Middle Atlantic farm families had abandoned the commercial production of wheat and corn and stopped tilling poor land. Instead, they improved their livestock, especially cattle, and specialized in vegetable and fruit production and dairy farming. They financed these initiatives through land sales and debt. Indeed, increasing land values, not farming, promised the greatest profit.

Farm families everywhere gradually adjusted to market conditions and began to welcome new opportunities. In 1820 about one-third of all produce was intended for market. By 1850 the amount surpassed 50 percent. Farmers shifted toward specialization and market-oriented production. The rewards for such flexibility were great. Produce sold at market financed land and equipment purchases and made credit arrangements possible. Middlemen specializing in the grain and food trades replaced the rural storekeepers who had once handled all transactions for local farmers, acting both as retailers and as marketing and purchasing agents.

Farm families who owned their own land flourished, but the rising cost of land and of farming made it harder to start up. By the 1840s it took more than ten years for a rural laborer to save enough money to farm for himself. Thus the number of tenant farmers and hired hands increased. Previously farmers had relied mostly on the labor of unpaid family members or enslaved workers; now they had to secure waged farm labor.

Farm women had a distinctive role in the market economy aside from their work in fields and barnyards.

WOMEN'S PAID LABOR Many sold eggs, dairy products, and garden produce in local markets, and their earnings became essential to household incomes. Butter and cheese making replaced spinning and weaving; farm women now sold commodities and bought cloth. The work was physically demanding and did not replace regular home and farm chores but added to them. Yet women took pride in their work, often gaining from it a sense of independence that was as valuable as their profits. Esther Lewis, a widow who sent from 75 to 100 pounds of butter monthly to Philadelphia in the 1830s, even hired other women to increase production.

Women's success at butter and cheese making led some farms to specialize in dairy production. After the Erie Canal opened, Ohio dairy farms had access to New York's export trade. Ohio entrepreneurs turned cheese into factory production in the 1840s, contracting to buy curd from local dairy farmers. Canals and railroads took the cheese to eastern ports, where wholesalers sold the cheese around the world, shipping it to California, England, and China. In 1844 Britain imported more than 5 million pounds of cheese from the United States.

Individually and collectively, Americans still valued agrarian life. State governments energetically promoted commercial agriculture to spur economic growth and sustain the values of an agrarian-based republic. Massachusetts in 1817 and New York in 1819 began to subsidize agricultural prizes and county fairs. New York required contestants to submit written descriptions of how they grew their prize crops; the state then published the essays to encourage new methods and specialization. The post office circulated farm journals that helped familiarize farmers with developments in agriculture.

Gradually the Old Northwest replaced the Northeast as the center of American family agriculture. Farms

MECHANIZATION OF AGRICULTURE in the Old Northwest were much larger, flatter, and better suited to the new mechanized farming implements than were their northeastern counterparts. Cyrus McCormick, a Virginia farmer, had invented the reaper in 1831. In one continuous motion, a revolving drum on the horse-drawn reaper positioned grain stalks in front of a blade and the cut grain fell onto

■ Women tended cows and chickens and sold dairy products and eggs in the growing market economy.   (Princeton University Library, Sinclair Hamilton Collection. Visual Materials Division, Department of Rare Books and Special Collections)

a platform. Though ridiculed by the *London Times* as "a cross between a flying machine, a wheelbarrow, and an Astly chariot," the reaper was a great success. McCormick patented his machine in 1834 and built a factory in Chicago that by 1847 sold a thousand reapers a year. Midwestern farmers bought reapers on credit and paid for them with the profits from their high yields. Similarly, John Deere's steel plow, invented in 1837, replaced the traditional iron plow; steel blades kept the soil from sticking and were tough enough to break the roots of prairie grass.

And just in time. The Midwest was becoming one of the leading agricultural regions of the world. Midwestern farms fed the growing cities in the East, bursting with growing immigrant populations, and still produced enough to export to Europe.

At the end of the eighteenth century, southern agriculture was diverse. The South grew sufficient grain to

THE COTTON SOUTH feed itself. Although debt plagued Virginia's tobacco growers, farther south, along the coast, slaves grew rice and some indigo for the market. Cotton was profitable only for the Sea Island planters in South Carolina and Georgia, who grew the luxurious long and silky variety. Short-staple cotton, which grew readily in the interior and in all kinds of soil, was unmarketable because its sticky seeds lay tangled in the fibers. Then, in 1793, Eli Whitney invented the cotton gin. The gin separated the cotton from the seeds fifty times faster than by hand and

■ This is a model of the reaper invented by McCormick in 1831. As Midwestern farmers mechanized in the 1840s, they bought factory-produced reapers. Increased production fed the growing eastern cities and led to grain export. (Smithsonian Institution, Washington, D.C.)

made possible the expansion of cotton production at the very time that new textile mills in England and New England were increasing demand for cotton cloth. The result transformed southern agriculture, revived and expanded slavery, and boosted export of both cotton and cloth.

After 1800 the cultivation of short-staple cotton spread rapidly. By the 1820s there were cotton plantations in the fertile lands of Louisiana, Mississippi, Alabama, Arkansas, and Tennessee, and the center of cotton production was moving west. From 1820 to 1840, South Carolina sank from first to fifth in cotton production, and Mississippi rose to first. In each decade after 1820, the total crop doubled. By 1825 the slave South was the world's dominant supplier of cotton, and the white fibers were America's largest export. Southerners with capital bought more land and more slaves and planted ever more cotton.

No region was more tied to international markets than the South, yet the region seemed immune to the transforming potential of foreign trade. The South produced cotton exclusively as a market crop. Though some cotton production became mechanized, with steam engines used in place of horses to power gins and presses, most southern capital remained concentrated in land and slaves. It could not shift easily to support manufacturing and commerce. In many ways the cotton economy resembled a colonial economy. Planters depended on distant agents, some in southern cities, many in the North, and even some in Europe, to represent them and handle finances, which often included loans. Thus critical market decisions were made by bankers, financiers, and brokers, all outside the South. The South was engaged in the new market economy, but at a distance.

The cotton boom, dependent on slave labor, defined both the southern economy and southern society as it moved westward. Slaveholders were oriented to the market economy, as were commercial farmers, merchants, and entrepreneurs in the North. But slaveholders did not pay wages for labor; they bought laborers. With capital tied to the slave system, the entire South—whites, free blacks, and slaves—were tied together and trapped by the cotton economy. Ultimately this "peculiar" system (see Chapter 13) would separate the South from the national economy and the nation.

The Rise of Manufacturing and Commerce

Though at first Americans imported machines or copied British designs, they soon built their own. Matthew Baldwin made steam engines in Philadelphia in the 1820s, but in 1834, with railroads expanding, Baldwin turned to making steam locomotives. By 1839 he had produced 140 of them, or 45 percent of all American-made locomotives. A visitor to his shop in 1838 found twelve engines in various states of construction. "Those parts of the engine, such as the cylinder, piston, valves . . . in which good fitting and fine workmanship are indispensable to the efficient action of the machine, were very highly finished," the British visitor reported. By 1840 the United States exported railroad engines to Russia, some German states, and even Britain.

British visitors to the 1851 London Crystal Palace Exhibition, the first modern world's fair, were equally impressed by American design and fine tooling of working parts. American companies displayed hundreds of American machines and wares—from farm tools to exotic devices such as the reaper and an ice-cream freezer—that

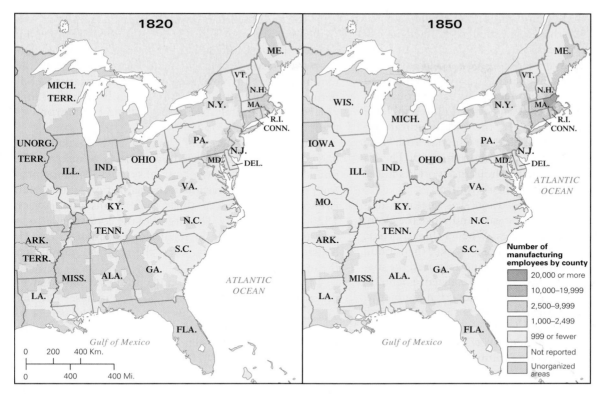

Map 10.3   U.S. Manufacturing Employment, 1820 and 1850

In 1820 manufacturing employment was concentrated mostly in the Northeast, where the first textile mills appeared. By 1850 the density of manufacturing in the Northeast had increased, but new manufacturing centers arose in Baltimore, Pittsburgh, and Cincinnati.   (Source: *Historical Atlas of the United States,* 2d ed. [Washington, D.C.: National Geographic Society, 1993], p. 148. Reprinted by permission of National Geographic Maps/National Geographic Society Image Collection.)

astonished observers. American manufacturers returned home with dozens of medals. Most impressive to the Europeans were three simple machines: Alfred C. Hobb's unpickable padlocks, Samuel Colt's revolvers, and Robbins and Lawrence's rifles fashioned with completely interchangeable parts. Like Baldwin's locomotives, all were machine-tooled rather than handmade, products of what the British called the American system of manufacturing.

The American system of manufacturing used precision machinery to produce interchangeable parts that did not require individual adjustment to fit. Eli Whitney, inventor of the cotton gin, had promoted the idea of interchangeable parts in 1798 when he contracted with the federal government to make ten thousand rifles in twenty-eight months. By the 1820s the United States Ordnance Department had contracted with private firms to introduce machine-made interchangeable parts for firearms. The American system

AMERICAN SYSTEM OF MANUFACTURING

quickly spread beyond the arsenals, producing the machine-tool industry—the manufacture of machines for the purposes of mass production. One outcome was an explosion in consumer goods. With the time and skill involved in manufacturing greatly reduced, the new system permitted mass production at low cost: Waltham watches, Yale locks, and other goods became household items, inexpensive yet of uniformly high quality.

Even larger than the machine-tool industry was the textile industry. New England mills began processing and weaving slave-grown cotton in the same decade that Whitney patented his gin. Boosted by embargo and war, then protected by the tariff, the textile industry boomed with the expansion of cotton cultivation after the war (see Map 10.3).

TEXTILE MILLS

The Boston Manufacturing Company, chartered in 1813, radically transformed textile manufacturing. Francis Cabot Lowell and other Boston merchants capitalized the corporation at $400,000—ten times the amount behind the first Rhode Island mills. The owners erected their factories in Waltham, Massachusetts, bringing all the manufacturing processes to a single location. They employed a resident manager to run the mill, thus separating ownership from management. Workers received wages, and the cloth they produced was sold throughout the United States. By the 1840s a cotton mill resembled a modern factory, and textiles were the most important industry in the nation. Cotton cloth production rose from 4 million yards in 1817 to 323 million in 1840. The industry employed around eighty thousand workers in the mid-1840s, more than half of them women.

The industry's great innovation was that the machines, not the women, spun the yarn and wove the cloth. Workers monitored the machines. When a thread broke, the machine stopped automatically; a worker then found the break, pieced the ends together, and restarted the machine. The mills increasingly used specialized machines. Their application of the American system of manufacturing enabled American firms to compete successfully with British cotton mills.

The early mills, dependent on waterpower, sprung up in rural areas. By erecting dams and watercourses, mill owners diverted water from farmers and destroyed fishing, an important source of income and protein in rural and village America. To protect their customary rights, fishermen and farmers fought the manufacturers in New England state legislatures, but petitions from job seekers in the mill environs supported the manufacturers. The ensuing compromises promoted mill development.

Textile manufacturing changed New England and had its greatest impact on Lowell, Massachusetts. The population of Lowell, the "city of spindles" and the prototype of early American industrialization, grew from twenty-five hundred to thirty-three thousand between 1826 and midcentury. The largest of the cotton-mill towns and the front runner in technological change, Lowell boasted the biggest work force, the greatest output, and the most capital invested.

The cloth New England mills produced was so inexpensive that many women began to purchase it rather than make their own. The success of the textile factories also spawned the ready-made clothing industry. Before the 1820s, women sewed most clothing

READY-MADE CLOTHING

■ In the 1830s an unknown artist painted *Middlesex Company Woolen Mills,* portraying the hulking mass of the mill buildings. The company organized all the manufacturing processes at a single location, in Lowell, Massachusetts, on the Merrimack River.   (Museum of American Textile History)

at home, and some people purchased used clothing. Tailors and seamstresses made wealthy men's and women's clothing to order. By the 1820s and 1830s, much clothing was mass-produced. Manufacturers used two methods, either separately or in combination. In one, the clothing was made in a factory; in the other, at home, through the putting-out system. In this arrangement, a journeyman tailor—a trained craftsman employed by a master tailor who owned the workshop—cut the fabric panels in the factory, and the masters "put out" the sewing at piece rates to women working in their own homes. In this way, women who formerly had spun their own yarn now received yarn from a master and returned finished cloth. The work itself was familiar, but the change was significant: women were operating their looms for wages and producing cloth for the market, not primarily for their families.

In 1832 Boston manufacturers employed three hundred journeyman tailors at $2 per day and thirteen hundred women and one hundred boys at 50 cents a day. Apprentices, if used at all, were no longer learning a trade; they were a permanent source of cheap labor. In the 1840s as many as a dozen different pairs of hands contributed to making a single pair of pants under the putting-out system.

Most of the early mass-produced clothes were made for men. Urban dwellers who lived in boarding and rooming houses, far from the female kin who previously would have made their garments, purchased the crudely made, loose-fitting clothing. Improvements in fit and changes in men's fashion eventually made ready-to-wear apparel more acceptable to clerks and professional men. In the 1840s the short sack coat, which did not taper at the waist, began to replace the embroidered waistcoat. This forerunner of the modern suit jacket fit loosely and needed little custom tailoring. Now even well-to-do men were willing to consider ready-made apparel. Most women made their own clothes, but those who could afford to do so employed seamstresses.

Retail clothing stores began to stock ready-made clothes in the 1820s. T. S. Whitmarsh of Boston advertised in 1827 that "he keeps constantly for Sale, from 5 to 10,000 Fashionable ready-made Garments." Such merchants often bought goods wholesale, though many manufactured shirts and trousers in their own factories. Lewis and Hanford of New York City boasted of cutting more than one hundred thousand garments in the winter of 1848–1849. The New York firm sold most of its clothing in the South and owned its own retail outlet in New Orleans. Paul Tulane, a New Orleans competitor, owned a New York factory that made goods for his

RETAIL MERCHANTS

Shirt Depot,
177 Washington Street,......Boston.
(Near Milk Street.)

SHIRTS FOR THE MILLION

TO LOCKE'S SHIRT DEPOT

F. B. LOCKE,
Manufacturer & Wholesale & Retail Dealer in
Shirts, Bosoms, Collars, Stocks, and Gent's Furnishing Goods of every description.
☞ FRENCH SHIRTS MADE TO ORDER. ☜

■ F. B. Locke adapted to the new market for ready-made clothing by becoming a manufacturer, wholesaler, and retailer of men's shirts. Although he continued to make shirts to order, the staple of his Shirt Depot was mass-produced shirts, as this advertisement from the *Boston Directory* for 1848–1849 indicates.   (Warshaw Collection of Business Americana, Smithsonian Institution, Washington, D.C.)

Louisiana store. In the West, Cincinnati became the center of the new men's clothing industry. By midcentury, Cincinnati's ready-to-wear apparel industry employed fifteen hundred men and ten thousand women. As in Boston, most of the women did outwork.

Commerce expanded hand in hand with manufacturing. Cotton, for instance, had once been traded by plantation agents, who sold the raw cotton and bought manufactured goods that they then sold to plantation owners, extending them credit when necessary. Cotton exports rose from 83 million pounds in 1815 to 298 million in 1830 to more than a billion pounds for the first time in 1849. Gradually, some agents came to specialize in finance alone: they were cotton brokers, who for a commission brought together buyers and sellers. Similarly, wheat and hog brokers sprang up in the West—in Cincinnati, Louisville, and St. Louis. The distribution of finished goods also became more specialized as wholesalers bought large quantities of particular items from manufacturers, and jobbers broke down the wholesale lots for retail stores and country merchants.

SPECIALIZATION OF COMMERCE

General merchants persisted longer in small towns than in cities. They continued to exchange some goods with local farm women—trading flour or pots and pans for eggs or other produce. And local craftsmen continued to sell their own finished goods, such as shoes and clothing. In some rural areas and on the frontier, peddlers acted as general merchants. But as transportation improved and towns grew, even small-town merchants began to specialize.

Commercial specialization transformed some traders in big cities, especially New York, into virtual merchant princes. After the Erie Canal opened, New York City became a stop on every major trade route from Europe, the southern ports, and the West. New York traders were the middlemen for southern cotton and western grain. Merchants in other cities played a similar role within their own regions. Some traders in turn invested their profits in factories, further stimulating urban manufacturing. Some cities specialized: Rochester became a milling center, and Cincinnati—"Porkopolis"—became the first meatpacking center.

Merchants who engaged in complex commercial transactions required large office staffs, mostly all male. At the bottom of the office hierarchy were messenger boys, often preteens, who delivered documents. Above them were copyists, on high stools, who hand-copied as many documents as needed. Clerks processed documents and shipping papers and did translations. Above them were the bookkeeper and the confidential chief clerk. Those seeking employment in such an office, called a countinghouse, often took a course from a writing master to acquire a "good hand." All hoped to rise someday to the status of partner, although their chances of doing so were slim.

Financial institutions played a significant role in the expansion of manufacturing and commerce. Banks, insurance companies, and corporations linked savers—those who deposited money in banks—with producers and speculators who wished to borrow money. After 1816, the Second Bank of the United States injected a national perspective into finance, but many farmers, local bankers, and politicians denounced the bank as a monster, blaming it for serving national, not local, interests. Western landowners suffered severe losses when the Second Bank reduced loans in the western states during the Panic of 1819. In 1836 critics finally succeeded in killing the bank (see page 286).

BANKING AND CREDIT SYSTEMS

The closing of the Second Bank in 1836 caused a nationwide credit shortage, which, in conjunction with the Panic of 1837, led to fundamental reforms in banking. Michigan and New York introduced charter laws promoting what was called free banking. Many other states soon followed suit. Previously, every new bank needed a special legislative charter to operate; thus each bank incorporation involved a political process. Under the new laws, any proposed bank that met certain minimum conditions—amount of capital invested, number of notes issued, and types of loans to be offered—would receive a state charter automatically. Banks in Michigan, New York, and, soon, other states could incorporate more easily.

Free banking proved to be a significant stimulus to the economy in the late 1840s and 1850s. New banks sprang up everywhere, providing merchants and manufacturers with the credit they needed. Free-banking laws also served as a precedent for general incorporation statutes that allowed manufacturing firms to receive state charters without special legislative acts.

Workers and the Workplace

Loud the morning bell is ringing,
  Up, up sleepers, haste away;
Yonder sits the redbreast singing,
  But to list we must not stay.

. . . .

Sisters, haste, the bell is tolling,
  Soon will close the dreadful gate;
Then, alas! We must go strolling,
  Through the counting-room too late.

. . . .

Now the sun is upward climbing,
  And the breakfast hour has come;
Ding, dong, ding, the bell is chiming,
  Hasten, sisters, hasten home.

The poet, writing in 1844 in the *Factory Girl's Garland*, uses the sound of the factory bell as a refrain to emphasize its incessant control, announcing when the workers are to wake, eat, begin and stop work, and go to sleep. Night and day the mill workers felt the stress of factory schedules.

But the first generation of young single women who left New England villages and farms to work in the mills had come with great optimism. The managers in rural Waltham recruited New England farm daughters with inducements including cash wages, company-run boarding houses, and cultural events such as evening lectures—none of which were available on the farm. This paternalistic approach, called the Waltham or Lowell system, spread to other mills erected alongside New England rivers. The mills offered steady work and good pay, airy rooms, prepared meals, and cultural activities. Though housekeepers enforced strict curfews, banned alcohol, and reported on workers' behavior and church attendance, mill work brought financial independence and friendship.

Sisters and cousins often worked and lived in the same mill and boarding house. They helped each other adjust, and their letters home drew kin to the mills. The benefits were not sufficient, however, to change their ambitions to be wives and mothers. Most arrivals were sixteen and stayed only about five years. When they left the mills to marry, other younger women interested in earning a wage took their places.

In the hard times from 1837 to 1842, demand for cloth declined, and most mills ran only part-time. Subsequently

BOOM AND BUST IN THE TEXTILE MILLS

managers pressured workers by means of the speed-up, the stretch-out, and the premium system. The speed-up increased the speed of the machines; the stretch-out increased the number of machines each worker had to operate; and premiums paid overseers whose departments produced the most cloth encouraged them to pressure workers for greater output. The result: between 1836 and 1850 the number of spindles and looms in Lowell increased 150 and 140 percent, respectively, while the number of workers increased by only 50 percent. The corporation's goal of building an industrial empire and maximizing profits took precedence over its paternalistic concern for workers' living conditions. In the race for profits, owners lengthened hours, cut wages, tightened discipline, and packed the boarding houses. Some mill workers began to think of themselves as slaves.

New England mill workers responded to their deteriorating working conditions by organizing and striking.

PROTESTS

In 1834, in reaction to a 25 percent wage cut, they unsuccessfully "turned out" (struck) against the Lowell mills. Two years later, when boarding house fees increased, they turned out again. As conditions continued to worsen, workers adopted new methods of resistance. In the 1840s, strikes gave way to a concerted effort to shorten the workday. Massachusetts mill women and other workers joined forces to press for state legislation mandating a ten-hour day. Eliza R. Hemingway, a three-year veteran of two different Lowell mills, told a Massachusetts House of Representatives committee in 1845 that workers' hours were too long. In the summer, work ran from 5:00 A.M. to 7:00 P.M., with time off for meals.

Women aired their complaints in worker-run newspapers: in 1842, the *Factory Girl* appeared in New Hampshire, the *Wampanoag and Operatives' Journal* in Massachusetts. Two years later they founded the *Factory Girl's Garland* and the *Voice of Industry,* nicknamed "the factory girl's voice." Even the *Lowell Offering,* the owner-sponsored paper that was the pride of mill workers and managers alike, became embroiled in controversy

■ This young mill girl at Waltham or Lowell, probably in the late 1840s, posed for an early daguerreotype. Her swollen and rough hands contrast with her youth, neat dress, and carefully tied, beribboned hair. Her hands suggest that she worked, as did most twelve- and thirteen-year-olds, as a warper, straightening the strands of cotton or wool as they entered the looms.   (Courtesy of Jack Naylor)

when workers charged that its editors had suppressed articles criticizing working conditions.

The women's labor organizations were weakened by worker turnover. Few militant native-born mill workers stayed on to fight the managers and owners, and gradually fewer New England daughters entered the mills. In the 1850s, Irish immigrant women who lived at home replaced them. Technological improvements in the looms and other machinery had made the work less skilled and more routine. The mills could thus pay lower wages and draw from a reservoir of unskilled labor.

A growing gender division in the workplace, especially in the textile, clothing, and shoemaking industries,

GENDER DIVISIONS IN WORK

was one important outcome of large-scale manufacturing. Although women and men in traditional agricultural and artisan households tended to perform different tasks, they worked as a family unit. As wage work spread, however, men's and women's work cultures became increasingly separate. The women and girls who left home for jobs in textile mills worked and lived in a mostly female world. In the clothing and shoemaking industries, whose male artisans had once worked at home assisted by unpaid family labor, men began working outside the home while women continued to work at home through the putting-out system. Tasks and wages, too, became rigidly differentiated: women sewed, whereas men shaped materials and finished products, receiving higher wages in shops employing men only.

The market economy had an impact on unpaid household labor as well. As home and workplace became separate and labor came to be defined in terms of wages (what could be sold in the marketplace) rather than production (what could be made by hand), the unpaid labor of women was devalued. Cash exchanged was the measure, and as families increasingly recorded their incomes and expenditures in account books, there was no category for women's unpaid services. Yet those labors were extensive; indeed, the family depended on women's work within the household, ever more so as sons and even daughters found wage work outside the home and had less time for household tasks. Thus gender defined household labor, and in the market economy it went unrecorded. Inevitably, it seemed to be worth little and was taken for granted.

The new textile mills, shoe factories, iron mills, and railroads were the antithesis of traditional workshop and household production. In factories, authority was hierarchically organized.

CHANGES IN THE WORKPLACE

Factory workers lost their sense of autonomy as impersonal market forces seemed to dominate their lives. Their jobs were insecure, as competition frequently led to layoffs and replacement by cheaper, less-skilled workers or children. Moreover, the formal rules of the factory contrasted sharply with the informal atmosphere of artisan shops and farm households. Journeymen recognized that the new system of manufacturing threatened them. When master craftsmen became managers in shoemaking and textiles as they turned their workshops into small factories, journeymen became factory operatives. In large factories, the workers never saw the owners, working under paid supervisors. The division of labor and the use of machines narrowed the skills required. Mill workers had to tolerate the roar of the looms, and all workers on power machines risked accidents that could maim or even kill. Perhaps most demoralizing, opportunities for advancement in the new system were virtually nil. And the bell, the steam whistle, or the clock governed the flow of work, as the *Factory Girl's Garland* poem anxiously described.

As a sense of distance from their employers took hold, so did deep-seated differences among workers. Initially, mill women drew on kinship, village, and gender ties to build supportive networks in factories. But in the 1840s, as recently arrived Irish immigrant women entered the mills, many workers found themselves working with total strangers. Wage workers felt distanced from traditional culture as well. As wage work became common, the republican virtues associated with independent craft traditions eroded. The rigid rules of factory work and the swings in employment brought on by boom-and-bust cycles restricted individual freedom. At every turn, workers were hemmed in by formidable forces.

In response, some workers organized to resist changes wrought by the market economy and factories and to regain control of their work and their

LABOR PARTIES

lives. Women textile workers organized into unions and demonstrated for better wages and conditions or lobbied legislatures for relief. Male workers, like shoemakers, also organized and protested, but because they were eligible to vote, they also organized political parties. Labor parties first formed in Pennsylvania, New York, and Massachusetts in the 1820s and then spread elsewhere; they advocated free public education and abolishing imprisonment for debt and opposed banks and monopolies. The interests of workers' parties often coincided with those of middle-class reformers: temperance, observance of the Sabbath, and suppression of vice (see Chapter 11). Ironically, however, reform politics also tended to divide workers. Many reforms—moral education, temperance, Sabbath closings—served the interests of merchants and industrialists seeking a more disciplined work force. Temperance and Sabbath closings pitted Protestants against Catholics who celebrated Sunday at public beer gardens. Anti-immigrant and anti-Catholic movements further divided workers.

Organized labor's greatest achievement during this period was to gain relief from the threat of conspiracy

EMERGENCE OF A LABOR MOVEMENT

laws. When journeyman shoemakers organized during the first decade of the century, their employers accused them of criminal conspiracy. The cordwainers' (shoemakers') cases between 1806 and 1815 left labor organizations in an uncertain position. Although the courts acknowledged the journeymen's right to organize, judges viewed strikes as illegal until a Massachusetts case, *Commonwealth v. Hunt* (1842), ruled that Boston journeyman bootmakers could strike "in such manner as best to subserve their own interests."

Yet workers found permanent labor organizations difficult to sustain. Most workers outside the crafts were unskilled or semiskilled at best. Moreover, religion, race, ethnicity, and gender divided workers, and labor organizations excluded African Americans and women. (Massachusetts mill women organized their own unions.) The first unions arose among urban journeymen in printing, woodworking, shoemaking, and tailoring. They tended to be local; the strongest resembled medieval guilds in that members sought to protect themselves against the competition of inferior workmen by regulating apprenticeship and establishing minimum wages. Umbrella organizations composed of individual craft unions, like the National Trades Union (1834), arose in several cities in the 1820s and 1830s. But the movement fell apart amid wage reductions and unemployment in the hard times of 1839–1843.

Labor organizations remained weak; individual producers—craftsmen, factory workers, and farmers—lost economic power; and workers increasingly forfeited control over their own work. While mill owners, corporate investors, large-scale landowners, and slaveholding planters reaped benefits from economic growth, workers' share of the national wealth declined after 1830.

Americans on the Move

After the War of 1812 the United States grew in size and population. The Louisiana Purchase (1803) doubled the land area of the United States, and acquisitions in the 1840s nearly doubled it again. Throughout the Atlantic world, population soared, and that of the United States grew by a third in each decade. Between 1820 and 1845, the U.S. population expanded by 10.6 million people, with immigration accounting for only a small percentage of this number; 89 percent of the population growth was from natural increase. In 1845, 20.2 million people lived in the United States.

The United States spread outward, mostly westward, from its original seaboard base (see Map 10.4). The admission of new states tells the story: Indiana (1816), Mississippi (1817), Illinois (1818), Alabama (1819), Maine (1820), and Missouri (1821) brought the Union to twenty-four states in the 1820s. Arkansas (1836) and Michigan (1837) soon followed, as did Florida and Texas (1845), Iowa (1846), and Wisconsin (1848) in the following decade.

WESTWARD MOVEMENT

Southerner and easterner, cotton raiser and grain farmer, black and white, slave and free person, owner and renter, investor and speculator, settler and transient marched across the Appalachians. In the first two decades of the century Americans poured into the Ohio River valley; then, starting in the 1820s they moved into the Mississippi River valley and beyond, doubling the population living beyond the Appalachians. By midcentury two-thirds of Americans lived west of the Appalachians. Mostly young and hard working, they had visions of establishing family farms and achieving economic security.

Some 5 to 10 percent of Americans moved each year, their travel made ever faster and easier by the expanding

Women who traveled west with their husbands found their domestic skills in great demand. In this watercolor entitled *Laying Out of Karns' City, Minnesota* (1856), E. Whitefield shows a woman preparing a meal out of her lean-to kitchen for her husband and their guests. (Chicago Historical Society)

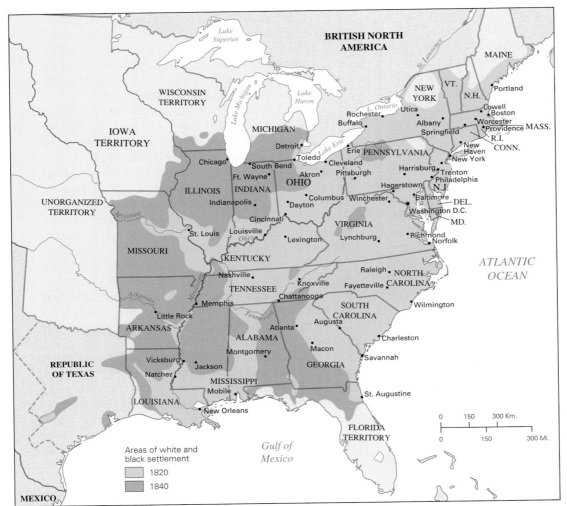

Map 10.4

Westward Movement, 1820 and 1840

Removal of Indians and a growing transportation network opened up land to white and black settlers in the West and in the Southeast, as the U.S. population grew from 9.6 million in 1820 to 17.1 million in 1840.

transportation networks. Restless, they settled only temporarily and then moved on. "There is more travelling in the United States than in any part of the world," observed a commentator in 1828. "Here the whole population is in motion, whereas, in old countries, there are millions who have never been beyond the sound of the parish bell." People tended to move short distances; thus long moves were made in stages. Though most people lived on farms, there was also a steady rural-to-urban migration.

After the 1820s the heart of cotton cultivation and the slave-based plantation system shifted from the coastal states to Alabama and the newly settled Mississippi valley—Tennessee, Louisiana, Arkansas, and Mississippi. Southerners brought their institutions with them; they forced slaves to move with them to the newer areas of the South, and yeoman farmers followed.

THE SOUTH

The shift was dramatic. The population of Mississippi soared from 73,000 in 1820 to 607,000 in 1850, with African American slaves in the majority. Across the Mississippi River, the population of Arkansas went from 14,000 in 1820 to 210,000 in 1850. Indian removal made this expansion possible. After the United States acquired Florida and attempted to colonize and suppress the Indian peoples there, southerners poured into the new territory.

The South and cotton continued westward into Texas. In 1830 the 7,000 American immigrants living in northwest Mexico outnumbered Mexicans there two to one. By 1835 the American population reached 35,000, including 3,000 slaves. The American settlers were restless for independence or U.S. annexation and chafed at Mexico's resistance toward Anglo domination in Texas. Independence in 1836 spurred further American immigration into Texas. By 1845 "Texas fever" had boosted the Anglo population to 125,000. Statehood that year opened the floodgates.

Not all moves were westward. A steady stream drifted from the Upper South to the Ohio valley, from slave to free states. Abraham Lincoln's family,

MOVES NORTH   for example, took this path in moving from Kentucky to Indiana Territory and, later, to Illinois. Though northern black people moved westward as well, thousands of free people of color moved to northern states and Canada in the 1830s following the adoption of black codes and mob violence in the South (see pages 321–322). Fugitives from slavery too went north. Hispanics in the Southwest continued to move north into areas of Texas and present-day New Mexico and Utah. Hispanics and Indians competed for control of the land, but when the U.S. Army suppressed the Comanches, Apaches, Navajos, and Utes, Hispanic migration spread.

Settlers needed land and credit. Reflecting the nationalist outlook, the federal government served as real estate

LAND GRANTS TO STATES   agent, transferring land to private hands, filling the West with non-Indian peoples, and promoting republican virtue. Some public lands were granted as rewards for military service; veterans of the War of 1812 received 160 acres. Until 1820, civilians could buy government land at $2 an acre (a relatively high price) on a liberal four-year payment plan, but the minimum purchase had been reduced in 1817 to 80 acres. After 1819 the government discontinued credit sales but reduced the price to an affordable $1.25 an acre.

Some eager pioneers settled land before it had been surveyed and offered for sale. Such illegal settlers, or squatters, then had to buy the land at auction and faced the risk of being unable to purchase it. In 1841, to facilitate settlement and end property disputes, Congress passed the Pre-emption Act, which legalized settlement prior to surveying.

Since most settlers needed to borrow money, private credit systems arose: banks, private investors, country

CREDIT   storekeepers, and speculators loaned money to farmers. Nearly all economic activity in the West involved credit, from land sales to produce shipments to railroad construction. In 1816 and 1836 easy credit boosted land prices. When tight credit, high interest, low prices, or destructive weather squeezed farmers' income, land values collapsed, ending the speculative bubble. Mortgage bankers and speculators then purchased land cheaply. As a consequence, many farmers became renters instead of owners of land; tenancy became more common in the West than it had been in New England.

A painting after William James Bennett's depiction of the busy, growing western port city of Detroit in 1836. It highlights the role cities played in western settlement and growth. The view is from Canada (present-day Windsor), looking south to Detroit, and the mostly rural Canadian shore contrasts sharply with booming Detroit. (Detroit Institute of Arts)

From the start, newly settled western areas depended on their links with towns and cities. Ohio River cities—

FRONTIER CITIES   Louisville and Cincinnati—and the old French settlements—Detroit on the Great Lakes, St. Louis on the Mississippi River—predated and promoted the earliest western settlements. So too in the South, from New Orleans to Natchez to Memphis, towns spearheaded settlement and economic growth. Steamboats connected the river cities with eastern markets and ports, carrying grain east and returning with finished goods. Like cities in the Northeast, these western cities eventually developed into manufacturing centers as merchants shifted their investments from commerce to industry. Louisville, for instance, became a textile center. Smaller cities specialized in flour mills, and all produced consumer goods for the hinterlands. As commerce, urban growth, and industrialization overtook the farmers' frontier, the West was wed to the Northeast.

American Indian Resistance and Removal

Indians were also on the move, but in forced migrations. To make way for white expansion, the indigenous cultures of the eastern and southern woodlands were uprooted. Perhaps 100,000 eastern and southern Indian people were removed between 1820 and

1850; about 30,000 died in the process. Those who remained became virtually invisible.

In theory, under the U.S. Constitution, the federal government recognized Indian sovereignty and treated

TREATY MAKING

Indian nations as foreign nations. Indeed the United States received Indian delegations with pomp and ceremony, exchanging presents as tokens of friendship. Agreements between Indian nations and the United States were signed, sealed, and ratified like other international treaties. In practice, however, treaty making and Indian sovereignty were fictions. The United States imposed conditions on Indian representatives, and as the United States expanded, new treaties replaced old ones, shrinking Indian land holdings. Eventually, under President Andrew Jackson, wholesale removal would be the order of the day.

Indians could delay but not prevent removal. Though Indian resistance persisted after the War of 1812, it only slowed the inevitable. In the 1820s native peoples in Ohio, southern Indiana and Illinois, southwestern Michigan, most of Missouri, central Alabama, and southern Mississippi ceded lands under federal pressure. They gave up nearly 200 million acres for pennies an acre.

To maintain independence and preserve traditional ways, many Indian nations tried to accommodate to the

INDIANS IN THE MARKET ECONOMY

expanding market economy. In the first three decades of the century, the Choctaw, Creek, and Chickasaw peoples in the lower Mississippi became suppliers and traders. Under treaty provisions, Indian commerce took place through trading posts and stores that provided Indians with supplies and purchased or bartered Indian-produced goods. Indians exchanged hides, skins, and beeswax for cloth, ammunition, manufactured goods, and illegal liquor. The trading posts extended credit to chiefs, and increasingly they fell into debt. With pelt prices falling, the debts grew enormously and often could be paid off only by selling land to the federal government. The Choctaws, Creeks, and Chickasaws found themselves in a cycle of trade debt and land cessions. By 1822 the Choctaw nation had sold 13 million acres but still carried a debt of $13,000. The Indians struggled to adjust, increasing agricultural production and hunting, working as farmhands and craftsman, and selling produce at market stalls in Natchez and New Orleans. Over time, however, they could not prevent the spread of the cotton economy that arose on their lands. With loss of land came dependency. The Choctaws came to rely on white Americans not only for manufactured goods but also for food.

Dependency facilitated removal of American Indian peoples to western lands. While the population of other groups increased by leaps and bounds, the Indian population fell. Alexis de Tocqueville noticed the contrast. "Not only have these wild tribes receded, but they are destroyed," Tocqueville concluded, after personally observing the tragedy of forced removal, "and as they give way or perish, an immense and increasing people fill their place. There is no instance upon record of so prodigious a growth or so rapid a destruction." War, forced removal, disease, especially smallpox, and malnutrition reduced many Indian nations by 50 percent. More than half of the Pawnees, Omahas, Otoes, Missouris, and Kansas died in the 1830s alone.

The wanderings of the Shawnees, the people of Prophet and Tecumseh (see pages 225–226), illustrate

SHAWNEES

the uprooting of Indian people. After giving up 17 million acres in Ohio in the 1795 Treaty of Greenville (see page 182), the Shawnees scattered to Indiana and eastern Missouri. After the War of 1812, Prophet's Indiana group withdrew to Canada under British protection. In 1822 other Shawnees sought Mexican protection and moved from Missouri to present-day eastern Texas. As the U.S. government promoted removal to Kansas, Prophet returned from Canada to lead a group to the new Shawnee lands in eastern Kansas in 1825. When Missouri achieved statehood in 1821, Shawnees living there were also forced to move to Kansas, where in the 1830s other Shawnees removed from Ohio or expelled from Texas joined them. By 1854 Kansas was open to white settlement, and the Shawnees had to cede seven-eighths of their land, or 1.4 million acres.

Removal had a profound impact on all Shawnees. The men lost their traditional role as providers; their methods of hunting and their knowledge of woodland animals were useless on the prairies of Kansas. As grain became the tribe's dietary staple, Shawnee women played a greater role as providers, supplemented by government aid under treaty provisions. (Typically, treaties required annual government distributions of grain, blankets, and cash payments.) Remarkably, the Shawnees preserved their language and culture in the face of these drastic changes. Although resistance proved incapable of protecting their lands, it did help maintain their culture.

Ever since the early days of European colonization, whites had sought the assimilation of American Indians

ASSIMILATION AND EDUCATION

through education and Christianity. This goal took on renewed urgency as the United States expanded westward. "Put into the hand of [Indian] children

■ Southern Indians attempted to remain in their ancestral lands in the South. Karl Bodmer's watercolor portrayed a Choctaw camp on the Mississippi River near Natchez, before the Indians were forced out of Mississippi and Alabama in 1830.   (Joslyn Art Museum, Omaha, Nebraska. Gift of the Enron Art Foundation)

the primer and the hoe," the House Committee on Indian Affairs recommended in 1818, "and they will naturally, in time, take hold of the plough; and, as their minds become enlightened and expand, the Bible will be their book, and they will grow up in habits of morality and industry . . . and become useful members of society." In 1819, in response to missionary lobbying, Congress appropriated $10,000 annually for "civilization of the tribes adjoining the frontier settlements." Protestant missionaries administered the "civilizing fund" and established mission schools. Catholic missions were already established in the Southwest and California.

Within five years thirty-two boarding schools enrolled Indian students. They substituted English for American Indian languages and taught agriculture alongside the Christian Gospel. The emphasis on agriculture taught the value of private property, hard work, adaptation to the market economy, and the nuclear family. But to settlers eyeing Indian land, assimilation through education seemed too slow a process. At the program's peak, schools across the United States enrolled fewer than fifteen hundred students; at that rate it would take centuries to assimilate all Indians. Thus wherever native peoples lived, illegal settlers disrupted their lives. Though obligated to protect the integrity of treaty lands, the federal government did so only halfheartedly. With government supporting westward expansion, legitimate Indian land rights gave way to the advance of white civilization.

In the 1820s it became apparent that neither economic dependency nor education nor Christianity could persuade Indians to cede enough acreage to satisfy land-hungry whites. Attention focused on southeastern tribes—Cherokees, Creeks, Choctaws, Chickasaws, and Seminoles—because much of their land remained intact after the War of 1812 and because they aggressively resisted white encroachment. Possessing some formal political institutions, they were better organized than the northern tribes to resist.

In his last annual message to Congress in late 1824, President James Monroe suggested that all Indians be moved beyond the Mississippi River.

INDIAN REMOVAL AS FEDERAL POLICY Three days later he sent a special message to Congress proposing removal. Monroe described his proposal as an "honorable" one that would protect Indians from invasion and provide them with independence for "improvement and civilization." Force would be unnecessary, he believed; Indians would willingly accept western land free from white encroachment.

Monroe's proposition targeted the Cherokees, Creeks, Choctaws, and Chickasaws, and they unanimously rejected it. Between 1789 and 1825 they had negotiated thirty treaties with the United States, and they had reached their limits. Most wished to remain on what little was left of their ancestral land.

Pressure from Georgia had prompted Monroe's policy. Cherokees and Creeks lived in northwestern

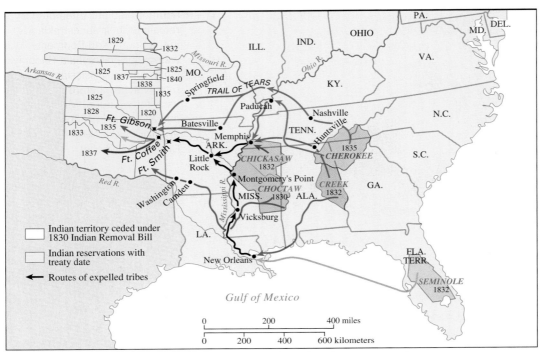

Map 10.5   Removal of Native Americans from the South, 1820–1840

Over a twenty-year period, the federal government and southern states forced Native Americans to exchange their traditional homes for western land. Some tribal groups remained in the South, but most settled in the alien western environment.   (Acknowledgment is due to Martin Gilbert and George Weidenfeld and Nicholson Limited for permission to reproduce this map, taken from *American History Atlas*)

Georgia, and in the 1820s the state accused the federal government of not fulfilling its 1802 promise to remove the Indians in return for the state's renunciation of its claim to western lands. Georgia remained unsatisfied by Monroe's removal messages and by further cessions by the Creeks. In 1826, under federal pressure, the Creek nation ceded all but a small strip of its Georgia acreage. Georgians were unmoved. Only the removal of the Georgia Creeks to the West could resolve the conflict between the state and the federal government.

For the Creeks the outcome was devastating. In an ultimately unsuccessful attempt to hold fast to the remainder of their traditional lands, which were in Alabama, they radically altered their political structure. In 1829, at the expense of traditional village autonomy, they centralized tribal authority and forbade any chief from ceding land. In the end, they lost not only their land but also their traditional forms of social and political organization.

Adapting to American ways seemed no more successful than resistance in forestalling removal. No people

CHEROKEES

met the challenge of civilizing themselves by American standards more

thoroughly than the Cherokees, whose traditional home centered on eastern Tennessee and northern Alabama and Georgia. Between 1819 and 1829 the tribe became economically self-sufficient and politically self-governing; during this Cherokee renaissance the twelve to fifteen thousand adult Cherokees came to think of themselves as a nation, not a collection of villages. In 1821 and 1822 Sequoyah, a self-educated Cherokee, devised an eighty-six-character phonetic alphabet that made possible a Cherokee-language Bible and a bilingual tribal newspaper, *Cherokee Phoenix* (1828). Between 1820 and 1823 the Cherokees created a formal government with a bicameral legislature, a court system, and a salaried bureaucracy. In 1827 they adopted a written constitution, modeled after that of the United States. Cherokee land laws, however, differed from U.S. law. The tribe collectively owned all Cherokee land and forbade land sales to outsiders. Nonetheless, the Cherokees assimilated American cultural patterns. Economic change paralleled political adaptation. Many became individual farmers and slaveholders; by 1833 they held fifteen hundred black slaves. They transformed their economy from hunting,

■ *The Trail of Tears,* by twentieth-century Pawnee artist Brummet Echohawk. About twenty thousand Cherokees were evicted in 1838–1839, and about one-quarter of them died on the forced march to present-day Oklahoma.   (Thomas Gilcrease Institute of American History and Art)

gathering, and subsistence agriculture to commodity trade based on barter, cash, and credit.

But Cherokees' political and economic changes failed to win respect or acceptance from southerners. In the 1820s, Georgia pressed them to sell the 7,200 square miles of land they held in the state. Congress appropriated $30,000 in 1822 to buy the Cherokee land in Georgia, but the Cherokees preferred to stay where they were. Impatient with their refusals to negotiate cession, Georgia annulled the Cherokees' constitution, extended the state's sovereignty over them, prohibited the Cherokee National Council from meeting except to cede land, and ordered their lands seized. The discovery of gold on Cherokee land in 1829 whetted Georgia's appetite for Cherokee territory.

Backed by sympathetic whites but not by the new president, Andrew Jackson, the Cherokees under Chief John Ross turned to the federal courts to defend their treaty with the United States and to prevent Georgia from seizing more land. Their legal strategy reflected their growing political sophistication. In *Cherokee Nation v. Georgia* (1831), Chief Justice John Marshall ruled that under the federal Constitution an Indian tribe was neither a foreign nation nor a state and therefore had no standing in federal courts. Nonetheless, said Marshall, the Indians had an unquestionable right to their lands; they could lose title only by

CHEROKEE NATION V. GEORGIA

voluntarily giving it up. A year later, in *Worcester v. Georgia,* Marshall defined the Cherokee position more clearly. The Indian nation was, he declared, a distinct political community in which "the laws of Georgia can have no force" and into which Georgians could not enter without permission or treaty privilege. The Cherokees cheered. *Phoenix* editor Elias Boudinot called the decision "glorious news." But Georgia refused to comply.

President Andrew Jackson, whose reputation had been built as an Indian fighter, refused to interfere because the case involved a state action. Newspapers widely reported that Jackson had said, "John Marshall has made his decision: now let him enforce it." Keen to open up new lands for settlement, Jackson favored expelling the Cherokees. In the Removal Act of 1830 Congress had provided Jackson with the funds he needed to negotiate new treaties and resettle the resistant tribes west of the Mississippi (see Map 10.5).

The Choctaws went first; they made the forced journey from Mississippi and Alabama to the West in the winter of 1831 and 1832. Alexis de Tocqueville was visiting Memphis when they passed through: "The wounded, the sick, newborn babies, and the old men on the point of death. . . . I saw them embark to cross the great river," he wrote, "and the sight will never fade from my memory. Neither sob nor complaint rose from that silent assembly. Their afflictions were of long standing, and they

TRAIL OF TEARS

felt them to be irremediable." Other tribes soon joined the forced march. The Creeks in Alabama resisted removal until 1836, when the army pushed them westward. A year later the Chickasaws followed.

Having fought removal in the courts, the Cherokees were divided. Some believed that further resistance was hopeless and accepted removal as the only chance to preserve their civilization. The leaders of this minority agreed in 1835 to exchange their southern home for western land in the Treaty of New Echota. Most, though, wanted to stand firm. John Ross, with petitions signed by fifteen thousand Cherokees, lobbied the Senate against ratification of the treaty. They lost. But when the time for evacuation came in 1838, most Cherokees refused to move. President Martin Van Buren sent federal troops to round them up. About twenty thousand Cherokees were evicted, held in detention camps, and marched to Indian Territory in present-day Oklahoma under military escort. Nearly one-quarter of them died of disease and exhaustion on what came to be known as the Trail of Tears.

When the forced march to the West ended, the Indians had traded about 100 million acres east of the Mississippi for 32 million acres west of the river plus $68 million. Only a few scattered remnants, among them the Seminoles in Florida and the Cherokees in the southern Appalachian Mountains, remained in the East and South.

Forced removal had a disastrous impact on the Cherokees and other displaced Indian nations. In the West they encountered an alien environment; lacking traditional ties, few felt at peace with the land. The animals and plants they found were unfamiliar. Unable to live off the land, many became dependent on government payments for survival. Removal also brought new internal conflicts. The Cherokees in particular struggled over their tribal government. In 1839 followers of John Ross assassinated the leaders of the protreaty faction. Violence continued sporadically until a new treaty in 1846 imposed a temporary truce.

Conflicts also arose among migrating American Indian groups from the South and East and Indians already living in the West, as they were forced to share land and scarce resources. Nearly one hundred thousand newcomers settled west of the Mississippi, and the existing game could not support them all. The Osages and Pawnees grittily fought the newcomers who, under U.S. Army escort, were invading their land and homes.

In Florida a small band of Seminoles continued to resist. Some Seminole leaders agreed in the 1832 Treaty of

SECOND SEMINOLE WAR

Payne's Landing to relocate to the West within three years, but others opposed the treaty, and some probably did not know it existed. A minority under Osceola, a charismatic leader, refused to vacate their homes and fought the pro-treaty group. When federal troops were sent to impose removal in 1835, Osceola waged a fierce guerrilla war against them.

The Florida Indians were a varied group that included many Creeks and mixed Indian–African Americans (ex-slaves or descendants of runaway slaves). The U.S. Army, however, considered them all Seminoles, subject to removal. General Thomas Jesup believed that the runaway slave population was the key to the war. "This, you may be assured, is a Negro, not an Indian war," he wrote a friend in 1836, "and if it be not speedily put down, the South will feel the effects of it on their slave population before the end of the next season."

Osceola was captured under a white flag of truce and died in an army prison in 1838, but the Seminoles fought on under Chief Coacoochee (Wild Cat) and other leaders. In 1842 the United States abandoned the removal effort. Most of Osceola's followers agreed to move west to Indian Territory in 1858, but many Seminoles remained in the Florida Everglades, proud of having resisted conquest.

Summary

*N*ationalism and self-confidence accompanied the end of the War of 1812. Under the Democratic-Republicans the federal government fostered expansion and economic growth through internal improvements, tariffs, the Second Bank of the United States, land sales, and Indian removal. The Supreme Court and American diplomats, too, asserted nationalism. John Quincy Adams negotiated peace and secure borders with Great Britain and Spain, and through the Monroe Doctrine insulated the Western Hemisphere from European conflict.

But sectionalism accompanied nationalism and geographical expansion. Conflicts over tariffs, economic hard times, and slavery brought discord. The Missouri Compromise, in preserving a balance between slave and free states, was a stopgap measure to avoid the explosive issue of slavery.

From 1816 through 1845 the United States experienced explosive growth. Population increased sixfold and moved westward. New farms grew cotton and grain for the market, and cities followed. In the process, Indians were pushed aside.

Agriculture remained the dominant industry, though by midcentury a booming manufacturing sector challenged farming. And agriculture itself was becoming market-oriented and mechanized. The market economy brought sustained growth; it also ushered in cycles of boom and bust. Americans became familiar with hard times and unemployment. The growing economy also meant larger-scale destruction of the environment: mills exploited New England waterways as a source of power.

Large-scale manufacturing also altered traditional patterns of production and consumption. Farm families began to purchase goods formerly made by wives and daughters and geared production to faraway markets. Farm women increasingly contributed income from market sales to the household purse. In New England many young women left the family farm to become the first factory workers in the new textile industry. As workshops and factories replaced home-based production, and the master-journeyman-apprentice system faded away, workplace relations became more impersonal, working conditions grew harsher, and men's and women's work became increasingly distinct. Industrial jobs began to attract large numbers of immigrants, and some workers organized labor unions.

LEGACY FOR A PEOPLE AND A NATION
A Mixed Economy

How active should the U.S. government be? Should it run, regulate, or leave to the market system healthcare, Social Security and private pensions, corporate concentration, and stock trading and investments? In other words, to what degree should the government be responsible for the well-being of the economy and individuals?

The Articles of Confederation limited government, the Constitution empowered it, and the Bill of Rights restricted it in specific areas. While Americans have continuously debated the appropriate role of government, the United States has generally occupied a middle ground: a mixed economy.

In the early nineteenth century, government played an active role in economic and social expansion. Federal and state governments built roads and canals, developed harbors, and operated post offices and the early telegraph. More commonly the government intervened to stimulate and regulate the private sector. In chartering corporations and banks and in land sales and grants, the United States created an infrastructure that laid the way for the market economy and industrialization.

In the late nineteenth century advocates of laissez-faire or hands-off government challenged the pre–Civil War traditions of an active government. Laissez faire dominated briefly until the 1880s and 1890s, when large corporations and trusts accumulated so much power that governments stepped in to regulate railroads and business concentration. After the turn of the century the federal government extended regulation to food, drugs, the environment, working conditions, and fair business practices. Probably the most innovative example of the mixed economy was the creation in 1913 of the Federal Reserve System—a public system for overseeing currency and banking that left control in private hands. After a revival of laissez faire in the 1920s, the crisis of the Great Depression of the 1930s and World War II would lead the federal government to establish the modern welfare state, which operates through a mixed public/private structure.

As the United States begins the twenty-first century, its people again debate the appropriate role of government. Conservatives view government as the problem rather than the solution, arguing that government regulation hampers individual freedom and distorts the law of supply and demand. Advocates of an activist government argue that only the government has the power and resources to check economic concentration and to protect health, safety, and the environment. The framework of this debate is a legacy from before the Civil War.

The *history companion* powered by Eduspace®
Your primary source for interactive quizzes, exercises, and more to help you learn efficiently.
http://history.college.hmco.com/students

REFORM AND POLITICS IN THE AGE OF JACKSON 1824–1845

"I proceed, Gentlemen, briefly to call your attention to the present state of Insane persons confined within this Commonwealth," Dorothea Dix petitioned the 1843 Massachusetts legislature, "in cages, closets, stalls, pens! Chained, naked, beaten with rods and lashed into obedience."

Dix revealed the netherworld she had uncovered in her two-year investigation of the treatment of the insane. She found appalling conditions in Massachusetts: men and women in cages, chained to walls, in dark dungeons, brutalized and held in solitary confinement. In a visit to a Newburyport almshouse in the summer of 1842, Dix expressed surprise at the comfortable conditions for the "one idiotic" and seven insane inhabitants. On the grounds she discovered, however, one man residing in a shed whose door opened to the local "dead room" or morgue; his only companions were corpses. Shocked, she heard from an attendant about another insane inmate of whom no one spoke openly: "a woman in a cellar."

Dix asked to see her. The superintendent warned Dix that the woman "was dangerous to be approached; that 'she had lately attacked his wife,' and was often naked." Dix pressed on. "If you will not go with me," she said, "give me the keys and I will go alone." They unlocked the doors and entered an underground cell. Beneath the staircase was a tiny door. In the shadows Dix saw "a female apparently wasted to a skeleton, partially wrapped in blankets." She was withered, wrote Dix, "not by age, but by suffering." When the inmate saw the visitors, she wailed with despair: "Why am I consigned to hell? dark—dark—I used to pray, I used to read the Bible—I have done no crime in my heart. I had friends; why have all forsaken me!—my God! my God! why hast thou forsaken me?"

Dix described in the most personal and vivid terms her visits to jails, almshouses, and private homes, and the cruel treatment of the insane. Her petition to the General Court of Massachusetts was so graphic and shocking that

◀ Dorothea Dix's powerful personal descriptions of the brutal treatment of the mentally ill propelled her from reform to politics. This painting of Dix portrays a sense of humanity and determination. (Courtesy, Special Collection/University Archives, Rutgers University Libraries)

the legislature voted to reprint it as a government pamphlet: *Memorial to the Massachusetts Legislature* (1843). Part petition, part sermon, and part autobiography, it made riveting reading.

The first-person narrative—"I tell what I have seen"—gave Dix's message power. She seemed, however, an unlikely herald. Reared in Massachusetts, she began teaching in Worcester at age fourteen in 1816. She wrote an elementary science text and children's devotional verse and poetry. Her appearance was somber: she wore dark dresses with starched white collars and pulled her hair back tightly. She never married and seemed aloof to other Bostonians, but she became an impassioned crusader for asylum reform, advocating hospitals for the mentally ill. In the 1840s she traveled more than 40,000 miles, exposing the inhumane treatment of the insane and petitioning state legislatures. From 1848 through 1856 she lobbied Congress annually to set aside 5 million acres to fund insane asylums. During the Civil War Dix recruited and supervised nurses for the federal government; afterward she resumed her efforts on behalf of the mentally ill. She died in 1887 in a hospital she had founded.

Dix epitomized much of early-nineteenth-century reform. She started with a religious belief in individual self-improvement and human perfectibility that led her to advocate collective responsibility, especially on behalf of those dependent on the kindness of others. She made reform her career, fearlessly entering the public arena. Investigating asylums, petitioning the Massachusetts legislature, and lobbying other states and Congress, Dix moved from reform to politics, and she helped create a new public role for women, in the process broadening the base of political participation.

The religious and reform fervor of the period arose both as part of the spiritual renewal known as the Second Great Awakening and as a response to the enormous transformation that the United States experienced after the War of 1812. Immigration, the market economy, growing inequality, the westward advance of settlement, and territorial expansion all contributed to remaking the United States. Many Americans had difficulty keeping up with the rapid pace of change and felt they no longer controlled their own fates.

Anxieties wrought by rapid change drove the impulse to reform society. Men and women organized to end the abuses of alcohol and prostitution, to improve conditions in prisons and asylums, to oppose secret and antidemocratic societies, to end slavery, and to achieve equal rights for women. Inevitably reform movements pushed men and women into politics, though only men voted. Opponents of reform, however, were equally concerned about social problems. What distinguished them from reformers was their skepticism about human perfectibility and their distrust of institutions and the exercise of power, both public and private. To them, government coercion was the greater evil. They sought to reverse, not shape, change.

Two issues in particular bridged reform and politics: the short-lived Antimasonry frenzy against secret societies; and the intense, uncompromising crusade for an immediate end to slavery. Though Antimasons organized the first third-party movement, abolition eventually overrode all other concerns. No single issue evoked the passion that slavery did. It pitted neighbor against neighbor and region against region.

The Jacksonians, too, saw themselves as reformers. They opposed special privileges and the Second Bank of the United States with the same vigor with which reformers opposed sin. President Andrew Jackson believed that a strong federal government restricted individual freedom by favoring one group over another. Social and religious reformers disagreed. Wanting a more active federal role, they rallied around the new Whig Party, which allied itself with humanitarian reform. Democrats and Whigs constituted a new party system, characterized by strong organizations, intense loyalty, and energetic religious and ethnic competition.

Both parties eagerly promoted expansionism during the prosperous 1840s. Democrats saw the agrarian West as an antidote to urbanization and industrialization; Whigs focused on the new commercial opportunities it offered. Expanding the nation to the Pacific seemed to be the manifest destiny of the United States. Texas, California, and Oregon, unknown to most Americans in 1800, had become familiar places by the 1830s and 1840s, and to annex them, the United States would challenge its neighbors north and south. ■

From Revival to Reform

*R*eligion was probably the strongest motivation behind organized benevolence and reform. Beginning in the late 1790s religious revivals galvanized Protestants, especially women, into social action. The most famous was at Cane Ridge, Kentucky, in 1801, and it became legendary. One report estimated twenty-five thousand people attended the August meetings, at a time when Kentucky's largest city, Lexington, had fewer than two thousand inhabitants. Revivals spread in waves, finding ready audiences in the countryside. At camp meetings, sometimes lasting a week with thousands in attendance, preachers exhorted sinners to repent and become genuine Christians. They offered salvation to all through personal conversion. At a time when only a minority could read and write, itinerant evangelists were democratizing American religion, making it available to all.

Resembling the Great Awakening of the eighteenth century (see pages 110–111), the movement came to be

SECOND GREAT AWAKENING

called the Second Great Awakening. It raised people's hopes for the Second Coming of the Christian messiah and the establishment of the Kingdom of God on earth. Revivalists resolved to speed the Second Coming by combating the forces of evil and darkness. Some believed that the United States had a special mission in God's design and a special role in eliminating evil. Under revivalist influence, the role of churches and ministers in community life diminished as lay participation increased, and evangelical Christians across the country tried to right the wrongs of the world. Visiting the United States in the 1830s, Alexis de Tocqueville noted that "there is no country in the world where the Christian religion retains greater influence" than in America.

In the South, huge numbers of people attended revivals, but they especially drew women and African Americans, free and slave. The call to personal repentance and conversion invigorated Protestantism, giving southern churches an evangelical base and giving evangelicalism a southern accent. In essence, the Second Great Awakening turned the South into the Bible belt. It also mostly ignored slavery, thus accommodating to it. In the North, New York lawyer Charles G. Finney led the revival movement. After his 1821 soul-shaking conversion, which he interpreted as "a retainer from the Lord Jesus Christ to plead his cause," Finney abandoned the law to convert souls, staging three- to four-day camp meetings in western New York, a region that experienced such continuous and heated waves of revivalism that it became known as "the burned-over district."

■ Samuel Waldo and William Jewett's oil portrait of Charles Finney around 1834 captures Finney at his peak. The charismatic Finney mesmerized his audiences, and contemporaries credited him with converting 500,000 people.   (Oberlin College Archives, Oberlin, OH)

ing "the democratic art of persuasion." Persuasion was at the core of democracy, of religious appeals to the heart, and of reform's influence on the head and the heart. Even nonevangelical Protestants and Catholics practiced persuasion in this era. Roman Catholics elevated the sermon to a central place in the church service, while in words and song, black preachers recalled the biblical exodus and the promise of escape from the land of slavery. Among Jews, Isaac Lesser, in a Philadelphia Sephardic congregation, introduced regular sermons in 1829, and Rabbi Isaac Meyer Wise, a German immigrant in 1846, later made it the hallmark of Reform Judaism.

As Methodists and Baptists moved west, migration patterns spread not only religion but also the impulse for moral reform. All revivalists shared a belief in individual self-improvement. The doctrine of perfectibility demanded that Christians actively organize and convert others. Thus the Second Great Awakening bred reform, and evangelical Protestants became missionaries for both religious and secular salvation. Wherever they preached, evangelists generated new religious groups and voluntary reform societies. New sects like the Mormons arose out of this ferment. So did associations to address the pressing issues of the day: temperance, education, Sabbath observance, dueling, and later slavery. Among the organizations created in the wake of revival were the American Sunday School Union (1824), the American Temperance Society (1826), the American Peace Society (1828), and the American Anti-Slavery Society (1833). Religious zeal led believers to support missionaries abroad, particularly in Asia and Africa. Collectively these groups constituted a national web of benevolent and moral-reform societies, and strengthened by numbers, they moved into the public sphere.

Salvation could be achieved, Finney preached, through spontaneous conversion like his own. He mesmerized his audiences. In everyday language, Finney preached that "God has made man a moral free agent." In other words, evil was avoidable: Christians were not doomed by original sin, and anyone could achieve salvation. Finney's brand of revivalism transcended sects, class, and race. At first a Presbyterian, he eventually found his home in Methodism with its doctrine of perfectibility. Revivalism had a particularly strong base among Methodists and Baptists, and in the 1820s the Methodists surpassed the Baptists as the most numerous denomination. These denominations grew the most because their structure maximized democratic participation and drew their ministers from ordinary folk.

Revivalist ministers and lay leaders were powerful preachers. Historian Nathan O. Hatch has called preach-

More women than men answered the call of Christianity, sustaining the Second Great Awakening and

EVANGELICAL WOMEN

invigorating local churches. Pious middle-class women in Rochester, New York, for instance, responded to Finney by spreading the word to other women while their husbands were at work. Gradually women brought their families and sometimes their husbands into church and reform. Although many businessmen recruited their employees to benevolent work, women more than men tended to feel personally responsible for counteracting the increasingly secular orientation of the expanding market economy. Emotionally charged conversions could return women to what they believed was the right path. It also offered them communal ties with other women.

Female missionary societies motivated organized religious and benevolent activity on an unprecedented scale.

For women and some men, reform represented their first political involvement at a time when women did not vote. In reform organizations women represented themselves; by participating directly in service activities, they pioneered new, visible, public roles for women. Within churches and society, they dissented and opposed traditional political leaders.

An exposé of prostitution in New York City illustrates how reform led to political action. John R. McDowall,

FEMALE REFORM SOCIETIES

a divinity student, published a report in 1830 documenting the prevalence of prostitution in New York City. Philip Hone, a prominent civic leader (see page 311), denounced McDowall's report as "a disgraceful document," and New York businessmen and politicians defended the city's good name against "those base slanders." Women, moved by the plight of "fallen women," revived the fight against prostitution in 1834. But whereas male reformers made prostitutes the target of their zeal, the newly organized Female Moral Reform Society focused on men who victimized young women, publicizing the names of brothel clients. They organized a shelter for refuge and an employment agency to find jobs for prostitutes.

During the 1830s, the New York society expanded its activities and geographical scope, calling itself the American Female Moral Reform Society. By 1840 it had 555 affiliated chapters across the nation. The society also entered the political sphere. In New York State in the 1840s, it successfully lobbied for criminal sanctions against men who seduced women into prostitution, as well as against the prostitutes themselves.

One of the most successful reform efforts was the campaign against alcohol. Drinking was widespread in

TEMPERANCE

the early nineteenth century. American men gathered in public houses and rural inns to gossip, talk politics, play cards, escape work and home, and drink whiskey, rum, and hard cider. Contracts were sealed, celebrations commemorated, and harvests toasted with liquor. Respectable women did not drink in public, but many regularly tippled alcohol-based patent medicines promoted as cure-alls. Why then did temperance become such a vital issue? And why were women especially active in the movement? Like all nineteenth-century reform, temperance had a strong religious foundation.

Evangelicals considered drinking sinful, and in many denominations, forsaking alcohol was part of conversion. Preachers condemned alcohol for violating the Sabbath; many workers labored six days and spent Sunday at the public house drinking and socializing. Alcoholism

As the temperance movement spread, the evils of alcohol became a major theme in popular culture. This 1830s lithograph, "Mortgaging the Farm," hints at drinking's potential destructiveness. Drunken, idyll farmers sit in the shadow of the gallows holding the tavern's signboard. (Old Sturbridge Village)

also destroyed families; it created poverty and crime. In the early 1840s thousands of ordinary women formed Martha Washington societies to protect families by reforming alcoholics, raising children as teetotalers, and spreading the temperance message. Popular culture of the time was laced with domestic images of the damage alcohol left: abandoned wives and children and drunken fathers. Timothy Shay Arthur dramatized these evils in *Ten Nights in a Barroom* (1853), a classic American melodrama, as did the lithograph "Mortgaging the Farm." Employers complained that drinkers took "St. Monday" as a holiday to recover from Sunday. In the new world of the factory, drinking was unacceptable.

As the temperance movement gained momentum, its goal shifted from moderation to voluntary abstinence and finally to prohibition. The American Society for the Promotion of Temperance, organized in 1826 to promote pledges of abstinence, became a pressure group for state prohibition legislation. By the mid-1830s five thousand state and local temperance societies touted teetotalism, and more than a million people had taken the pledge. Several hundred thousand children, for instance, enlisted in the Cold Water Army.

The temperance movement's success was reflected in a sharp decline in alcohol use. Per capita consumption fell from five gallons in 1800 to below two gallons in the 1840s. Success bred more victories. Maine prohibited the manufacture and sale of alcohol except for medicinal purposes in 1851, and by 1855 similar laws had been enacted throughout New England and in New York, Pennsylvania, and the Midwest.

Even as consumption declined, opposition to alcohol grew. From the 1820s on, many reformers expressed their prejudices by regarding alcohol as an evil introduced by Catholic immigrants. The Irish and Germans, the *American Protestant Magazine* complained in 1849, "bring the grog shops like the frogs of Egypt upon us." Demon rum became a prime target of reformers. Rum and immigrants defiled the Sabbath; rum and immigrants brought poverty; rum and immigrants supported the feared papacy. Many Catholics took the pledge of abstinence and formed their own organizations, such as the St. Mary's Mutual Benevolent Total Abstinence Society in Boston. But even Catholic teetotalers tended to oppose state regulation of drinking; temperance seemed to them a question of individual choice. They favored self-control, not state coercion.

As the career of Dorothea Dix demonstrated, moral reform also stimulated the construction of asylums and other institutions to house prisoners, the mentally ill, orphans, delinquent children, and the poor. Such institutions were needed, reformers argued, to shelter victims of society's turbulence and impose familial discipline on them. It was widely believed that criminals came from unstable families whose lack of restraint led to vice and drink. Idleness was both a symptom and a cause of crime; thus the clock governed a prisoner's day, and idleness was banished. Through discipline, inmates might become self-reliant and responsible. Even the most sinful could be redeemed.

PENITENTIARIES AND ASYLUMS

In the 1820s New York and Pennsylvania developed competing models for reforming criminals. Both rejected incarceration to punish criminals or to remove them from society, introducing instead disciplined regimens to rehabilitate them. New York's Auburn (1819–1823) and Ossining (1825) prisons placed prisoners in individual cells but brought them together in common workshops. Pennsylvania's Pittsburgh (1826) and Philadelphia (1829) prisons isolated prisoners completely, forcing them to eat, sleep, and work in their individual cells, allowing them contact only with guards and visitors.

Insane asylums, hospitals, and orphanages instituted similar approaches. Formerly the prescribed treatment removed disturbed individuals from society and isolated them among strangers, many with criminals. Dorothea Dix argued that this treatment was inhumane. The new asylums were clean and orderly. In response to Dix's crusade and reform societies, twenty-eight of thirty-three states had public institutions for the mentally ill by 1860.

Critical to reform movements was the building of networks. Reform and literary societies brought national speakers like Dorothea Dix, abolitionist Frederick Douglass, and hundreds of others to cities and towns to preach reform. Most reform organizations, like political parties, sponsored weekly newspapers, creating a virtual community of reformers. Annual conventions increased personal contacts and motivated supporters. Reformers made use of new technology—the new steam presses that permitted mass publication and the railroads that distributed their newspapers and pamphlets around the country—to spread their word.

ANTIMASONRY

More intense than moral reform movements but of shorter duration was the crusade against Freemasonry, a secret fraternity that had come to the United States from England in the eighteenth century. Sons of the Enlightenment such as Benjamin Franklin and George Washington were attracted to Masonry because it emphasized individual belief in a deity (as opposed to organized religion or a single church's doctrine). In the early nineteenth century Freemasonry attracted middle- and upper-class men prominent in commerce and civic affairs. For the ambitious, the Masons offered access to community leaders. Monumental lodges called attention to the Masons' affluence and prominence.

Opponents of Masonry believed that its secrecy and elite appeal were antidemocratic and antirepublican. Publications such as the *Anti Masonic Almanac* attacked Masonic initiation rites. Evangelicals labeled the order satanic. Antimasons argued that Masonry threatened the family because it excluded women and encouraged men to neglect their families for alcohol and ribald entertainment at Masonic lodges. As the temperance movement sought to liberate individuals from drink, Antimasons sought to liberate society from the grip of what they considered a powerful, antirepublican secret fraternity. To Antimasons, as penitentiaries and asylums would rehabilitate the criminal and insane, the abolition of Masonry would reestablish moral discipline. The political arena quickly absorbed Antimasonry, and its short life illustrates the close association of politics and reform in the period.

MORGAN AFFAIR

The catalyst for Antimasonry as an organized movement was the suspected murder of William Morgan, a disillusioned Mason who published an exposé in 1826, *The Illustration of Ma-*

No. IV.

ANTI MASONIC ALMANAC,

FOR THE YEAR

1831:

BY EDWARD GIDDINS.

The above plate represents " a poor blind candidate " taking the oath of an entered apprentice mason. He is divested of all clothing but a shirt, drawers, and one slipper; he kneels before the masonic altar on his naked knee, with a halter round his neck, and a hoodwink over his eyes; his left arm and breast are also bare; and in this humiliating posture he receives his oaths from the " worshipful master," wherein he binds himself to keep all masonic secrets, under the penalty of having his throat cut, his tongue torn out, and his body buried in the ocean. He is then taught the sign, grip, and word of that degree, and is presented with a little sheepskin apron, told he must wear it with the flap up, and that it is more honorable than the Star and Garter, or any other order that could be conferred upon him, except is a masonic lodge! and that it had been worn by kings, princes, and potentates, who were not ashamed to wear it. He is finally permitted to put his clothes on, and *thank the worshipful master, wardens, and brethren, for the honor they had conferred upon him!*

▪ Antimasonic publications, such as this 1831 almanac, made much of the allegedly sinister initiation rites that bound a new member "to keep all Masonic secrets, under the penalty of having his throat cut, his tongue torn out, and his body buried in the ocean." (Print collection, Miriam and Ira D. Wallach Division of Art, Prints, and Photographs, New York Public Library, Astor, Lenox and Tilden Foundations)

sonry, *By One of the Fraternity Who Has Devoted Thirty Years to the Subject.* Even before the book appeared, a group of Masons abducted Morgan in Canandaigua, New York. It was widely believed that his kidnappers murdered him, though his body was never found.

Events seemed to confirm Masonry's antidemocratic character. Prosecutors who were Masons appeared to obstruct the investigation of Morgan's abduction. The public pressed for justice, and a series of notorious trials from 1827 through 1831 led many to suspect a conspiracy. The cover-up became as much of an issue as Masonry itself, and the movement spread to other states. Antimasonry coalesced overnight in the burned-over district of western New York, and it quickly became a political movement.

With growing popular support, the Antimasons held conventions in 1827 to select candidates to oppose Masons running for office. The next year the conventions supported, for president, John Quincy Adams, and opposed Andrew Jackson because he was a Mason. The Antimasons held the first national political convention in Baltimore in 1831, and a year later they nominated William Wirt as their presidential candidate. Thus the Antimasons became a rallying point for anti-Jacksonians. Their electoral strength lay in New England and New York: in Vermont the Antimasons became the dominant party for a brief time in 1833; in Massachusetts they replaced the Democrats as the second major party. Antimasonry found little support, however, in the slave South.

CONVENTION SYSTEM

By the mid-1830s, Antimasonry had faded as a moral and political movement. A single-issue party, Antimasons declined along with Freemasonry. Yet Antimasonry left its mark on the politics of the era. As a moral crusade focused on public officeholders, it inspired broad participation in the political process. It drew new white voters into politics at a time when male suffrage was being extended, and it attracted the lower and middle classes by opposing the Masonic elite, exploiting their distrust of local political leaders. The Antimasons also changed party organization by pioneering the convention, rather than the caucus, for nominating candidates and by introducing the party platform.

Abolitionism and the Women's Movement

*a*ntimasonry foreshadowed and had much in common with abolitionism. Indeed, as Antimasonry waned, the antislavery movement gathered momentum. Abolitionist William Lloyd Garrison at first ignored the frenzy over the Morgan affair, but in 1832 he joined the ranks of Antimasons. Echoing his stand on emancipation, Garrison wrote: "I go for the immediate, unconditional and total abolition of Freemasonry." In his eyes, both slavery and Masonry undermined republican values. Eventually the issue of slavery became so compelling that it consumed all other reforms and threatened the nation itself. Those who advocated immediate emancipation saw slavery as, above all, a moral issue—the ultimate sin.

Free blacks in the North had demanded an end to slavery since the Revolution. Richard Allen, the first

■ Women played an activist role in reform, especially in abolitionism. A rare daguerreotype from August 1850 shows women and men, including Frederick Douglass, on the podium at an abolitionist rally in Cazenovia, New York. (Collection of J. Paul Getty Museum, Los Angeles, California)

AFRICAN AMERICAN ABOLITIONISTS

bishop of the African Methodist Episcopal (AME) Church, was outspoken on the issues. In 1800, for instance, he eulogized former president George Washington for freeing his slaves, and his sermon on immediatism—an immediate end to slavery—was widely circulated as a pamphlet. To free blacks slavery was both a moral issue and a personal one; while slavery was legal, they were always at risk of being seized as fugitives, and many had relatives who were slaves. David Walker's *Appeal . . . to the Colored Citizens* (1829), in language later imitated by Garrison, was a clarion call for immediatism and helped politicize many abolitionists. Walker, a southern-born free black, was Boston's leading abolitionist until his death in 1830. When Walker died, there were fifty black abolitionist societies in the United States assisting fugitive slaves, lobbying for emancipation, and exposing slavery as evil. African American newspapers spread the word.

Few whites, however, advocated the abolition of slavery before the 1830s. In the North, where by 1820 slavery had been virtually abolished (five states still had gradual emancipation plans that were freeing slaves in

GRADUAL EMANCIPATION

stages), whites took little interest in the issue. Antislavery sentiment appeared strongest in the Upper South, though northern involvement grew after the War of 1812. The American Colonization Society, founded in 1816, advocated gradual, voluntary emancipation and resettlement of former slaves in Africa, establishing the colony of Liberia for that purpose in the 1820s. Society members did not believe that free blacks had a place in the United States, and its members included Jefferson and other slaveholders, some evangelicals and Quakers, and (briefly) a few blacks.

During the 1830s, however, a small number of white reformers, driven by moral urgency, joined the black crusade for immediate emancipation. Soon the immediatists, who demanded immediate, complete, and uncompensated emancipation, surpassed the gradualists as the dominant strand of abolitionism. The most prominent and uncompromising immediatist, was the incendiary William Lloyd Garrison, a talented journalist who broke with moderate abolitionists in 1831. That year he began publishing *The Liberator,* which for thirty-five years would be his major weapon against slavery. He declared in its first issue, "I am in earnest—I will not equivocate—I will not excuse—I will not retreat a single inch—and *I will be heard.*"

Garrison's refusal to work with anyone who tolerated the delay of emancipation isolated him from other white opponents of slavery. He even forswore political action on the grounds that it was government that permitted slavery. Garrison burned a copy of the Constitution on July 4, 1854, proclaiming, "So perish all compromises with tyranny." By his actions and rhetorical power, Garrison helped to push antislavery onto the national agenda, though he had no specific plan for abolishing it. In essence, what Garrison called for was conversion of those who held slaves or cooperated with institutions that supported slavery; they must repent.

It is difficult to differentiate between those whites who became immediatists and those who did not. But

IMMEDIATISTS

immediatists like Garrison, Elizabeth Chandler, Amos Phelps, and Theodore Weld had much in common. They were young evangelicals active in benevolent societies in the 1820s; many became ordained ministers; and many had personal contact with free blacks and were sympathetic to African American rights. They were convinced that slaveholding was a sin. Motivated to abolish sin, they sought to change the institutions that harbored slavery. Finally, they shared great moral intensity. Because they were unwilling to compromise, their zeal made them forceful political activists. Their main organizational

The International Antislavery Movement

The heart of the international antislavery movement had been in Great Britain, but in the 1830s many of Britain's local antislavery societies thought they had accomplished their mission and disbanded. In 1833 Parliament ended slavery in the British Empire, and over the previous three decades the international slave trade had greatly diminished. At the same time, however, abolitionism in the United States was on the rise, and now American black abolitionists extended their work across the Atlantic. They revived the international movement to end slavery where it still existed—in Spanish possessions like Cuba, in independent and colonial South America, in Africa and Asia, and in the United States.

American abolitionism in the 1830s was invigorated by the militancy of these black abolitionists and by the conversion of William Lloyd Garrison to immediatism. Seeking to raise money and to put international pressure on the United States to abolish slavery, African American abolitionists in the 1840s toured Britain regularly. On the lecture circuit and in published narratives, they appealed for support. Especially effective were ex-slaves, who recounted their firsthand experiences of slavery and bared their scarred bodies.

Black abolitionists spoke in small towns and villages and in Britain's industrial centers. After fugitive slave Moses Gandy toured England, he published his autobiography, the first of dozens of slave narratives published in London. The next year, 1845, Frederick Douglass began a nineteen-month tour, giving three hundred lectures in Britain.

In 1849 black abolitionists William Wells Brown, Alexander Crummell, and J. W. C. Pennington were among the twenty American delegates at the international Paris Peace Conference. There Brown likened war and slavery, telling the eight hundred delegates from western Europe and the United States that "it is impossible to maintain slavery without maintaining war." His scheduled brief lecture tour in Britain turned into a five-year exile because, after passage of the 1850 Fugitive Slave Law, he feared being seized and sent back to slavery if he returned to the United States. In 1854 he became free when British abolitionists purchased his freedom from his former master.

Gandy, Douglass, Brown, and dozens of other former slaves helped revive abolitionism as an international issue. They energized the British and Foreign Anti-Slavery

■ William Wells Brown's autobiography stirred abolitionists in the United States and England. In 1849 Brown was among the American delegates to the Paris Peace Conference, then spent the next five years as an exile in Britain, fearing being sent back to slavery under the 1850 Fugitive Slave Act. He returned to the United States only after British abolitionists purchased his freedom from his former master. (Southern Historical Collection, The Library of the University of North Carolina, Chapel Hill)

Society, founded in 1839, and hundreds of more militant, local societies. By the early 1850s national abolitionist movements succeeded in abolishing slavery in Columbia, Argentina, Venezuela, and Peru. Though the United States continued to resist internal and international pressure, its black abolitionists were instrumental not only in reviving the worldwide antislavery movement but also, as advocates of woman's rights, international peace, temperance, and other reforms, in linking Americans to reform movements around the world.

vehicle was the American Anti-Slavery Society, founded in 1833.

In the 1840s escaped slaves Frederick Douglass and Harriet Tubman joined forces with white reformers in the American Anti-Slavery Society. Their militant and unrelenting campaign also won European support. "Brethren, arise, arise, arise!" Henry Highland Garnet commanded the 1843 National Colored Convention. "Strike for your lives and liberties. Now is the day and hour. Let every slave in the land do this and the days of slavery are numbered. Rather die freemen than live to be slaves."

Those who knew the experience of slavery firsthand, like Douglass and Sojourner Truth, wrote personal narratives that mobilized northerners. Most benevolent workers and reformers, however, kept their distance from the immediatists. They shared with immediatists the view that slavery was a sin but believed in gradual emancipation. They feared that if they moved too fast, attacked sinners too harshly, or interfered aggressively in time-honored customs and beliefs, they would destroy the harmony and order they sought to bring about through peaceful reform. But peace was at a premium: unlike temperance, the antislavery movement faced fierce opposition, even mob violence.

Immediatists' greatest recruitment successes resulted from defending their own constitutional rights, not the rights of slaves. Wherever they went, immediatists found their free speech threatened by hostile crowds. At Utica, New York, in 1835, merchants and professionals broke up the state Anti-Slavery Convention that had welcomed blacks and women. Mob violence peaked that year, with more than fifty riots aimed at abolitionists or African Americans. In 1837 in Alton, Illinois, a mob murdered abolitionist editor Elijah P. Lovejoy, who had been driven out of slaveholding Missouri, and rioters sacked his printing office. But public outrage at Lovejoy's murder only increased antislavery support in the North.

OPPOSITION TO ABOLITIONISTS

In the South, mobs blocked the distribution of antislavery tracts. Technological developments in mechanized papermaking and in steam-powered presses in the 1830s made it possible for the American Anti-Slavery Society to publish and distribute millions of pamphlets. The state of South Carolina intercepted and burned abolitionist literature, and President Andrew Jackson proposed a law prohibiting the mailing of antislavery tracts. In 1835 proslavery assailants killed four abolitionists in South Carolina and Louisiana and forty supposed insurrectionists in Mississippi and Louisiana that summer. Riots in the South, unchecked by authorities, were violent and deadly.

At a rally in Boston's Faneuil Hall in 1835, former Federalist Harrison Gray Otis portrayed abolitionists as subversives. Attacking Garrison's American Anti-Slavery Society as "revolutionary," he accused it of having women "turn their sewing parties into abolition clubs." Soon, Otis charged, school primers would teach "that A stands for abolition." Abolitionists, he predicted, would turn to politics, causing unforeseeable calamity. "What will become of the nation?" Otis asked. "What will become of the Union?"

But the furor between the abolitionists and their opponents had already entered the House of Representatives. Abolitionists bombarded Congress with petitions to abolish slavery and the slave trade in the District of Columbia, which Congress governed. The House in 1836 adopted what abolitionists labeled the "gag rule," which automatically tabled abolitionist petitions, effectively preventing debate on them. When the immediatists, in response, flooded Congress with nearly seven hundred thousand petitions, the gag rule gave new energy to the antislavery movement. In a dramatic defense of the right of petition, former president John Quincy Adams, now a representative from Massachusetts, took to the floor again and again to speak against the gag rule. (Its repeal in 1844 was anticlimactic.)

GAG RULE

The Missouri Compromise, censorship of the mails, and the gag rule represented attempts to keep the issue of slavery out of the political arena. Yet the more national leaders, especially Democrats, worked to avoid the issue, the more antislavery forces hardened their resolve. The unlawful and violent tactics used by opponents of abolition actually unified the movement by forcing factions to work together in mutual defense.

Abolition was highly factionalized, and its adherents fought one another as often as they fought the defenders of slavery. They were divided over Garrison's emphasis on "moral suasion"—winning over the hearts of slaveowners rather than coercing them—versus the practical politics of James G. Birney, the Liberty Party's candidate for president in 1840 and 1844, who sought to end slavery by electing abolitionists. They also disagreed about the place of free blacks in American society. And the movement split over support for other reforms, especially the roles and rights of women.

Women had been prominent in the antislavery movement from the start. They joined local female antislavery societies through their churches as part of the network of moral reform. In 1833 women in Boston founded the Female Anti-Slavery Society, and in many

WOMEN ABOLITIONISTS

antislavery organizations women were as active and politically involved as men. Lydia Maria Child, Maria Chapman, and Lucretia Mott served on the American Anti-Slavery Society's executive committee; Child edited its official paper, the *National Anti-Slavery Standard,* from 1841 to 1843, and Chapman coedited it from 1844 until 1848. Garrison's moral suasion attracted many women because it gave them a platform from which to oppose slavery. Yet some politically active societies excluded women because they could not vote and opposed women's roles in reform. In Boston in 1832, African American Maria Stewart was harshly criticized for addressing a mixed audience of abolitionist men and women. Opponents of such roles for women found her boldness—and her message that listeners should improve their own lives, their children's lives, and their communities—offensive. Stewart had to leave Boston for New York.

Later in the 1830s abolitionists Angelina and Sarah Grimké were similarly attacked for speaking to mixed audiences. One pastoral letter declared that women should obey, not lecture, men. This reaction turned the Grimkés' attention from the condition of slavers to the condition of women. Born into a Charleston, South Carolina, slaveholding family, both sisters had experienced conversion, became outspoken abolitionists, moved north, and found a home in Garrison's immediatism. Now they confronted the concept of "subordination to man," insisting that men and women had the "same rights and same duties." Sarah Grimké's *Letters on the Equality of the Sexes and the Condition of Women* and Angelina Grimké's *Letters to Catharine E. Beecher,* both published in 1838, initiated a new reform movement to secure legal and social equality of women.

Public participation in religious revival and reform had led some women to reexamine their positions in

WOMEN'S RIGHTS

society. As the predominant group in the Second Great Awakening, women began to challenge male domination in religion. During revivals women made public declarations of their faith and recounted their conversion experiences. Revivals brought ordinary women into the public sphere. Female societies and reform networks, convention participation, and advocacy opened new roles to women. The market economy also created new occupations for women outside their homes. Those factors, together, help explain why women's rights became an issue.

Women abolitionists were among the leaders on behalf of women's rights. In July 1848 Elizabeth Cady Stanton, Lucretia Mott, and Lucy Stone organized the Woman's Rights Convention at Seneca Falls, New York.

Elizabeth Cady Stanton posed in 1848 with two of her sons, Henry Jr., left, and Neil. Stanton, one of the organizers of the Seneca Falls Woman's Rights Convention, traveled widely and agitated for women's equality while raising five children. (Collection of Rhoda Jenkins)

Three hundred women and men reformers gathered to demand political, social, and economic equality for women. They protested women's legal disabilities—limited property rights and inability to vote—and their social restrictions, such as exclusion from advanced schooling and from many occupations. Their Declaration of Sentiments, modeled after the Declaration of Independence, broadcast the injustices suffered by women and launched the women's rights movement. "All men and women are created equal," the declaration proclaimed.

Advocates of women's rights were slow to garner support, especially from men, who held most of the political and legal power. In the 1840s the question of women's suffrage split the antislavery movement. Some men joined the ranks, notably Garrison and Frederick Douglass, but most men actively opposed a vote for women. Not everyone at Seneca Falls signed the resolution on women's suffrage. Of the one hundred who did, only two would live to see the passage of the Nineteenth Amendment to the Constitution seventy-two years later.

Jacksonianism and Party Politics

In the 1820s, reform pushed its way into politics. No less than reformers, politicians sought to control the direction of change in the expanding nation. The 1824 presidential election ignited a political barn fire that reformers, abolitionists, and expansionists would continuously stoke. By the 1830s, politics had become the great nineteenth-century American pastime.

The election of 1824, in which John Quincy Adams and Andrew Jackson faced off for the first time, heralded a more open political system. From 1800 through 1820 the system in which a congressional caucus (House and Senate members of the political party) chose Jefferson, Madison, and Monroe as the Democratic-Republican nominees had worked well. That it limited voters' involvement in choosing candidates was not an anomaly because in 1800 only five of the sixteen states selected presidential electors by popular vote. In most of the others, state legislatures selected the electors who voted for president. By 1824, however, eighteen out of twenty-four states chose electors at the polls.

The Democratic-Republican caucus in 1824 chose William H. Crawford of Georgia, secretary of the treasury,

ELECTION OF 1824

as its presidential candidate. But other Democratic-Republicans, emboldened by the chance to appeal directly to voters, put themselves forward as sectional candidates. John Quincy Adams drew support from New England, while westerners backed House Speaker Henry Clay of Kentucky. Secretary of War John C. Calhoun looked to the South for support and hoped to win Pennsylvania as well. The Tennessee legislature nominated Andrew Jackson, a popular military hero whose political views were unknown. Jackson had the most widespread support, but Crawford led in the party caucus. By boycotting the caucus and by attacking it as undemocratic, the four other candidates and their supporters ended the role of Congress in nominating presidential candidates.

In the four-way presidential election of 1824, Andrew Jackson led in both electoral and popular votes, but no candidate received a majority in the electoral college (see Map 11.1). Adams finished second, and Crawford and Clay trailed far behind (Calhoun had dropped out of the race before the election). Under the Constitution, the House of Representatives, voting by state delegation, one vote to a state, would select the next president from among the leaders in electoral votes. Clay, who had the fewest votes, was dropped. Crawford, who had a stroke

■ Presidential candidate Andrew Jackson is portrayed on a trinket or sewing box in 1824. This is an example of how campaigns entered popular culture and also illustrates the active role of women, excluded from voting, in politics. (Collection of David J. and Janice L. Frent)

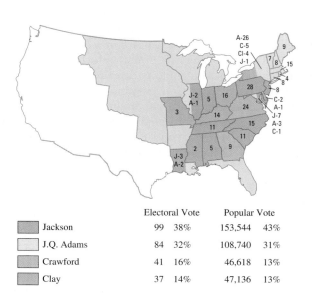

	Electoral Vote		Popular Vote	
Jackson	99	38%	153,544	43%
J.Q. Adams	84	32%	108,740	31%
Crawford	41	16%	46,618	13%
Clay	37	14%	47,136	13%

Map 11.1 Presidential Election, 1824

Andrew Jackson led in both electoral and popular votes but failed to win a majority of electoral college votes. The House elected John Quincy Adams president.

after the election, never received serious consideration. The influential Clay—Speaker of the House and leader of the Ohio valley states—backed Adams, who won with the votes of thirteen of the twenty-four state delegations. Clay became Adams's secretary of state, the traditional steppingstone to the presidency.

Angry Jacksonians denounced the outcome of the election as a "corrupt bargain" that had stolen the office. Jackson's bitterness reinforced his opposition to elitism and fueled his later emphasis on the people's will. The Democratic-Republican Party split. The Adams wing emerged as the National Republicans, and the Jacksonians became the Democrats; they immediately began planning for 1828.

After taking the oath of office, Adams proposed a strong nationalist policy incorporating Henry Clay's "American System," a program of protective tariffs, a national bank, and internal improvements. Adams believed the federal government should take an active role not only in the economy but also in education, science, and the arts. He proposed establishing a national university in Washington, D.C. Brilliant as a diplomat and secretary of state, Adams was an inept president. The political skills he had demonstrated in winning the office eluded him as chief executive. He underestimated the lingering effects of the Panic of 1819 and the resulting staunch opposition to a national bank and protective tariffs. Meanwhile, supporters of Andrew Jackson sabotaged Adams's administration at every opportunity.

The 1828 election pitted Adams against Jackson in a rowdy campaign. Voters displayed their enthusiasm for

ELECTION
OF 1828

Jackson with badges, medals, and other campaign paraphernalia, which were mass-produced for the first time. The contest was also intensely personal. Mudslinging was the order of the day. Jackson's supporters accused Adams of stealing the 1824 election and, when he was envoy to Russia, of having secured prostitutes for the czar. Anti-Jacksonians published reports that Rachel Jackson had had an affair with Jackson and married the young officer before her first husband divorced her in 1793; she was, they sneered, an adulterer and a bigamist. In 1806 Jackson had killed John Dickinson in a Kentucky duel defending Rachel's integrity, and the cry of murderer was revived in the election. After the election Rachel Jackson discovered a pamphlet defending her, and she was shocked by the extent of the charges. When she died of a heart attack in December 1828, Jacksonians charged that she was "murdered."

Although Adams kept the states he won in 1824, the opposition was unified, and Jackson swamped him (see

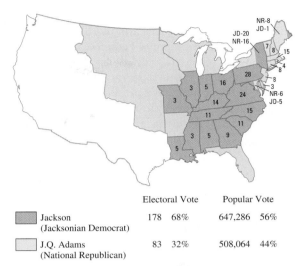

	Electoral Vote		Popular Vote	
Jackson (Jacksonian Democrat)	178	68%	647,286	56%
J.Q. Adams (National Republican)	83	32%	508,064	44%

Map 11.2   Presidential Election, 1828

Andrew Jackson avenged his 1824 loss of the presidency, sweeping the election in 1828.

Map 11.2). Jackson polled 56 percent of the popular vote and won in the electoral college by 178 to 83 votes. He and his supporters believed that the will of the people had finally been served. Through a lavishly financed coalition of state parties, political leaders, and newspaper editors, a popular movement had elected the president, and a new era began. The Democratic Party became the first well-organized national political party in the United States, and tight party organization became the hallmark of nineteenth-century American politics.

Nicknamed "Old Hickory" after the toughest of American hardwoods, Andrew Jackson was a rough-and-

ANDREW
JACKSON

tumble, ambitious man. Born in South Carolina in 1767, he rose from humble beginnings to become a wealthy Tennessee planter and slaveholder. Jackson was the first American president from the West and the first born in a log cabin; he was at ease among both frontiersmen and southern planters. Though vindictive and given to violent displays of temper, he could charm opposition into assent. A natural leader, Jackson inspired immense loyalty. He had an instinct for politics and picked both issues and supporters shrewdly.

Few Americans have been as celebrated as Jackson. Having served in the Revolution as a boy, he claimed a connection to the founding generation. In the Tennessee militia General Jackson led the campaign to remove Creeks from the Alabama and Georgia frontier (see pages

234–235). He burst onto the national scene in 1815 as the hero of the Battle of New Orleans and in 1818 enhanced his glory in an expedition against Seminoles in Spanish Florida. Jackson also served as a congressman and senator from Tennessee, and as the first territorial governor of Florida (1821), before running for president in 1824.

Jackson and his supporters offered an alternative to the strong federal government advocated by John

DEMOCRATS

Quincy Adams. The Democrats represented a wide range of views but shared a fundamental commitment to the Jeffersonian concept of an agrarian society. They viewed the central government as the enemy of individual liberty. The 1824 "corrupt bargain" had strengthened their suspicion of Washington politics. Jackson himself, a backwoodsman and farmer, symbolized simpler times.

Jacksonians feared the concentration of economic and political power. They believed that government intervention in the economy benefited special-interest groups and created corporate monopolies that favored the rich. They sought to restore the independence of the individual—the artisan and the ordinary farmer—by ending federal support of banks and corporations and restricting the use of paper currency, which they distrusted. Their definition of the proper role of government tended to be negative, and Jackson's political power was largely expressed in negative acts. He exercised the veto more than all previous presidents combined.

Jackson and his supporters also opposed reform as a movement. Reformers eager to turn their programs into legislation called for a more active government. But Democrats tended to oppose programs like educational reform and the establishment of a public education system. They believed, for instance, that public schools restricted individual liberty by interfering with parental responsibility and undermined freedom of religion by replacing church schools. Nor did Jackson share reformers' humanitarian concerns. He had no sympathy for American Indians, initiating the removal of the Cherokees along the Trail of Tears (see pages 267–268).

Jacksonians considered themselves reformers in a different way. By restraining government and emphasizing

JACKSONIANS
AS REFORMERS

individualism, they sought to restore traditional republican virtues, such as prudence and economy. No less zealous than reformers, Jackson sought to encourage self-discipline and self-reliance, traits undermined by economic and social change. In doing so, Jackson looked to Jefferson and the generation of the founders as models of traditional values. "My political creed," Jackson wrote to Tennessee congressman James

K. Polk in 1826, "was formed in the old republican school."

Like Jefferson, Jackson strengthened the executive branch of government even as he weakened the federal role. Given his popularity and the strength of his personality, this concentration of power in the presidency was perhaps inevitable, but in combining the roles of party leader and chief of state, he centralized power in the White House. Jackson relied on political friends, his "Kitchen Cabinet," for advice; he rarely consulted his official cabinet. Enamored of power, Jackson never hesitated to confront opponents with all the weapons at his disposal. He commanded enormous loyalty, and he rewarded his followers handsomely. Rotating officeholders, Jackson claimed, made government more responsive to the public will, but it allowed him to introduce a spoils system to appoint loyal Democrats to office. He removed fewer than one-quarter of the federal officeholders he inherited, but he used patronage to strengthen party organization and loyalty.

Jackson stressed rejection of elitism and special favors, rotation of officeholders—political appointees rather than a permanent bureaucracy—and belief in popular government. Time and again he declared that sovereignty resided with the people, not with the states or the courts. In this respect Jackson was a reformer; he returned government to majority rule. Yet it is hard to distinguish between Jackson's belief in himself as the instrument of the people and simple egotism and demagogic arrogance. After all, his opponents, too, claimed to represent the people.

Animosity grew year by year between Jacksonians and their opponents. Massachusetts senator Daniel Webster feared the men around the president; Henry Clay most feared Jackson himself. Rotation in office, they contended, corrupted government because appointments were based on political loyalty, not competency. Opponents mocked Jackson as "King Andrew I," charging him with abuse of power by ignoring the Supreme Court's ruling on Cherokee rights (see page 267), by using the spoils system, and by consulting his Kitchen Cabinet. Critics rejected his claim of restoring republican virtue and accused him of recklessly destroying the economy.

Amid this agitation, Jackson pursued his agenda. He invigorated the philosophy of limited government. In 1830 he vetoed the Maysville Road bill—which would have funded construction of a 60-mile turnpike from Maysville to Lexington, Kentucky. A federally subsidized internal improvement confined to one state was unconstitutional, he charged; such projects were properly a state responsibility. The veto undermined Henry Clay's nationalist program and personally embarrassed Clay because the project was in his home district. Such federal-state issues were to loom even larger in the nullification crisis.

Federalism at Issue: The Nullification and Bank Controversies

Soon Jackson had to face directly the question of the proper division of sovereignty between state and central governments. The slave South feared federal power, no state more so than South Carolina, where the planter class was strongest and slavery most concentrated. Southerners also resented protectionist tariffs, one of the foundations of Clay's American System, which in 1824 and 1828 protected manufactures by imposing import duties on manufactured cloth and iron. But in protecting northern factories, the tariff raised the costs of these goods to southerners, who quickly labeled the high tariff of 1828 the Tariff of Abominations.

South Carolina's political leaders went so far as to reject the 1828 tariff, invoking the doctrine of nullification, according to which a state had the right to overrule, or nullify, federal legislation. Nullification was based on the idea expressed in the Virginia and Kentucky Resolutions of 1798 (see page 208)—that the states, representing the people, have a right to judge the constitutionality of federal actions. Jackson's vice president, John C. Calhoun of South Carolina, argued in his unsigned *Exposition and Protest* that in any disagreement between the federal government and a state, a special state convention—like the conventions called to ratify the Constitution—should decide the conflict by either nullifying or affirming the federal law. Only the power of nullification, Calhoun asserted, could protect the minority against the tyranny of the majority.

NULLIFICATION

In public, Calhoun let others advance nullification. As Jackson's running mate in 1828, he had avoided endorsing nullification and thus embarrassing the Democratic ticket; he also hoped to win Jackson's support as the Democratic presidential heir apparent. Thus in early 1830 Calhoun presided silently over the Senate and its packed galleries when Senator Daniel Webster of Massachusetts and Senator Robert Y. Hayne of South Carolina debated states' rights. The debate started over a resolution to restrict western land sales and engaged the tariff issue by exploring sectional differences. It quickly

WEBSTER-HAYNE DEBATE

turned to the nature of the Union, with nullification a subtext. With Vice President Calhoun nodding in agreement, Hayne charged that the North was threatening to bring disunity, as it had done fifteen years earlier at the Hartford Convention (see pages 236, 237). Hayne accused reformers of wanting in "the spirit of false philanthropy" to destroy the South.

For two days Webster eloquently defended New England and the republic as he kept nullification on the defense. Though debating Hayne, he aimed his remarks at Calhoun. At the climax of the debate, Webster invoked two powerful images. One was the outcome of nullification: "states dissevered, discordant, belligerent; on a land rent with civil feuds, or drenched . . . in fraternal blood!" The other was a patriotic vision of a great nation flourishing under the motto "Liberty and Union, now and forever, one and inseparable."

Though sympathetic to states' rights and distrustful of the federal government, Jackson rejected the idea of state sovereignty. He strongly believed that sovereignty rested with the people. Believing deeply in the Union, he shared Webster's dread of nullification. Soon after the Webster-Hayne debate, the president made his position clear at a Jefferson Day dinner with the toast "Our Federal Union, it must and shall be preserved." Vice President Calhoun, when his turn came, toasted "The Federal Union—next to our liberty the most dear." Thus Calhoun revealed his adherence to states' rights. Calhoun and Jackson grew apart, and Jackson looked to Secretary of State Martin Van Buren, not Calhoun, as his successor.

Tension resumed when Congress passed a new tariff in 1832, reducing some duties but retaining high taxes on imported iron, cottons, and woolens. Though a majority of southern representatives supported the new tariff, South Carolinians refused to go along. In their eyes, the constitutional right to control their own destiny had been sacrificed to the demands of northern industrialists. More than the duties, they feared that the act could set a precedent for congressional legislation on slavery. In November 1832 a South Carolina state convention nullified both the 1828 and 1832 tariffs, declaring it unlawful for federal officials to collect duties in the state.

NULLIFICATION CRISIS

Old Hickory responded quickly. Privately he threatened to invade South Carolina and hang Vice President Calhoun; publicly he took measured steps. In December Jackson issued a proclamation opposing nullification. He moved troops to federal forts in South Carolina and prepared U.S. marshals to collect the required duties. At Jackson's request, Congress passed the Force Act, authorizing the president to call up troops but also offering a way to avoid force by collecting duties before foreign ships reached Charleston's harbor. At the same time, Jackson extended an olive branch by recommending tariff reductions.

Calhoun, disturbed by South Carolina's drift toward separatism, resigned as vice president and soon won election to represent South Carolina in the U.S. Senate. There he worked with Henry Clay to draw up the compromise Tariff of 1833. Quickly passed by Congress and signed by the president, the new tariff lengthened the list of duty-free items and reduced duties over nine years. Satisfied, South Carolina's convention repealed its nullification law. In a final salvo, it also nullified Jackson's Force Act. Jackson ignored the gesture.

Nullification offered a genuine debate on the nature and principles of the republic. Each side believed it was upholding the Constitution. Both sides felt they were opposing special privilege and subversion of republican values. South Carolina opposed the tyranny of the federal government and manufacturers that sought tariff protection. Jackson fought the tyranny of South Carolina, whose refusal to bow to federal authority threatened to split the republic. Neither side won a clear victory, though both claimed to have done so. It took another crisis, over a central bank, to define the powers of the federal government more clearly.

At stake was survival of the Second Bank of the United States, whose twenty-year charter was scheduled to expire in 1836. Like its predecessor, the bank served as a depository for federal funds and provided credit for businesses. Its bank notes circulated as currency throughout the country; they could be readily exchanged for gold, and the federal government accepted them as payment in all transactions. Through its twenty-five branch offices, the Second Bank acted as a clearing-house for state banks, keeping them honest by refusing to accept bank notes of any state bank lacking sufficient gold in reserve. Most state banks resented the central bank's police role: by presenting a state bank's notes for redemption all at once, the Second Bank could easily ruin a state bank. Moreover, with less money in reserve, state banks found themselves unable to compete on an equal footing with the Second Bank.

SECOND BANK OF THE UNITED STATES

Many state governments also regarded the national bank as unresponsive to local needs. Westerners and urban workers remembered with bitterness the bank's conservative credit policies during the Panic of 1819 (see page 245). As a private, profit-making institution, its policies reflected the interest of its owners, especially its president, Nicholas Biddle, who controlled the bank completely. An eastern patrician, Biddle symbolized all that westerners found wrong with the bank.

Rechartering was a volatile issue in the 1832 presidential campaign. The bank's charter was valid until 1836, but Henry Clay, the National Republican presidential candidate, persuaded Biddle to ask Congress to approve an early rechartering. This strategy was designed to pressure Jackson to sign the rechartering bill or to override his veto of it. The plan backfired, however. The president vetoed the bill, and the Senate failed to override. Jackson's veto message was an emotional attack on the undemocratic nature of the bank. "It is to be regretted," he wrote, "that the rich and powerful too often bend the acts of government to their selfish purposes."

The bank became the prime issue in the presidential campaign of 1832, with Jackson denouncing special privilege and economic power. With every state but South Carolina now choosing electors by popular vote, the Jacksonians used their party organization to mobilize voters by advertising the presidential election as the central event of the political system. When the Antimasons adopted a party platform, the first in the nation's history, the Democrats and the National Republicans quickly followed suit. The Democratic convention nominated Jackson and Martin Van Buren, Jackson's first secretary of state and then American minister to Great Britain; the National Republican convention selected Clay and John Sergeant. South Carolina nominated its own candidate, John Floyd. Jackson was reelected easily in a Democratic Party triumph.

After his sweeping victory and second inauguration, Jackson moved in 1833 to dismantle the Second Bank of the United States. He deposited federal funds in state-chartered banks (critics called them his "pet banks"). Without federal money, the Second Bank shriveled. When its federal charter expired in 1836, it became just another Pennsylvania-chartered private bank. Five years later it closed its doors.

JACKSON'S SECOND TERM

As Congress allowed the Bank of the United States to die, it passed the Deposit Act of 1836 with Jackson's support. The act authorized the secretary of the treasury to designate one bank in each state and territory to provide the services formerly performed by the Bank of the United States. The act provided that the federal surplus in excess of $5 million be distributed to the states as interest-free loans beginning in 1837. These loans were never repaid— a fitting Jacksonian restraint on the federal purse.

The surplus had derived from wholesale speculation in public lands: speculators borrowed money to purchase

■ This 1830 Ralph E. W. Earl oil painting of President Andrew Jackson, entitled *Tennessee Gentleman,* captures the complexity of Jackson's image. The first president from the West and the first born in a log cabin, Jackson nonetheless poses as an aristocrat with his plantation house, The Hermitage, in the background.   (Courtesy, The Hermitage—The Home of Andrew Jackson)

public land, used the land as collateral for credit to buy additional acreage, and repeated the cycle. Between 1834 and 1836 federal receipts from land sales rose from $5 million to $25 million. The state banks providing the loans issued bank notes. Jackson, an opponent of paper money, feared that the speculative craze threatened the stability of state banks and undermined the interests of settlers, who could not compete with speculators in bidding for the best land.

In keeping with his hard-money instincts and opposition to paper currency, the president ordered Treasury Secretary Levi Woodbury to issue the Specie Circular. It

SPECIE CIRCULAR provided that after August 1836 only specie—gold or silver—or Virginia scrip (paper money) would be accepted as payment for land. By ending credit sales, it significantly reduced purchases of public land and the federal budget surplus. As a result the government suspended payments to the states soon after they began.

The policy was a disaster. Although federal land sales fell sharply, speculation continued as land available for sale became scarce. The increased demand for specie squeezed banks, and many suspended the redemption of bank notes for specie. Credit contracted further as banks issued fewer notes and made fewer loans. Jackson aggravated the situation by instinctively pursuing a tight money policy. More important, the Specie Circular was similar to a bill defeated in the Senate just three months earlier. Jackson's opponents thus saw King Andrew at work. In the waning days of Jackson's administration, Congress voted to repeal the circular, but the president pocket-vetoed the bill by holding it unsigned until Congress adjourned. Finally in May 1838, a joint resolution of Congress overturned the circular. Sales of land resumed, but the speculative fervor had ended.

From George Washington to John Quincy Adams, the first six presidents had vetoed nine bills; Jackson alone vetoed twelve. Previous presidents believed that vetoes were justified only on constitutional grounds, but Jackson considered policy disagreements legitimate grounds as well. He made the veto an effective weapon for controlling Congress, since representatives and senators had to weigh the possibility of a presidential veto as they deliberated. In effect, Jackson made the executive for the first time a rival branch of government, equal in power to Congress.

The Whig Challenge and the Second Party System

*M*ost historians view the 1830s and 1840s as an age of reform and popularly based political parties. As the passions of reformers and abolitionists spilled over into politics, party differences became paramount and party loyalties solidified. For the first time in American history, grassroots political groups, organized from the bottom up, set the tone of political life. And both parties were national, drawing voters and winning counties in every region.

Opponents of the Democrats, including remnants of the National Republican Party, found shelter under a

WHIG PARTY common umbrella, the Whig Party, in the 1830s. Resentful of Jackson's domination of Congress, the Whigs borrowed the name of the British party that had opposed the tyranny of Hanoverian monarchs in the eighteenth century. From 1834 through the 1840s, the Whigs and the Democrats competed on a nearly equal footing. They fought at the city, county, state, and national levels and achieved a stability previously unknown in American politics. The political competition of this period—known as the second party system—was more intense and well organized than that of the first party system of Democratic-Republicans versus Federalists.

Reform and the party system changed politics. As political interest broadened, states expanded white male voting. By 1840 only seven of twenty-six states had property restrictions for male suffrage, though most excluded convicted felons. Some even allowed immigrants who had taken out citizenship papers to vote. Hotly contested elections further stimulated public interest in politics. The net effect was a sharp increase in the number of votes cast in presidential elections. Between 1824 and 1828 that number increased threefold, from 360,000 to over 1.1 million. In 1840, 2.4 million men cast votes. The proportion of eligible voters who cast ballots also increased, from about 27 percent in 1824 to more than 80 percent in 1840.

Increasingly the parties diverged. Whigs favored economic expansion through an activist government, Democrats through limited central government. *WHIGS AND REFORMERS* Whigs supported corporate charters, a national bank, and paper currency; Democrats were opposed to all three. Whigs also favored more humanitarian reforms than did Democrats, including public schools, abolition of capital punishment, prison and asylum reform, and temperance. Whigs were more optimistic than Democrats, generally speaking, and more enterprising. They did not object to helping a specific group if doing so would promote the general welfare. The chartering of corporations, they argued, expanded economic opportunity for everyone, laborers and farmers alike. Democrats, distrustful of concentrated economic power and of moral and economic coercion, held fast to the Jeffersonian principle of limited government.

Religion and ethnicity, not economics and class, most influenced party affiliation. The Whigs' support for energetic government and humanitarian and moral reform won the favor of evangelical Protestants, especially those involved in religious revivals. Methodists and Baptists were overwhelmingly Whigs, as were the small number of free black voters. The Whig Party was the vehicle of revivalist Protantism. In many locales the membership rolls of reform societies overlapped those of the party. Indeed, Whigs practiced a kind of political revivalism. Their rallies resembled camp meetings; in their speeches they employed pulpit rhetoric; their programs embodied the perfectionist beliefs of reformers. This potent blend of religion and politics—"intimately united" in America, according to Tocqueville—greatly intensified political loyalties.

In their appeal to evangelicals, Whigs alienated members of other faiths. The evangelicals' ideal Christian state had no room for nonevangelical Protestants, Catholics, Mormons, Unitarians, Universalists, or religious freethinkers. Those groups opposed Sabbath laws and temperance legislation in particular and state interference in moral and religious questions in general. In fact, they preferred to keep religion and politics separate. As a result, more than 95 percent of Irish Catholics, 90 percent of Reformed Dutch, and 80 percent of German Catholics voted Democratic.

Vice President Martin Van Buren, handpicked by Jackson, headed the Democratic ticket in the 1836 presidential election. Van Buren was a shrewd politician who had built a political machine—the Albany Regency—in New York and then left to join Jackson's cabinet in 1829. Having helped found the Democratic Party, Van Buren was a professional politician; he made his career in party politics. *ELECTION OF 1836*

Because the Whigs in 1836 had not yet coalesced into a national party, they entered three sectional candidates: Daniel Webster of New England, Hugh White of the South, and William Henry Harrison of the West. By splintering the vote, they hoped to throw the election into the House of Representatives. Van Buren, however, comfortably captured the electoral college even though he had only a 25,000-vote edge out of a total of 1.5 million votes cast. No vice-presidential candidate received a majority of electoral votes, and for the only time in American history the Senate decided a vice-presidential race, selecting Democratic candidate Richard M. Johnson of Kentucky.

Van Buren took office just weeks before the American credit system collapsed. In response to the impact of the Specie Circular, New York banks stopped redeeming paper currency with gold in mid-1837. Soon all banks suspended payments in hard coin. Thus began a downward economic spiral that curtailed bank loans and strangled business confidence. Credit contraction made things worse; after a brief recovery, hard times persisted from 1839 until 1843. *VAN BUREN AND HARD TIMES*

Ill advisedly, Van Buren followed Jackson's hard-money policies. He cut federal spending, which caused prices to drop further, and he opposed a national bank, which would have expanded credit. Even worse, the president proposed a new regional treasury system for government deposits. The proposed treasury branches would accept and pay out only gold and silver coin; they would not accept paper currency or checks drawn on state banks. Van Buren's independent treasury bill became law in 1840. By increasing the demand for hard coin, it deprived banks of gold and further accelerated price deflation. Whigs and Democrats faced off at the state level over these issues. Whigs favored new banks, more paper currency, and readily available corporate and bank charters. As the party of hard money, Democrats favored eliminating paper currency altogether. Increasingly the Democrats became distrustful even of state banks, and by the mid-1840s a majority favored eliminating all bank corporations.

With the nation in the grip of hard times, the Whigs prepared confidently for the election of 1840. Their

WILLIAM HENRY HARRISON AND THE ELECTION OF 1840

strategy was simple: hold on to loyal supporters and win over independents by blaming hard times on the Democrats. The Whigs rallied behind a military hero, General William Henry Harrison, conqueror of the Shawnees at Tippecanoe Creek in 1811 (see page 226). The Democrats renominated President Van Buren at a somber convention.

Harrison, or "Old Tippecanoe," and his running mate, John Tyler of Virginia, ran a "log cabin and hard cider" campaign—a people's crusade—against the aristocratic president in "the Palace." Though descended from a Virginia plantation family, Harrison presented himself as an ordinary farmer. The Whigs wooed supporters and independents alike with huge rallies, parades, songs, posters, campaign mementos, and a party newspaper, *The Log Cabin*. Harrison took the position that a presidential candidate should not be involved in the issues, earning himself the nickname "General Mum," but party hacks bluntly blamed the hard times on the Democrats. In a huge turnout, 80 percent of eligible voters cast ballots. Harrison won the popular vote by a narrow margin but swept the electoral college by 234 to 60.

Immediately after taking office in 1841, President Harrison convened a special session of Congress to pass the Whig program: repeal of the independent treasury system, a new national bank, and a higher protective tariff. But the sixty-eight-year-old Harrison caught pneumonia and died within a month of his inauguration. His successor, John Tyler, who had left the Democratic Party to protest Jackson's nullification proclamation, now found himself the first vice president to move up to the presidency on the death of a president.

In office, Tyler turned out to be more of a Democrat than a Whig. As critical of the Whigs' economic nationalism as he had been of Jackson's use of executive power, Tyler consistently opposed his own party's

Using patriotic and emotional images that look familiar to people today, General William Henry Harrison in 1840 ran a "log cabin and hard cider" campaign against Jackson's heir, President Martin Van Buren. The cotton bandana, presumably widely distributed given its practical use, shows Harrison, before a log cabin, welcoming a disabled veteran while another person draws hard cider. (Collection of Janice L. and David J. Frent)

PRESIDENT
TYLER

congressional agenda. He repeatedly vetoed Henry Clay's protective tariffs, internal improvements, and bills aimed at reviving the Bank of the United States. The only important measures that became law during his term were repeal of the independent treasury system and passage of a higher tariff. Two days after Tyler's second veto of a bank bill, the entire cabinet except Secretary of State Daniel Webster resigned; Webster, busy negotiating a new treaty with Great Britain, left shortly thereafter. Tyler became a president without a party, and the Whigs lost the presidency without losing an election. Disgusted Whigs referred to Tyler as "His Accidency."

Hard times in the late 1830s and early 1840s deflected attention from a renewal of Anglo-American tensions that had multiple sources: northern commercial rivalry with Britain, the default of state governments and corporations on British-held debts during the Panic of 1837, rebellion in Canada, boundary disputes, southern alarm over West Indian emancipation, and American expansionism.

One of the most troublesome disputes arose from the *Caroline* affair. A U.S. citizen, Amos Durfee, had been

ANGLO-
AMERICAN
TENSIONS

killed when Canadian militia set afire the privately owned steamer *Caroline* in the Niagara River. (The *Caroline* had supported an unsuccessful uprising against Great Britain in 1837.) Britain refused to apologize, and American newspapers called for revenge. Fearing that popular support for the Canadian rebels would ignite war, President Van Buren posted troops at the border to discourage raids. Tensions subsided in late 1840 when New York arrested Alexander McLeod, a Canadian deputy sheriff, for the murder of Durfee. McLeod eventually was acquitted. Had he been found guilty and executed, Lord Palmerston, the British foreign minister, might have sought war.

At almost the same time an old border dispute between Maine and New Brunswick disrupted Anglo-American relations. Great Britain had accepted an 1831 arbitration decision fixing a new boundary, but the U.S. Senate rejected it. Thus when Canadian lumbermen cut trees in the disputed region in the winter of 1838–1839, the citizens of Maine attempted to expel them. The lumbermen captured the Maine land agent and posse, both sides mobilized their militias, and Congress authorized a call-up of fifty thousand men. Ultimately, no blood was spilled. General Winfield Scott, who had patrolled the border during the *Caroline* affair, was dispatched to Aroostook, Maine, where he arranged a truce. The two sides compromised on their conflicting land claims in the Webster-Ashburton Treaty (1842).

These border disputes with Great Britain prefigured the conflicts that were to erupt in the 1840s over the expansion of the United States. With Tyler's succession to power in 1841 and James K. Polk's Democratic victory in the presidential election of 1844, federal activism in the domestic sphere ended for the rest of the decade, as attention turned to territorial expansion. Reform, however, was not dead. Its passions would resurface before the decade was over in the debate about slavery in the territories.

Manifest Destiny and Expansionism

The belief that American expansion westward and southward was inevitable, just, and divinely ordained was first labeled "manifest destiny" in 1845, by John L. O'Sullivan, editor of the *United States Magazine and Domestic Review*. The annexation of Texas, O'Sullivan wrote in 1845, was "the fulfillment of our manifest destiny to overspread the continent allotted by Providence for the free development of our yearly multiplying millions." Armed with such sentiments, expansionism reached a new fervor in the 1840s.

Since colonial days Americans had hungered for more land. Acquisition of the Louisiana Territory (1803) and Florida (1819) (see Map 9.1) and Indian removal (see pages 263–268) had set the process in motion. As the proportion of Americans living west of the Appalachians grew from one-quarter to one-half between 1830 and 1860, both national parties joined the popular clamor for expansion. Agrarian Democrats sought western land to balance urbanization. Enterprising Whigs looked to the new commercial opportunities the West offered. Southerners envisioned the extension of slavery and more slave states.

Fierce national pride spurred the quest for land. Subdued during hard times, it reasserted itself after 1843 when the economy recovered, and during the decade expansionism reached a new fervor. Americans were convinced that theirs was the greatest country on earth, with a special role to play in the world. As reform sought to perfect American society, so too expansion promised to extend the benefits of America's republican system of government to the unfortunate and the inferior.

In part, racism contributed to manifest destiny as well. The impulse to colonize and develop the West was based on the belief that Euro-Americans could use the land more productively than American Indians or Hispanics. Euro-Americans viewed Indians and Hispanics as inferior peoples, best controlled or conquered. Thus the same racial attitudes that justified discrimination against black people and slavery supported expansion in the West.

The desire to secure the nation from perceived external threats also fed expansionist fever. The internal enemies of the 1830s—banks, corporations, paper currency, alcohol—seemed pale in comparison to the opportunities Americans saw along their borders in the 1840s. Expansion, some believed, was necessary to preserve American independence, and no other nation should stop its westward movement.

Among the long-standing objectives of expansionists was Texas, Mexico's remote northern province that in
REPUBLIC OF TEXAS
addition to present-day Texas included parts of Oklahoma, Kansas, Colorado, Wyoming, and New Mexico (see Map 11.3). After winning its independence from Spain in 1821, Mexico had encouraged the development of Texas, offering large tracts of land virtually free to U.S. settlers called *empresarios*. The settlers in turn agreed to become Mexican citizens, adopt the Catholic religion, and bring hundreds of American families into the area. Moses and Stephen Austin, who had helped to formulate the policy, responded eagerly.

By 1835 thirty-five thousand Americans, including many slaveholders, lived in Texas. As the new settlers' numbers and power grew, they tended to ignore their commitments to the Mexican government. In response, dictator General Antonio López de Santa Anna tightened control over the region. In turn, the Anglo immigrants and *Tejanos*—Mexicans living in Texas—rebelled. At the Alamo mission in San Antonio in 1836, fewer than two hundred Texans made a heroic but unsuccessful stand against three thousand Mexicans under General Santa Anna. "Remember the Alamo" became the Texans' rallying cry. By the end of the year the Texans had won independence, delighting most Americans. Some saw the victory as a triumph of Protestants over Catholic Mexico; others cheered that proslavery Texans had defeated antislavery Mexicans.

Texas established the independent Lone Star Republic but soon sought annexation to the United States. Sam Houston, president of the Texas republic, opened negotiations with Washington, but the issue quickly became politically explosive. Southerners favored annexing proslavery Texas; abolitionists, many northerners, and most Whigs opposed annexation. In recognition of the political dangers, President Jackson had reneged on his promise to recognize Texas, and President Van Buren ignored annexation. Rebuffed by the United States, Texans talked about closer ties with the British and extending their republic to the Pacific coast. With Britain control-

■ Texans believed that their war for independence paralleled the Revolutionary War. The lady of liberty on this banner, carried by Texans in 1836, brings to mind similar images that stirred patriots during the American Revolution. (Archives Division, Texas State Library)

ling Canada, the prospect of a rival republic to the south caused some Americans to fear encirclement. If Texas reached the ocean and became an English ally, would not American independence be threatened?

President Tyler, committed to expansion, pushed for annexation. Eager to gain the 1844 Democratic nomination, Tyler hoped his position would build a political base in the South. Southerners also pressed for annexation. Former president Jackson agreed, stating that the United States must have Texas, "peacefully if we can, forcibly if we must." But the Senate rejected annexation in 1844. A letter from Secretary of State Calhoun to the British minister, justifying annexation to protect slavery, so outraged senators that the treaty was defeated 16 to 35.

As southerners sought expansion in the Southwest, northerners looked to the Northwest. "Oregon fever"
OREGON FEVER
struck thousands in 1841. Lured by the glowing reports of missionaries who seemed as enthusiastic about the Northwest's riches and beauty as about conversion of Indians, migrants in wagon trains took to the Oregon Trail. Their

Map 11.3 Westward Expansion, 1800–1860

Through exploration, purchase, war, and treaty, the United States became a continental nation, stretching from the Atlantic to the Pacific.

■ An unknown artist depicted, in rich detail, the election campaign of 1844. A team of Polk supporters offers a campaign handbill to the seated voter. Passions were so high and party organization was so extensive that door-to-door politicking became the norm.   (Courtesy, Nathan Liverant & Son)

enthusiasm was tempered by apprehension. Lavinia Porter feared that her husband did not have "the training to make a living on the plains of the West or the crossing of the continent in an ox team a successful venture." The 2,000-mile journey took six months or more, but within a few years five thousand settlers had arrived in the fertile Willamette valley south of the Columbia River.

Britain and the United States had jointly occupied the disputed Oregon Territory since the Convention of 1818 (see pages 242–243). Beginning with the administration of President John Quincy Adams, the United States had tried to fix the boundary at the 49th parallel, but Britain was determined to maintain access to Puget Sound and the Columbia River. Time only increased the American appetite. In 1843 a Cincinnati convention of expansionists demanded the entire Oregon Country for the United States, up to its northernmost border at latitude 54°40'. Soon "Fifty-four Forty or Fight" became the rallying cry of American expansionists.

Expansion into Oregon and rejection of the annexation of Texas, both favored by antislavery forces, worried southern leaders. Anxious about their diminishing ability to control the debate over slavery, they persuaded the 1844 Democratic convention to adopt a rule requiring the presidential nominee to receive two-thirds of the convention votes. In effect, the southern states acquired a veto, and they wielded it to block Van Buren as the nominee; most southerners objected to his opposition to slavery and

POLK AND THE
ELECTION OF
1844

Texas annexation. Instead, the party chose "Young Hickory," House Speaker James K. Polk, a hard-money Jacksonian, avid expansionist, and slaveholding cotton planter from Tennessee. The Whig leader Henry Clay, who opposed annexation, won his party's nomination handily. The Democratic platform called for occupation of the entire Oregon Territory and annexation of Texas. The Whigs, while favoring annexation, argued that the Democrats' belligerent nationalism would lead the nation into war with Great Britain or Mexico or both. Clay favored expansion through negotiation.

With a well-organized campaign, Polk and the Democrats won the election by 170 electoral votes to 105. (They won the popular vote by just 38,000 out of 2.7 million votes cast.) Polk won New York's 36 electoral votes by just 6,000 popular votes. Abolitionist James G. Birney, the Liberty Party candidate, had drawn almost 16,000 votes away from Clay, handing New York and the election to Polk. Abolitionist forces thus unwittingly brought about the choice of a slaveholder as president, but they viewed Polk as more moderate than Clay on slavery and the lesser of two evils.

Interpreting Polk's victory as a mandate for annexation, President Tyler proposed in his final days in office that Texas be admitted by joint resolution of Congress. The usual method of annexation, by treaty negotiation,

ANNEXATION OF TEXAS

required a two-thirds vote in the Senate—which expansionists clearly did not have, since there were sufficient opponents to slavery who would vote against annexation. Joint resolution required only a simple majority in each house. The resolution passed the House by 120 to 98 and the Senate by 27 to 25. Three days before leaving office, Tyler signed the measure. Mexico, which had never recognized Texas independence, immediately broke relations with the United States. In October the citizens of Texas ratified annexation, and Texas joined the Union in December 1845.

Summary

*R*eligion, reform, and expansionism shaped politics from 1824 through the 1840s. As the Second Great Awakening spread through villages and towns, the converts, especially women, organized to reform a rapidly changing society. Religion imbued men and women with zeal to right the wrongs of American society and the world. Reformers pursued perfectionism and republican virtue by battling with the evils of slavery, prostitution, and alcohol. As reformers, they sought to improve insane asylums and penitentiaries. In the process, women entered the public sphere as advocates of reform. Two issues elicited particular intensity: the comet of Antimasonry and the smoldering fire of abolitionism. The passions that both aroused were so potent, and success so elusive, that Antimasons and abolitionists transformed their moral crusades into political movements. Women's rights and nationalism contributed to the brew, and the new mixture made politics far more important, critical, and engaging than just voting at elections.

Reform remade politics, and politics remade public discourse. So too did American nationalism and economic cycles. As did reformers, President Adams raised expectations about an expanded governmental role. The organized parties of the 1820s and the struggles between the National Republicans and the Democrats, then between the Democrats and the Whigs, stimulated even greater interest in campaigns and political issues. The Democrats, who rallied around Andrew Jackson, and Jackson's opponents, who found shelter under the Whig tent, competed almost equally for the loyalty of voters. Both parties built strong organizations that faced off in national and local elections. And both parties favored economic expansion. Their world-views, however, were fundamentally different. Whigs were more optimistic and favored greater centralized government initiative. Democrats harbored a deep-seated belief in limited government. The controversies over the Second Bank of the United States and nullification allowed Americans to debate the principles of the republic. Jackson, however, did not hesitate to use presidential authority, and his opponents called him King Andrew.

Many Americans had caught the fever of expansionism. Euro-Americans wanted to colonize the continent, farmers sought land, slaveholders wished to extend slavery, and millions itched to move westward. The admission of Texas into the Union in 1845 seemed to fulfill one destiny—expansion—but brought divisiveness as well as the nation increasingly divided over the issue of slavery.

LEGACY FOR A PEOPLE AND A NATION
The Bible Belt

Had an eighteenth-century visitor to North America asked for the Bible belt, she would have been directed to New England, whose colonies were all founded for religious purposes. Early southerners tended to be more secular than religious. By the 1830s, however, the South was the most churched region, and southerners were the most devout. The Second Great Awakening, beginning with the Cane Ridge revival in 1801, spread like wildfire through the South. By the 1830s more than half of white and one-quarter of black southerners had undergone a conversion experience, and religion and the South formed a common identity. Embracing the Bible as the revealed word of God, the South became known as the Bible belt.

Religion helped define southern distinctiveness. Southern Protestant liturgy and cadences were as much African as European; thus southern and northern denominations grew apart. They formally separated in the 1840s when Southern Baptists and Methodists withdrew from the national organizations that had barred slaveowners from church offices. Presbyterians withdrew later. After the Civil War, evangelical denominations remained divided in northern and southern organizations.

Southern religion maintained tradition and resisted modern ways. Protestantism dominated, making the South more religiously homogeneous than other regions. Mostly evangelical, southern religion emphasized conversion and a personal battle against sin. By the twentieth century, fundamentalism, which stressed a literal reading of the Bible, reinforced resistance to modernism. Yet southern Protestantism lost ground as a political force in opposing evolution and in alliances with nativist, anti-immigrant groups.

But evangelicalism rose again in the 1960s, especially after a Catholic—John F. Kennedy—won the Democratic nomination for president. Many evangelicals began to vote their religion, moving to the Republican Party, and in 1964 Republican Barry Goldwater won the Bible belt states, breaking up the solid Democratic block. His conservative rhetoric resonated with southerners concerned about desegregation and erosion of religious values. *Time* called 1976 the "Year of the Evangelical" when born-again Southern Baptist Jimmy Carter was elected president.

In the 1980s and 1990s the Bible belt became the base of mobilized evangelical political action led by the Moral Majority. Religious and cultural issues rallied southern evangelicals: defending the traditional family, advocating prayer in schools, and opposing abortion, the Equal Rights Amendment, and gay rights legislation. In their own eyes, fundamentalist evangelical Protestants were defending biblical principles.

Thus the revivals that began in Kentucky in 1801 have rippled in ever wider circles across the South for two centuries, shaping the distinctive southern blend of culture and politics.

PEOPLE AND COMMUNITIES IN THE NORTH AND WEST 1830–1860

*a*t eight o'clock on a snowy St. Patrick's Day morning in Lowell, Massachusetts, in 1841, more than one hundred members of the Irish Benevolent Society pinned on large green and white flowers as they and a brass band prepared to march through the mill town. Across the United States—in Boston, New York, Philadelphia, Charleston, New Orleans, St. Louis— and around the world in Ireland, England, Canada, Argentina, and Australia, Irish settlers and their descendants expressed their Irish pride by celebrating.

St. Patrick's Day celebrations meant many things to different people. In colonial America, mostly Scots-Irish Protestants toasted Ireland and their mother country Britain at banquets. In the 1760s, in probably the first St. Patrick's Day parade in America, Irish Protestant soldiers in the British army marched with local residents in New York City. After the War of 1812, the ban- queters and marchers, mostly middle-class Irish, represented charities, and they raised money to assist immigrants. New arrivals were mostly Catholic, and the parades and banquets brought together Catholics and Protestants.

But events in Ireland made the American Irish community increasingly Catholic. A failed revolution against Britain in 1798, inspired by the American and French Revolutions, and the 1800 Act of Union, which merged Ireland into the United Kingdom, eliminated the Irish Parliament and disfranchised Catholics, making them powerless. Declining farm sizes and a population explosion made them impoverished. When Alexis de Tocqueville visited Ireland in 1835, four years after his trip to the United States, the contrast stunned him. "You cannot imagine," he wrote his father from Ireland, "what a complexity of miseries five centuries of oppression and disorders and religious hostility have piled up on this poor people."

While many struggled in Ireland for equal rights and economic survival, others left their country. In England, industrial Manchester and London offered

◀ New Yorkers celebrated St. Patrick's Day Parade in 1853, during the peak period of Irish immigration. Led by the mayor, the crowd reviewed the militia and the parading Irish marchers. Spectators came from all classes, including ordinary folk like the woman and child fruit sellers in the foreground. (Culver Pictures)

CHRONOLOGY

1827 • *Freedom's Journal,* first African American newspaper, appears

1830 • Smith founds Mormon Church
• First National Negro Convention

1830s–50s • Urban riots commonplace

1832 • Rice debuts in New York minstrel show

1835 • Arkansas passes first women's property law

1837 • Emerson delivers "The American Scholar" address
• Boston employs paid policemen

1837–48 • Mann heads the Massachusetts Board of Education

1838 • Mormons driven out of Missouri

1841–47 • Brook Farm combines spirituality, work, and play in a utopian rural community

1842 • Knickerbocker baseball club formed

1844 • Nativist riots peak in Philadelphia
• Smith brothers murdered in Illinois

1845 • Irish potato blight begins
• *Narrative of the Life of Frederick Douglass* appears

1846–47 • Mormon trek to the Great Salt Lake

1847–57 • Immigration at peak pre–Civil War levels

1848 • Abortive revolution in German states
• United States acquires Alta California in Treaty of Guadalupe Hidalgo
• Gold discovered in California

1849 • California gold rush transforms the West Coast

1852 • Stowe's *Uncle Tom's Cabin* published

1854 • Railroad reaches the Mississippi River
• Large-scale Chinese immigration begins
• Germans replace Irish as largest group of new arrivals

1855 • New York establishes Castle Garden as immigrant center

jobs, but more distant America offered political and religious freedom as well as economic opportunities. To the Irish, the United States offered the best hope.

Thus, in the 1820s and 1830s, in Lowell and elsewhere, St. Patrick's Day increasingly became identified with Irish Catholics. As a Catholic holiday, parades became more important than the banquets; recent immigrants were poorer, and they could not pay for banquets. But parades were an opportunity to express their solidarity as well as their appreciation for America. They marched against the British and its established Anglican Church, and for equal rights in Ireland. Increasingly they wore red, white, and blue as well as green, to demonstrate their identity. Both Americans and the Irish had suffered, they pointed out, from British tyranny. St. Patrick's Day speakers reminded audiences that "republicanism" was both an American and Irish principle. In 1837, on St. Patrick's Day, Dr. William James McNeven, who had been imprisoned following the 1798 insurrection, told his New York audience that the Irish sought only the rights Americans already possessed. Editor Thomas O'Connor, who described himself as an "Irishman by birth" and an "American by adoption," toasted "America as she is, Ireland as she ought to be." St. Patrick's Day linked American and Irish causes.

But increasingly American Irish Protestants stayed away from such events. They identified with Britain, not the Irish opposition. In the 1820s they began to skip St. Patrick's Day parades and march on July 12, commemorating English ascendancy—the victory of William of Orange in the Battle of the Boyne in 1690. They purposefully distanced themselves from the new immigrants, becoming Whigs while the new immigrants gravitated to Andrew Jackson. Then, in the 1840s and 1850s, as potato blight and famine stalked Ireland, nearly 2 million Irish immigrants—almost all Catholics—arrived in the United States. Now St. Patrick's Day marches attracted not hundreds but thousands, and nativists jeered the marchers, occasionally assaulting them. By the 1850s contingents of police had to accompany the paraders to protect them.

The huge Irish immigration was only part of a worldwide population movement. From the 1830s through the 1850s, millions of Europeans arrived on America's shores.

Immigration added to the rapidly growing population and transformed the American nation. Within large cities and in the countryside, whole districts became ethnic and religious enclaves.

What it meant to be an American was changing. The Revolution and early years of nation building diminished as sources of American identity. The cultural traditions of European immigrants differed from those in the American colonial past, and increasingly some white Americans came to see the differences as racial rather than cultural. Black Americans became racial outsiders, as did Hispanics in the Southwest. In a society growing ever more diverse and complex, conflict became common.

The market economy both energized and accentuated the differences among Americans. In the nation's cities, opulent mansions rose within sight of notorious slums, and both wealth and poverty reached extremes unknown in the countryside. Ethnicity, race, religion, and class divided Americans as well. Farm families attempted to maintain cohesive, rural villages, while utopians and groups like the Mormons sought to create self-governing communal havens.

The market economy altered family life too. As commerce and industry grew, the home lost its function as a workplace. Goods formerly made at home were now mass-manufactured in factories and bought in stores. Public schools took over much of the family's traditional role as prime educator. Leisure became a commodity to be purchased by those who could afford it. Families shrank in size, and more people lived outside family units. In the North and West, urban growth and immigration challenged economic and social conventions. ■

Country Life

Rural life changed significantly in the first half of the nineteenth century. Farm population in the coastal states declined as towns grew and manufacturing expanded. Farm families—native-born whites, blacks, and immigrants—sought more fertile and cheaper land in the West. Market-oriented communities arose there, linked to eastern markets by the new transportation networks. But not all accepted the market economy. The religious fervor of the Second Great Awakening inspired some to seek spiritual regeneration, rather than cash-crop profits, through the establishment of utopian communities.

In the 1850s, western settlement, technological improvements, competition, economic recovery, and a desire for national unity prompted development of regional and, eventually, national rail networks. By 1853 rail lines linked eastern cities to Chicago, and a year later track reached the Mississippi River. By 1860 rails stretched as far west as St. Joseph, Missouri, as railroad track tripled during the 1850s, reaching 30,600 miles in 1860.

RAILROAD LINKS

The railroad depot and post office in the farm village linked farmers with the world. But in these villages, with their churches, general stores, and taverns, communal values still ruled. Families gathered on one another's farms to accomplish as a community what they could not manage individually. Barn-raisings regularly brought people together. A farm family with the help of an itinerant carpenter would prepare the walls. The neighbors would come by buggy to help the family raise walls into position and build a roof. Afterward everyone celebrated with a hearty communal feast and sang, danced, and played games. They might compete in foot races, wrestling, or marksmanship, and on occasion they raced horses. Similar gatherings took place at harvest time and on special occasions.

FARM COMMUNITIES

Farm men and women had active social lives. Men met frequently at general stores, weekly markets, and taverns, and hunted and fished together. Some women also attended market, especially those engaged in dairy farming. More typically they met at after-church dinners, prayer groups, sewing and corn-husking bees, and quilting parties. These were cherished opportunities to exchange experiences, thoughts, and spiritual support, and to swap letters, books, and news.

Irene Hardy, who grew up in rural Ohio in the 1840s, left a memoir of the gatherings she had attended as a girl. Fifty years later she recalled apple bees at which neighbors gathered to make apple butter or preserves. After the day's work, Hardy remembered, the elders gossiped while the youngsters joked and teased each other and flirted. "Then came supper, apple and pumpkin pies, cider, doughnuts, cakes, cold chicken and turkey," Hardy wrote, "after which games, 'Forfeits,' 'Building a Bridge,' 'Snatchability,' even 'Blind Man's Bluff' and 'Pussy Wants a Corner.'" Traditional country bees had their town counterparts. Fredrika Bremer, a Swedish visitor, described a sewing bee in Cambridge, Massachusetts, in 1849, at which neighborhood women made clothes for

BEES

■ *The Lackawanna Valley* (1855) by George Inness. Hired by the Lackawanna Railroad to paint a picture showing the company's new roundhouse at Scranton, in northeastern Pennsylvania, Inness combined landscape and locomotive technology into an organic whole. Industrialism, Inness seems to say, belonged to the American landscape; it would neither overpower nor obliterate the land.
(Gift of Mrs. Huttleston Rogers, © 1996 Board of Trustees, National Gallery of Art, Washington, D.C.)

"a family who had lost all their clothing by fire." Yet town bees were not the all-day family affairs of the countryside, and when the Hardy family moved to Eaton, Ohio, Irene missed the country gatherings. The families of Eaton seldom held bees; instead, they purchased the goods country people made. They were wage earners and consumers, and the market economy shaped and controlled their daily lives.

Most Americans came to accept these changes as inevitable, but some tried to resist. One opposition path was to restore traditional work tasks and social cohesion by living in rural utopian communities. Some groups, like the Shakers, had originated in eighteenth-century Europe, while others, like the Mormons, arose in the wake of the religious ferment of the Second Great Awakening (see pages 273–274). What they shared in common was a commitment to rural communal living as members experimented with innovative (sometimes shocking) family arrangements and more egalitarian gender roles in a cooperative rather than competitive environment.

The Shakers, the largest of the communal utopian experiments, reached their peak between 1820 and 1860.

SHAKERS

In those years six thousand members lived in twenty settlements in eight states. Shaker communities emphasized agriculture and handcrafts; most managed to become self-sufficient and profitable enterprises. Shaker furniture became famous for its simplicity, beauty of design, and excellent construction. The community's craft tradition contrasted with the new factory regime.

But the Shakers were essentially a spiritual community. Founded in England in 1736 by Mother Ann Lee, they got their name from their worship service, which included singing and dancing. Ann Lee's children had died in infancy, and she believed that their deaths were retribution for her sin of intercourse; thus she advocated celibacy. After imprisonment in England in 1773–1774, she fulfilled a vision by settling in America.

In religious practice and social relations, Shakers offered an alternative to changes in urban and rural life. Shakers lived communally, abolishing individual families. Leadership tended to be in the hands of women. The settlements, however, depended on constant enlistment of new recruits, not only because the practice of celibacy meant that they could not reproduce themselves but also because most members only stayed a short time. Many Shaker settlements became temporary refuges for orphans, runaways, abused wives, and unemployed workers during hard times. And some families found themselves unsuited to communal living. Those who were not committed to the Shakers' spiritual message also moved on. In the middle of the nineteenth century, Shaker communities began a slow but steady decline.

The Church of Jesus Christ of Latter-day Saints, whose members were known as the Mormons, was the most

MORMONS successful communitarian experiment, and it, like the Shakers, restructured family life. During the religious ferment of the 1820s in western New York, Joseph Smith, a young farmer, reported that an angel called Moroni had given him divine engraved gold plates. Smith published his revelations as the *Book of Mormon* and organized a church in 1830. The next year the community moved west to Ohio to build a "New Jerusalem" and await the second coming of Jesus.

But angry mobs drove the Mormons from Ohio, and they settled in Missouri. There, too, the Mormons' rapid growth created antagonism, as did their claim that only Mormons would be saved upon Jesus' return. Anti-Mormons charged that Mormonism was fraudulent, a scam by Joseph Smith. Opponents also feared Mormon political power. In 1838 the governor of Missouri charged Smith with fomenting insurrection and gathered evidence to indict him and other leaders for treason.

Smith and his followers resettled in Nauvoo, Illinois. The state legislature gave them a city charter that made them self-governing and authorized a local militia. But again the community met antagonism, especially after Smith introduced the practice of polygamy in 1841, allowing men to have several wives at once. The next year Smith became mayor, and this consolidation of religious and political power, as well as Nauvoo's petition to the federal government to be a self-governing territory, further antagonized opponents, who now included some

former Mormons. After Smith and his brother were charged with treason and jailed, and then murdered, the Mormons left Illinois to seek security in the wilderness. In the Great Salt Lake valley, in the unorganized territory of Utah, they established a patriarchal, cooperative "community of saints." Now led by Brigham Young, they achieved religious freedom and political autonomy.

In Utah the Mormons distributed agricultural land according to family size. An extensive irrigation system, constructed by men who contributed their labor in proportion to the quantity of land they received and the amount of water they expected to use, transformed the arid valley into a rich oasis. As the colony developed, the church elders gained control of water, trade, industry, and eventually the territorial government of Utah.

Religious conviction fortified the Latter-day Saints to withstand persecution. The Mormons offered success and community in this world and salvation in the next to anyone who would join. Indeed, many recruits were poor and uneducated. To those who rejected existing churches, the Mormons also offered fellowship and religious certainty within a tight-knit society and cooperative economic system.

Not all utopian communities sought wilderness. Brook Farm cooperative in West Roxbury, Massachusetts, near

■ Violence stalked the Mormons until they found safety in the Great Salt Lake valley. Here a Mormon family—a father, three wives, and five children—poses for a photographer in the 1850s in Salt Lake City. (Church of Jesus Christ of Latter-Day Saints)

BROOK FARM   Boston, had a lasting impact although its achievements were more artistic than economic. Inspired by transcendentalism—the belief that the physical world is secondary to the spiritual realm, which human beings can reach not by custom and experience but only by intuition—Brook Farm's members rejected materialism. Their rural communalism combined spirituality, manual labor, intellectual life, and play. Founded in 1841 by the Unitarian minister George Ripley, a literary critic and friend of transcendentalist lecturer and essayist Ralph Waldo Emerson, Brook Farm attracted farmers, craftsmen, and writers, among them the novelist Nathaniel Hawthorne. Indeed, the fame of Brook Farm rested on the intellectual achievements of its members. Its school drew students from outside the community, and its residents contributed regularly to the *Dial*, the leading transcendentalist journal. In 1845 Brook Farm's hundred members organized themselves into model phalanxes (working-living units) suggested by French utopian Charles Fourier. Rigid regimentation replaced individualism, and membership dropped. After a disastrous fire in 1846, the experiment collapsed in 1847.

Though short-lived, Brook Farm played a significant role in the flowering of a national literature. During these years Hawthorne, Emerson, and *Dial*

AMERICAN
RENAISSANCE   editor Margaret Fuller joined Henry David Thoreau, Herman Melville, and others in a literary outpouring known today as the American Renaissance. In philosophical intensity and moral idealism, their work was both distinctively American and an outgrowth of the European romantic movement. Their themes were universal, their settings and characters American. Hawthorne, for instance, used Puritan New England as a backdrop, and Melville wrote of great spiritual quests as seafaring adventures.

The essayist Ralph Waldo Emerson was the prime mover of the American Renaissance and a pillar of the transcendental movement. Emerson had followed his father and grandfather into the ministry but quit his Boston Unitarian pulpit in 1831. After a two-year sojourn in Europe, he returned to lecture and write, preaching individualism and self-reliance. "We live in succession, in division, in parts, in particles," Emerson wrote. "We see the world piece by piece, as the sun, the moon, the animal, the tree; but the whole, of which these are the shining parts, is the soul." Intuitive experience of God is attainable, insisted Emerson, because "the Highest dwells" within every individual in the form of the "Over-soul." What gave Emerson's writings force was,

for his times, a simple, direct prose. In his first book, *Nature* (1836), and in "The American Scholar" (1837), a Phi Beta Kappa address at Harvard, Emerson explored human nature and American culture. Widely admired, he influenced Thoreau, Fuller, Hawthorne, and other members of Brook Farm.

Whether intellectual, spiritual, or economic in their origins, utopian communities can be seen as attempts to recapture the cohesiveness of traditional agricultural and artisan life in the face of the competitive pressures of the market economy and urbanization. Utopians resembled Puritan perfectionists; like the Separatists of seventeenth-century New England (see pages 49–50), they sought to begin anew in their own colonies.

The West

In the 1840s a trickling stream of migrants followed the Oregon Trail to the West Coast. Then, in 1848, gold was discovered in California. The next year a pioneer observed that the Oregon Trail "bore no evidence of having been much traveled." Traffic flowed south instead, and California drew population to the Pacific slope. One measure of this shift was the overland mail routes. In the 1840s the Oregon Trail had been the main communications link between the Midwest and the Pacific. Ten years later the post office routes terminated in California, not Oregon; in fact, in the 1850s there was no mail route north of Sacramento.

When the United States acquired Alta California from Mexico in the 1848 Treaty of Guadalupe Hidalgo

GOLD RUSH   (see page 358), the province was inhabited mostly by Indians, with some Mexicans living on large estates. A chain of small settlements surrounded military forts (*presidios*) and missions. That changed almost overnight after James Marshall, a carpenter, spotted gold particles in the millrace at Sutter's Mill (now Coloma, California, northwest of Sacramento) in January 1848. Word of the discovery spread, and Californians rushed to scrabble for instant fortunes. When the military explorer John C. Frémont reached San Francisco five months later, he found that "all its male inhabitants had gone to the mines." The town, "which a few months before was so busy and thriving, was then almost deserted."

By 1849 the news had sped around the world, and hundreds of thousands of fortune seekers, mostly young men, streamed in from Mexico, England, Germany, France, Ireland, and from all over the United States, including some African Americans. They mined the lodes

Gold in California

When James Marshall discovered gold in Sutter's Mill, California, in January 1848, word spread quickly—and quite literally around the world. Hundreds of millions of people thus learned of California for the first time. Within a year tens of thousands of adventurers from other countries had rushed to California, the new "land of opportunity." Soon it was as cosmopolitan as any other American place.

In an era before the telegraph crossed the oceans, it is surprising how fast the news traveled. Mexicans heard of the gold strike first. Next word spread to Chile, Peru, and throughout South America; then across the Pacific to Hawai'i, China, and Australia; and then to Europe—Ireland, France, and the German states. How did the news travel? Overland travelers brought the news south to Baja California and Sonora in Mexico. By spring 1849 some six thousand Mexicans were panning for gold around the newly established town of Sonora, California. Many of the Mexicans came north seasonally to seek gold, spreading news of California on every trip home.

Sailing ships brought news of California gold to Hawai'i. The newspaper *Honolulu Polynesian* announced it in the kingdom on June 24, 1848. "Honolulu has never before witnessed such an excitement as the gold fever has created," the *Polynesian* reported later that summer. Gold seekers and merchants sailed from Hawai'i to California, and their letters home recruited others to come. The constant traffic led to the introduction of regular steamship service between Hawai'i and California as early as 1853.

A ship brought news of California gold discoveries to Valparaiso, Chile, in August 1848. More dramatically, a few weeks later, another sailing vessel landed with $2,500 in gold dust aboard. Although Chilean newspapers initially ignored the discovery, the people in Chile's cities talked about nothing but gold. By November the newspapers were reporting rumors of overnight riches in California. Before the end of the year, two thousand Chileans had left for California, and many Chilean merchants opened branch stores in San Francisco.

Word of gold and California reached Australia in December 1848. Gold seekers quickly made travel arrangements, and by 1850 every ship in Sydney harbor was destined for California. News had already reached China in mid-1848. A San Francisco merchant headed for the gold fields, Chum Ming, had written a cousin about his hopes for wealth. Four months later the cousin arrived in San Francisco, with fellow villagers he had recruited. After the upheavals of the Taiping Revolution in 1850, Chinese migration soared. By the mid-1850s, one in five gold miners was Chinese.

Californians, new and old, foreign and native-born, expressed amazement at the ethnic variety. One described it as "the most curious Babel of a place imaginable." In 1850 the new state of California had nearly 40 percent foreign-born inhabitants, the majority non-European. Through word of mouth, rumor, letters home, and newspaper reports, the discovery of gold in 1848 linked California to millions of ordinary people around the globe.

This 1855 Frank Marryat drawing of a San Francisco saloon dramatizes the international nature of the California gold rush. Like theater performers, the patrons of the saloon dress their parts as Yankees, Mexicans, Asians, and South Americans. (© Collection of the New York Historical Society)

and washed away the surface soil with hydraulic works, leaving the land unsuitable for anything after they abandoned it.

Gold mining seemed to offer instant riches, and indeed, some made fortunes. In 1848 a California male servant earned $2,000 mining for gold and returned to Monterey a rich man. Peter Brown, a black man from Ste. Genevieve, Missouri, went to California alone, as did most "forty-niners." He wrote his wife in 1851 that "California is the best country in the world to make money. It is also the best place for black folks on the globe." He had earned $300 in two months.

Most forty-niners, however, never found enough gold to pay their expenses. "The stories you hear frequently in the States," one gold seeker wrote home, "are the most extravagant lies imaginable—the mines are a humbug." Another gold seeker called gold mining "Nature's Great Lottery scheme." Many found work in California's cities and agricultural districts more profitable. Meanwhile, enterprising merchants rushed to supply, feed, and clothe the new settlers. One such merchant was Levi Strauss, a German Jewish immigrant, whose tough mining pants found a ready market among the prospectors.

San Francisco, the former *presidio* and mission of Yerba Buena, had in 1848 been a small settlement of about a thousand Mexicans, Anglos, soldiers, friars, and Indians. As the West Coast gateway to the interior, it became an instant city, ballooning to thirty-five thousand people in 1850. Ships bringing people and supplies continuously jammed the harbor. A French visitor in that year wrote, "At San Francisco, where fifteen months ago one found only a half dozen large cabins, one finds today a stock exchange, a theater, churches of all Christian cults, and a large number of quite beautiful homes."

The forty-niners had their eyes on gold nuggets, but they had to be fed. Thus began the great California agricultural boom. Farmers preferred wheat; it required minimal investment, was easily planted, and offered a quick return at the end of a relatively short growing season. California farmers eagerly imported horse-drawn machines, since labor was scarce (and expensive). By the mid-1850s, California exported wheat and had become firmly linked, through commerce, to the rest of the United States. Farmers on the West Coast cleared the land and constructed log cabins. Success often depended on their access to water, and they sought to divert the streams and rivers of the West to irrigate their land.

FARMERS

In contrast to the Midwest, where family farms were the basic unit of production, in California men dominated mining, grazing, and large-scale wheat farming.

Most men came alone, drawn by a sense of adventure and personal opportunity. Women who accompanied their husbands—only one-seventh of the travelers on the overland trails were women—experienced migration differently. Their lives drastically changed as they left behind networks of friends and kin to journey, often with children, along an unknown and hazardous path to a strange environment. Yet in the West their domestic skills were in great demand. They received high fees for cooking, laundering, and sewing, and they ran boarding houses and hotels (men shunned domestic work).

City Life

Irish and other European immigrants and rural migrants made cities, especially northern ones, expand geometrically. The nation's population increased during this period from 12.9 million to 31.4 million. Europeans spread westward, and small rural settlements quickly became towns. In 1830 the nation had only 23 cities with 10,000 or more people and only 7 with more than 25,000. By 1860, 93 towns exceeded 10,000, 35 towns had more than 25,000, and 9 exceeded 100,000 (see Map 12.1). The Northeast was most heavily urban, and the percentage of people living in urban areas there grew from 14 to 35 percent between 1830 and 1860.

Some cities became great metropolitan centers. By 1830 New York City had been the nation's most populous city and major commercial center for twenty years. At midcentury, Baltimore and New Orleans dominated the South, and San Francisco was the leading West Coast city. In the Midwest, the new lake cities (Chicago, Detroit, and Cleveland) began to pass the frontier river cities (Cincinnati, Louisville, and Pittsburgh) founded a generation earlier. The largest cities of the North anchored a nationwide network linked by canals, roads, railroads, and the telegraph (see Chapter 10).

As the nation's premier city, New York grew from 202,000 people in 1830 to over 814,000 in 1860. The immigrant port city was mostly Irish and German by the 1850s. Across the East River, Brooklyn tripled in size between 1850 and 1860, becoming the nation's third-largest city, with a population of 279,000. Many people were short-term residents of the two cities; the majority did not stay ten years. Thus New York was ever changing, full of energy, reeking of sweat, horse dung, and garbage—and above all, teeming with people.

NEW YORK CITY

New York City literally had burst its boundaries around 1830. Until then New Yorkers could walk from

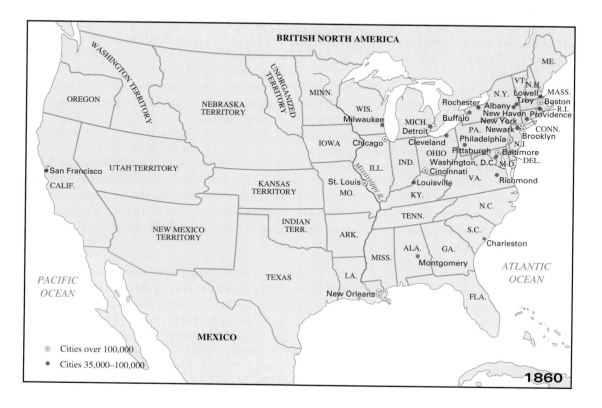

Map 12.1

Major American Cities in 1830 and 1860

The number of Americans who lived in cities increased rapidly between 1830 and 1860, and the number of large cities grew as well. In 1830 only New York City had a population exceeding one hundred thousand; thirty years later, eight more cities had surpassed that level.

one end to the other in an hour. In 1825, 14th Street was the city's northern boundary. By 1860, 400,000 people lived above that divide, and 42nd Street was the city's northern limit. Gone were the cow pastures, kitchen gardens, and orchards of the eighteenth century. George Templeton Strong, a New York lawyer, recorded in his diary in 1856 that he had attended a party on 37th Street: "It seems but the other day that thirty-seventh Street was an imaginary line running through a rural district and grazed over by cows." Mass transit made city expansion possible. Horse-drawn omnibuses appeared in New York in 1827, and the Harlem Railroad, completed in 1832, ran the length of Manhattan. By the 1850s all big cities had horse-drawn streetcars.

By modern standards nineteenth-century cities were disorderly, unsafe, and unhealthy. Expansion occurred so

URBAN PROBLEMS

rapidly that few cities could handle the problems it brought. For example, migrants from rural areas were accustomed to relieving themselves outside and throwing refuse in vacant areas. In the city, such waste smelled, spread disease, and polluted water. New York City partially solved the problem in the 1840s by abandoning wells in favor of reservoir water piped into buildings and outdoor fountains. In some districts, scavengers and refuse collectors carted away garbage and human waste, but in much of the city it just rotted on the ground. Only one-quarter of New York City's streets had sewers by 1857.

Cities lacked adequate taxing power to provide services for all. The best cities could do was to tax property adjoining new sewers, paved streets, and water mains. Thus new services and basic sanitation depended on residents' ability to pay. As a result, those most in need of services got them last. Another solution was to charter private companies to sell basic services. This plan worked well with gas service used for lights. Baltimore first chartered a private gas company in 1816; New York did so in 1842. By midcentury every major city was lit by a private gas supplier. The private sector, however, failed to supply the water the cities needed. Private firms lacked the capital to build adequate systems, and they laid pipe only in commercial and well-to-do residential areas, ignoring the poor. As population grew, city governments had to take over.

Cities led in offering public education. In 1800 only New England had public education; by 1860 every state offered some public education to whites.

HORACE MANN AND PUBLIC SCHOOLS

Under Horace Mann, secretary of the state board of education from 1837 to 1848, Massachusetts led the way. It established a minimum school year of six months and formalized the training of teachers.

Mann, an evangelist for public education and school reform, advocated free, state-sponsored education. "If we do not prepare children to become good citizens," Mann argued, "if we do not develop their capacities, imbue their hearts with the love of truth and duty, and a reverence for all things sacred and holy, then our republic must go down to destruction." Universal education, Mann proposed, would end misery and crime. Mann and others responded to the changes wrought by the market economy, urbanization, and immigration. The typical city dweller was a newcomer, whether from abroad or from the country. Public schools would take the children of strangers and give them shared values. But the system was distinctly racialized; few states included free black children in public schools.

Free public schools altered the scope of education. Schooling previously had focused on literacy, religious training, and discipline. Under Mann's leadership, the curriculum became more secular and appropriate for future American clerks, farmers, and workers. Students studied geography, American history, arithmetic, and science. Schools retained moral education, but they dropped direct religious indoctrination. Nonetheless, primers like *McGuffey's Eclectic Readers* still used Protestant Scripture to teach children to accept their positions in society. A good child, *McGuffey* taught, does not envy the rich: "It is God who makes some poor and others rich." *McGuffey* further preached that "the rich have troubles which we know nothing of; and . . . the poor, if they are good, may be very happy."

Catholics, immigrants, blacks, and workers sought to control their own schools, but the state legislatures established secular statewide standards under Protestant educators. Catholics in New York responded by building their own educational system over the next half-century. When Los Angeles became a city in 1850, it attempted to establish bilingual Spanish-English instruction. Trained bilingual teachers could not be found, however, and when the schools opened, they offered only English instruction.

Towns and cities created new patterns of leisure as well as work. In rural society, as Irene Hardy recalled,

LEISURE

social activities and work often took place at home. But in cities, dedicated spaces—streets, theaters, sports fields—constituted a public sphere for people to socialize. Through the sale of admission tickets or membership in associations, leisure became a commodity to be purchased. As the population became more diverse, leisure associations reflected ethnic, racial, and class divisions.

Traditional rural pursuits continued in the city. Men frequented taverns and spent spare time drinking and playing games of skill and strength—arm wrestling, ninepins, and pitching coins. Though city dwellers had less opportunity than their rural counterparts to ride and hunt, fishing remained popular among both men and women. Churches continued to serve as social centers, and the Second Great Awakening increased women's involvement. Church clubs combined socializing with good works.

Americans read more too. Thanks to the expansion of public education, the vast majority of native-born white Americans were literate by the 1850s. In cities, urban newspapers and magazines proliferated and bookstores spread. Power printing presses and better transportation made possible wide distribution of books and periodicals. The religious press—of both traditional sects and dissenters—produced pamphlets, hymnals, Bibles, and religious newspapers. Americans also read secular publications. Newspapers and magazines—political organs, literary journals, and the voices of specialized groups like mill workers—abounded in the 1830s and after. In Brookfield, Massachusetts, in 1798, the mails brought one weekly newspaper; fifty years later, in 1848, the post office delivered to subscribers fifty different newspapers and fifty-five monthly magazines.

READING

Fiction and autobiographies competed with religious tracts as popular literature. Newspapers and magazines printed fiction, and bookstores and stationers in large cities sold novels and autobiographies. Frederick Douglass's powerful attack on slavery in the *Narrative of the Life of Frederick Douglass, an American Slave, Written by Himself* (1845) sold widely. Many popular novels, some written by women, often for women, were set in the home and upheld Christian values. They reflected growing gender differences in American society in their exploration of the divisions between home and work, between emotion and authority, and between sentimentality and power. Yet in their support of traditional female moral roles, they also can be read as a challenge to prevailing values. Although Susan Warner's *The Wide, Wide, Wide World* (1850), Nathaniel Hawthorne's *The House of the Seven Gables* (1851), and Fanny Fern's *Ruth Hall* (1855) did not challenge women's traditional domestic roles, they gave women a special moral bearing. In giving a positive cast to notions of community and republican virtue, they implicitly criticized the growing market economy. By the 1850s popular fiction circulated widely. Harriet Beecher Stowe's antislavery novel, *Uncle Tom's Cabin, or Life Among the Lowly* (1852),

which appeared serially in 1851–1852, sold 300,000 copies in book form in its first year.

A major attraction, theater provided a social sphere in which both men and women gathered. A theater was often the second public building constructed in a town—after a church. Large cities boasted two or more theaters catering to different classes. In New York City the Park Theater enjoyed the patronage of the carriage trade, the Bowery drew the middle class, and the Chatham attracted workers. Some plays cut across class lines. Shakespeare was performed so often and appreciated so widely that even illiterate theatergoers knew his plays well. In the 1840s musical and dramatic presentations took on a more professional tone; like the Hutchinson Family (see pages 239–240), newly popular minstrel shows and traveling circuses offered carefully rehearsed routines. Dancing and music remained popular and took new forms, as in blackfaced minstrelsy.

THEATER

By the 1840s hundreds of traveling minstrel troupes performed a complete evening's entertainment in American theaters. Minstrel acts had first appeared two decades earlier, when white men, in burnt-cork makeup, imitated African Americans in song, dance, and patter. In the early 1830s Thomas D. Rice of New York became famous for his role as Jim Crow, an old southern slave. In ill-fitting patched clothing and torn shoes, the blackface Rice shuffled, danced, and sang on stage. Another stereotyped image soon joined him: Zip Coon, a black Bowery Boy. What minstrels presented was a European version of African American culture.

MINSTREL SHOWS

Minstrelsy combined contradictory elements. At one level, performers masked as people of color told jokes mocking economic and political elites. At the same time the actors stereotyped black people by exaggerating physical features. They also presented blacks as sensual and lazy, thus stoking the fires of racism with ridicule. In blending black culture with white humor, African dance with English folk tunes, and the African banjo with the Irish fiddle, minstrelsy seemed to represent the new urban potpourri. In portraying foils to sexual purity and work discipline, minstrelsy also constituted a resistance to the moral demands and factory regimens of the era. Ultimately, minstrelsy furthered growing racial divisions in the United States. The fictional representation of blacks on stage not only defined "blackness" but also defined "whiteness." Whiteness as a racial category took on meaning as laughing white audiences distinguished themselves from the black characters.

■ Thomas D. Rice playing "Jim Crow" in blackface at the Bowery Theater in New York City, 1833. The rowdy audience climbed on to the stage, leaving Rice little room to perform. In representing African Americans on stage, Rice and other minstrels contributed to establishing both black and white as racial categories.   (© Collection of the New York Historical Society)

Increasingly, urban recreation and sports became more formal commodities to be purchased. One had to buy a ticket to go to the theater, the circus, P. T. Barnum's American Museum in New York City, the racetrack, or the ballpark. Spectator sports surged. From 1831 enthusiasts could read the all-sports newspaper, *Spirit of the Times*. By 1849 news of boxing was so much in demand that a round-by-round account of a Maryland boxing match was telegraphed throughout the East. Horseracing, walking races, and, in the 1850s, baseball began to attract large urban male crowds.

SPORTS

Organized leagues replaced spontaneity. A group of Wall Street office workers formed the Knickerbocker Club in 1842 and in 1845 drew up rules for the game of baseball. Their rules were widely adopted and continue to serve as the basis for the game.

Ironically, public leisure soon developed a private dimension. Exclusive private clubs and associations provided space and occasions for leisure apart from the crowds and rowdiness in the public sphere. As cities grew, their pop-

CITY CULTURE

ulations seemed increasingly fragmented. Finding people similar to oneself required more of a conscious effort. The new associations that evolved served as a bulwark against the cultures of other groups—immigrants, migrants, blacks, and artisans. Middle- and upper-class New Yorkers who felt alienated in the city of their birth joined exclusive clubs. Some joined the Masonic order, which offered everything the bustling, chaotic city did not: an elaborate hierarchy, an orderly code of deference between ranks, harmony, and shared values. Members knew one another. Masons played a political role as well: they recruited officeholders and marched in the parades that were a regular feature of the city's life.

Ethnic, racial, and religious groups shared traditions in their own clubs and societies. The Irish formed the Hibernian Society and the Sons of Erin; Germans brought Turnvereine physical-cultural clubs from across the Atlantic; Jews founded B'nai B'rith as a men's club; and African Americans had chapters of the Prince Hall Masons in their communities. Women, too, organized their own associations, ranging from literary clubs to benevolent societies. Americans of all sorts—native- and foreign-born, black and white—also formed churches and church-associated clubs. Associations brought together like people, but they also formalized divisions.

Divisions seemed to occur naturally on city streets. In the 1840s, a youth culture developed on the Bowery, one of New York's entertainment strips. In the evenings the lamp-lit promenade, lined with theaters, dance halls, and cafés, became an urban midway. Older New Yorkers feared the "Bowery boys and gals," whose ostentatious dress and behavior seemed threatening to them. Around 1847 artist Nicholino Calyo depicted three Bowery boys in a watercolor painting (see below). A Bowery boy had long hair, often greased into a roll. He wore a broad-brimmed black hat, an open shirt collar, a black frock coat that reached below the knee, and as much jewelry as he could afford. His swaggering gait, especially when he had a girlfriend on his arm, frightened many in the middle class. Equally disturbing to old New Yorkers were the young working women who strolled the Bowery. They came in groups to enjoy each other's company and to meet Bowery boys. Unlike more genteel ladies who wore modest veils or bonnets, Bowery "gals" drew attention to themselves with outlandish costumes and ornate hats.

Much more than on the stage, racial, ethnic, and class divisions were played out in public space. Most working people spent much of their lives outdoors; they worked in the open air as laborers, shopped in public markets, paraded on city streets, and socialized on sidewalks. Young people courted, neighbors argued, and ethnic and racial groups defended their turf in public places. Urban streets served as a political arena as crowds listened to speakers, demonstrated, and sometimes took mob action.

Competition for jobs, often between native-born Americans and new immigrants, turned into violence on

URBAN RIOTS

city streets. In the 1830s riots became commonplace as economic, political, social, racial, and ethnic conflict erupted and professionals, merchants, craftsmen, and laborers vented their rage against political and economic rivals. "Gentlemen of property and standing," unnerved by antislavery proponents, sacked abolitionist and antislavery organizations, even murdering newspaper editor Elijah Lovejoy in Alton, Illinois, in 1837. In the 1840s "respectable" citizens drove the Mormons out of Missouri and Illinois. In Philadelphia native-born workers attacked Irish weavers in 1828, and whites and blacks fought on the docks in 1834 and 1835. Residents of North Philadelphia took to the streets continuously from 1840 to 1842 until the construction of a railroad through their neighborhood was abandoned. These disturbances came to a head in the Philadelphia riots of 1844, in which Protestant skilled workers attacked Irish Catholics. Smaller cities, too, became battlegrounds as nativist riots

■ Nicholino Calyo's watercolor *Soap-Locks, or Bowery Boys* (c. 1847) captured the bold body language and showy dress of the youths who controlled the sidewalks of the Bowery. (© Collection of The New York Historical Society)

peaked in the 1850s; Louisville, for instance, witnessed an anti-German riot in 1855. By 1840 more than 125 people had died in urban riots, and by 1860 fatalities exceeded 1,000.

As public disorder spread, Boston hired uniformed policemen in 1837 to supplement its part-time watchmen and constables, and New York in 1845 established a uniformed force. Nonetheless, middle-class city dwellers did not venture out alone at night. The police tried to control and suppress street activity. They used local laws against vagrancy and disturbing the peace to suppress free blacks and immigrants. The continuing inflow of immigrants to the cities worsened social tensions by pitting groups against one other in the contest for jobs, housing, and street space. In the midst of so much noise, crime, and conflict, the lavish uptown residences of the very rich rose like an affront to those struggling to survive.

Extremes of Wealth

*A*fter visiting all twenty-four states in 1831 and 1832, Alexis de Tocqueville characterized the United States as primarily a place of equality and opportunity for white males. He opened *Democracy in America,* his classic analysis of the American people and nation, with this observation: "No novelty in the United States struck me more vividly during my stay there than the equality of conditions."

Tocqueville attributed American equality—the relative fluidity of the social order—to Americans' mobility and restlessness. Geographic mobility, he felt, offered people a chance to start anew regardless of where they came from or who they were. Wealth and family mattered little; a person could be known by deeds alone. Indeed, Americans seemed driven by ambition and an itch to move. "An American will build a house in which to pass his old age," Tocqueville wrote, "and sell it before the roof is on; he will plant a garden and rent it just as the trees are coming into bearing; he will clear a field and leave others to reap the harvest; he will take up a profession and leave it, settle in one place and soon go off elsewhere with his changing desires."

Others disagreed with the egalitarian view of American life. *New York Sun* publisher Moses Yale Beach believed a new aristocracy based on wealth and power was forming. Author of twelve editions of *Wealth and Biography of the Wealthy Citizens of New York City,* Beach listed 750 New Yorkers with assets of $100,000 or more in 1845. John Jacob Astor, with a fortune of $25 million, led the list of 19 millionaires. Ten

GREAT
FORTUNES

■ This gouache, attributed to Nicholino Calyo, depicts the Haight family in their drawing room in 1848. Richard K. Wright was a wealthy New York City merchant, trading internationally, as the globe in the foreground suggests. Sarah Rogers Haight was a famous beauty and socialite, and the family's clothing, art, library, and furniture all stand in sharp contrast to the poverty, homelessness, and orphans found on the city's streets. (Museum of the City of New York. Bequest of Elizabeth Cushing Iselin)

years later, Beach reported more than 1,000 New Yorkers worth $100,000, among them 28 millionaires. Combining gossip-column items with wild guesses at people's wealth, Beach's publications suggest the enormous wealth of New York's upper class. Tocqueville himself, sensitive to conflicting trends in American life, had described the new industrial wealth. The rich and well educated "come forward to exploit industries," Tocqueville wrote, and become "more and more like the administrators of a huge empire. . . . What is this if not an aristocracy?"

Wealth throughout the United States was becoming concentrated in the hands of a relatively small number of people. In New York City between 1828 and 1845, the richest 4 percent of the city's population increased their holdings from an estimated 63 percent to 80 percent of all individual wealth. Meanwhile, the holdings of many ordinary people virtually disappeared. In Brooklyn between 1810 and 1841, the share of wealth held by the bottom two-thirds of families decreased from 10 percent to almost nothing. By 1860 the top 5 percent of American families owned more than half of the nation's wealth, and the top 10 percent owned nearly three-quarters.

From 1826 until his death in 1851 Philip Hone, one-time mayor of New York, kept a diary, meticulously recording the life of an American aris-

URBAN ELITE tocrat. On February 28, 1840, Hone attended a masked ball at the Fifth Avenue mansion of Henry Breevoort Jr. and Laura Carson Breevoort. The ball began at the fashionable hour of 10 P.M., and the five hundred invited ladies and gentlemen wore costumes adorned with ermine and gold. For more than a week, Hone believed, the affair "occupied the minds of people of all stations, ranks, and employments." Similar parties were held in Boston, Philadelphia, Baltimore, and Charleston. Hone regularly attended elegant dinners graced by fine cuisine and imported wines. The New York elite who filled the pages of Hone's diary—the 1 percent of the population who owned half of the city's wealth—lived in mansions attended by servants. Country estates, ocean resorts, mineral spas, and grand tours of Europe offered relief from the winter and spring social seasons and escape from the heat and smells of the summer.

Much of this wealth was inherited. For every John Jacob Astor who made millions in the western fur trade or George Law who left a farm to become a millionaire contractor and investor, ten others had inherited or married money. Andrew H. Mickle, a poor Irish immigrant who became a millionaire and mayor of New York City, derived his fortune from marrying the daughter of his

employer. Many of the wealthiest New Yorkers bore the names of the colonial commercial elite: Breevoort, Roosevelt, Van Rensselaer, and Whitney. These rich New Yorkers were not idle; they worked at increasing their fortunes and power. Urban capitalists like Philip Hone and the fashionable society, like their Boston counterparts who founded the Lowell mills, invested in and profited enormously from commerce and manufacturing. Wealth begat wealth, and marriage cemented upper-crust family ties.

But just a short walk from Hone's wealthy district were urban slums. There poor working men and women were continually anxious that hard times were imminent. They dreaded poverty, chronic illness, disability, old age, widowhood, and desertion. With good reason women did fear raising children without a spouse, as few women's jobs paid enough to support a family.

On crowded streets, the working poor jostled with newly arrived immigrants as well as free blacks, thieves, beggars, and prostitutes. New York

URBAN SLUMS City's Five Points, a few blocks from City Hall, lacked running water and sewers and was notorious for its physical and moral squalor. "I do think I saw more drunk folks, men and women, that day," frontiersman Davy Crockett recalled in 1835 of his visit to Five Points a year earlier, "than I ever saw before." Dominated by the Old Brewery, which had been converted to housing in 1837, the neighborhood was overwhelmingly immigrant, predominantly Irish but also with a few free black people. Contemporaries estimated that more than a thousand people lived in the Old Brewery's rooms and cellars. Throughout the city, workers' housing was at a premium. Houses built for two families often held four; tenements built for six families held twelve. Families took in lodgers to help pay the rent.

Meanwhile, a distinct middle class appeared on the urban scene. Small in number, they were the city businessmen, traders, and profession-

MIDDLE CLASS als in the market economy. The growth and specialization of trade rapidly increased their numbers. Middle-class families enjoyed the new consumer items: wool carpeting, fine wallpaper, and rooms full of furniture replaced the bare floors, whitewashed walls, and relative sparseness of eighteenth-century homes. Houses were large, often having from four to six rooms. Middle-class children slept one to a bed, and by the 1840s and 1850s middle-class families used indoor toilets. When Philadelphia publishing agent Joseph Engles died in 1861, an inventory of his estate indicated that his parlor contained two sofas, thirteen

A visible sign of urban poverty in the 1850s was the homeless and orphaned children, most of them immigrants, who wandered the streets of New York City. The Home for the Friendless Orphanage, at Twenty-ninth Street and Madison Avenue, provided shelter for some of the orphan girls. (© Collection of The New York Historical Society)

chairs, three card tables, a fancy table, a piano, a mirror, and a fine carpet. Other rooms were similarly furnished.

Middle-class families formed the backbone of the clubs and societies that Tocqueville had observed in America. They filled the family pews in church on Sundays; their male children went to college. They were as distant from Philip Hone's world as they were from the milieu of the working class and the poor. Increasingly they looked to the family and home as the core of middle-class life.

Family Life

Once primarily an economic unit, urban families in the nineteenth-century market economy began to lose their role as producers (see Chapter 10). The result was sweeping changes in the household economy as it adjusted to the market economy. As men increasingly worked for wages outside the home, and so did their offspring, the urban workplace and home became separate entities.

In the home men were economically dominant. English common law gave husbands absolute control over the family. Men owned their wives' personal property; they were legal guardians of the children; and they owned whatever family members produced or earned. A father still had the legal authority to oppose his daughter's choice of husband. Nonetheless, most American women, with their parents' blessing, chose their own marriage partners.

LEGAL RIGHTS

But the legal rights within families were beginning to change. Although married women still had limited legal rights and standing, they made modest gains in property and spousal rights from the 1830s on. Arkansas in 1835 passed the first married women's property law, and by 1860 sixteen more states had followed suit. In those states, women—single, married, or widowed—could own and convey property. When a wife inherited, earned, or acquired property, it was hers, not her husband's; and she could write a will. In the 1830s states began to liberalize divorce, adding cruelty and desertion as grounds for divorce. Nonetheless divorce was rare.

In working-class families, women left their parental homes as early as age twelve, earning wages most of their lives, with only short respites for bearing and rearing children. Primarily unmarried girls and women worked as domestic servants in other women's homes; married and widowed women worked as laundresses, seamstresses, and cooks. Some hawked food and wares on city streets; others did piecework sewing at home, earning wages in the putting-out system; and some became prostitutes. Few of these occupations enabled women to support themselves or a family at a respectable level.

WORKING WOMEN

Middle-class Americans, however, sought to keep women close to home. They idealized the family as a moral institution characterized by selflessness and cooperation, while the world of work—the market economy—was increasingly seen as an arena of conflict increasingly identified with men and dominated by base self-interest. If young girls left home to work—in New England's textile mills, in new urban stores as clerks—it was only for a brief interval before marriage.

The domestic ideal restricted the paying jobs available to middle-class women, but one occupation was considered consistent with genteel femininity: teaching. In 1823 the Beecher sisters, Catharine and Mary, established the Hartford Female Seminary and offered history and science in addition to the traditional women's curriculum of domestic arts and religion. A decade later Catharine Beecher successfully campaigned for teacher-training schools for women. By 1850 schoolteaching had become a woman's profession. "Females govern with less resort to physical force," Horace Mann asserted, "and exert a more kindly, humanizing and refining influence upon the dispositions and manners of their pupils." Many women worked for a time as teachers, usually for two to five years. Unmarried women earned about half the salary of male teachers.

TEACHERS

The market economy brought economic insecurity and altered family life. As the American population moved west, kin became separated and multigenerational families in the same household became less common. And all families, regardless of class or region, were shrinking in size. In 1830 American women bore an average of almost six children; by 1860 the figure had dropped to five. This decline occurred even though many immigrants with large-family traditions were settling in the United States; thus the birth rate among native-born women declined even more steeply. Although rural families re-

FAMILY SIZE

mained larger than their urban counterparts, birth rates among both groups declined comparably.

A number of factors account for reduced family size. Small families were viewed as increasingly desirable in an economy in which the family was a unit of consumption rather than production. In urban areas, children tended to become an economic burden rather than an asset as the family lost its role as a producer of goods. Children in smaller families, however, would have greater opportunities: parents could give them more attention, better

■ Rebecca Lukens pioneered in an unusual role for a woman in early-nineteenth-century America: she ran the Lukens Steel Company in eastern Pennsylvania from 1825 until she died in 1854. The deaths of her father in 1823 and of her husband in 1825 left her with the mill and large debts. She revived the steel company and soon was shipping iron plates as far away as Europe.   (Courtesy of Lukens, Inc., Coatesville, Pa.)

education, and more financial help. Evidence suggests many wives and husbands made deliberate decisions to limit the size of families. Where farmland was relatively expensive in eastern states, for instance, family size was smaller than in cheaper agricultural districts to the west.

The demographic data suggest that changes in childbearing reduced family size. Average age at marriage rose, thus shortening the period of potential childbearing. The age at which women bore their last child dropped from around forty in the mid-eighteenth century to around thirty-five in the mid-nineteenth.

But couples also limited their family size through birth control. Traditional practices continued—coitus interruptus (withdrawal of the male before completion of the sexual act), breast-feeding to prolong infertile periods, and rhythm methods. Traditional folk remedies from American Indian folk medicine to African societies spread as well. Although animal-skin condoms imported from France were too expensive for popular use, cheap rubber condoms became available in the 1850s. Douching after intercourse was also practiced. None of the methods was particularly reliable.

BIRTH CONTROL

As formerly private concerns began to be discussed publicly, women shared and purchased information on limiting reproduction. Reproductive controls were considered part of women's responsibilities. If all else failed, women resorted to abortions, especially after 1830. Ineffective folk methods of self-induced abortion had been around for centuries, but in the 1830s abortionists, mostly women, advertised surgical services in large cities. To protect women from unqualified abortionists, and in response to reformers opposed to abortion, states began to regulate the procedure. Between 1821 and 1841, ten states and one territory either restricted late-term abortions or prohibited abortion altogether; by 1860 twenty states had adopted such restrictions.

ABORTION

Smaller families and fewer births changed the family. At one time birth and infant care had occupied nearly the entire span of women's adult lives, and few mothers lived to see their youngest child reach maturity. In smaller families, individual children received greater attention, and childhood gradually came to be perceived as a distinct period in the life span. The expansion of public education in the 1830s and the policy of grouping schoolchildren by age reinforced this perspective.

Not everyone lived in traditional families. Many single men lived and worked outside of families. In urban areas rooming and boarding houses provided them with places to sleep and eat. The expansion of cities and the market economy led more women to live outside families as well. Lowell and other mill towns provided boarding houses for the single farm daughters who did factory work for a few years before marriage. Other women, like Louisa May Alcott (1832–1888), author of *Little Women* (1868), who lived most of her life in Massachusetts, followed an independent path. Her father, the philosopher Bronson Alcott, never adequately supported his family. Not even the family's participation in Brook Farm put enough food on the table. Louisa May Alcott supported the family by working as a seamstress, governess, teacher, and housemaid before her writing brought her success. "I think I shall come out right, and prove that though an Alcott, I can support myself," she wrote her father in 1856. "I like the independent feeling; and though not an easy life, it is a free one, and I enjoy it. I can't do much with my hands; so I will make a battering-ram of my head and make a way through this rough-and-tumble world."

SINGLE MEN AND WOMEN

Louisa May Alcott forswore marriage and a family. It was not easy in a society that considered family the foundation of a moral life and appropriate for women. But she and other unmarried women managed to pursue careers and lives defined by female relationships. Given the difficulty women had finding ways to support themselves, they undertook independence at great risk. Nonetheless, the proportion of single women in the population increased significantly in the nineteenth century. In Massachusetts in 1850, 17 percent of native-born women never married—a far larger percentage than in colonial days. Independent white women, in sum, were taking advantage of new opportunities offered by the market economy and urban expansion. At the same time communitarian ventures in rural America—exemplified by the Shakers, Mormons, and Brook Farm—offered experimentation in new family relationships.

Immigrant Lives in America

The United States continued to be a nation of newcomers. The 5 million immigrants who came to the United States between 1830 and 1860 outnumbered the entire population of the country recorded in the first census in 1790. The vast majority were European (see Figure 12.1). During the peak period of pre–Civil War immigration, from 1847 through 1857, 3.3 million immigrants entered the United States: 1.3 million from

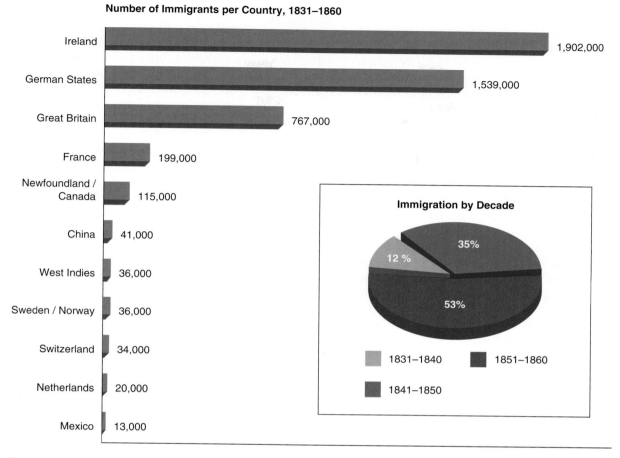

Figure 12.1 **Major Sources of Immigration to the United States, 1831–1860**

Most immigrants came from two areas: Great Britain, of which Ireland was a part, and the German states. These two areas sent more immigrants between 1830 and 1860 than the inhabitants of the United States enumerated at the first census in 1790. By 1860, 15 percent of the white population was of foreign birth.

(Source: Data from Stephan Thernstrom, ed., *Harvard Encyclopedia of American Ethnic Groups* [Cambridge, Mass., and London: Harvard University Press, 1980], 1047.)

Ireland and 1.1 million from the German states. By 1860, 15 percent of the white population was foreign-born.

This massive migration had been set in motion decades earlier. At the turn of the nineteenth century, the Napoleonic wars gave rise to one of the greatest population shifts in history; ultimately it lasted more than a century. War, revolution, famine, religious persecution, and the lure of industrialization led many Europeans to leave home. From the other side of the world, Asian immigration to the United States was just beginning; 41,000 Chinese, nearly all men, entered the United States from 1854 through 1860 to work mostly in heavy construction. The

United States attracted immigrants as the market economy offered jobs and its Constitution protected religious freedom. Not all planned to stay permanently, and many, like the Irish, saw themselves as exiles from their homeland.

The market economy needed workers. Large construction projects and mining operations sought strong young men, and textile mills sought young women. To fill these jobs both private firms and governments recruited European immigrants. Midwestern and western states lured potential settlers to promote economic growth. Two transplanted New Yorkers, Augustus and

PROMOTION OF
IMMIGRATION

Joe Kirby Allen, for instance, in 1836 set themselves up in what became Houston, Texas, and advertised in newspapers for settlers. In the 1850s Wisconsin appointed a commissioner of emigration, who advertised the state's advantages in European newspapers. Wisconsin also opened an office in New York and hired European agents to compete with other states and with firms like the Illinois Central Railroad in recruiting immigrants. Europeans' awareness of the United States grew as employers, states, and shipping companies promoted opportunities across the Atlantic. Often the message was stark: work and prosper in America or starve in Europe. The price of a ticket on the regularly scheduled sailing ships crossing the ocean after 1848 was within easy reach of millions of Europeans.

Success in America stimulated further emigration. "I wish, and do often say that we wish you were all in this happy land," wrote shoemaker John

LETTERS HOME

West of Germantown, Pennsylvania, to his kin in Corsley, England, in 1831, adding: "A man nor woman need not stay out of employment one hour here." John Down, a weaver from Frome, England, who immigrated to New York without his family, described for his wife in 1830 the bountiful meals he shared with a farmer's family. The farmhands sat at the same table with their masters and ate a banquet of puddings, pies, fruits and vegetables of the season, and preserves. Though Down sorely missed his family, he wrote, "I do not repent of coming, for you know that there was nothing but poverty before me." Such testimonials to the success of pauper immigrants in America circulated widely in Europe.

Immigrants endured the hardships of travel and of living in a strange land. The average transatlantic crossing took six weeks; in bad weather it could take three months. Disease spread unchecked among people packed together like cattle in steerage. More than seventeen thousand immigrants, mostly Irish, died from "ship fever" in 1847 alone. On arrival, con artists and swindlers preyed on newcomers. Boarding house and employment agents tried to lure them from their chosen destinations. In response, New York State established Castle Garden as an immigrant center in 1855. There, at the tip of Manhattan Island, the major port for European entry, immigrants were somewhat sheltered from fraud. Authorized transportation companies maintained offices in the large rotunda and assisted new arrivals with their travel plans.

Most immigrants gravitated toward cities, and many stayed in New York City itself. By 1855, 52 percent of its 623,000 inhabitants were immigrants, 28 percent from Ireland and 16 percent from the German states. Boston,

SETTLING IN

another major entry port for the Irish, took on a European tone; throughout the 1850s the city was about 35 percent foreign-born, of whom more than two-thirds were Irish. In the West, St. Louis's population was 61 percent foreign-born, and San Francisco had a foreign-born majority. Southern cities like Charleston and Savannah had significant Irish settlements. Many sought ethnic neighborhoods where their countrymen and women and their descendants lived.

Only a few immigrants had farming experience or the means to purchase land, but those who did settled in rural areas—though they tended to avoid the rural South, with its predominance of slave labor. German, Dutch, and Scandinavian farmers, in particular, headed toward the Midwest. Greater percentages of Scandinavians and Netherlanders took up farming than did other nationalities; both groups came mostly as religious dissenters and migrated in family units. The Dutch who founded colonies in western Michigan and Wisconsin, for instance, had seceded from the official Reformed Church of the Netherlands, fleeing persecution in their native land to establish new and more pious communities such as Holland and Zeeland in Michigan.

Not all new arrivals found success in the United States; hundreds of thousands returned to their homelands disappointed. Before the famine of the

IMMIGRANT DISENCHANTMENT

late 1840s hit Ireland, American recruiters had lured many Irish to swing picks and shovels on American canals and railroads and to work in construction. The promise that "he should soon become a wealthy man" lured Michael Gaugin, who had worked for thirteen years as an assistant engineer in the construction of a Dublin canal. The Irish agent for a New York firm convinced him to quit his job, which included a house and an acre of ground, to come to America. But Gaugin landed in New York City during the financial panic of 1837. He could not find work, and within two months he was broke, struggling to find the means to return to Ireland.

Before the great famine, caused by a blight that turned the potato crop—Ireland's food staple—rotten and inedible, there had been a substan-

IRISH IMMIGRANTS

tial outmigration from Ireland, mostly to English cities, but also a steady stream to the United States. From 1845 to 1849, death from starvation, malnutrition, and typhus spread in Ireland. In all, 1 million died and about 1.5 million scattered around the world, two-thirds of them to the United States. Ireland's major export became its people. At the peak of Irish immigration, from 1847 to 1854, 1.2 million Irish men and women entered the

United States. In every year but one between 1830 and 1854, the Irish constituted the largest group of immigrants. By the end of the nineteenth century there would be more Irish in the United States than in Ireland.

Though most Irish made an economic decision to leave their homeland, they often viewed themselves as political exiles, forced to flee because of British tyranny. While nature caused the potato blight, they blamed British misrule for the events that led to famine. Thus settlers of the Irish diaspora—in the United States, Canada, Australia, South Africa, Argentina, and even England— tended to be politically active. In the United States especially, as in St. Patrick's Day parades, they displayed their two national identities.

Most of the new immigrants from Ireland were young, female, poor, from rural districts, and Roman Catholic. In America, the women found work in textile mills and households. Young Irishmen worked in transportation and construction. The Irish supported their families back home and in Irish enclaves in cities, built Catholic churches and schools, and established networks of charitable and social organizations.

This wave of Irish immigrants, descended from the ancient Celts who spoke Gaelic, differed greatly from the Irish who had migrated earlier to the

RACIAL IDEAS

American colonies. In the eighteenth century (see page 92), the Protestant Scots-Irish predominated; they were considered British. But the Celts were considered inferior. The British had thought them barbaric, and they carried those views to America. Dr. Robert Knox of the Edinburgh College of Surgeons believed the British stood for liberty, whereas "the source of all evil lies in the race, the Celtic race of Ireland." "Race is everything," he declared in an 1850 study published in Philadelphia; "literature, science, art, in a word, civilization, depends upon it." Many Americans agreed, describing Irish immigrants in negative, racial terms. They talked about Celtic racial characteristics: a small upturned nose, high forehead, and black tint of skin. As scientists like Knox began to classify peoples into biological types, scientific theory buttressed the developing notion of race.

With the immigration of new groups to the United States (Celts, Jews, Catholics, and Chinese, for instance), with the black population growing, and with territorial expansion bringing Hispanics and more Indians into the United States as well, native-born white Americans were increasingly confronted with people who did not look like them. Many considered these non-British, non-European, non-Protestant people separate races, distinct from their own. Ralph Waldo Emerson, while rejecting the extremes

■ Though the popular slogan "No Irish Need Apply" excluded Irish immigrants from jobs and housing, it was used by Kathleen O'Neil to attack such exclusion in her lyrics and spirited melody. In the song the Irishman meets discrimination head on, and "No Irish Need Apply" is banished. (Special Collections, Milton S. Eisenhower Library, The Johns Hopkins University)

of Dr. Knox's argument, asserted the importance of race in *English Traits* (1856). To Emerson, as a son inherits his ancestors' "every mental and moral property," so too does a race pass on to its members its physical, intellectual, and moral characteristics. "Race avails . . . that all Celts are Catholics," Emerson wrote. "Race is a controlling influence in the Jew. . . . Race in the negro [sic] is of appalling importance. The French in Canada, cut off from all intercourse with the parent people, have held their national traits."

Were the Irish part of the white majority? In the 1840s and 1850s native-born white Americans and British and German immigrants often treated Irish men and women as if they were nonwhites. Posting placards warning "No Irish Need Apply," they excluded the Irish from many occupations. The Irish immigrants who lived with blacks in Five Points seemed to many observers to be much closer to black than white.

Closely related to racial stereotyping in its causes and nasty effects was anti-Catholicism, which became strident in the 1830s and was most overt and cruel in Boston, where a great many Irish had settled. Anti-Catholic riots were almost commonplace. In Charlestown, Massachusetts, a mob burned a convent in 1834; in Philadelphia a crowd attacked priests and nuns and vandalized churches in 1844; and in Lawrence, Massachusetts, a mob leveled the Irish neighborhood in 1854.

ANTI-CATHOLICISM

The native-born whites who rejected the Irish and hated Catholics were motivated in part by economic competition and anxiety. Competition was stiffest among the lowest-paid and least desirable jobs, from women's textile mill work to men's day-laboring jobs. To apprehensive workers, racializing the Irish as Celts was a way of keeping them out of the running. Irish Catholics were also blamed for nearly every social problem, from immorality and alcoholism to poverty and economic upheaval. Impoverished native-born workers complained to the Massachusetts legislature in 1845 that the Irish displaced "the honest and respectable laborers of the State . . . and from their manner of living . . . work for much less per day . . . being satisfied with food to support the animal existence alone." American workers, they claimed, "not only labor for the body but for the mind, the soul, and the State."

In emphasizing "the soul, and the State," native-born workers added a political dimension to their racial expression. Republicanism depended on broad participation and the consent of the governed, and it seemed to American nativists that the Irish, a nonwhite, non-British "race," were not fit to participate. The Know-Nothings turned these attitudes into a political movement in the 1850s (see page 368).

The experience of German immigrants differed from that of the Irish. By and large Americans viewed most Germans, especially the majority Protestant group, as white. They shared a racial stock with the English, who according to Emerson, "come mainly from the Germans." Americans stereotyped Germans as hard working, self-reliant, and intelligent, attributes also applied to white people. Many believed that Germans fit more easily than the Irish into American culture.

GERMAN IMMIGRANTS

In the ten years from 1846 to 1855, 977,000 immigrants from the German states entered the United States. In 1854 Germans replaced the Irish as the largest group of new arrivals. Potato blight also prompted emigration from the German states in the 1840s; other hardships added to the steady stream. Many came from regions where small landholdings made it hard to eke out a living. Craftsmen displaced by the industrial revolution sought jobs in the American expanding market economy. Political refugees—liberals, freethinkers, socialists, communists, and anarchists—fled to the United States after the abortive revolutions of 1848.

Germans shared the same language, though neither a single German state nor a common culture united them. While New York's sizable German population made it the world's third largest German-speaking city—after Vienna and Berlin—Germans settled elsewhere in the United States as well. In the South they were peddlers and merchants; in the North and West they worked as farmers, urban laborers, and businessmen. Their tendency to migrate as families and groups helped them maintain German customs and institutions. Many settled in small towns and rural areas where they could preserve their language and regional German cultures. In larger cities immigrants from the same German states tended to cluster together. Their presence transformed the tone of cities like Cincinnati and Milwaukee, as they became major producers of German beer and sausage and built shops and factories based on German craft skills, from cigar making to tool works.

Non-Protestant Germans did not fare so well, frequently encountering hostility fed by religious and racial prejudice. A significant number of German immigrants were Jewish, and Jews were considered a separate race. Anti-Catholics attacked the German immigrants who were Catholic. The Sunday tradition of urban German families gathering at beer gardens to eat and drink, to dance and sing, and sometimes to play cards outraged evangelical Protestants, who viewed this behavior as violating the sanctity of the Lord's day.

From Florida to Texas and the Southwest to California, Hispanic inhabitants of the borderlands became "immigrants" without actually moving; treaties placed them in the United States. Some Mexicans were unhappy to find themselves in a new country, while others welcomed the political self-government that the United States seemed to promise.

HISPANICS

But reality did not live up to promise. In Nueces County, Texas, at the time of the Texas Revolution (1836), Mexicans held all the land; twenty years later, they had lost it. The new Anglo owners produced crops for the market economy; *rancheros* and *vaqueros*—cowboys—became obsolete. Although many Texas Mexicans, called *Tejanos,* had fought for Texas's independence, new Anglo settlers tended to treat them as inferiors and foreigners. They became second-class citizens on land where they had lived for generations. Still they retained their culture. They held fast to their language, Roman Catholic religion, and cultural traditions. San Antonio, Mexican from 1821 to 1836 and thereafter a Texas city, illustrates *Tejano* persistence. The church, free public schools (established in 1827), newspapers, mutual aid societies, public holidays, and celebrations of life-cycle events from baptism to marriage to funerals all perpetuated *Tejano* culture.

In California—unlike in Texas, New Mexico, and Arizona—Hispanic society and political power quickly gave way to American and European culture. *Californios,* the Mexican population, numbered 10,000 in 1848, or two-thirds of the non-Indian population. By the end of the century the Hispanic population was 15,000 out of 1.5 million, and Hispanic culture was only a remnant, though Mexican immigrants would reestablish it in the twentieth century.

White Americans considered Hispanics, a group descended from Indians and Spaniards, as a separate, nonwhite race. Anglo-Americans also inherited the British view of Spaniards as inferior, lazy, and decadent, stereotypes they applied to Hispanics. Racializing Hispanics helped to justify the attitudes and actions of aggressive whites, who pushed aside any who stood in the way of expansion and settlement.

Free People of Color

*a*s Irish Americans marched on St. Patrick's Day, declaring their identities as Irish and Americans and demanding Ireland's liberation from the yoke of British colonialism, so too did African Americans celebrate freedom holidays, commemorating emancipation (where it took place) and protesting their own inequality and the persistence of slavery. Thus from 1834 through the Civil War, free people of color across the United States, from big cities like Boston, New York, Philadelphia, Cincinnati, and 1850s San Francisco to small towns like Troy, New York; Harrisburg, Ohio; and Niles, Michigan, celebrated August 1, the anniversary of West Indian emancipation, as a major holiday. "To many of us," Frederick Douglass said, "the first of August is like the white man's 4th of July." Celebrations were held in at least thirteen states, and New Bedford, Massachusetts's 1855 regional event topped them all with seven thousand attendees. And as on St. Patrick's Day, many whites saw such parades as provocative.

Blacks, slave and free, were the most visible nonwhite group in the early nineteenth century. As their

This painting (c. 1840) of Saint Isadore of Madrid, patron saint of farmers, is attributed to Rafael Aragon. Hispanic farmers in the Southwest sought the aid of Saint Isadore as they struggled to raise crops and preserve their culture.   (Courtesy of Dr. and Mrs. Ward Alan Minge)

GROWTH OF THE BLACK POPULATION numbers grew, from 2.3 million in 1830 to 4.4 million in 1860, whites increasingly viewed them as a racial group, a people apart from Europeans. In law and society most black people found themselves as outsiders in the land of their birth.

The free African American population grew from 320,000 in 1820 to almost 500,000 in 1860. Nearly half lived in the urban North, and almost an equal number in the Upper South, where outside of Baltimore—the nation's largest black community—most were rural. A scattering of free people of color lived in the Deep South. An estimated 60,000 free blacks lived in Canada as exiles from the United States. Despite differences in occupation, wealth, education, religion, and social status, the need for self-defense promoted solidarity among free blacks.

Ex-slaves constantly increased the ranks of free people of color in the North. Some, like Frederick Douglass and Harriet Tubman, were fugitives. Douglass, a Baltimore ship caulker, escaped in 1838 by bluffing his way to Philadelphia and freedom. Tubman, a slave in Maryland, escaped to Philadelphia in 1849 when it was rumored that she would be sold out of the state. Over the next two years she returned twice to free her two children, her sister, her mother, and her brother and his family. Some slaves received freedom in owners' wills when masters sought, at death, to rid themselves of the stain of owning slaves. Some owners released elderly slaves rather than support them in old age. Others freed their children, offspring of liaisons and forced relations with slaves. After Nat Turner's slave revolt in Virginia in 1831, when Upper South states further eroded the line between free and

■ Black churches—especially the African Methodist Episcopal Church, run by and for free people of color—were central in the communal and religious life of free people of color. Mrs. Juliann Jane Tillman, an AME minister in Philadelphia, was a popular preacher. Peter S. Duval printed this 1844 life drawing of Tillman by Alfred Hoffy. (Library of Congress)

slave by barring free blacks from learning to read, many families from the cities of Virginia moved to the Midwest. Even in the Midwest they were not full citizens: they could not vote, but at least they were free to educate their children.

Black people, free and slave, forged their own communities and culture in the early nineteenth century.

AFRICAN AMERICAN COMMUNITIES

Swept up by the Second Great Awakening, blacks turned increasingly to religion, most often to Christianity. But as they founded their own churches and independent denominations, like the African Methodist Episcopal (AME) Church (1816), they reshaped ritual and practice. Services reflected black musical traditions, from the "shout and call" to the spirituals, and they gave theological prominence to themes of equality, exodus, and freedom (see chapter 13). By 1846 there were 296 AME congregations in the United States and Canada. Black churches and preachers, both male and female, played central roles in their communities. Chapels and social halls functioned as town hall and school buildings. Ministers were political leaders, and their halls housed political forums, conventions, and protest meetings. Above all else they were abolitionists, united in their opposition to the enslavement of other black people, sometimes their own kin.

A network of voluntary associations became the hallmark of black communities. Besides the churches and reform societies—from abolition to temperance—men and women organized benevolent associations, literary societies, and schools. In Philadelphia in the 1840s, more than half of the black population belonged to mutual beneficiary societies. The Prince Hall Masons had more than fifty lodges in seventeen states by 1860. Many black leaders believed that these mutual aid societies would encourage thrift, industry, and morality, thus assisting their members to improve themselves. But no amount of effort could completely counteract the burden of white racism, which impinged on every aspect of their lives. For example, blacks in effect paid double for education: their taxes supported white public schools, which excluded black children; then they raised additional funds to educate their own children.

In the majority of states where free blacks were excluded from voting, they formed organizations to fight for equal rights. Among the early efforts to organize for self-defense was the Negro Convention movement. From 1830 to 1835, and irregularly thereafter, free blacks held national conventions with delegates drawn from city and state organizations. Under

POLITICAL ACTIVISM

middle-class leadership, which included the Philadelphia sail manufacturer James Forten and the orator Reverend Henry Highland Garnet, the convention movement served as a forum to attack slavery and agitate for equal rights. Militant new black newspapers joined the struggle. *Freedom's Journal*, the first black weekly, appeared in 1827; in 1837 the *Weekly Advocate* began publication in New York City. Both papers circulated throughout the North, disseminating African American political analysis and promoting activism.

Activists fought their second-class status and the continuation of slavery. The Constitution acknowledged slavery, but the Bill of Rights seemed to apply to free African Americans. The Fifth Amendment specified that "no person shall . . . be deprived of life, liberty, or property, without due process of law." But eighteenth-century political theory had defined the republic as being for whites only (see Chapter 7), and early federal legislation excluded blacks from common rights. The first naturalization law in 1790 limited citizenship to "free white persons." Thus from the start, legislation excluded free people of color from citizenship rights. When Congress created militias in 1792, they included only whites. After the admission of Missouri in 1821, every new state admitted until the Civil War, free and slave, banned blacks from voting. When Congress organized the Oregon and New Mexico Territories, it reserved public land grants for whites. Free people of color were defined as an alien race; they could not participate in the republican ideal that government rested on the consent of the governed.

DISCRIMINATION AND EXCLUSION

Even in the North, states attempted to exclude African Americans. Many northern and western states barred free blacks from entering or required them to post bonds ranging from $500 to $1,000 to guarantee their good conduct, as did Illinois (1819), Michigan (1837), and Oregon (1857). Only in Massachusetts, New Hampshire, Vermont, and Maine could blacks vote on an equal basis with whites throughout the early nineteenth century. In 1842 African Americans gained the right to vote in Rhode Island (where all voters faced restrictive property qualifications), but they had lost it earlier in Pennsylvania and Connecticut. Only Massachusetts permitted blacks to serve on juries. Four midwestern states and California did not allow African Americans to testify against whites. In Oregon blacks could not own real estate, make contracts, or sue in court. The laws were meant to render African Americans powerless.

Black people also faced economic restrictions. They were excluded from the new factory and clerical jobs of the expanding market economy. In the North and Upper South, black women, who were more likely to work for wages than white women, whether married or single, worked as house servants, cooks, washerwomen, and child nurses. Men worked as servants, waiters, cooks, barbers, janitors, and sailors. In service work wages were low but relatively immune from boom-and-bust cycles. Most black men, however, were construction workers, porters, longshoremen, and day laborers; all suffered frequent unemployment.

Some black men and women turned service occupations into businesses. In the growing cities blacks opened restaurants, taverns, hotels, barber shops, and employment agencies for domestic servants. Some became caterers. Others sold used clothing or were junk dealers or small-job contractors, especially in the Upper South. A few became very successful economically, like sail maker James Forten (Philadelphia), barbers William Johnson (Natchez) and Samuel Mordechai (St. Louis), and ship captain Paul Cuffee. They became wealthy, invested in real estate, and loaned money. With professionals—ministers, teachers, physicians and dentists, lawyers, and newspaper editors—they formed a growing black middle class.

While free people of color sought economic and political security, they forged their own cultural identity. They began to call themselves "Colored Americans" rather than "Africans," reflecting their growing participation in public life. Like the Irish who wore red, white, and blue on St. Patrick's Day, they acknowledged a dual consciousness, a dual identity, as African descendants and as Americans. There is much evidence that they mixed African and American cultures in distinct ways. They dressed up for church, wearing their "Sunday go-to-meetin' clothes." They modified African hairstyles in cutting, wrapping, and braiding their hair. Africans brought the banjo and drum to the New World, introducing new rhythms to Europeans. Black brass bands created what Walt Whitman called "grand American opera."

AFRICAN AMERICAN CULTURE

Most expressive was African American dance. From Congo Square in New Orleans on Sundays to the integrated "dives" in Five Points, New York, visitors observed African-based dance movements unknown to Europeans. European dance used arm and leg movements; but African dancers moved their entire bodies. "Single shuffle, double shuffle, cut and cross-cut; snapping his fingers, rolling his eyes, turning in his knees . . . , spinning about on his toes and heels like nothing but the man's fingers on the tambourine; dancing with two left legs, two right legs, two wooden legs, two wire legs, two spring legs—all sorts of legs and no legs," was Charles Dickens's 1842 attempt (in *American Notes*) to describe the flowing motion of Mr. Juba (William Henry Lane), "the greatest dancer known," in Five Points in 1842. Frederick Bremer in South Carolina in 1850 saw similar physical movements in a black church. They sang "with all their souls and with all their bodies in unison, for their bodies wagged, their heads nodded, their feet stamped, their knees shook, their elbows and their hands beat time to the tune." Here were the African traditions of polyrhythms, of improvisation, and intensive physicality. Over time, some white churches came to incorporate this style in their worship. And when whites parodied black styles in minstrel shows, they were acknowledging black culture.

In the late 1840s and 1850s the mood of many free blacks turned pessimistic. They felt frustrated by the failure of the abolitionist movement and angered by the passage of the stringent Fugitive Slave Act of 1850 (see page 362). Some fled to Canada, others became more militant, and a few joined John Brown in his plans for a slave uprising (see page 374). Many more were swept up in a wave of black nationalism that stressed racial solidarity, self-help, and a growing interest in Africa. Before this time, efforts to send African Americans "back to Africa" had originated with whites seeking to rid the United States of blacks, and nearly all African American leaders had been opposed. But in the 1850s some participated in emigrationist conventions led by abolitionists Martin Delany and Henry Bibb. Delany led an exploration party to the Niger valley as the emissary of a black convention, signing a treaty with Yoruba rulers to allow American settlers in their African kingdom.

Nothing better illustrates the difficult and ironic condition of free blacks in the United States than their flight to Canada and Africa in search of freedom while millions of European migrants came to the United States for liberty and opportunity. With the coming of the Civil War, the status of blacks would move onto the national political agenda.

Summary

*T*he American people and communities in the North and West were far more diverse and turbulent in the 1850s than they had been in the 1820s. The market economy and westward movement altered rural and urban life and class structure; heavy immigration, growing racial ideas, and the anguished position of free

people of color added to the tensions. Inequality increased, as did the gap between the haves and the have-nots. As the nation grew more populous and the market economy upset work and social relations, many felt a loss of tradition and community. Some longed to return to old values. Utopians like the Shakers, Mormons, and Brook Farmers sought to counter isolation and individualism.

Increasingly cities became the center of American life, with New York the predominant metropolis. Growing populations brought new problems, however, and cities struggled to provide adequate public health, safety, and education for their residents. Large cities offered rich leisure activities, from entertainment to sporting events. Increasingly, however, people divided along class, ethnic, and racial lines. Whether formal, as in the Masonic order, or informal as in the youth culture of the Bowery, divisions became more rigid. The gap between rich and poor widened.

In the midst of these changes, families adapted to the urban, market economy. They became consumers rather than producers, and they shrunk in size as women had fewer children. Middle-class families sought to insulate their homes from the competition of the market economy. Increasingly cities offered opportunities for people to live outside of families.

Famine and oppression in Europe propelled millions of people across the Atlantic, most from Ireland and the German states. American expansion added Hispanics to the nation. Diversity, competition, and religious and scientific thought fueled racial ideas. Many European descendants began to view and treat the Irish, Hispanics, and African Americans as inferior races rather than as cultural groups.

LEGACY FOR A PEOPLE AND A NATION
White Fascination with and Appropriation of Black Culture

White Americans' fascination with and appropriation of black culture blossomed in the early nineteenth century. Whites performed songs and dances from blackface minstrel reviews, while urban young people imitated black language, dress, and hairstyles. In the 1850s white songwriter Stephen Foster's "Old Folks at Home," "Susanna," and "Camptown Races" were enormously popular. Whites believed they were traditional black folk songs, though they romanticized the slave South.

American popular culture combined African, European, and African American traditions. Its emphasis on performance, improvisation, strong rhythms, vernacular language, multiple meanings, and integration into everyday life is evident of strong African ties. These elements appealed to whites because of their expressive powers. Whites also believed that black cultural forms were "exotic" and offered "natural" forms of expression.

Black traditions continue to influence twenty-first-century popular culture. Minstrelsy turned into vaudeville and Broadway theater, which gave birth to American popular music. Popular dance and music, performed mostly by whites, drew heavily on black gospel, slave spirituals, the blues, and jazz and spread through live performance, recorded music, and later radio and television. Black traditions influenced the swing bands of the 1930s, and after World War II, they shaped rhythm and blues, rock 'n' roll, and, later, rap, hip-hop, and ska.

Until recently, most whites experienced black culture as appropriated by whites. Minstrels in blackface and Stephen Foster's songs modified black culture for white audiences. But in the late twentieth century, a synthesis of black and white traditions became notable. In the early 1950s Bill Haley and the Comets, a white country-western group, combined black rhythm and blues with white country and western music. Their 1954 sensation, "Shake, Rattle & Roll," for instance, was a sanitized version of Big Joe Turner's rhythm and blues hit. White audiences responded enthusiastically, and when Haley and the Comets played "Rock Around the Clock" in the 1955 movie *Blackboard Jungle,* rock 'n' roll took off. Elvis Presley too synthesized rhythm and blues and gospel with country music and middle-of-the-road popular music. Rap and hip-hop built on the talking blues, call and response, and urban black and Chicano/a dance styles of the 1970s. White suburban youth made them dominant popular forms.

Popular music and dance, with its African American roots, is uniquely American. Young people fostered this popular culture and used its expressive elements to define themselves. Thus African American culture has given the people and nation a unique cultural legacy.

The **history companion** *powered by Eduspace®*
Your primary source for interactive quizzes, exercises, and more to help you learn efficiently.
http://history.college.hmco.com/students

PEOPLE AND COMMUNITIES IN A SLAVE SOCIETY: THE SOUTH 1830–1860

a slaveholder in debt was a dangerous man. Pierce Butler was broke. It was late winter of 1859, fear of disunion dominated national life, and Butler's slave auction had all of coastal Georgia and South Carolina talking. Butler was the grandson of Major Pierce Butler, a framer of the Constitution, a senator from South Carolina, and a wealthy planter. Butler the younger divided his time between the family's ostentatious home in Philadelphia and 1,500 acres of cotton plantations on Butler Island and St. Simons Island in Georgia, worked by eight hundred slaves. His marriage to the famous British actress Fanny Kemble had ended in divorce; she could not bear the realities of slavery on her husband's cotton plantations, and he could not bear her protests. By 1859 Butler had squandered a fortune of $700,000 through speculation and gambling. Allegedly, he blew $25,000 on one hand of cards.

Most of Butler's properties and possessions in Philadelphia were sold to satisfy his creditors. Then came the largest slave auction in American history. In the last week of February, 436 Butler slaves were taken to Savannah by railroad and steamboat. They were housed for several days in horse-and-carriage sheds at the Ten Broeck racetrack. People of all ages—infants, husbands, wives, children, grandparents—huddled in fearful expectation. Joseph Bryan, a slave broker and auctioneer, managed the sale. Among the planters and speculators who were there to buy was an undercover *New York Tribune* reporter who left a detailed account of the event. The auction, held in the racecourse's grandstand, lasted an agonizing two days in a driving rainstorm.

◀ Thomas S. Noble's painting *The Last Sale of Slaves* depicts the public drama and family horror of slave auctions. Noble's work stimulated a heated newspaper debate in St. Louis over its abolitionist message. The sight of people treated as property, and bills of sale signed on the table, leave slavery's most haunting images. (Missouri Historical Society)

If possible, families were sold intact for group prices; thus the old and infirm could still be liquidated, while the closest kin stayed together. A seventeen-year-old "Prime woman" named Dorcas and her three-month-old son, Joe, went for $2,200. A nineteen-year-old "prime young man," Abel, netted $1,295. Some families of four, such as Goin and Cassander and their two daughters, Emiline and Judy, brought only $1,600 together. At the end of the second day of what blacks in the region called the "weeping time," Butler had amassed $303,850 by selling 436 human beings. It would have been impossible to convince the numbed and despairing African Americans who traveled away from Savannah in wagons or railcars that their enslavement was not at the heart of the crisis dividing the nation.

As long as slavery was perceived as a peculiarly southern institution, even the ownership of humans as property, the threat of slave rebellion, and the divisions in southern society fostered by slave ownership did not seem to bother many northerners at first glance. But as slavery spread westward, its worst elements, such as the Butler auction, threatened and disturbed growing numbers of restless Americans. And on the ground in the South, as slaves' bodies, labor, and lives came to be defined more and more as chattel, they struggled to survive and resist, sometimes overtly, but more often in daily life and cultural expression.

By the 1830s the North was an emerging market economy embarking on an industrial revolution. Meanwhile, the South, with a different kind of growth and prosperity, also participated in the market revolution. New lands were settled, new states peopled, and steadily the South emerged as the world's most extensive and vigorous slave economy, linked to an international cotton trade and textile industry. Slavery had a far-reaching influence on all of southern society. The Old South's wealth came from export crops, land, and slaves; and its population was almost wholly rural. In the land where cotton became king, racial slavery affected not only economics but values, customs, laws, class structure, and the region's relationship to the nation. ■

The "Distinctive" South?

The South, the section composed of the slaveholding states from the Chesapeake region of Maryland and Virginia to Missouri and from Florida to Texas, has often been considered America's most distinctive region. Historians and other commentators have long asked the question: how was the Old South like or unlike the rest of the nation? Because of its unique history, has the South, in the words of poet Allen Tate, always been "Uncle Sam's other province"? Or as the southern writer W. J. Cash wrote in 1940, is the South "a tree with many age rings, with its limbs and trunk bent and twisted by all the winds of the years, but with its tap root in the Old South?" Figuring out just why the South seems more religious, more conservative, or more tragic than other regions of America has been an enduring practice in American thought.

Certain American values such as materialism, individualism, and faith in progress have been associated with the North in the nineteenth century, and values such as tradition, intolerance, and family loyalty with the South. The South, so the stereotype has it, was static, even "backward," and the North dynamic in the decades leading up to the Civil War. There are many measures of just how different South was from North in the antebellum era, and at the same time there were many Souths: low-country rice and cotton regions with dense slave populations; mountainous regions of small farmers, plantation culture, and subsistence agriculture; semitropical wetlands in the southeast; Texas grasslands; cities with bustling ports and merchants; and rural areas with only the rare homestead of hillfolk.

The South was distinctive because of its commitment to slavery, but it also shared much in common with the rest of the nation. The geographic sizes of the South and the North were roughly the same. By the 1830s, white southerners shared a heritage of heroes and ideology from the era of the American Revolution with their fellow free citizens in the North. With varying accents, southerners spoke the same language and worshiped the same Protestant God as northerners. Southerners lived under the same cherished Constitution as northerners, and they shared a common mixture of nationalism and localism in their attitudes toward government. Down to the 1840s, northerners and southerners invoked the doctrine of states' rights against federal authority with nearly equal frequency. A faith in the future fueled by a sense of American mission and the dreams in-

SOUTH-NORTH SIMILARITY

spired by the westward movement were as much a part of southern as of northern experience.

Indeed, some of the most eloquent visions of America as a land of independent, self-sufficient farmers expanding westward had come from a southerner, Thomas Jefferson. Jefferson believed that "virtue" rested in those who tilled the soil, that farmers made the best citizens. In 1804 Jefferson declared his "moral and physical preference of the agricultural over the manufacturing man." But as slavery and the plantation economy expanded (see Map 13.1), the South did not become a land of individual opportunity in the same manner as the North.

During the thirty years before the Civil War, the South shared in the nation's economic booms and busts. Research has shown that despite its enormous cruelties, slavery was a profitable labor system for planters. Southerners and northerners shared an expanding capitalist economy. As it grew, the slave-based economy of money-crop agriculture reflected the rational choices of planters. More land and more slaves generally converted into more wealth. By the eve of the Civil War in 1860, the distribution of wealth and property in the two sections was almost identical: 50 percent of free adult males owned only 1 percent of real and personal property, while the richest 1 percent owned 27 percent of the wealth. One study comparing Texas and Wisconsin in 1850 shows that the richest 2 percent of families in each state owned 31 to 32 percent of the wealth. So, both North and South had ruling classes, even if their wealth was invested in different kinds of property. Entrepreneurs in both sections, whether forging plantations out of Mississippi Delta land or shoe factories and textile mills in New England river towns, sought their fortunes in an expanding market economy.

But there were also important differences between the North and the South. The South's climate and longer growing season gave it an unmistakable rural and agricultural destiny. Its people, white and black, developed an intense attachment to place, to the ways people were related to the land and to one another. The South developed as a biracial society of brutal inequality, where the liberty of one race directly depended on the enslavement of another. White wealth was built on highly valued black labor.

SOUTH-NORTH DISSIMILARITY

Cotton growers spread out over as large an area as possible to maximize production and income. Population density was low; by 1860 there were only 2.3 people per square mile in vast and largely unsettled Texas, 15.6 in Louisiana, and 18.0 in Georgia. By contrast,

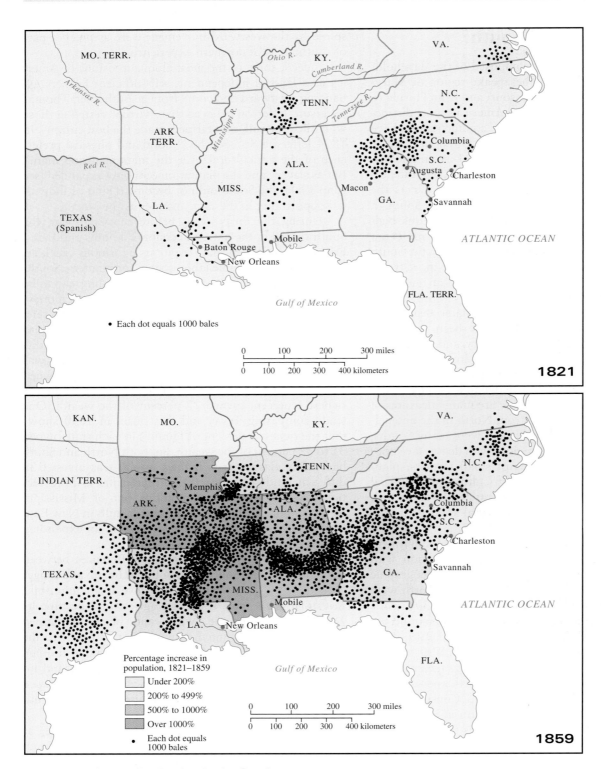

Map 13.1 Cotton Production in the South

These two maps reveal the rapid westward expansion of cotton production and its importance to the antebellum South.

■ A map, entitled "Historical Geography," produced in the 1850s, demonstrates from an abolitionist perspective the notion of historical and cultural differences between North and South. With the values of "liberty" emanating from Plymouth, and the values of slavery emanating from Jamestown, such simplistic but graphic depictions helped fuel sectional animosity. (Library of Congress)

population density in the nonslaveholding states east of the Mississippi River was almost three times higher. The Northeast had an average of 65.4 people per square mile. Massachusetts had 153.1 people per square mile, and New York City compressed 86,400 people into each square mile. When in the 1850s young Frederick Law Olmsted of Connecticut, later renowned as a landscape architect, toured the South as a journalist, he traveled mostly on horseback along primitive trails. Between Columbus, Georgia, and Montgomery, Alabama, Olmsted found "a hilly wilderness, with a few dreary villages, and many isolated cotton farms." For the designer of Central Park in New York City, this was just too much ruralness.

Where people were scarce, it was difficult to finance and operate schools, churches, libraries, or even inns and restaurants. Southerners were strongly committed to their churches, and some believed in the importance of universities, but all such institutions were far less developed than those in the North. Factories were rare be-

cause planters invested most of their capital in slaves. A few southerners did invest in iron or textiles on a small scale. But the largest southern "industry" was lumbering, and the largest factories used slave labor to make cigars. More decisively, the South was slower than the North to develop a unified market economy and a regional transportation network. Despite concerted efforts, the South had only 35 percent of the nation's railroad mileage in 1860.

The South lagged way behind the North in nearly any measure of industrial growth. It always had its reformist voices, however, who advocated commercial development. The South did have urban centers, especially ports like New Orleans and Charleston, which became crossroads of commerce and small-scale manufacturing. But slavery slowed urban growth. As a system of labor and racial control, slavery did not work well in cities. As one historian has said, southern urban centers were small market towns, dependent on agricultural trade— "urbanization without cities." Likewise, because of a lack of jobs, the South did not attract immigrants as readily as the North. By 1860 only 13 percent of the nation's foreign-born population lived in the slave states.

Like most northerners, antebellum southerners were adherents to evangelical Christianity. Americans from all regions held in common a faith in a personal God and in conversion and piety as the means to salvation. But southern evangelicalism was distinct from its northern practice. In the South, Baptists and Methodists concentrated on personal rather than social improvement. By the 1830s in the North, evangelicalism was a major wellspring of reform movements (see Chapter 11); but in the states where blacks were so numerous and unfree, and where the very social structure was under increasingly aggressive attacks from abolitionists, religion, as one scholar has written, preached "a hands-off policy concerning slavery." Although blacks themselves began to convert to Christianity in the early-nineteenth-century South, many southern whites feared a reform impulse that would foster what one historian has called an "interracial communion" in their churches and in their communities. Moreover, those women who may have been reform minded were prevented from developing frequent associations because of the sparse population. The only reform movements that did take hold in the emerging Bible belt of the South, such as temperance, focused on personal behavior, not social reform.

Within an inherently conservative social structure, antebellum southern law restricted the authority of the courts, reinforcing a tradition of planter control. Penitentiaries tended to house only whites, as most blacks were under the authority of personal masters. Lawbreaking in the South tended to be crimes of violence rather than crimes against property. Similarly, the rural character of the South and the significance of the plantation as a self-sufficient social unit meant that the section put few resources into improving disease control and public health. So, in a host of ways, the South was distinct.

Perhaps in no way was the South more distinctive than in its embrace of a particular world-view, a system

A SOUTHERN WORLD-VIEW AND THE PROSLAVERY ARGUMENT of thought and meaning held especially by the planter class, but also influencing all groups of whites. Like those of all people, southerners' values, beliefs, and rationalizations for slavery were not so different from those of any civilization trying to defend the institutions it inherits. But at the heart of the proslavery argument was a deep and abiding racism. The persistence of modern racism in all sections of the United States

is all the more reason to comprehend antebellum southerners' justifications for human slavery.

By 1830 white southerners defended slavery as a "positive good," and not merely a "necessary evil." They used the Bible and its many references to slaveholding, as well as the ancient roots of slavery, to foster a historical argument for bondage. Slavery, they deemed, was the natural status of blacks. Whites were the more intellectual race and blacks the race more inherently physical, and therefore destined for labor. Whites were the creators of civilizations, blacks the appointed hewers of wood and drawers of water. Proslavery writers did not mince words. In a proslavery tract written in 1851, John Campbell confidently declared that "there is as much difference between the lowest tribe of negroes and the white Frenchman, Englishman, or American, as there is between the monkey and the negro."

Some southerners defended slavery in practical terms; they simply saw their bondsmen as economic necessity and as symbols of their quest of prosperity. In 1845, James Henry Hammond of South Carolina argued that slaveholding was essentially a matter of property rights. He spoke for many southerners in his unwillingness to "deal in abstractions" about the "right and wrong" of slavery: property was sacred, protected by the Constitution, and slaves were legal property—end of argument.

The deepest root of the proslavery argument was a hierarchical view of the social order as slavery's defenders believed God or nature had prescribed it. Southerners cherished stability, duty, and honor, believing social change should come only in slow increments, if at all. As the Virginia legislature debated the gradual abolition of slavery in 1831–1832, in the wake of Nat Turner's rebellion, Thomas R. Dew, a slaveholder and professor of law and history at the College of William and Mary, contended that "that which is the growth of *ages* may require *ages* to remove." Dew's widely read work, *Abolition of Negro Slavery* (1832), ushered in an outpouring of proslavery writing that would intensify in volume and depth of commitment over the next thirty years. Until Turner's bloody rebellion, Dew admitted, emancipation in the South had "never been seriously discussed." But as slavery expanded westward and fueled national prosperity, Dew cautioned southerners that any degree of gradual abolition or colonization was impossible and threatened the whole region's "irremediable ruin." Writing one year after William Lloyd Garrison began publishing the antislavery *Liberator* in Boston, Dew declared black slavery part of the "order of nature," an indispensable part of the "deep and solid foundations of society," and the basis of the "well-ordered, well-established lib-

■ A slave woman with inventory number, unidentified photographer, c. 1860. This woman's humanity seems to survive in her expression despite the dehumanization represented in her worn clothing and her number. (The Burns Archive)

erty" of white Americans. Dew's well-ordered society also included his conception of the proper division of men and women into separate spheres and functions.

Proslavery advocates held very different views from those of northern reformers on the concepts of freedom, progress, and equality. They turned natural-law doctrine to their favor, arguing that the natural state of mankind was inequality of ability and condition, not equality. A former U.S. senator in South Carolina, William Harper, charged in 1837 that Jefferson's famous dictum about equality in the Declaration of Independence was no more than a "sentimental phrase." "Is it not palpably nearer the truth to say that no man was ever born free," Harper argued, "and that no two men were ever born equal?" Proslavery writers believed that people were born to certain stations in life; they stressed dependence over autonomy, and duty over rights, as the human condition. As the Virginia writer George Fitzhugh put it in 1854, "Men are not born entitled to equal rights. It would be far nearer

the truth to say, that some were born with saddles on their backs, and others booted and spurred to ride them."

Hence, however differently their slaves may have interpreted the relationship, many slaveholders believed that their ownership of people bound them to a set of paternal obligations. They saw themselves as guardians of a familial relationship between masters and slaves. Although contradicted by countless examples of slave resistance and escape, as well as by slave sales, planters needed to believe in, and exerted great energy in constructing, the idea of the contented slave. Slaveholders needed to endlessly justify how much the freedom and profits of whites depended on the bondage of blacks.

What the South had become by the 1830s, and grew even more fully into by 1860, was not merely a society with slaves, but a *slave society* (see pages 72–73). In this way, the region was most distinct within the larger American nation. Slavery and race affected everything in the Old South. Whites and blacks alike grew up, were socialized, married, reared children, worked, conceived of property, and honed their most basic habits of behavior under the influence of slavery. This was true of slaveholding and nonslaveholding whites, as well as of blacks who were slave and free. Slavery shaped the social structure of the South, fueled almost anything meaningful in its economy, and came to dominate its politics.

A Slave Society

The South was interdependent with the North, the West, and even with Europe in a growing capitalist market system. Southerners relied on northern banks, northern steamship companies working the great western rivers, and northern merchants to keep the cotton trade flowing. But there were elements of that system that southerners increasingly rejected during the antebellum era, especially urbanism, the wage labor system, a broadening right to vote, and any threats to the racial and class order on which they so depended.

In the antebellum era, as later, there were many Souths, but Americans have always been determined to define what one historian called the "Dixie difference." "The South is both American and something different," writes another historian, "at times a mirror or magnifier of national traits and at other times a counterculture." This was most acutely true in the decades before the Civil War.

Culturally, the South developed a proclivity to tell its own story. Its ruralness and its sense of tradition may have given southerners a special habit of telling tales. "Southerners . . . love a good tale," says Mississippi writer Eudora Welty. "They are born reciters, great memory retainers, diary keepers, letter exchangers, and letter savers, history tracers, and debaters, and—outstaying all the rest—great talkers." The South's tragic and distinct story begins in the Old South. The story was distinctive and national all at once.

Free Southerners: Farmers, Free Blacks, and Planters

a large majority of white southern families (three-quarters in 1860) owned no slaves. Some lived in towns and ran stores or businesses, but most were yeoman farmers who owned their own land and grew their own food. The social distance between different groups of whites was great. Still greater was the distance between whites and blacks.

These farmers were individualistic and hard working. Unlike their northern counterparts, their lives were not being transformed by improvements in transportation. They could be independent thinkers as well, but their status as a numerical majority did not mean that they set the political or economic direction of the slave society. Self-reliant and often isolated, always absorbed in the work of their farms, they operated both apart from and within the slave-based staple-crop economy.

YEOMAN FARMERS

Yeomen pioneered the southern wilderness, moving into undeveloped regions—or Indian land after removal—and building log cabins. After the War of 1812 they moved in successive waves down the southern Appalachians into the Gulf lands. In large sections of the South, especially inland from the coast and away from large rivers, small, self-sufficient farms were the norm. Lured by stories of good land, many men uprooted their wives and children repeatedly. So many shared the excitement over new lands that one North Carolinian wrote in alarm, "The Alabama Fever rages here with great violence. . . . I am apprehensive if it continues to spread as it has done, it will almost depopulate the country."

On the southern frontier men worked hard to clear fields and establish farms while their wives labored in the household economy and patiently re-created the social ties—to relatives, neighbors, fellow churchgoers—that enriched everyone's experience. Women seldom shared the men's excitement about moving. They dreaded the isolation and loneliness of the frontier. "We have been [moving] all our lives," lamented one woman. "As soon as ever we git comfortably settled, it is time to be off to something new."

Some yeomen acquired large tracts of level land, purchased slaves, and became planters. They forged part of the new wealth of the boom states of Mississippi and Louisiana, the region to which the southern political power base shifted by the 1840s and 1850s. Others clung to familiar mountainous areas or kept moving as independent farmers because, as one frontiersman put it, he disliked "seeing the nose of my neighbor sticking out between the trees." As one historian has put it, while they owned no slaves, yeomen were jealous of their independence, and "the household grounded their own claims to masterhood."

The yeomen enjoyed a folk culture based on family, church, and local region. Their speech patterns and inflections recalled their Scots-Irish and Irish backgrounds. They flocked to religious revivals called camp meetings, and in between they got together for house-raisings, logrollings, quilting bees, corn-shuckings, and hunting for both food and sport. Such occasions combined work with fun and fellowship, offering food in abundance, and usually liquor as well.

YEOMAN FOLK CULTURE

A demanding round of work and family responsibilities shaped women's lives in the home. They worked in the fields to an extent that astonished travelers such as Frederick Law Olmsted or Frances Trollope, who believed yeomen had rendered their wives "slaves of the soil." Throughout the year the care and preparation of food consumed much of women's time. Household tasks continued during frequent pregnancies and childcare. Primary nursing and medical care also fell to mothers, who often relied on folk wisdom. Women too wanted to be masters of their households, although it came at the price of their health.

Among the men there were many who aspired to wealth, eager to join the scramble for slaves and cotton profits. North Carolinian John F. Flintoff kept a diary of his struggle for success. At age eighteen in 1841, Flintoff went to Mississippi to seek his fortune. Like other aspiring yeomen, he worked as an overseer of slaves but often found it impossible to please his employers. At one point he gave up and returned to North Carolina, where he married and lived for a while in his parents' house. But Flintoff was "impatient to get along in the world," so he tried Louisiana next and then Mississippi again.

YEOMAN LIVELIHOODS

Flintoff's health suffered in the Gulf region and, routinely, "first rate employment" alternated with "very low wages." Moreover, as a young man working on isolated plantations, Flintoff often felt lonely. Even a revival

■ Eastman Johnson's *Fiddling His Way* (1866) depicts rural life by representing the visit of an itinerant black musician to a farm family. Expressions and gestures suggest remarkable ease between the races at the yeoman level of southern society. (The Chrysler Museum of Art, Norfolk, Virginia. Bequest of Walter P. Chrysler, Jr.)

meeting in 1844 proved "an extremely cold time" with "little warm feeling." His uncle and other employers found fault with his work, and in 1846 Flintoff concluded in despair that "managing negroes and large farms is soul destroying."

But a desire to succeed at this very economic proposition kept him going. At twenty-six, even before he owned any land, Flintoff bought his first slave, "a negro boy 7 years old." Soon he had purchased two more children, the cheapest slaves available. Conscious of his status as a slaveowner, Flintoff resented the low wages he was paid. In 1853, with nine young slaves and a growing family, Flintoff faced "the most unhappy time of my life." Fired by his uncle, he returned to North Carolina, sold some of his slaves, and purchased 124 acres with help from his in-laws. By 1860 he owned three horses, twenty-six hogs, ten head of cattle, and several slaves and was paying off his debts. As the Civil War approached, he looked forward to freeing his wife from labor, and possibly sending his sons to college. Although Flintoff demonstrated that a farmer could move in and out of the slaveholding class, he never achieved the cotton planter status he desired.

Probably more typical of the southern yeoman was Ferdinand L. Steel, who as a young man moved from North Carolina to Tennessee to work as a river boatman but eventually took up farming in Mississippi. Steel rose every day at five and worked until sundown. He and his family raised staple crops while cotton was his cash product: he sold five or six bales (about two thousand pounds) a year to obtain money for sugar, coffee, salt, calico, gunpowder, and a few other store-bought goods.

Thus Steel entered the market economy as a small farmer, but with mixed results. He picked his own cotton and complained that cotton cultivation was brutal work and not profitable. He felt like a serf in cotton's kingdom. When cotton prices fell, a small grower like Steel could be driven into debt and lose his farm.

Steel's life in Mississippi in the 1840s retained much of the flavor of the frontier. He made all the family's shoes; his wife and sister sewed dresses, shirts, and "pantaloons."

The Steel women also rendered their own soap and spun and wove cotton into cloth; the men hunted game. Steel doctored his illnesses with boneset tea and other herbs. As the nation fell deeper into crisis over the future of free or slave labor, this independent southern farmer never came close to owning a slave.

The focus of Steel's life was family and religion. Family members prayed together daily, and he studied Scripture for an hour after lunch. "My Faith increases, & I enjoy much of that peace which the world cannot give," he wrote in 1841. Seeking to prepare himself for Judgment Day, Steel borrowed histories, Latin and Greek grammars, and religious books from his church. Eventually he became a traveling Methodist minister. "My life is one of toil," he reflected, "but blessed be God that it is as well with me as it is."

Toil with even less security was the lot of two other groups of free southerners: landless whites and free

■ This formal photograph, ca. 1855, of a black woman attending to two mulatto children indicates how common mixed-race children were in domestic relations in the Old South.   (Photograph by James P. Bau; collection of Matthew Isenburg)

LANDLESS WHITES blacks. A sizable minority of white southern workers—from 25 to 40 percent, depending on the state—were unskilled laborers who owned no land and worked for others in the countryside and towns. Their property consisted of a few household items and some animals—usually pigs—that could feed themselves on the open range. The landless included some immigrants, especially Irish, who did heavy and dangerous work such as building railroads and digging ditches.

In the countryside, white farm laborers struggled to purchase land in the face of low wages or, if they rented, unpredictable market prices for their crops. By scrimping and saving and finding odd jobs, some managed to climb into the ranks of yeomen. When James and Nancy Bennitt of North Carolina succeeded in their ten-year struggle to buy land, they decided to avoid the unstable market in cotton; thereafter they raised extra corn and wheat as sources of cash. People like the Bennitts were both participants in and victims of an economy dominated by cotton producers who relied on slave labor.

Herdsmen who viewed pigs and livestock as a major economic asset always had a desperate struggle to succeed. By 1860, as the South anticipated war to preserve its society, between 300,000 and 400,000 white people in the four states of Virginia, North and South Carolina, and Georgia lived in genuine poverty, approximately one-fifth of the total white population. Their lives were harsh, to say the least. An early antebellum traveler in central South Carolina described the white folk he encountered in the countryside: "The people looked yellow, poor, and sickly. Some of them lived the most miserably I ever saw any poor people live." Land and slaves determined wealth in the Old South, and many whites possessed neither.

For the nearly quarter-million free blacks in the South in 1860, conditions were generally worse than the *FREE BLACKS* yeoman's and often little better than the slave's. The free blacks of the Upper South were usually descendants of men and women manumitted by their owners in the 1780s and 1790s. A remarkable number of slaveholders in Virginia and the Chesapeake region had freed their slaves because of religious principles and revolutionary ideals in the wake of American independence (see Chapter 7). Many free blacks also became free as runaways, especially by the 1830s, disappearing into the southern population; a few made their way northward.

White southerners were increasingly desperate to restrict this growing free black presence in their midst. "It seems the number of free Negroes," complained a Virginia slaveholder, "always exceeds the number of Negroes freed." Some free blacks worked in towns or cities, but most lived in rural areas and struggled to survive. They usually did not own land and had to labor in someone else's fields, often beside slaves. By law free blacks could not own a gun, buy liquor, violate curfew, assemble except in church, testify in court, or (throughout the South after 1835) vote. Despite these obstacles, a minority bought land, and others found jobs as skilled craftsmen.

A few free blacks prospered and bought slaves, most of them purchasing their own wives and children (whom they could not free, since laws required newly emancipated blacks to leave their states). In 1830 there were 3,775 free black slaveholders in the South; 80 percent lived in the four states of Louisiana, South Carolina, Virginia, and Maryland, and approximately one-half of the total lived in the two cities of New Orleans and Charleston. Hundreds of petitions survive in which black slaveholders asked to be exempted from antimanumission laws passed in most southern states. At the same time, a few mulattos in New Orleans were active slave traders in its booming market.

In the cotton and Gulf regions, a large proportion of free blacks were mulattos, the privileged offspring of wealthy white planters. Not all planters freed their mixed-race offspring, but those who did often recognized a moral obligation and gave their children a good education and financial backing. In a few cities like New Orleans, Charleston, and Mobile, extensive interracial sex, as well as migrations from the Caribbean, had produced a mulatto population that was recognized as a distinct class.

Free Black Communities

In many southern cities by the 1840s, free black communities formed, especially around an expanding number of churches. By the late 1850s, Baltimore had fifteen churches, Louisville nine, and Nashville and St. Louis four each, and most of them were African Methodist Episcopal. Class and race distinctions were important to southern free blacks, but outside a few cities, which developed fraternal orders of skilled craftsmen and fellowships of light-skinned people, most mulattos experienced hardship. In the United States, "one drop" of black "blood" (any observable racial mixture to white people's eyes) made them black, and potentially enslaveable.

At the top of the southern social pyramid were slaveholding planters. As a group they lived well, but most lived in comfortable farmhouses, not on the opulent scale that legend suggests. The grand plantation mansions, with fabulous gardens and long rows of out-

Planters

lying slave quarters, are an enduring symbol of the Old South. But a few statistics tell the fuller story: in 1850, 50 percent of southern slaveholders had fewer than five slaves; 72 percent had fewer than ten; 88 percent had fewer than twenty. Thus the average slaveholder was not a wealthy aristocrat but an aspiring farmer, usually a person of humble origins.

Consider the Louisiana cotton planter Bennet Barrow, a newly rich planter of the 1840s who was preoccupied with moneymaking. He worried constantly over his cotton crop, filling his diary with weather reports and gloomy predictions of his yields. Yet Barrow also strove to appear above such worries. He hunted frequently and had a passion for racing horses and raising hounds. He could report the loss of a slave without feeling, but emotion broke through his laconic manner when illness afflicted his sporting animals. "Never was a person more unlucky than I am," he mourned. "My favorite pup never lives." His strongest feelings surfaced when his horse Jos Bell—equal to "the best Horse in the South"—"broke down running a mile . . . ruined for Ever." The same day the distraught Barrow gave his human property a "general Whipping." In 1841 diary entries he worried about a rumored slave insurrection. He gave a "severe whipping" to several of his slaves when they disobediently killed a hog. And when a slave named Ginney Jerry "sherked" his cotton-picking duties and was rumored "about to run off," Barrow whipped him one day, and the next, recorded matter-of-factly: "took my gun found him in the Bayou behind the Quarter, shot him in his thigh—etc. raining all around."

The richest planters used their wealth to model genteel sophistication. Extended visits, parties, and balls to which women wore the latest fashions provided opportunities for friendship, courtship, and display. Such parties were held during the Christmas holidays, but also on such occasions a molasses stewing, a Bachelor's Ball, a horserace, or the crowning of the May Queen. These entertainments were especially important as diversions for plantation women, and at the same time they sustained a rigidly gendered society. Young women relished social events to break the monotony of their domestic lives. In 1826 a Virginia girl was ecstatic about the "week . . . I was in Town." "There were five beaux and as many belles in the house constantly," she declared, and all she and her companions did was "eat, visit, romp, and sleep."

Most of the planters in the cotton-boom states of Alabama and Mississippi were newly rich by the 1840s. As one historian put it, "a number of men mounted from log cabin to plantation mansion on a stairway of cotton

"King Cotton" in the World Economy

The economy of the Old South was deeply intertwined with international trade. Cash crops such as cotton were export, and the fate of this slave society depended on world trade, especially with Europe. Cotton planters and slaveholders constantly had their eyes on export prices.

The American South so dominated the world's supply of cotton that the size of the U.S. crop normally determined the price in an international market where demand continued to skyrocket. This circumstance gave southern planters enormous confidence that the cotton boom was permanent, and that the industrializing nations of England and France in particular would always bow to "King Cotton."

American cotton doubled in yield each decade after 1800 and provided three-fourths of the world's supply by the 1840s. Southern staple crops were fully three-fifths of all American exports by 1850, and one of every seven workers in England depended on American cotton for a job. Indeed, cotton production made slaves the single most valuable financial asset in the United States—greater in dollar value than all of America's banks, railroads, and manufacturing combined.

The Old South never developed its own banking and shipping capacity to any degree. If it had, its effort to be an international cartel might have succeeded longer. Most southern bank deposits were in the North, and southern cotton planters became ever more dependent on New York for shipping. As early as 1822 one-sixth of all southern cotton cleared for Liverpool or Le Havre from the port of New York and constituted two-fifths of all that city's exports.

A collapse of cotton prices in the Panic of 1837 prompted some southerners to try to establish more direct trade relations between themselves and Europe. In a series of economic conventions held from 1837 to 1839, delegates debated the nature of foreign trade, dependence on northern importers and financiers, and other alleged threats to their commercial independence and security. But nothing, save rhetoric, came of these conventions; it was the last time southern planters would organize to break from their Yankee middlemen and shippers.

"Cotton is King," the *Southern Cultivator* declared in 1859, "and wields an astonishing influence over the world's commerce." Until 1840 the cotton trade furnished much of the export capital to finance northern economic growth. After that date, however, the northern economy expanded without dependence on cotton profits. Nevertheless, southern planters and politicians continued to boast of King Cotton's supremacy. "Our cotton is the most wonderful talisman in the world," announced a planter in 1853. "By its power we are transmuting whatever we choose into whatever we want." "No power on earth dares...to make war on cotton," James Hammond lectured the U.S. Senate in 1858; "Cotton is king." Although the South produced 4.5 million bales in 1861, its greatest cotton crop ever, this link to the world was about to collapse in a civil war. Thereafter cotton was more a shackle to the South than a king.

■ Cotton traded to England would be returned to the United States in fabric collections called sample books, such as this Norwich Textile Sample Book. Orders were placed and then shipped to Americans. (Courtesy, The Henry Francis du Pont Winterthur Library: Joseph Downs Collection of Manuscripts & Printed Ephemera)

bales, accumulating slaves as they climbed." And many did not live like rich men. They put their new wealth into cotton acreage and slaves even as they sought refinement and high social status.

William Faulkner immortalized the new wealthy planter in a fictional character, Thomas Sutpen, in his novel *Absalom, Absalom!* (1936). Sutpen arrives in a Mississippi county in the 1830s, buys a huge plantation he calls Sutpen's Hundred, and with his troop of slaves converts it into a wealthy enterprise. Sutpen marries a local woman, and although he is always viewed as a mysterious outsider by many earlier residents of the county, he becomes a pillar of the slaveholding class, eventually an officer in the Confederate Army. But Sutpen is a self-made man of indomitable will and slave-based wealth. Although his ambition is ultimately his undoing, one of the earliest lessons he had learned about success in the South was that "you got to have land and niggers and a fine house. . . ."

The cotton boom in the Mississippi valley created one-generation aristocrats. A nonfictional case in point is Greenwood Leflore, a Chocktaw chieftain who owned a plantation in Mississippi with four hundred slaves. After selling his cotton on the world market, he spent $10,000 in France to furnish one room of his mansion with hand-woven carpets, furniture upholstered in gold leaf, tables and cabinets ornamented with tortoise-shell inlay, a variety of mirrors and paintings, and a clock and candelabra in brass and ebony.

Slaveholding men dominated society and, especially among the wealthiest and oldest families, justified their

SOUTHERN PATERNALISM

dominance over white women and black slaves through a paternalistic ideology. Instead of stressing the profitable aspects of commercial agriculture, they focused on their obligations, viewing themselves as custodians of the welfare of society in general, and of the black families they owned in particular. The paternalistic planter saw himself not as an oppressor but as the benevolent guardian of an inferior race. Even yeomen who moved in and out of the slaveowning class shared this attitude of racial paternalism.

Paul Carrington Cameron, who was North Carolina's largest slaveholder, exemplifies this mentality. After a period of sickness among his one thousand North Carolina slaves (he had hundreds more in Alabama and Mississippi), Cameron wrote, "I fear the Negroes have suffered much from the want of proper attention and kindness under this late distemper . . . no love of lucre shall ever induce me to be cruel. . . ." On another occasion he described to his sister the sense of responsibility he felt:

"Do you remember a cold & frosty morning, during [our mother's] illness, when she said to me 'Paul my son the people ought to be shod' this is ever in my ears, whenever I see any ones shoes in bad order; and in my ears it will be, so long as I am master."

It was comforting to rich planters to see themselves in this way, and slaves—accommodating to the realities of power—encouraged their masters to think their benevolence was appreciated. Paternalism also served as a defense against abolitionist criticism. Still, paternalism was often a matter of style, covering harsher assumptions. As talk of paternalistic duties increased, theories about the complete and permanent inferiority of blacks multiplied. In reality, paternalism grew as a give-and-take relationship between masters and slaves, each extracting from the other what they desired—owners took labor from the bondsmen, while slaves obligated masters to provide them a measure of autonomy and living space. But it also evolved as a theory of black slavery and white dominance. As one historian has argued, paternalism "grew out of the necessity to discipline and morally justify a system of exploitation, . . . a fragile bridge across the intolerable contradictions inherent" in a slave society dependent on "the willing reproduction and productivity of its victims."

Even Paul Cameron's benevolence vanished with changed circumstances. After the Civil War, he bristled at African Americans' efforts to be free and made sweeping economic decisions without regard to their welfare. Writing on Christmas Day 1865, Cameron showed little Christian charity (but a healthy profit motive) when he declared, "I am convinced that the people who gets rid of the free negro first will be the first to advance in improved agriculture. Have made no effort to retain any of mine [and] will not attempt a crop beyond the capacity of 30 hands." With that he turned off his land nearly a thousand black people, rented his fields to several white farmers, and invested in industry.

Relations between men and women in the planter class were similarly paternalistic. The upper-class southern woman was raised and educated to be a wife, mother, and subordinate companion to men. South Carolina's Mary Boykin Chesnut wrote of her husband, "He is master of the house. To hear is to obey. . . . All the comfort of my life depends upon his being in a good humor." In a social system based on the coercion of an entire race, women were not allowed to challenge society's rules on sexual or racial relations.

Planters' daughters usually attended one of the South's rapidly multiplying boarding schools. There they formed friendships with other girls and received an education.

Typically the young woman could entertain suitors whom her parents approved. But very soon she had to choose a husband and commit herself for life to a man whom she generally had known for only a brief time. Young women were often alienated and emotionally unfulfilled. They had to follow the wishes of their families, especially fathers. "It was for me best that I yielded to the wishes of papa," wrote a young North Carolinian in 1823. "I wonder when my best will cease to be painful and when I shall begin to enjoy life instead of enduring it."

Upon marriage, a planter-class woman ceded to her husband most of her legal rights, becoming part of his family. Most of the year she was isolated on a large plantation, where she had to oversee the cooking and preserving of food, manage the house, supervise care of the children, and attend sick slaves. All these realities were more rigid and confining on the frontier, where isolation was even greater. Women sought refuge in their extended families and associations with other women. In 1821 a Georgia woman wrote to her brother of the distress of a cousin's wife: "They are living . . . in the frontiers of the state and [a] perfectly uncivilized place. Cousin W. gets a good practice [the husband] but she is almost crazy to get to Alabama where one of her sisters is living." Men on plantations could occasionally escape into the public realm—to town, business, or politics. Women could retreat from rural plantation culture only into kinship.

It is not surprising that a perceptive young white woman sometimes approached marriage with anxiety.

MARRIAGE AND FAMILY AMONG PLANTER CLASS   Women could hardly help viewing their wedding day, as one put it in 1832, as "the day to fix my fate." Lucy Breckinridge, a wealthy Virginia girl of twenty, lamented the autonomy she surrendered at the altar. In her diary she recorded this unvarnished observation on marriage: "If [husbands] care for their wives at all it is only as a sort of servant, a being made to attend to their comforts and to keep the children out of the way. . . . A woman's life after she is married, unless there is an immense amount of love, is nothing but suffering and hard work."

Lucy loved young children but knew that childbearing often involved grief, poor health, and death. In 1840 the birth rate for white southern women in their childbearing years was almost 30 percent higher than the national average. The average southern white woman could expect to bear eight children in 1800; by 1860 the figure had decreased to only six, with one or more miscarriages likely. For those women who wanted to plan their fami-

■ Portrait of a planter's family and slave, New Market, Virginia, photographer unidentified, c. 1859-1864. The structure of life on a small plantation is vividly indicated here: the young black woman holding the baby, the white mistress with shawl and fan, and the planter as patriarch.   (Collection of William A. Turner)

lies, methods of contraception and medical care were uncertain. Complications of childbirth were a major cause of death, occurring twice as often in the hot, humid South as in the Northeast.

Sexual relations between planters and slaves were another source of problems that white women had to endure but were not supposed to notice. "Violations of the moral law . . . made mulattos as common as blackberries," protested a woman in Georgia, but wives had to play "the ostrich game." "A magnate who runs a hideous black harem," wrote Mrs. Chesnut, ". . . poses as the model of all human virtues to these poor women whom God and the laws have given him."

Southern men tolerated little discussion by women of the slavery issue. In the 1840s and 1850s, as abolitionist attacks on slavery increased, southern men published a barrage of articles stressing that women should restrict their concerns to the home. The *Southern Quarterly Review* declared, "The proper place for a woman is at home. One of her highest privileges, to be politically merged in the existence of her husband."

But some southern women were beginning to seek a larger role. A study of women in Petersburg, Virginia, a large tobacco-manufacturing town, revealed behavior that valued financial autonomy. Over several decades before 1860, the proportion of women who never married, or did not remarry after the death of a spouse, grew to exceed 33 percent. Likewise the number of women who worked for wages, controlled their own property, and ran millinery or dressmaking businesses increased. In managing property, these and other women benefited from legal changes such as the Mississippi Married Women's Property Act of 1839; to protect families from the husband's indebtedness during business panics and recessions, such reforms gave married women some property rights.

Slave Life and Labor

For African Americans, slavery was a burden that destroyed some people and forced others to develop modes of survival. Slaves knew a life of poverty, coercion, toil, and resentment. They provided the physical strength, and much of the know-how, to build an agricultural empire. But their daily lives embodied the nation's most basic contradiction: in the world's model republic, they were on the wrong side of a brutally unequal power relationship.

Southern slaves enjoyed few material comforts beyond the bare necessities. Although they generally had

SLAVES'
EVERYDAY
CONDITIONS

enough to eat, their diet was plain and monotonous, lacking in nutrition. Clothing too was plain, coarse, and inexpensive. Few slaves received more than one or two changes of clothing for hot and cold seasons and one blanket each winter. Children of both sexes ran naked in hot weather and wore long cotton shirts in winter. Many slaves had to go without shoes until December, even as far north as Virginia. The bare feet of slaves were often symbolic of their status, and one reason why, after freedom, many black parents were so concerned to provide their children with shoes.

Some of the richer plantations provided substantial houses, but the average slave lived in crude accommodations, usually one-room cabins. The gravest drawback of slave cabins was not lack of comfort but their unhealthfulness. Each dwelling housed one or two entire families. Crowding and lack of sanitation fostered the spread of infection and contagious diseases such as typhoid fever, malaria, and dysentery.

Hard work was the central fact of slaves' existence. The long hours and large work gangs that characterized

SLAVE WORK
ROUTINES

Gulf Coast cotton districts operated almost like factories in the field. Overseers rang the morning bell before dawn, and black people of varying ages, tools in hand, walked toward fields. Slaves who cultivated tobacco in the Upper South worked long hours picking the sticky, sometimes noxious, leaves under harsh discipline. And, as one woman recalled when interviewed in the 1930s, "it was way after sundown fore they could stop that field work. Then they had to hustle to finish their night work [such as watering livestock or cleaning cotton] in time for supper, or go to bed without it."

Working "from sun to sun" became a norm in much of the South. As one planter put it, slaves were the best labor because "you could command them and make them do what was right." Profit took precedence over paternalism. Slave women did heavy fieldwork, often as much as the men and even during pregnancy. Old people were kept busy caring for young children, doing light chores, or carding, ginning, and spinning cotton. The black abolitionist orator Frances Ellen Watkins captured this grinding economic reality of slavery in an 1857 speech, charging that slaveholders had "found out a fearful alchemy by which . . . blood can be transformed into gold. Instead of listening to the cry of agony, they listen to the ring of dollars and stoop down to pick up the coin."

Slave children were the future of the system and were widely valued as potential labor. "A child raised every

■ George Fuller, an itinerant painter from Massachusetts, worked from 1856 to 1858 in Alabama, where he made this sketch in ink and pencil of a mistress joining her slave at work on washday.
(Pocumtuck Valley Memorial Association)

two years," wrote Thomas Jefferson, "is of more profit than the crop of the best laboring man." And in 1858, an unidentified slaveowner writing in an agricultural magazine calculated that a slave girl he purchased in 1827 for $400 had borne three sons now worth $3,000 as his working field hands. Slave children gathered kindling, carried water to the fields, swept the yard, lifted cut sugar-cane stalks into carts, stacked wheat, chased birds away from sprouting rice plants, and labored at many levels of cotton and tobacco production. "Work," wrote one historian, "can be rightly called the thief who stole the childhood of youthful bond servants."

Incentives had to be part of the labor regime and the master-slave relationship as well. Planters in the South Carolina and Georgia low country used a task system whereby slaves were assigned measured amounts of work to be performed in a given amount of time. So much cotton on a daily basis was to be picked from a designated field, so many rows hoed or plowed in a particular slave's specified section. When the task system worked best, slaves and masters alike embraced it, fostering a degree of reciprocal trust.

By the 1830s slaveowners found that labor could be regulated and motivated by the clock. When their task and "clock time" was up, slaves' time was their own, for working in garden plots, tending to hogs, or even hiring out their own extra labor. The system's incentives afforded many slave families life-sustaining material and psychological benefits. From this experience and personal space, many slaves developed their own sense of property ownership.

Slaves could not demand much autonomy, of course, because the owner enjoyed a monopoly on force and violence. Whites throughout the South believed that slaves "can't be governed except with the whip." One South Carolinian frankly explained to a northern journalist that he whipped his slaves regularly, "say once a fortnight; . . . the fear of the lash kept them in good order." Evidence suggests that whippings were less frequent on small farms than on large plantations. But beatings symbolized authority to the master and tyranny to the slaves, who made them a benchmark for evaluating a master. In the words of former slaves, a good owner was one who did not "whip too much," whereas a bad owner "whipped till he's bloodied you and blistered you."

VIOLENCE AGAINST SLAVES

As these reports suggest, terrible abuses could and did occur. The master wielded virtually absolute authority on his plantation, and courts did not recognize the word of chattel. Slaveholders rarely had to answer to the law or to the state. Pregnant women were whipped, and there were burnings, mutilations, tortures, and murders. Yet physical cruelty may have been less prevalent in the United States than in other slaveholding parts of the New World. Especially in some of the sugar islands of the Caribbean, treatment was so poor and death rates were so high that the heavily male slave population shrank in size. In the United States, by contrast, the slave population experienced a steady natural increase as births exceeded deaths and each generation grew larger. Indeed, the North American slave population was the only one in the New World to naturally reproduce itself.

The worst evil of American slavery was not its physical cruelty but the nature of slavery itself: coercion, belonging to another person, virtually no hope for mobility or change. Recalling their time in bondage, some former slaves emphasized the physical abuse, or the "bullwhip days," as one woman described her past. But memories of physical punishment focused on the tyranny of whipping as much as the pain. Delia Garlic made the essential point: "It's bad to belong to folks that own you soul an' body. I could tell you 'bout it all day, but even then you couldn't guess the awfulness of it." Thomas Lewis put it this way: "There was no such thing as being good to slaves. Many people were better than others, but a slave belonged to his master and there was no way to get out of it." To be a slave was to be the object of another person's will and material gain, to be owned, as the saying went, "from the cradle to the grave."

As these comments reveal, the great majority of American slaves retained their mental independence and self-respect despite their bondage. Contrary to popular belief at the time, they were not loyal partners in their own oppression. They had to be subservient and speak honeyed words to their masters, but they talked and behaved quite differently among themselves. The evidence of their resistant attitudes comes from their actions and their own life stories. In *Narrative of the Life of Frederick Douglass, an American Slave, Written by Himself* (1845), Douglass wrote that most slaves, when asked about "their condition and the character of their masters, almost universally say they are contented, and that their masters are kind." Slaves did this, said Douglass, because they were governed by the maxim that "a still tongue makes a wise head," especially in the presence of unfamiliar people. Because they were "part of the human family," slaves often quarreled over who had the best master. But at the end of the day, Douglass remarked, when one had a bad master, he sought a better master; and when he had a better one, he wanted to "be his own master."

Some former slaves remembered warm feelings between masters and slaves, but the prevailing attitudes were distrust and antagonism. Slaves saw through acts of kindness. One woman said her mistress was "a mighty good somebody to belong to" but only "'cause she was raisin' us to work for her." A man recalled that his owners took good care of their slaves, "and Grandma Maria say, 'Why shouldn't they—it was their money.'" Slaves also resented being used as beasts of burden. One man observed that his master "fed us reg'lar on good, 'stantial food, just like you'd tend to your horse, if you had a real good one."

SLAVE-MASTER RELATIONSHIPS

Slaves were alert to the thousand daily signs of their degraded status. One man recalled the general rule that slaves ate cornbread and owners ate biscuits. If blacks did get biscuits, "the flour that we made the biscuits out of was the third-grade sorts." A former slave recalled, "Us catch lots of 'possums," but "the white folks at 'em." If the owner took his slaves' garden produce to town and sold it for them, the slaves often suspected him of pocketing part of the profits.

Suspicion often grew into hatred. When a yellow fever epidemic struck in 1852, many slaves saw it as God's retribution. An elderly ex-slave named Minnie Fulkes cherished the conviction that God was going to punish white people for their cruelty to blacks. She described the whippings that her mother had to endure, and then she exclaimed, "Lord, Lord, I hate white people and the flood waters goin' to drown some more."

On the plantation, of course, slaves had to keep such thoughts to themselves. Often they expressed one feeling to whites, another within their own households. In their daily lives slaves created many ways to survive and to sustain their humanity in this world of repression.

Slave Culture

a people is always "more than the sum of its brutalization," wrote the African American novelist Ralph Ellison in 1967. What people create in the face of hard luck and oppression is what provides hope. The resource that enabled slaves to maintain such defiance was their culture: a body of beliefs, values, and practices born of their past and maintained in the present. As best they could, they built a community knitted together by stories, music, a religious world-view, leadership, the smells of their cooking, the sounds of their own voices, and the tapping of their feet. "The values expressed in folklore," wrote the African American poet Sterling Brown, provided a "wellspring to which slaves . . . could return in times of doubt to be re-freshed." That they endured and found loyalty and strength among themselves is a tribute to their courage and triumph of the human spirit.

Slave culture changed significantly after 1800, as fewer and fewer slaves were African-born. For a few

AFRICAN CULTURAL SURVIVAL

years South Carolina reopened the international slave trade, but after 1808 Congress banned further importations. By the 1830s, the vast majority of slaves in the South were native-born Americans. Many blacks, in fact, can trace their American ancestry back further than most white Americans.

Despite lack of firsthand memory, African influences remained strong, especially in appearance and forms of expression. Some slave men plaited their hair into rows and fancy designs; slave women often wore their hair "in string"—tied in small bunches secured by a string or piece of cloth. A few men and many women wrapped their heads in kerchiefs of the styles and colors of West Africa. Some could remember the names of African ancestors passed on to them by family lore. In burial practices, slaves used jars and other glass objects to decorate graves, following similar African traditions.

Music, religion, and folktales were parts of daily life for most slaves. Borrowing partly from their African background, as well as forging new American folkways, they developed what scholars have called a "sacred world-view," which affected all aspects of work, leisure, and self-understanding. Slaves made musical instruments with carved motifs that resembled African stringed instruments. Their drumming and dancing followed African patterns that made whites marvel. One visitor to Georgia in the 1860s described a ritual dance of African origin: "A ring of singers is formed. . . . They then utter a kind of melodious chant, which gradually increases in strength, and in noise, until it fairly shakes the house, and it can be heard for a long distance." This observer of the "ring shout" also noted the agility of the dancers and the African call-and-response pattern in their chanting.

Many slaves continued to believe in spirit possession. Whites, too, believed in ghosts and charms, but the slaves' belief resembled the African concept of the living dead—the idea that deceased relatives visit the earth for many years until the process of dying is complete. Slaves also practiced conjuration and quasi-magical root medicine. By the 1850s the most notable conjurers and root doctors were reputed to live in South Carolina, Georgia, Louisiana, and other isolated coastal areas with high slave populations. But even in Maryland, a young Fred-

erick Douglass carried a special root that had to be positioned "always on the right side," given him by an "old advisor" who lived alone in the woods.

These cultural survivals provided slaves with a sense of their separate past. Such practices and beliefs were not static "Africanisms" or mere "retentions." They were cultural adaptations, living traditions re-formed in the Americas in response to new experience. African American slaves in the Old South were a people forged by two centuries of cultural mixture in the Atlantic world; and the South itself was a melding of many African and European cultural forces.

As they became African Americans, slaves also developed a sense of racial identity. In the colonial period, Africans had arrived in America from many different states and kingdoms, represented in distinctive languages, body markings, and traditions. Planters had used ethnic differences to create occupational hierarchies. By the early antebellum period, however, old ethnic identities gave way as American slaves increasingly saw themselves as a single group unified by race. Africans had arrived in the New World with virtually no concept of "race"; by the antebellum era, their descendants had learned through bitter experience that race was now the defining feature of their lives. They were a transplanted and transformed people.

As African culture gave way to a maturing African American culture, more and more slaves adopted

SLAVES' RELIGION AND MUSIC

Christianity. But they fashioned Christianity into an instrument of support and resistance. Theirs was a religion of justice and deliverance, quite unlike their masters' religious propaganda directed at them as a means of control. "You ought to have heard that preachin'," said one man. " 'Obey your master and mistress, don't steal chickens and eggs and meat,' but nary a word about havin' a soul to save." Slaves believed that Jesus cared about their souls and their plight. In their interpretations of biblical stories, as one historian has said, they were "literally willing themselves reborn." They rejected the idea that in heaven whites would have "the colored folks . . . there to wait on 'em." Instead, slaveholders would be "broilin' in hell for their sin" when God's justice came.

For slaves, Christianity was a religion of personal and group salvation. Devout men and women worshiped every day, "in the field or by the side of the road," or in special "prayer grounds" that afforded privacy. Some slaves held fervent secret prayer meetings that lasted far into the night. Many slaves nurtured an unshakable belief that God would enter history and end their bondage.

This faith—and the joy and emotional release that accompanied worship—sustained them.

Slaves also adapted Christianity to African practices. In West African belief, devotees are possessed by a god so thoroughly that the god's own personality replaces the human personality. In the late antebellum era, Christian slaves experienced possession by the Protestant "Holy Spirit." The combination of shouting, singing, and dancing that seemed to overtake black worshipers formed the heart of their religious faith. "The old meeting house caught fire," recalled an ex-slave preacher. "The spirit was there. . . . God saw our need and came to us. I used to wonder what made people shout but now I don't. There is a joy on the inside and it wells up so strong that we can't keep still. It is fire in the bones. Any time that fire touches a man, he will jump." Out in brush arbors or in meetinghouses, slaves took in the presence of God and sang away their woes. Some travelers observed "bands" of "Fist and Heel Worshippers." "He who could sing loudest and longest led the 'Band,'" said a suspicious black bishop from the North who opposed emotional religion, "a handkerchief in hand with which he kept time, while his feet resounded on the floor like the drumsticks of a bass drum." Many post-slavery black choirs could not perform properly without a good wooden floor to use as their "drum."

Rhythm and physical movement were crucial to slaves' religious experience. In their own preachers' chanted sermons, which reached out to gather the sinner into a narrative of meanings and cadences along the way to conversion, an American tradition was born. The chanted sermon was both a message from Scripture and a patterned form that required audience response punctuated by "yes sirs!" and "amens!" But it was in song that the slaves left their most sublime gift to American culture.

Through the spirituals, slaves tried to impose order on the chaos of their lives. Many themes run through the lyrics of slave songs. Often referred to later as the "sorrow songs," they also anticipate imminent rebirth. Sadness could give way immediately to joy: "Did you ever stan' on a mountain, wash yo hands in a cloud?" Rebirth was at the heart as well of the famous hymn "Oh, Freedom": "Oh, Oh, Freedom / Oh, Oh, Freedom over me— / But before I'll be a slave, / I'll be buried in my grave, / And go home to my Lord, / And Be Free!"

This tension and sudden change between sorrow and joy animates many songs: "Sometimes I feel like a motherless chile . . . / Sometimes I feel like an eagle in the air, / Spread my wings and fly, fly, fly!" Many songs also express a sense of intimacy and closeness with God. Some songs display an unmistakable rebelliousness, such as the enduring "He said, and if I had my way / If I had my

■ Drawing by Lewis Miller of a "Lynchburg Negro Dance," Lynchburg, Virginia, August 18, 1853. This work of art shows the slaves' use of elaborate costumes, string instruments, and the bones.   (Abby Aldrich Rockefeller Folk Art Collection, Colonial Williamsburg Foundation)

Lynchburg—negro dance, August 18th 1853.

way, if I had my way, / I'd tear this building down!" And some spirituals reached for a collective sense of hope in the black community as a whole:

> O, gracious Lord! When shall it be,
> That we poor souls shall all be free;
> Lord, break them slavery powers—
> Will you go along with me?
> Lord break them slavery powers,
> Go sound the jubilee!

In many ways, American slaves converted the Christian God to themselves. They sought an alternative world to live in—a home other than the one fate had given them on earth. In a thousand variations on the 'Brer Rabbit folktales—in which the weak survive by wit, and power is reversed—and in the countless refrains of their songs, they fashioned survival and resistance out of their own cultural imagination.

American slaves clung tenaciously to the personal relationships that gave meaning to life. Although American law did not recognize slave families, masters permitted them; in fact, slaveowners expected slaves to form families and have children. As a result, even along the rapidly expanding edge of the cotton kingdom, there was a normal ratio of men to women, young to old. Studies have shown that on some of the largest cotton plantations of South Carolina, when masters allowed their slaves increased autonomy working on the task system, the property accumulation thus fostered led to more stable and healthier families.

THE BLACK FAMILY IN SLAVERY

■ This photograph of five generations of a slave family, taken in Beaufort, South Carolina, in 1862, is silent but powerful testimony to the importance that enslaved African Americans placed on their ever-threatened family ties.   (Library of Congress)

Following African kinship traditions, African Americans avoided marriage between cousins (commonplace among aristocratic slaveowners). By naming their children after relatives of past generations, African Americans emphasized their family histories. If they chose to bear the surname of a slaveowner, it was often the name of the owner under whom their family had begun their bondage in America. Kinship networks and broadly extended families are what held life together in many slave communities.

For slave women sexual abuse and rape by white masters were ever-present threats to themselves and their family lives. By 1860 there were 405,751 mulattos in the United States, comprising 12.5 percent of the African American population, and the majority were the offspring of involuntary relationships. White planters were sometimes open with their behavior toward slave women, but not in the way they talked about it. As Mary Chesnut remarked, sex between slaveholding men and their slave women was "the thing we can't name." Buying slaves for sex was all too common at the New Orleans slave market. In what was called the "fancy trade" (a "fancy" was a young attractive slave girl or woman), females were often sold for prices as much as 300 percent higher than the average. At such auctions for young women, slaveholders exhibited some of the ugliest values at the heart of the slave system—patriarchal dominance demonstrated in paying $3,000 to $5,000 for female "companions."

Slave women had to negotiate this confused world of desire, threat, and shame. Harriet Jacobs, who spent much of her youth and early adult years dodging her owner's relentless sexual pursuit, descried this circumstance as "the war of my life." In recollecting her desperate effort to protect her children and help them find a way north to freedom, Jacobs asked a haunting question that many slave women carried with them to their graves: "Why does the slave ever love? Why allow the tendrils of the heart to twine around objects which may at any moment be wrenched away by the hand of violence?"

Separation from those they loved by violence, sexual appropriation, and sale was what slave families feared and hated most. Many struggled for years to keep their children together and, after emancipation, to reestablish contact with loved ones lost by forced migration and sale. Between 1820 and 1860 an estimated 2 million slaves were moved into the region extending from western Georgia to eastern Texas. When the Union Army registered thousands of black marriages

THE DOMESTIC SLAVE TRADE

in Mississippi and Louisiana in 1864 and 1865, fully 25 percent of the men over forty reported that they had been forcibly separated from a previous wife. Thousands of black families were disrupted every year to serve the needs of the expanding cotton economy. The Butler auction of 1859, described in the chapter-opening vignette, was only one gruesome chapter of a very long story.

Many antebellum white southerners made their living from the slave trade. In South Carolina alone by the 1850s, there were over one hundred slave-trading firms selling an annual average of approximately 6,500 slaves to southwestern states. Although southerners often denied it, vast numbers of slaves moved west by outright sale and not by migrating with their owners. A typical trader's advertisement read: "NEGROES WANTED. I am paying the highest cash prices for young and likely NEGROES, those having good front teeth and being otherwise sound."

Slave traders were practical, roving businessmen. They were sometimes considered degraded by white planters, but many slaveowners did business with them. Market forces, as the Butler auction indicates, drove this commerce in humanity. At slave "pens" in cities such as New Orleans, traders promoted "a large and commodious showroom . . . prepared to accommodate over 200 Negroes for sale." Traders did their utmost to make their slaves appear young, healthy, and happy, cutting gray whiskers off men, using "paddles" as discipline so as not to scar their merchandise, and forcing people to dance and sing as buyers arrived for an auction. When transported to the southwestern markets, slaves were often chained together in "coffles," which made journeys of 500 miles or more on foot.

The complacent mixture of racism and business among traders is evident in their own language. "I refused a girl 20 year[s] old at 700 yesterday," one trader wrote to another in 1853. "If you think best to take her at 700 I can still get her. She is very badly whipped but good teeth." Some sales were transacted at owners' requests. "Bought a cook yesterday that was to go out of state," wrote a trader; "she just made the people mad that was all." Some traders demonstrated how deeply slavery and racism were intertwined. "I have bought the boy Isaac for 1100," wrote a trader in 1854 to his partner. "I think him very prime. . . . He is a . . . house servant . . . first rate cook . . . and splendid carriage driver. He is also a fine painter and varnisher and . . . says he can make a fine panl door. . . . Also he performs well on the violin. . . . He is a genius and its strange to say I think he is smarter than I am."

A slave coffle on the march toward newly settled states of the Southwest. (Collection of William Loren Katz)

Slave Resistance and Rebellion

Slaves brought to their efforts at resistance the same common sense and determination that characterized their struggle to secure their family lives. The scales weighed heavily against overt revolution, and the slaves knew it. But they seized opportunities to alter their work conditions. They sometimes slacked off when they were not being watched. Thus owners complained that slaves "never would lay out their strength freely." These slave attitudes caused many whites to doubt the success of black free labor after the Civil War.

Daily discontent and desperation were also manifest in sabotage of equipment, in wanton carelessness about work, in theft of food, livestock, or crops, or in getting drunk on stolen liquor. Some slaves who were hired out

STRATEGIES OF RESISTANCE

might show their anger by hoarding their earnings. Or, they might just fall into recalcitrance. "I have a boy in my employ called Jim Archer," complained a Vicksburg, Mississippi, slaveholder in 1843. "Jim does not want to be under anyones control and says . . . he wants to go home this summer." A woman named Ellen, hired as a cook in Tennessee in 1856, quietly put mercury poison into a roasted apple for her unsuspecting mistress. And some slave women resisted as best they could by trying to control their own pregnancy, either by avoiding it or by seeking it as a way to improve their physical conditions.

Many male, and some female, slaves acted out their defiance by violently attacking overseers or even their owners. Southern court records and newspapers are full of accounts of these resistant slaves who gave the lie to the image of the docile bondsmen. The price they paid was high. Such lonely rebels were customarily secured and flogged, sold away, or hanged. One Louisiana planter reported strapping two especially uncooperative slaves to a stake and delivering 15 lashes to one and 175 to the other.

Many individual slaves attempted to run away to the North, and some received assistance from the loose network known as the Underground Railroad (see pages 363–364). But it was more common for slaves to run off temporarily to hide in the woods. Approximately 80 percent of runaways were male; women simply could not flee as readily because of their responsibility for children. Fear, disgruntlement over treatment, or family separation might motivate slaves to risk all in flight. Only a minority of those who tried such escapes ever made it to freedom in the North or Canada, but these fugitives made slavery a very insecure institution by the 1850s.

American slavery produced some fearless revolutionaries. Gabriel's Rebellion involved as many as a thousand slaves when it was discovered in 1800, just before it exploded in Richmond, Virginia (see pages 211–212). According to controversial court testimony, a similar conspiracy existed in Charleston in 1822, led by a free black named Denmark Vesey. Born a slave in the Caribbean, Vesey won a lottery of $1,500 in 1799, bought his own freedom, and became a religious leader in the black community. According to one long-argued interpretation, Vesey was a heroic revolutionary determined to free his people or die trying. But in a recent challenge, historian Michael Johnson points out that the court testimony is the only reliable source on the alleged insurrection. Could the testimony reveal less of reality than of white South Carolina's fears of slave rebellion? The court, says Johnson, built its case on rumors and intimidated witnesses, and "conjured into being" an insurrection not about to occur in reality. Whatever the facts, when the arrests and trials were over, thirty-seven "conspirators" were executed and more than three dozen others were banished from the state.

The most famous rebel of all, Nat Turner, struck for freedom in Southampton County, Virginia, in 1831. The

NAT TURNER'S INSURRECTION

son of an African woman who passionately hated her enslavement, Nat Turner was a precocious child who learned to read when he was very young. Encouraged by his first owner to study the Bible, he enjoyed certain privileges but also endured hard work and changes of masters. His father successfully escaped to freedom.

Eventually young Nat became a preacher with a reputation for eloquence and mysticism. After nurturing his plan for several years, Turner led a band of rebels from farm to farm in the predawn darkness of August 22, 1831. The group severed limbs and crushed skulls with axes or killed their victims with guns. Before

■ A bill of sale documents that this slave woman, Louisa, was owned by the young child whom she holds on her lap. In the future Louisa's life would be subject to the child's wishes and decisions.   (Missouri Historical Society, St. Louis)

alarmed planters stopped them, Nat Turner and his followers had slaughtered sixty whites of both sexes and all ages in forty-eight hours. The rebellion was soon put down, and in retaliation, whites killed slaves at random all over the region, including in adjoining states. Turner was eventually caught and then hanged. As many as two hundred African Americans, including innocent victims of marauding whites, lost their lives as a result of the rebellion.

Nat Turner remains one of the most haunting symbols in America's unresolved history with racial slavery and discrimination. While in jail awaiting execution, Turner was interviewed by a Virginia lawyer and slaveholder, Thomas R. Gray. Their intriguing creation, *The*

Confessions of Nat Turner, became a bestseller within a month of Turner's hanging. Turner told of his early childhood, his religious visions, his zeal to be free; Gray called the rebel a "gloomy fanatic," but in a manner that made him fascinating and produced one of the most remarkable documents in the annals of American slavery. In the wake of Turner's insurrection, many states passed stiffened legal codes against black education and religious practice.

Most importantly, in 1832 the state of Virginia, shocked to its core, held a full-scale legislative and public debate over gradual emancipation as a means of ridding itself of slavery and of blacks. The plan debated would not have freed any slaves until 1858, and it provided that eventually all blacks would be colonized outside Virginia. But when the House of Delegates voted, gradual abolition lost, 73 to 58. In the end, Virginia opted to do nothing except reinforce its own moral and economic defenses of slavery. It was the last time white southerners would debate any kind of emancipation until war forced their hand.

Harmony and Tension in a Slave Society

From 1830 to 1860, slavery impinged on laws and customs, individual values, and, increasingly, every aspect of southern politics. In all things, from their workaday movements to Sunday worship, slaves fell under the supervision of whites. State courts held that a slave "has no civil right" and could not hold property "except at the will and pleasure of his master." Revolts like Nat Turner's tightened the legal straitjacket even more. As political conflicts between North and South deepened, fears of slave revolt grew, and restrictions on slaves increased accordingly.

State and federal laws aided the capture of fugitive slaves and required nonslaveholders to support the slave system. All white male citizens had a legal duty to participate in slave patrols. Ship captains, harbor masters, and other whites were required to scrutinize the papers of African Americans who might be attempting to escape bondage.

Slavery deeply affected southern values precisely because it was the main determinant of wealth. Ownership

SLAVERY, WEALTH, AND SOCIAL STATUS of slaves guaranteed the labor to produce cotton and other crops on a large scale. Slaves were a commodity and an investment, much like gold; people bought them on speculation, hoping

for a steady rise in their market values. Across the South, variations in wealth from county to county corresponded very closely to variations in slaveholding. Wealth in slaves also translated into political power: a solid majority of political officeholders were slaveholders, and the most powerful were usually large-scale planters.

Slavery's influence spread throughout the social system until even the values and mores of nonslaveholders bore its imprint. The availability of slave labor tended to devalue free labor: where strenuous work under supervision was reserved for an enslaved race, few free people relished it. When Alexis de Tocqueville crossed from Ohio into Kentucky in his travels of 1831, he observed "the effect that slavery produces on society. On the right bank of the Ohio [River] everything is activity, industry; labor is honoured; there are no slaves. Pass to the left bank and the scene changes so suddenly that you think yourself on the other side of the world; the enterprising spirit is gone. There, work is not only painful; it is shameful." Tocqueville's own class impulses found a home in the South, however. There he found a "veritable aristocracy which . . . combines many prejudices with high sentiments and instincts."

The values of the aristocrat—lineage, privilege, pride, and refinement of person and manner—commanded respect throughout the South. Many of those qualities were in short supply, however, in the recently settled portions of the cotton kingdom, where frontier values of courage and self-reliance ruled. Thus independence and defense of one's honor became important traits for planter and frontier farmer alike.

ARISTOCRATIC VALUES AND FRONTIER INDIVIDUALISM

Instead of gradually disappearing as it did in the North, the Code Duello, which required men to defend their honor through violence, lasted much longer in the South. In North Carolina in 1851 a wealthy planter named Samuel Fleming responded to a series of disputes with the lawyer William Waightstill Avery by "cowhiding" (whipping) him on a public street. According to the code, Avery had two choices: to redeem his honor violently or to brand himself a coward through inaction. Three weeks later Avery shot Fleming dead at point-blank range during a session of the Burke County Superior Court, with Judge William Battle and numerous spectators looking on. A jury later took only ten minutes to find Avery not guilty, and the spectators gave him a standing ovation.

Other aristocratic values of the planter class were less acceptable to less wealthy whites. In their pride, planters expected not only to wield power but to receive deference from poorer whites. But the sternly independent yeoman class resented infringements of their rights, and many belonged to evangelical faiths that exalted values of simplicity and condemned the planters' love of wealth. Also conscious of national democratic ideals, yeomen sometimes challenged or rejected the political pretensions of planters. And much of the planters' power and their claims to a republican ideal of white men leading other white men was built on a foundation of black slave labor.

Class tensions emerged in the western, nonslaveholding parts of the seaboard states by the 1830s. There

YEOMAN DEMANDS AND WHITE CLASS RELATIONS

yeoman farmers resented their underrepresentation in state legislatures and the corruption in local government. After vigorous debate, the reformers won many battles. Voters in the more recently settled states of the Old Southwest adopted white manhood suffrage and other electoral reforms, including popular election of governors, legislative apportionment based on white population only, and locally chosen county government. Slaveowners knew that a more open government structure could permit troubling issues to arise. In Virginia, it was nonslaveholding westerners who petitioned and initiated the debate over abolition in the wake of Nat Turner's Rebellion in 1832.

Given such tensions, it was perhaps remarkable that slaveholders and nonslaveholders did not experience more overt conflict. Why were class confrontations among whites so infrequent? Historians have given several answers. One of the most important factors was race. The South's racial ideology stressed the superiority of all whites to blacks. Thus slavery became the basis of equality among whites, and racism inflated the status of poor whites and gave them a common interest with the rich. Moreover, family ties linked some nonslaveholders to wealthy planters, especially on the expanding frontier.

At the same time, the potential for upward mobility blunted some class conflict. The "Old South" was a fluid society in which many people rose in status by acquiring land or slaves, and those who did not wished they could. Even in cotton-rich Alabama in the 1850s, fewer than half of the richest families in a typical county belonged to its elite ten years later. Most did not die or lose their wealth; they merely moved on to some new state. This constant mobility in an expanding plantation economy meant that southern society did not settle into an utterly rigid social pattern.

Most importantly, in their daily lives yeomen and slaveholders were seldom in conflict. Before the Civil War most yeomen were able to pursue unhindered their independent lifestyle. They worked their farms, avoided debt, and marked progress for their families that in their rural habitats was unrelated to slaveholding. Likewise, slaveholders pursued their goals quite independently of yeomen. Planters farmed for the market but also for themselves.

Suppression of dissent also played an increasing role. After 1830 white southerners who criticized the slave system out of moral conviction or class resentment were intimidated, attacked, or legally prosecuted. By the 1850s the defense of slavery's interests exerted an ever more powerful influence on southern politics and society.

Still, there were signs that the relative lack of conflict between slaveholders and nonslaveholders was

HARDENING OF CLASS LINES

coming to an end in the late antebellum period. As cotton lands filled up, nonslaveholders saw their opportunities beginning to narrow; meanwhile, wealthy planters enjoyed expanding profits. The risks of entering cotton production were becoming too great and the cost of slaves too high for many yeomen to rise in society. From 1830 to 1860 the percentage of white southern families holding slaves declined steadily from 36 to 25 percent. Although slaveowners accounted for this smaller portion of the population, planters' share of the South's agricultural wealth remained at between 90 and 95 percent.

Urban artisans and mechanics felt the pinch acutely. Their numbers were few, and in bad times they were often the first to lose work as markets collapsed. Moreover, they faced stiff competition from urban slaves, whose masters wanted to hire them out to practice trades. White workers in some port cities staged protests demanding that economic competition from slaves be forbidden, but they were ignored. Such angry protests of white workers resulted in harsh restrictions on free African American laborers and craftsmen. Pre–Civil War politics reflected these tensions as well. Anticipating possible secession and the prospect of a war to defend slavery, slaveowners expressed growing fear about the loyalty of nonslaveholders. Schemes to widen the ownership of slaves were discussed, including reopening the African slave trade. In North Carolina, a prolonged and increasingly bitter controversy erupted over the combination of high taxes on land and low taxes on slaves. When nonslaveholder Hinton R. Helper denounced the slave system in *The Impending Crisis,* published in 1857, discerning planters feared the eruption of such controversies in every southern state.

But for the moment slaveowners stood secure. In the 1850s they occupied from 50 to 85 percent of the seats in state legislatures and a similarly high percentage of the South's congressional seats. Planters' interests controlled all the other major social institutions. Professors who criticized slavery had been dismissed from colleges and universities; schoolbooks that contained "unsound" ideas had been replaced. And almost all the Methodist and Baptist clergy had become slavery's most vocal defenders.

Summary

During the thirty years before the Civil War the South grew as part of America's westward expansion. Ideologically and economically, the southern states developed in many distinctive ways; at the same time, they were also deeply enmeshed in the nation's heritage and political economy. Far more than the North, the antebellum South was a biracial society; whites grew up directly influenced by black folkways and culture, and blacks, the vast majority of whom were slaves, became predominantly native-born Americans and the cobuilders with whites of a rural, agricultural society. From the Old South on to modern times, white and black southerners have always shared a tragic, mutual history.

With the sustained cotton boom, the South grew fatefully into a much larger slave society than it had been early in the century. The coercive influence of slavery affected virtually every element of southern life and politics, and increasingly produced a leadership determined to preserve a conservative, hierarchical social and racial order. Despite the white supremacy that united them, the democratic values of yeomen often clashed with the profit motives of aristocratic planters. The benevolent self-image and paternalistic ideology of slaveholders had to ultimately stand the test of the slaves' own judgments. African American slaves responded by fashioning over time a rich, expressive folk culture and a religion of personal and group deliverance. Their experiences could be profoundly different from one region and kind of labor to another. Some blacks were crushed by bondage; many others transcended it in an epic of survival and resistance.

By 1850, through their own wits and on the backs of African labor, white southerners had aggressively built one of the last profitable, expanding slave societies on earth. North of them, deeply intertwined with them in the same nation, market economy, constitutional system, and history, a different kind of society had grown even faster—one driven by industrialism and free labor. The clash of these two deeply connected, yet mutually fearful and divided societies was about to explode in political storms over how the nation would define its future.

LEGACY FOR A PEOPLE AND A NATION
Reparations for Slavery

How should the United States come to terms with 250 years of racial slavery? Is this period best forgotten as a terrible passage that African Americans as well as the country transcended over time? Or does the nation owe a long-overdue debt to black people for their oppression?

In the wake of emancipation in 1865, and rooted in vague federal promises, many former slaves believed they were entitled to "forty acres and a mule," but these never materialized. As the leader of a planters' association put it in 1865, "the emancipated slaves own nothing, because nothing but freedom has been given to them."

In 1897, Callie House, born in 1865 in a contraband camp for ex-slaves and a poor mother of four children, organized the National Ex-Slave Pension and Bounty Association, modeled after the pension system established for soldiers. House traveled all over the South, recruiting 250,000 members at 10-cent dues. Her lobbying of the federal government for slave pensions failed, and she was accused of mail fraud and imprisoned for one year in 1916.

More recently a widespread debate over "reparations" for slavery has emerged. As the history of slavery has been rewritten since the 1960s, Americans have learned a great deal about how slave labor created American wealth: how insurance companies insured slaves, how complicitous the U.S. government was in slavery's defense and expansion, and how slaves built the U.S. Capitol while their owners received $5 a month for their labor. And since 1989 Representative John Conyers Jr. has annually submitted an unsuccessful bill in Congress to establish a commission to study the legacies of slavery and racism.

The debate is fueled by a wealth of analogies: the reparations paid to Japanese Americans interned in World War II; the reparations paid to several Native American tribes for their stolen land; the reparations paid to thousands of Holocaust survivors and victims of forced labor; and a suit settled in 1999 that will pay an estimated $2 billion to some twenty thousand black farmers for discrimination practiced by the Agriculture Department in the early twentieth century.

On the other side, some argue that because there are no living former slaves or slaveholders, reparations for slavery can never take the form of money. But in 2002 a lawsuit was filed against three major corporations who allegedly profited from slavery, and the National Reparations Coordinating Committee promises a suit against the U.S. government itself. Critics argue that resources would be better spent "making sure black kids have a credible education" and in rebuilding inner cities. Advocates contend that when "government participates in a crime against humanity," it is "obliged to make the victims whole." The movement for reparations has strong support in grassroots black communities, and the issue has become the subject of a broad public debate. The legacy of slavery for a people and a nation promises to become America's most traumatic test of how to reconcile its history with justice.

The **history companion** *powered by Eduspace®*
Your primary source for interactive quizzes, exercises, and more to help you learn efficiently.
http://history.college.hmco.com/students

PRIZE BANNER
OBTAINED BY THE REPUBLICANS OF THE TOWNSHIP OF PEQUANNOC,
Septr 18th   1856.

FOR PRESIDENT
JOHN C. FREMONT,
FOR VICE PRESIDENT
WILLIAM L. DAYTON,

OUR STANDARD BEARER THEN,
THE BRAVE PATH FINDER BE!
FREE SPEECH, FREE PRESS, FREE SOIL,
FREE MEN,
FREMONT AND VICTORY,

E. Kranich, Pnt.
Morristown

SLAVERY AND AMERICA'S FUTURE: THE ROAD TO WAR 1845–1861

*a*s the delegates filed into the Musical Fund Hall in Philadelphia on June 17, 1856, they knew they had created something special in American politics. The first national nominating convention of the Republican Party met to approve a platform and select their presidential ticket. Formed just two years earlier, the party drew together a broad coalition of northern politicians who opposed the expansion of slavery, as well as the growing power of the South in the federal government. Most American political conventions in those years were raucous affairs; but at this gathering, according to a journalist, there was only "a slight quantity of liquor consumed, very little profane swearing . . . and . . . intense propriety." Republicans had come to Philadelphia for the solemn business of offering the American electorate a genuinely antislavery future.

Their coalition combined men who had been former Democrats; men who had been founding members of the American Party, a group that wanted to prohibit foreigners, especially Catholics, from settling in the United States; and many former Whigs, whose party had been shattered by the crisis over slavery and its expansion. They consisted of conservatives, moderates, and radicals; some believed slavery a moral evil, while others saw it as a political problem.

At this convention, a radical temper prevailed. The convention was only minutes old when the temporary chairman brought the delegates to their feet by using the Declaration of Independence to label slavery a great political danger to the nation's future. Permanent chairman Henry S. Lane of Indiana followed by declaring the "vital principle of the Republican party" to be "no more slave states," an aim he rooted in the "natural rights of man." Speaker after speaker declared that their party would render "freedom national" and "slavery sectional" by using the power of Congress to outlaw human bondage in all western territories.

◀ The Republican John C. Frémont's presidential campaign banner from Pequannoc Township, New Jersey, September 1856. The banner contains all the keywords of the Republican campaign except "free labor." (Library of Congress)

CHRONOLOGY

1846 • War with Mexico begins
• Oregon Treaty negotiated
• Wilmot Proviso inflames sectional divisions

1847 • Cass proposes idea of popular sovereignty

1848 • Treaty of Guadalupe Hidalgo gives United States new territory in the Southwest
• Free-Soil Party formed
• Taylor elected president

1849 • Gold discovered in California, which applies for admission to United States as free state

1850 • Compromise of 1850 passed in separate bills

1852 • Stowe publishes *Uncle Tom's Cabin*
• Pierce elected president

1854 • Publication of "Appeal of the Independent Democrats"
• Kansas-Nebraska Act wins approval and ignites controversy
• Republican Party formed
• Return of fugitive Burns from Boston to slavery in Virginia

1856 • Bleeding Kansas troubles nation
• Brooks attacks Sumner in Senate chamber
• Buchanan elected president, but Republican Frémont wins most northern states

1857 • *Dred Scott v. Sanford* endorses southern views on black citizenship and slavery in territories
• Economic panic and widespread unemployment begins

1858 • Kansas voters reject Lecompton Constitution
• Lincoln-Douglas debates attract attention
• Douglas proposes Freeport Doctrine

1859 • Brown raids Harpers Ferry

1860 • Democratic Party splits in two; southern Democrats demand "Slave Code for the Territories"
• Lincoln elected president
• Crittenden Compromise fails
• South Carolina secedes from Union

1861 • Six more Deep South states secede
• Confederacy established at Montgomery, Alabama
• Attack on Fort Sumter begins Civil War
• Four states in the Upper South join the Confederacy

The convention's platform committee was fittingly chaired by David Wilmot, a former Democrat who was no friend of black civil and political rights. But Wilmot, like others, was firmly opposed to slavery's expansion and endorsed the protection of free white men's labor and land ownership across the continent. The platform denounced the South's interest in the acquisition of Cuba, supported the building of a transcontinental railroad, and nodded gently against nativism. But these were all "like a tail to the antislavery kite," as one historian put it. At the heart of the platform was the short, direct credo calling upon Congress to "prohibit in the territories those twin relics of barbarism—polygamy and slavery." The Republicans nominated the famous western explorer and former California senator John C. Frémont for president. In the election that followed, Americans began to vote by section and not by party as never before. The Republican coalition began to unify the North around keeping the West free and alarmed the South, which now saw the future of its slave society endangered by a political movement determined to limit if not destroy slavery. Frémont would lose the 1856 election, but Republicans made the best showing in American history of a newly born party in its first presidential bid.

As the Republicans engaged in their near miss at winning the presidency in 1856, a larger drama of conflict and violence had begun to envelop the nation. In Kansas Territory, open warfare had exploded between proslavery and antislavery settlers. On the floor of the U.S. Senate a southern representative beat a northern senator senseless. A new fugitive slave law sent thousands of blacks fleeing into Canada in fear for their liberty and their lives. The tradition of compromise on political problems related to slavery teetered on the brink of complete collapse. Within a year the Supreme Court had issued a dramatic decision about slavery's constitutionality in westward expansion, and the status of African American citizenship—to the delight of most southerners and the dread of many northerners. And abolitionist John Brown was planning a raid into Virginia to start a slave rebellion.

The political culture of the American republic was disintegrating. As the 1850s advanced, slavery pulled

Americans, North and South, into a maelstrom of dispute that its best statesmen, ultimately, could not subdue. A prosperous nation, riven by stark contradictions, was on the road to a terrible war. Divergent economic and political aims, which had long been held in check, now flew apart over the issue of slavery. The old nationwide political parties fractured, and a realignment that reinforced sectional interests took their place. The means for compromise steadily slipped from the nation's grasp.

Slavery had aroused passions that could be neither contained nor resolved. What began as a dark cloud over the territories became a storm engulfing the nation. Between 1845 and 1853 the United States added Texas, California, Oregon Country, and the Southwest to its domain and launched the settlement of the Great Plains. During the administration of President James K. Polk alone (1845–1849), the nation increased its land mass by two-thirds. Each time the nation expanded, it confronted a thorny issue: should new territories and states be slave or free?

The ensuing political storms gave rise to a feeling in both North and South that America's future was at stake—the character of its economy, its labor system, its definition of liberty under the Constitution, and its racial self-definition. The new Republican Party believed that America's future depended on the unbounded labor of free men. They charged southerners with using the power of the federal government to make slavery legal throughout the Union. Southern leaders defended slavery and charged the North with unconstitutional efforts to destroy it.

For blacks, the growing dispute brought hope and despair. They could take heart that the country's political strife over slavery might somehow lead to their liberation. But in a nation now trying to define its future, blacks had to wonder whether they had a future at all in America. In 1855 Frederick Douglass spoke for slaves and former slaves when he wrote that "the thought of only being a creature of the present and the past, troubled me, and I longed to have a future—a future with hope in it." In those words, Douglass spoke as well to the nation's central dilemma. ■

The War with Mexico and Its Consequences

In the 1840s, territorial expansion surged forward under the leadership of President James K. Polk of North Carolina. The annexation of Texas (see pages 293–294) just before his inauguration did not necessarily make war with Mexico inevitable, but by design and through a series of calculated decisions, Polk brought the conflict on. Mexico broke off relations with the United States, and during the annexation process, Polk urged Texans to seize all land to the Rio Grande and claim the river as their southern and western border. Mexico held that the Nueces River was the border; hence the stage was set for conflict. Nothing could weaken Polk's determination to fulfill the nation's "manifest destiny" to rule the continent. He wanted Mexico's territory all the way to the Pacific, and all of Oregon Country, since 1818 jointly occupied with Britain, as well. He and his expansionist cabinet achieved their goals but were largely unaware of the price in domestic harmony that expansion would exact.

During the 1844 campaign, Polk's supporters had threatened war with Great Britain to gain all of Oregon.

OREGON
As president, however, Polk turned first to diplomacy. Not wanting to fight Mexico and Great Britain at the same time, he tried to avoid bloodshed in the Northwest, where America and Britain had for decades jointly occupied disputed territory. Dropping the demand for a boundary at latitude 54°40', he pressured the British to accept the 49th parallel. In 1846 Great Britain agreed. The Oregon Treaty gave the United States all of present-day Oregon, Washington, and Idaho and parts of Wyoming and Montana (see Map 14.1). Thus a new era of land acquisition and conquest had begun under the tenth president of the United States, the sixth to be a slaveholder, and one who secretly bought and sold slaves through an agent from the White House.

Toward Mexico, Polk was more aggressive. In early 1846, he ordered American troops under "Old Rough and Ready," General Zachary Taylor,

"MR. POLK'S WAR"
to march south and defend the contested border of the Rio Grande across from the town of Matamoros (see Map 14.2). Polk especially desired California as the prize in his expansionist strategy, and he attempted to buy from Mexico a huge tract of land extending to the Pacific. When that effort failed, Polk waited for war. Negotiations between troops on the Rio Grande were awkwardly

BRITISH NORTH AMERICA

54°40′

Natural boundary of Oregon

Fraser R.

VANCOUVER
ISLAND

49°   Vancouver

Line of 1846

Line of 1818

Missouri R.

Spokane

**UNITED
STATES**

Columbia R.

Ft. Walla Walla

*PACIFIC
OCEAN*

Portland

42°

Ft. Boise

Adams-Onís Treaty Line, 1819

SPANISH TERRITORY

British territory under 1846 treaty

United States territory under 1846 treaty

Map 14.1   American Expansion in Oregon

The slogan of Polk's supporters had been "Fifty-four forty or fight," but negotiation of a boundary at the 49th parallel avoided the danger of war with Great Britain.

conducted in French because no American officer spoke Spanish and no Mexican spoke English. After a three-week standoff, the tense situation came to a head. On April 24, 1846, Mexican cavalry ambushed a U.S. cavalry unit on the north side of the river; eleven Americans were killed and sixty-three taken captive. On April 26 Taylor sent a dispatch overland to Washington, D.C., which took two weeks to arrive, announcing: "Hostilities may now be considered as commenced."

Polk now drafted a message to Congress: Mexico had "passed the boundary of the United States, had invaded our territory and shed American blood on American soil." In the bill accompanying the war message, Polk deceptively declared that "war exists by the act of Mexico itself" and summoned the nation to arms. Two days later, on May 13, the House recognized a state of war with Mexico by a vote of 174 to 14, and the Senate by 40 to 2, with numerous abstentions. Some antislavery Whigs had tried to oppose the war but were barely allowed to gain the floor of Congress to speak. Since Polk withheld key facts, the full reality of what had happened on the distant Rio Grande was not known. But the theory and practice of manifest destiny had

launched the United States into its first major war on foreign territory.

The idea of war unleashed great public celebrations. Huge crowds gathered in southern cities such as Richmond and Louisville to voice support for the war effort. Twenty thousand Philadelphians and even more New Yorkers rallied in the same spirit. After news came of General Taylor's first two battlefield victories at Palo Alto and Resaca de la Palma, volunteers swarmed recruiting stations. From his home in Lansingburgh, New York, the writer Herman Melville remarked that "the people here are all in a state of delirium. . . . A military ardor pervades all ranks. . . . Nothing is talked of but the 'Halls of the Montezumas.'" Publishers rushed books about Mexican geography into print; "Palo Alto" hats and root beer went on sale. And the advent of daily newspapers, printed on new rotary presses, boosted sales by giving the war a romantic appeal.

*FOREIGN WAR
AND THE
POPULAR
IMAGINATION*

Here was an adventurous war of conquest in a far-off, exotic land. Here was the fulfillment of Anglo-Saxon–Christian destiny to expand and possess the North American continent and to take "civilization" to the "semi-Indian" Mexicans. For many, racism fueled the expansionist spirit. In 1846 an Illinois newspaper justified the war on the basis that Mexicans were "reptiles in the path of progressive democracy." For those who read newspapers, the War with Mexico became the first national event experienced with immediacy. The battles south of the border were reported by war correspondents. From Vera Cruz on the Gulf Coast of Mexico, ships carried news dispatches to New Orleans, whose nine daily newspapers ran a faster steamer out to meet them. With stories set in type before even reaching shore, the news was then sent by riders toward the North. Near the end of the war, news traveled by telegraph in only three days from New Orleans to Washington.

The war spawned an outpouring of poetry, song, drama, travel literature, and lithographs that captured the popular imagination and glorified the conflict. New lyrics to the tune "Yankee Doodle" proclaimed: "They attacked our men upon our land / and crossed our river too sir / now show them all with sword in hand / what yankee boys can do sir." Most of the war-inspired flowering in the popular arts was patriotic. But not everyone cheered. The abolitionist James Russell Lowell considered the war a "national crime committed in behoof of slavery, our common sin." Ralph Waldo Emerson confided to his journals in 1847: "The United States will conquer Mexico, but it will be as the man swallows ar-

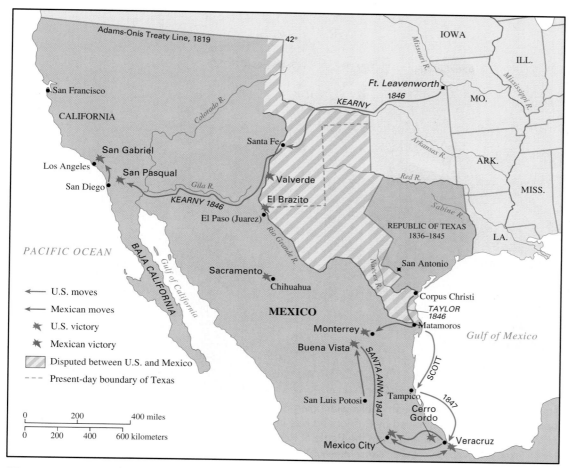

Map 14.2   The War with Mexico

This map shows the territory disputed between the United States and Mexico. After U.S. gains in northeastern Mexico and in New Mexico and California, General Winfield Scott captured Mexico City in the decisive campaign of the war.

senic, which brings him down in turn. Mexico will poison us." Even proslavery spokesman John C. Calhoun saw the perils of expansionism. Mexico, he said, was "the forbidden fruit; the penalty of eating it would be to subject our institutions to political death."

The troops proved unruly and undisciplined, and their politically ambitious commanders often quarreled among themselves. Nevertheless, progress was steady, and early in the war U.S. forces made significant gains. In May 1846 Polk ordered Colonel Stephen Kearny and a small detachment to invade the remote and thinly populated provinces of New Mexico and California. Taking Santa Fe without opposition, Kearny pushed into Cali-

CONQUEST

fornia, where he joined forces with rebellious American settlers led by Captain John C. Frémont and with a couple of U.S. naval units. General Zachary Taylor's forces attacked and occupied Monterrey, which surrendered in September, securing northeastern Mexico (see Map 14.2). And before the end of 1846 American soldiers had also established dominion over California. Because losses on the periphery of their large country had not broken Mexican resistance, General Winfield Scott carried the war to the enemy's heartland. Landing at Veracruz, he led fourteen thousand men toward Mexico City. This daring invasion proved the decisive campaign of the war. Scott's men, outnumbered and threatened by yellow fever, encountered a series of formidable Mexican

■ Enthusiastic publishers vied to furnish the American public with up-to-date news of the War with Mexico. This is one of three lithographs issued by Currier and Ives in 1846 to celebrate U.S. forces' capture of Mexico's General La Vega during the Battle of Resaca de la Palma, fought near the border of Texas and Mexico. (Amon Carter Museum, Fort Worth, Texas)

defenses, but engineers repeatedly discovered flanking routes around their foes. After a series of hard-fought battles, U.S. troops captured the Mexican capital.

Representatives of both countries signed the Treaty of Guadalupe Hidalgo in February 1848. The United States gained California and New Mexico (including present-day Nevada, Utah, and Arizona, and parts of Colorado and Wyoming) and recognition of the Rio Grande as the southern boundary of Texas. In return, the American government agreed to settle the claims of its citizens against Mexico ($3.2 million) and to pay Mexico a mere $15 million. On the day Polk received the treaty from the Senate, a mob in Paris forced Louis Philippe to abdicate the throne of France, and a German writer, Karl Marx, published a pamphlet, *The Communist Manifesto,* in London. The enormous influence of Marx's work would be many years away, but as the 1848 nationalistic revolutions against

TREATY OF GUADALUPE HIDALGO

monarchy spread to Italy, Austria, Hungary, and Germany, republican America seized an empire.

The costs of the war included the deaths of thirteen thousand Americans (mostly from disease) and fifty thousand Mexicans. Moreover, enmity endured between Mexico and the United States into the twentieth century. The domestic cost to the United States was even higher. Public opinion was sharply divided, despite widespread hostility toward Mexicans. Southwesterners were enthusiastic about the war, as were most southern planters; New Englanders strenuously opposed it. Whigs in Congress charged that Polk, a Democrat, had "provoked" an unnecessary war and "usurped the power of Congress." The aged John Quincy Adams denounced the war; and an Illinois Whig named Abraham Lincoln called Polk's justifications the "half insane mumbling of a fever-dream." Abolitionists and a small minority of antislavery Whigs charged that the war was no less than a plot to extend slavery. Congressman Joshua Giddings of Ohio charged that Polk's purpose was "to render slavery secure in Texas" and to extend slavery's dominion over the West.

These charges fed northern fear of the so-called Slave Power. Abolitionists had long warned of a slaveholding

"SLAVE POWER CONSPIRACY"

oligarchy that intended to dominate the nation through its hold on federal power. Slaveholders had gained control of the South by persecuting critics of slavery and suppressing dissent. They had forced the gag rule on Congress in 1836 (see page 280) and threatened northern liberties. To many white northerners, even those who saw nothing wrong with slavery, it was the battle over free speech that first made the idea of a Slave Power credible. The War with Mexico deepened such fears. Had this questionable war, asked antislavery northerners, not been launched for vast, new slave territory?

Northern opinion on slavery expansion began to shift, but the impact of the war on southern opinion was even more dramatic. At first some southern leaders had criticized the War with Mexico. Southern Whigs attacked the Democratic president for causing the war, and few southern congressmen saw slavery as the paramount issue. Many whites in both North and South feared that large land seizures would bring thousands of nonwhite Mexicans into the United States and upset the racial order. An Indiana politician did not want "any mixed races in our Union, nor men of any color except white, unless they be slaves." And the *Charleston Mercury* of South Carolina asked if the nation expected "to melt into our population eight millions of men, at war with us by race, by language, by religion, manners and laws." Yet despite their racism, many statesmen soon saw other prospects in the outcomes of a war of conquest in the Southwest.

In August 1846, David Wilmot, a Pennsylvania Democrat, proposed an amendment, or proviso, to a military

WILMOT PROVISO

appropriations bill: that "neither slavery nor involuntary servitude shall ever exist" in any territory gained from Mexico. Although the proviso never passed both houses of Congress, its repeated introduction by northerners transformed the debate over the expansion of slavery. Southerners suddenly circled their wagons to protect the future of a slave society. Alexander H. Stephens, only recently "no defender of slavery," now declared that slavery was based on the Bible and above moral criticism, and John C. Calhoun took an aggressive stand. The territories, Calhoun insisted, belonged to all the states, and the federal government could do nothing to limit the spread of slavery there. Southern slaveholders had a constitutional right rooted in the Fifth Amendment, Calhoun claimed, to take their slaves (as property) anywhere in the territories.

This position, often called "state sovereignty," which quickly became a test of orthodoxy among southern politicians, was a radical reversal of history. In 1787 the Confederation Congress had excluded slavery from the Northwest Territory (see pages 180–181); Article IV of the federal Constitution had authorized Congress to make "all needful rules and regulations" for the territories; and the Missouri Compromise had barred slavery from most of the Louisiana Purchase. Now, however, southern leaders demanded future guarantees for slavery.

In the North, the Wilmot Proviso became a rallying cry for abolitionists. Eventually the legislatures of fourteen northern states endorsed it—and not because all its supporters were abolitionists. David Wilmot, significantly, was neither an abolitionist nor an antislavery Whig. He denied having any "squeamish sensitiveness upon the subject of slavery" or "morbid sympathy for the slave." Instead, his goal was to defend "the rights of white freemen" and to obtain California "for free white labor." Wilmot's involvement in antislavery controversy is a measure of the remarkable ability of the territorial issue to alarm northerners of many viewpoints.

As Wilmot demonstrated, it was possible, however, to be both a racist and an opponent of slavery. The vast majority of white northerners were not active abolitionists, and their desire to keep the West free from slavery was often matched by their desire to keep blacks from settling there. Fear of the Slave Power was thus building a potent antislavery movement that united abolitionists and antiblack voters. At stake was an abiding version of the American Dream: the free individual's access to social mobility through acquisition of land and jobs in the West. This sacred ideal of *free labor,* and its dread of concentrated power, fueled a new political persuasion in America. A man's ownership and sale of his own labor, wrote the British economist Adam Smith, was "the most sacred and inviolable foundation of all property." Slave labor, thousands of northerners had come to believe, would degrade the honest toil of free men and render them unemployed and propertyless. The West must therefore be kept free of slaves and open to free white men.

The divisive slavery question could not be kept out of national politics. After Polk renounced a second term

THE ELECTION OF 1848 AND POPULAR SOVEREIGNTY

as president, the Democrats nominated Senator Lewis Cass of Michigan for president and General William Butler of Kentucky for vice president. Cass, a party loyalist who had served in Jackson's cabinet, had devised in 1847 the

TABLE 14.1
New Political Parties

Party	Period of Influence	Area of Influence	Outcome
Liberty Party	1839-1848	North	Merged with other antislavery groups to form Free-Soil Party
Free-Soil Party	1848-1854	North	Merged with Republican Party
Know-Nothings (American Party)	1853-1856	Nationwide	Disappeared, freeing most to join Republican Party
Republican Party	1854-present	North (later nationwide)	Became rival of Democratic Party and won presidency in 1860

idea of "popular sovereignty"—letting residents in the western territories decide the question of slavery for themselves. His party's platform declared that Congress lacked the power to interfere with slavery's expansion. The Whigs nominated General Zachary Taylor, a southern slaveholder and war hero; Congressman Millard Fillmore of New York was his running mate. The Whig convention similarly refused to assert that Congress had power over slavery in the territories.

But the issue could not be avoided. Many southern Democrats distrusted Cass and eventually voted for Taylor because he was a slaveholder. Among northerners, concern over slavery led to the formation of a new party. New York Democrats committed to the Wilmot Proviso rebelled against Cass and nominated former president Martin Van Buren. Antislavery Whigs and former supporters of the Liberty Party then joined them to organize the Free-Soil Party, with Van Buren as its candidate (see Table 14.1). This party, whose slogan was "Free Soil, Free Speech, Free Labor, and Free Men," won almost 300,000 northern votes. For a new third party to win 10 percent of the national vote was a signal achievement. Taylor polled 1.4 million votes to Cass's 1.2 million and won the White House, but the results were more ominous than decisive.

American politics had split along sectional lines as never before. Religious denominations, too, were splitting into northern and southern wings. Many Protestants, North and South, began to fear that God had an appointment with America, either to destroy the national sin of slavery or to help the South defend it as part of his divine order. As the 1850s dawned, the legacies of the War with Mexico and the conflicts of 1848 dominated national life and threatened the nature of the Union itself.

1850: Compromise or Armistice?

The first sectional battle of the new decade involved California. More than eighty thousand Americans flooded into California during the gold rush of 1849 (see page 302). With Congress unable to agree on a formula to govern the territories, President Taylor urged these settlers to apply directly for admission to the Union. They promptly did so, proposing a state constitution that did not allow for slavery. Because California's admission as a free state would upset the sectional balance of power in the Senate (the ratio of slave to free states was 15 to 15), southern politicians wanted to postpone admission and make California a slave territory, or at least to extend the Missouri Compromise line west to the Pacific. Representatives from nine southern states, meeting in Nashville, asserted the South's right to part of the territory.

Henry Clay, the venerable Whig leader, sensed that the Union was in peril. Twice before—in 1820 and 1833—Clay, the "Great Pacificator," had taken the lead in shaping sectional compromise; now he struggled one last time to preserve the nation. To hushed Senate galleries Clay presented a series of compromise measures in the winter of 1850. At one point Clay held up what he claimed was a piece of George Washington's coffin as a means of inspiring unity. Over the weeks that followed, he and Senator Stephen A. Douglas of Illinois, the "Little Giant," steered their omnibus bill, or compromise package, through debate and amendment.

DEBATE OVER SLAVERY IN THE TERRITORIES

The problems to be solved were numerous and difficult. Would California, or part of it, become a free state?

How should the territory acquired from Mexico be organized? Texas, which allowed slavery, claimed large portions of the new land as far west as Santa Fe. Southerners complained that fugitive slaves were not being returned as the Constitution required, and northerners objected to the sale of human beings in the nation's capital. Eight years earlier, in *Prigg v. Pennsylvania* (1842), the Supreme Court had ruled that enforcement of the fugitive slave clause in the Constitution was a federal obligation, buttressing long-standing southern desires to bring this issue to a head. Most troublesome of all, however, was the status of slavery in the territories.

Clay and Douglas hoped to avoid a specific formula, and in Lewis Cass's idea of popular sovereignty they discovered what one historian called a "charm of ambiguity" that appealed to practical politicians. Ultimately Congress would have to approve statehood for a territory, but "in the meantime," said Cass, it should allow the people living there "to regulate their own concerns in their own way."

Those simple words proved all but unenforceable. When could settlers prohibit slavery? To avoid dissension within their party, northern and southern Democrats explained Cass's statement to their constituents in two incompatible ways. Southerners claimed that neither Congress nor a territorial legislature could bar slavery. Only late in the territorial process, when settlers were ready to draft a state constitution, could they take that step, thus allowing time for slavery to take root. Northerners, however, insisted that Americans living in a territory were entitled to local self-government and thus could outlaw slavery at any time, especially early in the process.

The cause of compromise gained a powerful supporter when Senator Daniel Webster committed his prestige and eloquence to Clay's bill. "I wish to speak today," Webster declaimed on March 7 in a scene of high drama, "not as a Massachusetts man, nor as a Northern man, but as an American. I speak today for the preservation of the Union." Abandoning his earlier support for the Wilmot Proviso, Webster urged northerners not to "taunt or reproach" the South with antislavery measures. To southern firebrands he issued a warning that disunion inevitably would cause violence and destruction. For his efforts at compromise, Webster was condemned by many former abolitionist friends in New England who accused him of going over to the "devil."

Only three days earlier, with equal drama, Calhoun had been carried from his sickbed to deliver a speech opposing the compromise. Unable to stand and speak, his address was read for him by Senator James Mason of Virginia. Grizzled and dying, the South's intellectual defender warned that the "cords which bind these states" were "already greatly weakened." Calhoun did not address the specific measures in the bill; he predicted disunion if southern demands were not met, thereby frightening some into support of compromise.

Yet rising fear and Webster's influence were not enough. After months of labor, Clay and Douglas finally brought their legislative package to a vote, and lost. With Clay sick and absent from Washington, Douglas reintroduced the compromise measures one at a time. Though there was no majority for compromise, Douglas shrewdly realized that different majorities might be created for the separate measures. Because southerners favored some bills and northerners the rest, the small bloc for compromise could vote first with one section and then with the other. The strategy worked, and Douglas's resourcefulness alleviated the crisis as the Compromise of 1850 became law.

The compromise had five essential measures: California became a free state; the Texas boundary was set at **COMPROMISE OF 1850** its present limits (see Map 14.3) and the United States paid Texas $10 million in compensation for the loss of New Mexico territory; the territories of New Mexico and Utah were organized on a basis of popular sovereignty; the fugitive slave law was strengthened; and the slave trade was abolished in the District of Columbia. Jubilation greeted passage of the compromise; crowds in Washington and other cities celebrated the happy news. "On one glorious night," records a modern historian, "the word went abroad that it was the duty of every patriot to get drunk. Before the next morning many a citizen had proved his patriotism."

In reality, there was less cause for celebration than people hoped. At best, the Compromise of 1850 was an artful evasion. As one historian has argued, the legislation was more an "armistice," delaying greater conflict, than a compromise. Douglas had found a way to pass the five proposals without convincing northerners and southerners to agree on fundamentals. The compromise bought time for the nation, but it did not provide a real settlement of the territorial questions.

Furthermore, the compromise had two basic flaws. The first concerned the ambiguity of popular sovereignty. Southerners insisted there would be no prohibition of slavery during the territorial stage, and northerners declared that settlers could bar slavery whenever they wished. The compromise even allowed for the appeal of

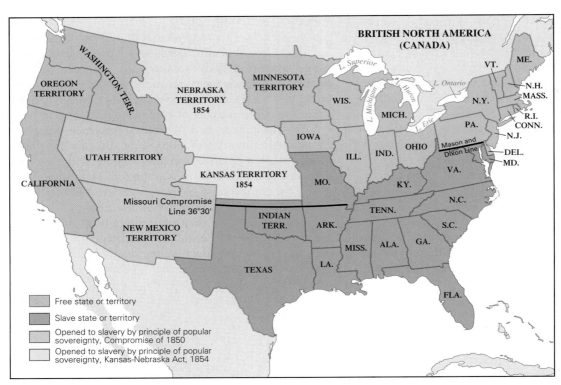

Map 14.3   The Kansas-Nebraska Act and Slavery Expansion, 1854

The vote on the Kansas-Nebraska Act (see also Table 14.2 on page 367) in the House of Representatives demonstrates the sectionalization of American politics due to the slavery question.

a territorial legislature's action to the Supreme Court. One witty politician remarked that the legislators had enacted a lawsuit instead of a law.

The second flaw lay in the Fugitive Slave Act, which gave new—and controversial—protection to slavery. The law empowered slaveowners to go into court in their own states to present evidence that a slave who owed them service had escaped. The resulting transcript and a description of the fugitive would then serve as legal proof of a person's slave status, even in free states and territories. Specially appointed court officials adjudicated the identity of the person described, not whether he or she was indeed a slave. Penalties made it a felony to harbor fugitives, and the law stated that northern citizens could be summoned to hunt fugitives. The fees paid to U.S. marshals favored slaveholders: $10 if the alleged fugitive was returned to the slaveowner, $5 if not returned.

FUGITIVE SLAVE ACT

Abolitionist newspapers quickly attacked the Fugitive Slave Act as a violation of fundamental American rights. Why were alleged fugitives denied a trial by jury? Why were they given no chance to present evidence or cross-examine witnesses? Why did the law give authorities a financial incentive to send suspected fugitives into bondage? These arguments convinced some northerners that all free blacks were vulnerable to kidnapping and enslavement. The "free" states were no longer a safe haven for black folk, whatever their origins.

Between 1850 and 1854, protests and violent resistance to slave catchers occurred in dozens of northern towns. Sometimes a captured fugitive was broken out of jail or from the clutches of slave agents by abolitionists, as in the case of Shadrach Minkins in 1851 in Boston, who was spirited by a series of wagons and trains across Massachusetts, up through Vermont, to Montreal, Canada. Also in 1851, a fugitive named Jerry McHenry was freed by an abolitionist mob in Syracuse, New York, and hurried into Canadian freedom. That same year as well, the small black community in Lancaster County, Pennsylvania, rose up in arms to defend four escaped slaves from a federal posse charged with reenslaving them. At this

"Christiana riot," the fugitives shot and killed Edward Gorsuch, the Maryland slaveowner who sought the return of his "property." Amid increasing border warfare over fugitive slaves, a headline reporting the Christiana affair screamed "Civil War, The First Blow Struck!"

Many abolitionists became convinced by their experience of resisting the Fugitive Slave Act that violence was a legitimate means of opposing slavery. In an 1854 column entitled "Is It Right and Wise to Kill a Kidnapper?" Frederick Douglass said that the only way to make the fugitive slave law "dead letter" was to make a "few dead slave catchers."

At this point a novel portrayed the humanity and suffering of slaves in a way that touched millions of

UNCLE TOM'S
CABIN

northerners. Harriet Beecher Stowe, whose New England family had produced many prominent ministers, wrote *Uncle Tom's Cabin* out of deep moral conviction. Her story, serialized in 1851 and published as a book in 1852, conveyed the agonies faced by slave families and described a mother's dash to freedom with her child across the frozen Ohio River. Stowe also portrayed slavery's evil effects on slaveholders, indicting the institution itself more harshly than she indicted the southerners caught in its web. Moreover, Stowe exposed northern racism and complicity with slavery by making the worst slaveholder a man of New England birth, and a visiting relative on a plantation a squeamish Vermont woman who could hardly cope with the near presence of blacks.

In nine months the book sold over three hundred thousand copies, by mid-1853 over a million. Countless people saw *Uncle Tom's Cabin* performed as a stage play or heard the story in dramatic readings or read similar novels inspired by it. Stowe brought home the evil of slavery to many who had never given it much thought. Indeed, for generations, the characters in *Uncle Tom's Cabin*—Eliza, Little Eva, Simon Legree, and Uncle Tom himself—entered the American imagination as symbols of the entire era of slavery and the Civil War.

The popularity of *Uncle Tom's Cabin* alarmed anxious southern whites. In politics and now in popular literature they saw threats to their way of life. Behind the South's aggressive claims about territorial rights lay the fear that if nearby areas outlawed slavery, they would be used as bases from which to spread abolitionism into the slave states. To most white southerners, a moral condemnation of slaveholding anywhere meant the same thing everywhere.

To protect slavery in the arena of ideas, southerners needed to counter indictments of the institution as a moral wrong. Accordingly, some fifteen to twenty

■ The Webb Family toured the North, presenting dramatic readings of *Uncle Tom's Cabin.* Performances by the Webbs and others deepened the already powerful impact of Harriet Beecher Stowe's novel.   (Harriet Beecher Stowe Center, Hartford, Conn.)

proslavery novels were published in the 1850s as responses to *Uncle Tom's Cabin.* Most of these anti–Uncle Tom books paled in comparison with Mrs. Stowe's masterpiece, but southern writers continued to defend their system as more humane than wage labor, and they blamed the slave trade on the "outside interference" of Yankee speculators. In awkward stories such as J. W. Page's *Uncle Robin in His Cabin and Tom Without One in Boston,* slaves were induced to run away by visiting abolitionists, and then all but starved in northern cities.

In reality, slaveholders were especially disturbed by the 1850s over what was widely called the Underground

THE
UNDERGROUND
RAILROAD

Railroad. This loose, illegal network of civil disobedience, spiriting runaways to freedom, had never been very organized. Thousands of slaves did escape by these routes, but largely through

■ In *Still Life of Harriet Tubman with Bible and Candle,* we see the youthful, calm, determined leader of the Underground Railroad. Appearing gentle, Tubman was in her own way a revolutionary who liberated nearly three hundred of her people. (© 2000 Louis Psihoyos/Matrix)

their own wits and courage and through the assistance of black vigilance committees in some northern cities. Lewis Hayden in Boston, David Ruggles in New York, William Still in Philadelphia, John Parker in Ripley, Ohio, and Jacob Gibbs in Washington, D.C., were only some of the many black abolitionists who managed fugitive slave escapes through their regions.

Moreover, Harriet Tubman, herself an escapee in 1848, returned to her native Maryland and to Virginia nearly twenty times and through clandestine measures helped as many as three hundred slaves to freedom, some of them her own family members. Maryland planters were so outraged at her heroic success that they offered a $40,000 reward for her capture.

In Ohio numerous white abolitionists, often Quakers, joined with blacks as agents of slave liberation at various points along the river border between slavery and freedom. In the wake of the Fugitive Slave Act, an estimated twenty thousand blacks, most of them fugitive slaves, moved from the northern states into Canada seeking security. The Underground Railroad also had numerous maritime routes, as coastal slaves escaped aboard ship out of Virginia or the Carolinas, or from New Orleans. Many slaves who escaped by sea ended up in northern port cities, and some went to the Caribbean or to England. Many fugitive slaves from the Lower South and in Texas had escaped over the decades to Florida and across the Mexican border. In Mexico they entered a country that had abolished slavery; in Florida many were fully assimilated into the Seminole communities and fought with them against the U.S. Army in the Seminole Wars of 1835–1842 and 1855–1858.

This constant, dangerous flow of humanity was a testament to human courage and the will for freedom. It never reached the scale believed by some angry slaveholders nor that of the countless safe houses and hideaways claimed by hundreds of northern towns and local historical societies today. But in reality and in legend the Underground Railroad applied pressure to the slavery crisis and provided slaves with a focus for hope.

The 1852 election gave southern leaders hope that slavery would be secure under the administration of a new president. Franklin Pierce, a Democrat from New Hampshire, won an easy victory over the Whig presidential nominee, General Winfield Scott. Pierce defended each section's rights as essential to the nation's unity, and southerners hoped that his firm support for the Compromise of 1850 might end the season of crisis. Because Scott's views on the compromise had been unknown and the Free-Soil candidate, John P. Hale of New Hampshire, had openly rejected it, Pierce's victory suggested widespread support for the compromise.

ELECTION OF 1852 AND THE COLLAPSE OF COMPROMISE

Pierce's victory, however, derived less from his strengths than from the Whig Party's weakness. The Whigs were a congressional and state-based party that had never achieved much success in presidential politics. By 1852 sectional discord had rendered the Whig Party all but dead.

President Pierce's embrace of the compromise appalled many northerners. His vigorous enforcement of the Fugitive Slave Act provoked outrage and fear of the Slave Power, especially in the case of the fugitive slave Anthony Burns, who had fled Virginia by stowing away on a ship in 1852. In Boston, thinking he was safe in a city known for abolitionism, Burns began a new life. But in 1854 federal marshals found and placed him under guard in Boston's courthouse. An interracial crowd of abolitionists attacked the courthouse, killing a jailor in an unsuccessful attempt to free Burns, whose case attracted nationwide attention.

Pierce moved decisively to enforce the Fugitive Slave Act. He telegraphed local officials to "incur any expense to insure the execution of the law" and sent marines, cavalry, and artillery to Boston. U.S. troops marched Burns to Boston harbor through streets draped in black and hung with American flags at half-mast. At a cost of $100,000, a single black man was returned to slavery through the power of federal law.

The national will to sustain the future of slavery was now tested at every turn. This demonstration of federal support for slavery radicalized opinion, even among many conservatives. Textile manufacturer Amos A. Lawrence observed that "we went to bed one night old fashioned, conservative, Compromise Union Whigs & waked up stark mad Abolitionists." Juries refused to convict the abolitionists who had stormed the Boston courthouse, and New England states began to pass personal-liberty laws designed to impede or block federal enforcement. In such laws local judges were absolved from enforcing the Fugitive Slave Act, in effect nullifying federal authority. What northerners now saw as evidence of a dominating Slave Power, outraged slaveholders saw as the legal defense of their rights.

Pierce seemed unable to avoid sectional conflict in other arenas as well. His proposal for a transcontinental railroad derailed when congressmen fought over its location, North or South. His attempts to acquire foreign territory stirred more trouble. An annexation treaty with Hawai'i failed because southern senators would not vote for another free state, and efforts to acquire slaveholding Cuba angered northerners. Events in the Pacific also caused division at home over just how far American expansion should extend. With two orchestrated landings in the Bay of Tokyo, in 1853 and 1854, Commodore Matthew Perry established U.S. intentions to trade with Japan, whether that country sought such contact or not. Offended and intrigued, the Japanese were impressed with Perry's steam-powered warships, the first such black-smoke-belching floating machines they had seen. Perry's Treaty of Kanagawa in March 1854 negotiated two ports as coaling stations for American ships. The much-sought-after trading arrangements were slow in coming, although this did not stop merchants and bankers from lavishing on Perry a hero's honors when he returned to the United States. In his meetings with the Japanese, the pompous Perry had given his hosts, whom

he considered an inferior people, a telegraph system, a quarter-scale railroad train, a bound history of the War with Mexico, and one hundred gallons of Kentucky whiskey.

Soon back home another territorial bill threw Congress and the nation into even greater turmoil, and the Compromise of 1850 fell into complete collapse.

Slavery Expansion and Collapse of the Party System

The new controversy began in a surprising way. Stephen A. Douglas, one of the architects of the Compromise of 1850, introduced a bill to establish the Kansas and Nebraska Territories. Talented and ambitious for the presidency, Douglas was known for compromise, not sectional quarreling. But he did not view slavery as a fundamental problem, and he was willing to risk some controversy to win economic benefits for Illinois, his home state. A transcontinental railroad would encourage settlement of the Great Plains and stimulate the economy of Illinois; but no company would build such a railroad before Congress organized the territories it would cross. Thus interest in promoting the construction of such a railroad drove Douglas to introduce a bill that inflamed sectional passions.

The Kansas-Nebraska bill exposed the conflicting interpretations of popular sovereignty. Douglas's bill left

THE KANSAS-NEBRASKA BILL "all questions pertaining to slavery in the Territories . . . to the people residing therein." Northerners and southerners, however, still disagreed violently over what territorial settlers could constitutionally do. Moreover, the Kansas and Nebraska Territories lay within the Louisiana Purchase, and the Missouri Compromise prohibited slavery in all that land from latitude 36°30' north to the Canadian border. If popular sovereignty were to mean anything in Kansas and Nebraska, it had to mean that the Missouri Compromise was no longer in effect and that settlers could establish slavery there.

Southern congressmen, anxious to establish slaveholders' right to take slaves into any territory, pressed Douglas to concede this point. They demanded an explicit repeal of the 36°30' limitation as the price of their support. During a carriage ride with Senator Archibald Dixon of Kentucky, Douglas debated the point at length. Finally he made an impulsive decision: "By God, Sir, you are right. I will incorporate it in my bill, though I know it will raise a hell of a storm."

Annexation of Cuba

One of the most contentious issues in antebellum American foreign relations was the annexation of Cuba. As a strategic bulwark against Britain and France in the Western Hemisphere, for its massive sugar wealth, and as a slave society that might reinforce the security of southern slavery, the Spanish-controlled island fired the imagination of manifest destiny. In the early republic, Presidents Jefferson and Madison explored acquisition. "I have ever looked on Cuba as the most interesting addition which could . . . be made to our system of states," wrote Jefferson. John Quincy Adams, speaking as secretary of state in 1823, considered Cuba "indispensable to the continuance . . . of the Union."

Until the 1840s the United States officially supported Spanish rule for stability and the preservation of slavery. Southerners feared a "second Haiti" if Cuba became independent through revolution. The prospect of slave insurrection and the spread of abolitionism throughout the upper Caribbean and the rim of the Deep South drove many southerners and three Democratic administrations to shift course and pursue acquisition of Cuba. Slaveholding politicians viewed Cuba as critical to expansion; human bondage, they believed, had to expand southward and westward or it might die.

In 1848 President Polk authorized $100 million to purchase Cuba. The Spanish foreign minister, however, told Polk's emissary that his government would rather see Cuba "sunk in the ocean" than sell it to the United States. During the crisis over the Kansas-Nebraska Act in 1854, as President Pierce revived the annexation scheme, some southerners planned to seize Cuba by force. Although the expedition never embarked, its prospect outraged antislavery Republicans eager to halt slavery's expansion and protect their claims for free labor as the basis of America's future.

Yet another aggressive American design on Cuba emerged in the Ostend Manifesto in October 1854. Written after a meeting among the American foreign ministers to Britain, France, and Spain, the document advocated conquest of Cuba if it could not be purchased. The ministers predicted that Cuba "would be Africanized and become a second St. Domingo, with all its attendant horrors to the white race." But antislavery northerners saw schemes of the "Slave Power," whose "will is the law of this administration." The Ostend controversy forced temporary abandonment of annexation efforts, but as the fires in Bleeding Kansas subsided in 1858, President Buchanan reignited Cuba fever. A fierce Senate debate over yet another purchase offer in early 1859 ended in bitter division over the extension of slavery's domain.

The failure of Cuban annexation was deeply intertwined with the meaning of the United States as a slaveholding republic. "I want Cuba, and I know that sooner or later we must have it . . . for the planting or spreading of slavery," said Mississippian Albert G. Brown in 1858. Too many northerners, however, understood Brown's intentions. In America's links to the world, in this case only 90 miles from the Florida coast, just as in domestic affairs, the expansion of slavery poisoned the body politic.

■ Despite the failure of filibustering expeditions, the effort to annex Cuba continued throughout James Buchanan's presidential administration. This cartoon portrays Sam Houston, the famed Texan and proponent of American expansion, rowing the boat for a harpoonist in quest of the whale, Cuba. The dream of appropriating Cuba to the United States died very hard in the antebellum era. *Vanity Fair*, New York, June 1860. (© Bettmann/Corbis)

TABLE 14.2

The Vote on the Kansas-Nebraska Act

The vote was 113–100 in favor.

	Aye	Nay
Northern Democrats	44	42
Southern Democrats	57	2
Northern Whigs	0	45
Southern Whigs	12	7
Northern Free-Soilers		4

■ Throughout the North the Kansas-Nebraska Act kindled fires of alarm over the Slave Power's "determination to extend its dominion" and "control the government of the nation." Public meetings like the one announced here, held in West Chester, Pennsylvania, aided the new Republican Party.   (American Antiquarian Society)

Perhaps Douglas underestimated the storm because he believed that conditions of climate and soil would keep slavery out of Kansas and Nebraska. Nevertheless, his bill threw open to slavery land from which it had been prohibited for thirty-four years. Opposition from Free-Soilers and antislavery forces was immediate and enduring; many considered this turn of events a betrayal of a sacred trust. The titanic struggle in Congress lasted three and a half months. Douglas won the support of President Pierce and eventually prevailed: the bill became law in May 1854 by a vote that demonstrated the dangerous sectionalization of American politics (see Map 14.3 and Table 14.2).

But the storm was just beginning. Abolitionists charged sinister aggression by the Slave Power, and northern fears of slavery's influence deepened. Opposition to the Fugitive Slave Act grew dramatically; between 1855 and 1859 Connecticut, Rhode Island, Massachusetts, Michigan, Maine, Ohio, and Wisconsin passed personal-liberty laws. These laws enraged southern leaders by providing counsel for alleged fugitives and requiring trial by jury. More important was the devastating impact of the Kansas-Nebraska Act on political parties. The weakened Whig Party broke apart into northern and southern wings that could no longer cooperate nationally. The Democrats survived, but their support in the North fell drastically in the 1854 elections. Northern Democrats lost sixty-six of their ninety-one congressional seats and lost control of all but two free-state legislatures.

The beneficiary of northern voters' wrath was a new political party. During debate on the Kansas-Nebraska bill, six congressmen had published an

BIRTH OF THE
REPUBLICAN
PARTY

"Appeal of the Independent Democrats." Joshua Giddings, Salmon Chase, and Charles Sumner—the principal authors of this protest—attacked Doug-

las's legislation as a "gross violation of a sacred pledge" (the Missouri Compromise) and a "criminal betrayal of precious rights" that would make free territory a "dreary region of despotism." Their appeal tapped a reservoir of deep concerns in the North, cogently expressed by Illinois's Abraham Lincoln.

Although Lincoln did not personally condemn southerners—"They are just what we would be in their situation"—he exposed the meaning of the Kansas-Nebraska Act. Denying "that there can be moral right in the enslaving of one man by another," Lincoln argued that the founders, from love of liberty, had banned slavery from the Northwest Territory, kept the word *slavery* out of the Constitution, and treated it overall as a "cancer" on the republic. Rather than encouraging liberty, the Kansas-Nebraska Act put slavery "on the high road to extension and perpetuity," and that constituted a "moral wrong and injustice." America's future, Lincoln warned, was being mortgaged to slavery and all its influences.

Thousands of ordinary white northerners agreed. During the summer and fall of 1854, antislavery Whigs and Democrats, Free-Soilers, and other reformers throughout the Old Northwest met to form the new Republican Party, dedicated to keeping slavery out of the territories. The influence of the Republicans rapidly spread to the East, and they won a stunning victory in the 1854 elections. In their first appearance on the ballot, Republicans captured a majority of northern House seats. Antislavery sentiment had created a new party and caused roughly a quarter of northern Democrats to desert their party.

For the first time, too, a sectional party had gained significant power in the political system. Now the Whigs were gone, and only the Democrats struggled to maintain national membership. The Republicans absorbed the Free-Soil Party and grew rapidly in the North. Indeed, the emergence of the Republican coalition of antislavery interests is the most rapid transformation in party allegiance and voter behavior in American history. This fact alone attests to the centrality of slavery expansion in the causation of the Civil War.

Republicans also drew into their coalition a fast-growing nativist movement that called itself the American

KNOW-
NOTHINGS

Party, or Know-Nothings (because its first members kept their purposes secret, answering "I know nothing" to all questions). This group exploited nativist fear of foreigners and Catholics. Between 1848 and 1860, nearly 3.5 million immigrants entered the United States—proportionally the heaviest inflow of foreigners ever in American history (see pages 314–319). Democrats courted the votes of these new citizens, but many native-born Anglo-Saxon Protestants believed that Irish and German Catholics would owe primary allegiance to the pope in Rome and not to the American nation.

In 1854 anti-immigrant fears gave the Know-Nothings spectacular success in some northern states. They triumphed especially in Massachusetts, electing 11 congressmen, a governor, all state officers, all state senators, and all but 2 of 378 state representatives. The temperance movement also gained new strength early in the 1850s with its promises to stamp out the evils associated with liquor and immigrants (a particularly anti-Irish campaign). In this context the Know-Nothings strove to reinforce Protestant morality and restrict voting and officeholding to the native-born. As the Whig Party faded from the scene, the Know-Nothings temporarily filled the void. But like the Whigs, the Know-Nothings could not keep their northern and southern wings to-

gether in the face of the slavery expansion issue, and they dissolved after 1856. The growing Republican coalition wooed the nativists with temperance ordinances and laws postponing suffrage for naturalized citizens (see Table 14.1).

With nearly half of the old electorate up for grabs, the demise of the Whig Party ensured a major realignment

PARTY
REALIGNMENT
AND THE
REPUBLICANS'
APPEAL

of the political system. The remaining parties made appeals to various segments of the electorate. Immigration, temperance, homestead bills, the tariff, internal improvements—all played important roles in attracting voters during the 1850s. The Republicans appealed strongly to those interested in the economic development of the West. Commercial agriculture was booming in the Ohio–Mississippi–Great Lake area, but residents of that region desired more canals, roads, and river and harbor improvements to reap the full benefit of their labors. Because credit was scarce, a homestead program attracted voters: its proponents argued that western land should be made available free to individual farmers. The Republicans seized on these political desires, promising internal improvements and land grants as well as backing higher tariffs for industrialists.

Partisan ideological appeals became the currency of the realigned political system. As Republicans preached "Free Soil, Free Labor, Free Men," they captured a self-image of many northerners. These phrases resonated with traditional ideals of equality, liberty, and opportunity under self-government—the heritage of republicanism. Invoking that heritage also undercut charges that the Republican Party was radical and unreliable.

"Free Soil, Free Labor, Free Men" seemed an appropriate motto for a northern economy that was energetic, expanding, and prosperous. Thousands of farmers had moved west to establish productive farms and growing communities. Midwesterners multiplied their yields by using new machines such as mechanical reapers. Railroads were carrying their crops to urban markets. And industry was beginning to perform wonders of production, making available goods that only recently had been beyond the reach of the average person. As northerners surveyed the general growth and prosperity, they thought they saw a reason for it.

The key to progress appeared, to many people, to be free labor—the dignity of work and the incentive of opportunity. Any hard-working and virtuous man, it was

REPUBLICAN
IDEOLOGY

thought, could improve his condition and achieve economic independence by seizing opportunities that the country had to offer. Republicans argued that the South, with little industry and slave labor, was backward by comparison. Their arguments captured the spirit of the age in the North.

Traditional republicanism hailed the virtuous common man as the backbone of the country. In Abraham Lincoln, a man of humble origins who had become a successful lawyer and political leader, Republicans had a symbol of that tradition. They portrayed their party as the guardian of economic opportunity, giving individuals a chance to work, acquire land, and attain success. In the words of an Iowa Republican, the United States was thriving because its "door is thrown open to all, and even the poorest and humblest in the land, may, by industry and application, gain a position which will entitle him to the respect . . . of his fellow-men."

At stake in the enveloping crises of the 1850s were thus two competing definitions of "liberty": southern planters' claims to protection of their liberty in the possession and transport of their slaves anywhere in the land, and northern workers' and farmers' claims to protection of their liberty to seek a new start on free land, unimpeded by a system that defined labor as slave and black. Thus, a growing number of northerners expressed the fear that the rising political storm was an "irrepressible conflict."

Opposition to the extension of slavery had brought the Republicans into being, but party members carefully broadened their appeal by adopting the causes of other groups. Their coalition ideology consisted of many elements: resentment of southern political power, devotion to unionism, antislavery based on free-labor arguments, moral revulsion to slavery, and racial prejudice. As the *New York Tribune* editor Horace Greeley wrote in 1856, "It is beaten into my bones that the American people are not yet anti-slavery." Four years later, Greeley again observed that "an Anti-Slavery man per se cannot be elected." But, he added, "a Tariff, River-and-Harbor, Pacific Railroad, Free Homestead man, may succeed although he is Anti-Slavery." As these elements joined the Republican Party, they also grew to fear slavery even more.

In the South, the disintegration of the Whig Party had left many southerners at loose ends politically; they

SOUTHERN DEMOCRATS

included a good number of wealthy planters, smaller slaveholders, and urban businessmen. Some gravitated to the American Party, but not for long. In the increasingly tense atmosphere of sectional crisis, these people were highly susceptible to strong states' rights positions and defense of slavery. The security of their own communities seemed at stake, and in the

1850s, most formerly Whig slaveholders converted to the Democrats.

Since Andrew Jackson's day, however, nonslaveholding small farmers had been the heart of the Democratic Party. Democratic politicians, though often slaveowners themselves, lauded the common man and argued that their policies advanced his interests. According to the southern version of republicanism, white citizens in a slave society enjoyed liberty and social equality because black people were enslaved. As Jefferson Davis put it in 1851, in other societies distinctions were drawn "by property, between the rich and the poor." But in the South, slavery elevated every white person's status and allowed the nonslaveholder to "stand upon the broad level of equality with the rich man." To retain the support of ordinary whites, southern Democrats emphasized this appeal to racism. The issue in the sectional crisis, they warned, was "shall negroes govern white men, or white men govern negroes?"

Southern leaders also portrayed sectional controversies as matters of injustice and insult to the South. The rights of all southern whites were in jeopardy, they argued, because antislavery and Free-Soil forces threatened an institution protected in the Constitution. The stable, well-ordered South was the true defender of constitutional principles, the rapidly changing North their destroyer.

Racial fears and traditional political loyalties helped keep the political alliance between yeoman farmers and planters largely intact through the 1850s. Across class lines, white southerners joined together in the interest of community security against what they perceived as the Republican Party's capacity to cause slave unrest in their midst. In the South no viable party emerged to replace the Whigs. The result was a one-party system that emphasized sectional issues and loyalty. In the South as in the North, political realignment sharpened sectional identities.

Political leaders of both sections used race in their arguments about opportunity, but northerners and southerners saw different futures. The *Montgomery* (Alabama) *Mail* warned southern whites in 1860 that the Republicans intended "to free the negroes and force amalgamation between them and the children of the poor men of the South. The rich will be able to keep out of the way of the contamination." Republicans warned northern workers that if slavery entered the territories, the great reservoir of opportunity for ordinary citizens would be poisoned.

In the territory of Kansas a succession of events, like hammer blows, deepened the conflict. The Kansas-Nebraska Act spawned hatred and violence as land-hungry partisans in the sectional struggle clashed repeatedly in Kansas Territory. Abolitionists and religious groups sent in armed Free-Soil settlers; southerners sent in their reinforcements to establish slavery and prevent "northern hordes" from stealing Kansas away. Conflicts led to bloodshed, and soon the whole nation was talking about "Bleeding Kansas."

Politics in the territory resembled war more than democracy. During elections for a territorial legislature in 1855, thousands of proslavery Missourians—known as Border Ruffians—invaded the polls and ran up a large but fraudulent majority for proslavery candidates. The resulting legislature legalized slavery, and in response Free-Soilers held an unauthorized convention at which they created their own government and constitution. In the spring of 1856, a proslavery posse sent to arrest the Free-Soil leaders sacked the Kansas town of Lawrence, killing several people. In revenge John Brown, a radical abolitionist with a band of followers, murdered five proslavery settlers living along Pottawatomie Creek. Soon, armed bands of guerrillas roamed the territory, battling over land claims as well as slavery.

BLEEDING KANSAS

These passions brought violence to the U.S. Senate in May 1856, when Charles Sumner of Massachusetts denounced "the Crime against Kansas." Radical in his antislavery views, Sumner bitterly assailed the president, the South, and Senator Andrew P. Butler of South Carolina. Soon thereafter Butler's cousin, Representative Preston Brooks, approached Sumner at the latter's Senate desk, raised his cane, and began to beat Sumner on the head. Trapped behind his desk, which was bolted in place, Sumner tried to rise, eventually wrenching the desk free before he collapsed, bleeding, on the floor.

Shocked northerners recoiled from what they saw as another southern assault on free speech and southerners' readiness to use violence. William Cullen Bryant, editor of the *New York Evening Post*, asked, "Has it come to this, that we must speak with bated breath in the presence of our southern masters?" As if in reply, the *Richmond Enquirer* denounced "vulgar Abolitionists in the Senate" who "have been suffered to run too long without collars. They must be lashed into submission." Popular opinion in Massachusetts strongly supported Sumner; South Carolina voters reelected Brooks and sent him dozens of commemorative canes. The country was becoming polarized.

The election of 1856 showed how extreme that polarization had become. When Democrats met to select a nominee, they shied away from prominent leaders whose views on the territories were well known. In-

■ Proslavery advocates and Free-Soilers clashed in open battle in Kansas Territory on September 13, 1856, captured in this sketch made by eyewitness S. J. Reader.
(Kansas State Historical Society)

SJ Reader, Del.

stead, they chose James Buchanan of Pennsylvania, whose chief virtue was that for the past four years he had been ambassador to Britain, uninvolved in territorial controversies. Superior party organization helped Buchanan win 1.8 million votes and the election, but he owed his victory to southern support. Hence, he was tagged with the label "a northern man with southern principles." Eleven of sixteen free states voted against him, and Democrats did not regain ascendancy in those states for decades. The Republican candidate, John C. Frémont, won those eleven free states and 1.3 million votes; Republicans had become the dominant party in the North after only two years of existence. The Know-Nothing candidate, Millard Fillmore, won almost 1 million votes, but this election was that party's last hurrah. The coming battle would pit a sectional Republican Party against an increasingly divided Democratic Party. With huge voter turnouts as high as 75–80 percent in many states, Americans were about to learn that elections really matter.

Slavery and the Nation's Future

For years the issue of slavery in the territories had convulsed Congress, and Congress had tried to settle the issue with vague formulas. In 1857 a different branch of government stepped into the fray. The Supreme Court took up this emotionally charged subject and attempted to silence controversy with a definitive verdict.

DRED SCOTT CASE

A Missouri slave named Dred Scott had sued his owner for his freedom. Scott based his claim on the fact that his former owner, an army surgeon, had taken him for several years into Illinois, a free state, and into the Wisconsin Territory, from which slavery had been barred by the Missouri Compromise. Scott first won and then lost his case as it moved on appeal through the state courts into the federal system and, finally, after eleven years, to the Supreme Court.

Normally Supreme Court justices were reluctant to inject themselves into political issues, and it seemed likely that the Court would stay out of this one. An 1851 decision had declared that state courts determined the status of Negroes who lived within their jurisdictions. The Supreme Court had only to follow this precedent to avoid ruling on substantive, and very controversial, issues: Was a black person like Dred Scott a citizen of the United States and thus eligible to sue in federal court? Had residence in a free state or territory made him free?

Did Congress have the power to prohibit slavery in a territory or to delegate that power to a territorial legislature?

After some initial reticence to take the case, the Supreme Court agreed to hear *Dred Scott v. Sanford* and decided to rule on the Missouri Compromise after all. Two northern justices indicated that they would dissent from the assigned opinion and argue for Scott's freedom and the constitutionality of the Missouri Compromise. Their decision emboldened southerners on the Court, who were growing eager to declare the 1820 geographical restriction on slavery unconstitutional. Southern sympathizers in Washington were pressing for a proslavery verdict, and several justices simply felt they should try to resolve sectional strife once and for all.

In March 1857, Chief Justice Roger B. Taney of Maryland delivered the majority opinion of a divided Court. Taney declared that Scott was not a citizen of either the United States or Missouri; that residence in free territory did not make Scott free; and that Congress had no power to bar slavery from any territory. The decision not only overturned a sectional compromise that had been honored for thirty-seven years; it also invalidated the basic ideas of the Wilmot Proviso and popular sovereignty as well.

The Slave Power seemed to have won a major constitutional victory. African Americans were especially dismayed, for Taney's decision asserted that the founders had never intended for black people to be citizens. At the nation's founding, the chief justice wrote, blacks had been regarded "as beings of an inferior order" with "no rights which the white man was bound to respect." Taney was mistaken, however. African Americans had been citizens in several of the original states, and had voted.

Nevertheless, the ruling seemed to shut the door permanently on black hopes for justice. After 1857, African Americans lived in the land of the *Dred Scott* decision. In northern black communities rage and despair prevailed. Many who were still fugitive slaves sought an uncertain refuge in Canada. Others considered emigration to the Caribbean or even to Africa. Mary Ann Shadd Cary, the leader of an emigration movement to Canada, advised her fellow blacks: "Your national ship is rotten and sinking, why not leave it?" Another black abolitionist said the *Dred Scott* decision had made slavery "the supreme law of the land and all descendants of the African race denationalized." In this state of social dislocation and fear, blacks contemplated whether they had any future in America.

Northern whites who rejected the decision's content were suspicious of the circumstances that produced it.

■ Dred Scott, a slave who brought suit in Missouri for his freedom, and Chief Justice Roger Taney, a descendant of Maryland's slaveholding elite, were principal figures in the most controversial Supreme Court decision of the nineteenth century. (Scott: Missouri Historical Society; Taney: Maryland Historical Society, Baltimore)

Five of the nine justices were southerners; three of the northern justices actively dissented or refused to concur in crucial parts of the decision. The only northerner who supported Taney's opinion, Justice Robert Grier of Pennsylvania, was known to be close to President Buchanan. In fact, Buchanan had secretly brought to bear improper but effective influence.

A storm of angry reaction broke in the North. The decision seemed to confirm every charge against the aggressive Slave Power. "There is such a thing as the slave power," warned the *Cincinnati Daily Commercial.* "It has marched over and annihilated the boundaries of the states. We are now one great homogenous slaveholding community." The *Cincinnati Freeman* asked, "What security have the Germans and the Irish that their children will not, within a hundred years, be reduced to slavery in this land of their adoption?" The poet James Russell Lowell expressed the racial and economic anxieties of poor northern whites when he had his Yankee character Ezekiel Biglow say in the language of the day:

> Wy, it's just ez clear ez figgers,
> Clear ez one an' one make two,
> Chaps thet make black slaves o' niggers,
> Want to make wite slaves o' you.

Republican politicians used these fears to strengthen their antislavery coalition. Abraham Lincoln stressed

that the territorial question affected every citizen. "The whole nation," he had declared as early as 1854, "is interested that the best use shall be made of these Territories. We want them for homes of free white people. This they cannot be, to any considerable extent, if slavery shall be planted within them." The territories must be reserved, he insisted, "as an outlet for free white people everywhere" so that immigrants could come to America and "find new homes and better their condition in life."

ABRAHAM LINCOLN AND THE SLAVE POWER

More importantly, Lincoln warned of slavery's increasing control over the nation. The founders had created a government dedicated to freedom, Lincoln insisted. Admittedly they had recognized slavery's existence, but the public mind, he argued in 1858, had always rested in the belief that slavery would die either naturally or by legislation. The next step in the unfolding Slave Power conspiracy, Lincoln alleged, would be a Supreme Court decision "declaring that the Constitution does not permit a State to exclude slavery from its limits. . . . We shall lie down pleasantly, dreaming that the people of Missouri are on the verge of making their State free; and we shall awake to the reality instead, that the Supreme Court has made Illinois a slave State." This charge was not hyperbole, for lawsuits soon challenged state laws that freed slaves brought within their borders.

Lincoln's most eloquent statement against the Slave Power was his famous "House Divided" speech, delivered as he announced his campaign for the U.S. Senate in 1858. Using biblical metaphor and extraordinary grace, he declared:

> "A house divided against itself cannot stand." I believe this government cannot endure, permanently half slave and half free. I do not expect the Union to be dissolved—I do not expect the House to fall—but I do expect it to cease to be divided. It will become all one thing or all the other. Either the opponents of slavery will arrest the further spread of it, and place it where the public mind shall rest in the belief that it is in the course of ultimate extinction; or its advocates will push it forward, till it shall become alike lawful in all the States, old as well as new, North as well as South.

Countless northerners heeded Lincoln's warnings, and events convinced them that slaveholders were nearing their goal of making slavery a national institution. Southerners, fatefully, never forgot Lincoln's use of the direct words "ultimate extinction."

Politically, these forceful Republican arguments offset the difficulties that the *Dred Scott* decision posed. By endorsing the South's doctrine of state sovereignty, the Court had in effect declared that the central position of the Republican Party—no extension of slavery—was unconstitutional. Republicans could only repudiate the decision, appealing to a "higher law," or hope to change the personnel of the Court. They did both and gained politically as fear of the Slave Power grew. But fear also deepened among free blacks. Frederick Douglass continued to try to fashion hope among his people but concluded a speech in the wake of the *Dred Scott* decision bleakly: "I walk by faith, not by sight."

For northern Democrats like Stephen Douglas, the Court's decision posed an awful dilemma. Northern voters were alarmed by the prospect

THE LECOMPTON CONSTITUTION AND SECTIONAL DISHARMONY AMONG DEMOCRATS

that the territories would be opened to slavery. To retain their support, Douglas had to find some way to reassure these voters. Yet, given his ambitions to lead the national Democratic Party and become president, Douglas could not afford to alienate southern Democrats.

Douglas chose to stand by his principle of popular sovereignty, even if the result angered southerners. In 1857 Kansans voted on a proslavery constitution that had been drafted at Lecompton. It was defeated by more than ten thousand votes in a referendum boycotted by

most proslavery voters. The evidence was overwhelming that Kansans did not want slavery, yet President Buchanan tried to force the Lecompton Constitution through Congress in an effort to hastily organize the territory.

Never had the Slave Power's influence over the government seemed more blatant; the Buchanan administration and southerners demanded a proslavery outcome, contrary to the popular will of the majority in Kansas. Breaking with the administration, Douglas threw his weight against the Lecompton Constitution. He gauged opinion in Kansas correctly, for in 1858 voters there rejected the constitution again. But his action infuriated southern Democrats. After the *Dred Scott* decision, southerners like Senator Albert G. Brown of Mississippi believed that slavery was protected in the territories: "The Constitution as expounded by the Supreme Court awards it. We demand it; we mean to have it." Increasingly, many southerners believed their sectional rights and slavery would be safe only in a separate nation. And northern Democrats, led by Douglas, found it harder to support the territorial protection for slavery that southern Democrats insisted was theirs as a constitutional right. Thus, in North and South the issue of slavery in the territories continued to destroy moderation and promote militancy.

Meanwhile, as the territorial process floundered in Kansas, it also collapsed in Utah. For their practice of

THE "MORMON WAR" IN UTAH

polygamy and their theocratic government, the Mormons who settled Utah were among the most persecuted peoples in America. Under the church-centered leadership of seer and prophet Brigham Young, the Mormons claimed the doctrine of popular sovereignty as their basis of independent rule while seeking recognition from Congress of territorial status and polygamy. But a series of corrupt territorial court justices appointed by Presidents Pierce and Buchanan failed to reign in the frontier society.

In 1857, Buchanan dispatched 2,500 troops, one-sixth of the U.S. Army, to suppress Young, who as one historian describes him, ruled "like a traitor in rebellion against the United States." Because of winter in the Rockies, the army never reached Utah. The massacre of a wagon train of 120 settlers by the Mormons and Indian allies notwithstanding, the "Mormon War" ended in Young withdrawing his forces and Buchanan sending peace commissioners and offering amnesty in 1858. The struggle over federal authority, as well as the Mormons' own "peculiar institution" in Utah, would continue for years.

Disunion

It is worth remembering that in the late 1850s most Americans were not caught up daily in the slavery crisis. They were preoccupied with personal affairs, especially coping with the effects of the economic panic that had begun in the spring of 1857. They were worried about widespread unemployment, the plummeting price of wheat, the declining wages at a textile mill, or sons who needed land. In the Midwest, clerks, mechanics, domestics, railroad hands, and lumber camp workers lost jobs by the thousands. Bankers were at a loss for what to do about a weak credit system caused by frenzied western land speculation that began early in the decade. In parts of the South, such as Georgia, the panic intensified class divisions between upcountry yeomen and coastal slaveholding planters. Farmers blamed the tight money policies of Georgia's budding commercial banking system on wealthy planters who controlled the state's Democratic Party.

The panic had been caused by several shortcomings of the unregulated American banking system, by frenzies of speculation in western lands and railroads, and by a weak and overburdened credit system. By 1858 Philadelphia had 40,000 unemployed workers, and New York City nearly 100,000. Fear of bread riots and class warfare gripped many cities in the North. True to form, blame for such economic woe became sectionalized, as southerners saw their system justified by the temporary collapse of industrial prosperity and northerners feared even more the incursions of the Slave Power on an insecure future.

Soon, however, the entire nation's focus would be thrown on a new dimension of the slavery question—

JOHN BROWN'S RAID ON HARPERS FERRY   armed rebellion, led by the abolitionist who had killed proslavery settlers along Pottawatomie Creek in "Bleeding Kansas." Born in Connecticut in 1800, John Brown had been raised by staunchly religious and antislavery parents. Between 1820 and 1855, he engaged in some twenty business ventures, including farming, nearly all of them failures. But Brown had a distinctive vision of abolitionism. He relied on an Old Testament conception of justice—"an eye for an eye"—and he had a puritanical obsession with the wickedness of others, especially southern slaveowners. Brown believed that slavery was an "unjustifiable" state of war conducted by one group of people against another. He also believed that violence in a righteous cause was a holy act, even a rite of purification for those who engaged in it. To Brown, the destruction of slavery in America required revolutionary ideology and revolutionary acts.

On October 16, 1859, Brown led a small band of whites and blacks (eighteen men in all) in an attack on the federal arsenal at Harpers Ferry, Virginia. Hoping to trigger a slave rebellion, Brown failed miserably and was quickly captured. In a celebrated trial in November and a widely publicized execution in December, in Charles Town, Virginia, Brown became one of the most enduring martyrs, as well as villains, of American history. His attempted insurrection struck fear into the South.

Then it became known that Brown had received financial backing from several prominent abolitionists. When northern intellectuals such as Emerson and Henry David Thoreau praised Brown as a holy warrior who "would make the gallows as glorious as the cross," white southerners' outrage multiplied. The South almost universally interpreted Brown's attack at Harpers Ferry as an act of midnight terrorism, as the fulfillment of their long-stated dread of "abolition emissaries" who would infiltrate the region to incite slave rebellion.

Perhaps most telling of all was the fact that the pivotal election of 1860 was less than a year away when Brown went so eagerly to the gallows, handing a note to

■ The earliest known photograph of John Brown, probably taken in 1846 in Massachusetts, shows him pledging his devotion to an unidentified flag, possibly an abolitionist banner. Already Brown was aiding runaway slaves and pondering ways to strike at slavery. (Ohio Historical Society)

his jailer with the famous prediction: "I John Brown am now quite certain that the crimes of this guilty land will never be purged away, but with blood." Most troubling to southerners, perhaps, was their awareness that while Republican politicians condemned Brown's crimes, they did so in a way that deflected attention onto the still greater crime of slavery.

Many Americans believed that the election of 1860 would decide the fate of the Union. The Democratic

ELECTION OF 1860

Party was the only party truly national in scope. "One after another," wrote a Mississippi editor, "the links which have bound the North and South together, have been severed . . . [but] the Democratic party looms gradually up . . . and waves the olive branch over the troubled waters of politics." But at its 1860 convention in Charleston, South Carolina, the Democratic Party split.

Stephen Douglas wanted his party's presidential nomination, but he could not afford to alienate northern voters by accepting the southern position on the territories. Southern Democrats, however, insisted on recognition of their rights—as the *Dred Scott* decision had defined them—and they moved to block Douglas's nomination. When Douglas obtained a majority for his version of the platform, delegates from the Deep South walked out of the convention. After efforts at compromise failed, the Democrats presented two nominees: Douglas for the northern wing, and Vice President John C. Breckinridge of Kentucky for the southern.

The Republicans nominated Abraham Lincoln at a rousing convention in Chicago. The choice of Lincoln reflected the growing power of the Midwest, and he was perceived as more moderate on slavery than the early front runner, Senator William H. Seward of New York. A Constitutional Union Party, formed to preserve the nation but strong only in the Upper South, nominated John Bell of Tennessee.

Bell's only issue in the ensuing campaign was the urgency of preserving the Union; Constitutional Unionists hoped to appeal to history, sentiment, and moderation to hold the country together. Douglas desperately sought to unite his northern and southern supporters, while Breckinridge quickly backed away from the appearance of extremism and his supporters in several states stressed his unionism. Although Lincoln and the Republicans denied any intent to interfere with slavery in the states where it existed, they stood firm against the extension of slavery into the territories.

The election of 1860 was sectional in character, and the only one in American history in which the losers refused to accept the result. Lincoln won, but Douglas, Breckinridge, and Bell together received a majority of the votes. Douglas had broad-based support but won few states. Breckinridge carried nine southern states, all in the Deep South. Bell won pluralities in Virginia, Kentucky, and Tennessee. Lincoln prevailed in the North, but in the four border states that ultimately remained loyal to the Union (Missouri, Kentucky, Maryland, and Delaware) he gained only a plurality, not a majority (see Table 14.3). Lincoln's victory was won in the electoral college. He polled only 40 percent of the total vote and was not even on the ballot in ten slave states.

Opposition to slavery's extension was the core issue of the Republican Party, and Lincoln's alarm over slavery's growing political power was genuine. Moreover, abolitionists and supporters of free soil in the North worked to keep the Republicans from compromising on their territorial stand. Meanwhile in the South, proslavery advocates and secessionists whipped up public opinion and demanded that state conventions assemble to consider secession.

Lincoln made the crucial decision not to soften his party's position on the territories. He wrote of the necessity of maintaining the bond of faith between voter and

TABLE 14.3

Presidential Vote in 1860 (by State)

Lincoln (Republican)	Carried all northern states and all electoral votes except 3 in New Jersey
Breckinridge (Southern Democrat)	Carried all slave states except Virginia, Kentucky, Tennessee, and Missouri
Bell (Constitutional Union)	Carried Virginia, Kentucky, Tennessee
Douglas (Northern Democrat)	Carried only Missouri

Lincoln received only 26,000 votes in the entire South and was not even on the ballot in ten slave states. Breckinridge was not on the ballot in three northern states.

candidate and of declining to set "the minority over the majority." Although many conservative Republicans—eastern businessmen and former Whigs who did not feel strongly about slavery—hoped for a compromise, the original and most committed Republicans—old Free-Soilers and antislavery Whigs—were adamant to stop the expansion of the peculiar institution.

In the winter of 1860–1861, Senator John J. Crittenden of Kentucky tried to craft a late-hour compromise. Hoping to don the mantle of Henry Clay and avert disunion, Crittenden proposed that the two sections divide the territories between them at latitude 36°30'. But the southerners would agree to this only if the Republicans did, too, for they wanted no less and knew that extremists in the South would demand much more. When Lincoln ruled out concessions on the territorial issue, Crittenden's peacemaking effort, based on old and discredited measures, collapsed.

Meanwhile, the Union was being destroyed. On December 20, 1860, South Carolina passed an ordinance of secession amid jubilation and cheering. This step marked the inaugural success of a strategy favored by secessionists: separate-state secession. Secessionists concentrated their efforts on the most extreme proslavery state, hoping that South Carolina's bold act would induce other states to follow, with each decision building momentum for disunion.

SECESSION AND THE CONFEDERATE STATES OF AMERICA

By reclaiming its independence, South Carolina raised the stakes in the sectional confrontation. No longer was secession an unthinkable step; the Union was broken. Secessionists now argued that other states should follow South Carolina and that those who favored compromise could make a better deal outside the Union than in it. Moderates found it difficult to dismiss such arguments, since most of them—even those who felt deep affection for the Union—were committed to defending southern rights and the southern way of life.

Southern extremists soon got their way in the Deep South. Overwhelming their opposition, they called separate state conventions and passed secession ordinances in Mississippi, Florida, Alabama, Georgia, Louisiana, and Texas. By February 1861 these states had joined South Carolina to form a new government in Montgomery, Alabama: the Confederate States of America. The delegates at Montgomery chose Jefferson Davis as their president, and the Confederacy began to function independently of the United States.

This apparent unanimity of action was deceiving. Confused and dissatisfied with the alternatives, many southerners who in 1860 had voted in the U.S. presidential election stayed home a few months later rather than vote for delegates who would decide on secession. Even so, in some state conventions the vote to secede was close, with secession decided by overrepresentation of plantation districts. Furthermore, the conventions were noticeably unwilling to let voters ratify their acts. Four states in

■ R. H. Howell, after Henry Cleenewerck, *The First Flag of Independence Raised in the South*. Lithograph, Savannah, Georgia, 1860. On the night of November 8, 1860, a huge crowd gathered in Johnson Square, Savannah, to protest Lincoln's election victory. The special banner on the obelisk reads "Our Motto Southern Rights, Equality of the States, Don't Tread on Me," drawing upon traditions from the Revolutionary War. (Library of Congress)

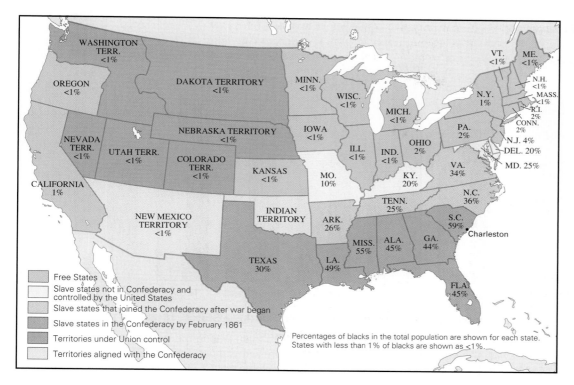

Map 14.4

The Divided Nation—Slave and Free Areas, 1861

After fighting began, the Upper South joined the Deep South in the Confederacy. How does the nation's pattern of division correspond to the distribution of slavery and the percentage of blacks in the population?

Free States
Slave states not in Confederacy and controlled by the United States
Slave states that joined the Confederacy after war began
Slave states in the Confederacy by February 1861
Territories under Union control
Territories aligned with the Confederacy

Percentages of blacks in the total population are shown for each state. States with less than 1% of blacks are shown as <1%.

the Upper South—Virginia, North Carolina, Tennessee, and Arkansas—flatly rejected secession and did not join the Confederacy until after fighting had begun. In the border states, popular sentiment was deeply divided; minorities in Kentucky and Missouri tried to secede, but these slave states ultimately came under Union control, along with Maryland and Delaware (see Map 14.4).

Such misgivings were not surprising. Secession posed new and troubling issues for southerners, especially the possibility of war, where it would be fought, and who would die. Analysis of election returns from 1860 and 1861 indicates that slaveholders and nonslaveholders were beginning to part company politically. Heavily slaveholding counties strongly supported secession. But nonslaveholding areas that had favored Breckinridge in the presidential election proved far less willing to support secession: most counties with few slaves took an antisecession position or were staunchly Unionist (see Figure 14.1). With war on the horizon, yeomen were beginning to consider their class interests and to ask themselves how far they would go to support slavery and slaveowners.

As for why the Deep South bolted, we need look no further than the speeches and writings of the secession commissioners sent out by the seven seceded states to try to convince the other slave states to join them. Repeat-

edly they stressed independence as the only way to preserve white racial security and the slave system against the hostile Republicans. Upon "slavery," said the Alabama commissioner, Stephen Hale, to the Kentucky legislature, rested "not only the wealth and prosperity of the southern people, but their very existence as a political community." Only secession, Hale contended, could sustain the "heaven-ordained superiority of the white over the black race."

The dilemma facing President Lincoln on inauguration day in March 1861 was how to maintain the authority of

FORT SUMTER AND OUTBREAK OF WAR

the federal government without provoking war. Proceeding cautiously, he sought only to hold on to forts in the states that had left the Union, reasoning that in this way he could assert federal sovereignty while waiting for a restoration. But Jefferson Davis, who could not claim to lead a sovereign nation if the Confederate ports were under foreign (that is, United States) control, was unwilling to be so patient. A collision was inevitable.

It arrived in the early morning hours of April 12, 1861, at Fort Sumter in Charleston harbor. A federal garrison there ran low on food, and Lincoln notified the South Carolinians that he was sending a ship to resupply the fort. For the Montgomery government, the

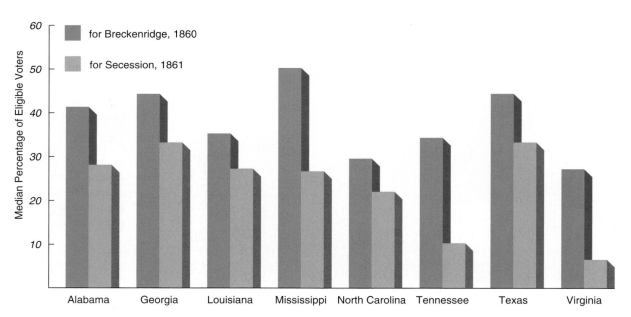

Figure 14.1   Voting Returns of Counties with Few Slaveholders, Eight Southern States, 1860 and 1861

This graph depicts voting in counties whose percentage of slaveholders ranked them among the lower half of the counties in their state. How does voters' support for secession in 1861 compare with support for John Breckinridge, the southern Democratic candidate in 1860? Why was their support for secession so weak? At this time counties with many slaveholders were giving increased support to secession.

alternatives were to attack the fort or to acquiesce to Lincoln's authority. After the Confederate cabinet met, the secretary of war ordered local commanders to obtain a surrender or attack the fort. After two days of heavy bombardment, the federal garrison finally surrendered. No one died in battle, though an accident during post-battle ceremonies killed two Union soldiers. Confederates permitted the U.S. troops to sail away on unarmed vessels while Charlestonians celebrated wildly. The Civil War—the bloodiest war in America's history—had begun.

Summary

Throughout the 1840s and 1850s many able leaders had worked diligently to avert this outcome. Most people, North and South, had hoped to keep the nation together. As late as 1858 even Jefferson Davis had declared, "This great country will continue united," saying that "to the innermost fibers of my heart I love it all, and every part." Secession dismayed northern editors and voters, and it also plunged some planters into depression. Paul Cameron, the largest slaveowner in North Carolina, confessed that he was "very unhappy. I love the Union." Many blacks, however, shared Freder-

ick Douglass's outlook. "The contest must now be decided," he wrote in March 1861, "and decided forever, which of the two, Freedom or Slavery, shall give law to this Republic. Let the conflict come."

Why had war broken out? Why had all efforts to prevent it failed? The conflict slavery generated was fundamental. The emotions bound up in attacking and defending slavery's future were too powerful, and the interests it affected too vital, for compromise. Even if one excludes extreme views, North and South had fundamentally different attitudes toward the institution. The logic of Republican ideology tended in the direction of abolishing slavery, even though Republicans denied any such intention. The logic of southern arguments led toward establishing slavery everywhere, though southern leaders too denied such a motive.

These positions hardened in American political life during the decade and a half before secession. Lincoln put these facts succinctly. In a post-election letter to his old friend Alexander Stephens of Georgia, soon to be vice president of the Confederacy, Lincoln offered assurance that Republicans would not attack slavery in the states where it existed. But Lincoln continued, "You think slavery is right and ought to be expanded; while we think it is wrong and ought to be restricted. That I suppose is the rub."

A nation may face unresolvable issues yet manage to get past them. New events can capture people's attention; time can alter interests and attitudes—this is why historians always remind us of the importance of "contingency" in human affairs. Change can occur when we least expect it and the best experts have not predicted it. Advocates of compromise hoped that the tradition of conciliation and sectional adjustment would yet again save the Union in 1860. They tried to contain conflict and buy time for the nation, but their efforts were doomed to failure.

Territorial expansion generated disputes so frequently that the nation never enjoyed an extended breathing space during the 1850s. Every southern victory increased fear of the Slave Power, and each new expression of Free-Soil sentiment made alarmed slaveholders more insistent in their demands. Eventually even those opposed to war could see no way to avoid it. In the profoundest sense, slavery was the root of the war. But as the fighting began, this, the war's central issue, was shrouded in confusion. How would the Civil War affect slavery, its place in the law, and African Americans' place in society? Would the institution survive a short war, but not a long war? As a people and a nation, Americans had reached the most fateful turning point in their history. Answers would now come from the battlefield and from the mobilization of two societies to wage war on a scale they had not imagined.

LEGACY FOR A PEOPLE AND A NATION
Terrorist or Freedom Fighter?

The greatest significance of John Brown's raid on Harpers Ferry in 1859 rests in its long aftermath in American memory. "Men consented to his death," wrote Frederick Douglass of Brown, "and then went home and taught their children to honor his memory." Brown is as important as a symbol as he is for his deeds. He has been at once one of the most beloved and most loathed figures in American history. In the song that bears his name, "John Brown's Body," a popular marching tune during the Civil War, his "soul goes marching on." As the poet Stephen Vincent Benet

wrote: "You can weigh John Brown's body well enough, / But how and in what balance weigh John Brown?"

In the wake of his execution, in painting, song, and poetry people constructed a John Brown mythology. Was he a Christ-like figure who died for the nation's sins, who had to commit crimes in order to expose the nation's larger crime? Or was he a terrorist, who murdered in the name of his own peculiar vision of God's will? Brown can be inspiring and disturbing, majestic and foolish, a warrior saint or a monster. He represents the highest ideals and the most ruthless deeds. He killed for justice and was hanged as a traitor. Perhaps Brown was one of the avengers of history who does the work the rest of us won't, or couldn't, or shouldn't.

Over the years many organizations have adopted John Brown as their justifying symbol, from left-wing students opposing American foreign policy to current anti-abortion groups who target clinics and doctors. In today's world, terrorism and revolutionary violence are more often in the news: an airliner is blown up over Lockerbie, Scotland; suicide bombers attack buses and restaurants in Israel; a federal building explodes in Oklahoma City; the Irish Republican Army plants explosives in London subways; American embassies are attacked in Africa and Europe; and on September 11, 2001, four hijacked passenger airplanes are turned into weapons of death that bring terrorism to American soil as never before. The story of John Brown's raid in 1859 forces us to ask when and how revolutionary violence—violence in the name of a political or spiritual end—is justified. That is his legacy for a people and a nation.

The *history companion* powered by Eduspace®
Your primary source for interactive quizzes, exercises, and more to help you learn efficiently.
http://history.college.hmco.com/students

TRANSFORMING FIRE: THE CIVIL WAR 1861–1865

He was an ordinary twenty-seven-year-old store clerk from a New England town. But he went off, as though directed by a manly compass, to seek the extraordinary experiences of comradeship and war. In the spring of 1861, Charles Brewster, a member of a militia unit in Northampton, Massachusetts, left his mother and two sisters behind and joined Company C of the Tenth Massachusetts Volunteers. At that moment, Brewster had no idea of his capacity for leadership or his ability to uphold such values as courage and manliness. But the war released him from the boredom and failure of his life.

On April 18, only three days after the surrender of Fort Sumter, a mustering of Company C turned into a large public rally. The next week seventy-five Northampton women committed their labor to sew uniforms for the company. Local poets came to the armory to recite patriotic verses to the would-be soldiers. Yesterday farmers, clerks, and mechanics, today they were the heroes who would "whip secesh." By June 10, after weeks of drilling, Brewster's company strode down Main Street amid a cheering throng of spectators. Flags waved everywhere, brass bands competed, and Brewster and his company boarded a train going south. En route the soldiers continued the joyous fervor of the day by singing "patriotic airs" to the accompaniment of a lone accordion.

Before their three-year enlistment ended, the Tenth Massachusetts participated in nearly every major battle fought by the Army of the Potomac from early 1862 to the summer of 1864. When the survivors of the Tenth were mustered out, only 220 of the nearly 1,000 in the original regiment were still on active duty. Their summer outing had transformed into the bloodiest war in history. They had seen thousands die of disease, practiced war upon civilians and the southern landscape, and loyally served the cause as variously defined, trying their best to fulfill their communities' expectations. In more than two hundred sometimes lyrical letters to his mother and sisters, Brewster, who rose to lieutenant and adjutant of his regiment, left a trove of commentary on the meaning

◀ War drastically altered the lives of millions of Americans. Many young men found in soldiering a combination of comradeship, devotion, boredom, and horror. Winslow Homer gave the ironic title *Home, Sweet, Home* to this painting of Union soldiers in camp about 1863.   (National Gallery of Art, Washington, D.C. Patron's Permanent Fund)

CHRONOLOGY

1861 • Battle of Bull Run
  • McClellan organizes Union Army
  • Union blockade begins
  • U.S. Congress passes first confiscation act
  • *Trent* affair

1862 • Union captures Fort Henry and Fort Donelson
  • U.S. Navy captures New Orleans
  • Battle of Shiloh shows the war's destructiveness
  • Confederacy enacts conscription
  • McClellan's Peninsula Campaign fails to take Richmond
  • U.S. Congress passes second confiscation act, initiating emancipation
  • Confederacy mounts offensive in Maryland and Kentucky
  • Battle of Antietam ends Lee's drive into Maryland in September
  • British intervention in the war on Confederate side is averted

1863 • Emancipation Proclamation takes effect
  • U.S. Congress passes National Banking Act
  • Union enacts conscription
  • African American soldiers join Union Army
  • Food riots occur in southern cities
  • Battle of Chancellorsville ends in Confederate victory but Jackson's death
  • Union wins key victories at Gettysburg and Vicksburg
  • Draft riots take place in New York City
  • Battle of Chattanooga leaves South vulnerable to Sherman's march into Georgia

1864 • Battles of the Wilderness and Spotsylvania produce heavy casualties on both sides in the effort to capture and defend Richmond
  • Battle of Cold Harbor continues carnage in Virginia
  • Lincoln requests Republican Party plank abolishing slavery
  • Sherman captures Atlanta
  • Confederacy begins to collapse on the home front
  • Lincoln wins reelection, eliminating any Confederate hopes for a negotiated end to war
  • Jefferson Davis proposes emancipation within the Confederacy
  • Sherman marches through Georgia to the sea

1865 • Sherman marches through Carolinas
  • U.S. Congress approves Thirteenth Amendment
  • Lee abandons Richmond and Petersburg
  • Lee surrenders at Appomattox Court House
  • Lincoln assassinated
  • Death toll in war reaches 620,000

of war, why slavery had to be destroyed, and especially the values of common, mid-nineteenth-century American men.

Brewster was as racist as many southerners in his perceptions of blacks. He was no "desperate hero" about battlefield courage, and he nearly died of dysentery twice. He was personally eager for rank and recognition, and eventually held only contempt for civilians who stayed at home. He was often miserably lonely and homesick, and he described battlefield carnage with an honest realism. The early romantic was transformed into a mature veteran by what he called the "terrible, terrible business" of war.

Most tellingly, Brewster's attitudes toward race transformed. In 1862 he defied orders and took in a seventeen-year-old ex-slave as his personal servant, patronizingly clothing him with his own old pants sent from home. In 1864, after surviving some of the worst battles of the war in Virginia, which destroyed his regiment, and frightened of civilian life, Brewster reenlisted to be a recruiter of black troops. In this new role, Brewster worked from an office in Norfolk, Virginia, where his principal job was writing "love letters" for illiterate black women to their soldier husbands at the front. In imagining Brewster sitting at a table with a lonely freedwoman, swallowing his prejudices toward blacks and women, and repeatedly writing or reciting the phrases "give my love to . . ." and "your Husband untall Death," we can glimpse the enormous potential for human transformation at work in this war.

The Civil War brought astonishing, unexpected changes to individuals everywhere in North and South. It obliterated the normal patterns of life. Millions of men were swept away into training camps and battle units. Armies numbering in the hundreds of thousands marched over the South, devastating once-peaceful countrysides. Families struggled to survive without their men; businesses tried to cope with the loss of workers. Women in both North and South took on extra responsibilities in the home and moved into new jobs in the work force. Many women joined the ranks of nurses and hospital workers. No sphere of life was untouched.

But southern soldiers, and their families, also experienced what few other groups of Americans have—utter defeat. For most of them, wealth changed to poverty and hope to despair as countless southern farms were ruined. Late in the war many southerners yearned only for an end to inflation, shortages, the escape of their slaves, and the death that visited nearly every family. Even the South's slaves, who hoped that they were witnessing the "coming of the jubilee," encountered unsympathetic liberators. When a Yankee soldier ransacked a slave woman's cabin, stealing her best quilts, she denounced him as a "nasty, stinkin' rascal" who had betrayed his cause of freedom. Angrily the soldier contradicted her, saying, "I'm fightin' for $14 a month and the Union."

Northern soldiers, though ultimately victorious, often resented the sacrifices demanded of them. Northern businessmen, however, viewed the economic effects of the war with optimism. The conflict ensured vast government expenditures, a heavy demand for goods, and lucrative federal contracts. *Harper's Monthly* reported that an eminent financier expected a long war, fostering huge purchases, paper money, active speculation, and rising prices. "The battle of Bull Run," predicted the financier, "makes the fortune of every man in Wall Street who is not a natural idiot."

Change was most drastic in the South, where secessionists had launched a conservative revolution for their section's national independence. Born of states' rights doctrine, the Confederacy now had to be transformed into a centralized nation to fight a vast war. Never were men more mistaken: their revolutionary means were fundamentally incompatible with their conservative purpose. Southern whites had feared that a peacetime government of Republicans would interfere with slavery and upset the routine of plantation life. Instead their own actions led to a war that turned southern life upside down and imperiled the very existence of slavery.

War altered the North as well, but less sharply. Because most of the fighting took place on southern soil, northern farms and factories remained largely unscathed and busy. Workers lost ground to inflation, but the economy hummed. A new pro-business atmosphere dominated Congress, where the seats of southern representatives were empty. To the alarm of many, the powers of the federal government and of the president increased during the war.

The war created social strains in both North and South. Disaffection was strongest in the Confederacy, where poverty and class resentment threatened the Confederacy from within as federal armies assailed it from without. In the North, dissent also flourished, and antiwar sentiment occasionally erupted into violence.

Ultimately, the Civil War forced on the nation a social and political revolution regarding race. Its greatest effect was to compel leaders and citizens to deal directly with the issue they had struggled over but had been unable to resolve: slavery. This issue, in a host of ways, had caused the war. Now the scope and demands of the war forced reluctant Americans to confront it. And blacks themselves embraced what was for them the most fundamental turning point in their experience as Americans. ■

America Goes to War, 1861–1862

Few Americans understood what they were getting into when the war began. The onset of hostilities sparked patriotic sentiments, optimistic speeches, and joyous ceremonies in both North and South. Northern communities, like Brewster's Northampton, raised companies of volunteers eager to save the Union and sent them off with fanfare. In the South, confident recruits boasted of whipping the Yankees and returning home before Christmas. Southern women sewed dashing uniforms for men who soon would be lucky to wear drab gray or butternut homespun. Americans went to war in 1861 with decidedly romantic notions of what they would experience.

Through the spring of 1861 both sides scrambled to organize and train their undisciplined armies. On July 21, 1861, the first battle took place outside Manassas Junction, Virginia, near a stream called Bull Run. General Irvin McDowell and 30,000 Union troops attacked General P. G. T. Beauregard's 22,000 southerners (see Map 15.1). As raw recruits struggled amid the confusion of their first battle, federal forces began to gain ground. Then they ran into a line of Virginia troops under General Thomas Jackson. "There is Jackson standing like a stone wall," shouted one Confederate. "Stonewall" Jackson's line held, and the arrival of 9,000 Confederate reinforcements won the day for the South. Union troops fled back to Washington, observed by shocked northern congressmen and spectators who had watched the battle; a few sightseers were actually captured for their folly.

FIRST BATTLE OF BULL RUN

■ In *Departure of the Seventh Regiment* (1861), flags and the spectacle of thousands of young men from New York marching off to battle give a deceptively gay appearance to the beginning of the Civil War.   (Museum of Fine Arts, Boston; M. and M. Karolik Collection)

The unexpected rout at Bull Run gave northerners their first hint of the nature of the war to come. While the United States enjoyed an enormous advantage in resources, victory would not be easy. Pro-Union feeling was growing in western Virginia, and loyalties were divided in the four border slave states—Missouri, Kentucky, Maryland, and Delaware. But the rest of the Upper South—the states of North Carolina, Virginia, Tennessee, and Arkansas—had joined the Confederacy in the wake of the attack on Fort Sumter. Moved by an outpouring of regional loyalty, half a million southerners volunteered to fight, so many that the Confederate government could hardly arm them all. The United States therefore undertook a massive mobilization of troops around Washington, D.C.

Lincoln gave command of the army to General George B. McClellan, an officer who proved to be better at organization and training than at fighting. McClellan put his growing army into camp and devoted the fall and winter of 1861 to readying a formidable force of a quarter-million men whose mission would be to take Richmond, established as the Confederate capital by July 1861. "The vast preparation of the enemy," wrote one southern soldier, produced a "feeling of despondency" in the South for the first time. But southern morale remained high early in the war.

While McClellan prepared, the Union began to implement other parts of its overall strategy, which called for a blockade of southern ports and eventual capture of the Mississippi River. Like a constricting snake, this "Anaconda plan" would strangle the Confederacy (see Map 15.2). At first the Union Navy had too few ships to patrol 3,550 miles of coastline and block the Confederacy's avenues of supply. Gradually, however, the navy increased the blockade's effectiveness, though it never stopped southern commerce completely.

GRAND STRATEGY

Confederate strategy was essentially defensive. A defensive posture was not only consistent with the South's claim of independence, but acknowledged the North's advantage in resources (see Figure 15.1). Furthermore, communities all across the South demanded their defense. But Jefferson Davis called the southern strategy an "offensive defensive," taking advantage of opportunities to attack and using its interior lines of transportation to concentrate troops at crucial points. In its war aims, the

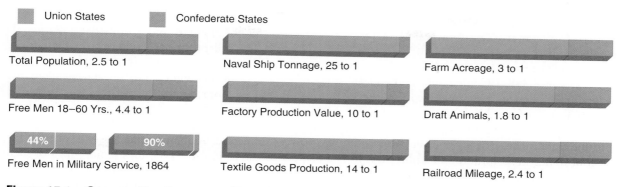

Figure 15.1   Comparative Resources, Union and Confederate States, 1861

The North had vastly superior resources. Although the North's advantages in manpower and industrial capacity proved very important, the South still had to be conquered, its society and its will crushed. (Source: *The Times Atlas of World History.* Time Books, London, 1978. Used with permission.)

Confederacy did not need to conquer the North; the Union effort, however, as time would tell, required conquest of the South.

Strategic thinking on both sides slighted the importance of "the West," that vast expanse of territory between Virginia and the Mississippi River and beyond. Guerrilla warfare broke out in 1861 in the politically divided state of Missouri, and key locations along the Mississippi and other major western rivers would prove to be crucial prizes in the North's eventual victory. Beyond the Mississippi River, the Confederacy hoped to gain an advantage by negotiating treaties with the Creeks, Choctaws, Chickasaws, Cherokees, Seminoles, and smaller tribes of Plains Indians. Meanwhile the Republican U.S. Congress carved the West into territories in anticipation of state making. But what began during the Civil War was the start of nearly three decades of offensive warfare against Indians, an enveloping strategy of conquest, relocation, and slaughter. All Americans would soon know they were in a war the scale of which few people had ever imagined.

The last half of 1861 brought no major land battles, but the North made gains by sea. Late in the summer

UNION NAVAL CAMPAIGN

Union naval forces captured Cape Hatteras and then seized Hilton Head, one of the Sea Islands off Port Royal, South Carolina. A few months later, similar operations secured vital coastal points in North Carolina, as well as Fort Pulaski, which defended Savannah. Federal naval operations established significant beachheads along the Confederate coastline (see Map 15.2).

The coastal victories off South Carolina foreshadowed a revolution in slave society. At the federal gun-

boats' approach, planters abandoned their lands and fled. For a while, Confederate cavalry tried to round up slaves and move them to the interior as well. But thousands of slaves greeted what they hoped to be freedom with rejoicing and broke the hated cotton gins. Some entered their masters' homes and took clothing and furniture, which they conspicuously displayed. A growing stream of runaways poured into the Union lines. Unwilling at first to wage a war against slavery, the federal government did not acknowledge the slaves' freedom— though it began to use their labor in the Union cause. This swelling tide of emancipated slaves, defined by many Union officers as "contraband" of war (confiscated enemy property), forced first a bitter and confused debate within the Union Army and government over how to treat the freedmen, and then a forthright attempt to harness their power.

The coastal incursions worried southerners, but the spring of 1862 brought even stronger evidence of the war's gravity. In March two ironclad ships—the *Monitor* (a Union warship) and the *Merrimack* (a Union ship seized by the Confederacy)—fought each other for the first time off the coast of Virginia; their battle, though indecisive, ushered in a new era in naval design. In April, Union ships commanded by Admiral David Farragut smashed through log booms blocking the Mississippi River and fought their way upstream to capture New Orleans.

Farther west three full Confederate regiments were organized, mostly of Cherokees, from Indian Territory,

WAR IN THE FAR WEST

but a Union victory at Elkhorn Tavern, Arkansas, shattered southern control of the region. Thereafter, dissension within Native American groups and a

Union victory the following year at Honey Springs, Arkansas, reduced Confederate operations in Indian Territory to guerrilla raids.

In the westernmost campaign of the war, from February to May 1862, some 3,000 Confederate and 4,000 Union forces fought for control of New Mexico Territory. The military significance of the New Mexico campaign was limited, but the Confederate invasion had grander aims: access to the trade riches of the Santa Fe Trail and possession of gold mines in Colorado and California. If the campaign had endured long enough, the Confederacy would have been much stronger with a western empire. But Colorado and New Mexico Unionists fought for their region, and in a series of battles at Glorieta Pass, 20 miles east of Santa Fe, on March 26–28, they blocked the Confederate invasion. By May 1, Confederate forces straggled down the Rio Grande River back into Texas, ending their effort to take New Mexico.

Meanwhile, in February 1862 land and river forces in northern Tennessee won significant victories for the Union. A Union commander named Ulysses S. Grant saw the strategic importance of Fort Henry and Fort Donelson,

GRANT'S TENNESSEE CAMPAIGN AND THE BATTLE OF SHILOH

the Confederate outposts guarding the Tennessee and Cumberland Rivers. If federal troops could capture these forts, Grant realized, they would open two prime routes into the heartland of the Confederacy. In just ten days he seized the forts, cutting off the Confederates completely and demanding "unconditional surrender" of Fort Donelson. A path into Tennessee, Alabama, and Mississippi now lay open before the Union Army. Grant's achievement of such a surrender from his former West Point roommate, Confederate commander Simon Bolivar Buckner, inspired northern public opinion.

Grant moved on into southern Tennessee and the first of the war's shockingly bloody encounters, the Battle of Shiloh (see Map 15.2). On April 6 Confederate general Albert Sidney Johnston caught federal troops with their backs to the water awaiting reinforcements along the Tennessee River. The Confederates attacked early in the morning and inflicted heavy damage all day. Close to victory, General Johnston was shot from his horse and killed. Southern forces almost achieved a break-

■ Both armies experienced religious revivals during the war. This photograph shows members of a largely Irish regiment from New York celebrating Mass at the beginning of the war. Notice the presence of some female visitors in the left foreground.
(Library of Congress)

through, but Union reinforcements arrived that night. The next day the tide of battle turned, and after ten hours of terrible combat, Grant's men forced the Confederates to withdraw.

Neither side won a victory at Shiloh, yet the losses were staggering. Northern troops lost 13,000 men (killed, wounded, or captured) out of 63,000; southerners sacrificed 11,000 out of 40,000. Total casualties in this single battle exceeded those in all three of America's previous wars combined. Now both sides were beginning to sense the true nature of the war. "I saw an open field," Grant recalled, "over which Confederates had made repeated charges . . . so covered with dead that it would have been possible to walk across the clearing, in any direction, stepping on dead bodies, without a foot touching the ground." Shiloh utterly changed Grant's thinking about the war. He had hoped that southerners soon would be "heartily tired" of the conflict. After Shiloh, "I gave up all idea of saving the Union except by complete conquest." Memories of the Shiloh battlefield, and many others to come, would haunt the soldiers who survived for the rest of their lives. Herman Melville's "Shiloh, A Requiem" captures the pathos of that spring day when armies learned the truth about war.

> Skimming lightly, wheeling still,
>   The swallows fly low
> Over the field in clouded days,
>   The forest-field of Shiloh—
> Over the field where April rain
> Solaced the parched ones stretched in pain
> Through the pause of night
> That followed the Sunday fight
>   Around the church of Shiloh—
> The church so lone, the log-built one,
> That echoed to many a parting groan
>   And natural prayer
>   Of dying foemen mingled there—
> Foemen at morn, but friends at eve—
>   Fame or country least their care:
> (What like a bullet can undeceive!)
>   But now they lie low,
> While over them the swallows skim,
>   And all is hushed at Shiloh.

On the Virginia front, President Lincoln had a different problem. General McClellan was slow to move.

MCCLELLAN AND THE PENINSULA CAMPAIGN

Only thirty-six, McClellan had already achieved notable success as an army officer and railroad president. Habitually overestimating the size of enemy forces, he called repeatedly for reinforcements

Map 15.1   McClellan's Campaign

The water route chosen by McClellan to threaten Richmond during the peninsular campaign.

and ignored Lincoln's directions to advance. McClellan advocated war of limited aims that would lead to a quick reunion. He intended no disruption of slavery, nor war on noncombatants. McClellan's conservative vision of the war was practically outdated before he ever moved his army into Virginia. Finally he chose to move by a water route, sailing his troops down the Chesapeake, landing them on the peninsula between the York and James Rivers, and advancing on Richmond from the east (see Map 15.1).

After a bloody but indecisive battle at Fair Oaks on May 31–June 1, the federal armies moved to within 7 miles of the Confederate capital. They could see the spires on Richmond churches. The Confederate commanding general, Joseph E. Johnston, was badly wounded at Fair Oaks, and President Jefferson Davis placed his chief military adviser, Robert E. Lee, in command. The fifty-five-year-old Lee was an aristocratic Virginian, a lifelong military officer, and a veteran of distinction from the War with Mexico. Although he initially opposed secession, Lee loyally gave his allegiance to his state and became a staunch Confederate nationalist. He soon foiled McClellan's legions.

First, Lee sent Stonewall Jackson's corps of 17,000 northwest into the Shenandoah valley behind Union forces, where they threatened Washington, D.C., and with rapid-strike mobility drew some federal troops away from Richmond to protect their own capital. Further, in mid-June, in an extraordinary four-day ride around the entire Union Army, Confederate cavalry under J. E. B. Stuart, a self-styled Virginia cavalier, with red cape and plumed hat, confirmed the exposed position of a major portion of McClellan's army north of the rain-swollen Chickahominy River. Then, in a series of engagements known as the Seven Days Battles, June 26–July 1, Lee struck at McClellan's army. Lee never managed to close his pincers around the retreating Union forces, but the daring move of taking the majority of his army northeast and attacking the Union right flank, while leaving only a small force to defend Richmond, forced McClellan (always believing he was outnumbered) to retreat toward the James River.

During the sustained fighting of the Seven Days, the Union forces suffered 20,614 casualties, and the Confederates 15,849. After repeated rebel assaults against entrenched positions on high ground at Malvern Hill, an officer concluded: "It was not war, it was murder." By August 3 McClellan withdrew his army back to the Potomac and the environs of Washington. Richmond remained safe for almost two more years.

Buoyed by these results, Jefferson Davis conceived an ambitious plan to turn the tide of the war and gain recognition of the Confederacy by European nations. He ordered a general offensive, sending Lee north into Maryland and Generals Kirby Smith and Braxton Bragg into Kentucky. Calling on residents of Maryland and Kentucky, still slave states, to make a separate peace with his government, Davis also invited northwestern states like Indiana, which sent much of their trade down the Mississippi to New Orleans, to leave the Union. This was a coordinated effort to take the war to the North, and to try to force a turning point.

CONFEDERATE OFFENSIVE IN MARYLAND AND KENTUCKY

The plan was promising, but every part of the offensive failed. In the bloodiest day of the entire war, September 17, 1862, McClellan turned Lee back from Sharpsburg, Maryland. In this Battle of Antietam 5,000 men died, and another 18,000 were wounded. Lee was lucky to escape destruction, for McClellan had intercepted a lost battle order, wrapped around cigars for each Confederate corps commander and inadvertently dropped by a courier. But McClellan moved slowly, failed to use his larger forces in simultaneous attacks, and allowed Lee's stricken army to retreat to safety across the Potomac. In the wake of Antietam, Lincoln removed McClellan from command.

■ In October 1862 in New York City, photographer Mathew Brady opened an exhibition of photographs from the Battle of Antietam. Although few knew it, Brady's vision was very poor, and this photograph of Confederate dead was actually made by his assistants, Alexander Gardner and James F. Gibson. (Library of Congress)

In Kentucky Generals Smith and Bragg secured Lexington and Frankfurt, but their effort to force the Yankees back to the Ohio River was stopped at the Battle of Perryville on October 8. Bragg's army retreated back into Tennessee, where on December 31, 1862, to January 2, 1863, they fought an indecisive but much bloodier battle at Murfreesboro. Casualties exceeded even those of Shiloh, and many lives were sacrificed on a bitter winter landscape.

Confederate leaders had marshaled all their strength for a breakthrough but had failed. Outnumbered and disadvantaged in resources, the South could not continue the offensive. Profoundly disappointed, Davis admitted to a committee of Confederate representatives that southerners were entering "the darkest and most dangerous period we have yet had."

But 1862 also brought painful lessons to the North. Confederate general J. E. B. Stuart executed a daring cavalry raid into Pennsylvania in October. Then on December 13 Union general Ambrose Burnside, now in command of the Army of the Potomac, unwisely ordered his soldiers to attack Lee's army, which held fortified positions on high ground at Fredericksburg, Virginia. Lee's men performed so efficiently in killing northerners that Lee was moved to say, "It is well that war is so terrible. We should grow too fond of it." Burnside's repeated assaults up Marye's Heights shocked even the opponents. "The Federals had fallen like the steady dripping of rain from the eaves of a house," remarked Confederate general James Longstreet. And a Union officer observed the carnage of 1,300 dead and 9,600 wounded Union soldiers: "The whole plain was covered with men, prostrate and dropping. . . . I had never before seen fighting like that . . . the next brigade coming up in succession would do its duty, and melt like snow coming down on warm ground."

The rebellion was far from being suppressed. Both sides were learning that they would have to pay a terrible price. And people on both home fronts had now to decide just what they would endure to win a war of one society against the other.

War Transforms the South

*T*he war caused tremendous disruptions in civilian life and altered southern society beyond all expectations. One of the first traditions to fall was the southern preference for local and limited government. States' rights had been a formative ideology for the Confederacy, but state governments were weak operations. The average citizen, on whom the hand of government had rested lightly, probably knew county authorities best. To withstand the massive power of the North, however, the South needed to centralize; like the colonial revolutionaries, southerners faced a choice of join together or die separately. Jefferson Davis quickly saw the necessity of centralization. If the states of the Confederacy insisted on fighting separately, said Davis, "we had better make terms as soon as we can."

Promptly Davis moved to bring all arms, supplies, and troops under his control. But by early 1862 the scope and duration of the conflict required something more. Tens of thousands of Confederate soldiers had volunteered for just one year's service, planning to return home in the spring to plant their crops. To keep southern armies in the field, the War Department encouraged reenlistments and called for new volunteers. However, as one official admitted, "the spirit of volunteering had died out." Finally, faced with a critical shortage of troops, in April 1862 the Confederate government enacted the first national conscription (draft) law in American history. Thus the war forced unprecedented change on states that had seceded out of fear of change.

THE CONFEDERACY AND CENTRALIZATION

Jefferson Davis was a strong chief executive. He adopted a firm leadership role toward the Confederate Congress, which raised taxes and later passed a tax-in-kind—paid in farm products. Almost three thousand agents dispersed to collect the tax, assisted by almost fifteen hundred appraisers. Where opposition arose, the government suspended the writ of habeas corpus (which prevented individuals from being held without trial) and imposed martial law. Despite Davis's unyielding stance, this tax system, however, proved inadequate to the South's war effort.

To replace the food that men in uniform would have grown, Davis exhorted state governments to require farmers to switch from cash crops to food crops. But the army remained short of food and labor. The War Department resorted to impressing slaves to work on fortifications, and after 1861 the government relied heavily on confiscation of food to feed the troops. Officers swooped down on farms in the line of march and carted away grain, meat, wagons, and draft animals. Such raids caused increased hardship for women managing farms in the absence of husbands and sons.

Soon the Confederate administration in Richmond gained virtually complete control over the southern economy. Because it controlled the supply of labor through conscription, the administration could compel industry to work on government contracts and supply the military's needs. The Confederate Congress also gave the central government almost complete control of the

■ Five Texans in the Confederate cavalry sitting for a formal photograph. Three have the "lone star" on their hats. Like thousands of others, these men posed to send their images to the folks back home, but also perhaps as an act of comradeship at the war front. (The Panhandle-Plains Historical Society, Canyon, Texas)

railroads. A large bureaucracy sprang up to administer these operations: over seventy thousand civilians staffed the Confederate administration. By the war's end, the southern bureaucracy was larger in proportion to population than its northern counterpart.

Historians have long argued over whether the Confederacy itself was a "rebellion," a "revolution," or the genuine creation of a "nation." Whatever label we apply, Confederates created a culture and an ideology of nationalism. Immediately, southerners tried to forge their own national symbols and identity. In flags, songs, language, seals, school readers, and other forms of "national characteristics," Confederates created their own story.

CONFEDERATE NATIONALISM

In its conservative crusade to preserve states' rights, the social order, and racial slavery, southerners believed the Confederacy was the true legacy of the American Revolution—in continuity with the War of American Independence and a bulwark against centralized power. In this view, southern "liberty" was no less a holy cause than that of the patriots of 1776. To southerners, theirs was a continuing revolution against the excesses of Yankee democracy; George Washington on horseback formed the center of the official seal of the Confederacy.

Also central to Confederate nationalism was a refurbished defense of slavery as a benign, protective institu-

tion. In wartime schoolbooks children were instructed in the divinely inspired, paternalistic character of slavery. And the idea of the "faithful slave" was key to southerners' nationalist cause. A poem popular among whites captured an old slave's rejection of the Emancipation Proclamation:

> Now, Massa, dis is berry fine, dese words
>   You've spoke to me,
> No doubt you mean it kindly, but ole Dinah
>   Won't be free . . .
> Ole Massa's berry good to me—and though I am
>   His slave,
> He treats me like I'se kin to him—and I would
>   Rather have
> A home in Massa's cabin, and eat his black
>   Bread too,
> Dan leave ole Massa's children and go and
>   Lib wid you.

In the face of defeat and devastation, this and other forms of Confederate nationalism collapsed in the final year of the war. But much of the spirit and substance of Confederate nationalism would revive in the postwar period in a new ideology of the Lost Cause.

Clerks and subordinate officials crowded the towns and cities where Confederate departments set up their offices. Clerks had always been males, but now "government girls" staffed the Confederate bureaucracy.

SOUTHERN
CITIES AND
INDUSTRY

The sudden population booms that resulted overwhelmed the housing supply and stimulated new construction. The pressure was especially great in Richmond, whose population increased 250 percent. Mobile's population jumped from 29,000 to 41,000; Atlanta began to grow; and 10,000 people poured into war-related industries in little Selma, Alabama.

As the Union blockade disrupted imports of manufactured products, the traditionally agricultural South forged industries. Many planters shared Davis's hope that industrialization would bring "deliverance, full and unrestricted, from all commercial dependence" on the North or the world. Indeed, beginning almost from scratch, the Confederacy achieved tremendous feats of industrial development. Chief of Ordnance Josiah Gorgas increased the capacity of Richmond's Tredegar Iron Works and other factories to the point that by 1865 his Ordnance Bureau was supplying all Confederate small arms and ammunition. Meanwhile, the government constructed new railroad lines and ironworks, much of the labor for which consisted of slaves relocated from farms and plantations.

White women, restricted to narrow roles in antebellum society, gained substantial new responsibilities in

CHANGING
ROLES OF
WOMEN

wartime. The wives and mothers of soldiers now headed households and performed men's work, including raising crops and tending animals. Women in nonslaveowning families cultivated fields themselves, while wealthier women suddenly had to perform as overseers and manage field work. In the cities, white women—who had been virtually excluded from the labor force—found a limited number of respectable paying jobs, and female schoolteachers appeared in the South for the first time.

Women experienced both confidence and agony from their new responsibilities. Among them was Janie Smith, a young North Carolinian. Raised in a rural area by prosperous parents, she now faced grim realities as the war reached her farm and troops turned her home into a hospital. "It makes me shudder when I think of the awful sights I witnessed that morning," she wrote to a friend. "Ambulance after ambulance drove up with our wounded. . . . Under every shed and tree, the tables were carried for amputating the limbs. . . . The blood lay in puddles in the grove; the groans of the dying . . . were horrible." But Janie Smith learned to cope with crisis. She ended her account with the proud words, "I can dress amputated limbs now and do most anything in the way of nursing wounded soldiers."

Patriotic sacrifice appealed to some women, but others resented their new burdens. A Texas woman who had struggled to discipline slaves pronounced herself "sick of trying to do a man's business." Others grew angry over shortages and resented cooking and unfamiliar contact with lower-class women. Some women grew scornful of the war and demanded that their men return to help provide for families.

For millions of ordinary southerners, change brought privation and suffering. Mass poverty descended for the

HUMAN
SUFFERING,
HOARDING,
AND INFLATION

first time on a large minority of the white population. Many yeoman families had lost their breadwinners to the army. As a South Carolina newspaper put it, "The duties of war have caled away from home the sole supports of many, many families. . . . Help must be given, or the poor will suffer." Women on their own sought help from relatives, neighbors, friends, anyone. Sometimes they pleaded their cases to the Confederate government. "In the name of humanity," begged one woman, "discharge my husband he is not able to do your government much good and he might do his children some good . . . my poor children have no home nor no Father." To the extent that the South eventually lost the will to fight in the face of defeat, women played a key role in demanding an end to the war.

The South was in many places so sparsely populated that the conscription of one skilled craftsman could work a hardship on the people of an entire county. Often they begged in unison for the exemption or discharge of the local miller or the neighborhood tanner or wheelwright. Physicians also were in short supply. Most serious, however, was the loss of a blacksmith. As a petition from Alabama explained, "Our Section of County [is] left entirely Destitute of any man that is able to keep in order any kind of Farming Tules."

The blockade of Confederate shipping created shortages of important supplies—salt, sugar, coffee, nails—and speculation and hoarding made the shortages worse. Greedy businessmen cornered the supply of some commodities; prosperous citizens stocked up on food. The *Richmond Enquirer* criticized a planter who purchased so many wagonloads of supplies that his "lawn and paths looked like a wharf covered with a ship's loads." North Carolina's Governor Zebulon Vance worried about "the cry of distress . . . from the poor wives and children of our soldiers. . . . What will become of them?"

Inflation raged out of control, fueled by the Confederate government's heavy borrowing and inadequate taxes, until prices had increased almost 7,000 percent. Inflation particularly imperiled urban dwellers without their own sources of food. As early as 1861 and 1862, newspapers reported that "want and starvation are staring thousands in the face," and troubled officials predicted that "women and children are bound to come to suffering if not starvation." Some families came to the aid of their neighbors, and "free markets," which disbursed goods as charity, sprang up in various cities. But hoarding continued, and a rudimentary relief program organized by the Confederacy failed to meet the need.

As their fortunes declined, people of once-modest means looked around and found abundant evidence that all classes were not sacrificing equally.

INEQUITIES OF THE CONFEDERATE DRAFT

And they noted that the Confederate government enacted policies that favored the upper class. Until the last year of the war, for example, prosperous southerners could avoid military service by hiring substitutes. Prices for substitutes skyrocketed until it cost a man $5,000 or $6,000 to send someone to the front in his place. Well over 50,000 upper-class southerners purchased such substitutes. Mary Boykin Chesnut knew of one young aristocrat who "spent a fortune in substitutes. . . . He is at the end of his row now, for all able-bodied men are ordered to the front. I hear he is going as some general's courier." The rich traded on their social connections to avoid danger.

Anger at such discrimination exploded in October 1862 when the Confederate Congress exempted from military duty anyone who was supervising at least twenty slaves. "Never did a law meet with more universal odium," observed one representative. "Its influence upon the poor is most calamitous." Protests poured in from every corner of the Confederacy, and North Carolina's legislators formally condemned the law. Its defenders argued, however, that the exemption preserved order and aided food production, and the statute remained on the books. The twenty-slave law is indicative of the racial fears many Confederates felt as the war threatened to overturn southern society.

Dissension spread, and alert politicians and newspaper editors warned of class warfare. The bitterness of letters to Confederate officials suggests the depth of the people's anger. "If I and my little children suffer [and] die while there Father is in service," threatened one woman, "I invoke God Almighty that our blood rest upon the South." Another woman swore to the secretary of war that unless help was provided to poverty-stricken wives and mothers "an allwise god . . . will send down his fury . . . [on] those that are in power." War magnified existing social tensions in the Confederacy, and created a few new ones.

Wartime Northern Economy and Society

With the onset of war, a tidal wave of change rolled over the North as well. Factories and citizens' associations geared up to support the war, and the federal government and its executive branch gained new powers. The energies of an industrializing society were harnessed to serve the cause of the Union. Idealism and greed flourished together, and the northern economy proved its awesome productivity. Unlike the experience of the South, northern farms and factories came through the war unharmed.

At first the war was a shock to business. Northern firms lost their southern markets, and many companies had to change their products and find new customers to remain open. Southern debts became uncollectable, jeopardizing not only northern merchants but also many western banks. In farming regions, families struggled with an aggravated shortage of labor caused by army enlistments. A few enterprises never pulled out of the tailspin caused by the war. Cotton mills lacked cotton; construction declined; shoe manufacturers sold few of the cheap shoes that planters had bought for their slaves.

NORTHERN BUSINESS, INDUSTRY, AND AGRICULTURE

But certain entrepreneurs, such as wool producers, benefited from shortages of competing products, and soaring demand for war-related goods swept some businesses to new success. To feed the hungry war machine, the federal government pumped unprecedented sums into the economy. The Treasury issued $3.2 billion in bonds and paper money called "greenbacks," and the War Department spent over $360 million in revenues from new taxes, including the nation's first income tax. Government contracts soon totaled more than $1 billion. Secretary of War Edwin M. Stanton's list of the supplies needed by the Ordnance Department indicates the scope of government demand: "7,892 cannon, 11,787 artillery carriages, 4,022,130 small-arms, . . . 1,022,176,474 cartridges for small-arms, 1,220,555,435 percussion caps, . . . 26,440,054 pounds of gunpowder, . . . and 90,416,295 pounds of lead." Stanton's list covered only weapons; the government also purchased huge quantities of uniforms, boots, food, camp equipment, saddles, ships, and other necessities. War-related spending revived business in many northern states. In 1863 a merchants' magazine examined the effects of the war in Massachusetts: "Seldom, if ever, has the business of Massachusetts been more active or profitable than during the past year. . . . In every department of labor the

Despite initial problems, the task of supplying a vast war machine kept the northern economy humming. This photograph shows businesses on the west side of Hudson Street in New York City in 1865. (© Collection of The New York Historical Society)

government has been, directly or indirectly, the chief employer and paymaster." Government contracts saved Massachusetts shoe manufacturers from ruin.

Nothing illustrated the wartime partnership between business and government better than the work of Jay Cooke, a wealthy New York financier. Cooke threw himself into the marketing of government bonds to finance the war effort. With imagination and energy, he convinced both large investors and ordinary citizens to invest enormous sums, and in the process earning hefty commissions for himself. But the financier's profit served the Union cause, as the interests of capitalism and government merged.

War aided some heavy industries in the North as well, especially iron and steel production. Although new railroad construction slowed, repairs helped the manufacture of rails to increase. Of considerable significance for the future was the railroad industry's adoption of a standard gauge (width) for track, which eliminated the unloading and reloading of boxcars and created a unified transportation system.

The northern economy also grew because of a complementary relationship between agriculture and industry. Mechanization of agriculture had begun before the war. Wartime recruitment and conscription, however, gave western farmers an added incentive to purchase labor-saving machinery. The shift from human labor to machines created new markets for industry and expanded the food supply for the urban industrial work force. The boom in the sale of agricultural tools was tremendous. Cyrus and William McCormick built an industrial empire in Chicago from the sale of their reapers. Between 1862 and 1864 the manufacture of mowers and reapers doubled to 70,000 yearly; by war's end 375,000 reapers were in use, triple the number in 1861. Thus northern farm families whose breadwinners went to war did not suffer as much as their counterparts did in the South. "We have seen," one magazine observed, "a stout matron whose sons are in the army, cutting hay with her team . . . and she cut seven acres with ease in a day, riding leisurely upon her cutter."

Northern industrial and urban workers did not fare as well. After the initial slump, jobs became plentiful, but inflation ate up much of a worker's paycheck. The price of coffee had tripled; rice and sugar had doubled; and clothing, fuel, and rent had all climbed. Between 1860 and 1864 consumer prices

NORTHERN WORKERS' MILITANCY

rose at least 76 percent, while daily wages rose only 42 percent. Workers' families consequently suffered a substantial decline in their standards of living.

As their real wages shrank, industrial workers lost job security. To increase production, some employers replaced workers with labor-saving machines. Other employers urged the government to promote immigration to secure cheap labor. Workers responded by forming unions and sometimes by striking. Skilled craftsmen organized to combat the loss of their jobs and status to machines; women and unskilled workers, who were excluded by the craftsmen, formed their own unions. Indeed, thirteen occupational groups—including tailors, coal miners, and railway engineers—formed national unions during the Civil War, and the number of strikes climbed steadily.

Employers reacted with hostility to this new labor independence. Manufacturers viewed labor activism as a threat to their freedom of action and accordingly formed statewide or craft-based associations to cooperate and pool information. These employers shared blacklists of union members and required new workers to sign "yellow dog" contracts (promises not to join a union). To put down strikes, they hired strikebreakers from among blacks, immigrants, and women, and sometimes used federal troops to break the will of unions.

Labor militance, however, did not prevent employers from making profits, nor from profiteering on government contracts. Unscrupulous businessmen took advantage of the suddenly immense demand for army supplies by selling clothing and blankets made of "shoddy"—wool fibers reclaimed from rags or worn cloth. Shoddy goods often came apart in the rain; most of the shoes purchased in the early months of the war were worthless. Contractors sold inferior guns for double the usual price and passed off tainted meat as good. Corruption was so widespread that it led to a year-long investigation by the House of Representatives. Those who romanticize the Civil War era rarely learn of these historical realities in the daily lives of Americans.

Legitimate enterprises also made healthy profits. The output of woolen mills increased so dramatically that dividends in the industry nearly tripled.

ECONOMIC NATIONALISM AND GOVERNMENT-BUSINESS PARTNERSHIP Some cotton mills made record profits on what they sold, even though they reduced their output. Brokerage houses worked until midnight and earned unheard-of commissions. Railroads carried immense quantities of freight and passengers, increasing their business to the point that railroad stocks skyrocketed in value.

Railroads also were a leading beneficiary of government largesse. With southern representatives absent from Congress, the northern route of the transcontinental railroad quickly prevailed. In 1862 and 1864 Congress chartered two corporations, the Union Pacific Railroad and the Central Pacific Railroad, and assisted them financially in connecting Omaha, Nebraska, with Sacramento, California. For each mile of track laid, the railroads received a loan of from $16,000 to $48,000 in government bonds plus 20 square miles of land along a free 400-foot-wide right of way. Overall, the two corporations gained approximately 20 million acres of land and nearly $60 million in loans.

Other businessmen benefited handsomely from the Morrill Land Grant Act (1862). To promote public education in agriculture, engineering, and military science, Congress granted each state 30,000 acres of federal land for each of its congressional districts. The states could sell the land, as long as they used the income for the purposes Congress had intended. The law eventually fostered sixty-nine colleges and universities, but one of its immediate effects was to enrich a few prominent speculators. At the same time, the Homestead Act of 1862 offered cheap, and sometimes free, land to people who would settle the West and improve their property.

Before the war, there was no adequate national banking, taxation, or currency. Banks operating under state charters issued no fewer than seven thousand different kinds of notes, which were difficult to distinguish from forgeries. During the war, Congress and the Treasury Department established a national banking system empowered to issue national bank notes, and by 1865 most state banks were forced to join the national system by means of a prohibitive tax. This process created sounder currency, but also inflexibility in the money supply and an eastern-oriented financial structure that, later in the century, pushed farmers in need of credit and cash to revolt.

In response to the war, the Republicans created an activist federal government. They converted the sale of war bonds into a crusade, affirming that the country could absorb any level of debt or expense for the cause of union. Indeed, with agricultural legislation, the land grant colleges, higher tariffs, and railroad subsidies, the federal government entered the economy forever. Moreover, Republican economic policies bonded people to the nation as never before. Economic nationalism eventually helped buttress public opinion for the controversial cause of slave emancipation.

The powers of the federal government and the president grew steadily during the crisis. Abraham Lincoln, like Jefferson Davis, found that war required active presidential leadership.

EXPANSION OF PRESIDENTIAL POWER At the beginning of the conflict, Lincoln launched a major shipbuilding program without waiting for Congress to assemble. The lawmakers later approved his decision, and Lincoln continued to act in advance of Congress when he deemed such action necessary. In one striking exercise of executive power, Lincoln suspended the writ of habeas corpus for everyone living between Washington, D.C., and Philadelphia. There was scant legal justification for this act, but the president's motive was practical: to ensure the loyalty of Maryland, which surrounded the capital on three sides. Later in the war, with congressional approval, Lincoln repeatedly suspended habeas corpus and invoked martial law. Between fifteen and twenty thousand U.S. citizens were arrested on suspicion of disloyal acts. Through such measures Lincoln expanded the powers of wartime presidents.

On occasion Lincoln used his wartime authority to bolster his own political fortunes. He and his generals proved adept at furloughing soldiers so they could vote in close elections; those whom Lincoln furloughed, of course, usually voted Republican. He also came to the aid of other officeholders in his party. When the Republican governor of Indiana, who was battling Democrats in his legislature that sought a negotiated end to the war, ran short of funds, Lincoln had the War Department supply $250,000. This procedure lacked constitutional sanction, but it advanced the Union cause.

In thousands of self-governing towns and communities, northern citizens felt a personal connection to representative government. Secession threatened to destroy their system, and northerners rallied to its defense. Secular and church leaders supported the cause, and even ministers who preferred to separate politics and pulpit denounced "the iniquity of causeless rebellion." In the first two years of the war, northern morale remained remarkably high for a cause that today may seem abstract—the Union—but at the time meant the preservation of a social and political order that people cherished.

THE UNION CAUSE

But in the excitement of moneymaking, an eagerness to display one's wealth flourished in the largest cities. *Harper's Monthly* reported that "the suddenly enriched contractors, speculators, and stock-jobbers . . . are spending money with a profusion never before witnessed in our country. . . . The men button their waistcoats with diamonds . . . and the women powder their hair with gold and silver dust." The *New York Herald* summarized that city's atmosphere: "This war has entirely changed the American character. . . . The individual who makes the most money—no matter how—and spends the most—no matter for what—is considered the greatest man."

Yet idealism coexisted with ostentation. Many churches endorsed the Union cause as God's cause. One Methodist newspaper described the war as a contest between "equalizing, humanizing Christianity" and "disunion, war, selfishness, [and] slavery." Abolitionists campaigned to turn the war into a crusade against slavery. Free black communities and churches both black and white responded to the needs of slaves who flocked to the Union lines, sending clothing, ministers, and teachers to aid the freedpeople. Indeed, northern blacks gave wholehearted support to the war, volunteering by the thousands at first and in spite of the initial rejection they received from the Lincoln administration.

Thus northern society embraced strangely contradictory tendencies. Materialism and greed flourished alongside idealism, religious conviction, and self-sacrifice. In decades to come Americans would commemorate and build monuments to soldiers' sacrifice and idealism, not to opportunism, and sometimes not even to the causes for which they fought, which was a way of forgetting the deeper nature of the conflict.

Northern women, like their southern counterparts, took on new roles. Those who stayed home organized over ten thousand soldiers' aid societies, rolled bandages, and raised $3 million to aid injured troops. Women were instrumental in pressing for the first trained ambulance corps in the Union armies, and they formed the backbone of the U.S. Sanitary Commission, a civilian agency officially recognized by the War Department in 1861. The Sanitary Commission provided crucial nutritional and medical aid to soldiers. Although most of its officers were men, the bulk of its volunteers who ran its seven thousand auxiliaries were women. Women organized elaborate "Sanitary Fairs" all across the North to raise money and awareness for soldiers' health and hygiene.

NORTHERN WOMEN ON HOME FRONT AND BATTLEFRONT

Approximately 3,200 women also served as nurses in frontline hospitals, where they pressed for better care of the wounded. Yet women had to fight for a chance to serve at all; the professionalization of medicine since the Revolution had created a medical system dominated by men, and many male physicians did not want women's aid. Even Clara Barton, famous for her persistence in working in the worst hospitals at the front, was ousted from her post in 1863. But with Barton, women such as the stern Dorothea Dix (see pages 271–272), well known for her efforts to reform asylums for the insane, and an Illinois widow, Mary Ann Bickerdyke, who served tirelessly in Sherman's army in the West, established a heroic tradition for Civil War nurses. They also advanced the professionalization of nursing as several schools of nursing were established in northern cities during or after the war.

Women also wrote popular fiction about the war. In sentimental war poetry, short stories, and novels, and in printed war songs that reached thousands of readers, women produced a commercial literature in illustrated weeklies, monthly periodicals, and special "story papers." In many stories women characters seek recognition for their loyalty and service to the Union, while countless others probed the suffering and death of loved ones at the front. And by 1863, women writers found the liberation of slaves an irresistible subject. At its heart, what one historian has called a "feminized war literature," explored the relationship between individual and national needs, between "home" and the "cause."

The poet Walt Whitman left a record of his experiences as a volunteer nurse in Washington, D.C. As

WALT WHITMAN'S WAR

he dressed wounds and tried to comfort suffering and lonely men, Whitman found "the marrow of the tragedy concentrated in those Army Hospitals." But despite "indescribably horrid wounds," he also found inspiration in such suffering and a deepening faith in American democracy. Whitman cel-

■ Walt Whitman, now America's most celebrated wartime poet. His *Drum Taps* series, part of his evolving masterpiece *Leaves of Grass,* left some of the most haunting and moving poetic images of both the death and new life wrought by the war.   (National Portrait Gallery, Smithsonian Institution, Washington, D.C.)

ebrated the "incredible dauntlessness" and sacrifice of the common soldier who fought for the Union. As he had written in the preface to his great work *Leaves of Grass* (1855), "The genius of the United States is not best or most in its executives or legislatures, but always most in the common people." Whitman worked this idealization of the common man into his poetry, which also explored homoerotic themes and rejected the lofty meter and rhyme of European verse to strive for a "genuineness" that would appeal to the masses.

In "The Wound Dresser," Whitman meditated unforgettably on the deaths he witnessed on both sides:

> On, on I go, (open doors of time! open hospital doors!)
> The crush'd head I dress, (poor crazed hand tear not
>   the bandage away,)
> The neck of the cavalry-man with the bullet through
>   and through I examine,
> Hard the breathing rattles, quite glazed already the eye,
>   yet life struggled hard,
> (Come sweet death! be persuaded O beautiful death!
>   In mercy come quickly.)

Whitman mused for millions in the war who suffered the death of a husband, brother, father, or friend. Indeed, the scale of death in this war shocked many Americans into believing that this conflict had to be for purposes larger than themselves.

The Advent of Emancipation

Despite the sense of loyalty to cause that animated soldiers and civilians on both sides, the governments of the United States and the Confederacy lacked clarity about the purpose of the war. Throughout the first several months of the struggle, both Davis and Lincoln studiously avoided references to slavery. Davis realized that emphasis on the issue could increase class conflict in the South. To avoid identifying the Confederacy only with the interests of slaveholders, he articulated a broader, traditional ideology. Davis told southerners that they were fighting for constitutional liberty: northerners had betrayed the founders' legacy, and southerners had seceded to preserve it. As long as Lincoln also avoided making slavery an issue, Davis's line seemed to work.

Lincoln had his own reasons for not mentioning slavery. It was crucial at first not to antagonize the Union's border slave states, whose loyalty was tenuous. Also for many months Lincoln hoped that a pro-Union majority would assert itself in the South. It might be possible, he thought, to coax the South back into the Union and stop the fighting, short of what he later called "the result so fundamental and astounding"—emancipation. Raising the slavery issue would severely undermine both goals. Powerful political considerations also dictated Lincoln's reticence. The Republican Party was a young and unwieldy coalition. Some Republicans burned with moral outrage over slavery; others were frankly racist, dedicated to protecting free whites from the Slave Power and the competition of cheap slave labor. A forthright stand by Lincoln on the subject of slavery could split the party. No northern consensus on what to do about slavery existed early in the war.

The president's hesitancy ran counter to some of his personal feelings. Lincoln was a compassionate man whose humility and moral anguish during the war were evident in his speeches and writings. But as a politician, Lincoln distinguished between his own moral convictions and his official acts. His political positions were studied and complex, calculated for maximum advantage.

LINCOLN AND EMANCIPATION

Many blacks furiously attacked Lincoln during the first year of the war for his refusal to convert the struggle into an "abolition war." When Lincoln countermanded General John C. Frémont's order of liberation for slaves owned by disloyal masters in Missouri in September 1861, the *Anglo-African* declared that the president, by his actions, "hurls back into the hell of slavery thousands . . . rightfully set free." As late as July 1862, Frederick Douglass condemned Lincoln as a "miserable tool of traitors and rebels," and characterized administration policy as reconstruction of "the old union on the old and corrupting basis of compromise, by which slavery shall retain all the power that it ever had." Douglass wanted the old union destroyed and a new one created in the crucible of a war that would destroy slavery and rewrite the Constitution in the name of human equality. To his own amazement, within a year, just such a profound result began to take place.

Lincoln first broached the subject of slavery in a substantive way in March 1862, when he proposed that the states consider emancipation on their own. He asked Congress to promise aid to any state that decided to

■ A group of "contrabands" (liberated slaves), photographed at Cumberland Landing, Virginia, May 14, 1862, at a sensitive point in the war when their legal status was still not fully determined. The faces and generations of the women, men, and children represent the human drama of emancipation.   (Library of Congress)

emancipate, appealing especially to border state representatives. What Lincoln proposed was gradual emancipation, with compensation for slaveholders and colonization of the freed slaves outside the United States. To a delegation of free blacks he explained that "it is better for us both . . . to be separated."

Until well into 1864 Lincoln's administration promoted an impractical scheme to colonize blacks in Central America or the Caribbean. Lincoln saw colonization as one option among others in dealing with the impending freedom of America's 4.2 million slaves. As yet, he was unconvinced that America had any prospect as a truly biracial society, and he desperately feared that white northerners might not support a war for black freedom. Led by Frederick Douglass, black abolitionists vehemently opposed these machinations by the Lincoln administration.

Other politicians had much greater plans for a struggle against slavery. A group of Republicans in Congress, known as the Radicals and led by men such as George Julian, Charles Sumner, and Thaddeus Stevens, dedicated themselves to a war for emancipation. They were instrumental in creating a special House-Senate committee on the conduct of the war, which investigated Union reverses, sought to make the war effort more efficient, and prodded the president to take stronger measures against slavery.

In August 1861, at the Radicals' instigation, Congress passed its first confiscation act. Designed to punish the Confederates, the law confiscated all property used for "insurrectionary purposes." Thus if the South used slaves in a hostile action, those slaves were declared seized and liberated as contraband of war. A second confiscation act (July 1862) went much further: it confiscated the property of anyone who supported the rebellion, even those who merely resided in the South and paid Confederate taxes. Their slaves were declared "forever free of their servitude." These acts stemmed from the logic that in order to crush the southern rebellion, the government had to use extraordinary powers.

CONFISCATION ACTS

Lincoln refused to adopt that view in the summer of 1862. He stood by his proposal of voluntary gradual emancipation by the states and made no effort to enforce the second confiscation act. His stance provoked a public protest from Horace Greeley, editor of the powerful *New York Tribune*. In an open letter to the president entitled "The Prayer of Twenty Millions," Greeley pleaded with Lincoln to "execute the laws" and declared, "On the face of this wide earth, Mr. President, there is not one . . . intelligent champion of the Union cause who does not feel that all attempts to put down the Rebellion

and at the same time uphold its inciting cause are preposterous and futile." Lincoln's reply was an explicit statement of his calculated approach to the question. He disagreed, he said, with all those who would make slavery the paramount issue of the war. "I would save the Union," announced Lincoln. "If I could save the Union without freeing any slave I would do it, and if I could save it by freeing all the slaves I would do it; and if I could save it by freeing some and leaving others alone I would also do that. What I do about slavery, and the colored race, I do because I believe it helps to save the Union." Lincoln closed with a personal disclaimer: "I have here stated my purpose according to my view of official duty; and I intend no modification of my oft-expressed personal wish that all men everywhere could be free."

When he wrote those words, Lincoln had already decided to boldly issue a presidential Emancipation Proclamation. He was waiting, however, for a Union victory so that it would not appear to be an act of desperation. Yet the letter to Greeley was not simply an effort to stall; it was an integral part of Lincoln's approach to the future of slavery, as the text of the Emancipation Proclamation would show. Lincoln was concerned to condition public opinion as best he could for the coming social revolution, and he needed to delicately consider international opinion as well.

On September 22, 1862, shortly after Union success at the Battle of Antietam, Lincoln issued the first part of his two-part proclamation. Invoking his powers as commander-in-chief of the armed forces, he announced that on January 1, 1863, he would emancipate the slaves in the states "in rebellion." Lincoln made plain that he would judge a state to be in rebellion in January if it lacked bona fide representatives in the U.S. Congress. Thus his September proclamation was less a declaration of the right of slaves to be free than a threat to southerners: unless they put down their arms and returned to Congress, they would lose their slaves. "Knowing the value that was set on the slaves by the rebels," said Garrison Frazier, a black Georgia minister, "the President thought that his proclamation would stimulate them to lay down their arms . . . and their not doing so has now made the freedom of the slaves a part of the war." Lincoln had little expectation that southerners would give up their effort, but he was careful to offer them the option, thus trying to put the onus of emancipation on them.

EMANCIPATION PROCLAMATIONS

In the fateful January 1 proclamation, Lincoln excepted (as areas in rebellion) every Confederate county or city that had fallen under Union control. Those areas, he declared, "are, for the present, left precisely as if this proclamation were not issued." Nor did Lincoln liberate slaves in the border slave states that remained in the Union. "The President has purposely made the proclamation inoperative in all places where . . . the slaves [are] accessible," charged the anti-administration *New York World.* "He has proclaimed emancipation only where he has notoriously no power to execute it." Partisanship aside, even Secretary of State Seward said sarcastically, "We show our sympathy with slavery by emancipating slaves where we cannot reach them and holding them in bondage where we can set them free." A British official, Lord Russell, commented on the "very strange nature" of the document, noting that it did not declare "a principle adverse to slavery." Russell may have missed the point.

Lincoln was worried about the constitutionality of his acts. Making the liberation of the slaves "a fit and necessary war measure" raised a variety of legal questions. How long did a war measure remain in force? Did it expire with the suppression of a rebellion? The proclamation did little to clarify the status or citizenship of the freed slaves, although it did open the possibility of military service for blacks. How indeed would this change the character and purpose of the war?

Thus the Emancipation Proclamation was an ambiguous document. But if as a legal document it was wanting, as a moral and political document it had great meaning. Because the proclamation defined the war as a war against slavery, radicals could applaud it, even if the president had not gone as far as Congress. Yet at the same time it protected Lincoln's position with conservatives, leaving him room to retreat if he chose and forcing no immediate changes on the border slave states. It was a delicate balancing act, but one from which there was no real turning back.

Most important, though, thousands of slaves had already reached Union lines in various sections of the South. They had "voted with their feet" for emancipation, as many said, well before the proclamation. And now, every advance of federal forces into slave society was a liberating step. This Lincoln knew in taking his own initially tentative, and then forthright, steps toward emancipation.

Across the North and in Union-occupied sections of the South, blacks and their white allies celebrated the Emancipation Proclamation with unprecedented fervor. Full of praise songs, these celebrations demonstrated that whatever the fine print of the proclamation, black folks knew that they had lived to see a new day. At a large "contraband camp" in Washington, D.C., some six hundred black men, women, and children gathered at the superintendent's headquarters on New Year's Eve and sang through the night. In chorus after chorus of "Go Down, Moses," they announced the magnitude of their painful but beautiful exodus. One newly supplied verse concluded with "Go down, Abraham, away down in Dixie's land, tell Jeff Davis to let my people go!"

The need for men soon convinced the administration to recruit northern and southern blacks for the Union Army. By the spring of 1863, African American troops were answering the call of a dozen or more black recruiters barnstorming the cities and towns of the North. Lincoln came to see black soldiers as "the great available and yet unavailed of force for restoring the Union." African American leaders hoped that military service would secure equal rights for their people. Once the black soldier had fought for the Union, wrote Frederick Douglass, "there is no power on earth which can deny that he has earned the right of citizenship in the United States." If black soldiers turned the tide, asked another man, "would the nation refuse us our rights?"

In June 1864 Lincoln gave his support to a constitutional ban on slavery. On the eve of the Republican national convention, Lincoln called the party's chairman to the White House and instructed him to have the party "put into the platform as the keystone, the amendment of the Constitution abolishing and prohibiting slavery forever." The party promptly called for the Thirteenth Amendment. Republican delegates probably would have adopted such a plank without his urging, but Lincoln demonstrated his commitment by lobbying Congress for quick approval of the measure. The proposed amendment passed in early 1865 and was sent to the states for ratification. The war to save the Union had also become the war to free the slaves.

It has long been debated whether Abraham Lincoln deserved the label (one he never claimed for himself) of

WHO FREED THE SLAVES?

"Great Emancipator." Was Lincoln ultimately a reluctant emancipator, following rather than leading Congress and public opinion? Or did Lincoln give essential presidential leadership to the most transformative and sensitive aspect of the war by going slow on emancipation, but once moving, never backpedaling on black freedom. Once he had realized the total character of the war and decided to prosecute it to the unconditional surrender of the Confederates, Lincoln made the destruction of slavery central to the war's purpose.

Others have argued, however, that the slaves themselves are the central story in the achievement of their own freedom. When they were in proximity to the war zones, or had opportunities as traveling laborers, slaves fled for their freedom by the thousands. Some worked as camp laborers for the Union armies, and eventually more than 180,000 black men served in the Union Army and Navy. Sometimes freedom came as a combination of confusion, fear, and joy in the rural hinterlands of the South. Some found freedom as individuals in 1861, and some not until 1865 as members of trains of refugees trekking great distances to reach contraband camps.

However freedom came to individuals, emancipation was a historical confluence of two essential forces: one, a policy directed by and dependent on the military authority of the president in his effort to win the war; and two, the will and courage necessary for acts of self-emancipation. In his annual message in December 1862, Lincoln asserted that "in giving freedom to the slave, we assure freedom to the free." Likewise, most blacks understood the long-term meaning in those words—in the midst of total war they comprehended their freedom as both given and taken, but also as their fundamental human right.

Before the war was over, the Confederacy, too, addressed the issue of emancipation. Jefferson Davis himself

A CONFEDERATE PLAN OF EMANCIPATION

offered a proposal for black freedom of a kind. Late in the war he was willing to sacrifice slavery to achieve independence. He proposed that the Confederate government purchase forty thousand slaves to work for the army as laborers, with a promise of freedom at the end of their service. Soon Davis upgraded the idea, calling for the recruitment and arming of slaves as soldiers, who likewise would gain their freedom at war's end. The wives and children of these soldiers, he made plain, must also receive freedom from the states. Davis and his advisers envisioned an "intermediate" status for ex-slaves of "serfage or peonage." Thus at the bitter end, a few southerners were willing to sacrifice some of the racial, if not class, destiny for which they had launched their revolution.

Bitter debate over Davis's plan resounded through the Confederacy. When the Confederate Congress approved slave enlistments without the promise of freedom in March 1865, Davis insisted on more. He issued an executive order to guarantee that owners would emancipate slave soldiers and eventually their families.

The war ended before much could come of these desperate policy initiatives on the part of the Confederacy. By contrast, Lincoln's Emancipation Proclamation stimulated a vital infusion of forces into the Union armies. Before the war was over, 134,000 former slaves (and 52,000 free blacks) had fought for freedom and the Union. Their participation was pivotal in northern victory. As both policy and process, emancipation had pro-

found practical and moral implications for the new nation to be born out of the war.

The Soldiers' War

The intricacies of policymaking and social revolutions were far from the minds of most ordinary soldiers. Military service completely altered their lives. Enlistment took young men from their homes and submerged them in large organizations whose military discipline ignored their individuality. Army life meant tedium, physical hardship, and separation from loved ones. Yet the military experience had powerful attractions as well. It molded men on both sides so thoroughly that they came to resemble one another far more than they resembled civilians back home. Many soldiers forged amid war a bond with their fellows and a connection to a noble purpose that they cherished for years afterward.

Union soldiers may have sensed most clearly the massive scale of modern war. Most were young; the average soldier was between eighteen and twenty-one. Many went straight from small towns and farms into large armies supplied by extensive bureaucracies. By late 1861 there were 640,000 volunteers in arms, a stupendous increase over the regular army of 20,000 men.

Soldiers benefited from certain new products, such as canned condensed milk, but blankets, clothing, and

HOSPITALS AND CAMP LIFE

arms were often of poor quality. Hospitals were badly managed at first. Rules of hygiene in large camps were scarcely enforced; latrines were poorly made or carelessly used. One investigation turned up "an area of over three acres, encircling the camp as a broad belt, on which is deposited an almost perfect layer of human excrement." Water supplies were unsafe and typhoid epidemics common. About 57,000 men died from dysentery and diarrhea; in fact, 224,000 Union troops died from disease or accidents, far more than the 140,000 who died as a result of battle. Confederate troops were less well supplied, especially in the latter part of the war, and they had no sanitary commission. Still, an extensive network of hospitals, aided by many white female volunteers and black women slaves, sprang up to aid the sick and wounded.

On both sides troops quickly learned that soldiering was far from glorious. "The dirt of a camp life knocks all its poetry into a cocked hat," wrote a North Carolina volunteer in 1862. One year later he marveled at his earlier innocence. Fighting had taught him "the realities of a

These two Ohio soldiers posed with pieces of hardtack, mess equipment, and their ever-present knapsacks, which doubled as dining tables. Such a photo provided a special expression about life in camp for families back home. (James C. Frasca Collection)

soldier's life. We had no tents after the 6th of August, but slept on the ground, in the woods or open fields. . . . I learned to eat fat bacon raw, and to like it. . . . Without time to wash our clothes or our persons . . . the whole army became lousy more or less with body lice." Union troops "skirmished" against lice by boiling their clothes but, reported one soldier, "I find some on me in spite of all I can do."

Few had seen violent death before, but war soon exposed them to the blasted bodies of their friends and comrades. "Any one who goes over a battlefield after a battle," wrote one Confederate, "never cares to go over another. . . . It is a sad sight to see the dead and if possible more sad to see the wounded—shot in every possible way you can imagine." Many men died gallantly; there were innumerable striking displays of courage. But more often soldiers gave up their lives in mass sacrifice, in tactics that made little sense.

Still, Civil War soldiers developed deep commitments to each other and to their task. As campaigns dragged on, most soldiers who did not desert grew determined to see the struggle through. "We now, like true Soldiers go determined not to yield one inch," wrote a New York corporal. When at last the war was over, "it seemed like breaking up a family to separate," one man observed. Another admitted, "We shook hands all around, and

laughed and seemed to make merry, while our hearts were heavy and our eyes ready to shed tears."

Advances in technology made the Civil War particularly deadly. By far the most important were the rifle and the "minie ball." Bullets fired from a smoothbore musket tumbled and wobbled as they flew through the air and thus were not accurate at distances over 80 yards. Cutting spiraled grooves inside the barrel gave the projectile a spin and much greater accuracy, but rifles remained difficult to load and use until the Frenchman Claude Minie and the American James Burton developed a new kind of bullet. Civil War bullets were sizable lead slugs with a cavity at the bottom that expanded upon firing so that the bullet "took" the rifling and flew accurately. With these bullets, rifles were accurate at 400 yards and useful up to 1,000 yards.

THE RIFLED MUSKET

This meant, of course, that soldiers assaulting a position defended by riflemen were in greater peril than ever before. Even though Civil War rifles were cumbersome to load, the defense gained a significant advantage. While artillery now fired from a safe distance, there was no substitute for the infantry assault or the popular turning movements aimed at an enemy's flank. Thus advancing soldiers had to expose themselves repeatedly to accurate rifle fire. Because medical knowledge was rudimentary, even minor wounds often led to amputation, and to death through infection. Never before in Europe or America had such massive forces pummeled each other with weapons of such destructive power. As losses mounted, many citizens wondered at what Union soldier (and future Supreme Court justice) Oliver Wendell Holmes Jr. called "the butcher's bill."

At the outset of the war, racism in the Union Army was strong. Most white soldiers wanted nothing to do with black people and regarded them as inferior. "I never came out here for to free the black devils," wrote one soldier, and another objected to fighting beside African Americans because "We are a too superior race for that." For many, acceptance of black troops grew only because they could do heavy labor and "stop Bullets as well as white people." A popular song celebrated "Sambo's Right to Be Kilt" as the only justification for black enlistments.

THE BLACK SOLDIER'S FIGHT FOR MANHOOD

But among some a change occurred. While recruiting black troops in Virginia in late 1864, Charles Brewster sometimes denigrated the very men he sought to enlist. But he was delighted at the sight of a black cavalry unit because it made the local "secesh" furious, and he praised black soldiers who "fought nobly" and filled hospitals with "their wounded and mangled bodies." White officers who volunteered to lead black units only to gain promotion found that experience altered their opinions. After just one month with black troops, a white captain informed his wife, "I have a more elevated opinion of their abilities than I ever had before. I know that many of them are vastly the superiors of those . . . who would condemn them all to a life of brutal degradation." One general reported that his "colored regiments" possessed "remarkable aptitude for military training," and another observer said, "They fight like fiends."

Black troops created this change through their own dedication. They had a mission to destroy slavery and demonstrate their equality. "When Rebellion is crushed," wrote a black volunteer from Connecticut, "who will be more proud than I to say, 'I was one of the first of the despised race to leave the free North with a rifle on my shoulder, and give the lie to the old story that the black man will not fight.'" Corporal James Henry Gooding of Massachusetts's black Fifty-fourth Regiment explained that his unit intended "to live down all prejudice against its color, by a determination to do well in any position it is put." After an engagement he was proud that "a regiment of white men gave us three cheers as we were passing them," because "it shows that we did our duty as men should."

Through such experience under fire the blacks and whites of the Fifty-fourth Massachusetts forged deep bonds. Just before the regiment launched its costly as-

■ Company E, 4th U.S. Colored Infantry, photographed at Fort Lincoln, Virginia, in 1864. Nothing so symbolized the new manhood and citizenship among African Americans in the midst of the war as such young black men in blue. (Chicago Historical Society)

sault on Fort Wagner in Charleston harbor, in July 1863, a black soldier called out to abolitionist Colonel Robert Gould Shaw, who would perish that day, "Colonel, I will stay by you till I die." "And he kept his word," noted a survivor of the attack. "He has never been seen since." Indeed, the heroic assault on Fort Wagner was celebrated for demonstrating the valor of black men. This bloody chapter in the history of American racism proved many things, not least of which was that black men had to die in battle to be acknowledged as men.

Such valor emerged despite persistent discrimination. Off-duty black soldiers were sometimes attacked by northern mobs; on duty, they did most of the heavy labor. The Union government, moreover, paid white privates $13 per month plus a clothing allowance of $3.50, whereas black privates earned only $10 per month less $3 for clothing. Outraged by this injustice, several regiments refused to accept any pay whatsoever, and Congress eventually remedied the inequity. In this instance, at least, the majority of legislators agreed with a white private that black troops had "proved their title to manhood on many a bloody field fighting freedom's battles."

1863: The Tide of Battle Turns

The fighting in the spring and summer of 1863 did not settle the war, but it began to suggest the outcome. The campaigns began in a deceptively positive way for Confederates, as Lee's army performed brilliantly in battles in central Virginia.

For once, a large Civil War army was not slow and cumbersome but executed tactics with speed and precision.

BATTLE OF CHANCELLORSVILLE On May 2 and 3, west of Fredericksburg, Virginia, some 130,000 members of the Union Army of the Potomac bore down on fewer than 60,000 Confederates. Boldly, Lee and Stonewall Jackson divided their forces, ordering 30,000 men under Jackson on a day-long march westward to prepare a flank attack.

This classic turning movement was carried out in the face of great numerical disadvantage. Arriving at their position late in the afternoon, Jackson's seasoned "foot cavalry" found unprepared Union troops laughing, smoking, and playing cards. The Union soldiers had no idea they were under attack until frightened deer and rabbits bounded out of the forest, followed by gray-clad troops. The Confederate attack drove the entire right side of the Union Army back in confusion. Eager to press his advantage, Jackson rode forward with a few officers to study the ground. As they returned at twilight, south-

ern troops mistook them for federals and fired, fatally wounding their commander. The next day Union forces left in defeat. Chancellorsville was a remarkable southern victory but costly because of the loss of Stonewall Jackson, who would forever remain a legend in Confederate memory.

July brought crushing defeats for the Confederacy in two critical battles—Vicksburg and Gettysburg—that severely damaged Confederate hopes for independence. Vicksburg was a vital western citadel, the last major fortification on the Mississippi River in southern hands (see Map 15.2). After months of searching through swamps and bayous, General Ulysses S. Grant found an advantageous approach to the city. He laid siege to Vicksburg in May, bottling up the defending army of General John Pemberton. If Vicksburg fell, Union forces would control the river, cutting the Confederacy in two and gaining an open path into its interior. To stave off such a result, Jefferson Davis gave command of all other forces in the area to General Joseph E. Johnston and beseeched him to go to Pemberton's aid. Meanwhile, at a council of war in Richmond, General Robert E. Lee proposed a Confederate invasion of the North. Although such an offensive would not relieve Vicksburg directly, it could stun and dismay the North and, if successful, possibly even lead to peace. By invading the North a second time, Lee hoped to take the war out of war-weary Virginia, garner civilian support in Maryland, win a major victory on northern soil, threaten major cities, and thereby force a Union capitulation on his terms.

SIEGE OF VICKSBURG

As Lee's emboldened army advanced through western Maryland and into Pennsylvania, Confederate prospects to the south along the Mississippi darkened. Davis repeatedly wired General Johnston, urging him to concentrate his forces and attack Grant's army. Johnston, however, did little, telegraphing back, "I consider saving Vicksburg hopeless." Grant's men, meanwhile, were supplying themselves from the abundant crops of the Mississippi River valley and could continue their siege indefinitely. Their rich meat-and-vegetable diet became so tiresome, in fact, that one day, as Grant rode by, a private looked up and muttered, "Hardtack," referring to the dry biscuits that were the usual staple of soldiers' diets. Soon a line of soldiers was shouting "Hardtack! Hardtack!" demanding respite from turkey and sweet potatoes.

In such circumstances the fall of Vicksburg was inevitable, and on July 4, 1863, its commander surrendered. The same day a battle that had been raging for three days concluded at Gettysburg, Pennsylvania (see Map 15.3).

BATTLE OF GETTYSBURG

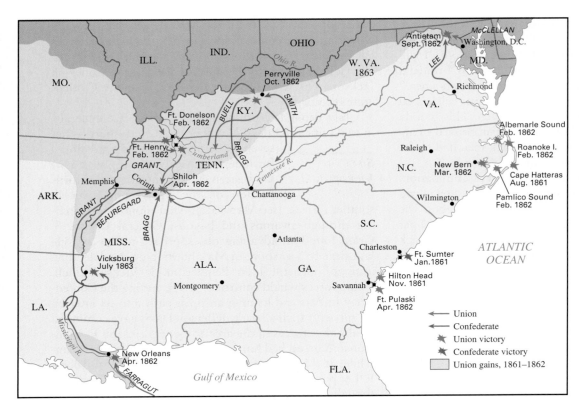

Map 15.2   War in the West, 1861–1863

Here is an overview of the Union's successful campaigns in the West and its seizure of key points on the Mississippi River, as well as along the Atlantic coast in 1862 and 1863. These actions were decisive in paving the way for ultimate northern victory.

On July 1 Confederate forces hunting for a supply of shoes had collided with part of the Union Army. Heavy fighting on the second day over two steep hills left federal forces in possession of high ground along Cemetery Ridge, running more than a mile south of the town. There they enjoyed the protection of a stone wall and a clear view of their foe across almost a mile of open field.

Undaunted, Lee believed his reinforced troops could break the Union line, and on July 3 he ordered a direct assault. Full of foreboding, General James Longstreet warned Lee that "no 15,000 men ever arrayed for battle can take that position." But Lee stuck to his plan. Virginians under General George E. Pickett and North Carolinians under General James Pettigrew methodically marched up the slope in a doomed assault known as Pickett's Charge. For a moment a few hundred Confederates breached the enemy's line, but most fell in heavy slaughter. On July 4 Lee had to withdraw, having suffered almost 4,000 dead and about 24,000 missing and wounded. The Confederate general reported to President Davis that "I am alone to blame" and offered to resign. Davis replied that to find a more capable commander was "an impossibility." The Confederacy had reached what many consider its "high water mark" on that ridge at Gettysburg.

Southern troops displayed unforgettable courage and dedication at Gettysburg, and the Union Army, which suffered 23,000 casualties (nearly one-quarter of the force), under General George G. Meade exhibited the same bravery in stopping the Confederate invasion. But the results there and at Vicksburg were disastrous for the South. The Confederacy was split in two; west of the Mississippi General E. Kirby Smith had to operate on his own, virtually independent of Richmond. Moreover, the heartland of Louisiana, Tennessee, and Mississippi lay exposed to invasion. Far to the north, Lee's defeat spelled the end of major southern offensive actions. Too weak to prevail in attack, the Confederacy henceforth would have to conserve its limited resources and rely on a prolonged defense. By refusing to be beaten, and wearing down northern morale, the South might yet win, but its prospects were darker than ever before.

Disunity, South, North, and West

Both northern and southern governments waged the final two years of the war in the face of increasing opposition at home. Dissatisfactions that had surfaced earlier grew more intense and sometimes vi-

Map 15.3   Battle of Gettysburg

In the war's greatest battle, fought around a small market town in southern Pennsylvania, Lee's invasion of the North was repulsed. Union forces had the advantage of high ground, shorter lines, and superior numbers. The casualties for the two armies—dead, wounded, and missing—exceeded 50,000 men.

olent. The gigantic costs of a civil war that neither side seemed able to win fed the unrest. But protest also arose from fundamental stresses in the social structures of North and South.

The Confederacy's problems were more deeply rooted than the North's. Vastly disadvantaged in industrial capacity, natural resources, and labor, southerners felt the cost of the war more directly and more painfully than northerners. But even more fundamental were the Confederacy's internal problems; the southern class system threatened the Confederate cause.

DISINTEGRATION OF CONFEDERATE UNITY

One ominous development was the planters' increasing opposition to their own government. Not only did the Richmond government impose new taxes but Con-

federate military authorities also impressed slaves to build fortifications. And when Union forces advanced on plantation areas, Confederate commanders burned stores of cotton that lay in the enemy's path. Such interference with plantation routines and financial interests was not what planters had expected of their government, and they complained bitterly.

Nor were the centralizing policies of the Davis administration popular. The increasing size and power of the Richmond government startled and alarmed planters who had condemned federal usurpations. In fact, the Confederate constitution had granted substantial powers to the central government, especially in time of war. But many planters assumed with R. B. Rhett, editor of the *Charleston Mercury,* that the Confederate constitution "leaves the States untouched in their Sovereignty, and commits to the Confederate Government only a few simple objects, and a few simple powers to enforce them." Governor Joseph E. Brown of Georgia took a similar view of the importance of the states. During the brief interval between Georgia's secession from the Union and its admission to the Confederacy, Brown sent an ambassador to Europe to seek recognition for the sovereign republic of Georgia from Queen Victoria, Napoleon III, and the king of Belgium.

Years of opposition to the federal government within the Union had frozen southerners in a defensive posture. Now they erected the barrier of states' rights as a defense against change, hiding behind it while their capacity for creative statesmanship atrophied. Planters sought, above all, a guarantee that their plantations and their lives would remain untouched. As secession revolutionized their world, and hard war took so many lives, some never could fully commit to the cause.

Confused and embittered planters struck out at Jefferson Davis. Conscription, thundered Governor Brown, was "subversive of [Georgia's] sovereignty, and at war with all the principles for the support of which Georgia entered into this revolution." Searching for ways to frustrate the law, Brown bickered over draft exemptions and ordered local enrollment officials not to cooperate with the Confederacy. The *Charleston Mercury* told readers that "conscription . . . is . . . the very embodiment of Lincolnism, which our gallant armies are today fighting." In a gesture of stubborn selfishness, Robert Toombs of Georgia, a former U.S. senator, refused to switch from cotton to food crops, defying the wishes of the government, the newspapers, and his neighbors' petitions. His action bespoke the inflexibility of the southern elite at a crucial point in the Confederacy's struggle to survive.

The southern courts ultimately upheld Davis's power to conscript. Despite his cold formality and inability to

■ The impoverishment of nonslaveholding white families was a critical problem for the Confederacy. The sale of this sheet music was intended not only to boost morale but also to raise money that could be used to aid the hungry and needy. This effort and larger government initiatives, however, failed to solve the problem. (Chicago Historical Society)

disarm critics, Davis possessed two important virtues: iron determination and total dedication to independence. These qualities kept the Confederacy afloat. But his actions earned him the hatred of influential and elite citizens.

Meanwhile, for ordinary southerners, the dire predictions of hunger and suffering were becoming a reality. Food riots occurred in the spring of 1863 in Atlanta, Macon, Columbus, and Augusta, Georgia, and in Salisbury and High Point, North Carolina. On April 2 a crowd assembled in Richmond to demand relief. A passerby, noticing the excitement, asked a young girl, "Is there some celebration?" "We celebrate our right to live," replied the girl. "We are starving. As soon as enough of us get together we are going to the bakeries and each of us will take a loaf of bread." Soon they did just that, sparking a riot that Davis ordered quelled at gunpoint.

FOOD RIOTS IN SOUTHERN CITIES

Throughout the rural South, ordinary people resisted more quietly—by refusing to cooperate with conscription, tax collection, and impressments of food. "In all the States impressments are evaded by every means which ingenuity can suggest, and in some openly resisted," wrote a high-ranking commissary officer. Farmers who did provide food for the army refused to accept payment in certificates of credit or government bonds, as required by law. Conscription officers increasingly found no one to draft. "The disposition to avoid military service is general," observed one of Georgia's senators in 1864. In some areas tax agents were killed in the line of duty.

Jefferson Davis was ill equipped to deal with such discontent. Austere and private by nature, he failed to communicate with the masses. Often he buried himself in military affairs or administrative details. His class perspective also distanced him from the sufferings of the common people. While his social circle in Richmond dined on duck and oysters, ordinary southerners recovered salt from the drippings on their smokehouse floors and went hungry. Davis failed to reach out to the plain folk and thus lost their support.

Such discontent was certain to affect the Confederate armies. "What man is there that would stay in the army and no that his family is sufring at home?" an angry citizen wrote anonymously to the secretary of war. Worried about their loved ones and resentful of what they saw as a rich man's war, large numbers of men did indeed leave the armies. Their friends and neighbors gave them support. Mary Chesnut observed a man being dragged back to the army as his wife looked on. "Desert agin, Jake!" she cried openly. "You desert agin, quick as you kin. Come back to your wife and children."

DESERTIONS FROM THE CONFEDERATE ARMY

Desertion did not become a serious problem for the Confederacy until mid-1862, and stiffer policing solved the problem that year. But from 1863 on, the number of men on duty fell rapidly. By mid-1863, John A. Campbell, the South's assistant secretary of war, wondered whether "so general a habit" as desertion could be considered a crime. Campbell estimated that 40,000 to 50,000 troops were absent without leave and that 100,000 were evading duty in some way. Furloughs, amnesty proclamations, and appeals to return had little effect; by November 1863 Secretary of War James Seddon admitted that one-third of the army could not be accounted for.

The defeats at Gettysburg and Vicksburg dealt a heavy blow to Confederate morale. When the news reached Josiah Gorgas, the genius of Confederate ordnance operations, he confided to his diary, "Today absolute ruin seems our portion. The Confederacy totters to its destruction." In desperation President Davis and several state governors resorted to threats and racial scare tactics to drive southern whites to further sacrifice. Defeat, Davis warned, would mean "extermination of yourselves, your wives, and children." Governor Charles Clark of Mississippi predicted "elevation of the black race to a position of equality—aye, of superiority, that will make them your masters and rulers."

From this point on, the internal disintegration of the Confederacy quickened. A few newspapers began to call openly for peace. "We are for peace," admitted the *Raleigh* (North Carolina) *Daily Progress*, "because there has been enough of blood and carnage, enough of widows and orphans." Similar proposals were made in several state legislatures, though they were presented as plans for independence on honorable terms. Confederate leaders began to realize that they were losing the support of the common people. Governor Zebulon Vance of North Carolina wrote privately that victory would require more "blood and misery . . . and our people will not pay this price I am satisfied for their independence."

In North Carolina a peace movement grew under the leadership of William W. Holden, a popular Democratic politician and editor. Over one hundred public meetings took place in the summer of 1863 in support of peace negotiations, and many seasoned political observers believed that Holden had the majority of the people behind him. In Georgia early in 1864, Governor Brown and Alexander H. Stephens, vice president of the Confederacy, led a similar effort. Ultimately, however, these movements came to naught. The lack of a two-party system threw into question the legitimacy of any criticism of the government; even Holden and Brown could not entirely escape the taint of dishonor and disloyalty.

ANTIWAR SENTIMENT, SOUTH AND NORTH

The results of the 1863 congressional elections strengthened dissent in the Confederacy. Everywhere secessionists and supporters of the administration lost seats to men not identified with the government. In the last years of the war, Davis's support in the Confederate Congress dwindled. Only a few editors and a core of courageous, determined soldiers, especially in Lee's Army of Northern Virginia, kept the Confederacy alive in spite of disintegrating popular support.

By 1864 much of the opposition to the war had moved entirely outside the political sphere. Southerners were simply giving up the struggle and withdrawing their cooperation from the government. Deserters dominated whole towns and counties. Active dissent was particu-

larly common in upland and mountain regions. "The condition of things in the mountain districts of North Carolina, South Carolina, Georgia, and Alabama," admitted Assistant Secretary of War Campbell, "menaces the existence of the Confederacy as fatally as either of the armies of the United States." The government was losing the support of its citizens.

In the North, opposition to the war was similar but less severe. Alarm intensified over the growing centralization of government, and by 1863 war-weariness was widespread. Resentment of the draft sparked protest, especially among poor citizens, and the Union Army struggled with a desertion rate as high as the Confederates'. But the Union was so much richer than the South in human resources that none of these problems ever threatened the effectiveness of the government. Fresh recruits were always available, especially after black enlistments in 1863.

Also, Lincoln possessed a talent that Davis lacked: he knew how to stay in touch with the ordinary citizen. Through letters to newspapers and to soldiers' families, he reached the common people and demonstrated that he had not forgotten them. The daily carnage, the tortuous political problems, and the ceaseless criticism weighed heavily on him. But this president—a self-educated man of humble origins—was able to communicate his suffering. His moving words helped to contain northern discontent, though they could not remove it.

Much of the wartime protest in the North was political in origin. The Democratic Party fought to regain power by blaming Lincoln for the war's death toll, the expansion of federal powers, inflation and the high tariff, and the emancipation of blacks. Appealing to tradition, its leaders called for an end to the war and reunion on the basis of "the Constitution as it is and the Union as it was." The Democrats denounced conscription and martial law and defended states' rights. They charged repeatedly that Republican policies were designed to flood the North with blacks, depriving white males of their status, their jobs, and their women. In the 1862 congressional elections, the Democrats made a strong comeback, and peace Democrats—who would go much further than others in their party to end the war—had influence in New York State and majorities in the legislatures of Illinois and Indiana.

PEACE DEMOCRATS

Led by outspoken men like Representative Clement L. Vallandigham of Ohio, the peace Democrats made themselves highly visible. Vallandigham criticized Lincoln as a "dictator" who had suspended the writ of habeas corpus without congressional authority and had arrested thousands of innocent citizens. He condemned both conscription and emancipation and urged voters to use their power at the polls to depose "King Abraham." Vallandigham stayed carefully within legal bounds, but his attacks seemed so damaging to the war effort that military authorities arrested him for treason. Lincoln wisely decided against punishment—and martyr's status—for the Ohioan and exiled him to the Confederacy. (Eventually Vallandigham returned to the North through Canada.)

Lincoln believed that antiwar Democrats were linked to secret organizations that harbored traitorous ideas. These societies, he feared, encouraged draft resistance, discouraged enlistment, sabotaged communications, and plotted to aid the Confederacy. Likening such groups to a poisonous snake, Republicans sometimes branded them—and by extension the peace Democrats—as "Copperheads." Although some Confederate agents were active in the North and Canada, they never genuinely threatened the Union war effort.

More violent opposition to the government arose from ordinary citizens facing the draft, which became

New York City Draft Riots

law in 1863. While some soldiers risked their lives willingly out of a desire to preserve the Union or extend freedom, many others openly sought to avoid service. Under the law, a draftee could stay at home by providing a substitute or paying a $300 commutation fee. Many wealthy men chose these options, and in response to popular demand, clubs, cities, and states provided the money for others to escape conscription. In all, 118,000 substitutes were provided and 87,000 commutations paid before Congress ended the commutation system in 1864.

The urban poor and immigrants in strongly Democratic areas were especially hostile to conscription. Federal enrolling officers made up the lists of eligibles, a procedure open to personal favoritism and prejudice. Many men, including some of modest means, managed to avoid the army by hiring a substitute or paying commutation, but the poor viewed the system as discriminatory, and many immigrants suspected (wrongly, on the whole) that they were called in disproportionate numbers. (Approximately 200,000 men born in Germany and 150,000 born in Ireland served in the Union Army.)

As a result, there were scores of disturbances. Enrolling officers received rough treatment in many parts of the North, and riots occurred in New Jersey, Ohio, Indiana, Pennsylvania, Illinois, and Wisconsin. By far the most serious outbreak of violence occurred in New York City in July 1863. The war was unpopular in that Democratic stronghold, and racial, ethnic, and class tensions

■ Mobs in the New York City draft riots directed much of their anger at African Americans. Rioters burned an orphanage for black children and killed scores of blacks. This wood engraving, which appeared in the *Illustrated London News* on August 8, 1863, depicts a lynching in Clarkson Street.   (Chicago Historical Society)

ran high. Shippers had recently broken a longshoremen's strike by hiring black strikebreakers to work under police protection. Working-class New Yorkers feared an inflow of black labor from the South and regarded blacks as the cause of the war. Poor Irish workers resented being forced to serve in the place of others who could afford to avoid the draft.

Military police officers came under attack first, and then mobs crying "Down with the rich" looted wealthy homes and stores. But blacks became the special target. Those who happened to be in the rioters' path were beaten; soon the mob rampaged through African American neighborhoods, destroying an orphan asylum. At least seventy-four people died in the violence, which raged out of control for three days. Only the dispatch of army units directly from Gettysburg ended this tragic episode of racism and class resentment.

East and West, and over race, land, and culture, America was a deeply divided country. A civil war of

War Against Indians in the Far West

another kind raged on the Great Plains and in the Southwest. By 1864 U.S. troops under the command of Colonel John Chivington waged full-scale war against the Sioux, Arapaho, and Cheyennes in order to eradicate Indian title to all of eastern Colorado. Indian chiefs sought peace, but American commanders had orders to "burn villages and kill Cheyennes whenever and wherever found." A Cheyenne chief, Lean Bear, was shot from his horse as he rode toward U.S. troops, holding in his hand papers given him by President Lincoln during a visit to Washington, D.C. Another chief, Black Kettle, was told by the U.S. command that by moving his people to Sand Creek, Colorado, they would find a safe haven. But on November 29, 1864, 700 cavalrymen, many drunk, attacked the Cheyenne village. With most of the men absent hunting, the slaughter included 105 Cheyenne women and children and 28 men. American soldiers scalped and mutilated their victims, carrying women's body parts on their saddles or hats back to Denver. The Sand Creek Massacre, and the retaliation against white ranches and stagecoaches by Indians in 1865, would live in western historical memory forever.

In New Mexico and Arizona Territories an authoritarian and brutal commander, General James Carleton, waged war on the Apaches and the Navajos. Both tribes had engaged for generations in raiding the Pueblo Indians and Hispanic peoples of the region to maintain their security and economy. During the Civil War years, Anglo-American farms also became Indian targets. In 1863, the New Mexico Volunteers, commanded in the field by former mountain man Kit Carson, defeated the Mescalero Apaches and forced them onto a reservation at Bosque Redondo in the Pecos River valley.

But the Navajos, who lived in a vast region of canyons and high deserts, resisted. In a "scorched earth" campaign, Carson destroyed the Navajos' livestock, orchards, and crops. On the run, starving and demoralized, the Navajos began to surrender for food in January 1864. Three-quarters of the twelve thousand Navajos were rounded up and forced to march 400 miles (the "Long Walk") to the Bosque Redondo Reservation, suffering malnutrition and death along the way. When General William T. Sherman visited the reservation in 1868 he found the Navajos "sunk into a condition of absolute poverty and despair." Permitted to return to a fraction of their homelands later that year, the Navajos carried with them searing memories of the federal government's ruthless policies of both removal and eradication of Indian peoples.

Back east, war-weariness reached a peak in the summer of 1864, when the Democratic Party nominated the popular General George B. McClellan for president and inserted a peace plank into its platform. The plank, written by Vallandigham, called for an armistice, and spoke vaguely about preserving the Union. The Democrats made racist appeals to white insecurity, calling

ELECTION
OF 1864

Lincoln "Abe the nigger-lover" and "Abe the widow-maker." Lincoln concluded that it was "exceedingly probable that this Administration will not be reelected." No incumbent president had been reelected since 1832, and no nation had ever held a general election in the midst of all-out civil war. Some radical Republicans worked to dump Lincoln from their ticket in favor of either Salmon P. Chase or John C. Frémont, although little came of either effort. Even a relatively unified Republican Party, declaring itself for "unconditional surrender" of the Confederacy and a constitutional amendment abolishing slavery, faced the horrible casualty lists and battlefield stalemate of the summer of 1864.

The fortunes of war soon changed the electoral situation. With the fall of Atlanta and Union victories in the Shenandoah valley by early September, Lincoln's prospects rose. Decisive in the election was that eighteen states allowed troops to vote at the front, and Lincoln won an extraordinary 78 percent of the soldier vote. In taking 55 percent of the total popular vote, Lincoln's reelection—a referendum on the war and emancipation—had a devastating impact on southern morale. Without such a political outcome in 1864, a Union military victory, and a redefined nation, may never have been possible.

1864–1865: The Final Test of Wills

During the final year of the war, the Confederates could still have won their version of victory if military stalemate and northern antiwar sentiment had forced a negotiated settlement to end the war. But events and northern determination prevailed as Americans endured the bloodiest nightmare in their history.

The North's long-term diplomatic strategy succeeded in 1864. From the outset, the North had pursued one paramount goal: to prevent recognition of the Confederacy by European nations. Foreign recognition would belie Lincoln's claim that the United States was fighting an illegal rebellion and would open the way to the financial and military aid that could ensure Confederate independence. Both England and France stood to benefit from a divided and weakened America. Thus to achieve their goal, Lincoln and Secretary of State Seward needed to avoid both serious military defeats and controversies with the European powers.

NORTHERN
DIPLOMATIC
STRATEGY

Aware that the textile industry employed one-fifth of the British population directly or indirectly, southerners banked on British recognition of the Confederacy. But

The Civil War in Britain

So engaged was the British public with America's disunion and war that an unemployed weaver, John Ward, frequently trekked many miles from Britain's Low Moor to Clitheroe just to read newspapers about the strife.

Because of the direct reliance of the British textile industry on southern cotton (cut off by the war), as well as the many ideological and familial ties between the two nations, the American war was decisive in Britain's economy and domestic politics. The British aristocracy and most cotton mill owners were solidly pro-Confederate and proslavery, while a combination of clergymen, shopkeepers, artisans, and radical politicians worked for the causes of Union and emancipation. Most British workers saw their futures at stake in a war for slave emancipation. "Freedom" to the huge British working class (who could not vote) meant basic political and civil rights, as well as the bread and butter of secure jobs in an industrializing economy, now damaged by a "cotton famine" that threw millhands out of work.

English aristocrats saw Americans as untutored, wayward cousins and took satisfaction in America's troubles. Conservatives believed in the superiority of the British system of government and looked askance at America's leveling tendencies. And some aristocratic British Liberals also saw Americans through their class bias and sympathized with the Confederacy's demand for "order" and independence. English racism also intensified in these years, exemplified by the popularity of minstrelsy and the employment of science in the service of racial theory.

The intensity of the British propaganda war over the American conflict is evident in the methods of their debate: public meetings organized by both sides were huge affairs, with cheering and jeering, competing banners, carts and floats, orators and resolutions. In a press war the British argued over when rebellion is justified, whether secession was right or legal, whether slavery was at the heart of the conflict, and especially over the democratic image of America itself. This bitter debate over America's trial became a test over reform in Britain: those eager for a broadened franchise and increased democracy were pro-Union, and those who preferred to preserve Britain's class-ridden political system favored the Confederacy.

The nature of the internal British debate was no better symbolized than by the dozens of African Americans who served as pro-Union agents. The most popular was William Andrew Jackson, Confederate president Jefferson Davis's former coachman, who had escaped from Richmond in September 1862. Jackson's articulate presence at public meetings countered pro-Confederate arguments that the war was not about slavery.

In the end the British government did not recognize the Confederacy, and by 1864 the English cotton lords had found new sources of the crop in Egypt and India. But in this link between America and its English roots at its time of greatest travail, we can see that the Civil War was a transformation of international significance.

Some southern leaders pronounced that cotton was "king" and would bring Britain to their cause. This British cartoon shows King Cotton brought down in chains by the American eagle, anticipating the cotton famine to follow and the intense debate in Great Britain over the nature and meaning of the American Civil War. (Granger Collection)

at the beginning of the war, British mills had a 50 percent surplus of cotton on hand, and they later found new sources of supply in India, Egypt, and Brazil. And throughout the war, some southern cotton continued to reach Europe, despite the Confederacy's embargo on cotton production, an ill-fated policy aimed at securing British support. Refusing to be stampeded into recognition of the Confederacy, the British government kept its eye on the battlefield. France, though sympathetic to the South, was unwilling to act independently of Britain. Confederate agents managed to purchase valuable arms and supplies in Europe and obtained loans from European financiers, but they never achieved a diplomatic breakthrough.

■ Both General Grant (*left*) and General Lee (*right*) were West Point graduates and had served in the U.S. Army during the War with Mexico. Their bloody battles against each other in 1864 stirred northern revulsion to the war even as they brought its end in sight. (National Archives)

More than once the Union strategy nearly broke down. An acute crisis occurred in 1861 when the over-zealous commander of an American frigate stopped the British steamer *Trent* and removed two Confederate ambassadors, James Mason and John Slidell, sailing to Britain. When they were imprisoned in Boston, northerners cheered, but the British interpreted the capture as a violation of freedom of the seas and demanded the prisoners' release. Lincoln and Seward waited until northern public opinion cooled and then released the two southerners. Soon forgotten, the incident nevertheless strained U.S.-British relations.

Then the sale to the Confederacy of warships constructed in England sparked vigorous protest from U.S. ambassador Charles Francis Adams. A few English-built ships, notably the *Alabama,* reached open water to serve the South. Over a period of twenty-two months, without entering a southern port (because of the Union blockade), the *Alabama* destroyed or captured more than sixty U.S. ships, leaving a bitter legal legacy to be settled in the postwar period.

On the battlefield, the northern victory was far from won in 1864. General Nathaniel Banks's Red River

BATTLEFIELD STALEMATE AND A UNION STRATEGY FOR VICTORY

campaign, designed to capture more of Louisiana and Texas, quickly fell apart, and the capture of Mobile Bay in August did not cause the fall of Mobile. Union general William Tecumseh Sherman commented that the North had to "keep the war South until they are not only ruined, exhausted, but humbled in pride and spirit." Sherman soon brought total war to the southern heartland. On the eastern front during the winter of 1863–1864, the two armies in Virginia settled into a stalemate awaiting yet another spring offensive by the North.

Military authorities throughout history have agreed that deep invasion is very risky: the farther an army penetrates enemy territory, the more vulnerable are its own communications and supply lines. Moreover, observed the Prussian expert Karl von Clausewitz, if the invader encountered a "truly national" resistance, his troops would be "everywhere exposed to attacks by an insurgent population." The South's vast size and a determined resistance could yet make a northern victory improbable.

General Grant, by now in command of all the federal armies, decided to test these conditions—and southern

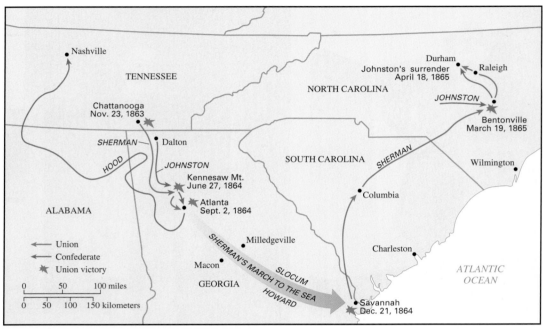

Map 15.4   Sherman's March to the Sea

The West proved a decisive theater at the end of the war. From Chattanooga, Union forces drove into Georgia, capturing Atlanta. Following the fall of Atlanta, General Sherman embarked on his march of destruction through Georgia to the coast and then northward through the Carolinas.

will—with a strategic innovation of his own: raids on a massive scale. Less tied to tradition and by-the-book maneuver than most other Union commanders, Grant proposed to use whole armies to destroy Confederate railroads, thus ruining the enemy's transportation and damaging the South's economy. Abandoning their lines of support, Union troops would live off the land while laying waste all resources useful to the military and to the civilian population of the Confederacy. After General George H. Thomas's troops won the Battle of Chattanooga in November 1863, the heartland of Georgia lay open. Grant entrusted General Sherman with 100,000 men for an invasion deep into the South, toward the rail center of Atlanta.

Jefferson Davis countered by positioning the army of General Joseph E. Johnston in Sherman's path. Davis's

FALL OF ATLANTA

entire political strategy for 1864 was based on demonstrating Confederate military strength and successfully defending Atlanta. Davis hoped that southern resolve would lead to the political defeat of Lincoln and the election of a president who would sue for peace. When General Johnston slowly but steadily fell back toward Atlanta, Davis grew anxious and sought assurances that Atlanta would be held. From a purely military point of view, Johnston maneuvered skillfully. But when Johnston fell silent and continued to retreat, Davis replaced him with the one-legged General John Hood, who knew his job was to fight. "Our all depends on that army

at Atlanta," wrote Mary Chesnut. "If that fails us, the game is up."

For southern morale, the game was up. Hood attacked but was beaten, and Sherman's army occupied Atlanta on September 2, 1864. The victory buoyed northern spirits and ensured Lincoln's reelection. A government clerk in Richmond wrote, "Our fondly-cherished visions of peace have vanished like a mirage of the desert." Davis exhorted southerners to fight on and win new victories before the federal elections, but he had to admit that "two-thirds of our men are absent . . . most of them absent without leave." In a desperate diversion, Hood's army marched north to cut Sherman's supply lines and force him to withdraw, but Sherman began to march sixty thousand of his men straight to the sea, planning to live off the land and destroying Confederate resources as he went (see Map 15.4).

Sherman's army was an unusually formidable force, composed almost entirely of battle-tested veterans and

SHERMAN'S MARCH TO THE SEA

officers who had risen through the ranks from the midwestern states. Before the march began, army doctors weeded out any men who were weak or sick. Tanned, bearded, tough, and unkempt, the remaining veterans were determined, as one put it, "to Conquer this Rebelien or Die." They believed "the South are to blame for this war" and were ready to make the South pay. Although many harbored racist attitudes, most had come to support emancipation because, as one said, "Slavery stands in the way of putting down the rebellion." Confederate General Johnston later commented, "There has been no such army since the days of Julius Caesar."

As Sherman's men moved across Georgia, they cut a path 50 to 60 miles wide and more than 200 miles long. The totality of the destruction they caused was awesome. A Georgia woman described the "Burnt Country" this way: "The fields were trampled down and the road was lined with carcasses of horses, hogs, and cattle that the invaders, unable either to consume or to carry with them, had wantonly shot down to starve our people. . . . The stench in some places was unbearable." Such devastation diminished the South's material resources and sapped its will to resist.

After reaching Savannah in December, Sherman marched his armies north into the Carolinas. To his soldiers, South Carolina was "the root of secession." They burned and destroyed as they moved through, encountering little resistance. The opposing army of General Johnston was small, but Sherman's men should have been prime targets for guerrilla raids and harassing attacks by local defense units. The absence of both led South Carolina's James Chesnut Jr. (a politician and the husband of Mary Chesnut) to write that his state "was shamefully and unnecessarily lost. . . . We had time, opportunity and means to destroy him. But there was wholly wanting the energy and ability required by the occasion." Southerners had lost the will to continue the struggle.

Sherman's march drew additional human resources to the Union cause. In Georgia alone as many as nineteen thousand slaves gladly took the opportunity to escape bondage and join the Union troops as they passed through the countryside. Others remained on the plantations to await the end of the war, either from an ingrained wariness of whites or negative experiences with federal soldiers. The destruction of food harmed slaves as well as white rebels, and many blacks lost livestock, clothing, crops, and other valuables to their liberators. In fact, the brutality of Sherman's troops shocked some liberated slaves. "I've seen them cut the hams off of a live pig or ox and go off leavin' the animal groanin'," recalled one man. "The master had 'em kilt then, but it was awful."

It was awful, too, in Virginia, where the path to victory proved protracted and ghastly. Throughout the spring and summer of 1864, intent on capturing Richmond, Grant hurled his troops at Lee's army in Virginia

VIRGINIA'S BLOODY SOIL and suffered appalling losses: almost 18,000 casualties in the Battle of the Wilderness, where skeletons poked out of the shallow graves dug one year be-

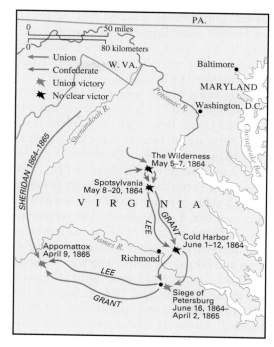

Map 15.5 The War in Virginia, 1864–1865
At great cost, Grant hammered away at Lee's army until the weakened southern forces finally surrendered at Appomattox Court House.

fore; more than 8,000 at Spotsylvania; and 12,000 in the space of a few hours at Cold Harbor (see Map 15.5).

Before the assault at Cold Harbor (which Grant later admitted was a grave mistake), Union troops pinned scraps of paper bearing their names and addresses to their backs, certain they would be mowed down as they rushed Lee's trenches. In four weeks in May and June, Grant lost as many men as were enrolled in Lee's entire army. From early May until July, when Union forces had marched and fought all the way from forests west of Fredericksburg to Petersburg, south of Richmond, which they besieged, the two armies engaged each other nearly every day. The war had reached a horrible modern scale. Wagon trains carrying thousands of Union wounded crawled back toward Washington. "It was as if war," wrote historian Bruce Catton, "the great clumsy machine for maiming people, had at last been perfected. Instead of turning out its gist spasmodically, with long waits between each delivery, it was at last able to produce every day, without any gaps at all."

Undaunted, Grant kept up the pressure, saying, "I propose to fight it out along this line if it takes all summer." Though costly, and testing northern morale to its limits, these battles prepared the way for eventual victory:

Lee's army shrank until offensive action was no longer possible, while Grant's army kept replenishing its forces with new recruits. The siege of Petersburg, with the armies facing each other in miles of trenches, lasted throughout the winter of 1864–1865.

The end finally came in the spring of 1865. Grant kept battering Lee, who tried but failed to break through the Union line. With the numerical superiority of Grant's army now greater than two to one, Confederate defeat was inevitable. On April 2 Lee abandoned Richmond and Petersburg. On April 9, hemmed in by Union troops, short of rations, and with fewer than thirty thousand men left, Lee surrendered at Appomattox Court House. Grant treated his rival with respect and paroled the defeated troops, allowing cavalrymen to keep their horses and take them home. The war was over at last. Within weeks, Confederate forces under Johnston surrendered, and Davis, who had fled Richmond but wanted the war to continue, was captured in Georgia. The North rejoiced, and most southerners fell into despair, expecting waves of punishment. In the profound relief and stillness of the surrender field at Appomattox, no one could know the tasks of healing and justice that lay ahead.

SURRENDER AT APPOMATTOX

With Lee's surrender, Lincoln knew that the Union had been preserved, yet he lived to see but a few days of war's aftermath. On the evening of Good Friday, April 14, he accompanied his wife to Ford's Theatre in Washington to enjoy a popular comedy. There John Wilkes Booth, an embittered southern sympathizer, shot the president in the head at point-blank range. Lincoln died the next day. Twelve days later, troops tracked down and killed Booth. The Union had lost its wartime leader, and millions publicly mourned the martyred chief executive along the route of the funeral train that took his body home to Illinois. Relief at the war's end mingled hauntingly with a renewed sense of loss and anxiety about the future. Millions never forgot where they were and how they felt at the news of Lincoln's assassination.

Property damage and financial costs were enormous, though difficult to tally. U.S. loans and taxes during the conflict totaled almost $3 billion, and interest on the war debt was $2.8 billion. The Confederacy borrowed over $2 billion but lost far more in the destruction of homes, crops, livestock, and other property. In southern war zones the landscape was desolated. Over wide regions fences and crops were destroyed; houses, barns, and bridges burned; and fields abandoned and left to erode. Union troops had looted factories and put two-thirds of the South's railroad system out of service.

FINANCIAL TALLY

Estimates of the total cost of the war exceed $20 billion—five times the total expenditures of the federal government from its creation to 1861. By 1865, the federal government's spending had soared to twenty times the

■ At the war's end, the U.S. flag flew over the state capitol in Richmond, Virginia, which bore many marks of destruction.   (National Archives)

■ The death of President Lincoln caused a vast outpouring of grief in the North. As this Currier and Ives print shows, on its way to Illinois, his funeral train stopped at several cities to allow local services to be held.   (Anne S. K. Brown Military Collection, John Hay Library, Brown University)

prewar level and accounted for over 26 percent of the gross national product. Many of these changes were more or less permanent, as wartime measures left the government more deeply involved in manufacturing, banking, and transportation. If southerners had hoped to remove government from the economy, the war had now irrepressibly bound them together, a lesson of note for our twenty-first-century debates over the same issues.

The human costs of the Civil War were especially staggering. The total number of military casualties on both sides exceeded 1 million—a frightful toll for a nation of 31 million people. Approximately 360,000 Union soldiers died, 110,000 of them from wounds suffered in battle. Another 275,175 Union soldiers were wounded but survived. On the Confederate side, an estimated 260,000 lost their lives, and almost as many suffered wounds. More men died in the Civil War than in all other American wars combined until Vietnam. Of an estimated 194,743 northerners in southern prisons, 30,218 died; of 214,865 southerners in northern prisons, 25,976 died. The prison story from the war was one in which neither side could claim pride, and it caused embittered debate in war memory for decades.

DEATH TOLL

These unprecedented losses flowed from fundamental strife over the nature of the Union and the liberty of black people. Both sides saw vital interests in the struggle. As Julia Ward Howe wrote in her famous "Battle Hymn," they had heard "the trumpet that shall never call retreat." And so the war took its horrifying course. The first great legacy of the war in the lives of its survivors was, therefore, death itself. Although precise figures on enlistments are impossible to obtain, it appears that 700,000 to 800,000 men served in the Confederate armies. Far more, possibly 2.3 million, served in the Union armies. All these men were taken from home, family, and personal goals; their lives, if they survived at all, were disrupted in ways that were never repaired.

Summary

The Civil War altered American society forever. During the war, in both North and South, women had taken on new roles as they struggled to manage the hardships of the home front, to grieve, and to work for the prosecution of the war. Industrialization and large economic enterprises grew in power. Ordinary citizens found that their futures were increasingly tied to huge organizations. The character and extent of government power changed markedly. Under Republican leadership, the federal government had expanded its power not only to preserve the Union but also to extend freedom. A social revolution and government authority emancipated the slaves, and Lincoln had called for "a new birth of freedom" in America. A republic desperately divided against itself had survived, but in new constitutional forms yet to take shape during Reconstruction.

It was unclear how or whether the nation would use its power to protect the rights of the former slaves. Secession was dead, but whether Americans would continue to embrace a centralized nationalism remained to be seen.

The war ended decisively after tremendous sacrifice, but it left many unanswered questions. How would white southerners, embittered and impoverished, respond to efforts to reconstruct the nation? How would the country care for the maimed, the orphans, the farming women without men to work their land, and all the dead who had to be found and properly buried? What would be the place of black men and women in American life?

In the West, two civil wars raged, one between Union and Confederate forces, and the other resulting in a conquest of southwestern Indians by U.S. troops and land-hungry settlers. On the diplomatic front, the Union government had delicately managed to keep Great Britain and other foreign powers out of the war. Dissent flourished in both North and South, playing a crucial role in the ultimate collapse of the Confederacy, while the Union cause was only marginally affected by sabotage and draft riots.

In the Civil War Americans had undergone an epic of destruction and survival—a transformation like nothing else in their history. White southerners had experienced defeat as few other Americans have ever faced. Blacks were walking proudly but anxiously from slavery to freedom. White northerners were, by and large, self-conscious victors in a massive war for the nation's existence and for new definitions of freedom. The war, including all its drama, sacrifice, and social and political changes, left a compelling memory in American hearts and minds for generations.

LEGACY FOR A PEOPLE AND A NATION
The Confederate Battle Flag

The most widespread and controversial symbol to emerge from the Civil War era is the Confederate flag. Rather than the official flag of the Confederacy, it was a battle flag that soldiers carried to mark the center of a unit's position in the confusion of combat. Over time, this flag has taken on powerful emotional meanings.

At Confederate veterans' reunions and parades from the 1870s well into the twentieth century, the flag was an emblem of the South's Lost Cause. After extended controversy, many captured Confederate flags were returned by the federal government to southern states in 1905 as a gesture of reconciliation. Increasingly, Confederate remembrance merged with white supremacy at the turn of the twentieth century, and African Americans resented the flag.

In the late 1940s the flag became a fixture of popular culture with heightened racial meanings. In 1948 it was a symbol of the States' Rights ("Dixiecrat") Party. By the 1950s waving the Confederate flag became a demonstration of defiance among southern whites against the civil rights revolution. With the spread of American popular culture abroad, the Confederate flag can now be found all over the world, as a symbol of racism and vague demonstrations of defiance against power.

What does this flag mean as a symbol? Some southern whites argue that it is merely a marker of regional pride and identity. Some stress the flag's value as a symbol of rebellion against the establishment, or "political correctness." But to most blacks and to many whites, it expresses racism. The flag is loaded with coded meanings that can be interpreted in opposite ways. Some claim it represents the "nobility" of southern military tradition; others conclude that it stands for the hatred embodied in the history of the Ku Klux Klan.

In recent times, the Confederate flag has been the center of legal and political controversy. Disputes have emanated from city councils, high schools, and universities over public and private uses of the flag. Most visible of all have been the debates in the states of Georgia, South Carolina, Alabama, and Mississippi over whether to cease flying the Confederate flag at official sites, or as part of state flags. The debate over the legacy of the Confederate flag may never end. At issue are important questions: free speech, equal protection under law, perception versus reality, official government endorsement of collective symbols, the significance of race and racism in our national memory, and the meaning of the Civil War itself.

The **history companion** *powered by Eduspace®*
Your primary source for interactive quizzes, exercises, and more to help you learn efficiently.
http://history.college.hmco.com/students

RECONSTRUCTION: AN UNFINISHED REVOLUTION 1865–1877

*T*he lower half of the city of Charleston, South Carolina, the seedbed of secession, lay in ruin when most of the white population evacuated on February 18, 1865. A prolonged bombardment by Union batteries and gunboats around Charleston harbor had already destroyed many of the lovely town homes of the low-country planters. Then, as the city was abandoned, fires broke out everywhere, ignited in bales of cotton left in huge stockpiles in public squares. To many observers the flames were the funeral pyres of a dying civilization.

Among the first Union troops to enter Charleston was the Twenty-first U.S. Colored Regiment, which received the surrender of the city from its mayor. For black Charlestonians, most of whom were former slaves, this was a time of celebration. In symbolic ceremonies they proclaimed their freedom and announced their rebirth. Whatever the postwar order would bring, the freedpeople of Charleston converted Confederate ruin into a vision of Reconstruction based on Union victory and black liberation.

Still, in Charleston, as elsewhere, death demanded attention. During the final year of the war, the Confederates had converted the planters' Race Course, a horseracing track, and its famed Jockey Club, into a prison. Union soldiers were kept in terrible conditions in the interior of the track, without shelter. The 257 who died of exposure and disease were buried in a mass grave behind the judges' stand. After the fall of the city, Charleston's blacks organized to create a proper burial ground for the Union dead. During April more than twenty black workmen reinterred the dead in marked graves, and built a high fence around the cemetery. They built an archway over the entrance to the gravesite, and painted an inscription, "Martyrs of the Race Course."

◀ "Entrance of the 55th Massachusetts (Colored) Regiment into Charleston, S.C., February 21, 1865." Thomas Nast, pencil, oil, and wash on board, 1865. Black troops celebrated as they marched into the Confederate stronghold, hoisting their caps on their bayonets, and singing "John Brown's Body" as they marched up Meeting Street, Charleston's main thoroughfare. (Museum of Fine Arts, Boston)

And then they planned an extraordinary ceremony. On the morning of May 1, 1865, a procession of ten thousand people marched around the planters' Race Course, led by three thousand children carrying armloads of roses and singing "John Brown's Body." They were followed by black women with baskets of flowers and wreaths, and then by black men. The parade concluded with members of black and white Union regiments and white missionaries and teachers, led by James Redpath, the supervisor of freedmen's schools in the region. All who could fit assembled at the gravesite; five black ministers read from Scripture, and a black children's choir sang "America," "We'll Rally Around the Flag," the "Star-Spangled Banner," and Negro spirituals. When the ceremony ended, the large crowd retired to the Race Course for speeches, picnics, and military festivities.

The war was over in Charleston, and "Decoration Day"—now Memorial Day, the day to remember the war dead and decorate their graves with flowers—had been founded by African Americans. Black people—by their labor, their words, their songs, and their marching feet on the old planters' Race Course—had created an American tradition. In their vision, they were creating the Independence Day of a Second American Revolution.

Reconstruction would bring revolutionary circumstances, but revolutions can go backward. The Civil War and its aftermath wrought unprecedented changes in American society, law, and politics, but the underlying realities of economic power, racism, and judicial conservatism limited Reconstruction's revolutionary potential. As never before, the nation had to determine the nature of federal-state relations, whether confiscated land could be redistributed, how to bring justice to the freedpeople and to aggrieved white folk whose property and lives were devastated. And at the end of the day, Americans faced the harrowing challenge of psychological healing from a bloody and fratricidal war. How they would negotiate this tangled relationship between healing and justice would determine the extent of change during Reconstruction.

Nowhere was the turmoil of Reconstruction more evident than in national politics. Lincoln's successor, Andrew Johnson, fought bitterly with Congress over the shaping of Reconstruction policies. Although a southerner, Johnson had always been a foe of the South's wealthy planters, and his first acts as president suggested that he would be tough on "traitors." Before the end of 1865, however, Johnson's policies changed direction, and he became the protector of southern interests. Jefferson Davis stayed in prison for two years, but Johnson quickly pardoned other rebel leaders and allowed them to occupy high offices. He also ordered the return of plantations to their original owners, including abandoned coastal lands of Georgia and South Carolina on which forty thousand freed men and women had settled by order of General William Tecumseh Sherman early in 1865.

Johnson imagined a lenient and rapid "restoration" of the South to the Union rather than the fundamental "reconstruction" that Republican congressmen favored. Between 1866 and 1868, the president and the Republican leadership in Congress engaged in a bitterly antagonistic power struggle over how to put the United States back together again. Before these struggles were over, Congress had impeached the president, enfranchised the freedmen, and given them a role in reconstructing the South. The nation also adopted the Fourteenth and Fifteenth Amendments, ushering equal protection of the law, a definition of citizenship, and universal manhood suffrage into the Constitution. But little was done to open the doors of economic opportunity to black southerners, and the cause of equal rights for African Americans as the central aim of Reconstruction fell almost as fast as it rose.

By 1869 the Ku Klux Klan employed extensive violence and terror to thwart Reconstruction and undermine black freedom. As white Democrats in the South recaptured state governments, they encountered little opposition from the North. Moreover, as the 1870s advanced, industrial growth accelerated, creating new opportunities and priorities. The West, its seemingly limitless potential and its wars against Indians, drew American resources and consciousness like never before. Political corruption became a nationwide scandal, bribery a way of doing business.

Thus Reconstruction became a revolution eclipsed. The white South's desire to take back control of their states and of race relations overwhelmed the national interest in stopping them. But Reconstruction left enduring legacies the nation has struggled with ever since. ■

Wartime Reconstruction

Civil wars leave immense challenges of healing, justice, and physical rebuilding. Anticipating that process, Reconstruction of the Union was an issue as early as 1863, well before the war ended. Many key questions loomed on the horizon when and if the North succeeded on the battlefield. How would the nation be restored? How would southern states and leaders be treated? As errant brothers, or as traitors? What was the constitutional basis for readmission of states to the Union and where, if anywhere, could American statesmen look for precedence or guidance? More specifically, four vexing problems compelled early thinking and would haunt the Reconstruction era throughout. One, who would rule in the South once it was defeated? Two, who would rule in the federal government, Congress or the president? Three, what were the dimensions of black freedom, and what rights under law would the freedmen enjoy? And four, would Reconstruction be a preservation of the old republic, or a second revolution, a reinvention of a new republic?

Abraham Lincoln had never been antisouthern, though he had grown to become the leader of an anti-slavery war. He lost three brothers-in-law killed in the war on the Confederate side. His worst fear was that the war would collapse at the end into guerrilla warfare across the South, with surviving bands of Confederates carrying on resistance. Lincoln insisted that his generals give lenient terms to southern soldiers once they surrendered. In his Second Inaugural Address, delivered only a month before his assassination, Lincoln promised "malice toward none; with charity for all," as Americans strove to "bind up the nation's wounds."

LINCOLN'S 10 PERCENT PLAN

Lincoln planned early for a swift and moderate Reconstruction process. In his "Proclamation of Amnesty and Reconstruction," issued in December 1863, he proposed to replace majority rule with "loyal rule" as a means of reconstructing southern state governments before hostilities ended. He proposed pardons to all ex-Confederates except the highest-ranking military and civilian officers. Then, as soon as 10 percent of the voting population in the 1860 general election in a given state had taken an oath to the United States and established a government, the new state would be recognized. Lincoln did not consult Congress in these plans, and "loyal" assemblies (known as "Lincoln governments") were created in Louisiana, Tennessee, and Arkansas in 1864, states largely occupied by Union troops. These governments were weak and dependent on northern armies for survival.

Congress responded with great hostility to Lincoln's moves to readmit southern states in what seemed such a premature manner. Many Radical Republicans, strong proponents of emancipation and aggressive prosecution of the war against the South, considered the 10 percent plan a "mere mockery" of democracy. Led by Thaddeus Stevens of Pennsylvania in the House and Charles Sumner of Massachusetts in the Senate, congressional Republicans locked horns with Lincoln and proposed a longer and harsher approach to Reconstruction. Stevens advocated a "conquered provinces" theory, and Sumner employed an argument of "state suicide." Both contended that southerners had organized as a foreign nation to make war on the United States and, by secession, had destroyed their status as states. They therefore must be treated as "conquered foreign lands" and reverted to the status of "unorganized territories" before any process of readmission could be entertained (by Congress).

CONGRESS AND THE WADE-DAVIS BILL

In July 1864, the Wade-Davis bill, named for its sponsors, Senator Benjamin Wade of Ohio and Congressman Henry W. Davis of Maryland, emerged from Congress with three specific conditions for southern readmission: one, it demanded a "majority" of white male citizens participating in the creation of a new government; two, to vote or be a delegate to constitutional conventions, men had to take an "iron-clad" oath (declaring they had never aided the Confederate war effort); and three, all officers above the rank of lieutenant, and all civil officials in the Confederacy, would be disfranchised and deemed "not a citizen of the United States." The Confederate states were to be defined as "conquered enemies," said Davis, and the process of readmission was to be harsh and slow. Lincoln, ever the adroit politician, pocket-vetoed the bill and issued a conciliatory proclamation of his own announcing that he would not be inflexibly committed to any "one plan" of Reconstruction.

This exchange came during Grant's bloody campaign in Virginia against Lee, when the outcome of the war and Lincoln's reelection were still in doubt. Radical members of his own party, indeed, were organizing a dump-Lincoln campaign for the 1864 election. On August 5, Radical Republicans issued the "Wade-Davis Manifesto" to newspapers; an unprecedented attack on a sitting president by members of his own party, it accused Lincoln of usurpation of presidential powers and disgraceful leniency toward an eventually conquered South.

What emerged in 1864–1865 was a clear-cut debate and a potential constitutional crisis. Lincoln saw Reconstruction as a means of weakening the Confederacy and winning the war; the Radicals saw it as a longer-term transformation of the political and racial order of the country.

In early 1865, Congress and Lincoln joined in two important measures that recognized slavery's centrality to the war. On January 31, with strong administration backing, Congress passed the Thirteenth Amendment, which had two provisions: first, it abolished involuntary servitude everywhere in the United States; second, it declared that Congress shall have power to enforce this outcome by "appropriate legislation." When the measure passed by 119 to 56, a mere two votes more than the necessary two-thirds, rejoicing broke out in Congress. A Republican recorded in his diary: "Members joined in the shouting and kept it up for some minutes. Some embraced one another, others wept like children. I have felt ever since the vote, as if I were in a new country."

THIRTEENTH AMENDMENT

But the Thirteenth Amendment had emerged from a long congressional debate and considerable petitioning and public advocacy. One of the first and most remarkable petitions for a constitutional amendment abolishing slavery was submitted early in 1864 by Elizabeth Cady Stanton, Susan B. Anthony, and the Women's Loyal National League. Women throughout the Union accumulated thousands of signatures, even venturing into staunchly pro-Confederate regions of Kentucky and Missouri to secure supporters. It was a long road from the Emancipation Proclamation to the Thirteenth Amendment—through treacherous constitutional theory, a bedrock of belief that the sacred document ought never be altered, and partisan politics. But the logic of winning the war by crushing slavery, and of securing a new beginning for the nation under law that so many had now died to save, won the day.

Potentially as significant, on March 3, 1865, Congress created the Bureau of Refugees, Freedmen, and Abandoned Lands—the Freedmen's Bureau, an unprecedented agency of social uplift, necessitated by the ravages of the war. Americans had never engaged in federal aid to citizens on such a scale. With thousands of refugees, white and black, displaced in the South, the government continued what private freedmen's aid societies had started as early as 1862. In the mere four years of its existence, the Freedmen's Bureau

FREEDMEN'S BUREAU

supplied food and medical services, built several thousand schools and some colleges, negotiated several hundred thousand employment contracts between freedmen and their former masters, and tried to manage confiscated land.

The Bureau would be a controversial aspect of Reconstruction, within the South, where whites generally hated it, and within the federal government, where politicians divided over its constitutionality. Some Bureau agents were devoted to freedmen's rights, while others were opportunists who exploited the chaos of the postwar South. The war had forced into the open an eternal question of republics: What are the social welfare obligations of the state toward its people, and what do people owe their governments in return? Apart from their conquest and displacement of the eastern Indians, Americans were relatively inexperienced at the Freedmen's Bureau's task—social reform through military occupation.

The Meanings of Freedom

Black southerners entered into life after slavery with hope and circumspection. A Texas man recalled his father telling him, even before the war was over, "Our forever was going to be spent living among the Southerners, after they got licked." Freed men and women tried to gain as much as they could from their new circumstances. Often the changes they valued the most were personal—alterations in location, employer, or living arrangements.

For America's former slaves, Reconstruction had one paramount meaning: a chance to explore freedom. A southern white woman admitted in her diary that the black people "showed a natural and exultant joy at being free." Former slaves remembered singing far into the night after federal troops, who confirmed rumors of their emancipation, reached their plantations. The slaves on a Texas plantation shouted for joy, their leader proclaiming, "We is free—no more whippings and beatings." A few people gave in to the natural desire to do what had been impossible before. One angry grandmother dropped her hoe and ran to confront her mistress. "I'm free!" she yelled. "Yes, I'm free! Ain't got to work for you no more! You can't put me in your pocket now!" Another man recalled that he and others "started on the move," either to search for family members or just to exercise the human right of mobility.

THE FEEL OF FREEDOM

■ "The Armed Slave," William Sprang, oil on canvas, c. 1865. This remarkable painting depicts an African American veteran soldier, musket with fixed bayonet leaning against the wall, cigar in hand indicating a new life of safety and leisure, reading a book to demonstrate his embrace of education and freedom. The man's visage leaves the impression of satisfaction and dignity.
(The Civil War Library and Museum, Philadelphia)

Many freed men and women reacted more cautiously and shrewdly, taking care to test the boundaries of their new condition. "After the war was over," explained one man, "we was afraid to move. Just like terrapins or turtles after emancipation. Just stick our heads out to see how the land lay." As slaves they had learned to expect hostility from white people, and they did not presume it would instantly disappear. Life in freedom might still be a matter of what was allowed, not what was right. One sign of this shrewd caution was the way freed people evaluated potential employers. "Most all the Negroes that had good owners stayed with 'em, but the others left. Some of 'em come back and some didn't," explained one man. After considerable wandering in search of better circumstances, a majority of blacks eventually settled as agricultural workers back on their former farms or plantations. But they relocated their houses and did their utmost to control the conditions of their labor.

Former slaves concentrated on improving their daily lives. Throughout the South they devoted themselves to reuniting their families, separated during slavery by sale or hardship, and during the war by dislocation and the emancipation process. With only shreds of information to guide them, thousands of freed people embarked on odysseys in search of a husband, wife, child, or parent. By relying on the black community for help and information, and placing ads in black newspapers that continued to appear well into the 1880s, some succeeded in their quest, while others trudged through several states and never found loved ones.

REUNION OF AFRICAN AMERICAN FAMILIES

Husbands and wives who had belonged to different masters established homes together for the first time, and, as they had tried under slavery, parents asserted the right to raise their own children. A mother bristled when her old master claimed a right to whip her children. She informed him that "he warn't goin' to brush none of her chilluns no more." The freed men and women were too much at risk to act recklessly, but, as one man put it, they were tired of punishment and "sure didn't take no more foolishment off of white folks."

Many black people wanted to minimize contact with whites because, as Reverend Garrison Frazier told General Sherman in January 1865, "There is a prejudice against us . . . that will take years to get over." To avoid contact with overbearing whites who were used to supervising them, blacks abandoned the slave quarters and fanned out to distant corners of the land they worked. "After the war my stepfather come," recalled Annie Young, "and got my mother and we moved out in the piney woods." Others described moving "across the creek" or building a "saplin house . . . back in the woods." Some rural dwellers established small all-black settlements that still exist today along the back roads of the South.

BLACKS' SEARCH FOR INDEPENDENCE

Even once-privileged slaves desired such independence and social separation. One man turned down the master's offer of the overseer's house and moved instead to a shack in "Freetown." He also declined to let the former owner grind his grain for free because it "make him feel like a free man to pay for things just like anyone else."

In addition to a fair employer, what freed men and women most wanted was the ownership of land. Land represented self-sufficiency and a chance to gain compensation for generations of bondage. General Sherman's special Field Order Number 15, issued in February 1865, set aside 400,000 acres of land in the Sea Islands region for the exclusive settlement of the freedpeople. Hope swelled among ex-slaves as forty-acre plots, mules, and "possessary titles" were promised to them. But President Johnson ordered them removed in October and returned the land to its original owners under army enforcement. A northern observer noted that slaves freed in the Sea Islands of South Carolina and Georgia made "plain, straight-forward" inquiries as they settled on new land. They wanted to be sure the land "would be theirs after they had improved it." Everywhere, blacks young and old thirsted for homes of their own.

FREEDPEOPLE'S DESIRE FOR LAND

But most members of both political parties opposed genuine land redistribution to the freedmen. Even northern reformers who with Lincoln's encouragement had administered the Sea Islands during the war showed little sympathy for black aspirations. The former Sea Island slaves wanted to establish small, self-sufficient farms. Northern soldiers, officials, and missionaries of both races brought education and aid to the freedmen but also insisted that they grow cotton. They emphasized profit, cash crops, and the values of competitive capitalism.

"The Yankees preach nothing but cotton, cotton!" complained one Sea Island black. "We wants land," wrote another, but tax officials "make the lots too big, and cut we out." Indeed, the U.S. government sold thousands of acres in the Sea Islands, 90 percent of which went to wealthy investors from the North. At a protest against evictions from a contraband camp in Virginia in 1866, freedman Bayley Wyatt made black desires and claims clear: "We has a right to the land where we are located. For why? I tell you. Our wives, our children, our husbands, has been sold over and over again to purchase the lands we now locates upon; for that reason we have a divine right to the land."

Ex-slaves reached out for valuable things in life that had been denied them. One of these was education. Blacks of all ages hungered for the knowledge in books that had been permitted only to whites. With freedom, they started schools and filled classrooms both day and night. On log seats and dirt floors, freed men and women studied their letters in old almanacs and discarded dictionaries. Young children brought infants to school with them, and adults attended

BLACK EMBRACE OF EDUCATION

African Americans of all ages eagerly pursued the opportunity in freedom to gain an education. This young woman in Mt. Meigs, Alabama, is helping her mother learn to read. (Smithsonian Institute, photo by Rudolf Eickemeyer)

thropy. The Yankee schoolmarm—dedicated, selfless, and religious—became an agent of progress in many southern communities. Thus did African Americans seek a break from their pasts through learning. More than 600,000 were enrolled in elementary school by 1877.

Blacks and their white allies also saw the need for colleges and universities to train teachers, ministers, and professionals for leadership. The American Missionary Association founded seven colleges, including Fisk and Atlanta Universities, between 1866 and 1869. The Freedmen's Bureau helped to establish Howard University in Washington, D.C., and northern religious groups such as the Methodists, Baptists, and Congregationalists supported dozens of seminaries and teachers' colleges.

During Reconstruction, African American leaders often were highly educated individuals; many were from the prewar elite of free people of color. This group had benefited from its association with wealthy whites, many of whom were blood relatives; some planters had given their mulatto children an outstanding education. Francis Cardozo, who held various offices in South Carolina, had attended universities in Scotland and England. P. B. S. Pinchback, who became lieutenant governor of Louisiana, was the son of a planter who had sent him to school in Cincinnati. Both of the two black senators from Mississippi, Blanche K. Bruce and Hiram Revels, possessed privileged educations. Bruce was the son of a planter who had provided tutoring at home; Revels was the son of free North Carolina blacks who had sent him to Knox College in Illinois. These men and many self-educated former slaves brought to political office not only fervor but experience.

Freed from the restrictions and regulations of slavery, blacks could build their own institutions as they saw fit. The secret churches of slavery came into the open; in countless communities throughout the South, ex-slaves "started a brush arbor." A brush arbor was merely "a sort of . . . shelter with leaves for a roof," but the freed men and women worshiped in it enthusiastically. "Preachin' and shouting sometimes lasted all day," they recalled, for the opportunity to worship together freely meant "glorious times."

GROWTH OF BLACK CHURCHES

Within a few years independent branches of the Methodist and Baptist denominations had attracted the great majority of black Christians in the South. By 1877, in South Carolina alone, the African Methodist Episcopal (A.M.E.) Church had 1,000 ministers, 44,000 members, and its own school of theology, while the A.M.E.

at night or after "the crops were laid by." Many a teacher had "to make herself heard over three other classes reciting in concert" in a small room. The desire to escape slavery's ignorance was so great that, despite their poverty, many blacks paid tuition, typically $1 or $1.50 a month. These small amounts constituted major portions of a person's agricultural wages and added up to more than $1 million by 1870.

The federal government and northern reformers of both races assisted this pursuit of education. In its brief life the Freedmen's Bureau founded over four thousand schools, and idealistic men and women from the North established others funded by private northern philan-

Churches became a center of African American life, both social and political, during and after Reconstruction. Churches, big and small, like this one, Faith Memorial Church, in Hagley Landing, South Carolina, became the first black-owned institutions for the postfreedom generation. (*Aunt Phebe, Uncle Tom and Others: Character Studies Among the Old Slaves of the South Fifty Years After* by Essie Collins Matthews)

Zion Church had 45,000 members. In the rapid growth of churches, some of which became the wealthiest and the most autonomous institutions in black life, the freedpeople demonstrated their most secure claim on freedom as they created enduring communities.

The desire to gain as much independence as possible also shaped the former slaves' economic arrangements.

RISE OF THE SHARECROPPING SYSTEM

Since most of them lacked money to buy land, they preferred the next best thing: renting the land they worked. But the South had a cash-poor economy with few sources of credit, and few whites would consider renting land to blacks. Most blacks had no means to get cash before the harvest, and thus other alternatives had to be tried.

Black farmers and white landowners therefore turned to sharecropping, a system in which farmers kept part of their crop and gave the rest to the landowner while living on his property. The landlord or a merchant "furnished" food and supplies, such as draft animals and seed, needed before the harvest, and he received payment from the crop. Although landowners tried to set the laborers' share at a low level, black farmers had some bargaining power, at least at first. Sharecroppers would hold out, or move and try to switch employers from one year to another. As the system matured during the 1870s and 1880s, most sharecroppers worked "on halves"—half for the owner and half for themselves.

The sharecropping system, which materialized as early as 1868 in parts of the South, originated as a desirable compromise. It eased landowners' problems with cash and credit, and provided them a permanent, dependent labor force; blacks accepted it because it gave them more freedom from daily supervision. Instead of working in the hated gangs under a white overseer, as in slavery, they farmed their own plot of land in family groups. But sharecropping later proved to be a disaster. Owners and merchants developed a monopoly of control

■ Sharecropping became an oppressive system in the postwar South. At plantation stores like this one, photographed in Mississippi in 1868, merchants recorded in their ledger books debts that few sharecroppers were able to repay. (Recordbook: Smithsonian Institute, Division of Community Life; Plantation store: Amistad Foundation Collection at the Wadsworth Athenaeum, Hartford, Connecticut)

over the agricultural economy, as sharecroppers found themselves riveted into ever-increasing debt (see page 554).

The fundamental problem, however, was that southern farmers as a whole still concentrated on cotton, a crop with a bright past and a dim future. In freedom, black women often stayed away from the fields and cotton picking, allowing them to concentrate on domestic chores. Given the diminishing incentives of the system, they placed greater value on independent choices about gender roles and family organization than on reaching higher levels of production. By 1878 the South had recovered its prewar share of British cotton purchases. But even as southerners grew more cotton, their reward diminished. Cotton prices began a long decline, as world demand fell off.

Thus southern agriculture slipped deeper and deeper into depression. Black sharecroppers struggled under a growing burden of debt that reduced their independence and bound them to landowners and to furnishing merchants almost as oppressively as slavery had bound them to their masters. Many white farmers became debtors, too, gradually lost their land, and joined the ranks of

sharecroppers. This economic transformation took place as the nation struggled to put its political house back in order.

Johnson's Reconstruction Plan

*W*hen Reconstruction began under President Andrew Johnson, many expected his policies to be harsh. Throughout his career in Tennessee he had criticized the wealthy planters and championed the small farmers. When an assassin's bullet thrust Johnson into the presidency, many former slaveowners shared the dismay of a North Carolina woman who wrote, "Think of Andy Johnson [as] the president! What will become of us—'the aristocrats of the South' as we are termed?" Northern Radicals also had reason to believe that Johnson would deal sternly with the South. When one of them suggested the exile or execution of ten or twelve leading rebels to set an example, Johnson replied, "How are you going to pick out so small a number? . . . Treason is a crime; and crime must be punished."

■ Combative and inflexible, President Andrew Johnson contributed greatly to the failure of his own Reconstruction program. (Library of Congress)

Like his martyred predecessor, Johnson followed a path in antebellum politics from obscurity to power. With

ANDREW
JOHNSON OF
TENNESSEE

no formal education, he became a tailor's apprentice. But from 1829, while in his early twenties, he held nearly every office in Tennessee politics: alderman, state representative, congressman, two terms as governor, and U.S. senator by 1857. Although elected as a southern Democrat, Johnson was the only senator from a seceded state who refused to follow his state out of the Union. Lincoln appointed him war governor of Tennessee in 1862, hence his symbolic place on the ticket in the president's bid for reelection in 1864.

Johnson's political beliefs made him look a little like a Republican, but at heart he was an old Jacksonian Democrat. And as they said in the mountainous region of east Tennessee, where Johnson established a reputation as a stump speaker, "Old Andy never went back on his 'raisin'." Although a staunch Unionist, Johnson was also an ardent states' rightist. Before the war, he had supported tax-funded public schools and homestead legislation, fashioning himself as a champion of the common man. Although he vehemently opposed secession, Johnson advocated limited government. He shared none of the Radicals' expansive conception of federal power. His philosophy toward Reconstruction may be summed up in the slogan he adopted: "The Constitution as it is, and the Union as it was."

Through 1865 Johnson alone controlled Reconstruction policy, for Congress recessed shortly before he became president and did not reconvene until December. In the following eight months, Johnson put into operation his own plan, forming new state governments in the South by using his power to grant pardons. Johnson followed Lincoln's leniency by extending even easier terms to former Confederates.

Johnson had owned house slaves, although he had never been a planter. He accepted emancipation as a result

JOHNSON'S
RACIAL VIEWS

of the war, but he did not favor black civil and political rights. Johnson believed that black suffrage could never be imposed on a southern state by the federal government, and that set him on a collision course with the Radicals. When it came to race, Johnson was a thoroughgoing white supremacist. He held what one politician called "unconquerable prejudices against the African race." In perhaps the most blatantly racist official statement ever delivered by an American president, Johnson declared in his annual message of 1867 that blacks possessed less "capacity for government than any other race of people. No independent government of any form has ever been successful in their hands; . . . wherever they have been left to their own devices they have shown a constant tendency to relapse into barbarism."

Such racial views had an enduring effect on Johnson's policies. Where whites were concerned, however, Johnson seemed to be pursuing changes in class relations. He proposed rules that would keep the wealthy planter class at least temporarily out of power.

White southerners were required to swear an oath of loyalty as a condition of gaining amnesty or pardon, but

JOHNSON'S
PARDON POLICY

Johnson barred several categories of people from taking the oath: former federal officials, high-ranking Confederate officers, and political leaders or graduates of West Point or Annapolis who joined or aided the Confederacy. To this list Johnson added another important group: all ex-Confederates whose taxable property was worth more than $20,000. These individuals had to apply personally to the president for pardon and restoration of their political rights.

Thus it appeared that the leadership class of the Old South would be removed from power, for virtually all the rich and powerful whites of prewar days needed Johnson's special pardon. The president, it seemed, meant to take revenge on the haughty aristocrats and thereby promote a new leadership of deserving yeomen.

Johnson appointed provisional governors, who began the Reconstruction process by calling constitutional conventions. The delegates chosen for these conventions had to draft new constitutions that eliminated slavery and invalidated secession. After ratification of these constitutions, new governments could be elected, and the states would be restored to the Union with full congressional representation. But only those southerners who had taken the oath of amnesty and been eligible to vote on the day the state seceded could participate in this process. Thus unpardoned whites and former slaves were not eligible.

If Johnson intended to strip the old elite of its power, he did not hold to his plan. The old white leadership proved resilient and influential; prominent Confederates (a few with pardons but many without) won elections and turned up in various appointive offices. Then, surprisingly, Johnson started pardoning aristocrats and leading rebels. He hired additional clerks to write out the necessary documents and then began to issue pardons to large categories of people. By September 1865 hundreds were being issued in a single day. These pardons, plus the rapid return of planters' abandoned lands, restored the old elite to power and quickly gave Johnson the image as the South's champion. He further gained southern loyalty with his hostility to the Freedmen's Bureau.

PRESIDENTIAL RECONSTRUCTION

Why did Johnson allow the planters to regain power? Perhaps vanity betrayed his judgment. Too long an isolated outsider, Johnson may have succumbed to the flattery of the pardon seekers. He was also determined on a rapid Reconstruction in order to deny the Radicals the opportunity for the more thorough racial and political changes they desired in the South. And Johnson needed southern support in the 1866 elections; hence, he declared Reconstruction complete only eight months after Appomattox. Thus in December 1865 many Confederate congressmen traveled to Washington to claim seats in the U.S. Congress. Even Alexander Stephens, vice president of the Confederacy, returned to Capitol Hill as a senator-elect.

The election of such prominent rebels troubled many northerners. So did other results of Johnson's program. Some of the state conventions were slow to repudiate secession; others admitted only grudgingly that slavery was dead.

Furthermore, to define the status of freed men and women and control their labor, some legislatures merely revised large sections of the slave codes by substituting the word *freedmen* for *slaves*. The new black codes compelled the former slaves to carry passes, observe a curfew, live in housing provided by a landowner, and give up hope of entering many desirable occupations. Stiff vagrancy laws and restrictive labor contracts bound freedpeople to plantations, and "anti-enticement" laws punished anyone who tried to lure these workers to other employment. State-supported schools and orphanages excluded blacks entirely.

BLACK CODES

It seemed to northerners that the South was intent on returning African Americans to servility and that Johnson's Reconstruction policy held no one responsible for the terrible war. But memories of the war—not yet a year over—were still raw, and would dominate political behavior for several elections to come. Thus the Republican majority in Congress decided to call a halt to the results of Johnson's plan. On reconvening, the House and Senate considered the credentials of the newly elected southern representatives and decided not to admit them. Instead, they bluntly challenged the president's authority and established a joint committee to study and investigate a new direction for Reconstruction.

The Congressional Reconstruction Plan

Northern congressmen were hardly unified, but they did not doubt their right to shape Reconstruction policy. The Constitution mentioned neither secession nor reunion, but it gave Congress the primary role in the admission of states. Moreover, the Constitution declared that the United States shall guarantee to each state a republican form of government. This provision, legislators believed, gave them the authority to devise policies for Reconstruction.

They soon found that other constitutional questions affected their policies. What, for example, had rebellion done to the relationship between southern states and the Union? Lincoln had always insisted that states could not secede—they had engaged in an "insurrection"—and that the Union remained intact. Not even Andrew Johnson, however, accepted the southern position that state governments of the Confederacy could simply reenter the nation. Congressmen who favored vigorous Reconstruction measures argued that the war had broken the Union, and that the South was subject to the victor's will. Moderate congressmen held that the states had forfeited their rights through rebellion and thus had come under congressional supervision.

These theories mirrored the diversity of Congress itself. Northern Democrats, weakened by the war most of them had opposed in its final year, denounced any idea of racial equality and supported Johnson's policies. Conservative Republicans, despite their party loyalty, favored a limited federal role in Reconstruction. The Radical Republicans, led by Thaddeus Stevens, Charles Sumner, and George Julian, wanted to transform the South. Although a minority in their party, they had the advantage of clearly defined goals. They believed it was essential to democratize the South, establish public education, and ensure the rights of the freedpeople. They favored black suffrage, supported some land confiscation and redistribution, and were willing to exclude the South from the

THE RADICALS

Union for several years if necessary to achieve their goals. Born of the war and its outcome, the Radicals brought a new civic vision to American life; they wanted to create an activist federal government and the beginnings of racial equality. A large group of moderate Republicans did not want to go as far as the Radicals but opposed Johnson's leniency.

One overwhelming political reality faced all four groups: the 1866 elections. Having questioned Johnson's program, Congress needed to develop an alternative plan. Ironically, Johnson and the Democrats sabotaged the possibility of a conservative coalition. They refused to cooperate with conservative or moderate Republicans and insisted that Reconstruction was over, that the new state governments were legitimate, and that southern representatives should be admitted to Congress. Among the Republicans, the Radicals' influence grew in proportion to Johnson's intransigence.

Trying to work with Johnson, Republicans believed a compromise had been reached in the spring of 1866. Under its terms Johnson would agree to two modifica-

■ In 1866, as Congress reviewed the progress of Reconstruction, news from the South had a considerable impact. Violence against black people, like the riot in Memphis depicted here, helped convince northern legislators that they had to modify President Johnson's policies. (Library of Congress)

CONGRESS VS. JOHNSON

tions of his program: extension of the Freedmen's Bureau for another year and passage of a civil rights bill to counteract the black codes. This bill would force southern courts to practice equality before the law by allowing federal judges to remove from state courts cases in which blacks were treated unfairly. Its provisions applied to public, not private, acts of discrimination. The civil rights bill of 1866 was the first statutory definition of the rights of American citizens.

Johnson destroyed the compromise, however, by vetoing both bills (they later became law when Congress overrode the president's veto). Denouncing any change in his program, the president condemned Congress's action and revealed his own racism. Because the civil rights bill defined U.S. citizens as native-born persons who were taxed, Johnson claimed it discriminated against "large numbers of intelligent, worthy, and patriotic foreigners . . . in favor of the negro." The bill, he said, operated "in favor of the colored and against the white race."

All hope of presidential-congressional cooperation was now dead. In 1866 newspapers reported daily violations of blacks' rights in the South and carried alarming accounts of antiblack violence—notably in Memphis and New Orleans, where police aided brutal mobs in their attacks. In Memphis forty blacks were killed and twelve schools burned by white mobs, and in New Orleans the toll was thirty-four African Americans dead and two hundred wounded. Such violence convinced Republicans, and the northern public, that more needed to be done. A new Republican plan took the form of the Fourteenth Amendment to the Constitution, forged out of a compromise between radical and conservative elements of the party.

Of the four parts of the Fourteenth Amendment, the first would have the greatest legal significance in later years. It conferred citizenship on the freedmen and prohibited states from abridging their constitutional "privileges and immunities" (see the Appendix for the Constitution and all amendments). It also barred any state from taking a person's life, liberty, or property "without due process of law" and from denying "equal protection of the laws." These resounding phrases became powerful guarantees of African Americans' civil rights—indeed, of the rights of all citizens—in the twentieth century.

FOURTEENTH AMENDMENT

Nearly universal agreement emerged among Republicans on the amendment's second and third provisions. The second declared the Confederate debt null and void and guaranteed the war debt of the United States. Northerners rejected the notion of paying taxes to reimburse those who had financed a rebellion, and business groups agreed on the necessity of upholding the credit of the U.S. government. The third provision barred Confederate leaders from holding state and federal office. Only Congress, by a two-thirds vote of each house, could remove the penalty. The amendment thus guaranteed a degree of punishment for the leaders of the Confederacy.

The fourth part of the amendment dealt with representation and embodied the compromises that produced the document. Northerners disagreed about whether black citizens should have the right to vote. As a citizen of Indiana wrote to a southern relative, there was strong feeling in favor of "humane and liberal laws for the government and protection of the colored population." But there was prejudice, too. "Although there is a great deal [of] profession among us for the relief of the darkey yet I think much of it is far from being sincere. I guess we want to compel you to do right by them while we are not willing ourselves to do so." Those arched words are indicative of not only how revolutionary Reconstruction had become, but also how far the public will lagged behind the enactments that became new constitutional cornerstones.

Emancipation made every former slave a full rather than three-fifths of a person, which would increase southern representation. Thus the postwar South stood to gain power in Congress, and if white southerners did not allow blacks to vote, former secessionists would derive the political benefit from emancipation. That was more irony than most northerners could bear. So Republicans determined that if a southern state did not grant black men the vote, their representation would be reduced proportionally. If they did enfranchise black men, their representation would be increased proportionally. This compromise avoided a direct enactment of black suffrage, but would deliver future black voters to the Republican Party.

The Fourteenth Amendment specified for the first time that voters were "male," and ignored female citizens, black and white. For this reason it provoked a strong reaction from the women's rights movement. Advocates of women's equality had worked with abolitionists for decades, often subordinating their cause to that of the slaves. During the drafting of the Fourteenth Amendment, however, female activists demanded to be heard. Prominent leaders such as Elizabeth Cady Stanton and Susan B. Anthony ended their alliance with abolitionists and fought more determinedly for themselves, while others remained committed to the idea that it was "the Negro's hour." Thus the amendment infused new life into the women's rights movement and caused considerable strife among old allies. Many male former abolitionists, white and black, were willing to delay the day of woman suffrage in favor of securing freedmen the right to vote in the South.

In 1866, however, the major question in Reconstruction politics was how the public would respond to the congressional initiative. Johnson did his best to block the Fourteenth Amendment in both North and South. Condemning Congress for its refusal to seat southern representatives, the president urged state legislatures in the South to vote against ratification. Every southern legislature except Tennessee's rejected the amendment by a wide margin.

THE SOUTH'S AND JOHNSON'S DEFIANCE, 1866

To present his case to northerners, Johnson organized a National Union Convention and took to the stump himself. In an age when active personal campaigning was rare for a president, Johnson boarded a special train for a "swing around the circle" that carried his message into the Northeast, the Midwest, and then back to Washington. In city after city, he criticized the Republicans in a ranting, undignified style. Increasingly, audiences rejected his views and hooted and jeered at him. In this whistle-stop tour, Johnson began to hand out American flags with thirty-six rather than twenty-five stars, declaring that the Union was already restored. At many towns he likened himself to a "persecuted" Jesus who might now be martyred "upon the cross" for his magnanimity toward the South. And, repeatedly, he labeled the Radicals "traitors" for their efforts to take over Reconstruction.

The elections of 1866 were a resounding victory for Republicans in Congress. Radicals and moderates whom Johnson had denounced won reelection by large margins, and the Republican majority grew to two-thirds of both houses of Congress. The North had spoken clearly: Johnson's policies were prematurely giving the advan-

Map 16.1   The Reconstruction

This map shows the five military districts established when Congress passed the Reconstruction Act of 1867. As the dates within each state indicate, conservative Democratic forces quickly regained control of government in four southern states. So-called Radical Reconstruction was curtailed in most of the others as factions within the weakened Republican Party began to cooperate with conservative Democrats.

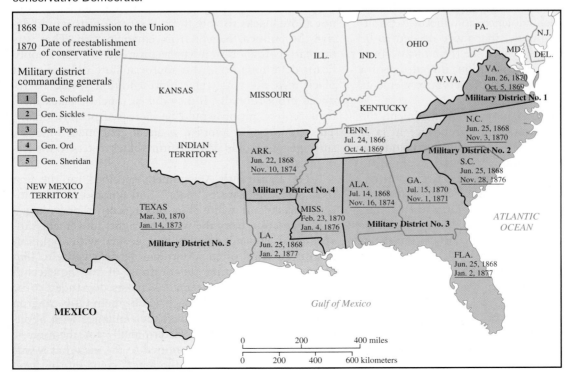

tage to rebels and traitors. Although the Radicals may have been out ahead of public opinion, most northerners feared for "the future peace and safety of the Union" if Johnson's approach to Reconstruction prevailed. Thus Republican congressional leaders won a mandate to pursue their Reconstruction plan.

But, thanks to Johnson and southern intransigence, that plan had reached an impasse. Nothing could be accomplished as long as the "Johnson governments" existed and the southern electorate remained exclusively white. Republicans resolved to form new state governments in the South and enfranchise the freedmen.

After some embittered debate in which Republicans and the remaining Democrats in Congress argued over

RECONSTRUCTION ACTS OF 1867–1868

the meaning and memory of the Civil War itself, the First Reconstruction Act passed in March 1867. This plan, under which the southern states were actually readmitted to the Union, incorporated only a part of the Radical program. Union generals, commanding small garrisons of troops and charged with supervising all elections, assumed control

in five military districts in the South (see Map 16.1). Confederate leaders designated in the Fourteenth Amendment were barred from voting until new state constitutions were ratified. The act guaranteed freedmen the right to vote in elections for state constitutional conventions and in subsequent elections. In addition, each southern state was required to ratify the Fourteenth Amendment, to ratify its new constitution by majority vote, and to submit it to Congress for approval (see Table 16.1).

Thus African Americans gained an opportunity to fight for a better life through the political process, and ex-Confederates were given what they interpreted as a bitter pill to swallow in order to return to the Union. The Second, Third, and Fourth Reconstruction Acts, passed between March 1867 and March 1868, provided the details of operation for voter registration boards, the adoption of constitutions, and the administration of "good faith" oaths on the part of white southerners.

In the words of one historian, the Radicals succeeded in "clipping Johnson's wings." But they had hoped Congress could do much more. Thaddeus Stevens, for

TABLE 16.1

Plans for Reconstruction Compared

	Johnson's Plan	Radicals' Plan	Fourteenth Amendment	Reconstruction Act of 1867
Voting	Whites only; high-ranking Confederate leaders must seek pardons	Give vote to black males	Southern whites may decide but can lose representation if they deny black suffrage	Black men gain vote; whites barred from office by Fourteenth Amendment cannot vote while new state governments are being formed
Officeholding	Many prominent Confederates regain power	Only loyal white and black males eligible	Confederate leaders barred until Congress votes amnesty	Fourteenth Amendment in effect
Time out of Union	Brief	Several years; until South is thoroughly democratized	Brief	3–5 years after war
Other change in southern society	Little; gain of power by yeomen not realized; emancipation grudgingly accepted, but no black civil or political rights	Expand public education; confiscate land and provide farms for freedmen; expansion of activist federal government	Probably slight, depending on enforcement	Considerable, depending on action of new state governments

FAILURE OF LAND REDISTRIBUTION

example, argued that economic opportunity was essential to the freedmen. "If we do not furnish them with homesteads from forfeited and rebel property," Stevens declared, "and hedge them around with protective laws . . . we had better left them in bondage." Stevens therefore drew up a plan for extensive confiscation and redistribution of land. Only one-tenth of the land affected by his plan was earmarked for freedmen, in forty-acre plots. The rest was to be sold to generate money for Union veterans' pensions, compensation to loyal southerners for damaged property, and payment of the federal debt.

But plans for property redistribution were unpopular measures, and virtually all failed to gain legitimacy. Northerners were accustomed to a limited role for government, and the business community staunchly opposed any interference with private-property rights, even for former Confederates. Thus black farmers were forced to seek work in a hostile environment in which landowners opposed their acquisition of land, even as renters.

Congress's quarrels with Andrew Johnson grew even more bitter. To restrict Johnson's influence and safeguard its plan, Congress passed a number of

CONSTITUTIONAL CRISIS

controversial laws. First, it limited Johnson's power over the army by requiring the president to issue military orders through the General of the Army, Ulysses S. Grant, who could not be dismissed without the Senate's consent. Then Congress passed the Tenure of Office Act, which gave the Senate power to approve changes in the president's cabinet. Designed to protect Secretary of War Stanton, who sympathized with the Radicals, this law violated the tradition that a president controlled appointments to his own cabinet.

All of these measures, as well as each of the Reconstruction Acts, were passed by a two-thirds override of presidential vetoes. The situation led some to believe that the federal government had reached a stage of "congressional tyranny," and others to conclude that Johnson had become an obstacle to the legitimate will of the people in reconstructing the nation on a just and permanent basis.

Johnson took several belligerent steps of his own. He issued orders to military commanders in the South limiting their powers and increasing the powers of the civil governments he had created in 1865. Then he removed military officers who were conscientiously enforcing Congress's new law, preferring commanders who allowed disqualified Confederates to vote. Finally, he tried to remove Secretary of War Stanton. With that attempt the confrontation reached its climax.

Impeachment is a political procedure provided for in the Constitution as a remedy for crimes or serious abuses of power by presidents, federal judges,

IMPEACHMENT OF PRESIDENT JOHNSON

and other high officials in the government. Those who are impeached (judged or politically indicted) in the House are then tried in the Senate. Historically, this power has generally not been used as a means to investigate and judge the private lives of presidents, although in recent times it was used in this manner in the case of President Bill Clinton.

Twice in 1867, the House Judiciary Committee had considered impeachment of Johnson, rejecting the idea

■ Thomas Waterman Wood, who had painted portraits of society figures in Nashville before the war, sensed the importance of Congress's decision in 1867 to enfranchise the freedmen. This oil painting, one of a series on suffrage, emphasizes the significance of the ballot for the black voter.   (Cheekwood Museum of Art, Nashville, Tennessee)

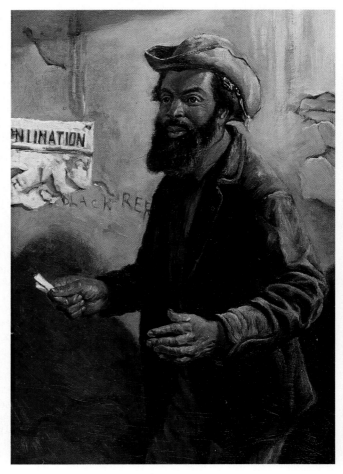

once and then recommending it by only a 5-to-4 vote. That recommendation was decisively defeated by the House. After Johnson tried to remove Stanton, however, a third attempt to impeach the president carried easily in early 1868. The indictment concentrated on his violation of the Tenure of Office Act, though many modern scholars regard his efforts to impede enforcement of the Reconstruction Act of 1867 as a far more serious offense.

Johnson's trial in the Senate lasted more than three months. The prosecution, led by Radicals such as Thaddeus Stevens and Benjamin Butler, attempted to prove that Johnson was guilty of "high crimes and misdemeanors." But they also argued that the trial was a means to judge Johnson's performance, not a judicial determination of guilt or innocence. The Senate ultimately rejected such reasoning, which could have made removal from office a political weapon against any chief executive who disagreed with Congress. Although a majority of

senators voted to convict Johnson, the prosecution fell one vote short of the necessary two-thirds majority. Johnson remained in office, politically weakened and with only a few months left in his term. Some Republicans backed away from impeachment because they had their eyes on the 1868 election and did not want to hurt their prospects of regaining the White House.

In the 1868 presidential election Ulysses S. Grant, running as a Republican, defeated Horatio Seymour, a

ELECTION OF 1868

New York Democrat. Grant was not a radical, but his platform supported congressional Reconstruction and endorsed black suffrage in the South. (Significantly, Republicans stopped short of endorsing black suffrage in the North.) The Democrats, meanwhile, vigorously denounced Reconstruction and thus renewed the sectional conflict. Indeed, in the 1868 election, the Democrats conducted the most openly racist campaign to that time in American history. Both sides waved the "bloody

■ A Republican Party brass band in action during the 1868 election campaign in Baton Rouge, Louisiana. The Union regimental colors and soldier caps demonstrate the strong federal presence in the South at this pivotal moment in radical Reconstruction.   (Andrew D. Lytle Collection, Louisiana and Lower Mississippi Valley Collections, LSU Libraries, Louisiana State University, Baton Rouge, La.)

shirt," accusing each other as the villains of the war's sacrifices. By associating themselves with rebellion and with Johnson's repudiated program, the Democrats went down to defeat in all but eight states, though the popular vote was fairly close. Participating in their first presidential election ever on a wide scale, blacks decisively voted en masse for General Grant.

In office Grant acted as an administrator of Reconstruction but not as its enthusiastic advocate. He vacillated in his dealings with the southern states, sometimes defending Republican regimes and sometimes currying favor with Democrats. On occasion Grant called out federal troops to stop violence or enforce acts of Congress. But he never imposed a true military occupation on the South. Rapid demobilization had reduced a federal army of more than 1 million to 57,000 within a year of the surrender at Appomattox. Thereafter the number of troops in the South continued to fall, until in 1874 there were only 4,000 in the southern states outside Texas. The later legend of "military rule," so important to southern claims of victimization during Reconstruction, was steeped in myth.

In 1869, in an effort to write democratic principles into the Constitution, the Radicals passed the Fifteenth

FIFTEENTH AMENDMENT

Amendment. This measure forbade states to deny the right to vote "on account of race, color, or previous condition of servitude." Such wording did not guarantee the right to vote. It deliberately left states free to restrict suffrage on other grounds so that northern states could continue to deny suffrage to women and certain groups of men—Chinese immigrants, illiterates, and those too poor to pay poll taxes.

Although several states outside the South refused to ratify, three-fourths of the states approved the measure, and the Fifteenth Amendment became law in 1870. It too had been a political compromise, and though African Americans rejoiced all across the land at its enactment, it left open the possibility for states to create countless qualification tests to obstruct voting in the future.

With passage of the Fifteenth Amendment, many Americans, especially supportive northerners, considered Reconstruction essentially completed. "Let us have done with Reconstruction," pleaded the *New York Tribune* in April 1870. "The country is tired and sick of it. . . . Let us have Peace!" But some northerners, like radical abolitionist Wendell Phillips, worried. "Our day," he warned, "is fast slipping away. Once let public thought float off from the great issue of the war, and it will take . . . more than a generation to bring it back again."

Reconstruction Politics in the South

*F*rom the start, Reconstruction encountered the resistance of white southerners. In the black codes and in private attitudes, many whites stubbornly opposed emancipation, and the former planter class proved especially unbending because of their tremendous financial loss in slaves. In 1866 a Georgia newspaper frankly observed that "most of the white citizens believe that the institution of slavery was right, and . . . they will believe that the condition, which comes nearest to slavery, that can now be established will be the best."

Fearing loss of control over their slaves, some planters attempted to postpone freedom by denying or misrepresenting events. Former slaves

WHITE RESISTANCE

reported that their owners "didn't tell them it was freedom" or "wouldn't let [them] go." Agents of the Freedmen's Bureau reported that "the old system of slavery [is] working with even more rigor than formerly at a few miles distant from any point where U.S. troops are stationed." To hold onto their workers, some landowners claimed control over black children and used guardianship and apprentice laws to bind black families to the plantation.

Whites also blocked blacks from acquiring land. A few planters divided up plots among their slaves, but most condemned the idea of making blacks landowners. A Georgia woman whose family was known for its support of religious education for slaves was outraged that two property owners planned to "rent their lands to the Negroes!" Such action was, she declared, "injurious to the best interest of the community."

Adamant resistance by propertied whites soon manifested itself in other ways, including violence. In one North Carolina town a local magistrate clubbed a black man on a public street, and bands of "Regulators" terrorized blacks in parts of that state and in Kentucky. Amidst their defeat, many planters believed, as a South Carolinian put it, that blacks "can't be governed except with the whip." And after President Johnson encouraged the South to resist congressional Reconstruction, some white conservatives worked hard to capture the new state governments, while others boycotted the polls in an attempt to defeat Congress's plans.

Very few black men stayed away from the polls. Enthusiastically and hopefully, they voted Republican. Most agreed with one man who felt he should "stick to the end with the party that freed me." Illiteracy did not

Thanks to a large black turnout and the restrictions on prominent Confederates, a new southern Republican Party came to power in the constitutional conventions of 1868–1870. Republican delegates consisted of a sizable contingent of blacks (265 out of the total of just over 1,000 delegates throughout the South), some northerners who had moved to the South, and native southern whites who favored change. Together these Republicans brought the South into line with progressive reforms adopted earlier in the rest of the nation. The new constitutions were more democratic. They eliminated property qualifications for voting and holding office, and they turned many appointed offices into elective posts. They provided for public schools and institutions to care for the mentally ill, the blind, the deaf, the destitute, and the orphaned.

The conventions broadened women's rights in property holding and divorce. Usually, the goal was not to make women equal with men but to provide relief to thousands of suffering debtors. In families left poverty-stricken by the war and weighed down by debt, it was usually the husband who had contracted the debts. Thus giving women legal control over their own property provided some protection to their families. The goal of some delegates, however, was to elevate women with the right to vote.

■ Thomas Nast, in this 1868 cartoon, pictured the combination of forces that threatened the success of Reconstruction: southern opposition and the greed, partisanship, and racism of northern interests.
(Library of Congress)

Under these new constitutions the southern states elected Republican-controlled governments. For the first time, the ranks of state legislators in 1868 included some black southerners. It remained to be seen now how much social change these new governments would bring about. Contrary to what white southerners would later claim, the Republican state governments did not disfranchise ex-Confederates as a group. The vexing questions of land reform and enforcement of racial equality all but overwhelmed the Republican governments.

TRIUMPH OF REPUBLICAN GOVERNMENTS

Land reform largely failed because in most states whites were in the majority and former slaveowners controlled the best land and other sources of economic power. James Lynch, a leading black politician from Mississippi, explained why African Americans shunned the "folly" of disfranchising whites. Unlike northerners who "can leave when it becomes too uncomfortable," landless former slaves "must be in friendly relations with the great body of the whites in the state. Otherwise . . . peace can be maintained only by a standing army." Despised and lacking economic or social power, southern Republicans strove for acceptance and legitimacy.

Far from being vindictive toward the race that had enslaved them, most southern blacks treated leading

BLACK VOTERS AND THE SOUTHERN REPUBLICAN PARTY

prohibit blacks (or uneducated whites) from making intelligent choices. Although Mississippi's William Henry could read only "a little," he testified that he and his friends had no difficulty selecting the Republican ballot. "We stood around and watched," he explained. "We saw D. Sledge vote; he owned half the county. We knowed he voted Democratic so we voted the other ticket so it would be Republican." Women, who could not vote, encouraged their husbands and sons, and preachers exhorted their congregations to use the franchise. With such group spirit, zeal for voting spread through entire black communities.

rebels with generosity and appealed to white southerners to adopt a spirit of fairness and cooperation. In this way the South's Republican Party condemned itself to defeat if white voters would not cooperate. Within a few years Republicans were reduced to the embarrassment of making futile appeals to whites while ignoring the claims of their strongest supporters, blacks. But for a time some propertied whites accepted congressional Reconstruction as a reality and declared themselves willing to compete under the new rules. All sides found an area of agreement in economic policies.

Reflecting northern ideals and southern necessity, the Reconstruction governments enthusiastically promoted industry. Confederates had seen how in-

INDUSTRIALIZATION dustry aided the North during the war. Accordingly, Reconstruction legislatures encouraged investment with loans, subsidies, and exemptions from taxation for periods up to ten years. The southern railroad system was rebuilt and expanded, and coal and iron mining made possible Birmingham's steel plants. Between 1860 and 1880, the number of manufacturing establishments in the South nearly doubled.

This emphasis on big business, however, produced higher state debts and taxes, drew money away from schools and other programs, and multiplied possibilities for corruption. It also locked Republicans into a conservative strategy. In courting elite whites who never joined the Republican Party, Republicans lost the opportunity of building support among poorer whites.

Policies appealing to African American voters never went beyond equality before the law. In fact, the whites

REPUBLICANS AND RACIAL EQUALITY who controlled the southern Republican Party were reluctant to allow blacks a share of offices proportionate to their electoral strength. Aware of their weakness, black leaders did not push very far for revolutionary economic or social change. In every southern state, they led efforts to establish public schools, although they did not press for integrated facilities. In 1870 South Carolina passed the first comprehensive school law in the South. By 1875, 50 percent of black school-age children in that state were enrolled in school, and approximately one-third of the three thousand teachers were black.

■ One notable success in Reconstruction efforts to stimulate industry was Birmingham, Alabama. Here workers cast molten iron into blocks called pigs. (Birmingham Public Library)

Some African American politicians did fight for civil rights and integration. Many were from cities such as New Orleans or Mobile, where large populations of light-skinned free blacks had existed before the war. Their experience in such communities had made them sensitive to issues of status, and they spoke out for open and equal public accommodations. Laws requiring equal accommodations won passage throughout the Deep South, but they often went unenforced or required expensive legal action.

Economic progress was uppermost in the minds of most freedpeople and black representatives from rural districts. Black southerners needed land, and much land did fall into state hands for nonpayment of taxes and was offered for sale in small lots. But most freedmen had too little cash to bid against investors or speculators. South Carolina established a land commission, but it could help only those with money to buy. Any widespread redistribution of land had to arise from Congress, which never supported such action. The lack of genuine land redistribution remained the significant lost opportunity of Reconstruction.

Within a few years, as centrists in both parties met with failure, white hostility to congressional Reconstruction

MYTH OF "NEGRO RULE"

began to dominate. Some conservatives had always desired to fight Reconstruction through pressure and racist propaganda. They put economic and social pressure on blacks: one black Republican reported that "my neighbors will not employ me, nor sell me a farthing's worth of anything." Charging that the South had been turned over to ignorant blacks, conservatives deplored "black domination," which became a rallying cry for a return to white supremacy.

Such attacks were inflammatory propaganda, and part of the growing myth of "Negro rule," which would serve as a central theme in battles over the memory of Reconstruction. African Americans participated in politics but hardly dominated or controlled events. They were a majority in only two out of ten state constitutional writing conventions (transplanted northerners were a majority in one). In the state legislatures, only in the lower house in South Carolina did blacks ever constitute a majority; among officeholders, their numbers generally were far fewer than their proportion in the population. Sixteen blacks won seats in Congress before Reconstruction was over, but none was ever elected governor. Only eighteen served in a high state office such as lieutenant governor, treasurer, superintendent of education, or secretary of state. In all, some four hundred blacks served in political office during the Reconstruc-

tion era. Although they never dominated the process, they established a rich tradition of government service and civic activism. Elected officials, such as Robert Smalls in South Carolina, labored tirelessly for cheaper land prices, better healthcare, access to schools, and the enforcement of civil rights for their people. For too long the black politicians of Reconstruction were the forgotten heroes of this seedtime of America's long civil rights movement.

Conservatives also assailed the allies of black Republicans. Their propaganda denounced whites from

CARPETBAGGERS AND SCALAWAGS

the North as "carpetbaggers," greedy crooks planning to pour stolen tax revenues into their sturdy luggage made of carpet material. Immigrants from the North, who held the largest share of Republican offices, were all tarred with this brush.

In fact, most northerners who settled in the South had come seeking business opportunities as schoolteachers or to find a warmer climate and never entered politics. Those who did enter politics generally wanted to democratize the South and to introduce northern ways, such as industry, public education, and the spirit of enterprise. Carpetbaggers' ideals were tested by hard times and ostracism by white southerners.

In addition to tagging northern interlopers as carpetbaggers, conservatives invented the term *scalawag* to discredit any native white southerner who cooperated with the Republicans. A substantial number of southerners did so, including some wealthy and prominent men. Most scalawags, however, were yeoman farmers, men from mountain areas and nonslaveholding districts who had been restive under the Confederacy. They saw that they could benefit from the education and opportunities promoted by Republicans. Banding together with freedmen, they pursued common class interests and hoped to make headway against the power of long-dominant planters. Cooperation even convinced a few white Republicans that "there is but little if any difference in the talents of the two races," as one observed, and that all should have "an equal start." Yet this black-white coalition was vulnerable to the race issue, and most scalawags did not support racial equality.

Taxation was a major problem for the Reconstruction governments. Republicans wanted to maintain

TAX POLICY AND CORRUPTION AS POLITICAL WEDGES

prewar services, repair the war's destruction, stimulate industry, and support important new ventures such as public schools. But the Civil War had destroyed much of the South's tax base. One category of valuable

■ "Ku Klux Klansman," unidentified photographer, c. 1869. This Klansman posed in full regalia, including flowing cuffs on pants, a complete mask, and a club. The Ku Klux Klan offered some whites the opportunity to enact political terror and express their white supremacy in ritualistic, secret ways. Costumes were essential parts of this violent organization. (Gilman Paper Company, New York, NY)

property—slaves—had disappeared entirely. And hundreds of thousands of citizens had lost much of the rest of their property—money, livestock, fences, and buildings—to the war. Thus an increase in taxes (sales, excise, and on property) was necessary even to maintain traditional services, and new ventures required still-higher taxes. Inevitably, Republican tax policies aroused strong opposition, especially among the yeomen.

Corruption was another serious charge levied against the Republicans. Unfortunately, it often was true. Many carpetbaggers and black politicians engaged in fraudulent schemes, sold their votes, or padded expenses, taking part in what scholars recognize was a nationwide surge of corruption in an age ruled by "spoilsmen" (see pages 545–546). Corruption carried no party label, but the Democrats successfully pinned the blame on unqualified blacks and greedy carpetbaggers among southern Republicans.

All these problems hurt the Republicans, whose leaders also allowed factionalism along racial and class lines to undermine party unity. But in *KU KLUX KLAN* many southern states the deathblow came through violence. The Ku Klux Klan (its members altered the Greek word for "circle," *kuklos*), a secret veterans' club that began in Tennessee in 1866, spread through the South, and rapidly evolved into a terrorist organization. Violence against African Americans occurred from the first days of Reconstruction but became far more organized and purposeful after 1867. Klansmen sought to frustrate Reconstruction and keep the freedmen in subjection. Nighttime harassment, whippings, beatings, rapes, and murder became common, and terrorism dominated some counties and regions.

Although the Klan persecuted blacks who stood up for their rights as laborers or individuals, its main purpose was political. Lawless nightriders made active Republicans the target of their attacks. Leading white and black Republicans were killed in several states. After freedmen who worked for a South Carolina scalawag started voting, terrorists visited the plantation and, in the words of one victim, "whipped every . . . [black] man they could lay their hands on." Klansmen also attacked Union League clubs—Republican organizations that mobilized the black vote—and schoolteachers who were aiding the freedmen.

Klan violence was not a spontaneous outburst of racism; very specific social forces shaped and directed it. In North Carolina, for example, Alamance and Caswell Counties were the sites of the worst Klan violence. Slim Republican majorities there rested on cooperation between black voters and white yeomen, particularly those whose Unionism or discontent with the Confederacy had turned them against local Democratic officials. Together, these black and white Republicans had ousted officials long entrenched in power. The wealthy and powerful men in Alamance and Caswell who had lost their accustomed political control were the Klan's county officers and local chieftains. They organized a deliberate campaign of terror, recruiting members and planning atrocities. By intimidation and murder, the Klan weakened the Republican coalition and restored a Democratic majority.

Klan violence injured Republicans across the South. One of every ten black leaders who had been delegates to the 1867–1868 state constitutional conventions was attacked, seven fatally. In one judicial district of North Carolina the Ku Klux Klan was responsible for twelve murders, over seven hundred beatings, and other acts of violence, including rape and arson. A single attack on Alabama Republicans in the town of Eutaw left four blacks dead and fifty-four wounded. In South Carolina five hundred masked Klansmen lynched eight black prisoners at the Union County jail, and in nearby York County the Klan committed at least eleven murders and hundreds of whippings. According to historian Eric Foner, the Klan "made it virtually impossible for Republicans to campaign or vote in large parts of Georgia."

Thus a combination of difficult fiscal problems, Republican mistakes, racial hostility, and terror brought

FAILURE OF RECONSTRUCTION

down the Republican regimes. In most southern states, "Radical Reconstruction" lasted only a few years (see Map 16.1). The most enduring failure of Reconstruction, however, was not political; it was social and economic. Reconstruction failed to alter the South's social structure or its distribution of wealth and power. Without land of their own, freed men and women were at the mercy of white landowners. Armed only with the ballot, freedmen in the South had little chance to effect significant changes.

To reform the southern social order, Congress would have had to redistribute land, but most lawmakers opposed an attack on private property. Radical Republicans like Albion Tourgée, a former Union soldier who moved to North Carolina and was elected a judge, condemned Congress's timidity. Turning the freedman out on his own without protection, said Tourgée, constituted "cheap philanthropy." Indeed, many African Americans believed that during Reconstruction, the North "threw all the Negroes on the world without any way of getting along." Moreover, without careful supervision by Congress, the situation of the freed men and women deteriorated. As the North lost interest, Reconstruction collapsed.

Reconstruction Reversed

*N*ortherners had always been more interested in suppressing rebellion than in aiding southern blacks, and by the early 1870s the North's commitment to bringing about change in the South weakened. Criticism of the southern governments grew, new issues captured public attention, and sentiment for national reconciliation gained popularity in politics. In one southern state after another, Democrats regained control, and they threatened to defeat Republicans in the North as well. Whites in the old Confederacy referred to this decline of Reconstruction as "southern redemption," and during the 1870s, "redeemer" Democrats

■ Albion Winegar Tourgée, a former Union soldier severely wounded at the Battle of Bull Run in 1861, became a carpetbagger and was elected a district judge in North Carolina during Reconstruction. In 1879 he published a best-selling novel, *A Fool's Errand,* which told his own story of travail as a Yankee immigrant in the South confronting the Ku Klux Klan and implementing freedmen's rights.
(Chautauqua County Historical Society, Westfield, N.Y.)

claimed to be the saviors of the South from alleged "black domination" and "carpetbag rule." And for one of only a few times in American history, violence and terror emerged as a tactic in normal politics.

In 1870 and 1871 the violent campaigns of the Ku Klux Klan forced Congress to pass two Enforcement

POLITICAL IMPLICATIONS OF KLAN TERRORISM

Acts and an anti-Klan law. These laws made actions by individuals against the civil and political rights of others a federal criminal offense for the first time. They also provided for election supervisors and permitted martial law and suspension of the writ of habeas corpus to combat murders, beatings, and threats by the Klan. Federal prosecutors used the laws rather selectively. In 1872 and 1873 Mississippi and the Carolinas saw many prosecutions; but in other states where violence flourished, the laws were virtually ignored. Southern juries sometimes refused to convict Klansmen; out of a total of 3,310 cases, only 1,143 ended in convictions. Though many Klansmen (roughly two thousand in South Carolina alone) fled their states to avoid prosecution, and the Klan officially

The Grants' Tour of the World

On May 17, 1877, two weeks after his presidency ended, Ulysses S. Grant and his wife Julia embarked from Philadelphia on a grand tour of the world that would last twenty-six months. Portrayed as a private vacation, the trip was a very public affair. The taint of corruption in Grant's second term could only be dissipated in the air of foreign lands reached by steamship. The small entourage included John Russell Young, a reporter for the *New York Herald* who recorded the journeys in the two-volume illustrated *Around the World with General Grant*. Their expenses were paid by banker friends and by Grant's personal resources accumulated in gifts.

The Grants spent many months in England attending a bewildering array of banquets, one with Queen Victoria. In Newcastle, thousands of workingmen conducted a massive parade in Grant's honor. He was received as the odd American cousin, simple and great, the conqueror and warrior statesmen. In an age that worshipped great men, Grant was viewed as the savior of the American nation, the liberator of slaves, and as a celebrity—a measure of the American presence on the world stage.

On the European continent the pattern continued as every royal or republican head of state hosted the Grants. In Belgium, France, Switzerland, Italy, Russia, Poland, Austria, and Spain the Grants reveled in princely attentions. In Berlin, Grant met Otto von Bismarck, the chancellor of Germany. The two got along well discussing war, world politics, and the abolition of slavery.

The Grants next went to Egypt, where they rode donkeys into remote villages along the Nile, and then traveled by train to the Indian Ocean, where they embarked for India. They encountered British imperialism in full flower in Bombay, and that of the French in Saigon. Northward in Asia the grand excursion went to China and Japan. In Canton, Grant passed before an assemblage of young men who, according to a reporter, "looked upon the barbarian with . . . contempt in their expression, very much as our young men in New York would regard Sitting Bull or Red Cloud." In Japan the Grants had a rare audience with Emperor Mutsuhito in the imperial palace. Grant found Japan "beautiful beyond description," and the receptions were the most formal of all.

"I am both homesick and dread going home," Grant wrote in April 1879. Sailing across the Pacific, the Grants landed in San Francisco in late June. Why had Grant taken such a prolonged trip? Travel itself had its own rewards, but the tour became an unusual political campaign. Grant sought publicity abroad to convince his countrymen back home that they should reelect him president in 1880. But the strategy failed; Grant had developed no compelling issue or reason why Americans should choose him again. He would spend his final years, however, a war hero and a national symbol. No American president would again establish such personal links to the world until Woodrow Wilson at the end of World War I.

■ On their tour of the world, Ulysses and Julia Grant sat here with companions and guides in front of the Great Yppostyle Hall at the Temple of Amon-Ra in Karnak in Luxor, Egypt, 1878. The Grants' extraordinary tour included many such photo opportunities, often depicting the plebeian American president's presence in exotic places with unusual people. Whether he liked it or not, Grant was a world celebrity. (Library of Congress)

disbanded, the threat of violence did not end. Paramilitary organizations known as Rifle Clubs and Red Shirts often took the Klan's place.

Klan terrorism openly defied Congress, yet even on this issue there were ominous signs that the North's commitment to racial justice was fading. Some conservative but influential Republicans opposed the anti-Klan laws. Rejecting other Republicans' arguments that the Thirteenth, Fourteenth, and Fifteenth Amendments had made the federal government the protector of the rights of citizens, these dissenters echoed an old Democratic charge that Congress was infringing on states' rights. Senator Lyman Trumbull of Illinois declared that the states remained "the depositories of the rights of the individual." If Congress could punish crimes like assault or murder, he asked, "what is the need of the State governments?" For years Democrats had complained of "centralization and consolidation"; now some Republicans seemed to agree with them. This opposition foreshadowed a more general revolt within Republican ranks in 1872.

Disenchanted with Reconstruction, a group calling itself the Liberal Republicans bolted the party in 1872 and nominated Horace Greeley, the well-known editor of the *New York Tribune,* for president. The Liberal Republicans were a varied group, including civil service reformers, foes of corruption, and advocates of a lower tariff. Normally such disparate elements would not cooperate with one another, but two popular and widespread attitudes united them: distaste for federal intervention in the South and an elitist desire to let market forces and the "best men" determine events, both in the South and in Washington.

LIBERAL REPUBLICAN REVOLT

The Democrats also gave their nomination to Greeley in 1872. The combination was not enough to defeat Grant, who won reelection, but it reinforced Grant's desire to avoid confrontation with white southerners. Greeley's campaign for North-South reunion, for "clasping hands across the bloody chasm," was a bit premature to win at the polls, but was a harbinger of the future of American politics. Organized Blue-Gray fraternalism (gatherings of Union and Confederate veterans) began as early as 1874 in some states. Grant continued to use military force sparingly and in 1875 refused a desperate request for troops from the governor of Mississippi to quell racial and political terrorism in that state.

Dissatisfaction with Grant's administration grew during his second term. Strong-willed but politically naive, Grant made a series of poor appointments. His secretary of war, his private secretary, and officials in the Treasury and Navy Departments were involved in bribery or tax-cheating scandals. Instead of exposing the corruption, Grant defended the culprits. In 1874, as Grant's popularity and his party's prestige declined, the Democrats recaptured the House of Representatives, signaling the end of the Radical Republican vision of Reconstruction. The Republican Party faced more unfavorable publicity in 1875, when several of Grant's appointees were indicted for corruption.

The effect of Democratic gains in Congress was to weaken legislative resolve on southern issues. Congress had already lifted the political disabilities of the Fourteenth Amendment from many former Confederates. In 1872 it had adopted a sweeping Amnesty Act, which pardoned most of the remaining rebels and left only five hundred barred from political office holding. In 1875 Congress passed a Civil Rights Act, partly as a tribute to the recently deceased Charles Sumner, purporting to guarantee black people equal accommodations in public places, such as inns and theaters, but the bill was watered down and contained no effective provisions for enforcement. (The Supreme Court later struck down this law; see page 551.)

GENERAL AMNESTY

Democrats regained control of four state governments before 1872 and in a total of eight by January 1876 (see Map 16.1). In the North Democrats successfully stressed the failure and scandals of Reconstruction governments. As opinion shifted, a prominent northern historian published an article condemning the enfranchisement of blacks as "a wholesale creation of the most ignorant mass of voters to be found in the civilized world." Many Republicans sensed that their constituents were tiring of southern issues and the legacies of the war. Sectional reconciliation now seemed crucial for commerce. The nation was expanding westward rapidly, and the South was a new frontier for investment.

Both industrialization and immigration were surging, hastening the pace of change in national life. Within only eight years, postwar industrial production increased by an impressive 75 percent. For the first time, nonagricultural workers outnumbered farmers, and only Britain's industrial output was greater than that of the United States. Government financial policies did much to bring about this rapid growth. Low taxes on investment and high tariffs on manufactured goods aided industrialists. With such help, the northern economy quickly recovered its prewar rate of growth. And between 1865 and 1873, 3 million

RECONCILIATION AND INDUSTRIAL EXPANSION

immigrants entered the country, most settling in the industrial cities of the North and West. As the number of foreigners rose, so did suspicion and hostility among native-born white Americans.

Then the Panic of 1873 ushered in over five years of economic contraction. Three million people lost their jobs, and the clash between labor and capital became the major issue of the day (see Chapter 18). Class attitudes diverged, especially in the large cities. Debtors and the unemployed sought easy-money policies to spur economic expansion (workers and farmers desperately needed cash). Businessmen, disturbed by the widespread strikes and industrial violence that accompanied the panic, fiercely defended property rights and demanded "sound money" policies. The chasm between farmers and workers and wealthy industrialists grew ever wider.

Nowhere did the new complexity and violence of American race relations play out so vividly as in the

■ Anti-Chinese prejudice, intimidation, and violence is depicted in this cartoon of the Native American expressing a sense of solidarity with the Chinese immigrant. Both were the subjects of "banishment" in the face of American expansion.   (*Harper's Weekly*, February 8, 1879)

"EVERY DOG" (NO DISTINCTION OF COLOR) "HAS HIS DAY."
RED GENTLEMAN TO YELLOW GENTLEMAN: "Pale face 'fraid you crowd him out, as he did me."

THE WEST, RACE, AND RECONSTRUCTION

West. As the Fourteenth Amendment and other enactments granted to blacks the beginnings of citizenship, other nonwhite peoples faced continued persecution. Across the West, the federal government pursued a policy of containment against Native Americans. In California, where white farmers and ranchers often forced Indians into captive labor, some civilians practiced a more violent form of "Indian hunting." By 1880, thirty years of such violence left an estimated 4,500 California Indians dead at the hands of white settlers.

In Texas and the Southwest, the rhetoric of national expansion still deemed Mexicans and other mixed race Hispanics to be debased, "lazy," and incapable of self-government. And in California and other states of the Far West, thousands of Chinese immigrants became the victims of brutal violence. Few whites had objected to the Chinese who did the dangerous work of building railroads through the Rocky Mountains. But when the Chinese began to compete for urban, industrial jobs, great conflict emerged. Anticoolie clubs appeared in California in the 1870s, seeking laws against Chinese labor, fanning the flames of racism, and organizing vigilante attacks on Chinese workers and the factories that employed them. Western politicians sought white votes by pandering to prejudice, and in 1879 the new California constitution denied the vote to Chinese.

If we view America from coast to coast, and not merely on the North-South axis, the Civil War and Reconstruction years both dismantled racial slavery and fostered a volatile new racial complexity, especially in the West. During the same age when early anthropologists employed elaborate theories of "scientific" racism to determine a hierarchy of racial types, the West was a vast region of racial mixing and conflict. Some African Americans, despite generations of mixture with Native Americans, asserted that they were more like whites than the nomadic, "uncivilized" Indians, while others, like the Creek freedmen of Indian Territory, sought an Indian identity. In Texas, whites, Indians, blacks, and Hispanics had mixed for decades, and by the 1870s forced reconsideration in law and custom of just who was white and who was not.

During Reconstruction, America was undergoing what one historian has called a "reconstruction" of the very idea of "race" itself. And as it did so, tumbling into some of the darkest years of American race relations, the turbulence of the expanding West reinforced a resurgent white supremacy, a new nationalism, and the reconciliation of North and South.

Following the Civil War, pressure for expansion reemerged (see Chapter 22), and in 1867 Secretary of

FOREIGN EXPANSION State William H. Seward arranged a vast addition of territory to the national domain through the purchase of Alaska from the Russian government. Opponents ridiculed Seward's $7.2 million venture, calling Alaska Frigidia, the Polar Bear Garden, and Walrussia. But Seward convinced important congressmen of Alaska's economic potential, and other lawmakers favored the dawning of friendship with Russia.

Also in 1867 the United States took control of the Midway Islands, a thousand miles northwest of Hawai'i. And in 1870 President Grant tried unsuccessfully to annex the Dominican Republic. Seward and his successor, Hamilton Fish, also resolved troubling Civil War grievances against Great Britain. Through diplomacy they arranged a financial settlement of claims on Britain for damage done by the *Alabama* and other cruisers built in England and sold to the Confederacy.

Meanwhile, the Supreme Court played its part in the northern retreat from Reconstruction. During the Civil War the Court had been cautious and inactive. Reaction to the *Dred Scott* decision (1857) had been so violent, and the Union's wartime emergency so great, that the Court avoided interference with government actions. The justices breathed a collective sigh of relief, for example, when legal technicalities prevented them from reviewing the case of Clement Vallandigham, a Democratic opponent of Lincoln's war effort, who had been convicted by a military tribunal of aiding the enemy. But in 1866 a similar case, *Ex parte Milligan,* reached the Court through proper channels.

JUDICIAL RETREAT FROM RECONSTRUCTION

Lambdin P. Milligan of Indiana had plotted to free Confederate prisoners of war and overthrow state governments. For these acts a military court sentenced Milligan, a civilian, to death. Milligan challenged the authority of the military tribunal, claiming that he had a right to a civil trial. The Supreme Court declared that military trials were illegal when civil courts were open and functioning, and its language indicated that the Court intended to reassert its authority.

In the 1870s the Court successfully renewed its challenge to Congress's actions when it narrowed the meaning and effectiveness of the Fourteenth Amendment. The *Slaughter-House* cases (1873) began in 1869, when the Louisiana legislature granted one company a monopoly on the slaughtering of livestock in New Orleans. Rival butchers in the city promptly sued. Their attorney, former Supreme Court justice John A. Campbell, argued that Louisiana had violated the rights of some of its citizens in favor of others. The Fourteenth Amendment, Campbell contended, had revolutionized the constitutional system by bringing individual rights under federal protection. Campbell thus articulated an original goal of the Republican Party: to nationalize civil rights and guard them from state interference.

But in the *Slaughter-House* decision, the Supreme Court dealt a stunning blow to the scope and vitality of the Fourteenth Amendment. Refusing to accept Campbell's argument, the Court declared state citizenship and national citizenship separate. National citizenship involved only matters such as the right to travel freely from state to state and to use the navigable waters of the nation, and only these narrow rights, held the Court, were protected by the Fourteenth Amendment.

The Supreme Court also concluded that the butchers who sued had not been deprived of their rights or property in violation of the due-process clause of the amendment. Shrinking from a role as "perpetual censor upon all legislation of the States, on the civil rights of their own citizens," the Court's majority declared that the framers of the recent amendments had not intended to "destroy" the federal system, in which the states exercised "powers for domestic and local government, including the regulation of civil rights." Thus the justices severely limited the amendment's potential for securing and protecting the rights of black citizens—its original intent.

The next day the Court decided *Bradwell v. Illinois,* a case in which Myra Bradwell, a female attorney, had been denied the right to practice law in Illinois on account of her gender. Pointing to the Fourteenth Amendment, Bradwell's attorneys contended that the state had unconstitutionally abridged her "privileges and immunities" as a citizen. The Supreme Court rejected her claim, alluding to women's traditional role in the home.

In 1876 the Court weakened the Reconstruction era amendments even further by emasculating the enforcement clause of the Fourteenth Amendment and revealing deficiencies inherent in the Fifteenth Amendment. In *U.S. v. Cruikshank* the Court overruled the conviction under the 1870 Enforcement Act of Louisiana whites who had attacked a meeting of blacks and conspired to deprive them of their rights. The justices ruled that the Fourteenth Amendment did not give the federal government power to act against these whites. The duty of protecting citizens' equal rights, the Court said, "rests alone with the States." Such judicial conservatism had a profound impact down through the next century, blunting the revolutionary potential in the Civil War amendments.

As the 1876 elections approached, most political observers saw that the nation was increasingly focused on

DISPUTED ELECTION OF 1876 AND THE COMPROMISE OF 1877

economic issues and that the North was no longer willing to pursue the goals of Reconstruction. The results of a disputed presidential election confirmed this fact. Samuel J. Tilden, the Democratic governor of New York, ran strongly in the South and needed only one more electoral vote to triumph over Rutherford B. Hayes, the Republican nominee. Nineteen electoral votes from Louisiana, South Carolina, and Florida (the only southern states not yet under Democratic rule) were disputed; both Democrats and Republicans claimed to have won in those states despite fraud committed by their opponents. One vote from Oregon was undecided because of a technicality (see Map 16.2).

To resolve this unprecedented situation, on which the Constitution gave little guidance, Congress established a fifteen-member electoral commission. In the interest of impartiality, membership on the commission was to be balanced between Democrats and Republicans. Since the Republicans held the majority in Congress, they prevailed, 8 to 7, on every attempt to count the returns, with commission members voting along strict party lines. Hayes would become president if Congress accepted the commission's findings.

Congressional acceptance was not certain. Democrats controlled the House and could filibuster to block action on the vote. Many citizens worried that the nation had entered a major constitutional crisis and would slip once again into civil war, as some southerners vowed, "Tilden or Fight." The crisis was resolved when Democrats acquiesced in the election of Hayes based on a "deal" cut in a Washington hotel between Hayes's supporters and southerners who wanted federal aid to railroads, internal improvements, federal patronage, and removal of troops from southern states. Northern and southern Democrats simply decided they could not win and did not contest the election of a Republican who was not going to continue Reconstruction policies in the South. Thus Hayes became president, inaugurated privately inside the White House to avoid any threat of violence, southerners relished their promises of economic aid, and Reconstruction was unmistakably over.

Southern Democrats rejoiced, but African Americans grieved over the betrayal of their hopes for equality.

BETRAYAL OF BLACK RIGHTS

Tens of thousands considered leaving the South, where real freedom was no longer a possibility. "[We asked] whether it was possible we could stay

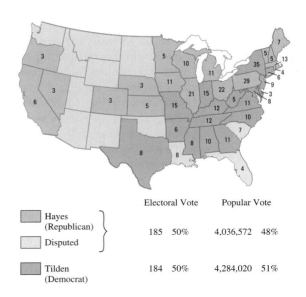

Electoral Vote   **Popular Vote**

Hayes (Republican)

Disputed

     185   50%   4,036,572   48%

Tilden (Democrat)   184   50%   4,284,020   51%

Map 16.2   Presidential Election of 1876 and the Compromise of 1877

In 1876 a combination of solid southern support and Democratic gains in the North gave Samuel Tilden the majority of popular votes, but Rutherford B. Hayes won the disputed election in the electoral college, after a deal satisfied Democratic wishes for an end to Reconstruction.

under a people who had held us in bondage," said Henry Adams. In South Carolina, Louisiana, Mississippi, and other southern states, thousands gathered up their possessions and, like Adams, migrated to Kansas. They were called Exodusters, disappointed people still searching for their share in the American dream. Even in Kansas they met disillusionment, as the welcome extended by the state's governor soon gave way to hostility among much of the white population.

Blacks now had to weigh their options, which were not much wider than they had ever been. The Civil War had brought emancipation, and Reconstruction had guaranteed their rights under law. But events and attitudes in larger white America were foreboding. In a Fourth of July speech in Washington, D.C., in 1875, Frederick Douglass anticipated this predicament. He reflected anxiously on the American centennial to be celebrated the following year. The nation, Douglass feared, would "lift to the sky its million voices in one grand Centennial hosanna of peace and good will to all the white race . . . from gulf to lakes and from sea to sea." Douglass looked back on fifteen years of unparalleled change for his people and worried about the hold of white supremacy on America's historical memory: "If war among the whites brought peace and liberty to the blacks, what will peace among the whites bring?" Douglass's question would echo down through American political culture for decades.

Summary

*R*econstruction left a contradictory record. It was an era of tragic aspirations and failures, but also of unprecedented legal, political, and social change. The Union victory brought about an increase in federal power, stronger nationalism, sweeping federal intervention in the southern states, and landmark amendments to the Constitution. But northern commitment to make these changes endure had eroded, and the revolution remained unfinished. The mystic sense of promise for new lives and liberties among the freedpeople, demonstrated in that first Decoration Day in Charleston, had fallen in a new, if temporary, kind of ruin.

The North embraced emancipation, black suffrage, and constitutional alterations strengthening the central government. But it did so to defeat the rebellion and secure the peace. As the pressure of these crises declined, strong underlying continuities emerged and placed their mark on Reconstruction. The American people and the courts maintained a preference for state authority and a distrust of federal power. The ideology of free labor dictated that property should be respected and that individuals should be self-reliant. Racism endured and transformed into the even more virulent forms of Klan terror and theories of black degeneration. Concern for the human rights of African Americans was strongest when their plight threatened to undermine the interests of whites, and reform frequently had less appeal than moneymaking in an individualistic, enterprising society.

As Reconstruction policies sought for a time to remake the South, industrialization challenged American society and values. How would the country develop its immense resources in an increasingly interconnected national economy? How would farmers, industrial workers, immigrants, and capitalists fit into the new social system? Industrialization not only promised a higher standard of living but wrought increased exploitation of labor. Moreover, industry increased the nation's power and laid the foundation for an enlarged American role in international affairs. The American imagination again turned to the conquest of new frontiers.

In the wake of the Civil War Americans faced two profound tasks—the achievement of healing and the dispensing of justice. Both had to occur, but they never developed in historical balance. Making sectional reunion compatible with black freedom and equality overwhelmed the imagination in American political culture, and the nation still faced much of this dilemma more than a century later.

LEGACY FOR A PEOPLE AND A NATION
The Fourteenth Amendment

Before the Civil War, no definition of civil rights existed in America. Reconstruction legislation, especially the Fourteenth Amendment, changed that forever. Approved by Congress in 1866, and ratified by 1868, the Fourteenth Amendment enshrined in the Constitution the ideas of birthright citizenship and equal rights. The Fourteenth Amendment was designed to secure and protect the rights of the freedpeople. But over time, the "equal protection of the law" clause became one of the most important and malleable provisions in the Constitution. It has been used at times to support the rights of states, cities, corporations, immigrants, women, religious organizations, gays and lesbians, students, and labor unions. It has advanced both tolerance and intolerance, affirmative action and anti-affirmative-action programs. It provides the legal wellspring for the generations-old civil rights movement in the United States.

The amendment as originally written required individuals to pursue grievances through private litigation, alleging state denial of a claimed federal right. At first the Supreme Court interpreted it conservatively, especially on racial matters, and by 1900 the idea of color-blind liberty in America was devastated by segregation laws, disfranchisement, and unpunished mob violence.

But Progressive reformers used the equal-protection clause to advocate government support of health, union organizing, municipal housing, a progressive income tax, and the protection of woman and child laborers. In the 1920s and 1930s, a judicial defense of civil liberties and free speech took hold, especially from Justice Louis Brandeis. The Supreme Court expanded the amendment's guarantee of equality by a series of decisions upholding the rights of immigrant groups to resist "forced Americanization," especially Catholics in their creation of parochial schools.

And, from its inception in 1910, the NAACP waged a long campaign to reveal the inequality of racial segregation in schooling and every other kind of public facility. Led by Charles Houston and Thurgood Marshall, this epic legal battle culminated in the *Brown v. Board of Education* desegregation decision of 1954.

In the multilayered Civil Rights Act of 1964, the equal-protection tradition was reenshrined into American law. Since 1964 Americans have lived in a society where the Fourteenth Amendment's legacy is the engine of expanded liberty for women and all minorities, as well as a political battleground for defining the nature and limits of human equality, and for redistributing justice long denied.

The **history companion** *powered by Eduspace®*

Your primary source for interactive quizzes, exercises, and more to help you learn efficiently.
http://history.college.hmco.com/students

THE DEVELOPMENT OF THE WEST 1877–1900

*I*n 1893 a young historian named Frederick Jackson Turner delivered a stunning lecture at the Columbian Exposition in Chicago. In it, Turner expounded a theory that would preoccupy the textbooks of high school and college students for several generations. Titled "The Significance of the Frontier in American History," the paper argued that the existence of "free land, its continuous recession, and the advancement of American settlement westward" had created a distinctively American spirit of democracy and egalitarianism. The conquest of a succession of frontier Wests, in other words, explained American progress and character.

At a covered arena across the street from this world's fair, the folk character Buffalo Bill Cody staged two performances daily of an extravaganza called "The Wild West." Though Cody also dramatized the conquest of frontiers and the creation of an American identity, his perspective differed markedly from Turner's. While Turner described a relatively peaceful settlement of largely empty western land, Cody portrayed violent conquest of territory occupied by savage Indians. Turner's heroes were persevering farmers who tamed the wilderness with axes and plows. Buffalo Bill's heroes were rugged scouts who braved danger and defeated Indians with firepower and blood. Turner used images of log cabins, wagon trains, and wheat fields to argue that the frontier fashioned a new, progressive race. Cody, who used a cast of actual Indians and soldiers (plus himself) to stage scenes of Indian attacks and clashes between native warriors and white cavalry, depicted the West as a place of brutal aggression and heroic victory.

Turner's thesis and Cody's spectacle contained exaggerations and inaccuracies, yet both Turner and Cody were to some degree correct. The American West inspired material and cultural progress, and it also witnessed the forceful domination of one group of humans over another and over the environment. Both

◀ Thomas Moran (1837-1926) painted numerous scenes like this one of a lone Indian dwarfed by nature. Yet the West's raw bounty was luring countless white settlers even as Moran depicted the region's wilderness and immensity. (*Mist in Kanab Canyon, Utah*, Thomas Moran, 1892, oil, Smithsonian American Art Museum, Bequest of Mrs. Bessie B. Croffut)

C H R O N O L O G Y

1862 • Homestead Act grants free land to citizens who live on and improve the land
   • Morrill Land Grant Act gives states public land to finance agricultural and industrial colleges

1864 • Chivington's militia massacres Black Kettle's Cheyennes at Sand Creek

1869 • First transcontinental railroad completed, with connection at Promontory Point, Utah

1872 • Yellowstone becomes first national park

1873 • Barbed wire invented, enabling western farmers to enclose and protect fields cheaply

1876 • Sioux annihilate Custer's federal troops at Little Big Horn

1877 • Nez Percé Indians under Young Joseph surrender to U.S. troops

1878 • Timber and Stone Act allows citizens to buy timberland cheaply but also enables large companies to acquire huge tracts of forest land

1879 • Carlisle School for Indians established in Pennsylvania

1880–81 • Manypenny's *Our Indian Wards* and Jackson's *A Century of Dishonor* influence public conscience about poor government treatment of Indians

1881 • Shootout at OK Corral between Clantons and Earps

1881–82 • Chinese Exclusion Acts prohibit Chinese immigration to the United States

1883 • National time zones standardized

1884 • U.S. Supreme Court first defines Indians as wards under government protection

1887 • Dawes Severalty Act ends communal ownership of Indian lands and grants land allotments to individual Native American families
   • Hatch Act provides for agricultural experiment stations in every state
   • California passes law permitting farmers to organize into districts

1887–88 • Devastating winter on Plains destroys countless livestock and forces farmers into economic hardship

1890 • Final suppression of Plains Indians by U.S. Army at Wounded Knee
   • Census Bureau announces closing of the frontier
   • Yosemite National Park established

1892 • Muir helps found Sierra Club

1893 • Turner presents "frontier thesis" at Columbian Exposition

1896 • Rural Free Delivery made available

1902 • Newlands Reclamation Act passed

Turner and Cody believed that by the 1890s the frontier era had come to an end. In fact, Turner's essay had been sparked by an announcement from the superintendent of the 1890 census that "at present the unsettled area [of the West] has been so broken into by isolated bodies of settlement that there can be hardly said to be a frontier line." Over time, Turner's theory was abandoned (even by Turner himself) as too simplistic, and Buffalo Bill was relegated to the gallery of rogues and showmen (though he subsequently became an advocate of irrigated farming). Even so, both Wests that they depicted persist in the romance of American history, while they obscured the more complex real story of western development in the late nineteenth century.

One fact is certain. Much of the West was never empty, and its inhabitants utilized its resources in quite different ways. Indians had managed the environment and sustained their needs long before white settlers arrived on the scene. On the Plains, for example, Pawnee Indians planted crops in the spring, left their fields in summer to hunt buffalo, then returned for harvesting. They sometimes battled with Cheyennes and Arapahos, who wanted hunting grounds and crops for their own purposes. Pawnee technology was simple. Though they sometimes splurged feasting on buffalo, they survived by developing and using natural resources in limited ways. Concepts of private property and profit had little meaning for them.

For white Americans, however, expanses of land and water were assets to be utilized for economic gain. As whites settled the West in the late nineteenth century, they exploited the environment for profit far more extensively than did Indians. They excavated deep into the earth to remove valuable minerals, felled forests to construct homes and other buildings, pierced the countryside with railroads to carry goods and link markets, and dammed rivers and plowed soil with machines to grow crops. Their goal was not mere survival; it included buying, selling, and opening markets nationally and internationally through corporate big business. As they transformed the landscape, the triumph of their market economies transformed the entire nation.

The West, which by 1870 referred to the expanse between the Mississippi River and the Pacific Ocean, actually consisted of several regions and a variety of economic potential. Abundant rainfall along the northern

Pacific Coast fed huge forests. Farther south into California, woodlands and grasslands provided fertile valleys suitable for vegetable fields and orange groves. Eastward, from the Cascades and Sierra Nevada to the Rocky Mountains, is a series of deserts and plateaus known as the Basin and Range province, where gold, silver, and other minerals lay buried. East of the Rockies, the Great Plains divided into a semiarid western side of few trees and tough buffalo grass and an eastern sector of ample rainfall and tall grasses. The Plains could support grain crops and livestock.

Much of the West had long been the scene of great migrations. Before contact with whites, Indian peoples had moved around and through the region. As they searched for food and shelter, they warred, traded, and negotiated with one another. In parts of the Southwest, natives built towns, farms, and ranches. After the Civil War, white people flooded into the West, overwhelming the native peoples. Between 1870 and 1890, the population living in the region swelled from 7 million to nearly 17 million.

The West's abundance of exploitable land and raw materials filled white Americans with faith that anyone eager and persistent enough could succeed. But this confidence rested on a belief that white people were somehow special, and individual advantage often asserted itself at the expense of people of color and the poor, as well as the environment. Though eventually some people came to realize the benefits of protecting the environment, Americans rarely thought about conserving resources because there always seemed to be more territory to develop and bring into the market economy.

By 1890 farms, ranches, mines, towns, and cities could be found in almost every corner of the present-day continental United States. Though of symbolic importance, the fading of the frontier had little direct impact on people's behavior, for vast stretches of land remained unsettled. Pioneers who failed in one locale rarely perished; they moved on and tried again somewhere else. Although life in the West could be challenging, a surplus of seemingly uninhabited land gave Americans a feeling that they would always have a second chance. It was this belief in an infinity of second chances, more than Turner's theory of frontier democracy or Cody's reenactments of heroic battles, that left a deep imprint on the American character. ■

The Economic Activities of Native Peoples

*H*istorians once defined the American frontier as "the edge of the unused," implying, as Frederick Jackson Turner had, that the frontier disappeared once white migrants arrived to occupy supposedly open land for farming or the building of cities. Scholars now recognize that Native Americans settled and developed the West before other Americans migrated there. Neither passive nor powerless in the face of nature, Indians had been shaping their environment—for better and for worse—for centuries. Nevertheless, almost all native economic systems weakened in the late nineteenth century. Why and how did these declines happen?

Western Indian cultures varied. Some Indians lived in permanent settlements; others moved their camps and villages. Seldom completely isolated, most Indians were participants and recipients in a large-scale flow of goods, culture, language, and disease carried by migrating bands that moved from one region to another. Regardless of their type of settlement, all Indians based their economies to differing degrees on four activities: crop growing; livestock raising; hunting, fishing, and gathering; and trading and raiding. Corn was the most common crop; sheep and horses, acquired from Spanish colonizers and from other Indians, were the livestock; and buffalo (American bison) were the primary prey of hunts. Indians raided one another for food, tools, hides, and horses, which in turn they used in trading with other Indians and with whites. They also attacked to avenge wrongs and to displace competitors from hunting grounds. To achieve their standards of living, Indians tried to balance their economic systems. When a buffalo hunt failed, they subsisted on crops. When crops failed, they could still hunt buffalo and steal food and horses in a raid or trade livestock and furs for necessities.

SUBSISTENCE CULTURES

For Indians on the Great Plains, whether they were nomads such as the Lakotas or village dwellers such as the Pawnees, everyday life focused on the buffalo. They cooked and preserved buffalo meat; fashioned hides into clothing, shoes, and blankets; used sinew for thread and bowstrings; and carved tools from bones and horns. Buffalo were so valuable that the Pawnees and Lakotas often came into conflict over access to herds. The Plains Indians also depended on horses, which they used for transportation and hunting, and as symbols of wealth. To provide food for their herds, Pawnees and other Plains Indians altered the environment by periodically setting fire to tall-grass prairies. The fires burned away dead plants, facilitating the growth of new grass in the spring so horses could feed all summer.

In the Southwest, Indians were herders and placed great value on sheep, goats, and horses. Old Man Hat, a Navajo, explained, "The herd is money. . . . You know that you have some good clothing; the sheep gave you that. And you've just eaten different kinds of food; the sheep gave that food to you. Everything comes from the sheep." He was not speaking of money in a business sense, though. To Navajos, the herds provided status and security. Like many Indians, the Navajos emphasized generosity and distrusted private property and wealth. Within the family, sharing was expected; outside the family, gifts and reciprocity governed personal relations. southwestern Indians, too, altered the environment, building elaborate irrigation systems to maximize use of scarce water supplies.

What buffalo were to the Plains Indians and sheep were to southwestern Indians, salmon were to Indians of the Northwest. Before the mid-nineteenth century, the Columbia River and its tributaries supported the densest population of native peoples in North America, all of whom fished the river for salmon in the summer and stored dried fish for the winter. The Clatsops, Klamathets, and S'Klallam applied their technology of stream diversion, platform construction over the water, and special baskets to better harvest fish. Like natives of other regions, many of these Indians traded for horses, buffalo robes, beads, cloth, and knives.

On the Plains and in parts of the Southwest, this native world began to dissolve after 1850 when whites entered and competed with Indians for access to and control over natural resources. Perceiving buffalo and Indians as hindrances to their ambitions, whites endeavored to eliminate both. Railroads sponsored buffalo hunts in which eastern sportsmen shot at the bulky targets from slow-moving trains. The army refused to enforce treaties that reserved hunting grounds for exclusive Indian use. Some hunters collected from $1 to $3 from tanneries for hides that were sent east to be used mainly as belts to drive industrial machinery; others did not even stop to pick up their kill.

SLAUGHTER OF BUFFALO

Unbeknownst to both Indians and whites, however, a complex combination of circumstances had already doomed the buffalo before the slaughter of the late 1800s. Indians themselves were contributing to the depletion of the herds by increasing their kills, especially to obtain hides for trade with whites and other Indians. Also, a period of generally dry years in the 1840s and 1850s had forced Indians to set up camps in more fertile river basins, where they competed with buffalo for space and water. As a result, the bison were pushed out of important grazing territory and faced threats of starvation.

■ The horses, sometimes numbering more than one hundred, and the women and children, usually twenty or thirty, were a liability as well as a help to a Plains Indian camp. The horses competed with buffalo for valuable pasturage, and the women and children made camps vulnerable when white soldiers attacked. (Denver Public Library, Western History Division)

When whites arrived on the Plains, they too sought to settle in the same river basin areas, thereby further forcing buffalo away from nutritious grasslands. At the same time, lethal animal diseases such as anthrax and brucellosis, brought in by white-owned livestock, decimated buffalo, many of whom had been weakened by malnutrition and drought. Increased numbers of horses, oxen, and sheep owned by white newcomers, as well as by some Indians, also upset the bison's grazing patterns by devouring grasses that buffalo depended on at certain times of the year. In sum, a convergence of human and environmental shocks created vulnerability among the buffalo to which the mass killing only struck the final blow. By the 1880s only a few hundred remained of the 25 million bison estimated on the Plains in 1820.

In the Northwest, the basic wild source of Indian food supply, salmon, suffered a fate similar to that of the buffalo, but for different reasons. *DECLINE OF SALMON* White commercial fishermen and canneries moved into the Columbia and Willamette River valleys during the 1860s and 1870s, and by the 1880s they had greatly diminished the salmon runs on the Columbia. Increasing numbers of salmon running up river to spawn were being caught before they laid their eggs, so the fish supply was not being replenished. By the twentieth century, the construction of dams on the river and its tributaries further impeded the salmon's ability to reproduce. The government protected Indian fishing rights on the river, and hatcheries helped restore some of the fish supply, but the need for electrical power from dams, combined with depletion of the salmon from overfishing and pollution, curtailed the supply of this resource in the Northwest.

The Transformation of Native Cultures

Buffalo slaughter and salmon reduction undermined Indian subsistence, but a unique mix of human demography contributed as well. For most of the nineteenth century, the white population that migrated into western lands inhabited by Indians was overwhelmingly young and male. In 1870 white men outnumbered white women by three to two in California, two to one in Colorado, and two to one in Dakota Territory. By 1900, preponderances of men remained throughout these places. Most of these males were unmarried and in their twenties and thirties, the stage of life when they were most prone to violent behavior. In other words, the whites that Indians were most

likely to come into contact with first were explorers, traders, trappers, soldiers, prospectors, and cowboys—almost all of whom possessed guns and had few qualms about using their weapons against animals and humans who got in their way.

Moreover, these men subscribed to prevailing attitudes that Indians were primitive, lazy, devious, and cruel. Such contempt made exploiting and killing natives all the easier, and violence was often "justified" by claims of preempting threats to life and property. When Indians raided white settlements, they sometimes mutilated bodies, burned buildings, and kidnapped women, acts that were embellished in campfire stories, pamphlets, and popular fiction—all of which reinforced images of Indians as savages. Among the bachelor society of saloons and cabins, men boasted of their exploits in Indian fighting and showed off trophies of scalps and other body parts taken from victims.

Indian warriors also were young, armed, and prone to violence. Valuing bravery and vengeance, they boasted of fighting white interlopers. But Indian communities contrasted with those of whites in that they contained excesses of women and children, making native bands less mobile and therefore vulnerable to attack. They also were vulnerable to the bad habits of the bachelor white society. Indians copied white behavior of bingeing on cheap whiskey and indulging in prostitution. The syphilis and gonorrhea that Indian men contracted from Indian women infected by whites killed many and reduced the ability of natives to reproduce, a consequence that their population, already declining from smallpox and other diseases spread by whites, could not afford. Thus the age and gender structure of the white frontier population, combined with attitudes of racial contempt, created a further threat to Indian existence in the West.

Government policy reinforced efforts to remove Indians from the path of white ambitions. North American natives were organized not so much *LACK OF NATIVE UNITY* into tribes, as whites believed, but rather into hundreds of bands and confederacies in the Plains and into villages in the Southwest and Northwest. Some two hundred distinct languages and dialects separated these groups and made it difficult for Indians to unite against white invaders. Although a language group could be defined as a tribe, separate bands and clans within each language group had their own leaders, and seldom did a tribal chief hold widespread power. Moreover, bands usually spent more time quarreling among themselves than with white settlers, and sometimes bands from completely different peoples, such as Kiowas and Comanches in the southern plains, lived together.

Nevertheless, the U.S. government needed some way of categorizing Indians so as to fashion a policy toward

TERRITORIAL TREATIES

them. It did so by imputing more meaning to tribal organization than was warranted. After the Treaty of Greenville in 1795, American officials considered Indian tribes to be separate nations with which they could make treaties that ensured peace and defined boundaries between Indian and white lands. But the U.S. government did not understand that a chief or chiefs who agreed to a treaty did not speak for all members of a band and that the group would not necessarily abide by an agreement. Moreover, whites seldom accepted treaties as guarantees of Indians' future land rights. In the Northwest, whites considered treaties pro-

■ Using buffalo hides to fashion garments, Indians often exhibited artistic skills in decorating their apparel. This Ute Indian hide dress shows symbolic as well as aesthetic representations.   (Denver Art Museum)

tecting Indians' fishing rights on the Columbia River to be nuisances and ousted Indians from the best locations so they could use mechanical devices that harvested thousands of fish a day. On the Plains, whites assumed that they could settle wherever they wished, and they rarely hesitated to commandeer choice farmland along river basins. As white settlers pressed into Indian territories, treaties made one week were violated the next.

From the 1860s to the 1880s, the federal government tried to force western Indians onto reservations,

RESERVATION POLICY

where, it was thought, they could be "civilized." Reservations usually consisted of those areas of a group's previous territory that were least desirable to whites. When assigning Indians to such parcels, the government promised protection from white encroachment and agreed to provide food, clothing, and other necessities.

The reservation policy helped make way for the market economy. In the early years of contact in the West, trade had benefited both Indians and whites and had taken place on a nearly equal footing, much as it had between eastern Indians and whites in the years before the American Revolution. Indians had acquired clothing, guns, and horses in return for furs, jewelry, and, sometimes, military assistance to whites against other Indians. In the West, however, whites' needs and economic power grew disproportionate to Indians' needs and power. Indians became more dependent, and whites increasingly dictated what was to be traded and on what terms. For example, white traders persuaded Navajo weavers in the Southwest to produce heavy rugs suitable for eastern customers and to adopt new designs and colors to boost sales. Meanwhile, Navajos raised fewer crops and were forced to buy food because the market economy undermined their subsistence agriculture. Soon they were selling land and labor to whites as well, and their dependency made it easier to force them onto reservations.

Reservation policy had degrading consequences. First, Indians had no say over their own affairs on reservations. Supreme Court decisions in 1884 and 1886 defined them as wards (falling, like helpless children, under government protection) and denied them the right to become U.S. citizens. Thus they were unprotected by the Fourteenth and Fifteenth Amendments, which had extended to African Americans the privileges and legal protections of citizenship. Second, pressure from white farmers, miners, and herders who continually sought Indian lands made it difficult for the government to preserve reservations intact. Third, the government ignored native history, even combining on the same reservation

Indian bands that habitually had waged war against each other. Rather than serving as civilizing communities, reservations weakened every aspect of Indian life, except the resolve of some to survive.

NATIVE RESISTANCE

Not all Indians succumbed to market forces and reservation restrictions. Pawnees in the Midwest, for example, resisted the disadvantageous deals that white traders tried to impose on them. And some natives tried to preserve their cultures even as they became dependent on whites. Pawnees, for example, agreed to leave their Nebraska homelands for a reservation in the hope that they could hunt buffalo and grow corn in their own way.

INDIAN WARS

As they had done earlier in the East, whites responded to western Indian recalcitrance and defiance with organized military aggression. In 1864, for example, in order to eliminate Indians who blocked white ambitions in the Sand Creek region of Colorado, a militia force led by Methodist minister John Chivington attacked a Cheyenne band under Black Kettle, killing almost every Indian. In 1877 four detachments of troops, aided by Crow and Cheyenne scouts, chased 800 Nez Percé Indians over rugged terrain in the Northwest, finally surrounding and killing many before one of their leaders, Young Joseph, surrendered. In 1879 4,000 U.S. soldiers forced a surrender from Utes, who already had given up most of their ancestral territory in western Colorado but were resisting further concessions.

The most infamous of Indian battles occurred in June 1876 when 2,500 Lakotas led by Chiefs Rain-in-the-Face, Sitting Bull, and Crazy Horse surrounded and annihilated 256 government troops led by the rash Colonel George A. Custer near the Little Big Horn River in southern Montana. Though Indians consistently demonstrated military skill in such battles, shortages of supplies and relentless pursuit by U.S. soldiers, including all–African American units of Union Army veterans called Buffalo Soldiers (so named by the Cheyenne and Comanche they fought), eventually overwhelmed armed Indian resistance. Native Americans were not so much conquered in battle as they were harassed and starved into submission.

REFORM OF INDIAN POLICY

In the 1870s and 1880s, officials and reformers sought more peaceful means of dealing with western natives. Instead of battling Indians as foreign enemies, whites would "civilize" and "uplift" them through landholding and education. This meant changing their identities and outlawing customs deemed by the government to be "savage and barbarous." In this

■ Plains Indians did not write books or letters as whites did, but they did tell stories and spread news through art. They painted scenes on hides and notebooks to represent events such as this one, which depicts the Indians' annihilation of General George A. Custer's soldiers at Little Big Horn in 1876. (Smithsonian Institution, Western History Division)

regard, the United States copied imperialist policies of other nations such as the French, who banned native religious ceremonies in their Pacific island colonies, and the British, who jailed African religious leaders. The United States government determined to persuade Indians to abandon their traditional cultures and adopt values of the American work ethic: ambition, thrift, and materialism. At the same time, other forces argued for sympathetic—and sometimes patronizing—treatment. Reform treatises, such as George Manypenny's *Our Indian Wards* (1880) and Helen Hunt Jackson's *A Century of Dishonor* (1881), and unfavorable comparison with Canada's management of Indian affairs aroused the American conscience. Canada had granted native peoples the rights of British subjects and proceeded more slowly than the United States in efforts to acculturate Indians. A high rate of intermarriage between Indians and Canadian whites also promoted smoother relations.

In the United States, the two most active Indian reform organizations were the Women's National Indian Association (WNIA) and the Indian Rights Association (IRA). The WNIA, composed mainly of white women who sought to use domestic skills to help people in need, urged gradual assimilation of Indians. The IRA, which was more influential but numbered few Native Americans among its members, supported citizenship and landholding by individual Indians. Most reformers believed Indians were culturally inferior to whites and assumed Indians could succeed economically only if they embraced middle-class values of diligence and education.

Reformers particularly deplored Indians' sexual division of labor. Women seemed to do all the work—tending crops, raising children, cooking, curing hides, making tools and clothes—while being servile to men, who hunted but were otherwise idle. Ignoring the fact that white men sometimes mistreated white women, groups such as the WNIA and IRA wanted Indian men to bear more responsibilities, to treat Indian women more respectfully, and to resemble male heads of white middle-class households. But when Indian men and women adopted the model of white society, in which women were supposed to be submissive and private, Indian women lost much of the economic independence and power over daily life that they once had.

In 1887 Congress reversed its reservation policy and passed the Dawes Severalty Act. The act, which achieved a goal recommended by reformers, authorized dissolution of community-owned Indian property and granted land allotments to individual Indian families. The government held that land in trust for twenty-five years, so families could not sell their allot-

DAWES SEVERALTY ACT

ments. The law also awarded citizenship to all who accepted allotments (an act of Congress in 1906 delayed citizenship for those Indians who had not yet taken their allotment). It also entitled the government to sell unallocated land to whites.

Indian policy, as carried out by the Interior Department, now took on two main features, both of which aimed at assimilating Indians into white American forms of culture. First and foremost, as required by the Dawes Act, the federal government distributed reservation land to individual families in the belief that the American institution of private property would create useful citizens and integrate Indians into the larger society. As one official stated, the goal was to "weaken and destroy (Indians') tribal relations and individualize them by giving each a separate home and having them subsist by industry." Second, officials believed that Indians would abandon their "barbaric" habits more quickly if their children were educated in boarding schools away from the reservations.

The Dawes Act reflected a Euro-American and Christian world-view, an earnest but narrow belief that a society of families headed by men was the most desired model. Government agents and reformers were joined by professional educators who viewed schools as tools to create a patriotic, industrious citizenry. Using the model of Hampton Institute, founded in Virginia in 1869 for the education of newly freed slaves, educators helped establish the Carlisle School in Pennsylvania in 1879, which served as the flagship of the government's Indian school system. In keeping with Euro-American custom, the boarding schools imposed white-defined sex roles: boys were taught farming and carpentry while girls learned sewing, cleaning, and cooking.

In 1890 the government made one last show of force. With active resistance having been suppressed, some Lakotas and other groups turned to the religion of the Ghost Dance as a spiritual means of preserving native culture. Inspired by a Paiute prophet named Wovoka, the Ghost Dance involved movement in a circle until the dancers reached a trancelike state and envisioned dead ancestors. Some dancers believed these ancestral visitors heralded a day when buffalo would return to the Plains and all elements of white civilization, including guns and whiskey, would be buried. The Ghost Dance expressed this messianic vision in a ritual involving several days of dancing and meditation.

GHOST DANCE

Ghost Dancers forswore violence but appeared aggressive when they donned sacred shirts that they believed would repel the white man's bullets. As the religion spread, government agents became alarmed about the

■ White reformers believed children at Indian boarding schools needed to adopt "civilized" dress as necessary to their education. Thus the eleven Chirachua Apache girls and boys who were wearing native dress when they reached the Carlisle (Pennsylvania) School in November 1883 (top) had their hair cut and wore uniforms and dresses for the (bottom) photograph taken after their supposed transformation four months later. (Both photos, Cumberland County Historical Society, Carlisle, PA)

possibility of renewed Indian uprisings. Charging that the cult was anti-Christian, they began arresting Ghost Dancers. Late in 1890, the government sent the Seventh Cavalry, Custer's old regiment, to detain some Lakotas moving toward Pine Ridge, South Dakota. Though the Indians were starving and seeking shelter, the army assumed they were armed for revolt. Overtaking the band at a creek called Wounded Knee, the troops massacred an estimated three hundred men, women, and children in the snow.

The Dawes Act effectively accomplished what whites wanted and Indians feared: it reduced native control over land. Eager speculators induced Indians to sell their newly acquired property, in spite of federal safeguards against such practices. Between 1887 and the 1930s, Indian landholdings dwindled from 138 million acres to 52 million. Land-grabbing whites were particularly cruel to the Ojibwas of the northern plains. In 1906 Senator Moses E. Clapp of Minnesota attached to an Indian

THE LOSING OF THE WEST

appropriations bill a rider declaring that mixed-blood adults on the White Earth reservation were "competent" (meaning educated in white ways) enough to sell their land without having to observe the twenty-five-year waiting period stipulated in the Dawes Act. When the bill became law, speculators duped many Ojibwas into signing away their land in return for counterfeit money and worthless merchandise. The Ojibwas lost more than half their original holdings, and economic ruin overtook them.

The government's policy had other injurious effects on Indians' ways of life. The boarding-school program enrolled thousands of children and tried to teach them that their inherited customs were inferior, but most returned to their families demoralized and confused rather than ready to assimilate into white society. Polingaysi Qoyawayma, a Hopi woman forced to take the Christian name Elizabeth Q. White, recalled after four years spent at the Sherman Institute in Riverside, California, "As a Hopi, I was misunderstood by the white man; as a convert of the missionaries, I was looked upon with suspicion by the Hopi people."

Ultimately, political and ecological crises overwhelmed most western Indian groups. White violence and military superiority alone did not defeat them. Their economic systems had started to break down before the military campaigns occurred. Buffalo extinction, enemy raids, and disease, in addition to force, combined to hobble subsistence culture to the point that Native Americans had no alternative but to yield their lands to market-oriented whites. Believing their culture to be superior, whites determined to transform Indians into successful farmers by teaching them the value of private property, educating them in American ideals, and eradicating their "backward" languages, lifestyles, and religions. Although Indians tried to retain their culture by both adapting and yielding to the various demands they faced, by the end of the century they had lost control of the land and were under increasing pressure to shed their group identity. The West was won at their expense, and to this day they remain casualties of an aggressive age.

The Extraction of Natural Resources

*I*n contrast to Indians, who used natural resources mostly to meet subsistence needs and small-scale trading, most whites who migrated to the West and the Great Plains were driven by the desire for material success. To their eyes, the vast stretches of territory lay as untapped sources of wealth that could bring about a better life (see Map 17.1). Extraction of these resources advanced settlement and created new markets at home and abroad; it also fueled revolutions in transportation, agriculture, and industry that swept across the United States in the late nineteenth century. At the same time, extraction of nature's wealth gave rise to wasteful interaction with the environment and fed habits of racial and sexual oppression.

In the mid-1800s, eager prospectors began to comb western forests and mountains for gold, silver, timber, and copper. The mining frontier advanced rapidly, drawing thousands of people to Nevada, Idaho, Montana, Utah, and Colorado. California, where a gold rush helped populate a thriving state with more than three hundred thousand people by 1860, furnished many of the miners, who traveled to nearby states in search of riches. Others followed traditional routes, moving from the East and Midwest to western mining regions.

MINING AND LUMBERING

Prospectors tended to be restless optimists, willing to climb mountains and trek across deserts in search of a telltale glint of precious metal. They shot game for food and financed their explorations by convincing merchants to advance credit for equipment in return for a share of the as-yet-undiscovered lode. Unlucky prospectors whose credit ran out took jobs and saved up for another search.

Digging for and transporting minerals was extremely expensive, so prospectors who did discover veins of metal seldom mined them. Instead, they sold their claims to large mining syndicates such as the Anaconda Copper Company. Financed by eastern capital, these companies could bring in engineers, heavy machinery, railroad lines, and work crews. In doing so, they made western mining corporate, just like eastern manufacturing. Although discoveries of gold and silver first drew attention to the West and its resources, mining companies usually exploited less romantic but equally lucrative bonanzas of lead, zinc, tin, quartz, and copper.

Cutting fir and spruce trees for lumber to satisfy the demand for construction and heating materials needed vast tracts of forest land to be profitable. Because forests in the upper Midwest and South had been depleted—aided by inventions such as bandsaws and feeding machines that quickened the pace of timber cutting—lumber corporations moved into the Northwest. They often grabbed millions of acres under the Timber and Stone Act, passed by Congress in 1878 to stimulate settlement in California, Nevada, Oregon, and Washington. It allowed private citizens to buy, at a low price, 160-acre plots "unfit for cultivation" and "valuable chiefly for

Map 17.1   The Development and Natural Resources of the West

By 1890 mining, lumbering, and cattle ranching had penetrated many areas west of the Mississippi River, and railroads had linked together the western economy. These characteristics, along with the spread of agriculture, contributed to the Census Bureau's observation that the frontier had disappeared; yet, as the map shows, large areas remained undeveloped.

By the 1880s, large-scale operations had replaced solitary prospectors in the extraction of minerals from western territories. Here, powerful sprays of water are being used to wash silver from a deposit in Alma, Colorado.   (Colorado Historical Society)

timber." Lumber companies hired seamen from waterfront boarding houses to register private claims to timberland and then transfer those claims to the companies. By 1900 private citizens had bought over 3.5 million acres, but most of that land belonged to corporations.

While mining corporations were acquiring western mineral deposits and lumber corporations were acquiring Northwest timberlands, oil companies were beginning to drill for wells in the Southwest. In 1900 most of the nation's petroleum still came from the Appalachians and the Midwest, but rich oil reserves had been discovered in southern California and eastern Texas. Although oil and kerosene were still used mostly for lubrication and lighting, oil discovered in the Southwest later became a vital new source of fuel.

The West became a rich multiracial society, including not only Native Americans and native-born white migrants but also Hispanics, African Americans, and

A COMPLEX POPULATION

Asians. A crescent of territory, a borderland stretching from western Texas through New Mexico and Arizona to northern California, supported Hispanic ranchers and sheepherders, descendants of the Spanish who originally had claimed the land. In New Mexico, Spaniards mixed with Indians to form a *mestizo* population of small farmers and ranchers. All along the Southwest frontier, Mexican immigrants moved into American territory to find work. Some returned to Mexico seasonally; others stayed.

Before federal law excluded them in 1881 and 1882, some two hundred thousand Chinese immigrants—mostly young, single males—came to the United States and built communities in California, Oregon, and Washington. By the 1870s, Chinese composed half of California's agricultural work force. The state's fertile fields and citrus groves demanded a huge migrant work force, and Chinese laborers moved from one ripening crop to another working as pickers and packers.

Japanese, Mexican, and European immigrants also moved from place to place as they worked in mining and agricultural communities. The region consequently developed its own migrant economy, with workers shifting within a large geographical area as they took short-term jobs in mining, farming, and railroad construction.

African Americans tended to be more settled in the West, many of them "exodusters" who inhabited all-black towns. Nicodemus, Kansas, for example, was founded in 1877 by African American migrants from Lexington, Kentucky, and grew to six hundred residents within two years. Early experiences were challenging; however, the town managed to survive with the aid of food, firewood, and other staples furnished by nearby Osage Indians.

Though unmarried men numerically dominated the western natural-resource frontier, many communities contained populations of white women who had come for the same reason as men: to find a fortune. But on the mining frontier as elsewhere, women's independence was limited; they usually accompanied a husband or father and seldom prospected themselves. Even so, many women used their labor as a resource and earned money by cooking and laundering and in some cases providing sexual services for the miners in houses of prostitution. In the Northwest, they worked in canneries, cleaning and salting the fish that their husbands caught.

To control labor and social relations within this complex population, white settlers made race an important distinguishing social characteristic in the West. They usually identified four nonwhite races: Indians,

SIGNIFICANCE
OF RACE

Mexicans (both Mexican Americans, who had originally inhabited western lands, and Mexican immigrants), "Mongolians" (a term applied to Chinese), and "Negroes." In creating these categories, whites imposed racial distinctions on people who, with the possible exception of African Americans, had never before considered themselves to be a "race." Whites using these categories ascribed demeaning characteristics to all nonwhites, judging them to be permanently inferior. In 1878, for example, a federal judge in California ruled that Chinese could not become U.S. citizens because they were not "white persons."

Racial minorities in western communities occupied the bottom half of a two-tiered labor system. Whites dominated the top tier of managerial and skilled labor positions. Unskilled laborers, often Irish, Chinese, and Mexicans, worked in mines, on railroad construction, and as agricultural and domestic laborers. Blacks also worked in railroad and mining camps, doing cooking and cleaning, while Indians barely participated in the white-controlled labor system at all. All nonwhite groups plus the Irish encountered prejudice, especially as whites tried to reserve for themselves whatever riches the West might yield. Anti-Chinese violence erupted during hard times. When the Union Pacific Railroad tried to replace white workers with lower-waged Chinese in Rock Springs, Wyoming, in 1885, whites invaded the Chinese part of town, burned it down, and killed twenty-eight. Mexicans, many of whom had been the original owners of the land, saw their property claims ignored or stolen by white miners and farmers. In California, many Mexicans moved to cities, where they could get only unskilled, low-paying jobs.

The multiracial quality of western society, however, also included a cross-racial dimension. Because so many white male migrants were single, intermarriage with Mexican and Indian women was common. Such intermarriage was acceptable for white men, but not for white women, especially where Asian immigrants were involved. Most miscegenation laws passed by western legislatures were intended to prevent Chinese and Japanese men from marrying white women.

A number of white women helped to bolster family and community life as members of the home mission movement. Protestant missions had long sponsored benevolent activities abroad, such as in China, and had aided the settlement of Oregon in the 1840s. But in the mid-nineteenth century a number of women broke away from male-dominated missionary organizations. Their efforts focused on helping women in countries where

Born in China, Polly Bemis, pictured here, came to America when her parents sold her as a slave. An Idaho saloon-keeper bought her, and she later married a man named Charlie Bemis, who won her in a card game. Her life story was common among the few Chinese women who immigrated to the United States in the 1860s and 1870s (most Chinese immigrants were men). Unlike many Chinese, however, she lived peacefully after her marriage until her death in 1933.   (Idaho Historical Society Library and Archives)

"barbaric" practices such as polygamy and female infanticide existed. Soon, these women—middle-class and white—were establishing missionary societies in the United States to fulfill their slogan, "Woman's work for woman." In the West, they exercised moral authority by building homes to rescue women—unmarried mothers, Mormons, Indians, and Chinese—who they believed had fallen prey to men or who had not yet accepted the principles of Christian virtue.

As whites were wresting control of the land from the Indians and Mexican inhabitants of the Southwest and

CONSERVATION
MOVEMENT

California, questions arose over control of the nation's animal, mineral, and timber resources. Much of the remaining undeveloped land west of the Mississippi was in the public domain, and some people believed that the federal government, as its owner, should limit its exploitation. Others, however, believed that their own and the nation's prosperity depended on unlimited use of the land.

Questions about natural resources caught Americans between a desire for progress and a fear of spoiling the land. After the Civil War, people eager to protect the natural landscape began to organize a conservation movement. Sports hunters, concerned about loss of wildlife, opposed market hunting and lobbied state legislatures to pass hunting regulations. Artists and tourists in 1864 persuaded Congress to preserve the beautiful Yosemite Valley by granting it to the state of California, which reserved it for public use. Then, in 1872 Congress designated the Yellowstone River region in Wyoming as the first national park. And in 1891, conservationists, led by naturalist John Muir, pressured Congress to authorize President Benjamin Harrison to create forest reserves—public lands protected from private-interest cutting. Such policies met with strong objections from lumber companies, lumber dealers, railroads, and householders accustomed to cutting timber freely for fuel and building material. Despite Muir's activism and efforts by the Sierra Club (which Muir helped found in 1892), and by corpo-

rations such as the Southern Pacific railroad, which supported rational resource development, opposition was loudest in the West, where people remained eager to take advantage of nature's bounty. Moreover, national parks induced some spoiling of the land they were intended to preserve, as tourist services necessitated the building of roads, hotels, restaurants, and sewers in the wilderness.

Development of mining and forest regions, and of the farms and cities that followed, brought western territories to the threshold of statehood (see Map 17.2). In 1889 Republicans seeking to solidify control of Congress passed an omnibus bill granting statehood to North Dakota, South Dakota, Washington, and Montana. Wyoming and Idaho, both of which allowed women to vote, were admitted the following year. Congress denied statehood to Utah until 1896, wanting assurances from the Mormons, who constituted a majority of the territory's population and controlled its government, that they would give up polygamy.

ADMISSION OF NEW STATES

Those states' mining towns and lumber camps spiced American folk culture and fostered a go-getter optimism

Map 17.2   The United States, 1876–1912

A wave of admissions between 1889 and 1912 brought remaining territories to statehood and marked the final creation of new states until Alaska and Hawai'i were admitted in the 1950s.

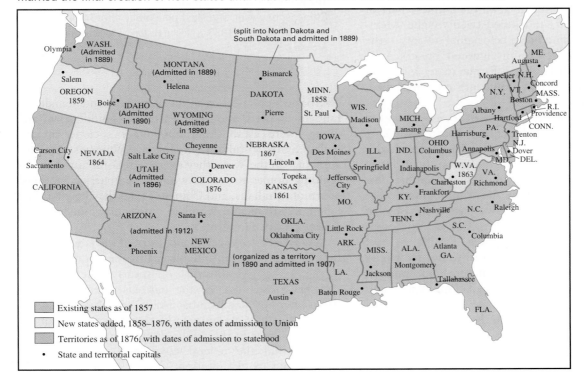

that distinguished the American spirit. The lawlessness and hedonism of places such as Deadwood, in Dakota Territory, and Tombstone, in Arizona Territory, gave the West notoriety and romance. Legends grew up almost immediately about characters whose lives both typified and magnified western experience. Cowboys, especially, captivated popular imagination, not only in the United States but in Europe as well, and promoters like Buffalo Bill enhanced the appeal of western folklore.

Arizona's mining towns, with their free-flowing cash and loose law enforcement, attracted gamblers, thieves, and opportunists whose names came to stand for the Wild West. Near Tombstone, the infamous Clanton family and their partner John Ringgold (known as Johnny Ringo) engaged in smuggling and cattle rustling. Inside the town, the Earp brothers—Wyatt, Jim, Morgan, Virgil, and Warren—and their friends William ("Bat") Masterson and John Henry ("Doc") Holliday operated on both sides of the law as gunmen, gamblers, and politicians. A feud between the Clantons and Earps climaxed on October 26, 1881, in a shootout at the OK Corral, where three Clantons were killed and Holliday and Morgan Earp were wounded. These characters and their exploits provided material for many cowboy movies and television programs in future years.

Mark Twain, Bret Harte, and other writers captured for posterity the flavor of western life, and characters like Buffalo Bill, Annie Oakley, Wild Bill Hickok, Poker Alice, and Bedrock Tom became western folk heroes. But violence and eccentricity were far from common. Most miners and lumbermen worked long hours, often for corporations rather than as rugged individuals, and had little time, energy, or money for gambling, carousing, or gunfights. Women worked as long or longer as teachers, laundresses, storekeepers, and housewives. Only a few were sharpshooters or dancehall queens. For most, western life was a matter of adapting and surviving.

Irrigation and Transportation

Glittering gold, tall trees, and gushing oil shaped popular images of the West, but water gave it life. If western territories and states promised wealth from mining, cutting, and drilling, their agricultural potential promised more—but only if settlers could find a way to bring water to the arid land. Western economic development is the story of how public and private interests used technology and organization to develop the region's river basins and make the land agriculturally

productive. Just as control of land was central to western development, so too was control of water.

For centuries, Indians irrigated southwestern lands to sustain their subsistence farming. When the Spanish arrived, they began tapping the Rio Grande River to irrigate farms in southwest Texas, New Mexico, and California. Later they channeled water to the California mission communities of San Diego and Los Angeles. The first Americans of northern European ancestry to practice extensive irrigation were the Mormons. Arriving in Utah in 1847, they quickly diverted streams and rivers into networks of canals, whose water enabled them to farm the hard-baked soil. By 1890 Utah boasted over 263,000 irrigated acres supporting more than two hundred thousand people.

Efforts at land reclamation through irrigation in Colorado and California raised controversies over rights to the precious streams that flowed through the West. Americans had inherited the English common-law principle of riparian rights, which held that only those who owned land along a river's banks could appropriate from the water's flow. The stream itself, according to riparianism, belonged to God; those who lived near it could take water for normal needs but were not to diminish the river. This principle, intended to protect nature, discouraged economic development because it prohibited each property owner from damming or diverting water at the expense of others who lived along the banks.

RIGHTS TO WATER

Americans who settled the West rejected riparianism in favor of the doctrine of prior appropriation, which awarded a river's water to the first person who claimed it. Westerners, taking cues in part from eastern Americans who had diverted waterways to power mills and factories, asserted that water, like timber, minerals, and other natural resources, existed to serve human needs and advance profits. They argued that anyone intending a beneficial or "reasonable" (economically productive) use of river water should have the right to appropriation, and the courts generally agreed.

Under appropriation, those who dammed and diverted water often reduced the flow of water downstream. People disadvantaged by such action could protect their interests either by suing those who deprived them of water or by establishing a public authority to regulate water usage. Thus in 1879 Colorado created several water divisions, each with a commissioner to determine and regulate water rights. In 1890 Wyoming enlarged the concept of control with a constitutional provision declaring that the state's rivers were public property subject to state supervision.

America's frontier West was not unique. Australia, founded like the United States as a European colony, underwent a parallel frontier society that resembled the American experience in several ways, especially in its mining development, its folk society, and its treatment of indigenous people. Australia experienced a gold rush in 1851, just two years after the United States did, and large-scale mining companies quickly moved into its western regions to extract lucrative mineral deposits. In 1897, future U.S. president Herbert Hoover, who at that time was a twenty-two-year-old geology graduate, went to work in Australia and began his successful career as a mining engineer.

A promise of mineral wealth lured thousands of immigrants to Australia in the late nineteenth century. Many of the newcomers arrived from China, and, as in the United States, these immigrants, almost all of whom were men, encountered abusive treatment. Anti-Chinese riots erupted in debarkation ports in New South Wales in 1861 and 1873, and beginning in 1854 Australia passed several laws restricting Chinese immigration. When the country became an independent British federation in 1901, one of its first acts applied a strict literacy test that virtually terminated Chinese immigration for over fifty years.

As in the American West, the Australian frontier bred folk heroes who came to symbolize white masculinity. In a society where men vastly outnumbered women, Australians glorified the rugged, aggressive individual who displayed self-reliance and quick judgment. An ethos of freedom and opportunity intertwined with the idea of masculine ruggedness, and the Australian backcountry man became as idealized as the American cowboy. Australian outlaws such as Ned Kelly, an infamous bushranger hanged in 1880, achieved the same notoriety as Americans Jesse James and Billy the Kid.

As Australians lauded "white men" who brought a spirit of personal liberty and opportunism to a new country, they also considered native peoples, whom they called "Aborigines" rather than Indians, as savages needing to be conquered and civilized. Some whites considered Aborigines "living fossils," akin to prehistoric humans. Christian missionaries viewed natives as lost in pagan darkness and tried to convert them. In 1869 the government of Victoria passed an Aborigine Protection Act that encouraged removal of native children from their families so they could learn European customs in schools run by whites. Aborigines tried in their own ways to adapt. They formed cricket teams, and those with light skins sometimes hid their identity by reporting themselves as white for the census. In the end, though, assimilation did not work, and Australians resorted to reservations as a means of "protecting" Aborigines, just as Americans isolated native peoples on reserved land. Like the Americans, Australians could not find a place for Aborigines in a land of opportunity for whites.

Much like the American counterpart, the Australian frontier was populated by natives before Anglo colonists arrived. The aborigines, as the Australian natives were called, lived in villages and utilized their own culture to adapt to the environment. This photo shows a native camp in the Maloga reserve. (National Library of Australia)

■ Water, aided by human resolve, coaxed crops from the dry soil and helped make the West habitable for whites. On this Colorado farm, a windmill pumps water for irrigation.   (Longmont Museum, Longmont, Colorado)

Destined to become the most productive agricultural state, California devised a dramatic settlement to the problem of water rights, sometimes called the "California Solution." In the 1860s a few individuals controlled huge tracts of land in the fertile Sacramento and San Joaquin River valleys, which they used for speculating in real estate, raising cattle, and growing wheat. But around the edges of the wheat fields lay unoccupied lands that could profitably support vegetable and fruit farming if irrigated properly.

Unlike western states that had favored appropriation rights over riparian rights, California maintained a mixed legal system that upheld riparianism while allowing for some appropriation. This system disadvantaged irrigators and prompted them to seek to change state law. In 1887 the legislature passed a bill permitting farmers to organize into districts that would construct and operate irrigation projects. An irrigation district could use its public authority to purchase water rights, seize private property to build irrigation canals, and finance projects through taxation or by issuing bonds. As a result of this legislation, California became the nation's leader in irrigated acreage, with more than 1 million irrigated acres by 1890, and the state's fruit and vegetable crops made its agriculture the most profitable in the country.

Though state irrigation provisions stimulated development, the federal government still owned most of western lands in the 1890s, ranging from 64 percent of California to 96 percent of Nevada. Prodded by land-hungry developers, states wanted the federal government to transfer to them at least part of the public domain lands. States claimed that they could make these lands profitable through reclamation—providing them with irrigated water. Congress generally refused such assignments because of the controversies they raised. If one state sponsored irrigation to develop its own land, who would regulate waterways that flowed through more than one state or that potentially could provide water to a nearby state? If, for example, California assumed control of the Truckee River, which flowed westward out of Lake Tahoe on the California-Nevada border, how would Nevadans be assured that California would give them sufficient water? Only the federal government, it seemed, had power to regulate regional water development.

NEWLANDS RECLAMATION ACT

In 1902, after years of debates, Congress passed the Newlands Reclamation Act. Named for Nevada congressman Francis Newlands, the act allowed the federal government to sell western public lands to individuals in parcels not to exceed 160 acres, and to use proceeds from such sales to finance irrigation projects. The Newlands Act provided for control but not conservation of water, because three-fourths of the water used in open-ditch irrigation, the most common form, was lost to evaporation. Thus the legislation fell squarely within the tradition of development of nature for human profit. Often identified as an example of sensitivity to natural-resource conservation, the Newlands Reclamation Act in fact represented a decision by the federal government to aid the agricultural and general economic development of the West, just as state and federal subsidies to railroads during the 1850s and 1860s aided settlement of the West.

RAILROAD CONSTRUCTION

Between 1865 and 1890, railroad construction boomed, as total track in the United States grew from 35,000 to 200,000 miles, mostly from construction west of the Mississippi River (see Map 17.1). By 1900, the United States contained one-third of all railroad track in the world. A diverse mix of workers made up construction crews. The Central Pacific, built eastward from San Francisco, imported seven thousand Chinese to build its tracks; the Union Pacific, extending westward from Omaha, Nebraska, used mainly Irish construction gangs. Workers lived in shacks and tents that were dismantled, loaded on flatcars, and relocated at intervals of about 60 or 70 miles. After 1880, when steel rails began to replace iron rails, railroads helped to boost the nation's steel industry to international leadership. Railroad expansion also spawned related industries, including coal production, passenger- and freight-car manufacture, and depot construction. Influential and essential, railroads also gave important impetus to western urbanization. With their ability to transport large loads of people and freight, lines such as the Union Pacific and Southern Pacific accelerated the growth of western hubs such as Omaha, Kansas City, Cheyenne, Los Angeles, Portland, and Seattle.

RAILROAD SUBSIDIES

Railroads accomplished these feats with help from some of the largest government subsidies in American history. Executives argued that because railroads were a public benefit, the government should aid them by giving them land from the public domain, which they could then sell to finance railroad construction. During the Civil War, Congress, dominated by business-minded Republicans and in the absence of representatives from the seceded southern states, was sympathetic, as it had been when it aided steamboat companies earlier in the nineteenth century. As a result, the federal government granted railroad corporations over 180 million acres, mostly for interstate routes. These grants usually consisted of a right of way, plus alternate sections of land in a strip 20 to 80 miles wide along the right of way. Railroads funded construction by using the land as security for bonds or by selling it for cash. States and localities heaped on further subsidies. State legislators, many of whom had financial interests in a railroad's success, granted some 50 million acres. Cities and towns also assisted, usually by offering loans or by purchasing railroad bonds or stocks.

Government subsidies had mixed effects. Though capitalists often opposed government involvement in economic matters of private companies, privately owned railroads nevertheless accepted public aid and pressured governments into meeting their needs. The Southern Pacific, for example, threatened to bypass Los Angeles unless the city paid a bonus and built a depot. Localities that could not or would not pay suffered. Without public help, few railroads could have prospered sufficiently to attract private investment, yet such aid was not always salutary. During the 1880s, the policy of generosity haunted communities whose zeal had prompted them to commit too much to railroads that were never built or that defaulted on loans. Some laborers and farmers fought subsidies, arguing that companies like Southern Pacific would become too powerful. Many communities boomed, however, because they had linked their fortunes to the iron horse. Moreover, railroads helped attract investment into the West and drew farmers into the market economy.

STANDARD GAUGE; STANDARD TIME

Railroad construction brought about important technological and organizational reforms. By the late 1880s, almost all lines had adopted standard-gauge rails so their tracks could connect with one another. Air brakes, automatic car couplers, standardized handholds on freight cars, and other devices made rail transportation safer and more efficient. The need for gradings, tunnels, and bridges spurred the growth of the American engineering profession. Organizational advances included systems for coordinating complex passenger and freight schedules and the adoption of uniform freight-classification systems.

Railroads also altered conceptions of time and space. First, by surmounting physical barriers to travel, railroads transformed space into time. Instead of expressing

■ Train schedules not only changed the American economy but also altered how Americans timed their daily lives. As people and businesses ordered their day according to the arrival and departure of trains, distances became less important than hours and minutes.   (Library of Congress)

the distance between places in miles, people began to refer to the amount of time it took to travel from one place to another. Second, railroad scheduling required nationwide standardization of time. Before railroads, local church bells and clocks struck noon when the sun was directly overhead, and people set clocks and watches accordingly. But because the sun was not overhead at exactly the same moment everywhere, time varied from place to place. Boston's clocks, for instance, differed from those in New York by almost twelve minutes. To impose regularity, railroads created their own time zones. By 1880 there were nearly fifty different standards, but in 1883 the railroads, without authority from Congress, agreed to establish four standard time zones for the whole country. Most communities adjusted their clocks accordingly, and railroad time became national time.

Farming the Plains

Western agriculture in the late nineteenth century exemplified two important achievements: the transforming of arid, windswept prairies into arable land that would yield crops to benefit hu-

mankind, and the transformation of agriculture into big business by means of mechanization, long-distance transportation, and scientific cultivation. These feats did not come easily. The climate and terrain of the Great Plains presented formidable challenges, and overcoming them did not guarantee success. Technological innovation and the mechanization of agriculture enabled farmers to feed the nation's burgeoning population and turned the United States into the world's breadbasket, but the experience also scarred the lives of countless men and women who made that accomplishment possible.

During the 1870s and 1880s, hundreds of thousands of hopeful farmers streamed into the Great Plains region.

SETTLEMENT OF THE PLAINS

More acres were put under cultivation in states such as Kansas, Nebraska, and Texas during these two decades than in the entire country during the previous 250 years. The number of farms tripled from 2 million to over 6 million between 1860 and 1910. Several states opened offices in the East to lure migrants westward. Land-rich railroads were especially aggressive, advertising cheap land, arranging credit terms, offering reduced fares, and promising instant success. Railroad agents—often former immigrants—traveled to Denmark, Sweden, Germany, and other European nations to recruit settlers and greeted newcomers at eastern ports.

Most families who settled western farmlands migrated because opportunities in the West seemed to promise a second chance, a better existence than their previous one. Railroad expansion gave farmers in remote regions a way to ship produce to market, and the construction of grain elevators eased problems of storage. As a result of worldwide as well as national population growth, demand for farm products grew rapidly, and the prospects for commercial agriculture—growing crops for profit and for shipment to distant, including international, markets—became more favorable than ever.

Life on the farm, however, was much harder than advertisements and railroad agents suggested. Migrants

HARDSHIP ON THE PLAINS

often encountered scarcities of essentials they had once taken for granted, and they had to adapt to the environment. The open prairies contained little lumber for housing and fuel, so pioneer families had to build houses of sod and burn buffalo dung for heat. Water for cooking and cleaning was sometimes as scarce as timber. Few families were lucky or wealthy enough to buy land near a stream that did not dry up in summer and freeze in winter. Machinery for drilling wells was expensive, as were windmills for drawing water to the surface.

■ Posing in front of their sod house, this proud Nebraska family displays the seriousness that derived from their hard lives on the Great Plains. Though bushes and other growth appear in the background, the absence of trees is notable.   (Nebraska State Historical Society, Solomon D. Butcher Collection)

The weather was even more formidable than the terrain. The climate between the Missouri River and the Rocky Mountains divides along a line running from Minnesota southwest through Oklahoma, then south, bisecting Texas. West of this line, annual rainfall averages less than twenty-eight inches, not enough for most crops or trees (see Map 17.3), and even that scant life-giving rain was never certain. Heartened by adequate water one year, farmers gagged on dust and broke plows on hardened limestone soil the next.

Weather seldom followed predictable cycles. In summer, weeks of torrid heat and parching winds suddenly gave way to violent storms that washed away crops and property. The wind and cold of winter blizzards piled up mountainous snowdrifts that halted outdoor movement. During the Great Blizzard that struck Nebraska and the Dakota Territory in January 1888, the temperature plunged to 36 degrees below zero, and the wind blew at 56 miles per hour. Thousands of livestock perished. In springtime, melting snow swelled streams, and floods threatened millions of acres. In the fall, a week without rain turned dry grasslands into tinder, and the slightest spark could ignite a raging prairie fire. Though

early Plains settlers encountered a wet-weather cycle that prompted optimism, the climate changed abruptly in 1886, beginning a drought that lasted until the mid-1890s and drove many farmers off the land.

Nature could be cruel even under good conditions. Weather that was favorable for crops was also good for breeding insects. Worms and flying pests ravaged fields. In the 1870s and 1880s swarms of grasshoppers virtually ate up entire farms. Heralded only by the din of buzzing wings, a mile-long cloud of insects would smother the land and devour everything: plants, tree bark, and clothes. As one farmer lamented, the "hoppers left behind nothing but the mortgage."

Settlers also had to cope with social isolation. In New England and Europe, farmers lived in villages and traveled daily to nearby fields. This pattern was rare in the vast expanses of the Plains—and in the Far West and South as well—where peculiarities of land division compelled rural dwellers to live apart from each other. The Homestead Act of 1862 and other measures to encourage western settlement offered cheap or free plots to people who would reside on and improve

SOCIAL ISOLATION

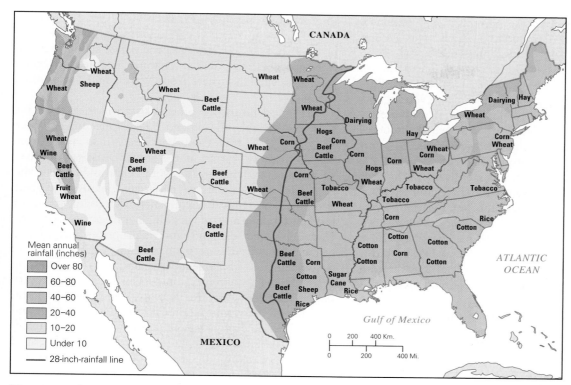

Map 17.3   Agricultural Regions of the United States, 1890

In the Pacific Northwest and east of the 28-inch-rainfall line, farmers could grow a greater variety of crops. Territory west of the line was either too mountainous or too arid to support agriculture without irrigation. The grasslands that once fed buffalo herds now could feed beef cattle.

their property. Because most plots acquired by small farmers were rectangular—usually encompassing 160 acres—at most four families could live near each other, but only if they congregated around the shared four-corner intersection. In practice, farm families usually lived back from their boundary lines, and at least a half-mile separated farmhouses.

Letters that Ed Donnell, a young Nebraska home-steader, wrote to his family in Missouri reveal how time and circumstances could dull optimism. In the fall of 1885, Donnell rejoiced to his mother: "I like Nebr first rate. . . . I have saw a pretty tuff time a part of the time since I have been out here, but I started out to get a home and I was determined to win or die in the attempt. . . . Have got a good crop of corn, a floor in my house and got it ceiled overhead." Already, though, Donnell was lonely. He went on: "There is lots of other bachelors here but I am the only one I know who doesn't have kinfolks living handy. . . . You wanted to know when I was going to get married. Just as quick as I can get money ahead to get a cow."

A year and a half later, Donnell's dreams were dis-solving and, still a bachelor, he was beginning to look for a second chance elsewhere. He wrote to his brother, "The rats eat my sod stable down. . . . I may sell out this summer, land is going up so fast. . . . If I sell I am going west and grow up with the country." By fall conditions had worsened. Donnell lamented, "We have been having wet weather for 3 weeks. . . . My health has been so poor this summer and the wind and the sun hurts my head so. I think if I can sell I will . . . move to town for I can get $40 a month working in a grist mill and I would not be exposed to the weather." Donnell's doubts and hardships, shared by thousands of other people, fed the cityward migration of farm folk that fueled late-nineteenth-century urban growth (see Chapter 19).

Farm families survived by sheer resolve and by or-ganizing churches and clubs where they could social-ize a few times a month. By 1900 two developments had brought rural settlers into closer contact with modern consumer society (though people in sparsely settled re-gions west of the twenty-eight-inch-rainfall line remained

MAIL-ORDER COMPANIES AND RURAL FREE DELIVERY

isolated for several more decades). First, mail-order companies such as Montgomery Ward and Sears, Roebuck made new products available to almost everyone by the 1870s and 1880s. Emphasizing personal attention to customers, Ward's and Sears were outlets for sociability as well as material goods. Letters from customers to Mr. Ward often reported family news and sought advice on needs from gifts to childcare. A Washington man wrote, "As you advertise everything for sale that a person wants, I thought I would write you, as I am in need of a wife, and see what you could do for me." Another reported: "I suppose you wonder why we haven't ordered anything from you since the fall. The cow kicked my arm and broke it and besides my wife was sick, and there was the doctor bill. But now, thank God, that is paid, and we are all well again, and we have a fine new baby boy, and please send plush bonnet number 29d8077."

Second, after farmers petitioned Congress for extension of the postal service, in 1896 the government made Rural Free Delivery (RFD), which had begun earlier in West Virginia, widely available. Farmers previously had to go to town to pick up mail. Now, they could receive letters, newspapers, and catalogues in a roadside mailbox nearly every day. In 1913 the postal service inaugurated parcel post, which enabled people to receive packages, such as orders from Ward's and Sears, more cheaply.

The agricultural revolution that followed the Civil War was driven by the expanded use of machinery. When the Civil War drew men away from *MECHANIZATION* farms in the upper Mississippi River *OF AGRICULTURE* valley, the women and older men who remained behind began using reapers and other mechanical implements to satisfy demand for food and to take advantage of high grain prices. After the war, continued demand and high prices encouraged farmers to depend more on machines, and inventors developed new implements in planting and harvesting grain. Seeders, combines, binders, mowers, and rotary plows, carried westward by railroads, improved grain growing on the Plains and in California in the 1870s and 1880s. Technology also aided dairy and poultry farming. The centrifugal cream separator, patented in 1879, sped the process of skimming cream from milk, and a mecha-

■ By the late nineteenth century, the industrial revolution was making a significant impact on farming. This scene from a Colorado wheat farm shows a harvest aided by a steam tractor and belt-driven thresher, equipment that made large-scale commercial crop production possible.   (Colorado Historical Society)

nized incubator, invented in 1885, made chicken raising more profitable.

For centuries, the acreage of grain a farmer could plant was limited by the amount that could be harvested by hand. Machines—driven first by animals, then by steam—significantly increased productivity. Before mechanization, a farmer working alone could harvest about 7.5 acres of wheat. Using an automatic binder that cut and bundled the grain, the same farmer could harvest 135 acres. Machines dramatically reduced the time and cost of farming other crops as well (see Table 17.1).

Meanwhile, Congress and scientists worked to improve existing crops and develop new ones. The 1862 Morrill Land Grant Act gave each state federal lands to sell in order to finance educational institutions that aided agricultural development. The act prompted establishment of state universities in Wisconsin, Illinois, Minnesota, California, and other states. A second Morrill Act in 1890 aided more schools, including a number of black colleges. The Hatch Act of 1887 provided for agricultural experiment stations in every state, further encouraging the advancement of farming science and technology.

LEGISLATIVE AND SCIENTIFIC AIDS

Science also enabled farmers to use the soil more efficiently. Researchers developed dry farming, a technique of plowing and harrowing that minimized evaporation of precious moisture. Botanists perfected varieties of "hard" wheat whose seeds could withstand northern winters, and millers invented a process for grinding the tougher wheat kernels into flour. Agriculturists also adapted new varieties of alfalfa from Mongolia, corn from North Africa, and rice from Asia. Horticulturist Luther Burbank developed hundreds of new food plants and flowers at a garden laboratory in Sebastopol, California. George Washington Carver, a son of slaves who became a chemist and taught at Alabama's Tuskegee Institute, created new products from peanuts, soybeans, sweet potatoes, and cotton wastes and developed industrial applications from agricultural products. Other scientists developed means of combating plant and animal diseases. Just as in mining and manufacturing, science and technology provided American farming with means for expanding productivity in the market economy.

The Ranching Frontier

While commercial farming was overspreading the West, it ran headlong into one of the region's most romantic industries—ranching. Beginning in the sixteenth century, Spanish landholders engaged in cattle raising in Mexico and what would become the American Southwest. They employed Indian and Mexican cowboys, known as *vaqueros*, to tend their herds and round up free-roaming cattle to be branded and slaughtered. American immigrant ranchers moving into Texas and California in the early nineteenth century hired *vaqueros*, who in turn taught their skills in roping, branding, horse training, and saddle making to white Anglo and African American cowboys. By the 1860s, cattle raising became increasingly profitable as population growth boosted the demand for beef and railroads simplified the transportation of food. By 1870 drovers were herding thousands of Texas cattle northward to Kansas, Missouri, and Wyoming (see Map 17.1). At the northern terminus—usually Abilene, Dodge City, or Cheyenne—the cattle were sold to northern ranches or loaded onto trains bound for Chicago and St. Louis for slaughter and distribution to national and international markets.

The long drive gave rise to romantic lore of bellowing cattle, buckskin-clad cowboys, and smoky campfires under starry skies, but the process was not very efficient. Trekking 1,000 miles or more for two to three months made cattle sinewy and tough. Herds traveling through Indian lands and farmers' fields were sometimes shot at and later prohibited from such trespass by state laws. Ranchers adjusted by raising herds nearer to railroad routes. When ranchers discovered that crossing Texas longhorns with heavier Hereford and Angus breeds produced animals better able to survive northern winters, cattle raising expanded northward. Between 1860 and 1880 the cattle population of Kansas, Nebraska,

TABLE 17.1

Time and Cost of Farming an Acre of Land by Hand and by Machine, 1890

Crop	Hours Required		Labor Cost	
	Hand	Machine	Hand	Machine
Wheat	61	3	$3.65	$.66
Corn	39	15	$3.62	$1.51
Oats	66	7	$3.73	$1.07
Loose hay	21	4	$1.75	$.42

Source: Ray Allan Billington, *Westward Expansion: A History of the American Frontier,* 2d ed. (New York: Macmillan, 1960), p. 697. Used by permission of Macmillan Publishing Company.

■ A group of cowboys prepare for a roundup. Note the presence of African Americans, who, along with Mexicans, made up one-fourth of all cowboys. Though they rarely became trail bosses or ranch owners, black cowboys enjoyed an independence on the trails that was unavailable to them on tenant farms and city streets. (Nebraska State Historical Society)

Colorado, Wyoming, Montana, and the Dakotas increased from 130,000 to 4.5 million, crowding out already declining buffalo herds. Profits were considerable. A rancher could purchase a calf for $5, let it feed at no cost on the Plains for a few years, recapture it in a roundup and sell it at a market price of $40 or $45.

Cattle raisers needed vast pastures to graze their herds while incurring as little expense as possible in using such land. Thus they often bought a few acres bordering a stream and turned their herds loose on adjacent public domain that no one wanted because it lacked water access. By this method, called open-range ranching, a cattle raiser could utilize thousands of acres by owning only a hundred or so. Neighboring ranchers often formed associations and allowed their herds to graze together. Owners identified their cattle by burning a brand into each animal's hide. Each ranch had its own brand—a shorthand method for labeling movable property. But as demand for beef kept rising and as ranchers and capital flowed into the Great Plains, cattle began to overrun the range and ranchers began to have trouble controlling the land.

THE OPEN RANGE

Meanwhile, sheepherders from California and New Mexico also were using the public domain, sparking territorial clashes. Ranchers complained that sheep ruined grassland by eating down to the roots and that cattle refused to graze where sheep had been because the "woolly critters" left a repulsive odor. Armed conflict occasionally erupted when cowboys and sheepherders resorted to violence rather than settle disagreements in court, where a judge might discover that both were using public land illegally.

More importantly, however, the advancing farming frontier was generating new demands for land. Devising a way to organize property resulted in an unheralded but highly significant change in land management. The problem was fencing. Lacking sufficient timber and stone for traditional fencing, western settlers could not easily define and protect their property. Tensions flared when farmers accused cattle raisers of allowing their herds to trespass on cropland and when herders in turn charged that farmers should fence their property against grazing animals. But ranchers and farmers alike lacked an economical means of enclosing their herds and fields.

■ Bordered by the product it was promoting, this advertisement conveyed the message that railroads and farmers could protect their property from each other by utilizing a new type of fencing. (Elwood House Museum, DeKalb, Illinois)

The solution was barbed wire. Invented in 1873 by Joseph F. Glidden, a DeKalb, Illinois, farmer, this fencing consisted of two wires held in place by sharp spurs twisted around them. Mass-produced by the Washburn and Moen Manufacturing Company of Worcester, Massachusetts—80.5 million pounds worth in 1880 alone—barbed wire provided a cheap and durable means of enclosure. It opened the Plains to homesteaders by enabling them to protect their farms from grazing cattle. It also ended open-range ranching and made roundups unnecessary because it enclosed private land that often had been used illegally for grazing and because it enabled large-scale ranchers to isolate their herds within massive stretches of private property. As well, the development of the round silo for storing and making feed (silage) enabled cattle raisers to feed their herds without grazing them on vast stretches of land.

BARBED WIRE

By 1890 big businesses were taking over the cattle industry and applying scientific methods of breeding and feeding. As well, big corporations used technology to squeeze larger returns out of meatpacking. Like buffalo, all parts of a cow had uses. Its hide was valuable for leather, and about half of it consisted of salable meat. Meatpackers' largest profits came from livestock by-products: blood for fertilizer, hooves for glue, fat for candles and soap, and the rest for sausages. But the processing of cattle also had notable environmental impact. What meatpackers and leather tanners could not sell was dumped into nearby rivers and streams. By the late nineteenth century, the Chicago River, which flowed past the city's mammoth meatpacking plants, created such a powerful stench that nearby residents became sick in the summer.

RANCHING AS BIG BUSINESS

Open-range ranching had made beef a staple of the American diet and created a few fortunes, but its features could not survive the spurs of barbed wire and the rush of history. Moreover, another environmental impact, the brutal winters of 1886–1887, destroyed 90 percent of some herds and drove small ranchers out of business. Most ranchers now owned or leased the land they used, though some illegal fencing persisted. Cowboys formed labor organizations and participated in strikes for higher pay. The myth of the cowboy's freedom and individualism lived on, but ranching, like mining and farming, quickly became a corporate business.

Summary

The reality of history proved Frederick Jackson Turner's image of the West as the home of democratic spirit and Buffalo Bill's depiction of the West as the stage of the white man's victory to be incomplete at best. Interaction between people and the environment proved to be far more intricate than either understood.

The land of the American West exerted a lasting influence, through both its dominance and its fragility, on the complex mix of people who settled it. Indians, the original inhabitants, had used, and sometimes abused, the land to support subsistence cultures that included trade and war as well as hunting and farming. Living mostly in small groups, they depended heavily on delicate resources such as buffalo herds and salmon runs. When they came into contact with commerce-minded, migratory Euro-Americans, their resistance to the market economy, diseases, and violence that whites brought into the West failed.

Mexicans, Chinese and other immigrants, African Americans, and Anglos discovered a reciprocal relationship between human activities and the nonhuman world that they had not always anticipated. Miners, timber cutters, farmers, and builders extracted raw minerals to supply eastern factories, used irrigation and mechanization to bring forth agricultural abundance from the land, filled pastures with cattle and sheep to expand food sources, and constructed railroads to tie the nation together. In doing so, they transformed half of the continent within a few decades. But the environment also exerted its own power over humans through its climate, its insects and predators, its undesirable plant growths, and its impenetrable hazards and barriers to human movement and agriculture.

The West's settlers, moreover, employed force, violence, and greed that sustained discrimination within a multiracial society, left many farmers feeling cheated and

betrayed, provoked contests over use of water and pastures, and sacrificed environmental balance for market profits. The region's raw materials and agricultural products improved living standards and hastened the industrial progress of the Machine Age, but not without human and environmental costs.

LEGACY FOR A PEOPLE AND A NATION
The West and Rugged Individualism

Though born in New York State, Theodore Roosevelt, twenty-sixth president of the United States, thought of himself as a westerner. In 1884, at age twenty-five, he moved to Dakota Territory to live on ranches he had bought there. He loved what he called "vast silent spaces, a place of grim beauty," where he could mingle with cowboys, gamblers, and gunmen. In the West, Roosevelt believed, he developed a character of "rugged individualism," an ability to conquer challenges through independent strength and fortitude. He once wrote of his experience that he "knew toil and hardship and hunger and thirst . . . but we felt the beat of hardy life in our veins, and ours was the glory of work and the joy of living."

Americans have long shared Roosevelt's fascination with the West and its reputation for rugged individualism. They have popularized western settings and characters in movies and on television. The film *Cimarron* (1930) was one of the first to win an Academy Award, and *Gunsmoke* held the record as one of the longest-running television series (1955–1975). Movie star John Wayne epitomized the rugged westerner in dozens of films. From *The Virginian*, first published in 1902, to the recent novels of Larry McMurtry, Americans have made stories about the West bestsellers. In many stories, a lone individual, usually male and white, overcomes danger and hardship with solitary effort. In their appreciation of this quality, Americans have not only infused political and moral rhetoric with references to rugged individualism but have sought to reenact the cowboy role, dressing in wide-brimmed hats and boots, denim jeans, and buckskin jackets.

Western reality, however, is far different from the myth of rugged individualism. Migrants to the West traveled on railroads built with government subsidies, acquired land cheaply from the federal government under the Homestead and Timber and Stone Acts, depended on the army to remove Indians, and cut forests and diverted rivers with federal support. More recently, western politicians who oppose big government have received votes from constituents who depend on federal farm subsidies and price supports, free or subsidized water, and government-financed disaster relief from droughts, floods, and tornadoes.

The West could not have been settled and developed without both individualism *and* government assistance—what might be called "rugged cooperation." Here was the West's true legacy to a people and a nation. The federal government, with state assistance, created opportunities that tenacious miners, ranchers, and farmers took advantage of. Those who populated the West had to be rugged, but they had—and continue to need—help.

The **history companion** *powered by Eduspace*®
Your primary source for interactive quizzes, exercises, and more to help you learn efficiently.
http://history.college.hmco.com/students

THE MACHINE AGE 1877–1920

*I*n 1911, iron molders at the Watertown Arsenal, a government weapons factory near Boston, went on strike after one of their number was fired. Joseph Cooney had objected to having his work timed by an efficiency expert with a stopwatch, and the molders knew that the time study was the first step in the imposition of new work routines. Questioned about why the workers struck, iron molders union president John Frey explained, "The workman believes when he goes on strike that he is defending his job." Frey meant that the molders felt a property right to their labor, that a job was not something that could be changed or removed from them without their consent.

The army officers who ran the factory believed differently. They thought that they owned the molders' labor and that the output was "not much more than one-half what it should be." To increase production, the managers had installed an incentive-pay system, but when that did not work they hired Dwight Merrick, an expert in a new field called "scientific management," to time workers' tasks and suggest ways to speed their performance.

The day Merrick began his time study, a molder named Perkins secretly timed the same task. Merrick reported that the job should take twenty-four minutes; Perkins found that to do the job right required fifty minutes. Merrick concluded that the workers were wasting time and materials in making molds; Perkins maintained that the molders knew more about making molds than Merrick did. That evening, the molders met to discuss how they should respond to the discrepancy between Merrick's report and their own sense of their job. Joseph Cooney argued that they should not submit to the system of scientific management, and the workers drew up a petition expressing their views. So when the next day Cooney confronted Merrick, they were ready to walk out.

Eventually, a compromise was reached between molders and their bosses at the Watertown Arsenal, but this small incident reveals one of the important consequences of the industrialization that was making so many new products

◀ Building parts for mowing machines at the McCormick farm implements factory, these workers are engaged in mechanized, mass production. Machines, standardized parts, and assembly-line production transformed American industrialization, the status of labor, and the availability of consumer goods. (Navistar Archives)

479

CHRONOLOGY

1869 • Knights of Labor founded

1873–78 • Economic decline

1876 • Bonsack invents machine for rolling cigarettes

1877 • Widespread railroad strikes protest wage cuts

1878 • Edison Electric Light Company founded

1879 • George's *Progress and Poverty* argues against economic inequality

1881 • First federal trademark law begins spread of brand names

1882 • Standard Oil Trust formed

1884–85 • Economic decline

1886 • Haymarket riot in Chicago protests police brutality against labor demonstrators
  • American Federation of Labor (AFL) founded

1888 • Bellamy's *Looking Backward* depicts utopian world free of monopoly, politicians, and class divisions

1890 • Sherman Anti-Trust Act outlaws "combinations in restraint of trade"

1892 • Homestead (Pennsylvania) steelworkers strike against Carnegie Steel Company

1893–97 • Economic depression causes high unemployment and business failures

1894 • Workers at Pullman Palace Car Company strike

1895 • *U.S. v. E. C. Knight Co.* limits Congress's power to regulate manufacturing

1896 • *Holden v. Hardy* upholds law regulating miners' work hours

1898 • Taylor promotes scientific management as efficiency measure in industry

1901–03 • U.S. Steel Corporation founded
  • E. I. du Pont de Nemours and Company reorganized
  • Ford Motor Company founded

1903 • Women's Trade Union League founded

1905 • *Lochner v. New York* overturns law limiting bakery workers' work hours and limits labor protection laws
  • Industrial Workers of the World (IWW) founded

1908 • *Muller v. Oregon* upholds law limiting women to ten-hour workday
  • First Ford Model T built

1911 • Triangle Shirtwaist Company fire in New York City leaves 146 workers dead

1913 • Ford begins moving assembly line

1919 • Telephone operator unions strike in New England

available in the late 1800s. The new order was both exciting and demoralizing. To increase production, factories and machines divided work routines into minute, repetitive tasks and organized work according to dictates of the clock. Workers (employees) like the Watertown molders who had long thought of themselves as valued for their skills now struggled to avoid becoming slaves to machines. Meanwhile, in their quest for productivity and profits, corporations (employers) merged and amassed great power. Defenders of the new system devised theories to justify it, while critics and laborers tried to combat what they thought were abuses of power.

Industrialization is a complex process whose chief feature is production of goods by machine rather than by hand. In the mid-nineteenth century, an industrial revolution swept through parts of the United States, and the mechanization that characterized it set the stage for a second round in the late 1800s and early 1900s. Three technological developments propelled this new process: the harnessing of electricity, the internal combustion engine, and new applications in the use of chemicals. These technologies followed from earlier industrialization. Steam engines, which had reached their peak of utility, generated demand for a new power source—electricity. The railroads' mechanization of transportation spurred progress in automobile manufacture. And the textile industry's experiments with dyes, bleaches, and cleaning agents advanced chemical research.

In 1860 only one-fourth of the American labor force worked in manufacturing and transportation; by 1900 over half did so. As the twentieth century dawned, the United States was not only the world's largest producer of raw materials and food but also the most productive industrial nation (see Map 18.1). Between 1880 and 1920, migrants from farms and abroad swelled the industrial work force (see Chapter 19); but labor-saving machines, more than people, boosted productivity. Innovations in business organization and marketing also fueled the drive for profits.

These developments had momentous effects on standards of living and everyday life. Between 1877 and 1920, a new consumer society took shape as goods that had once been accessible to a few became available to many. Former luxuries were becoming necessities. Products such as canned foods and machine-made clothing that had hardly existed before the Civil War became common by the turn of the century. The accomplishments of industrialism provided an additional chapter to the extraction of natural resources and the expansion of agriculture (see Chapter 17). Together, these processes brought together people, the environment, and technology in a mix that gave rise to both constructive and destructive forces. ■

Technology and the Triumph of Industrialism

n 1876 Thomas A. Edison and his associates set up a laboratory in a wooden shed in Menlo Park, New Jersey. There they intended to turn out "a minor invention every ten days and a big thing every six months or so." Edison envisioned his lab as an invention factory, where creative people pooled ideas and skills to fashion marketable products. Here he would blend brash enthusiasm with a systematic work ethic. If Americans wanted new products, Edison believed, they had to

Map 18.1   Industrial Production, 1919

By the early twentieth century, each state could boast of at least one kind of industrial production. Although the value of goods produced was still highest in the Northeast, states like Minnesota and California had impressive dollar values of outputs.   (Source: Data from U.S. Bureau of the Census, *Fourteenth Census of the United States,* 1920, Vol. IX, *Manufacturing* [Washington, D.C.: U.S. Government Printing Office, 1921].)

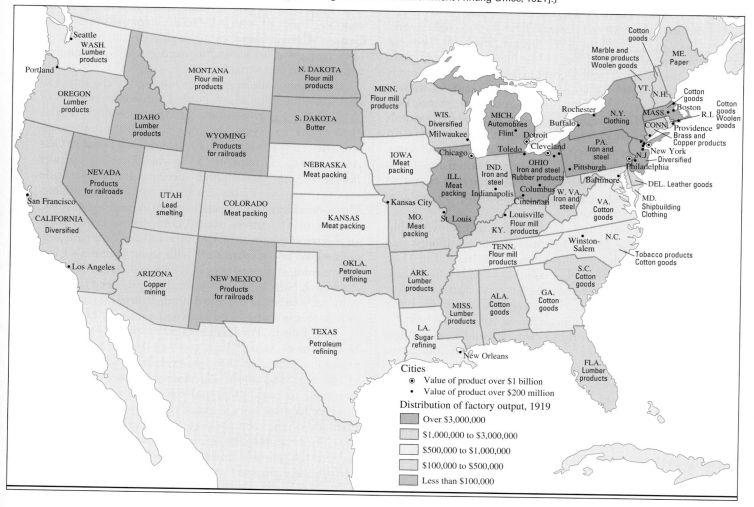

organize and work purposefully to bring about progress. Such efforts reflected the forward-looking spirit that enlivened American industrialization at the end of the nineteenth century.

Americans long thought of themselves as a mechanical people, willing to replace old technologies with new ones. Like the image of second chances represented by the West, the machine symbolized opportunity. The patent system, created by the Constitution to "promote the Progress of science and useful Arts," testifies to an outburst of American mechanical inventiveness. Between 1790 and 1860 the U.S. Patent Office granted a total of 36,000 patents. In 1897 alone, however, it granted 22,000, and between 1860 and 1930 it registered 1.5 million. Inventions often sprang from a marriage between technology and business organization. The harnessing of electricity, internal combustion, and industrial chemistry illustrates how this marriage worked.

Most of Edison's more than one thousand inventions used electricity to transmit light, sound, and images.

BIRTH OF THE ELECTRICAL INDUSTRY Perhaps his biggest "big thing" project began in 1878 when the Edison Electric Light Company embarked on a search for a cheap, efficient means of indoor lighting. After tedious experiments, Edison perfected an incandescent bulb that used a vacuum and tungsten to prevent the filament from burning up when electric current passed through it. At the same time, he devised a system of power generation and distribution—an improved dynamo and a parallel circuit of wires—to provide electricity conveniently to a large number of customers.

To market his ideas, Edison acted as his own publicist. During the 1880 Christmas season he illuminated Menlo Park with forty incandescent bulbs, and in 1882 he built a power plant that could light eighty-five buildings in New York's Wall Street financial district. A *New York Times* reporter marveled that working in his office at night now "seemed almost like writing in daylight."

Edison's system of direct current could transmit electric power only a mile or two because it lost voltage the farther it was transmitted. George Westinghouse, an inventor from Schenectady, New York, who had won fame by devising an air brake for railroad cars, solved the problem. Westinghouse purchased European patent rights to generators that used alternating current and transformers that reduced high-voltage power to lower voltage levels, thus making long-distance transmission more efficient.

Other entrepreneurs utilized new business practices to market Edison's and Westinghouse's technological breakthroughs. Samuel Insull, Edison's private secretary, organized Edison power plants across the country, amassing an electric-utility empire. In the late 1880s and early 1890s financiers Henry Villard and J. P. Morgan bought up patents in electric lighting and merged small equipment-manufacturing companies into the General Electric Company. Equally important, General Electric and Westinghouse Electric encouraged practical applications of electricity by establishing research laboratories that paid scientists to create electrical products for everyday use.

While corporations organized company labs, individual inventors continued to work independently and tried, sometimes successfully and sometimes not, to sell their handiwork and patents to manufacturers. One such inventor, Granville T. Woods, an engineer sometimes called the "black Edison," patented thirty-five devices vital to electronics and communications. Among his inventions, most of which he sold to companies such as General Electric, were an automatic circuit breaker, an electromagnetic brake, and instruments to aid communications between railroad trains.

Early innovations in the technology of the internal-combustion engine, which powers a piston by a series of

HENRY FORD AND THE AUTOMOBILE INDUSTRY explosions within a confined space, were undertaken by European engineers. Major progress occurred in Germany in 1885, when Gottlieb Daimler built a high-speed internal-combustion engine driven by vaporized gasoline. These developments inspired one of America's most visionary manufacturers, Henry Ford. In the 1890s Ford, an electrical engineer in Detroit's Edison Company, experimented in his spare time with using Daimler's gasoline-burning engine to power a vehicle. George Selden, a Rochester, New York, lawyer, had already been tinkering with such engines, but Ford applied organizational genius to this invention and spawned a massive industry.

Like Edison, Ford had a scheme as well as a product. In 1909 he declared, "I am going to democratize the automobile. When I'm through, everybody will be able to afford one, and about everyone will have one." Ford proposed to reach this goal by mass-producing thousands of identical cars in exactly the same way. Adapting methods of the meatpacking and metalworking industries, Ford engineers set up assembly lines that drastically reduced the time and cost of producing autos. Instead of performing numerous tasks, each worker was assigned

The Atlantic Cable

During the late nineteenth century, as American manufacturers expanded their markets overseas, their ability to communicate with customers and investors improved immeasurably as a result of a telegraph cable laid beneath the Atlantic Ocean. The telegraph was an American invention, and Cyrus Field, the man who came up with the idea to lay a cable across the Atlantic, was an American. Yet most of the engineers who worked on the Atlantic cable, as well as most of the capitalists involved in the venture, were British. In 1851, a British company laid the world's first successful undersea telegraph cable from Dover, England, to Calais, France, proving that an insulated wire could carry signals underwater. The effectiveness of this venture, which connected Reuters news service to the European continent and allowed French investors to receive instantaneous messages from the London Stock Exchange, inspired British and American businessmen to attempt a larger project across the Atlantic.

The first attempts to build a transatlantic cable failed, but in 1866 a British ship, funded by British investors, successfully laid a telegraph wire that operated without interruption. The project was designed by cooperative efforts of American and British electrical engineers. Thereafter, England and the United States grew more closely linked in their diplomatic relations, and citizens of both nations developed greater concern for each other as a result of their ability to receive international news more quickly. When American president James Garfield was assassinated in 1881, the news traveled almost instantly to Great Britain, and Britons mourned the death more profusely than they had mourned the passing of Abraham Lincoln, whose death was not known in England until eleven days after it occurred because transatlantic messages at that time traveled by steamship.

Some people lamented the stresses that near-instant international communications now created. One observer remarked that the telegraph tended "to make every person in a hurry, and I do not believe that with our business it is very desirable that it should be so." But financially savvy individuals experienced welcome benefits as a result of the cable's link. Rapid availability of stock quotes boomed the businesses of the New York and London stock exchanges, much to investors' delight. Newspaper readers enjoyed reading about events on the other side of the ocean the next day instead of a week after they occurred. And the success of the Atlantic cable inspired similar ventures in the Mediterranean Sea, the Indian Ocean, and, eventually, across the Pacific. By 1902 underwater cables circled the globe, and the age of global telecommunications had begun.

Laid by British ships across the ocean in 1866, the Atlantic cable linked the United States with England and continental Europe so that telegraph communications could be sent and received much more swiftly than ever before. Now Europeans and Americans could exchange news about politics, business, and military movements almost instantly, whereas previously such information could take a week or more to travel from one country to another.   (Library of Congress)

■ The assembly line broke the production process down into simple tasks that individual workers could efficiently repeat hour after hour. Here, assembly-line workers at the Ford plant in Highland Park, Michigan, outside Detroit, are installing pistons in engines of the Model T around 1914.   (Henry Ford Museum and Greenfield Village)

only one task, performed repeatedly, using the same specialized machine. A conveyor belt moved past stationary workers who fashioned each component part and progressively assembled the entire car.

The Ford Motor Company began operation in 1903. In 1908, the first year it built the Model T, Ford sold 10,000 cars. In 1913 the company's first full assembly line began producing automobiles in Highland Park, outside Detroit, and the next year, 248,000 Fords were sold. Rising automobile production created more jobs, higher earnings, and greater profits in related industries such as oil, paint, rubber, and glass, which in turn necessitated increased extraction of resources from the West and abroad. As well, the internal-combustion engine helped give birth to the manufacture of trucks, buses, and, ultimately, airplanes. These industries, as well as many others, would not have been possible without precision machine tools to create standardized parts. Advances in grinding and cutting materials in this era made production processes accurate to one-thousandth of an inch.

By 1914 many Ford cars cost $490, about one-fourth of their price a decade earlier. Yet even $490 was too expensive for many workers, who earned at best $2 a day. That year, however, Ford tried to spur productivity, prevent high labor turnover, head off unionization, and better enable his workers to buy the cars they produced by offering them the Five-Dollar-Day plan—a combination of wages and profit sharing.

The du Pont family did for the chemical industry what Edison and Ford did for the electrical and automobile industries. The du Ponts had been manufacturing gunpowder since the early 1800s. In 1902, fearing antitrust prosecution for the company's near-monopoly of the American explosives industry, three cousins, Alfred, Coleman, and Pierre, took over E. I. du Pont de Nemours and Company and broadened production into fertilizers, dyes, and other chemical products. In 1911 du Pont scientists and engineers working in the nation's first research labo-

THE DU PONTS AND THE CHEMICAL INDUSTRY

Tobacco production was one southern industry that traditionally hired African American laborers. This scene from a Richmond tobacco factory around 1880 shows women and children preparing leaves for curing by tearing off the stems.   (Valentine Museum)

ratory adapted cellulose to the production of new materials such as photographic film, rubber, lacquer, textile fibers, and plastics; the innovation wrought a significant transformation in consumer products. Du Pont research into dyestuffs, which are organic compounds, also aided the pharmaceutical industry. The du Pont company pioneered methods of management, accounting, and reinvestment of earnings, all of which contributed to efficient production, better recordkeeping, and higher profits.

The South's two major staple crops, tobacco and cotton, propelled that region into the machine age. Before

TECHNOLOGY AND SOUTHERN INDUSTRY

the 1870s, Americans used tobacco mainly for snuff, cigars, and chewing. But in 1876 James Bonsack, an eighteen-year-old Virginian, invented a machine for rolling cigarettes. Sales soared when James B. Duke of North Carolina, who popularized cigarettes just as Edison and Ford popularized their products, began marketing cigarettes by enticing consumers with free samples, trading cards, and billboards. By 1900 his American Tobacco Company was a nationwide business, employing Jewish immigrant cigar makers who trained laborers in the mass production of cigarettes.

Cigarette factories, located in southern cities, employed black and white workers (including women), though in separate locations of the plant.

New technology helped relocate the textile industry to the South. Electricity had made the water-powered mills in New England obsolete. New factories with electric looms were more efficient, and local investors built them in small towns along the Carolina Piedmont and elsewhere in the South, where a cheap labor force was available as well. Women and children who worked in these mills earned 50 cents a day for twelve or more hours of work—about half the wages northern workers received. New textile machinery needed fewer workers with fewer skills, and electric lighting expanded the hours of production.

By 1900 the South had more than four hundred textile mills, with a total of 4 million spindles. Many companies built villages around their mills, where they controlled housing, stores, schools, and churches. Inside these towns, owners banned criticism of the company and squelched attempts at union organization.

Northern and European capitalists financed other southern industries. Between 1890 and 1900, northern lumber syndicates moved into pine forests of the Gulf states, boosting production 500 percent. During the 1880s, northern investors developed southern iron and steel manufacturing, much of it in the boom city of Birmingham, Alabama. Except for some modernized plants, however, the South lacked technological innovations, such as in the machine-tool industry, that had enabled northern industries to compete with those of other industrializing nations.

Nevertheless, southern boosters heralded the emergence of a New South. Henry Grady, editor of the *Atlanta Constitution* and a passionate voice of southern progress, proclaimed, "We have sowed towns and cities in the place of theories, and put business in place of politics. We have challenged your spinners in Massachusetts and your iron-makers in Pennsylvania. . . . We have fallen in love with work." Grady's optimism was premature. A New South would eventually emerge, but not until after the First World War.

In all regions, the timing of technological innovation varied from one industry to another, but machines broadly altered the economy and everyday life.

CONSEQUENCES OF TECHNOLOGY Telephones and typewriters made face-to-face communication less important and facilitated correspondence and recordkeeping in the growing insurance, banking, and advertising firms. Electric sewing machines made mass-produced clothing available to almost everyone. Refrigeration changed dietary habits by enabling the preservation and shipment of meat, fruit, vegetables, and dairy products. Cash registers and adding machines revamped accounting and created new clerical jobs. At the same time, American universities established programs in engineering, making it less necessary for manufacturers like Edison and the du Ponts to depend on European universities for graduates in chemistry and physics.

Profits resulted from higher production at lower costs. As technological innovations made large-scale production more economical, owners replaced small factories with larger ones. Between 1850 and 1900, average capital investment in a manufacturing firm increased from $700,000 to $1.9 million. Only large companies could afford to buy complex machines and operate them at full capacity. And large companies could best take advantage of discounts for shipping products in bulk and for buying raw materials in quantity. Economists call such advantages economies of scale.

Profitability depended as much on how production was arranged as on the machines in use. Where once shop-floor workers such as the Watertown molders had control over how a product was made, by the 1890s engineers and managers with specialized knowledge had assumed this responsibility. They planned every task to increase output. By standardizing production, they reduced the need for worker skills and judgment, boosting profits at the expense of worker independence.

The most influential advocate of efficient production was Frederick W. Taylor. As foreman and engineer for the

FREDERICK W. TAYLOR AND EFFICIENCY Midvale Steel Company in the 1880s, Taylor concluded that the best way a company could reduce fixed costs and increase profits was to apply scientific studies of "how quickly the various kinds of work . . . ought to be done." The "ought" in Taylor's formulation signified producing more for lower cost per unit, usually by eliminating unnecessary workers. Similarly, "how quickly" signified that time and money were equivalent. Above all, efficiency was a science.

In 1898 Taylor took his stopwatch to the Bethlehem Steel Company to illustrate how his principles of scientific management worked. His experiments, he explained, required studying workers and devising "a series of motions which can be made quickest and best." Applying this technique to the shoveling of ore, Taylor designed fifteen kinds of shovels and prescribed the proper motions for using each one. He succeeded in reducing a crew of 600 men to 140. Soon, other companies, including the Watertown Arsenal, began applying Taylor's theories to their production lines.

■ Taken at the historic moment of liftoff, this photograph shows the first airplane flight at Kitty Hawk, North Carolina, December 17, 1903. With Orville Wright lying at the controls and brother Wilbur standing nearby, the plane was airborne only twelve seconds and traveled 120 feet. Even so, the flight marked the beginning of one of the twentieth century's most influential industries.   (Library of Congress)

As a result of Taylor's writings and experiments, time, as much as quality, became the measure of acceptable work, and science rather than experience determined the ways of doing things. As integral elements of the assembly line, which divided work into specific time-determined tasks, employees like the Watertown molders feared that they were becoming another kind of interchangeable part.

Mechanization and the Changing Status of Labor

By 1900, the status of labor had shifted dramatically in just a single generation. Technological innovation and assembly-line production created new jobs, but because most machines were labor saving, fewer workers could produce more in less time. Moreover, workers could no longer accurately be termed producers, as farmers and craftsmen had traditionally thought of themselves. The working class now consisted mainly of employees—men, women, and children who worked only when someone hired them. Producers had been paid in accordance with the quality of what they produced; now, employees received wages for time spent on the job.

As mass production subdivided manufacturing into small tasks, workers continually repeated the same

MASS PRODUCTION

specialized operation. One investigator found that the worker became "a mere machine. . . . Take the proposition of a man operating a machine to nail on 40 to 60 cases of heels in a day. That is 2,400 pairs, 4,800 shoes in a day. One not accustomed to it would wonder how a man could pick up and lay down 4,800 shoes in a day, to say nothing of putting them . . . into a machine. . . . That is the driving method of the manufacture of shoes under these minute subdivisions."

Assembly lines and scientific management also deprived employees of their independence. Workers could no longer decide themselves when to begin and end the workday, when to rest, and what tools and techniques to use. The clock and production experts regulated them. As a Massachusetts factory operative testified in 1879, "During working hours the men are not allowed to speak to each other, though working close together, on pain of instant discharge. Men are hired to watch and patrol the shop." And workers were now surrounded by others who labored at the same rate for the same pay, regardless of the quality of their effort.

Workers affected by these changes, such as the Watertown iron molders, struggled to retain independence and self-respect in the face of employers' ever-increasing power. As new groups encountered the industrial system, they resisted in various ways. Artisans such as cigar

■ The rise of new clerical occupations at the beginning of the twentieth century gave women countless employment opportunities. Employers hired women to file company records and type letters and paid them less than they paid male employees. The floor-to-ceiling file cases in the records room of Metropolitan Life Insurance Company in New York was the largest outfit of steel file cases in the world.   (Museum of the City of New York, Gift of Donald Beggs)

makers, glass workers, and coopers (barrel makers), caught in the transition from hand labor to machine production, fought to preserve their work pace and customs, such as appointing a fellow worker to read a newspaper aloud while they worked. When immigrants went to work in factories, they tried to persuade foremen to hire their relatives and friends, thus preserving on-the-job family and village ties. Off the job, workers continued to gather in saloons and parks for leisure-time activities such as social drinking and holiday celebrations, ignoring employers' attempts to control their social lives.

Employers, concerned with efficiency and productivity, wanted certain standards of behavior upheld. Thus, they supported temperance and moral-reform societies, dedicated to combating immoderate drinking and debauchery. Ford Motor Company required workers to satisfy the company's behavior code before becoming el-

igible for the profit-sharing segment of the Five-Dollar-Day plan. To increase worker incentives, some employers established piecework rates, paying laborers an amount per item produced, rather than an hourly wage. These efforts to increase productivity and maximize use of machines were intended to make workers docile (like the machines they operated).

As machines and assembly lines reduced the need for skilled workers, employers found they could cut labor costs by hiring women and children for low-skill, low-wage jobs. Between 1880 and 1900, the numbers of employed women soared from 2.6 million to 8.6 million. At the same time their occupational patterns underwent striking changes (see Figure 18.1). The proportion of women in domestic service (maids, cooks, laundresses)—the most common and

RESTRUCTURING OF THE WORK FORCE

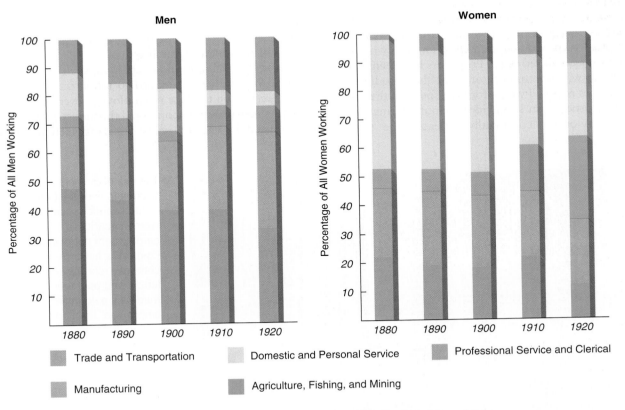

Figure 18.1   Distribution of Occupational Categories Among Employed Men and Women, 1880–1920

The changing lengths of the bar segments of each part of this graph represent trends in male and female employment. Over the forty years covered by this graph, the agriculture, fishing, and mining segment for men and the domestic service segment for women declined the most, while notable increases occurred in manufacturing for men and services (especially store clerks and teachers) for women.   (Source: U.S. Bureau of the Census, *Census of the United States, 1880, 1890, 1900, 1910, 1920* [Washington, D.C.: U.S. Government Printing Office].)

lowest-paid form of female employment—dropped as jobs opened in other sectors. In manufacturing, women usually held menial positions in textile mills and food-processing plants that paid as little as $1.56 a week for seventy hours of labor. (Unskilled men received $7 to $10 for a similar workweek.) Though the number of female factory hands tripled between 1880 and 1900, the proportion of women workers in these jobs remained about the same.

General expansion of the clerical and retail sectors, however, caused the numbers and percentages of women who were typists, bookkeepers, and sales clerks to skyrocket. Previously, when sales and office positions had required accounting and letter-writing skills, men had dominated such jobs. Then new inventions such as the typewriter, cash register, and adding machine simplified these tasks. By 1920 women filled nearly half of all clerical jobs; in 1880 only 4 percent had been women. Companies eagerly hired women who had taken trade-school courses in typing and shorthand and were looking for the better pay and conditions that clerical jobs offered compared with factory and domestic work. An official of a sugar company observed in 1919 that "all the bookkeeping of this company . . . is done by three girls and three bookkeeping machines . . . one operator takes the place of three men." Though paid low wages, women also were attracted to sales jobs because of the respectability, pleasant surroundings, and contact with affluent customers that such positions offered. Nevertheless, sex discrimination pervaded the clerical sector. In department stores, male cashiers took in cash and made change; women were seldom given responsibility for billing or counting money. Women held some low-level supervisory positions, but males dominated the managerial ranks.

Although most children who worked toiled on their parents' farms, the number in nonagricultural occupations tripled between 1870 and 1900. In 1890 over 18 percent of all children between ages ten and fifteen were gainfully employed (see Figure 18.2). Textile and shoe factories in particular employed workers below age sixteen. Mechanization created numerous light tasks, such as running errands and helping machine operators, that children could handle at a fraction of adult wages. Conditions were especially hard for child laborers in the South, where growing numbers of textile mills needed unskilled hands. Mill owners induced white sharecroppers and tenant farmers, who desperately needed extra income, to bind their children over to factories at miserably low wages.

Several states, especially in the Northeast, passed laws specifying minimum ages and maximum workday

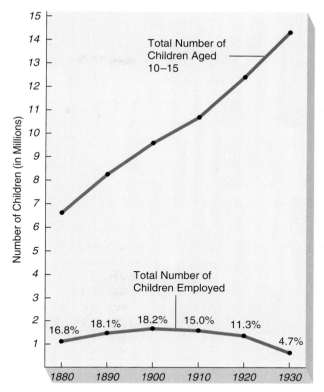

Figure 18.2   Children in the Labor Force, 1880–1930
The percentage of children in the labor force peaked around the turn of the century. Thereafter, the passage of state laws requiring children to attend school until age fourteen and limiting the ages at which children could be employed caused child labor to decline.   (Source: Data from *The Statistical History of the United States from Colonial Times to the Present* [Stamford, Conn.: Fairfield Publishers, 1965].)

hours for child labor. But large companies could evade regulations because such statutes regulated only firms operating within state borders, not those engaged in interstate commerce. Enforcing age requirements proved difficult because many parents, needing income from child labor, lied about their children's ages and employers rarely asked. After 1900, state laws and automation, along with compulsory school attendance laws, began to reduce the number of children employed in manufacturing, but many more worked at street trades—shining shoes and peddling newspapers and other merchandise—and as helpers in stores. After 1910 Progressive era reformers sought federal legislation to control child labor (see Chapter 21).

Industrial work was highly dangerous. Repetitive tasks using high-speed machinery dulled concentration,

■ Factories employed children from the early nineteenth century well into the twentieth. In textile mills like the one pictured here, girls operated machines, and boys ran messages and carried materials back and forth. Mill girls had to tie up their hair to keep it from getting caught in the machines. The girl posing here with a shawl over her head would not have worn that garment while she was working. (National Archives)

INDUSTRIAL ACCIDENTS

and the slightest mistake could cause serious injury. Industrial accidents rose steadily before 1920, killing or maiming hundreds of thousands of people each year. In 1913, for example, after factory owners had installed safety devices, some 25,000 people died in industrial mishaps, and 1 million were injured. For those with mangled limbs, infected cuts, and chronic illnesses, there was no disability insurance to replace lost income, and families stricken by such misfortunes suffered acutely.

Sensational disasters, such as explosions and mine cave-ins, aroused public clamor for better safety regulations. The most notorious tragedy was a fire at New York City's Triangle Shirtwaist Company in 1911, which killed 146 workers, most of them teenage Jewish immigrant women trapped in locked workrooms.

Despite public clamor, prevailing free-market views hampered passage of legislation that would regulate working conditions, and employers denied responsibility for employees' well-being. As one railroad manager declared, "The regular compensation of employees covers all risk or liability to accident. If an employee is disabled by sickness or any other cause, the right to claim compensation is not recognized."

Although factory workers endured unhealthy and dangerous working conditions, low wages caused the most suffering. Many employers believed in the "iron law of wages," which dictated that wage rates be set by the laws of supply and demand. In theory, because laborers were free to make their own choices, and because employers competed for labor, workers would receive the highest wages an employer could afford. In reality, under the "iron law," employers could pay as little as workers were willing to accept. Employers justified the system by invoking individual freedom: a worker who did not like the wages being paid was free to quit and find a job elsewhere.

"IRON LAW OF WAGES"

Courts regularly denied labor the right to organize and bargain collectively on grounds that wages should be individually negotiated between employee and employer. In contrast, wage earners believed the system trapped

■ On March 25, 1911, the worst factory fire in U.S. history occurred at the Triangle Shirtwaist Company, which occupied the top three floors of a building in New York City. Fed by piles of fabric, the fire spread quickly, killing 146 of the 500 young women, mostly Jewish immigrants, employed in the factory. Many of the victims, lined up at the morgue in this scene, were trapped inside rooms locked by their employer; others plunged to their death out of the upper-story windows.   (Juanita Hadwin Collector. Triangle Fire Lantern Slides, Kheel Center, Cornell University, Ithaca, NY 14853-3901)

them. A factory worker told Congress in 1879, "The market is glutted, and we have seasons of dullness; advantage is taken of men's wants, and the pay is cut down; our tasks are increased, and if we remonstrate, we are told our places can be filled. I work harder now than when my pay was twice as high."

Reformers and union leaders lobbied Congress for laws to improve working conditions, but the Supreme Court limited the scope of such legislation by narrowly defining which jobs were dangerous and which workers needed protection. In *Holden v. Hardy* (1896), the Court upheld a law regulating working hours of miners because overly long hours would increase the threat of injury. In *Lochner v. New York* (1905), however, the Court voided a law limiting bakery workers to a sixty-hour week and ten-hour day. Responding to the argument that states had authority to protect workers' health and safety, the Court ruled that baking was not a dangerous enough occupation to justify restricting workers' right to sell their labor freely. Such restriction, according to the Court, violated the Fourteenth Amendment's guarantee that no state could "deprive any person of life, liberty, or property without due process of law."

In *Muller v. Oregon* (1908), the Court used a different rationale to uphold a law limiting women to a ten-

COURT RULINGS ON LABOR REFORM

hour workday in laundries. In this case the Court set aside its *Lochner* argument that a state could not interfere with an individual's right of contract to assert that a woman's well-being "becomes an object of public interest and care in order to preserve the strength and vigor of the race." The case represented a victory for labor reformers, who had sought government regulation of hours and working conditions. As a result of the *Muller* decision, however, later laws barred women from occupations, such as printing and transportation, that required heavy lifting, long hours, or night work, thus further confining women to low-paying, dead-end jobs.

Labor Violence and the Union Movement

*W*orkers adjusted to mechanization as best they could. Some people submitted to the demands of the factory, machine, and time clock. Some tried to blend old ways of working into the new system. Some never adjusted and wandered from place to place, job to job. Others, however, turned to organized resistance. Anxiety over the loss of independence and a desire for better wages, hours, and working conditions pushed more workers into unions. Trade unions, which included only skilled workers in particular crafts such as printing and iron molding, dated from the early nineteenth century, but the narrowness of their membership left them without widespread influence. The National Labor Union, founded in 1866, claimed 640,000 members from a variety of industries but collapsed during the hard times of the 1870s.

In the economic slump that followed the Panic of 1873, railroad managers cut wages, increased workloads,

RAILROAD STRIKES OF 1877

and laid off workers, especially those who had joined unions. Such actions drove workers to strike and riot. The year 1877 marked a crisis for labor. In July unionized railroad workers organized a series of strikes to protest wage cuts. Violence spread from Pennsylvania and West Virginia to the Midwest, Texas, and California. Venting pent-up anger, rioters attacked railroad property, derailing trains and burning rail yards. State militia companies, organized and commanded by employers, broke up picket lines and fired into threatening crowds. In several communities, factory workers, wives, and merchants aided the strikers, while railroads enlisted strikebreakers to replace union men.

The worst violence occurred in Pittsburgh, where on July 21 state troops bayoneted and fired on rock-throwing demonstrators, killing ten and wounding many more. Infuriated, the mob drove the troops into a railroad roundhouse and set fires that destroyed 39 buildings, 104 engines, and 1,245 freight and passenger cars. The next day, the troops shot their way out of the roundhouse and killed twenty more citizens before fleeing the city. After more than a month of unprecedented carnage, President Rutherford B. Hayes sent in federal soldiers—the first significant use of the army to quell labor unrest.

Laborers in other industries sympathized with the strikers, as did residents of their communities. A Pittsburgh state militiaman, ordered out to break the 1877 strike, recalled, "I talked to all the strikers I could get my hands on, and I could find but one spirit and one purpose among them—that they were justified in resorting to any means to break down the power of the corporations."

The only broad-based labor organization to survive that depression was the Knights of Labor. Founded in

KNIGHTS OF LABOR

1869 by Philadelphia garment cutters, the Knights began recruiting other workers in the 1870s. In 1879 Terence V. Powderly, a machinist and mayor of Scranton, Pennsylvania, was elected grand master. Under his forceful guidance, Knights membership grew rapidly, peaking at 730,000 in 1886. In contrast to most craft unions, Knights welcomed unskilled and semiskilled workers, including women, immigrants, and African Americans.

The Knights tried to avert the bleak future that they believed industrialism portended by building a workers' alliance that offered an alternative to profit-oriented industrial capitalism. They believed they could eliminate conflict between labor and management by establishing a cooperative society in which laborers, not capitalists, owned the industries in which they worked for themselves. The goal, argued Powderly, was to "eventually make every man his own master—every man his own employer. . . . There is no good reason why labor cannot, through cooperation, own and operate mines, factories, and railroads." This view simultaneously strengthened and weakened the organization. The cooperative idea, attractive in the abstract, was unattainable because employers held the economic leverage and could outcompete laborers who might try to establish their own businesses. Strikes offered one means of achieving immediate goals, but Powderly and other Knights leaders argued that strikes tended to divert attention from the long-term goal of a cooperative society and that workers tended to lose more by striking than they won.

Some Knights, however, did support militant action. In 1886 the Knights demanded higher wages and union recognition from railroads in the Southwest. Railroad magnate Jay Gould refused to negotiate, and a strike began in Texas and spread to Kansas, Missouri, and Arkansas. As violence increased, Powderly met with Gould and called off the strike, hoping to reach a settlement. But Gould again rejected concessions, and the Knights gave in. Militant craft unions began to desert the Knights, upset by Powderly's compromise and confident that they could attain more on their own. Knights membership dwindled, although the union survived in a few small towns, where it made a brief attempt to unite with Populists in the 1890s (see Chapter 20). The special interests of craft unions replaced the Knights' broad-based but often vague appeal, and dreams of labor unity faded.

At the same time that Knights went on strike in the Southwest, several groups calling for an eight-hour

HAYMARKET RIOT

workday generated mass strikes and the largest spontaneous labor demonstration in the country's history. On May 1, 1886, in Chicago, some one hundred thousand workers turned out, including radical anarchists who believed in using violence to replace all government with voluntary cooperation. In Europe, labor radicals had made May 1 a day of special demonstration, and Chicago police, fearing that European radicals were transplanting their tradition of violence to the United States, mobilized to prevent disorder, especially among striking workers at the huge McCormick

■ The Haymarket Riot of 1886 was one of the most violent incidents of labor unrest in the late nineteenth century. This drawing, from *Frank Leslie's Illustrated Newspaper,* shows workers fleeing while police beat demonstrators with nightsticks. As this clash was occurring, a bomb, allegedly set off by anarchists, exploded, killing both police and workers.   (Library of Congress)

reaper plant. The day passed calmly, but two days later police stormed an area near the factory and broke up a battle between striking unionists and nonunion strikebreakers. Police shot and killed two unionists and wounded several others.

The next evening, labor groups rallied at Haymarket Square, near downtown Chicago, to protest police brutality. As a police company approached, a bomb exploded, killing seven and injuring sixty-seven. In reaction, authorities made mass arrests of anarchists and unionists. Eventually a court convicted eight anarchists of the bombing, though evidence of their guilt was questionable. Four were executed, and one committed suicide in prison. The remaining three were pardoned in 1893 by Illinois governor John P. Altgeld, who believed they had been victims of the "malicious ferocity" of the courts. Denounced by capitalists as a friend of anarchy, Altgeld found that his act of conscience ruined his political career.

The Haymarket bombing, like the 1877 railroad strikes, drew attention to labor's growing discontent and heightened fear of radicalism. The participation of anarchists and socialists, many of them foreign-born, created a feeling that forces of law and order had to act swiftly to prevent social turmoil. To protect their city, private Chicago donors helped to establish a military base at Fort Sheridan and the Great Lakes Naval Training Station. Elsewhere, governments strengthened police forces and armories. Employer associations, coalitions of manufacturers in the same industry, countered labor militancy by drawing up blacklists of union activists whom they would not employ, and by hiring private detectives to suppress strikes.

The American Federation of Labor (AFL), founded in 1886, emerged from the upheavals of that year as the

AMERICAN FEDERATION OF LABOR

major workers' organization. An alliance of national craft unions, the AFL had about 140,000 members, most of them skilled workers. Led by Samuel Gompers, a pragmatic and opportunistic immigrant who headed the Cigar Makers' Union, the AFL avoided the Knights' and anarchists' idealism to press for concrete goals: higher wages, shorter hours, and the right to bargain collectively. In contrast to the Knights, the AFL accepted the industrial system and worked to improve conditions within it.

AFL member unions retained autonomy in their own areas of skill but tried to develop a general policy that would suit all members. The national organization required constituent unions to hire organizers to expand membership, and it collected dues for a fund to aid members on strike. The AFL avoided party politics, adhering instead to Gompers's dictum to support labor's friends and oppose its enemies, regardless of party.

AFL membership grew to 1 million by 1901 and 2.5 million by 1917, when it represented 111 national unions and 27,000 local unions. But because member unions tried to protect skilled workers by organizing by craft rather than by workplace, they had little interest in recruiting unskilled workers. Nor did they recruit women. Of 6.3 million employed women in 1910, fewer than 2 percent belonged to unions. Male unionists often rationalized women's exclusion by insisting that women should not be employed. According to one labor leader, "Woman is not qualified for the conditions of wage labor. . . . The mental and physical makeup of woman is in revolt against wage service. She is competing with the man who is her father or husband or is to become her husband." Mostly, unionists worried that because women were paid less than men, their own wages would be lowered or that they would lose jobs if women invaded the workplace. Moreover, male workers, accustomed to sex segregation in employment, could not imagine working side by side with women.

Organized labor also excluded most immigrant and African American workers, often fearing that such groups would depress wages. Some trade unions welcomed skilled immigrants—foreign-born craftsmen were prominent leaders of several unions—but only the more radical unions had explicit policies of accepting immigrants and blacks. Blacks were prominent in the coal miners' union and were partially unionized in trades such as construction, barbering, and dock work, which had large numbers of African American workers. But they could belong only to segregated local unions in the South, and the majority of northern AFL unions had exclusion policies. Long-held prejudices were reinforced when blacks and immigrants, eager for any work they could get, worked as strikebreakers, hired to replace striking whites.

The AFL and the labor movement suffered a series of setbacks in the early 1890s, when once again labor violence stirred public fears. In July 1892 the AFL-affiliated Amalgamated Association of Iron and Steelworkers refused to accept pay cuts and went on strike in Homestead, Pennsylvania. Henry C. Frick, president of Carnegie Steel Company, then closed the plant. Shortly thereafter, Frick tried to protect the plant by hiring three hundred guards from the Pinkerton Detective Agency and floating them in by barge under cover of darkness. Lying in wait on the shore of the Monongahela River, angry workers attacked and routed the guards. State troops intervened, and after five months the strikers gave in. By then public opinion had turned against the union, after a young anarchist who was not a striker attempted to assassinate Frick.

HOMESTEAD STRIKE

In 1894 workers at the Pullman Palace (railroad passenger) Car Company walked out in protest over exploitative policies at the company town near Chicago. The paternalistic George Pullman provided everything for the twelve thousand residents of the so-called model town named after him. His company owned and controlled all land and buildings, the school, the bank, and the water and gas systems. It paid wages, fixed rents, and spied on disgruntled employees. As one laborer grumbled, "We are born in a Pullman house, fed from the Pullman shop, taught in the Pullman school, catechized

PULLMAN STRIKE

in the Pullman church, and when we die we shall be buried in the Pullman cemetery and go to the Pullman hell."

One thing Pullman would not do was negotiate with workers. When hard times began in 1893, Pullman tried to protect profits and stock dividends by cutting wages 25 to 40 percent while holding firm on rents and prices in the town. Hard-pressed workers sent a committee to Pullman to protest his policies. He reacted by firing three members of the committee. Enraged workers, most of them from the American Railway Union, called a strike; Pullman retaliated by closing the factory. The union, led by the charismatic Eugene V. Debs, voted to aid the strikers by refusing to handle any Pullman cars attached to any trains. Pullman still rejected arbitration. The railroad owners' association then enlisted aid from U.S. Attorney General Richard Olney, a former railroad attorney, who obtained a court injunction to prevent the union from "obstructing the railways and holding up the mails." President Grover Cleveland ordered federal troops to Chicago, ostensibly to protect rail-carried mail but in reality to crush the strike. Within a month strikers gave in, and Debs went to prison for defying the court injunction. The Supreme Court upheld Debs's six-month sentence on grounds that the federal government had the power to remove obstacles to interstate commerce.

In the West, Colorado miners engaged in several bitter struggles and violent strikes. In 1905 they helped form a new, radical labor organization, the Industrial Workers of the World (IWW). Unlike the AFL, the IWW strove like the Knights of Labor to unite all laborers, including the unskilled and African Americans who were excluded from craft unions. Its motto was "An injury to one is an injury to all," and its goal was "One Big Union." But the "Wobblies," as IWW members were known, exceeded the goals of the Knights by espousing tactics of violence and sabotage.

IWW

Embracing the rhetoric of class conflict—"The final aim is revolution," according to IWW creed—and an ideology of socialism, Wobblies believed workers should seize and run the nation's industries. "Mother" Jones, an Illinois coalfield union organizer; Elizabeth Gurley Flynn, a fiery orator known as the "Joan of Arc of the labor movement"; and William D. (Big Bill) Haywood, the brawny, one-eyed founder of the Western Federation of Miners, led a series of strife-torn strikes. Demonstrations erupted in western lumber and mining camps, in the steel town of McKees Rocks, Pennsylvania (1907), and in the textile mills of Lawrence, Massachusetts (1912). Though the Wobblies' anticapitalist goals and aggressive tactics attracted considerable publicity, IWW membership probably never exceeded 150,000. The organization collapsed during the First World War when federal prosecution sent many of its leaders to jail and local police forces and mobs violently harassed IWW members.

Despite their general exclusion from the union movement, women employees did organize and fight employers as strenuously as men did. Since the early years of industrialization, female workers had formed their own labor associations. Some, such as the Collar Laundry Union of Troy, New York, organized in the 1860s, had successfully struck for higher wages. The "Uprising of the 20,000" in New York City, a 1909 strike by male and female immigrant members of the International Ladies Garment Workers Union (ILGWU), was one of the country's largest strikes to that time. Women were also prominent in the 1912 Lawrence, Massachusetts, textile workers' strike. Female trade-union membership swelled during the 1910s, but men monop-

WOMEN UNIONISTS

olized national trade-union leadership, even in industries with large female work forces, such as garment manufacturing, textiles, and boots and shoes.

Women, however, did dominate one union: the Telephone Operators' Department of the International Brotherhood of Electrical Workers. Organized in Montana and San Francisco early in the twentieth century, the union spread throughout the Bell system, the nation's monopolistic telephone company and single largest employer of women. To promote solidarity among their mostly young members, union leaders organized dances, excursions, and bazaars. They also sponsored educational programs to enhance members' leadership skills. The union focused mainly on workplace issues. Intent on developing pride and independence among telephone operators, the union resisted scientific management techniques and tightening of supervision. In 1919 several militant union branches paralyzed the phone service of five New England states, but the union collapsed after a failed strike, again in New England, in 1923.

■ In 1919, telephone operators, mostly female, went out on strike and shut down phone service throughout New England. These workers, who interrupted their picketing to pose for the photograph, showed that women could take forceful action in support of their labor interests.   (Corbis-Bettmann)

The first women's organization seeking to promote interests of laboring women was the Women's Trade Union League (WTUL), founded in 1903 and patterned after a similar organization in England. The WTUL sought workplace protection legislation and reduced hours for female workers, sponsored educational activities, and campaigned for women's suffrage. It helped telephone operators organize their union, and in 1909 it supported the ILGWU's massive strike against New York City sweatshops. Initially the union's highest offices were held by middle-class women who sympathized with female wage laborers, but control shifted in the 1910s to forceful working-class leaders, notably Agnes Nestor, a glove maker; Rose Schneiderman, a cap maker; and Mary Anderson, a shoe worker. The WTUL advocated opening apprenticeship programs to women so they could enter skilled trades and training female workers to assume leadership roles. It served as a vital link between the labor and women's movements into the 1920s.

The dramatic labor struggles in the half-century following the Civil War make it easy to forget that only a small fraction of American wage workers belonged to unions. In 1900 about 1 million out of a total of 27.6 million workers were unionized. By 1920 total union membership had grown to 5 million, still only 13 percent of the work force. Unionization was strong in construction trades, transportation, communications, and, to a lesser extent, manufacturing. For many workers, getting and holding a job took priority over wages and hours. Job instability and the seasonal nature of work seriously hindered union-organizing efforts. Few companies employed a full work force all year round; most employers hired workers during peak seasons and laid them off during slack periods. Thus employment rates fluctuated wildly. The 1880 census showed that in some communities 30 percent of adult males had been jobless at some time during the previous year. Moreover, union organizers took no interest in large segments of the industrial labor force and intentionally barred others.

THE EXPERIENCE OF WAGE WORK

The millions of men, women, and children who were not unionized tried in their own ways to cope with pressures of the machine age. Increasing numbers, both native-born and immigrant, turned to fraternal societies such as the Polish Roman Catholic Union and the Jewish B'nai B'rith. For small monthly or yearly contributions these organizations provided members with life insurance, sickness benefits, and funeral expenses and had become widespread by the early twentieth century.

For most American workers, the machine age had mixed benefits. Industrial wages, though rarely generous, rose between 1877 and 1914, boosting purchasing power and creating a mass market for standardized goods. Yet in 1900 most employees worked sixty hours a week at wages that averaged 20 cents an hour for skilled work and 10 cents an hour for unskilled. And workers found that even as their wages rose, living costs increased even faster.

Standards of Living

Some Americans, like the Watertown molders, distrusted a system that treated them like machines, but few could resist the experts' claims that efficiency and mechanization were improving everyday life. The expansion of railroad, postal, and telephone service drew even isolated communities into the orbit of a consumer-oriented society. American ingenuity combined with mass production and mass marketing to make available myriad goods that previously had not existed or had been the exclusive property of the wealthy. The new material well-being, symbolized by canned foods, ready-made clothes, and home appliances, had a dual effect. It blended Americans of differing status into consumer communities defined not by place of residence or class but by possessions, and it accentuated differences between those who could afford goods and services and those who could not.

If a society's affluence can be measured by how it converts luxuries into commonplace articles, the United States was indeed becoming affluent in the years between 1880 and 1920. In 1880 smokers rolled their own cigarettes; only wealthy women could afford silk stockings; only residents of Florida, Texas, and California could enjoy fresh oranges; and people made candy and soap at home. By 1899 manufactured goods and perishable foodstuffs had become increasingly available. That year Americans bought 2 billion machine-produced cigarettes and 151,000 pairs of silk stockings, consumed oranges at the rate of 100 crates for every 1,000 people, and spent an average of $1.08 per person on store-bought candy and 63 cents per person on soap. By 1921 the transformation had advanced even further. Americans smoked 43 billion cigarettes that year (403 per person), bought 217 million pairs of silk stockings, ate 248 crates of oranges per 1,000 people, and spent $1.66 per person on confectionery goods and $1.40 on soap.

COMMONPLACE LUXURIES

What people can afford obviously depends on their resources and incomes. Data for the period show that incomes rose broadly. The expanding economy spawned massive fortunes and created a new industrial elite. An 1891 magazine article estimated that 120 Americans were worth at least $10 million. By 1920 the richest 5 percent of the population received almost one-fourth of all earned income. Incomes also rose among the middle class. For example, average pay for clerical workers rose 36 percent between 1890 and 1910 (see Table 18.1). At the turn of the century, employees of the federal executive branch averaged $1,072 a year, and college professors $1,100 (between $20,000 and $25,000 in modern dollars), not handsome sums, but much more than manual workers received. With such incomes, the middle class, whose numbers were increasing as a result of new job opportunities, could afford relatively comfortable housing. A six- or seven-room house cost around $3,000 to buy or build (about $85,000 to $90,000 in current dollars) and from $15 to $20 per month ($450 to $550 in current dollars) to rent.

Though wages for industrial workers increased, their income figures were deceptive because jobs were not always secure and workers had to expend a disproportionate amount of income on necessities. On average, annual wages of factory workers rose about 30 percent, from $486 in 1890 (about $12,000 to $14,000 in modern dollars) to $630 in 1910 (about $15,000 to $17,000 in current dollars). In industries with large female work forces, such as shoe and paper manufacturing, hourly rates remained lower than in male-dominated industries such as coal mining and iron production. Regional variations were also wide. Nevertheless, as Table 18.1 shows, most wages moved upward. Income for farm laborers followed the same trend, though wages remained relatively low because farm workers generally received free room and board.

Wage increases mean little, however, if living costs rise as fast or faster. That is what happened. The weekly cost of living for a typical wage earner's

COST OF LIVING family of four rose over 47 percent between 1889 and 1913. In other words, a combination of food and other goods that cost $6.78 in 1889 increased, after a slight dip in the mid-1890s, to $10 by 1913. In few working-class occupations did income rise as fast as cost of living.

How then could working-class Americans afford machine-age goods and services? Many could not. The daughter of a textile worker, recalling her school days, described how "some of the kids would bring bars of chocolate, others an orange. . . . I suppose they were richer than a family like ours. My father used to buy a bag of candy and a bag of peanuts every payday. . . . And

TABLE 18.1

American Living Standards, 1890–1910

	1890	1910
Income and earnings		
Annual income		
Clerical worker	$848	$1,156
Public school teacher	256	492
Industrial worker	486	630
Farm laborer	233	336
Hourly wage		
Soft-coal miner	0.18[a]	0.21
Iron worker	0.17[a]	0.23
Shoe worker	0.14[a]	0.19
Paper worker	0.12[a]	0.17
Labor statistics		
Number of people in labor force	28.5 million	41.7 million[b]
Average workweek in manufacturing	60 hours	51 hours

a. 1892
b. 1920

that's all we'd have until the next payday." Another woman explained how her family coped with high prices and low wages: "My mother made our clothes. People then wore old clothes. My mother would rip them out and make them over."

Still, a family could raise its income and partake modestly in consumer society by sending children and
SUPPLEMENTS TO women into the labor market (see
FAMILY INCOME pages 488–489). In a household where the father made $600 a year, wages of other family members might lift total family income to $800 or $900. Many families also rented rooms to boarders and lodgers, a practice that could yield up to $200 a year and provide housewives with vital roles in the family economy. These means of increasing family income enabled people to spend more and save more. Between 1889 and 1901, working-class families markedly increased expenditures for life insurance and union dues as well as for new leisure activities (see Chapter 19). Workers were thus able to improve their living standards, but not without sacrifices.

More than ever, American working people lived within a highly developed wage and money economy. Between 1890 and 1920, the labor force increased by 50 percent, from 28 million workers to 42 million. These figures, however, are misleading: in general, they represent a change in the nature of work as much as an increase in the number of available jobs. In the rural society that predominated in the nineteenth century, women and children performed jobs crucial to a family's daily existence—cooking, cleaning, planting, and harvesting—but they seldom appeared in employment figures because they earned no wages. As the nation industrialized and the agricultural sector's share of national income and population declined, paid employment became more common. Jobs in industry and commerce were easier to define and easier to count. The proportion of Americans who worked—whether in fields, households, factories, or offices—probably did not increase markedly. Most Americans, male and female, had always worked. What was new was the increase in paid employment, making purchases of consumer goods and services more affordable.

Science and technology eased some of life's struggles, and their impact on living standards strengthened after

HIGHER LIFE EXPECTANCY

1900. Medical advances, better diets, and improved housing sharply reduced death rates and extended life. Between 1900 and 1920, life expectancy rose by fully six years and the death rate dropped by 24 percent. Notable declines occurred in deaths from typhoid, diphtheria, influenza (except for a harsh pandemic in 1918 and 1919), tuberculosis, and intestinal ailments—diseases that had been scourges of earlier generations. There were, however, significantly more deaths from cancer, diabetes, and heart disease, afflictions of an aging population and of new environmental factors such as smoke and chemical pollution. Americans also found more ways to kill one another: although suicide rates remained stable, homicides and automobile-related deaths—effects of a fast-paced urban society—increased dramatically.

Not only were amenities and luxuries more available than in the previous half-century, but means to upward mobility seemed more accessible as well. Though inequities that had pervaded earlier eras remained in place, and race, gender, religion, and ethnicity still affected access to opportunity, education increasingly became the key to success. Public education, aided by construction of new schools and passage of laws that required children to stay in school to age fourteen, equipped young people to achieve a living standard higher than their parents'. Between 1890 and 1922, the number of students enrolled in public high schools rose dramatically, though by today's standards graduation rates among young people were low—16.3 percent in 1920, up from 3.5 percent in 1890. The creation of managerial and sales jobs in service industries helped to counter the downward mobility that resulted when mechanization pushed skilled workers out of their crafts. And the resulting

goods of mass production meant that even workers found life more convenient.

At the vanguard of a revolution in American lifestyles stood the toilet. The chain-pull washdown water closet,

FLUSH TOILETS

invented in England around 1870, reached the United States in the 1880s. Shortly after 1900 the flush toilet appeared; thanks to mass production of enamel-coated fixtures, it became common in American homes and buildings. The toilet, cheap and easy to install, brought about a shift in habits and attitudes. Before 1880 only luxury hotels and estates had private indoor bathrooms. By the 1890s the germ theory of disease had raised fears about carelessly disposed human waste as a source of infection and water contamination. Much more rapidly than Europeans did, Americans combined a desire for cleanliness with an urge for convenience, and began including water closets in middle-class urban houses. By the 1920s, they were prevalent in many working-class homes too. Bodily functions took on an unpleasant image, and the home bathroom became a place of utmost privacy. Edward and Clarence Scott, who produced white tissue in perforated rolls, provided Americans a more convenient form of toilet paper than the rough paper they had previously used. At the same time, toilets and private bathtubs gave Americans new ways to use—and waste—water. Plumbing advances belonged to a broader democratization of convenience that accompanied mass production and consumerism.

The tin can also altered lifestyles. Before the mid-nineteenth century, Americans typically ate only foods

PROCESSED AND PRESERVED FOODS

that were in season. Drying, smoking, and salting could preserve meat for a short time, but the availability of fresh meat and fresh milk was limited; there was no way to prevent spoilage. A French inventor developed the cooking-and-sealing process of canning around 1810, and in the 1850s an American man named Gail Borden devised a means of condensing and preserving milk. Availability of canned goods and condensed milk increased during the 1860s, but processing some foods was difficult, and container supplies remained low because cans had to be made by hand. In the 1880s, technology solved production problems. Inventors fashioned machines to peel fruits and vegetables and to process salmon, as well as stamping and soldering machines to mass-produce cans from tin plate. Now, even people remote from markets, like sailors and cowboys, could readily consume tomatoes, milk, oysters, and other alternatives to previously monotonous diets. Housewives preserved their own fruits and vegetables, "putting up" foods in sealed glass jars.

Other trends and inventions broadened Americans' diets. Growing urban populations created demands that encouraged fruit and vegetable farmers to raise more produce. Railroad refrigerator cars enabled growers and meatpackers to ship perishables greater distances and to preserve them for longer periods. By the 1890s northern city dwellers could enjoy southern and western strawberries, grapes, and tomatoes for several months of the year. Home iceboxes enabled middle-class families to store perishables. An easy means of producing ice commercially was invented in the 1870s, and by 1900 the nation had two thousand commercial ice plants, most of which made home deliveries.

Availability of new foods also inspired health reformers to correct the American diet. In the 1870s John

DIETARY REFORM H. Kellogg, nutritionist and manager of the Western Health Reform Institute in Battle Creek, Michigan, began serving patients new health foods, including peanut butter and wheat flakes. Several years later his brother, William K. Kellogg, invented corn flakes, and Charles W. Post introduced Grape-Nuts, revolutionizing breakfast by replacing eggs, potatoes, and meat with ready-to-eat cereal, which supposedly was healthier. Just before the First World War, scientists discovered the dietetic value of vitamins A and B (C and D were discovered after the war). Growing numbers of published cookbooks and the opening of cooking schools reflected heightened interest in food and its possibilities for health and enjoyment. As well, home gardens in urban backyards became easier to tend, aided by the Burpee Company, founded in Philadelphia in 1876, which mailed flower and vegetable seeds to gardeners who bought them through mail-order catalogues—just as they bought goods from Sears Roebuck.

Even the working class enjoyed a more diversified diet. As in the past, the poorest people still consumed cheap foods, heavy in starches and carbohydrates. Southern textile workers, for example, ate corn mush and fatback (the strip of meat from a hog's back) almost every day. Poor urban families seldom could afford meat. Now, though, many of them could purchase previously unavailable fruits, vegetables, and dairy products. Workers had to spend a high percentage of their income on food—almost half of a breadwinner's wages—but they never suffered the severe malnutrition that plagued other developing nations.

Just as cans and iceboxes made many foods widely available, the sewing machine sparked a revolution in

Using color, large-scale scenes, and fanciful images, manufacturers of consumer goods advertised their products to a public eager to buy. This ad from the W. K. Kellogg Company, maker of breakfast foods, shows the increasingly common practice of using an attractive young woman to capture attention.   (Picture Research Consultants & Archives)

READY-MADE CLOTHING clothing. Before 1850 nearly all clothes Americans wore were made at home or by seamstresses and tailors, and a person's social status was apparent in what he or she wore. Then in the 1850s the sewing machine, invented in Europe but refined by Americans Elias Howe Jr. and Isaac M. Singer, came into use in clothing and shoe manufacture. Demand for uniforms during the Civil War boosted the ready-made (as opposed to custom-made) clothing industry, and by 1890 annual retail sales of machine-made garments reached $1.5 billion. Mass production enabled manufacturers to turn out good-quality apparel at relatively low cost and to standardize sizes to fit different body shapes. By 1900 only the poorest families could not afford "ready-to-wear" clothes. Tailors and seamstresses, once the main clothing producers, were relegated to repair work. Many women continued to make clothing at home, to save money or as a hobby,

■ Advertising, which developed into a powerful medium in the late nineteenth century, used explicit and implicit domestic images to reinforce a wife's role as homemaker. This ad implies that a devoted wife lovingly assumes tasks such as sewing and mending clothing, guided into her role by a strong and superior husband. (Library of Congress)

1900s, long hair tied behind the neck was the most popular style. By the First World War, when many women worked in hospitals and factories, shorter and less hindering hairstyles had become acceptable.

Men's clothes, too, became lightweight and stylish. Before 1900 men in the middle and well-off working classes would have owned two suits, one for Sundays and special occasions and one for everyday wear. After 1900, however, manufacturers began to produce garments from fabrics of different weights and for different seasons. Men replaced derbies with felt hats, and stiff collars and cuffs with soft ones; somber, dark-blue serge gave way to lighter shades and more intricate weaves. Workingmen still needed durable, inexpensive overalls, shirts, and shoes. But even for males of modest means, clothing was becoming something to be bought instead of made and remade at home.

Department and Chain Stores
Department stores and chain stores helped to create and serve this new consumerism. Between 1865 and 1900, Macy's in New York, Wanamaker's in Philadelphia, Marshall Field in Chicago, and Rich's in Atlanta became urban landmarks. Previously, working classes bought goods in stores with limited inventories, and wealthier people patronized fancy shops; price, quality of goods, and social custom discouraged each from shopping at the other's establishments. Now department stores, with their open displays of clothing, housewares, and furniture—all available in large quantities to anyone with the purchase price—caused a merchandising revolution. They offered not only a wide variety but also home deliveries, exchange policies, and charge accounts.

Meanwhile, the Great Atlantic Tea Company, founded in 1859, became the first grocery chain. Renamed the Great Atlantic and Pacific Tea Company in 1869 (and known as A&P), the firm's stores bought in volume and sold to the public at low prices. By 1915 there were eighteen hundred A&P stores, and twelve thousand more were built in the next ten years. Other chains, such as Woolworth's dime stores that sold inexpensive personal items and novelties, grew rapidly during the same period.

Advertising
A society of scarcity does not need advertising: when demand exceeds supply, producers have no trouble selling what they market. But in a society of abundance such as industrial America, supply frequently outstrips demand, necessitating a means to increase and create demand. Thus advertising assumed a new scale and function. In 1865 retailers spent about $9.5 million on advertising;

but commercial dress patterns intended for use with a sewing machine simplified home production of clothing and injected another form of standardization into everyday life.

Mechanized mass-produced garments and dress patterns altered clothing styles. Restrictive Victorian styles still dominated female fashions, but women were abandoning the most burdensome features. As women's participation in work and leisure activities became more active, dress designers placed greater emphasis on comfort. In the 1890s long sleeves and skirt hemlines receded, and high-boned collars disappeared. Women began wearing tailored blouses called shirtwaists, manufactured by such companies as the Triangle Shirtwaist Factory. Designers used less fabric; by the 1920s a dress required three yards of material instead of ten. Petite prevailed as the ideal: the most desirable waist measurement was 18 to 20 inches, and corsets were big sellers. In the early that sum reached $95 million by 1900 and nearly $500 million by 1919.

In the late nineteenth century, large companies that mass-produced consumer goods hired advertisers to create "consumption communities," bodies of consumers loyal to a particular brand name. In 1881 Congress passed a trademark law enabling producers to register and protect brand names. Thousands of companies registered products as varied as Hires Root Beer, Uneeda Biscuits, and Carter's Little Liver Pills. Advertising agencies—a service industry pioneered by N. W. Ayer & Son of Philadelphia—in turn offered expert advice to compa-

nies that wished to cultivate brand loyalty. Newspapers served as the prime instrument for advertising. In the mid-nineteenth century, publishers began to pursue higher revenues by selling more ad space. Wanamaker's placed the first full-page ad in 1879, and advertisers began to use large print and to include elaborate illustrations and photographs of products. Such attention-getting techniques transformed advertising into news. More than ever before, people read newspapers to find out what was for sale as well as what was happening.

Outdoor billboards and electrical signs rivaled newspapers as important advertising organs. Advertisers posted signs in railroad and subway stations, and billboards on city buildings and alongside roads promoted national products such as Gillette razors, Kodak cameras, Wrigley chewing gum, and Budweiser beer. In the mid-1890s, electricity made lighted billboards more dynamic and appealing. Commercial districts were lit up by what one spokesman called "a medium of motion, of action, of *life*, of *light*, of compulsory attraction." The flashing electric signs on New York City's Broadway—such as a forty-five-foot Heinz pickle in green bulbs and a huge illuminated chariot race atop the Hotel Normandie—gave the street its label "the Great White Way." Soon "talking" signs were installed, with reading matter moving along signboards providing news as well as advertising copy in a multitude of colors. Americans now had a variety of inducements to consume.

The Corporate Consolidation Movement

*N*either new products nor new marketing techniques could mask certain unsettling factors in the American economy. The huge capital investment in new technology meant that factories had to operate at near capacity to recover costs. But the more manufacturers produced, the more they had to sell. To sell more, they had to reduce prices. To increase profits and compensate for reduced prices, they further expanded production and often reduced wages. To expand, they borrowed money. And to repay loans, they had to produce and sell even more. This spiraling process strangled small firms that could not keep pace and thrust workers into constant uncertainty. The same cycle affected commerce, banking, and transportation as well as manufacturing.

In this environment, optimism could dissolve at the hint that debtors could not meet their obligations. Indeed, financial panics afflicted the economy during every decade in the late nineteenth century, ruining businesses and destroying workers' security. Economic declines that began in 1873, 1884, and 1893 lingered for several years. Business leaders disagreed on what caused them. Some blamed overproduction; others pointed to underconsumption; still others blamed lax credit and investment practices. Whatever the explanation, businesspeople began seeking ways to combat the uncertainty of boom-and-bust business cycles. Many adopted centralized forms of business organization, notably corporations, pools, trusts, and holding companies.

Unlike laborers, industrialists never questioned the capitalist system. They sought new ways to build on the base that had supported economic growth since the early 1800s, when states adopted incorporation laws to encourage commerce and industry. Under such laws, almost anyone could start a company and raise money by selling stock to investors. Stockholders shared in profits without personal risk because laws limited their liability for company debts to the amount of their own investment; the rest of their wealth was protected should the company fail. Nor did investors need to concern themselves with a firm's day-to-day operation; responsibility for company administration rested with its managers.

RISE OF CORPORATIONS

Corporations proved to be the best instruments to raise capital for industrial expansion, and by 1900 two-thirds of all goods manufactured in the United States were produced by corporate firms such as General Electric and the American Tobacco Company. Corporations won judicial protection in the 1880s and 1890s when the Supreme Court ruled that they, like individuals, are protected by the Fourteenth Amendment. That is, states could not deny corporations equal protection under the law and could not deprive them of rights or property without due process of law. Such rulings insulated corporations against government interference in their operations.

As downward swings of the business cycle threatened profits, corporation managers sought greater stability in new and larger forms of economic concentration. Between the late 1880s and early 1900s, an epidemic of business consolidation swept the country, resulting in massive conglomerates that have since dominated the nation's economy. At first such alliances were tentative and informal, consisting mainly of cooperative agreements among firms that manufactured the same product or offered the same service. Through these arrangements, called pools, competing companies tried to control the market by agreeing how much each should produce and sharing profits. Used by railroads (to divide up traffic), steel producers, and whiskey distillers, pools depended on their members' honesty. Such "gentlemen's agreements" worked during good times when there was enough business for all; but during slow periods, desire for profits often tempted pool members to secretly reduce prices or sell more than the agreed quota. The Interstate Commerce Act of 1887 outlawed pools among railroads (see page 546), but by then the pooling strategy's usefulness was already fading.

POOLS

■ Believing that Rockefeller's Standard Oil monopoly was exercising dangerous power, this political cartoonist depicts the trust as a greedy octopus whose sprawling tentacles already ensnare Congress, state legislatures, and the taxpayer, and are reaching for the White House. (Library of Congress)

John D. Rockefeller, boss of Standard Oil, disliked pools, calling them weak and undependable. In 1879 one

TRUSTS

of his lawyers, Samuel Dodd, devised a more stable means of dominating the market. Because state laws prohibited one corporation from holding stock in another corporation, Dodd adapted an old device called a trust, a legal arrangement whereby a responsible individual would manage the financial affairs of a person unwilling or unable to handle them alone. Dodd reasoned that one company could control an industry by luring or forcing stockholders of smaller companies in that industry to yield control of their stock "in trust" to the larger company's board of trustees. This device allowed Rockefeller to achieve horizontal integration—the acquisition of several similar companies—of the profitable petroleum industry in 1882 by combining his Standard Oil Company of Ohio with other refineries he bought up.

In 1888 New Jersey adopted new laws allowing corporations chartered there to own property in other states

HOLDING COMPANIES

and to own stock in other corporations. (Trusts provided for trusteeship, not ownership.) This liberalization facilitated creation of the holding company,

which owned a partial or complete interest in other companies. Holding companies could in turn merge their companies' assets (buildings, equipment, inventory, and cash) as well as their management. Under this arrangement, Rockefeller's holding company, Standard Oil of New Jersey, merged forty refining companies. By 1898 Standard Oil refined 84 percent of all oil produced in the nation, controlled most pipelines, and engaged in natural-gas production and ownership of oil-producing properties.

Standard Oil's expansion into operations besides refining exemplified a new form of economic combination. To dominate their markets, many holding companies sought control over all aspects of their operations, including raw-materials extraction, product manufacture, and distribution. A model of such vertical integration, which fused related business under unified management, was Gustavus Swift's meat-processing operation. During the 1880s, Swift invested in livestock, slaughterhouses, refrigerator cars, and marketing to ensure profits from the sale of his beef at prices he could control. With their widespread operations, both Swift and Standard Oil extended the economic tentacles of single companies that connected West to East, North to South.

Mergers provided answers to industry's search for order and profits. Between 1889 and 1903, some three hundred combinations were formed, most of them trusts and holding companies. The most spectacular was U.S. Steel Corporation, financed by J. P. Morgan in 1901. This enterprise, made up of iron-ore properties, freight carriers, wire mills, and other firms, was capitalized at over $1.4 billion. Other mammoth combinations included the Amalgamated Copper Company, American Sugar Refining Company, and U.S. Rubber Company. In 1896 fewer than a dozen corporations were worth over $10 million; by 1903 three hundred were worth that much, and seventeen had assets exceeding $100 million. At the same time, these huge companies ruthlessly put thousands of competitors out of business.

The merger movement created a new species of businessman, one whose vocation was financial organizing rather than producing a particular good or service. Shrewd operators sought opportunities for combination, formed a holding company, then persuaded producers to sell their firms to the new company. These financiers raised money by selling stock and borrowing from banks. Their attention ranged widely. W. H. Moore organized the American Tin Plate Company, Diamond Match Company, and National Biscuit Company, and he acquired control of the Rock Island Railroad. Elbert H. Gary similarly participated in consolidation of the barbed-wire industry and of U.S. Steel. Investment bankers like J. P. Morgan and Jacob Schiff piloted the merger movement, inspiring awe with their financial power and organizational skills.

FINANCIERS

Growth of corporations in the late nineteenth century turned stock and bond exchanges into hubs of activity. In 1886 trading on the New York Stock Exchange passed 1 million shares a day. By 1914 the number of industrial stocks traded reached 511, compared with 145 in 1869. Between 1870 and 1900, foreign investment in American companies rose from $1.5 billion to $3.5 billion. Personal savings and institutional investment also mushroomed: assets of savings banks, concentrated in the Northeast and West Coast, rose by 700 percent between 1875 and 1897 to a total of $2.2 billion. States loosened regulations to enable banks to invest in railroads and industrial enterprises. Commercial banks, insurance companies, and corporations also invested heavily. As one journal proclaimed, "Nearly the whole country (including the typical widow and orphan) is interested in the stock market." This exaggeration reflected what optimistic capitalists wanted to believe.

The Gospel of Wealth and Its Critics

Business leaders used corporate consolidation not to promote competition but to minimize it. To justify their tactics to a public committed to the free market, they invoked the doctrine of Social Darwinism. Developed by British philosopher Herbert Spencer and preached in the United States by Yale professor William Graham Sumner, Social Darwinism loosely grafted Charles Darwin's theory of the survival of the fittest onto laissez faire, the doctrine that government should not interfere in private economic affairs. Social Darwinists reasoned that, in an unconstrained economy, power and wealth would flow naturally to the most capable people. Acquisition and possession of property were thus sacred and hard-earned rights. Civilization depended on this system, explained Sumner. "If we do not like the survival of the fittest," he wrote, "we have only one possible alternative, and that is survival of the unfittest." In this view, monopolies represented the natural accumulation of economic power by those best suited for wielding it.

Social Darwinists reasoned, too, that wealth carried moral responsibilities to provide for those less fortunate or less capable. Steel baron Andrew Carnegie asserted what he called "the Gospel of Wealth": he and other industrialists were guardians of society's wealth and as such had a duty to serve society in humane ways. Over his lifetime, Carnegie donated more than $350 million to libraries, schools, peace initiatives, and the arts. Such philanthropy, however, also implied a right for benefactors like Rockefeller and Carnegie to define what was good and necessary for society; it did not translate into paying workers decent wages.

Like western entrepreneurs who lauded rugged individualism while seeking public subsidies in their mining, transportation, and agricultural businesses, leaders in the corporate consolidation movement extolled individual initiative and independence but also pressed for government assistance. While denouncing efforts to legislate maximum working hours or regulate factory conditions as interference with natural economic laws, they lobbied forcefully and successfully for subsidies, loans, and tax relief to encourage business growth. Grants to railroads (see Chapter 17) were one form of such assistance. Tariffs, which raised prices of foreign products by placing import taxes on

GOVERNMENT ASSISTANCE TO BUSINESS

them, were another. When Congress imposed high tariffs on foreign goods such as kerosene, steel rails, woolen goods, and tin plate, American producers could raise prices on their own kerosene, rails, woolens, and tin to just under what comparable foreign goods would sell for with the tariff included. Since the inception of tariffs in the early nineteenth century, industrialists argued that tariff protection encouraged the development of new products and new enterprises. But tariffs also forced consumers to pay artificially high prices for many goods.

While defenders insisted that trusts and other forms of big business were a natural and efficient outcome of

DISSENTING VOICES

economic development, critics charged that these forms were unnatural because they stifled opportunity and originated from greed. Such charges emanating from farmers, workers, and intellectuals reflected an ardent fear of monopoly—the domination of an economic activity (such as oil refining) by one powerful company (such as Standard Oil). Those who feared monopoly believed that large corporations fixed prices, exploited workers by cutting wages, destroyed opportunity by crushing small businesses, and threatened democracy by corrupting politicians—all of which was not only unnatural but immoral. To critics, ethics eclipsed economics.

Many believed in a better path to progress. By the mid-1880s, a number of intellectuals began to challenge Social Darwinism and laissez-faire economics. Sociologist Lester Ward attacked the application of evolutionary theory to social and economic relations. In *Dynamic Sociology* (1883), Ward argued that human control of nature, not natural law, accounted for civilization's advance. A system that guaranteed survival only to the fittest was wasteful and brutal; instead, Ward reasoned, cooperative activity fostered by government intervention was more moral. Economists Richard Ely, John R. Commons, and Edward Bemis agreed that natural forces should be harnessed for the public good. They denounced the laissez-faire system for its "unsound morals" and praised the positive assistance that government could offer.

While academics endorsed intervention in the natural economic order, others more directly questioned why the United States had to have so many poor people while a few became fabulously wealthy. Henry George was a San Francisco printer and writer who had fallen into desperate poverty during the depression of the 1870s. Alarmed at the exploitative power of large enterprises, he came to believe that inequality stemmed from the ability of a few to profit from rising land values. George argued that such profits made speculators rich simply

because of increased demand for living and working space, especially in cities. To prevent profiteering, George proposed to replace all taxes with a "single tax" on the "unearned increment"—the rise in property values caused by increased market demand rather than by owners' improvements. George's scheme, argued forcefully in *Progress and Poverty* (1879), had great popular appeal and almost won him the mayoralty of New York City in 1886.

Unlike George, who accepted private ownership, novelist Edward Bellamy believed competitive capitalism promoted waste. Instead, he proposed a state in which government owned the means of production. Bellamy outlined his dream in *Looking Backward* (1888). The novel, which sold over a million copies, depicted Boston in the year 2000 as a peaceful community where everyone had a job and a technological elite managed the economy according to scientific principles. Though a council of elders ruled and ordinary people could not vote in this utopia, Bellamy tried to convince readers that a "principle of fraternal cooperation" could replace vicious competition and wasteful monopoly. His vision, which he called "Nationalism," sparked formation of Nationalist clubs across the country and kindled popular appeals for political reform, social welfare measures, and government ownership of railroads and utilities.

Few people supported the universal government ownership envisioned by Bellamy, but several states took

ANTITRUST LEGISLATION

steps to prohibit monopolies and regulate business. By 1900, fifteen states had constitutional provisions outlawing trusts, and twenty-seven had laws forbidding pools. Most were agricultural states in the South and West that were responding to antimonopolistic pressure from farm organizations. But state governments lacked staff and judicial support for an effective attack on big business, and corporations found ways to evade restrictions. Only national legislation, it seemed, could work.

Congress moved hesitantly toward such legislation but in 1890 passed the Sherman Anti-Trust Act. Introduced by Senator John Sherman of Ohio, the law made illegal "every contract, combination in the form of trust or otherwise, or conspiracy in the restraint of trade." Those found guilty of violating the law faced fines and jail terms, and those wronged by illegal combinations could sue for triple damages. However, the law, which had been watered down when it was rewritten by pro-business eastern senators, was left purposely vague. It did not clearly define "restraint of trade" and consigned interpretation of its provisions to the courts, which at the time were strong allies of business.

Judges used the law's vagueness to blur distinctions between reasonable and unreasonable restraints of trade. When in 1895 the federal government prosecuted the so-called Sugar Trust for owning 98 percent of the nation's sugar-refining capacity, eight of nine Supreme Court justices ruled in *U.S. v. E. C. Knight Co.* that control of manufacturing did not necessarily mean control of trade. According to the Court, the Constitution empowered Congress to regulate interstate commerce, but manufacturing (which in the Knight case took place entirely within the state of Pennsylvania) did not fall under congressional control.

Between 1890 and 1900 the federal government prosecuted only eighteen cases under the Sherman Anti-Trust Act. The most successful involved railroads directly involved in interstate commerce. Ironically, the act equipped the government with a tool for breaking up labor unions: courts that did not consider monopolistic production a restraint on trade willingly applied antitrust provisions to boycotts encouraged by striking unions.

Summary

*M*echanization and new inventions thrust the United States into the vanguard of industrial nations and immeasurably altered daily life between 1877 and 1920. But in industry, as in farming and mining, massive size and aggressive consolidation engulfed the individual, changing the nature of work from individual activity undertaken by skilled producers to mass production undertaken by wage earners. Laborers fought to retain control of their work but struggled to develop well-organized unions that could meet their needs. The outpouring of products created a mass society based on consumerism and dominated by technology and the communications media.

The problems of enforcing the Sherman Anti-Trust Act reflected the uneven distribution of power. Corporations consolidated to control resources, production, and politics. Laborers and reformers had numbers and ideas but lacked influence. They benefited from material gains that technology and mass production provided, but they accused businesses of acquiring too much influence and profiting at their expense. In factories and homes, some people celebrated the industrial transformation while others struggled with the dilemma of industrialism: whether a system based on ever-greater profits was the best way for Americans to fulfill the nation's democratic destiny.

The march of industrial expansion proved almost impossible to stop, however, because so many powerful and ordinary people were benefiting from it. Moreover, the waves of people pouring into the nation's cities were increasingly providing both workers and consumers for America's expanding productive capacity. The dynamo of American vitality now rested in its urban centers.

LEGACY FOR A PEOPLE AND A NATION
Industrialization, Smoke, and Pollution Control

Coal fueled the steel mills and iron foundries of America's industrial era, and the burning of coal meant smoke. Skies over cities such as Pittsburgh and St. Louis became clogged with choking pollution not just from factories but also from coal-burning railroads, steamboats, and home furnaces. Dark fogs turned light-colored clothing black and covered marble statues with inky dust. The heaviest smoke came from burning soft, bituminous coal, which has a higher heat content, is available in greater supply, and is cheaper than hard, cleaner-burning anthracite coal. Prior to the First World War, the United States used four times as much bituminous coal as anthracite coal, and industrial centers of Pennsylvania and the Midwest depended heavily on bituminous coal. As well, new chemical plants began spewing pollutants other than coal dust into the air.

Many Americans assumed that air was a free resource that did not need protection. They accepted air pollution as a necessary nuisance. But others knew some of the dangers of coal smoke and began campaigns to curb the worst pollution. By 1900, doctors reported a link between coal smoke and respiratory diseases such as bronchitis and pneumonia. Women's groups and health reformers argued that air contamination undermined efforts to keep cities clean. As early as 1881, Chicago and a few other cities passed antismoke legislation and hired smoke inspectors, but courts often declared such laws unconstitutional, and judges were reluctant to enforce regulations that remained on the books. San Francisco burned natural gas as a fuel, and New York City tried to ban use of bituminous coal, but most cities could do little, especially since electric plants, as well as factories, burned coal to produce energy.

As the twentieth century advanced, air pollution from coal decreased as technological innovations reduced smoke output. By midcentury, many industries had converted to natural gas and petroleum, but governments refrained from direct control of emissions because industries and ordinary citizens were reluctant to pay added costs for more efficient combustion equipment or costlier fuel. At the same time, however, automobile emissions were creating pollution problems that may have seemed more innocuous than health hazards caused by smoke but were in reality just as dangerous.

In the late 1960s, air pollution became the defining issue of the new environmental reform movement, and it drove federal environmental policy. The Clean Air Act amendment of 1970 recognized for the first time that pollution was a national problem and subject to federal authority. That act and subsequent legislation established federal power to set air quality standards and prompted states and cities to pass their own laws. Since then, business interests and environmentalists have scuffled over how strict regulations should be, often bouncing the issue of air pollution between urges of health and cleanliness on one hand and economic progress, convenience, and job creation on the other. Thus an unwanted legacy of industrial progress—air pollution—remains an unresolved problem.

The *history companion* powered by Eduspace®

Your primary source for interactive quizzes, exercises, and more to help you learn efficiently.

http://history.college.hmco.com/students

THE VITALITY AND TURMOIL OF URBAN LIFE 1877–1920

*I*t reads like a movie story line. Rahel Gollop grew up in a shtetl, a Jewish village in western Russia. Her father, driven to desperation by poverty and anti-Jewish pogroms (violent persecutions by Russian officials), left his family in 1890 to find a better life. Arrested by Russian soldiers, he escaped into Germany and found passage on a steamship bound for New York City. After two and a half years in the United States, he had saved enough to purchase tickets so Rahel and her aunt could join him in America. A year later, Rahel's mother, brothers, and sisters arrived.

Rahel's first impression of the American city was one of awe. "I was dazed by all there was to see," she recalled. "I looked with wonder at the tall houses, the paved streets, the street lamps. As I had never seen a large city and had had only a glimpse of a small one, I thought these things true only of America." But soon the Gollops' landlady, an immigrant who had been in the United States for several years, gave Rahel a dose of reality. Rahel wrote:

> When she asked us how we liked America, and we spoke of it with praise, she smiled a queer smile. "Life here is not all that it appears to the 'green horn' (new immigrant)," she said. She told us that her husband was a presser of coats and earned twelve dollars when he worked a full week. Aunt Masha thought twelve dollars a good deal. Again Mrs. Felesberg smiled. "No doubt it would be," she said, "where you used to live. You had your own house, and most of the food came from the garden. Here you will have to pay for everything; the rent!" she sighed, "for the light, for every potato, every grain of barley."

Like other immigrant families, the Gollops coped with this urban world where a family could not afford their own house and where they had to pay for everything. To help her parents and enable her brothers to attend school, Rahel,

◀ With hope and apprehension, millions of foreign immigrants poured into America's pulsing cities between 1880 and 1920. Bringing with them values, habits, and attire from the Old World, they faced a multitude of new experiences, expectations, and products in the New World and tried to negotiate their existence by combining the new with the old. (Albanian Woman, Ellis Island, 1905. © Collection for Creative Photography, The University of Arizona) dors by drunken nativists. Like other immigrants, Rahel sought security by associating with her own kind, rarely mingling with strangers.

Gradually Rahel broke away. Health problems brought her into a Protestant hospital, where she was exposed to another culture. She learned to read English and acquired an education. Rejecting the man whom her parents had selected for her husband, she married a grocer and became a writer. She published her autobiography in 1918 and died in 1925 at the age of forty-five, possibly of suicide.

The experiences of Rahel Gollop illustrate many themes characterizing American urban life in the late nineteenth and early twentieth centuries. Where to live, where to work, how to support the family, the cash-based economy, ethnic consciousness and bigotry, the quest for individual independence and respectability—all these and more made cities places of hope, frustration, comfort, and conflict. Their clanging trolleys, smoky air, crowded streets, and jumble of languages contrasted with the quiet pace of village and farm life.

Cities had exerted significant influence on the nation's history since its inception, but not until the 1880s did the United States begin to become a fully urban nation. The new industrialization and technological innovations of the late nineteenth century (see Chapter 18) fueled widespread economic and geographical expansion that funneled millions of people into cities. By 1920 a milestone of urbanization was passed: that year's census showed that, for the first time, a majority of Americans (51.2 percent) lived in cities (settlements with more than 2,500 people). This new fact of national life was as symbolically significant as the disappearance of the frontier in 1890.

Cities served as marketplaces and forums, bringing together the people, resources, and ideas responsible for many changes in neighborhoods, politics, commerce, and leisure that American society was experiencing. By 1900 a network of small, medium, and large cities spanned every section of the country. Some people relished the opportunities and excitement cities offered; others found American cities disquieting and threatening. But whatever people's personal impressions, cities had become central to American life. The ways people built cities and adjusted to the urban environment have shaped American society. ■

only twelve years old, went to work in a garment sweatshop. Before she was twenty she had held a variety of jobs, mostly doing tailoring work. She witnessed—and went through—many of the travails suffered by other immigrants, including the beating of eastern European Jews on election night and the harassment of street ven-

Growth of the Modern City

*T*hough their initial functions had been commercial, cities became the main arenas for industrial growth in the late nineteenth century. As centers of labor, transportation, and communication, cities supplied everything factories needed. Capital accumulated by urban mercantile enterprises fed industrial investment. City dwellers also acted as consumers for myriad new products. Thus urban growth and industrialization wound together in a mutually advantageous spiral. The further industrialization advanced, the more opportunities it created for jobs and investment. Increased opportunities in turn drew more people to cities; as workers and as consumers, they fueled yet more industrialization. Urban growth in modern America was a dynamic process involving all groups of Americans, including those already settled and new arrivals from Europe and Asia.

Most cities housed a variety of industrial enterprises, but product specialization gradually became common. Mass production of clothing concentrated in New York, the shoe industry in Philadelphia, textiles in New Eng-

INDUSTRIAL DEVELOPMENT

land cities. Other cities processed products from surrounding agricultural regions: flour in Minneapolis, cottonseed oil in Memphis, beef and pork in Chicago. Still others processed natural resources: gold and copper in Denver, fish and lumber in Seattle, coal and iron in Pittsburgh and Birmingham, oil in Houston and Los Angeles. Such activities increased cities' magnetic attraction for people in search of steady employment.

Urban and industrial growth transformed the national economy and freed the United States from dependence on European capital and manufactured goods. Imports and foreign investments still flowed into the United States. But by 1900, cities and their factories, stores, and banks were converting America from a debtor agricultural nation into an industrial, financial, and exporting power.

At the same time, the compact city of the early nineteenth century, where residences mingled among shops, factories, and warehouses, burst open. From Boston to Los Angeles, the built environment sprawled several miles beyond the original settlement. No longer did walking distance determine a city's size. No longer did different social groups live close together. Instead, cities

■ Electric trolley cars and other forms of mass transit enabled middle-class people like these women and men to reside on the urban outskirts and ride into the city center for work, shopping, and entertainment.   (Museum of the City of New York, The Byron Collection)

subdivided into distinct districts: working-class and ethnic neighborhoods, downtown, and a ring of suburbs. Two forces were responsible for this new arrangement. One, mass transportation, was centrifugal, propelling people and enterprises outward. The other, economic change, was centripetal, drawing human and material resources inward.

Mass transportation moved people faster and farther. By the 1870s, horse-drawn vehicles began sharing

MECHANIZATION OF MASS TRANSPORTATION

city streets with motor-driven conveyances. At first, commuter railroads carried commuters to and from outlying communities. In the 1880s, cable cars (carriages that moved by clamping onto a moving underground wire) started operating in Chicago, San Francisco, and other cities. Then in the 1890s, electric-powered streetcars began replacing horse cars and cable cars. Designed in Montgomery, Alabama, and Richmond, Virginia, electric trolleys spread to nearly every large American city. Between 1890 and 1902, total electrified track grew from 1,300 to 22,000 miles. In a few cities, companies raised track onto trestles, enabling vehicles to travel above jammed downtown streets. In Boston, New York, and Philadelphia, transit firms dug underground subway tunnels, also to avoid traffic congestion. Because elevated railroads and subways were extremely expensive to construct, they appeared only in the few cities where companies could amass necessary capital and where there were enough riders to ensure profits.

Another form of mass transit, the electric interurban railway, linked nearby cities. Usually built over shorter distances than steam railroads, interurbans operated between cities with growing suburban populations and furthered urban development by making outlying regions attractive for home buyers and businesses. The extensive Pacific Electric Railway network in southern California, for example, facilitated travel and economic development in that region.

Mass transit launched urban dwellers into remote neighborhoods and created a commuting public. Those

URBAN SPRAWL

who could afford the fare—usually 5 cents—could live beyond the crowded central city and commute there for work, shopping, and entertainment. Working-class families, who needed every cent, found streetcars unaffordable. But the growing middle class could escape to quiet, tree-lined neighborhoods on the outskirts and live in bungalows with their own yards. Real-estate development boomed around city borders. Between 1890 and 1920, for example, developers in the Chicago area opened 800,000 new lots—enough to house at least three times

the city's 1890 population. A home several miles from downtown was inconvenient, but benefits outweighed costs. As one suburbanite wrote in 1902, "It may be a little more difficult for us to attend the opera, but the robin in my elm tree struck a higher note and a sweeter one yesterday than any prima donna ever reached."

Urban sprawl was essentially unplanned, but certain patterns did emerge. Eager to capitalize on commuting possibilities, thousands of small investors who bought land in anticipation of settlement paid little attention to the need for parks, traffic control, and public services. Guided by profit motives, construction of mass transit benefited the urban public unevenly. Streetcar lines serviced mainly districts that promised the most riders— those whose fares would increase company revenues.

Streetcars, elevateds, and subways altered commercial as well as residential patterns. When consumers moved outward, businesses followed. New business centers sprouted at trolley-line intersections and near elevated-railway stations. Branches of department stores and banks joined groceries, theaters, taverns, and shops to create neighborhood shopping centers, forerunners of today's suburban malls. Meanwhile, the urban core became a work zone, where tall buildings loomed over streets clogged with people, horses, and vehicles. Districts such as Chicago's Loop and New Orleans's Canal Street employed thousands in commerce and finance.

Between 1870 and 1920, the number of Americans living in cities increased from 10 million to 54 million.

POPULATION GROWTH

During this period, the number of cities with more than 100,000 people swelled from fifteen to sixty-eight; the number with more than 500,000 rose from two to twelve (see Map 19.1). These figures, dramatic in themselves, represent millions of stories of dreams and frustration, coping and confusion, success and failure.

During these years, American urban growth came not from natural increase (excess of births over deaths) but through the annexation of bordering land and people and mostly by net migration (excess of in-migrants over out-migrants). Every city grew territorially. The most notable such enlargement occurred in 1898 when New York City, which previously consisted of only Manhattan and the Bronx, merged with Brooklyn, Staten Island, and part of Queens and doubled from 1.5 million to 3 million people. Suburbs often desired annexation for the schools, water, fire protection, and sewer systems that cities could provide. Sometimes annexation preceded settlement, adding vacant land where new residents could live. In the 1880s, Chicago, Minneapolis, and Los Ange-

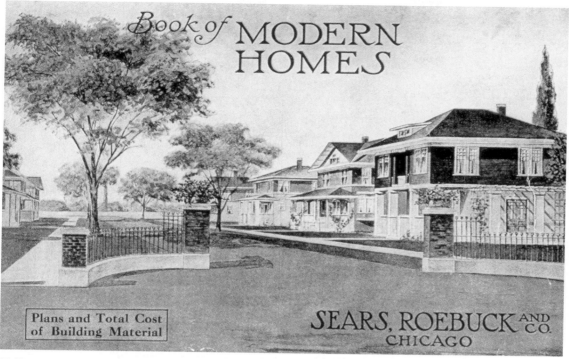

■ Along with mass-produced consumer goods such as clothing and appliances, Sears, Roebuck and Company marketed architectural plans for middle-class suburban housing. This drawing, taken from the Sears catalogue for 1911, illustrates the kind of housing developed on the urban outskirts in the early twentieth century.   (Sears, Roebuck and Company)

les incorporated hundreds of undeveloped square miles into their borders.

But in-migration from the countryside and immigration from abroad made by far the greatest contribution to urban population growth. In fact, movement to cities nearly matched the massive migration to the West that was occurring at the same time. Urban newcomers arrived from two major sources: the American countryside and Europe. Asia, Canada, and Latin America also supplied immigrants, though in smaller numbers.

URBAN IN-
MIGRATION

Despite land rushes in the West, rural populations declined as urban populations burgeoned. Low crop prices and high debts dashed white farmers' hopes and drove them toward opportunities that cities seemed to offer. Such migration peopled major cities such as Detroit, Chicago, and San Francisco but also secondary cities such as Indianapolis, Salt Lake City, Nashville, and San Diego. The thrill of city life beckoned especially to young people. A character in the play *The City* (1920) spoke for many youths when she exclaimed, "Who wants to smell new-mown hay, if he can breathe in gasoline on Fifth Avenue instead! Think of the theaters! The crowds! Think of being able to go out on the street and see someone you didn't know by sight!" Despair drove farm boys to cities, but for every four men who migrated cityward, five women did the same, often to escape unhappy home-life. But young women also were drawn by the independence that urban employment offered.

In the 1880s and 1890s, thousands of rural African Americans also moved cityward, seeking better employment and fleeing crop liens, ravages of the boll weevil on cotton crops, racial violence, and political oppression. Though black migration accelerated after 1915, thirty-two cities already had more than ten thousand black residents by 1900. Black populations of southern cities such as Baltimore, Atlanta, and Birmingham increased, but northern places such as New York, Cleveland, and Chicago also received thousands of African American migrants. These urban newcomers resembled other migrants in their rural backgrounds and economic motivations, but they differed in several important ways. Because few factories would employ African Americans, most found

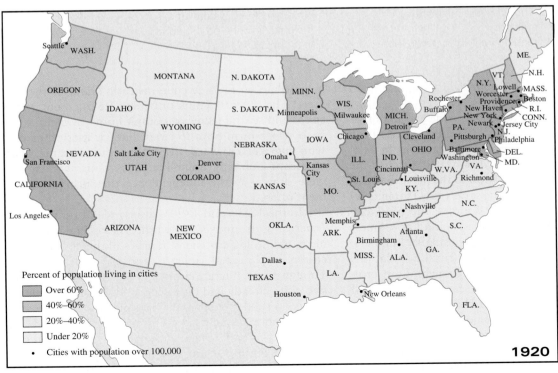

Map 19.1   Urbanization, 1880 and 1920

In 1880 the vast majority of states still were heavily rural. By 1920 only a few had less than 20 percent of their population living in cities.

jobs in the service sector—cleaning, cooking, and driving—rather than in industrial trades. Also, because most service openings were traditionally female jobs, black women outnumbered black men in cities such as New York, Baltimore, and New Orleans. In the South, African Americans migrating from the countryside became an important source of unskilled labor in the region's growing cities. By 1900 almost 40 percent of the total population of both Atlanta, Georgia, and Charlotte, North Carolina, were blacks.

In the West, many Hispanics, once a predominantly rural population, moved into cities. They took unskilled construction and grading jobs previously held by Chinese laborers who had been driven from southern California cities, and in some Texas cities native Mexicans (called *Tejanos*) held the majority of all unskilled jobs. In

■ The Caribbean as well as Europe sent immigrants to the United States. Proud and confident on arrival from their homeland of Guadeloupe, these women perhaps were unprepared for the double disadvantage they faced as both blacks and foreigners. (William Williams Papers, Manuscripts & Archives Division, The New York Public Library)

places such as Los Angeles, males often left home for long periods to take temporary agricultural jobs, leaving behind female heads of household.

Even more newcomers were foreign immigrants who fled villages and cities in Europe, Asia, Canada, and Latin America for the United States.

FOREIGN IMMIGRATION Many never intended to stay; they wanted only to make enough money to return home and live in greater comfort and security. For every hundred foreigners who entered the country, around thirty ultimately left. Still, like Rahel Gollop the Russian garment maker, most of the 26 million immigrants who arrived between 1870 and 1920 remained, and the great majority settled in cities, where they helped reshape American culture.

Immigration to the United States was part of a worldwide movement pushing people away from traditional means of support and pulling them toward better opportunities. Population pressures, land redistribution, and industrialization induced millions of peasants, small farmers, and craftsmen to leave Europe and Asia for Canada, Australia, Brazil, and Argentina, as well as the United States. Religious persecution, too, particularly the merciless pogroms and military conscription that Jews suffered in eastern Europe, forced people like Rahel Gollop's father to escape across the Atlantic. Migration has always characterized human history, but in the late nineteenth century technological advances in communications and transportation spread news of opportunities and made travel cheaper, quicker, and safer.

Immigrants from northern and western Europe had long made the United States their main destination, but

THE NEW IMMIGRATION after 1880 economic and demographic changes propelled a second wave of immigrants from other regions. Northern and western Europeans continued to arrive, but increased numbers came from eastern and southern Europe, plus smaller bands from Canada, Mexico, and Japan (see Map 19.2 and Figure 19.1). Two-thirds of newcomers who arrived in the 1880s came from Germany, England, Ireland, and Scandinavia; between 1900 and 1909, when the new wave peaked, two-thirds came from Italy, Austria-Hungary, and Russia. By 1910 arrivals from Mexico outnumbered arrivals from Ireland, and numerous Japanese had moved to the West Coast and Hawai'i. Foreign-born blacks, chiefly from the West Indies, also came. (See the Appendix for the nationalities of immigrants.)

Many long-settled Americans feared those they called "new immigrants," whose customs, Catholic and Jewish faiths, and poverty made them seem more alien. Unlike earlier arrivals from Great Britain and Ireland, new immigrants did not speak English, and more than half worked in low-skilled occupations. Yet old and new immigrants closely resembled each other in their strategies for coping. The majority of both groups hailed from societies that made family the focus of all undertakings. As Rahel Gollop's case illustrates, whether and when to emigrate was decided in light of family needs, and family bonds remained tight after immigrants reached America. New arrivals usually knew where they wanted to go and how to get there because they received aid from relatives who had already immigrated. Workers often helped kin obtain jobs, and family members pooled resources to maintain, if not improve, their standard of living.

Map 19.2 Sources of European-Born Population, 1900 and 1920

In just a few decades, the proportion of European immigrants to the United States who came from northern and western Europe decreased (Ireland and Germany) or remained relatively stable (England and Scandinavia), while the proportion from eastern and southern Europe dramatically increased. (Data from U.S. Census Bureau, "Historical Census Statistics on the Foreign-born Population of the United States: 1850–1990," Feb. 1999. Retrieved Feb. 12, 2000, http://www.census.gov/population.)

Figure 19.1   Composition of Population, Selected Cities, 1920

Immigration and migration made native-born whites of native-born parents minorities in almost every major city by the early twentieth century. Moreover, foreign-born residents and native-born whites of foreign parents (combining the green and purple segments of a line) constituted absolute majorities in numerous places.

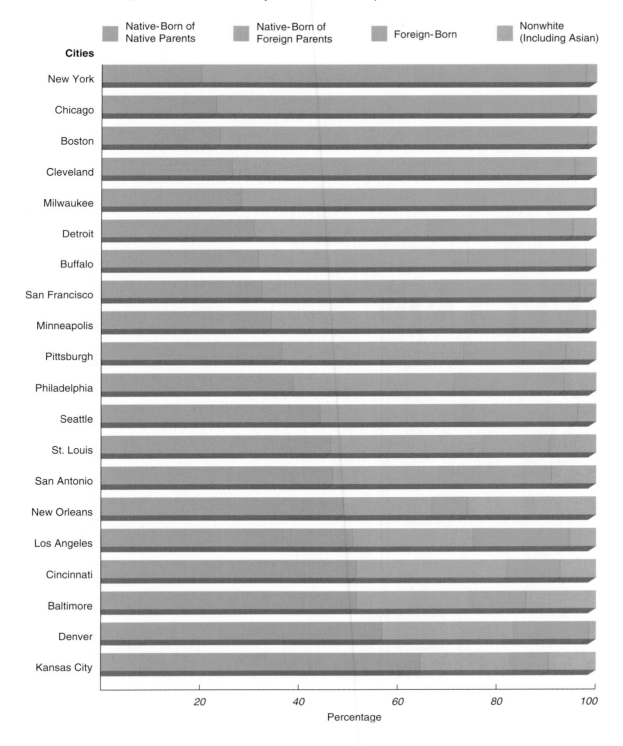

Once they arrived, in-migrants and immigrants rarely stayed put. Each year millions of families packed up and moved elsewhere. Some moved to another neighborhood; others left town. A railroad ticket for another city cost only a few dollars, and many had little to lose by moving. Transience affected every region, every city. From Boston to San Francisco, from Minneapolis to San Antonio, more than half the families residing in a city at any one time were gone ten years later. Even within a city, it was not un-common for a family to live at three or more different addresses over a ten- or fifteen-year period. Overall, one in every three or four families moved every year (today the rate is one in five). Population turnover affected almost every neighborhood, every ethnic and occupational group.

GEOGRAPHIC AND SOCIAL MOBILITY

Migration offered one path to improved opportunity; occupational change offered another. An advance up the social scale through occupational mobility to new jobs was mostly available to white males. Thanks to urban and industrial expansion, thousands of businesses were needed to supply goods and services to burgeoning urban populations, and as corporations grew and centralized operations, they required new managerial personnel. Capital for a large business was hard to amass, but an aspiring merchant could open a saloon or shop for a few hundred dollars. Knowledge of accounting could qualify one for white-collar jobs with higher incomes than manual labor. Thus nonmanual work and the higher social status and income that tended to accompany it were attainable.

Such advancement occurred often. To be sure, only a very few could accumulate large fortunes. The vast majority of the era's wealthiest businessmen began their careers with distinct advantages: American birth, Protestant religion, superior education, and relatively affluent parents. Yet considerable movement occurred along the road from poverty to moderate success, from manual to nonmanual jobs. Personal successes like that of Meyer Grossman, a Russian immigrant to Omaha, Nebraska, who worked as a teamster before saving enough to open a successful furniture store, were common.

Rates of upward occupational mobility were slow but steady between 1870 and 1920. In fast-growing cities such as Atlanta, Los Angeles, and Omaha, approximately one in five white manual workers rose to white-collar or owner's positions within ten years—provided they stayed in the city that long. In older cities such as Boston and Philadelphia, upward mobility averaged closer to one in six workers in ten years. Some men slipped from a higher to lower rung on the occupational ladder, but rates of upward movement usually doubled those of downward movement. Though patterns were not consistent, immigrants generally experienced less upward and more downward mobility than the native-born did. Still, regardless of birthplace, the chances for a white male to rise occupationally over the course of his career or to hold a higher-status job than his father were relatively good.

What constitutes a better job, however, depends on one's definition of improvement. Many immigrant artisans, such as a German carpenter or Italian shoemaker,

■ Those who wished to Americanize the immigrants believed the public schools could provide the best setting for assimilation. This 1917 poster from the Cleveland Board of Education and the Cleveland Americanization Committee used the languages most common to the new immigrants—Slovene, Italian, Polish, Hungarian, and Yiddish—as well as English to invite newcomers to free classes where they could learn "the language of America" and "citizenship." (National Park Service Collection, Ellis Island Immigration Museum. Photo: Chermayeff & Geismar/ MetaForm)

considered an accountant's job demeaning. People with traditions of pride in manual skills neither desired non-manual jobs nor encouraged their children to seek them. As one Italian tailor explained, "I learned the tailoring business in the old country. Over here, in America, I never have trouble finding a job because I know my business from the other side [Italy]. . . . I want that my oldest boy learn my trade because I tell him that you could always make at least enough for the family."

Business ownership, moreover, entailed risks. Failure rates were high among saloon owners and other small proprietors in working-class neighborhoods because the low incomes of their customers made business uncertain. Many manual workers sought security rather than mobility, preferring a steady wage to the risks of ownership. A Sicilian who lived in Bridgeport, Connecticut, observed that "the people that come here they afraid to get in business because they don't know how that business goes. In Italy these people don't know much about these things because most of them work on farms or in [their] trade."

Many women held paying jobs and migrated within and between cities, but often with fathers or husbands whose economic standing usually defined their social position. Women could improve status by marrying men with wealth or potential, but other avenues were mostly closed. Laws limited what women could inherit; educational institutions blocked their training in professions such as medicine and law; and prevailing assumptions attributed higher aptitude for manual skills and business to men than to women. For African Americans, American Indians, Mexican Americans, and Asian Americans opportunities were even fewer. Assigned to lowest-paying occupations by prejudice, they could make few gains.

In addition to advancing occupationally, a person might achieve social mobility by acquiring property such as building or buying a house. But property was not easy to acquire. Banks and savings-and-loan institutions had strict lending practices, and mortgage loans carried high interest rates and short repayment periods. Thus renting, even of single-family houses, was common, especially in big cities. Nevertheless many families were able to amass savings, which they could use as down payments on property. Ownership rates varied regionally—higher in western cities, lower in eastern cities—but 36 percent of all urban American families owned their homes in 1900, the highest homeownership rate of any western nation except for Denmark, Norway, and Sweden.

Many who migrated, particularly unskilled workers, did not improve their status; they simply floated from one low-paying job to another. Others did find greener pastures. Studies of Boston, Omaha, Atlanta, and other cities show that most men who rose occupationally or

acquired property had migrated from somewhere else. Thus while cities frustrated the hopes of some, they offered opportunities to others. The possibilities for upward mobility seemed to temper people's dissatisfaction with the tensions and frustrations of city life. For every story of rags to riches, there were a multitude of small triumphs mixed with dashed hopes and discrimination, small successes mixed with disappointment. Although the gap between the very rich and the very poor widened, for those in between, the expanding economies of American cities created room.

Urban Neighborhoods

Despite the constant turnover that made them dynamic places, American cities were characterized by collections of subcommunities where people, most of whom had migrated from somewhere else, coped with daily challenges to their cultures. Rather than yield completely to pressures to assimilate, migrants and immigrants interacted with the urban environment in a complex way that enabled them to retain their identity while also altering both their own outlook and the social structure of cities themselves.

In their new surroundings—where the English language was a struggle, where the clock regulated their

CULTURAL RETENTION AND CHANGE

workday, and where housing and employment were uncertain—immigrants first anchored their lives to the rock they knew best: their culture. Old World customs persisted in immigrant districts of Italians from the same province, Japanese from the same island district, or Russian Jews from the same *shtetl*. Newcomers re-created mutual aid societies they had known in their homelands. For example, in western cities Japanese transferred *ken* societies, which organized social celebrations and relief services, and Chinese used loan associations, called *whey*, which raised money to help members acquire businesses. Chinese also transplanted village associations called *fongs*, which rented apartments for homeless members; *kung saw*, which were assistance organizations of people with the same family name regardless of what part of China they came from; and *tongs*, which were secret societies designed to aid people but which often acted as gangs that extorted protection money from businesses. Southern Italians transplanted the system whereby a *padrone* (boss) found jobs for unskilled workers by negotiating with—and receiving a payoff from—an employer. People practiced religion as they always had, held traditional feasts and pageants, married within their group, and pursued old feuds with people from rival villages. Among Orthodox Jews from eastern Europe, men grew earlocks, women wore wigs, and children attended afternoon religious training.

In industrial cities such as Chicago, Philadelphia, and Detroit, European immigrants initially clustered in inner-city neighborhoods where low-skill jobs and cheap housing were most available. In these cities, immigrants inhabited multiethnic neighborhoods, places historians have called "urban borderlands," where a diversity of people, identities, and lifestyles coexisted. Even within districts identified with a certain group, such as Little Italy, Jewtown, Polonia, or Greektown, rapid mobility constantly undermined residential homogeneity as former inhabitants dispersed to other neighborhoods and new inhabitants moved in. Often a particular area would be inhabited by several ethnic groups, and the local businesses and institutions, such as the bakeries, butcher shops, churches, and club headquarters—which usually would be operated by and for one ethnic group—gave a neighborhood its identity.

URBAN BORDERLANDS

Though different groups jointly inhabited urban borderlands, members of the same group often tried to exclude outsiders from their neighborhood space and institutions. Some Europeans, such as Italians, Jews, and Poles, deliberately tried to maintain separate religious, linguistic, and cultural lifestyles. For such groups, their neighborhoods acted as havens until individuals were ready to cross from the borderland into the majority society.

But these borderland experiences often dissolved, sometimes in a generation, sometimes in just a few years. The expansion of mass transportation and outward movement of factories enabled people to move to other neighborhoods, where they interspersed with families of their own socioeconomic class but not necessarily of their own ethnicity. European immigrants did encounter prejudice, such as the exclusion of Jews from certain neighborhoods, professions, and clubs, or the inability of Italians to break into urban politics, but discrimination rarely was systematic or complete. For people of color, however—African Americans, Asians, and Mexicans—the borderlands kept a more persistent character that, because of discrimination, became less multiethnic over time.

Though the small numbers of African Americans who inhabited American cities in the eighteenth and early nineteenth centuries may have lived near to or interspersed with whites, by the late nineteenth century rigid racial discrimination forced them into relatively permanent, highly segregated ar-

RACIAL SEGREGATION IN CITIES

eas later labeled as ghettos. By 1920 in Chicago, Detroit, Cleveland, and other cities where tens of thousands of blacks now lived, two-thirds or more of the total African American population inhabited only 10 percent of the residential area. The only way blacks could relieve the pressures of crowding resulting from increasing migration was to expand residential borders into surrounding, previously white neighborhoods, a process often resulting in harassment and attacks on black families by white residents whose intolerant attitudes were intensified by fears that black neighbors would cause property values to decline.

Within their neighborhoods, African Americans, like other urban people, nurtured cultural institutions that helped them cope with urban life: shops, schools, clubs, theaters, dance halls, newspapers, and saloons. Churches, particularly those of the Baptist and African Methodist Episcopal (AME) branches of Protestantism, were especially influential. Pittsburgh blacks boasted twenty-eight such churches in the early 1900s. Membership in Cincinnati's black Baptist churches doubled between 1870 and 1900. In Louisville, blacks pooled their resources and built their own theological institute. In virtually all cities, black religious activity not only dominated local life but also represented cooperation across class and regional lines.

Asians encountered similar discrimination and isolated residential experience. Although Chinese immigrants often preferred to live apart from Anglos in the Chinatowns of San Francisco, Los Angeles, and New York City, where they created their own business, government, and protective institutions, Anglos made every effort to keep them separated. In San Francisco, anti-Chinese hostility was fomented by Denis Kearney, an Irish immigrant who blamed Chinese for massive unemployment in California in the late 1870s. Using the slogan "The Chinese must go," Kearney and his followers intimidated employers into refusing to hire Chinese and drove hundreds of Asians out of the city. San Francisco's government prohibited Chinese laundries (which were social centers as well as commercial establishments) from locating in white neighborhoods and banned the wearing of queues, the traditional Chinese hair braid. In 1882, Congress passed the Chinese Exclusion Act, which suspended Chinese immigration and prohibited naturalization of those Chinese already residing in the United States. And in 1892, Congress approved the Geary Act, which extended immigration restriction and required Chinese Americans to carry certificates of residence issued by the Treasury Department. A San Francisco–based organization called the Chinese Six Companies

■ Though Chinese immigrants struggled, like other immigrants, to succeed in American society, they often faced severe discrimination because of their different lifestyles. As this photo of a San Francisco grocery shows, Chinese looked, dressed, and ate differently than did white Americans. Occasionally, they suffered from racist violence that caused them to fear not only for their personal safety but also for the safety of establishments like this one that might suffer damage from resentful mobs.   (The Bancroft Library, University of California)

fought the law, but in 1893 the U.S. Supreme Court upheld the Geary Act in *Fong Yue Ting v. United States.* Japanese immigrants, called *Issei,* most of whom settled in or near Los Angeles, were prevented by law from becoming American citizens and, like the Chinese, developed communities with their own economic and residential character.

Mexicans in southwestern cities experienced somewhat more complex residential patterns. In places such as Los Angeles, Santa Barbara, and Tucson, Mexicans had been the original inhabitants, and Anglos were migrants who overtook the city, pushing Mexicans into adjoining areas. Here, Mexicans became increasingly isolated in residential and commercial districts called *barrios.* Frequently, real-estate covenants, by which property owners pledged not to sell homes to Mexicans (or to African Americans, or to Jews), kept Mexican families confined in *barrios* of Los Angeles, Al-

MEXICAN BARRIOS

buquerque, and San Antonio. These areas tended to be located away from central-city multiethnic borderlands housing European immigrants. To a considerable extent, then, racial bias, more than any other factor, made urban experiences of nonwhites unique compared with those of whites.

Everywhere, Old World culture mingled with New World realities. As Rahel Gollop discovered, the diversity of American cities prompted immigrants to modify their attitudes and habits. With so many people moving about, interacting on streets and in workplaces, cultural change was hard to avoid. Few newcomers could avoid contact with people different from themselves, and few could prevent such contacts from altering old ways of life.

CULTURAL ADAPTATION

Immigrants struggled to maintain native languages and to pass them down to younger generations. But English, taught in schools and needed on the job, soon penetrated nearly every community. Foreigners fashioned homeland garments from American fabrics. Italians went to American doctors but still carried traditional amulets to ward off evil spirits. Unavailability of Asian vegetables and spices forced Chinese American cooks to improvise by using local ingredients in a dish called "chop suey" to serve their Asian customers. Music especially revealed adaptations. Polka bands entertained at Polish social gatherings, but their repertoires blended American and Polish folk music; once dominated by violins, bands added accordions, clarinets, and trumpets so they could play louder. Mexican ballads acquired new themes that described adventures of border crossing and hardships of labor in the United States.

The influx of so many immigrants between 1870 and 1920 transformed the United States from a basically Protestant nation into a diverse collection of Protestants, Catholics, Orthodox Christians, Jews, Buddhists, and Muslims. Newcomers from Italy, Hungary, Polish lands, and Slovakia joined Irish and Germans to boost the proportion of Catholics in many cities. In Buffalo, Cleveland, Chicago, and Milwaukee, Catholic immigrants and their offspring approached a majority of the population. Catholic Mexicans constituted over half of the population of El Paso. German and Russian immigrants gave New York one of the largest Jewish populations in the world.

Although many foreigners identified themselves by their village or region of birth, native-born Americans simplified by categorizing them by nationality. People from County Cork and County Limerick were merged into Irish; those from Schleswig and Württemberg into Germans; those from Calabria and Campobasso into Italians. Immigrant institutions, such as newspapers and churches, found they had to appeal to the entire nationality in order to survive.

Partly in response to Protestant charges that they could not retain Old World religious beliefs and were a hindrance to assimilation, many Catholics and Jews tried to accommodate their faiths to the new environment. Catholic and Jewish leaders from earlier immigrant groups supported liberalizing trends—use of English in sermons, phasing-out of Old World rituals such as saints' feasts, and a preference for public over religious schools. As long as new immigrants continued to arrive, however, these trends met stiff resistance.

Newcomers usually held on to familiar practices, whether the folk Catholicism of southern Italy or the Orthodox Judaism of eastern Europe. Because Catholic parishes served distinct geographical areas, immigrants wanted parish priests of their own kind in spite of church attempts to make American Catholicism more uniform. Bishops acceded to pressures from predominantly Polish congregations for Polish- rather than German-born priests. Eastern European Jews, convinced that Reform Judaism sacrificed too much to American ways, established the Conservative branch, which retained traditional ritual, though it abolished the segregation of women in synagogues and allowed English prayers.

Each of the three major migrant groups that peopled American cities—native-born whites, foreigners of various races, and native-born blacks—helped to mold modern American culture. The cities nurtured rich cultural variety: American folk music and literature, Italian and Mexican cuisine, Irish comedy, Yiddish theater, African American jazz and dance, and much more. Newcomers in the late nineteenth century changed their environment as much as they were changed by it.

Living Conditions in the Inner City

In spite of the cultural contributions of their inhabitants in the late nineteenth and early twentieth centuries, the central sections of American cities seemed to harbor every affliction that plagues modern society: poverty, disease, crime, and other unpleasant conditions that occur when large numbers of people live close together. City dwellers coped as best they could, and technology, private enterprise, and public authority achieved some remarkable successes. But even today, many problems still await solution.

One of the most persistent shortcomings—the scarcity of adequate housing for all who need it—has its origins in nineteenth-century urban development. In spite of massive construction in the 1880s and early 1900s, population growth outpaced housing supplies. Lack of inexpensive housing especially afflicted working-class families who, because of low wages, had to rent their living quarters. As cities grew, landlords took advantage of shortages in low-cost rental housing by splitting up existing buildings to house more people, constructing multiple-unit tenements, and hiking rents. Low-income families adapted to high costs and short supply by sharing space and expenses. It became common in many big cities for a one-family apartment to be occupied by two or three families or by a single family plus several boarders.

The result was unprecedented crowding. In 1890 New York City's immigrant-packed Lower East Side,

INNER-CITY HOUSING

where the Gollop family lived, averaged 702 people per acre, one of the highest population densities in the world. Inner districts had distinctive physical appearances in different cities: six- to eight-story barracks-like buildings in New York; dilapidated row houses in Baltimore and Philadelphia; converted slave quarters in Charleston and New Orleans; and crumbling two- and three-story frame houses in Seattle and San Francisco.

Inside these structures, conditions were harsh. The largest rooms were barely ten feet wide, and interior rooms either lacked windows or opened onto narrow shafts that bred vermin and rotten odors. Describing such a duct, one immigrant housekeeper revealed, "It's damp down there, and the families, they throw out garbage and dirty papers and the insides of chickens, and other unmentionable filth. . . . I just vomited when I first cleaned up the air shaft." Few buildings had indoor plumbing; the only source of heat was dangerous, polluting coal-burning stoves.

Housing problems sparked widespread reform campaigns. New York State took the lead by applying light,

HOUSING REFORM

ventilation, and safety codes for new tenement buildings with laws passed in 1867, 1879, and 1901. These and similar measures in other states could not remedy ills of existing buildings, but they did impose minimal obligations on landlords. A few reformers, such as journalist Jacob Riis and humanitarian Lawrence Veiller, advocated housing low-income families in "model tenements," with more spacious rooms and better facilities. Model tenements, however, required landlords to accept lower profits, a sacrifice few were willing to make. Both reformers and public officials opposed government financing of better housing, fearing that such a step would undermine private enterprise. Still, new housing codes and regulatory commissions strengthened the power of local government to oversee construction.

Eventually, technology brought about momentous changes in home life. Advanced systems of central heating (furnaces), artificial lighting, and modern indoor plumbing created a new kind of consumption, first for middle-class

NEW HOME TECHNOLOGY

■ Inner-city dwellers used not only indoor space as efficiently as possible but also what little outdoor space was available to them. Scores of families living in this cramped block of six-story tenements in New York strung clotheslines behind the buildings. Notice that there is virtually no space between buildings, so only rooms at the front and back received daylight and fresh air.   (Library of Congress)

households and later for most others. Whereas formerly families bought coal or chopped wood for cooking and heating, made candles for light, and hauled water for bathing, they increasingly connected to outside pipes and wires for gas, electricity, and water. Moreover, these utilities helped create new attitudes about privacy. Middle-class bedrooms and bathrooms became comfortable private retreats. Even children could have their own bedrooms, complete with individualized decoration. Also, though not affordable for the poor, central heat and artificial light made it possible for the middle class to enjoy a steady, comfortable temperature and turn night into day, while indoor plumbing removed unpleasant experiences of the outhouse.

Better housing for the poor came later, but scientific and technological advances eventually enabled city dwellers and the entire nation to live in greater comfort and safety. By the 1880s, doctors had begun to accept the theory that microorganisms (germs) cause disease. In response, cities established more efficient systems of water purification and sewage disposal. Although disease and death rates remained higher in cities than in the countryside, and tuberculosis and other respiratory ills continued to plague inner-city districts, public health regulations as applied to water purity, sewage disposal, and food quality helped to control dread diseases such as cholera, typhoid fever, and diphtheria.

Meanwhile, street paving, modernized firefighting equipment, and electric street lighting spread rapidly across urban America. Steel-frame construction, which supports a building with a metal skeleton rather than with masonry walls, made possible the erection of skyscrapers—and thus more efficient vertical use of scarce and costly urban land. Electric elevators and steam-heating systems serviced these buildings. Steel-cable suspension bridges, developed by John A. Roebling and epitomized by his Brooklyn Bridge (completed in 1883), linked metropolitan sections more closely.

None of these improvements, however, lightened the burden of poverty. The urban economy, though generally expanding, advanced erratically. Em-

POVERTY RELIEF ployment, especially for unskilled workers in manufacturing and construction, rose and fell with business cycles and changing seasons. An ever-increasing number of families lived on the margins of survival.

Since colonial days, Americans have disagreed about how much responsibility the public should assume for poor relief. According to traditional beliefs, still widespread at the beginning of the twentieth century, anyone could escape poverty through hard work and clean living;

indigence existed only because some people were morally weaker than others. Such reasoning bred fear that aid to poor people would encourage paupers to rely on public support rather than their own efforts. As business cycles fluctuated and poverty increased, this attitude hardened, and city governments discontinued direct grants of food, fuel, and clothing to needy families. Instead, cities provided relief in return for work on public projects and sent special cases to state-run almshouses, orphanages, and homes for the blind, deaf, and mentally ill.

Efforts to rationalize relief fostered some change in attitude. Between 1877 and 1892, philanthropists in ninety-two cities formed Charity Organization Societies, an attempt to make social welfare (like business) more efficient by merging disparate charity groups into coordinated units. Believing poverty to be caused by personal defects such as alcoholism and laziness, members of these organizations spent most of their time visiting poor families and encouraging them to be thriftier and more virtuous. These visits also were intended to identify the "deserving" poor.

Close observation of the poor, however, prompted some humanitarians to conclude that people's environments, not their shortcomings, caused poverty and that society ought to shoulder greater responsibility for improving social conditions. They had faith that they could reduce poverty by improving housing, education, sanitation, and job opportunities rather than admonishing the poor to be more moral. This attitude fueled campaigns for building codes, factory regulations, and public health measures in the Progressive era of the early twentieth century (see Chapter 20). Still, most middle- and upper-class Americans continued to endorse the creed that in a society of abundance only the unfit were poor and that poverty relief should be tolerated but never encouraged. As one charity worker put it, relief "should be surrounded by circumstances that shall . . . repel every one . . . from accepting it."

Crime and disorder, as much as crowding and poverty, nurtured fears that cities, especially their slums,

CRIME AND VIOLENCE threatened the nation. The more cities grew, it seemed, the more they shook with violence. While homicide rates declined in industrialized nations such as England and Germany, those in America rose alarmingly: 25 murders per million people in 1881; 107 per million in 1898. Pickpockets, swindlers, and burglars roamed every city. Urban outlaws, such as Rufus Minor, acquired as much notoriety as western desperadoes. Short, stocky, and bald, Minor resembled a shy clerk, but one police chief labeled him "one of the smartest bank sneaks in

America." A sometime associate of Billy "The Kid" Burke, Minor often grew a beard before holding up a bank, then shaved afterward to avoid identification by eyewitnesses. Minor was implicated in bank heists in New York City, Cleveland, Detroit, Providence, Philadelphia, Albany, Boston, and Baltimore—all between 1878 and 1882.

Despite fears, however, urban crime and violence may simply have become more conspicuous and sensational rather than more prevalent. To be sure, concentrations of wealth and the mingling of different peoples provided opportunities for larceny, vice, and assault. But urban lawlessness and brutality probably did not exceed that of backwoods mining camps and southern plantations. Nativists were quick to blame immigrants for urban crime, but the criminal rogues' gallery included native-born Americans as well as foreigners. One investigation of jails in 1900 concluded that "we have ourselves evolved as cruel and cunning criminals as any that Europe may have foisted upon us."

The cityward movement of African Americans especially sparked white violence, and as the twentieth century dawned, a series of race riots spread across the nation. In 1898 citizens of Wilmington, North Carolina, resenting African Americans' involvement in local politics, rioted and killed dozens of blacks. In the fury's wake, whites expelled black officeholders and instituted restrictions to prevent blacks from voting. In Atlanta in 1906, newspaper accounts alleging attacks by black men on white women provoked an outburst of shooting and killing that left twelve blacks dead and seventy injured. An influx of African American unskilled laborers and strikebreakers into East St. Louis, Illinois, heightened racial tensions that erupted in 1917 when blacks fired back at a car whose occupants they believed had shot into their homes. When whites discovered that the blacks had mistakenly killed two policemen riding in the car, a full-scale riot erupted that ended only after nine whites and thirty-nine blacks had been killed and over three hundred buildings destroyed. In addition to mass violence, innumerable disruptions, ranging from domestic violence to muggings to gang fights, made cities scenes of constant turbulence.

Managing the City

Those concerned with managing cities faced daunting challenges in the late nineteenth century. Burgeoning populations, business expansion, and technological change created urgent needs for sewers, police and fire protection, schools, parks, and other services. Such needs strained municipal resources beyond their capacities, and city governments were poorly organized to handle them. Legislative and administrative functions were typically scattered among a mayor, city council, and independent boards that administered health regulations, public works, and poverty relief. Philadelphia at one time had thirty different boards, plus a mayor and council. Also, state governments often interfered in local matters, appointing board members and limiting cities' abilities to levy taxes and borrow money.

Finding sources of clean water and a way to dispose of waste became increasingly urgent challenges. Earlier in the nineteenth century, urban households used privies (outdoor toilets) to dispose of human excrement, and factories dumped untreated sewage into nearby rivers, lakes, and bays. By the late nineteenth century, most cities had replaced private wells and water companies with public water supplies, but these services did not guarantee pure water. The installation of sewer systems and flush toilets, plus use of water as coolant in factories, overwhelmed waterways, contaminating drinking water sources and sending pollution to communities downstream. The stench of rivers was often unbearable, and pollution bred disease. Memphis and New York experienced yellow-fever epidemics in the 1870s and 1880s, and typhoid fever threatened many cities. By 1900, the Pasaic River in northern New Jersey, once a popular recreation and fishing site, had been ruined by discharge from the several cities along its banks.

WATER SUPPLY AND SEWAGE DISPOSAL

Acceptance in the 1880s of the germ theory of disease prompted cities to take steps to reduce chances that human waste and other pollutants would endanger water supplies, but the task proved difficult. Some states passed laws prohibiting discharge of raw sewage into rivers and streams, and a few cities began the expensive process of chemically treating sewage. Gradually, water managers installed mechanical filters, and cities, led by Jersey City, began purifying water supplies by adding chlorine. These efforts dramatically reduced death rates from typhoid fever.

But disposal of waste, magnified by industrial as well as population expansion, remained a thorny problem. Experts in 1900 estimated that every New Yorker generated annually some 160 pounds of garbage (food and bones); 1,200 pounds of ashes (from stoves and furnaces); and 100 pounds of rubbish (shoes, furniture, and other discarded items). Europeans of that era produced about half as much trash. Solid waste dumped from factories and businesses included tons of scrap metal, wood, and other materials. In addition, each of the estimated

■ This scene, taken by a Philadelphia photographer sent to record the extent of trash littering city streets and sidewalks, illustrates the problems of disposal confronting inner-city, immigrant neighborhoods and the necessity for some form of public service to remove the refuse. Seemingly oblivious to the debris, the residents pose for the photographer. (Philadelphia City Archives, Department of Records)

3.5 million horses in American cities in 1900 dropped about 20 pounds of manure and a gallon of urine daily—a serious environmental pollution. When horses died, the disposal of carcasses brought more environmental problems. In past eras, excrement, trash, and dead animals could be dismissed as nuisances; by the twentieth century they became health and safety hazards.

Citizen groups, led by women's organizations, began discussing the dilemma in the 1880s and 1890s, and by the turn of the century urban governments hired sanitary engineers, such as New York's George Waring, to set up efficient systems of garbage collection and disposal, mostly in incinerators and landfills. Engineers also were solving other urban problems and making cities more livable. Providing street lighting, bridge and street construction, fire protection, and other such needs required technological creativity, and in addressing these critical issues, the American engineering profession developed new systems and standards of worldwide significance. Elected officials came to depend on the ex-

URBAN ENGINEERS

pertise of engineers, who seemed best qualified to supervise a city's expansion. Insulated within bureaucratic agencies away from tumultuous party politics, engineers generally carried out their responsibilities efficiently and made some of the most lasting contributions to urban management.

After the mid-nineteenth century, urban dwellers increasingly depended on professional police to protect life and property, but law enforcement became complicated and controversial as various groups now crowding the cities differed in their views of the law and how it should be enforced. Ethnic and racial minorities were more likely to be arrested than those with economic or political influence. And police officers applied the law less harshly to members of their own ethnic groups and to people who bought exemptions with bribes.

LAW ENFORCEMENT

As urban law enforcers, police, often poorly trained and prone to corruption, were caught between demands for swift and severe action on one hand and for leniency on the other. As urban society diversified, some people

■ "Big Tim" Sullivan, a New York City ward boss, rewarded "repeat voters" with a new pair of shoes. Sullivan once explained, "When you've voted 'em with their whiskers on, you take 'em to a barber and scrape off the chin fringe. Then you vote 'em again. . . . Then to a barber again, off comes the sides and you vote 'em a third time with the mustache. . . . [Then] clean off the mustache and vote 'em plain face. That makes every one of 'em for four votes." (Library of Congress)

clamored for crackdowns on drunkenness, gambling, and prostitution; at the same time, others favored loose law enforcement so they could indulge in these customer-oriented crimes. Achieving balance between the idealistic intentions of criminal law and people's desire for individual freedom grew increasingly difficult, and it has remained so to this day.

Out of the apparent confusion surrounding urban management arose political machines, organizations whose main goals were the rewards—money, influence, and prestige—of getting and keeping power. Machine politicians routinely used fraud and bribery to further their ends. But they also provided relief, security, and services to the crowds of newcomers who voted for them and kept them in power. By meeting people's needs, machine politicians accomplished things that other agencies had been unable or unwilling to attempt.

POLITICAL MACHINES

Machines bred leaders, called bosses, who catered to urban working classes and especially to new immigrant voters, who provided their power base. Most bosses had immigrant backgrounds and had grown up in the inner city; they knew their constituents' needs firsthand. Bosses held power because they tended to problems of everyday life. Martin Lomasney, boss of Boston's South End, explained, "There's got to be in every ward somebody that any bloke can come to—no matter what he's done—and get help. Help, you understand, none of your law and justice, but help." In return for votes, bosses provided jobs, built parks and bathhouses, distributed food and clothing to the needy, and helped when someone ran afoul of the law. Pittsburgh's Christopher Magee gave his city a zoo and a hospital. Brooklyn's Hugh McLaughlin provided free burial services. Such personalized service cultivated mass attachment to the boss; never before had public leaders assumed such responsibility for people in need. Bosses, moreover, were genuinely public people and they made politics a full-time profession. They attended weddings and wakes, joined clubs, and held open house in saloons where neighborhood folk could speak to them personally. According to George Washington Plunkitt, a neighborhood boss in New York City who published his memoirs in 1905, "As a rule [the boss] has no business or occupation other than politics. He plays politics every day and night in the year and his headquarters bears the inscription, 'Never closed.'"

To finance their activities and campaigns, bosses exchanged favors for votes and money. Power over local government enabled machines to control the awarding of public contracts, the granting of utility and streetcar franchises, and distribution of city jobs. Recipients of city business and jobs were expected to repay the machine with a portion of their profits or salaries and to cast supporting votes on election day. Critics called this process graft; bosses called it gratitude.

Bosses such as Philadelphia's "Duke" Vare, Kansas City's Tom Pendergast, and New York's Richard Croker lived like kings, though their official incomes were slim. Yet machines were rarely as dictatorial or corrupt as critics charged. Rather, several machines, like businesses, evolved into highly organized political structures, such as New York's Tammany Hall organization (named after a society that originally began as a patriotic and fraternal club), that wedded public accomplishments with personal gain. The system rested on a popular base and was held together by loyalty and service. A few bosses had no permanent organization; they were freelance opportunists who bargained for power, sometimes winning and sometimes losing. But most machines were coalitions of smaller organizations that derived power directly from inner-city neighborhoods. Bosses also could boast major accomplishments. Machine-led governments constructed urban infrastructures—public buildings, sewer systems, schools, bridges, and mass-transit lines—and expanded urban services—police, firefighting, and public health departments.

Machine politics, however, was neither neutral nor fair. Racial minorities and new immigrant groups such as Italians and Poles received only token jobs and nominal favors, if any. And bribes and kickbacks made machine projects and services costly to taxpayers. Cities could not ordinarily raise enough revenue for their construction projects from taxes and fees, so they financed expansion with loans from the public in the form of municipal bonds. Critics of bosses charged that these loans were inflated or unnecessary. Necessary or not, municipal bonds caused public debts to soar, and taxes had to be raised to repay their interest and principal. In addition, machines dispensed favors to legal and illegal businesses. Payoffs from gambling, prostitution, and illicit liquor traffic became important sources of machine revenue. But in an age of economic individualism, bosses were no more guilty of discrimination and self-interest than were business leaders who exploited workers, spoiled the landscape, and manipulated government in pursuit of profits. Sometimes humane and sometimes criminal, bosses acted as brokers between various sectors of urban society and an uncertain world.

While bosses were consolidating their power, others were trying to destroy them. Many middle- and upper-class Americans feared that immigrant-based political machines menaced democracy and that unsavory alliances between bosses and businesses wasted municipal finances. Anxious over the poverty, crowding, and disorder that accompanied city growth, and convinced that urban services were making taxes too high, civic reformers organized to install more responsible leaders at the helm of government.

CIVIC REFORM

Urban reform arose in part from the industrial system's emphasis on eliminating inefficiency. Business-minded reformers believed government should run like a company. The way to achieve this goal, they concluded, was to elect officials who would hold down expenses and prevent corruption. Thus they advocated reducing city budgets, making public employees work more efficiently, and cutting taxes.

To implement business principles in government, civic reformers supported structural changes such as city-manager and commission forms of government, which would place administration in the hands of experts rather than politicians, and nonpartisan, citywide rather than neighborhood-based election of officials. Armed with such strategies, reformers believed they could cleanse party politics and weaken bosses' power bases in the neighborhoods. They rarely realized, however, that bosses succeeded because they used government to meet people's needs. Reformers noticed only the waste and corruption that machines bred.

A few reform mayors moved beyond structural changes to address social problems. Hazen S. Pingree of Detroit, Samuel "Golden Rule" Jones of Toledo, and Tom Johnson of Cleveland worked to provide jobs to poor people, reduce charges by transit and utility companies, and promote governmental responsibility for the welfare of all citizens. They also supported public ownership of gas, electric, and telephone companies, a quasi-socialist reform that alienated their business allies. But Pingree, Jones, and Johnson were exceptions. Civic reformers could not match the bosses' political savvy; they achieved some successes but rarely held office for very long.

A different type of reform arose outside politics. Driven to improve as well as manage society, social reformers—mostly young and middle class—embarked on campaigns to identify and solve urban problems. Housing reformers pressed local governments for building codes to ensure safety in tenements. Educational reformers sought to use public schools as a means of preparing immigrant children for citizenship by teaching them American values.

Social Reform

Perhaps the most ambitious urban reform movement was the settlement house. Located in inner-city neighborhoods and run mostly by young, middle-class women who went to live and work among poor people in order to bridge the gulf between social classes, settlements sponsored programs for better education, jobs, and housing. The first American settlement, patterned after London's Toynbee Hall, opened in New York City in 1886, and others quickly appeared in cities across the country. Early settlement included leaders such as Jane Addams, founder of Hull House in Chicago in 1889 and one of the country's most influential women, and Florence Kelley, who pioneered laws to protect consumers and working women. Although working-class and immigrant neighborhood residents sometimes mistrusted them as outsiders, settlement workers undertook successful activities such as vocational classes, childcare, and ethnic pageants.

As they broadened their scope to fight for school nurses, building and factory safety codes, and public playgrounds, settlement workers became reform leaders in cities and in the nation. Their efforts to involve national and local governments in the solution of social problems put them in the vanguard of the Progressive era, when a reform spirit swept the nation (see Chapter 21). Moreover, settlement-house programs created new professional opportunities for women in social work, public health, and child welfare. These professions enabled female reformers to build a dominion of influence over social policy independent of male-dominated professions and to make valuable contributions to national as well as inner-city life.

Like much in American life, the settlement-house movement was segregated. Middle-class white women lobbied for government programs to aid mostly white immigrant and native-born working classes. Black women reformers, excluded from white settlements, raised funds from private donors and focused on helping members of their own race. African American women were especially active in founding schools, old-age homes, and hospitals, but they also worked for racial advancement and protection of black women from sexual exploitation. Their ranks included Jane Hunter, who founded a home for unmarried black working women in Cleveland in 1911 and inspired the establishment of similar homes in other cities, and Modjeska Simkins, who worked to overcome health problems among blacks in South Carolina.

While female activists tried to revive neighborhoods, a group of male reformers organized the City Beautiful movement to improve cities' attractiveness. Inspired by the Columbian Exposition of 1893, a dazzling world's fair held in a "White City" built on Chicago's South Side, architects and planners aimed to redesign the urban landscape. Led by architect Daniel Burnham, City Beautiful advocates built civic centers, parks, and boulevards that would make cities economically efficient as well as beautiful. "Make no little plans," Burnham urged. "Make big plans; aim high in hope and work." This attitude spawned beautifying projects in Chicago, San Francisco, and Washington, D.C., in the early 1900s. Yet most big plans existed mostly as big dreams. Neither government nor private businesses could finance large-scale projects, and planners disagreed among themselves and with social reformers over whether beautification would truly solve urban problems.

The City Beautiful Movement

Regardless of their focus, urban reformers wanted to save cities, not abandon them. They believed they could improve urban life by restoring cooperation among all citizens. They often failed to realize, however, that cities were places of great diversity and that different people held very different views about what reform actually meant. To civic reformers, appointing government workers on the basis of civil service exams rather than party loyalty meant progress, but to working-class men civil service signified reduced employment opportunities. Moral reformers believed that restricting the sale of alcoholic beverages would prevent working-class breadwinners from squandering wages and ruining their health, but immigrants saw such crusades as interference in their private lives. Planners saw new streets and civic buildings as modern necessities, but such structures often displaced the poor. Well-meaning humanitarians criticized immigrant mothers for the way they shopped, dressed, did housework, and raised children, without regard for these mothers' inability to afford products that the consumer economy created. Thus urban reform merged idealism with naiveté and insensitivity.

Family Life

*A*lthough the vast majority of Americans lived within families, this basic social institution suffered strain during the era of urbanization and industrialization. New institutions—schools, social clubs, political organizations, unions—increasingly competed with the family to provide nurture, education, and security. Clergy and journalists warned that the growing separation between home and work, rising divorce rates, the entrance of women into the work force, and loss of parental control over children spelled peril for home and family. Yet the family retained its fundamental role as a cushion in a hard, uncertain world.

Throughout modern Western history, most people have lived in two overlapping social units: household

FAMILY AND HOUSEHOLD STRUCTURES

and family. A household is a group of people, related or unrelated, who share the same residence. A family is a group related by kinship, some members of which typically live together. In the late nineteenth and early twentieth centuries, different patterns characterized the two institutions.

Since colonial times, most American households (75 to 80 percent) have consisted of nuclear families—usually a married couple, with or without children. About 15 to 20 percent of households consisted of extended families—usually a married couple, with or without children, plus one or more relatives such as parents, adult siblings, grandchildren, aunts, and uncles. About 5 percent of households consisted of people living alone or in boarding houses and hotels. Despite slight variations, this pattern held relatively constant among ethnic, racial, and socioeconomic groups.

Several factors explain this pattern. Because immigrants tended to be young, the American population as a whole was young. In 1880 the median age was under twenty-one, and by 1920 it was still only twenty-five. (Median age at present is about thirty-three.) Moreover, in 1900 the death rate among people aged forty-five to sixty-four was double what it is today. As a result, there were relatively few aged people: only 4 percent of the population was sixty-five or older, compared with about 13 percent today. Thus few families could form extended three-generation households, and fewer children than today had living grandparents. Migration split up many families, and the ideal of a home of one's own encouraged nuclear household organization.

The average size of nuclear families did change over time, though. Most of Europe and North America

DECLINING BIRTH RATES

experienced falling birth rates in the nineteenth century. The decline in the United States began early in the 1800s and accelerated toward the end of the century. In 1880 the birth rate was 40 live births per 1,000 people; by 1900 it had dropped to 32; by 1920 to 28. Although fertility was higher among blacks, immigrants, and rural people than among white native-born city dwellers, birth rates of all groups fell. Several factors explain this decline.

First, the United States was becoming an urban nation, and birth rates are historically lower in cities than in rural areas. On farms, where young children worked at home or in the fields, each child born represented an addition to the family work force. In the wage-based urban economy, children could not contribute significantly to the family income for many years, and a new child represented another mouth to feed. Second, infant mortality fell as diet and medical care improved, and families did not have to bear many children to ensure that some would survive. Third, awareness that smaller families meant improved quality of life seems to have stimulated decisions to limit family size—either by abstaining from sex during the wife's fertile period or by using contraception and abortion. Families with six or eight children became rare; three or four became more usual. Birth-control technology—diaphragms and condoms—had been utilized for centuries, but in this era new materials made devices more convenient and dependable. Use of rubber rather than animal membranes for condoms after 1869 inspired British playwright and philosopher George Bernard Shaw to exclaim that new birth-control devices were "the greatest invention of the nineteenth century."

The household tended to expand and contract over the lifetime of a given family. Its size increased as children

BOARDING

were born. Then it shrank as children left home before they were twenty years old, especially in working-class families, usually to work. The process of leaving home altered household composition; large numbers of young people—and some older people—lived as boarders and lodgers. Middle- and working-class families commonly took in boarders to occupy rooms vacated by grown children and to get additional income. Immigrants such as Rahel Gollop often lodged with relatives and fellow villagers until they could establish themselves. By 1900, as many as 50 percent of city residents had lived either as, or with, boarders at some point during their lifetime. Housing reformers charged that boarding caused overcrowding and loss of privacy. Yet the practice was highly useful.

■ The Hedlund family of St. Paul, Minnesota, celebrates the Fourth of July together in 1911 with flags and fireworks. Consisting of two parents and three children, the family represents the modern household of two generations and limited family size.

For people on the move, boarding was a transitional stage, providing a quasi-family environment until they set up their own households. Especially in communities where economic hardship or rapid growth made housing expensive or scarce, newlyweds sometimes lived temporarily with one spouse's parents. Families also took in widowed parents or unmarried siblings who otherwise would have lived alone, and many young unmarried men and women continued to live at home although they had jobs and independent social lives.

At a time when welfare agencies were rare, the family was the institution to which people could turn in times of need. Even when relatives did not live together, they often resided nearby and aided one another with childcare, meals, shopping, advice, and consolation. They also obtained jobs for each other. Factory foremen who had responsibility for hiring often recruited new workers recommended by their employees. According to one new arrival, "After two days my brother took me to the shop he was working in and his boss saw me and he gave me the job."

But obligations of kinship were not always welcome. Immigrant families pressured last-born children to stay at home to care for aging parents, a practice that stifled opportunities for education, marriage, and economic independence. As an aging Italian-American father confessed, "One of our daughters is an old maid [and] causes plenty of troubles. . . . It may be my fault because I always wished her to remain at home and not to marry for she was of great financial help." Tensions also developed between generations, such as when immigrant parents and American-born children clashed over the abandonment of Old World ways or the amount of wages employed children should contribute to the household. Nevertheless, for better or worse, kinship provided people a means of coping with the stresses caused by urban-industrial society. Social and economic change did not sever family ties.

Large numbers of city dwellers were unmarried. In 1890 almost 42 percent of adult American men and 37 percent of women were single, almost twice as high as the figures for 1960 but slightly lower than they are

UNMARRIED PEOPLE

today. About half of them still lived in their parents' household, but many others inhabited boarding houses or rooms in the homes of strangers. Mostly young, these men and women constituted a separate subculture that helped support institutions like dance halls, saloons, cafés, and the Young Men's Christian Association (YMCA) and Young Women's Christian Association (YWCA).

Some unmarried people were part of the homosexual populations that thrived especially in large cities like New York, San Francisco, and Boston. Though numbers are difficult to estimate, gay men had their own subculture of clubs, restaurants, coffeehouses, theaters, and support networks. A number of same-sex couples, especially women, formed lasting marital-type relationships, sometimes called "Boston marriages." Some men cruised in the sexual underground of streets and bars. People in this subculture were categorized more by how they acted—men acting like women, women acting like men—than by who their sexual partners were. The term *homosexual* was not used. Men who dressed and acted like women were called "fairies," and men who displayed masculine traits could be termed "normal" even though they might have sexual relations with fairies. Gay women remained even more hidden, and a lesbian subculture of clubs and commercial establishments was rare until the 1920s. The gay world, then, was a complex one that included a variety of relationships and institutions.

Although the family remained resilient and adaptable, subtle but significant changes began to occur in individual life patterns. Before the late

STAGES OF LIFE

nineteenth century, stages of life were less distinct than they are today, and generations blended together with relatively little differentiation. Childhood, for instance, had been regarded as a period during which young people prepared for adulthood by gradually assuming more roles and responsibilities. The subdivisions of youth—toddlers, schoolchildren, teenagers, and the like—were not recognized or defined. Because married couples had more children over a longer time span than is common today, active parenthood occupied most of adult life. Older children who cared for younger siblings might begin parenting even before reaching adulthood. And because relatively few people lived to advanced age or left work voluntarily, and because old-age homes were rare, older people were not isolated from other age groups.

In the late nineteenth century, demographic and social changes altered these patterns. Decreasing birth rates shortened the period of parental responsibility, so more middle-aged couples experienced an "empty nest" when all their children had grown up and left home. Longer life expectancy and a tendency by employers to force aged workers to retire separated the old from the young. At the same time, work became more specialized and education in graded schools more formalized, especially after states passed compulsory school-attendance laws in the 1870s and 1880s. Childhood and adolescence became more distinct from adulthood. As a result of these and other trends (including the fact that lower birth rates gave people fewer sisters and brothers to relate to), Americans grew more conscious of age and peer influence. People's roles in school, in the family, on the job, and in the community came to be determined by age more than by any other characteristic.

Thus by 1900, family life and functions were both changing and holding firm. New institutions were assuming tasks formerly performed by the family. Schools made education a community responsibility. Employment agencies, personnel offices, and labor unions were taking responsibility for employee recruitment and job security. Age-based peer groups exerted greater influence over people's values and activities. Migration and divorce seemed to be splitting families apart. Yet in the face of these pressures, the family adjusted by expanding and contracting to meet temporary needs, and kinship remained a dependable though not always appreciated institution.

An emphasis on family togetherness became especially visible at holiday celebrations. Middle-class moralists

HOLIDAY CELEBRATIONS

helped make Thanksgiving, Christmas, and Easter special times for family reunion and child-centered activities, and female relatives made special efforts to cook and decorate the home. Birthdays, too, took on an increasingly festive quality, both as an important family occasion and as a milestone for measuring the age-related norms that accompanied intensified consciousness of life stages. New holidays were created as well. In 1914, President Woodrow Wilson signed a proclamation designating the second Sunday in May as Mother's Day, capping a six-year campaign by Anna Jarvis, a schoolteacher who believed grown children too often neglected their mothers. Ethnic and racial groups made efforts to fit national celebrations to their cultures, using holidays as occasions for preparing special ethnic foods and engaging in special ceremonies. For many, holiday celebrations were a testimony to the vitality of family life. "As I grew up, living conditions were a bit crowded," one woman reminisced, "but no one minded because we were a family . . . thankful we all lived together."

The New Leisure and Mass Culture

*O*n December 2, 1889, as hundreds of workers paraded through Worcester, Massachusetts, in support of shorter working hours, a group of carpenters hoisted a banner proclaiming "Eight Hours for Work, Eight Hours for Rest, Eight Hours for What We Will." That last phrase was significant, for it laid claim to a special segment of daily life that belonged to the individual. Increasingly, among all urban social classes, leisure activities, doing "what we will," filled this time segment.

American inventors had long tried to create labor-saving devices, but not until the late 1800s did technology become truly time-saving. Mechanization and assembly-line production cut the average workweek in manufacturing from sixty-six hours in 1860 to sixty in 1890 and forty-seven in 1920. These reductions meant shorter workdays and freer weekends. White-collar employees spent eight to ten hours a day on the job and often worked only half a day or not at all on week-

INCREASE IN LEISURE TIME

ends. To be sure, thousands of laborers in steel mills and sweatshops still endured twelve- or fourteen-hour shifts and had no time or energy for leisure. But as the economy shifted from one of scarcity and production to one of surplus and consumption, more Americans began to engage in a variety of diversions, and a substantial segment of the economy provided for—and profited from—leisure. By the early 1900s, many Americans were enmeshed in the business of play.

After the Civil War, amusement became an organized, commercial activity. Production of games, toys, and musical instruments for indoor family entertainment expanded. Games such as checkers and backgammon had long histories, but improvements in printing and paper production and the rise of manufacturers such as Milton Bradley and Parker Brothers increased the popularity of board games. Significantly, the content of board games shifted from moral lessons to topics involving transportation, finance, and sports. Also, by the 1890s, middle-class families were buying mass-produced pianos and sheet music that made singing of popular songs a common form of home entertainment. The vanguard of new leisure pursuits, however, was sports. Formerly a

■ Amusement centers such as Luna Park, at Coney Island in New York City, became common and appealing features of the new leisure culture. One of the most popular Coney Island attractions was a ride called Shooting the Chutes, which resembled modern-day giant water slides. In 1904, Luna Park staged an outrageous stunt when an elephant slid down the chute. It survived, apparently unfazed. (Picture Research Consultants and Archives)

SHOOTING THE CHUTES, CONEY ISLAND, N. Y.

fashionable indulgence of elites, organized sports became a favored pastime of all classes, attracting countless participants and spectators. Even those who could not play or watch got involved by reading about sports in the newspapers.

The most popular organized sport was baseball. Derived from older bat, ball, and base-circling games,

BASEBALL

baseball was formalized in 1845 by the Knickerbocker Club of New York, which codified the rules of play. By 1860 at least fifty baseball clubs existed, and youths played informal games on city lots and rural fields across the nation. In 1869 a professional club, the Cincinnati Red Stockings, went on a national tour, and other clubs followed suit. The National League of Professional Baseball Clubs, founded in 1876, gave the sport a stable, businesslike structure. Not all athletes benefited, however; as early as 1867 a "color line" excluded black players from professional teams. Nevertheless, by the 1880s professional baseball was big business. In 1903 the National League and competing American League (formed in 1901) began a World Series between their championship teams, entrenching baseball as the national pastime. The Boston Red Sox beat the Pittsburgh Pirates in that first series.

Baseball appealed mostly to men. But croquet, which also swept the nation, attracted both sexes. Middle- and

CROQUET AND CYCLING

upper-class people held croquet parties and outfitted wickets with candles for night contests. In an era when the departure of paid work from the home had separated men's from women's spheres, croquet increased opportunities for social contact between the sexes.

Meanwhile, cycling achieved popularity rivaling that of baseball, especially after 1885, when the cumbersome velocipede, with its huge front wheel and tall seat, gave way to safety bicycles with pneumatic tires and wheels of identical size. By 1900 Americans owned 10 million bicycles, and clubs like the League of American Wheelmen were petitioning state governments to build more paved roads. One journal boasted that cycling "cured dyspepsia, headaches, insomnia, and sciatica" and gave "a vigorous tone to the whole system." Organized cycle races enabled professional riders such as Major Taylor, an African American, to win fame in Europe and the United States. Like croquet, cycling brought men and women together, combining opportunities for exercise and courtship. Moreover, the bicycle played an influential role in freeing women from constraints of Victorian fashions. In order to ride the dropped-frame female models, women had to wear divided skirts and simple undergarments. Gradually, cycling costumes influenced everyday

fashions. As the 1900 census declared, "Few articles . . . have created so great a revolution in social conditions as the bicycle."

Other sports had their own patrons. Tennis and golf attracted both sexes but remained pastimes of the

FOOTBALL

wealthy. Played mostly at private clubs, these sports lacked baseball's team competition and cycling's informality. American football, as an intercollegiate competition, mostly attracted players and spectators wealthy enough to have access to higher education. By the late nineteenth century, however, the game was appealing to a broader audience. The 1893 Princeton-Yale game drew fifty thousand spectators, and informal games were played in yards and playgrounds throughout the country.

Soon, however, college football became a national scandal because of its violence and use of "tramp athletes," nonstudents whom colleges hired to help their teams win. Critics accused football of mirroring undesirable features of American society. An editor of *The Nation* charged in 1890 that "the spirit of the American Youth, as of the American man, is to win, to 'get there,' by fair means or foul; and the lack of moral scruple which pervades the struggles of the business world meets with temptations equally irresistible in the miniature contests of the football field."

The scandals climaxed in 1905, when 18 players died from game-related injuries and over 150 were seriously injured. President Theodore Roosevelt, a strong advocate of athletics, convened a White House conference to discuss ways to eliminate brutality and foul play. The gathering founded the Intercollegiate Athletic Association (renamed the National College Athletic Association in 1910) to police college sports. In 1906 the association altered the game to make it less violent and more open. New rules outlawed "flying wedge" rushes, extended from five to ten yards the distance needed to earn a first down, legalized the forward pass, and tightened player eligibility requirements.

As more women enrolled in college, they pursued physical activities besides croquet and cycling. Believing that intellectual success required active and healthy bodies, college women participated in sports such as rowing, track, and swimming. Eventually women made basketball their most popular intercollegiate sport. Invented in 1891 as a winter sport for men, basketball received women's rules (which limited dribbling and running and encouraged passing) from Senda Berenson of Smith College.

Paralleling the rise of sports, American show business also became a mode of leisure created by and for

CIRCUSES

common people. Circuses—traveling shows of acrobats and animals—had

Japanese Baseball

Baseball, the "American pastime," was one of the new leisure-time pursuits that Americans took with them into different parts of the world. The Shanghai Base Ball Club was founded by Americans in China in 1863, but few Chinese paid much attention to the sport, largely because the Imperial Court renounced the game as spiritually corrupting. However, when Horace Wilson, an American teacher, taught the rules of baseball to his Japanese students some time around 1870, the game received enthusiastic welcome as a reinforcement of traditional virtues. In fact baseball quickly became so much a part of Japanese culture that one Japanese writer commented, "Baseball is perfect for us. If the Americans hadn't invented it, we probably would have."

During the 1870s, Japanese high schools and colleges organized baseball games, and in 1883 Hiroshi Hiraoka, a railroad engineer who had studied in Boston, founded the first official local team, the Shimbashi Athletic Club Athletics. Fans displayed wild devotion to this and similar teams as they developed over the next several years.

Before Americans introduced baseball to Japan, the Japanese had no team sports and no concept of recreational athletics. When they learned about baseball, they found that the idea of a team sport fit into their culture very well. But the Japanese had difficulty applying the American concept of leisure to the game. For them, baseball was serious business, involving hard and often brutal training. Practices at Ichiko, one of Japan's two great high school baseball teams in the late nineteenth century, were dubbed "Bloody Urine" because many players passed blood after a day of drilling. There was a spiritual quality as well, linked to Buddhist values. According to one Japanese coach, "The purpose of [baseball] training is not health but the forging of the soul, and a strong soul is only born from strong practice. . . . Student baseball must be the baseball of self-discipline, or trying to attain the truth, just as in Zen Buddhism." This attitude prompted Japanese to consider baseball as a new method to pursue the spirit of Bushido, the way of the samurai.

When Americans played baseball in Japan, the Japanese thought them to be strong and talented but lacking in discipline and respect. Americans insulted the Japanese by refusing to remove their hats and bow when they stepped up to bat. An international dispute occurred in 1891 when William Imbrie, an American professor at Meijo University in Tokyo, arrived late for a local game. Finding the gate locked, he climbed over the fence in order to watch the game. The fence, however, had sacred meaning and some Japanese fans attacked Imbrie for his sacrilege. Imbrie suffered facial injuries, prompting the American embassy to lodge a formal complaint. Americans assumed that their game would encourage Japanese to become like westerners to some extent, but the Japanese transformed the American pastime into an expression of team spirit, discipline, and nationalism that was uniquely Japanese.

■ Replete with bats, gloves, and uniforms, this Japanese baseball team of 1890 very much resembles its American counterpart of that era. The Japanese adopted baseball soon after Americans became involved in their country, but also added its their cultural qualities to the game. (Japanese Baseball Hall of Fame)

535

existed since the 1820s. But after the Civil War, railroads enabled them to reach cities and towns across the country. Circuses offered two main attractions: oddities of nature, both human and animal, and the temptation and conquest of death. At the heart of their appeal was the astonishment that trapeze artists, lion tamers, acrobats, and clowns aroused.

Three branches of American show business—popular drama, musical comedy, and vaudeville—matured with the growth of cities. Theatrical performances offered audiences escape into melodrama, adventure, and comedy. Plots were simple, the heroes and villains recognizable. For urban people unfamiliar with the frontier, popular plays made the mythical Wild West and Old South come alive through stories of Davy Crockett, Buffalo Bill, and the Civil War. Virtue and honor always triumphed in melodramas such as *Uncle Tom's Cabin* and *The Old Homestead*, reinforcing faith that in an uncertain and disillusioning world, goodness would prevail.

POPULAR DRAMA AND MUSICAL COMEDY

Musical comedies entertained audiences with song, humor, and dance. The American musical derived from lavishly costumed operettas common in Europe. By introducing American themes (often involving ethnic groups), folksy humor, and catchy tunes, these shows spawned the nation's most popular songs and entertainers. George M. Cohan, a spirited singer, dancer, and songwriter born into an Irish family of entertainers, became master of American musical comedy after the turn of the century. Drawing on patriotism and traditional values in songs like "Yankee Doodle Boy" and "You're a Grand Old Flag," Cohan helped bolster morale during the First World War. Comic opera, too, became popular. Initially, American comic operas imitated European musicals, but by the early 1900s composers like Victor Herbert were writing for American audiences. Shortly thereafter Jerome Kern began composing more sophisticated musicals, and American musical comedy became more unique.

Because of its variety, vaudeville was probably the most popular mass entertainment in early twentieth-century America. Shows included, in rapid succession, acts of jugglers, pantomimists, magicians, puppeteers, acrobats, comedians, singers, and dancers. Around 1900, the number of vaudeville theaters and troupes skyrocketed. Shrewd entrepreneurs, who promoted entertainment as Edison and Ford promoted technology, made vaudeville big business. The famous producer Florenz Ziegfeld brilliantly packaged shows in a stylish format—the Ziegfeld Follies—and gave the nation a new model of

VAUDEVILLE

■ Joe Weber and Lew Fields were one of the most popular comic teams in vaudeville. They and similar comedians used fast-paced dialogue to entertain audiences with routines such as this one: Doctor: Do you have insurance? Patient: I ain't got one nickel insurance. Doctor: If you die, what will your wife bury you with? Patient: With pleasure. (Corbis-Bettmann)

femininity, the Ziegfeld Girl, whose graceful dancing and alluring costumes suggested a haunting sensuality.

Show business provided new opportunities for female, African American, and immigrant performers, but it also encouraged stereotyping and exploitation. Comic opera diva Lillian Russell, vaudeville singer-comedienne Fanny Brice, and burlesque queen Eva Tanguay attracted intensely loyal fans, commanded handsome fees, and won respect for their talents. In contrast to the demure Victorian female, they conveyed an image of pluck and creativity. There was something both shocking and refreshingly confident about Eva Tanguay when she sang earthy songs like "It's All Been Done Before but Not the Way I Do It" and "I Don't Care." But lesser female performers and showgirls (called "soubrettes") were often exploited by male promoters and theater owners, many of whom wanted only to profit by titillating the public with the sight of scantily clad women.

Before the 1890s, the chief form of commercial entertainment that employed African American performers was the minstrel show, but vaudeville opened new opportunities to them. As stage settings shifted from the plantation to the city, music shifted from folk tunes to ragtime (music with a syncopated melody). Pandering to prejudices of white audiences, composers and performers of both races ridiculed blacks. As songs like "He's Just a Little Nigger, but He's Mine All Mine" and "You May Be a Hawaiian on Old Broadway, but You're Just Another Nigger to Me" confirm, blacks were demeaned on stage much as they were in society. Burt Williams, a talented and highly paid black comedian and dancer, achieved success by playing stereotypical roles of darky and dandy but was tormented by the humiliation he had to suffer.

An ethnic flavor gave much of American mass entertainment its uniqueness. Indeed, immigrants occupied the core of American show business. Vaudeville in particular utilized ethnic humor, exaggerating dialects and other national traits. Skits and songs reinforced stereotypes and made fun of ethnic groups, but such distortions were more self-conscious and sympathetic than those directed at blacks. Ethnic humor often involved everyday difficulties that immigrants faced. A typical scene involving Italians, for example, highlighted a character's uncertain grasp of English, which caused him to confuse *mayor* with *mare*, *diploma* with the *plumber*, and *pallbearer* with *polar bear*. Such scenes allowed audiences to laugh with, rather than at, foibles of the human condition. The conditions of African Americans, however, were subject to more vicious jokes.

Shortly after 1900, live entertainment began to yield to a more accessible form of commercial amusement: motion pictures. Perfected by Thomas Edison in the 1880s, movies began as slot-machine peepshows in penny arcades and billiard parlors. Eventually images were projected onto a screen so that large audiences could view them, and a new medium was born. At first, subjects of films hardly mattered; scenes of speeding trains, acrobats, and writhing belly dancers were thrilling enough.

Producers soon discovered that a film could tell a story in exciting ways. Thanks to creative directors like D. W. Griffith, motion pictures became a distinct art form. Griffith's *Birth of a Nation* (1915), an epic film about the Civil War and Reconstruction, fanned racial prejudice by depicting African Americans as threats to white moral values. The National Association for the Advancement of Colored People (NAACP), formed in 1909, led organized protests against it. But the film's innovative techniques—close-ups, fade-outs, and battle

MOVIES

■ Dick Merriwell and his brother, Frank, were fictional heroes of hundreds of stories written in the early 1900s by Burt Standish (the pen name used by Gilbert Patten). In a series of adventures, mostly involving sports, these popular character models used their physical skills, valor, and moral virtue to lead by example, accomplish the impossible, and influence others to behave in an upstanding way. (Collection of Picture Research Consultants, Inc.)

scenes—heightened the drama. By 1920, movies appealed to all classes (admission usually cost a nickel), and audiences idolized film stars such as Mary Pickford, Lillian Gish, and Charlie Chaplin.

By making it possible to mass-produce sound and images, technology made entertainment a highly desirable consumer good. The still camera, modernized by inventor George Eastman, enabled ordinary people to record their own visual images, especially useful for preserving family memories. The phonograph, another Edison invention, brought musical performances into the home. Moreover, the spread of movies, photography, and phonograph meant that access to live performances no longer limited people's exposure to art and entertainment.

News also became a consumer product. Using high-speed printing presses, cheap paper, and profits from growing advertisement revenues, shrewd publishers created a medium that made people crave news and ads just as they craved amusements. City life and increased leisure time seemed to nurture a fascination with the sensational, and from the 1880s onward popular urban newspapers increasingly whetted that appetite.

Joseph Pulitzer, a Hungarian immigrant who bought the *New York World* in 1883, pioneered journalism as a branch of mass culture. Believing that newspapers should be "dedicated to the cause of the people rather

than to that of the purse potentates," Pulitzer filled the *World* with stories of disasters, crimes, and scandals and printed screaming headlines, set in large bold type like that used for advertisements. Pulitzer's journalists not only reported news but sought it out and created it. *World* reporter Nellie Bly (real name, Elizabeth Cochrane) faked her way into an insane asylum and wrote a brazen exposé of the sordid conditions she found. Other reporters staged stunts and hunted down heart-rending human-interest stories. Pulitzer also popularized comics, and the yellow ink they were printed in gave rise to the term *yellow journalism* as a synonym for sensationalism.

Pulitzer's strategy was immensely successful. In one year the *World*'s circulation increased from 20,000 to 100,000, and by the late 1890s it reached 1 million. Soon other publishers, such as William Randolph Hearst, who bought the *New York Journal* in 1895 and started an empire of mass-circulation newspapers, adopted Pulitzer's techniques. Pulitzer, Hearst, and their rivals boosted circulation further by emphasizing sports and women's news. Newspapers had previously reported sporting events, but yellow-journalism papers gave such stories greater prominence by printing separate, expanded sports pages. Sports news re-created a game's drama through narrative and statistics and promoted sports as a leisure-time attraction. Newspapers also added special sections devoted to household tips, fashion, decorum, and club news to capture female readers. Like crime and disaster stories, sports and women's sections helped to make news a mass commodity.

By the early twentieth century, mass-circulation magazines overshadowed expensive elitist journals of earlier

eras. Publications such as *McClure's, Saturday Evening Post,* and *Ladies' Home Journal* offered human-interest stories, muckraking exposés (see page 571), titillating fiction, photographs, colorful covers, and eye-catching ads to a growing mass market. Meanwhile, the total number of published books more than quadrupled between 1880 and 1917. This rising consumption of news and books reflected growing literacy. Between 1870 and 1920, the proportion of Americans over age ten who could not read or write fell from 20 percent to 6 percent.

Other forms of communication also expanded. In 1891 there was less than 1 telephone for every 100 people in the United States; by 1901 the number had grown to 2.1, and by 1921 it swelled to 12.6. In 1900

Americans used 4 billion postage stamps; in 1922 they bought 14.3 billion. The term *community* took on new dimensions, as people used the media, mail, and telephone to extend their horizons far beyond their immediate localities. More than ever before, people in different parts of the country knew about and discussed the same news event, whether it was a sensational murder, a sex scandal, or the fortunes of a particular entertainer or athlete. America was becoming a mass society where the same products, the same technology, and the same information dominated everyday life, regardless of region.

To some extent, the cities' new amusements and media had a homogenizing influence, allowing ethnic and social groups to share common experiences. Parks, ball fields, vaudeville shows, most movies, and feature sections of newspapers and magazines were nonsectarian and apolitical. Yet, different consumer groups used them to reinforce their own cultural habits. Immigrant groups, for example, often occupied parks and amusement areas as sites for special ethnic gatherings. To the dismay of reformers who hoped that public recreation and holidays would assimilate newcomers and teach them habits of restraint, immigrants used picnics and Fourth of July celebrations as occasions for boisterous drinking and sometimes violent behavior. Young working-class men and women resisted parents' and moralists' warnings and frequented urban dance halls, where they explored their own forms of courtship and sexual behavior. And children often used streets and rooftops to create their own entertainment rather than participate in adult-supervised games in parks and playgrounds. Thus as Americans learned to play, their leisure—like their work and politics—expressed, and was shaped by, the pluralistic forces that thrived in urban life.

Summary

*M*uch of what American society is today originated in the urbanization that occurred between 1877 and 1920. Though their governments and neighborhoods may have seemed chaotic, American cities experienced an "unheralded triumph" by the early 1900s. Amid corruption and political conflict, urban engineers modernized local infrastructures with sewer, water, and lighting services, and urban governments made the environment safer by expanding professional police and fire departments. When native inventiveness met the traditions of European, African, and Asian cultures, a new kind of society emerged. This society seldom functioned smoothly; there really was no coherent urban community, only a collection of subcommunities. The jumble of social classes, ethnic and racial groups, political organizations, and professional experts sometimes lived in harmony, sometimes not. Generally, cities managed to thrive because of rather than in spite of their diverse fragments.

Amid bewildering diversity, fearful yet confident native-born whites tried to Americanize and uplift immigrants, but newcomers stubbornly protected their cultures. Optimists had envisioned the American nation as a melting pot, where various nationalities would fuse into a unified people. Instead, many ethnic groups proved unmeltable, and racial minorities got burned on the bottom of the pot. As a result of immigration and urbanization, the United States became a pluralistic society—not so much a melting pot as a salad bowl, where ingredients retained their original flavor and occasionally blended. Often the results were compound identifications: Irish American, Italian American, Polish American, and the like.

Pluralism and interest-group loyalties enhanced the importance of politics. If America was not a melting pot, then different groups were competing for power, wealth, and status. Some people carried polarization to extremes and tried to suppress everything allegedly un-American. Efforts to enforce homogeneity generally failed, however, because the country's cultural diversity prevented domination by a single ethnic majority. By 1920, immigrants and their offspring outnumbered the native-born in many cities, and the national economy depended on these new workers and consumers. Migrants and immigrants transformed the United States into an urban nation. They gave American culture its rich and varied texture, and they laid the foundations for the liberalism that characterized American politics in the twentieth century.

LEGACY FOR A PEOPLE AND A NATION
Ethnic Food

Today, an ordinary American might eat a bagel for breakfast, a gyro sandwich for lunch, and wonton soup, shrimp creole, and rice pilaf for dinner, followed by chocolate mousse and espresso. An evening snack might consist of nachos and lager beer. These items, each identified with a different ethnic group, serve as tasty reminders that immigrants have made important and lasting contributions to the nation's culinary culture. The American diet also represents one of the few genuine ways that the multicultural nation has served as a melting pot.

The American taste for ethnic food has a complicated history. Since the nineteenth century, the food business has offered immigrant entrepreneurs lucrative opportunities, many of which involved products unrelated to their own ethnic background. The industry is replete with success stories linked to names such as Hector Boiardi (Chef Boyardee), William Gebhardt (Eagle Brand chili and tamales), Jeno Paulucci (Chun-King), and Alphonse Biardot (Franco-American), all of whom immigrated to the United States in the late nineteenth or early twentieth century. But Americans have also supported unheralded local immigrant merchants and restaurateurs who have offered special and regional fare—German, Chinese, Italian, Tex-Mex, "soul food," or Thai—in every era.

Unlike the strife that occurred over housing, jobs, schools, and politics when different nationalities collided, the evolution of American eating habits has been peaceful. Occasionally, criticisms developed, such as when dietitians and reformers in the early twentieth century charged that Mexican immigrants were harming their digestion by overusing tomatoes and peppers and that the rich foods of eastern European Jews made them overly emotional and less capable of assimilating. But as historian Donna Gabaccia has observed, relatively conflict-free sharing and borrowing have characterized American food ways far more than "food fights" and intolerance. The sensory pleasure of eating has always overridden cultural loyalty, and mass marketers have been quick to capitalize.

As each wave of immigrants has entered the nation—and especially as these newcomers have occupied the cities, where cross-cultural contact has been inevitable—food has given them certain ways of becoming American, of finding some form of group acceptance, while also giving them a means of confirming their identity. At the same time, those who already thought of themselves as Americans have willingly made the cuisine of the newcomers' legacy a part of the existing culture and a part of themselves.

The **history Companion** *powered by Eduspace®*

Your primary source for interactive quizzes, exercises, and more to help you learn efficiently.
http://history.college.hmco.com/students

GILDED AGE POLITICS 1877–1900

She had a sharp tongue and a combative spirit. Known to friends as the "People's Joan of Arc" and to enemies as the "Kansas Pythoness," Mary Elizabeth Lease was such an electrifying orator that, according to one observer, "she could recite the multiplication table and set a crowd hooting and harrahing at her will." She was born in 1853 in Pennsylvania but lived most of her adult life in Kansas. Married at age twenty, she bore five children but somehow found time to study law while she took in washing, pinning her notes above her washtub.

In 1885, Mary became the first woman admitted to the Kansas bar and began an activist career. Joining the Women's Christian Temperance Union and an organization called the Farmers' Alliance, she became a spokesperson for the Populist party and made more than 160 speeches in 1890 on behalf of downtrodden rural folk and laboring people. She later ran for the U.S. Senate and campaigned for James B. Weaver, presidential candidate of the new Populist party. But she damaged her party's fortune by stubbornly refusing to unite with Democrats sympathetic to her opposition to big business and political corruption. Yet Lease's reputation for powerful language inspired her causes, which ranged beyond Populism to prohibition, woman suffrage, and birth control. She once proclaimed, "This is a nation of inconsistencies. . . . We fought England for our liberty and put chains on four million blacks. We wiped out slavery and [then] by our tariff laws and national banks began a system of white wage slavery worse than the first." Though she denied urging Kansas farmers to "raise less corn and more hell," she admitted that it "was a good bit of advice."

Lease's turbulent career paralleled an eventful era, one that can be characterized by three themes: special interest ascendancy, legislative accomplishment, and political exclusion. When she attacked railroads, Wall Street, and businessmen whom she accused of exploiting farmers, Lease expressed the growing dissatisfaction with the ways in which powerful private interests—manufacturers,

◀ Politics in the late nineteenth century was a major community activity. In an age before movies, television, shopping malls, and widespread professional sports, forceful orators such as Socialist Party leader Eugene V. Debs, shown speaking in a railroad yard, attracted large audiences for speeches that sometimes lasted for hours. (Brown Brothers)

C H R O N O L O G Y

1873 • Congress ends coinage of silver dollars

1873–78 • Economic hard times hit

1876 • Hayes elected president

1877 • Georgia passes poll tax to disfranchise African Americans in the South

1878 • Bland-Allison Act requires Treasury to buy between $2 and $4 million in silver each month

1880 • Garfield elected president

1881 • Garfield assassinated; Arthur assumes the presidency

1883 • Pendleton Civil Service Act introduces merit system
• Supreme Court strikes down 1875 Civil Rights Act

1884 • Cleveland elected president

1886 • *Wabash* case declares that only Congress can limit interstate commerce rates

1887 • Farmers' Alliances form
• Interstate Commerce Commission begins regulating rates and practices of interstate shipping

1888 • B. Harrison elected president

1890 • McKinley Tariff raises tariff rates
• Sherman Silver Purchase Act commits Treasury to buying 4.5 million ounces of silver each month
• "Mississippi Plan" uses poll taxes and literacy tests to prevent African Americans from voting
• National American Woman Suffrage Association formed

1892 • Populist convention in Omaha draws up reform platform
• Cleveland elected president

1893 • Sherman Silver Purchase Act repealed

1893–97 • Major economic depression hits United States

1894 • Wilson-Gorman Tariff passes
• Coxey's army marches on Washington, D.C.

1895 • Cleveland deal with bankers saves gold reserves

1896 • McKinley elected president
• *Plessy v. Ferguson* establishes separate-but-equal doctrine

1898 • Louisiana implements "grandfather clause"

1899 • *Cummins v. County Board of Education* applies separate-but-equal doctrine to schools

1900 • Gold Standard Act requires all paper money to be backed by gold
• McKinley reelected president

railroad managers, bankers, and wealthy men in general—were exercising damaging greed in large corporations. The era's venality seemed so widespread that when, in 1874, Mark Twain and Charles Dudley Warner satirized America as a land of shallow money grubbers in their novel *The Gilded Age,* the name stuck. Historians have used the expression "Gilded Age" to characterize the late nineteenth century.

At the same time, Lease's rhetoric obscured economic and political accomplishments at both the state and national levels. Between 1877 and 1900, industrialization, urbanization, and the commercialization of agriculture altered national politics and government as much as they shaped everyday life. Congress achieved legislative landmarks in railroad regulation, tariff and currency reform, civil service, and other important issues in spite of partisan and regional rivalries. Meanwhile, the judiciary actively supported big business by defending property rights against state and federal regulation. The presidency was occupied by honest, respectable men who, though not as exceptional as Washington, Jefferson, or Lincoln, prepared the office for its more activist character after the turn of the century. Even so, exclusion—the third phenomenon—prevented the majority of Americans—including women, southern blacks, Indians, uneducated whites, and unnaturalized immigrants—from voting and from access to the tools of democracy. This exclusion simmered within the hearts of Mary Elizabeth Lease and many others.

Until the 1890s, those three phenomena of special interests, accomplishment, and exclusion existed within a delicate political equilibrium characterized by a stable party system and balance of power among geographical sections. Then in the 1890s rural discontent rumbled through the West and South, and a deep economic depression bared flaws in the industrial system. Though she feuded with those most able to support her, Lease helped awaken rural masses with her fiery rhetoric. Amid economic and political disruption, a presidential campaign in 1896 stirred Americans as they had not been stirred for a generation. A new party arose, old parties split, sectional unity dissolved, and fundamental disputes about the nation's future climaxed. The nation emerged from the turbulent 1890s with new economic configurations and new political alignments. ■

The Nature of Party Politics

*a*t no other time in the nation's history was public interest in elections more avid than between 1870 and 1896. Consistently, around 80 percent of eligible voters (white and black males in the North, somewhat lower rates among mostly white males in the South) cast ballots in local and national elections. (Under 50 percent typically do so today.) Politics served as a form of recreation, more popular than baseball or circuses. Actual voting provided only the final step in a process that included parades, picnics, and speeches. As one observer remarked, "What the theatre is to the French, or the bull fight . . . to the Spanish . . . [election campaigns] and the ballot box are to our people."

Political rivalry and party loyalty in part reflected American pluralism. As different groups competed for

CULTURAL-
POLITICAL
ALIGNMENTS

power, wealth, and status, they formed coalitions to achieve their goals. But such alliances were fragile; their memberships shifted according to the issue in question. With some exceptions, groups who opposed government interference in matters of personal liberty identified with the Democratic Party; those who believed government could be an agent of moral reform identified with the Republican Party. Democrats included immigrant Catholics and Jews, who followed ritual and sacraments to guide personal behavior and prove one's faith in God. Republicans consisted mostly of native-born Protestants, who believed that salvation was best achieved by purging the world of evil and that legislation could protect people from sin. Democrats would restrict government power. Republicans believed in direct government action.

At state and local levels, adherents of these two cultural traditions battled over how much government should control people's lives. The most contentious issues were use of leisure time and celebration of Sunday, the Lord's day. Protestant Republicans tried to keep the Sabbath holy through legislation that prohibited bars, stores, and commercial amusements from being open on Sundays. Immigrant Democrats, accustomed to feasting and playing after church, fought saloon closings and other restrictions on the only day they had free from work. Similar splits developed over public versus parochial schools and prohibition versus the free availability of liquor.

These issues made politics a personal as well as a community activity. In an era before movie stars and media heroes, people formed strong loyalties to individual politicians, loyalties that often overlooked crassness and corruption. James G. Blaine—Maine's flamboyant and powerful congressman, senator, presidential aspirant, and two-time secretary of state—typified this appeal. Followers called him the "Plumed Knight," composed songs and organized parades in his honor, and sat mesmerized by his long speeches, while disregarding his corrupt alliances with businessmen and his animosity toward laborers and farmers.

Allegiances to national parties and candidates were so evenly divided that no faction gained control for any sustained period of time. Between 1877 and 1897, Republicans held the presidency for three terms, Democrats for two. Rarely did the same party control both the presidency and Congress simultaneously. From 1876 through 1892, presidential elections were extremely close. The outcome often hinged on the popular vote in a few populous northern states—Connecticut, New York, New Jersey, Ohio, Indiana, and Illinois. Both parties tried to gain advantages by nominating presidential and vice-presidential candidates from these states (and also by committing vote fraud on their candidates' behalf).

Moreover, internal quarrels split both the Republican and Democratic Parties. Among Republicans,

PARTY FACTIONS

New York's pompous senator Roscoe Conkling led one faction, known as "Stalwarts." A physical-fitness devotee labeled "the finest torso in public life," Conkling worked the spoils system to win government jobs for his supporters. The Stalwarts' rivals were the "Half Breeds," led by James G. Blaine, who pursued influence as blatantly as Conkling did. On the sidelines stood more idealistic Republicans, or "Mugwumps" (supposedly an Indian term meaning "mug on one side of the fence, wump on the other"). Mugwumps such as Senator Carl Schurz of Missouri scorned the political roguishness that tainted Republican leaders and believed that only righteous, educated men like themselves should govern. Meanwhile, Democrats subdivided into white-supremacy southerners, immigrant-stock and working-class urban political machines, and business-oriented advocates of low tariffs. Like Republicans, Democrats avidly pursued the spoils of office.

In each state, one party usually dominated, and within that party a few men typically held dictatorial power. Often the state "boss" was a senator who parlayed his state power into national influence. Until the Seventeenth Amendment to the Constitution was ratified in 1913, state legislatures elected U.S. senators, and a senator could wield enormous influence with his command of federal jobs. Besides Conkling and Blaine, the senatorial ranks included Thomas C. Platt of New York, Nelson W. Aldrich of Rhode Island, Mark A. Hanna of Ohio, Matthew S. Quay of Pennsylvania, and William Mahone

Missionaries

While many Americans during the Gilded Age engaged in partisan politics, they also devoted themselves to another, often-overlooked form of commitment: spreading the Gospel to the world. American Christians from most denominations contributed far more money toward missionary work than they did toward other popular political and social causes, and American missionaries sailed to nearly every part of the globe. First intended to teach native peoples about the Bible, missionary projects focused increased attention on overseas undertakings as the nineteenth century progressed, sending funds and volunteers to the Middle East, Africa, and China. Expanding beyond pure preaching, mission organizations sponsored construction of schools and hospitals and taught secular subjects as well as biblical learning.

American missionaries altered the educational climate in several countries. In Syria, for example, they opened the American University of Beirut (first called the Syrian Protestant College), and the school soon developed departments of medicine, pharmacy, and commerce. Its nursing program was one of the few places in the Middle East where women could receive technical training. Missionaries' educational efforts in the Middle East also helped increase interest in Arabic literature. Their use of Arabic printing presses to translate the Bible advanced the mass production of books for consumption by Middle Easterners.

In Africa, almost all leaders of the earliest independent African states had been educated in schools founded and taught by European and American missionaries, many of whom were African American. Protestant denominations believed that African American missionaries would be more effective than white missionaries in Africa, and though African American missionaries shared white convictions in the superiority of Western culture, they did not share their racial prejudices.

Lay persons as well as clergy went abroad and helped expand the realm of missionary work. By 1890, there were one hundred missionary physicians in China, who brought American medical techniques to 350,000 patients per year. Many other missionaries to China were unmarried American women whose feminist impulses prompted them to take action against practices such as foot binding, which they considered debasing to women.

American foreign missionaries in the late nineteenth century did not come close to realizing their goal of converting the world to Christ, but they did achieve modest results. When, like European missionaries, they tried to impose Western customs in the places to which they traveled, they were often rejected and sometimes even persecuted. Yet they established churches that lasted for decades, and the schools they founded influenced native educational efforts. In the United States, divisions between liberals and fundamentalists in the 1920s destroyed the evangelical unity that had enabled the creation of large missionary societies in the nineteenth century, and though many American religious organizations are still active in missionary work, by the 1930s the heyday of foreign missions linking Americans to the world was over.

Missionary work enabled American women to undertake humanitarian projects in foreign lands. Using both her gentility and her strength of character, Dr. Kate Woodall, shown in this photo from 1895, carried out her missionary work in China by training female medical students.   (ABCFM Pictures. Courtesy of Houghton Library, Harvard University)

of Virginia. These men exercised their power brazenly. Quay once responded to an inquiry about using secret information from a Senate investigation to profit from an investment in the American Sugar Refining Company by pronouncing, "I do not feel that there is anything in my connection with the Senate to interfere with my buying or selling stock when I please, and I propose to do so in the future."

Issues of Legislation

I n Congress, the issues of sectional controversies, patronage abuses, railroad regulation, tariffs, and currency provoked heated debates but also important legislation. Well into the 1880s, bitter hostilities from the Civil War and Reconstruction continued to divide Americans. Republicans capitalized on war memories by "waving the bloody shirt" at Democrats. As one Republican orator harangued in 1876, "Every man that tried to destroy this nation was a Democrat. . . . Soldiers, every scar you have on your heroic bodies was given you by a Democrat." In the South, Democratic candidates also waved the bloody shirt, calling Republicans traitors to white supremacy and states' rights.

Other Americans also sought advantages by invoking war memories. The Grand Army of the Republic, an organization of 400,000 Union Army veterans, allied with the Republican Party and cajoled Congress into providing generous pensions for former Union soldiers and their widows. Many pensions were deserved: Union troops had been poorly paid, and thousands of wives had been widowed. But for some veterans, the war's emotional memories furnished an opportunity to profit at public expense. Though the Union Army spent $2 billion to fight the Civil War, pensions to veterans ultimately cost $8 billion, one of the largest welfare commitments the federal government has ever made. By 1900 soldiers' pensions accounted for roughly 40 percent of the federal budget. Confederate veterans received none of this money, though some southern states funded small pensions and built old-age homes for ex-soldiers.

Few politicians dared oppose Civil War pensions, but some attempted to dismantle the spoils system. The

CIVIL SERVICE REFORM

practice of awarding government jobs to party workers, regardless of their qualifications, had taken root before the Civil War and flourished afterward. As the postal service, diplomatic corps, and other government agencies expanded, so did the public payroll. Between 1865 and 1891, the number of federal jobs tripled, from 53,000 to 166,000. Elected officials scram-

■ Before the Pendleton Act of 1883, many government positions were filled by patronage; hat in hand, job seekers beseeched political leaders to find a place for them. Here a member of Congress presents office-seeking friends to President Hayes. (Library of Congress)

bled to control these jobs as a means to benefit themselves and their party. In return for comparatively short hours and high pay, appointees to federal positions pledged votes and a portion of their earnings to their patrons.

Shocked by such corruption, especially after the revelation of scandals in the Grant administration, some reformers began advocating appointments and promotions based on merit rather than political connections. Civil service reform accelerated in 1881 with the formation of the National Civil Service Reform League, led by editors E. L. Godkin and George W. Curtis. That year, the assassination of President James Garfield by a distraught job seeker hastened the drive for change. The Pendleton Civil Service Act, passed by Congress in 1882 and signed by President Chester Arthur in 1883, created the Civil Service Commission to oversee competitive examinations for government positions. The act gave the commission jurisdiction over only 10 percent of federal jobs, though the president could expand the list. Because the Constitution barred Congress from interfering in state affairs, civil service at the state and local levels developed in a more haphazard manner. Nevertheless, the Pendleton Act marked a beginning and provided a model for further reform.

Veterans' pensions and civil service reform were not the main issues of the Gilded Age, however. Rather, economic policy occupied congressional business more than ever before. Railroads particularly provoked controversy. As rail networks spread, so did competition. In their quest for customers, railroad lines reduced rates to outmaneuver rivals, but rate wars hurt profits and inconsistent freight charges angered shippers and farmers. On noncompetitive routes, railroads often boosted charges as high as possible to compensate for unprofitably low rates on competitive routes, making pricing disproportionate to distance. Charges on short-distance shipments served by only one line could exceed those on long-distance shipments served by competing lines. Railroads also played favorites, reducing rates to large shippers and offering free passenger passes to preferred customers and politicians.

Such favoritism stirred farmers, small merchants, and reform politicians to demand rate regulation. Their efforts succeeded first at the state level.

RAILROAD REGULATION By 1880 fourteen states had established commissions to limit freight and storage charges of state-chartered lines. Railroads fought these measures, arguing that the Constitution guaranteed them freedom to acquire and use property without government restraint. But in 1877, in *Munn v. Illinois,* the Supreme Court upheld the principle of state regulation, declaring that grain warehouses owned by railroads acted in the public interest and therefore must submit to regulation for "the common good."

State legislatures, however, could not regulate interstate lines, a limitation affirmed by the Supreme Court in the *Wabash* case of 1886, in which the Court declared that only Congress could limit rates involving interstate commerce. Reformers thereupon demanded federal action. Congress responded in 1887 by passing the Interstate Commerce Act. The law prohibited pools, rebates, and long-haul/short-haul rate discrimination, and it created the Interstate Commerce Commission (ICC), the nation's first regulatory agency, to investigate railroad rate-making methods, issue cease-and-desist orders against illegal practices, and seek court aid to enforce compliance. The legislation's weak provisions for enforcement, however, left railroads room for evasion, and federal judges chipped away at ICC powers. In the *Maximum Freight Rate* case (1897), the Supreme Court ruled that the ICC lacked power to set rates; and in the *Alabama Midlands* case (1897), the Court overturned prohibitions against long-haul/short-haul discrimination. Even so, the principle of regulation, though weakened, remained in force.

The economic issue of tariffs carried strong political implications. In 1816, Congress initially created a tariff,

TARIFF POLICY which levied duties (taxes) on imported goods, to protect American manufactures and agricultural products from European competition. But tariffs quickly became a tool by which special interests could enhance their profits. By the 1880s these interests had succeeded in obtaining tariffs on more than four thousand items. A few economists and farmers argued for free trade, but most politicians still insisted that tariffs were a necessary form of government assistance to support industry and preserve jobs.

The Republican Party put protective tariffs at the core of its political agenda to support economic growth. Democrats complained that tariffs made prices artificially high by keeping out less expensive foreign goods, thereby benefiting domestic manufacturers while hurting farmers whose crops were not protected and consumers who had to buy manufactured goods. For example, a yard of flannel produced abroad might cost 10 cents, but an 8-cent import duty raised the price paid by American consumers to 18 cents. An American manufacturer of a similar yard of flannel, also costing 10 cents, could charge 17 cents, underselling foreign competition by 1 cent yet still pocketing a 7 cent profit because he did not have to pay the tariff.

During the Gilded Age, revenues from tariffs and other levies created a surplus in the federal budget. Most Republicans, being businessmen, liked the idea that the government was earning more than it spent and hoped to keep the extra money as a Treasury reserve or to spend it on projects like harbor improvements that would aid commerce. Democrats, however, asserted that the federal government should not be a profit-making business. They wanted to eliminate surplus by reducing tariffs. Democrats acknowledged a need for protection of some manufactured goods and raw materials, but they favored lower tariff duties to encourage foreign trade and to reduce the Treasury surplus.

Manufacturers and their congressional allies firmly controlled tariff policy. The McKinley Tariff of 1890 boosted already-high rates by another 4 percent. When House Democrats supported by President Grover Cleveland passed a bill to trim tariffs in 1894, Senate Republicans, aided by southern Democrats eager to protect their region's infant industries, particularly textiles and steel, added six hundred amendments restoring most cuts (Wilson-Gorman Tariff). In 1897 the Dingley Tariff raised rates further. Attacks on duties, though unsuccessful, made tariffs a symbol of privileged business in the public mind and a continuing target of reformers.

Monetary policy inflamed even stronger emotions than tariffs did. When increased industrial and agricultural production caused prices to fall after the Civil War, debtors and creditors had opposing reactions. Farmers suffered because the prices they received for crops were dropping, but because high demand for a relatively limited amount of available money raised interest rates on loans, it was costly for them to borrow funds to pay mortgages and other debts. They favored schemes like the coinage of silver to increase the amount of currency in circulation. An expanded money supply, they reasoned, would reduce interest rates, making their debts less burdensome. Small businessmen, needing loans to start new operations, agreed with farmers. Large merchants, manufacturers, and bankers favored a more stable, limited money supply backed only by gold. They feared that the value of currency not backed by gold would fluctuate; the resulting uncertainty would threaten investors' confidence in the U.S. economy.

MONETARY POLICY

Arguments over the quantity and quality of money, however, transcended economics. Creditor-debtor tension translated into class divisions between haves and have-nots. The debate also reflected sectional cleavages: western silver-mining areas and agricultural regions of the South and West against the more conservative industrial Northeast. And the issue carried moral, almost religious, overtones. Some Americans believed the beauty, rarity, and durability of gold gave it magical potency. Others believed the gold standard for currency was too limiting; sustained prosperity, they insisted, demanded new attitudes.

By the 1870s, the currency controversy boiled down to gold versus silver. Previously, the government had bought both gold and silver to back the national currency, setting a ratio that made a gold dollar worth sixteen times more than a silver dollar. Mining discoveries after the gold rush of 1848, however, increased the gold supply and lowered its market price relative to that of silver. Consequently, silver dollars disappeared from circulation—because of their inflated value relative to gold, owners hoarded them—and in 1873 Congress officially stopped coining silver dollars. European governments also stopped buying silver, and the United States and many of its trading partners unofficially adopted the gold standard, meaning that their currency was backed chiefly by gold.

But within a few years, new mines in the American West began to flood the market with silver, and its price dropped. Because gold now was relatively less plentiful, it became worth more than sixteen times the value of sil-

■ Taking advantage of the new fad of bicycling (see Chapter 19), a cartoonist in an 1886 issue of the humor magazine *Puck* illustrates the controversy over silver coinage. Depicting two uncoordinated wheels, one a silver coin and the other a gold coin, the illustration conveys the message of how hard it was to proceed with conflicting kinds of currency.   (Private Collection)

ver (the ratio reached twenty to one by 1890), and it became worthwhile to spend rather than hoard silver dollars. Silver producers wanted the government to resume buying silver at the old sixteen-to-one ratio, which amounted to a subsidy because they could sell silver to the government above market price. Debtors, hurt by the economic hard times of 1873–1878, saw silver as a means of expanding the currency supply. They joined silver producers to press for resumption of silver coinage at the old sixteen-to-one ratio.

With both parties split into silver and gold factions, Congress first tried to compromise. The Bland-Allison Act (1878) authorized the Treasury to buy between $2 million and $4 million worth of silver each month, and the Sherman Silver Purchase Act (1890) increased the government's monthly silver purchase by specifying weight (4.5 million ounces) rather than dollars. Neither measure satisfied the different interest groups. Creditors wanted the government to stop buying silver, while for debtors, the legislation failed to expand the money supply satisfactorily and did not erase the impression that the government favored creditors' interests. The issue would become even more emotional during the presidential election of 1896 (see pages 561–564).

National politics was not a glamorous field of endeavor in the Gilded Age. Senators and representatives earned small salaries and usually had the financial burden of maintaining two residences: one in their home district and one in Washington. Weather in the nation's capital was oppressively hot in summer, muddy and icy in winter. Most members of Congress had no private office space, only a desk. They worked long hours responding to constituents' requests, wrote their own speeches, and paid for staff out of their own pockets. Yet, cynics to the contrary, most politicians were principled and dedicated. They managed to deal with important issues and pass some significant legislation pertaining to civil service, railroad regulation, and monetary issues under difficult conditions.

LEGISLATIVE ACCOMPLISHMENTS

The Presidency Restrengthened

*O*perating under the cloud of Andrew Johnson's impeachment, Grant's scandals, and doubts about the legitimacy of the 1876 election (see Chapter 16), American presidents between 1877 and 1900 moved gingerly to restore authority to their office. Proper and honest, Presidents Rutherford Hayes (1877–1881), James Garfield (1881), Chester Arthur (1881–1885), Grover Cleveland (1885–1889 and 1893–1897), Benjamin Harrison (1889–1893), and William McKinley (1897–1901) tried to act as legislative as well as administrative leaders. Like other politicians, they used symbols. Hayes served lemonade at the White House to emphasize that he, unlike his predecessor Ulysses Grant, was no hard drinker. McKinley set aside his cigar in public so photographers would not catch him setting a bad example for youth. More important, each president initiated legislation and used the veto to guide national policy.

Rutherford B. Hayes had been a Union general and an Ohio congressman and governor before his disputed election to the presidency, an event that prompted opponents to label him "Rutherfraud." Though his party expected him to serve business interests, Hayes played a quiet role as reformer and conciliator. He emphasized national harmony over sectional

HAYES, GARFIELD, AND ARTHUR

rivalry and opposed racial violence. He tried to overhaul the spoils system by appointing civil service reformer Carl Schurz to his cabinet and by battling New York's patronage king, Senator Conkling. (He fired Conkling's protégé, Chester Arthur, from the post of New York customs house collector.) Though averse to using government power to aid the oppressed, Hayes believed society should not ignore needs of the American Chinese and Indians, and after retiring from the presidency he worked diligently to aid former slaves.

When Hayes declined to run for reelection in 1880, Republicans nominated another Ohio congressman and Civil War hero, James A. Garfield, who defeated Democrat Winfield Scott Hancock, also a Civil War hero, by just 40,000 votes out of 9 million cast. By winning the pivotal states of New York and Indiana, however, Garfield carried the electoral college by a comfortable margin, 214 to 155. A solemn and cautious man, Garfield spent most of his brief presidency trying to secure an independent position among party potentates. He hoped to reduce the tariff and develop economic relations with Latin America and pleased civil service reformers by rebuffing Conkling's patronage demands. But his chance to make lasting contributions ended in July 1881 when Charles Guiteau shot him in a Washington railroad station. Garfield lingered for seventy-nine days while doctors tried vainly to remove a bullet lodged in his back, but he succumbed to infection and died September 19.

Garfield's successor was Vice President Chester A. Arthur, the New York spoilsman whom Hayes had fired in 1878. Republicans had nominated Arthur for vice president only to help Garfield win New York State's electoral votes. Though his elevation to the presidency made reformers shudder, Arthur became a dignified and temperate executive. He signed the Pendleton Civil Service Act, urged Congress to modify outdated tariff rates, and supported federal regulation of railroads. He wielded the veto aggressively, killing several bills that excessively benefited railroads and corporations. But congressional partisans frustrated his plans for reducing the tariff and strengthening the navy. Arthur wanted to run for president in 1884 but lost the nomination to James G. Blaine at the Republican national convention.

To oppose Blaine, Democrats named New York's governor, Grover Cleveland, a bachelor who had tainted his reputation when he fathered an illegitimate son—a fact he admitted during the campaign. Both parties focused on the sordid. (Alluding to Cleveland's bastard son, Republicans chided him with catcalls of "Ma! Ma! Where's my pa?" To which Democrats replied, "Gone to the White House, Ha! Ha! Ha!") Distaste for Blaine prompted some Mugwump Republicans to desert their party for Cleveland. On election day Cleveland beat Blaine by only 29,000 popular votes; his tiny margin of 1,149 votes in New York gave him that state's 36 electoral votes, enough for a 219-to-182 victory in the electoral college. Cleveland may have won New York thanks to last-minute remarks of a local Protestant minister, who equated Democrats with "rum, Romanism, and rebellion." Democrats eagerly publicized the slur among New York's large Irish-Catholic population, urging voters to protest by supporting Cleveland.

Cleveland, the first Democratic president since James Buchanan (1857–1861), tried to exert vigorous leadership.

CLEVELAND AND HARRISON

He expanded civil service, vetoed hundreds of private pension bills, and urged Congress to cut tariff duties. When advisers warned that his stand might weaken his chances for reelection, the president retorted, "What is the use of being elected or reelected, unless you stand for something?" But the Mills tariff bill of 1888, passed by the House in response to Cleveland's wishes, died in the Senate. When Democrats renominated Cleveland for the presidency in 1888, businessmen in the party convinced him to moderate his attacks on high tariffs.

Republicans in 1888 nominated Benjamin Harrison, former senator from Indiana and grandson of President William Henry Harrison (1841). During the campaign, some Republicans manipulated a British diplomat into stating that Cleveland's reelection would be good for England. Irish Democrats, who hated England's colonial rule over Ireland, took offense, as intended, and Cleveland's campaign was weakened. Perhaps more beneficial to Harrison were the bribery and multiple voting that helped him win Indiana by 2,300 votes and New York by 14,000. (Democrats also indulged in such cheating, but Republicans proved more successful at it.) Those states ensured Harrison's victory. Though Cleveland outpolled Harrison by 90,000 popular votes, Harrison carried the electoral vote by 233 to 168.

The first president since 1875 whose party had majorities in both houses of Congress, Harrison used a variety of methods, ranging from threats of vetoes to informal dinners and consultations with politicians, to influence the course of legislation. Partly in response, the Congress of 1889–1891 passed 517 bills, 200 more than the average passed by Congresses between 1875 and 1889. Harrison showed support for civil service by appointing the reformer Theodore Roosevelt as civil service commissioner, but neither the president nor Congress could resist pressures from special interests, especially those waving the bloody shirt. Harrison signed the Dependents' Pension Act, which provided pensions for Union

■ A paper lantern and wooden whistle represent just two of countless types of items used to expose voters to candidates for election—in this instance, Benjamin Harrison, the Republic presidential candidate in 1888. In an age before television advertising, such knickknacks brought candidates before the public in a unique way. (Collection of David J. and Janice L. Frent)

veterans who had suffered war-related disabilities and granted aid to their widows and minor children. The bill doubled the number of welfare recipients from 490,000 to 966,000.

The Pension Act and other appropriations in 1890 pushed the federal budget past $1 billion for the first time in the nation's history. Democrats blamed the "Billion-Dollar Congress" on spendthrift Republicans. Voters reacted by unseating seventy-eight Republicans in congressional elections of 1890. Seeking to capitalize on voter unrest, Democrats nominated Grover Cleveland to run against Harrison again in 1892. This time Cleveland attracted large contributions from business and beat Harrison by 370,000 popular votes (3 percent of the total) and easily won the electoral vote.

In office again, Cleveland moved boldly to address problems of currency, tariffs, and labor unrest. His actions reflected a narrow orientation toward business interests and bespoke political weakness. During his campaign Cleveland had promised sweeping tariff reform, but he made little effort to line up support in the Senate, where protectionists undercut efforts to reduce rates. And when 120,000 boycotting railroad workers paralyzed commerce in the Pullman strike of 1894, Cleveland bowed to requests from railroad managers and Attorney General Richard Olney (a former railroad lawyer) to send in troops (see page 494). In spite of Cleveland's attempts at initiative, major events—particularly economic downturn and agrarian ferment—shoved him from the limelight.

Discrimination, Disfranchisement, and Response

*T*hough the scope of government activity expanded during the Gilded Age, policies of discrimination and exclusion continued to haunt more than half of the nation's population. Just as before the Civil War, issues of race gave a peculiar quality to politics in the South. There, poor whites, facing economic losses, feared that newly enfranchised African American men would challenge whatever political and social superiority (real and imagined) they enjoyed. Wealthy white landowners and merchants fanned these fears, using racism to divide whites and blacks and to distract poor whites from protesting their own economic subjugation.

The majority of the nation's African Americans lived in the South and worked in agriculture. Although the abolition of slavery altered their legal status, it did not markedly improve their economic opportunities. In 1880, 90 percent of all southern blacks depended for a

VIOLENCE
AGAINST
AFRICAN
AMERICANS

living on farming or personal and domestic service—the same occupations they had held as slaves. The New South, moreover, proved to be as violent for blacks as the Old South had been. Weapons, including a gun commonly known as a "nigger killer," were plentiful, and whites seldom hesitated to use them. More dramatically, between 1889 and 1909, more than seventeen hundred African Americans were lynched in the South. Most lynchings were acts of terror that occurred in sparsely populated districts where whites felt threatened by an influx of migrant blacks who had no friends, black or white, to vouch for them. Most lynching victims were accused of assault—rarely proved—on a white woman.

Blacks did not suffer such violence silently, however. Protests arose on several fronts. In Memphis, for example, Ida B. Wells, a teacher in an African American school, reacted to the lynching of a local black store-owner in 1892 by establishing a newspaper, called *The Free Speech and Headlight*, that published attacks against the evils of lynching. After urging local blacks to migrate to the West, Wells was forced to flee to England to escape threats against her life. But she soon returned and wrote *A Red Record* (1895), which tabulated statistics on racial lynchings and served as a foundation for further protest campaigns.

With slavery dead, white supremacists fashioned new ways to keep blacks in an inferior position. Southern leaders, embittered by northern interference in race relations during Reconstruction and eager to reassert authority over people whom they believed to be inferior, instituted measures to prevent blacks from voting and to segregate them legally from whites.

The end of Reconstruction had not stopped blacks from voting. Despite threats and intimidation, blacks still formed the backbone of the southern Republican Party and won numerous elective offices. In North Carolina, for example, eleven African Americans served in the state Senate and forty-three in the House between 1877 and 1890. Rather than trying to influence whom blacks voted for, white politicians sought to impose restrictions that would disenfranchise blacks, that is, deprive them of their right to vote. Beginning with Tennessee in 1889 and Arkansas in 1892, southern states levied taxes of $1 to $2 on all citizens wishing to vote. These poll taxes proved prohibitive to most blacks, who were so poor and deep in debt that they rarely had cash for any purpose. Other schemes disfranchised blacks who could not read.

DISFRANCHISEMENT

Disfranchisement was accomplished in other devious

ways. The Supreme Court determined in *U.S. v. Reese* (1876) that Congress had no control over local and state elections other than the explicit provisions of the Fifteenth Amendment, which prohibits states from denying the vote "on account of race, color, or previous condition of servitude." State legislatures found ways to exclude black voters without mentioning race, color, or servitude. For instance, an 1890 state constitutional convention established the "Mississippi Plan," requiring all voters to pay a poll tax eight months before each election, to present the tax receipt at election time, and to prove that they could read and interpret the state constitution. Registration officials applied stiffer standards to blacks than to whites, even declaring black college graduates ineligible on grounds of illiteracy. In 1898 Louisiana enacted the first "grandfather clause," which established literacy and property qualifications for voting but exempted sons and grandsons of those eligible to vote before 1867, the year the Fifteenth Amendment had gone into effect. Other southern states initiated similar measures.

Such restrictions proved highly effective. In South Carolina, for example, 70 percent of eligible blacks voted in the 1880 presidential election; by 1896 the rate had dropped to 11 percent. By the 1900s African Americans had effectively lost political rights in the South. More importantly, because voting is often considered a common right of citizenship, disfranchisement stripped African American men of their social standing as U.S. citizens. Disfranchisement also affected poor whites, few of whom could meet poll tax, property, and literacy requirements. Thus the total number of eligible voters in Mississippi shrank from 257,000 in 1876 to 77,000 in 1892.

Racial discrimination also stiffened in areas beyond mere voting as existing customs of racial separation were expanded in law. In a series of cases

LEGAL SEGREGATION

during the 1870s, the Supreme Court opened the door to discrimination by ruling that the Fourteenth Amendment protected citizens' rights only against infringement by state governments. The federal government, according to the Court, lacked authority over what individuals or organizations might do. If blacks wanted legal protection from individual prejudice, the Court said, they must seek it from state laws because under the Tenth Amendment states retained all powers not specifically assigned to Congress. These rulings climaxed in 1883 when in the *Civil Rights* cases the Court struck down the 1875 Civil Rights Act, which prohibited segregation in public facilities such as streetcars, theaters, and parks. Again the Court declared that the federal government could not

In the years after Reconstruction, lynchings of African American men occurred with increasing frequency, chiefly in sparsely populated areas where whites looked on strangers, especially black strangers, with fear and suspicion. (© R. P. Kingston/Index Stock Imagery, Picture Cube Division)

regulate behavior of private individuals in matters of race relations.

States, however, still could segregate on a "separate but equal" basis, as upheld by the Supreme Court in the famous case of *Plessy v. Ferguson* (1896). This case began in 1892 when the Citizens Committee, a New Orleans organization of prominent African Americans, chose Homer Plessy, a dark-skinned Creole who was only one-eighth black (but still considered black by Louisiana law), as a volunteer to violate a state law by sitting in a separate whites-only railroad car. The Citizens Committee hoped to challenge the law through Plessy's arrest. But in upholding Plessy's conviction, the Court stated that a state law providing for separate facilities for the two races was not unconstitutional because "a distinction which is founded in the color of the two races, and which must always exist so long as white men are distinguished from the other race by color—has no tendency to destroy the legal equality of the two races." In 1899, the Court applied the separate-but-equal doctrine to schools in *Cummins v. County Board of Education,* legitimating school segregation until it was overturned by *Brown v. Board of Education* in 1954.

Segregation laws—known as Jim Crow laws—multiplied throughout the South, confronting African Americans with daily reminders of inferior status. State and local statutes restricted them to the rear of streetcars, to separate public drinking fountains and toilets, and to separate sections of hospitals and cemeteries. A Birmingham, Alabama, ordinance required that the races be "distinctly separated . . . by well defined physical barriers" in "any room, hall, theatre, picture house, auditorium, yard, court, ballpark, or other indoor or outdoor place." Mobile, Alabama, passed a curfew requiring blacks to be off the streets by 10 P.M., and Atlanta mandated separate Bibles for the swearing-in of black witnesses in court.

African American women and men challenged the political climate in several ways. Some boycotted discriminatory businesses; others considered moving to Africa. Still others promoted "Negro business enterprise," in which African Americans tried to establish

AFRICAN AMERICAN ACTIVISM

their own businesses and factories. In 1898, Atlanta University professor John Hope called upon blacks to become their own employers and supported formation of Negro Business Men's Leagues. In the optimistic days following Reconstruction, a number of blacks used higher education as a means of elevating their status. In all-black teachers' colleges, most of which were coeducational, blacks sought opportunities for themselves and their race. Education also seemed to present a way to foster interracial cooperation. But the white supremacy campaigns that Jim Crow laws reflected taught southern blacks that they would have to negotiate in a biracial, rather than interracial, society.

While disfranchisement pushed African American men, who in contrast to women had previously been able to vote, out of public life, African American women used traditional roles as mothers, educators, and moral guardians to seek services and reforms that signified a kind of political activity that was more subtle than voting. They successfully lobbied local and state governments in the South for reforms such as cleaner city streets, better public health, expanded charity services, and vocational education. Ida B. Wells moved to Chi-

■ Livingstone College in North Carolina was one of several institutions of higher learning established by and for African Americans in the late nineteenth century. With a curriculum that emphasized training for educational and religious work in the South and in Africa, these colleges were coeducational, operating on the belief that both men and women could have public roles. (Courtesy of Heritage Hall, Livingstone College, Salisbury, North Carolina)

cago and continued her crusade for equal rights by founding the Women's Era Club, the first civic organization for African American women. In less threatening means than casting ballots, black women found ways to join with white women in campaigns to improve the general community and to negotiate with the white male power structure to achieve their goals. In many instances, however, white women joined men in support of white supremacy campaigns.

In the North, white women contended head-on with male power structures. Their goal was the vote; their successes in reaching this goal were limited. Prior to 1869, each state determined who was qualified to vote. The Fifteenth Amendment, adopted that year, forbade states to deny the vote "on account of race, color or previous condition" but omitted any reference to sex. For the next twenty years, two organizations—the National Woman Suffrage Association (NWSA) and the American Woman Suffrage Association (AWSA)—crusaded for female suffrage. The NWSA, led by militants Elizabeth Cady Stanton and Susan B. Anthony, advocated women's rights in courts and workplaces as well as at the ballot box. The AWSA, led by former abolitionists Lucy Stone and Thomas Wentworth Higginson, focused more narrowly on suffrage.

WOMAN SUFFRAGE

In 1878 Susan B. Anthony, who had lost in the courts when she tried to vote in 1872, persuaded Senator A. A. Sargent of California to introduce a constitutional amendment stating that "the right of citizens of the United States to vote shall not be denied or abridged by the United States or by any state on account of sex." A Senate committee killed the bill, but the NWSA had it reintroduced repeatedly over the next eighteen years. On the few occasions when the bill reached the Senate floor, it was voted down by senators who claimed that suffrage would interfere with women's family obligations.

While the NWSA fought for suffrage on the national level, the AWSA worked to amend state constitutions. (The groups merged in 1890 to form the National American Woman Suffrage Association.) Though these campaigns succeeded only slightly, they helped train a corps of female leaders in political organizing and public speaking. Women did win partial victories. Between 1870 and 1910, eleven states (mostly in the West) legalized limited woman suffrage. By 1890 nineteen states allowed women to vote on school issues, and three granted suffrage on tax and bond issues. The right to vote in national elections awaited a later generation, but the activities of women such as Mary E. Lease, Ida B. Wells, Susan B. Anthony, and Lucy Stone proved that women did not have to vote to be politically active.

HOW WOMEN'S SUFFRAGE WILL INCREASE THE POWER OF THE WARD HEELER.

■ This anti-woman suffrage cartoon implies that if women were to be allowed to vote, the inferior types among them—in this case, ugly, slovenly immigrants—would outweigh—and outvote their more distinguished sisters. The artist, drawing for *Judge* magazine in 1894, was not only expressing anti-female and anti-immigrant views but also using a fear that female voters would only entrench corrupt politicians. (William L. Clements Library)

Agrarian Unrest and Populism

*W*hile voting and racial segregation concerned those suffering from political exclusion, economic inequities sparked a mass movement that would shake American society. The agrarian revolt—a mixture of strident rhetoric, nostalgic dreams, and hard-headed egalitarianism—began in Grange organizations in the early 1870s. It accelerated when Farmers' Alliances formed in Texas in the late 1870s and spread across the Cotton Belt and Great Plains in the 1880s. The Alliance movement flourished chiefly in areas where tenancy, debt, weather, and insects endangered struggling farmers. Once under way, the agrarian rebellion inspired visions of a truly cooperative and democratic society.

Southern agriculture, unlike that of the Midwest, did not benefit much from mechanization (see Chapter 17).

SHARECROPPING AND TENANT FARMING IN THE SOUTH

Tobacco and cotton, the principal southern crops, required constant hoeing and weeding by hand. Tobacco could not be harvested all at once because the leaves matured at different rates and because the stems were too fragile for machines. Thus after the Civil War, southern agriculture remained labor-intensive, except that labor-lords, who had once utilized slaves, were replaced by landlords, who employed sharecroppers and tenant farmers.

Sharecropping and tenant farming entangled millions of black and white southerners in a web of debt and humiliation, at whose center stood the crop lien. Most farmers, too poor to have ready cash, borrowed in order to buy necessities. They could offer as collateral only what they could grow. A farmer in need of supplies dealt with a "furnishing merchant," who would exchange supplies for a lien, or legal claim, on the farmer's forthcoming crop. After the crop was harvested and brought to market, the merchant collected his debt by claiming the portion of the crop that would satisfy the loan. All too often, however, the debt exceeded the crop's value. The farmer could pay off only part of the debt to the merchant but still needed food and supplies for the coming year. The only way he could get these supplies was to sink deeper into debt by reborrowing and giving the merchant a lien on his next crop.

Merchants frequently took advantage of indebted farmers' powerlessness by inflating prices and charging interest ranging from 33 to 200 percent on the advances farmers received. Suppose, for example, that a cash-poor farmer needed a 20-cent bag of seed or 20-cent piece of cloth. The furnishing merchant would sell him the goods on credit but would boost the price to 28 cents. At year's end that 28-cent loan would have accumulated interest, raising the farmer's debt to 42 cents—more than double the item's original cost. The farmer, having pledged more than his crop's worth against scores of such debts, fell behind in payments and never recovered. If he fell too far behind, he could be evicted.

The crop-lien system caused hardship in former plantation areas where tenants and sharecroppers grew cotton for the same markets that had existed before the Civil War. In the southern backcountry, which in antebellum times had been characterized by small farms, few slaves, and diversified agriculture, the crop-lien problem was compounded by other economic changes. New spending habits of backcountry farmers illustrate these changes. In 1884 Jephta Dickson of the northern Georgia hills bought $55.90 worth of flour, potatoes, peas, meat, corn, and syrup from merchants. Such expenditures would have been rare before the Civil War, when farmers grew almost all the food they needed. But after the war, yeomen like Dickson shifted to commercial farming; in the South that meant raising cotton. This move to the market economy came about for two reasons: debts incurred during the war and Reconstruction forced farmers to grow crops that would bring in cash, and railroads enabled them to transport cotton to markets more easily than before. As backcountry yeomen devoted more acres to cotton, they raised less of what they needed on a daily basis and found themselves more frequently at the mercy of merchants.

In the Midwest, as growers cultivated more land, as mechanization boosted productivity, and as foreign competition increased, supplies of agri-

HARDSHIP IN THE MIDWEST AND WEST

cultural products exceeded national and worldwide demand. Consequently, prices for staple crops dropped steadily. A bushel of wheat that sold for $1.45 in 1866 brought only 80 cents in the mid-1880s and 49 cents by the mid-1890s. Meanwhile, transportation and storage fees remained high relative to other prices. Expenses for seed, fertilizer, manufactured goods, taxes, and mortgage interest trapped many farm families in stressful and sometimes desperate circumstances. In order to buy necessities and pay bills, farmers had to produce more. But the spiral wound ever more tightly: the more farmers produced, the lower prices for their crops dropped (see Figure 20.1).

The West suffered from special hardships. In Colorado absentee capitalists seized control of access to transportation and water, and concentration of technology in the hands of large mining companies pushed out small firms. Charges of monopolistic control by railroads echoed among farmers, miners, and stockmen in

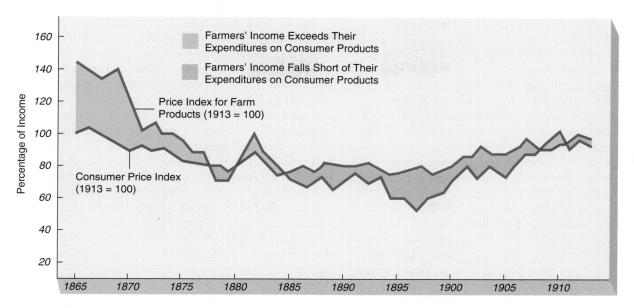

Figure 20.1   Consumer Prices and Farm Product Prices, 1865–1913

Until the late 1870s, in spite of falling farm prices, farmers were able to receive from their crops more income than they spent on consumer goods. But beginning in the mid-1880s, consumer prices leveled off and then rose while prices for farm products continued to drop. As a result, farmers found it increasingly difficult to afford consumer goods, a problem that plagued them well into the twentieth century.

Wyoming and Montana. In California, Washington, and Oregon, wheat and fruit growers found their opportunities blocked by railroads' control of transportation and storage rates.

Even before they felt the full impact of these developments, farmers began to organize. With aid from Oliver H. Kelley, a clerk in the Department of Agriculture, farmers in almost every state during the 1860s and 1870s founded a network of local organizations called Granges. By 1875 the Grange had twenty thousand branches and a million members. Like voluntary organizations throughout the country, Granges had constitutions, elected officers, and membership oaths. Strongest in the Midwest and South, Granges at first served a chiefly social function, sponsoring meetings and educational events to relieve the loneliness of farm life. Family-oriented, local Granges welcomed women's participation.

GRANGE MOVEMENT

As membership flourished, Granges turned to economic and political action. Local branches formed cooperative associations to buy supplies and to market crops and livestock. In a few instances, Grangers operated farm-implement factories and insurance companies. Most enterprises failed, however, because farmers lacked capital for large-scale buying and because competition from large manufacturers and dealers undercut them. For example, the mail-order firm Montgomery Ward could furnish rural customers with cheaper products more conveniently than could Granges.

Despite their efforts, Granges declined in the late 1870s. They achieved some political successes, convincing states to establish agricultural colleges, electing sympathetic legislators, and pressing state legislatures for so-called Granger laws to regulate transportation and storage rates. But these ventures faltered when corporations won court support to overturn Granger laws in the *Wabash* case of 1886. Granges disavowed party politics and thus would not challenge the power of business interests within the two major parties. After a brief assertion of economic and political influence, Granges again became farmers' social clubs.

In the Southwest, migrations of English-speaking ranchers into pastureland used communally by Mexican farmers and villagers sparked another kind of agrarian protest. In the late 1880s, a group calling itself Las Gorras Blancas, or White Hats, struggled to control lands that their Mexican ancestors had once held. They harassed Anglo ranchers and destroyed fences

THE WHITE HATS

that Anglos had erected on public land. Sounding like the Grangers and Knights of Labor before them and the Populists after them, the White Hats proclaimed in 1889, "Our purpose is to protect the rights and interest of the people in general and especially those of the helpless classes." Their cause, however, could not halt Anglos from legally buying and using public land, and by 1900 many Hispanics had given up farming to work as agricultural laborers or to migrate into the cities.

By 1890 rural activism shifted to the Farmers' Alliances, two networks of organizations—one in the Great Plains, one in the South—that constituted a new mass movement. (The West also had Alliance groups, but they tended to be smaller and more closely linked to labor radicals and antimonopoly organizations.) The first Farmers' Alliances arose in Texas, where hard-pressed small farmers rallied against crop liens, merchants, and railroads in particular, and against money power in general. Using traveling lecturers to recruit members, Alliance leaders extended the movement into other southern states. By 1889 the southern Alliance boasted 2 million members, and a separate Colored Farmers' National Alliance claimed 1 million black members.

FARMERS' ALLIANCES

A similar movement flourished in the Plains, which in the late 1880s organized 2 million members in Kansas, Nebraska, and the Dakotas.

Like Granges, Farmers' Alliances fostered community loyalty through rallies, educational meetings, and cooperative buying and selling agreements. Women participated actively in Alliance activities. Alliances also proposed a new economic remedy, a subtreasury plan to relieve shortages of cash and credit, the most serious rural problems. The plan had two parts. One called for the federal government to construct warehouses where farmers could store nonperishable crops while awaiting higher prices; the government would then loan farmers Treasury notes amounting to 80 percent of the market price that the stored crops would bring. Farmers could use these notes as legal tender to pay debts and make purchases. Once the stored crops were sold, farmers would repay the loans plus small interest and storage fees. This provision would enable farmers to avoid the exploitative crop-lien system.

The subtreasury plan's second part would provide low-interest government loans to farmers who wanted to buy land. These loans, along with the Treasury notes loaned to farmers who temporarily stored crops in gov-

■ Exhibited at the Chicago World's Fair of 1893, this cabin was the site of the first Farmers' Alliance meeting in Lampasas County, Texas. Using recruiters, rallies, and meetings replete with slogans such as "We Are All Mortgaged but Our Votes," the organization voiced the grievances of rural America and laid the groundwork for formation of the Populist party in the 1890s. (Private Collection)

ernment warehouses, would inject cash into the economy and encourage the kind of inflation that advocates hoped would raise crop prices without raising other prices. If the government subsidized business through tariffs and land grants, reasoned Alliance members, why should it not help farmers earn a decent living, too?

If all Farmers' Alliances had been able to unite, they could have made a formidable force; but racial and sectional differences and personality

PROBLEMS IN ACHIEVING ALLIANCE UNITY

clashes thwarted early attempts at merging. Racial barriers weakened Alliance voter strength because, as noted earlier, southern white Democrats had succeeded in creating voting restrictions that prevented African Americans from becoming a political force. Second, raw racism impeded acceptance of blacks by white Alliances. Some southern leaders, such as Georgia's Tom Watson, did try to unite distressed black and white farmers, realizing that both races suffered from similar burdens. But poor white farmers could not forgo their racism. Many came from families that had supported the Ku Klux Klan during Reconstruction. Some had owned slaves, considered African Americans a permanently inferior people, and took comfort in the belief that there always would be people worse off than they were. Thus few white Alliance men addressed the needs of black farmers, and many used white-supremacist rhetoric to guard against accusations that they encouraged race-mixing. At an 1889 meeting in St. Louis, white southerners, fearing reprisals from landowners and objecting to participation by blacks, rejected uniting with northern Alliances because such a merger would have ended secret Alliance activities and whites-only membership rules. Northern Alliances declined to merge with southerners, renounced amalgamation, fearing domination by more experienced southern leaders.

Differences on regional issues also prevented unity. Northern farmers, mostly Republicans, wanted protective tariffs to keep out foreign grain. White southerners, mostly Democrats, wanted low tariffs to hold down costs of foreign manufactured goods. Northern and southern Alliances both favored government regulation of transportation and communications, equitable taxation, currency reform, and prohibition of landownership by foreign investors.

In spite of their initial divisions, growing membership and rising confidence drew Alliances into politics.

RISE OF POPULISM

By 1890 farmers had elected several officeholders sympathetic to their cause, especially in the South, where Alliances controlled four governorships, eight state legislatures, and forty-seven seats in Congress (forty-four in the House, three in the Senate). In the Mid-

west, Alliance candidates often ran on third-party tickets and achieved some success in Kansas, Nebraska, and the Dakotas. Leaders crisscrossed the country organizing meetings to solidify support for a new party. During the summer of 1890, the Kansas Alliance held a "convention of the people" and nominated candidates who swept the state's fall elections. Formation of this People's, or Populist, Party gave a title to Alliance political activism. (Populism, derived from *populus*, the Latin word for "people," is the political doctrine that asserts the rights and powers of the common people in their struggle with the privileged elite.) The Alliance election successes in 1890 energized efforts to unite Alliance groups into a single Populist party. A meeting in 1891 of northern and southern Alliances in Cincinnati failed when southerners chose to remain Democrats rather than risk joining a third party. But by 1892 southern Alliance members were ready for independent action. Meeting with northern counterparts in St. Louis, they summoned a People's Party convention in Omaha, Nebraska, on July 4 to draft a platform and nominate a presidential candidate.

The new party's platform was a sweeping reform document. Its preamble charged that the nation had been "brought to the verge of moral, political, and material ruin. Corruption dominates the ballot box, the legislatures, the Congress, and touches . . . even the [courts]." Charging that inequality (between white classes) threatened to splinter American society, the platform declared, "The fruits of the toil of millions are boldly stolen to build up colossal fortunes for a few." Claiming that "wealth belongs to him that creates it," the document addressed three central sources of rural unrest: transportation, land, and money. Frustrated with weak state and federal regulation, Populists demanded government ownership of railroad and telegraph lines. They urged the federal government to reclaim all land owned for speculative purposes by railroads and foreigners. The monetary plank called on the government to expand the currency by making more money available for farm loans and by basing money on free and unlimited coinage of silver. Other planks advocated a graduated income tax, postal savings banks, direct election of U.S. senators, and a shorter workday. As its presidential candidate, the party nominated James B. Weaver of Iowa, a former Union general and supporter of an expanded money supply.

The Populist campaign featured dynamic personalities and vivid rhetoric. The Kansas plains rumbled with

POPULIST SPOKESPEOPLE

speeches not only by the inflammatory Mary Elizabeth Lease but also by "Sockless Jerry" Simpson, an unschooled but canny rural reformer who got his nickname after he ridiculed wealthy people for their silk stockings, causing a reporter to carp that Simpson probably wore no stockings at all. The South produced equally dynamic leaders, such as Texas's Charles W. Macune, Georgia's Tom Watson, and North Carolina's Leonidas Polk. Colorado's governor Davis "Bloody Bridles" Waite attacked mine owners with prolabor and antimonopolist rhetoric. Minnesota's Ignatius Donnelly, pseudoscientist and writer of apocalyptic novels, became chief ideologue of the northern plains and penned the Omaha platform's thunderous language. The campaign also attracted opportunists such as James Hogg, the three-hundred-pound governor of Texas, and one-eyed, sharp-tongued "Pitchfork Ben" Tillman of South Carolina, who were not genuine Populists but used agrarian fervor for their own political ends.

Weaver garnered 8 percent of the popular vote in 1892, majorities in four states, and twenty-two electoral votes. Not since 1856 had a third party done so well in its first national effort. Nevertheless, the party faced a dilemma of whether to stand by its principles at all costs or compromise in order to gain power. The election had been successful for Populists only in the West. The vote-rich Northeast ignored Weaver, and Alabama was the only southern state that gave Populists as much as one-third of its votes. More ominously, Populist politics were diverting Alliance attention from social and economic reform.

Still, Populism gave rural dwellers in the South and West emotional faith in the future. Although Populists were flawed egalitarians—they mistrusted blacks and foreigners—they sought change in order to fulfill their version of American ideals. Amid hardship and desperation, millions of people came to believe that a cooperative democracy in which government would ensure equal opportunity could overcome corporate power. A banner draped above the stage at the Omaha convention captured the movement's spirit: "We do not ask for sympathy or pity. We ask for justice." With this goal in mind, Populists looked forward to the presidential election of 1896 with hope.

The Depression and Protests of the 1890s

Before that election took place, however, the nation suffered some major disruptions. In 1893, shortly before Grover Cleveland's second presidency, the Philadelphia and Reading Railroad, once a thriving and profitable line, went bankrupt. Like other railroads, the Philadelphia and Reading had borrowed heavily to lay track and build stations and bridges. But overexpansion cut into profits, and ultimately the company was unable to pay its debts.

The same problem beset manufacturers. For example, output at McCormick farm machinery factories was nine times greater in 1893 than in 1879, but revenues had only tripled. To compensate, the company bought more equipment and squeezed more work out of fewer laborers. This strategy, however, only enlarged debt and unemployment. Jobless workers found themselves in the same plight as employers: they could not pay their bills. Banks suffered, too, when their customers defaulted. The failure of the National Cordage Company in May 1893 sparked a chain reaction of business and bank closings. By year's end, five hundred banks and sixteen hundred businesses had failed. An adviser warned President Cleveland, "We are on the eve of a very dark night." He was right. Between 1893 and 1897, the nation suffered a devastating economic depression.

Personal hardship followed business collapse; nearly 20 percent of the labor force were jobless for a significant time during the depression. Falling demand caused prices to drop between 1892 and 1895, but layoffs and wage cuts more than offset declining living costs. Many people

■ Mary E. Lease (1850–1933) was one of the founders of the Populist party in Kansas. Tall and intense, she had a deep, almost hypnotic voice that made her an effective publicist for the farmers' cause. She gave a seconding speech to the presidential nomination of James B. Weaver in 1892. (The Kansas State Historical Society, Topeka, Kansas)

could not afford basic necessities. The New York police estimated that twenty thousand homeless and jobless people roamed the city's streets. Surveying the impact on Boston, Henry Adams wrote, "Men died like flies under the strain, and Boston grew suddenly old, haggard, and thin."

As the depression deepened, the currency dilemma reached a crisis. The Sherman Silver Purchase Act of

CONTINUING CURRENCY PROBLEMS

1890 had committed the government to use Treasury notes (silver certificates) to buy 4.5 million ounces of silver each month. Recipients could redeem these certificates for gold, at the ratio of one ounce of gold for every sixteen ounces worth of silver. But a western mining boom made silver more plentiful, causing its market value relative to gold to fall and prompting holders of Sherman silver notes and greenback currency issued during the Civil War to cash in their notes in exchange for more valuable gold. As a result, the nation's gold reserve dwindled, falling below $100 million in early 1893.

The $100 million level had psychological importance. If investors believed that the country's gold reserve was disappearing, they would lose confidence in America's economic stability and refrain from investing. British capitalists, for example, owned some $4 billion in American stocks and bonds. If dollars were to depreciate because there was too little gold to back them up, the British would stop investing in American economic growth. In fact, the lower the gold reserve dropped, the more people rushed to redeem their money—to get gold before it disappeared. Panic spread, causing more bankruptcies and unemployment.

Vowing to protect the gold reserves, President Cleveland called a special session of Congress to repeal the Sherman Silver Purchase Act. Repeal passed in late 1893, but the run on gold continued through 1894. In early 1895 reserves fell to $41 million. In desperation, Cleveland accepted an offer of 3.5 million ounces of gold in return for $65 million worth of federal bonds from a banking syndicate led by financier J. P. Morgan. When the bankers resold the bonds to the public, they made a $2 million profit. Cleveland claimed that he had saved the reserves, but discontented farmers, workers, silver miners, and even some of Cleveland's Democratic allies saw only humiliation in the president's deal with big businessmen. "When Judas betrayed Christ," charged Senator Tillman, "his heart was not blacker than this scoundrel, Cleveland, in betraying the [Democratic Party]."

Few people knew what the president was really enduring. At about the time Cleveland called Congress into special session, doctors discovered a malignant tumor on his palate that required immediate removal. Fearful that

publicity of his illness would hasten the run on gold, and intent on preventing Vice President Adlai E. Stevenson, a silver supporter, from gaining influence, Cleveland kept his condition a secret. He announced that he was going sailing, and doctors removed his cancerous upper left jaw while the yacht floated outside New York City. Outfitted with a rubber jaw, Cleveland resumed a full schedule five days later, hiding terrible pain to dispel rumors that he was seriously ill. He eventually recovered, but those who knew of his surgery believed it had sapped his vitality.

The deal between Cleveland and Morgan did not end the depression. After improving slightly in 1895, the economy plunged again. Farm income, declining since 1887, continued to slide; factories closed; banks that remained open restricted withdrawals. The tight money supply depressed housing construction, drying up jobs and reducing immigration. Cities such as Detroit allowed citizens to cultivate "potato patches" on vacant land to help alleviate food shortages. Each night urban police stations filled up with vagrants who had no place to stay.

The depression ultimately ran its course. In the final years of the century, gold discoveries in Alaska, good

CONSEQUENCES OF THE DEPRESSION

harvests, and industrial growth brought relief. But the downturn hastened the crumbling of the old economic system and the emergence of a new one. The American economy had become national rather than sectional; the fate of a large business in one part of the country had repercussions elsewhere. When farmers in the West fell into debt and lost purchasing power, their depressed condition in turn affected the economic health of railroads, farm-implement manufacturers, and banks in other regions. Moreover, the corporate consolidation and trend toward bigness that characterized the new business system were beginning to solidify just when the depression hit. Many companies had expanded too rapidly. When contraction occurred, their reckless debts dragged them down, and they pulled other industries with them.

A new global marketplace was emerging, forcing American farmers to contend not only with discriminatory transportation rates and falling crop prices at home, but also with Canadian and Russian wheat growers, Argentine cattle ranchers, Indian and Egyptian cotton manufacturers, and Australian wool producers. More than ever before the condition of one country's economy affected the economies of other countries. In addition, the glutted domestic market persuaded American businessmen to seek new markets abroad (see Chapter 22).

The depression exposed fundamental tensions in the industrial system. Technological and organizational changes had been widening the gap between employees

DEPRESSION-ERA PROTESTS and employers for half a century (see Chapter 18), and a wave of dissent emerged from this gap. The era of protest began with the railroad strikes of 1877 (see page 492). The vehemence of those strikes, and the support they drew from working-class people, raised fears that the United States would experience a popular uprising like one in Paris six years earlier, which had briefly overturned the government and introduced communist principles. The Haymarket riot of 1886, a general strike in New Orleans in 1891, and a prolonged strike at the Carnegie Homestead Steel plant in 1892 (see page 494) heightened anxieties. In the West, embittered workers also rebelled. In 1892 violence erupted at a silver mine in Coeur d'Alene, Idaho. Angered by wage cuts and a lockout, striking miners seized the mine and battled federal troops sent to subdue them.

To many, it seemed like worker protests portended an economic and political explosion. In 1894, the year the economy plunged into depression, there were over thirteen hundred strikes and countless riots. Contrary to accusations of business leaders, few protesters were anarchists or communists come from Europe to sabotage American democracy. Rather, the disaffected included thousands of men and women who believed that in a democracy their voices should be heard.

Small numbers of socialists did participate in these and other confrontations. Furthermore, personal experience *SOCIALISTS* convinced many workers who never became socialists to agree with Karl Marx (1818–1883), the German philosopher and father of communism, that whoever controls the means of production determines how well people live. Marx wrote that industrial capitalism generates profits by paying workers less than the value of their labor and that mechanization and mass production alienate workers from their labor. Thus, Marx contended, capitalists and laborers engage in an inescapable conflict over how much workers will benefit from their efforts. According to Marx, only by abolishing the return on capital—profits—could labor receive its true value, an outcome possible only if workers owned the means of production. Marx predicted that workers worldwide would become so discontented that they would revolt and seize factories, farms, banks, and transportation lines. This revolution would establish a socialist order of justice and equality. Marx's vision appealed to some workers because it promised independence and abundance. It appealed to some intellectuals because it promised to end class conflict and crude materialism.

In America, socialism suffered from lack of strong leadership and disagreement over how to achieve Marx's vision. Much of the movement consisted of ideas brought in by immigrants, first from Germany but also by Russian Jews, Italians, Hungarians, and Poles. It splintered into small groups, such as the Socialist Labor Party, led by Daniel DeLeon, a fiery West Indian–born lawyer. DeLeon and other socialist leaders failed to attract the mass of unskilled laborers because they often focused on fine points of doctrine while ignoring workers' everyday needs. They could not rebut the clergy and business leaders who celebrated opportunity, self-improvement, and consumerism. Social mobility and the philosophy of individualism also undermined socialist aims. Workers hoped that they or their children would benefit through education and acquisition of property or by becoming their own boss; thus most American workers sought individual advancement rather than the betterment of all.

Events in 1894 triggered changes within the socialist movement. That year an inspiring leader arose in response *EUGENE V. DEBS* to the government's quashing of the Pullman strike and of the newly formed American Railway Union. Eugene V. Debs, the union's intense and animated president, converted to socialism while serving a six-month prison term for defying an injunction against the strike (see page 494). Once released, Debs became the leading spokesman for American socialism, combining visionary Marxism with Jeffersonian and Populist antimonopolism. Debs captivated audiences with passionate eloquence and indignant attacks on the free-enterprise system. "Many of you think you are competing," he would lecture. "Against whom? Against Rockefeller? About as I would if I had a wheelbarrow and competed with the Santa Fe [railroad] from here to Kansas City." By 1900 the group soon to be called the Socialist Party of America was uniting around Debs. It would make its presence felt more forcefully in the new century.

In 1894 Debs shared public attention with Jacob S. Coxey, a quiet businessman from Massillon, Ohio. Like *COXEY'S ARMY* Debs, Coxey had a vision. He was convinced that, to aid debtors, the government should issue $500 million of "legal tender" paper money, make low-interest loans to local governments, and use the loaned money to pay the unemployed to build roads and other public works. He planned to publicize his scheme by leading a march from Massillon to Washington, D.C., gathering a "petition in boots" of unemployed workers along the way. Coxey even christened his newborn son Legal Tender and proposed that his teenage daughter lead the procession on a white horse.

Coxey's army, about 200 strong, left in March 1894. Moving across Ohio into Pennsylvania, the marchers received food and housing in depressed industrial towns and rural villages, and they attracted new recruits. Elsewhere, a dozen similar marches from places such as Seattle, San Francisco, and Los Angeles also began the trek eastward. Sore feet prompted some marchers to commandeer trains, but most processions were peaceful and law-abiding. One public official called the marchers the "idle, useless dregs of humanity," but the troops kept themselves and their camps clean and well organized.

While other marchers were still on the road, Coxey's band of 500, including women and children, entered Washington on April 30. The next day (May Day, a date traditionally associated with socialist demonstrations), the group, armed with "war clubs of peace," marched to the Capitol. When Coxey and a few others vaulted the wall surrounding the Capitol grounds, mounted police moved in and routed the crowd. Coxey tried to speak from the Capitol steps, but police dragged him away. As arrests and clubbings continued, Coxey's dream of a demonstration of 400,000 jobless workers dissolved. Like the strikes, the first people's march on Washington yielded to police muscle.

Unlike socialists, who wished to replace the capitalist system, Coxey's troops merely wanted more jobs and better living standards. Today, in an age of union contracts, regulation of business, and government-sponsored unemployment relief, their goals do not appear radical. The brutal reactions of officials, however, reveal how threatening dissenters such as Coxey and Debs seemed to defenders of the existing social order.

The Silver Crusade and the Election of 1896

*a*mid the tumults of social protest and economic depression, it appeared that the presidential election of 1896 would be pivotal. Debates over money and power were climaxing, Democrats and Republicans continued their battle over control of Congress and the presidency, and the Populist party stood at the center of the political whirlwind.

Populists did not suffer the suppression that unions and Coxey's army experienced, but, like earlier third parties, they encountered roadblocks.
POPULIST PARTY As late as 1894, Populist candidates made good showings in elections in the West and South, but the party was underfinanced and underorganized. It had strong and colorful candidates, but not enough of them to effectively challenge the major parties. Voters remained reluctant to abandon old loyalties to Republicans or Democrats.

mercilessly scourges the money changers in the Temple of the Republic.
—*New York Recorder.*

This book tells its readers more about gold, silver and currency generally than any other publication we know of, and in a way that every man can fully comprehend. —*Chicago Inter Ocean.*

PUBLISHERS
COIN PUBLISHING COMPANY

■ Published in 1894, *Coin's Financial School* by William H. Harvey expressed the position of free silver in simple language and illustrations. Written in the form of lectures on the money question given by "Professor Coin," Harvey's book had enormous appeal to distressed farmers.
(Trustees of the Boston Public Library)

The Populist crusade against "money power" settled on the issue of silver, which many people saw as a simple solution to the nation's complex ills. To them, free coinage of silver symbolized an end to special privileges for the rich and the return of government to the people because it would lift the common people out of debt, increase the amount of cash in circulation, and reduce interest rates. Populists agreed and made free coinage of silver their political battle cry.
FREE SILVER

As the election of 1896 approached, Populists had to decide how to translate their few previous electoral victories into larger success. Should they join with sympathetic factions of the major parties, thus risking a loss of identity, or should they remain an independent third party and settle for minor wins at best? Except in mining areas of the Rocky Mountain states, where free coinage of silver had strong support, Republicans were unlikely allies because their support for the gold standard and big-business orientation represented what Populists opposed.

In the North and West, alliance with Democrats was more plausible. There, the Democratic Party retained vestiges of antimonopoly ideology and sympathy for a looser currency system, though "gold Democrats" such as President Cleveland and Senator David Hill of New York held powerful influence. Populists assumed they shared common interests with Democratic urban workers, who they believed suffered the same oppression that beset farmers. In the South, fusion with Democrats seemed less likely, since there the party constituted the very power structure against which farmers had revolted in the late 1880s. Whichever option they chose, fusion or independence, Populists ensured that the election campaign of 1896 would be the most issue oriented since 1860.

As they prepared to nominate their presidential candidate, each party was divided. Republicans, guided by Ohio industrialist Marcus A. Hanna, had only minor problems. For a year, Hanna had been maneuvering to

REPUBLICAN NOMINATION OF MCKINLEY

win the nomination for Ohio's governor, William McKinley. By the time the party convened in St. Louis, Hanna had corralled enough delegates to succeed. "He had advertised McKinley," quipped Theodore Roosevelt, "as if he were a patent medicine." The Republicans' only distress occurred when they adopted a moderate platform supporting gold, rejecting a prosilver stance proposed by Colorado senator Henry M. Teller. Teller, who had been among the party's founders forty years earlier, walked out of the convention in tears, taking a small group of silver Republicans with him.

At the Democratic convention, prosilver delegates wearing silver badges and waving silver banners paraded through the Chicago Amphitheatre. Observing their tumultuous demonstrations, one delegate wrote, "For the first time I can understand the scenes of the French Revolution!" A *New York World* reporter remarked that "all the silverites need is a Moses." They found one in William Jennings Bryan.

■ During the 1896 presidential campaign, Republicans depicted their candidate, William McKinley, as holding the key to prosperity for both the working man and the white-collar laborer, shown here raising their hats to the candidate. Republicans successfully made this economic theme, rather than the silver crusade of McKinley's unsuccessful opponent, William Jennings Bryan, the difference in the election's outcome.   (Collection of David J. and Janice L. Frent)

THE LOCKOUT IS ENDED; HE HOLDS THE KEY.

Bryan, age thirty-six, arrived at the Democratic convention as a member of a contested Nebraska delegation.

WILLIAM JENNINGS BRYAN A former congressman whose support for coinage of silver had annoyed President Cleveland, Bryan found the depression's impact on midwestern farmers distressing. Shortly after the convention seated Bryan and his colleagues instead of a competing faction that supported the gold standard, Bryan joined the party's resolutions committee and helped write a platform calling for free coinage of silver. When the committee presented the platform to the full convention, Bryan rose to speak on its behalf. His now-famous closing words ignited the delegates:

> Having behind us the producing masses of this nation and the world, supported by the commercial interests, the laboring interests, and the toilers everywhere, we will answer [the wealthy classes'] demand for a gold standard by saying to them: You shall not press down upon the brow of labor this crown of thorns, you shall not crucify mankind upon a cross of gold.

The speech could not have been better timed. Delegates who backed Bryan for president now had no trouble enlisting support. It took five ballots to win the nomination, but the magnetic "Boy Orator" proved irresistible. In accepting the silverite goals of southerners and westerners and repudiating Cleveland's policies in its platform, the Democratic Party became more attractive to discontented farmers. But like the Republicans, it, too, alienated a dissenting minority wing. Some gold Democrats withdrew and nominated their own candidate.

Bryan's nomination presented the Populist party convention with a dilemma. Should Populists join Democrats in support of Bryan, or should they nominate their own candidate? Tom Watson, who opposed fusion with Democrats, warned that "the Democratic idea of fusion [is] that we play Jonah while they play whale." Others reasoned that supporting a different candidate would split the anti-McKinley vote and guarantee a Republican victory. In the end the convention compromised, first naming Watson as its vice-presidential nominee to preserve party identity (Democrats had nominated Maine shipping magnate Arthur Sewall for vice president) and then nominating Bryan for president.

The campaign, as Kansas journalist William Allen White observed, "took the form of religious frenzy . . . as the crusaders of the revolution rode home, praising the people's will as though it were God's will and cursing wealth for its iniquity." The speeches rang with emotionalism. Bryan preached that "every great economic ques-

William Jennings Bryan (1860–1925) posed for this photograph in 1896, when he first ran for president at the age of thirty-six. Bryan's emotional speeches turned agrarian unrest and the issue of free silver into a moral crusade.   (Library of Congress)

tion is in reality a great moral question." Republicans countered Bryan's attacks on privilege by predicting chaos if he won. While Bryan raced around the country giving twenty speeches a day, Hanna invited thousands of people to McKinley's home in Canton, Ohio, where the candidate plied them with homilies on moderation and prosperity, promising something for everyone. In an appeal to working-class voters, Republicans stressed the new jobs that a protective tariff would create.

The election results revealed that the political standoff had finally ended. McKinley, symbol of urban and

ELECTION RESULTS corporate ascendancy, beat Bryan by over 600,000 popular votes and won in the electoral college by 271 to 176 (see Map 20.1). It was the most lopsided presidential election since 1872.

Bryan worked hard to rally the nation, but obsession with silver undermined his effort and prevented Populists from building the urban-rural coalition that would have expanded their political appeal. The silver issue diverted voters from focusing on broader reforms deriving from the Alliance movement and the 1892 Omaha platform. Reformer Henry Demarest Lloyd summarized the matter succinctly: "Free silver," he wrote, "is the cowbird of the

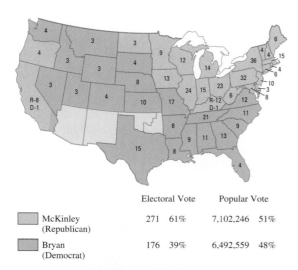

		Electoral Vote		Popular Vote	
▪	McKinley (Republican)	271	61%	7,102,246	51%
▪	Bryan (Democrat)	176	39%	6,492,559	48%

Map 20.1 Presidential Election, 1896

William Jennings Bryan had strong voter support in the South and West, but the numerically superior industrial states, plus California, created majorities for William McKinley.

reform movement. It waited till the nest had been built by the sacrifices and labor of others, and then it laid its eggs in it, pushing out the others which it smashed to the ground." Urban workers, who might have benefited from Populist goals, shied away from the silver issue out of fear that free coinage would shrink the value of their wages. Labor leaders such as the AFL's Samuel Gompers, though partly sympathetic, would not commit themselves fully because they viewed farmers as businessmen, not workers. And socialists such as Daniel DeLeon denounced Populists as "retrograde" because they, unlike socialists, believed in free enterprise. Thus the Populist crusade collapsed. Although Populists and fusion candidates won a few state and congressional elections, the Bryan-Watson ticket of the Populist party polled only 222,600 votes nationwide.

As president, McKinley signed the Gold Standard Act (1900), requiring that all paper money be backed by gold. A seasoned and personable politician, McKinley was best known for crafting protective tariffs; as a congressman from Ohio, he had guided passage of record-high tariff rates in 1890. He accordingly supported the Dingley Tariff of 1897, which raised duties even higher. Domestic tensions subsided during McKinley's presidency; an upward swing of the business cycle and a money supply enlarged by gold discoveries in

THE MCKINLEY PRESIDENCY

Alaska, Australia, and South Africa helped restore prosperity. A believer in opening new markets abroad to sustain prosperity at home, McKinley encouraged imperialistic ventures in Latin America and the Pacific (see Chapter 22). Good times and victory in the Spanish-American War enabled him to beat Bryan again in 1900, using the slogan "The Full Dinner Pail."

Summary

Politicians during the Gilded Age succeeded in making many modest, and some major, accomplishments. Guided by well-meaning, generally competent people, much of what occurred in statehouses, the halls of Congress, and the White House prepared the nation for the twentieth century. Laws encouraging economic growth with some principles of regulation, measures expanding government agencies while reducing crass patronage, federal intervention in trade and currency issues, and a more active presidency all evolved during the 1870s and 1880s.

True to Mary Lease's characterization, the United States remained a "nation of inconsistencies." Those who supported disfranchisement of African Americans and continued discrimination against both blacks and women still polluted politics. Nor could the system tolerate radical views such as those expressed by socialists, Coxey, or Populists. But many politicians concerned themselves with more than patronage and influence; most genuinely wanted to create what they believed was a good society.

The 1896 election realigned national politics. The Republican Party, founded in the 1850s amid a crusade against slavery, became the majority party by emphasizing government aid to business, expanding its social base to include urban workers, and playing down its moralism. The Democratic Party miscalculated on the silver issue and held its traditional support only in the South. After 1896, however, loyalties lacked the potency they once had. Suspicion of party politics increased, and voter participation rates declined. A new kind of politics was brewing, one in which technical experts and scientific organization would attempt to supplant the backroom deals and favoritism that had characterized the previous age.

In retrospect, it is easy to see that the Populists never had a chance. The political system lacked ability to accept third parties. The structure of Congress was such that the two-party system had enormous power, making it difficult for the few Populist representatives even to speak, let alone serve on important committees and promote reform legislation.

Nevertheless, by 1920 many Populist goals were achieved, including regulation of railroads, banks, and utilities; shorter workdays; a variant of the subtreasury plan; a graduated income tax; direct election of senators; and the secret ballot. These reforms succeeded because a variety of groups united behind them. Immigration, urbanization, and industrialization had transformed the United States into a pluralistic society in which compromise among interest groups had become a political fact of life. As the Gilded Age ended, business was still in the ascendancy, and large segments of the population were still excluded from political and economic opportunity. But the winds of dissent and reform had begun to blow more strongly.

LEGACY FOR A PEOPLE AND A NATION
Interpreting a Fairy Tale

The Wizard of Oz, one of the most popular movies of all time, began as a work of juvenile literature penned by journalist L. Frank Baum in 1900. Originally titled *The Wonderful Wizard of Oz,* the story used memorable characters to create a fun-filled and adventurous quest.

While children could view the tale and film as an adventure, adults were tempted to search for hidden meanings. In 1964, one scholar, Henry M. Littlefield, published an article in which he asserted that Baum really intended to write a Populist parable about the conditions of overburdened farmers and laborers. The characters in *The Wonderful Wizard,* Littlefield opined, supported his theory. Dorothy symbolized the well-intentioned common person; the Scarecrow, the struggling farmer; the Tin Man, the industrial worker. Hoping for a better life, these friends, along with the Cowardly Lion (William Jennings Bryan with a loud roar but little power), followed a yellow brick road (the gold standard) that led nowhere. The Emerald City they find is presided over by a wizard, who rules from behind a screen. A typical politician, the wizard

tries to be all things to all people, but Dorothy reveals him as a fraud. Dorothy is able to leave this muddled society and return to her simple Kansas farm family of Aunt Em and Uncle Henry by using her magical silver slippers (representing coinage of silver, though the movie made them red).

Subsequent theorists, while sometimes qualifying Littlefield, found additional supportive symbols, such as Oz being the abbreviation for ounces (oz.), the chief measurement of gold; the Wicked Witch of the East—who, Baum wrote, kept the little people (Munchkins) "in bondage, . . . making them slaves for her night and day"—could be seen as representing the forces of industrial capitalism. Baum's story, seen in film by most Americans, became a useful tool for explaining Populism to students, and by the 1970s its apparent message had strong appeal to critics of "the Establishment."

But then investigators began to take another look and offer different conclusions. In 1983, historian William R. Leach asserted that Baum's masterpiece actually was a celebration of urban consumer culture. Its language exalted the opulence of Emerald City, which to Leach resembled the "White City" of the Chicago World's Fair of 1893, and Dorothy's upbeat nature symbolized the optimism of the age. Moreover, Baum's career supported this new interpretation. Before he was a writer, he designed display windows and was involved in theater—activities that gave him an appreciation of modern urban life.

Rather than confusion, the real legacy of *The Wonderful Wizard of Oz* has been its ability to provoke differing interpretations. It does not matter which view is correct; instead, what matters is that Baum's fairy tale, the first real American work of this sort, has bequeathed to the present so many fascinating images about the diversity and contradictions of American culture.

The **history Companion** *powered by Eduspace®*
Your primary source for interactive quizzes, exercises, and more to help you learn efficiently.
http://history.college.hmco.com/students

THE PROGRESSIVE ERA 1895–1920

a coworker once described Florence Kelley as a "guerrilla warrior" in the "wilderness of industrial wrongs." A woman of sharp wit and commanding presence, Kelley accomplished as much as anyone in guiding the United States out of the tangled swamp of unregulated industrial capitalism into the uncharted seas of the twentieth-century welfare state.

Kelley's career traced a remarkable odyssey. Raised in middle-class comfort in Philadelphia, the daughter of a Republican congressman, Kelley graduated from Cornell University in 1883. She prepared to study law, but the University of Pennsylvania denied her admission to its graduate school because of her gender. Instead, she traveled to Europe. In Zurich, Kelley joined a group of socialists who alerted her to the plight of the underprivileged. She married a socialist Russian medical student and returned to New York City in 1886. When the marriage collapsed from debts and physical abuse, Kelley took her three children to Chicago in 1891. Later that year she moved into Hull House, a settlement house residence in the slums where middle-class reformers went to live in order to help and learn from working-class immigrants. There her transforming work truly began.

Until the 1890s, Kelley's life had been male oriented, influenced first by her father, then by her husband. She had tried to enter public life by attending law school and participating in socialist organizations, but men blocked her path at every turn. At Hull House, however, Kelley entered a female-dominated environment, where women sought to apply helping skills to the betterment of society. This environment encouraged Kelley to assert her powerful abilities.

Over the next decade, Kelley became the nation's most ardent advocate of improved conditions for working-class women and children. She investigated and publicized the exploitative sweatshop system in Chicago's garment industry, lobbied for laws to prohibit child labor and regulate women's working hours, and served as Illinois's first factory inspector. Her work helped create new professions for women in social service, and her strategy of investigating, publicizing, and crusading for action became a model for reform. Perhaps most

◀ During the Progressive era, reformers advocated new ways of thinking and new techniques to achieve progress in a variety of fields. Progressive educators, for example, cast aside rigid methods of memorization and discipline in favor of encouraging children to use their minds and hands in ways that were relevant to their lives. (Library of Congress)

CHRONOLOGY

1895 • Booker T. Washington gives Atlanta Compromise speech
• National Association of Colored Women founded

1898 • *Holden v. Hardy* upholds limits on miners' working hours

1900 • McKinley reelected

1901 • McKinley assassinated; T. Roosevelt assumes the presidency

1904 • T. Roosevelt elected president
• *Northern Securities* case dissolves railroad trust

1905 • *Lochner v. New York* removes limits on bakers' working hours

1906 • Hepburn Act tightens ICC control over railroads
• Meat Inspection Act passed
• Pure Food and Drug Act passed

1908 • Taft elected president
• *Muller v. Oregon* upholds limits on women's working hours

1909 • NAACP founded

1910 • Mann-Elkins Act reinforces ICC powers
• White Slave Traffic Act (Mann Act) prohibits transportation of women for "immoral purposes"
• Taft fires Pinchot

1911 • Society of American Indians founded

1912 • Woodrow Wilson elected president

1913 • Sixteenth Amendment ratified, legalizing federal income tax
• Seventeenth Amendment ratified, providing for direct election of U.S. senators
• Underwood Tariff institutes income tax
• Federal Reserve Act establishes central banking system

1914 • Federal Trade Commission created to investigate unfair trade practices
• Clayton Anti-Trust Act outlaws monopolistic business practices

1916 • Wilson reelected
• Adamson Act mandates eight-hour workday for railroad workers

1919 • Eighteenth Amendment ratified, establishing prohibition of alcoholic beverages

1920 • Nineteenth Amendment ratified, giving women the vote in federal elections

significant, she and fellow reformers like Jane Addams and Lillian Wald enlisted government to aid in the solution of social problems.

During the 1890s economic depression, labor violence, political upheaval, and foreign entanglements shook the nation. Technology had fulfilled many promises, but great numbers of Americans continued to suffer from poverty and disease. Some critics regarded industrialists as monsters who controlled markets, wages, and prices for the sole purpose of maximizing profits. Others believed government was corroded by bosses who enriched themselves through politics. Tensions created by urbanization and industrialization seemed to be fragmenting society into conflicting interest groups.

By 1900, however, the previous decade's political tumult had calmed, and economic depression seemed to be over. The nation emerged victorious from a war against Spain (see Chapter 22), and a new era of dynamic political leaders such as Theodore Roosevelt and Woodrow Wilson was dawning. A sense of renewal served both to intensify anxiety over continuing social and political problems and to raise hopes that somehow such problems could be fixed and democracy could be reconciled with capitalism.

From these circumstances there emerged a complex and many-sided reform campaign. By the 1910s reformers were calling themselves "Progressives"; in 1912 they formed a political party by that name to embody their principles. Historians have uniformly used the term *Progressivism* to refer to the era's spirit while disagreeing over its meaning and over which groups and individuals actually were Progressive. Nonetheless, the era between 1895 and 1920 included a series of movements, each aiming in one way or another to renovate or restore American society, values, and institutions.

The reform impulse had many sources. Industrial capitalism had created awesome technology, unprecedented productivity, and a cornucopia of consumer goods. But it also brought harmful overproduction, domineering monopolies, labor strife, and the spoiling of natural resources. Burgeoning cities facilitated the amassing and distribution of goods, services, and cultural amenities; they also bred poverty, disease, and crime. Inflows of immigrants and the rise of a new class of managers and professionals reconfigured the social order. And the depression of the 1890s forced leading citizens to realize what working people already knew: the central promise of American life was not being kept; equality of opportunity was a myth.

In addressing these problems, Progressives organized their ideas and actions around three goals. First, they sought to end abuses of power. Attacks on privilege, monopoly, and corruption were not new; Jacksonian reformers of the 1830s and 1840s and Populists of the 1890s belonged to the same tradition. Progressives, however, broadened the offensive. Trustbusting, consumers' rights, and good government became compelling political issues.

Second, Progressives aimed to supplant corrupt power with humane institutions such as schools and medical clinics. Though eager to protect individual rights, they abandoned individualistic notions that hard work and good character automatically ensured success and that the poor had only themselves to blame for their plight. Instead, Progressives acknowledged that society had responsibility and power to improve individual lives, and they believed that government, acting for society at large, must intervene in social and economic affairs to protect the common good and elevate public interest above self-interest. Their revolt against fixed categories of thought challenged entrenched views on women's roles, race relations, education, legal and scientific thought, and morality.

Third, Progressives wanted to apply scientific principles and efficient management to economic, social, and political institutions. Their aim was to establish bureaus of experts that would end wasteful competition and promote social and economic order. Science and the scientific method—planning, control, and predictability—were their central values. Just as corporations applied scientific management techniques to achieve economic efficiency, Progressives advocated expertise and planning to achieve social and political efficiency.

Befitting their name, Progressives had faith in the ability of humankind to create a better world. They voiced such phrases as "humanity's universal growth" and "the upward spiral of human development." Rising incomes, new educational opportunities, and increased availability of goods and services created an aura of confidence that social improvement would follow. Judge Ben Lindsey of Denver, who spearheaded reform in the treatment of juvenile delinquents, expressed the Progressive creed when he wrote, "In the end the people are bound to do the right thing, no matter how much they fail at times." ■

■ This painting (1904) by Everett Shinn depicts the disastrous consequences of poverty and the unkept promise of American life. Unable to pay the rent, thousands of families, along with their meager belongings, were forced into the streets. A painter of the so-called Ashcan School, Shinn captured the distress of poverty-stricken families forced to experience this humiliation. (National Museum of American Art, Washington, D.C./Art Resource, N.Y.)

The Varied Progressive Impulse

Progressive reformers addressed vexing issues that had surfaced in the previous half-century, but they did so in a new political climate. As the twentieth century dawned, party loyalty eroded and voter turnout declined. In northern states, voter participation in presidential elections dropped from Gilded Age levels of 80 percent of the eligible electorate to less than 60 percent. In southern states, where poll taxes and literacy tests excluded most African Americans and many poor whites from the polls, it fell below 30 percent. Parties and elections, it seemed, lost influence over government policies. At the same time, the political system was opening to new interest groups, each of which championed its own cause.

Local voluntary associations had existed since the 1790s, but many organizations became nationwide in scope after 1890 and tried to shape public policy to meet their goals. These organizations included professional associations such as the American Bar Association; women's organizations such as the National American Woman Suffrage Association; issue-oriented groups such as the National Consumers League; civic clubs such as the National Municipal League; and minority-group associations, such as the National Negro Business League and the Society of American Indians. Because they usually acted independently of established political parties, such groups made politics more fragmented and issue focused than in earlier eras.

NATIONAL ASSOCIATIONS AND FOREIGN INFLUENCES

Also, American reformers adapted foreign models and ideas for reorganizing society. A variety of proposals traveled across the Atlantic; some were introduced by Americans such as Florence Kelley who had observed reforms in England, France, and Germany, others by foreigners traveling in the United States. (Europeans also learned from Americans, but the balance of the idea flow tilted toward the United States.) Americans directly copied ideas such as the settlement house, which came directly from England. Such reforms as old-age insurance, subsidized workers' housing, city planning, and rural reconstruction originated abroad and were adopted or modified in America. Although goals of the rural-based Populist movement lingered—moral regeneration, political democracy, and antimonopolism—the Progressive quest for social justice, educational and legal reform, and government streamlining had a largely urban bent. Also, by utilizing advances in mail, telephone, and telegraph communications, urban reformers exchanged information and coordinated efforts.

Progressive goals—ending abuse of power, reforming social institutions, and promoting bureaucratic

■ Judge Ben Lindsey (1869–1943) of Denver was a Progressive reformer who worked for children's legal protection. Like many reformers of his era, Lindsey had an earnest faith in the ability of humankind to build a better world. (Library of Congress)

THE NEW MIDDLE CLASS AND MUCKRAKERS

and scientific efficiency—existed in all levels of society. But the new middle class—men and women in professions of law, medicine, engineering, settlement house and social work, religion, teaching, and business—formed the vanguard of reform. Offended by inefficiency and immorality in business, government, and human relations, these people determined to apply rational techniques they learned in their professions to problems of the larger society.

Their indignation motivated many middle-class Progressive reformers to seek an end to abuses of power. Their views were voiced by journalists whom Theodore Roosevelt dubbed muckrakers (after a character in the Puritan allegory *Pilgrim's Progress* who, rather than looking heavenward at beauty, looked downward and raked the muck to find what was wrong with life). Muckrakers fed public taste for scandal and sensation by exposing social, economic, and political wrongs. Their investigative articles in *McClure's, Cosmopolitan,* and other popular magazines attacked adulterated foods, fraudulent insurance, prostitution, and political corruption. Lincoln Steffens's articles in *McClure's,* later published as *The Shame of the Cities* (1904), epitomized muckraking style. Steffens hoped his exposés of bosses' misrule would inspire mass outrage and, ultimately, reform. Other well-known muckraking works included Upton Sinclair's *The Jungle* (1906), a novel that disclosed outrages of the meatpacking industry; Ida M. Tarbell's critical history of Standard Oil (first published in *McClure's,* 1902–1904); Burton J. Hendrick's *Story of Life Insurance* (1907); and David Graham Phillips's *Treason of the Senate* (1906).

To improve politics, Progressives advocated nominating candidates through direct primaries instead of party caucuses and holding nonpartisan elections to prevent fraud and bribery bred by party loyalties. To make officeholders more responsible, Progressives urged adoption of the initiative, which permitted voters to propose new laws; the referendum, which enabled voters to accept or reject a law; and the recall, which allowed voters to remove offending officials and judges from office. The goal, like that of the business-consolidation movement, was efficiency: Progressives would reclaim government by replacing the boss system with accountable managers chosen by a responsible electorate.

The Progressive spirit also stirred some male business leaders and wealthy females. Executives like Alexander Cassatt of the Pennsylvania Railroad supported some government regulation and political reforms to protect

UPPER-CLASS REFORMERS

their interests from more radical reformers. Others, like E. A. Filene, founder of a Boston department store, and Tom Johnson, a Cleveland streetcar magnate, were humanitarians who worked unselfishly for social justice. Business-dominated organizations like the Municipal Voters League and U.S. Chamber of Commerce thought that running schools, hospitals, and local government like efficient businesses would help stabilize society. Elite women led organizations like the Young Women's Christian Association (YWCA), which aided unmarried working women, and they joined middle- and working-class women in the Woman's Christian Temperance Union (WCTU), the largest women's organization of its time, which supported numerous causes besides abstinence from drinking.

Vital elements of what became modern American liberalism derived from working-class urban experiences. By 1900 many urban workers were pressing for government intervention to ensure safety and security. They advocated "bread-and-butter reforms" such as safe factories, shorter workdays, workers' compensation, better housing, and health safeguards. Often these were the same people who supported political bosses, supposedly the enemies of reform. In fact, bossism was not necessarily at odds with humanitarianism. When "Big Tim" Sullivan, an influential boss in New York City's Tammany Hall political machine, was asked why he supported a shorter workday for women, he explained, "I had seen me sister go out to work when she was only fourteen and I know we ought to help these gals by giving 'em a law which will prevent 'em from being broken down while they're still young."

WORKING-CLASS REFORMERS

After 1900, voters from urban working-class districts elected several Progressive legislators who had trained in the trenches of machine politics. New York's Alfred E. Smith and Robert F. Wagner, Massachusetts's David I. Walsh, and Illinois's Edward F. Dunne—all from immigrant backgrounds—earnestly supported reform at the state and national levels. They wanted government to take responsibility for alleviating hardships that resulted from urban-industrial growth, but they did not subscribe to all reforms. As protectors of individual liberty, they opposed reforms such as prohibition, Sunday closing laws, civil service, and nonpartisan elections, which conflicted with their constituents' interests. On the other hand, they joined with other reformers to pass laws aiding labor and promoting social welfare.

Some disillusioned people wanted a different society altogether. A blend of immigrant intellectuals, industrial

■ Though their objectives sometimes differed from those of middle-class Progressive reformers, socialists also became a more active force in the early twentieth century. Socialist parades on May Day, such as this one in 1910, were meant to express the solidarity of all working people.   (Library of Congress)

SOCIALISTS workers, disaffected Populists, miners, and women's rights activists, they turned to socialism. Taking a cue from European counterparts, especially in Germany, England, and France, where the government sponsored such projects as low-cost housing, social insurance and old-age pensions, public ownership of municipal services, and labor reform, they advocated that similar measures be adopted in the United States. Rarely, however, did these reforms gain wide acceptance. Labor unions, for example, opposed social insurance because it would increase taxes on members' wages. Real-estate interests opposed any government intervention in housing.

In politics, the majority of socialists united behind Eugene V. Debs (see page 560), the American Railway Union organizer who drew nearly 100,000 votes as the Socialist Party's presidential candidate in the 1900 presidential election. A spellbinding spokesman for radical causes such as peace and antimaterialism, Debs won 400,000 votes in 1904, and in 1912, at the pinnacle of his and his party's career, he polled over 900,000. With stinging rebukes of exploitation and unfair privilege, Debs and socialists like Milwaukee's Victor Berger and

New York's Morris Hilquit made compelling overtures to reform-minded people. Some Progressives, such as Florence Kelley, joined the Socialist Party. But most Progressives had too much at stake in capitalism to want to overthrow it. Municipal ownership of public utilities represented their limit of drastic change. In Wisconsin, where Progressivism was most advanced, reformers refused to ally with Berger's more radical group. California Progressives temporarily allied with conservatives to prevent socialists from gaining power in Los Angeles. And few Progressives objected when Debs was jailed in 1918 for giving an antiwar speech.

In some ways, Progressive reform in the South resembled that of other regions. Essentially urban and middle

SOUTHERN PROGRESSIVISM class in nature, it included the same strategies for railroad and utility regulation, factory safety, pure food and drug legislation, and moral reform that existed in Wisconsin, California, and New York. The South pioneered some political reforms; the direct primary originated in North Carolina; the city-commission plan arose in Galveston, Texas; and the city-manager plan began in Staunton, Virginia. Progressive governors, such as Braxton Bragg Comer of Alabama and Hoke Smith of Georgia, introduced business regulation and other reforms that rivaled actions inspired by northern counterparts.

Yet racial discrimination did not lessen in the South just because reformers held office. Racial bitterness tainted southern Progressive politics, excluding African Americans from most benefits of reform. The exclusion of black men from voting through poll taxes, literacy requirements, and other means (see pages 550–551) meant that electoral reforms affected only whites—and then only white men with enough cash and education to satisfy voting prerequisites. Governors such as Smith, Comer, Charles B. Aycock of North Carolina, and James K. Vardamann of Mississippi rested their power on appeals to white supremacy.

At the same time, however, southern women, white and black, made notable contributions to Progressive causes, just as they did in the North. To be sure, southern women's reform efforts remained racially distinct. White women crusaded against child labor, founded social service organizations, and challenged unfair wage rates. African American women, using a nonpolitical guise as homemakers and religious leaders—roles that whites found more acceptable than political activism—served their communities by acting as advocates for street cleaning, better education, and health reforms.

It would be a mistake to assume that a Progressive spirit captured all of American society between 1895 and
1920. Large numbers of people, heavily represented in Congress, disliked government interference in economic affairs and found no fault with existing power structures. Defenders of free enterprise opposed regulatory measures out of fear that government programs undermined the individual initiative and competition that they believed were basic to a free-market system. Government intervention, they contended, contradicted the natural law of survival of the fittest. "Old-guard" Republicans like Senator Nelson W. Aldrich of Rhode Island and House Speaker Joseph Cannon of Illinois championed this ideology. Outside Washington, D.C., tycoons like J. P. Morgan and John D. Rockefeller insisted that progress would result only from maintaining the profit incentive and an unfettered economy.

OPPONENTS OF PROGRESSIVISM

Moreover, prominent Progressives were not "progressive" in every respect. Governor Hiram Johnson of California, a leading western Progressive, promoted discrimination against Japanese Americans; New Jersey's Woodrow Wilson had no sympathy for African Americans; and settlement houses in northern cities kept blacks and whites apart in separate programs and buildings.

Nevertheless, Progressive reformers generally occupied the center of the ideological spectrum. Moderate, socially aware, sometimes contradictory, they believed on one hand that laissez faire was obsolete and on the other that a radical departure from free enterprise was dangerous. Like Thomas Jefferson, they expressed faith in the conscience and will of the people; like Alexander Hamilton, they desired a strong central government to act in the interest of conscience. Their goals were both idealistic and realistic. As minister-reformer Walter Rauschenbusch wrote, "We shall demand perfection and never expect to get it."

Governmental and Legislative Reform

*M*istrust of tyranny had traditionally prompted most Americans to believe that democratic government should be small and unobtrusive, should interfere in private affairs only in unique circumstances, and should withdraw when balance had been restored. But in the late 1800s this viewpoint weakened when problems resulting from economic change seemed to overwhelm individual effort. Corporations pursued government aid and protection for their enterprises. Discontented farmers sought government regulation of railroads and other monopolistic businesses. And city dwellers, accustomed to favors performed by political machines, came to expect government to act on their behalf.

Progressive reformers endorsed the principle that government should ensure justice and well-being. Increasingly aware that a simple, inflexible government was inadequate in a complex industrial age, they reasoned that public authority needed to counteract inefficiency and exploitation. But before activists could effectively use such power, they would have to reclaim government from politicians whose greed they believed had soiled the democratic system. Thus eliminating corruption from government was a central thrust of Progressive activity.

RESTRUCTURING GOVERNMENT

Prior to the Progressive era, reformers had attacked corruption in cities (see Chapter 19). Between 1870 and 1900, opponents of urban bosses tried to restructure government through such reforms as civil service, nonpartisan elections, and tight scrutiny of public expenditures. A few reformers advocated poverty relief, housing improvement, and labor regulations, but most worked for efficient—meaning economical—government. After

Robert M. La Follette (1855–1925) was one of the most dynamic of Progressive politicians. As governor of Wisconsin, he sponsored a program of political reform and business regulation known as the Wisconsin Plan. In 1906 he entered the U.S. Senate and continued to champion Progressive reform. The National Progressive Republican League, which La Follette founded in 1911, became the core of the Progressive Party. (State Historical Society of Wisconsin)

1900 reform campaigns installed city-manager and commission forms of government (in which urban officials were chosen for professional expertise, rather than political connections) and public ownership of utilities (to prevent gas, electric, and transit companies from profiting at public expense).

Reformers found the city too small an arena, however, for the changes they sought. Frustrated by limited victories, they theorized that state and federal governments offered more opportune locations for needed legislation. Goals tended to vary regionally. In the Plains and West, reformers rallied behind railroad regulation and government control of natural resources. In the South, they continued the Populist crusade against big business and autocratic politicians. In the Northeast and Midwest, they attacked corrupt politics and unsafe labor conditions.

Faith in a strong, fair-minded executive prompted Progressives to support a number of skillful and charismatic governors. Georgia's Hoke Smith and California's Hiram Johnson were examples of such governors; Wisconsin's Robert M. La Follette was another. A self-made small-town lawyer, La Follette rose through the state Republican Party to become governor in 1900. In office, he initiated a multipronged reform program including direct primaries, more equitable taxes, and regulation of railroad rates. He also appointed commissions staffed by experts, who supplied him with facts and figures he used in fiery speeches to arouse support for his policies. After three terms as governor, La Follette was elected to the U.S. Senate and carried his ideals into national politics. "Battling Bob" displayed a rare ability to approach reform scientifically while still exciting people with moving rhetoric. His goal, he asserted, was "not to 'smash' corporations, but to drive them out of politics, and then to treat them exactly the same as other people are treated."

ROBERT M. LA FOLLETTE

Crusades against corrupt politics produced modest changes. By 1916 all but three states had direct primaries, and many had adopted the initiative, referendum, and recall. Political reformers achieved a major goal in 1913 with adoption of the Seventeenth Amendment, which provided for direct election of U.S. senators (they previously had been elected by state legislatures, many of which Progressives thought were corrupt). Such measures did not always succeed. Party bosses, better organized and more experienced than reformers, were still able to control elections. Efforts to use the initiative, referendum, and recall often failed because special-interest groups spent large sums to influence the voting. Moreover, courts usually aided rather than reined in entrenched power.

State laws passed as a result of Progressive effort to improve labor conditions had more long-term impact than did Progressive political reforms because middle-class and working-class reformers could sometimes agree on issues affecting working people. At the instigation of a middle-class/working-class coalition, many states used their constitutional police power to protect public health and safety and to enact factory inspection laws. By 1916 nearly two-thirds of the states required compensation for victims of industrial accidents. A coalition of labor and humanitarian groups even induced some legislatures to

LABOR REFORM

Russian Temperance

When American temperance advocates, including some Progressive reformers, succeeded in obtaining nationwide prohibition with a constitutional amendment in 1919, they were not the first in the world to do so. In Russia, vodka and other spirits had been outlawed since 1914, when Czar Nicholas II decreed nationwide prohibition. A reform campaign had begun there twenty-seven years earlier, when author Leo Tolstoy started a temperance society.

While American reformers feared the moral and economic consequences of drunkenness, some Russians linked alcohol to deficiencies in strength and valor, believing Russia had lost the war with Japan in 1905 because excessive drinking rendered their soldiers unfit to fight. Others were sensitive to European and American criticism of their country's cultural acceptance of heavy drinking, and they wanted to rid their homeland of that negative image. Both Russians and Americans, however, agreed that alcohol had negative effects on health. Adopting American treatments, Russian doctors opened clinics to help alcoholics overcome their addiction.

In contrast to the United States, where the American Woman's Christian Temperance Union played a large role in temperance reform, in Russia most of the organized temperance workers were men. Russian women never formed their own temperance society. Rather, upper-class Russian women were more interested in joining suffrage societies and fighting to get the vote, while working-class Russian women opted for personal persuasion and impromptu action. One group of peasant women even resorted to installing a lock on the door of the village liquor store to prevent their husbands from buying any more vodka. Moreover, women of all classes were hesitant about the way a ban on alcohol might undermine Russian customs of hospitality, which required a hostess to serve vodka and wine to guests.

When Bolsheviks seized power in 1917, they extended prohibition and appointed a special commissar of temperance to enforce the law. But, as later in the United States, Russian prohibition did not prohibit drinking. Russians who wanted to drink found substitutes, some of them dangerous, such as wood alcohol, cologne, or varnish. Eventually, the Bolshevik regime abandoned prohibition for one of the same reasons that Americans did: they needed the tax revenues from the sale of alcoholic beverages.

In 1925, Russia halted its experiment and restored the state vodka monopoly, which guaranteed the government a steady flow of income. Alcohol abuse increased, as did alcohol-related diseases such as liver cancer and fetal alcohol syndrome, problems that continue to plague the country in the twenty-first century. Though on a lesser scale, similar problems resulted after Americans ended their prohibition experiment by ratifying the Twenty-first Amendment in 1933. The dilemma of excessive drinking and alcoholism linked the United States to Russia, but both countries discovered that their populations wanted their drinks and that prohibition was not the best way to fight alcohol's resulting problems.

Like the Americans, other people—in this instance, Ukrainians—used posters as propaganda for a cause. Here, the temperance movement in the Ukraine in the early twentieth century depicted a dissolute alcoholic with bottle in hand, and the text links his drinking with the work of the Devil. (© Rykoff Collection/Corbis)

grant aid to mothers with dependent children. Under pressure from the National Child Labor Committee, nearly every state set a minimum age for employment (varying from twelve to sixteen) and prohibited employers from making children work more than eight or ten hours a day. Such laws had limited effect, though, because they seldom provided for the close inspection of factories that enforcement required. And families that needed extra income evaded the laws by encouraging their children to lie about their ages when seeking employment.

Several groups united to achieve restricted working hours for women. After the Supreme Court, in *Muller v. Oregon,* upheld Oregon's ten-hour limit in 1908 (see page 491), more states passed laws protecting female workers. Meanwhile, in 1914 efforts of the American Association for Old Age Security showed signs of success when Arizona established old-age pensions. Judges struck down the law, but demand for pensions continued, and in the 1920s many states enacted laws to provide for needy elderly people.

Reformers themselves did not always agree about what was Progressive, especially on whether state intervention should regulate drinking habits and sexual behavior. For example, the Anti-Saloon League, formed in 1893, intensified the long-standing campaign against drunkenness and its costs to society. This organization allied with the Women's Christian Temperance Union (founded in 1874) to publicize alcoholism's role in causing liver disease and other health problems. The League was especially successful in shifting attention from individual responsibility for temperance to the alleged link between the drinking that saloons encouraged and the accidents, poverty, and poor productivity that were consequences of drinking.

TEMPERANCE AND PROHIBITION

The war on saloons prompted many states and localities to restrict liquor consumption. By 1900 almost one-fourth of the nation's population lived in "dry" communities (which prohibited the sale of liquor). But consumption of alcohol, especially beer, increased after 1900, convincing prohibitionists that a nationwide ban was the best solution. They enlisted support from notables such as Supreme Court Justice Louis D. Brandeis and former president William Howard Taft, and in 1918 Congress passed the Eighteenth Amendment (ratified in 1919 and implemented in 1920), outlawing the manufacture, sale, and transportation of intoxicating liquors. Not all prohibitionists were Progressive reformers, and not all Progressives were prohibitionists. Nevertheless, the Eighteenth Amendment can be seen as an expression of the Progressive goal to protect family and workplace through reform legislation.

Moral outrage erupted when muckraking journalists charged that international gangs were kidnapping young women and forcing them into prostitution, a practice called white slavery. Charges were more imagined than real, but they alarmed some moralists who falsely perceived a link between immigration and prostitution and feared that prostitutes were producing genetically inferior children. Though a number of women voluntarily entered "the profession" because it offered them much higher incomes than any other form of work and other women only occasionally performed sexual favors in return for male gifts, those fearful about the social consequences of prostitution prodded governments to investigate and pass corrective legislation. The Chicago Vice Commission, for example, undertook a "scientific" survey and published its findings as *The Social Evil in Chicago* in 1911. The report concluded that poverty, gullibility, and desperation drove women into prostitution.

PROSTITUTION AND WHITE SLAVERY

Such investigations found rising numbers of prostitutes but failed to prove that criminal organizations deliberately lured women into "the trade." Reformers nonetheless believed they could attack prostitution by punishing those who promoted it. In 1910 Congress passed the White Slave Traffic Act (Mann Act), prohibiting interstate and international transportation of a woman for immoral purposes. By 1915 nearly every state had outlawed brothels and solicitation of sex. Such laws ostensibly protected young women from exploitation, but in reality they failed to address the more serious problem of sexual violence that women suffered at the hands of family members and presumed friends and at the workplace.

Like prohibition, the Mann Act reflected growing sentiment that government could improve behavior by restricting it. Reformers believed that the source of evil was not original sin or human nature but the social environment. If evil was created by human will, it followed that it could be eradicated by human effort. Intervention in the form of laws could help create a heaven on earth.

New Ideas in Social Institutions

In addition to legislative paths, reform impulses opened new vistas in the ways social institutions were organized. Preoccupation with efficiency and scientific management infiltrated realms of education, law, religion, and the social sciences. Darwin's theory of evolution had challenged traditional beliefs in a God-created world; immigration had created complex social diversity; and technology had made old habits of production obsolete. Thoughtful people in several professions grappled with how to respond to the new era yet preserve what was best from the past.

Changing patterns of school attendance required new ways of educational thinking. As late as 1870, when families needed children at home to do farm work, Americans attended school for an average of only a few months a year for four years. By 1900, however, urban life gave children more time for school. Laws required children to attend school to age fourteen, and swelling populations of immigrant and migrant children jammed schoolrooms. Meanwhile, the number of public high schools grew from five hundred in 1870 to ten thousand in 1910. Before the Civil War, curricula had consisted chiefly of moralistic pieties from *McGuffey's Reader*. But in the late nineteenth century, psychologist G. Stanley Hall and philosopher John Dewey asserted that modern education ought to prepare children differently. They insisted that

JOHN DEWEY AND PROGRESSIVE EDUCATION

personal development, not subject matter, should be the focus of the curriculum.

Progressive education, based on Dewey's *The School and Society* (1899) and *Democracy and Education* (1916), was a uniquely American phenomenon. Dewey believed that learning should involve real-life problems and that children should be taught to use intelligence and ingenuity as instruments for controlling their environments. From kindergarten through high school, Dewey asserted, children should learn through direct experience, not by rote memorization. Dewey and his wife, Alice, put these ideas into practice in their own Laboratory School located at the University of Chicago.

A more practical curriculum became the driving principle behind reform in higher education as well. Previously, the purpose of American colleges and universities had resembled that of European counterparts: to train a select few for careers in law, medicine, and religion. But in the late 1800s, institutions of higher learning multiplied, aided by land grants and by an increase in people who could afford tuition. Between 1870 and 1910 the number of colleges and

GROWTH OF COLLEGES AND UNIVERSITIES

■ Poised and proud, these members of the University of Michigan's Class of 1892 represent the student body of a publicly funded college in the late nineteenth century. With their varied curricula, inclusion of women, and increasing enrollments, such schools transformed American higher education in the Progressive era.   (University of Michigan)

universities in the United States grew from 563 to nearly 1,000. Curricula expanded as educators sought to make learning more appealing and to keep up with technological and social changes. Harvard University, under President Charles W. Eliot, pioneered in substituting electives for required courses and experimenting with new teaching methods. The University of Wisconsin and other state universities achieved distinction in new areas of study such as political science, economics, and sociology. Many schools, private and public, considered athletics vital to a student's growth, and intercollegiate sports became a permanent feature of student life as well as source of school pride.

Southern states, in keeping with separate-but-equal policies, set up segregated land-grant colleges for blacks in addition to institutions for whites. Separate was a more accurate description of these institutions than equal. African Americans continued to suffer from inferior educational opportunities. Nevertheless, African American men and women found intellectual stimulation in all-black colleges and hoped to use their education to promote the uplifting of their race.

As higher education expanded, so did female enrollments. Between 1890 and 1910 the number of women in colleges and universities swelled from 56,000 to 140,000. Of these, 106,000 attended coeducational institutions (mostly state universities); the rest enrolled in women's colleges. By 1920, 283,000 women attended college, accounting for 47 percent of total enrollment. But discrimination lingered in admissions and curriculum policies. Women were encouraged (indeed, they usually sought) to take home economics and education courses rather than science and mathematics, and, as Florence Kelley discovered, most medical schools, including Harvard and Yale, refused to admit women. Barred from many private institutions, women attended separate schools, most of which were founded in the late nineteenth century—institutes such as Women's Medical College of Philadelphia and colleges such as Smith, Mount Holyoke, and Wellesley.

American educators adopted the prevailing attitude of business: more is better. They justifiably congratulated themselves for increasing enrollments and making instruction more meaningful. By 1920, 78 percent of children between ages five and seventeen were enrolled in public elementary and high schools; another 8 percent attended private and parochial schools. These figures represented a huge increase over 1870 attendance rates. There were 600,000 college and graduate students in 1920, compared with only 52,000 in 1870. Yet few people looked beyond the numbers to assess how well schools were doing their jobs. Critical analysis seldom tested the faith that schools could promote equality and justice as well as personal growth and responsible citizenship.

The legal profession also embraced new emphases on experience and scientific principles. Harvard law professor Roscoe Pound, an influential proponent of the new outlook, urged that social reality should influence legal thinking. Oliver Wendell Holmes Jr., associate justice of the Supreme Court between 1902 and 1932, led the attack on the traditional view of law as universal and unchanging. "The life of the law," said Holmes, sounding like Dewey, "has not been logic; it has been experience." The opinion that law should reflect society's needs challenged the practice of invoking inflexible legal precedents that often obstructed social legislation. Louis D. Brandeis, a lawyer who later joined Holmes on the Supreme Court, insisted that judges' opinions be based on scientifically gathered information about social realities. Using the Progressive approach to problems, Brandeis collected extensive data on harmful effects of long working hours to convince the Supreme Court, in *Muller v. Oregon* (1908), to uphold Oregon's ten-hour limit to women's workday.

PROGRESSIVE LEGAL THOUGHT

New legal thinking met with some resistance. Judges raised on laissez-faire economics and strict interpretation of the Constitution overturned laws Progressives thought necessary for effective reform. Thus despite Holmes's forceful dissent, in 1905 the Supreme Court, in *Lochner v. New York*, revoked a New York law limiting bakers' working hours. As in similar cases, the Court's majority argued that the Fourteenth Amendment protected an individual's right to make contracts without government interference and that this protection superseded police power. Judges weakened other federal regulations by invoking the Tenth Amendment, which prohibited the federal government from interfering in matters reserved to the states.

Courts did uphold some regulatory measures, particularly those protecting public safety. A string of decisions beginning with *Holden v. Hardy* (1898), in which the Supreme Court sustained a Utah law regulating working hours for miners, confirmed the use of state police power to protect health, safety, and morals. Judges also affirmed federal police power and Congress's authority over interstate commerce by upholding federal legislation such as the Pure Food and Drug Act, the Meat Inspection Law (see page 586), and the Mann Act. In these instances citizens' welfare took precedence over the Tenth Amendment.

But the concept of general welfare often conflicted with the concept of equal rights when local majorities imposed their will on minorities. Even if one agreed that laws should address society's needs, whose needs should prevail? The United States was (and remains) a mixed nation; gender, race, religion, and ethnicity deeply influenced law. In many localities a native-born Protestant majority imposed Bible reading in public schools (offending Catholics and Jews), required businesses to close on Sundays, limited women's rights, restricted religious practices of Mormons and other groups, prohibited interracial marriage, and enforced racial segregation. Justice Holmes asserted that laws should be made for "people of fundamentally differing views," but were such laws possible in a nation of so many different interest groups? The debate continues to this day.

Social science—the study of society and its institutions—experienced changes similar to those affecting
SOCIAL SCIENCE education and law. In economics, a group of young scholars used statistics to argue that laws governing economic relationships were not timeless. Instead, they claimed, theory should reflect prevailing social conditions. Richard T. Ely of Johns Hopkins University and the University of Wisconsin, reflecting this opinion, argued that poverty and impersonality resulting from industrialization required intervention by "the united efforts of Church, state, and science." A new breed of sociologists led by Lester Ward, Albion Small, and Edward A. Ross agreed, adding that citizens should actively work to cure social ills rather than passively wait for problems to solve themselves. Academics like Ely and Small believed their ideas to be "socialistic," not in the European sense of the term but rather considering "socialistic" as the ethical opposite of competitive "individualistic."

Meanwhile, Progressive historians Frederick Jackson Turner, Charles A. Beard, and Vernon L. Parrington examined the past to explain present American society. Beard, like other Progressives, believed that the Constitution was a flexible document amenable to growth and change, not a sacred code imposed by wise forefathers. His influential *Economic Interpretation of the Constitution* (1913) argued that a group of merchants and business-oriented lawyers created the Constitution to defend private property. If the Constitution had served special interests in one age, it could be changed to serve broader interests in another age. Meanwhile, political scientists like Woodrow Wilson emphasized the practical over the theoretical, advocating expansion of government power to ensure justice and progress.

In public health, organizations such as the National Consumers League (NCL) joined physicians and social scientists to bring about some of the most far-reaching

Progressive reforms. Founded by Florence Kelley in 1899, NCL activities included woman suffrage, protection of female and child laborers, and elimination of potential health hazards. After aiding in the success of *Muller v. Oregon,* the organization became active in sponsoring court cases on behalf of women workers and joined with reform lawyers Louis Brandeis and Felix Frankfurter in support of these cases. Local branches united with women's clubs to advance consumer protection measures such as the licensing of food vendors and inspection of dairies. They also urged city governments to fund neighborhood clinics that provided health education and medical care to the poor.

Much of Progressive reform rested on religious underpinnings. The distresses of modern society especially
THE SOCIAL GOSPEL sparked new thoughts about fortifying social relations with moral principles. Particularly, a movement known as the Social Gospel, led by Protestant ministers Walter Rauschenbusch, Washington Gladden, and Charles Sheldon, would counter the brutality of competitive capitalism by interjecting Christian churches into practical, worldly matters such as arbitrating industrial harmony and improving the environment of the poor. Believing that service to fellow humans provided the way to securing individual salvation and to creating God's kingdom on earth, Social Gospelers actively participated in social reform and governed their lives by asking, "What would Jesus do?"

The Social Gospel served as a response to Social Darwinism, the application of biological natural selection
EUGENICS and survival of the fittest to human interactions (see page 504). But another movement that flourished during the Progressive era, eugenics, sought to apply Darwinian principles to society in a more scientific way. The brainchild of Francis Galton, an English statistician and cousin of Charles Darwin, eugenics rested on the belief that human character and habits could be inherited. If good traits could be inherited, so could bad traits such as criminality, insanity, and feeblemindedness. Just as some Progressives believed that to create a better world, society had an obligation to intervene and erase poverty and injustice, eugenicists believed society had an obligation to prevent the reproduction of the mentally defective, the criminally inclined, and people generally deemed to be inferior. Inevitably such ideas targeted immigrants and people of color.

Followers of eugenics advocated two basic means to prevent the proliferation of people whose offspring might threaten American progress. One was to sterilize those identified as unfit to reproduce. Beginning in the early twentieth century, several state legislatures considered laws to sterilize (mostly through vasectomy) certain criminal and insane men. In 1907 Indiana enacted the country's first statute permitting involuntary sterilization of "confirmed criminals, idiots, imbeciles, and rapists" when a committee of experts considered such action advisable. By 1915 thirteen states had such laws, and by 1930 the number reached thirty. The other method of protecting American society from inferior people involved restricting immigration. Though not strictly a work of eugenics, Madison Grant's *The Passing of the Great Race* (1916) strongly bolstered theories that immigrants from southern and eastern Europe threatened to weaken American society because they were inferior mentally and morally to earlier Nordic immigrants. Thus, many people, including some Progressives, concluded that new laws should curtail the influx of Poles, Italians, Jews, and other eastern and southern Europeans, as well as Asians. Such efforts reached fruition in the 1920s when restrictive legislation, often backed by eugenics theories, drastically closed the door to "new" immigrants. Not all support for sterilization and immigration restriction came from eugenicists, but in the Progressive era, eugenics arose as an invidious way of applying science to social organization.

Thus a new breed of men and women pressed for institutional change and political reform in the two decades before the First World War. Largely middle class, trained in new professional standards, confident that new ways of thinking could bring about progress, these people helped broaden government's role to meet the needs of a mature industrial society. But their questioning of prevailing assumptions also unsettled conventional attitudes toward race and gender.

Challenges to Racial and Sexual Discrimination

*T*he white male reformers of the Progressive era dealt primarily with issues of politics and institutions, and in so doing ignored issues directly affecting former slaves, nonwhite immigrants, Indians, and women. Yet activists within these groups caught the Progressive spirit, challenged entrenched ideas and customs, and made strides toward their own advancement. Their efforts, however, posed a dilemma. Should women and nonwhites aim to imitate white men, with white men's values as well as their rights? Or was there something unique about racial and sexual cultures that they should

preserve at the risk of sacrificing broader gains? Both groups fluctuated between attraction to and rejection of the culture that excluded them.

In 1900 nine-tenths of African Americans lived in the South, where repressive Jim Crow laws had multiplied in the 1880s and 1890s (see page 552).

CONTINUED DISCRIMINATION FOR AFRICAN AMERICANS

Denied legal and voting rights and officially segregated in almost all walks of life, southern blacks faced constant exclusion. In 1910 only 8,000 out of 970,000 high-school-age blacks in the South were enrolled in high schools. And blacks met with relentless violence from lynching and countless acts of intimidation.

Many African Americans moved northward in the 1880s, accelerating their migration after 1900. The conditions they found represented relative improvement over rural sharecropping, but job discrimination, inferior schools, and segregated housing prevailed in northern as well as southern cities. White authorities perpetuated segregation by confining blacks to separate and inferior schools, hospitals, and other institutions. A half-century after slavery's abolition, most whites still agreed with historian James Ford Rhodes, who wrote that blacks were "innately inferior and incapable of citizenship."

African American leaders differed sharply over how—and whether—to pursue assimilation. In the wake of emancipation, ex-slave Frederick Douglass urged "ultimate assimilation through self-assertion, and on no other terms." Others favored separation from white society and supported emigration to Africa or the establishment of all-black communities in Oklahoma Territory and Kansas. Others, as bitter as white racists, advocated militancy, believing, as one writer stated, "Our people must die to be saved and in dying must take as many along with them as it is possible to do with the aid of firearms and all other weapons."

Most blacks could neither escape nor conquer white society. They sought other routes to economic and social improvement. Self-help, a strategy articulated by educator Booker T. Washington, offered one popular alternative. Born into slavery in backcountry Virginia in 1856, Washington obtained an education and in 1881 founded Tuskegee Institute in Alabama, an all-black vocational school. There he developed a philosophy that blacks' best hopes for assimilation lay in at least temporarily accommodating to whites. Rather than fighting for political rights, Washington counseled African Americans to work hard, acquire property, and prove they were worthy of respect. Washington voiced

■ Booker T. Washington's Tuskegee Institute helped train young African Americans in useful crafts such as shoemaking and shoe repair, as illustrated here. At the same time, however, Washington's intentions and the Tuskegee curriculum reinforced what many whites wanted to believe: that blacks were unfit for anything except manual labor. (Tuskegee University Library)

his views in a speech at the Atlanta Exposition in 1895. "Dignify and glorify common labor," he urged in what became known as the Atlanta Compromise. "Agitation of questions of racial equality is the extremest folly." Envisioning a society where blacks and whites would remain apart but share similar goals, Washington observed that "in all things that are purely social we can be as separate as the fingers, yet one as the hand in all matters essential to mutual progress."

Whites welcomed Washington's accommodation policy because it advised patience and reminded black people to stay in their place. Because he said what they wanted to hear, white businesspeople, reformers, and politicians chose to regard Washington as representative of all African Americans. Yet though Washington endorsed a separate-but-equal policy, he projected a subtle racial pride that would find more direct expression in black nationalism in the twentieth century, when some African Americans advocated control of their own businesses and schools. Washington never argued that blacks were inferior to whites; he asserted that they could enhance their dignity through self-improvement.

Some blacks concluded that Washington favored a degrading second-class citizenship. His southern-based philosophy did not appeal to educated northern African Americans, such as William Monroe Trotter, fiery editor of the *Boston Guardian,* or social scientist T. Thomas

Fortune. In 1905 a group of "anti-Bookerites" convened near Niagara Falls and pledged militant pursuit of such rights as unrestricted voting, economic opportunity, integration, and equality before the law. Representing the Niagara movement was W. E. B. Du Bois, an outspoken critic of the Atlanta Compromise.

A New Englander and first black to receive a Ph.D. degree from Harvard, Du Bois was both a Progressive

W. E. B. DU BOIS AND THE "TALENTED TENTH"

and a member of the black elite. He held an undergraduate degree from all-black Fisk University and had studied in Germany, where he learned about scientific investigation. While a faculty member at Atlanta University, Du Bois compiled fact-filled sociological studies of black urban life and wrote poetically in support of civil rights. He treated Washington politely but could not accept white domination. "The way for a people to gain their reasonable rights," Du Bois asserted, "is not by voluntarily throwing them away." Instead, blacks must agitate for what was rightfully theirs.

Dissatisfied with Washington's strategy, Du Bois believed that an intellectual vanguard of cultured, highly trained blacks, the "Talented Tenth," could advance the race by using their skill to pursue racial equality. In 1909, he joined with white liberals who also were discontented with Washington's accommodationism to form the

National Association for the Advancement of Colored People (NAACP). Du Bois and his allies aimed to use the organization to end racial discrimination and obtain voting rights through legal redress in the courts. By 1914 the NAACP had fifty branch offices and six thousand members.

Whatever their views, African Americans faced continued oppression. Those who managed to acquire property and education encountered white resentment, especially when they fought for equality. The federal government only aggravated biases. During Woodrow Wilson's presidency, southern cabinet members preserved racial separation in restrooms, restaurants, and government office buildings and balked at hiring black workers. Wilson, himself a southerner, condoned segregation. Commenting on Wilson's racism in 1913, Booker T. Washington wrote, "I have never seen the colored people so discouraged and so bitter as they are at the present time."

Though they were making strides on their own, African Americans struggled with questions about identity and their place in white society. Du Bois voiced this dilemma poignantly, observing that "one ever feels his twoness—an American, a Negro, two souls, two thoughts, two unreconciled strivings, two warring ideals in one dark body." Somehow blacks had to reconcile that "twoness" by combining racial pride with national identity. As Du Bois wrote in 1903, a black "would not Africanize America, for America has too much to teach the world and Africa. He would not bleach his Negro soul in a flood of white Americanism, for he knows that Negro blood has a message for the world. He simply wishes to make it possible for a man to be both a Negro and an American." That simple wish would haunt the nation for decades to come.

The dilemma of identity bedeviled American Indians as well, but it had an added tribal dimension. Since the 1880s, Native American reformers had belonged to white-led organizations. In 1911 educated, middle-class Indians formed their own association, the Society of American Indians (SAI), to work for better education, civil rights, and healthcare. It also sponsored "American Indian Days" to cultivate pride and offset images of savage peoples promulgated in Wild West shows.

SOCIETY OF AMERICAN INDIANS

The SAI's emphasis on racial pride, however, was squeezed between pressures for assimilation from one side and tribal allegiance on the other. Its small membership did not fully represent the diverse and unconnected Indian nations, and its attempt to establish a governing body fizzled. Some tribal governments no longer existed to select representatives, and most SAI members simply promoted their self-interest. At the same time, the goal of achieving acceptance in white society proved elusive. Individual hard work was not enough to overcome white prejudice and condescension, and attempts to redress grievances through legal action faltered for lack of funds. Ultimately, SAI had to rely on rhetoric and moral exhortation, which had little effect on poverty-stricken Indians who seldom knew that SAI even existed. Torn by internal disputes, the association folded in the early 1920s.

Challenges to established social assumptions also raised questions of identity among women. The ensuing quandaries resembled those faced by racial minorities: What tactics should women use to achieve equality? What should be women's role in society? Could women achieve equality with men and at the same time change male-dominated society?

"THE WOMAN MOVEMENT"

The answers that women found involved a subtle but important shift in women's politics. Before 1910, crusaders for women's rights referred to themselves as "the woman movement." This label applied to middle-class women who strived to move beyond the household into higher education and paid professions in social welfare. Like African American and Indian leaders, women argued that legal and voting rights were indispensable to such moves. These women's rights advocates based their claims on the theory that women's special, even superior, traits as guardians of family and morality would humanize all of society. Settlement-house founder Jane Addams, for example, endorsed woman suffrage by asking, "If women have in any sense been responsible for the gentler side of life which softens and blurs some of its harsher conditions, may not they have a duty to perform in our American cities?"

Women's clubs represented a unique dimension of the woman movement. Originating as middle-class literary and educational organizations, women's clubs began taking stands on public affairs in the late nineteenth century. Because female activists were generally barred from holding public office (except in a few western states), they asserted traditional female responsibilities for home and family as the rationale for reforming society through an enterprise called social housekeeping. Rather than advocate reforms such as trustbusting and direct primaries, these women worked for factory inspection, regulation of children's and women's labor, improved housing and education, and consumer protection.

WOMEN'S CLUBS

Such efforts were not confined to white women. Mostly excluded from white women's clubs, African American women had their own club movement, including the Colored Women's Federation, which sought to establish a training school for "colored girls." Founded in 1895, the National Association of Colored Women was the nation's first African American social service organization; it concentrated on establishing nurseries, kindergartens, and retirement homes. Black women also developed reform organizations within Black Baptist and African Methodist Episcopal churches.

Around 1910 some of those concerned with women's place in society began using the term *feminism* to represent

FEMINISM

their ideas. Whereas the woman movement spoke generally of duty and moral purity, feminists, more explicitly conscious of their identity as women, emphasized rights and self-development. Feminism, however, contained an inherent contradiction. On one hand feminists argued that all women should unite in the struggle for rights because of their shared disadvantages as women. On the other, feminists insisted that sex-typing—treating women differently from men—must end because it resulted in discrimination. Thus feminists advocated the contradictory position that women should unite as a gender group for the purpose of abolishing all gender-based distinctions.

Feminism focused primarily on economic and sexual independence. Charlotte Perkins Gilman, a major figure in the movement, denounced Victorian notions of womanhood and articulated feminist goals in her numerous writings. Her book *Women and Economics* (1898) declared that domesticity and female innocence were obsolete and attacked men's monopoly on economic opportunity. Arguing that paid employees should handle domestic chores such as cooking, cleaning, and childcare, Gilman asserted that modern women must take jobs in industry and the professions.

Feminists also supported a single standard of behavior for men and women, and several feminists joined the

MARGARET SANGER'S CRUSADE

birth-control movement led by Margaret Sanger. A former visiting nurse who believed in woman's right to sexual pleasure and to determine when to have a child, Sanger helped reverse state and federal "Comstock laws"—named after a nineteenth-century New York moral reformer—that had banned publication and distribution of information about sex and contraception. Though Sanger later gained acceptance, her speeches and actions initially aroused opposition from those who saw birth control as a threat to family and morality. Sanger persevered and in 1921 formed the American Birth Control League, enlisting physicians and social workers to convince judges to al-

■ The rise of the settlement house movement and of the Visiting Nurse Association provided young middle-class women with opportunities to aid inner-city working-class neighborhoods and formed the basis of the social work profession. Here a group of visiting nurses prepare to apply their medical training to the disadvantaged. (Corbis-Bettmann)

low distribution of birth-control information. Most states still prohibited the sale of contraceptives, but Sanger succeeded in introducing the issue into public debate.

During the Progressive era, a generation of feminists, represented by Harriot Stanton Blatch, daughter of nineteenth-century suffragist Elizabeth

WOMAN SUFFRAGE

Cady Stanton, carried on women's battle for the vote. Blatch, whose chief goal was improvement of women's working conditions, agreed with those who saw the vote as the means by which women could bring about such improvement. Declaring that all women worked, whether they performed paid labor or unpaid housework, Blatch believed that all women's efforts contributed to society's betterment. In her view, achievement rather than wealth and refinement was the best criterion for public status. Thus women should exercise the vote not to enhance the power of elites but to promote and protect women's economic roles.

Despite internal differences, suffragists united behind their single goal and achieved some successes. Nine states, all in the West, allowed women to vote in state and local elections by 1912, and women continued to press for national suffrage (see Map 21.1). Their tactics ranged from moderate but persistent letter-writing and publications of the National American Woman Suffrage Association, led by Carrie Chapman Catt, to spirited meetings and militant marches of the National Woman's Party, led by Alice Paul. All these activities heightened public awareness. More decisive, however, was women's service during the First World War as factory laborers, medical volunteers, and municipal workers. By convincing legislators that women could shoulder public responsibilities, women's wartime contributions gave final impetus to passage of the national suffrage amendment (the Nineteenth) in 1920.

In spite of these accomplishments, the activities of women's clubs, feminists, and suffragists failed to create an interest group united or powerful enough to overcome men's political, economic, and social control. Like blacks, women knew that voting rights would mean little until society's attitudes changed. The Progressive era helped women to clarify issues that concerned them, but major reforms were not achieved until a later era. As feminist Crystal Eastman observed in the aftermath of the suffrage crusade: "Men are saying perhaps, 'Thank God, this everlasting women's fight is over!' But women, if I know them, are saying, 'Now at last we can begin.'... Now they can say what they are really after, in common with all the rest of the struggling world, is freedom."

Theodore Roosevelt and the Revival of the Presidency

*T*he Progressive era's theme of reform in politics, institutions, and social relations drew attention to government, especially the federal government, as the foremost agent of change. Though the federal gov-

Map 21.1   Woman Suffrage Before 1920

Before Congress passed and the states ratified the Nineteenth Amendment, woman suffrage already existed, but mainly in the West. Several midwestern states allowed women to vote only in presidential elections, but legislatures in the South and Northeast generally refused such rights until forced to do so by constitutional amendment.

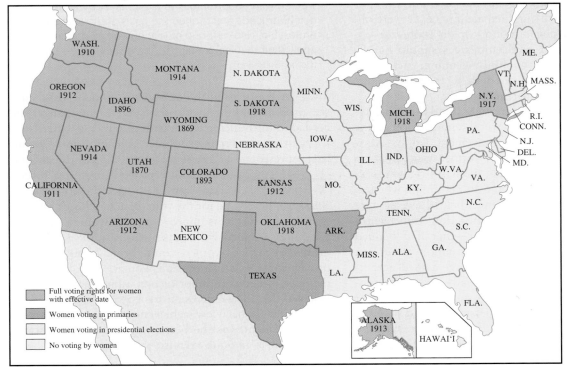

ernment had notable accomplishments during the preceding Gilded Age (see Chapter 20), its role mainly had been to support rather than control economic expansion, as when it transferred western public lands and resources to private ownership. Then, in September 1901, the political climate suddenly shifted. The assassination of President William McKinley by anarchist Leon Czolgosz vaulted Theodore Roosevelt, the vigorous young vice president, into the White House. As governor of New York, Roosevelt had angered Republican bosses by showing sympathy for regulatory legislation, so they rid themselves of their pariah by pushing him into national politics. Little did they anticipate that they provided the steppingstone for the nation's most forceful president since Lincoln and a president who bestowed the office with much of its twentieth-century character.

As a youth Roosevelt suffered from asthma and near-sightedness. Driven throughout his life by an obsession to overcome his physical limitations, he exerted what he and his contemporaries called "manliness," meaning a zest for action and display of courage in a "strenuous life." In his teens he became an expert marksman and horseman and later competed

THEODORE ROOSEVELT

on Harvard's boxing and wrestling teams. In the 1880s he went to live on a Dakota ranch, where he roped cattle and brawled with cowboys. Descended from a Dutch aristocratic family, Roosevelt had wealth to indulge in such pursuits. But he also inherited a sense of civic responsibility that guided him into a career in public service. He served three terms in the New York State Assembly, ran for mayor of New York City in 1886 (finishing third), sat on the federal Civil Service Commission, served as New York City's police commissioner, and was assistant secretary of the navy. In these offices Roosevelt earned a reputation as a combative, politically crafty leader. In 1898 Roosevelt thrust himself into the Spanish-American War by organizing a volunteer cavalry brigade, called the Rough Riders, to fight in Cuba. Though his dramatic act had little impact on the war's outcome, it excited public imagination and made him a media hero.

Only forty-two years old when he assumed the presidency, Roosevelt carried his youthful exuberance into the White House. (A British diplomat once quipped, "You must always remember that the president is about 6.") Considering himself a Progressive, he concurred with his allies that a small, uninvolved government

■ Theodore Roosevelt (1858–1919) liked to think of himself as a great outdoorsman. He loved most the rugged countryside and believed that he and his country should serve as examples of "manliness." (California Museum of Photography, University of California)

would not suffice in the industrial era. Instead, economic development necessitated a government powerful enough to guide national affairs broadly. "A simple and poor society," he observed, "can exist as a democracy on the basis of sheer individualism. But a rich and complex society cannot so exist." Especially in economic matters, he wanted the government to act as an umpire, deciding when big business was good and when it was bad. But his brash patriotism and dislike of qualities he considered effeminate also recalled earlier eras of unbridled expansion when raw power prevailed in social and economic affairs.

The federal regulation of the economy that characterized twentieth-century American history began with

REGULATION OF TRUSTS

Roosevelt's presidency. Roosevelt turned his attention first to big business, where consolidation had created massive, monopolistic trusts. Although labeled a "trustbuster," Roosevelt actually considered business consolidation an efficient means to achieve material progress. He believed in distinguishing between good and bad trusts and preventing bad ones from manipulating markets. Thus he instructed the Justice Department to use antitrust laws to prosecute railroad, meatpacking, and oil trusts, which he believed unscrupulously exploited the public. Roosevelt's policy triumphed in 1904 when the Supreme Court, convinced by the government's arguments, ordered the breakup of Northern Securities Company, the huge railroad combination created by J. P. Morgan and his business allies (*Northern Securities* case). Roosevelt chose, however, not to attack other trusts, such as U.S. Steel, another of Morgan's creations.

When prosecution of Northern Securities began, Morgan reportedly collared Roosevelt and offered, "If we have done anything wrong, send your man to my man and they can fix it up." The president refused but was more sympathetic to cooperation between business and government than his rebuff might suggest. Rather than prosecute at every turn, he urged the Bureau of Corporations (part of the newly created Department of Labor and Commerce) to assist companies to merge and expand. Through investigation and cooperation, the administration cajoled businesses to regulate themselves; corporations often accepted regulation because it helped them operate more efficiently and reduced overproduction.

Roosevelt also supported regulatory legislation, especially after his resounding electoral victory in 1904, in which he won votes from Progressives and businesspeople alike. After a year of wrangling, Roosevelt persuaded Congress to pass the Hepburn Act (1906), which gave the Interstate Commerce Commission (ICC) greater authority to set railroad freight and storage rates, though it did allow courts to overturn rate decisions. Progressive senator Robert La Follette complained that Roosevelt had compromised with congressional business allies to ensure the bill's passage. But Roosevelt chose to reaffirm the principle of regulation rather than risk defeat over unreachable, idealistic objectives.

Roosevelt showed similar willingness to compromise on legislation to ensure the purity of food and drugs. For

PURE FOOD AND DRUG LAWS

decades reformers had been urging government regulation of processed meat and patent medicines. Public outrage at fraud and adulteration flared in 1906 when Upton Sinclair published *The Jungle,* a fictionalized exposé of Chicago meatpacking plants. Sinclair, a socialist whose objective was to improve working conditions, shocked public sensibilities with his vivid descriptions:

> There would be meat stored in great piles in rooms; and the water from the leaky roofs would drip over it, and thousands of rats would race about on it. It was too dark in these storage places to see well, but a man could run his hand over these piles of meat and sweep off handfuls of dried dung of rats. These rats were a nuisance, and the packers would put poisoned bread out for them; they would die, and then rats, bread, and meat would go into the hoppers together.

After reading the novel, Roosevelt ordered an investigation. Finding Sinclair's descriptions accurate, he supported the Meat Inspection Act, which passed Congress in 1906. Like the Hepburn Act, this law reinforced the principle of government regulation, requiring that government agents monitor the quality of processed meat. But as part of a compromise to pass the bill, the government, rather than the meatpackers, had to finance inspections, and meatpackers could appeal adverse decisions in court. Nor were companies required to provide date-of-processing information on canned meats. Most large meatpackers welcomed the legislation anyway, because it helped them force out smaller competitors and restored foreign confidence in American meat products.

The Pure Food and Drug Act (1906) not only prohibited dangerously adulterated foods but also addressed abuses in the patent medicine industry. Makers of tonics and pills had long been making undue claims about their products' effects and liberally using alcohol and narcotics as ingredients. Ads in popular publications, such as one for a "Brain Stimulator and Nerve Tonic" in the Sears, Roebuck catalogue, made wildly exaggerated claims. Al-

HIMROD'S CURE
—FOR—

ROSE COLD,   **DIPHTHERIA,**

ASTHMA,

Catarrh, Hay Fever,

CROUP, INFLUENZA
AND
Ordinary Colds.

PRICE ONE DOLLAR.

■ Makers of unregulated patent medicines advertised that their products had exorbitant abilities to cure almost any ailment. The Pure Food and Drug Act of 1906 did not ban such products but tried to prevent manufacturers from making such unsubstantiated claims.   (© Bettmann/Corbis)

though the law did not ban such products, it required that labels list the ingredients—a goal consistent with Progressive confidence that if people knew the truth they would make wiser purchases.

Roosevelt's approach to labor resembled his stance toward business. When the United Mine Workers struck against Pennsylvania coal mine owners in 1902 over an eight-hour workday and higher pay, the president employed Progressive tactics of investigation and arbitration. Owners, however, stubbornly refused to recognize the union or arbitrate grievances. As winter approached and fuel shortages threatened, Roosevelt roused public opinion. He threatened to use federal troops to reopen the mines, thus forcing management to accept arbitration of the dispute by a special commission. The commission decided in favor of higher wages and reduced hours. It also required management to deal with grievance committees elected by the miners but did not mandate recognition of the union. The decision, according to

Roosevelt, provided a "square deal" for all. The settlement also embodied Roosevelt's belief that the president or his representatives should determine which labor demands were legitimate and which were not. In Roosevelt's mind there were good and bad labor organizations (socialists, for example, were bad), just as there were good and bad business combinations.

Roosevelt combined the Progressive impulse for efficiency with his love for the great outdoors to make lasting and original contributions to modern resource conservation. Government involvement in this endeavor, especially the establishment of national parks, had begun in the late nineteenth century (see pages 463–464). But Roosevelt advanced the movement by favoring *conservation* over *preservation*. Thus he not only exercised presidential power to declare national monuments of such natural wonders as the Olympic Peninsula in Washington and the Petrified Forest and Grand Canyon in Arizona but also backed a policy of "wise use" of forests, waterways, and other resources for beneficial purposes. Previously, the government had transferred ownership and control of natural resources on federal land to the states and to private interests. Roosevelt, however, believed the most efficient way to use and conserve resources would be for the federal government to retain management over lands that remained in the public domain.

CONSERVATION

Roosevelt exerted federal authority over resources in several ways. He protected waterpower sites from sale to private interests and charged permit fees for users who wanted to produce hydroelectricity. He also supported the Newlands Reclamation Act of 1902, which controlled sale of irrigated federal land in the West (see page 467). And he tripled the number and acreage of national forests and supported conservationist Gifford Pinchot in creating the U.S. Forest Service.

As chief forester and principal advocate of the "wise use" policy, Pinchot promoted scientific management of the nation's woodlands. He asserted, "All the resources of forest reserves are for *use* [so that] water, wood, and forage of the reserves are conserved and wisely used for the benefit of the home builder first of all." He obtained Roosevelt's support for transferring management of the national forests from the Interior Department to his bureau in the Agriculture Department, arguing that forests were crops grown on "tree farms." Under his guidance, the Forest Service charged fees for grazing livestock within the national forests, supervised bidding for the cutting of timber, and hired university-trained foresters as federal employees.

GIFFORD PINCHOT

Pinchot and Roosevelt did not seek to lock up—preserve—resources permanently; rather they wanted to guarantee—conserve—their efficient use and prevent big corporations from demanding release of more federal land. Although antifederal, anticonservation attitudes still prevailed in the West, many of those involved in natural-resource exploitation welcomed such a policy because, like regulation of food and drugs, it enabled them to minimize overproduction and to restrict competition. They benefited from Roosevelt and Pinchot's efforts, such as their encouragement of large lumber companies to engage in reforestation. Mostly, corporations tried to influence federal bureaucracies and Congress to act in their behalf while at the same time denouncing federal interference. As a result of new federal policies, the West and its resources fell under the Progressive spell of management.

In 1907 Roosevelt had to compromise his principles in the face of economic crisis. That year a financial panic

PANIC OF 1907 — caused by reckless speculation forced some New York banks to close to prevent frightened depositors from withdrawing money. J. P. Morgan helped stem the panic by persuading financiers to stop dumping their stocks. In return for Morgan's aid, Roosevelt approved a deal allowing U.S. Steel to absorb the Tennessee Iron and Coal Company—a deal at odds with Roosevelt's trustbusting aims.

During his last year in office, Roosevelt retreated from the Republican Party's traditional friendliness to big business. He lashed out at irresponsible "malefactors of great wealth" and supported stronger business regulation and heavier taxation of the rich. Having promised that he would not seek reelection, Roosevelt backed his friend Secretary of War William Howard Taft for the Republican nomination in 1908, hoping that Taft would continue his initiatives. Democrats nominated William Jennings Bryan for the third time, but the "Great Commoner" lost again. Aided by Roosevelt, who still enjoyed great popularity, Taft won by 1.25 million popular votes and a 2-to-1 margin in the electoral college.

Early in 1909 Roosevelt traveled to Africa to shoot game (his passion for the manly activity of hunting

TAFT ADMINISTRATION — outweighed his support for conservation), leaving Taft to face political problems that Roosevelt had managed to postpone. Foremost among them was the tariff; rates had risen to excessive levels. Honoring Taft's pledge to cut rates, the House passed a bill sponsored by Representative Sereno E. Payne that provided for numerous reductions. Protectionists in the Senate prepared, as in the past, to amend the House bill and revise rates upward. But Senate Progressives, led by La Follette, organized a stinging attack on the tariff for benefiting special interests, trapping Taft between reformers who claimed to be preserving Roosevelt's antitrust campaign and protectionists who still dominated the Republican Party. In the end, Senator Aldrich and other protectionists restored many of the cuts the Payne bill had made, and Taft—who believed the bill had some positive provisions and understood that more extreme cuts were not politically possible—signed what became known as the Payne-Aldrich Tariff (1909). In the eyes of Progressives, Taft had failed the test of filling Roosevelt's shoes.

Progressive and conservative wings of the Republican Party rapidly drifted apart. Soon after the tariff controversy, a group of insurgents in the House led by Nebraska's George Norris challenged Speaker "Uncle Joe" Cannon of Illinois, whose power over committee assignments and the scheduling of debates could make or break a piece of legislation. Taft first supported, then abandoned, the insurgents, who nevertheless managed to liberalize procedures by enlarging the influential Rules Committee and removing selection of its members from Cannon's control. In 1910 Taft also angered conservationists by firing Gifford Pinchot, who had protested Secretary of the Interior Richard A. Ballinger's plan to reduce federal supervision of western waterpower sites and Ballinger's sale of coal lands in Alaska, both of which were intended to make private development easier.

In reality Taft was as sympathetic to reform as Roosevelt was. He prosecuted more trusts than Roosevelt, expanded national forest reserves, signed the Mann-Elkins Act (1910), which bolstered regulatory powers of the ICC, and supported labor reforms such as the eight-hour workday and mine safety legislation. The Sixteenth Amendment, which legalized the federal income tax as a permanent part of federal power, and the Seventeenth Amendment, which provided for direct election of U.S. senators, were initiated during Taft's presidency (and ratified in 1913). Like Roosevelt, Taft compromised with big business, but unlike Roosevelt he lacked ability to manipulate the public with spirited rhetoric. Roosevelt had expanded presidential power and infused the presidency with vitality. "I believe in a strong executive," he once asserted. "I believe in power." Taft, by contrast, believed in the strict restraint of law. He had been a successful lawyer and judge and returned to the bench as chief justice of the United States between 1921 and 1930. His caution and unwillingness to offend disappointed those accustomed to Roosevelt's impetuosity.

In 1910, when Roosevelt returned from Africa boasting three thousand animal trophies, he found his party torn and tormented. Reformers, angered by Taft's apparent insensitivity to their causes, formed the National Progressive Republican League and rallied behind Robert La Follette for president in 1912, though many hoped Roosevelt would run. Another wing of the party remained loyal to Taft. Disappointed by Taft's performance (particularly his firing of Pinchot), Roosevelt began to speak out. He filled speeches with references to "the welfare of the people" and stronger regulation of business. When La Follette became ill early in 1912, Roosevelt, proclaiming himself fit as a "bull moose," threw his hat into the ring for the Republican presidential nomination.

Taft's supporters controlled the Republican convention and nominated him for a second term. In protest, Roosevelt's supporters bolted the convention to form a third party—the Progressive, or Bull Moose, Party—and nominated the fifty-three-year-old former president. Meanwhile, Democrats took forty-six ballots to select their candidate, New Jersey's Progressive governor Woodrow Wilson. Socialists, by now an organized and growing party, again nominated Eugene V. Debs. The ensuing campaign exposed voters to the most thorough debate on the nature of the American system since 1896.

In accepting the Progressive Party's nomination, Theodore Roosevelt proclaimed, "We stand at Armageddon and we battle for the Lord." Central to his campaign was a scheme called the "New Nationalism," a term coined by reform editor Herbert Croly. Roosevelt foresaw an era of national unity in which government would coordinate and regulate economic activity. He would not destroy big business, which he viewed as an efficient organizer of production. Instead, he would establish regulatory commissions of experts who would protect citizens' interests and ensure wise use of economic power. "The effort at prohibiting all combinations has substantially failed," he claimed. "The way out lies . . . in completely controlling them."

Wilson offered a more idealistic proposal, the "New Freedom," based on ideas of Progressive lawyer Louis Brandeis. Wilson argued that concentrated economic power threatened individual liberty and that monopolies should be broken up so the marketplace could become genuinely open. But he would not restore laissez faire. Like Roosevelt, Wilson would enhance government authority to protect and regulate. "Freedom today," he declared, "is something more than being let alone. Without the watchful . . . resolute interference of the government, there can be no fair play between individuals and such

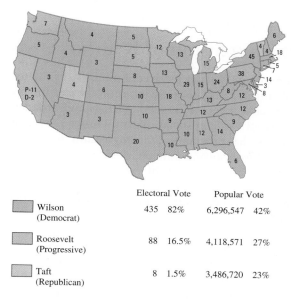

	Electoral Vote		Popular Vote	
Wilson (Democrat)	435	82%	6,296,547	42%
Roosevelt (Progressive)	88	16.5%	4,118,571	27%
Taft (Republican)	8	1.5%	3,486,720	23%

Map 21.2   Presidential Election, 1912

Though he won a minority of the popular votes, Woodrow Wilson captured so many states that he achieved an easy victory in the electoral college.

powerful institutions as the trust." Wilson stopped short, however, of advocating the cooperation between business and government inherent in Roosevelt's New Nationalism.

Roosevelt and Wilson stood closer together than their rhetoric implied. Despite his faith in experts as regulators, Roosevelt harbored a belief in individual freedom as strong as Wilson's. And Wilson was not completely hostile to concentrated economic power. Both men supported equality of opportunity (chiefly for white males), conservation of natural resources, fair wages, and social betterment for all. Neither would hesitate to expand government activity through strong personal leadership and bureaucratic reform.

Amid passionate moral pronouncements from Roosevelt and Wilson, as well as a hard-hitting critique from Debs and a low-key defense of conservatism from Taft, the popular vote was inconclusive. The victorious Wilson won just 42 percent, though he did capture 435 out of 531 electoral votes (see Map 21.2). Roosevelt received 27 percent of the popular vote. Taft finished third, polling 23 percent of the popular vote and only 8 electoral votes. Debs won 901,000 votes, 6 percent of the total, but no electoral votes. One major outcome was evident, however; three-quarters of the electorate supported some alternative to the view of restrained government that Taft represented.

Woodrow Wilson and the Extension of Reform

E ven though Wilson received a minority of the total vote in 1912, he could interpret the election results as a mandate to subdue trusts and broaden the government's role in social reform. On inauguration day in 1913, he proclaimed, "The Nation has been deeply stirred by a solemn passion. . . . The feelings with which we face this new age of right and opportunity sweep across our heartstrings like some air out of God's own presence, where justice and mercy are reconciled and the judge and the brother are one."

The public fondly called Roosevelt "Teddy" and "TR," but Thomas Woodrow Wilson was too aloof ever

WOODROW WILSON

to be nicknamed "Woody" or "WW." Born in Virginia in 1856 and raised in the South, Wilson was the son of a Presbyterian minister. He earned a B.A. degree at Princeton University, studied law at the University of Virginia, received a Ph.D. degree from Johns Hopkins University, and became a professor of history, jurisprudence, and political economy. Between 1885 and 1908, he published several respected books on American history and government.

Wilson's manner reflected his background. He exuded none of Roosevelt's brashness, yet he was a charismatic leader. A superb orator, he could inspire intense loyalty with religious imagery and eloquent expressions of American ideals. Wilson's convictions led him early into reform. In 1902 he became president of Princeton and upset tradition with curricular reforms and battles against the university's aristocratic elements. In 1910 New Jersey's Democrats, eager for respectability, nominated Wilson for governor. After winning the election, Wilson repudiated the party bosses and promoted Progressive legislation. A poor administrator, he often lost his temper and stubbornly refused to compromise. His accomplishments nevertheless attracted national attention and won him the Democratic nomination for president in 1912.

As president, Wilson found it necessary to blend New Freedom competition with New Nationalism regulation;

WILSON'S POLICY ON BUSINESS REGULATION

in so doing he set the direction of future federal economic policy. The corporate merger movement had made restoration of open competition impossible; Wilson could only try to prevent corporate abuses by expanding government's regulatory powers. His administration moved toward that end with passage in 1914 of the Clayton Anti-Trust Act and a bill creating the Federal Trade Commission (FTC). The Clayton Act corrected deficiencies of the Sherman Anti-Trust Act of 1890 (see page 505) by outlawing such practices as price discrimination (efforts to destroy competition by lowering prices in some regions but not in others) and interlocking directorates (management of two or more competing companies by the same executives). The FTC could investigate companies and issue cease-and-desist orders against unfair trade practices. Accused companies could appeal FTC orders in court; nevertheless, the FTC represented another step toward consumer protection.

Wilson expanded banking regulation with the Federal Reserve Act (1913), which established the nation's first central banking system since 1836, when the Second Bank of the United States expired. The act intended to break the power that banking syndicates such as that of J. P. Morgan held over money supply and credit. It created twelve district banks to hold reserves of member banks throughout the nation. The district banks, supervised by the Federal Reserve Board, would lend money to member banks at a low interest rate called the discount rate. By adjusting this rate (and thus the amount a bank could afford to borrow), district banks could increase or decrease the amount of money in circulation. In other words, in response to the nation's needs, the Federal Reserve Board could loosen or tighten credit. Monetary affairs no longer would depend on the gold supply, and interest rates would be fairer, especially for small borrowers.

Wilson attempted to restore competition in commerce with the Underwood Tariff, passed in 1913. By the

TARIFF AND TAX REFORM

1910s, prices for some consumer goods had become unnaturally high because tariffs discouraged the importation of cheaper foreign materials and manufactured goods. By reducing or eliminating certain tariff rates, the Underwood Tariff encouraged imports. To replace revenues lost because of tariff reductions, the act levied a graduated income tax on U.S. residents—an option made possible when the Sixteenth Amendment was ratified earlier that year. The income tax was tame by today's standards. Incomes under $4,000 were exempt; thus almost all factory workers and farmers escaped taxation. Individuals and corporations earning between $4,000 and $20,000 had to pay a 1 percent tax; thereafter rates rose gradually to a maximum of 6 percent on earnings over $500,000.

The outbreak of the First World War (see Chapter 23) and the approaching presidential election campaign prompted Wilson to support stronger reforms in 1916. Concerned that farmers needed a better system of long-term mortgage credit, the president backed the Federal Farm Loan Act. This measure created twelve federally supported banks (not to be confused with the Federal Reserve banks) that could lend money at moderate interest to farmers who belonged to credit institutions—a watered-down version of the subtreasury plan that Populists had proposed a generation earlier (see page 556).

To forestall railroad strikes that might disrupt transportation at a time of national emergency, Wilson in 1916 also pushed passage of the Adamson Act, which mandated eight-hour workdays and time-and-a-half overtime pay for railroad laborers. He pleased Progressives by appointing Brandeis, the "people's advocate," to the Supreme Court, though an anti-Semitic backlash almost blocked Senate approval of the Court's first Jewish justice. Also, Wilson courted support from social reformers by backing laws that regulated child labor and provided workers' compensation for federal employees who suffered work-related injuries or illness.

In selecting a candidate to oppose Wilson in 1916, Republicans snubbed Theodore Roosevelt in favor of

ELECTION OF 1916

Charles Evans Hughes, Supreme Court justice and former reform governor of New York. Acutely aware of the First World War's impact on national affairs (Europe had been at war since 1914), Wilson ran on a platform of peace, Progressivism, and preparedness; his supporters used the campaign slogan "He Kept Us Out of War." Hughes and his party could not muzzle Roosevelt, whose bellicose speeches suggested that Republicans would drag Americans into war. The election outcome was close. Wilson received 9.1 million votes to Hughes's 8.5 million and barely won in the electoral college, 277 to 254. The Socialist candidate drew only 600,000 votes, down from 901,000 in 1912, largely because Wilson's reforms had won over some socialists and because the ailing Eugene Debs was no longer the party's standard-bearer.

During Wilson's second term, U.S. involvement in the First World War increased government regulation of the economy. In his first term Wilson had become convinced that regulatory commissions, which could easily fall under the influence of the interests they were meant to regulate, were often ineffective. Mobilization for war, he came to believe, required coordination of production and cooperation between the public and private sectors. The War Industries Board exemplified this cooperation: private businesses regulated by the board submitted to its control on condition that their profit motives would continue to be satisfied. After the war, Wilson's administration dropped most cooperative and regulatory measures,

■ Depicted here as a stern Roman consul, Woodrow Wilson was a former professor (his university background is represented here by the scholarly owl at his side) who as president used a stubborn moralism to guide the nation toward his ideals.   (Picture Research Consultants & Archives)

including farm price supports, guarantees of collective bargaining, and high taxes. This retreat from regulation, prompted in part by the election of a Republican Congress in 1918, stimulated a new era of business ascendancy in the 1920s.

Summary

By 1920 a quarter-century of reform had wrought momentous changes. Government, economy, and society as they had existed in the nineteenth century were gone forever. In their efforts to achieve goals of ending abuses of power, reforming institutions, and applying scientific and efficient management, Progressives established the principle of public intervention to ensure fairness, health, and safety. Concern over poverty and injustice reached new heights. For every American who suffered some form of deprivation, three or four enjoyed unprecedented material comforts. But amid growing affluence, reformers could not sustain their efforts indefinitely. Although Progressive values lingered after the First World War, a mass-consumer society began to refocus people's attention away from reform to materialism.

Multiple and sometimes contradictory goals characterized the Progressive era. By no means was there a single Progressive movement. Programs on the national level ranged from Roosevelt's faith in big government as a coordinator of big business to Wilson's promise to dissolve economic concentrations and legislate open competition. At state and local levels, reformers pursued causes as varied as neighborhood improvement, government reorganization, public ownership of utilities, betterment of working conditions, and control of morality. National associations coordinated efforts on specific issues, but reformers with different goals often worked at cross-purposes. New consciousness about identity confronted women and African Americans, and although women made some inroads into public life, both groups still found themselves in confined social positions and dependent on their own resolve in their quest for dignity and recognition.

In spite of their remarkable successes, the failure of many Progressive initiatives indicates the strength of the opposition, as well as weaknesses within the reform movements themselves. Courts asserted constitutional and liberty-of-contract doctrines in striking down key Progressive legislation, notably the federal law prohibiting child labor. In states and cities, adoption of the initiative, referendum, and recall did not encourage greater participation in government as had been hoped; those mechanisms either were seldom used or became tools of special interests. On the federal level, regulatory agencies rarely had enough resources for thorough investigations; they had to depend on information from the very companies they policed. Progressives thus failed in many respects to redistribute power. In 1920, as in 1900, government remained under the influence of business, a state of affairs that many people considered quite satisfactory.

Yet the reform movements that characterized the Progressive era reshaped the national outlook. Trust-busting, however faulty, forced industrialists to become more sensitive to public opinion, and insurgents in Congress partially diluted the power of dictatorial politicians. Progressive legislation equipped government with tools to protect consumers against price fixing and dangerous products. The income tax, created to redistribute wealth, also became a source of government revenue. Social reformers relieved some ills of urban life. And per-haps most important, Progressives challenged old ways of thinking. Although the questions they raised about the quality of American life remained unresolved, Progressives made the nation acutely aware of its principles and promises.

LEGACY FOR A PEOPLE AND A NATION
Margaret Sanger, Planned Parenthood, and the Birth-Control Controversy

Some reforms of the Progressive era illustrate how earnest intentions to help can become tangled in divisive issues of morality. Such is the legacy of birth-control advocate Margaret Sanger. In 1912, Sanger began writing an advice column on sex education in the *New York Call* titled "What Every Girl Should Know." Almost immediately, censors accused her of writing obscene literature because she discussed venereal disease in a public way. The issue of limiting family size, however, occupied more of her attention, and she began counseling poor women on New York's Lower East Side about how to avoid the pain of frequent childbirth, miscarriage, and bungled abortion. In 1914, Sanger published the first issue of *The Woman Rebel*, a radical monthly that advocated a woman's right to practice birth control. Indicted for distributing obscenity through the mails, Sanger fled to England to avoid prosecution. There, she joined a set of radicals and gave speeches on behalf of birth control and a woman's need to enjoy sexual fulfillment without fear of pregnancy.

Returning to the United States, Sanger opened the country's first U.S. birth-control clinic, in Brooklyn in 1916. She was arrested and jailed, but when a court exempted physicians from a law prohibiting dissemination of contraceptive information, she set up a doctor-run clinic in 1923. Staffed by female doctors and social workers, the Birth Control Clinical Research Bureau acted as a model for other clinics. At the same time, Sanger organized the American Birth Control League (1921) and tried to win support from medical and social reformers, including some from the eugenics movement, for legalized birth control. Eventually, her radical views caused her to fall out with some of her allies, and she resigned from the American Birth Control League in 1928.

The movement continued, however, and in 1938 the American Birth Control League and the Birth Control Clinical Research Bureau merged to form the Birth Control Federation of America, renamed the Planned Parenthood Federation of America (PPFA) in 1942. The organization's name defined its mission to strengthen the family and stabilize society with the help of governmental support, rather than to focus more directly on the feminist issue of whether or not a woman should have the right of voluntary motherhood. Throughout the 1940s, PPFA emphasized family planning through making contraceptives more accessible. In 1970, it began receiving funds under a federal program to provide family planning services.

In the 1960s, the emergence of new feminist agitation for women's rights and rising concerns about overpopulation expanded issues of birth control and moved abortion into an arena of high controversy. Though PPFA had initially dissociated itself from abortion as a means of family planning, the intense debate between a woman's "choice" and an unborn child's "right to life" drew the organization into the fray, especially after 1973, when the Supreme Court validated women's right to an abortion in *Roe v. Wade*. The national PPFA and its local branches fought legislative and court attempts to make abortions illegal, and in 1989 it helped organize a women's march on Washington for equality and abortion rights. At the same time, some Latino and African American groups attacked PPFA's stance, charging that abortion was a kind of eugenics program meant to reduce births among nonwhite races.

Because of PPFA's involvement in abortion politics, several of its clinics have been targets of constant picketing and even violence by those who believe abortion to be immoral. PPFA now operates nearly nine hundred health centers providing medical services and education nationwide and has fulfilled Margaret Sanger's dream of legalized contraception and family planning. But, as with other reforms dealing with issues of morality and individual rights, birth control has left a legacy to a people and a nation of disagreement over whose rights and whose morality should prevail.

The **history companion** powered by Eduspace®

Your primary source for interactive quizzes, exercises, and more to help you learn efficiently.
http://history.college.hmco.com/students

*T*HE QUEST FOR EMPIRE 1865–1914

*D*evil!" they angrily shouted at Lottie Moon. "Foreign devil!" The Southern Baptist missionary, half a world away from home, braced herself against the Chinese "rabble" she vowed to convert to Christianity. On a day in the 1880s, she walked "steadily and persistently" through the hecklers, vowing silently to win their acceptance and then their souls.

Born in 1840 in Virginia and educated at what is now Hollins College, Charlotte Diggs Moon volunteered in 1873 for "woman's work" in northern China. There she taught and proselytized, largely among women and children because women seldom preached to men and men were forbidden to preach to women. This compassionate, pious, and courageous single woman, "putting love into action," worked in China until her death in 1912.

Lottie Moon (Mu Ladi, or 幕拉第) made bold and sometimes dangerous evangelizing trips in the 1870s and 1880s to isolated Chinese hamlets. "O! The torture of human eyes upon you; scanning every feature, every look, every gesture!" Curious peasant women pinched her, pulling on her skirt, purring, "How white her hand is!" They peppered her with questions: "How old are you?" and "Where do you get money to live on?" Speaking in Chinese, she held high a picture book on Jesus Christ's birth and crucifixion, drawing the chattering crowd's attention to the "foreign doctrine" that she hoped would displace Confucianism, Buddhism, and Taoism.

In the 1890s a "storm of persecution" against foreigners swept China. Missionaries, because they were upending traditional ways and authority, became hated targets. One missionary conceded that in "believing Jesus," girls and women alarmed men who worried that "disobedient wives and daughters" would no longer "worship the idols when told." In the village of Shaling in early 1890, Lottie Moon's Christian converts were beaten and the "foreign devils" ordered to move out. Fearing for her life, she had to flee. For several months in 1900, during the violent Boxer Rebellion, she had to leave China altogether as a multinational force (that included U.S. troops) intervened to save foreign missionaries, diplomats, and merchants.

◀ The missionary Lottie Moon (1840–1912) is surrounded in 1901 by English-language students in Japan during her refuge from the Boxer Rebellion in China. (Virginia Baptist Historical Society & University Archives)

CHRONOLOGY

1861–69 • Seward sets expansionist course

1867 • United States acquires Alaska and Midway

1876 • Pro-U.S. Díaz begins thirty-four-year rule in Mexico

1878 • U.S. gains naval rights in Samoa

1885 • Strong's *Our Country* celebrates Anglo-Saxon destiny of dominance

1887 • U.S. gains naval rights to Pearl Harbor, Hawai'i

1890 • Alfred Thayer Mahan publishes *The Influence of Sea Power upon History*
• McKinley Tariff hurts Hawaiian sugar exports

1893 • Economic crisis leads to business failures and mass unemployment
• Pro-U.S. interests stage successful coup against Queen Lili'uokalani of Hawai'i

1895 • Cuban revolution against Spain begins
• Japan defeats China in war, annexes Korea and Formosa (Taiwan)

1898 • United States formally annexes Hawai'i
• U.S. battleship *Maine* blows up in Havana harbor
• United States defeats Spain in Spanish-American War

1899 • Treaty of Paris enlarges U.S. empire
• United Fruit Company forms and becomes influential in Central America
• Philippine insurrection breaks out, led by Emilio Aguinaldo

1901 • McKinley assassinated; Theodore Roosevelt becomes president

1903 • Panama grants canal rights to United States
• Platt Amendment subjugates Cuba

1904 • Roosevelt Corollary declares U.S. a hemispheric "police power"

1905 • Portsmouth Conference ends Russo-Japanese War

1906 • San Francisco School Board segregates Asian schoolchildren
• U.S. invades Cuba to quell revolt

1907 • "Great White Fleet" makes world tour

1910 • Mexican revolution threatens U.S. interests

1914 • U.S. troops invade Mexico
• First World War begins
• Panama Canal opens

Lottie Moon and thousands of other missionaries managed to convert to Christianity only a very small minority of the Chinese people. Although she, like other missionaries, probably never shed the Western view that she represented a superior religion and culture, she seldom wavered from her affection for the Chinese people and from her devotion to the foreign missionary project—from her "rejoicing to suffer." In frequent letters and articles directed to a U.S. audience, she lobbied to recruit "a band of ardent, enthusiastic, and experienced Christian women," to stir up "a mighty wave of enthusiasm for Woman's Work for Woman." To this day, the Lottie Moon Christmas Offering in Southern Baptist churches raises millions of dollars for missions abroad.

Like so many other Americans who went overseas in the late nineteenth and early twentieth centuries, Lottie Moon helped spread American culture and implant U.S. influence abroad. In this complex process, other peoples sometimes adopted and sometimes rejected American ways. At the same time, American participants in this cultural expansion, and the cultural collisions it generated, became transformed. Lottie Moon, for example, strove to understand the Chinese people and learn their language. She abandoned the derogatory phrases "heathen Chinese" and "great unwashed" and even assumed their dress. She reminded other, less sensitive missionaries that the Chinese rightfully took pride in their own ancient history and thus had no reason to "gape in astonishment at Western civilization."

Lottie Moon also changed—again, in her own words—from "a timid self-distrustful girl into a brave self-reliant woman." As she questioned the Chinese confinement of women, most conspicuous in arranged marriages, foot binding, and sexual segregation, she advanced women's rights. She understood that she could not convert Chinese women unless they had the freedom to listen to her appeals. Bucking the gender ideology of the times, she also uneasily rose to challenge the male domination of America's religious missions. When the Southern Baptist Foreign Mission Board denied women missionaries the right to vote in meetings, she resigned in protest. The board soon reversed itself.

In later decades critics labeled the activities of Lottie Moon and other missionaries as "cultural imperialism," accusing them of seeking to subvert indigenous traditions and sparking destructive cultural clashes. Defenders of missionary work, on the other hand, have celebrated their efforts to break down cultural barriers and to bring the world's peoples closer together. Either way, Lottie Moon's story illustrates how Americans in the late nineteenth century interacted with the world in diverse ways, how through their experiences the categories "domestic" and "foreign" intersected, and how they expanded abroad not only to seek land, trade, investments, and strategic bases but also to promote American culture, including the Christian faith.

Between the Civil War and the First World War, an expansionist United States joined the ranks of the great world powers. Before the Civil War, Americans had repeatedly extended the frontier: they bought Louisiana; annexed Florida, Oregon, and Texas; pushed Indians out of the path of white migration westward; seized California and other western areas from Mexico; and acquired southern parts of present-day Arizona and New Mexico from Mexico (the Gadsden Purchase). Americans had also developed a lucrative foreign trade with most of the world and promoted American culture wherever they traveled. They rekindled their expansionist course after the Civil War, building, managing, and protecting an overseas empire.

It was an age of empire. By the 1870s, most of Europe's powers were carving up Africa and large parts of Asia and Oceania for themselves. By 1900 the powers had conquered more than 10 million square miles (one-fifth of the earth's land), and 150 million people. As the century turned, France, Russia, and Germany were spending heavily on modern steel navies, challenging an overextended Great Britain. In Asia, meanwhile, a rapidly modernizing Japan expanded at the expense of both China and Russia.

Engineering advances altered the world's political geography through the Suez Canal (1869), the British Trans-Indian railroad (1870), and the Russian Trans-Siberian Railway (1904), while steamships, machine guns, telegraphs, and malaria drugs greatly facilitated the imperialists' task. Simultaneously, the optimistic spirit that had characterized European political discourse in the 1850s and 1860s gave way to a brooding pessimism and a sense of impending warfare informed by notions of racial conflict and survival of the fittest.

This transformation of world politics did not escape notice by observant Americans, and some argued the United States risked being "left behind" if it failed to join the scramble for territory and markets. Republican senator Henry Cabot Lodge of Massachusetts, claiming that the "great nations" were seizing "the waste areas of the world," advised that "the United States must not fall out of the line of march," because "civilization and the advancement of the [Anglo-Saxon] race" were at stake. Such thinking helped fuel the desire of Americans in the years after the Civil War to exert their influence beyond the continental United States, to reach for more space, more land, more markets, more cultural penetration, and more power.

By 1900 the United States had emerged as a great power with particular clout in Latin America, especially as Spain declined and Britain disengaged from the Western Hemisphere. In the Pacific, the new U.S. empire included Hawai'i, American Samoa, and the Philippines. Theodore Roosevelt, who in the 1890s was a leading spokesman for the imperialist cause, would as president in the decade that followed seek to consolidate this newfound power.

Most Americans applauded expansionism—the outward movement of goods, ships, dollars, people, and ideas—as a traditional feature of their nation's history. But many became uneasy whenever expansionism gave way to imperialism—the imposition of control over other peoples, undermining their sovereignty and usurping their freedom to make their own decisions. Abroad, native nationalists, commercial competitors, and other imperial nations tried to block the spread of U.S. influence. ■

Imperial Dreams

Foreign policy assumed a new importance for Americans in the closing years of the nineteenth century. For much of the Gilded Age, they had been preoccupied by internal matters such as industrialization, the construction of the railroads, and the settlement of the West. Over time, however, increasing numbers of political and business leaders began to look outward, and to advocate a more activist approach to world affairs. The motives of these expansionists were complex and varied, but all of them emphasized the supposed benefits of such an approach to the country's domestic health.

■ As one expression of the theme of economic expansion, this poster, advertising the Uncle Sam stove manufactured in New York by the Abendroth Bros. company, announces that food links the United States with the rest of the world. Although the foods on the long list are international—potatoes from Ireland and macaroni from Italy, for example—the message here is that the United States itself is "feeding the world." The turkey being removed from the oven seems to be the only unique American offering, but many of the items on the list were also produced in the United States. The poster was issued in 1876, which explains the image of the Centennial building in Philadelphia and the patriotic red, white, and blue colors. (© Collection of The New York Historical Society)

That proponents of expansion stressed the benefits that would accrue at home should come as no surprise, for foreign policy has always sprung from the domestic setting of a nation—its needs and moods, ideology and culture. The leaders who guided America's expansionist foreign relations were the same people who guided the economic development of the machine age, forged the transcontinental railroad, built America's bustling cities and giant corporations, and shaped a mass culture. They unabashedly espoused the idea that the United States was an exceptional nation, so different from and superior to others because of its Anglo-Saxon heritage and its God-favored and prosperous history.

Exceptionalism was but one in an intertwined set of ideas that figured prominently in the American march toward empire. Nationalism, capitalism, Social Darwinism, and a paternalistic attitude toward foreigners influenced American leaders as well. "They are children and we are men in these deep matters of government," the future president Woodrow Wilson announced in 1898. The very words he chose reveal the gender and age bias of American attitudes. Where these attitudes intersected with foreign cultures, there came not only adoption but rejection, not only imitation but clash, as Lottie Moon learned.

It would take time for most Americans to grasp the changes under way. "The people" may influence domestic policy directly, but the making of foreign policy is usually dominated by what scholars have labeled the "foreign policy elite"—opinion leaders in politics, journalism, business, agriculture, religion, education, and the military. In the post–Civil War era, this small group, whom Secretary of State Walter Q. Gresham called "the thoughtful men of the country," expressed the opinions that counted. Better read and better traveled than most Americans, more cosmopolitan in outlook, and politically active, they believed that U.S. prosperity and security depended on the exertion of U.S. influence abroad. Increasingly in the late nineteenth century, and

*FOREIGN POLICY
ELITE*

especially in the 1890s, the expansionist-minded elite urged both formal and informal imperialism. Ambitious and clannish, the imperialists often met in Washington, D.C., at the homes of the historian Henry Adams and the writer and diplomat John Hay (who became secretary of state in 1898) or at the Metropolitan Club. They talked about building a bigger navy and digging a canal across Panama, Central America, or Mexico, establishing colonies, and selling surpluses abroad. Theodore Roosevelt, appointed assistant secretary of the navy in 1897, was among them; so were Senator Henry Cabot Lodge, who joined the Foreign Relations Committee in 1896, and the corporate lawyer Elihu Root, who later would serve as both secretary of war and secretary of state. Such well-positioned luminaries kept up the drumbeat for empire.

These American leaders believed that selling, buying, and investing in foreign marketplaces were important to the United States. Why? One reason was profits from foreign sales. "It is my dream," declared the governor of Georgia in 1878, to see "in every valley . . . a cotton factory to convert the raw material of the neighborhood into fabrics which shall warm the limbs of Japanese and Chinese." Fear helped make the case for foreign trade as well because the nation's farms and factories produced more than Americans could consume, all the more so during the 1890s depression. Foreign commerce might serve as a safety valve to relieve overproduction, unemployment, economic depression, and the social tension that arose from them. Surpluses had to be exported, the economist David A. Wells warned, or "we are certain to be smothered in our own grease." Economic ties also permitted political influence to be exerted abroad and helped spread the American way of life, especially capitalism, creating a world more hospitable to Americans. In an era when the most powerful nations in the world were also the greatest traders, vigorous foreign economic expansion symbolized national stature.

Though most business leaders remained focused on the domestic marketplace, foreign trade figured prominently in the tremendous economic growth of **FOREIGN TRADE** the United States after the Civil War. **EXPANSION** Foreign commerce, in turn, stimulated the building of a larger protective navy, the professionalization of the foreign service, calls for more colonies, and a more interventionist foreign policy. In 1865 U.S. exports totaled $234 million; by 1900 they had climbed to $1.5 billion (see Figure 22.1). By 1914, at the outbreak of the First World War, exports had reached $2.5 billion, prompting some Europeans to protest an American "invasion" of goods. In 1874 the United States reversed its historically unfavorable balance of trade (im-

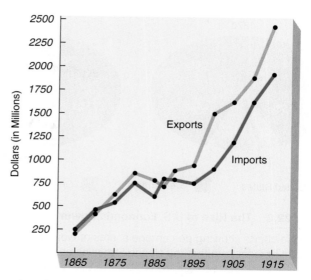

Figure 22.1   U.S. Trade Expansion, 1865–1914

This figure illustrates two key characteristics of U.S. foreign trade: first, that the United States began in the 1870s to enjoy a favorable balance of trade (exporting more than it imported); second, that U.S. exports expanded tremendously, making the United States one of the world's economic giants.   (Source: Thomas G. Paterson, J. Garry Clifford, and Kenneth J. Hagan, *American Foreign Relations: A History,* 5th ed. Copyright © 2000 by Houghton Mifflin Company.)

porting more than it exported) and began to enjoy a long-term favorable balance (exporting more than it imported)—though the balance of payments remained in the red. Most of America's products went to Britain, continental Europe, and Canada, but increasing amounts flowed to new markets in Latin America and Asia. Meanwhile, direct American investments abroad reached $3.5 billion by 1914, placing the United States among the top four investor countries.

Agricultural goods accounted for about three-fourths of total exports in 1870 and about two-thirds in 1900, with grain, cotton, meat, and dairy products topping the export list that year. More than half of the annual cotton crop was exported each year. Midwestern farmers transported their crops by railroad to seaboard cities and then on to foreign markets. Farmers' livelihoods thus became tied to world-market conditions and the outcomes of foreign wars. Wisconsin cheesemakers shipped to Britain; the Swift and Armour meat companies exported refrigerated beef to Europe. To sell American grain abroad, James J. Hill of the Great Northern Railroad distributed wheat cookbooks translated into several Asian languages.

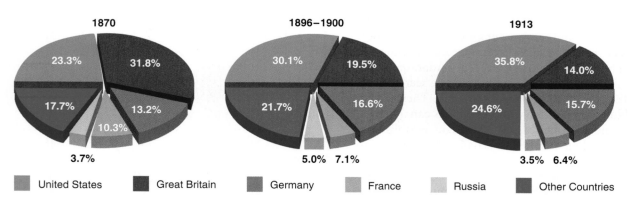

Figure 22.2   The Rise of U.S. Economic Power in the World

These pie charts showing percentage shares of world manufacturing production for the major nations of the world demonstrate that the United States came to surpass Great Britain in this significant economic measurement of power.   (Source: League of Nations data presented in Aaron L. Friedberg, *The Weary Titan: Britain and the Experience of Relative Decline, 1895–1905* [Princeton, N.J.: Princeton University Press, 1988], p. 26.)

In 1913, when the United States outranked both Great Britain and Germany in manufacturing production (see Figure 22.2), manufactured goods led U.S. exports for the first time. Substantial proportions of America's steel, copper, and petroleum were sold abroad, making many workers in those industries dependent on American exports. George Westinghouse marketed his air brakes in Europe; almost as many Singer sewing machines were exported as were sold at home; and Cyrus McCormick's "reaper kings" harvested the wheat of Russian fields.

In promoting the expansion of U.S. influence overseas, many officials championed a nationalism based on

RACE THINKING AND THE MALE ETHOS

notions of American supremacy. Some, echoing the articulations of European imperialists (who had their own conceptions of national supremacy), found justification for expansionism in racist theories then permeating Western thought and politics. For decades, the Western scientific establishment had classified humankind by race, and students of physical anthropology drew on phrenology and physiognomy— the measurement of skull size and the comparison of facial features—to produce a hierarchy of superior and inferior races. One prominent French researcher, for example, claimed that blacks represented a "female race" and "like the woman, the black is deprived of political and scientific intelligence; he has never created a great state . . . he has never accomplished anything in industrial mechanics. But on the other hand he has great virtues of sentiment. Like women he also likes jewelry, dancing, and singing."

The language of U.S. leaders was also weighted with words such as *manliness* and *weakling*. Member of Congress, son-in-law of Senator Lodge, and Spanish-American War veteran Augustus P. Gardner extolled the "arena of lust and blood, where true men are to be found." The warrior and president Theodore Roosevelt viewed people of color (or "darkeys," as he called them) as effeminate weaklings who lacked the ability to govern themselves and could not cope with world politics. Americans regularly debased Latin Americans as half-breeds needing close supervision, distressed damsels begging for manly rescue, or children requiring tutelage. The gendered imagery prevalent in U.S. foreign relations joined race thinking to place women, people of color, and nations weaker than the United States in the low ranks of the hierarchy of power and, hence, in a necessarily dependent status justifying U.S. dominance.

Reverend Josiah Strong's popular and influential *Our Country* (1885) celebrated an Anglo-Saxon race destined to lead others. "As America goes, so goes the world," he declared. A few years later he wrote that "to be a Christian and an Anglo-Saxon and an American . . . is to stand at the very mountaintop of privilege." Social Darwinists saw Americans as a superior people certain to overcome all competition. Secretary of State Thomas F. Bayard (1885–1889) applauded the "overflow of our population and capital" into Mexico to "saturate those regions with Americanism." But, he added, "we do not want them" until "they are fit."

The magazine *National Geographic*, which published its first issue in 1888, chronicled with photographs America's new overseas involvements in Asia and the Pacific. The editors chose pictures that reflected prevailing American ethnocentric attitudes toward foreigners. Even when smiling faces predominated, the image portrayed was that of strange, exotic, premodern people who had not become "Western." Emphasizing this point, *National Geographic* regularly pictured women with naked breasts.

Fairs, too, stereotyped other peoples as falling short of civilization. Fair managers not only celebrated the impressive technology of "Western civilization"; they also put people of color on display in the "freaks" or "midway" section. Alongside bearded women and the fattest man in the world were exhibits—as at the 1895 Atlanta and 1897 Nashville fairs—of Cubans and Mexicans in primitive village settings. Dog-eating Filipinos aroused particular comment at the 1904 St. Louis World's Fair.

Race thinking—popularized in world's fairs, magazine cartoons, postcards, school textbooks, museums, and political orations—reinforced notions of American greatness, influenced the way U.S. leaders dealt with other peoples, and obviated the need to think about the subtle textures of other societies. Such racism downgraded diplomacy and justified domination and war, because self-proclaimed superiors do not negotiate with people ranked as inferiors.

The same thinking permeated attitudes toward immigrants, whose entry into the United States was first restricted in these years. Although the Burlingame Treaty (1868) had provided for free immigration between the United States and China, for example, in the American West riots against Chinese immigrants erupted again and again—in Los Angeles (1871), San Francisco (1877), Denver (1880), and Seattle (1886). A new treaty in 1880 permitted Congress to suspend Chinese immigration to the United States, and it did so two years later. A violent incident occurred in Rock Springs, Wyoming, in 1885, when white coal miners and railway workers rioted and massacred at least twenty-five Chinese.

In 1906 the San Francisco School Board, reflecting the anti-Asian bias of many West Coast Americans, ordered the segregation of all Chinese, Koreans, and Japanese in special schools. Tokyo protested the discrimination against its citizens. The following year, President Roosevelt quieted the crisis by striking a "gentleman's agreement" with Tokyo restricting the inflow of Japanese immigrants; San Francisco then rescinded its segregation order. Relations with Tokyo were jolted again in 1913 when the California legislature denied Japanese residents the right to own property in the state.

With a mixture of self-interest and idealism typical of American thinking on foreign policy, expansionists believed that empire benefited both Americans and those who came under their control. When the United States intervened in other lands or lectured weaker states, Americans claimed that

THE "CIVILIZING" IMPULSE

■ As part of "Anthropology Days" during the 1904 St. Louis World's Fair, organizers put on a series of athletic events showing "primitive" people participating in games such as running, high-jumping, archery, and spear throwing. In this photo by Jessie Tarbox Beals, Igorots from the Philippines compete in a spear-throwing contest. The winners were given American flags. Meanwhile, the 1904 Olympic Games took place on an irregular basis during the fair featuring white "civilized" athletes (the vast majority from the United States) who received gold medals for their victories. (Special Collections, St. Louis Public Library)

■ The missionaries Charles and Anna Hartwell, brother and sister, travel in 1901 on their "gospel boat," working out of the Fuzhou mission in China.   (ABCFM Pictures, courtesy of Houghton Library, Harvard University)

in remaking foreign societies they were extending liberty and prosperity to less fortunate people. William Howard Taft, as civil governor of the Philippines (1901–1904), described the United States's mission in its new colony as lifting up Filipinos "to a point of civilization" that will make them "call the name of the United States blessed." Later, after becoming secretary of war (1904–1908), Taft said about the Chinese that "the more civilized they become . . . the wealthier they become, and the better market they become for us." "The world is to be Christianized and civilized," declared Reverend Josiah Strong. "And what is the process of civilizing but the creating of more and higher wants."

Missionaries dispatched to Asia and Africa (like Lottie Moon in the chapter-opening vignette) helped spur the transfer of American culture and power abroad—"the peaceful conquest of the world," as Reverend Frederick Gates put it. One organization, the Student Volunteers for Foreign Missions, began in the 1880s on college cam-

puses and by 1914 had placed some 6,000 missionaries abroad. In 1915 a total of 10,000 American missionaries worked overseas. In China, by 1915 more than 2,500 American Protestant missionaries—most of them female—labored to preach the gospel, to teach school, and to administer medical care.

Ambitions and Strategies

The U.S. empire grew gradually, sometimes haltingly, as American leaders defined guiding principles and built institutions to support overseas ambitions. William H. Seward, one of its chief architects, argued relentlessly for extension of the American frontier as senator from New York (1849–1861) and secretary of state (1861–1869). "There is not in the history of the Roman Empire an ambition for aggrandizement so marked as that which characterizes the American people," he once said. Seward envisioned a large, coordinated U.S. empire encompassing Canada, the Caribbean, Cuba, Central America, Mexico, Hawai'i, Iceland, Greenland, and the Pacific islands. This empire would be built not by war but by a natural process of gravitation toward the United States. Commerce would hurry the process, as would a canal across Central America, a transcontinental American railroad to link up with Asian markets, and a telegraph system to speed communications.

Most of Seward's grandiose plans did not reach fruition in his own day. In 1867, for example, he signed a treaty with Denmark to buy the Danish West Indies (Virgin Islands), but his domestic political foes in the Senate and a hurricane that wrecked St. Thomas scuttled his effort. The Virgin Islanders, who had voted for annexation, had to wait until 1917 for official U.S. status. Also failing was Seward's scheme with unscrupulous Dominican Republic leaders to gain a Caribbean naval base at Samaná Bay. The stench of corruption rising over this unsavory deal-making wafted into the Ulysses S. Grant administration and foiled Grant's initiative in 1870 to buy the entire island nation. The Senate rejected annexation.

SEWARD'S QUEST FOR EMPIRE

Anti-imperialism, not just politics, blocked Seward. Anti-imperialists such as Senator Carl Schurz and E. L. Godkin, editor of the magazine *The Nation,* argued that the country already had enough unsettled land and that creating a showcase of democracy and prosperity at home would best persuade other peoples to adopt American institutions and principles. Some anti-imperialists, sharing the racism of the times, opposed the annexation of territory populated by dark-skinned people.

■ Beginning in the late nineteenth century, Standard Oil (the forerunner of Exxon Mobil Corporation) sent agents to China to persuade the Chinese to use American-made kerosene in their lamps and cooking stoves. To promote sales, the American entrepreneurs gave away small lamps, which the Chinese called *Mei Foo* (Beautiful Companion). One agent who popularized the lamp was William P. Coltman, shown here with Chinese business associates. At right is one of the advertisements.   (Exxon Mobil Corporation)

Seward did enjoy some successes. In 1866, citing the Monroe Doctrine (see page 244), he sent troops to the border with Mexico and demanded that France abandon its puppet regime there. Also facing angry Mexican nationalists, Napoleon III abandoned the Maximilian monarchy that he had installed by force three years earlier. In 1867 Seward paid Russia $7.2 million for the 591,000 square miles of Alaska—land twice the size of Texas. Some critics lampooned "Seward's Icebox," but the secretary of state extolled the Russian territory's rich natural resources, and the Senate voted overwhelmingly for the treaty. That same year, Seward laid claim to the Midway Islands (two small islands and a coral atoll northwest of Hawai'i) in the Pacific Ocean.

Seward realized his dream of a world knit together by a giant communications system. In 1866, through the persevering efforts of the financier Cyrus Field, an underwater transatlantic cable linked European and American telegraph networks. Backed by J. P. Morgan's capital, the communications pioneer James A. Scrymser strung telegraph lines to Latin America, entering Chile in 1890. In 1903 a submarine cable reached across the Pacific to the Philippines; three years later it

INTERNATIONAL COMMUNICATIONS

extended to Japan and China. Information about markets, crises, and war flowed steadily and quickly. Wire telegraphy—like radio (wireless telegraphy) later—shrank the globe. Nellie Bly, a reporter for the *New York World,* accented the impact of new technology in 1890 when she completed a well-publicized trip around the world in seventy-two days. Drawn closer to one another through improved communications and transportation, nations found that faraway events had more and more impact on their prosperity and security. Because of the communications revolution, "every nation elbows other nations to-day," observed Amherst College professor Edwin Grosvenor in 1898.

More and more, American diplomats found that they could enter negotiations with their European counterparts on roughly equal terms—a sure sign that the United States had arrived on the international stage. Seward's successor Hamilton Fish (1869–1887), for example, achieved a diplomatic victory in resolving the knotty problem of the *Alabama* claims. The *Alabama* and other vessels built in Great Britain for the Confederacy during the Civil War had preyed on Union shipping. Senator Charles Sumner demanded that Britain pay $2 billion in damages or cede Canada to the United States, but Fish favored negotiations. In 1871 Britain and America signed the Washington Treaty, whereby the British apologized and agreed to the creation of a tribunal, which later awarded the United States $15.5 million.

Washington officials also confronted European powers in a contest over Samoa, a group of beautiful South Pacific islands 4,000 miles from San Francisco on the trade route to Australia. In 1878 the United States gained exclusive right to a coaling station at Samoa's coveted port of Pago Pago. Eyeing the same prize, Britain and Germany began to cultivate ties with Samoan leaders. Year by year tensions grew as the powers dispatched warships to Samoa and aggravated factionalism among Samoa's chiefs. War seemed possible. At the eleventh hour, however, Britain, Germany, and the United States met in Berlin in 1889 and, without consulting the Samoans, devised a three-part protectorate that limited Samoa's independence. Ten years later the three powers partitioned Samoa: the United States received Pago Pago through annexation of part of the islands (now called American Samoa and administered by the U.S. Department of the Interior); Germany took what is today independent Western Samoa; and Britain, for renouncing its claims to Samoa, obtained the Gilbert Islands and Solomon Islands.

With eyes on all parts of the world, even on Africa, where U.S. interests were minimal, ardent expansionists embraced navalism—the campaign to

ALFRED T. MAHAN AND NAVALISM

build an imperial navy. Calling attention to the naval buildup by the European powers, notably Germany, they argued for a bigger, modernized navy, adding the "blue water" command of the seas to its traditional role of "brown water" coastline defense and riverine operations. Captain Alfred Thayer Mahan became a major popularizer for this "New Navy." Because foreign trade was vital to the United States, he argued, the nation required an efficient navy to protect its shipping; in turn, a navy required colonies for bases. "Whether they will or no," Mahan wrote, "Americans must now begin to look outward. The growing production of the country demands it." Mahan's lectures at the Naval War College in Newport, Rhode Island, where he served as president, were published as *The Influence of Sea Power upon History* (1890). This book sat on every serious expansionist's shelf, and foreign leaders turned its pages. Theodore Roosevelt and Henry Cabot Lodge

eagerly consulted Mahan, sharing his belief in the links between trade, navy, and colonies, and his growing alarm over "the aggressive military spirit" of Germany.

Moving toward naval modernization, Congress in 1883 authorized construction of the first steel-hulled warships. American factories went to work to produce steam engines, high-velocity shells, powerful guns, and precision instruments. The navy shifted from sail power to steam and from wood construction to steel. Often named for states and cities to kindle patriotism and local support for naval expansion, New Navy ships such as the *Maine*, *Oregon*, and *Boston* thrust the United States into naval prominence, especially during crises in the 1890s.

Crises in the 1890s: Hawai'i, Venezuela, and Cuba

In the depression-plagued 1890s, crises in Hawai'i and Cuba gave expansionist Americans opportunities to act on their zealous arguments for what Senator Lodge called a "large policy." Belief that the frontier at home had closed accentuated the expansionist case. In 1893 the historian Frederick Jackson Turner postulated that an ever-expanding continental frontier had shaped the American character. That "frontier has gone," Turner pronounced, "and with its going has closed the first period of American history." He did not explicitly say that a new frontier had to be found overseas in order to sustain the American way of life, but he did claim that "American energy will continually demand a wider field for its exercise."

Hawai'i, the Pacific Ocean archipelago of eight major islands located 2,000 miles from the West Coast of

ANNEXATION OF HAWAI'I

the United States, emerged as a new frontier for Americans. The Hawaiian Islands had long commanded American attention—commercial, religious, missionary, naval, and diplomatic. Wide-eyed U.S. expansionists envisioned ships sailing from the eastern seaboard through a Central American canal to Hawai'i and then on to the fabled China market. Already by 1881 Secretary of State James Blaine had declared the Hawaiian Islands "essentially a part of the American system." By 1890 Americans owned about three-quarters of Hawai'i's wealth and subordinated its economy to that of the United States through sugar exports that entered the U.S. marketplace duty-free.

In Hawai'i's multiracial society Chinese and Japanese nationals far outnumbered Americans, who represented a mere 2.1 percent of the population. Prominent

Queen Lili'uokalani (1838–1917), ousted from her throne in 1893 by wealthy revolutionaries, vigorously protested in her autobiography and diary, as well as in interviews, the U.S. annexation of Hawai'i in 1898. For years she defended Hawaiian nationalism and emphasized that American officials in 1893 had conspired with Sanford B. Dole and others to overthrow the native monarchy.   (Courtesy of the Lili'uokalani Trust)

Americans on the islands—lawyers, businessmen, and sugar planters, many of them the sons of missionaries—organized secret clubs and military units to contest the royal government. In 1887 they forced the king to accept a constitution that granted foreigners the right to vote and shifted decision-making authority from the monarchy to the legislature. The same year, Hawai'i granted the United States naval rights to Pearl Harbor. Many native Hawaiians (53 percent of the population in 1890) believed that the *haole* (foreigners)—especially Americans—were taking their country from them.

The McKinley Tariff of 1890 created an economic crisis for Hawai'i that further undermined the native government. The tariff eliminated the duty-free status of Hawaiian sugar exports in the United States. Suffering declining sugar prices and profits, the American island elite pressed for annexation of the islands by the United States so that their sugar would be classified as domestic rather than foreign. When Princess Lili'uokalani assumed the throne in 1891, she sought to roll back the political power of the *haole*. The next year, the white oligarchy—questioning her moral rectitude, fearing Hawaiian nationalism, and reeling from the McKinley Tariff—formed the subversive Annexation Club.

The annexationists struck in January 1893 in collusion with John L. Stevens, the chief American diplomat in Hawai'i, who dispatched troops from the U.S.S. *Boston* to occupy Honolulu. The queen, arrested and confined, surrendered. However, rather than yield to the new provisional regime, headed by Sanford B. Dole, son of missionaries and a prominent attorney, she relinquished authority to the U.S. government. Up went the American flag. "The Hawaiian pear is now fully ripe and this is the golden hour to pluck it," a triumphant Stevens informed Washington. Against the queen's protests and those of Japan, President Benjamin Harrison hurriedly sent an annexation treaty to the Senate.

Sensing foul play, incoming President Grover Cleveland ordered an investigation, which confirmed a conspiracy by the economic elite in league with Stevens and noted that most Hawaiians opposed annexation. Down came the American flag. But when Hawai'i gained renewed attention as a strategic and commercial way station to Asia and the Philippines during the Spanish-American War, President William McKinley maneuvered annexation through Congress on July 7, 1898, by means of a majority vote (the Newlands Resolution) rather than by a treaty, which would have required a two-thirds count. Under the Organic Act of June 1900, the people of Hawai'i became U.S. citizens with the right to vote in local elections and to send a nonvoting delegate to Congress. Statehood for Hawai'i came in 1959.

The Venezuelan crisis of 1895 also saw the United States in an expansive mood. For decades Venezuela and

VENEZUELAN BOUNDARY DISPUTE

Great Britain had quarreled over the border between Venezuela and British Guiana. The disputed territory contained rich gold deposits and the mouth of the Orinoco River, a commercial gateway to northern South America. Venezuela asked for U.S. help. President Cleveland decided that the "mean and hoggish" British had to be warned away. In July 1895, Secretary of State Richard Olney brashly lectured the British that the Monroe Doctrine prohibited European powers from denying self-government to nations in the Western Hemisphere. He aimed his spread-eagle words at an international audience, proclaiming the United States "a civilized state" whose "fiat is law" in the

Americas. The United States, he declared, is "master of the situation and practically invulnerable as against any or all other powers." The British, seeking international friends to counter intensifying competition from Germany, quietly retreated from the crisis. In 1896 an Anglo-American arbitration board divided the disputed territory between Britain and Venezuela. The Venezuelans were barely consulted. Thus the United States displayed a trait common to imperialists: disregard for the rights and sensibilities of small nations.

REVOLUTION IN CUBA

In 1895 came another crisis forced by U.S. policy, this one in Cuba. From 1868 to 1878 the Cubans had battled Spain for their independence. Slavery was abolished but independence denied. While the Cuban economy suffered depression, repressive Spanish rule continued. Insurgents committed to *Cuba libre* waited for another chance, and José Martí, one of the heroes of Cuban history, collected money, arms, and men in the United States.

American financial support of the Cuban cause was but one of the many ways the lives of Americans and Cubans intersected. Their cultures, for example, melded. Cubans of all classes settled in Baltimore, New York, Boston, and Philadelphia. Prominent Cubans on the island sent their children to schools in the United States. When Cuban expatriates returned home, many came in American clothes, spoke English, had American names, played baseball, and jettisoned Catholicism for Protestant denominations. Struggling with competing identities, Cubans admired American culture but resented U.S. economic hegemony (predominance).

The Cuban and U.S. economies were also intertwined. American investments of $50 million, most in sugar plantations, dominated the Caribbean island. More than 90 percent of Cuba's sugar was exported to the United States, and most island imports came from the United States. Havana's famed cigar factories relocated to Key West and Tampa to evade protectionist U.S. tariff laws. Martí, however, feared that "economic union means political union," for "the nation that buys, commands" and "the nation that sells, serves." Watch out, he warned, for a U.S. "conquering policy" that reduced Latin American countries to "dependencies."

Martí's fears were prophetic. In 1894, the Wilson-Gorman Tariff imposed a duty on Cuban sugar, which had been entering the United States duty-free under the McKinley Tariff. The Cuban economy, highly dependent on exports, plunged into deep crisis, hastening the island's revolution against Spain and its further incorporation into "the American system."

In 1895, from American soil, Martí launched a revolution against Spain that mounted in human and material costs. Rebels burned sugar-cane fields and razed mills, conducting an economic war and using guerrilla tactics to avoid head-on clashes with Spanish soldiers. "It is necessary to burn the hive to disperse the swarm," explained the insurgent leader Máximo Gomez. U.S. investments went up in smoke, and Cuban-American trade dwindled. To separate the insurgents from their supporters among the Cuban people, Spanish general Valeriano Weyler instituted a policy of "reconcentration." Some 300,000 Cubans were herded into fortified towns and camps, where hunger, starvation, and disease led to tens of thousands of deaths. As reports of atrocity and destruction became headline news in the American yellow press (see page 538), Americans sympathized increasingly with the insurrectionists. In late 1897 a new government in Madrid modified reconcentration and promised some autonomy for Cuba, but the insurgents continued to gain ground.

SINKING OF THE MAINE

President William McKinley had come to office as an imperialist who advocated foreign bases for the New Navy, the export of surplus production, and U.S. supremacy in the Western Hemisphere. Vexed by the turmoil in Cuba, he came to believe that Spain should give up its colony. At one point he explored the purchase of Cuba by the United States for $300 million. Events in early 1898 caused McKinley to lose faith in Madrid's ability to bring peace to Cuba. In January, when antireform pro-Spanish loyalists and army personnel rioted in Havana, Washington ordered the battleship *Maine* to Havana harbor to demonstrate U.S. concern and to protect American citizens.

On February 15 an explosion ripped the *Maine,* killing 266 of 354 American officers and crew. Just a week earlier, William Randolph Hearst's inflammatory *New York Journal* had published a stolen private letter written by the Spanish minister in Washington, Enrique Dupuy de Lôme, who belittled McKinley as a "cheap politician" and suggested that Spain would fight on. Congress soon complied unanimously with McKinley's request for $50 million in defense funds. The naval board investigating the *Maine* disaster then reported that a mine had caused the explosion. Vengeful Americans blamed Spain. (Later, official and unofficial studies attributed the sinking to an accidental internal explosion.)

The impact of these events narrowed McKinley's diplomatic options. Though reluctant to go to war, he decided to send Spain an ultimatum. In late March the United States insisted that Spain accept an armistice, end

On July 1, 1898, U.S. troops stormed Spanish positions on San Juan Hill near Santiago, Cuba. Both sides suffered heavy casualties. A *Harper's* magazine correspondent reported a "ghastly" scene of hundreds killed and thousands wounded. The American painter William Glackens (1870–1938) put to canvas what he saw. Because Santiago surrendered on July 17, propelling the United States to victory in the war, and because Rough Rider Theodore Roosevelt fought at San Juan Hill and later gave a self-congratulatory account of the experience, the human toll has often gone unnoticed. (Wadsworth Atheneum, Hartford, Gift of Henry Schnakenberg)

MCKINLEY'S ULTIMATUM AND WAR DECISION

reconcentration altogether, and designate McKinley as arbiter. Madrid made concessions. It abolished reconcentration and rejected, then accepted, an armistice. The weary president hesitated, but he would no longer tolerate chronic disorder just 90 miles off the U.S. coast. On April 11 McKinley asked Congress for authorization to use force "to secure a full and final termination of hostilities between . . . Spain and . . . Cuba, and to secure in the island the establishment of a stable government, capable of maintaining order." American intervention, he said, meant "hostile constraint upon both the parties to the contest."

McKinley listed the reasons for war: the "cause of humanity"; the protection of American life and property; the "very serious injury to the commerce, trade, and business of our people"; and, referring to the destruction of the *Maine,* the "constant menace to our peace." At the end of his message, McKinley mentioned Spain's recent concessions but made little of them. On April 19 Congress declared Cuba free and independent and directed the president to use force to remove Spanish authority from the island. The legislators also passed the Teller Amendment, which disclaimed any U.S. intention to annex Cuba or control the island except to ensure its "pacification" (by which they meant the suppression of any actively hostile elements of the population). McKinley beat back a congressional amendment to recognize the rebel government. Believing that the Cubans were not ready for self-government, he argued that they needed a period of American tutoring.

The Spanish-American War and the Debate over Empire

*D*iplomacy had failed. By the time the Spanish concessions were on the table, events had already pushed the antagonists to the brink. Washington might have been more patient, and Madrid might have faced the fact that its once-grand empire had disintegrated. Still, prospects for compromise appeared dim because the advancing Cuban insurgents would settle for nothing less than full independence, and no Spanish government could have given up and remained in office. Nor did the United States welcome a truly independent Cuban government that might attempt to reduce U.S. interests. As the historian Louis A. Pérez Jr. has argued, McKinley's decision for war may have been "directed as much against Cuban independence as it was against Spanish sovereignty." Thus came a war some have titled (awkwardly, but accurately) the "Spanish-American-Cuban-Filipino War" so as to represent all the major participants and to identify where the war was fought and whose interests were most at stake.

The motives of Americans who favored war were mixed and complex. McKinley's April message expressed

MOTIVES FOR WAR

a humanitarian impulse to stop the bloodletting, a concern for commerce and property, and the psychological need to end the nightmarish anxiety once and for all. Republican politicians advised McKinley that their party would lose the upcoming congressional elections unless he solved the Cuban question. Many businesspeople, who had been hesitant before the

crisis of early 1898, joined many farmers in the belief that ejecting Spain from Cuba would open new markets for surplus production.

Inveterate imperialists saw the war as an opportunity to fulfill expansionist dreams, while conservatives, alarmed by Populism and violent labor strikes, welcomed war as a national unifier. One senator commented that "internal discord" was disappearing in the "fervent heat of patriotism." Sensationalism also figured in the march to war, with the yellow press exaggerating stories of Spanish misdeeds. Assistant Secretary of the Navy Theodore Roosevelt and others too young to remember the bloody Civil War looked on war as adventure and used masculine rhetoric to trumpet the call to arms.

More than 263,000 regulars and volunteers served in the army and another 25,000 in the navy during the war. Most of them never left the United States. The typical volunteer was young (early twenties), white, unmarried, native-born, and working-class. Deaths numbered 5,462—but only 379 in combat. The rest fell to yellow fever and typhoid, and most died in the United States, especially in camps in Tennessee, Virginia, and Florida, where in July and August a typhoid epidemic devastated

■ The Spanish fleet in the Caribbean was commanded by Admiral Pascual Cervera y Topete. His squadron entered Santiago Bay, Cuba, May 19, 1898, where it was immediately blockaded by Admiral William T. Sampson's fleet. On July 3 Cervera, following orders from Madrid, tried a heroic but unsuccessful escape from the U.S. blockade. This painting by Henry Reuterdahl depicts the destruction of the squadron. Cervera survived and became a prisoner of war. (From *The Story of the Spanish-American War of 1898* as told by W. Newphew King, Lieutenant U.S.N.)

the ranks. About 10,000 African American troops, assigned to segregated regiments, found no relief from racism and Jim Crow, even though black troops played a key role in the victorious battle for Santiago de Cuba. For all, food, sanitary conditions, and medical care were bad. Still, Roosevelt could hardly contain himself. Although his Rough Riders, a motley unit of Ivy Leaguers and cowboys, proved undisciplined and often ineffective, they nonetheless received a good press largely because of Roosevelt's self-serving publicity efforts.

To the surprise of most Americans, the first war news actually came from faraway Asia, from the Spanish

DEWEY IN THE PHILIPPINES

colony of the Philippine Islands. Here, too, Madrid faced a rebellion from Filipinos seeking independence. On May 1, 1898, Commodore George Dewey's New Navy ship *Olympia* led an American squadron into Manila Bay and wrecked the outgunned Spanish fleet. Dewey and his sailors had been on alert in Hong Kong since February, when he received orders from imperial-minded Washington to attack the islands if war broke out. Manila ranked with Pearl Harbor and Pago Pago as a choice harbor, and the Philippines sat significantly on the way to China and its potentially huge market.

Facing Americans and rebels in both Cuba and the Philippines, Spanish resistance collapsed rapidly. U.S. ships blockaded Cuban ports to prevent Spain from resupplying its army, which suffered hunger and disease because Cuban insurgents had cut off supplies from the countryside. American troops saw their first ground-war action on June 22, the day several thousand of them landed near Santiago de Cuba and laid siege to the city. On July 3 U.S. warships sank the Spanish Caribbean squadron in Santiago harbor. American forces then assaulted the Spanish colony of Puerto Rico to obtain another Caribbean base for the navy and a strategic site to help protect a Central American canal. Losing on all fronts, Madrid sued for peace.

On August 12 Spain and the United States signed an armistice to end the war. In Paris, in December 1898,

TREATY OF PARIS

American and Spanish negotiators agreed on the peace terms: independence for Cuba from Spain; cession of the Philippines, Puerto Rico, and the Pacific island of Guam to the United States; and American payment of $20 million to Spain for the territories. The U.S. empire now stretched deep into Asia; and the annexation of Wake Island (1898), Hawai'i (1898), and Samoa (1899) gave American traders, missionaries, and naval promoters other steppingstones to China.

During the war with Spain, the *Washington Post* detected "a new appetite, a yearning to show our strength. . . . The taste of empire is in the mouth of the people." But as the nation debated the Treaty of Paris, anti-imperialists such as author Mark Twain, Nebraska politician William Jennings Bryan, intellectual William Graham Sumner, reformer Jane Addams, industrialist Andrew Carnegie, and Senator George Hoar of Massachusetts argued vigorously against annexation of the Philippines. They were disturbed that a war to free Cuba had led to empire, and they stimulated a momentous debate over the fundamental course in American foreign policy.

Imperial control could be imposed either formally (by military occupation, annexation, or colonialism) or

ANTI-IMPERIALIST ARGUMENTS

informally (by economic domination, political manipulation, or the threat of intervention). Anti-imperialist ire focused mostly on the formal kind of imperial control, involving an overseas territorial empire comprised of people of color living far from the mainland. Some critics appealed to principle, citing the Declaration of Independence and the Constitution: the conquest of people against their wills violated the right of self-determination. Philosopher William James charged that the United States was throwing away its special place among nations; it was, he warned, about to "puke up its heritage."

Other anti-imperialists predicted that the very character of the American people was being corrupted by the imperialist zeal. Jane Addams, seeing children play war games in the streets of Chicago, pointed out that they were not freeing Cubans but rather slaying Spaniards. Hoping to build a distinct foreign policy constituency out of networks of women's clubs and organizations, prominent women such as Addams championed peace and an end to imperial conquest.

Still other anti-imperialists protested that the United States was practicing a double standard—"offering liberty to the Cubans with one hand, cramming liberty down the throats of the Filipinos with the other, but with both feet planted upon the neck of the negro," as an African American politician from Massachusetts put it. Some white anti-imperialists, believing in a racial hierarchy, warned that annexing people of color would undermine Anglo-Saxon purity and supremacy at home.

For Samuel Gompers and other anti-imperialist labor leaders the issue was jobs: they worried that what Gompers called the "half-breeds and semi-barbaric people" of the new colonies would undercut American labor. Might not the new colonials be imported as cheap contract labor to drive down the wages of American workers? Would not exploitation of the weak abroad become contagious and lead to further exploitation of the weak at home? Would not an overseas empire drain interest and resources from pressing domestic problems, delaying reform?

The anti-imperialists entered the debate with many handicaps and never launched an effective campaign. Although they organized the Anti-Imperialist League in November 1898, they differed so profoundly on domestic issues that they found it difficult to speak with one voice on a foreign question. They also appeared inconsistent: Gompers favored the war but not the postwar annexations; Carnegie would accept colonies if they were not acquired by force; Hoar voted for annexation of Hawai'i but not of the Philippines; Bryan backed the Treaty of Paris but only, he said, to hurry the process toward Philippine independence. Finally, possession of the Philippines was an established fact, very hard to undo.

The imperialists answered their critics with appeals to patriotism, destiny, and commerce. They sketched a

IMPERIALIST ARGUMENTS

scenario of American greatness: merchant ships plying the waters to boundless Asian markets; naval vessels cruising the Pacific to protect American interests; missionaries uplifting inferior peoples. It was America's duty, they insisted, quoting a then-popular Rudyard Kipling poem, to "take up the white man's burden." Furthermore, Filipino insurgents were beginning to resist U.S. rule, and it seemed cowardly to pull out under fire. Germany and Japan, two powerful international competitors, were snooping around the Philippines, apparently ready to seize them if the United States's grip loosened. National honor dictated that Americans keep what they had shed blood to take. Republican Senator Albert Beveridge of Indiana asked: "Shall [history] say that, called by events to captain and command the proudest, ablest, purest race of history in history's noblest work, we declined that great commission?"

In February 1899, by a 57-to-27 vote (just 1 more than the minimum two-thirds majority), the Senate passed the Treaty of Paris, ending the war with Spain. Most Republicans voted yes and most Democrats no. An amendment promising independence as soon as the Filipinos formed a stable government lost only by the tie-breaking ballot of the vice president. The Democratic presidential candidate Bryan carried the anti-imperialist case into the election of 1900, warning that repudiation of self-government in the Philippines would weaken the principle at home. But the victorious McKinley refused to apologize for American imperialism. "It is no longer a question of expansion with us," he asserted. "If there is any question at all it is a question of contraction; and who is going to contract?"

Asian Encounters: War in the Philippines, Diplomacy in China

*a*s McKinley knew, however, the Philippine crisis was far from over. He said he intended to "uplift and civilize" the Filipinos, but they denied that they needed U.S. paternalism. Emilio Aguinaldo, the Philippine nationalist leader who had been battling the Spanish for years, believed that American officials had promised independence for his country. But after the victory, U.S. officers ordered Aguinaldo out of Manila and isolated him from decisions affecting his nation. In early 1899, feeling betrayed by the Treaty of Paris, he proclaimed an independent Philippine Republic and took up arms. U.S. officials soon set their jaws against the rebellion.

In a war fought viciously by both sides, American soldiers burned villages and tortured captives, while Filipino

PHILIPPINE INSURRECTION AND PACIFICATION

forces staged hit-and-run guerrilla ambushes that were often brutally effective. Americans spoke of the "savage" Filipino; one soldier declared that the Philippines "won't be pacified until the niggers [Filipinos] are killed off like the Indians." U.S. troops introduced a variant of the Spanish reconcentration policy—in the province of Batangas, for instance, U.S. troops forced residents to live in designated zones in an effort to separate the insurgents from local supporters. Disaster followed. Poor sanitation, starvation, and malaria and cholera killed several thousand people. Outside the secure areas, Americans destroyed food supplies to starve out the rebels. At least one-quarter of the population of Batangas died or fled.

Before the Philippine insurrection was suppressed in 1902, more than 200,000 Filipinos and 5,000 Americans lay dead. Resistance to U.S. rule, however, did not disappear. The fiercely independent, vehemently anti-Christian, and often violent Muslim Filipinos of Moro Province refused to knuckle under. The U.S. military ordered them to submit or be exterminated. In 1906 the Moros finally met defeat; 600 of them, including many women and children, were slaughtered at the Battle of Bud Dajo. As General Leonard Wood, the Moro provincial governor, wrote the president, "Work of this kind has its disagreeable side."

U.S. officials, with a stern military hand, soon tried to Americanize the Philippines. Architect Daniel Burnham, leader of the City Beautiful movement (see page 529), planned modern Manila. U.S. authorities instituted a new education system, with English as the main language of instruction. The Philippine economy grew as an American satellite, and a sedition act silenced critics of U.S. authority by sending them to prison. In 1916 the Jones Act vaguely promised independence once the Philippines established a "stable government." The United States finally ended its rule in 1946 during an intense period of decolonization after the Second World War.

In China, McKinley opted for an approach that emphasized negotiations, with greater success. Outsiders had been pecking away at China since the 1840s, but the

CHINA AND THE OPEN DOOR POLICY

Japanese onslaught intensified the international scramble. Taking advantage of the Qing (Manchu) dynasty's weakness, the major powers carved out spheres of influence (regions over which

the outside powers claimed political control and exclusive commercial privileges): Germany in Shandong; Russia in Manchuria; France in Yunnan and Hainan; Britain in Kowloon and Hong Kong. Then, in 1895, the same year as the outbreak of the Cuban revolution, Japan claimed victory over China in a short war and assumed control of Formosa and Korea as well as parts of China proper (see Map 22.1). American religious and business leaders petitioned Washington to halt the dismemberment of China before they were closed out.

Secretary of State John Hay knew that the United States could not force the imperial powers out of China,

Map 22.1   Imperialism in Asia: Turn of the Century

China and the Pacific region had become imperialist hunting grounds by the turn of the century. The European powers and Japan controlled more areas than the United States, which nonetheless participated in the imperial race by annexing the Philippines, Wake, Guam, Hawai'i, and Samoa; announcing the Open Door policy; and expanding trade. As the spheres of influence in China demonstrate, that besieged nation succumbed to outsiders despite the Open Door policy.

The U.S. System of Education in the Philippines

In the Philippines, U.S. officials moved swiftly after 1898 to create a school system based on the American notion of universal education. Under the Spanish, education had been severely limited and largely in the hands of the Catholic Church. By establishing more and better schools U.S. leaders hoped to convince Filipinos of America's goodwill and thereby expedite the task of pacifying the archipelago (chain of islands). By 1901, a national education system from elementary school through teacher's colleges had been established. Most instruction would be in English rather than native Philippine languages (only a small minority spoke Spanish), a decision that rankled many Filipinos.

To help overcome a massive shortage of teachers, the U.S. government recruited thousands of young American educators. They would enter Manila on cattle cruisers from San Francisco, more than a thousand arriving in 1901–1902 alone. One ship, the U.S.S. *Thomas*, carried 540 teachers, both male and female. These "Thomasites," as they and those who followed them became known, fanned out to communities all over the country, where they opened local schoolhouses.

Also in these years American officials arranged for promising Filipinos to be sent to study at universities in the United States. Upon their return these students, known in the Philippines as *pensionados*, provided a cadre of well-trained medical doctors, engineers, and other professionals and were installed in leadership positions in both the public and private sectors. Other Filipinos earned their degrees at home, many of them at the University of the Philippines, founded in 1908 as the country's premier educational institution.

For female students, in particular, changes brought about by the new policies were profound. The establishment of public school instruction for both boys and girls, and the opening up of higher education to women—both at home and as *pensionados/pensionadas* in the United States—allowed women to qualify as professionals for the first time. Many seized the chance. They earned degrees, entered the public sphere, and founded and led their own universities and colleges. Although male students outnumbered female students in both high school and college in the early decades, by the end of the twentieth century women outnumbered men at the university level.

But not all Filipinos could take advantage of the new educational opportunities. The U.S. goal of truly universal education never became a reality. From the start schools varied widely in quality, and Filipino elites proved better able than the less privileged to take advantage of the system. In poor and rural areas access to schools was often difficult. The result was a widening gap between the entitled few and the masses in the decades of U.S. colonial rule (which ended in 1946) and postcolonial independence.

Still, it remains true that for millions in the Philippines the arrival of the Americans linked the two countries through a world of learning and advancement. Whatever the motives behind the new education policy, it was progressive, an irony that was not lost on educated Filipinos. They knew they owed their education partly to the colonial power.

■ Boys in Normal High School, Manila, Philippines, 1900. (Library of Congress)

but he was determined to protect American commerce and missionaries such as Lottie Moon. He knew that missionaries had become targets of Chinese nationalist anger, and that American oil and textile companies had been disappointed in the results of their investments in the country. Thus in September 1899 Hay sent the nations with spheres of influence in China a note asking them to respect the principle of equal trade opportunity—an Open Door. The recipients sent evasive replies, privately complaining that the United States was seeking for free in China the trade rights that they had gained at considerable military and administrative cost.

The next year, a Chinese secret society called the Boxers (so named in the Western press because some members were martial artists) incited riots that killed foreigners, including missionaries, and laid siege to the foreign legations in Beijing. The Boxers sought ultimately to expel all foreigners from China. The United States, applauded by American merchants and missionaries alike, joined the other imperial nation powers in sending troops to lift the siege. Hay also sent a second Open Door note in July that instructed other nations to preserve China's territorial integrity and to honor "equal and impartial trade." Hay's protests notwithstanding, China continued for years to be fertile soil for foreign exploitation, especially by the Japanese.

Though Hay's foray into Asian politics settled little, the Open Door policy became a cornerstone of U.S. diplomacy. The "open door" had actually been a long-standing American principle, for as a trading nation the United States opposed barriers to international commerce and demanded equal access to foreign markets. After 1900, however, when the United States began to emerge as the premier world trader, the Open Door policy became an instrument first to pry open markets and then to dominate them, not just in China but throughout the world. The Open Door also developed as an ideology with several tenets: first, that America's domestic well-being required exports; second, that foreign trade would suffer interruption unless the United States intervened abroad to implant American principles and keep markets open; and third, that the closing of any area to American products, citizens, or ideas threatened the survival of the United States itself.

TR's World

*T*heodore Roosevelt played an important role in shaping U.S. foreign policy in the McKinley administration. As assistant secretary of the navy (1897–1898), as a Spanish-American War hero, and then as vice president in McKinley's second term, Roosevelt worked tirelessly to make the United States a key member of the great power club. He had long had a fascination with power and its uses. He also relished hunting and killing. After an argument with a girlfriend in his youth, he vented his anger by shooting a neighbor's dog. When he killed his first buffalo in the West, he danced crazily around the carcass as his Indian guide watched in amazement. Roosevelt justified the slaughtering of Amerian Indians, if necessary, and took his Rough Riders to Cuba, desperate to get in on the fighting. He was not disappointed. "Did I tell you," he wrote Henry Cabot Lodge afterward, "that I killed a Spaniard with my own hands?"

Like many other Americans of his day, Roosevelt took for granted the superiority of Protestant Anglo-American culture, and he believed in the importance of using American power to shape world affairs (a conviction he summarized by citing the West African proverb "Speak softly and carry a big stick, and you will go far"). In TR's world there were "civilized" and "uncivilized" nations; the former, primarily white and Anglo-Saxon or Teutonic, had a right and a duty to intervene in the affairs of the latter (generally nonwhite, Latin, or Slavic, and therefore "backward") to preserve order and stability. If violent means had to be used to accomplish this task, so be it.

Roosevelt's love of the good fight caused many to rue his ascension to the presidency after McKinley's

PRESIDENTIAL AUTHORITY

assassination in September 1901. But there was more to this "cowboy" than mere bluster; he was also an astute analyst of foreign policy and world affairs. TR understood that American power, though growing year by year, remained limited, and that in many parts of the world the United States would have to rely on diplomacy and nonmilitary means to achieve satisfactory outcomes. It would have to work in concert with other powers.

Roosevelt sought to centralize foreign policy in the White House. The president had to take charge of foreign relations, he believed, in the same way he took the lead in formulating domestic priorities of reorganization and reform. Congress was too large and unwieldy. As for public opinion, it was, Roosevelt said, "the voice of the devil, or what is still worse, the voice of the fool." This conviction that the executive branch should be supreme in foreign policy was to be shared by most presidents who followed TR in office, down to the present day.

With this bald assertion of presidential and national power, Roosevelt stepped onto the international stage. His first efforts were focused on Latin America, where

U.S. economic and strategic interests and power towered (see Map 22.2), and on Europe, where repeated political and military disputes persuaded Americans to develop friendlier relations with Great Britain while avoiding entrapment in the continent's troubles, many of which Americans blamed on Germany.

As U.S. economic interests expanded in Latin America, so did U.S. political influence. Exports to Latin America, which exceeded $50 million in the 1870s, had risen to more than $120 million when Roosevelt became president in 1901, and then reached $300 million in 1914. Investments by U.S. citizens in Latin America climbed to a commanding $1.26 billion in 1914. In 1899 two large banana importers had merged to form the United Fruit Company. United Fruit owned much of the land in Central America (more than a million acres in 1913), as well as the railroad and steamship lines, and the firm became an influential economic and political force in the region. The company worked to eradicate yellow fever and malaria at the same time that it manipulated Central American politics, partly by bankrolling favored officeholders.

After the destructive war in Cuba, U.S. citizens and corporations continued to dominate the island's economy, controlling the sugar, mining, tobacco, and utilities industries and most of the rural lands. Private U.S. investments in Cuba grew from $50 million before the revolution to $220 million by 1913, and U.S. exports to the island rose from $26 million in 1900 to $196 million in 1917. The Teller Amendment outlawed the annexation of Cuba, but officials in Washington soon used the document's call for "pacification"

CUBA AND THE PLATT AMENDMENT

Map 22.2 U.S. Hegemony in the Caribbean and Latin America

Through many interventions, territorial acquisitions, and robust economic expansion, the United States became the predominant power in Latin America in the early twentieth century. The United States often backed up the Roosevelt Corollary's declaration of a "police power" by dispatching troops to Caribbean nations, where they met nationalist opposition.

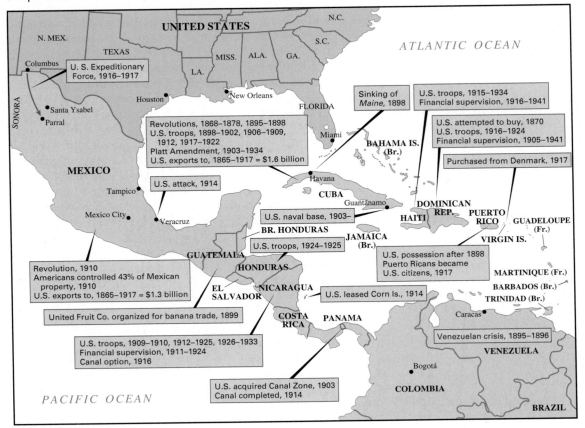

to justify U.S. control. American troops remained there until 1902.

Favoring the "better classes," U.S. authorities restricted voting rights largely to propertied Cuban males, excluding two-thirds of adult men and all women. American officials also forced the Cubans to append to their constitution a frank avowal of U.S. hegemony known as the Platt Amendment. This statement prohibited Cuba from making a treaty with another nation that might impair its independence; in practice, this meant that all treaties had to have U.S. approval. Most important, another Platt Amendment provision granted the United States "the right to intervene" to preserve the island's independence and to maintain domestic order. The amendment also required Cuba to lease a naval base to the United States (at Guantánamo Bay, and still under U.S. jurisdiction today). Formalized in a 1903 treaty, the amendment governed Cuban-American relations until 1934. "There is, of course, little or no independence left Cuba under the Platt Amendment," General Wood, military governor of the island until 1902, told President Roosevelt.

The Cubans, like the Filipinos, chafed under U.S. mastery. Widespread demonstrations protested the Platt Amendment, and a rebellion against the Cuban government in 1906 prompted Roosevelt to order another invasion of Cuba. The marines stayed until 1909, returned briefly in 1912, and occupied the island again from 1917 to 1922. All the while, U.S. officials helped to develop a transportation system, expand the public school system, found a national army, and increase sugar production. When Dr. Walter Reed's experiments, based on the theory of the Cuban physician Carlos Juan Finlay, proved that mosquitoes transmitted yellow fever, sanitary engineers controlled the insect and eradicated the disease.

Puerto Rico, the Caribbean island taken as a spoil of war in the Treaty of Paris, also developed under U.S. tutelage. Although no Puerto Rican sat at the negotiating table for that treaty, the Puerto Rican elite at first welcomed the United States as an improvement over Spain. But disillusionment soon set in. The condescending U.S. military governor, General Guy V. Henry, regarded Puerto Ricans as naughty, ill-educated children who needed "kindergarten instruction in controlling themselves without allowing them too much liberty." Some residents warned against the "Yankee peril"; others applauded the "Yankee model" and futilely anticipated statehood (see pages 618–619).

Panama, meanwhile, became the site of a bold U.S. expansionist venture. In 1869 the world had marveled at

PANAMA CANAL the completion of the Suez Canal, a waterway in Northeast Africa that greatly facilitated travel between the Indian Ocean and Mediterranean Sea and enhanced the power of the British Empire. Surely that feat could be duplicated in the Western Hemisphere, possibly in Panama, a province of Colombia. One expansionist, U.S. navy captain Robert W. Shufeldt, predicted that a new canal would convert "the Gulf of Mexico into an American lake." Business interests joined politicians, diplomats, and navy officers in insisting that the United States control such an interoceanic canal.

■ In a suit and hat, President Theodore Roosevelt occupies the controls of a 95-ton power shovel at a Panama Canal worksite. Roosevelt's November 1906 trip to inspect the massive project was the first time a sitting president left the United States. *(AP/Wide World)*

To construct such a canal, however, the United States had to overcome daunting obstacles. The Clayton-Bulwer Treaty with Britain (1850) had provided for joint control of a canal. The British, recognizing their diminishing influence in the region and cultivating friendship with the United States as a counterweight to Germany, stepped aside in the Hay-Pauncefote Treaty (1901) to permit a solely U.S.-run canal. When Colombia hesitated to meet Washington's terms, Roosevelt encouraged Panamanian rebels to declare independence and ordered American warships to the isthmus to back them.

In 1903 the new Panama awarded the United States a canal zone and long-term rights to its control. The treaty also guaranteed Panama its independence. (In 1922 the United States paid Colombia $25 million in "conscience money" but did not apologize.) The completion of the Panama Canal in 1914 marked a major technological achievement. During the canal's first year of operation, more than one thousand merchant ships squeezed through its locks.

As for the rest of the Caribbean, Theodore Roosevelt resisted challenges to U.S. hegemony. Worried that Latin American nations' defaults on debts owed to European banks were provoking European intervention (England, Germany, and Italy sent warships to Venezuela in 1902), the president in 1904 issued the Roosevelt Corollary to the Monroe Doctrine. He warned Latin Americans to stabilize their politics and finances. "Chronic wrongdoing," the corollary lectured, might require "intervention by some civilized nation," and "in flagrant cases of such wrongdoing or impotence," the United States would have to assume the role of "an international police power." Laced with presumptions of superiority, Roosevelt's declaration provided the rationale for frequent U.S. interventions in Latin America.

ROOSEVELT COROLLARY

From 1900 to 1917, U.S. presidents ordered American troops to Cuba, Panama, Nicaragua, the Dominican Republic, Mexico, and Haiti to quell civil wars, thwart challenges to U.S. influence, gain ports and bases, and forestall European meddling (see Map 22.2). U.S. authorities ran elections, trained national guards that became politically powerful, and renegotiated foreign debts, shifting them to U.S. banks. They also took over customs houses to control tariff revenues and government budgets (as in the Dominican Republic, from 1905 to 1941).

U.S. officials focused particular attention on Mexico, where long-time dictator Porfirio Díaz (1876–1910) aggressively recruited foreign investors through tax incentives and land grants. American capitalists came to own Mex-

U.S.-MEXICO RELATIONS

ico's railroads and mines and invested heavily in petroleum and banking. By the early 1890s, the United States dominated Mexico's foreign trade. By 1910 Americans controlled 43 percent of Mexican property and produced more than half of the country's oil; in the state of Sonora, 186 of 208 mining companies were American owned. The Mexican revolutionaries who ousted Díaz in 1910, like nationalists elsewhere in Latin America, set out to reclaim their nation's sovereignty by ending their economic dependency on the United States.

The revolution descended into a bloody civil war with strong anti-Yankee overtones, and the Mexican government intended to nationalize extensive American-owned properties. Washington leaders worked to thwart this aim, with President Woodrow Wilson twice ordering troops onto Mexican soil: once in 1914, at Veracruz, to avenge a slight to the U.S. uniform and flag and to overthrow the nationalistic government of President Victoriano Huerta, who was also trying to import German weapons; and again in 1916, in northern Mexico, where General John J. "Black Jack" Pershing spent months pursuing Pancho Villa after the Mexican rebel had raided an American border town. Having failed to capture Villa and facing another nationalistic government led by Venustiano Carranza, U.S. forces departed in January 1917.

As the United States reaffirmed the Monroe Doctrine against European expansion in the hemisphere and demonstrated the power to enforce it, European nations reluctantly honored U.S. hegemony in Latin America. In turn, the United States held to its tradition of standing outside European embroilments. The balance of power in Europe was precarious, and seldom did an American president involve the United States directly. Theodore Roosevelt did help settle a Franco-German clash over Morocco by mediating a settlement at Algeciras, Spain (1906). But the president drew American criticism for entangling the United States in a European problem. Americans endorsed the ultimately futile Hague peace conferences (1899 and 1907) and negotiated various arbitration treaties but on the whole stayed outside the European arena, except to profit from extensive trade with it.

In East Asia, though, both Roosevelt and his successor William Howard Taft took an activist approach. Both sought to preserve the Open Door and to contain Japan's rising power in the region. Many race-minded Japanese interpreted the U.S. advance into the Pacific as an attempt by whites to gain ascendancy over Asians. Japanese leaders nonetheless urged their citizens to go to America to study it as a model for industrializing and achieving world power. Although some

PEACEMAKING IN EAST ASIA

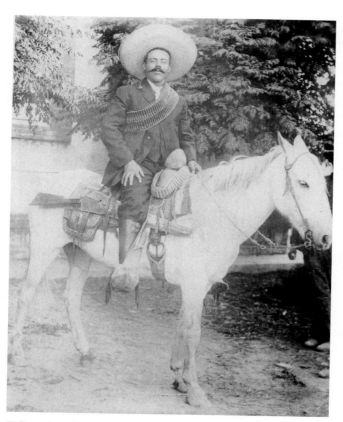

■ Francisco "Pancho" Villa presented himself as a selfless Mexican patriot. Americans living along the border thought otherwise, particularly after Villa's forces murdered more than 30 U.S. civilians. American troops pursued Villa more than 300 hundred miles into Mexico but never caught him.   (John O. Hardman Collection)

dorsed the Open Door in China. Roosevelt also built up American naval power to deter the Japanese; in late 1907 he sent on a world tour the navy's "Great White Fleet" (so named because the ships were painted white for the voyage). Duly impressed, the Japanese began to build a bigger navy of their own.

President Taft, for his part, thought he might counter Japanese advances in Asia through dollar diplomacy—

DOLLAR DIPLOMACY the use of private funds to serve American diplomatic goals and at the same time garner profits for American financiers. In this case, Taft induced American bankers to join an international consortium to build a railway in China. Taft's venture, however, seemed only to embolden Japan to solidify and extend its holdings in China, where internal discord continued after the nationalist revolution of 1911 overthrew the Qing dynasty.

In 1914, when the First World War broke out in Europe, Japan seized Shandong and some Pacific islands from the Germans. In 1915 Japan issued its Twenty-One Demands, virtually insisting on hegemony over all of China. The Chinese door was being slammed shut, but the United States lacked adequate countervailing power in Asia to block Japan's imperial thrusts. A new president, Woodrow Wilson, worried about how the "white race" could blunt the rise of "the yellow race."

In London, British officials shared this concern, though their primary attention was focused on rising tensions in

ANGLO-AMERICAN RAPPROCHEMENT Europe. A special feature of American-European relations in the TR-Taft years was the flowering of an Anglo-American cooperation that had been growing throughout the late nineteenth century. One outcome of the intense German-British rivalry and the rise of the United States to world power was London's quest for friendship with Washington. Already prepared by racial ideas of Anglo-Saxon kinship, a common language, and respect for representative government and private-property rights, Americans appreciated British support in the 1898 war and the Hay-Pauncefote Treaty, and London's virtual endorsement of the Roosevelt Corollary and withdrawal of British warships from the Caribbean. As Mark Twain said of the two imperialist powers: "We are kin in sin."

British-American trade and U.S. investment in Britain also secured ties. By 1914 more than 140 American companies operated in Britain, including H. J. Heinz's processed foods and F. W. Woolworth's "penny markets." Many Britons decried an Americanization of British culture. One journalist complained that a Briton "wakes in the morning at the sound of an American alarm clock;

Americans proudly proclaimed the Japanese the "Yankees of the East," the United States gradually had to make concessions to Japan to protect the vulnerable Philippines and to sustain the Open Door policy. Japan continued to plant interests in China and then smashed the Russians in the Russo-Japanese War (1904–1905). President Roosevelt mediated the negotiations at the Portsmouth Conference in New Hampshire and won the Nobel Peace Prize for this effort to preserve a balance of power in Asia and shrink Japan's "big head."

In 1905, in the Taft-Katsura Agreement, the United States conceded Japanese hegemony over Korea in return for Japan's pledge not to undermine the U.S. position in the Philippines. Three years later, in the Root-Takahira Agreement, Washington recognized Japan's interests in Manchuria, whereas Japan again pledged the security of the Pacific possessions held by the United States and enrises from his New England sheets, and shaves with . . . a Yankee safety razor. He . . . slips his Waterbury watch into his pocket [and] catches an electric train made in New York. . . . At his office . . . he sits on a Nebraskan swivel chair, before a Michigan roll-top desk." Such exaggerated fears and the always prickly character of the Anglo-American relationship, however, gave way to cooperation in world affairs, most evident in 1917 when the United States threw its weapons and soldiers into the First World War on the British side against Germany.

Summary

In the years from the Civil War to the First World War, expansionism and imperialism elevated the United States to world power status. By 1914 Americans held extensive economic, strategic, and political interests in a world made smaller by modern technology. The victory over Spain in 1898 was but the most dramatic moment in the long process. The outward reach of U.S. foreign policy from Seward to Wilson sparked opposition from domestic critics, other imperial nations, and foreign nationalists, but expansionists prevailed, and the trend toward empire endured.

From Asia to Latin America, economic and strategic needs and ideology motivated and justified expansion and empire. The belief that the United States needed foreign markets to absorb surplus production to save the domestic economy joined missionary zeal to reform other societies through the promotion of American products and culture. Notions of racial and male supremacy and appeals to national greatness also fed the appetite for foreign adventure and commitments. The greatly augmented navy became a primary means for satisfying American ideas and wants.

Revealing the great diversity of America's intersection with the world, missionaries such as Moon in China, generals such as Wood in Cuba, companies such as Singer in Africa and Heinz in Britain, and politicians such as Taft in the Philippines carried American ways, ideas, guns, and goods abroad to a mixed reception. The conspicuous declarations of Olney, Hay, Roosevelt, and other leaders became the guiding texts for U.S. principles and behavior in world affairs. A world power with far-flung interests to protect, the United States had to face a tough test of its self-proclaimed greatness and reconsider its political isolation from Europe when a world war broke out in August 1914.

LEGACY FOR A PEOPLE AND A NATION
The Status of Puerto Rico

Ever since the U.S. invasion of their island in July 1898 and their transfer under the Treaty of Paris from Spain to the United States, Puerto Ricans have debated their status, their very identity. Colony? territory? nation? state? or the "Commonwealth of Puerto Rico" that the U.S. Congress designated in 1952? A small Caribbean island with 3.8 million people (another 3.4 million Puerto Ricans live in the United States), Puerto Rico has held nonbinding plebiscites in 1967, 1993, and 1998, each time rejecting both statehood and independence in favor of commonwealth. In the 1998 referendum, 46.5 percent voted for statehood and 2.5 percent for independence. The U.S. Congress, which holds the constitutional authority to set the rules by which Puerto Ricans live, stands as sharply divided as the islanders, rejecting independent nationhood, unwilling to force statehood if Puerto Ricans do not want it, yet uneasy with the ambivalence that commonwealth status promotes.

Although a plurality of Puerto Ricans have narrowly endorsed commonwealth status, they remain troubled by their incomplete self-government. The island governs itself, and Puerto Ricans are U.S. citizens (made so by the Jones Act of 1916). They pay no federal income taxes, though they do contribute to Social Security, and they cannot elect representatives to Congress or vote in U.S. elections. Yet Puerto Ricans can make their presence felt in the halls of power in Washington. In 1999, many of them marched in protest against the U.S. Navy's decades-long use of one of Puerto Rico's islands, Vieques, as a bombing range. Two years later, after additional protests and a wave of press reports in the United States, President George W. Bush announced that the United States would vacate the military installation by May 2003.

The issue of cultural nationalism dominates the debate over Puerto Rico's political status. A majority of Puerto Ricans have rejected statehood because they fear it would mean giving up their Latin American culture and Spanish language. Most Puerto Ricans today, although bilingual, prefer Spanish over English, and many oppose the mandatory school courses in English. Commonwealthers warn that if Puerto Rico became a state, mainland conservatives might make English the official U.S. language. Puerto Rico's uncertain status persists as a legacy of the era of empire building. Then, as now, the issue centered on the rights of self-determination—in this case, the right of a people to sustain their own culture.

The *history companion* powered by Eduspace®

Your primary source for interactive quizzes, exercises, and more to help you learn efficiently.

http://history.college.hmco.com/students

ENLIST

AMERICANS IN THE GREAT WAR 1914–1920

*O*n May 7, 1915, Secretary of State William Jennings Bryan was having lunch with several cabinet members at the Shoreham Hotel in Washington when he received a bulletin: the luxurious British ocean liner *Lusitania* had been sunk, apparently by a German submarine. He rushed to his office, and at 3:06 P.M. came the confirmation from London: "THE LUSITANIA WAS TORPEDOED OFF THE IRISH COAST AND SANK IN HALF AN HOUR. NO NEWS YET OF PASSENGERS." In fact, 1,198 people had perished, including 128 Americans. The giant vessel had taken not half an hour to go down but just eighteen minutes. Bryan was deeply distraught, but not altogether surprised. The European powers were at war, and he had feared precisely this kind of calamity. Britain had imposed a naval blockade against Germany, and the Germans had responded by launching submarine warfare against Allied shipping. Berlin authorities had proclaimed the North Atlantic a danger zone, and German submarines had already sunk numerous British and Allied ships. As a passenger liner, the *Lusitania* was supposed to be spared, but German officials had placed notices in U.S. newspapers warning that Americans who traveled on British or Allied ships did so at their own risk; passenger liners suspected of carrying munitions or other contraband were subject to attack. For weeks Bryan had urged President Woodrow Wilson to stop Americans from booking passage on British ships; Wilson had refused.

That evening Bryan mused to his wife, "I wonder if that ship carried munitions of war. . . . If she did carry them, it puts a different phase on the whole matter! England has been using our citizens to protect her ammunition!" The *Lusitania*, it soon emerged, was carrying munitions, and Bryan set about urging a restrained U.S. response. Desperate to keep the United States out of the war, he urged Wilson to couple his condemnation of the German action with an equally tough note to Britain protesting its blockade and to ban Americans from

◀ This poster by Fred Spear, published in Boston not long after the *Lusitania* sinking, captured the anger Americans felt at the loss of 123 of their fellow citizens, among them women and children. Nearly two years before U.S. entry in the war, posters like this one urged Americans to enlist as preparation for the day when they must surely confront the German enemy. (Library of Congress)

CHRONOLOGY

1914 • First World War begins in Europe

1915 • Germans sink *Lusitania* off the coast of Ireland

1916 • After torpedoing the *Sussex,* Germany pledges not to attack merchant ships without warning
• National Defense Act expands military

1917 • Germany declares unrestricted submarine warfare
• Russian Revolution ousts the czar; Bolsheviks later take power
• United States enters the First World War
• Selective Service Act creates the draft
• Espionage Act limits First Amendment rights
• Race riot breaks out in East St. Louis, Illinois

1918 • Wilson announces Fourteen Points for new world order
• Sedition Act further limits free speech
• U.S. troops at Château-Thierry help blunt German offensive
• U.S. troops intervene in Russia against Bolsheviks
• Spanish flu pandemic kills 20 million worldwide
• Armistice ends the First World War

1919 • Paris Peace Conference punishes Germany and launches League of Nations
• May Day bombings help instigate Red Scare
• American Legion organizes for veterans' benefits and antiradicalism
• Wilson suffers stroke after speaking tour
• Senate rejects Treaty of Versailles and U.S. membership in League of Nations
• *Schenck v. U.S.* upholds Espionage Act

1920 • Palmer Raids round up suspected radicals

that he would not ban Americans from travel on belligerent ships, and that he intended to send a second protest note to Germany, Bryan resigned. Privately, Wilson called Bryan a traitor.

The division between the president and his secretary of state reflected divisions within the American populace over Europe's war. The split could be seen in the reaction to Bryan's resignation. Eastern newspapers charged him with "unspeakable treachery" and of stabbing the country in the back. In the Midwest and South, however, Bryan was accorded respect, and he won praise from pacifists and German American groups for his "act of courage." A few weeks later, speaking to a capacity crowd of fifteen thousand at Madison Square Garden (another fifty thousand tried to get in), Bryan was loudly applauded when he warned against "war with any of the belligerent nations." While many Americans felt, like President Wilson, that honor was more important than peace, others joined Bryan in thinking that some sacrifice of neutral rights was reasonable if the country could thereby stay out of the fighting. The debate would continue up until U.S. entry into the war in 1917, and the tensions would still ripple thereafter.

Like most Americans, Bryan had been stunned by the outbreak of the Great War (as it quickly became known) in 1914. For years the United States had participated in the international competition for colonies, markets, and weapons supremacy. But full-scale war seemed unthinkable. The new machine guns, howitzers, submarines, and dreadnoughts were such awesome death engines that leaders surely would not use them. When they did, lamented one social reformer, "civilization is all gone, and barbarism come."

For almost three years President Wilson kept America out of the war. During this time, he sought to protect U.S. trade interests and to improve the nation's military posture. He lectured the belligerents to rediscover their humanity and to respect international law. But American property, lives, and neutrality fell victim to British and German naval warfare. When, two years after the *Lusitania* went down, the president finally asked Congress for a declaration of war, he did so with his characteristic crusading zeal. America entered the battle not just to win the war but to reform the postwar world: to "make the world safe for democracy."

traveling on belligerent ships. Wilson hesitated. Others, including former president Theodore Roosevelt, called the sinking "an act of piracy" and pressed for war. Wilson did not want war, but neither did he accept Bryan's argument that the British and German violations should be treated the same. He sent a strong protest note to Berlin, calling on the German government to end its submarine warfare.

For the next several weeks, as Bryan continued to press his case, he sensed his growing isolation within the administration. When in early June Wilson made it clear

A year and a half later, the Great War would be over. It exacted a terrible cost on Europe, for a whole generation of young men was cut down—some 10 million soldiers perished. Europeans looked at their gigantic cemeteries and could scarcely believe what had happened. They experienced an acute spiritual loss in the destruction of ideals, confidence, and goodwill. Economically, too, the damage was immense. Most portentous of all for the future of the twentieth century, the Great War toppled four empires of the Old World—German, Austro-Hungarian, Russian, and Ottoman Turkish—and left two others, British and French, drastically weakened.

For the United States the human and material cost was comparatively small, yet Americans could rightly claim to have helped tip the scales in favor of the Allies with their infusion of war materiel and troops, as well as their extension of loans and food supplies. The war years also witnessed a massive international transfer of wealth from Europe across the Atlantic, as the United States went from being the world's largest debtor nation to its largest creditor nation. The conflict marked the coming of age of the United States as a world power. In these and other respects the Great War was a great triumph for Americans.

In other ways, though, World War I was a difficult, painful experience. It accentuated and intensified social divisions. Racial tensions accompanied the northward migration of southern blacks, and pacifists and German Americans were harassed. The federal government, eager to stimulate patriotism, trampled on civil liberties to silence critics. And following a communist revolution in Russia, a Red Scare in America repressed radicals and tarnished America's reputation as a democratic society. After the war, groups that sought to consolidate wartime gains vied with those who wanted to restore the prewar status quo. Although reformers continued to devote themselves to issues such as prohibition and woman suffrage, the war experience helped splinter the Progressive movement. Jane Addams sadly remarked that "the spirit of fighting burns away all those impulses . . . which foster the will to justice."

Abroad, Americans who had marched to battle as if on a crusade grew disillusioned with the peace process. They recoiled from the spectacle of the victors squabbling over the spoils, and they chided Wilson for failing to deliver the "peace without victory" he promised. As in the 1790s, the 1840s, and the 1890s, Americans once again engaged in a searching national debate about the fundamentals of their foreign policy. After negotiating the Treaty of Versailles at Paris following World War I, the president urged U.S. membership in the new League of Nations, which he promoted as a vehicle for reforming world politics. The Senate rejected his appeal (the League nonetheless organized without U.S. membership) because many Americans feared that the League might threaten the U.S. empire and entangle Americans in Europe's problems. ■

Precarious Neutrality

The war that erupted in August 1914 grew from years of European competition over trade, colonies, allies, and armaments. Two powerful alliance systems had formed: the Triple Alliance of Germany, Austria-Hungary, and Italy, and the Triple Entente of Britain, France, and Russia. All had imperial holdings and ambitions for more, but Germany seemed particularly bold as it rivaled Great Britain for world leadership. Many Americans saw Germany as a threat to U.S. interests in the Western Hemisphere and viewed Germans as an excessively militaristic people who embraced autocracy and spurned democracy.

Strategists said that Europe enjoyed a balance of power, but crises in the Balkan countries of southeastern

OUTBREAK OF THE FIRST WORLD WAR

Europe triggered a chain of events that shattered the "balance." Slavic nationalists sought to enlarge Serbia, an independent Slavic nation, by annexing regions such as Bosnia, then a province of the Austro-Hungarian Empire (see Map 23.1). On June 28, 1914, Archduke Franz Ferdinand, heir to the Austro-Hungarian throne, was assassinated by a Serbian nationalist while on a state visit to Sarajevo, the capital of Bosnia. Alarmed by the prospect of an engorged Serbia on its border, Austria-Hungary consulted its Triple Alliance partner Germany, which urged toughness. When Serbia called on its Slavic friend Russia for help, Russia in turn looked for backing from its ally France. In late July, Austria-Hungary declared war against Serbia. Russia then began to mobilize its armies.

Germany—having goaded Austria-Hungary toward war and believing war inevitable—struck first, declaring war against Russia on August 1 and against France two days later. Britain hesitated, but when German forces

Map 23.1   Europe Goes to War, Summer 1914

Bound by alliances and stirred by turmoil in the Balkans, where Serbs repeatedly upended peace, the nations of Europe descended into war in the summer of 1914. Step by step a Balkan crisis escalated into the "Great War."

slashed into neutral Belgium to get at France, London declared war against Germany on August 4. Eventually Turkey (the Ottoman Empire) joined Germany and Austria-Hungary as the Central Powers, and Italy (switching sides) and Japan teamed up with Britain, France, and Russia as the Allies. Japan took advantage of the European war to seize Shandong, Germany's sphere of influence in China.

President Wilson at first sought to distance America from the conflagration by issuing a proclamation of neutrality—the traditional U.S. policy toward European wars. He also asked Americans to refrain from taking sides, to exhibit "the dignity of self-control." In private, the president said, "We definitely have to be neutral, since otherwise our mixed populations would wage war on each other." The United States, he fervently hoped, would stand apart as a sane, civilized nation in a deranged international system.

Wilson's lofty appeal for American neutrality and unity at home collided with several realities between August 1914 and April 1917. First, ethnic groups in the

TAKING SIDES United States did take sides. Many German Americans and anti-British Irish Americans (Ireland was then trying to break free from British rule) cheered for the Central Powers. Americans of British and French ancestry and others with roots in Allied nations tended to champion the Allied cause. Germany's attack on Belgium confirmed in many people's minds that Germany had become the archetype of unbridled militarism.

The pro-Allied sympathies of Wilson's administration also weakened the U.S. neutrality proclamation. Honoring Anglo-American rapprochement (see page 617), Wilson shared the conviction with British leaders that a German victory would destroy free enterprise and government by law. If Germany won the war, he prophesied, "it would change the course of our civilization and make the United States a military nation." Several of Wilson's chief advisers and diplomats—his assistant Col. Edward House, ambassador to London Walter Hines Page, and Robert Lansing, a counselor in the State Department who later became secretary of state—held similar anti-German views that often translated into pro-Allied policies.

U.S. economic links with the Allies also rendered neutrality difficult, if not impossible. England had long been one of the nation's best customers. Now the British flooded America with new orders, especially for arms. Sales to the Allies helped pull the American economy out of its recession. Between 1914 and 1916, American exports to England and France grew 365 percent, from $753 million to $2.75 billion. In the same period, however, largely because of Britain's naval blockade, exports to Germany dropped by more than 90 percent, from $345 million to only $29 million. Loans to Britain and France from private American banks—totaling $2.3 billion during the neutrality period—financed much of U.S. trade with the Allies. Germany received only $27 million in the same period. The Wilson administration, which at first frowned on these transactions, came to see them as necessary to the economic health of the United States.

From Germany's perspective, the linkage between the American economy and the Allies meant that the United States had become the Allied arsenal and bank. Americans, however, faced a dilemma: cutting their economic ties with Britain would constitute an unneutral act in favor of Germany. Under international law, Britain—which controlled the seas—could buy both contraband (war-related goods) and noncontraband from neutrals. It was Germany's responsibility, not America's, to stop such trade in ways that international law prescribed—

that is, by an effective blockade of the enemy's territory, by the seizure of contraband from neutral (American) ships, or by the confiscation of goods from belligerent (British) ships. Germans, of course, judged the huge U.S. trade with the Allies an act of unneutrality that had to be stopped.

The president and his aides believed, finally, that Wilsonian principles stood a better chance of international acceptance if Britain, rather than the Central Powers, sat astride the postwar world. "Wilsonianism," the cluster of ideas Wilson espoused, consisted of traditional American principles (such as democracy and the Open Door) and a conviction that the United States was a beacon of freedom to the world. Only the United States could lead the convulsed world into a new, peaceful era of unobstructed commerce, free-market capitalism, democratic politics, and open diplomacy. American Progressivism, it seemed, was to be projected onto the world.

WILSONIANISM

"America had the infinite privilege of fulfilling her destiny and saving the world," Wilson claimed. Empires had to be dismantled to honor the principle of self-determination. Armaments had to be reduced. Critics charged that Wilson often violated his own credos in his eagerness to force them on others—as his military interventions in Mexico in 1914, Haiti in 1915, and the Dominican Republic in 1916 testified. All agreed, though, that such ideals served American commercial purposes; in this way idealism and self-interest were married.

To say that American neutrality was never a real possibility given ethnic loyalties, economic ties, and Wilsonian preferences is not to say that Wilson sought to enter the war. He emphatically wanted to keep the United States out. Time and again, he tried to mediate the crisis to prevent one power from crushing another. In early 1917, the president remarked that "we are the only one of the great white nations that is free from war today, and it would be a crime against civilization for us to go in." But go in the United States finally did. Why?

The short answer is that Americans got caught in the Allied–Central Power crossfire. British naval policy aimed to sever neutral trade with Germany in order to cripple the German economy. The British, "ruling the waves and waiving the rules," declared a blockade of water entrances to Germany and mined the North Sea. They also harassed neutral shipping by seizing cargoes and defining a broad list of contraband (including foodstuffs) that they prohibited neutrals from shipping to Germany. American commerce with Germany dwindled rapidly. Furthermore, to counter German submarines,

VIOLATIONS OF NEUTRAL RIGHTS

Initially underestimated as a weapon, the German U-boat proved to be frighteningly effective against Allied ships. At the beginning of the war, Germany had about twenty operational submarines in its High Seas Fleet, but officials moved swiftly to speed up production. This photograph shows a German U-boat under construction in 1914. (Bibliothek fur Zeitgeschichte, Stuttgart)

the British flouted international law by arming their merchant ships and flying neutral (sometimes American) flags. Wilson frequently protested British violations of neutral rights, pointing out that neutrals had the right to sell and ship noncontraband goods to belligerents without interference. But London often deftly defused Washington's criticism by paying for confiscated cargoes, and German provocations made British behavior appear less offensive by comparison.

Unable to win the war on land and determined to lift the blockade and halt American-Allied commerce, Germany looked for victory at sea by using submarines. In February 1915 Berlin declared a war zone around the British Isles, warned neutral vessels to stay out so as not to be attacked by mistake, and advised passengers from neutral nations to stay off Allied ships. President Wilson informed Germany that the United States would hold it to "strict accountability" for any losses of American life and property.

Wilson was interpreting international law in the strictest possible sense. The law that an attacker had to warn a passenger or merchant ship before attacking, so that passengers and crew could disembark safely into lifeboats, predated the submarine. The Germans thought the slender, frail, and sluggish *Unterseebooten* (U-boats) should not be expected to surface to warn ships, for surfacing would cancel out the U-boats' advantage of surprise and leave them vulnerable to attack. Berlin protested that Wilson was denying it the one weapon that could break the British economic stranglehold, disrupt the Allies' substantial connection with U.S. producers and bankers, and win the war. To all concerned—British, Germans, and Americans—naval warfare became a matter of life and death.

The Decision for War

*U*ltimately, it was the war at sea that doomed the prospect of U.S. neutrality. In the early months of 1915 German U-boats sank ship after ship, most notably the British liner *Lusitania* on May 7. In mid-August, after a lull following Germany's promise to refrain from attacking passenger liners, another British vessel, the *Arabic*, was sunk off Ireland. Three Americans died. The Germans quickly pledged that an unarmed passenger ship would never again be attacked without warning. But the sinking of the *Arabic* fueled debate over American passengers on belligerent vessels. Why not require Americans to sail on American craft? asked critics, echoing Bryan's plea from the previous spring (see the chapter-opening vignette). From August 1914 to March 1917, after all, only 3 Americans died on an American ship (the tanker *Gulflight,* sunk by a German U-boat in May 1915), whereas about 190 were killed on belligerent ships.

In March 1916 a U-boat attack on the *Sussex,* a French vessel crossing the English Channel, took the United States a step closer to war. Four Americans were injured on that ship, which the U-boat commander mistook for a minelayer. Stop the marauding submarines, Wilson lectured Berlin, or the United States will sever diplomatic relations. Again the Germans retreated, pledging not to attack merchant vessels without warning. At about the same time, U.S. relations with Britain soured. The British crushing of the Easter Rebellion in Ireland and further British restriction of U.S. trade with the Central Powers aroused American anger.

As the United States became more entangled in the Great War, many Americans urged Wilson to keep the

PEACE ADVOCATES

nation out. In early 1915, Jane Addams, Carrie Chapman Catt, and other suffragists helped found the Woman's Peace Party, the U.S. section of the Women's International League for Peace and Freedom. "The mother half of humanity," claimed women peace advocates, had a special role as "the guardians of life." Later that same year, some pacifist Progressives—including Oswald Garrison Villard, Paul Kellogg, and Lillian Wald—organized an antiwar coalition, the American Union Against Militarism. The businessman Andrew Carnegie, who in 1910 had established the Carnegie Endowment for International Peace, helped finance peace groups. So did Henry Ford, who in late 1915 sent a "peace ship" to Europe to propagandize for a negotiated settlement. Socialists such as Eugene Debs added their voices to the peace movement.

Antiwar advocates emphasized several points: that war drained a nation of its youth, resources, and reform impulse; that it fostered repression at home; that it violated Christian morality; and that wartime business barons reaped huge profits at the expense of the people. Militarism and conscription, Addams pointed out, were what millions of immigrants had left behind in Europe. Were they now—in the United States—to be forced into the decadent system they had escaped? Although the peace movement was splintered—some wanted to keep the United States out of the conflict but did not endorse the pacifists' claim that intervention could never be justi-

fied—it carried political and intellectual weight that Wilson could not ignore, and it articulated several ideas that he shared. In fact, he campaigned on a peace platform in the 1916 presidential election. After his triumph, Wilson futilely labored once again to bring the belligerents to the conference table. In early 1917 he advised them to temper their acquisitive war aims, appealing for "peace without victory."

In Germany, Wilson's overture went unheeded. Since August 1916, leaders in Berlin had debated whether to

UNRESTRICTED SUBMARINE WARFARE

resume the unrestricted U-boat campaign. Opponents feared a break with the United States, but proponents claimed there was no choice. Only through an all-out attack on Britain's supply shipping, they argued, could Germany win the war before the British blockade and trench warfare in France had exhausted Germany's ability to keep fighting. If the U-boats could sink 600,000 tons of Allied shipping per month, the German admiralty estimated, Britain would be brought to the brink of starvation. True, the United States might enter the war, but that was a risk worth taking. Victory might be achieved before U.S. troops could be ferried across the Atlantic in sizable numbers. It proved a winning argument. In early February 1917, Germany launched unrestricted submarine warfare. All warships and merchant vessels—belligerent or neutral—would be attacked if sighted in the declared war zone. Wilson quickly broke diplomatic relations with Berlin.

This German challenge to American neutral rights and economic interests was soon followed by a German threat to U.S. security. In late February, British intelligence intercepted and passed to U.S. officials a telegram addressed to the German minister in Mexico from German foreign secretary Arthur Zimmermann. Its message: If Mexico joined a military alliance against the United States, Germany would help Mexico recover the territories it had lost in 1848, including several western states. Zimmermann hoped to "set new enemies on America's neck—enemies which give them plenty to take care of over there."

The Zimmermann telegram stiffened Wilson's resolve. Even though Mexico City rejected Germany's offer, the Wilson administration judged Zimmermann's telegram "a conspiracy against this country." Mexico still might let German agents use Mexican soil to propagandize against the United States, if not sabotage American properties. The prospect of a German-Mexican collaboration helped turn the tide of opinion in the American Southwest, where antiwar sentiment had been strong.

WAR MESSAGE
AND WAR
DECLARATION
"warfare against mankind." Passionately and eloquently, Wilson enumerated U.S. grievances: Germany's violation of freedom of the seas, disruption of commerce, interference with Mexico, and breach of human rights by killing innocent Americans. The "Prussian autocracy" had to be punished by "the democracies." Russia was now among the latter, he was pleased to report, because the Russian Revolution had ousted the czar just weeks before. Congress declared war against Germany on April 6 by a vote of 373 to 50 in the House and 82 to 6 in the Senate. (This vote was for war against Germany only; a declaration of war against Austria-Hungary came several months later, on December 7.) Montana's Jeannette Rankin, the first woman ever to sit in Congress, cast a ringing "no" vote. "Peace is a woman's job," she declared, "because men have a natural fear of being classed as cowards if they oppose war" and because mothers should protect their children from death-dealing weapons.

For principle, for morality, for honor, for commerce, for security, for reform—for all of these reasons, Wilson took the United States into the Great War. The submarine was certainly the culprit that drew a reluctant president and nation into the maelstrom. Yet critics did not attribute the U.S. descent into war to the U-boat alone. They emphasized Wilson's rigid definition of international law, which did not accommodate the submarine's tactics. They faulted his contention that Americans should be entitled to travel anywhere, even on a belligerent ship loaded with contraband. They criticized his policies as unneutral. But they lost the debate. Most Americans came to accept Wilson's view that the Germans had to be checked to ensure an open, orderly world in which U.S. principles and interests would be safe.

America went to war to reform world politics, not to destroy Germany. Wilson once claimed that the United States was "pure air blowing in world politics, destroying illusions and cleaning places of morbid miasmic gasses." By early 1917 the president concluded that America would not be able to claim a seat at the postwar peace conference unless it became a combatant. At the peace conference, Wilson intended to promote the principles he thought essential to a stable world order, to advance democracy and the Open Door, and to outlaw revolution and aggression. Wilson tried to preserve part of his country's status as a neutral by designating the United States an "Associated" power rather than a full-fledged Allied nation, but this was akin to a hope of being only partly pregnant.

■ Jeannette Rankin (1880–1973) of Montana was the first woman to sit in the House of Representatives (elected in 1916) and the only member of Congress to vote against U.S. entry into both world wars (in 1917 and 1941). A lifelong pacifist, she led a march in Washington, D.C.—at age eighty-seven—against U.S. participation in the Vietnam War. (Brown Brothers)

Soon afterward, Wilson asked Congress for "armed neutrality" to defend American lives and commerce. He requested authority to arm American merchant ships and to "employ any other instrumentalities or methods that may be necessary." In the midst of the debate, Wilson released Zimmermann's telegram to the press. Americans were outraged. Still, antiwar senators Robert M. La Follette and George Norris, among others, saw the armed-ship bill as a blank check for the president to move the country to war, and they filibustered it to death. Wilson proceeded to arm America's commercial vessels anyway. The action came too late to prevent the sinking of several American ships. War cries echoed across the nation. In late March, an agonized Wilson called Congress into special session.

On April 2, 1917, the president stepped before a hushed Congress. Solemnly he accused the Germans of

Winning the War

Even before the U.S. declaration of war, the Wilson administration—encouraged by such groups as the National Security League and the Navy League and by mounting public outrage against Germany's submarine warfare—had been strengthening the military under the banner of "preparedness." When the pacifist song "I Didn't Raise My Boy to Be a Soldier" became popular, preparedness proponents retorted, "I Didn't Raise My Boy to Be a Coward." The National Defense Act of 1916 provided for increases in the army and National Guard and for summer training camps modeled on the one in Plattsburgh, New York, where a slice of America's social and economic elite had trained in 1915 as "citizen soldiers." The Navy Act of 1916 started the largest naval expansion in American history.

To raise an army after the declaration of war, Congress in May 1917 passed the Selective Service Act,

THE DRAFT AND THE SOLDIER

requiring all males between the ages of twenty-one and thirty (later changed to eighteen and forty-five) to register. National service, proponents believed, would not only prepare the nation for battle but instill patriotism and respect for order, democracy, and personal sacrifice. Critics feared it would lead to the militarization of American life.

On June 5, 1917, more than 9.5 million men signed up for the "great national lottery." By war's end, 24 million men had been registered by local draft boards. Of this number, 4.8 million had served in the armed forces, 2 million of that number in France. Among them were hundreds of thousands who had volunteered before December 1917, when the government prohibited enlistment because the military judged voluntarism too inefficient (many volunteers were more useful in civilian factories than in the army) and too competitive (enlistees got to choose the service they wanted, thus setting off recruiting wars). Millions of laborers received deferments from military duty because they worked in war industries or had dependents.

The typical soldier was a draftee in his early to mid-twenties, white, single, American-born, and poorly educated (most had not attended high school, and perhaps 30 percent could not read or write). Tens of thousands of women enlisted in the army Nurse Corps, served as "hello girls" (volunteer bilingual telephone operators) in the army Signal Corps, and became clerks in the navy and Marine Corps On college campuses; 150,000 students joined the Student Army Training Corps or similar navy and marine units. At officer training camps, the army turned out "ninety-day wonders."

Some 400,000 African Americans also served in the military. Although many southern politicians feared arming African Americans, the army drafted them into segregated units, where they were assigned to menial labor and endured crude abuse and miserable conditions. Ultimately more than 42,000 blacks would see combat in Europe, however, and several black units served with distinction in various divisions of the French army. The all-black 369th Infantry Regiment, for example, spent more time in the trenches—191 days—and received more medals than any other American outfit. The French government awarded the entire regiment the Croix de Guerre.

■ Some 15,000 Native Americans served in the military in World War I. Most of them were enlistees who sought escape from restrictive Indian schools and lives of poverty, opportunities to develop new skills, and chances to prove their patriotism. This photo shows Fast Fred Horse, a Rosebud Sioux, as he recuperates in a New York hospital after suffering injury and paralysis during the Meuse-Argonne campaign of fall 1918. Unlike African Americans, Native Americans were not assigned to segregated units during the war. Native Americans participated in all major battles against German forces and suffered a high casualty rate in large part because they served as scouts, messengers, and snipers.   (William Hammond Mathers Museum, Indiana University)

Though French officers had their share of racial prejudice and often treated the soldiers from their own African colonies poorly, black Americans serving with the French reported a degree of respect and cooperation generally lacking in the American army. They also spoke of getting a much warmer reception from French civilians than they were used to in the United States. The irony was not lost on African American leaders such as W. E. B. Du Bois, who had endorsed the support of the National Association for the Advancement of Colored People (NAACP) for the war and echoed its call for blacks to volunteer for the fight so they might help make the world safe for democracy and help blur the color lines at home.

Not everyone eligible for military service was eager to sign up, however. Approximately 3 million men evaded draft registration. Some were arrested, and others fled to Mexico or Canada, but most stayed at home and were never discovered. Another 338,000 men who had registered and been summoned by their draft boards failed to show up for induction. According to arrest records, most of these "deserters" and the more numerous "evaders" were lower-income agricultural and industrial laborers. Some simply felt overwhelmed by the government bu-

reaucracy and stayed away; others were members of minority or ethnic groups who felt alienated. Although nearly 65,000 draftees initially applied for conscientious-objector status (refusing to bear arms for religious or pacifistic reasons), some changed their minds or, like so many others, failed preinduction examinations. Quakers and Mennonites were numerous among the 4,000 inductees actually classified as conscientious objectors (COs). They did not have it easy. General Leonard Wood called COs "enemies of the Republic," and the military harassed them. COs who refused noncombat service, such as in the medical corps, faced imprisonment.

The U.S. troops who shipped out to France would do their fighting under American command. General

TRENCH WARFARE

John J. Pershing, head of the American Expeditionary Forces (AEF), insisted that his "sturdy rookies" remain a separate, independent army. He was not about to turn over his "doughboys" (so termed, apparently, because the large buttons on American uniforms in the 1860s resembled a deep-fried bread of that name) to Allied commanders, who had become wedded to unimaginative and deadly trench warfare, producing a military stalemate and ghastly casualties on the western

A U.S. soldier of Company K, 110th Infantry Regiment, receives aid during fighting at Verennes, France. (National Archives)

front. Since the fall of 1914, zigzag trenches fronted by barbed wire and mines stretched across France. Between the muddy, stinking trenches lay "no man's land," denuded by artillery fire. When ordered out, soldiers would charge enemy trenches. If machine-gun fire did not greet them, poison gas might.

First used by the Germans in April 1915, chlorine gas stimulated overproduction of fluid in the lungs, leading to death by drowning. One British officer tending to troops who had been gassed reported that "quite 200 men passed through my hands. . . . Some died with me, others on the way down. . . . I had to argue with many of them as to whether they were dead or not." Gas in a variety of forms (mustard and phosgene, in addition to chlorine) would continue in use throughout the war, sometimes blistering, sometimes incapacitating, often killing.

The extent of the dying in the trench warfare is hard to comprehend. At the Battle of the Somme in 1916, the British and French suffered 600,000 dead or wounded to earn only 125 square miles; the Germans lost 400,000 men. At Verdun that same year, 336,000 Germans perished, while at Passchendaele in 1917 more than 370,000 British men died to gain about 40 miles of mud and barbed wire. Ambassador Page grew sickened by what Europe had become—"a bankrupt slaughter-house inhabited by unmated women."

The first American units landed in France on June 26, 1917, marched in a Fourth of July parade in Paris, and then moved by train toward the *SHELL SHOCK* front. They soon learned about the horrors caused by advanced weaponry. Some suffered shell shock, a form of mental illness also known as war psychosis. Symptoms included a fixed empty stare, violent tremors, paralyzed limbs, listlessness, jabbering, screaming, and haunting dreams. The illness could strike anyone; even those soldiers who appeared most manly and courageous cracked after days of incessant shelling and inescapable human carnage. "There was a limit to human endurance," one lieutenant explained. Providing some relief were Red Cross canteens, staffed by women volunteers, which gave soldiers way stations in a strange land and offered haircuts, food, and recreation. Some ten thousand Red Cross nurses also cared for the young warriors, while the American Library Association distributed 10 million books and magazines.

In Paris, where forty large houses of prostitution thrived, it became commonplace to hear that the British were drunkards, the French were whoremongers, and the *AMERICAN UNITS IN FRANCE* Americans were both. Venereal disease became a serious problem. French prime minister Georges Clemenceau offered licensed, inspected prostitutes

■ During the First World War, the War Department promoted a film to combat sexually transmitted diseases. After the war, the New York State Board of Censors declared the film obscene. (Social Welfare History Archives Center, University of Minnesota)

in "special houses" to the American army. When the generous Gallic offer reached Washington, Secretary of War Newton Baker gasped, "For God's sake . . . don't show this to the President or he'll stop the war." By war's end, about 15 percent of America's soldiers had contracted venereal disease, costing the army $50 million and 7 million days of active duty. Periodic inspections, chemical prophylactic treatments, and the threat of court-martial for infected soldiers kept the problem from being even greater.

The experience of being in Europe enlarged what for many American draftees had been a circumscribed world. Soldiers filled their diaries and letters with descriptions of the local customs and "ancient" architecture and noted how the grimy and war-torn French countryside bore little resemblance to the groomed landscapes they had seen before in paintings. Some mixed admiration for the spirit of endurance they saw in the populace with irritation that the locals were not more grateful for the Americans' arrival. "Life in France for the American soldier meant marching in the dirt and mud, living in cellars in filth, being wet and cold and fighting," the chief of staff of the Fourth Division remarked. "He had come to help France in the hour of distress and he was glad he came but these French people did not seem to appreciate him at all."

The influx of American men and materiel—and the morale blow they delivered to the Central Powers—decided the outcome of the First World War. With both sides virtually exhausted, the Americans tipped the balance toward the Allies. It took time, though, for the weight of the American military machine to make itself felt. From an early point, the U.S. Navy battled submarines and escorted troop carriers, and pilots in the U.S. Air Service, flying mostly British and French aircraft, saw limited action, mostly against German ground troops and transport. American "aces" such as Eddie Rickenbacker took on their German counterparts in aerial "dogfights" and became heroes, as much in France as in their own country. But only ground troops could make a decisive difference, and American units actually did not engage in much combat until after the lull in the fighting during the harsh winter of 1917–1918.

By then, the military and diplomatic situation had changed dramatically, because of an event that was arguably the most important political

THE BOLSHEVIK REVOLUTION

development of the twentieth century: the Bolshevik Revolution in Russia. In November 1917, the liberal-democratic government of Aleksander Kerensky, which had led the country since the czar's abdication early in the year, was overthrown by radical socialists led by V. I. Lenin. Lenin seized power vowing to change world politics and end imperial rivalries on terms that challenged Woodrow Wilson's. Lenin saw the war as signaling the impending end of capitalism and looked for a global revolution, carried out by workers, that would sweep away the "imperialist order." For Western leaders, the prospect of Bolshevik-style revolutions spreading worldwide was too frightening to contemplate. The ascendancy of the world's laboring classes working in unity would destroy governments everywhere.

In the weeks following their takeover, the Bolsheviks attempted to embarrass the capitalist governments and incite world revolution by publishing several secret agreements among the Allies for dividing up the colonies and other territories of the Central Powers in the event of an Allied victory. Veteran watchers of world affairs found nothing particularly shocking in the documents, and Wilson had known of them, but the disclosures belied the noble rhetoric of Allied war aims. Wilson confided to Colonel House that he really wanted to tell the Bolsheviks to "go to hell," but he accepted the colonel's argument that he would have to address Lenin's claims that there was little to distinguish the two warring sides and that socialism represented the future.

The result was the Fourteen Points, unveiled in January 1918, in which Wilson reaffirmed America's commit-

FOURTEEN POINTS

ment to an international system governed by laws and renounced territorial gains as a legitimate war aim. The first five points called for diplomacy "in the public view," freedom of the seas, lower tariffs, reductions in armaments, and the decolonization of empires. The next eight points specified the evacuation of foreign troops from Russia, Belgium, and France and appealed for self-determination for nationalities in Europe, such as the Poles. For Wilson, the fourteenth point was the most important—the mechanism for achieving all the others: "a general association of nations," or League of Nations.

Wilson's appeal did not impress Lenin, who called for an immediate end to the fighting, the eradication of colonialism, and self-determination for all peoples. Lenin also made a separate peace with Germany—the Treaty of Brest-Litovsk, signed on March 3, 1918. The deal erased centuries of Russian expansion, as Poland, Finland, and the Baltic states were taken from Russia and Ukraine was granted independence. One of Lenin's motives was to allow Russian troops loyal to the Bolsheviks to return home to fight anti-Bolshevik forces, who had launched a civil war to oust the new government.

In March 1918, with German troops released from the Russian front and transferred to France, the Germans

AMERICANS IN BATTLE

launched a major offensive. By May they had pushed to within 50 miles of Paris. Late that month, troops of the U.S. First Division helped blunt the German advance at Cantigny (see Map 23.2). In June the Third Division and French forces held positions along the Marne River at Château-Thierry, and the Second Division soon attacked the Germans in the Belleau Wood. American soldiers won the battle after three weeks of fighting, but thousands died or were wounded after they made almost sacrificial frontal assaults against German machine guns.

Allied victory in the Second Battle of the Marne in July 1918 stemmed all German advances. In September, French and American forces took St. Mihiel in a ferocious battle in which American gunners fired 100,000 rounds of phosgene gas shells. Then the Allies began their massive Meuse-Argonne offensive. More than 1 million Americans joined British and French troops in weeks of fierce combat; some 26,000 Americans died be-

fore the Allies claimed the Argonne Forest on October 10. For Germany—its ground and submarine war stymied, its troops and cities mutinous, its allies Turkey and Austria dropping out, its Kaiser abdicated, and facing the prospect of endless American troop reinforcements—peace became imperative. The Germans accepted a punishing armistice that took effect on the morning of November 11, 1918, at the eleventh hour of the eleventh day of the eleventh month.

The cost of the war is impossible to compute, but the scale is clear enough: the belligerents counted 10 million soldiers and 6.6 million civilians dead and 21.3 million people wounded. Fifty-three thousand American soldiers died in battle, and another 62,000 died from disease. Many of the latter died from the virulent strain of influenza that ravaged the world in late 1918 and would ultimately claim more victims than the Great War itself. The economic damage was colossal as well, helping to

CASUALTIES

Map 23.2

American Troops at the Western Front, 1918
America's 2 million troops in France met German forces head-on, ensuring the defeat of the Central Powers in 1918.

The Influenza Pandemic of 1918

In the summer and fall of 1918, as World War I neared its end, a terrible plague swept the earth. It was a massive outbreak of influenza, and it would kill more than twice as many as the Great War itself—somewhere between 25 and 40 million people. In the United States, 675,000 people died.

The first cases were identified in midwestern military camps in early March. Soldiers complained of flulike symptoms—headache, sore throat, fever—and many did not recover. At Fort Riley, Kansas, 48 men died. But with the war effort in full swing, few in government or the press took notice. Soldiers shipped out to Europe in large numbers (84,000 in March), some unknowingly carrying the virus in their lungs. The illness appeared on the western front in April. By the end of June, an estimated 8 million Spaniards were infected, thereby giving the disease its name, the Spanish flu.

In August, after a midsummer lull, a second, deadlier form of the influenza began spreading. This time, the epidemic erupted simultaneously in three cities on three continents: Freetown, Sierra Leone, in Africa; Brest, France, the port of entry for many American soldiers; and Boston, Massachusetts. In September, the disease swept down the East Coast to New York, Philadelphia, and beyond. That month, 12,000 Americans died.

It was a flu like no other. People could be healthy at the start of the weekend and dead by the end of it. Some experienced a rapid accumulation of fluid in the lungs and would quite literally drown. Others died more slowly, of secondary infections with bacterial pneumonia. Mortality rates were highest for twenty- to twenty-nine-year-olds—the same group dying in huge numbers in the trenches.

In October, the epidemic hit full force. It spread to Japan, India, Africa, and Latin America. In the United States, 200,000 perished. There was a nationwide shortage of caskets and gravediggers. Stores were forbidden to hold sales, and funerals were limited to fifteen minutes. Schools and cinemas closed. Bodies were left in gutters or on front porches, to be picked up by trucks that drove the streets. Army surgeon general Victor Vaughan made a frightening calculation: "If the epidemic continues its mathematical rate of acceleration, civilization could easily disappear from the face of the earth within a few weeks."

Then, suddenly, in November, for reasons still unclear, the epidemic eased, though the dying continued into 1919.

In England and Wales, the final toll was 200,000. Samoa lost a quarter of its population, while in India, the epidemic may have claimed a staggering 20 million. It was, in historian Roy Porter's words, "the greatest single demographic shock mankind has ever experienced."

World War I had helped spread the disease, but so had technological improvements that in previous decades facilitated global travel. The world was a smaller, more intimate place, often for good but sometimes for ill. Americans, accustomed to thinking that two great oceans could isolate them, were reminded that they were immutably linked to humankind.

A nurse at a special camp for influenza victims on the grounds of Corey Hill Hospital in Brookline, Massachusetts, September 1918. The gauze mask she and countless others wore that autumn proved to be useless—the microbe could pass right through. (© Underwood & Underwood/Corbis)

account for the widespread starvation Europe experienced in the winter of 1918–1919. Economic output on the continent dwindled, and transport over any distance was in some countries virtually nonexistent. "We are at the dead season of our fortunes," wrote one British observer. "Never in the lifetime of men now living has the universal element in the soul of man burnt so dimly."

The German, Austro-Hungarian, Ottoman, and Russian empires were no more, themselves casualties of the conflagration. For a time it appeared the Bolshevik Revolution might spread westward, as communist uprisings shook Germany and parts of central Europe. Even before the armistice, revolutionaries temporarily took power in the German cities of Bremen, Hamburg, and Lübeck. In Hungary, a government actually held power for several months, while Austria was racked by left-wing demonstrations. In Moscow, meanwhile, the new Soviet state sought to consolidate its power. "We are sitting upon an open powder magazine," Colonel House worried, "and some day a spark may ignite it."

Mobilizing the Home Front

"It is not an army that we must shape and train for war," declared President Wilson, "it is a nation." The United States was a belligerent for only nineteen months, but the war had a tremendous impact at home. The federal government moved swiftly to expand its power over the economy to meet war needs and intervened in American life as never before. The vastly enlarged Washington bureaucracy managed the economy, labor force, military, public opinion, and more. Federal expenditures increased tremendously as the government spent more than $760 million a month from April 1917 to August 1919. As tax revenues lagged behind, the administration resorted to deficit spending (see Figure 23.1). The total cost of the war was difficult to calculate, since future generations would have to pay veterans' benefits and interest on loans. To Progressives of the New Nationalist persuasion (see page 589), the wartime expansion and centralization of government power were welcome. To others, these changes seemed excessive, leading to concentrated, hence dangerous, federal power.

The federal government and private business became partners during the war. So-called dollar-a-year executives flocked to the nation's capital from major companies, retaining their corporate salaries while serving in official administrative and consulting capaci-

BUSINESS-
GOVERNMENT
COOPERATION

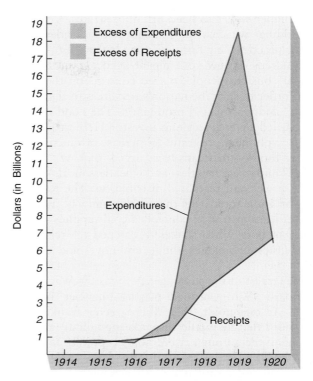

Figure 23.1   The Federal Budget, 1914–1920

During the First World War, the federal government spent more money than it received from increased taxes. It borrowed from banks or sold bonds through Liberty Loan drives. To meet the mounting costs of the war, in other words, the federal government had to resort to deficit spending. Expenditures topped receipts by more than $13 billion in 1919. Given this wartime fiscal pattern, moreover, the U.S. federal debt rose from $1 billion in 1914 to $25 billion in 1919.   (Source: U.S. Department of Commerce, *Historical Statistics of the United States: Colonial Times to 1957* [Washington, D.C., Bureau of the Census, 1960], p. 711.)

ties. Early in the war, the government relied on several industrial committees for advice on purchases and prices. But evidence of self-interested businesspeople cashing in on the national interest aroused public protest. The head of the aluminum advisory committee, for example, was also president of the largest aluminum company. The assorted committees were disbanded in July 1917 in favor of a single manager, the War Industries Board. But the federal government continued to work closely with business through trade associations, which grew significantly to two thousand by 1920. The government also suspended antitrust laws and signed cost-plus contracts, which guaranteed companies a healthy profit and a means to pay higher wages to head off labor strikes. Competitive bidding was virtually abandoned. Under such wartime practices, big business grew bigger.

Hundreds of new government agencies, staffed primarily by businesspeople, placed controls on the economy in order to shift the nation's resources to the Allies, the AEF, and war-related production. The Food Administration, led by engineer and investor Herbert Hoover, launched voluntary programs to increase production and conserve food—Americans were urged to grow "victory gardens" and to eat meatless and wheatless meals—but it also set prices and regulated distribution. The Railroad Administration took over the snarled railway industry. The Fuel Administration controlled coal supplies and rationed gasoline. When strikes threatened the telephone and telegraph companies, the federal government seized and ran them.

The largest of the superagencies was the War Industries Board (WIB), headed by the financier Bernard Baruch. At one point, this Wall Streeter frankly told Henry Ford that he would dispatch the military to seize his plants if the automaker did not accept WIB limits on car production. Ford relented. Although the WIB seemed all-powerful, in reality it had to conciliate competing interest groups and compromise with the business executives whose advice it so valued. Designed as a clearinghouse to coordinate the national economy, the WIB made purchases, allocated supplies, and fixed prices at levels that business requested. The WIB also ordered the standardization of goods to save materials and streamline production. The varieties of automobile tires, for example, were reduced from 287 to 3.

The performance of the mobilized economy was mixed, but it delivered enough men and materiel to France to ensure the defeat of the Central Powers. About a quarter of all American production was diverted to war needs. As farmers enjoyed boom years of higher prices, they put more acreage into production and mechanized as never before. From 1915 to 1920 the number of tractors in American fields jumped tenfold. Gross farm income for the period from 1914 to 1919 increased more than 230 percent. Although manufacturing output leveled off in 1918, some industries realized substantial growth because of wartime demand. Steel reached a peak production of 45 million tons in 1917, twice the prewar figure. As U.S. soldiers popularized American brands in Europe, tobacconists profited from a huge increase in cigarette sales: from 26 billion cigarettes in 1916 to 48 billion in 1918. Overall, the

ECONOMIC PERFORMANCE

■ During the First World War, the United States Fuel Administration promoted economic mobilization at home in this poster printed in several languages.   (National Park Service Collection, Ellis Island Immigration Museum. Photo Chermayeff and Geismar MetaForm)

gross national product in 1920 stood 237 percent higher than in 1914.

The rush to complete massive assignments caused mistakes to be made. Weapons deliveries fell short of demand; the bloated bureaucracy of the War Shipping Board failed to build enough ships. In the severe winter of 1917–1918, millions of Americans could not get coal. Coal companies held back on production to raise prices; railroads did not have enough coal cars; and harbors froze, closing out coal barges. In January, blizzards shut down midwestern railroads and factories, impeding the war effort. People died from pneumonia and freezing. A Brooklyn man went out in the morning to forage for coal and returned to find his two-month-old daughter frozen to death in her crib.

To help pay its bills during the war, the government dramatically increased tax rates. The Revenue Act in 1916 started the process by raising the surtax on high incomes and corporate profits, imposing a federal tax on large estates, and significantly increasing the tax on munitions manufacturers. Still, the government financed only one-third of the war through taxes. The other two-thirds came from loans, including Liberty bonds sold to the American people through aggressive campaigns. The War Revenue Act of 1917 provided for a more steeply graduated personal income tax, a corporate income tax, an excess-profits tax, and increased excise taxes on alcoholic beverages, tobacco, and luxury items.

Although these taxes did curb excessive corporate profiteering, several loopholes tempted the unscrupulous. Sometimes companies inflated costs to conceal profits or paid high salaries and bonuses to their executives. Four officers of Bethlehem Steel, for example, divided bonuses of $2.3 million in 1917 and $2.1 million the next year. Corporate net earnings for 1913 totaled $4 billion; in 1917 they reached $7 billion; and in 1918, after the tax bite and the war's end, they still stood at $4.5 billion. Profits and patriotism went hand in hand in America's war experience. The abrupt cancellation of billions of dollars' worth of contracts at the end of the war, however, caused a brief economic downturn, a short boom, and then an intense decline (see Chapter 24).

For American workers, the full-employment wartime economy brought undoubted benefits. It increased their total earnings and gave many of them time-and-a-half pay for overtime work. Given the higher cost of living, however, workers saw minimal improvement in their economic standing. Turnover rates were high as workers switched jobs for higher pay and better conditions. Sometimes employers practiced "scamping," the pirating of laborers from other companies. Some employers sought to overcome labor shortages by expanding welfare and social programs and by establishing personnel departments—"specialized human nature engineers to keep its human machinery frictionless," as General Electric explained.

LABOR SHORTAGE

To meet the labor crisis, the Department of Labor's U.S. Employment Service matched laborers with job vacancies, especially attracting workers from the South and Midwest to war industries in the East. The department also temporarily relaxed the literacy-test and head-tax provisions of immigration law to attract farm labor, miners, and railroad workers from Mexico. Because the labor crisis also generated a housing crisis as workers

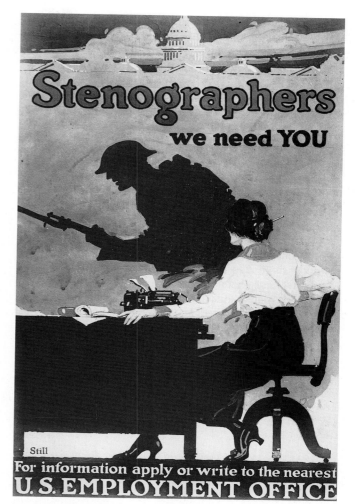

■ Using posters, many government agencies appealed to the American people to help win the war. This one, from the U.S. Employment Service, encouraged women to enter the work force. (National Archives)

crammed into cities, the U.S. Housing Corporation and Emergency Fleet Corporation, following British example, built row houses in Newport News, Virginia, and Eddystone, Pennsylvania.

The tight wartime labor market had another consequence: new work opportunities for women. Business targeted women to fill job vacancies. In Connecticut, a special motion picture, *Mr. and Mrs. Hines of Stamford Do Their Bit*, appealed to housewives' patriotism, urging them to take factory jobs. Although the total number of women in the work force increased slightly, the real story was that many changed jobs, sometimes moving into formerly male domains. Some white women left domestic service for factories, shifted from clerking in department stores to stenography and typing, or departed textile mills for employment in firearms plants. At least 20 percent of all workers in the wartime electrical-machinery, airplane, and food industries were women. Some one hundred thousand women worked in the rail-

■ Stella Young (1896–1989), a Canadian-born woman from Chelsea, Massachusetts, became widely known as the "Doughnut Girl" because of her service during the First World War with the American branch of the Salvation Army, an international organization devoted to social work. She arrived in France in March 1918 and worked in emergency canteens near the battle front, providing U.S. troops with coffee, cocoa, sandwiches, doughnuts, pie, and fruit. Stella Young became famous when this picture of her wearing a khaki uniform and a "doughboy" steel helmet was widely circulated as a postcard. A piece of sheet music was even written about her. She served again in World War II. Chelsea named a city square in her honor in 1968.   (Picture Research Consultants & Archives)

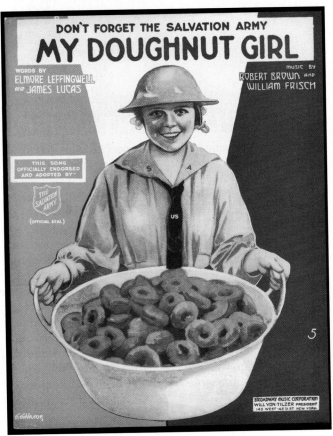

road industry. As white women took advantage of these new opportunities, black women took some of their places in domestic service and in textile factories. For the first time, department stores employed black women as elevator operators and cafeteria waitresses. Most working women were single and remained concentrated in sex-segregated occupations, serving as typists, nurses, teachers, and domestic servants.

Women also participated in the war effort in other ways. As volunteers, they made clothing for refugees and soldiers, served at Red Cross facilities, and taught French to nurses assigned to the war zone. Many worked for the Women's Committee of the Council of National Defense, whose leaders included Ida Tarbell and Carrie Chapman Catt. A vast network of state, county, and town volunteer organizations, the council publicized government mobilization programs, encouraged home gardens, sponsored drives to sell Liberty bonds, and continued the push for social welfare reforms. This patriotic work won praise from men and improved the prospects for passage of the Nineteenth Amendment granting woman suffrage (see pages 583–584). "We have made partners of women in this war," Wilson said as he endorsed woman suffrage in 1918. "Shall we admit them only to a partnership of suffering and sacrifice . . . and not to a partnership of privilege and right?"

Among African Americans, war mobilization wrought significant change as southern blacks undertook a great migration to northern cities to work in railroad yards, packing houses, steel mills, shipyards, and coal mines. Between 1910 and 1920, Cleveland's black population swelled by more than 300 percent, Detroit's by more than 600 percent, and Chicago's by 150 percent. Much of the increase occurred between 1916 and 1919. All told, about a half-million African Americans uprooted themselves to move to the North. Families sometimes pooled savings to send one member; others sold their household goods to pay for the journey. Most of the migrants were males—young (in their early twenties), unmarried, and skilled or semiskilled. Wartime jobs in the North provided an escape from low wages, sharecropping, tenancy, crop liens, debt peonage, lynchings, and political disfranchisement. To a friend back in Mississippi, one African American wrote: "I just begin to feel like a man. . . . I don't have to humble to no one. I have registered. Will vote the next election."

To keep factories running smoothly, Wilson instituted the National War Labor Board (NWLB) in early

NATIONAL WAR LABOR BOARD

1918. The NWLB discouraged strikes and lockouts and urged management to negotiate with existing unions. In

July, after the Western Union Company fired eight hundred union members for trying to organize the firm's workers and then defied an NWLB request to reinstate the employees, the president nationalized the telegraph lines and put the laborers back to work. That month, too, the NWLB directed General Electric to raise wages and stop discriminating against metal trades union members in Schenectady, New York. On the other hand, in September the NWLB ordered striking Bridgeport, Connecticut, machinists back to munitions factories, threatening to revoke their draft exemptions (granted earlier because they worked in an "essential" industry).

Many labor leaders hoped the war would offer opportunities for recognition and better pay through partnership with government. Samuel Gompers threw the AFL's loyalty to the Wilson administration, promising to deter strikes. He and other moderate labor leaders accepted appointments to federal agencies. The antiwar Socialist Party blasted the AFL for becoming a "fifth wheel on [the] capitalist war chariot," but union membership climbed from roughly 2.5 million in 1916 to more than 4 million in 1919.

The AFL, however, could not curb strikes by the radical Industrial Workers of the World (IWW, also known as "Wobblies") or rebellious AFL locals, especially those controlled by labor activists and socialists. In the nineteen war months, more than six thousand strikes expressed workers' demands for a "living wage" and improved working conditions (many called for an eight-hour workday). Exploiting Wilsonian wartime rhetoric, workers and their unions also sought to "de-Kaiser" American industry—that is, to create "industrial democracy," a more representative workplace with a role for labor in determining job categories and content and with workplace representation through shop committees. By 1920, in defiance of the national AFL, labor parties had sprung up in twenty-three states.

Civil Liberties Under Challenge

Gompers's backing of the call to arms meant a great deal to Wilson and his advisers, and they noted with satisfaction that most newspapers, religious leaders, and public officials were similarly supportive. They were less certain, however, about the attitudes of ordinary Americans. "Woe be to the man that seeks to stand in our way in this day of high resolution," the president warned. An official and unofficial campaign soon began to silence dissenters who questioned

Wilson's decision for war or who protested the draft. In the end, the Wilson administration compiled one of the worst civil liberties records in American history.

The targets of governmental and quasi-vigilante repression were the hundreds of thousands of Americans and aliens who refused to support the war: pacifists from all walks of life, conscientious objectors, socialists, radical labor groups, the debt-ridden tenant farmers of Oklahoma who staged the Green Corn Rebellion against the draft, the Non-Partisan League, reformers such as Robert La Follette and Jane Addams, and countless others. In the wartime process of debating the question of the right to speak freely in a democracy, the concept of "civil liberties" for the first time in American history emerged as a major public policy issue (see "Legacy for a People and a Nation," pages 648–649).

The centerpiece of the administration's campaign to win support for the war was the Committee on Public Information (CPI), formed in April 1917 and headed by Progressive journalist George Creel. Employing some of the nation's most talented writers and scholars, the CPI used propaganda to shape and mobilize public opinion. Pamphlets and films demonized the Germans, and CPI "Four-Minute Men" spoke at movie theaters, schools, and churches to pump up a patriotic mood. Encouraged by the CPI to promote American participation in the war, film companies and their trade association, the National Association of the Motion Picture Industry, produced documentaries, newsreels, and anti-German movies such as *The Kaiser, the Beast of Berlin* (1918) and *To Hell with the Kaiser* (1918).

THE COMMITTEE ON PUBLIC INFORMATION

The committee also urged the press to practice "self-censorship" and encouraged people to spy on their neighbors. "Not a pin dropped in the home of anyone with a foreign name," Creel claimed with satisfaction, "but that it rang like thunder on the inner ear of some listening sleuth." Exaggeration, fear-mongering, distortion, half-truths—such were the stuff of the CPI's "mind mobilization."

Encouraged by official behavior, ultrapatriotic groups such as the Sedition Slammers and the American Defense Society sought to cleanse the nation through vigilantism. A German American miner in Illinois was wrapped in a flag and lynched. In Hilger, Montana, citizens burned history texts that mentioned Germany. By the end of the war, sixteen states had banned the teaching of the German language. To avoid trouble, the Kaiser-Kuhn grocery in St. Louis changed its name to Pioneer Grocery. Germantown, Nebraska, became Garland, while

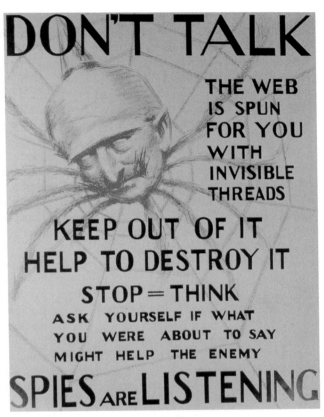

DON'T TALK

THE WEB IS SPUN FOR YOU WITH INVISIBLE THREADS

KEEP OUT OF IT
HELP TO DESTROY IT
STOP = THINK
ASK YOURSELF IF WHAT YOU WERE ABOUT TO SAY MIGHT HELP THE ENEMY

SPIES ARE LISTENING

■ Through its concerted propaganda effort, the Committee on Public Information helped sell to the American people U.S. participation in the First World War. In this 1917 poster, the committee also warned against German spies, perhaps even German American spies, who might pick up secrets from unsuspecting citizens.   (Private Collection)

the townspeople in Berlin, Iowa, henceforth hailed from Lincoln. The German shepherd became the Alsatian shepherd.

Because towns had Liberty Loan quotas to fill, they sometimes bullied "slackers" into purchasing bonds. Nativist advocates of "100% Americanism" exploited the emotional atmosphere to exhort immigrants to throw off their Old World cultures. Companies offered English-language and naturalization classes in their factories and refused jobs and promotions to those who did not make adequate strides toward learning English. Even labor's drive for compulsory health insurance, which before the war had gained advocates in several states, including New York and California, became victimized by the poisoned war atmosphere. Many physicians and insurance companies had for years denounced health insurance as

"socialistic"; after the United States entered the war, they discredited it as "Made in Germany."

Even institutions that had long prided themselves on tolerance became contaminated by the spirit of coercion. At Wellesley College, economics professor Emily Greene Balch was fired because of her pacifist views (she won the Nobel Peace Prize in 1946). Three Columbia University students were apprehended in mid-1917 for circulating an antiwar petition. Columbia also fired Professor J. M. Cattell, a distinguished psychologist, for his antiwar stand. His colleague Charles Beard, a historian with a prowar perspective, resigned in protest, stating: "If we have to suppress everything we don't like to hear, this country is resting on a pretty wobbly basis." In a number of states, local school boards dismissed teachers who questioned the war.

The Wilson administration also guided through an obliging Congress the Espionage Act (1917) and the

ESPIONAGE AND SEDITION ACTS

Sedition Act (1918). The first statute forbade "false statements" designed to impede the draft or promote military insubordination, and it banned from the mails materials considered treasonous. The Sedition Act made it unlawful to obstruct the sale of war bonds and to use "disloyal, profane, scurrilous, or abusive" language to describe the government, the Constitution, the flag, or the military uniform. These loosely worded laws gave the government wide latitude to crack down on critics. Fair-minded people could disagree over what constituted false or abusive language, but in the feverish home-front atmosphere of the First World War, the Justice Department's definition prevailed. More than two thousand people were prosecuted under the acts, and many others were intimidated into silence.

The war emergency gave Progressives and conservatives alike an opportunity to throttle the Industrial Workers of the World and the Socialist Party. Government agents raided IWW meetings, and the army marched into western mining and lumber regions to put down IWW strikes. By the end of the war most of the union's leaders were in jail. The Socialist Party fared little better. In summer 1918, with a government stenographer present, Socialist Party leader Eugene V. Debs delivered a spirited oration extolling socialism and freedom of speech—including the freedom to criticize the Wilson administration for taking America into the war. Federal agents arrested him. Debs told the court what many dissenters—and, later, many jurists and scholars—thought of the Espionage Act: it was "a despotic enactment in flagrant conflict with democratic principles and with the spirit of free institutions." Handed a ten-year sentence,

Debs remained in prison until late 1921, when he received a pardon.

The Supreme Court endorsed such convictions. In *Schenck v. U.S.* (1919), the Court unanimously upheld the conviction of a Socialist Party member who had mailed pamphlets urging resistance to the draft. In time of war, Justice Oliver Wendell Holmes wrote, the First Amendment could be restricted: "Free speech would not protect a man falsely shouting 'fire' in a theater and causing panic." If, according to Holmes, words "are of such a nature as to create a clear and present danger that they will bring about the substantial evils that Congress has a right to prevent," free speech could be limited.

Red Scare, Red Summer

The line between wartime suppression of dissent and the postwar Red Scare is not easily drawn. In the name of patriotism, both harassed suspected internal enemies and deprived them of their constitutional rights; both had government sanction. Together they stabbed at the Bill of Rights and wounded radicalism in America. Yet in at least two respects the phenomena were different. Whereas in wartime the main fear had been of subversion, after the armistice it was revolution; and whereas in 1917 the target had often been German Americans, in 1919 it was frequently organized labor. The Russian Revolution and the communist risings elsewhere in Europe alarmed many Americans, and the fears grew when in 1919 the Soviet leadership announced the formation of the Communist International (or Comintern), whose purpose was to export revolution throughout the world. Terrified conservatives responded by looking for pro-Bolshevik sympathizers (or "Reds," from the red flag used by communists) in the United States, especially in immigrant groups and labor unions.

Labor union leaders emerged out of the war determined to secure higher wages for workers, to meet rising prices and to retain wartime bargaining rights. Employers instead rescinded benefits they had been forced to grant to labor during the war, including recognition of unions. The result was a rash of labor strikes in 1919 that sparked the Red Scare. All told, more than thirty-three hundred strikes involving 4 million laborers jolted the nation that year, including the Seattle general strike in January. On May 1, a day of celebration for workers around the world, bombs were sent through the mails to prominent Americans. Most of the devices were intercepted and dismantled, but police never captured the

LABOR STRIKES

conspirators. Most people assumed, not unreasonably, that anarchists and others bent on the destruction of the American way of life were responsible. Next came the Boston police strike in September. Some sniffed a Bolshevik conspiracy, but others thought it ridiculous to label Boston's Irish American Catholic cops "radicals." The conservative governor of Massachusetts, Calvin Coolidge, gained national attention by proclaiming that nobody had the right to strike against the public safety. State guardsmen soon replaced the striking policemen.

Unrest in the steel industry in September stirred more ominous fears. Many steelworkers worked twelve hours a day, seven days a week, and lived in squalid housing. They looked to local steel unions, organized by the National Committee for Organizing Iron and Steel Workers, to help them improve their lives. When postwar unemployment in the industry climbed and the U.S. Steel Corporation refused to meet with committee representatives, some 350,000 workers walked off the job demanding the right to collective bargaining, a shorter workday, and a living wage. The steel barons hired strikebreakers and sent agents to club strikers. Worried about both the 1919 strikes and Bolshevism, President Wilson warned against "the poison of disorder" and the "poison of revolt." But in the case of steel, the companies won; the strike collapsed in early 1920.

One of the leaders of the steel strike was William Z. Foster, an IWW member and militant labor organizer who later joined the Communist Party. His presence in a labor movement seeking bread-and-butter goals permitted political and business leaders to dismiss the steel strike as a foreign threat orchestrated by American radicals. There was in fact no conspiracy, and the American left was badly splintered. Two defectors from the Socialist Party, John Reed and Benjamin Gitlow, founded the Communist Labor Party in 1919. The rival Communist Party of the United States of America, composed largely of aliens, was launched the same year. Neither party commanded many followers—their combined membership probably did not exceed seventy thousand—and in 1919 the harassed Socialist Party could muster no more than thirty thousand members.

Although divisiveness among radicals actually signified weakness, both Progressives and conservatives interpreted the advent of the new parties as strengthening the radical menace. That is certainly how the American Legion saw the question. Organized in May 1919 to lobby for veterans' benefits, the Legion soon preached an antiradicalism that fueled the Red Scare. By 1920, 843,000 Legion members, mostly middle- and upper-class, had

AMERICAN LEGION

become stalwarts of an impassioned Americanism that demanded conformity.

Wilson's attorney general, A. Mitchell Palmer, also insisted that Americans think alike. A Progressive reformer, Quaker, and ambitious politician, Palmer declared that "revolution" was "eating its way into the homes of the American workmen, licking the altars of the churches, leaping into the belfry of the school bell." Palmer appointed J. Edgar Hoover to head the Radical Division of the Department of Justice. The zealous Hoover compiled index cards bearing the names of allegedly radical individuals and organizations. During 1919 agents jailed IWW members; Palmer also saw to it that 249 alien radicals, including the anarchist Emma Goldman, were deported to Russia.

Again, state and local governments took their cue from the Wilson administration. States passed peacetime sedition acts under which hundreds of people were arrested. Vigilante groups and mobs flourished once again, their numbers swelled by returning veterans. In November 1919, in Centralia, Washington, American Legionnaires broke from a parade to storm the IWW hall. Several were wounded. A number of Wobblies were soon arrested, and one of them, an ex-soldier, was taken from jail by a mob, then beaten, castrated, and shot. The New York State legislature expelled five duly elected Socialist Party members in early 1920.

The Red Scare reached a climax in January 1920 in the Palmer Raids. Hoover planned and directed the operation; government agents in thirty-three cities broke into meeting halls and homes without search warrants. *PALMER RAIDS* More than four thousand people were jailed and denied counsel. In Boston some four hundred people were kept in detainment on bitterly cold Deer Island; two died of pneumonia, one leaped to his death, and another went insane. Because of court rulings and the courageous efforts of Assistant Secretary of Labor Louis Post, who deliberately held up paperwork, most of the arrestees were released, although in 1920–1921 nearly six hundred were deported.

Palmer's disregard for elementary civil liberties drew criticism. Civil libertarians and lawyers charged that his tactics violated the Constitution. Many of the arrested "communists" had committed no crimes. When Palmer called for a peacetime sedition act, he alarmed both liberal and conservative leaders. His dire prediction that serious violence carried out by pro-Soviet radicals would mar May Day 1920 proved mistaken—not a single disturbance occurred anywhere in the country. Palmer, who had taken to calling himself the "Fighting Quaker," was jeered as the "Quaking Fighter."

Just as Palmer insisted that communists were behind the labor strife of the postwar period, so he maintained *RACIAL UNREST* that they were responsible for the racial violence that also gripped the nation in these years. Here again, the charge was baseless. For African Americans, it was clear well before the end of the war that their participation in the war effort had not led to a meaningful change in white attitudes; they continued to experience discrimination in both North and South. When the United States entered the First World War, there was not one black judge in the entire country. Segregation remained social custom. The Ku Klux Klan was reviving, and racist films such as D. W. Griffith's *The Birth of a Nation* (1915) fed prejudice with its celebration of the Klan and its demeaning depiction of blacks. Lynching statistics exposed the wide gap between wartime declarations of humanity and the American practice of inhumanity at home: between 1914 and 1920, 382 blacks were lynched, some of them in military uniform.

Northern whites who resented "the Negro invasion" vented their anger in riots, as in East St. Louis, Illinois, in July 1917 (see page 525). The next month, in Houston, where African American soldiers faced white harassment and refused to obey segregation laws, whites and blacks exchanged gunfire. Seventeen whites and two African Americans died, and the army sentenced thirteen black soldiers to death and forty-one to life imprisonment for mutiny. During the bloody "Red Summer" of 1919 (so named by black author James Weldon Johnson for the blood that was spilled), race riots rocked two dozen cities and towns. The worst violence occurred in Chicago, a favorite destination for migrating blacks. In the very hot days of July 1919, a black youth swimming at a segregated white beach was hit by a thrown rock and drowned. Rumors spread, tempers flared, and soon blacks and whites were battling one another. Stabbings, burnings, and shootings went on for days until state police restored some calm. Thirty-eight people died, twenty-three African Americans and fifteen whites.

By the time of this tragedy, a disillusioned W. E. B. Du Bois had already concluded that black support for the war had not diminished whites' adherence to inequality and segregation. That spring he vowed a struggle: "We return. We return from fighting. We return fighting." Or as poet Claude McKay put it after the Chicago riot in a poem he titled "If We Must Die":

Like men we'll face the murderous cowardly pack.
Pressed to the wall, dying, but fighting back.

The exhortations of Du Bois and McKay reflected a newfound militancy that could be observed among black

■ An African American is confronted by state militia members during the race riots in Chicago in 1919. The troops were called in after Mayor Bill Thompson determined that the city police could not restore order.   (Chicago Historical Society photo by Jun Fujita)

BLACK MILITANCY

veterans and the growing black communities in the North. Editorials in African American newspapers subjected white politicians, including the president, to increasingly harsh criticism and at the same time implored readers to embrace their own prowess and beauty: "The black man is a power of great potentiality upon whom consciousness of his own strength is about to dawn." The NAACP stepped up its campaign for civil rights and equality, vowing at a 1919 conference on lynching to publicize the terrors of the lynch law and to seek legislation to stop "Judge Lynch." Other blacks, doubtful of the NAACP's claim that they would one day be accepted as equal citizens, turned instead to a charismatic Jamaican immigrant named Marcus Garvey (see page 659), who called on African Americans to abandon their hopes for integration and to seek a separate black nation.

The crackdown on laborers and radicals and the resurgence of racism in 1919 were signs of how the high hopes among these groups during the war years had been dashed. Reform suffered as reformers either joined in the suppression or became victims of it. Though the passage

of the Nineteenth Amendment in 1920, guaranteeing women the right to vote, showed that reform could happen, it was the exception to the rule. Unemployment, inflation, racial conflict, labor upheaval, a campaign against free speech—all combined in the immediate post-war years to create a broad feeling of disillusionment.

The Defeat of Peace

President Wilson seemed more focused on confronting the threat of radicalism abroad than at home. Throughout the final months of the war he fretted about the Soviet takeover in Russia, and he watched with apprehension the communist uprisings in various parts of central Europe. Months earlier, in mid-1918, Wilson had revealed his ardent anti-Bolshevism when he ordered five thousand American troops to northern Russia and ten thousand more to Siberia, where they joined other Allied contingents in fighting what was now a Russian civil war. Wilson did not consult Congress. He said the military expeditions would guard

Allied supplies and Russian railroads from German seizure and would also rescue a group of Czechs who wished to return home to fight the Germans.

Worried that the Japanese were building influence in Siberia and closing the Open Door, Wilson also hoped to deter Japan from further advances in Asia. Mostly, though, he wanted to smash the infant Bolshevik government, a challenge to his new world order. Thus he backed an economic blockade of Russia, sent arms to anti-Bolshevik forces, and refused to recognize Lenin's government. The United States also secretly passed military information to anti-Bolshevik forces and used food relief to shore up opponents of the Soviets in the Baltic region. Later, at the Paris Peace Conference, Russia was denied a seat. U.S. troops did not leave Siberia until spring 1920, after the Bolsheviks had demonstrated their staying power.

As if Lenin's challenge were not serious enough, Wilson also faced a monumental task in securing a postwar settlement. When he departed for the Paris Peace Conference in December 1918, he faced obstacles erected by his political enemies, by the Allies, and by himself. Some observers suggested that a cocky Wilson underestimated his task. During the 1918 congressional elections, Wilson committed the blunder of suggesting that patriotism required the election of a Democratic Congress; Republicans had a field day blasting the president for questioning their love of country. The GOP gained control of both houses, signaling trouble for Wilson in two ways. First, a peace treaty would have to be submitted for approval to a potentially hostile Senate. Second, the election results at home diminished Wilson's stature in the eyes of foreign leaders. Wilson aggravated his political problems by not naming a senator to his advisory American Peace Commission. He also refused to take any prominent Republicans with him to Paris or to consult with the Senate Foreign Relations Committee before the conference. It did not help that the president denounced his critics as "blind and little provincial people."

Upon arriving in Europe Wilson was greeted with huge and adoring crowds in Paris, London, and Rome. Behind closed doors, however, the leaders of these countries—Georges Clemenceau of France, David Lloyd George of Britain, and Vittorio Orlando of Italy (with Wilson, the Big Four)—became formidable adversaries. Clemenceau mused: "God gave man the Ten Commandments, and he broke every one. Wilson has given us Fourteen Points. We shall see." After four years of horrible war, the Allies were not about to be cheated out of the fruits of victory. Wilson could wax lyrical about a "peace without victory," but the late-arriving Americans

had not suffered the way the peoples of France and Great Britain had suffered. Germany would have to pay, and pay big, for the calamity it had caused.

At the conference, held at the ornate palace of Versailles, the Big Four tried to work out an agreement. Critics quickly pointed out that Wilson had immediately abandoned the first of his Fourteen Points, diplomacy "in the public view." The victors demanded that Germany (which had not been invited to the proceedings) pay a huge reparations bill. Wilson instead called for a small indemnity, fearing that a resentful and economically hobbled Germany might turn to Bolshevism or disrupt the postwar community in some other way. Unable to moderate the Allied position, the president reluctantly gave way, agreeing to a clause blaming the war on the Germans and to the creation of a commission to determine the amount of reparations (later set at $33 billion). Wilson acknowledged that the peace terms were "hard," but he also came to believe that "the German people must be made to hate war."

PARIS PEACE CONFERENCE

As for the breaking up of empires and the principle of self-determination, Wilson could deliver on only some of his goals. Creating a League-administered "mandate" system, the conferees placed former German and Turkish colonies under the control of other imperial nations. Japan gained authority over Germany's colonies in the Pacific, while France and Britain obtained parts of the Middle East—the French obtained what became Lebanon and Syria, while the British received the three former Ottoman provinces that became Iraq. Britain also secured Palestine, on the condition that it uphold its wartime promise to promote "the establishment in Palestine of a national home for the Jewish people" without prejudice to "the civil and religious rights of existing non-Jewish communities"—the so-called Balfour Declaration of 1917.

In other arrangements, Japan replaced Germany as the imperial overlord of China's Shandong Peninsula, and France was permitted occupation rights in Germany's Rhineland. Elsewhere in Europe, Wilson's prescriptions fared better. Out of Austria-Hungary and Russia came the newly independent states of Austria, Hungary, Yugoslavia, Czechoslovakia, and Poland. Wilson and his colleagues also built a *cordon sanitaire* (buffer zone) of new westward-looking nations (Finland, Estonia, Latvia, and Lithuania) around Russia to quarantine the Bolshevik contagion (see Map 23.3).

Wilson worked hardest on the charter for the League of Nations. The League represented the centerpiece of his plans for the postwar world, and not merely because the

Map 23.3   Europe Transformed by War and Peace

After President Wilson and the other conferees at the Paris Peace Conference negotiated the Treaty of Versailles, empires were broken up. In eastern Europe, in particular, new nations emerged.

LEAGUE OF
NATIONS AND
ARTICLE 10

organization would regulate the final peace treaty. The League of Nations Wilson envisioned would have power over all disputes among states, including those that did not arise from the peace agreement; as such, the organization could, he believed, have a truly transformative effect on international relations. Even so, the great powers would have preponderant say: the organization would have an influential council of five permanent members and elected delegates

■ In October 1919 President Woodrow Wilson (1856–1924) receives assistance after his massive stroke, which made it difficult for him to maintain his train of thought and manage government affairs. Historians continue to debate the influence of Wilson's poor health on the president's losing battle for U.S. membership in the League of Nations. (Library of Congress)

from smaller states, an assembly of all members, and a World Court.

Wilson identified Article 10 as the "kingpin" of the League covenant: "The Members of the League undertake to respect and preserve as against external aggression the territorial integrity and existing political independence of all Members of the League. In case of any such aggression or in case of any threat or danger of such aggression the Council shall advise upon the means by which this obligation shall be fulfilled." This collective-security provision, along with the entire League charter, became part of the peace treaty because Wilson insisted that there could be no future peace with Germany without a league to oversee it.

German representatives at first refused to sign the punitive treaty but submitted in June 1919. They gave up 13 percent of Germany's territory, 10 percent of its population, all of its colonies, and a huge portion of its national wealth. Many people wondered how the League could function in the poisoned postwar atmosphere of humiliation and revenge. But Wilson waxed euphoric: "The stage is set, the destiny disclosed. It has come about by no plan of our conceiving, but by the hand of God."

Critics in the United States were not so sure. In March 1919, thirty-nine senators (enough to deny the treaty the necessary two-thirds vote) had signed a petition stating that the League's structure did not adequately protect U.S. interests. Wilson denounced his critics as "pygmy" minds, but he persuaded the peace conference to exempt the Monroe Doctrine and domestic matters from League jurisdiction. Having made these concessions to senatorial advice, Wilson would budge no more. Compromises with other nations had been necessary to keep the conference going, he insisted, and the League would rectify wrongs. Could his critics not see that membership in the League would give the United States "leadership in the world"?

Critics of the Treaty

In the summer months, criticism of the peace process and the treaty mounted: Wilson had bastardized his own principles. He had conceded Shandong to Japan. He personally had killed a provision affirming the racial equality of all peoples. The treaty did not mention freedom of the seas, and tariffs were not reduced. Reparations on Germany promised to be punishing. Senator La Follette and other critics on the left protested that the League would perpetuate empire. Conservative critics feared that the League would limit American freedom of action in world affairs, stymie U.S. expansion, and intrude on domestic questions. And Article 10 raised serious questions: Would the United States be *obligated* to use armed force to ensure collective security? And what about colonial rebellions, such as in Ireland or India? Would the League feel compelled to crush them? "Were a League of Nations in existence in the days when George Washington fought and won," an Irish American editor wrote, "we would still be an English colony."

Senator Henry Cabot Lodge of Massachusetts led the Senate opposition to the League. A Harvard-educated Ph.D. and partisan Republican who also had an intense personal dislike of Wilson, Lodge packed the Foreign Relations Committee with critics and prolonged public hearings. He introduced several reservations to the treaty, the most important of which held that Congress had to approve any obligation under Article 10.

In September 1919 Wilson embarked on a speaking tour of the United States. Growing more exhausted every day, he dismissed his antagonists as "contemptible quitters." Provoked by Irish American and German American hecklers, he lashed out in Red Scare terms: "Any man who carries a hyphen about him carries a dagger which he is ready to plunge into the vitals of the Republic." While doubts about Article 10 multiplied, Wilson tried to highlight neglected features of the League charter—such as the arbitration of disputes and an international conference to abolish child labor. In Colorado, a day after delivering another passionate speech, the president awoke to nausea and uncontrollable facial twitching. "I just feel as if I am going to pieces," he said. A few days later, he suffered a massive stroke that paralyzed his left side. He became peevish and even more stubborn, increasingly unable to conduct presidential business. Advised to placate Lodge and other "Reservationist" senatorial critics so the Versailles treaty would have a chance of being approved by Congress, Wilson rejected "dishonorable compromise." From Senate Democrats he demanded utter loyalty—a vote against all reservations.

Twice in November the Senate rejected the Treaty of Versailles and thus U.S. membership in the League. In

SENATE REJECTION OF THE TREATY AND LEAGUE

the first vote, Democrats joined sixteen "Irreconcilables," mostly Republicans who opposed any treaty whatsoever, to defeat the treaty with reservations (39 for and 55 against). In the second vote, Republicans and Irreconcilables turned down the treaty without reservations (38 for and 53 against). In March 1920 the Senate again voted; this time a majority (49 for and 35 against) favored the treaty with reservations, but the tally fell short of the two-thirds needed. Had Wilson permitted Democrats to compromise—to accept reservations—he could have achieved his fervent goal of membership in the League, which, despite the U.S. absence, came into being.

At the core of the debate lay a basic issue in American foreign policy: whether the United States would endorse collective security or continue to travel the more solitary path articulated in George Washington's Farewell Address and in the Monroe Doctrine. In a world dominated by imperialist states unwilling to subordinate their strategic ambitions to an international organization, Americans preferred their traditional nonalignment and freedom of choice over binding commitments to collective action. That is why so many of Wilson's critics targeted Article 10. Wilson countered that this argument amounted to embracing the status quo—the European imperialist states are selfish, so the United States should be too. Acceptance of Article 10 and membership in the League promised something better, he believed, for the United States and for the world; it promised collective security in place of the frail protection of alliances and the instability of a balance of power.

In the end, World War I did not make the world safe for democracy. Wilson failed to create a new world order

AN UNSAFE WORLD

through reform. Still, the United States emerged from the First World War an even greater world power. By 1920 the United States had become the world's leading economic power, producing 40 percent of its coal, 70 percent of its petroleum, and half of its pig iron. It also rose to first rank in world trade. American companies took advantage of the war to nudge the Germans and British out of foreign markets, especially in Latin America. Meanwhile, the United States shifted from being a debtor to a creditor nation, becoming the world's leading banker.

After the disappointment of Versailles, appeals for arms control accelerated and the peace movement revitalized. At the same time, the military became better armed and more professional. The Reserve Officers Training Corps (ROTC) became permanent; military "colleges" provided upper-echelon training; and the Army Industrial College, founded in 1924, pursued business-military cooperation in the area of logistics and planning. The National Research Council, created in 1916 with government money and Carnegie and Rockefeller funds, continued after the war as an alliance of scientists and businesspeople engaged in research relating to national defense. Tanks, quick-firing guns, armor-piercing explosives, and oxygen masks for high-altitude-flying pilots were just some of the technological advances that emerged from the First World War.

The international system born in these years was unstable and fragmented. Espousing decolonization and taking to heart the Wilsonian principle of self-determination, nationalist leaders active during the First World War, such as Ho Chi Minh of Indochina and Mohandas K. Gandhi of India, vowed to achieve independence for their peoples. Communism became a disruptive force in world politics, and the Soviets bore a grudge against those invaders who had tried to thwart their revolution. The new states in central and eastern Europe proved weak, dependent on outsiders for security. Germans bitterly resented the harsh peace settlement, and German war debts and reparations problems dogged international order for years. As it entered the 1920s, the international system that Woodrow Wilson had vowed to reform wobbled.

Summary

*a*t the close of the First World War, historian Albert Bushnell Hart observed that "it is easy to see that the United States is a new country." Actually, America came out of the war an unsettled mix of the old and the new. The war years marked the emergence of the United States as a world power, and Americans could take justifiable pride in the contribution they made to the Allied victory. At the same time, the war exposed deep divisions among Americans: white versus black, nativist versus immigrant, capital versus labor, men versus women, radical versus Progressive and conservative, pacifist versus interventionist, nationalist versus internationalist. It is little wonder that Americans—having experienced race riots, labor strikes, disputes over civil liberties, and the League fight—wanted to escape to what President Warren G. Harding called "normalcy."

During the war the federal government intervened in the economy and influenced people's everyday lives as never before. Centralization of control in Washington, D.C., and mobilization of the home front served as a model for the future. Although the Wilson administration shunned reconstruction or reconversion plans (war housing projects, for example, were sold to private investors) and quickly dismantled the many governmental agencies, the World War I experience of the activist state served as guidance for 1930s reformers battling the Great Depression (see Chapter 25). The partnership of government and business in managing the wartime economy advanced the development of a mass society through the standardization of products and the promotion of efficiency. Wilsonian wartime policies also nourished the concentration of corporate ownership through the suspension of antitrust laws. Business power dominated the next decade. American labor, by contrast, entered lean

years, although new labor management practices, including corporate welfare programs, survived.

Although the disillusionment evident after Versailles did not cause the United States to adopt a policy of isolationist withdrawal (see Chapter 26), skepticism about America's ability to right wrongs abroad marked the postwar American mood. The war was grimy and ugly, far less glorious than Wilson's lofty rhetoric suggested. People recoiled from photographs of shell-shocked faces and of bodies dangling from barbed wire. American soldiers, tired of idealism, craved the latest baseball scores and their regular jobs. Those Progressives who had believed that entry into the war would deliver the millennium later marveled at their naiveté. Many lost their enthusiasm for crusades, and many others turned away in disgust from the bickering of the victors. Some felt betrayed. The journalist William Allen White angrily wrote to a friend that the Allies "have—those damned vultures—taken the heart out of the peace, taken the joy out of the great enterprise of the war, and have made it a sordid malicious miserable thing like all the other wars in the world."

By 1920 Woodrow Wilson's idealism seemed to many Americans to be a spent force, both at home and abroad. Aware of their country's newfound status as a leading world power, they were unsure what this reality meant for the nation, or for their individual lives. With a mixed legacy from the Great War, and a sense of uneasiness, the country entered the new era of the 1920s.

LEGACY FOR A PEOPLE AND A NATION
Freedom of Speech and the ACLU

Though freedom of speech is enshrined in the U.S. Constitution, for more than a century after the nation's founding the concept had little standing in American jurisprudence. Before World War I, those with radical views often met with harsh treatment for exercising what today would be termed their freedom of speech. During the war, however, the Wilson administration's suppression of dissidents led some Americans to reformulate the traditional definition of allowable speech. Two key figures in this movement were Roger Baldwin, a conscientious objector, and woman suffrage activist Crystal Eastman. Baldwin and Eastman were among the first to advance the idea that the content of political speech could be separated from the identity of the speaker and that patriotic Americans could—indeed should—defend the right of others to express political beliefs abhorrent to their own. After working during the war to defend the rights of conscientious objectors, Baldwin and Eastman—joined by activists such as Jane Addams, Helen Keller, and Norman Thomas—formed the American Civil Liberties Union (ACLU).

Since 1920 the ACLU, which today has some 300,000 members in three hundred chapters nationwide, has aimed to protect the basic civil liberties of all Americans and to extend them to those to whom they have traditionally been denied. The organization has been involved in almost every major civil liberties case contested in U.S. courts, among them the John Scopes "monkey trial" (1925) concerning the teaching of evolution at a Tennessee school, and the landmark *Brown v. Board of Education* case (1954) that ended federal tolerance of racial segregation. More recently, the ACLU was involved in a 1997 case in which the Supreme Court decided that the 1996 Communications Act banning "indecent speech" violated First Amendment rights.

Conservatives have long criticized the ACLU for its opposition to official prayers in public schools and its support of the legality of abortion, as well as for what they see as its selectivity in deciding whose freedom of speech to defend. Backers of the organization counter that it has also defended those on the right, such as Oliver North, a key figure in the Iran-contra scandal of the 1980s.

Either way, the principle of free speech is today broadly accepted by Americans, so much so that even ACLU bashers take it for granted. Ironically, the Wilson administration's crackdown on dissent produced an expanded commitment to freedom of speech for a people and a nation.

The **history companion** *powered by Eduspace®*

Your primary source for interactive quizzes, exercises, and more to help you learn efficiently.
http://history.college.hmco.com/students

CHAPTER 24

THE NEW ERA 1920–1929

*E*ager to win $25,000 offered by a hotel owner to the first person to fly an airplane nonstop between New York and Paris, three different crews stood ready to go at Roosevelt Airfield in the spring of 1927. One man, Charles A. Lindbergh, young, handsome, and the only one piloting his plane solo, decided to risk drizzly weather and start the trip May 20. For thirty-three hours, his craft, *The Spirit of St. Louis,* bounced across the Atlantic skies. The flight seized the attention of practically every American as newspaper and telegraph reports followed Lindbergh's progress. He reached the Irish coast! He crossed over England! He entered France! And when he landed at Le Bourget Airfield, the nation rejoiced. The *New York Evening World* sold 114,000 extra newspapers on May 21; the *St. Louis Post-Dispatch* sold 40,000 extra. President Calvin Coolidge dispatched a warship to bring "Lucky Lindy" back home. Celebrants sent Lindbergh 55,000 telegrams and dropped 1,800 tons of shredded paper on him during a triumphant homecoming parade.

Charles Lindbergh was one of the most celebrated heroes in American history. Though his was not the first transatlantic flight (in 1919 two men piloted a plane from Newfoundland to Ireland, and a crew of five reached Europe by way of the Azores), Lindbergh's venture made a stunt pilot into an American idol. During his flight, forty thousand spectators at New York's Yankee Stadium watching a boxing match stood in silence and prayed for Lindbergh's safety. One newspaper exclaimed that Lindbergh had accomplished "the greatest feat of a solitary man in the history of the human race." Among countless prizes, Lindbergh received the Distinguished Flying Cross and the Congressional Medal of Honor. Promoters offered him millions of dollars to tour the world by air and $700,000 for a movie contract. Texas named a town after him.

Through it all, Lindbergh, nicknamed "The Lone Eagle," remained dignified, even aloof. His flight and its aftermath, however, open insights into his era. The burst of publicity and thrill of celebration point to the impacts of commercialism, new technology, and mass entertainment. Yet Lindbergh himself epito-

◀ Landing in France on May 21, 1927, Charles Lindbergh completed a flight across the Atlantic Ocean and instantly became one of the nation's most revered heroes. His accomplishment and the publicity surrounding it represented much of what made the 1920s a New Era. (Corbis/Bettmann)

C H R O N O L O G Y

1920 • Nineteenth Amendment ratified, legalizing the vote for women in federal elections
• Harding elected president
• KDKA transmits first commercial radio broadcast

1920–21 • Postwar deflation and depression occurs

1921 • Federal Highway Act funds national highway system
• Emergency Quota Act establishes immigration quotas
• Sacco and Vanzetti convicted
• Sheppard-Towner Act allots funds to states to set up maternity and pediatric clinics

1922 • Economic recovery raises standard of living
• *Coronado Coal Company v. United Mine Workers* rules that strikes may be illegal actions in restraint of trade
• *Bailey v. Drexel Furniture Company* voids restrictions on child labor
• Federal government ends strikes by railroad shop workers and miners
• Fordney-McCumber Tariff raises rates on imports

1923 • Harding dies; Coolidge assumes the presidency
• *Adkins v. Children's Hospital* overturns a minimum-wage law affecting women

1923–24 • Government scandals (Teapot Dome) exposed

1924 • National Origins Act revises immigration quotas
• Coolidge elected president

1925 • Scopes trial highlights battle between religious fundamentalists and modernists

1927 • Sacco and Vanzetti executed
• Lindbergh pilots solo transatlantic flight
• Ruth hits sixty home runs
• *The Jazz Singer*, the first movie with sound, is released

1928 • Stock market soars
• Hoover elected president

1929 • Stock market crashes; Great Depression begins

mized individual achievement, self-reliance, and courage—old-fashioned values that also vied for public allegiance in an era contemporaries themselves identified as "new."

During the 1920s, consumerism flourished. Though poverty beset small farmers, workers in declining industries, and nonwhites in inner cities, most other people enjoyed a high standard of living relative to previous generations. Spurred by advertising and installment buying, Americans eagerly acquired radios, automobiles, real estate, and stocks. As in the Gilded Age, government—embodied in Congress, the presidency, and the Supreme Court—maintained a favorable climate for business. And in contrast to the Progressive era, few people worried about abuses of private power. Yet state and local governments, extending the reach of public authority, undertook important reforms.

As Charles Lindbergh's adventure reveals, it was an era of contrast and complexity. Fads and frivolities coincided with creativity in the arts and notable advances in science and technology. Changes in work habits, family responsibilities, and healthcare fostered new uses of time and new attitudes about behavior. While material bounty and leisure enticed Americans into new amusements, winds of change also stirred up waves of reaction. Those who held tight to traditional beliefs scorned liberal ideas. The era's modernism and materialism were both appealing and unsettling, prompting both enthusiasm and rejection.

An unseen storm lurked on the horizon, however. The glitter of consumer culture that dominated everyday life blinded Americans to rising debts and uneven prosperity. Just before the decade closed, a devastating depression brought the era to a brutal close. ■

Big Business Triumphant

The 1920s began with a jolting economic decline. Shortly after the First World War ended, industrial output dropped and unemployment rose as wartime orders dried up, consumer spending dwindled, and demobilized soldiers flooded the work force. As European agriculture recovered from war, American exports contracted and farm income plunged. Unemployment, around 2 percent in 1919, passed 12 percent in

1921. Railroads and mining industries suffered in the West. Layoffs spread through New England as textile companies abandoned outdated factories for the convenient raw materials and cheap labor of the South.

Aided by electric energy, a recovery began in 1922 and continued unevenly until 1929. By decade's end,

NEW ECONOMIC EXPANSION factories using electric motors dominated industry, increasing productivity and sending thousands of steam engines to the scrap heap. Electric power helped manufacturers produce new metal alloys such as aluminum and synthetic materials such as rayon. As well, most urban households now had electric lighting and could utilize new appliances such as refrigerators, toasters, and vacuum cleaners.

As Americans acquired spending money and leisure time, service industries such as restaurants, beauty salons, and movie theaters boomed. Installment, or time-payment, plans ("A dollar down and a dollar forever," one critic quipped) drove the new consumerism. Of 3.5 million automobiles sold in 1923, some 80 percent were bought on credit.

Economic expansion brought a continuation of corporate consolidation that had created trusts and holding

OLIGOPOLIES AND "NEW LOBBYING" companies in the late nineteenth century. Although Progressive era trust-busting had reined in big business, it had not eliminated oligopoly, the control of an entire industry by a few large firms. By the 1920s oligopolies dominated not only production but also marketing, distribution, and finance. In basic industries such as steel production and electrical equipment, a few sprawling companies such as U.S. Steel and General Electric predominated.

Business and professional organizations that had arisen around 1900 also expanded in the 1920s. Retailers and manufacturers formed trade associations to swap information and coordinate planning. Farm bureaus promoted scientific agriculture and tried to stabilize markets. Lawyers, engineers, and social scientists expanded their professional societies. These special-interest groups participated in what is called the "new lobbying." In a complex society in which government was playing an increasingly influential role, hundreds of organizations sought to convince federal and state legislators to support their interests. One Washington, D.C., observer contended that "lobbyists were so thick they were constantly falling over one another."

Government policies helped business thrive, and legislators came to depend on lobbyists' expertise in making decisions. Prodded by lobbyists, Congress cut taxes on corporations and wealthy individuals in 1921 and the next year raised tariff rates in the Fordney-McCumber Tariff Act. Presidents Warren G. Harding, Calvin Coolidge, and Herbert Hoover appointed cabinet officers who took favorable stances toward business. Regulatory agencies such as the Federal Trade Commission and Interstate Commerce Commission monitored company activities but, under the influence of lobbyists, cooperated with corporations more than they regulated them.

The Supreme Court, led by Chief Justice William Howard Taft, the former president, protected business and private property as aggressively as in the Gilded Age and abandoned its Progressive era antitrust stance. Key decisions sheltered business from government regulation and hindered organized labor's ability to achieve its ends through strikes and legislation. In *Coronado Coal Company v. United Mine Workers* (1922), Taft ruled that a striking union, like a trust, could be prosecuted for illegal restraint of trade. Yet in *Maple Floor Association v. U.S.* (1929), the Court decided that trade associations that distributed anti-union information were not acting in restraint of trade. The Court also voided restrictions on child labor (*Bailey v. Drexel Furniture Company,* 1922) and overturned a minimum-wage law affecting women because it infringed on liberty of contract (*Adkins v. Children's Hospital,* 1923).

Organized labor suffered other setbacks during the 1920s. Fearful of communism allegedly brought into the

SETBACKS FOR ORGANIZED LABOR country by radical immigrants, public opinion turned against workers who disrupted everyday life with strikes. Perpetuating tactics used during the Red Scare (see pages 641–643), the Harding administration in 1922 obtained a sweeping court injunction to quash a strike by 400,000 railroad shop workers. The same year, the Justice Department helped put down a nationwide strike by 650,000 miners. Courts at both the state and federal level issued injunctions to prevent strikes and permitted businesses to sue unions for damages suffered from labor actions.

Meanwhile, some corporations countered the appeal of unions by offering pensions, profit sharing (which amounted to withholding wages for later distribution), and company-sponsored picnics and sporting events—a policy known as welfare capitalism. State legislators aided employers by prohibiting closed shops (workplaces where union membership was mandatory) and permitting open shops (which could discriminate against unionized workers). Labor leaders, especially of unions affiliated with the American Federation of Labor, tended to be conservative and, as in the Progressive era, were reluctant to organize unskilled workers. As a result of court action, welfare capitalism, and indifferent leadership, union membership fell from 5.1 million in 1920 to 3.6 million in 1929.

Agriculture was one sector of the national economy that languished during the 1920s. Pressed into competition

LANGUISHING AGRICULTURE

with growers in other countries and trying to increase productivity by investing in new machines such as plows, harvesters, and tractors, American farmers found themselves further beset by debt. As in the 1880s and 1890s, overproduction and foreign competition depressed crop and livestock prices, in turn reducing incomes. Early in the decade, for example, the price that farmers could get for cotton dropped by two-thirds and that of hogs and cattle fell by half. As a result, farm income never recovered after the First World War, and the gap between a farmer's income and that of an urban worker widened. Many farmers became tenants because they lost their land; more quit farming altogether.

Politics and Government

a series of Republican presidents extended Theodore Roosevelt's notion of government-business cooperation, but they made government a compliant coordinator rather than the active manager Roosevelt had advocated. A symbol of government's goodwill toward business was President Warren G. Harding, elected in 1920 when the populace no longer desired national or international crusades. Democrats had nominated Ohio's Governor James M. Cox, who supported Woodrow Wilson's fading hopes for U.S. membership in the League of Nations. But Cox and his running mate, Franklin D. Roosevelt, governor of New York, failed to excite voters. Harding, who kept his position on the League vague, captured 16 million popular votes to 9 million for Cox. (The total vote in the 1920 presidential election was 36 percent higher than in 1916, reflecting participation of women voters for the first time.)

A small-town newspaperman and senator from Ohio who was an engaging public speaker, Harding appointed some capable assistants who helped promote business growth, notably Secretary of State Charles Evans Hughes, Secretary of Commerce Herbert Hoover, Secretary of the Treasury Andrew Mellon, and Secretary of Agriculture Henry C. Wallace. Harding also backed some reforms. His administration helped streamline federal spending with the Budget and Accounting Act of 1921 (which created the Bureau of the Budget), supported antilynching legislation (rejected by Congress),

and approved bills assisting farm cooperatives and liberalizing farm credit.

Harding's problem was that he had personal weaknesses. Married to an insecure, domineering woman, he

SCANDALS OF HARDING ADMINISTRATION

had affairs with other women. As a senator, he had a long-term liaison with Carrie Phillips, the wife of an Ohio merchant. In 1917, he began a relationship with Nan Britton, who was thirty-one years his junior. A daughter was born from the affair in 1919, and Britton reputedly continued to visit Harding in the White House after he became president. Unlike Grover Cleveland, however, Harding never acknowledged his illegitimate offspring.

Of more consequence than his sexual escapades, Harding said yes too often to predatory friends, appointing cronies who saw office holding as an invitation to personal gain. Charles Forbes of the Veterans Bureau went to federal prison, convicted of fraud and bribery in connection with government contracts. Attorney General Harry Daugherty was implicated in bribery and other fraudulent schemes; he escaped prosecution by refusing to testify against himself. Most notoriously, a congressional inquiry in 1923 and 1924 revealed that Secretary of the Interior Albert Fall had accepted bribes to lease oil-rich government property to private oil companies. For his role in the affair—called the Teapot Dome scandal after a Wyoming oil reserve that he turned over to the Mammoth Oil Company—Fall was fined $100,000 and spent a year in jail, the first cabinet officer ever to be so disgraced.

By mid-1923, Harding had become disillusioned. Amid rumors of mismanagement and crime, he told a journalist, "My God, this is a hell of a job. I have no trouble with my enemies. . . . But my friends, my God-damned friends . . . they're the ones that keep me walking the floor nights." On a speaking tour that summer, Harding became ill and died in San Francisco on August 2. Though his death preceded revelation of the Teapot Dome scandal, some people speculated that to avoid an embarrassing impeachment Harding committed suicide or was poisoned by his wife. Most evidence, however, points to death from natural causes, probably a heart attack. At any rate, Harding was truly mourned. A warm, dignified-looking man who relished a good joke and an evening of poker, he seemed suited to a nation recovering from world war and domestic hard times.

Vice President Calvin Coolidge, Harding's successor, was far more closemouthed. (Alice Roosevelt Longworth, Teddy's daughter, quipped that Coolidge looked as if he had been weaned on a pickle.) As governor of Massachusetts, Coolidge attracted national attention in

1919 with his active stand against striking Boston policemen, a policy that won him business support and the vice-presidential nomination in 1920. Ordinarily, however, he was content to let events take their course, prompting columnist Walter Lippmann to remark on the "grim, determined, alert inactivity, which keeps Mr. Coolidge occupied constantly."

Coolidge's presidency coincided with business prosperity. Respectful of private enterprise and aided by Andrew Mellon, who was retained as secretary of the treasury, Coolidge's administration reduced federal debt, lowered income-tax rates (especially for the wealthy), and began construction of a national highway system. Congress took little initiative during these years, except in regard to farm policy. Responding to farmers' complaints of falling prices, Congress twice passed bills to establish government-backed price supports for staple crops (the McNary-Haugen bills of 1927 and 1928). Resembling the subtreasury scheme that Farmers' Alliances had advocated in the 1890s (see page 556), these bills were to establish a complex system whereby the government would buy surplus farm products and either hold them until prices rose or sell them abroad. Farmers argued that they deserved as much gov-

COOLIDGE PROSPERITY

ernment protection as manufacturers got. Coolidge, however, vetoed the measures both times as improper government interference in the market economy.

"Coolidge prosperity" was the decisive issue in the presidential election of 1924. Both major parties ran candidates who favored private initiative over government intervention. Republicans nominated Coolidge with little dissent. At their national convention, Democrats first debated whether to condemn the revived Ku Klux Klan (see page 666), voting 542 to 541 against condemnation. They then endured 103 ballots, deadlocked between southern prohibitionists, who supported former secretary of the treasury William G. McAdoo, and antiprohibition easterners, who backed New York's governor Alfred E. Smith. They finally compromised on John W. Davis, a New York corporation lawyer.

Remnants of the Progressive movement, along with various farm, labor, and socialist groups, formed a new Progressive Party and nominated Robert M. La Follette, the aging Wisconsin reformer. The new party stressed issues of the previous two decades: public ownership of utilities, aid to farmers, rights for organized labor, and regulation of business. The election results endorsed Coolidge prosperity. Coolidge beat Davis by 15.7 million to 8.4 million popular votes, and 382 to 136 electoral

■ President Calvin Coolidge liked to hobnob with business leaders yet also display his Vermont background. He is shown here at his home in Plymouth, Vermont, in 1925 holding a bucket of maple syrup and sitting with Harvey Firestone (of the tire company) on his right, Henry Ford on his left, and Thomas Edison on Ford's left. (Calvin Coolidge Memorial Room, Forbes Library, Northampton, MA)

votes. La Follette finished third, receiving 4.8 million popular votes and only 13 electoral votes.

Impressed by the triumph of business influence, political analysts claimed that Progressivism had died. They

EXTENSIONS OF PROGRESSIVE REFORM

were partly right. The urgency for political and economic reform that had moved the previous generation faded in the 1920s. Much reform, however, occurred at state and local levels. Following initiatives begun before the First World War, thirty-four states instituted or expanded workers' compensation laws in the 1920s. Many states established employee-funded old-age pensions and welfare programs for the indigent. In cities, social workers strived for better housing and poverty relief. By 1926 every major city and many smaller ones had planning and zoning commissions to harness physical growth to the common good. The nation's statehouses, city halls, and universities trained a new generation of reformers who later influenced national affairs.

The federal government's generally apathetic Indian policy disturbed some reformers. Organizations such as

INDIAN AFFAIRS

the Indian Rights Association, the Indian Defense Association, and the General Federation of Women's Clubs worked to obtain justice and social services, including better education and return of tribal lands. But Native Americans, no longer a threat to whites' ambitions, were treated by the general population like other minorities: as objects of discrimination who nevertheless were expected to assimilate. Severalty, the policy created by the Dawes Act of 1887 (see page 458) of allotting land to individuals rather than to tribes, failed to make Indians self-supporting. Indian farmers had to suffer poor soil, lack of irrigation, scarce medical care, and cattle thieves. Deeply attached to their land, they showed little inclination to move to cities. Whites still hoped to convert native peoples into "productive" citizens, but in a way that ignored indigenous cultures. Reformers were especially critical of Indian women, who refused to adopt middle-class homemaking habits and balked at sending their children to boarding schools.

Meanwhile, the federal government struggled to clarify Indians' citizenship status. The Dawes Act had conferred citizenship on all Indians who accepted land allotments but not on those who remained on reservations. Also, the government retained special control over Indian citizens that it did not exercise over other citizens. For example, because of alleged drunkenness on reservations, federal law prevented the sale of liquor to Indians even before ratification of prohibition. After several court challenges, Congress finally passed a law in 1924 granting full citizenship to all Indians who previously had not received it. Also, President Herbert Hoover's administration reorganized the Bureau of Indian Affairs and increased expenditures for health, education, and welfare. Much of the money, however, went to enlarge the bureaucracy rather than into Indian hands.

Even after achieving suffrage in 1920 with ratification of the Nineteenth Amendment, politically active

WOMEN AND POLITICS

women remained excluded from local and national power structures. But their voluntary organizations used tactics that advanced modern pressure-group politics. Whether the issue was birth control, peace, education, Indian affairs, or opposition to lynching, women in these associations publicized their causes and lobbied legislators rather than trying to elect their own candidates. For example, though the League of Women Voters, reorganized out of the National American Woman Suffrage Association, did encourage women to run for office, it worked more actively as lobbyists for laws to improve conditions for employed women, the mentally ill, and the urban poor.

Action by women's groups persuaded Congress to pass the Sheppard-Towner Act (1921), which allotted funds to states to create maternity and pediatric clinics. (The measure ended in 1929, when Congress, under pressure from private physicians, canceled funding.) The Cable Act of 1922 reversed the law under which an American woman who married a foreigner assumed her husband's citizenship, allowing such a woman to retain U.S. citizenship. At the state level, women achieved rights, such as the ability to serve on juries.

As new voters, however, women accomplished relatively little; most women pursued diverging interests. Women in the National Association of Colored Women, for example, fought for the rights of minority women and men without support from either the National Woman's Party or the newly organized League of Women Voters. Some groups, such as the National Woman's Party, pressed for an equal rights amendment to ensure women's equality with men under the law. But such activity alienated the National Consumers League, the Women's Trade Union League, the League of Women Voters, and other organizations that supported special protective legislation to limit the hours and improve conditions for employed women. Though no polls were taken, it appears that percentages of women who voted were lower compared with those of men (which were dropping during the decade). But like men, women of all types seemed preoccupied with the new era's materialism.

Materialism Unbound

Between 1919 and 1929, the gross national product—the total value of all goods and services produced in the United States—swelled by 40 percent. Wages and salaries also grew (though not as drastically), while the cost of living remained relatively stable. People had more purchasing power, and they spent as Americans had never spent (see Table 24.1). Technology's benefits were reaching more people than ever before. By 1929 two-thirds of all Americans lived in dwellings that had electricity, compared with one-sixth in 1912. In 1929 one-fourth of all families owned vacuum cleaners, and one-fifth had toasters. Many could afford such goods as radios, washing machines, and movie tickets only because more than one family member earned wages or because the breadwinner took a second job. Nevertheless, new products and services were available to more than just the rich.

The automobile stood as vanguard of all the era's material wonders. During the 1920s automobile registrations

EFFECTS OF THE
AUTOMOBILE

soared from 8 million to 23 million, and by 1929 there was one car on the roads for every five Americans. Mass production and competition brought down prices, making cars affordable even to some working-class families. A Ford Model T cost less than $300, and a Chevrolet sold for $700 by 1926—when factory workers earned about $1,300 a year and clerical workers about $2,300. Used cars cost less. At those prices, people could consider the car a necessity rather than a luxury. "There is no such thing as a 'pleasure automobile,'" proclaimed one newspaper ad in 1925. "You might as well talk of 'pleasure fresh air,' or of 'pleasure beef steak.' . . . The automobile increases length of life, increases happiness, represents above all other achievements the progress and the civilization of our age."

Cars altered American life as much as railroads had seventy-five years earlier. City streets became cleaner as autos replaced the horses that had dumped tons of manure every day. Women who learned to drive achieved newfound independence, taking touring trips by themselves or with female friends, conquering muddy roads, and making repairs when their vehicles broke down. Families created "homes on wheels," packing food and camping equipment to "get away from it all." By 1927 most autos were enclosed (they previously had open tops), creating new private space for courtship and sex. A vast choice of models (there were 108 automobile manufacturers in 1923) and colors allowed owners to express personal tastes. Some owners customized their

TABLE 24.1	
Consumerism in the 1920s	
1900	
2 bicycles	$ 70.00
wringer and washboard	5.00
brushes and brooms	5.00
sewing machine (mechanical)	25.00
TOTAL	$ 105.00
1928	
automobile	$ 700.00
radio	75.00
phonograph	50.00
washing machine	150.00
vacuum cleaner	50.00
sewing machine (electric)	60.00
other electrical equipment	25.00
telephone (per year)	35.00
TOTAL	$1,145.00

From *Another Part of the Twenties,* by Paul Carter. Copyright 1977 by Columbia University Press. Reprinted with permission of the publisher.

Note: These figures, taken from an article in *Survey Magazine* in 1928, contrast one family's expenditures on consumer goods in 1900 with those of 1928.

cars, installing beds and mechanical gadgets such as special horns and starters. Most importantly, the car was the ultimate symbol of social equality. As one writer observed in 1924, "It is hard to convince Steve Popovich, or Antonio Branca, or plain John Smith that he is being ground into the dust by Capital when at will he may drive the same highways, view the same scenery, and get as much enjoyment from his trip as the modern Midas."

Americans' passion for driving necessitated extensive construction of roads and abundant supplies of fuel. Since the late 1800s farmers and bicyclists had been lobbying for improved roads. After the First World War motorists joined the campaign, and in the 1920s government aid made "automobility" truly feasible. In 1921 Congress passed the Federal Highway Act, providing funds for state roads, and in 1923 the Bureau of Public Roads planned a national highway system. Roadbuilding in turn inspired technological developments such as mechanized road graders and concrete mixers, and mass-produced tires and plate glass. The oil refining industry, aided by chemistry, became vast and powerful. In 1920 the United States produced about 65 percent of the

■ During the 1920s, the desire to own an automobile spread to members of all classes, races, and ethnic groups. Low prices and available credit enabled this family from Beaumont, Texas, to own a "touring car." (Tyrrell Historical Library)

world's oil. Automobiles also forced public officials to pay more attention to safety and traffic control. General Electric Company produced the first timed stop-and-go traffic light in 1924.

By 1929 more money was spent on advertising automobiles and other goods and services than on all types of formal education. Blending psychological theory with practical cynicism, advertising theorists asserted confidently that any person's tastes could be manipulated, and they employed new techniques to achieve their ends. For example, cosmetics manufacturers such as Max Factor, Helena Rubenstein, and the African American entrepreneur Madame C. J. Walker used movie stars and beauty advice in magazines to induce women to buy their products. Baseball star Babe Ruth was hired to endorse food and sporting goods.

ADVERTISING

Radio became one of the era's most influential advertising and entertainment media. By 1929 over 10 million families owned radios, and Americans spent $850 million a year on radio equipment. In the early 1920s, Congress decided that radio should be a private enterprise, not a tax-supported public service as in Great Britain. As a result, American programming focused on entertain-

RADIO

ment and public spectacle—such as Lindbergh's flight—rather than on educational content, because entertainment attracted larger audiences and therefore higher profits from advertisers. Station KDKA in Pittsburgh, at first noncommercial, pioneered broadcasting in 1920. Then, in 1922, an AT&T-run station in New York ran advertisements—"commercials"—for a Long Island real estate developer. Soon other stations began airing advertisements, and by 1922 there were 508 such stations. In 1929 the National Broadcasting Company began to assemble a network of stations and soon was charging advertisers $10,000 to sponsor an hour-long show.

Radio also transformed political culture. In 1924, the presidential nominating conventions of both political parties were the first to be broadcast, enabling candidates and issues to reach more Americans simultaneously than ever before. And as a result of its mass marketing and standardized programming, radio had the effect of blurring ethnic boundaries and creating—at least in one way—a homogeneous "American" culture, an effect that television and other mass media extended throughout the twentieth century.

Although low-income people could not afford all modern products and services, some new trends benefited the working classes, especially those living in cities.

■ The spread of electric service to households gave families access to new forms of entertainment, such as recorded music. The Victrola Talking Machine Company, with its trademark of a little fox terrier looking into the horn of a Gramophone, became one of the world's most recognized advertisers, even after it was purchased by RCA in 1929. (Picture Research Consultants & Archives)

Indoor plumbing and electricity became more common in private residences, and canned foods and ready-made clothes were more affordable. A little cash and a lot of credit enabled many wage earners to purchase an automobile. Spending became a national pastime. No wonder many Americans wanted Henry Ford to run for president in 1924.

Cities, Migrants, and Suburbs

Consumerism signified not merely an economically mature nation but an urbanized one. The 1920 federal census revealed that for the first time a majority of Americans lived in urban areas (defined as places with 2,500 or more people); the city had become the focus of national experience. Growth in manufactur-

ing and services helped propel urbanization. Industries such as steel, oil, and auto production energized Birmingham, Houston, and Detroit; services and retail trades boosted expansion in Seattle, Atlanta, and Minneapolis. Explosive growth also occurred in warm-climate cities—notably Miami and San Diego—where promises of comfort and profit attracted thousands of speculators.

During the 1920s, 6 million Americans left their farms for the city. Irrigation and mechanization had created "factories in the fields," making large-scale farming so efficient that fewer farmers could produce more crops than ever before. As a result, crop prices plummeted and small landholders and tenants could not make a living. Midwesterners, particularly young single people who felt stifled when they compared their existence with the flashy openness of urban life, moved to regional centers like Kansas City and Indianapolis or to the West. Between 1920 and 1930, California's population increased 67 percent, and California became one of the most urbanized states while retaining its status as a leading agricultural state. Meanwhile, streams of rural southerners moved to that region's burgeoning industrial cities or rode railroads northward to Chicago and Cleveland.

African Americans, in what has come to be called the Great Migration, made up a sizable portion of people on

AFRICAN AMERICAN MIGRATION

the move. Pushed from cotton farming by a boll weevil plague and lured by industrial jobs, 1.5 million blacks moved cityward during the 1920s, doubling the African American populations of New York, Chicago, Detroit, and Houston. Race still distinguished social and economic affairs. Forced by low wages and discrimination to seek the cheapest housing, black newcomers squeezed into low-rent ghettos. Unlike white migrants, who were free to move out from the inner city when they could afford to, blacks found better housing closed to them. The only way they could expand their housing opportunities was to spill into nearby white neighborhoods, a process that sparked resistance and violence. Fears of such "invasion" prompted white neighborhood associations to adopt restrictive covenants, whereby homeowners pledged not to sell or rent property to blacks.

In response to discrimination, threats, and violence, thousands of urban blacks joined movements that glorified

MARCUS GARVEY

racial independence. The most influential of these nationalist groups was the Universal Negro Improvement Association (UNIA), headed by Marcus Garvey, a Jamaican immigrant who believed blacks should separate from corrupt white society. Proclaiming "I am the equal of any

Pan American Airways

Air transportation and air mail service between the United States and Latin America began in the 1920s, but establishing the connections was not easy at first because of anti-American hostility in the region. In 1926, the U.S. government, fearful that German aircraft might drop bombs on the Panama Canal if the United States were ever again to go to war with Germany, signed a treaty with Panama giving American airplanes exclusive rights to operate in Panamanian airports. But America's hero of the air, Charles Lindbergh, and a formerly obscure pilot, Juan Trippe, played key roles in changing sentiments and expanding American air service to other parts of Latin America.

Trippe dreamed of creating an international airline. With help from his father-in-law, a banking partner of J. P. Morgan, he established Pan American Airways (informally known as Pan Am) in 1927, invested in modern airplane technology, and won a contract to carry mail between Florida and Cuba. In December of that year, still basking in fame from his transatlantic heroics, Lindbergh flew to Mexico and used his charm to win over the Mexicans to accept airline links to the United States. The next year, Lindbergh joined Pan Am and began flying company planes to destinations in Central and South America. Welcomed wildly everywhere he landed, Lindbergh helped Trippe initiate mail and passenger service to Panama, Mexico, and other Latin American countries in 1929. Trippe advertised to wealthy Americans the opportunity to escape prohibition and enjoy Caribbean beaches by taking Pan Am flights to Havana and beyond, and he offered in-flight meals to travelers.

Needing landing facilities in order to operate, Pan Am built some of the airports that became essential connections between Latin America and the rest of the world, and Trippe's employees created aerial maps that provided navigational aids for many years. Pan Am not only linked Latin America more closely with the United States but also helped unite parts of Latin America that previously were divided by impenetrable mountain ranges. Yet also, Pan Am was willing to resort to almost any tactic to build an airport and start service. As a result, it cooperated with unsavory dictators, engaged in bribery, and violated human rights, in one case helping Bolivian police to corral local Indians behind barbed wire for several days in order to clear land for a new airport.

Still, Pan Am not only enabled Americans (mostly the wealthy) to travel abroad more conveniently but also brought more foreigners to the United States. In 1942, one of its aircraft became the first to fly around the world. In the 1940s, the company began offering flights to Europe and Africa and in 1950 changed its name to Pan American World Airways to emphasize its global character. Until its demise in 1991, Pan Am provided a leading link between the United States and the rest of the world.

Providing air transport connections to the Caribbean, Central America, and South America, Pan American Airways established the first major passenger and cargo links between the United States and other nations. By the early 1930s, flights were so numerous that the time-table announced in this illustration consisted of twelve pages. (The Pan American Heritage Web Site)

[Cropped images provided separately]

white man," Garvey cultivated racial pride with mass meetings and parades. He also promoted black-owned businesses. *Negro World,* Garvey's newspaper, refused to publish ads for products foreign to black culture, such as hair straightening and skin-lightening cosmetics, and he founded the Black Star shipping line to help blacks emigrate to Africa.

The UNIA declined in the mid-1920s after ten UNIA leaders were arrested on charges of anarchism, and Garvey was deported for mail fraud involving the bankrupt Black Star line—the company's main problem was that unscrupulous dealers had sold it dilapidated ships. Middle-class black leaders like W. E. B. Du Bois and several ministers of black churches opposed the UNIA, fearing that its extremism would undermine their efforts and influence. Nevertheless, in New York, Chicago, Detroit, and other big cities, the organization attracted a large following (contemporaries estimated 500,000; Garvey claimed 6 million), and Garvey's speeches instilled many African Americans with a heightened sense of racial pride.

The newest immigrants to American cities came from Mexico and Puerto Rico, where, as in rural North America, declining fortunes pushed people off the land.

NEWCOMERS FROM MEXICO AND PUERTO RICO

During the 1910s, Anglo farmers' associations encouraged Mexican immigration to provide cheap agricultural labor, and by the 1920s Mexican migrants comprised three-fourths of farm labor in the American West. Regarding the migrants as simple peasants, growers treated Mexican laborers as slaves, providing them low wages and poor healthcare. Also, however, many Mexicans were drawn to growing cities like Denver, San Antonio, Los Angeles, and Tucson. Resembling other immigrant groups, they generally lacked resources and skills, and men outnumbered women. Though some achieved middle-class status, most crowded into low-rent districts plagued by poor sanitation, poor police protection, and poor schools. Both rural and urban Mexicans moved constantly back and forth across the border between their homeland and the United States, creating a way of life that Mexicans called *sin fronteras*—without borders.

The 1920s also witnessed an influx of Puerto Ricans to the mainland. Puerto Rico had been a U.S. possession since 1898, and its natives were granted U.S. citizenship in 1916. A shift in the island's economy from sugar to

■ Over a half million Mexicans immigrated to the United States during the 1920s. Many of them traveled in families and worked together in fields and orchards of California and other western states. This family is shown pitting apricots in Los Angeles County in 1924. (Seaver Center for Western History Research, Natural History Museum of Los Angeles County)

coffee production created a labor surplus. Attracted by contracts from employers seeking cheap labor, most Puerto Rican migrants moved to New York City, where they created *barrios* (communities) in Brooklyn and Manhattan and found jobs in manufacturing and in hotels, restaurants, and domestic service.

Within their communities, both Puerto Ricans and Mexicans maintained traditional customs and values and developed businesses—*bodegas* (grocery stores), cafés, boarding houses—and social organizations to help them adapt to American society. Educated elites—doctors, lawyers, business owners—tended to become community leaders.

As urbanization peaked, suburban growth accelerated. Although towns had sprouted around cities since the nation's earliest years, prosperity and automobile transportation in the 1920s made suburbs more accessible to those wishing to flee congested urban neighborhoods. Between 1920 and 1930, suburbs of Chicago (such as Oak Park and Evanston), Cleveland (Shaker Heights), and Los Angeles (Burbank and Inglewood) grew five to ten times faster than did the nearby central cities. These communities sparked an outburst of home construction; Los Angeles builders alone opened 3,200 subdivisions and erected 250,000 homes for auto-owning suburbanites. Most suburbs were middle- and upper-class bedroom communities; some, like Highland Park (near Detroit) and East Chicago, were industrial satellites.

GROWTH OF SUBURBS

Increasingly, suburbs resisted annexation to core cities. Suburbanites wanted to escape big-city crime, grime, and taxes, and they fought to preserve control over their own police, schools, and water and gas services. Particularly in the Northeast and Midwest, the suburbs' fierce independence choked off expansion by the central city and prevented central cities from access to the resources and tax bases of wealthier suburban communities. Moreover, automobiles and the dispersal of population spread the environmental problems of city life—trash, pollution, noise—across the entire metropolitan area.

■ Wide highways, cheap land, and affordable housing allowed automobile commuters to move to the urban periphery. In this photo, young women wearing 1920s flapper-style outfits celebrate the phenomenal growth of Culver City, outside Los Angeles. Notice the strong presence of the motor car. (Security Pacific National Bank Collection, Los Angeles Public Library)

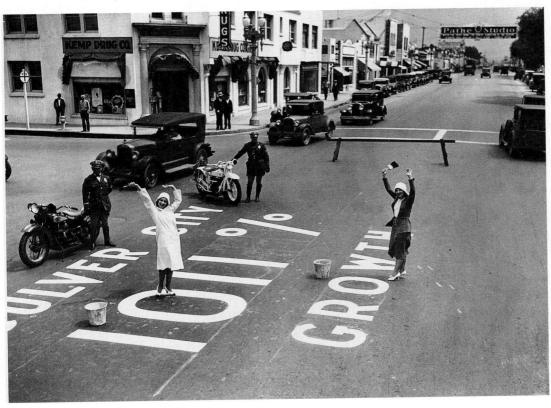

Cities and suburbs fostered the mass culture that gave the decade its character. Most of the consumers who jammed shops, movie houses, and sporting arenas and who embraced fads like crossword puzzles, miniature golf, and marathon dancing lived in or around cities. These were the places where people defied law and tradition by patronizing speakeasies (illegal saloons during prohibition), wearing outlandish clothes, and listening to jazz. They were also the places where devout moralists strained to resist modernism. Yet the ideal of small-town society survived. While millions thronged cityward, Americans reminisced about the innocence and simplicity of a world gone by. This was the dilemma the modern nation faced: how does one anchor oneself in a world of rampant materialism and rapid social change?

New Rhythms of Everyday Life

*A*mid changes to modern society, Americans developed new ways of using time. People increasingly split daily life into distinct compartments: work, family, and leisure. Each type of time was altered in the 1920s. For many, time on the job shrank. Though strikes following the First World War failed to reduce working hours, increased mechanization and higher productivity enabled employers to shorten the workweek for many industrial laborers from six days to five and a half. White-collar employees often worked a forty-hour week, enjoyed a full weekend off, and received annual vacations as a standard job benefit.

Family time is hard to measure, but certain trends are clear. Family size decreased between 1920 and 1930 as birth control became more widely practiced. Among American women who married in the 1870s and 1880s, well over half who survived to age fifty had five or more children; of their counterparts who married in the 1920s, however, just 20 percent had five or more children. Meanwhile, the divorce rate rose. In 1920 there was 1 divorce for every 7.5 marriages; by 1929 the national ratio was 1 in 6, and in many cities it was 2 in 7. In conjunction with longer life expectancy, lower birth rates and more divorce meant that adults were devoting a smaller portion of their lives to raising children.

Housewives still worked long hours cleaning, cooking, and raising children, but machines now lightened some of their tasks and enabled them to use time differently than their forebears had. Especially in middle-class households, electric irons and washing machines simplified some chores. Gas- and oil-powered central heating and hot-water heaters eliminated the

HOUSEHOLD
MANAGEMENT

hauling of wood, coal, and water, the upkeep of a kitchen fire, and the removal of ashes.

Even as technology and economic change made some tasks simpler, they also created new demands on a woman's time. As daughters of working-class families stayed in school longer and as alternative forms of employment caused a shortage of servants in wealthier households, those who formerly had helped housewives with cleaning, cooking, and childcare were less available. The availability of washing machines, hot water, vacuum cleaners, and commercial soap put greater pressure on wives to keep everything clean. Indeed, advertisers of these products tried to make women feel guilty for not giving enough attention to cleaning the home. No longer a producer of food and clothing as her ancestors had been, a housewife now also became the chief shopper, responsible for making sure her family spent money wisely. And the automobile made the wife a family's chief chauffeur. One survey found that urban housewives spent on average 13 percent of their work time, seven and a half hours per week, driving to shop and to transport children.

New emphasis on nutrition added a scientific dimension to housewives' responsibilities. With the discovery of vitamins between 1915 and 1930, nutritionists began advocating consumption of certain foods to prevent illness. Giant food companies scrambled to advertise their products as filled with vitamins and minerals beneficial to growth and health. Not only did producers of milk and canned fruits and vegetables exploit the vitamin craze, but other companies made lofty claims that were hard to dispute because little was known about these invisible, tasteless ingredients. Welch's Grape Juice, for example, avoided mentioning its excess of sugars when it advertised that it was "Rich in Health Values," containing vitamins, minerals, and "the laxative properties you cannot do without." Even chocolate candy manufacturers plugged their bars as vitamin-packed.

HEALTH
AND LIFE
EXPECTANCY

Better diets and improved hygiene made Americans generally healthier. Life expectancy at birth increased from fifty-four to sixty years between 1920 and 1930, and infant mortality decreased by two-thirds. Public sanitation and research in bacteriology and immunology combined to reduce risks of life-threatening diseases such as tuberculosis and diphtheria. But medical progress did not benefit all groups equally; race mattered in health trends as well as in everything else. Rates of infant mortality were 50 to 100 percent higher among nonwhites than among whites, and tuberculosis in inner-city slums remained alarmingly common. Moreover, fatalities from car accidents rose 150 percent, and deaths from heart

Your Children ___
___ is their food safe ?

YOU, as a conscientious mother, buy the best food for your children, prepare it with scrupulous care and cook it correctly. Yet, in spite of all, you may be giving your children food which is not wholesome—possibly dangerous!

For even the best food becomes unsafe to eat unless it is *kept* at the proper degree of cold, which medical authorities agree should be 50 degrees or less—always. Above that temperature, bacteria multiply, food is contaminated—becomes a menace to health.

There is only one way to be sure that your children's food is fresh and healthful—correct refrigeration. There is one refrigerator that assures you of scientifically perfect refrigeration at all times —the General Electric. Faithfully, quietly, day and night, it maintains a

temperature safely below the danger point—50 degrees.

The General Electric is ideal for the home. Its simple mechanism which you never need to oil, is mounted on top

The price of this new all-steel refrigerator— the small-family model—is now
$215 AT THE FACTORY

of the cabinet and hermetically sealed in a steel casing. It has a simple and accessible temperature control, makes a generous supply of ice cubes, creates no radio interference. It has the only *all-steel*, warp-proof cabinet—easily cleaned, sanitary.

Your dealer will be glad to explain the spaced payment plan, which makes it so easy to own this faithful watchman of the family health. Let him help you select the particular model that fits your needs. If there is not a dealer near you, write Electric Refrigeration Dept., General Electric Co., Hanna Building, Cleveland, Ohio, for booklet Q-9.

An unmatched record
There are now more than 300,000 homes enjoying the comfort and protection of General Electric Refrigerators—and not one of the owners has ever had to pay a single dollar for repairs or service.

GENERAL ✧ ELECTRIC
ALL-STEEL REFRIGERATOR

■ While electric appliances gave mothers and housewives more convenient ways to carry out their roles, producers tried to sell their products by creating guilt among women who were concerned over their families' safety. Here, the General Electric Company warns a mother that she needs a GE refrigerator if she is to be "conscientious" and "scrupulous" about giving her children wholesome and healthy food.   (Picture Research Consultants & Archives)

disease and cancer—diseases of old age—increased 15 percent. Nevertheless, Americans in general were living longer: the total population over age sixty-five grew 35 percent between 1920 and 1930, while the rest of the population increased only 15 percent.

Longer life and the worsening economic status of the elderly stirred interest in government pensions and other

OLDER AMERICANS AND RETIREMENT

forms of old-age assistance. Industrialism put premiums on youth and agility, pushing older people into poverty from forced retirement and reduced income.

Recognizing the needs of aging citizens, most European countries established state-supported pension systems in the early 1900s. Many Americans, however, believed that individuals should prepare for old age by saving in their youth; pensions, they felt, smacked of socialism. As late as 1923 the Pennsylvania Chamber of Commerce labeled old-age assistance "un-American and socialistic . . . an entering wedge of communistic propaganda."

Yet conditions were alarming. Most inmates in state poorhouses were older people, and almost one-third of Americans age sixty-five and older depended financially on someone else. Few employers, including the federal government, provided for retired employees. Noting that the government fed retired horses until they died, one postal worker complained, "For the purpose of drawing a pension, it would have been better had I been a horse than a human being." Resistance to pension plans finally broke at the state level in the 1920s. Led by Isaac Max Rubinow and Abraham Epstein, reformers persuaded voluntary associations, labor unions, and legislators to endorse old-age assistance through pensions, insurance, and retirement homes. By 1933 almost every state provided at least minimal support to needy elderly people, and a path had been opened for a national program of old-age insurance.

As people encountered new influences in their time away from work and family, altered habits and values

SOCIAL VALUES

were inevitable. Aided by new fabrics and chemical dyes, clothes became a means of self-expression and personal freedom. Women and men wore more casual and gaily colored styles than their parents would have considered. The line between acceptable and inappropriate behavior blurred as smoking, drinking, swearing, and frankness about sex became fashionable. Birth-control advocate Margaret Sanger, who a decade earlier had been accused of promoting race suicide, gained a large following in respectable circles. Newspapers, magazines, motion pictures, and popular songs (such as "Hot Lips" and "Burning Kisses") made certain that Americans did not suffer from "sex starvation." A typical movie ad promised "brilliant men, beautiful jazz babies, champagne baths, midnight revels, petting parties in the purple dawn, all ending in one terrific smashing climax that makes you gasp."

Other trends weakened inherited customs. Because child-labor laws and compulsory-attendance rules kept children in school longer than ever before, peer groups played a more influential role in socializing youngsters. In earlier eras, different age groups often shared the same activities: children worked with older people in fields and kitchens, and young apprentices toiled in workshops be-

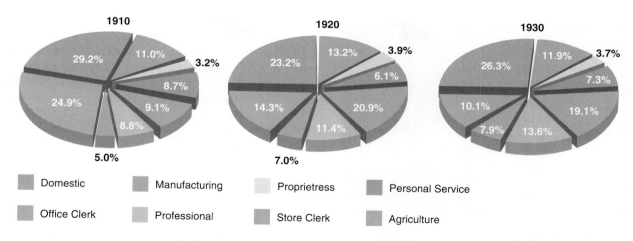

Figure 24.1 Changing Dimensions of Paid Female Labor, 1910–1930

These charts reveal the extraordinary growth in clerical and professional occupations among employed women and the accompanying decline in agricultural labor in the early twentieth century. Notice that manufacturing employment peaked in 1920 and that domestic service fluctuated as white immigrant women began to move out of these jobs and were replaced by women of color.

side older journeymen and craftsmen. Now, graded school classes, sports, and clubs constantly brought together children of the same age, separating them from the company and influence of adults. Meanwhile, parents tended to rely less on traditions of childcare and more on experts who wrote manuals on how best to raise children.

After the First World War, women continued to stream into the labor force. By 1930, 10.8 million women held paying jobs, an increase of 2 million since war's end. Most notably, the proportion of women working in agriculture shrank, while proportions in categories of urban jobs grew or held steady (see Figure 24.1). The sex segregation that had long characterized workplaces persisted; most women took jobs that men seldom sought and vice versa. Over 1 million women were in the professional category, but most were teachers and nurses. In the office clerk category, some 2.2 million women were typists, bookkeepers, and filing clerks, a tenfold increase since 1920. Another 736,000 were store clerks, and growing numbers could be found in the personal service category as waitresses and hairdressers. Though almost 2 million women worked in manufacturing, their numbers grew very little over the decade. Wherever women were employed, their wages seldom exceeded half of those paid to men.

WOMEN IN THE WORK FORCE

Although women worked outside the home for a variety of reasons, their families' economic needs were paramount. The consumerism of the 1920s tempted working-class and middle-class families to satisfy their wants and needs by living beyond their means or by sending women into the labor force. In previous eras, most people whose earnings supplemented those of the primary breadwinner had been young and single. Even though the vast majority of married women did not work outside the home (only 12 percent were employed in 1930), married women as a proportion of the work force rose by 30 percent, and the number of employed married women swelled from 1.9 million to 3.1 million. These figures omit countless widowed, divorced, and abandoned women who held jobs and who, like married women, often had children to support.

The proportion of women of racial minorities in paid labor was double that of white women. Often they entered the labor force because their husbands were unemployed or underemployed. The majority of employed African American women held domestic jobs doing cooking, cleaning, and laundry. The few who held factory jobs, such as in cigarette factories and meatpacking plants, performed the least desirable, lowest-paying tasks. Some opportunities opened for educated black women in social work, teaching, and nursing, but even these women faced discrimination and low incomes. Grandmothers and aunts helped with childcare when mothers took outside employment, but such arrangements did not lessen the economic burdens on households beset by lack of skills, poverty, and prejudice.

EMPLOYMENT OF MINORITY WOMEN

■ The expansion of service-sector jobs and new technology opened new opportunities for women in the 1920s. This telephone operator handled scores of phone calls at the same time and monitored a huge switchboard. Her dress and jewelry contrasted with the simpler styles worn by factory women, who had to be more careful in working with dangerous machines.   (George Eastman House)

havior, chaste, modest heroines were eclipsed by movie temptresses like Clara Bow, known as the "It Girl," and Gloria Swanson, notorious for torrid love affairs on and off the screen. Many women were asserting a new social equality with men. One observer described "the new woman" as intriguingly independent:

> She takes a man's point of view as her mother never could. . . . She will never make you a hatband or knit you a necktie, but she'll drive you from the station . . . in her own little sports car. She'll don knickers and go skiing with you, . . . she'll dive as well as you, perhaps better, she'll dance as long as you care to, and she'll take everything you say the way you mean it.

The era's openness regarding sexuality also enabled the underground homosexual culture to surface a little more than in previous eras. In nontra-

HOMOSEXUAL CULTURE — ditional city neighborhoods, such as New York's Greenwich Village and Harlem, cheap rents and an apparent tolerance of alternate lifestyles attracted gay men and lesbians who patronized dance halls, speakeasies, cafés, and other gathering places. Such establishments that catered to a gay clientele remained targets for police raids, however, demonstrating that homosexual men and women could not expect acceptance from the rest of society.

These trends represented a break with the more restrained culture of the nineteenth century. But social change rarely proceeds smoothly. As the decade wore on, various groups mobilized to defend older values.

Lines of Defense

Early in 1920 the leader of a newly formed organization, using a tactic adopted by modern associations, hired two public relations experts to recruit members. The experts, Edward Clarke and Elizabeth Tyler, canvassed communities in the South, Southwest, and Midwest, where they found thousands of men eager to pay a $10 membership fee and $6 for a white uniform. Clarke and Tyler pocketed $2.50 from each membership they sold. Their success helped build the organization to 5 million members by 1923.

No ordinary civic club like the Lions or Kiwanis, this was the Ku Klux Klan, a revived version of the hooded

KU KLUX KLAN — order that terrorized southern communities after the Civil War. Its appeal was based on fear, and it vowed to protect female purity as well as racial and ethnic purity. As one pamphlet distributed by Clarke and Tyler declared, "Every criminal, every gambler, every thug, every liber-

Economic necessity also drew thousands of Mexican women into wage labor, although their tradition resisted female employment. Exact figures are difficult to uncover, but it is certain that many Mexican women in the Southwest worked as field laborers, operatives in garment factories, and domestic servants. Next to black women, Japanese American women were the most likely to hold paying jobs. They too worked as field hands and domestics, jobs in which they encountered racial bias and low pay.

Employed or not, some women remade the image of femininity. In contrast to heavy, floor-length dresses and long hair of previous generations, the

ALTERNATIVE IMAGES OF FEMININITY — short skirts and bobbed hair of the 1920s "flapper" symbolized independence and sexual freedom. Though few women lived the flapper life, the look became fashionable among office workers and store clerks as well as college coeds. As models of female be-tine, every girl ruiner, every home wrecker, every wife beater, every dope peddler, every moonshiner, every white slaver, every Rome-controlled newspaper, every black spider—is fighting the Klan. Think it over, which side are you on?"

Reconstituted in 1915 by William J. Simmons, an Atlanta evangelist and insurance salesman, the Klan was the most sinister reactionary movement of the 1920s. It revived the hoods, intimidating tactics, and mystical terminology of its forerunner (its leader was the Imperial Wizard, its book of rituals the Kloran). But the new Klan had broader membership and broader objectives than the old (see pages 440–441). It fanned outward from the Deep South and for a time wielded frightening power in places as diverse as Oregon, Oklahoma, and Indiana. Its membership included many from the middle class who were fearful of losing social and economic gains achieved from postwar prosperity and nervous about a new youth culture that seemed to be eluding family control. As well, an estimated half-million women joined, some of them having moved out of women's organizations such as the Women's Christian Temperance Union and Young Women's Christian Association.

One phrase summed up Klan goals: "Native, white, Protestant supremacy." Native meant no immigration, no "mongrelization" of American culture. According to Imperial Wizard Hiram Wesley Evans, white supremacy was a matter of survival. "The world," he warned, "has been so made so that each race must fight for its life, must conquer, accept slavery, or die. The Klansman believes the whites will not become slaves, and he does not intend to die before his time." Evans praised Protestantism for promoting "unhampered individual development," and he accused the Catholic Church of discouraging assimilation and enslaving people to priests and a foreign pope.

Using threatening assemblies, violence, and political and economic pressure, the Klan menaced many communities in the early 1920s. Klansmen meted out vigilante justice to suspected bootleggers, wife beaters, and adulterers; forced schools to adopt Bible reading and to stop teaching the theory of evolution; campaigned against Catholic and Jewish political candidates; pledged members not to buy from merchants who did not share their views; and fueled racial tensions against Mexicans in Texas border cities. Klan women not only joined male members in activities to promote native white Protestantism but also worked for suffrage and other women's rights. By 1925, however, the Invisible Empire was weakening, as scandal undermined its moral base. In 1925 Indiana grand dragon David Stephenson was

convicted of second-degree murder after he kidnapped and raped a woman who later died either from taking poison or from infection caused by bites on her body. More generally, the Klan's negative, exclusive brand of patriotism and purity could not compete in a pluralistic society.

The Ku Klux Klan had no monopoly on bigotry in the 1920s; intolerance pervaded American society. Nativists had been urging an end to free immigration since the 1880s. They charged that Catholic and Jewish immigrants clogged city slums, flouted community norms, and stubbornly held to alien religious and political beliefs. As naturalist Madison Grant, whose study of zoology prompted him to believe that certain human races, mainly Nordics, were superior to others, wrote in *The Passing of the Great Race* (1916): "These immigrants adopt the language of the native American, they wear his clothes, they steal his name and they are beginning to take his women, but they seldom adopt his religion or understand his ideals."

Guided by such sentiments, the movement to restrict immigration gathered support. Labor leaders warned

IMMIGRATION QUOTAS

that floods of aliens would depress wages and raise unemployment. Business executives, who formerly had opposed restrictions because they desired cheap immigrant laborers, changed their minds, having realized that they could keep wages low by mechanizing and by hiring black workers. Drawing support from such groups, Congress reversed previous policy and set yearly immigration quotas for each nationality. The limits favored northern and western Europeans, reflecting nativist prejudices in favor of white Anglo-Saxon or Teuton Protestant immigrants and against Catholic and Jewish immigrants from southern and eastern Europe. By stipulating that annual immigration of a given nationality could not exceed 3 percent of the number of immigrants from that nation residing in the United States in 1910, the Emergency Quota Act of 1921 discriminated against immigrants from southern and eastern Europe, whose numbers were small in 1910 relative to those from northern Europe.

The Quota Act was a temporary measure, and in 1924 Congress replaced it with the National Origins Act. This law restricted the influx to 150,000 people by setting quotas at 2 percent of each nationality residing in the United States in 1890, except for Asians, who were banned completely. (Chinese already had been excluded by legislation in 1882.) The act further restricted southern and eastern Europeans, since fewer of those groups lived in the United States in 1890 than in 1910, though

Anti-immigrationists used songs, as well as speeches and posters, to promote their cause. This 1923 tune urges the government to "Close the Gates" lest foreigners betray the hard-won rights of Americans and "drag our Colors down." (National Park Service Collection, Ellis Island Immigration Museum)

the law did allow wives and children of U.S. citizens to enter as nonquota immigrants. As a result, the 1921 quotas for southern and eastern Europeans fell by 84 percent while those northern and western Europeans dropped by only 29 percent. In 1927 a revised National Origins Act apportioned new quotas to begin in 1929. It retained the limit of 150,000 possible immigrants, but redefined quotas to be distributed among European countries in proportion to the "national-origins" (country of birth or descent) of American inhabitants in 1920. People from Canada, Mexico, and Puerto Rico did not fall under the quotas (except for those whom the Labor Department defined as potential paupers), and soon they became the largest immigrant groups (see Figure 24.2).

Fear of immigrant radicalism, persisting from the Red Scare of 1919, fueled antiforeign flames. Controversy arose in 1921 when a court convicted Nicola Sacco and Bartolomeo Vanzetti, two immigrant anarchists, of

SACCO AND VANZETTI CASE murdering a guard and paymaster during a robbery in South Braintree, Massachusetts. Sacco and Vanzetti's main offenses seem to have been their political beliefs and Italian origins. Though evidence failed to prove their guilt, Judge Webster Thayer openly sided with the prosecution and privately called the defendants "anarchist bastards." Appeals and protests failed to win a new trial, and the prisoners, who remained calm and dignified throughout their ordeal, were executed in 1927. Their deaths touched off rallies and riots in Europe, Asia, and South America, leaving doubts about the United States as the land that nurtured freedom of belief.

While nativists lobbied for racial purity, the pursuit of spiritual purity stirred religious fundamentalists.

FUNDAMENTALISM Millions of Americans sought certainty and salvation against what they perceived as the skepticism and irreverence of a materialistic, hedonistic society by following evangelical denominations of Protestantism that accepted literal interpretation of the Bible. Resolutely believing that God's miracles created life and the world, they were convinced that Darwin's theory of evolution was speculation, and that if fundamentalists constituted a majority of a community, as they did throughout the South, they should be able to determine what would be taught in schools. Their enemies were "modernists," who interpreted "truths" critically, using reasoning from psychology and anthropology. To modernists, the Bible's accuracy did not matter; what was important was the historical relevance of God in culture and the role of science in advancing knowledge.

In 1925 Christian fundamentalism clashed with modernism in a celebrated case in Dayton, Tennessee.

SCOPES TRIAL Early that year the state legislature passed a law forbidding public school instructors to teach the theory that humans had evolved from lower forms of life rather than descended from Adam and Eve. Shortly thereafter, high school teacher John Thomas Scopes volunteered to serve in a test case and was arrested for violating the law. Scopes's trial that summer became a headline event. William Jennings Bryan, former secretary of state and three-time presidential candidate, argued for the prosecution, and a team of civil liberties lawyers headed by Clarence Darrow represented the defense. News correspondents crowded into town, and radio stations broadcast the trial from coast to coast.

Although Scopes was convicted—clearly he had broken the law—modernists claimed victory. The testimony, they believed, showed fundamentalism to be illogical. The trial's climax occurred when Bryan himself took the

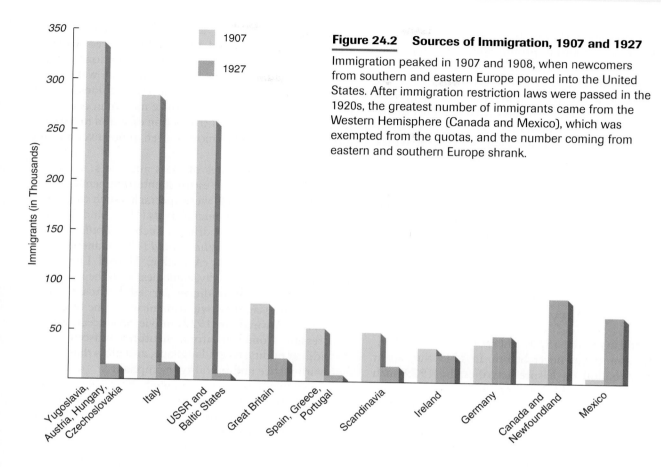

Figure 24.2   Sources of Immigration, 1907 and 1927

Immigration peaked in 1907 and 1908, when newcomers from southern and eastern Europe poured into the United States. After immigration restriction laws were passed in the 1920s, the greatest number of immigrants came from the Western Hemisphere (Canada and Mexico), which was exempted from the quotas, and the number coming from eastern and southern Europe shrank.

witness stand as an expert on religion and science. Responding to Darrow's probing, Bryan asserted that Eve really had been created from Adam's rib, that the Tower of Babel was responsible for the diversity of languages, and that a biblical "day" could have lasted thousands of years. Spectators in Dayton cheered Bryan for his testimony, but the liberal press mocked him and his allies. Humorist Will Rogers quipped, "I see you can't say that man descended from the ape. At least that's the law in Tennessee. But do they have a law to keep a man from making a jackass of himself?" Nevertheless, fundamentalists convinced many school boards to limit the teaching of evolution and influenced the content of high school biology books. As well, they created an independent subculture, with their own schools, camps, radio ministries, and missionary societies.

Klan rallies, immigration restriction, and fundamentalist literalism might appear as last gasps of a rural society struggling against modern urban-industrial values. Yet city dwellers swelled the ranks of all these movements. Nearly half the Klan's members lived in cities, especially in working-class neighborhoods where fear of invasion by racial minorities and foreigners was strong.

Even urban reformers backed immigration restriction as a means of controlling poverty and quickening the assimilation of immigrants.

Cities also housed hundreds of Pentecostal churches, which attracted both blacks and whites struggling with economic insecurity, nervous about modernism's attack on old-time religion, and swayed by the pageantry and personal God such churches depicted. Using modern advertising techniques and elaborately staged services broadcast on radio, magnetic preachers such as flamboyant Aimee Semple McPherson of Los Angeles, former baseball player Billy Sunday, and Father Divine (George Baker, an African American who amassed an interracial following especially in eastern cities) stirred revivalist fervor. Revivalism represented one, but not the only, attempt to sustain old-fashioned values and find anchors in a fast-moving, materialistic world. Some Americans lashed out at "different" cultures and hedonistic behavior. Millions firmly believed that nonwhites and immigrants were inferior people who imperiled national welfare. Clergy and teachers of all faiths condemned drinking, dancing, new

SAVING OLD-FASHIONED VALUES

dress styles, and sex in movies and in parked cars. Many urban dwellers supported prohibition, believing that eliminating the temptation of drink would help win the battle against poverty, vice, and corruption. Yet even while mourning a lost past, most Americans sincerely sought some kind of balance as they tried to adjust to the modern order in one way or another. Few refrained from listening to the radio and attending movies, activities that proved less corrupting than critics feared. More than ever, Americans sought fellowship in civic organizations. Membership swelled in Rotary, Elks, and women's clubs, and the number of Community Chests—associations that coordinated local welfare projects—grew from 12 in 1919 to 361 in 1930. Perhaps most important, more people were finding release in recreation and new uses of leisure time.

The Age of Play

*a*mericans in the 1920s embraced commercial entertainment as never before. In 1919 they spent $2.5 billion on leisure activities; by 1929 such expenditures topped $4.3 billion, a figure not again equaled until after the Second World War. Spectator amusements—movies, music, and sports—accounted for 21 percent of the 1929 total; the rest involved participatory recreation, such as games, hobbies, and travel.

Entrepreneurs responded quickly to an appetite for fads, fun, and "ballyhoo"—a blitz of publicity that lent exaggerated importance to some person or event, such as Charles Lindbergh's flight. Games and fancies particularly attracted newly affluent middle-class families. Early in the 1920s, mahjong, a Chinese tile game, was the craze. In the mid-1920s devotees popularized crossword puzzles, printed in mass-circulation newspapers and magazines. Next, funseekers adopted miniature golf as their new fad. By 1930 the nation boasted thirty thousand miniature golf courses featuring tiny castles, windmills, and waterfalls. Dance crazes like the Charleston were practiced throughout the country, aided by live and recorded music on radio and the growing popularity of jazz.

In addition to indulging actively, Americans were avid spectators, particularly of movies and sports. In total

MOVIES AND SPORTS

capital investment, motion pictures became one of the nation's leading industries. Nearly every community had at least one theater, whether it was a hundred-seat Bijou on Main Street or a big-city "picture palace" with ornate lobbies and thousands of cushioned

seats. In 1922 movies attracted 40 million viewers weekly; by decade's end the number neared 100 million—at a time when the nation's population was 120 million and total weekly church attendance was 60 million. Between 1922 and 1927, the Technicolor Corporation developed a means to produce movies in color. This process, along with the introduction of sound in *The Jazz Singer* in 1927, made movies even more exciting and realistic.

Responding to tastes of mass audiences, the movie industry produced more escapist entertainment than art. The most popular films were spectacles such as Cecil B. DeMille's *The Ten Commandments* (1923) and *The King of Kings* (1927); lurid dramas such as *Souls for Sale* (1923) and *A Woman Who Sinned* (1924); and slapstick comedies starring Fatty Arbuckle, Harold Lloyd, and Charlie Chaplin. Ironically, comedies, with their poignant satires of the human condition, carried the most thought-provoking messages. Movie content was tame by current standards, however. In 1927, movie producers, bowing to pressure from legislators, instituted self-censorship, forbidding nudity, rough language, and plots that did not end with justice and morality triumphant.

Spectator sports also boomed. Each year millions packed stadiums and parks to cheer athletic events. Gate receipts from college football surpassed $21 million by the late 1920s. In an age when technology and mass production had robbed experiences and objects of their uniqueness, sports provided unpredictability and drama that people craved. Newspapers and radio magnified this tension, feeding news to an eager public and glorifying events with such unrestrained narrative that sports promoters did not need to buy advertising.

Baseball's drawn-out suspense, variety of plays, and potential for keeping statistics attracted a huge following. After the "Black Sox scandal" of 1919, when eight members of the Chicago White Sox were banned from the game for allegedly throwing the World Series to the Cincinnati Reds (even though a jury acquitted them), baseball regained respectability by transforming itself. Discovering that home runs excited fans, the leagues redesigned the ball to make it livelier. Game attendance skyrocketed. A record 300,000 people attended the six-game 1921 World Series between the New York Giants and New York Yankees. Millions gathered regularly to watch local teams, and even more listened to professional games on the radio.

Sports, movies, and the news created a galaxy of heroes. As technology and mass society made the individual less significant, people clung to heroic personalities as a means of identifying

SPORTS HEROES

with the unique. Names such as Bill Tilden in tennis, Gertrude Ederle in swimming (in 1926 she became the first woman to swim across the English Channel), and Bobby Jones in golf were household words. The power and action of boxing, football, and baseball produced the most popular sports heroes. Heavyweight champion Jack Dempsey, the "Manassa (Colorado) Brawler," attracted the first of several million-dollar gates in his fight with French boxer Georges Carpentier in 1921. Harold "Red" Grange, running back for the University of Illinois football team, thrilled fans and sportswriters with his speed and agility.

Baseball's foremost hero was George Herman "Babe" Ruth, who began his career as a pitcher but found he could use his prodigious strength to better advantage hitting home runs. Ruth hit twenty-nine in 1919, fifty-four in 1920 (the year the Boston Red Sox traded him to the New York Yankees), fifty-nine in 1921, and sixty in

1927—each year a record. His talent and boyish grin endeared him to millions. Known for overindulgence in food, drink, and sex, he charmed fans into forgiving his excesses by appearing at public events and visiting hospitalized children.

While admiring physical exploits of sports heroes, Americans fulfilled a yearning for romance and adventure through movie idols. The films and personal lives of Douglas Fairbanks, Gloria Swanson, and Charlie Chaplin were discussed in parlors and pool halls across the country. One of the decade's most ballyhooed personalities was Rudolph Valentino, whose suave manner made women swoon and men imitate his pomaded hairdo and slick sideburns. Valentino's image exploited the era's sexual liberalism and flirtation with wickedness. In his most famous film, Valentino played a passionate sheik who carried away

MOVIE STARS AND PUBLIC HEROES

■ Babe Ruth had widespread appeal as one of the country's first sports superstars. Here a photograph of his mighty home run swing appears on a school notebook, showing the new link between sports and consumerism. (Private Collection)

■ Rudolph Valentino became the idol of men and women alike in *The Sheik,* his most famous movie. With flashing eyes and wanton smile, Valentino carries a swooning woman to his tent. This immensely popular movie earned $1 million for Paramount Pictures. (Museum of Modern Art Film Still Archive)

beautiful women to his tent, combining the roles of abductor and seducer. When he died at thirty-one of complications from ulcers and appendicitis, the press turned his funeral into a public extravaganza. Mourners lined up for over a mile to file past his coffin.

In their quest for fun and self-expression, some Americans became lawbreakers by refusing to give up drinking.

PROHIBITION The Eighteenth Amendment (1919) and federal law (1920) that prohibited the manufacture, sale, and transportation of alcoholic beverages (see page 576) worked well at first. Per capita consumption of liquor dropped, as did arrests for drunkenness, and the price of illegal booze rose above what average workers could afford. But legislators mostly refrained from enforcing prohibition. In 1922 Congress gave the Prohibition Bureau only three thousand employees and less than $7 million for nationwide enforcement.

After 1925 the so-called noble experiment of prohibition broke down as thousands of people made their own wine and bathtub gin, and bootleg importers along the country's borders and shorelines easily evaded the few patrols that attempted to intercept them. Moreover, drinking, like gambling and prostitution, was a business with willing customers, and criminal organizations quickly capitalized on public demand. The most notorious of such mobs belonged to Al Capone, a burly tough who seized control of illegal liquor and vice in Chicago, maintaining his grip on both politicians and the vice business through intimidation, bribery, and violence. But Capone contended, in a statement revealing of the era, "Prohibition is a business. All I do is supply a public de-

mand." Americans wanted their liquor and beer, and until 1931 when a federal court convicted and imprisoned him for income-tax evasion (the only charge for which authorities could obtain hard evidence), Capone supplied them. Reflecting on the contradictions inherent in prohibition, columnist Walter Lippmann wrote in 1931, "The high level of lawlessness is maintained by the fact that Americans desire to do so many things which they also desire to prohibit."

Cultural Currents

*I*ntellectuals like Lippmann were quick to point to the era's hypocrisy. Serious writers and artists felt at odds with society, and their rejection of materialism and conformity was both biting and bitter.

Several writers from the so-called Lost Generation, including novelist Ernest Hemingway and poets Ezra Pound and T. S. Eliot, abandoned the United States for Europe. Others, such as novelists William Faulkner and Sinclair Lewis, remained in America but, like the expatriates, expressed disillusionment with the materialism that they witnessed. F. Scott Fitzgerald's *This Side of Paradise* (1920) and *The Great Gatsby* (1925); Lewis's *Babbitt* (1922), *Arrowsmith* (1925), and *Elmer Gantry* (1927); and Eugene O'Neill's plays exposed and derided Americans' preoccupation with money. Edith Wharton explored the clash of old and new moralities in novels such as *The Age of Innocence* (1920). Ellen Glasgow, one of the South's leading literary figures, lamented

LITERATURE OF ALIENATION

the trend toward impersonality in *Barren Ground* (1925). John Dos Passos's *Three Soldiers* (1921) and Hemingway's *A Farewell to Arms* (1929) interwove antiwar sentiment with critiques of the emptiness in modern relationships.

Spiritual discontent quite different from that of white writers inspired a new generation of African American

HARLEM RENAISSANCE

artists. Middle-class, educated, and proud of their African heritage, black writers rejected white culture and exalted the militantly assertive "New Negro." Most of them lived in New York's Harlem; in this "Negro Mecca" black intellectuals and artists, aided by a few white patrons, celebrated black culture during what became known as the Harlem Renaissance.

The popular 1921 musical comedy *Shuffle Along* is often credited with launching the Harlem Renaissance. The musical showcased talented African American artists such as lyricist Noble Sissle, composer Eubie Blake, and singers Florence Mills, Josephine Baker, and Mabel Mercer. Harlem in the 1920s also fostered a number of gifted writers, among them poets Langston Hughes, Countee Cullen, and Claude McKay; novelists Zora Neale Hurston, Jessie Fauset, and Jean Toomer; and essayist Alain Locke. As well, the movement included visual artists such as Aaron Douglas, James A. Porter, and Augusta Savage.

These artists and intellectuals grappled with notions of identity. Though cherishing their African heritage, they realized that blacks had to come to terms with themselves as Americans. Thus Alain Locke urged that the New Negro should become "a collaborator and participant in American civilization." But Langston Hughes wrote, "We younger Negro artists who create now intend to express our individual dark-skinned selves without fear or shame. If white people are pleased, we are glad. If they are not, it doesn't matter. We know we are beautiful."

The Jazz Age, as the 1920s is sometimes called, owes its name to the music of black culture. Evolving from

JAZZ

African and black American folk music, early jazz communicated exuberance, humor, and authority that African Americans seldom experienced in their public and political lives. With emotional rhythms and emphasis on improvisation, jazz blurred the distinction between composer and performer and created intimacy between performer and audience. As African Americans moved northward, jazz traveled with them. Urban dance halls and bars often featured jazz, and gifted performers like trumpeter Louis Armstrong, trombonist Kid Ory, and blues singer Bessie Smith enjoyed wide fame thanks to

■ Florence Mills was a talented performer whose singing career received a major boost from her appearance in the musical comedy *Shuffle Along,* a show that heralded the beginning of the Harlem Renaissance.   (Howard Greenburg Galleries, © 1997 Donna VanDer Zee)

phonograph records and radio. Music recorded by black artists and aimed at black consumers (sometimes called "race records") gave African Americans a place in consumer culture. More importantly, jazz endowed America with its most distinctive serious and popular art form.

In many ways the 1920s were the most creative years the nation had yet experienced. Painters such as Georgia O'Keeffe, Aaron Douglas, and John Marin forged a uniquely American style of painting. European composers and performers still dominated classical music, but American composers such as Henry Cowell pioneered electronic music, and Aaron Copland built orchestral works around native folk motifs. George Gershwin blended jazz rhythms, classical forms, and folk melodies in serious compositions (*Rhapsody in Blue*, 1924, and the Piano Concerto in F, 1925), musical dramas (*Funny Face*, 1927), and hit tunes such as "Summertime" and "Someone to Watch Over Me." In architecture the skyscraper boom drew worldwide attention to American forms. At the beginning of the decade, essayist Harold Stearns had complained that "the most . . . pathetic fact in the social life of America today is emotional and aesthetic starvation." By 1929 that contention had been disproved.

■ This painting by the African American artist Archibald Motley represented the "Ash-Can" style, which considered no subject too undignified to paint, as well as the sensual relationship between jazz music and dancing within African American culture. (Collection of Archie Motley and Valerie Gerrard Browne. Photo courtesy of The Art Institute of Chicago)

The Election of 1928 and the End of the New Era

Intellectuals' uneasiness about materialism seldom affected the confident rhetoric of politics. Herbert Hoover voiced that confidence when he accepted the Republican nomination for president in 1928. "We in America today," Hoover boasted, "are nearer to the final triumph over poverty than ever before in the history of any land. . . . We have not yet reached the goal, but, given a chance to go forward with the policies of the last eight years, we shall soon, with the help of God, be in sight of the day when poverty will be banished from this nation."

Hoover was an apt Republican candidate in 1928 (Coolidge chose not to seek reelection) because he fused the traditional value of individual hard work with modern emphasis on collective action. A Quaker from Iowa, orphaned at age ten, Hoover worked his way through Stanford University and became a wealthy mining engineer. During and after the First World War, he distinguished himself as U.S. food administrator and head of food relief for Europe.

HERBERT HOOVER

As secretary of commerce under Harding and Coolidge, Hoover had what has been called "associational-

ism." Recognizing the extent to which nationwide associations dominated commerce and industry, Hoover wanted to stimulate cooperation between business and government. He took every opportunity to make the Commerce Department a center for the promotion of business, encouraging the formation of trade associations, holding conferences, and issuing reports, all aimed at improving productivity, marketing, and profits. His active leadership prompted one observer to quip that Hoover was "Secretary of Commerce and assistant secretary of everything else."

As their candidate, Democrats chose New York's governor Alfred E. Smith, whose background contrasted sharply with Hoover's. Hoover had rural, native-born, Protestant, business roots and had never run for public office. Smith was an urbane, gregarious politician of immigrant stock with a career embedded in New York City's Tammany Hall political machine. His relish for the give-and-take of city streets is apparent in his response to a heckler during the campaign. When the heckler shouted, "Tell them all you know, Al. It won't take long!" Smith unflinchingly retorted, "I'll tell them all we both know, and it won't take any longer!"

AL SMITH

Smith was the first Roman Catholic to run for president on a major party ticket. His religion enhanced his appeal among urban ethnics, who were voting in increasing numbers, but intense anti-Catholic sentiments lost him southern and rural votes. Smith had compiled a strong record on Progressive reform and civil rights during his governorship, but his campaign failed to build a coalition of farmers and city dwellers because he stressed issues unlikely to unite these groups, particularly his opposition to prohibition.

Smith waged a spirited campaign, directly confronting anti-Catholic critics, but Hoover, who emphasized national prosperity under Republican administrations, won the popular vote by 21 million to 15 million, the electoral vote by 444 to 87. Smith's candidacy nevertheless had beneficial effects on the Democratic Party. He carried the nation's twelve largest cities, which formerly had given majorities to Republican candidates, and he lured millions of foreign-stock voters to the polls for the first time. For the next forty years or so, the Democratic Party solidified this urban base, which in conjunction with its traditional strength in the South made the party a formidable force in national elections.

At his inaugural, Hoover proclaimed a New Day, "bright with hope." His cabinet, composed mostly of

HOOVER'S ADMINISTRATION

businessmen committed to the existing order, included six millionaires. To the lower ranks of government Hoover appointed young professionals who agreed with him that scientific methods could solve national problems. If Hoover was optimistic, so were most Americans. The belief was widespread that individuals were responsible for their own success and that unemployment and poverty suggested personal weakness. Prevailing opinion also held that ups and downs of the business cycle were natural and therefore not to be tampered with by government.

This trust dissolved in the fall of 1929 when stock market prices suddenly plunged after soaring in 1928.

STOCK MARKET CRASH

Analysts explained the drop as temporary. But on October 24, "Black Thursday," panic selling set in. Prices of many stocks hit record lows; some sellers could find no buyers. Stunned crowds gathered outside the frantic New York Stock Exchange. At noon, leading bankers met at the headquarters of J. P. Morgan and Company. To restore faith, they put up $20 million and ceremoniously began buying stocks. The mood brightened and some stocks rallied. The bankers, it seemed, had saved the day.

But as news of Black Thursday spread, panicked investors decided to sell stocks rather than risk further losses. On "Black Tuesday," October 29, prices plummeted again. Hoover, who never had approved of what he called "the fever of speculation," assured Americans that "the crisis will be over in sixty days." Three months later, he still believed that "the worst is over without a doubt." He shared the popular assumptions that the stock market's ills could be quarantined and that the economy was strong enough to endure until the market righted itself. Instead, the crash ultimately helped to unleash a devastating depression.

The economic weakness that underlay the Great Depression had several interrelated causes. One was

DECLINING DEMAND

declining demand. Since mid-1928, demand for new housing had faltered, leading to declining sales of building materials and unemployment among construction workers. Growth industries such as automobiles and electric appliances had been able to expand as long as consumers bought their products. Frenzied expansion, however, could not continue unabated. When demand leveled off, factory owners had to curtail production and could not hire more workers. Instead, unsold inventories stacked up in warehouses, and laborers were laid off. Retailers also had amassed large inventories that were going unsold, and in turn they started ordering less from manufacturers. Farm prices continued to sag, leaving farmers with less income to purchase new machinery and goods. As wages and purchasing power stagnated, workers who produced consumer products could not afford to buy them. Thus by 1929 a sizable population of underconsumers was causing serious repercussions.

Underconsumption also resulted from widening divisions in income distribution. As the rich grew richer, middle- and lower-income Americans made modest gains at best. Though average per capita disposable income (income after taxes) rose about 9 percent between 1920 and 1929, income of the wealthiest 1 percent rose 75 percent, accounting for most of the increase. Much of this increase was put into stock market investments, not consumer goods.

Furthermore, in their eagerness to increase profits, many businesses overloaded themselves with debt. To

CORPORATE DEBT

obtain loans, they manipulated or misrepresented their assets in ways that weakened their ability to repay if forced to do so. Such practices, overlooked by lending agencies, put the nation's banking system on precarious footing. When one part of the edifice collapsed, the entire structure crumbled.

The depression also resulted from risky stock market speculation. Not only had corporations invested huge

STOCK MARKET SPECULATION

sums in stocks, but individuals also bought heavily on margin, meaning that they purchased stock by placing a

■ As the stock market tumbled on October 24, 1929, a crowd of concerned investors gathered outside the New York Stock Exchange on Wall Street, unprepared for an unprecedented economic decline that would send the country into a tailspin for the next decade. (Corbis-Bettmann)

down payment of only a fraction of the stock's actual price and then used stocks they had bought, but not fully paid for, as collateral for more stock purchases. When stock prices stopped rising, people tried to sell holdings they had bought on margin to minimize their losses. But numerous investors selling at the same time caused prices to drop. As stock values collapsed, brokers demanded full payment for stocks bought on margin. Investors attempted to comply by withdrawing savings from banks or selling stocks at a loss for whatever they could get. Bankers in turn needed cash and pressured businesses to pay back their loans, tightening the vise further. The more obligations went unmet, the more the system tottered. Inevitably, banks and investment companies collapsed.

International economic conditions also contributed to the depression. During the First World War and post-war reconstruction, Americans loaned billions of dollars to European nations. By the late 1920s, however, American investors were keeping their money at home, investing instead in the more lucrative U.S. stock market. Europeans, unable to borrow more funds and unable to sell goods in the American market because of high tariffs, began to buy less from the United States. Moreover, the Allied nations depended on German war reparations to pay their own war debts to the United States, and the German government depended on American bank loans to pay war reparations to the Allies. When the crash choked off American loans, the Germans could not pay reparations debts to the Allies, and in turn the Allies were unable to pay war debts to the United States. The world economy ground to a halt.

INTERNATIONAL ECONOMIC TROUBLES

Government policies also underlay the crisis. The federal government refrained from regulating wild speculation, contenting itself with occasionally scolding bankers and businesspeople. In keeping with government support of business expansion, the Federal Reserve Board pursued easy credit policies before the crash, charging low discount rates (interest rates on its loans to member banks) even though easy money was financing the speculative mania.

FAILURE OF FEDERAL POLICIES

Partly because of optimism and partly because of the relatively undeveloped state of economic analysis, neither the experts nor people on the street realized what really had happened in 1929. Conventional wisdom, based on experiences from previous depressions, held that little could be done to correct economic problems; they simply had to run their course. So in 1929 people waited for the tailspin to ease, never realizing that the era of expansion and frivolity had come to an end and that society and politics, as well as the economy, would have to be rebuilt.

Summary

Two disturbing events, the end of the First World War and the beginning of the Great Depression, marked the boundaries of the 1920s. In the war's aftermath, traditional customs weakened as women and men sought ways to balance new liberation with old-fashioned values. A host of new effects from modern science and technology, the automobile, conveniences such as electric appliances, and broadened exposure from mass media, movies, and travel touched the lives of rich and poor alike. Moreover, the decade's general prosperity and freewheeling attitudes enabled ordinary Americans to emulate wealthier people not only by consuming more but also by trying to get rich through stock market speculation. The depression stifled some of these habits, but others were hard to break.

Beneath the "era of excess" lurked two important phenomena rooted in previous eras. One was the continued resurfacing of prejudice and intergroup tensions that had long tainted the American dream. As prohibitionists, Klansmen, and immigration restrictionists made their voices heard, they encouraged discrimination against racial minorities and slurs against supposedly inferior ethnic groups. Meanwhile, the distinguishing forces of twentieth-century life—technological change, bureaucratization, mass culture, and growth of the middle class—accelerated, making the decade truly a "new era." Both phenomena would recur as major themes in the nation's history for the rest of the twentieth century.

LEGACY FOR A PEOPLE AND A NATION
Intercollegiate Athletics

In 1924 scandals of brutality, academic fraud, and illegal payments to recruits prompted the Carnegie Foundation for the Advancement of Higher Education to undertake a five-year investigation of college sports. Its 1929 report condemned coaches and alumni supporters for violating the amateur code. The report had minimal effect, however. As the career of Red Grange illustrated, football had become big-time during the 1920s, and other sports followed suit as scores of colleges and universities built stadiums and arenas to attract spectators, bolster alumni allegiance, enhance revenues, and promote school spirit.

For most of the twentieth century and into the twenty-first, intercollegiate athletics, with highly paid coaches and highly recruited student-athletes, ranked as one of the nation's major commercial entertainments. At the same time, American colleges and universities have struggled to reconcile conflicts between the commercialism of athletic competition on one hand and the restraints of educational objectives and athletic amateurism on the other. Supposedly, cultivation of the mind is the mission of higher education. But the economic potential of college sports coupled with burgeoning of athletic departments—including administrators, staffs, and tutors as well as coaches and trainers—has created programs that compete with and sometimes overshadow the academic operations of the institutions that sponsor intercollegiate athletics.

Since the 1920s, recruiting scandals, cheating incidents, and academic fraud in college sports have sparked continual controversy and criticism. In 1952, after revelations of point-shaving (fixing the outcome) of basketball games involving several colleges in New York and elsewhere, the American Council on Education undertook a study of college sports similar to that of the Carnegie Foundation a generation earlier. Its recommendations, including the abolition of football bowl games, went largely unheeded. In 1991, further abuses, especially in academics, prompted the Knight Foundation Commission on Intercollegiate Athletics to conduct a study that urged college presidents to take the lead in reforming intercollegiate athletics. After a follow-up study with recommendations in 2001, few significant changes resulted.

The most sweeping reforms followed court rulings in the 1990s that mandated under Title IX of the Educational Amendments Act of 1972 that women's sports be treated equally with men's sports. Enforcement, however, provoked a backlash that resulted in suggested changes to prevent men's teams from being cut in order to satisfy Title IX requirements. As long as millions of dollars are involved and sports remain a vital component of college as well as national culture, the system established in the 1920s has shown the ability to withstand most pressures for change.

The *history* *Companion* powered by Eduspace®

Your primary source for interactive quizzes, exercises, and more to help you learn efficiently.
http://history.college.hmco.com/students

THE GREAT DEPRESSION AND THE NEW DEAL 1929–1941

*I*n 1931, the rain stopped in the Great Plains. Montana and North Dakota became as arid as the Sonora Desert. Temperatures reached 115 degrees in Iowa. The soil baked. Farmers watched rich black dirt turn to gray dust.

Then the winds began to blow. Farmers had stripped the Plains of native grasses in the 1920s, using tractors to put millions of acres of new land into production. Now, with nothing to hold the earth, it began to blow away. The dust storms began in 1934—and worsened in 1935. Dust obscured the noonday sun; some days it was pitch black at noon. Cattle, blinded by blowing grit, ran in circles until they died. A seven-year-old boy in Smith Center, Kansas, suffocated in a dust drift. Boiling clouds of dust filled the skies in parts of Kansas, Colorado, Oklahoma, Texas, and New Mexico—the Dust Bowl.

In late 1937 on a farm near Stigler, Oklahoma, Marvin Montgomery counted up his assets: $53 and a car—a 1929 Hudson he had just bought. "The drought and such as that, it just got so hard," he said later, "I decided it would help me to change countries." So on December 29, 1937, Montgomery and his wife and four children—along with their furniture, bedding, pots, and pans—squeezed into the Hudson. "I had that old car loaded to the full capacity," Marvin told a congressional committee conducting hearings in a migratory labor camp in 1940, "on top, the sides, and everywhere else." Traveling west on Route 66, the Montgomerys headed for California.

They were not alone. At least a third of farms in the Dust Bowl were abandoned in the 1930s, and many families made the westward trek, lured by circulars and newspaper advertisements promising work in the fields of California. Some 300,000 people migrated to California in the 1930s. Most of these were not displaced and poverty-stricken farm families like the Montgomerys; many were white-collar workers seeking better opportunities in California's cities. It was the plight of families like the Montgomerys, however, captured in the

◀ This 1939 photograph, titled "Mother and Children on the Road," was taken in Tule Lake, California, by Farm Security Administration photographer Dorothea Lange. The FSA used photos like this one to build public support for New Deal programs to assist migrant workers and the rural poor.   (Library of Congress)

679

CHRONOLOGY

1929 • Stock market crash (Oct.); Great Depression begins

1930 • Hawley-Smoot Tariff raises rates on imports

1931 • "Scottsboro Boys" arrested in Alabama

1932 • Banks fail throughout nation
• Bonus Army marches on Washington
• Hoover's Reconstruction Finance Corporation tries to stabilize banks, insurance companies, and railroads
• Roosevelt elected president

1933 • 13 million Americans unemployed
• "First Hundred Days" of Roosevelt administration offers major legislation for economic recovery and poor relief
• National bank holiday halts run on banks
• Agricultural Adjustment Act (AAA) encourages decreased farm production
• National Industrial Recovery Act (NIRA) attempts to spur industrial growth
• Tennessee Valley Authority established

1934 • Long starts Share Our Wealth Society
• Townsend proposes old-age pension plan
• Indian Reorganization (Wheeler-Howard) Act restores lands to tribal ownership

1935 • National Labor Relations (Wagner) Act guarantees workers' right to unionize
• Social Security Act establishes insurance for the aged, the unemployed, and needy children
• Works Progress Administration creates jobs in public works projects
• Revenue (Wealth Tax) Act raises taxes on business and the wealthy

1936 • 9 million Americans unemployed
• United Auto Workers win sit-down strike against General Motors

1937 • Roosevelt's court-packing plan fails
• Memorial Day massacre of striking steelworkers
• "Roosevelt recession" begins

1938 • 10.4 million Americans unemployed
• 80 million movie tickets sold each week

1939 • Marian Anderson performs at Lincoln Memorial
• Social Security amendments add benefits for spouses and widows

federal-government-sponsored Farm Security Administration photographs and immortalized in John Steinbeck's bestselling 1938 novel *The Grapes of Wrath*, that came to represent the human suffering of the Great Depression.

The Montgomerys' trip was not easy. The family ran out of money somewhere in Arizona and worked in the cotton fields there for five weeks before they moved on. Once in California, "I hoed beets some; hoed some cotton, and I picked some spuds," Marvin reported, but wages were low, and migrant families found little welcome. As they took over the agricultural labor formerly done by Mexicans and Mexican Americans, they learned that by doing fieldwork they had forfeited their "whiteness" in the eyes of many rural Californians. "Negroes and 'Okies' upstairs," read a sign in a San Joaquin valley movie theater.

Most migrants to rural California lived in squalid makeshift camps, but the Montgomerys were lucky. They got space in housing provided for farm workers by the federal government through the Farm Security Administration (FSA). The FSA camp at Shafter in Kern County had 240 tents and 40 small houses. For nine months the Montgomery family of six lived in a 14-by-16-foot tent, which rented for 10 cents a day plus four hours of volunteer labor a month. Then they proudly moved into an FSA house, "with water, lights, and everything, yes sir; and a little garden spot furnished." Marvin, homesick for the farm, told the congressional committee that he hoped to return to Oklahoma, but his seventeen-year-old son Harvey saw a different future. "I like California," he said. "I would rather stay out here." And soon there were plentiful employment opportunities in California, not only for Harvey Montgomery but for many other newcomers, in aircraft factories and shipyards mobilizing for the Second World War.

The Montgomerys' experience shows the human costs of the Great Depression, but statistics are necessary to give a sense of its magnitude. In the 1930s, as nations worldwide plunged into depression, the United States confronted a crisis of enormous proportions. Between 1929 and 1933, the gross national product was cut in half. Corporate profits fell from $10 billion to $1 billion; 100,000 businesses shut their doors altogether. As businesses failed or cut back, they laid off workers. Every day, thousands of men and women lost their jobs. Four million workers were unemployed in January 1930; by November the number had jumped to 6 million. When President Herbert Hoover left office in 1933, 13 million workers—about one-fourth of the labor force—were idle, and millions more had only part-time work. There was no national safety net: no welfare system, no unemployment compensation, no Social Security. And as banks failed by the thousands, with no federally guaranteed deposit insurance, families' savings simply disappeared.

Herbert Hoover, who had been elected president in the prosperity and optimism of the late 1920s, looked first to private enterprise for solutions. By the end of his term, he had extended the federal government's role in managing an economic crisis further than any of his predecessors. Still, the economy had not improved and, as the depression deepened, the mood of the country became increasingly desperate. The economic catastrophe exacerbated existing racial and class tensions, and law and order seemed to be breaking down. In Germany, the international economic crisis propelled Adolf Hitler to power. While America's leaders did not really expect the United States to turn to fascism, they also knew that the German people had not anticipated Hitler's rise, either. By late 1932 the depression seemed more than just "hard times." Many feared it was a crisis of capitalism, and even of democracy itself.

In 1932 voters turned Hoover out of office, replacing him with a man who promised a New Deal and projected hope in a time of despair. Franklin Delano Roosevelt showed a willingness to experiment, and while his scattershot approach did not end the economic depression (only the massive mobilization for World War II did that), New Deal programs did provide many Americans with jobs or other means of financial support. For the first time, the federal government assumed responsibility for the nation's economy and the welfare of its citizens. New federal agencies regulated a financial system badly in need of reform; Franklin Roosevelt's administration gave legitimacy to labor unions and collective bargaining. Social Security guaranteed assistance to many of America's elderly citizens and to others who could not support themselves. In the process, the power of the federal government was strengthened in relation to states and local authorities.

As it transformed the role and power of the federal government, however, the New Deal maintained America's existing economic and social systems. Though some Americans saw the depression crisis as an opportunity for major economic change—even revolution—Roosevelt's goal was to save capitalism. New Deal programs increased federal government regulation of the economy, but they did not fundamentally alter the existing capitalist system or the distribution of wealth in the nation. And despite pressure (even within his own administration) to attack the social system that denied equality to African Americans, Roosevelt never directly challenged legal segregation in the south—in part because he relied on the votes of southern white Democrats to pass New Deal legislation.

Despite its limits, the New Deal preserved America's democratic experiment through a time of uncertainty and crisis. By the end of the decade, the widening force of world war shifted America's focus from domestic to foreign policy. But the changes set in motion by the New Deal continued to transform the United States for decades to come. ■

Hoover and Hard Times: 1929–1933

By the early 1930s, as the depression continued to deepen, tens of millions of Americans were desperately poor. In the cities, hungry men and women lined up at soup kitchens. People survived on potatoes, crackers, or dandelion greens; some scratched through garbage cans for bits of food. In West Virginia and Kentucky hunger was so widespread—and resources so limited—that the American Friends Service Committee distributed food only to those who were at least 10 percent below the normal weight for their height. Reports of starvation and malnutrition spread. In November 1932, *The Nation* told its readers that one-sixth of the American population risked starvation over the coming winter. Social workers in New York reported there was "no food at all" in the homes of many of the city's black children. In Albany, New York, a ten-year-old girl died of starvation in her elementary school classroom.

Families, unable to pay rent, were evicted from houses and apartments. The new homeless poured into shantytowns, called "Hoovervilles" in ironic tribute to the formerly popular president, that had sprung up in most cities. Over a million men took to the road or the rails in desperate search for any sort of work. Teenage boys and girls (the latter called "sisters of the road") also left destitute families to strike out on their own. With uncertain futures, many young couples delayed marriage. The average age at which people married rose by more than two years during the 1930s. Married people put off having children, and in 1933 the birth rate sank below replacement rates. (Contraceptive sales, with condoms costing at least $1 per dozen, did not fall during the depression.) More than 25 percent of women who were between the ages of twenty and thirty during the Great Depression never had children.

Farmers were hit especially hard by the economic crisis. The agricultural sector, which employed almost

FARMERS AND INDUSTRIAL WORKERS

a quarter of American workers, had never shared in the good times of the 1920s. But as urbanites cut back on spending and foreign competitors dumped their own agricultural surpluses into the global market, prices for agricultural products hit rock bottom. Individual farmers tried to make up for lower prices by producing more, thus adding to the surplus and depressing prices even further. By 1932, a bushel of wheat that cost North Dakota farmers 77 cents to produce brought only 33 cents. Throughout the nation, cash-strapped farmers could not pay their property taxes or mortgages. Banks, facing their own ruin, refused to extend deadlines and foreclosed on the mortgages. In Mississippi, it was reported in 1932, on a single day in April approximately one-fourth of all the farmland in the state was being auctioned off to meet debts. By the middle of the decade, the ecological crisis of the Dust Bowl would drive thousands of farmers from their land.

Unlike farmers, America's industrial workers had seen a slow but steady rise in their standard of living during the 1920s, and their spending on consumer goods had bolstered the nation's economic growth. In 1929, almost every urban American who wanted a job had one. But as Americans had less money to spend, sales of manufactured goods plummeted and factories closed—more than seventy thousand had gone out of business by 1933. As car sales dropped from 4.5 million in 1929 to 1 million in 1933, Ford laid off more than two-thirds of its workers in Detroit. All of the remaining workers at U.S. Steel, America's first billion-dollar corporation, were put on "short hours"; the huge steel company had no full-time workers in 1933. Almost a quarter of industrial workers were unemployed, and those who managed to hang onto a job saw the average wage fall by almost one-third.

For workers who had long been marginal, discriminated against, or relegated to the lowest rungs of the

MARGINAL WORKERS

employment ladder, the depression was a crushing blow. In the South, where employment opportunities for African Americans were already most limited, pressure for "Negro removal" grew. The jobs that most white men had considered below their dignity before the depression—street cleaners, bellhops, garbage collectors—seemed suddenly desirable as other jobs disappeared. In 1930, a short-lived fascist-style organization, the Black Shirts, recruited forty thousand members with the slogan "No Jobs for Niggers Until Every White Man Has a Job!" African Americans living in the North did not fare much better. As industry cut production, African Americans were the first fired. An Urban League survey of 106 cities found black unemployment rates averaged 30 to 60 percent higher than rates for whites. By 1932, African American unemployment reached almost 50 percent.

Mexican Americans and Mexican nationals trying to make a living in the American Southwest also felt the twin impacts of economic depression and racism. Concentrated in agricultural work, they saw their wages at California farms fall from a miserable 35 cents an hour in 1929 to a cruel 14 cents an hour by 1932. Throughout the Southwest, Anglo-Americans claimed that foreign workers were stealing their jobs. Campaigns against "foreigners" hurt not only Mexican immigrants but also American citizens of Hispanic background whose families had lived in the Southwest for centuries, long before the land belonged to the United States. In 1931, the Labor Department announced that the United States would deport illegal immigrants to free jobs for American citizens. This policy fell hardest on people of Mexican origin. Even those who had immigrated legally often lacked full documentation. Officials often ignored the fact that children born in the United States were U.S. citizens. The U.S. government officially deported eighty-two thousand Mexicans between 1929 and 1935, but a much larger number—almost half a million people—repatriated to Mexico during the 1930s. Some left voluntarily, but many were coerced or tricked into believing they had no choice.

Women of all classes and races shared status as marginalized workers. Even before the economic crisis, women were barred altogether from many jobs and paid at significantly lower rates than men. As the economy worsened, working women faced heightened discrimina-

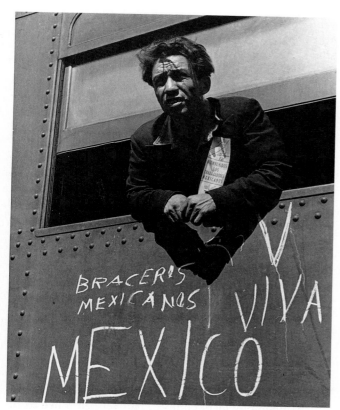

■ Many Mexican farm workers *(braceros)* were deported in the early 1930s, but by the end of the decade growers eager for the return of this source of cheap labor began to recruit trainloads of Mexicans as farm laborers in southwestern states. This photo, taken by Dorothea Lange in 1938, shows one of these workers.   (Dorothea Lange Collection, Oakland Museum of California, City of Oakland. Gift of Paul S. Taylor)

The depression had a mixed impact on women workers. At first, women lost jobs more quickly than men. Women in low-wage manufacturing jobs were laid off before male employees, who were presumed to be supporting families. Hard times hit domestic workers especially hard, as middle-class families economized by dispensing with household help. Almost a quarter of women in domestic service—a high percentage of them African American—were unemployed by January 1931. And as jobs disappeared, women of color lost even these poorly paid positions to white women who were newly willing to do domestic labor. Despite discrimination and a poor economy, however, the number of women working outside the home rose during the 1930s. "Women's jobs," such as teaching, clerical work, and switchboard operators, were not hit so hard as "men's jobs" in heavy industry, and women—including married women who previously did not work for wages—increasingly sought employment to keep their families afloat during hard times. Still, by 1940 only 15.2 percent of married women worked outside the home.

Though unemployment rates climbed to 25 percent, most Americans did not lose their homes or their jobs during the depression. Professional and white-collar workers did not fare as badly as industrial workers and farmers. Many middle-class families, however, while never hungry or homeless, "made do" with less. "Use it up, wear it out, make it do, or do without," the saying went, and middle-class women cut back on household expenses by canning food or making their own clothes; newspapers offered imaginative suggestions for cooking cheap cuts of meat ("Liverburgers") or for using "extenders," cheap ingredients to make food go further ("Cracker-Stuffed Cabbage"). Though most families' incomes fell, the impact was cushioned by the falling cost of consumer goods, especially food. In early 1933, for example, a café in Omaha offered a ten-course meal, complete with a rose for ladies and cigar for gentlemen, for 60 cents.

MIDDLE-CLASS WORKERS AND FAMILIES

As housewives scrambled to make do, men who could no longer provide well for their families often blamed themselves for their "failures." But even for the relatively affluent, the psychological impact of the depression was inescapable. The human toll of the depression was visible everywhere, and no one took economic security for granted anymore. Suffering was never equal, but all Americans had to contend with years of uncertainty and with fears about the future of their families and their nation.

tion. Most Americans already believed that men should be breadwinners and women homemakers. With widespread male unemployment, it was easy to believe that women who worked took jobs from men. In fact, men laid off from U.S. Steel would not likely have been hired as elementary school teachers, secretaries, "sales girls," or maids. The job market was heavily segregated. Nonetheless, when a 1936 Gallup poll asked whether wives should work if their husbands had jobs, 82 percent of the respondents (including 75 percent of the women) answered no. Such beliefs translated into policy. Of fifteen hundred urban school systems surveyed by the National Education Association in 1930 and 1931, 77 percent refused to hire married women as teachers, and 63 percent fired female teachers who married while employed.

5 ways to use
ARMOUR'S FIXED FLAVOR STAR HAM
LEFTOVERS

ARMOUR HIGHEST QUALITY FOODS
"BETTER BUY ARMOUR'S AND BE SURE"

■ As the economic depression deepened, Americans had less money to spend, even on necessities, and manufacturers of consumer goods struggled to sell their products and stay in business. In this 1932 *Ladies' Home Journal* advertisement, Armour Foods tried to convince housewives who were "making do" with less that it was economical—"often as low as 10¢ a serving"—to purchase a whole ham instead of cheaper cuts of meat. (Picture Research Consultants & Archives)

Although Herbert Hoover, "the Great Engineer," had a reputation as a problem solver, the economic crisis was not easily solved and no one, including Hoover, really knew what to do. Experts and leaders disagreed about the causes of the depression, and they disagreed about the proper course of action, as well. Many prominent business leaders believed that financial panics and depressions, no matter how painful, were part of a natural and ultimately beneficial "business cycle." Economic depressions, according to this theory, brought down inflated prices and cleared the way for real economic growth. As one banker told a Senate committee investigating the rise in unemployment in 1931, "You are always going to have, once in so many

HOOVER'S LIMITED SOLUTIONS

years, difficulties in business, times that are prosperous and times that are not prosperous. There is no commission or any brain in the world that can prevent it."

Herbert Hoover disagreed. "The economic fatalist," he said, "believes that these crises are inevitable. . . . I would remind these pessimists that exactly the same thing was once said of typhoid, cholera, and smallpox." Hoover had great faith in "associationalism": business organizations and professional groups, coordinated by the federal government, working together to solve the nation's problems. The federal government's role was limited to gathering information and serving as a clearinghouse for ideas and plans. State and local governments, along with private industry, could then choose—voluntarily—to implement these plans.

To many Americans, it seemed as if Hoover was doing nothing to fight the economic downturn. In fact, Hoover stretched his core beliefs about the proper role of government to their limit. He tried voluntarism, exhortation, and limited government intervention. First, he sought voluntary pledges from hundreds of business groups that they would keep wages stable and renew economic investment. But when individual businessmen looked at their own bottom lines, few were able to live up to their promises.

As unemployment climbed, Hoover continued to encourage voluntary responses to mounting need, creating the President's Organization on Unemployment Relief (POUR) to generate private contributions for relief of the destitute. Though 1932 saw record charitable contributions, they were nowhere near adequate. By mid-1932 one-quarter of New York's private charities, funds exhausted, had closed their doors. Atlanta's Central Relief Committee could provide only $1.30 per family per week to those seeking help. State and city officials found their treasuries drying up, too. Hoover, however, held firm. "It is not the function of the government to relieve individuals of their responsibilities to their neighbors," he insisted.

Hoover feared that government "relief" would destroy the spirit of self-reliance among the poor. Thus he authorized the use of federal funds to feed the drought-stricken livestock of Arkansas farmers but rejected a smaller federal grant that would have provided food for impoverished farm families. Many Americans were becoming angry at what seemed like Hoover's insensitivity. When Hoover, trying to restore confidence to the increasingly anxious nation, said: "What this country needs is a good big laugh. . . . If someone could get off a good joke every ten days, I think our troubles would be over," the resulting jokes were not exactly what he had in mind. "Business is improving," one man tells another. "Is Hoover dead?" asks his companion. In the two short years since his election, Hoover had become the most hated man in the nation.

Hoover eventually endorsed limited federal action to combat the economic crisis, but it was much too little. Federal public works projects, such as the Grand Coulee Dam in Washington, created some jobs. The Federal Farm Board, created under the Agricultural Marketing Act of 1929, supported crop prices by lending money to cooperatives to buy crops and keep them off the market. But the board soon ran short of money, and unsold surpluses jammed warehouses.

Hoover also signed into law the Hawley-Smoot Tariff (1930), which was meant to support American farmers and manufacturers by raising import duties on foreign goods to a staggering 40 percent. Instead it hampered international trade as other nations created their own protective tariffs. And as other nations sold fewer goods to the United States, they had less money to repay their debts to the United States or to buy American products. Fearing the collapse of the international monetary system, Hoover in 1931 announced a moratorium on the payment of First World War debts and reparations.

In January 1932, the administration took its most forceful action. The Reconstruction Finance Corporation (RFC) provided federal loans to banks, insurance companies, and railroads, an action Hoover hoped would shore up those industries and halt the disinvestment in the American economy. New York mayor Fiorello La Guardia called this provision of taxpayers' dollars to private industry "a millionaire's dole." But with the RFC, Hoover had compromised his ideological principles. This was direct government intervention, not "voluntarism." If he would support direct assistance to private industries, why not direct relief to the millions of unemployed?

More and more Americans, in fact, had begun to ask that question. Though most met the crisis with bewilderment or quiet despair, social unrest and violence began to surface as the depression deepened. In scattered incidents, farmers and unemployed workers took direct action against what they saw as the causes of their plight. Others lashed out in anger, scapegoating those even weaker than themselves. Increasing violence raised the specter of popular revolt, and Chicago mayor Anton Cermak told Congress that if the federal government did not send his citizens aid, it would have to send troops instead.

PROTEST AND SOCIAL UNREST

Throughout the nation, tens of thousands of farmers took the law into their own hands. Angry crowds forced auctioneers to accept just a few dollars for foreclosed property, and then returned it to the original owners. Farmers also tried to stop produce from reaching the market. In August 1932 a new group, the Farmers' Holiday Association, encouraged farmers to take a "holiday"—to hold back agricultural products as a way to limit supply and drive prices up. In the Midwest, farmers barricaded roads with spiked logs and telegraph poles to stop other farmers' trucks, and then dumped the contents in roadside ditches. In Iowa, strikers shot four other farmers who tried to run a roadblock.

In the cities, also, protest grew. The most militant actions came from Unemployed Councils, local groups similar to unions for unemployed workers that were created and led by Communist Party members. Communist leaders believed that the depression demonstrated the failure of capitalism and offered an opportunity for revolution. Few of the quarter-million Americans who joined the local Unemployed Councils sought revolution, but they did demand action. "Fight, Don't Starve," read banners in a Chicago demonstration. Demonstrations often turned ugly. When three thousand members of Detroit Unemployment Councils marched on Ford's River Rouge plant in 1932, Ford security guards opened fire on the crowd, killing four men and wounding fifty. Battles between protesters and police broke out in cities from East to West Coasts, but rarely were covered as national news.

As social unrest spread, so, too, did racial violence. Vigilante committees offered bounties in an attempt to force African American workers from the Illinois Central Railroad's payroll: $25 for maiming and $100 for killing black workers. Ten men were murdered and at least seven more wounded. With the worsening economy, the Ku Klux Klan reemerged, and at least 140 attempted lynchings were recorded between January 1930 and February 1933. In most cases local authorities were able to prevent the lynchings, but white mobs tortured, hung, and mutilated thirty-eight black men during the early years of the Great Depression. Racial violence was not restricted to the South; lynchings took place in Pennsylvania, Minnesota, Colorado, and Ohio as well.

The worst public confrontation shook the nation in the summer of 1932. More than fifteen thousand unemployed World War I veterans and their families converged on the nation's capital as Congress debated a bill authorizing immediate payment of cash "bonuses" that veterans had been scheduled to receive in 1945. Calling themselves the Bonus Expeditionary Force, or Bonus Army, they set up a sprawling "Hooverville" shantytown

BONUS ARMY

■ In June 1932 unemployed veterans of the First World War board a truck in Girard, Alabama, and Columbus, Georgia, and travel to Washington, D.C., to join the "Bonus Army" and demand payment of their soldiers' bonuses.   (Wide World Photos, Inc.)

in Anacostia Flats, just across the river from the Capitol. Concerned about the impact on the federal budget, President Hoover threw his weight against the bonus bill, and after much debate the Senate voted it down. "We were heroes in 1917, but we're bums today," one veteran shouted after the Senate vote.

Most of the Bonus Marchers left Washington after this defeat, but several thousand stayed on. Some were simply destitute, with nowhere to go; others stayed to press their case. The president called them "insurrectionists" and set a deadline for their departure. On July 28, Hoover sent in the U.S. Army, led by General Douglas MacArthur. Four infantry companies, four troops of cavalry, a machine gun squadron, and six tanks converged on the veterans and their families. What followed shocked the nation. Men and women were chased down by horsemen; children were tear-gassed; shacks were set afire. The next day, newspapers carried photographs of U.S. troops attacking their own citizens. Hoover was unrepentant, insisting in a campaign speech, "Thank God we still have a government that knows how to deal with a mob."

While desperation-driven social unrest raised fears of revolution, some saw an even greater danger in the growing disillusionment with democracy itself. As the depression worsened, the appeal of a strong leader—

someone who would take decisive action, unencumbered by constitutionally mandated checks and balances—grew. In early 1933, media magnate William Randolph Hearst released the film *Gabriel over the White House*, in which a political hack of a president is possessed by the archangel Gabriel and, divinely inspired, assumes dictatorial powers to end the misery of the Great Depression. More significantly, in February 1933 the U.S. Senate passed a resolution calling for newly elected president Franklin D. Roosevelt to assume "unlimited power." The rise to power of Hitler and his National Socialist Party in depression-ravaged Germany was an obvious parallel, adding to the sense of crisis that would come to a head in early 1933.

Franklin D. Roosevelt and the Launching of the New Deal

In the presidential campaign of 1932, voters were presented with a clear choice. In the face of the Great Depression, incumbent Herbert Hoover held to a platform of limited federal intervention. Democratic challenger Franklin Delano Roosevelt insisted that the federal government had to play a much greater role. He supported direct relief payments for the unemployed,

Map 25.1 Presidential Election, 1932

One factor above all decided the 1932 presidential election: the Great Depression. Roosevelt won forty-two states, Hoover six.

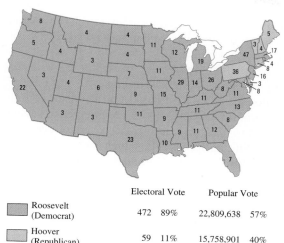

	Electoral Vote		Popular Vote	
Roosevelt (Democrat)	472	89%	22,809,638	57%
Hoover (Republican)	59	11%	15,758,901	40%

declaring that such aid "must be extended by Government, not as a matter of charity, but as a matter of social duty." He pledged "a new deal for the American people." During the campaign, he was never very explicit about the outlines of his "New Deal." His most concrete proposals, in fact, were sometimes contradictory (in a nation without national news media, this was less a problem than it would be today). But all understood that he had committed to use the power of the federal government to combat the economic crisis that was paralyzing the nation. Voters chose Roosevelt over Hoover overwhelmingly: Roosevelt's 22.8 million popular votes far outdistanced Hoover's 15.8 million (see Map 25.1). Third-party Socialist candidate Norman Thomas drew nearly 1 million votes.

Franklin Roosevelt, the twentieth-century president most beloved by America's "common people," had been

FRANKLIN D. ROOSEVELT

born into a world of old money and upper-class privilege. The talented son of a politically prominent family, he seemed destined for political success. After graduating from Harvard College and Columbia Law School, he had married Eleanor Roosevelt, Theodore Roosevelt's niece and his own fifth cousin, once removed. He served in the New York State legislature, was appointed assistant secretary of the navy by Woodrow Wilson and, at the age of thirty-eight, ran for vice president in 1920 on the Democratic Party's losing ticket.

Then, in 1921, Roosevelt was stricken with polio. For two years he was bedridden, fighting one of the most

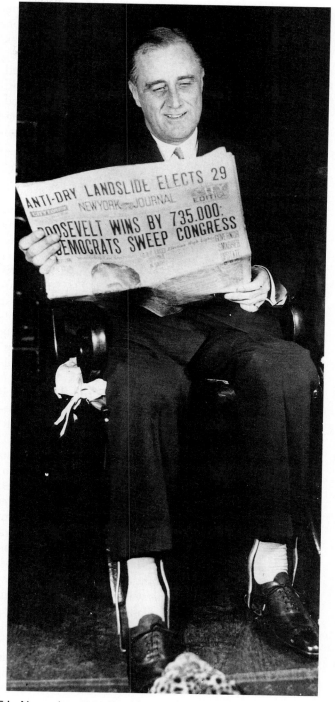

■ In November 1930 Franklin D. Roosevelt (1882–1945) read the good news. Reelected governor of New York by 735,000 votes, he immediately became a leading contender for the Democratic presidential nomination. Notice Roosevelt's leg braces, rarely shown because of an unwritten agreement by photographers to shoot him from the waist up. (© Bettmann/Corbis)

feared diseases of the early twentieth century. He lost the use of his legs but gained, according to his wife Eleanor, a new strength of character that would serve him well as he reached out to depression-scarred America. As Roosevelt explained it, "If you had spent two years in bed trying to wiggle your big toe, after that anything would seem easy." By 1928 Roosevelt was sufficiently recovered to run for—and win—the governorship of New York, and then to accept the Democratic Party's presidential nomination in 1932.

Elected in November 1932, Roosevelt would not take office until March 4, 1933. (The Twentieth Amendment to the Constitution—the so-called Lame Duck Amendment, ratified in 1933—shifted all future inaugurations to January 20.) In this long interregnum, the American banking system reached the verge of collapse.

The origins of the banking crisis lay in the flush years of World War I and the 1920s, when American banks

BANKING CRISIS

made countless risky loans. After real-estate and stock market bubbles burst in 1929 and agricultural prices collapsed, many of these loans went bad. As a result, many banks lacked sufficient funds to cover their customers' deposits. Fearful of losing their savings in a bank collapse, depositors pulled money out of banks and put it into gold or under mattresses. "Bank runs," in which crowds of angry, frightened customers lined up to demand their money, became a common sight in economically ravaged towns throughout the nation.

By the election of 1932, the bank crisis was escalating rapidly. Hoover, the lame-duck president, refused to take action without Roosevelt's support, while Roosevelt called Hoover's request for support "cheeky" and refused to endorse actions he could not control. Meanwhile, the situation worsened. By March 4, the day of Roosevelt's inauguration, every state in the union had either suspended banking operations or restricted depositors' access to their money in some fashion. The new president understood that this was more than a test of his administration. The total collapse of the U.S. banking system would threaten the survival of the nation.

Roosevelt (who reportedly saw the film *Gabriel over the White House* several times before his inauguration) used his inaugural address to promise the American people decisive action. Standing in a cold rain on the Capitol steps, he vowed to face the crisis "frankly and boldly." The lines we best remember from his speech are words of comfort: "[L]et me assert my firm belief," the new president told the thousands gathered on the Capitol grounds and the millions gathered around their radios, "that the only thing we have to fear is fear

itself—nameless, unreasoning, unjustified terror." But the only loud cheers that day came when Roosevelt invoked "the analogue of war," asserting that, if need be, "I shall ask the Congress for the one remaining instrument to meet the crisis—broad Executive power to wage a war against the emergency, as great as the power that would be given to me if we were in fact invaded by a foreign foe."

The next day Roosevelt, using powers legally granted by the World War I "Trading with the Enemy" Act, shut down the nation's banks for a four-day "holiday" and summoned Congress to an emergency session beginning March 9. He immediately introduced the Emergency Banking Relief Bill, which was passed sight unseen by unanimous House vote, approved 73 to 7 in the Senate, and signed into law the same day. This bill provided federal authority to reopen solvent banks and reorganize the rest. It also authorized federal money to shore up private banks. In his inaugural address, Roosevelt had attacked "unscrupulous money changers," and many critics of the failed banking system had hoped he planned to remove the banks from private hands. Instead, as one North Dakota congressman complained, "the President drove the money changers out of the Capitol on March 4th and they were all back on the 9th." In fact, Roosevelt's banking policy was much like Hoover's—a fundamentally conservative approach that upheld the status quo.

The banking bill alone, however, could not save the U.S. banking system. Unless Americans were confident enough to deposit money in the reopened banks, the crisis would continue. The president went directly to the American people. In the first of his radio "Fireside Chats," he used clear, simple language to explain his actions and ask for support. "We have provided the machinery to restore our financial system," he said. "It is up to you to support and make it work." The next morning the banks opened their doors. People lined up—but the majority of them waited to deposit money. It was an enormous triumph for the new president. It also demonstrated that Roosevelt, while unafraid to take bold action, was not as radical as some wished or as others feared.

During the ninety-nine-day-long special session of Congress, dubbed by journalists "The First Hundred

FIRST HUNDRED DAYS

Days," the federal government took on dramatically new roles. Roosevelt, aided by a group of advisers—lawyers, university professors, and social workers, who were collectively nicknamed "the Brain Trust"—and by the enormously capable First Lady, set out to revive the American economy. These "New Dealers" had no single, coherent plan, and Roosevelt's economic policies fluctuated between attempts to balance the budget and massive deficit spending (spending more than is taken in in taxes, and borrowing the difference). But with a strong mandate for action and the support of a Democrat-controlled Congress, the new administration produced a flood of legislation. The first priority was economic recovery. Two basic strategies emerged during the First Hundred Days. New Dealers experimented with forms of national economic planning, and they also created a range of "relief" programs to help those in need.

At the heart of the New Deal experiment in planning were the National Industrial Recovery Act (NIRA) and

NATIONAL
INDUSTRIAL
RECOVERY ACT

the Agricultural Adjustment Act (AAA). The NIRA was based on the belief that "destructive competition" had worsened industry's economic woes. Skirting antitrust regulation, the NIRA authorized competing businesses to cooperate in crafting industrywide "codes." Thus automobile manufacturers, for example, would cooperate to limit production, establish industrywide prices for their goods, and set workers' wages. Competition among these manufacturers would no longer drive down prices and wages. According to this logic, with wages and prices stabilized, consumer spending would increase, and rising consumer demand would allow industries to rehire workers.

Individual businesses' participation in this program, administered by the National Recovery Administration (NRA), was voluntary—with one catch. Businesses that adhered to the industrywide "codes" could display the "Blue Eagle," the NRA symbol; the government urged consumers to boycott businesses that did not fly the Blue Eagle. This voluntary program, while larger in scale than any previous government–private-sector cooperation, was not very different from Hoover-era "associationalism."

From the beginning, the NRA faced serious problems. As small-business owners had feared, big business easily dominated the NRA-mandated cartels. NRA staff did not have the training or experience to stand up to the representatives of corporate America. The twenty-six-year-old NRA staffer who oversaw the creation of the petroleum industry code was "helped" in his work by twenty highly paid oil industry lawyers. The majority of the 541 codes eventually approved by the NRA reflected the interests of major corporations, not small-business owners, labor, or consumers. Most fundamentally, the NRA did not deliver economic recovery. In 1935, the Supreme Court put an end to the fragile, floundering system. Using an old-fashioned—what Roosevelt called a

"horse-and-buggy" definition—of interstate commerce, the Supreme Court found that the NRA extended federal power past its constitutional bounds.

The Agricultural Adjustment Act (AAA), with tighter federal control of economic planning, had a more endur-

AGRICULTURAL
ADJUSTMENT
ACT

ing effect on the United States. Establishing a national system of crop controls, the AAA offered subsidies to farmers who agreed to limited production

■ Under the Agricultural Adjustment Act, farmers received government payments for not planting crops or for destroying crops they already had planted. Some farmers, however, needed help of a different kind. The Resettlement Administration, established by executive order in 1935, was authorized to resettle destitute farm families from areas of soil erosion, flooding, and stream pollution to homestead communities. This poster was done by Ben Shahn.   (Library of Congress)

of specific crops. (Overproduction drove crop prices down.) The subsidies, funded by taxing the processors of agricultural goods, were meant to provide farmers the same purchasing power they had had during the prosperous period before World War I. In 1933, to reduce production already under way, the nation's farmers agreed to destroy 8.5 million piglets and to plow under crops in the fields. While this strategy made sense as a way to raise prices for agricultural goods, millions of Americans who were hungry or malnourished found it difficult to understand the economic theory behind this waste of food.

Government crop subsidies had unintended consequences: they were a disaster for tenant farmers and sharecroppers. The AAA's hopes that landlords would keep their tenants on the land even while cutting production were not fulfilled. In the South the number of sharecropper farms dropped by almost a third between 1930 and 1940. The result was a homeless population of dispossessed Americans—many of them African American—heading to cities and towns in all parts of the nation. But the subsidies did help many. In the depression-ravaged Dakotas, for example, government payments accounted for almost three-quarters of the total farm income for 1934.

In 1936 the Supreme Court found that the AAA, like the NRA, was unconstitutional. But the AAA (unlike the NRA) was too popular with its constituency, American farmers, to disappear. The legislation was rewritten to meet the Supreme Court's objections, and farm subsidies continue into the twenty-first century.

With millions of Americans in desperate poverty, Roosevelt also moved quickly to implement programs to help the poor. By 1935, $3 billion in federal funds went

TABLE 25.1

New Deal Achievements

Year	Labor	Agriculture and Environment	Business and Industrial Recovery	Relief	Reform
1933	Section 7(a) of NIRA	Agricultural Adjustment Act Farm Credit Act	Emergency Banking Relief Act Economy Act Beer-Wine Revenue Act Banking Act of 1933 (guaranteed deposits) National Industrial Recovery Act	Civilian Conservation Corps Federal Emergency Relief Act Home Owners Refinancing Act Public Works Administration Civil Works Administration	TVA Federal Securities Act
1934	National Labor Relations Board	Taylor Grazing Act			Securities Exchange Act
1935	National Labor Relations (Wagner) Act	Resettlement Administration Rural Electrification Administration		Works Progress Administration National Youth Administration	Social Security Act Public Utility Holding Company Act Revenue Act (wealth tax)
1937		Farm Security Administration		National Housing Act	
1938	Fair Labor Standards Act	Agricultural Adjustment Act of 1938			

Source: Adapted from Charles Sellers, Henry May, and Neil R. McMillen, *A Synopsis of American History,* 6th ed. Copyright © 1985 by Houghton Mifflin Company. Reprinted by permission.

Figure 25.1   The Economy Before and After the New Deal, 1929–1941

The New Deal reduced bank closings, business failures, and unemployment, and it increased farm prices, wages, and salaries. Some of the nation's most persistent economic problems, however, did not disappear until the advent of the Second World War.

RELIEF PROGRAMS

to poor relief. New Dealers, however—like many other Americans—disapproved of direct relief payments to the poor. "Give a man a dole and you save his body and destroy his spirit; give him a job and pay him an assured wage and you save both the body and the spirit," wrote Harry Hopkins, Roosevelt's trusted adviser and head of the president's major relief agency, the Federal Emergency Relief Administration (FERA). Thus New Deal programs emphasized "work relief." By January 1934, the Civil Works Administration gave work to 4 million people, most of whom earned $15 a week. And the Civilian Conservation Corps (CCC) paid unmarried young men (young women were not eligible) $1 a day to do hard outdoor labor: building dams and reservoirs, creating trails in national parks. The program was segregated by race but brought together young men from very different backgrounds. By 1942 the CCC had employed 2.5 million young men, including 80,000 Native Americans who worked on western Indian reservations.

The Public Works Administration (PWA), created by Title II of the National Industrial Recovery Act, appropriated $3.3 billion for public works in 1933. PWA workers built the Grand Coulee Dam (begun during Hoover's administration) and the Triborough Bridge in New York City, as well as hundreds of public buildings. But the main purpose of the PWA was to pump federal money into the economy. As federal revenues for 1932 had totaled only $1.9 billion, this huge appropriation shows the Roosevelt administration was willing to use the controversial technique of deficit spending in an attempt to stimulate the economy.

The special session of Congress adjourned on June 16, 1933. In just over three months, Roosevelt had delivered fifteen messages to Congress proposing major legislation, and Congress had passed fifteen significant laws (see Table 25.1). The United States had rebounded from near collapse. As columnist Walter Lippmann wrote, at the time of Roosevelt's inauguration the country was a collection of "disorderly panic-stricken mobs and factions. In the hundred days from March to June we became again an organized nation confident of our power to provide for our own security and to control our own destiny." Throughout the remainder of 1933 and the spring and summer of 1934, more New Deal bills became law. And as New Deal programs were implemented, unemployment fell steadily from 13 million in 1933 to 9 million in 1936. Farm prices rose, along with wages and salaries, and business failures abated (see Figure 25.1).

Political Pressure and the Second New Deal

Roosevelt's New Deal had enjoyed unprecedented popular and congressional support, but that would not last. The dramatic actions of the First Hundred Days were possible as responses to a national emergency, but the unity of the First Hundred Days masked deep divides within the nation. Once the immediacy of the crisis was averted, the struggle over solutions began in earnest. Some sought to stop the expansion of government power; others pushed for increased governmental action to combat continuing poverty and inequality. Pressure came from all directions as the president considered the next phase of New Deal action.

With the arrival of partial economic recovery, many wealthy business leaders became vocal critics of the New Deal. Some charged that there was too much taxation and government regulation. Others condemned the deficit financing of relief and public works. In 1934 the leaders of several major corporations joined with former presidential candidate Al Smith and disaffected conservative Democrats to establish the American Liberty League. This group mounted a highly visible campaign against New Deal "radicalism." In an attempt to turn southern whites against the New Deal and so splinter the Democratic Party, the Liberty League also secretly channeled funds to a racist group in the South, which circulated incendiary pictures of the First Lady with African Americans.

BUSINESS OPPOSITION

While many prominent business leaders fought the New Deal, many other Americans (sometimes called populists) thought the government favored business too much and paid too little attention to the needs of the common people. Unemployment had decreased—but 9 million people were still without work. In 1934 a wave of strikes hit the nation, affecting 1.5 million workers. In 1935, enormous dust storms enveloped the southern plains states, killing livestock and driving families like the Montgomerys from their land. Millions of Americans still suffered. As their dissatisfaction mounted, so too did the appeal of various demagogues, who sought power by playing to the prejudices and unreasoning passions of the people and who presented simple explanations for their plight.

DEMAGOGUES AND POPULISTS

Father Charles Coughlin, a Roman Catholic priest whose weekly radio sermons reached up to 30 million listeners, appealed to the fears and frustrations of people who felt they'd lost control of their lives to distant elites and impersonal forces. Increasingly anti–New Deal, he also was increasingly anti-Semitic, telling his listeners that the cause of their woes was an international conspiracy of Jewish bankers.

Another challenge came from Dr. Francis E. Townsend, a public health officer in Long Beach, California, who was thrown out of work at age sixty-seven with only $100 in savings. His situation was not unusual. With social welfare left to the states, only about 400,000 of the 6.6 million elderly Americans received any sort of state-supplied pension. And as employment and savings disappeared with the depression, many older people fell into desperate poverty. Townsend proposed that Americans over the age of sixty should receive a government pension of $200 a month, financed by a new "transaction" (sales) tax. In fact, Townsend's plan was fiscally impossible (almost three-quarters of working Americans earned just $200 a month or less) and profoundly regressive (because sales tax rates are the same for everyone, they take a larger share of income from those who earn least). Thus, Townsend actually proposed a massive transfer of income from the working poor to the nonworking elderly. Nonetheless, 20 million Americans, or one in five American adults—concerned about the plight of the elderly and not about details of funding—signed petitions supporting this plan.

Then there was Huey Long, perhaps the most successful populist demagogue in American history. Long was elected governor of Louisiana in 1928 with the slogan "Every Man a King, but No One Wears a Crown." As a U.S. senator, Long at first supported the New Deal, but he began to believe that Roosevelt had fallen captive to big business. Long countered in 1934 with the Share Our Wealth Society, which advocated the seizure (by taxation) of all income exceeding $1 million a year and of wealth in excess of $5 million per family. From these funds, the government would provide each American family an annual income of $2,000 and a one-time homestead allowance of $5,000. (Long's plan was fiscally impossible, but definitely not regressive.) By mid-1935 Long's movement claimed 7 million members, and few doubted that Long aspired to the presidency. An assassin's bullet extinguished his ambition in September 1935.

While populist critics pushed at Franklin Roosevelt, the political left was gaining ground. In Wisconsin the left-wing Progressive Party reelected Robert La Follette Jr. to the Senate in 1934, provided seven of the state's ten representatives to Congress, and placed

LEFT-WING CRITICS

■ In the 1930s, Senator Huey Long *(center)* had a mass following and presidential ambitions. But he was assassinated in 1935, the evening this photograph was taken. When Long was shot, he fell into the arms of James O'Connor *(left),* a political crony. Louisiana governor O. K. Allen *(right)* seized a pistol and dashed into the corridor in pursuit of the murderer shouting, "If there's shooting, I want to be in on it." (Wide World Photos, Inc.)

■ Mary McLeod Bethune, pictured here with her friend and supporter Eleanor Roosevelt, became the first African American woman to head a federal agency as director of the Division of Negro Affairs of the National Youth Administration.
(© Bettmann/Corbis)

La Follette's brother Philip in the governorship. Muckraker and socialist Upton Sinclair won the Democratic gubernatorial nomination in California in 1934 with the slogan "End Poverty in California." Even the U.S. Communist Party found new support. Changing its strategy to disclaim any intention of overthrowing the U.S. government, the party proclaimed that "Communism Is Twentieth Century Americanism," and began to cooperate with left-wing labor unions, student groups, and writers' organizations in a "Popular Front" against fascism abroad and racism at home. In 1938, at its high point for the decade, the party had fifty-five thousand members.

It was not only populists and socialists who pushed Roosevelt to focus on social justice. Largely owing to Eleanor Roosevelt's influence, the administration included activists who were committed to progressive causes. Frances Perkins, America's first woman cabinet member, came from a social work background, as did Roosevelt's close adviser Harold Ickes. A circle of women activists in government and the Democratic Party, attached to Eleanor Roosevelt, were strong advocates for social reform. Even African Americans had an unprecedented voice in this White House. By 1936 at least fifty African Americans

SHAPING THE SECOND NEW DEAL

held relatively important positions in New Deal agencies and cabinet-level departments. Journalists called these officials—who met on Friday evenings at the home of Mary McLeod Bethune, a distinguished educator who served as Director of Negro Affairs for the National Youth Administration—the "black cabinet." Finally, Eleanor Roosevelt herself worked tirelessly to put social justice issues at the center of the New Deal agenda.

Influenced by these advisers, Roosevelt also drew political lessons from the success of populist demagogues and leftist politicians. Many Americans who had been hit hard by the depression looked to the New Deal for help and for social justice. If that help was not forthcoming, Roosevelt would lose their support. Other Americans—not the poorest, but those with a tenuous hold on the middle class—were afraid of the continued chaos and disorder. They wanted security and stability. Still others, with more to lose, were frightened by the populist promises of people like Long and Coughlin. They wanted the New Deal to preserve American capitalism (see Figure 25.2). With these lessons in mind, Roosevelt looked ahead to the presidential election of 1936 and took the initiative once more.

During the period historians call "the Second New Deal," Roosevelt introduced a range of progressive pro-

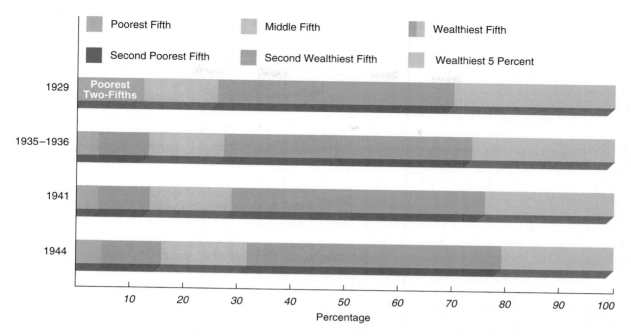

Figure 25.2   Distribution of Total Family Income Among the American People, 1929–1944 (Percentage)

Although the New Deal provided economic relief to the American people, it did not, as its critics so often charged, significantly redistribute income downward from the rich to the poor.   (Source: Adapted from U.S. Bureau of the Census, *Historical Statistics of the United States, Colonial Times to 1970,* 2 parts [Washington, D.C.: U.S. Government Printing Office, 1975], Part 1, p. 301.)

grams aimed at providing, as he said in a 1935 address to Congress, "greater security for the average man than he has ever known before in the history of America." The first triumph of the Second New Deal was an innocuous-sounding but momentous law that Roosevelt called "the Big Bill." The Emergency Relief Appropriation Act provided $4 billion in new deficit spending, primarily to establish massive public works programs for the jobless. Among the programs funded by the Emergency Relief Appropriation Act were the Resettlement Administration, which resettled destitute families and organized rural homestead communities and suburban greenbelt towns for low-income workers; the Rural Electrification Administration, which brought electricity to isolated rural areas; and the National Youth Administration, which sponsored work-relief programs for young adults and part-time jobs for students.

The largest and best-known program funded by the Emergency Relief Appropriation Act was the Works Progress Administration (WPA), later renamed the Work Projects Administration. The WPA ultimately employed more than 8.5 million people. Its workers built 650,000

WORKS PROGRESS ADMINISTRATION miles of highways and roads and 125,000 public buildings, as well as bridges, reservoirs, irrigation systems, sewage treatment plants, parks, playgrounds and swimming pools throughout the nation. Many WPA projects helped local communities: WPA workers built or renovated schools and hospitals, operated nurseries for preschool children, and taught 1.5 million adults to read and write.

The WPA also sponsored a multitude of cultural programs, which not only provided employment for artists, musicians, writers, and actors but offered art in myriad forms to the people. The WPA's Federal Theater Project brought vaudeville, circuses, and theater, including African American and Yiddish plays, to cities and towns across the country; its Arts Project hired painters and sculptors to teach their crafts in rural schools and commissioned artists to decorate post office walls with murals depicting ordinary life in America past and present. The Federal Music Project employed 15,000 musicians in government-sponsored orchestras, and collected folk songs from around the nation. Perhaps the most ambitious of the New Deal's cultural programs was the WPA's Federal Writers Project (FWP), which hired talented authors such as John Steinbeck and Richard Wright. FWP writers created guidebooks for every state and territory, and they wrote about the plain people of the United States. More than two thousand elderly men and women who had been freed from slavery by the Civil War told their stories to FWP writers, who collected these "slave narratives"; life stories of sharecroppers and textile workers were published as *These Are Our Lives* (1939). These and other WPA arts projects were controversial, for many of the WPA artists, musicians, actors, and writers sympathized with the political struggles of workers and farmers. Critics assailed them as left-wing propaganda, and in fact some of these artists were communists. However, the goal of this "Popular Front" culture was not to overthrow the government, but to recover a tradition of American radicalism through remembering, and celebrating artistically, the lives and labor of America's plain folk.

The programs and agencies created by the Big Bill were part of a short-term "emergency" strategy, meant to address the immediate needs of the nation. Roosevelt's long-term strategy centered around the second major piece of Second New Deal legislation, the Social Security Act. The Social Security Act created, for the first time, a federal system to provide for the social welfare of American citizens. Its key provision was a federal pension system in which eligible workers paid mandatory Social Security taxes on their wages and their employers contributed an equivalent amount; these

SOCIAL SECURITY ACT

■ Enacted in 1935, Social Security has been one of the most enduring of all New Deal programs. This poster urges eligible Americans to apply promptly for their Social Security cards. (Library of Congress)

workers then received federal retirement benefits. The Social Security Act also created several welfare programs, including a cooperative federal-state system of unemployment compensation and Aid to Dependent Children (later renamed Aid to Families with Dependent Children, AFDC) for needy children in families without fathers present. Over the course of the twentieth century, benefits provided through the Social Security system would save tens of millions of Americans, especially the elderly, from lives of poverty and despair.

Compared with the national systems of social security already in place in most western European nations, the U.S. Social Security system was fairly conservative. First, the government did not pay for old-age benefits; workers and their bosses did. Second, the tax was regressive in that the more workers earned, the less they were taxed proportionally. Finally, the law did not cover agricultural labor, domestic service, and "casual labor not in the course of the employer's trade or business" (for example, janitorial work at a hospital). Thus a disproportionally high number people of color, who worked as farm laborers, as domestic servants, and in service jobs in hospitals and restaurants, received no benefits. The act also excluded public sector employees, so that many teachers, nurses, librarians, and social workers, the majority of whom were women, went uncovered. (Although the original Social Security Act provided no retirement benefits for spouses or widows of covered workers, Congress added these benefits in 1939.) Despite these limitations, the Social Security Act was a highly significant development. With its passage, the federal government took responsibility not only for the economic security of the aged but also for the temporarily jobless, dependent children, and people with disabilities.

As the election of 1936 approached, Roosevelt began to use the populist language of his critics. He made scathing attacks on big business. De-

ROOSEVELT'S POPULIST STRATEGIES

nouncing "entrenched greed" and the "unjust concentration of wealth and power," he proposed that government should "cut the giants down to size" through antitrust suits and heavy corporate taxes. He also supported the Wealth Tax Act, which some critics saw as the president's attempt to "steal Huey Long's thunder." The tax act helped achieve a slight redistribution of income by raising the income taxes of the wealthy. It also imposed a new tax on business profits and increased taxes on inheritances, large gifts, and profits from the sale of property.

In November 1936, Roosevelt won the presidency by a huge landslide, defeating the Republican nominee, Governor Alf Landon of Kansas, by a margin of 27.8 million votes to 16.7 million. The Democrats also won huge majorities in the House and Senate. Some observers even worried that the two-party system was about to collapse. Roosevelt and the Democrats had forged a powerful "New Deal coalition." This new alliance consisted of the urban masses—especially immigrants from southern and eastern Europe and their sons and daughters—organized labor, the eleven states of the Confederacy (the "Solid South"), and northern blacks. By this time, there were sufficient numbers of African Americans in northern cities to constitute voting blocks, and New Deal benefits drew them away from the Republican Party, which they had long supported as the party of Lincoln. With the New Deal coalition, the Democratic Party came to dominate the two-party system and would occupy the White House for most of the next thirty years.

Labor

During the worst years of the depression, American workers continued to organize and to struggle for the rights of labor. Management, however, resisted unionization vigorously. Many employers refused to recognize unions, and some hired armed thugs to intimidate workers. One business publication declared that "a few hundred funerals will have a quieting influence." As employers refused to negotiate with union representatives, workers walked off the job. Employers tried to replace striking workers with strikebreakers—and workers tried to keep the strikebreakers from crossing their picket lines. The situation often turned violent. Local police or National Guard troops frequently intervened on the side of management, smashing workers' picket lines. As strikes spread throughout the nation, violence erupted in the steel, automobile, and textile industries, among lumber workers in the Pacific Northwest, and among teamsters in the Midwest. In 1934 a strike of longshoremen was met with violence by police on the docks of San Francisco; two union members were killed, and workers' anger spread to other industries. Eventually 130,000 workers joined the general strike.

Workers pushed the Roosevelt administration for support, which came in the 1935 National Labor Relations (Wagner) Act. This act guaranteed workers the right to organize unions and to bargain collectively. It outlawed "unfair labor practices" such as firing workers who joined unions, prohibited management from sponsoring company unions, and required employers to bargain with labor's elected union representatives to set

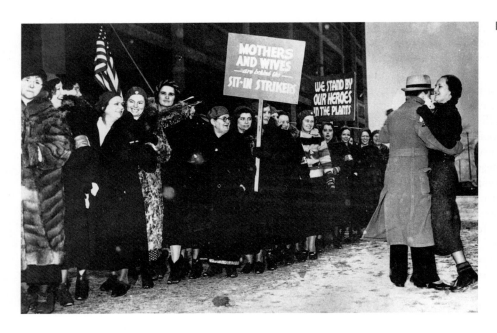

During the 1937 sit-down strike by automobile workers in Flint, Michigan, a women's "emergency brigade" of wives, mothers, daughters, sisters, and sweethearts conducted daily demonstrations at the plants. When the police sought to force the men out of Chevrolet Plant No. 9 by filling it with tear gas, the women armed themselves with clubs and smashed out the plant's windows to let in fresh air.   (Wide World Photos, Inc.)

wages, hours, and working conditions. Critically for its success, the Wagner Act created a mechanism for enforcement: the National Labor Relations Board (NLRB). Though labor-management conflict continued, by the end of the decade the NLRB played a key role in mediating disputes. And with federal protection, union membership grew. Organizers in the coal fields told miners that "President Roosevelt wants you to join the union," and join they did—along with workers in dozens of industries. In 1929 union membership stood at 3.6 million; in mid-1938 it surpassed 7 million.

The Wagner Act further alienated business leaders from the New Deal. "No Obedience," proclaimed an editorial in a leading business magazine. The business-sponsored Liberty League insisted that the Supreme Court would soon find the Wagner Act unconstitutional.

Conflict existed not only between labor and management, but within the labor movement itself. The rapid growth and increasing militancy of the movement exacerbated an existing division between "craft" and "industrial" unions in the United States. Craft unions represented labor's elite, the skilled workers in a particular trade, such as carpentry. Industrial unions represented all the workers, skilled and unskilled, in a given industry, such as automobile manufacture. In the 1930s, it was the industrial unions that had grown dramatically.

Craft unions dominated the American Federation of Labor, the powerful umbrella organization for specific

RIVALRY BETWEEN CRAFT AND INDUSTRIAL UNIONS

unions. Most AFL leaders offered little support for industrial organizing. Many looked down on the industrial workers, disproportionately immigrants from southern and eastern Europe—"the rubbish at labor's door," in the words of the Teamsters' president. Skilled workers had different economic interests from the great mass of unskilled workers, and more conservative craft unionists were often alarmed at what they saw as the radicalism of industrial unions.

In 1935, the industrial unionists made their move. John L. Lewis, head of the United Mine Workers and the nation's most prominent labor leader, resigned as vice president of the AFL. He and other industrial unionists created the Committee for Industrial Organization (CIO); the AFL responded by suspending all CIO unions. In 1938 the slightly renamed Congress of Industrial Organizations had 3.7 million members, slightly more than the AFL's 3.4 million. Unlike the AFL, the CIO included women and people of color in its membership. Union membership gave these "marginal" workers greater employment security and the benefits of collective bargaining.

The most decisive labor conflict of the decade came in late 1936, when the United Auto Workers (UAW), an industrial union, demanded recognition from General Motors (GM), Chrysler, and Ford. When GM refused, UAW organizers responded with a relatively new tactic: a "sit-down strike." On December 30, 1936, workers at the Fisher Body plant in Flint, Michigan, went on strike *inside* the Fisher One factory. They re-

SIT-DOWN STRIKES

fused to leave the building, thus immobilizing a key part of the GM production system. GM tried to force the workers out by turning off the heat. When police attempted to take back the plant, strikers hurled steel bolts, coffee mugs, and bottles. The police tried tear gas. Strikers turned the plant's water hoses on the police.

As the sit-down strike spread to adjacent plants, auto production plummeted. General Motors obtained a court order to evacuate the plant, but the strikers stood firm, risking imprisonment and fines. In a critical decision, Michigan's governor refused to send in the National Guard to clear workers from the buildings. After forty-four days, the UAW triumphed. GM agreed to recognize the union, and Chrysler quickly followed. Ford held out until 1940.

On the heels of this triumph, however, came a grim reminder of the costs of labor's struggle. On Memorial Day 1937, a group of picnicking work-

MEMORIAL DAY MASSACRE

ers and their families marched toward the Republic Steel plant in Chicago, intending to show support for strikers on a picket line in front of the plant. Police blocked their route and ordered them to disperse. One of the marchers threw something at the police, and the police attacked. Ten men were killed, seven of them shot in the back. Thirty marchers were wounded, including a woman and three children. Many Americans, fed up with labor strife and violence, showed little sympathy for the workers. The anti-labor *Chicago Tribune* blamed the marchers and praised police for repelling "a trained military unit of a revolutionary body."

At great cost, organized labor made great gains during the 1930s. Gradually, the violence that had erupted during the depression years receded as the National Labor Relations Board proved effective in mediating disputes. And unionized workers—about 23 percent of the nonagricultural work force—saw their standards of living rise. By 1941, the average steelworker could afford to buy a new coat for himself and his wife every six years, and every other year, a pair of shoes for each of his children.

Federal Power and the Nationalization of Culture

In the 1930s, national culture, politics, and policies played an increasingly important role in the lives of Americans from different regions, classes, and ethnic backgrounds. This happened, in large part, because of the expansion of the power of the federal government. During the decade-long economic crisis, politi-

cal power moved from the state and local level to the White House and Congress. Individual Americans, in new ways, found their lives bound up with the federal government. In 1930, with the single exception of the post office, Americans had little direct contact with the federal government. By the end of the 1930s, almost 35 percent of the population had received some sort of federal government benefit, whether crop subsidies through the federal AAA or a WPA job or relief payments through FERA. As political analyst Michael Barone argues, "The New Deal changed American life by changing the relationship between Americans and their government." Americans in the 1930s began to look to the federal government to play a major and active role in the life of the nation.

The New Deal changed the American West more than any other region, as federally sponsored construction of

NEW DEAL IN THE WEST

dams and other public works projects reshaped the region's economy and environment. During the 1930s the federal Bureau of Reclamation, an obscure agency created in 1902 to provide irrigation for small farms and ranches, expanded its mandate dramatically to build large multipurpose dams that controlled entire river systems. The Boulder Dam (later renamed for Herbert Hoover) harnessed the Colorado River, providing water to southern California municipalities and using hydroelectric power to produce electricity for Los Angeles and southern Arizona. The Central Valley Project dammed the Sacramento River and its tributaries; at a cost of $2.3 billion, it was not meant simply to help small farmers irrigate their land. Instead, large factory farms consolidated their hold in the region with water from these massive projects, which were paid for by taxpayers across the nation and by regional consumers of municipal water and electricity.

The water from these dams opened new areas to agriculture and allowed western cities to expand; the cheap electricity they produced attracted industry to the region. These federally managed projects also gave the federal government an unprecedented role in the West. Especially after the completion of Washington State's Grand Coulee Dam in 1941, the federal government controlled both a great deal of water and hydroelectric power in the region. And in the West, control of water meant control over the region's future.

The federal government also brought millions of acres of western land under its control in the 1930s, limiting agricultural production not only to keep crop and livestock prices from falling further but also to combat the environmental disaster of the Dust Bowl. To reduce

■ In 1930, 90 percent of American farms did not have electricity. This 1936 cover from *Fortune* magazine celebrates the work of the Rural Electrification Administration, which brought power to some of America's most remote regions. (*Fortune* magazine, March 1936)

pressure on the land from overgrazing, the federal government bought 8 million cattle from farmers in a six-month period in 1934–1935 and transported the healthy cattle out of the region. In 1934, the Taylor Grazing Act imposed new restrictions on ranchers' use of public lands for grazing stock. Federal stock reduction programs probably saved the western cattle industry, but they destroyed the traditional economy of the Navajos by forcing them to reduce the size of their sheep herds on their federally protected reservation lands. The large farms and ranches of the West benefited immensely from federal subsidies and crop supports through the AAA, but such programs also increased federal government control in the region. As western historian Richard White argues, by the end of the 1930s "federal bureaucracies were quite literally remaking the American West."

New federal activism extended to the West's people, as well. Over the past several decades, federal policy

NEW DEAL FOR NATIVE AMERICANS toward Native Americans, especially those on western Indian reservations, had been disastrous. The Bureau of Indian Affairs (BIA) was riddled with corruption; in its attempts to "assimilate" Native Americans it had separated children from their parents, suppressed native languages, and outlawed tribal religious practices. Such BIA-enforced assimilation was not successful. Division of tribal lands had failed to promote individual land ownership—almost half of those living on reservations in 1933 owned no land. In the early 1930s, Native Americans were the poorest group in the nation, plagued by epidemics and malnutrition, with an infant mortality rate twice that of white Americans.

In 1933, Roosevelt named one of the BIA's most vocal critics to head the agency. John Collier, founder of the American Indian Defense Agency, meant to completely reverse the course of America's Indian policy, and his initiatives had many positive results. The Indian Reorganization Act (1934) went a long way toward ending the forced assimilation of native peoples and restoring Indian lands to tribal ownership. It also gave federal recognition to tribal governments. Indian tribes had regained their status as semisovereign nations, guaranteed "internal sovereignty" in all matters not specifically limited by acts of Congress.

Not all Indian peoples supported the IRA. Some saw it as a "back-to-the-blanket" measure based on romantic notions of "authentic" Indian culture. The tribal government structure specified by the IRA was culturally alien—and quite perplexing—to tribes such as the Papagos, whose language had no word for "representative." The Navajo nation also refused to ratify the IRA; in a terrible case of bad timing, the vote took place during the federally mandated destruction of Navajo sheep herds. Eventually, however, 181 tribes organized under the IRA. Collier had succeeded in reversing some of the destructive policies of the past, and the IRA laid the groundwork for future economic development and limited political autonomy among native peoples.

New Dealers did not set out to transform the American West, but they did intend to transform the American South. Well before the Great Depression, the South was mired in widespread and debilitating poverty. In 1929, the South's per capita income of $365 per year was less than half of the West's $921. More than half of the region's farm families were tenants or sharecroppers with no land of their own. "Sickness, misery, and unnecessary death" (in the words of a contemporary

NEW DEAL IN THE SOUTH

■ As the commissioner of Indian affairs, John Collier *(right)* reversed long-standing U.S. policy, insisting that "the cultural history of Indians is in all respects to be considered equal to that of any non-Indian group." However, some of the reforms he introduced were at odds with traditional practices, as in the case of the Hopi, whose tradition of independent villages did not fit the model of centralized tribal control mandated by the Indian Reorganization Act. Here, Hopi leaders Loma Haftowa *(left)* and Chaf Towa *(middle)* join Collier at the opening ceremonies for the new Department of the Interior building in Washington, D.C.   (Wide World Photos, Inc.)

study) plagued the southern poor. Almost 15 percent of South Carolina's people could not read or write.

Roosevelt, who sought a cure for his polio in the pools of Warm Springs, Georgia, had seen southern poverty firsthand and understood its human costs. But in describing the South as "the Nation's No. 1 economic problem" in 1938, he was referring to the economic theory that underlay many New Deal programs. So long as its people were too poor to participate in the nation's mass consumer economy, the South would be a drag on national economic recovery.

The largest federal intervention in the South was the Tennessee Valley Authority (TVA), authorized by Congress during Roosevelt's First Hundred Days. The TVA was created to develop a water and hydroelectric power project similar to the multipurpose dams of the West; dams would not only control flooding but produce electric power for the region (see Map 25.2). However, confronted with the poverty and hopelessness of the Tennessee River Valley region (which included parts of Virginia, North Carolina, Tennessee, Georgia, Alabama, Mississippi, and Kentucky), the TVA quickly extended its focus. Through the TVA, the federal government promoted economic development, helped bring electricity to rural areas, restored fields worn out from overuse, and fought the curse of malaria.

The TVA achieved its goals but, in the process, became a major polluter. TVA strip mining caused soil ero-

sion. Its coal-burning generators released sulfur oxides, which combined with water vapor to produce acid rain. Above all, the TVA degraded the water by dumping untreated sewage, toxic chemicals, and metal pollutants from strip mining into streams and rivers. Though an economic miracle, over time the TVA proved to be a monumental disaster in America's environmental history.

During the 1930s, the Roosevelt administration faced a very difficult political situation in the South. The southern senators whose support Roosevelt needed so desperately benefited from the flow of federal dollars to their states. But they were also suspicious of federal intervention and determined to preserve "states' rights." Especially when federal action threatened the South's racial hierarchy, they resisted passionately. As the nation's poorest and least educated region, the South would not easily be integrated into the national culture and economy. But New Deal programs began that process, and in so doing improved the lives of at least some of the region's people.

It was not only federal government programs that broke down regional boundaries and fostered national connections during the 1930s. The national mass medium of radio helped millions survive hard times, and America's national popular culture played a critical role in the life of Americans throughout the 1930s.

MASS MEDIA AND POPULAR CULTURE

Map 25.2   The Tennessee Valley Authority

To control flooding and to generate electricity, the Tennessee Valley Authority constructed dams along the Tennessee River and its tributaries from Paducah, Kentucky, to Knoxville, Tennessee.

The sound of the radio filled the days and nights of the depression era. Manufacturers rushed to produce cheaper models, and a 1937 study found that Americans were buying radios at the rate of twenty-eight a minute. By the end of the decade 27.5 million households owned radios, and families listened on average five hours a day. Roosevelt understood the importance of the radio in American life, going directly to the American people with radio "Fireside Chats" throughout his presidency. Americans, in fact, put him eleventh in a ranking of America's top "radio personalities" in 1938.

The radio offered Americans many things. In a time of uncertainty, radio gave citizens immediate access—as never before—to the political news of the days and to the actual voices of their elected leaders. During hard times, radio offered escape: for children, the adventures of *Flash Gordon* and of *Jack Armstrong, the All American Boy;* for housewives, the new soap operas such as *The Romance of Helen Trent* and *Young Widder Brown.* Entire families gathered to listen to the comedy of ex-vaudevillians George Burns and Gracie Allen, and Jack Benny.

Radio also gave people a chance to participate—however vicariously—in events they could never have experienced before: listeners were carried to New York City for performances of the Metropolitan Opera on Saturday afternoons; to the Moana Hotel on the beach at Waikiki through the live broadcast of *Hawaii Calls;* to major league baseball games (begun by the St. Louis Cardinals in 1935) in distant cities. Millions shared the horror of the kidnapping of aviator Charles Lindbergh's son in 1932; black Americans in the urban North and the rural South shared the triumphal moment when African American boxer Joe Louis knocked out white heavyweight champion James Braddock in 1937. Radio lessened the isolation of individuals and communities. It helped to create a more homogeneous mass culture, as children throughout the nation acted out the same stories they'd learned from the radio, but by offering a set of shared experiences, it also lessened the gulfs among Americans from different regions and class backgrounds.

The shared popular culture of 1930s America also centered around Hollywood movies. Though the film industry suffered in the initial years of the depression—almost one-third of all movie theaters closed, and ticket prices fell from 30 cents to 20 cents—it rebounded after 1933. In a nation of fewer than 130 million people, between 80 and 90 million movie tickets were sold each

The 1936 Olympic Games

GERMANY
XIᵗʰ OLYMPIC GAMES
1936
1ˢᵗ—16ᵗʰ AUGUST
BERLIN

The 1936 Olympic Games that were scheduled to take place in Berlin, under the Nazi regime, created a dilemma for the United States and for other nations. Should they go to Berlin? Would participation in the Nazi-orchestrated spectacle lend credence to Hitler's regime? Or would victories won by other nations undermine Hitler's claims about the superiority of Germany's "Aryan race"?

Although the modern Olympic Games had been founded in 1896 with high hopes that they might help unite the nations of the world in peace and understanding, international politics were never far from the surface. Germany had been excluded from the 1920 and 1924 games following its aggression and defeat in World War I, and the International Olympic Committee's choice (in 1931) of Berlin for the XI Olympiad was intended to welcome Germany back into the world community. However, with Hitler's rise to power in 1933, Germany determined to use the games as propaganda for the Nazi state and to demonstrate the superiority of its pure "Aryan" athletes. Soon thereafter, campaigns to boycott the Berlin Olympics emerged in several nations, including Great Britain, Sweden, France, Czechoslovakia, and the United States.

The American people were divided over the question of a boycott. Some U.S. Jewish groups led campaigns against U.S. participation in Berlin, while others took no public position, concerned that their actions might lead to increased anti-Semitic violence within Germany. African Americans, overwhelmingly, opposed boycotting the games. Well aware of Hitler's attitudes toward "mongrel" peoples, many looked forward to demonstrating on the tracks and fields of Berlin just how wrong Hitler's notions of Aryan superiority were. Some also pointed out the hypocrisy of American officials who criticized Germany while ignoring U.S. discrimination against black athletes.

The debate over the Berlin Olympics also revealed pockets of American anti-Semitism. Faced with the prospect of a boycott, the president of the American Olympic Committee (AOC), Avery Brundage, first insisted that the "Games belong to the athletes and not to the politicians." When the boycott movement continued, however, he attributed it to a "conspiracy" of Jews and communists and instructed American athletes not to get involved in the "present Jew-Nazi altercation." Despite such rhetoric, Brundage remained head of the AOC.

In the end, the United States sent 312 athletes to Berlin. Eighteen were African American. These athletes won fourteen medals, or almost one-quarter of the U.S. total of fifty-six. Track and field star Jesse Owens came home with four gold medals.

Despite the initial controversy, the XI Olympiad was a public relations triumph for Germany in the United States, and the *New York Times* proclaimed that the XI Olympiad had put Germany "back in the fold of nations." As participants and spectators flocked to swastika-bedecked Berlin, Hitler's vow that the Olympic Games would thereafter take place in Germany "for all time to come" seemed suddenly possible.

The idealistic vision of nations linked together through peaceful athletic competition hit a low point at the 1936 Olympics. The 1940 Olympic Games, scheduled for Tokyo, were cancelled because of the escalating world war.

The eleventh summer Olympic Games in Berlin were carefully crafted as propaganda for the Nazi state. And the spectacle of the 1936 games, as represented in the poster above, was impressive. But on the athletic fields, Nazi claims of Aryan superiority were challenged by athletes such as African American Jesse Owens, who is shown breaking the Olympic record in the 200-meter race. (Above: © Leonard de Selva/Corbis; left: © Corbis-Bettmann)

■ Radio provided the backdrop for family life and household chores during the 1930s, with programs ranging from operas to soap operas. The largest audience for any single program during the decade listened to the Joe Louis–Max Schmeling boxing match in June 1938.   (Wide World Photo, Inc.)

week by the mid-1930s. Comedies were especially popular, from the slapstick of the Marx Brothers to the sophisticated banter of *My Man Godfrey* or *It Happened One Night*. While many Americans sought escape from grim reality at the movies, the appeal of upbeat movies was in the context of economic hard times. The song "Who's Afraid of the Big Bad Wolf?" from Disney's *Three Little Pigs*, was a big hit in 1933—as the economy hit bottom. Hollywood film, like radio, helped to consolidate a national culture by offering Americans a shared set of vicarious experiences.

Finally, in an unintended consequence, federal policies intended to channel jobs to male heads of households strengthened the power of national popular culture. During Roosevelt's first two years in office 1.5 million youths lost jobs; many young people who would have gone to work at the age of fourteen in better times decided to stay in school. By the end of the decade, three-quarters of American youth went to high school—up from one-half in 1920—and graduation rates doubled. School was free, classrooms were warm, and education seemed to promise a better future. The exuberant, fad-driven peer cultures that had developed in 1920s high schools and colleges were no more, but consumer-oriented youth culture had not died out. And as more young people went to high school, more participated in that national youth culture. Increasingly, young people

listened to the same music. More than ever before, they adopted the same styles of clothing, of dance, of speech. Paradoxically, the hard times of the depression did not destroy youth culture; instead, they caused youth culture to spread more widely among America's young.

The Limits of the New Deal

Roosevelt began his second term with great optimism and a strong mandate for reform. Almost immediately, however, the president's own actions undermined his New Deal agenda. Labor strife and racial issues divided the American people. As fascism spread in Europe, the world inched toward war and domestic initiatives lost ground to foreign affairs and defense. By late 1938, New Deal reform had ground to a halt. But the New Deal, in six years, had had a profound impact on the United States.

Following his landslide electoral victory in 1936, Roosevelt set out to safeguard his progressive agenda.

COURT-PACKING PLAN

The greatest danger he saw was from the U.S. Supreme Court. In ruling unconstitutional both the National Industrial Recovery Act (in 1935) and the Agricultural Adjustment Act (in 1936), the Court rejected not only specific provisions of hastily drafted New

Deal legislation but the expansion of presidential and federal power such legislation entailed. Only three of the nine justices were consistently sympathetic to New Deal "emergency" measures, and Roosevelt was convinced the Court would invalidate most of the Second New Deal legislation. Citing the advanced age and heavy workload of the nine justices, he asked Congress for authority to appoint up to six new justices to the Supreme Court. But in an era that had seen the rise to power of Hitler, Mussolini, and Stalin, many Americans saw Roosevelt's plan as an attack on constitutional government. Even those sympathetic to the New Deal worried about politicizing the Court. "Assuming, which is not at all impossible," wrote prominent journalist William Allen White, "a reactionary president, as charming, as eloquent and as irresistible as Roosevelt, with power to change the court, and we should be in the devil's own fix." Congress rebelled, and Roosevelt experienced his first major congressional defeat.

The episode had a final, ironic twist. During the long public debate over court packing, the ideological center of the Court shifted. Key swing-vote justices on the Supreme Court began to vote in favor of liberal, pro–New Deal rulings. In short order the Court upheld both the Wagner Act (*NLRB v. Jones & Laughlin Steel Corp.*), ruling that Congress's power to regulate interstate commerce also involved the power to regulate the production of goods for interstate commerce, and the Social Security Act. Moreover, a new judicial pension program encouraged older judges to retire, and the president was able to appoint seven new associate justices in the next four years, including notables such as Hugo Black, Felix Frankfurter, and William O. Douglas. In the end, Roosevelt got what he wanted from the Supreme Court, but the court-packing plan damaged his political credibility.

Another New Deal setback was the renewed economic recession of 1937–1939, sometimes called the Roosevelt recession. Despite his use of deficit spending, Roosevelt had never abandoned his commitment to a balanced budget. In 1937, confident that the depression had largely been cured, he began to cut back government spending. At the same time the Federal Reserve Board, concerned about a 3.6 percent inflation rate, tightened credit. The two actions sent the economy into a tailspin: unemployment climbed from 7.7 million in 1937 to 10.4 million in 1938. Soon Roosevelt resumed deficit financing.

The New Deal was in trouble in 1937 and 1938, and New Dealers struggled over the direction of liberal reform. Some urged vigorous trustbusting; others advocated the resurrection of national economic planning as it had existed under the National Recovery Administration. But in the end Roosevelt rejected these alternatives and chose deficit financing as a means to stimulate consumer demand and create jobs. And in 1939, with conflict over the world war that had begun in Europe commanding more and more of the nation's attention, the New Deal came to an end. Roosevelt sacrificed further domestic reforms in return for conservative support for his programs of military rearmament and preparedness.

No president had ever served more than two terms, and as the presidential election of 1940 approached, many Americans speculated about whether Franklin Roosevelt would run for a third term. Roosevelt seemed undecided until the spring of 1940, when Adolf Hitler's military advances in Europe apparently convinced him to stay on. Roosevelt preempted the critique of his opponent, Republican Wendell Willkie, by expanding military and naval contracts, thereby reducing unemployment. Roosevelt also promised Americans, "Your boys are not going to be sent into any foreign wars."

On election day, the New Deal coalition held, though it did not deliver the landslide victory it had in the 1936 election (see Map 25.3). As in 1936, however, Roosevelt

Map 25.3 Presidential Election, 1940

Roosevelt won an unprecedented third term in the 1940 presidential election. He did not repeat his landslide 1936 victory, in which he won all but two states. But he did capture thirty-eight states in 1940 to Republican Wendell Willkie's ten.

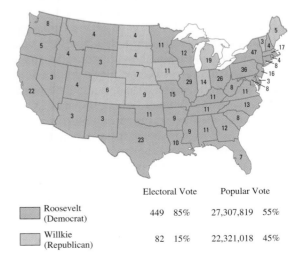

	Electoral Vote	Popular Vote
Roosevelt (Democrat)	449 85%	27,307,819 55%
Willkie (Republican)	82 15%	22,321,018 45%

won in the cities, primarily among blue-collar workers, ethnic Americans, and African Americans. He also carried every state in the South. Although New Deal reform was over at home, Roosevelt was still riding a wave of public approval.

While the New Deal directly touched the lives of a great many Americans, not all benefited equally. More than anything else, differences were based on race. The New Deal fell short of equality for people of color for two major reasons. First was the relationship between local and national power. Over and over, in the South and the West, national New Deal programs confronted local custom, and local custom won. In the South, African Americans received lower relief payments than whites and were paid lower wages in WPA jobs. The situation was similar in the Southwest. In Tucson, Arizona, for example, Federal Emergency Relief Agency officials divided applicants into four groups—Anglos, Mexican Americans, Mexican immigrants, and Indians—and allocated relief payments in descending order.

RACE AND THE LIMITS OF THE NEW DEAL

Such discriminatory practices were rooted not only in racism but also in the economic interests of whites/Anglos. The majority of African American and Mexican American workers were paid so poorly they *earned* less than impoverished whites got for "relief." Why would these workers take low-paying private jobs if government relief or government work programs provided more income? Local communities understood that federal programs threatened a political, social, and economic system based on racial hierarchies.

The case of the Scottsboro Boys illustrates the power of racism in the conflict between local and national power in 1930s America. One night in March 1931 a fight broke out between groups of young black and white "hobos" on a Southern Railroad freight train as it passed through Alabama. The black youths won the fight and tossed the whites off the train. Not long afterwards a posse stopped the train, arrested the black youths, and threw them in the Scottsboro, Alabama, jail. The posse also discovered two white women "riding the rails"; they claimed these young men had raped them. Word spread, and the youths were barely saved from a lynch mob. Medical evidence later showed that the women were lying. But within two weeks, eight of the so-called Scottsboro Boys were convicted of rape by all-white juries and sentenced to death. The ninth, a boy of thirteen, was saved from the death penalty by one vote. The case—so clearly a product of southern racism—became a cause

célèbre, both in the nation and, through the efforts of the Communist Party, around the world.

The Supreme Court intervened, ruling that Alabama deprived black defendants of equal protection under the law by systematically excluding African Americans from juries and that the defendants had been denied counsel. Alabama, however, staged new trials. Five of the young men were convicted and spent almost two decades in prison. Despite federal action through the Supreme Court, Alabama prevailed. Southern resistance to federal intervention, centered around issues of race, would not yield easily to federal power.

The political realities of southern resistance would limit the gains made by all people of color under the New Deal. Roosevelt could not secure passage of his legislative program without the support of southern Democrats, and they were willing to hold him hostage over race. For example, in 1938, southern Democrats blocked an antilynching bill with a six-week-long filibuster in the Senate—thus paralyzing the government. Roosevelt refused to use his political capital to break the filibuster and pass the bill. Politically, he had much to lose and little to gain. He knew that blacks would not desert the Democratic Party, but without southern senators, his legislative agenda was dead. Roosevelt wanted all Americans to enjoy the benefits of democracy, but he had no strong commitment to the cause of civil rights. As the NAACP's Roy Wilkins put it, "Mr. Roosevelt was no friend of the Negro. He wasn't an enemy, but he wasn't a friend."

Why, then, did African Americans support Roosevelt and the New Deal? Because, despite discriminatory policies, the New Deal helped African Americans. By the end of the 1930s, almost one-third of African American households survived on income from a WPA job. African Americans held some significant positions in the Roosevelt administration. Finally, there was the First Lady. When the acclaimed black contralto Marian Anderson was barred from performing in Washington's Constitution Hall by its owners, the Daughters of the American Revolution, Eleanor Roosevelt arranged for Anderson to sing at the Lincoln Memorial on Easter Sunday, 1939. Such public commitment to racial equality was enormously important to African American citizens.

Despite widespread support for Roosevelt and the New Deal, many African Americans were well aware of the limits of New Deal reform. Some concluded that they could depend only on themselves and organized self-help and direct-action movements. In 1934 black tenant farmers and sharecroppers joined with poor whites to form

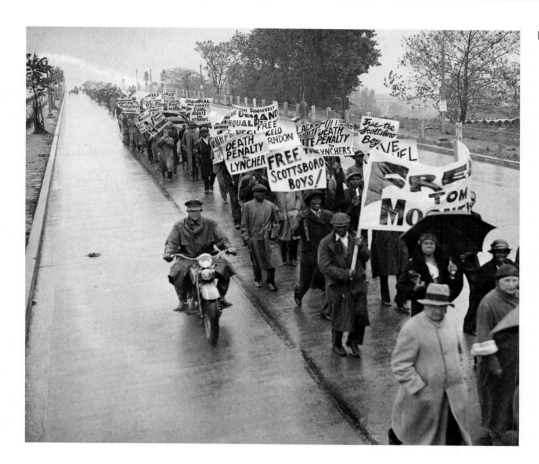

■ Marchers in Washington (January 1, 1934) demand freedom for the "Scottsboro boys," who were falsely accused and convicted of raping two white women in Alabama, and call upon President Roosevelt for "Equal Rights for Negroes." The case of the Scottsboro boys came to symbolize not only the racism and violence of the Jim Crow South, but also the discriminatory policies and practices that harmed African Americans throughout the nation. (© Corbis/Bettmann)

the Southern Tenant Farmers' Union. In the North, the militant Harlem Tenants League fought rent increases and evictions, and African American consumers began to boycott white merchants who refused to hire blacks as clerks. Their slogan was "Don't Buy Where You Can't Work." And the Brotherhood of Sleeping Car Porters, under the astute leadership of A. Philip Randolph, fought for the rights of black workers. Such actions, along with the limited benefits of New Deal programs, helped to improve the lives of black Americans during the 1930s.

Any analysis of the New Deal must begin with Franklin Delano Roosevelt himself. Assessments of Roosevelt varied widely during his presidency: he was passionately hated, and just as passionately loved. Roosevelt personified the presidency for the American people. When he spoke directly to Americans in his Fireside Chats, hundreds of thousands wrote to him, sharing their problems, asking for his help, offering their advice.

AN ASSESSMENT OF THE NEW DEAL

Eleanor Roosevelt, the nation's First Lady, played a crucial and unprecedented role in the Roosevelt administration. As First Lady, she worked tirelessly for social justice and human rights, bringing reformers, trade unionists, and advocates for the rights of women and African Americans to the White House. Described by some as the conscience of the New Deal, she took public positions—especially on African American civil rights— far more progressive than those of her husband's administration. In some ways she served as a lightning rod, deflecting conservative criticism from her husband to herself. But her public stances also cemented the allegiance of other groups, African Americans in particular, to the New Deal.

Most historians and political scientists consider Franklin Roosevelt a truly great president, citing his courage and buoyant self-confidence, his willingness to experiment, and his capacity to inspire the nation during the most somber days of the depression. Some, who see the New Deal as a squandered opportunity for true political and economic change, charge that Roosevelt lacked vision and courage. They judge Roosevelt by goals that were not his own: Roosevelt was a pragmatist whose goal was to preserve the system. But even scholars who criticize Roosevelt's performance agree that he transformed the presidency. "Only Washington, who made the office, and Jackson, who remade it, did more than Roosevelt to raise it to its present condition of strength, dignity, and independence," claims political scientist Clinton Rossiter. Some find this transformation troubling, tracing the roots of "the imperial presidency" to the Roosevelt administration.

During his more than twelve years in office, Roosevelt strengthened not only the presidency but the federal government. In the past, the federal government had exercised little control over the economy. Through New Deal programs, the government greatly added to its regulatory responsibilities, including overseeing the nation's financial systems. For the first time the federal government assumed a responsibility to offer relief to the jobless and the needy, and for the first time it used deficit spending to stimulate the economy. Millions of Americans benefited from government programs that are still operating today. The New Deal laid the foundation of the Social Security system on which subsequent presidential administrations would build.

New Deal programs pumped money into the economy and saved millions of Americans from hunger and misery. However, as late as 1939, more than 10 million men and women were still jobless, and the nation's unemployment rate stood at 19 percent. In the end it was not the New Deal but massive government spending during the Second World War that brought full economic recovery. In 1941, as a result of mobilization for war, unemployment declined to 10 percent, and in 1944, at the height of the war, only 1 percent of the labor force was jobless. World War II, not the New Deal, would reinvigorate the American economy.

Summary

In the 1930s, a major economic crisis threatened the future of the nation. By 1933, almost a quarter of America's workers were unemployed. Millions of people did not have enough to eat or adequate places to live. Herbert Hoover, elected president in 1928, believed that government should play only a limited role in managing and regulating the nation's economy. He tried to solve the nation's economic problems through a voluntary partnership of businesses and the federal government known as associationalism. In the 1932 presidential election, voters turned to the candidate who promised them a "New Deal." President Franklin Delano Roosevelt acted decisively to stabilize America's capitalist system, and then worked to ameliorate its harshest impacts on the nation's people.

The New Deal was a liberal reform program that developed within the parameters of America's capitalist and democratic system. Most fundamentally, it expanded the role and power of the federal government. Because of New Deal reforms, banks, utilities, stock markets, farms, and most businesses operated in accord with rules set by the federal government. The federal government guaranteed workers' right to join unions without fear of employer reprisals, and federal law required employers to negotiate with workers' unions to set wages, hours, and working conditions. Many unemployed workers, elderly and disabled Americans, and dependent children were protected by a national welfare system, administered through the federal government. And the president, through the power of the mass media and his own charisma, became an important presence in the lives of ordinary Americans.

The New Deal faced challenges from many directions. As the depression wore on, populist demagogues blamed scapegoats or offered overly simple explanations for the plight of the American people. Business leaders attacked the New Deal for its new regulation of business and support of organized labor. As the federal government expanded its role throughout the nation, tensions between national and local authority sometimes flared up, and differences in regional ways of life and social and economic structures presented challenges to national policymakers. Both the West and the South were transformed by federal government action, but citizens of both regions were suspicious of federal intervention, and white southerners strongly resisted any attempt to challenge the racial system of Jim Crow. The political realities of a fragile New Deal coalition and strong opposition shaped—and limited—New Deal programs of the 1930s and the social welfare systems Americans still live with today.

It was the economic boom created by America's entry into World War II that ended the Great Depression, not the New Deal. However, New Deal programs helped many of America's people live better, more secure lives. And the New Deal fundamentally changed the way that the U.S. government would deal with future economic downturns and with the needs of its citizens in good times and in bad.

LEGACY FOR A PEOPLE AND A NATION
Social Security

The New Deal's Social Security system has created a more secure and enjoyable old age for millions of Americans who might otherwise have lived in poverty. Although Social Security initially excluded some of America's neediest citizens, such as farm and domestic workers, amendments to the law have expanded eligibility. Today, almost 99 percent of American workers are covered by Social Security.

Despite its successes, today's Social Security system faces an uncertain future. Its troubles are due, in part, to decisions made during the 1930s. President Franklin Roosevelt did not want Social Security to be confused with poor relief. Therefore, he rejected the European model of government-funded pensions and instead created a system financed by payments from workers and their employers. This system, however, presented a short-term problem. If benefits came from their own contributions, workers who began receiving Social Security payments in 1940 would have received less than a dollar a month. Therefore, Social Security payments from current workers paid the benefits of those already retired.

Over the years, this system of financing has become increasingly unstable. In 1935, when the system was created, average life expectancy was lower than sixty-five years, the age one could begin to collect ben-efits. Today, on average, American men live almost sixteen years past the retirement age of sixty-five, while women come close to twenty years past retirement age. In 1935, there were 16 current workers paying into the system for each person receiving retirement benefits. In 2000, there were fewer than 3.5 workers per retiree. Almost 77 million baby boomers born in the 1940s, 1950s, and 1960s will retire in the first decades of the twenty-first century. Unless the system is reformed, many argue, the retirement of the baby-boom cohort could bankrupt the system.

While the stock market was rising rapidly during the 1990s, some proposed that since Social Security paid only a fraction of what individuals might have earned by investing their Social Security tax payments in the stock market, Americans be allowed to do just that. Some opponents declared this proposal too risky; others simply pointed to the structure of Social Security retirement. If current workers kept their money to invest, where would benefits for current retirees come from? The stock market's huge decline beginning in 2001 (and the losses sustained by private pension funds) slowed the push for privatization. But with the oldest baby boomers beginning to retire, questions about the future of the Social Security system will become increasingly important in the years to come.

The **history Companion** powered by Eduspace®
Your primary source for interactive quizzes, exercises, and more to help you learn efficiently.
http://history.college.hmco.com/students

PEACESEEKERS AND WARMAKERS: AMERICANS IN THE WORLD 1920–1941

*I*n 1921 the Rockefeller Foundation declared war on the mosquito in Latin America. As the carrier of yellow fever, the biting insect *Aedes aegypti* transmitted a deadly virus that caused severe headaches, vomiting, jaundice (yellow skin), and, for many, death. With clearance from the U.S. Department of State, the foundation dedicated several million dollars for projects to control yellow fever in Latin America, beginning with Mexico. Learning from the pioneering work of Carlos Juan Finlay of Cuba, Oswaldo Cruz of Brazil, and U.S. Army surgeon Walter Reed, scientists sought to destroy the mosquito in its larval stage, before it became an egg-laying adult.

Nothing less than U.S. dominance in the hemisphere seemed at stake. U.S. diplomats, military officers, and business executives agreed with foundation officials that the disease threatened public health, which in turn disturbed political and economic order. When outbreaks occurred, ports were closed and quarantined, disrupting trade and immigration. The infection struck down American officials, merchants, investors, and soldiers stationed abroad. Workers became incapacitated, reducing productivity. Throughout Latin America, insufficient official attention to yellow-fever epidemics stirred public discontent against regimes the United States supported. When the Panama Canal opened its gates to ships from around the world in 1914, some leaders feared that the death-dealing disease would spread, even reinfecting the United States, which had suffered its last epidemic in 1905.

In Veracruz, a Mexican province of significant U.S. economic activity where American troops had invaded in 1914, a yellow-fever outbreak in 1920 killed 235 people. The next year, gradually overcoming strong local anti-U.S. feelings, Rockefeller personnel painstakingly inspected breeding places in houses and deposited larvae-eating fish in public waterworks. In 1924 La Fundación Rockefeller

◀ Officials of the Brazilian Federal Health Service, in cooperation with the Rockefeller Foundation, spray houses in Bahía to control mosquitoes during a campaign in the 1920s to battle yellow fever. (Courtesy of the Rockefeller Archive Center)

CHRONOLOGY

1921–22 • Washington Conference limits naval arms
• Rockefeller Foundation begins battle against yellow fever in Latin America

1922 • Mussolini comes to power in Italy

1924 • Dawes Plan eases German reparations

1928 • Kellogg-Briand Pact outlaws war

1929 • Great Depression begins
• Young Plan reduces German reparations

1930 • Hawley-Smoot Tariff raises duties

1931 • Japan seizes Manchuria

1933 • Adolf Hitler becomes chancellor of Germany
• United States extends diplomatic recognition to Soviet Union
• U.S. announces Good Neighbor policy for Latin America

1934 • Fulgencio Batista comes to power in Cuba

1935 • Italy invades Ethiopia
• Congress passes first Neutrality Act

1936 • Germany reoccupies the Rhineland
• Spanish Civil War breaks out

1937 • Sino-Japanese War breaks out
• Roosevelt makes "quarantine speech" against aggressors

1938 • Mexico nationalizes American-owned oil companies
• Munich Conference grants part of Czechoslovakia to Germany

1939 • Germany and Soviet Union sign nonaggression pact
• Germany invades Poland, and Second World War begins

1940 • Germany invades Denmark, Norway, Belgium, the Netherlands, and France
• Selective Training and Service Act starts first U.S. peacetime draft

1941 • Lend-Lease Act gives aid to Allies
• Germany attacks Soviet Union
• U.S. freezes Japanese assets
• Roosevelt and Churchill sign Atlantic Charter
• Japanese flotilla attacks Pearl Harbor, Hawai'i, and U.S. enters Second World War

declared yellow fever eradicated in Mexico. Elsewhere in Latin America, the foundation's antimosquito campaign proved successful in maritime and urban areas but less so in rural and jungle regions. Rockefeller Foundation efforts in the 1920s and 1930s also carried political effects: strengthening central governments by providing a national public health infrastructure and helping diminish anti-U.S. sentiment in a region known for virulent anti-Yankeeism.

The Rockefeller Foundation's drive to eradicate the mosquito offers insights into Americans' fervent but futile effort to build a stable international order after the First World War. The United States did not cut itself off from international affairs, despite the tag "isolationist" that is sometimes still applied to U.S. foreign relations during the interwar decades. Americans remained very active in world affairs in the 1920s and 1930s—from gunboats on Chinese rivers, to negotiations in European financial centers, to marine occupations in Haiti and Nicaragua, to oil wells in the Middle East, to campaigns against diseases in Africa and Latin America. President Wilson had it right when he said after the First World War that the United States had "become a determining factor in the history of mankind, and after you have become a determining factor you cannot remain isolated, whether you want to or not."

Even so, a majority of Americans came out of World War I deeply suspicious of foreign entanglements, of using collective action to address the world's ills. The most apt description of interwar U.S. foreign policy is "independent internationalism." That is, the United States was active on a global scale but retained its independence of action, its traditional unilateralism. Notwithstanding the nation's far-flung overseas projects—colonies, spheres of influence, naval bases, investments, trade, missionary activity, humanitarian projects—many Americans did think of themselves as isolationists, by which they meant that they wanted no part of Europe's political squabbles, military alliances and interventions, or the League of Nations, which might drag them unwillingly into war. More internationalist-minded Americans—a group that included most senior officials—were equally desirous of staying out of any future European war but were more willing than isolationists to work to shape the world to their liking.

Such a world would be peaceful and stable, the better to facilitate American prosperity and security. In the interwar years American diplomats increasingly sought to exercise the power of the United States through conferences, humanitarian programs, cultural penetration ("Americanization"), moral lectures and calls for peace, nonrecognition of disapproved regimes, arms control, and economic and financial ties under the Open Door principle. In Latin America, for example, U.S. leaders downgraded military interventions to fashion a Good Neighbor policy.

But a stable world order proved elusive. Some nations schemed to disrupt it, and severe economic problems undercut it. Public health projects saved countless lives but could not address the low living standards and staggering poverty of dependent peoples across the globe. The debts and reparations bills left over from the First World War bedeviled the 1920s, and the Great Depression of the 1930s shattered world trade and finance. The depression threatened America's prominence in international markets; it also spawned totalitarianism and political extremism, militarism, and war in Europe and Asia. As Nazi Germany marched toward world war, the United States tried to protect itself from the conflict by adopting a policy of neutrality. At the same time, the United States sought to defend its interests in Asia against Japanese aggression by invoking the Open Door policy.

In the late 1930s, and especially after the outbreak of European war in September 1939, many Americans came to agree with President Franklin D. Roosevelt that Germany and Japan imperiled the U.S. national interest because they were building exclusive, self-sufficient spheres of influence based on military power and economic domination. Roosevelt first pushed for American military preparedness and then for the abandonment of neutrality in favor of aiding Britain and France. A German victory in Europe, he reasoned, would undermine Western political principles, destroy traditional economic ties, threaten U.S. influence in the Western Hemisphere, and place at the pinnacle of European power a fanatical man—Adolf Hitler—whose ambitions and barbarities seemed limitless.

At the same time, Japan seemed determined to dismember America's Asian friend China, to destroy the Open Door principle by creating a closed economic sphere in Asia, and to endanger a U.S. colony—the Philippines. To deter Japanese expansion in the Pacific, the United States ultimately cut off supplies of vital American products such as oil. But economic warfare only intensified antagonisms. Japan's surprise attack on Pearl Harbor, Hawai'i, in December 1941 finally brought the United States into the Second World War. ■

Searching for Peace and Order in the 1920s

The First World War left Europe in shambles. Between 1914 and 1921, Europe suffered tens of millions of casualties from world war, civil wars, massacres, epidemics, and famine. Germany and France both lost 10 percent of their workers. Crops, livestock, factories, trains, forests, bridges—little was spared. The American Relief Administration and private charities delivered food to needy Europeans, including Russians wracked by famine in 1921 and 1922. Americans hoped not only to feed desperate Europeans but also to dampen any appeal political radicalism might have for them. As Secretary of State Charles Evans Hughes put it in the early 1920s, "There will be no permanent peace unless economic satisfactions are enjoyed." Hughes and other leaders expected American economic expansion to promote international stability—that is, out of economic prosperity would spring a world free from ideological extremes, revolution, arms races, aggression, and war.

Collective security, as envisioned by Woodrow Wilson (see page 646), elicited far less enthusiasm among Hughes and other Republican leaders. Senator Henry Cabot Lodge gloated in 1920 that "we have destroyed Mr. Wilson's League of Nations and . . . we have torn up Wilsonism by the roots." Not quite. The Geneva-headquartered League of Nations, envisioned as a peacemaker, did prove feeble, not just because the United States did not join but because members failed to utilize the new organization to settle important disputes. Still, starting in the mid-1920s, American officials participated discreetly in League meetings on public health, prostitution, drug and arms trafficking, counterfeiting of currency, and other questions. American jurists served on the Permanent Court of International Justice (World Court), though the United States also refused to join that League body. The Rockefeller Foundation, meanwhile, donated $100,000 a year to the League to support its work in public health.

Wilson's legacy was felt in other ways as well. In the United States, peace societies worked for international

PEACE GROUPS stability, many of them keeping alive the Wilsonian preference for a world body. During the interwar years, peace groups such as the Fellowship of Reconciliation and the National Council for Prevention of War drew widespread public support. Women peace advocates gravitated to several of their own organizations because they lacked influence in the male-dominated groups and because of the popular assumption that women—as life givers and nurturing

■ The Women's Peace Union (WPU) distributed this flier in the 1920s to remind Americans of the human costs of the First World War. One of many peace societies active in the interwar years, the WPU lobbied for a constitutional amendment requiring a national referendum on a declaration of war. In the 1930s Representative Louis Ludlow (Democrat of Indiana) worked to pass such a measure in Congress, but he failed.   (Schwimmer-Lloyd Collection, Freida Langer Lazarus Papers. The New York Public Library, Astor, Lenox, and Tilden Foundations)

War Is a Crime Against Humanity

Gassed; Near Dun-sur-Meuse, in the Woods, France

To you who are filled with horror at the sufferings of war-ridden mankind;

To you who remember that **ten million men** were slaughtered in the last war;

To you who have the courage to face the reality of **war, stripped of its sentimental "glory"**;

We make this appeal:—

Eight years since the signing of the Armistice! And peace is still hard beset by preparations for war. In another war men, women and children would be more wantonly, more cruelly massacred, by death rays, gas, disease germs, and machines more fiendish than those used in the last war. Those whom you love must share in its universal destruction.

Can You Afford Not To Give Your Utmost To Cleanse The World Of This Black Plague Of Needless Death and Suffering?

Send your contribution to an uncompromising Peace organization

THE WOMEN'S PEACE UNION
39 Pearl Street, New York

mothers—had a unique aversion to violence and war. Carrie Chapman Catt's moderate National Conference on the Cure and Cause of War, formed in 1924, and the more radical U.S. Section of the Women's International League for Peace and Freedom (WILPF), organized in 1915 under the leadership of Jane Addams and Emily Greene Balch, became the largest women's peace groups (see page 627). When Addams won the Nobel Peace Prize in 1931, she transferred her award money to the League of Nations.

Most peace groups pointed to the carnage of the First World War and the futility of war as a solution to international problems, but they differed over strategies to ensure world order. Some urged cooperation with the League of Nations and the World Court. Others championed the arbitration of disputes, disarmament and arms reduction, the outlawing of war, and strict neutrality during wars. The WILPF called for an end to U.S. economic imperialism, which, the organization claimed, compelled the United States to intervene militarily in Latin America to protect U.S. business interests. The Women's Peace Union (organized in 1921) lobbied for a constitutional amendment to require a national referendum on a declaration of war. The Carnegie Endowment for International Peace (founded in 1910) promoted peace education through publications. Quakers, YMCA officials, and Social Gospel clergy in 1917 created the American Friends Service Committee to identify pacifist alternatives to warmaking. All in all, peaceseekers believed that their various reform activities could and must deliver a world without war.

The urgings of these peace advocates influenced the administration of Warren G. Harding to convene the Washington Naval Conference of November 1921–February 1922. Delegates from Britain, Japan, France, Italy, China, Portugal, Belgium, and the Netherlands joined a U.S. team led by Secretary of State Charles Evans Hughes to discuss limits on naval armaments. Britain, the United States, and Japan were facing a naval arms race whose huge military spending endangered economic rehabilitation. American leaders also worried that an expansionist Japan, with the world's third largest navy, would overtake the United States, ranked second behind Britain.

WASHINGTON NAVAL CONFERENCE

Hughes opened the conference by making a stunning announcement: he proposed to achieve real disarmament by offering to scrap thirty major U.S. ships, totaling 846,000 tons. He then turned to the shocked British and Japanese delegations and urged them to do away with somewhat smaller amounts. The final limit, Hughes declared, should be 500,000 tons each for the Americans and the British; 300,000 tons for the Japanese; and 175,000 tons each for the French and the Italians (that is, a ratio of 5:3:1.75). These totals were agreed to in the Five-Power Treaty, which also set a ten-year moratorium on the construction of capital ships (battleships and aircraft carriers). The governments also pledged not to build new fortifications in their Pacific possessions (such as the Philippines).

In a second agreement, the Nine-Power Treaty, the conferees reaffirmed the Open Door in China, recognizing Chinese sovereignty. Finally, in the Four-Power Treaty, the United States, Britain, Japan, and France agreed to re-spect one another's Pacific possessions. The three treaties did not limit submarines, destroyers, or cruisers; nor did they provide enforcement powers for the Open Door declaration. Still, the conference was a major achievement for Hughes. He achieved genuine arms limitation and at the same time improved America's strategic position in the Pacific vis-à-vis Japan.

Peace advocates also welcomed the Locarno Pact of 1925, a set of agreements among European nations that sought to reduce tensions between Germany and France, and the Kellogg-Briand Pact of 1928. In the latter document, named for its chief promoters U.S. secretary of state Frank B. Kellogg and French premier Aristide Briand, sixty-two nations agreed to "condemn recourse to war for the solution of international controversies, and renounce it as an instrument of national policy." The accord passed the Senate 85 to 1, but many lawmakers considered it little more than a statement of moral preference because it lacked enforcement provisions. Although weak—skeptics called it a mere "international kiss"—the Kellogg-Briand Pact reflected popular opinion that war was barbaric and wasteful, and the agreement stimulated serious public discussion of peace and war. But arms limitations, peace pacts, and efforts by peace groups and international institutions all failed to muzzle the dogs of war, which fed on the economic troubles that upended world order.

KELLOGG-BRIAND PACT

■ French foreign minister Aristide Briand (1862–1932) *(left)* and U.S. secretary of state Charles Evans Hughes (1862–1948) join other diplomats at the Washington Conference of 1921–1922, where they negotiated a naval arms control agreement. Years later Briand helped craft the Kellogg-Briand Pact outlawing war. A graduate of Brown University and Columbia Law School, Hughes also served on the Supreme Court at two different times: 1910–1916 (associate justice) and 1930–1941 (chief justice). Conservative and reserved (Theodore Roosevelt called him "the bearded iceberg"), Hughes argued that the United States must be internationalist, leading the world to respect law and order.   (National Archives)

The World Economy, Cultural Expansion, and Great Depression

*W*hile Europe struggled to recover from the ravages of the First World War, the international economy wobbled and then, in the early 1930s, collapsed. The Great Depression set off a political chain reaction that carried the world to war. Cordell Hull, secretary of state under President Franklin D. Roosevelt from 1933 to 1944, often pointed out that political extremism and militarism sprang from maimed economies. "We cannot have a peaceful world," he warned, "until we rebuild the international economic structure." Hull proved right.

For leaders such as Hughes and Hull, who believed that economic expansion by the United States would stabilize world politics, America's prominent position in the international economy seemed opportune. Because of World War I, the United States became a creditor nation and the financial

ECONOMIC AND CULTURAL EXPANSION

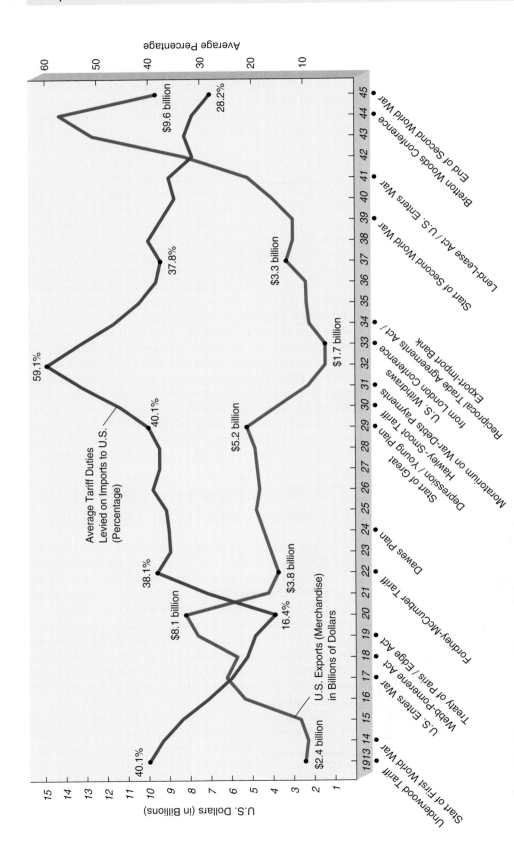

Figure 26.1 **The United States in the World Economy**

In the 1920s and 1930s, global depression and war scuttled the United States's hope for a stable economic order. This graph suggests, moreover, that high American tariffs meant lower exports, further impeding world trade. The Reciprocal Trade Agreements program initiated in the early 1930s was designed to ease tariff wars with other nations. (Source: U.S. Bureau of the Census, *Historical Statistics of the United States, Colonial Times to 1970* [Washington, D.C., 1975].)

capital of the world (see Figure 26.1). From 1914 to 1930, private investments abroad grew fivefold to more than $17 billion. By the late 1920s the United States produced nearly half of the world's industrial goods and ranked first among exporters ($5.2 billion worth of shipments in 1929). For example, General Electric invested heavily in Germany, American companies began to exploit Venezuela's rich petroleum resources, and U.S. firms began to challenge British control of oil resources in the Middle East. Britain and Germany lost ground to American businesses in Latin America, where Standard Oil operated in eight nations and the United Fruit Company became a huge landowner.

America's economic prominence facilitated the export of American culture. Hollywood movies saturated the global market and stimulated interest in American ways and products. In Britain, where American silent and talkie films dominated, one woman from a mining town recalled seeing on the screen "all these marvelous [American] film stars. Everything was bright. I just wanted to go there and be like them." Although some foreigners warned against "Americanization," others aped American mass-production methods and emphasis on efficiency and modernization. Coca-Cola opened a bottling plant in Essen, Germany, and Ford built an automobile assembly plant in Cologne. The German writer

Hans Joachim claimed that this cultural adoption might help deliver a peaceful, democratic world because "our interest in elevators, radio towers, and jazz was . . . an attitude that wanted to convert the flame thrower into a vacuum cleaner."

Germans marveled at Henry Ford's economic success and industrial techniques ("Fordismus"), buying out copies of his translated autobiography, *My Life and Work* (1922). In the 1930s, the Nazi leader Adolf Hitler sent German car designers to Detroit before he launched the Volkswagen. Further advertising the American capitalist model were the Phelps-Stokes Fund, exporting to black Africa Booker T. Washington's Tuskegee philosophy of education, and the Rockefeller Foundation, battling diseases in Latin America and Africa, supporting colleges to train doctors in Lebanon and China, and funding medical research and nurses' training in Europe.

The U.S. government assisted this cultural and economic expansion. The Webb-Pomerene Act (1918) excluded from antitrust prosecution those combinations set up for export trade; the Edge Act (1919) permitted American banks to open foreign-branch banks; and the overseas offices of the Department of Commerce gathered and disseminated valuable market information. The federal government also stimulated foreign loans by American investors, discouraging those that might be

■ John D. Rockefeller Jr. (1874–1960), second from right, traveled to China in 1921 for the dedication of the Peking Union Medical College, a project of the Rockefeller Foundation, the philanthropic organization founded in 1913 by the oil industrialist John D. Rockefeller Sr. At the center of this photograph is Xu Shi Chang (1855–1939), China's president. (Courtesy of the Rockefeller Archive Center)

used for military purposes. "In these days of competition," an American diplomat explained, "capital, trade, agriculture, labor, and statecraft all go hand in hand if a country is to profit." U.S. government support for the expansion of the telecommunications industry helped International Telegraph and Telephone (IT&T), Radio Corporation of America (RCA), and the Associated Press (AP) become international giants by 1930. The

■ In the early 1930s, treatments of the Soviet Union in the American press were generally mild and polite. The March 1932 issue of Henry Luce's *Fortune* magazine, appearing a year before the U.S. government extended recognition to the Soviet Union, featured this cover illustration by Diego Rivera and a special thirty-page section entitled "Russia, Russia, Russia." One appendix explicated the teachings of Karl Marx, while another listed dozens of U.S. businesses that had sold more than a million dollars worth of goods to the Soviet Union in 1930, among them Ford Motor Co., Westinghouse, Caterpillar, John Deere, American Express, and RCA.   (The Michael Barson Collection/Past Perfect)

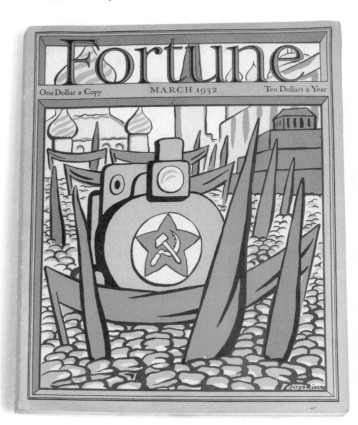

U.S. Navy's cooperation with Juan T. Trippe's Pan American Airline Company helped its "flying boats" reach Asia.

Europeans watched American economic expansion with wariness and branded the United States stingy for

WAR DEBTS AND GERMAN REPARATIONS

its handling of World War I debts and reparations. Twenty-eight nations became entangled in the web of inter-Allied government debts, which totaled $26.5 billion ($9.6 billion of it owed to the U.S. government). Europeans owed private American creditors another $3 billion. Europeans urged Americans to erase the government debts as a magnanimous contribution to the war effort. During the war, they angrily charged, Europe had bled while America profited. "There is only one way we could be worse with the Europeans," remarked the humorist Will Rogers, "and that is to have helped them out in two wars instead of one." American leaders insisted on repayment, some pointing out that the victorious European nations had gained vast territory and resources as war spoils. Senator George Norris of Nebraska, emphasizing domestic priorities, declared that the United States could build highways in "every county seat" if only the Europeans would pay their debts.

The debts question became linked to Germany's $33 billion reparations bill—an amount some believed Germany had the capacity but not the willingness to pay. In any case, hobbled by inflation and economic disorder, Germany began to default on its payments. To keep the nation afloat and to forestall the radicalism that might thrive on economic troubles, American bankers loaned millions of dollars. A triangular relationship developed: American investors' money flowed to Germany, Germany paid reparations to the Allies, and the Allies then paid some of their debts to the United States. The American-crafted Dawes Plan of 1924 greased the financial tracks by reducing Germany's annual payments, extending the repayment period, and providing still more loans. The United States also gradually scaled down Allied obligations, cutting the debt by half during the 1920s.

But the triangular arrangement depended on continued German borrowing in the United States, and in 1928 and 1929 American lending abroad dropped sharply in the face of more lucrative opportunities in the stock market at home (see Chapters 24 and 25). The U.S.-negotiated Young Plan of 1929, which reduced Germany's reparations, salvaged little as the world economy sputtered and collapsed. That year Britain rejected an offer from President Herbert Hoover to trade its total debt for British Honduras (Belize), Bermuda, and Trinidad. By 1931, when Hoover declared a moratorium on payments, the Allies had paid back only $2.6 billion. Staggered by the Great Depression—an international catastrophe—they defaulted on the rest. Annoyed with Europe, Congress in 1934 passed the Johnson Act, which forbade U.S. government loans to foreign governments in default on debts owed to the United States.

As the depression deepened, tariff wars revealed a reinvigorated economic nationalism. By 1932 some

DECLINE IN TRADE

twenty-five nations had retaliated against rising American tariffs (created in the Fordney-McCumber Act of 1922 and the Hawley-Smoot Act of 1930) by imposing higher rates on foreign imports. From 1929 to 1933, world trade declined in value by some 40 percent. Exports of American merchandise slumped from $5.2 billion to $1.7 billion.

Who was responsible for the worldwide economic cataclysm? There was blame to go around. The United States might have lowered its tariffs so that Europeans could sell their goods in the American market and thus earn dollars to pay off their debts. Americans also might have worked for a comprehensive, multinational settlement of the war debts issue. Instead, at the London Conference in 1933, President Roosevelt barred U.S. cooperation in international currency stabilization. Vengeful Europeans might have trimmed Germany's huge indemnity. The Germans might have borrowed less from abroad and taxed themselves more. The Soviets might have agreed to pay rather than repudiate Russia's $4 billion debt.

For Secretary of State Hull, finding a way out of the crisis depended on reviving world trade. Increased trade, he insisted, not only would help the United States pull itself out of the economic doldrums but also would boost the chances for global peace. Calling the protective tariff the "king of evils," he successfully pressed Congress to pass the Reciprocal Trade Agreements Act in 1934. This important legislation empowered the president to reduce U.S. tariffs by as much as 50 percent through special agreements with foreign countries. The central feature of the act was the most-favored-nation principle, whereby the United States was entitled to the lowest tariff rate set by any nation with which it had an agreement. If, for example, Belgium and the United States granted each other most-favored-nation status, and Belgium then negotiated an agreement with Germany that reduced the Belgian tariff on German typewriters, American typewriters would receive the same low rate.

In 1934 Hull also helped create the Export-Import Bank, a government agency that provided loans to foreigners for the purchase of American goods. The bank stimulated trade and became a diplomatic weapon, allowing the United States to exact concessions through the approval or denial of loans. But in the short term, Hull's ambitious programs—examples of America's independent internationalism—brought only mixed results.

Economic imperatives also lay behind another major policy decision in these years: the move by the Roosevelt

U.S. RECOGNITION OF THE SOVIET UNION

administration to extend diplomatic recognition to the Soviet Union. Throughout the 1920s the Republicans had refused to open diplomatic relations with the Soviet government, which had failed to pay $600 million for confiscated American-owned property and had repudiated preexisting Russian debts. To many Americans, the communists ranked as godless, radical malcontents bent on destroying the American way of life through world revolution. Nonetheless, in the late 1920s American businesses such as General Electric and International Harvester entered the Soviet marketplace, and Henry Ford signed a contract to build an automobile plant there. By 1930 the Soviet Union had become the largest buyer of American farm and industrial equipment.

Upon entering the White House Roosevelt concluded that nonrecognition had failed to alter the Soviet system, and he speculated that closer Soviet-American relations might help the economy and also deter Japanese expansion. In 1933 Roosevelt granted U.S. diplomatic recognition to the Soviet Union in return for Soviet agreement to discuss the debts question, to forgo subversive activities in the United States, and to grant Americans in the Soviet Union religious freedom and legal rights.

U.S. Dominance in Latin America

ne of the assumptions behind Hughes's Washington Treaty system of 1921–1922 was that certain powers would be responsible for maintaining order in their regions—Japan in East Asia, for example, and the United States in Latin America. Through the Platt Amendment, the Roosevelt Corollary, the Panama Canal, military intervention, and economic preeminence the United States had thrown an imperial net over Latin America in the early twentieth century (see Chapter 22). U.S. dominance in the hemisphere grew apace after the First World War. A prominent State Department officer patronizingly remarked that Latin Americans were incapable of political progress because of their "low racial quality." They were, however, "very easy people to deal with if properly managed."

And managed they were. American-made schools, roads, telephones, and irrigation systems dotted Caribbean and Central American nations. American "money doctors" in Colombia and Peru helped reform tariff and tax laws and invited U.S. companies to build public works. Washington forced private high-interest loans on the Dominican Republic and Haiti as ways to wield influence there. In El Salvador, Honduras, and Costa Rica, the State Department pressed governments to silence anti-imperialist intellectuals. For a time, Republican administrations curtailed U.S. military intervention in the hemisphere, withdrawing troops from the Dominican Republic (1924) and Nicaragua (1925) that had been committed in the previous decade (see page 616). But the marines returned to Nicaragua in 1926 to end fighting between conservative and liberal Nicaraguans and to protect American property. In Haiti, the U.S. troop commitment made under Woodrow Wilson in 1915 lasted until 1934, the soldiers there to keep pro-Washington governments in power. All the while, U.S. authorities maintained Puerto Rico as a colony (see Map 26.1).

By 1929 direct American investments in Latin America (excluding bonds and securities) totaled $3.5 billion, while U.S. exports dominated the trade of the area. Country after country experienced the repercussions of U.S. economic and political decisions. For example, the price that Americans set for Chilean copper determined the health of Chile's economy. North American oil executives bribed Venezuelan politicians for tax breaks.

Latin American nationalists protested that their resources were being drained away as profits for U.S. companies, leaving too many nations in a status of dependency. A distinguished Argentine writer, Manuel Ugarte, asserted that the United States had become a new Rome that annexed wealth rather than territory, but unapologetic Americans believed that they were bringing not only material improvements to Latin American neighbors but also the blessings of liberty.

DEPENDENCY STATUS

Criticism of U.S. imperialism in the region mounted in the interwar years. In 1928, at the Havana Inter-American conference, U.S. officials unsuccessfully tried to kill a resolution stating that "no state has a right to intervene in the internal affairs of another." Two years later, a prominent Chilean newspaper warned that the American "Colossus" had "financial might" without "equal in history," and that its aim was "Americas for the Americans—of the North." In the United States, Senator William Borah of Idaho urged that Latin Americans be granted the right of self-determination, letting them decide their own futures. Business leaders feared that Latin American nationalists would direct their anti-Yankee feelings against American-owned property. Some Americans also became troubled by the double standard that prevailed. Hoover's secretary of state, Henry L. Stimson,

PRIVATE WHARF, W. F. McLAUGHLIN & CO., SANTOS, BRAZIL.

■ Among the U.S. companies with large holdings in Latin America in the interwar period was F. W. McLaughlin & Co. of Chicago. Here, workers on a private company wharf in Santos, Brazil, prepare to load coffee for shipment to the United States. (© Curt Teich Postcard Archives, Lake County Museum)

Map 26.1   The United States and Latin America Between the Wars

The United States often intervened in other nations to maintain its hegemonic power in Latin America, where nationalists resented outside meddling in their sovereign affairs. The Good Neighbor policy decreased U.S. military interventions, but U.S. economic interests remained strong in the hemisphere.

acknowledged the problem in 1932 when he was protesting Japanese incursions in China: "If we landed a single soldier among those South Americans now . . . it would put me absolutely in the wrong in China, where Japan has done all this monstrous work under the guise of protecting her nationals with a landing force."

Renouncing unpopular military intervention, the United States shifted to other methods to maintain its influence in Latin America: Pan-Americanism (a concept dating back some fifty years that aimed to bring about closer ties between North and South America), support for strong local leaders, the training of national guards, economic and cultural penetration, Export-Import Bank loans, financial supervision, and political subversion. Although this general approach predated his presidency, Franklin Roosevelt gave it a name in 1933: the Good Neighbor policy. It meant that the United States would be less blatant in its domination—less willing to defend exploitative business practices, less eager to launch military expeditions, and less reluctant to consult with Latin Americans.

GOOD NEIGHBOR POLICY

"Give them a share," Roosevelt said, as he took several measures to show he meant business. Most notably, he ordered home the U.S. military forces that had been stationed in Haiti (since 1915) and Nicaragua (since 1912, with a hiatus in 1925–1926), and he restored some sovereignty to Panama and increased that nation's income from the canal. Such acts greatly enhanced Roosevelt's popularity in Latin America, and his image was further boosted when, in a series of pan-American conferences, he joined in pledging that no nation in the hemisphere would intervene in the "internal or external affairs" of any other.

Here Roosevelt promised more than he was prepared to deliver. His administration continued to support and to bolster dictators in the region, believing that they would promote stability and preserve U.S. economic interests. ("He may be an S.O.B.," Roosevelt supposedly remarked of the Dominican Republic's ruthless leader Rafael Leonidas Trujillo, "but he is our S.O.B.") And when a revolution brought a radical government to power in Cuba in 1933, FDR proved unwilling to let the matter be. Though he refrained from sending U.S. ground troops to Cuba, he instructed the American ambassador in Havana to work with conservative Cubans to replace the new government with a regime more friendly to U.S. interests. With Washington's support, army sergeant Fulgencio Batista took power in 1934.

During the Batista era, which lasted until Fidel Castro dethroned Batista in 1959, Cuba attracted and protected U.S. investments while it aligned itself with U.S. foreign policy goals. In return, the United States provided military aid and Export-Import Bank loans, abrogated the unpopular Platt Amendment, and gave Cuban sugar a favored position in the U.S. market. Cuba became further incorporated into the North American consumer culture, and American tourists flocked to Havana's night life of rum, rhumba, prostitution, and gambling. Nationalistic Cubans protested that their nation had become a mere extension—a dependency—of the United States.

Another test for the Good Neighbor policy came in Mexico later in the decade; once again, Roosevelt showed a level of restraint that his predecessors had lacked. Since Woodrow Wilson sent troops to Mexico in 1914 and again in 1916, U.S.-Mexican relations had endured several difficult periods as the two governments wrangled over the rights of U.S. economic interests. Still, throughout the post–World War I period the United States stood as Mexico's chief trading partner, accounting for 61 percent of Mexico's imports and taking 52 percent of its exports in 1934. That year, however, a new government under Lázaro Cárdenas pledged "Mexico for the Mexicans" and promptly strengthened trade unions so they could strike against foreign corporations.

CLASH WITH MEXICAN NATIONALISM

In 1937, workers struck foreign oil companies for higher wages and recognition, but the companies, including Standard Oil, rejected union appeals, hoping to send a message across the hemisphere that economic nationalism could never succeed. In a statement of economic independence the following year, the Cárdenas government boldly expropriated the property of all foreign-owned petroleum companies, calculating that the approaching war in Europe would restrain the United States from attacking Mexico. The United States countered by reducing purchases of Mexican silver and promoting a multinational business boycott against the nation. But Roosevelt rejected appeals from some business leaders that he intervene militarily and instead decided to compromise, in part because he feared that the Mexicans would increase oil sales to Germany and Japan. Negotiations were long and difficult, but in 1942 an agreement was reached whereby the United States conceded that Mexico owned its raw materials and could treat them as it saw fit, and Mexico compensated the companies for their lost property.

All in all, then, under Roosevelt the Good Neighbor policy can be said to have gone a considerable distance toward living up to its name—or at least the United

■ Ambassador Josephus Daniels (1862–1948) *(second from left)* and Mexican president Lázaro Cárdenas (1895–1970) *(second from right)* enjoy a cordial moment during the often stormy relations between the United States and Mexico in the 1930s. When Cárdenas attempted to regain control of his nation's oil resources from multinational corporations through expropriation, Daniels defended him as a "New Dealer" seeking to improve his country's living standards. Accepting Daniels's description and calling Cárdenas "one of the few Latin leaders who was actually preaching and trying to practice democracy," President Roosevelt compromised with Mexico in 1941.   (Library of Congress)

States was now a Markedly Better Neighbor. Even as it remained the dominant power in the hemisphere, its newfound restraint created hopes among Latin Americans that a new era had dawned. Yet the more sober-minded nationalists in the region knew that Washington might be acting differently were it not for the deepening tensions in Europe and Asia. These threats created a sense that all the nations in the Western Hemisphere should stand together.

The Course to War in Europe

The main threat came from a revitalized Germany. On March 5, 1933, one day after the inauguration of Franklin Roosevelt, Germany's parliament granted dictatorial powers to the new chancellor Adolf Hitler, leader of the Nazi Party. The act marked the culmination of a stunning rise to power for Hitler, whose Nazis very likely would have remained a fringe party had the Great Depression not hit Germany with such force. Production plummeted 40 percent, and unemployment ballooned to 6 million, meaning two workers out of five

did not have jobs. Together with a disintegrating banking system, which robbed millions of their savings, as well as widespread resentment among Germans over the post–World War I Versailles peace settlement, the plummeting employment figures brought mass discontentment to the country. While the communists preached a workers' revolution, German business executives and property owners threw their support to Hitler and the Nazis, many of them believing they could manipulate him once he had thwarted the communists. They were wrong.

Like Benito Mussolini, who had gained control of Italy in 1922, Hitler was a fascist. Fascism (called Nazism, or National Socialism, in Germany) was a collection of ideas and prejudices that celebrated supremacy of the state over the individual; of dictatorship over democracy; of authoritarianism over freedom of speech; of a regulated, state-oriented economy over a free-market economy; and of militarism and war over peace. The Nazis vowed not only to revive German economic and military strength but also to cripple communism and "purify" the German "race" by destroying Jews and other people, such as homosexuals and Gypsies, whom Hitler disparaged as inferiors. The Nuremberg Laws of

1935 stripped Jews of citizenship and outlawed intermarriage with Germans. Teachers, doctors, and other professionals could not practice their craft, and half of all German Jews were without work.

Determined to get Germany out from under the Versailles treaty system, Hitler withdrew Germany from the League of Nations, ended reparations payments, and began to rearm. While secretly laying plans for the conquest of neighboring states, he watched admiringly as Mussolini's troops invaded the African nation of Ethiopia in 1935. The next year Hitler ordered his own goose-stepping troopers into the Rhineland, an area that the Versailles treaty had demilitarized. When Germany's timid neighbor France did not resist this act, Hitler crowed: "The world belongs to the man with guts!"

GERMAN AGGRESSION UNDER HITLER

■ The German leader Adolf Hitler (1889–1945) is surrounded in this propagandistic painting by images that came to symbolize hate, genocide, and war: Nazi flags with emblems of the swastika, the iron cross on the dictator's pocket, Nazi troops in loyal salute. The anti-Semitic Hitler denounced the United States as a "Jewish rubbish heap" of "inferiority and decadence" that was "incapable of conducting war." (U.S. Army Center of Military History)

Soon the aggressors joined hands. In 1936 Italy and Germany formed an alliance called the Rome-Berlin Axis. Shortly thereafter Germany and Japan united against the Soviet Union in the Anti-Comintern Pact. To these events Britain and France responded with a policy of appeasement, hoping to curb Hitler's expansionist appetite by permitting him a few territorial nibbles. The policy of appeasing Hitler, though not altogether unreasonable in terms of what could be known at the time, proved disastrous, for the hate-filled German leader continually raised his demands.

Hitler also made his presence felt in Spain, where a civil war broke out in 1936. Beginning in July, the Loyalists defended Spain's elected republican government against Francisco Franco's fascist movement. About three thousand American volunteers, known as the Abraham Lincoln Battalion of the "International Brigades," joined the fight on the side of the Loyalist republicans, which also had the backing of the Soviet Union. Hitler and Mussolini sent military aid to Franco, who won in 1939, tightening the grip of fascism on the European continent.

Early in 1938 Hitler once again tested the limits of European tolerance when he sent soldiers into Austria to annex the nation of his birth. Then in September he seized the largely German-speaking Sudeten region of Czechoslovakia. Appeasement reached its apex that month when France and Britain, without consulting the Czechs, agreed at Munich to allow Hitler this territorial bite, in exchange for a pledge that he would not take more. British prime minister Neville Chamberlain returned home to proclaim "peace in our time," confident that Hitler was satiated. In March 1939 Hitler swallowed the rest of Czechoslovakia (see Map 26.3).

THE MUNICH CONFERENCE

Americans had watched this buildup of tension in Europe with apprehension. Many sought to distance themselves from the tumult by embracing isolationism, whose key elements were abhorrence of war and fervent opposition to U.S. alliances with other nations. Americans had learned powerful negative lessons from the First World War: that war damages reform movements, undermines civil liberties, dangerously expands federal and presidential power, disrupts the economy, and accentuates racial and class tensions (see Chapter 23). A 1937 Gallup poll found that nearly two-thirds of the respondents thought U.S. participation in World War I had been a mistake.

ISOLATIONIST VIEWS IN THE UNITED STATES

Conservative isolationists feared higher taxes and increased executive power if the nation went to war again. Liberal isolationists worried that domestic problems might go unresolved as the nation spent more on the military. Many isolationists predicted that in attempting to spread democracy abroad or to police the world, Americans would lose their freedoms at home. The vast majority of isolationists opposed fascism and condemned aggression, but they did not think the United States should have to do what Europeans themselves refused to do: block Hitler. Isolationist sentiment was strongest in the Midwest and among anti-British ethnic groups, especially Americans of German or Irish descent, but it was a nationwide phenomenon that cut across socioeconomic, ethnic, party, and sectional lines and attracted a majority of the American people.

Some isolationists charged that corporate "merchants of death" had promoted war and were assisting the

NYE COMMITTEE HEARINGS

aggressors. A congressional committee headed by Senator Gerald P. Nye held hearings from 1934 to 1936 on the role of business and financiers in the U.S. decision to enter the First World War. The Nye committee did not prove that American munitions makers had dragged the nation into that war, but it did uncover evidence that corporations practicing "rotten commercialism" had bribed foreign politicians to bolster arms sales in the 1920s and 1930s and had lobbied against arms control.

Isolationists grew suspicious of American business ties with Nazi Germany and fascist Italy that might endanger U.S. neutrality. Twenty-six of the top one hundred American corporations, including DuPont, Standard Oil, and General Motors, had contractual agreements in 1937 with German firms. And after Italy attacked Ethiopia in 1935, American petroleum, copper, scrap iron, and steel exports to Italy increased substantially, despite Roosevelt's call for a moral embargo on such commerce. A Dow Chemical official stated: "We do not inquire into the uses of the products. We are interested in selling them." Not all American executives thought this way. The Wall Street law firm of Sullivan and Cromwell, for example, severed lucrative ties with Germany to protest the Nazi persecution of Jews.

Reflecting the popular desire for distance from Europe's disputes, Roosevelt signed a series of neutrality

NEUTRALITY ACTS

acts. Congress sought to protect the nation by outlawing the kinds of contacts that had compromised U.S. neutrality during World War I. The Neutrality Act of 1935 prohibited arms shipments to either side in a war once the president had declared the existence of belligerency. Roosevelt had wanted the authority to name the aggressor and apply an arms embargo against it alone, but Congress would not grant the president such discretionary power. The Neutrality Act of 1936 forbade loans to belligerents. After a joint resolution in 1937 declared the United States neutral in the Spanish Civil War, Roosevelt embargoed arms shipments to both sides. The Neutrality Act of 1937 introduced the cash-and-carry principle: warring nations wishing to trade with the United States would have to pay cash for their nonmilitary purchases and carry the goods from U.S. ports in their own ships. The act also forbade Americans from traveling on the ships of belligerent nations.

President Roosevelt shared isolationist views in the early 1930s. Although prior to World War I he was an

ROOSEVELT'S EVOLVING VIEWS

expansionist and interventionist like his older cousin Theodore, during the interwar period FDR talked less about preparedness and more about disarmament and the horrors of war, less about policing the world and more about handling problems at home. In a passionate speech delivered in August 1936 at Chautauqua, New York, Roosevelt expressed prevailing isolationist opinion and made a pitch for the pacifist vote in the upcoming election: "I have seen war. . . . I have seen blood running from the wounded. I have seen men coughing out their gassed lungs. . . . I have seen the agony of mothers and wives. I hate war." The United States, he promised, would remain unentangled in the European conflict. During the crisis over Czechoslovakia in 1938, Roosevelt endorsed appeasement and greeted the Munich accord with a "universal sense of relief."

All the while, Roosevelt grew troubled by the arrogant behavior of Germany, Italy, and Japan—aggressors he tagged the "three bandit nations." He condemned the Nazi persecution of the Jews and the Japanese slaughter of Chinese civilians. Privately he chastised the British and French for failing to collar Hitler. Yet he himself also moved cautiously in confronting the German leader. In November 1938, Hitler launched *Kristallnacht* (or "Crystal Night," so named for the shattered glass that littered the streets after the attack on Jewish synagogues, businesses, and homes) and sent tens of thousands of Jews to concentration camps. Roosevelt expressed his shock, recalled the U.S. ambassador to Germany, and allowed fifteen thousand refugees on visitor permits to remain longer in the United States. But he would not do more, such as break trade relations with Hitler or push Congress to loosen tough immigration laws enacted in the 1920s. Congress, for its part, rejected all measures, including a bill to admit twenty thousand children under the age of fourteen. Motivated by economic concerns and widespread anti-Semitism, more than 80 percent of

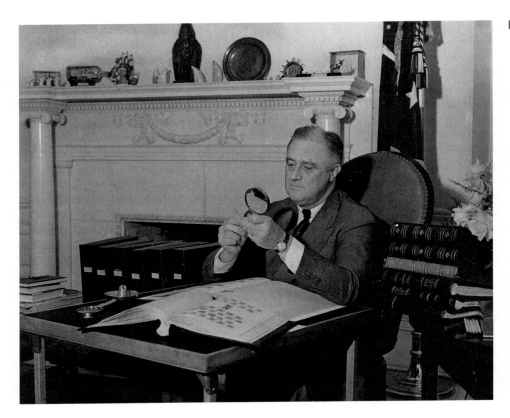

⬛ President Franklin D. Roosevelt relaxes with his favorite hobby, stamp collecting, from which he said he learned history and geography. During World War II he once showed British prime minister Winston Churchill a stamp from "one of your colonies." Churchill asked: "Which one?" Roosevelt replied: "One of your last. . . . You won't have them much longer, you know."
(Franklin D. Roosevelt Library)

Americans supported Congress's decision to uphold immigration restrictions.

Even the tragic voyage of the *St. Louis* did not change government policy. The vessel left Hamburg in mid-1939 carrying 930 desperate Jewish refugees who lacked proper immigration documents. Denied entry to Havana, the *St. Louis* headed for Miami, where Coast Guard cutters prevented it from docking. The ship was forced to return to Europe. Some of those refugees took shelter in countries that later were overrun by Hitler's legions. "The cruise of the *St. Louis*," wrote the *New York Times*, "cries to high heaven of man's inhumanity to man."

Quietly, though, Roosevelt had begun moving to ready the country for war. In early 1938 he successfully pressured the House of Representatives to defeat a constitutional amendment proposed by Indiana Democrat Louis Ludlow to require a majority vote in a national referendum before a congressional declaration of war could go into effect (unless the United States were attacked). Later that year, in the wake of the Munich crisis, Roosevelt asked Congress for funds to build up the air force, which he believed essential to deter aggression. In Janu-

ary 1939 the president secretly decided to sell bombers to France, saying privately that "our frontier is on the Rhine." Although the more than five hundred combat planes delivered to France did not deter war, French orders spurred growth of the U.S. aircraft industry.

For Roosevelt as for other Western leaders, Hitler's swallowing of the whole of Czechoslovakia in March 1939 proved a turning point, forcing them to face a stark new reality. Until now, they had been able to explain away Hitler's actions by saying he was only trying to reunite German-speaking peoples. That argument no longer worked. Leaders in Paris and London realized that if the German leader was to be stopped, it would have to be by force. When Hitler began eyeing his neighbor Poland, London and Paris announced they would stand by the Poles. Undaunted, Berlin signed a nonaggression pact with Moscow in August 1939. Soviet leader Joseph Stalin believed that the West's appeasement of Hitler had left him no choice but to cut a deal with Berlin. But Stalin also coveted territory: a top-secret protocol attached to the pact carved eastern Europe into German and Soviet zones and permitted the Soviets to grab the eastern half of Poland and the three Baltic states of Lithuania, Estonia, and Latvia, formerly part of the Russian Empire.

In the early morning hours of September 1 German tank columns rolled into Poland. German fighting planes

POLAND AND THE OUTBREAK OF WORLD WAR II

covered the advance, thereby launching a new type of warfare, the *blitzkrieg* (lightning war)—highly mobile land forces and armor combined with tactical aircraft. Within forty-eight hours Britain and France responded by declaring war on Germany. "It's come at last," Franklin Roosevelt murmured. "God help us all."

When Europe descended into the abyss of war in September 1939, Roosevelt declared neutrality and pressed

REPEAL OF THE ARMS EMBARGO

for repeal of the arms embargo. Isolationist senator Arthur Vandenberg of Michigan roared back that the United States could not be "an arsenal for one belligerent without becoming a target for the other." After much debate, however, Congress in November lifted the embargo on contraband and approved cash-and-carry exports of arms. Using "methods short of war," Roosevelt thus began to aid the Allies. Hitler sneered that a "half Judaized, half negrified" United States was "incapable of conducting war."

Japan, China, and a New Order in Asia

hile Europe succumbed to political turmoil and war, Asia suffered the aggressive march of Japan. The United States had interests at stake in Asia: the Philippines and Pacific islands, religious missions, trade and investments, and the Open Door in China. In traditional missionary fashion, Americans also believed that they were China's special friend and protector. "With God's help," Senator Kenneth Wherry of Nebraska once proclaimed, "we will lift Shanghai up and up, ever up, until it is just like Kansas City." Pearl Buck's best-selling novel *The Good Earth* (1931), made into a widely distributed film six years later, countered prevailing images of the very different—and thus deviant—"heathen Chinee" by representing the Chinese as noble, persevering peasants. The daughter of Presbyterian missionaries, Buck helped shift negative American images of China to positive ones. By contrast, the aggressive Japan loomed as a threat to American attitudes and interests. The Tokyo government seemed bent on subjugating China and unhinging the Open Door doctrine of equal trade and investment opportunity.

The Chinese themselves were uneasy about the U.S. presence in Asia. Like the Japanese, they wished to reduce the influence of westerners. The Chinese Revolution of 1911 still rumbled in the 1920s as antiforeign riots damaged American property and imperiled American missionaries. Chinese nationalists criticized Americans for the imperialist practice of extraterritoriality (the exemption of foreigners accused of crimes from Chinese legal jurisdiction), and they demanded an end to this affront to Chinese sovereignty.

In the late 1920s, civil war broke out in China when Jiang Jieshi (Chiang Kai-shek) ousted Mao Zedong and

JIANG JIESHI

his communist followers from the ruling Guomindang Party. Americans applauded this display of anti-Bolshevism and Jiang's conversion to Christianity in 1930. Jiang's new wife, Soong Meiling, also won their hearts. American-educated, Madame Jiang spoke flawless English, dressed in Western fashion, and cultivated ties with prominent Americans. Warming to Jiang, U.S. officials abandoned one imperial vestige by signing a treaty in 1928 restoring control of tariffs to the Chinese. U.S. gunboats and marines still remained in China to protect American citizens and property.

The Japanese grew increasingly suspicious of U.S. ties with China. In the early twentieth century, Japanese-American relations steadily deteriorated as Japan gained influence in Manchuria, Shandong, and Korea. The Japanese sought not only to oust Western imperialists from Asia but also to dominate Asian territories that produced the raw materials that their import-dependent island nation required. The Japanese also resented the discriminatory immigration law of 1924, which excluded them from emigrating to the United States and declared they were "aliens ineligible to citizenship." Secretary Hughes urged Congress not to pass the act; when it rejected his counsel, he sadly called the law "a lasting injury" to Japanese-American relations. Despite the Washington Conference treaties, naval competition continued. Also, although the volume of Japanese-American trade was twice that of Chinese-American trade, commercial rivalry strained relations between Japan and the United States. In the United States the importation of inexpensive Japanese goods, especially textiles, spawned "Buy America" campaigns and boycotts.

Relations further soured in 1931 after the Japanese military seized Manchuria from China (see Map 26.2),

MANCHURIAN CRISIS

weakened by civil war and unable to resist. Larger than Texas, Manchuria served Japan both as a buffer against the Soviets and as a vital source of

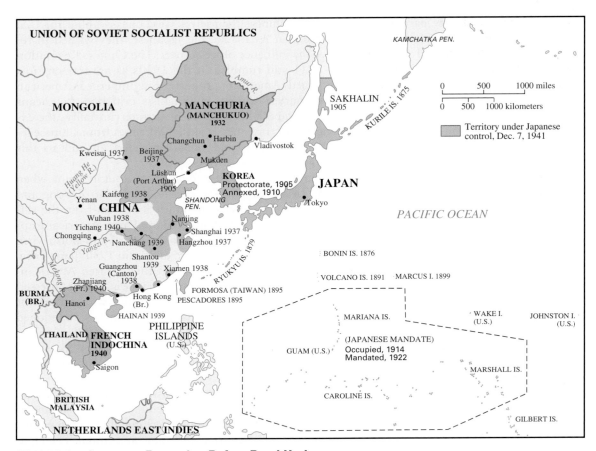

Map 26.2 Japanese Expansion Before Pearl Harbor

The Japanese quest for predominance began at the turn of the century and intensified in the 1930s. China suffered the most at the hands of Tokyo's military. Vulnerable U.S. possessions in Asia and the Pacific proved no obstacle to Japan's ambitions for a Greater East Asia Co-Prosperity Sphere.

coal, iron, timber, and food. More than half of Japan's foreign investments rested in Manchuria. "We are seeking room that will let us breathe," said a Japanese politician, arguing that his heavily populated island nation (65 million people in an area slightly smaller than California) needed to expand in order to survive. Although the seizure of Manchuria violated the Nine-Power Treaty and the Kellogg-Briand Pact, the United States did not have the power to compel Japanese withdrawal, and the League of Nations did little but condemn the Tokyo government. The American response came as a moral lecture known as the Stimson Doctrine: the United States would not recognize any impairment of China's sovereignty or of the Open Door policy, Secretary Stimson declared in 1932. He himself later described his policy as largely "bluff."

Japan continued to pressure China. In mid-1937, owing to Japanese provocation, the Sino-Japanese War erupted. Japanese forces seized Beijing and cities along the coast. The gruesome bombing of Shanghai intensified anti-Japanese sentiment in the United States. Senator Norris, an isolationist who moved further away from isolationism with each Japanese thrust, condemned the Japanese as "disgraceful, ignoble, barbarous, and cruel, even beyond the power of language to describe." In an effort to help China by permitting it to buy American arms, Roosevelt refused to declare the existence of war, thus avoiding activation of the Neutrality Acts.

In a speech denouncing the aggressors on October 5, 1937, the president called for a "quarantine" to curb the "epidemic of world lawlessness." People who thought Washington had been too gentle with Japan cheered.

ROOSEVELT'S QUARANTINE SPEECH   Isolationists warned that the president was edging toward war. On December 12 Japanese aircraft sank the American gunboat *Panay*, an escort for Standard Oil Company tankers on the Yangtze River. Two American sailors died during the attack. Roosevelt was much relieved when Tokyo apologized and offered to pay for damages.

■ After the outbreak of the Sino-Japanese War (termed the "China Incident" by Japan) in 1937, Japanese postcard publishers churned out large numbers of postcards showing the newly conquered territories, or weaponry, or scenes of army life. Soldiers would send the postcards back to family members in Japan. This image appeared on the cover of a packet of eight postcards in the late 1930s. The text reads: "China Incident Postcard—Fourth Set." (Eric Politzer/Curt Teich Postcard Archives, Lake County Museum)

Japan's declaration of a "New Order" in Asia, in the words of one American official, "banged, barred, and bolted" the Open Door. Alarmed, the Roosevelt administration during the late 1930s gave loans and sold military equipment to Jiang's Chinese government. Secretary Hull declared a moral embargo on the shipment of airplanes to Japan. Meanwhile, the U.S. Navy continued to grow, aided by a billion-dollar congressional appropriation in 1938. In mid-1939 the United States abrogated its trade treaty with Tokyo, yet Americans continued to ship oil, cotton, and machinery to Japan. The administration hesitated to initiate economic sanctions because such pressure might spark a Japanese-American war at a time when Germany posed a more serious threat and the United States was unprepared for war. When war broke out in Europe in the late summer of 1939, Japanese-American relations were stalemated.

U.S. Entry into World War II

a stalemate was just fine with many Americans if it served to keep the United States out of war. But how long could the country stay out? Roosevelt remarked in 1939 that the United States could not "draw a line of defense around this country and live completely and solely to ourselves." Thomas Jefferson had tried that with his 1807 embargo—"the damned thing didn't work" and "we got into the War of 1812." America, the president insisted, could not insulate itself from world war. Polls showed that Americans strongly favored the Allies and that most supported aid to Britain and France, but the great majority emphatically wanted the United States to remain at peace. Troubled by this conflicting advice—oppose Hitler, aid the Allies, but stay out of the war—the president gradually moved the nation from neutrality to undeclared war against Germany and then, after the Japanese attack on Pearl Harbor, to full-scale war itself.

Because the stakes were so high, Americans vigorously debated the direction of their foreign policy from 1939 through 1941. Unprecedented numbers of Americans spoke out on foreign affairs and joined organizations that addressed the issues. Spine-chilling events and the widespread use of radio, the nation's chief source of news, helped stimulate this high level of public interest. So did ethnic affiliations with the various belligerents and victims of aggression. The American Legion, the League of Women Voters, labor unions, and local chapters of the Committee to Defend America by Aiding the Allies and the isolationist America First Committee (both

Radio News

In radio's early years, stations broadcast little news. Network executives believed their job was to entertain Americans, and that current affairs should be left to newspapers. Yet radio could do something that no previous medium of communication could do: it could report not merely what had happened, but what was happening as it happened.

Franklin Roosevelt was among the first to grasp radio's potential in this regard. As governor of New York he occasionally went on the air, and soon after becoming president he commenced his Fireside Chats. With a voice perfectly suited to the medium, he reassured Americans suffering through the depression that, although current conditions were grim, the government was working hard to help them. So successful were these broadcasts that, in the words of one journalist, "The President has only to look toward a radio to bring Congress to terms."

Across the Atlantic, another leader also understood well the power of radio. Adolf Hitler determined early that he would use German radio to carry speeches directly to the people. The message came through loud and clear: Germany had been wronged by enemies abroad and by Marxists and Jews at home. But the Nazis under Hitler's direction would lead the country back to its former greatness. The Third Reich would last a thousand years. As "Sieg Heil!" thundered over the airwaves, millions of Germans came to see Hitler as their salvation.

In 1938, as events in Europe reached a crisis, American radio networks increased their news coverage. When Hitler annexed Austria in March, NBC and CBS broke into scheduled programs to deliver news bulletins. Then, on the evening of Saturday, March 13, CBS went its rival one better by broadcasting the first international news roundup, a half-hour show featuring live reports on the annexation from the major capitals of Europe. A new era in American radio was born. In the words of author Joseph Persico, what made the broadcast revolutionary "was the listener's sensation of being on the scene," even though the event was taking place in far-off Europe.

When leaders from France and Britain met with Hitler in Munich later that year, millions of Americans listened to live radio updates with rapt attention. Correspondents soon became well known, none more so than Edward R. Murrow of CBS. During the Nazi air "blitz" of London in 1940–1941, Murrow's rich, understated, nicotine-scorched voice kept Americans spellbound. "This—is London," he would begin each broadcast, then proceed to give graphic accounts that tried, as he put it, to "report suffering to people [Americans] who have not suffered."

Murrow was resolutely pro-Allies, and there is little doubt his reports strengthened the interventionist voices in Washington by emphasizing Winston Churchill's greatness and England's bravery. More than that, though, radio reports from Europe made Americans feel more closely linked than before to the experiences of people living thousands of miles and an ocean away.

Edward R. Murrow at his typewriter in wartime London.
(Library of Congress)

Map 26.3   The German Advance, 1939–1942

Hitler's drive to dominate Europe pushed German troops deep into France and the Soviet Union. Great Britain took a beating but held on with the help of American economic and military aid before the United States itself entered the Second World War in late 1941.

organized in 1940) provided outlets for citizen participation in the national debate. African American churches organized anti-Italian boycotts to protest Mussolini's pummeling of Ethiopia.

In March 1940 the Soviet Union invaded Finland. In April Germany conquered Denmark and Norway (see Map 26.3). "The small countries are *FALL OF FRANCE* smashed up, one by one, like matchwood," sighed Winston Churchill, who became Britain's prime minister on May 10, 1940, the day Germany attacked Belgium, the Netherlands, and France. German divisions ultimately pushed French and British forces back to the English Channel. At Dunkirk, France, between May 26 and June 6, more than 300,000 Allied soldiers frantically escaped to Britain on a flotilla of small boats. The Germans occupied Paris a week later. A new French government located in the town of Vichy

decided to collaborate with the conquering Nazis and, on June 22, surrendered France to Berlin. With France knocked out of the war, the German Luftwaffe (air force) launched massive bombing raids against Great Britain in preparation for a full-scale invasion. Stunned Americans asked, Could Washington or New York be the Luftwaffe's next target?

Alarmed by the swift defeat of one European nation after another, Americans gradually shed their isolationist sentiment. Some liberals left the isolationist fold; it became more and more the province of conservatives. Emotions ran high. Roosevelt called the isolationists "ostriches" and charged that some were pro-Nazi subversives. Assuring Americans that New Deal reforms would not have to be sacrificed to achieve military preparedness, the president began to aid the beleaguered Allies to prevent the fall of Britain. In May 1940 he ordered the

your BRITAIN · fight for it now

ISSUED BY A·B·C·A

■ Guns, tanks, and bombs were the principal weapons of the war, but there were other, more subtle forms of warfare as well. Words, posters, and films waged a constant battle for the hearts and minds of the citizenry of each belligerent nation just as surely as military weapons engaged the enemy. This scene of the South Downs in England sought to arouse feelings for an idealized pastoral Britain. (Frank Newbould)

sale of old surplus military equipment to Britain and France. In July he cultivated bipartisan support by naming Republicans Henry L. Stimson and Frank Knox, ardent backers of aid to the Allies, secretaries of war and the navy, respectively. In September, by executive agreement, the president traded fifty over-age American destroyers for leases to eight British military bases, including Newfoundland, Bermuda, and Jamaica.

Two weeks later Roosevelt signed into law the hotly debated and narrowly passed Selective Training and

First Peacetime Military Draft

Service Act, the first peacetime military draft in American history. The act called for the registration of all men between the ages of twenty-one and thirty-five. Soon more than 16 million men had signed up, and draft notices began to be delivered. Meanwhile, Roosevelt won reelection in November 1940 with promises of peace: "Your boys are not going to be sent into any foreign wars." Republican candidate Wendell Willkie, who in the emerging spirit of bipartisanship had not made an issue of foreign policy, snapped, "That hypocritical son of a bitch! This is going to beat me!" It did.

Roosevelt claimed that the United States could stay out of the war by enabling the British to win. The United States, he said, must become the "great arsenal of democracy." In January 1941 Congress debated the president's Lend-Lease bill. Because Britain was broke, the president explained, the United States should lend rather than sell weapons, much as a neighbor lends a garden

hose to fight a fire. Most lawmakers needed little persuasion. In March 1941, with pro-British sentiment running high, the House passed the Lend-Lease Act by 317 votes to 71; the Senate followed with a 60-to-31 tally. The initial appropriation was $7 billion, but by the end of the war the amount had reached $50 billion, more than $31 billion of it for Britain.

To ensure the safe delivery of Lend-Lease goods, Roosevelt ordered the U.S. Navy to patrol halfway across the Atlantic, and he sent American troops to Greenland. In July, arguing that Iceland was also essential to the defense of the Western Hemisphere, the president dispatched marines there. He also sent Lend-Lease aid to the Soviet Union, which Hitler had attacked in June (thereby shattering the 1939 Nazi-Soviet nonaggression pact). If the Soviets could hold off two hundred German divisions in the east, Roosevelt calculated, Britain would gain some breathing time. Churchill, who had long thundered against communists, now applauded aid to the Soviets: "If Hitler invaded Hell, I would make at least a favorable reference to the Devil in the House of Commons."

In August 1941 Churchill and Roosevelt met for four days on a British battleship off the coast of Newfoundland. They got along well, trading naval stories and enjoying

Atlantic Charter

the fact that Churchill was half American (his mother was from New York). The two leaders issued the Atlantic Charter, a set of war aims reminiscent

■ President Franklin D. Roosevelt *(left)* and British prime minister Winston Churchill (1874–1965) confer on board a ship near Newfoundland during their summit meeting of August 1941. During the conference, they signed the Atlantic Charter. Upon his return to Great Britain, Churchill told his advisers that Roosevelt had promised to "wage war" against Germany and do "everything" to "force an incident."   (Franklin D. Roosevelt Library)

of Wilsonianism (see page 625): collective security, disarmament, self-determination, economic cooperation, and freedom of the seas. Churchill later recalled that the president told him in Newfoundland that he could not ask Congress for a declaration of war against Germany but "he would wage war" and "become more and more provocative."

Within days, German and American ships came into direct contact in the Atlantic. On September 4, a German submarine launched torpedoes at (but did not hit) the American destroyer *Greer*. Henceforth, Roosevelt said, the U.S. Navy would shoot on sight. He also announced a policy he already had promised Churchill in private: American warships would convoy British merchant ships across the ocean. Thus the United States entered into an undeclared naval war with Germany. When in early October a German submarine torpedoed the U.S. destroyer *Kearny* off the coast of Iceland, the president announced that "the shooting has started. And history has recorded who fired the first shot." Later that month, when the destroyer *Reuben James* went down with the loss of more than one hundred American lives, Congress scrapped the cash-and-carry policy and further revised the Neutrality Acts to permit transport of munitions to Britain on armed American merchant ships. The United States was edging very close to being a belligerent.

It seems ironic, therefore, that the Second World War came to the United States by way of Asia. Roosevelt had wanted to avoid war with Japan in order to concentrate American resources on the defeat of Germany. In

U.S. DEMANDS ON JAPAN September 1940, after Germany, Italy, and Japan had signed the Tripartite Pact (to form the Axis powers), Roosevelt slapped an embargo on shipments of aviation fuel and scrap metal to Japan. Because the president believed the Japanese would consider a cutoff of oil a life-or-death matter, he did not embargo that vital commodity. But after Japanese troops occupied French Indochina in July 1941, Washington froze Japanese assets in the United States, virtually ending trade (including oil) with Japan. "The oil gauge and the clock stood side by side" for Japan, wrote one observer.

Tokyo recommended a summit meeting between President Roosevelt and Prime Minister Prince Konoye, but the United States rejected the idea. American officials insisted that the Japanese first agree to respect China's sovereignty and territorial integrity and to honor the Open Door policy—in short, to get out of China. According to polls taken in fall 1941, the American people seemed willing to risk war with Japan to thwart further aggression. For Roosevelt, Europe still claimed first priority, but he supported Secretary Hull's hard-line policy against Japan's pursuit of the Greater East Asia Co-Prosperity Sphere—the name Tokyo gave to the vast Asian region it intended to dominate.

Roosevelt told his advisers to string out ongoing Japanese-American talks to gain time—time to fortify the Philippines and check the fascists in Europe. By breaking the Japanese diplomatic code and deciphering intercepted messages through Operation MAGIC, American officials learned that Tokyo's patience with diplomacy was fast dissipating. In late November the Japanese rejected American demands that they withdraw from Indochina. An intercepted message that American experts decoded on December 3 instructed the Japanese embassy in Washington to burn codes and destroy cipher machines—a step suggesting that war was coming.

The Japanese plotted a daring raid on Pearl Harbor in Hawai'i. An armada of sixty Japanese ships, with a **SURPRISE ATTACK ON PEARL HARBOR** core of six carriers bearing 360 airplanes, crossed 3,000 miles of the Pacific Ocean. To avoid detection, every ship maintained radio silence. In the early morning of December 7, some 230 miles northwest of Honolulu, the carriers unleashed their planes, each stamped with a red sun representing the Japanese flag. They swept down on the unsuspecting American naval base and nearby airfields, dropping torpedoes and bombs and strafing buildings.

The battleship U.S.S. *Arizona* fell victim to a Japanese bomb that ignited explosives below deck, killing more than one thousand sailors. The U.S.S. *Nevada* tried to escape the inferno by heading out to sea, but a second wave of aerial attackers struck the ship. Altogether the invaders sank or damaged eight battleships and many smaller vessels and smashed more than 160 aircraft on the ground. Huddled in an air-raid shelter, sixteen-year-old Mary Ann Ramsey watched the injured come in "with filthy black oil covering shredded flesh. With the first sailor, so horribly burned, personal fear left me; he brought me the full tragedy of the day." A total of 2,403 died; 1,178 were wounded. By chance, three aircraft carriers at sea escaped the disaster. The Pearl Harbor tragedy, from the perspective of the war's outcome, amounted to a military inconvenience more than a disaster.

How could the stunning attack on Pearl Harbor have happened? After all, American cryptanalysts had broken the Japanese diplomatic code. **EXPLAINING PEARL HARBOR** Although the intercepted Japanese messages told policymakers that war lay ahead, the intercepts never revealed naval or military plans and never specifically mentioned Pearl Harbor. Roosevelt did not, as some critics charged, conspire to leave the fleet vulnerable to attack so that the United States could enter the Second World War through the "back door" of Asia. The base at Pearl Harbor was not on red alert because a message sent from Washington warning of the imminence of war had been too casually transmitted by a slow method and had arrived too late. Base commanders were too relaxed, believing Hawai'i too far from Japan to be a target for all-out attack. Like Roosevelt's advisers, they expected an assault against British Malaya, Thailand, or the Philippines (see Map 26.2). The Pearl Harbor calamity stemmed from mistakes and insufficient information, not from conspiracy.

On December 8, referring to the previous day as "a date which will live in infamy," Roosevelt asked Congress for a declaration of war against Japan. He noted that the Japanese had also attacked Malaya, Hong Kong, Guam, the Philippines, Wake, and Midway, and he expressed the prevailing sense of revenge when he vowed that Americans would never forget "the character of the onslaught against us." A unanimous vote in the Senate and a 388-to-1 vote in the House thrust America into war. Representative Jeannette Rankin of Montana voted no, repeating her vote against entry into the First World War. Britain declared war on Japan, but the Soviet Union did not. Three days later, Germany and Italy, honoring the Tripartite Pact they had signed with Japan in September 1940, declared war against the United States. "Hitler's fate was sealed," Churchill later wrote. "Mus-

■ The stricken U.S.S. *West Virginia* was one of eight battleships caught in the surprise Japanese attack at Pearl Harbor, Hawai'i, on December 7, 1941. In this photograph, sailors on a launch attempt to rescue a crew member from the water as oil burns around the sinking ship. (U.S. Army)

solini's fate was sealed. As for the Japanese, they would be ground to powder. . . . I went to bed and slept the sleep of the saved and thankful."

A fundamental clash of systems explains why war came. Germany and Japan preferred a world divided into closed spheres of influence. The United States sought a liberal capitalist world order in which all nations enjoyed freedom of trade and investment. American principles manifested respect for human rights; fascists in Europe and militarists in Asia defiantly trampled such rights. The United States prided itself on its democratic system;

Germany and Japan embraced authoritarian regimes backed by the military. When the United States protested against German and Japanese expansion, Berlin and Tokyo charged that Washington was applying a double standard, conveniently ignoring its own sphere of influence in Latin America and its own history of military and economic aggrandizement. Americans rejected such comparisons and claimed that their expansionism had benefited not just themselves but the rest of the world. So many incompatible objectives and outlooks obstructed diplomacy and made war likely.

Likely, but perhaps not inevitable. At least with respect to the Japanese, there is the tantalizing question of

AVOIDABLE WAR?

whether a more flexible American negotiating posture in the fall of 1941 might have averted a U.S.-Japan war. Privately, after all, American planners admitted that they were largely powerless to affect Japan's moves in China; they further conceded among themselves that any Japanese withdrawal from China would take many months to carry out. So why the public insistence that Japan had to get out, and get out now? Why not assent, grudgingly, to the Japanese presence in China and also reopen at least limited trade with the Tokyo government, in order to forestall further Japanese expansion in Southeast Asia? Such a policy would have delayed any showdown with Japan, allowed continued concentration on the European war, and also given Washington more time to rearm. Writes historian David M. Kennedy: "Whether under those circumstances a Japanese-American war might have been avoided altogether is among the weightiest of might-have-beens, with implications for the nature and timing of America's struggle against Hitler and for the shape of postwar Europe as well as Asia." It was not to be, though, and the United States now prepared to wage war in two theaters half a world apart.

Summary

In the 1920s and 1930s, Americans proved unable to create a peaceful and prosperous world order. The Washington Conference treaties failed to curb a naval arms race or to protect China, and both the Dawes Plan and the Kellogg-Briand Pact proved ineffective. Philanthropic activities fell short of need, and the process of cultural "Americanization" provided no panacea. In the era of the Great Depression, U.S. trade policies, shifting from protectionist tariffs to reciprocal trade agreements, only minimally improved U.S. or international commerce. Recognition of the Soviet Union barely improved relations. Most ominous of all, the aggressors Germany and Japan ignored repeated U.S. protests, from the Stimson Doctrine onward; as the 1930s progressed, the United States became more entangled in the crises in Europe and Asia. Even where American power and policies seemed to work to satisfy Good Neighbor goals—in Latin America—nationalist resentments simmered and Mexico challenged U.S. dominance.

During the late 1930s and early 1940s, President Roosevelt hesitantly but steadily moved the United States from neutrality to aid for the Allies, to belligerency, and finally to a declaration of war after the attack on Pearl Harbor. Congress gradually revised and retired the Neutrality Acts in the face of growing danger and receding isolationism. Independent internationalism and economic and nonmilitary means to peace gave way to alliance building and war.

The Second World War offered yet another opportunity for Americans to set things right in the world. As the publisher Henry Luce wrote in *American Century* (1941), the United States must "exert upon the world the full impact of our influence, for such purposes as we see fit and by such means as we see fit." As they had so many times before, Americans flocked to the colors. Isolationists joined the president in spirited calls for victory. "We are going to win the war, and we are going to win the peace that follows," Roosevelt predicted.

LEGACY FOR A PEOPLE AND A NATION
Presidential Deception of the Public

Before U-652 launched two torpedoes at the *Greer,* heading for Iceland on September 4, 1941, the U.S. destroyer had stalked the German submarine for hours. Twice the *Greer* signaled the U-boat's location to British patrol bombers, one of which dropped depth charges on the submarine. After the torpedo attack, which missed its mark, the *Greer* also released depth charges. But when President Roosevelt described the encounter in a dramatic radio "Fireside Chat" on September 11, he declared that the German submarine, without warning, had fired the first shot, and he protested German "piracy" as a violation of the principle of freedom of the seas.

Roosevelt did not tell the American people the full truth about the events of September 4, and what he did tell was misleading. The incident had little to do with freedom of the seas—which related to neutral merchant ships, not to U.S. warships operating in a war zone. Roosevelt's words amounted to a call to arms, yet he never asked Congress for a declaration of war against Germany. The president believed that he had to deceive the public in order to move hesitant Americans toward noble positions that they would ultimately see as necessary. Public opinion polls soon demonstrated that the practice worked, as most Americans approved the shoot-on-sight policy Roosevelt announced as a consequence of the *Greer* incident.

Several years later, in his book *The Man in the Street* (1948), Thomas A. Bailey defended Roosevelt. The historian argued that "because the masses are notoriously shortsighted, and generally cannot see danger until it is at their throats, our statesmen are forced to deceive them into an awareness of their own long-term interests." Roosevelt's critics, on the other hand, even those who agreed with him that Nazi Germany had to be stopped, have seen in his methods a danger to the democratic process, which cannot work in an environment of dishonesty and a usurping of congressional powers. In the 1960s, during America's descent into the Vietnam War, Senator J. William Fulbright of Arkansas recalled the *Greer* incident: "FDR's deviousness in a good cause made it easier for LBJ to practice the same kind of deviousness in a bad cause." Indeed,

during the Tonkin Gulf crisis of 1964, President Lyndon B. Johnson shaded the truth in order to gain from Congress wide latitude in waging war. In the 1980s Reagan administration officials, in the Iran-contra affair, consciously and publicly lied about U.S. arms sales to Iran and about covert aid to Nicaraguan terrorists.

Following Roosevelt, presidents have found it easier to exaggerate, distort, withhold, or even lie about the facts of foreign relations in order to shape a public opinion favorable to their policies. One result: the growth of the "imperial presidency"—the president's grabbing of power from Congress, and use of questionable means to reach his objectives. The practice of deception—for an end the president calls noble—was one of Roosevelt's legacies for a people and a nation.

The **history companion** *powered by Eduspace®*

Your primary source for interactive quizzes, exercises, and more to help you learn efficiently.

http://history.college.hmco.com/students

THE SECOND WORLD WAR AT HOME AND ABROAD 1941–1945

*W*illiam Dean Wilson was only sixteen in 1942 when U.S. Marine Corps recruiters came to Shiprock, New Mexico, where he was a student at the Navajo boarding school, but he was eager to fight the war. Five years too young to be drafted and a year too young to volunteer for the marines, he lied about his age. His parents did not want him to drop out of school and go to war, but he removed the note reading "Parents will not consent" from his recruiting file and was inducted into the Marine Corps.

Despite his youth, Wilson was recruited for one of the most important projects of the war. Battles were won or lost because nations broke the codes in which their enemies transmitted messages. The marines sought to use a code based on Diné, the Navajo language, which is extremely complex because of its syntax and tonal qualities. In 1942 it did not exist in written form, and there were fewer than thirty non-Navajos in the world—none of them Japanese—who could understand it. Unlike written ciphers, this code promised to be unbreakable.

Wilson and his fellow Navajo recruits trained as radio operators and helped devise a basic code. Navajo words represented the first letter of their English translations; thus *wol-la-chee* ("ant") stood for the letter *A*. Each also memorized a special dictionary of Navajo words that represented 413 basic military terms and concepts. *Dah-he-tih-hi* ("hummingbird") meant fighter plane; *ne-he-mah,* "our mother," was the United States; *beh-na-ali-tsosie,* "slant-eye," stood for Japan.

By the time Wilson's seventeenth birthday arrived, he was fighting in the Pacific. Beginning with the Battle of Guadalcanal, he and others from the corps of 420 code talkers took part in every assault the marines conducted in the Pacific from 1942 to 1945. Usually, two code talkers were assigned to a battalion, one going ashore with the assault forces and the other remaining on ship to receive

◀ Navajo "code talkers," who were U.S. Marines, were among the first assault forces to land on Pacific beaches. Dodging enemy fire, they set up radio equipment and transmitted vital information to headquarters, including enemy sightings and targets for American shelling. The Japanese never broke the special Navajo code. The artist is Colonel C. H. Waterhouse, U.S. Marine Corps (retired). (U.S. Marine Corps Art Collection/Colonel C. H. Waterhouse)

CHRONOLOGY

1941
- Government war-preparedness study concludes U.S. not ready for war before June 1943
- Roosevelt issues Executive Order No. 8802, forbidding racial discrimination by defense industry
- Japan attacks Pearl Harbor
- United States enters World War II

1942
- War Production Board created to oversee conversion to military production
- Millions of Americans move to take jobs in war industries
- Allies losing war in Pacific to Japan; U.S. victory at Battle of Midway in June is turning point
- Office of Price Administration creates rationing system for food and consumer goods
- U.S. pursues "Europe First" war policy; Allies reject Stalin's demands for a second front and invade North Africa
- West Coast Japanese Americans relocated to internment camps
- Manhattan Project set up to create atomic bomb
- Congress of Racial Equality established

1943
- Soviet Army defeats German troops at Stalingrad
- Congress passes War Labor Disputes (Smith-Connally) Act following coal miners strike
- Zoot suit riots in Los Angeles; race riots break out in Detroit, Harlem, and forty-five other cities
- Allies invade Italy
- Roosevelt, Churchill, and Stalin meet at Teheran Conference

1944
- Allied troops land at Normandy on D-Day, June 6
- Roosevelt elected to fourth term as president
- U.S. retakes Philippines

1945
- Roosevelt, Stalin, and Churchill meet at Yalta Conference
- British and U.S. forces firebomb Dresden, Germany
- Battles of Iwo Jima and Okinawa result in heavy Japanese and American losses
- Roosevelt dies; Truman becomes president
- Germany surrenders; Allied forces liberate Nazi death camps
- Potsdam Conference calls for Japan's "unconditional surrender"
- U.S. uses atomic bombs on Hiroshima and Nagasaki
- Japan surrenders
- More than 55 million people worldwide have perished in WWII

messages. Often under hostile fire, code talkers set up their radio equipment and began transmitting, reporting sightings of enemy forces and directing shelling by American detachments. Their work required great courage, and it paid off. "Were it not for the Navajos," declared Major Howard Conner, Fifth Marine Division signal officer, "the Marines would never have taken Iwo Jima. The entire operation was directed by Navajo code. . . . I had six Navajo radio sets operating around the clock. In that period alone they sent and received over eight hundred messages without an error."

As it did for millions of other American fighting men and women, wartime service changed the Navajo code talkers' lives, broadening their horizons and often deepening their ambitions. Many became community leaders. William Dean Wilson, for example, became a tribal judge. From "the service," recalled Raymond Nakai, a navy veteran who became chairman of the Navajo nation, "the Navajo got a glimpse of what the rest of the world is doing." But in 1945 most Navajo war veterans were happy to return to their homes and traditional culture. And in accordance with Navajo ritual, the returning veterans participated in purification ceremonies to dispel the ghosts of the battlefield and invoke blessings for the future.

The Second World War marked a turning point in the lives of millions of Americans, as well as in the history of the United States. Most deeply affected were those who fought the war, on the beaches and battlefields, in the skies and at sea. For forty-five months Americans fought abroad to subdue the German, Italian, and Japanese aggressors. Though the war began badly for the United States, by mid-1942 the Allies had halted the Axis powers' advance. In June 1944 American troops, together with Canadian, British, and Free French units, launched a massive invasion across the English Channel, landing at Normandy and pushing into Germany by the following spring. Battered by merciless bombing raids, leaderless after Adolf Hitler's suicide, and pressed by a Soviet advance from the east, the Nazis capitulated in May 1945. In the Pacific, Americans drove Japanese forces back, island by island, toward Japan. America's devastating conventional bombing of Japanese cities, followed by the atomic bombs that demolished Hiroshima and Nagasaki in August 1945, led to the surrender of Japan.

Throughout the war the "Grand Alliance"—Britain, the Soviet Union, and the United States—stuck together to defeat Germany. But they disagreed about how best to fight the war and had profound differences over how to shape the postwar world. Prospects for postwar international cooperation seemed bleak, and the advent of the atomic age frightened everyone.

Though the war was fought far from the United States, it had a major impact on American society. America's leaders sought to fight the war on the "production front" as well as on the battlefield, and committed the United States to become the "arsenal of democracy," producing vast quantities of arms for the war against the Axis. Essential to victory was the mobilization of all sectors of the economy—industry, finance, agriculture, labor. America's big businesses got even bigger, as did its central government, labor unions, and farms. The federal government had the monumental task of coordinating activity in these spheres, as well as in two new ones: higher education and science.

During the war nearly one of every ten Americans moved permanently to another state. Most headed for war-production centers, especially cities in the North and on the West Coast. Japanese Americans moved, too, but involuntarily, as they were rounded up by the army and placed in internment camps. And while the war offered new economic and political opportunities for African Americans, encouraging them to demand their full rights as citizens, competition for jobs and housing created the conditions for an epidemic of race riots. For women, the war offered new job opportunities in the armed forces and in war industries. For some, work was an economic necessity; for others, it was a patriotic obligation; for all, it brought greater financial independence and self-esteem.

On the home front, the American people united behind the war effort, collecting scrap iron, rubber, and newspapers for recycling and planting "victory gardens." Though commodities such as food and gasoline were rationed, the war had brought prosperity back to the United States. At war's end, although many Americans grieved loved ones lost in battle and worried about the stability of the emerging postwar order, the United States enjoyed unprecedented power and unmatched prosperity among the world's nations. ■

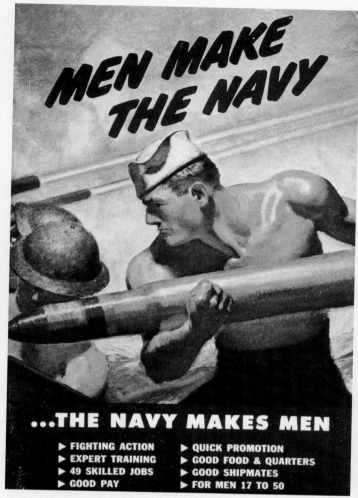

■ "MEN MAKE THE NAVY . . . ," proclaims this U.S. Navy recruiting booklet, which encourages men to enlist by highlighting the good pay, food, and shipmates, as well as the possibility of "fighting action." One hundred thousand women also responded to the navy's recruiting efforts by joining the WAVES.   (Private Collection)

The United States at War

*a*s Japanese bombs fell in the United States territory of Hawai'i, American antiwar sentiment evaporated. Franklin Roosevelt summoned the nation to war with Japan on December 8, proclaiming that "the American people in their righteous might will win through to absolute victory." When Germany formally declared war on the United States on December 11, America joined British and Soviet Allied nations in the ongoing war against the Axis powers of Japan, Germany, and Italy. The American public's shift from caution—even isolationism—to fervent support for war was sudden and dramatic. Some former critics of intervention, seeking a persuasive explanation, turned to the popular children's story *Ferdinand the Bull*. Ferdinand, though huge and powerful, just liked to "sit and smell the flowers"—until the day he was stung by a bee. It was a comforting tale, but not accurate. As the world went to war, the United States had not been, like Ferdinand, just "smell[ing] the flowers." America's embargo of shipments to Japan and refusal to accept Japan's expansionist policies had brought the two nations to the brink of war, and the United States was deeply involved in an undeclared naval war with Germany well before Japan's attack on Pearl Harbor. By December 1941, Roosevelt had long since instituted a peacetime draft, created war mobilization agencies, and commissioned war plans for simultaneous struggle in Europe and the Pacific. America's entry into World War II was not a surprise.

Nonetheless, the nation was not ready for war. Throughout the 1930s, funding for the military had been a low priority. In September 1939 (when Hitler invaded Poland and the Second World War began), the U.S. army ranked forty-fifth in size among the world's armies and could fully equip only one-third of its 227,000 men. A peacetime draft instituted in 1940 expanded the U.S. military to 2 million men, but Roosevelt's 1941 survey of war preparedness, the "Victory Plan," estimated that the United States could not be ready to fight before June 1943.

A Nation Unprepared

In December 1941, U.S. victory was not a foregone conclusion. In Europe, the Allies were losing the war (see Map 26.3). Hitler had claimed Austria, Czechoslovakia, Poland, the Netherlands, Denmark, and Norway. Romania was lost, then Greece and Bulgaria. France had fallen in 1940. Britain fought on, but German planes rained bombs on London. More than 3 million soldiers under German command had penetrated deep into the Soviet Union and into Africa. German U-boats controlled the Atlantic from the Arctic to the Caribbean. Within months of America's entry into the war, German submarines sank 216 vessels—some so close to American shores that coastal residents could see the glow of burning ships.

In the Pacific, the war was largely America's to fight. The Soviets had not declared war on Japan, and though British troops protected Great Britain's Asian colonies, they were too few to make much difference. By late spring of 1942 Japan had captured most of the European colonial possessions in Southeast Asia: the

War in the Pacific

Dutch East Indies (Indonesia); French Indochina (Vietnam); and the British colonies of Malaya, Burma, Western New Guinea, Hong Kong, and Singapore. In the American Philippines, the struggle went on longer, but also in vain. The Japanese attacked the Philippines hours after their success at Pearl Harbor and, finding the entire force of B-17 bombers sitting on the airfields, destroyed U.S. air capability in the region. American and Filipino troops fell back to the Bataan Peninsula in an attempt to hold the main island, Luzon, but Japanese forces were superior. In March 1942, under orders from Roosevelt, General Douglas MacArthur, the commander of U.S. forces in the Far East, departed the Philippines for the safety of Australia, proclaiming, "I shall return."

Left behind were almost eighty thousand American and Filipino troops. Starving and decimated by disease, they held on for almost another month before surrendering. Those who survived long enough to surrender faced worse horror. The Japanese troops, lacking supplies themselves, were unprepared to deal with such a large number of prisoners, and most believed the prisoners had forfeited honorable treatment by surrendering. In what came to be known as the Bataan Death March, the Japanese force-marched their captives to prison camps 80 miles away. Guards denied the prisoners food and water, and bayoneted or beat to death those who fell behind. As many as ten thousand Filipinos and six hundred Americans died on the march. Filipino civilians suffered horribly. Tens of thousands of refugees and prisoners of war died under Japanese occupation.

As losses mounted, the United States began to strike back. On April 18, sixteen American B-25s appeared in the skies over Japan. The American flyers released bombs above Tokyo and other cities and then, having exhausted their fuel, crashed their planes just inside China. The Doolittle raid (named after the mission's leader) did little harm to Japan, but it had an enormous psychological impact on Japanese leaders. The image of American bombers over Japan's home islands pushed Japanese commander Yamamoto to bold action. Instead of consolidating control close to home, Yamamoto concluded, Japan must move quickly to lure the weakened United States into a "decisive battle." The target was Midway—two tiny islands about 1,000 miles northwest of Honolulu, where the U.S. Navy had a base. If Japan could take Midway—not implausible, given Japan's string of victories—it would have a secure defensive perimeter far from the home islands (see Map 27.1). By using Guam, the Philippines, and perhaps even Australia as hostages, Japan could dictate a negotiated peace with the United States.

What General Yamamoto did not know was that America's MAGIC codebreaking machines could deci-

Map 27.1   The Pacific War

The strategy of the United States was to "island-hop"—from Hawai'i in 1942 to Iwo Jima and Okinawa in 1945. Naval battles were also decisive, notably the Battles of the Coral Sea and Midway in 1942. The war in the Pacific ended with Japan's surrender on August 15, 1945 (V-J Day).   (Source: Thomas G. Paterson, J. Garry Clifford, Kenneth J. Hagan, *American Foreign Policy: A History*, vol. 2, 3d ed. Copyright © 1991 by D. C. Heath Company. Used by permission of Houghton Mifflin Company.)

pher Japanese messages. This time, surprise was on the side of the United States, and the Japanese fleet found the U.S. Navy and its carrier-based dive bombers lying in wait. The Battle of Midway in June 1942 was a turning point in the Pacific war. Japan's only hope had been that early victories would convince the United States to withdraw, leaving Japan to control the Pacific. That outcome was no longer a possibility. Now Japan was on the defensive.

Despite the importance of these early battles in the Pacific, America's war strategy was "Europe First." Germany,

"EUROPE FIRST" STRATEGY

American war planners recognized, was a greater threat to the United States than Japan. Roosevelt and his military advisers believed that if Germany conquered the Soviet Union, it might directly threaten the United States. Furthermore, Roosevelt feared that the

coalition of major Allies might not hold much longer. The Soviet Union, suffering almost unimaginable losses as its military battled Hitler's invading army, might pursue a separate peace. Therefore, U.S. war plans called for the United States to work first with Britain and the USSR to defeat Germany, then to deal with an isolated Japan.

British prime minister Winston Churchill and Soviet premier Joseph Stalin disagreed vehemently, however, over how to wage the war against Germany. By late 1941, before the fierce Russian winter stalled their onslaught, German troops had nearly reached Moscow and Leningrad (present-day St. Petersburg) and had slashed deeply into Ukraine, taking Kiev. Over a million Soviet soldiers had died defending their country. Stalin pressed for British and American troops to attack Germany from the west, through France, to draw German troops away from the Soviet front. Roosevelt believed "with heart and mind" that Stalin was right, and promised to open a "second front" to Germany's west before the end of 1942. Churchill, however, blocked this plan. In part because of experience with the agonies of prolonged trench warfare in World War I, British military commanders did not want a large-scale invasion of Europe. Churchill argued that it was essential to win control of the North Atlantic shipping lanes first, and promoted air attacks on Germany and a smaller, safer attack on Axis positions in North Africa. Churchill meant to halt the Germans in North Africa and so protect British imperial possessions in the Mediterranean and the oil-rich Middle East.

Against the urging of his advisers, Roosevelt accepted Churchill's plan. The U.S. military was not yet ready for a major campaign, and Roosevelt needed to show the American public some success in the European war before the end of 1942. Thus, instead of coming to the rescue of the USSR, the British and Americans made a joint landing in North Africa in November 1942. American troops, facing relatively light resistance, won quick victories in Algeria and Morocco. In Egypt, the British confronted General Erwin Rommel and his Afrika Korps in a struggle for control of the Suez Canal and the oil fields of the Middle East. After six months of fighting, trapped between British and American troops, Rommel's army surrendered. On the Soviet front, against all odds, the Soviet army hung on, fighting block by block for control of Stalingrad in the deadly cold, to defeat the German Sixth Army in early 1943. By the spring of 1943, German advances had been stalled and, like Japan, from this point on Germany was on the defensive. Relations among the Allies remained precarious as the United States and Britain continued to resist Stalin's demand for a second front. The death toll, already in the millions, continued to mount.

The Production Front and American Workers

I n late December 1940—almost a year before the United States entered the war—Franklin Roosevelt pledged that America would serve as the world's "great arsenal of democracy," making the machines that would win the war for the Allies. After December 7, 1941, U.S. strategy remained much the same. The United States would prevail through a "crushing superiority of equipment," Roosevelt told Congress. Though the war would be fought on the battlefields of Europe and the Pacific, the nation's strategic advantage lay on the "production front" at home.

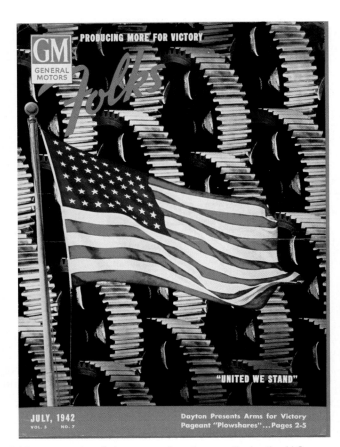

■ Unprepared to fight a war of such magnitude, the U.S. government turned to the nation's largest and most efficient corporations to produce the planes and ships and guns that would make America "the great arsenal of democracy," and General Motors received 8 percent of the value of all government war contracts. With no new cars to sell, GM continued to advertise in national magazines, proclaiming "Victory is Our Business." Pictured here is GM's in-house magazine for employees, reminding these "production soldiers" of the importance of their work. (Courtesy, Collection of Peter Kreitler/General Motors)

Goals for military production were staggering. In 1940, with war looming, American factories had built only 3,807 airplanes. Following Pearl Harbor, Roosevelt asked for 60,000 aircraft in 1942 and double that number in 1943. Plans called for the manufacture of 16 million tons of shipping and 120,000 tanks. The military needed supplies to train and equip an armed forces that would grow to 16 million men. Thus, for the duration of the war, military production took precedence over the manufacture of civilian goods. Automobile plants built tanks and airplanes instead of cars; dress factories sewed military uniforms. The War Production Board, established by Roosevelt in early 1942, had the enormous task of allocating resources and coordinating production among thousands of independent factories.

During the war, American businesses overwhelmingly cooperated with government war-production plans.

BUSINESSES, UNIVERSITIES, AND THE WAR EFFORT

Patriotism was one reason, but generous incentives were another. Major American industries had at first resisted government pressure to shift to military production. Beginning in 1940, as the U.S. produced armaments for the Allies, the American economy had begun to recover from the depression. Rising consumer spending built industrial confidence. Auto manufacturers, for example, expected to sell 4 million cars in 1941, a more than 25 percent increase over 1939. The massive retooling necessary to produce planes or tanks instead of cars would be enormously expensive and leave manufacturers totally dependent on a single client—the federal government. Moreover, many major industrialists, such as General Motors head Alfred Sloan, remained suspicious of Roosevelt and what they saw as his antibusiness policies.

Government, however, met business more than half way. The federal government paid for expensive retooling and factory expansions; it guaranteed profits to industry by allowing them to charge the government for the cost of producing items plus a fixed amount as profit; it created generous tax write-offs and exemptions from antitrust laws. War mobilization did not require America's businesses to sacrifice profits. Instead, corporations doubled their net profits between 1939 and 1943. As Secretary of War Henry Stimson explained, when a "capitalist country" goes to war, it must "let business make money out of the process or business won't work."

Most military contracts went to America's largest corporations, which had the facilities and experience to guarantee rapid, efficient production. From mid-1940 through September 1944 the government awarded contracts totaling $175 billion, no less than two-thirds of which went to the top one hundred corporations. General Motors alone received 8 percent of the total. This approach made sense for a nation that wanted enormous quantities of war goods manufactured in the shortest possible time; most small businesses just did not have the necessary capacity. However, government contracts for war production further consolidated American manufacturing in the hands of a few giant corporations.

Wartime needs also created a new relationship between science and the U.S. military. As the federal government mobilized scientists and engineers for the war effort,

MANHATTAN PROJECT

millions of dollars went to America's largest universities: $117 million to Massachusetts Institute of Technology (MIT) alone. These federally sponsored research programs developed important new technologies of warfare, such as radar and the proximity fuse. The most important focus of government-sponsored scientific research, however, was the Manhattan Project, a secret effort to build an atomic bomb, into which the government poured more than $2 billion. Roosevelt had been convinced by scientists fleeing the Nazis in 1939 that Germany was working to create an atomic weapon, and he resolved to beat them at their own efforts. The world's first sustained nuclear chain reaction was achieved by the Manhattan Project at the University of Chicago in 1942, and in 1943 the federal government set up a secret community for atomic scientists and their families at Los Alamos, New Mexico. In this remote, sparsely populated, and beautiful setting, some of America's most talented scientists worked with Jewish refugees from Nazi Germany to develop the weapon that would change the world. Although the expression "military-industrial complex" had not yet been coined (president and former five-star general Dwight Eisenhower would do so in 1961) the web of military-business-university interdependence had begun to be woven.

America's new defense factories, running round the clock, required millions of workers. At first workers were

NEW OPPORTUNITIES FOR WORKERS

plentiful: 9 million Americans were still unemployed in 1940 when war mobilization began, and 3 million remained without work in December 1941. But during the war, the armed forces took 16 million men out of the potential civilian labor pool, forcing industry to look elsewhere for workers. Women, African Americans, Mexican Americans, poor whites from the isolated mountain hollows of Appalachia and the tenant farms of the Deep South—all streamed into jobs in defense plants.

In some cases, federal action eased their path. In 1941, as the federal government poured billions of dollars into war industries, many industries refused to hire African Americans. "The Negro will be considered only as janitors and other similar capacities," one executive notified black applicants. A. Philip Randolph, head of the Brotherhood of Sleeping Car Porters, proposed a march on Washington, D.C., to demand equal access to jobs in defense industries. Roosevelt, fearing that the march might provoke race riots and also that communists might infiltrate the movement, offered the March on Washington movement a deal. In exchange for canceling the march, he issued Executive Order No. 8802, which prohibited discrimination in war industries and in the government. Officially guaranteed the right to war industry jobs on an equal basis with white workers, more than 1.5 million black Americans migrated from the South to the industrial cities of the North and West during the war.

In addition, Mexican workers filled wartime jobs in the United States. Although the U.S. government had deported Mexicans as unemployment rose during the Great Depression, about 200,000 Mexican farm workers, or *braceros*, were offered short-term contracts to fill agricultural jobs left vacant as Americans sought well-paid war work. Mexican and Mexican American workers alike faced discrimination and segregation, but they seized the economic opportunities newly available to them. In 1941, not a single Mexican American worked in the Los Angeles shipyards. By 1944, seventeen thousand people of Mexican descent were employed there.

Women, also, played an important role on the production front. At first, employers had insisted the women were not suited for industrial jobs. As labor shortages began to threaten the war effort, however, employers did an about-face. "Almost overnight," said

WOMEN AT WORK

Mary Anderson, head of the Women's Bureau of the Department of Labor, "women were reclassified by industrialists from a marginal to a basic labor supply for munitions making." Posters and billboards urged women to "Do the Job HE Left Behind." The government's War Manpower Commission glorified the invented worker "Rosie the Riveter," who was featured on posters, in magazines, and in the recruiting jingle "Rosie's got a boyfriend, Charlie / Charlie, he's a marine / Rosie is protecting Charlie / Working overtime on the riveting machine."

Rosie the Riveter was an inspiring image, but she did not accurately represent women in the American work force. Only 16 percent of women workers held jobs in defense plants, and only 4.4 percent of the jobs classified as "skilled" (such as riveting) were held by women. Nonetheless, during the war years, more than 6 million women entered the labor force, and the number of working women increased by 57 percent. Many did take advantage of the new employment opportunities. More than 400,000 African American women quit work as domestic servants to enjoy the higher pay and union benefits of industrial employment. Seven million women moved to war-production areas, such as Willow Run, Michigan, site of a massive bomber plant, and southern California,

■ Women workers mastered numerous job skills during the war. In 1942 crews of women cared for Long Island commuter trains like this one. (© Bettmann/Corbis)

home of both shipyards and aircraft factories. And the majority of women workers who did not hold war-production jobs—whether they took traditional "women's jobs" as clerical workers or filled traditionally male jobs as bus drivers or even "lumberjills" as men left for military service or better-paid factory jobs—kept the American economy going and freed other workers for the demanding work in the war-production plants.

Workers in defense plants were often expected to work ten days for every day off, or to accept difficult night shifts. Recognizing the importance of keeping people on the job, both businesses and the federal government provided workers new forms of support. The West Coast Kaiser shipyards offered not only high pay, but also childcare, subsidized housing, and healthcare: the Kaiser Permanente Medical Care Program, a forerunner of the health maintenance organization (HMO), supplied medical care to workers for a weekly payroll deduction of 50 cents. The federal government also funded childcare centers and before- and after-school programs. At its peak, 130,000 preschoolers and 320,000 school-age children were enrolled in federally sponsored childcare.

Because industrial production was key to America's war strategy, the federal government attempted to make

ORGANIZED LABOR DURING WARTIME

sure that labor strikes, so common in the 1930s, would not interrupt production. Less than a week after Pearl Harbor, a White House labor-management conference agreed to a no-strike/no-lockout pledge. In 1942 Roosevelt created the National War Labor Board (NWLB) to settle labor disputes. The NWLB forged a temporary compromise between labor union demands for a "closed shop," in which only union members could work, and management's desire for "open" shops. Workers could not be required to join a union, but unions could enroll as many members as possible. Between 1940 and 1945, union membership ballooned from 8.5 million to 14.75 million.

However, the government did not hesitate to restrict union power if it threatened war production. When coal miners in the United Mine Workers union went on strike in 1943, following an attempt by the NWLB to limit wage increases to a cost-of-living adjustment, lack of coal halted railroads and shut down steel mills essential to war production. Few Americans supported this action. An air force pilot said, "I'd just as soon shoot down one of those strikers as shoot down Japs—they're doing as much to lose the war for us." Congress responded with the War Labor Disputes (Smith-Connally) Act, which gave the president authority to seize and operate any strike-bound plant deemed necessary to the national security.

For close to four years, American factories operated twenty-four hours a day, seven days a week, fighting the

SUCCESS ON THE PRODUCTION FRONT

war on the production front. Between 1940 and 1945, American factories turned out roughly 300,000 airplanes; 102,000 armored vehicles; 77,000 ships; 20 million small arms; 40 billion bullets; and 6 million tons of bombs. By war's end, the United States was producing 40 percent of the world's weaponry. This amazing feat depended on transforming formerly skilled work in industries such as shipbuilding into an assembly-line process of mass production. Henry Ford, now seventy-eight years old, created a massive bomber plant on farmland along Willow Run Creek not far from Detroit. Willow Run's assembly lines, almost a mile long, turned out B-24 Liberator bombers at the rate of one an hour. On the West Coast, William Kaiser used mass-production techniques to cut construction time for Liberty ships—the huge, 440-foot-long cargo ships that transported the tanks and guns and bullets overseas—from 355 to 56 days. (As a publicity stunt, Kaiser's Richmond shipyard, near San Francisco, built one Liberty ship in 4 days, 15 hours, and 26 minutes.) The ships were not well made; welded hulls sometimes split in rough seas, and one ship foundered while still docked at the pier. However, as the United States struggled to produce cargo ships faster than German U-boats could sink them, speed of production was more important than quality.

A visitor to the Willow Run plant described "the roar of the machinery, the special din of the riveting gun absolutely deafening nearby, the throbbing crash of the giant metal presses . . . the far-reaching line of half-born skyships growing wings under swarms of workers." His words reveal the might of American industry but also offer a glimpse of the experience of workers, who did dirty, repetitive, and physically exhausting work day after day "for the duration." Though American propaganda during the war badly overstated the contributions of well-paid war workers as being equal to those of men in combat, the American production front played a critical role in winning the war.

Life on the Home Front

The United States was the only major combatant in World War II that did not experience warfare directly (Hawai'i was a U.S. territory, and the Philippines a U.S. possession, but neither was part of the nation proper). Americans worried about loved ones fighting in distant places; they grieved the loss of sons and brothers and fathers and husbands and friends. Their lives were disrupted. But the United States, protected by two oceans from its enemies, was spared the war that other nations experienced. Bombs did not fall on American cities; invading armies did not burn and rape and kill. Instead, war mobilization ended the Great Depression and brought prosperity. American civilians experienced the paradox of good times amid global conflagration.

Though the war was distant, it was a constant presence in the lives of Americans on what was called "the home front." Civilians supported the *SUPPORTING THE* war effort in many ways. Families *WAR EFFORT* planted 20 million "victory gardens" to free up food supplies for the armed forces. Housewives saved fat from cooking and returned it to butchers, for cooking fat yielded glycerin to make black powder used in shells or bullets. Children collected scrap metal, aware that the iron in one old shovel blade was enough for four hand grenades and that every tin can helped make a tank or Liberty ship.

Many consumer goods were rationed or unavailable during the war. To save wool for military use, the War Production Board basically redesigned men's suits, narrowing lapels, shortening jackets, and dispensing with vests and pant cuffs. Bathing suits, the WPB specified, must shrink by 10 percent. When silk and nylon were diverted from stockings to parachutes, women used makeup on their legs and drew in the "stocking" seam with eyebrow pencil. The Office of Price Administration (OPA), created by Congress in 1942, established a nationwide rationing system for consumer goods such as sugar, coffee, and gasoline. By early 1943, the OPA had instituted a point system for rationing food. Every citizen—regardless of age—received two ration books each month. Blue stamps were for canned fruits and vegetables; red for meat, fish, and dairy. To buy a pound of meat, for example, consumers had to pay its cost in dollars and in points. With only 48 blue points and 64 red points per person per month, in September 1944 a small bottle of ketchup "cost" 20 blue points, while "creamery butter" cost 20 red points and sirloin steak 13 red points a pound. Pork shoulder, however, required only dollars. Sugar was tightly rationed, and people saved for months to make a special birthday cake or holiday dessert. Feeding a family required complex calculations. A black market for counterfeit ration books and scarce consumer goods existed, but most Americans understood that sugar produced alcohol for weapons manufacture and that meat went to feed "our boys" overseas.

Despite near unanimous support for the war effort, government leaders worried that, in a long war, public willingness to sacrifice might lag. To *PROPAGANDA* build public support, in 1942 Roo- *AND POPULAR* sevelt created the Office of War Infor- *CULTURE* mation (OWI), which took charge of domestic propaganda and hired Hollywood filmmakers and New York copywriters to sell the war at home. Striking OWI posters exhorted Americans to save and sacrifice and reminded them to watch what they said, for "loose lips sink ships."

Popular culture also reinforced wartime messages. An advertisement for vacuum cleaners (unavailable for the duration) in the *Saturday Evening Post* urged women war workers to fight "for freedom and all that means to women everywhere. You're fighting for a little house of your own, and a husband to meet every night at the door. You're fighting for the right to bring up your children without the shadow of fear." Popular songs urged Americans to "Remember December 7th" or to "Accentuate the Positive." Others made fun of America's enemies ("You're a sap, Mr. Jap / You make a Yankee cranky / You're a sap, Mr. Jap / Uncle Sam is gonna spanky") or, like "Cleanin' My Rifle (and Dreamin' of You)," dealt with the hardship of wartime separation.

Movies drew 90 million viewers a week in 1944—out of a total population of 132 million. Many Hollywood films sought to meet Eleanor Roosevelt's challenge to "Keep 'em laughing." *A WAVE, a WAC, and a Marine* promised "no battle scenes, no message, just barrels of fun and jive to make you happy you're alive." Others, such as *Bataan* or *Wake Island*, portrayed actual—if sanitized—events in the war. Even in the most frivolous comedies, however, the war was always present. Theaters held "plasma premieres," offering free admission to those who donated a half-pint of blood to the Red Cross. Audiences rose to sing "The Star Spangled Banner," then watched newsreels featuring carefully censored footage of recent combat before the feature film began. On D-Day, June 6, 1944, as Allied troops landed at Normandy, theater managers across the nation led audiences in the Lord's Prayer or the Twenty-third Psalm ("The Lord is my shepherd . . ."). It was in movie theaters that Americans saw the horror of Nazi death camps in May 1945. The Universal newsreel narrator ordered audiences: "Don't turn away. Look."

The war demanded sacrifices from Americans, but it also rewarded them with new highs in personal income. Between 1939 and the end of the war, per *WARTIME* capita income rose from $691 to $1,515. *PROSPERITY* Wages and salaries increased more than

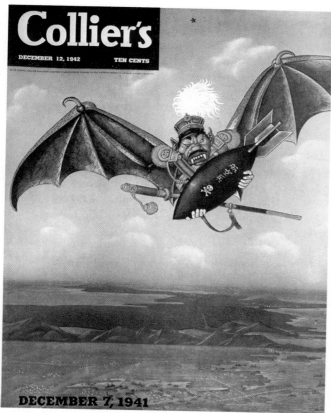

DECEMBER 7, 1941

■ In the days following the attack on Pearl Harbor, the Japanese were often pictured as subhuman—buck-toothed, nearsighted rodents and other vermin. Racial stereotyping would affect how both the Americans and the Japanese waged war. The Americans badly underestimated the Japanese, leaving themselves open for the surprise attack on Pearl Harbor and American forces in the Philippines. And the Japanese, believing Americans were barbarians who lacked a sense of honor, mistakenly expected the United States would withdraw from East Asia once confronted with Japanese power and determination. *(Collier's,* December 12, 1942)

135 percent from 1940 to 1945. OPA-administered price controls kept inflation in the single digits so that wage increases didn't disappear to higher costs. With few consumer goods to buy, the savings rate rose.

Though fighting World War II was enormously expensive, costing approximately $304 billion (more than $3 trillion in today's dollars), the United States chose not to finance the war primarily through taxation. Instead, the government relied on deficit spending, borrowing money in the form of war bonds sold to patriotic citizens and fi-

nancial institutions and sending the national debt skyrocketing, from $49 billion in 1941 to $259 billion in 1945 (the debt was not paid off until 1970). However, wartime revenue acts did increase the number of Americans paying personal income tax from 4 million to 42.6 million—at rates ranging from 6 to 94 percent—and introduced a new system in which employers "withheld" taxes from employee paychecks. For the first time, individual Americans paid more in taxes than did corporations.

Despite hardships and fears, the war offered home-front Americans new opportunities, and millions of Americans took them. More than 15 million civilians moved during the war (see Map 27.2). More than half moved to another state, and half of that number moved to another region. People who had never traveled farther than the next county found themselves on the other side of the country—or of the world. People moved for defense jobs or to be close to loved ones at stateside military postings. Southerners moved north, northerners moved south, and 1.5 million people moved to California.

A NATION IN MOTION

The rapid influx of war workers to major cities and small towns strained the resources of surrounding communities. Migrants crowded into substandard housing, such as woodsheds, tents, or cellars, or into trailer parks without adequate sanitary facilities. Disease spread: scabies and ringworm, polio, tuberculosis. Many native citizens found the war workers—especially the unmarried men—a rough bunch. In the small town of Lawrence, Kansas, leaders bragged of the economic boost a new war plant gave the town but fretted over the appearance of bars, "dirty windowed dispensaries" that sold alcohol to the war workers.

In and around Detroit, where car factories now produced tanks and planes, established residents called war workers freshly arrived from southern Appalachia "hill-billies" and "white trash." A new joke circulated: "How many states are there in the Union? Forty-five. Tennessee and Kentucky moved to Michigan, and Michigan went to hell." Many of these migrants knew little about urban life. One young man from rural Tennessee, unfamiliar with traffic lights and street signs, navigated by counting the number of trees between his home and the war plant where he worked. Some Appalachian "trailer-ites" appalled their neighbors by building outdoor privies or burying garbage in their yards.

As people from different backgrounds confronted one another under difficult conditions, tensions rose. Widespread racism made things worse. In 1943 almost 250 racial conflicts exploded in forty-seven cities.

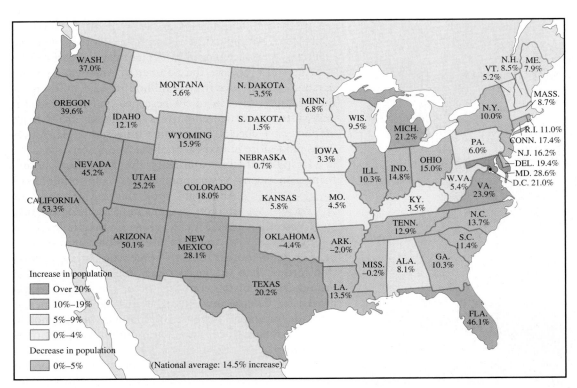

Map 27.2   A Nation on the Move, 1940–1950

American migration during the 1940s was the largest on record to that time. The farm population dropped dramatically as men, women, and children moved to war-production areas and to army and navy bases, particularly on the West Coast. Well over 30 million Americans (civilian and military) migrated during the war. Many returned to their rural homes after the war, but 12 million migrants stayed in their new locations. Notice the population increases on the West Coast, as well as in the Southwest and Florida.

RACIAL CONFLICTS

Outright racial warfare bloodied the streets of Detroit in June. White mobs, undeterred by police, roamed the city attacking blacks. Blacks hurled rocks at police and dragged white passengers off streetcars. At the end of thirty hours of rioting, twenty-five blacks and nine whites lay dead. Surveying the damage, an elderly black woman said, "There ain't no North anymore. Everything now is South."

The heightened racial and ethnic tensions of wartime also led to riots in Los Angeles in 1943. Young Mexican American gang members, or *pachucos*, had adopted the zoot suit: a long jacket with wide padded shoulders, loose pants "pegged" below the knee, a wide-brimmed hat, and dangling watch chain. With cloth rationed, wearing pants requiring five yards of fabric was a political statement, and some young men wore the zoot suit as a purposeful rejection of wartime ideals of service and sacrifice. Though in fact a high percentage of Mexican

Americans served in the armed forces, many white servicemen believed otherwise. Racial tensions were not far from the surface in overcrowded L.A., and rumors that *pachucos* had attacked white sailors quickly led to violence. For four days, mobs of white men—mainly soldiers and sailors—roamed the streets attacking zoot-suiters and stripping them of their clothes. The city of Los Angeles outlawed zoot suits and arrested men who wore them, but the "zoot suit riots" ended only when naval personnel were removed from the city.

The dislocations of war also had profound impacts on the nation's families. Despite policies that exempted

FAMILIES IN WARTIME

married men and fathers from the draft during most of the war, almost 3 million families were broken up. Young children grew up not knowing their fathers. The divorce rate of 16 per 1,000 marriages in 1940 almost doubled to 27 per 1,000 in 1944. At the same time, hundreds of thousands of men and women were

■ Members of the Vega family pose for the camera in uniforms of the Marine Corps, National Guard, and U.S. Navy. (Los Angeles Public Library)

giving their all to men in uniform. Many young men and women, caught up in the emotional intensity of war, behaved in ways they never would have done in peacetime. Often that meant hasty marriages to virtual strangers, especially if a baby was on the way. Taboos against unwed motherhood remained strong, however, and the percentage of babies born to unmarried women in the United States increased only from 0.7 percent to 1 percent of all births during the war. Wartime mobility also increased opportunities for young men and women to explore sexual attraction to members of the same sex, and gay communities grew in such cities as San Francisco.

In many ways, the war reinforced traditional gender roles that had been weakened during the depression, when many men had been unable to fulfill roles as breadwinners. Now men defended their nation while women "kept the home fires burning." Some women took "men's jobs," but those few who did so from patriotism rather than need understood their work to be "for the duration"—the home-front equivalent to men's wartime military service. Even so, women who worked were frequently blamed for neglecting their children and creating an "epidemic" of juvenile delinquency—seen in the "victory girl." Nonetheless, millions of women took on new responsibilities in wartime, whether on the factory floor or within their families. Many husbands returned home to find that the lives of their wives and children seemed complete without them, and some women found that they enjoyed the greater freedom and independence they had during that time. By war's end, many Americans were changed by their wartime experiences.

getting married. The number of marriages rose from 73 per 1,000 unmarried women in 1939 to 93 in 1942. Some couples scrambled to get married so they could live together before the man was sent overseas; others doubtless married and had children to qualify for military deferments. As might be expected, the birth rate also climbed: total births rose from about 2.4 million in 1939 to 3.1 million in 1943. Many births were "goodbye babies," conceived as a guarantee that the family would be perpetuated even if the father died in battle.

On college campuses, some virtually stripped of male students, women complained along with the song lyrics: "There is no available male." But other young women found an abundance of male company, sparking concern about wartime threats to sexual morality. *Youth in Crisis*, a newsreel shown throughout the nation in 1943, featured a girl with "experience far beyond her age" necking with a soldier on the street. These "victory girls" or "cuddle bunnies" were said to support the war effort by

The Limits of American Ideals

During the war, the U.S. government worked hard to explain to its citizens the reasons for their sacrifices. In 1941 Roosevelt had pledged America to defend "four essential human freedoms"—freedom of speech; freedom of religion, freedom from want, and freedom from fear—and government-sponsored films contrasted democracy and totalitarianism, freedom and fascism, equality and oppression.

Despite such confident proclamations, as America fought the totalitarian regimes of the Axis powers, the nation confronted questions with no easy answers. What limits on civil liberties were justified in the interest of national security? How freely could information flow to the nation's citizens without revealing military secrets to the enemy and costing American lives? How could the United States protect itself against the threat of spies or

LINKS TO THE WORLD

War Brides

During and immediately after World War II, more than 60,000 American servicemen married women from other nations, both those the United States had fought alongside and those it had fought against. The U.S. government promised these servicemen that it would deliver their wives and babies to their doorsteps, free of charge.

The U.S. Army's "Operation War Bride," which would eventually transport more than 70,000 women and children, began in Britain in early 1946. The first batch of war brides—455 British women and their 132 children—arrived in the United States on February 4, 1946. As the former WWII transport *Argentina* sailed into New York harbor in the predawn darkness, the Statue of Liberty was specially illuminated to greet them. Women who had sung "There'll Always Be an England" as they set sail from Southampton, England, gathered on the deck to attempt "The Star Spangled Banner." These women, many of them teenagers, had left their homes and families behind to join their new husbands in a strange land. Mrs. Edna Olds Butler, "nearly seventeen," practiced a southern accent in hope that her new in-laws in Roanoke Rapids, North Carolina, would be

able to understand her. Two young British women had married African American soldiers, and one carried with her a letter from her husband promising that she would be the "white queen of Atlanta."

Women fanned out to every state of the union. Women from war-destroyed cities were impressed by the material abundance of American society and pleased by the warm welcome they received. But America's racial prejudice shocked Shanghai native Helen Chia Wong, wife of Staff Sgt. Albert Wong of Fourteenth Air Force Service Command, when she and her husband were turned away from a house by a rental agent with the explanation: "The neighbors wouldn't like it." The file of one young woman who sought passage back to England showed another kind of distress. An American official noted that she was "too shocked to bring her baby up on the black tracks of a West Virginia [coal] mining town as against her own home in English countryside of rose-covered fences." It wasn't always easy, but most of the war brides settled into their new families and communities, becoming part of their new nation and helping to forge an intimate link between America and other nations of the world.

The army's "Operation War Bride" (sometimes called "Operation Mother-in-Law" or "the Diaper Run") began in Britain in early 1946. Employing eleven former World War II troopships, including the *Queen Mary,* the U.S. government relocated the wives and babies of U.S. servicemen from dozens of nations to the U.S. These English war brides, with babies their fathers have not yet seen, are waiting to be reunited with their husbands in Massachusetts, Missouri, and Iowa. (© Bettmann/Corbis)

saboteurs, especially from German, Italian, or Japanese citizens living in the United States? And what about America's ongoing domestic problems—particularly the problem of race? Could the nation address its own citizens' demands for reform as it fought the war against the Axis? The answers to these questions often revealed tensions between the nation's democratic ideals and its wartime practices.

For the most part, America handled the issue of civil liberties well. American leaders embraced a "strategy of truth," declaring that citizens of a democratic nation required a truthful accounting of the war's progress. However, the government closely controlled information about military matters. Censorship was serious business, as even seemingly unimportant details might tip off enemies about troop movements or invasion plans. Government-created propaganda sometimes dehumanized the enemy. Nonetheless, the American government resorted to hate mongering much less frequently than during the First World War.

More complex was the question of how to handle dissent, and how to guard against the possibility that enemy agents were operating within the nation's borders. The Alien Registration (Smith) Act, passed in 1940, made it unlawful to advocate the overthrow of the U.S. government by force or violence or to join any organization that did so. After Pearl Harbor, the government drew upon this authority to take thousands of Germans, Italians, and other Europeans into custody as suspected spies and potential traitors. During the war, the government interned 14,426 Europeans in Enemy Alien Camps. Fearing subversion, the government also prohibited ten thousand Italian Americans from living or working in restricted zones along the California coast, including San Francisco and Monterey Bay.

In March 1942, Roosevelt ordered that all the 112,000 foreign-born Japanese and Japanese Americans

INTERNMENT OF JAPANESE AMERICANS

living in California, Oregon, and the state of Washington (the vast majority of the mainland population) be removed from the West Coast to "relocation centers" for the duration of the war. While individual German and Italian nationals were interned because of specific charges against them, that was not the case here. There were no individual charges; Japanese and Japanese Americans were imprisoned as a group, under suspicion solely because they were of Japanese descent.

American anger at Japan's "sneak attack" on Pearl Harbor fueled the calls for internment, as did fears that

In February 1942 President Franklin D. Roosevelt ordered that all Japanese Americans living on the West Coast be rounded up and placed in prison camps. These families were awaiting a train to take them to an assembly center in Merced, California; from there, they would be sent to relocation camps in remote inland areas.   (National Archives)

West Coast cities might yet come under enemy attack. Long-standing racism also played a critical role, and General John L. DeWitt, chief of the Western Defense Command, warned, "The Japanese race is an enemy race." Finally, people in economic competition with Japanese Americans were among the strongest supporters of internment. Though Japanese nationals were forbidden to gain U.S. citizenship or own property, American-born Nissei (second generation) and Sansei (third generation) were increasingly successful in business and agriculture. The relocation order forced Japanese Americans to sell property valued at $500 million for a fraction of its worth. West Coast Japanese Americans also lost their positions in the truck-garden, floral, and fishing industries.

The internees were sent to flood-damaged lands at Relocation, Arkansas; to the intermountain terrain of Wyoming and the desert of western Arizona; and to other arid and desolate spots in the West. The camps were bleak and demoralizing. Behind barbed wire stood tarpapered wooden barracks where entire families lived in a single room furnished only with cots, blankets, and a bare light bulb. Toilets and dining and bathing facilities were communal; privacy was almost nonexistent. In such difficult circumstances, people nonetheless attempted to sustain community life, setting up schools for the children and clubs for adults to battle monotony.

Betrayed by their government, almost 6,000 internees renounced U.S. citizenship and demanded to be sent to Japan. Some Japanese Americans sought legal remedy, but the Supreme Court upheld the government's action in *Korematsu v. U.S.* (1944). Still others sought to demonstrate their loyalty. The all–Japanese American 442nd Regimental Combat Team, drawn heavily from young men in internment camps, was the most decorated unit of its size. Suffering heavy casualties in Italy and France, members of the 442nd were awarded a Congressional Medal of Honor, 47 Distinguished Service Crosses, 350 Silver Stars, and more than 3,600 Purple Hearts. In 1988, Congress issued a public apology and largely symbolic payment of $20,000 to each of the 60,000 surviving Japanese American internees.

As America mobilized for war, some African American leaders attempted to force the nation to confront the uncomfortable parallels between the racist doctrines of the

AFRICAN AMERICANS AND "DOUBLE V"

Nazis and the persistence of Jim Crow segregation in the United States. Proclaiming a "Double V" campaign (victory at home and abroad), influential groups such as the National Associa-

tion for the Advancement of Colored People (NAACP) saw the war as an opportunity "to persuade, embarrass, compel and shame our government and our nation . . . into a more enlightened attitude toward a tenth of its people." Membership in civil rights organizations soared during the war. The NAACP, 50,000 strong in 1940, had 450,000 members by 1946. And in 1942 civil rights activists influenced by the philosophy of India's Mohandas Gandhi founded the Congress of Racial Equality (CORE), which stressed "nonviolent direct action" and staged sit-ins to desegregate restaurants and movie theaters in northern cities and Washington, D.C.

Military service was a key issue for African Americans, who understood the traditional link between the duty to defend one's country and the rights of full citizenship. But the United States military remained segregated by race and strongly resisted efforts to use black units as combat troops. As late as 1943, less than 6 percent of the armed forces was African American, compared with more than 10 percent of the population. The marines at first refused to accept African Americans at all, and the navy approximated segregation by assigning black men to service positions in which they would rarely interact with nonblacks as equals or superiors.

Why did the United States fight a war for democracy with a segregated military? The United States military

A SEGREGATED MILITARY

understood that its sole priority was to stop the Axis and win the war, and the federal government and War Department decided that the midst of world war was no time to try to integrate the armed forces. The majority of Americans (approximately 89 percent of Americans were white) opposed integration, many of them vehemently. As a sign of how deeply racist beliefs penetrated the United States, the Red Cross segregated blood plasma during the war. In most southern states, racial segregation was not simply custom; it was the law. Integration of military installations and training camps, the majority of which were in the South, would have provoked a crisis as federal power contradicted state law. Pointing to outbreaks of racial violence in southern training camps as evidence, government and military officials argued that wartime integration would almost certainly have provoked even more racial violence, created disorder within the military, and hindered America's war effort. Such resistance might have been short-term, but the War Department did not take that chance. Justifying its decision, the War Department argued that it could not "act outside the law, nor contrary to the will of the majority of the citizens of the Nation." General

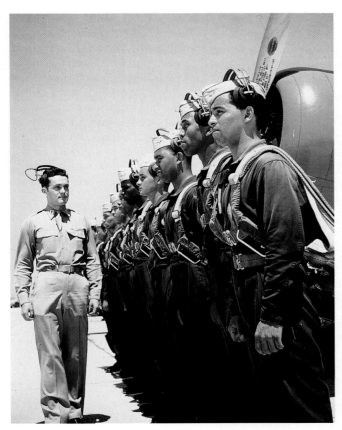

■ During World War II, for the first time, the War Department sanctioned the training and use of African American pilots. These members of the 99th Pursuit Squadron—known as "Tuskegee Airmen" because they trained at Alabama's all-black Tuskegee Institute—joined combat over North Africa in June 1943. Like most African American units in the racially segregated armed forces, the men of the 99th Pursuit Squadron were under the command of white officers.   (National Archives)

Marshall himself proclaimed that it was not the job of the army to "solve a social problem that has perplexed the American people throughout the history of this nation. . . . The army is not a sociological laboratory." Hopes for racial justice, so long deferred, were another casualty of the war.

Despite such discrimination, many African Americans stood up for their rights. Lt. Jackie Robinson refused to move to the back of the bus while training at the army's Camp Hood, Texas, in 1944—and faced court-martial, even though military regulations forbade racial discrimination on military vehicles, no matter local law or custom. Black sailors disobeyed orders to return to work after surviving an explosion that destroyed two ships, killed 320 men, and shattered windows 35 miles away—an explosion caused by navy practice of assigning black stevedores, completely untrained in handling high explosives, to load bombs from the munitions depot at Port Chicago, near San Francisco, onto Liberty ships. When they were court-martialed for mutiny, future Supreme Court justice and chief counsel for the NAACP Thurgood Marshall asked why only black sailors did this work. He proclaimed: "This is not fifty men on trial for mutiny. This is the Navy on trial for its whole vicious policy toward Negroes."

As the war wore on, African American servicemen did fight on the front lines, and fought well. The Marine Corps commandant in the Pacific proclaimed that "Negro Marines are no longer on trial. They are Marines, period." The "Tuskegee Airmen," pilots trained at the Tuskegee Institute in Alabama, saw heroic service in all-black units such as the Ninety-ninth Pursuit Squadron, which won eighty Distinguished Flying Crosses. After the war, African Americans—as some white Americans had feared—called upon their wartime service to claim the full rights of citizenship. Black men and women shared fully in the benefits offered to veterans under the GI Bill (see page 799). African Americans' wartime experiences were mixed, but the war was a turning point in the movement for equal rights.

America's most tragic failure to live up to its democratic ideas was in refusing to assist European Jews and others attempting to flee Hitler's Germany (see page 725). As early as 1942, American papers reported the "mass slaughter" of Jews and other "undesirables" (Gypsies, homosexuals, the physically and mentally handicapped) under Hitler. Roosevelt knew about the existence of Nazi death camps capable of killing up to two thousand people an hour using the gas Zyklon-B. However, American leaders chose not to divert airpower from principal targets in Germany to destroy the camps or the rail access to them.

AMERICA AND THE HOLOCAUST

British and American representatives met in Bermuda in 1943 to discuss the situation but took no concrete action. Appalled, Secretary of the Treasury Henry Morgenthau Jr. charged that the State Department's foot dragging made the United States an accessory to murder. "It takes months and months to grant the visa and then it usually applies to a corpse," he wrote bitterly. Early in 1944, stirred by Morgenthau's well-documented plea, Roosevelt created the War Refugee Board, which set up

■ When the British liberated the Bergen-Belsen concentration camp near Hanover, Germany, in April 1945, they found this mass grave. It held the remains of thousands of Holocaust victims who had been starved, gassed, and machine-gunned by their Nazi jailers. This photograph and many others provide irrefutable proof of the Holocaust's savagery. (Imperial War Museum)

refugee camps in Europe and played a crucial role in saving 200,000 Jews from death. But, lamented one American official, "by that time it was too damned late to do too much." By war's end, the Nazis had systematically murdered almost 11 million people.

Life in the Military

More than 16 million men and approximately 350,000 women served in the U.S. armed forces during World War II. Eighteen percent of American families had a father, son, or brother in the armed forces. Some of these men (and all of the women) volunteered, eager to defend their nation. But most who served—more than 10 million—were draftees. Compared with the draft in both the Civil War and the Vietnam War, the World War II draft reached broadly and fairly equitably through the American population. Almost 10,000 Princeton students or alumni served—as did all four of Franklin and Eleanor Roosevelt's sons—

while throughout the nation judges offered minor criminal offenders the choice of the military or jail.

The Selective Service Act provided for deferments, but they did not disproportionately benefit the well-to-do. The small number of college deferments was more than balanced by deferments for a long list of "critical occupations," including not only war industry workers but also almost 2 million agricultural workers. Most deferments were for those deemed physically or mentally unqualified for military service. Army physicians discovered what a toll the depression had taken on the nation's youth as draftees arrived with rotted teeth and deteriorated eyesight—signs of malnutrition. Army dentists pulled 15 million teeth and fitted men with dentures; optometrists prescribed 2.5 million pairs of glasses. Hundreds of thousands of men with venereal diseases were cured by sulfa drugs, developed in 1942. Military examiners also found evidence of the impact of racism and poverty. Half of African American draftees had no schooling beyond the sixth grade, and up

SELECTIVE SERVICE

to one-third were functionally illiterate. Forty-six percent of African Americans and almost a third of European Americans called for the draft were deferred, classified "4-F"—unfit for service.

Nonetheless, almost 12 percent of America's total population served in the military. Regiments were created rapidly, throwing together men from very different backgrounds. Regional differences were profound, and northerners and southerners—literally—often could not understand one another. Ethnic differences complicated things further. Though African Americans and Japanese Americans served in their own separate units, Hispanics, Native Americans—including the Navajo code talkers—and Chinese Americans served in "white" units. Furthermore, the differences among "whites"—the "Italian" kid from Brooklyn and the one from rural Mississippi (or rural Montana)—were profound. The result was often tension, but many Americans became less prejudiced and less provincial as they served with men unlike themselves.

Military service was widespread, but the burdens of combat were not equally shared. Though women served their nation honorably and often courageously, women's roles in the U.S. military were much more restricted than in the British or Soviet militaries, where women served as anti-aircraft gunners and in other combat-related positions. Many U.S. women volunteers served as nurses, in communications offices, and as typists or cooks. In the United States, the recruiting slogan for the WACs (Women's Army Corps) was "Release a Man for Combat." However, most men in the armed forces never saw combat, either; one-quarter never left the United States. The United States had the lowest "teeth-to-tail" ratio of any of the combatants, with each combat soldier backed up by eight or more support personnel. Japan's ratio was close to one to one. One-third of U.S. military personnel served in clerical positions, with well-educated men most likely to be slotted into noncombat positions. African Americans, though assigned dirty and dangerous tasks, were largely kept from combat service. In World War II, lower-class, less-educated white men bore the brunt of the fighting.

For those who fought, combat in World War II was as horrible as anything humans have experienced. Home-front audiences for the war films Hollywood churned out saw men die bravely, shot cleanly through the heart and comforted by their buddies in their last moments. What men experienced was carnage. Fewer than 10 percent of casualties were caused by bullets. Most men were killed or wounded by mortars, bombs,

FIGHTING THE WAR

or grenades. Seventy-five thousand American men remained missing in action at the end of the war, blown into fragments of flesh too small to identify. Combat meant days and weeks of unrelenting rain in malarial jungles, sliding down a mud-slicked hill to land in a pile of putrid corpses. It meant drowning in the waters of the frigid North Atlantic amid burning wreckage of a torpedoed ship. It meant using flamethrowers that burned at 2,000 degrees Fahrenheit on other human beings. It meant being violently ill on a landing craft steering through floating body parts of those who had attempted the landing first, knowing that if you tripped you would likely drown under the sixty-eight-pound weight of your pack, and that if you made it ashore you would likely be blown apart by artillery shells. Service was "for the duration" of the war. Only death, serious injury, or victory offered release. In this hard world, men fought to victory.

In forty-five months of war, close to 300,000 American servicemen died in combat. Almost 1 million American troops were wounded, half of them seriously. Medical advances, such as the development of penicillin and the use of blood plasma to prevent shock, helped wounded men survive—but many never fully recovered from those wounds. Between 20 and 30 percent of combat casualties were psychoneurotic, as men were pushed past the limits of endurance. The federal government strictly censored images of American combat deaths for most of the war, consigning them to a secret file known as "the chamber of horrors." Americans at home rarely understood what combat had been like, and many men, upon return, never talked about their experiences in the war.

Winning the War

Axis hopes for victory depended on a short war. Leaders in Germany and Japan were well aware that if the United States had time to fully mobilize, flooding the theaters of war with armaments and reinforcing Allied troops with fresh, trained men, the war was lost. However, powerful factions in the Japanese military and German leadership believed that the United States would concede if it met with early, decisive defeats. Hitler, blinded by racial arrogance, stated shortly after declaring war on the United States, "I don't see much future for the Americans. . . . It's a decayed country. . . . American society [is] half Judaized, and the other half Negrified. How can one expect a State like that to hold together." By mid-1942 the Axis powers understood that they had underestimated not only American resolve but also the willingness of other Allies to sacrifice their citizens to stop the Axis …7.3). The chance of an Axis victory …gly slim as months passed, but though the outcome was virtually certain after spring 1943, two years of bloody fighting lay ahead.

As the war continued, the Allies concentrated on defeating the aggressors, but their suspicions of one another undermined cooperation. The Soviets continued to press Britain and the United States to open a second front to the west of Germany and so draw Ger-

TENSIONS AMONG THE ALLIES

man troops away from the USSR. The English-speaking Allies, however, continued to delay. Stalin was not mollified by the massive "thousand bomber" raids on Germany begun by Britain's Royal Air Force in 1942, nor by the Allied invasion of Italy in the summer of 1943. When Italy surrendered in September to American and British officers, Stalin grumbled that the arrangement smacked of a separate peace.

With the alliance badly strained, Roosevelt sought reconciliation through personal diplomacy. The three Allied leaders met in Teheran, Iran, in December 1943.

Map 27.3   The Allies on the Offensive in Europe, 1942–1945

The United States pursued a "Europe First" policy: first defeat Germany, then focus on Japan. American military efforts began in North Africa in late 1942 and ended in Germany in 1945 on May 8 (V-E Day).

Stalin dismissed Churchill's repetitious justifications for further delaying the second front. Roosevelt had had enough, too; he also rejected Churchill's proposal for another peripheral attack, this time through the Balkans to Vienna. The three finally agreed to launch Operation Overlord—the cross-Channel invasion of France—in early 1944. And the Soviet Union promised to aid the Allies against Japan once Germany was defeated.

The second front opened in the dark morning hours of June 6, 1944—D-Day. In the largest amphibious landing in history, 200,000 Allied troops under the command of American general Dwight D. Eisenhower scrambled ashore at Normandy, France. Thousands of ships ferried the men within a hundred yards of the sandy beaches. Landing craft and soldiers immediately encountered the enemy; they triggered mines and were pinned down by fire from cliffside pillboxes. Meanwhile, Allied airborne troops dropped behind German lines. Although heavy aerial and naval bombardment and the

WAR IN EUROPE

clandestine work of saboteurs had softened the German defenses, the fighting was ferocious.

Allied troops soon spread across the countryside, liberating France and Belgium and entering Germany itself in September. In December, German armored divisions counterattacked in Belgium's Ardennes Forest, hoping to push on to Antwerp to halt the flow of Allied supplies through that Belgian port. After weeks of heavy fighting in what has come to be called the Battle of the Bulge—because of a "bulge" 60 miles deep and 40 miles wide where German troops had pushed back the Allied line—the Allies gained control in late January 1945. Meanwhile, battle-hardened Soviet troops marched through Poland and cut a path to Berlin. American forces crossed the Rhine River in March 1945 and captured the heavily industrial Ruhr valley. Several units peeled off to enter Austria and Czechoslovakia, where they met up with Soviet soldiers.

Even as Allied forces faced the last, desperate resistance from German troops in the Battle of the Bulge, Allied leaders began planning the peace. In early 1945 Franklin

■ The first wave of U.S. troops hits Omaha Beach during the D-Day invasion on June 6, 1944. More than 200,000 men were wounded or killed on Omaha beach that day, some drowned when they lost their footing in the rough surf and were pulled under by the weight of their 68-pound packs; others were torn by artillery or machine gun fire from German gun batteries on the cliffs that rose steeply from the beach. This photo—one of the first D-Day photos released—was taken by daring war photographer Robert Capa, who landed in Normandy with the first troops.   (© Bettmann/Corbis)

YALTA CONFERENCE Roosevelt, by this time very ill, called for a summit meeting to discuss a host of political questions—including what to do with Germany. The three Allied leaders met at Yalta, in the Russian Crimea, in February 1945. Each of the Allies arrived at Yalta with definite goals that reflected their desires for the shape of the postwar world. Britain, its formerly powerful empire now vulnerable and shrinking, sought to protect its colonial possessions and to limit Soviet power, in part by insisting that France be included in plans for postwar control of Germany, thus reducing the Soviet sphere of influence from one-third to one-quarter of the defeated nation. The Soviet Union, with 21 million dead, wanted reparations from Germany to assist in the massive task of rebuilding at home. The Soviets hoped to expand their sphere of influence throughout eastern Europe and to guarantee their national security; Germany, Stalin insisted, must be permanently weakened so that the Soviet Union never again suffered a German attack.

The United States, like the other powers, hoped to expand its influence and control the peace. To that end, Roosevelt lobbied for the United Nations Organization, which had been approved in principle at a meeting the previous year at Dumbarton Oaks in Washington, D.C., and through which the United States believed it could exercise influence. The lessons of World War I also shaped American proposals; seeking long-term peace and stability, the United States hoped to avoid the debts-reparations fiasco that had plagued Europe after the First World War. U.S. goals included self-determination for liberated peoples; gradual and orderly decolonization; and management of world affairs by what Roosevelt once called the Four Policemen: the Soviet Union, Great Britain, the United States, and China. (Roosevelt hoped China might help stabilize Asia after the war; the United States abolished the Chinese Exclusion Act in 1943 in an attempt to consolidate ties between the two nations.) The United States was also determined to limit Soviet influence in the postwar world. Obviously, there was much about which to disagree.

Military positions at the time of the Yalta conference helped to shape the negotiations. Soviet troops occupied those countries in eastern Europe that they had liberated, including Poland, where Moscow had installed a pro-Soviet regime despite a British-supported Polish government-in-exile in London. With Soviet troops in place, the ability of Britain and the United States to negotiate over the future of eastern Europe was limited. As for Germany, the Big Three agreed that some eastern German territory would be transferred to Poland, and the remainder divided into four zones (the fourth zone to be administered by France). Berlin, within the Soviet zone, would also be divided among the four victors. Yalta

■ The three Allied leaders— Winston Churchill, Franklin D. Roosevelt, and Joseph Stalin— met at Yalta in February 1945. Having been president for twelve years, Roosevelt showed signs of age and fatigue. Two months later, he died of a massive cerebral hemorrhage. (Franklin D. Roosevelt Library)

marked the high point of the Grand Alliance; in the tradition of diplomatic give-and-take, each of the Allies came away with something it wanted. In exchange for U.S. promises to support Soviet claims on territory lost to Japan in the Russo-Japanese War of 1904–1905, Stalin agreed to sign a treaty of friendship with Jiang Jieshi (Chiang Kai-shek), America's ally in China, rather than with the communist Mao Zedong (Mao Tse-tung), and to declare war on Japan two or three months after Hitler's defeat.

Franklin D. Roosevelt, reelected to an unprecedented fourth term in November 1944, did not live to see

HARRY TRUMAN

the war's end. He died on April 12, and Vice President Harry S Truman became president and commander-in-chief. Truman, who had replaced former vice president Henry Wallace as Roosevelt's running mate in 1944, was inexperienced in foreign policy. He was not even informed about the top-secret atomic weapons project until after he became president. The day after Roosevelt's death, Truman sought out old friends, Democrats and Republicans, in Congress, to ask their help in this "terrible job." Shortly afterward, he told reporters: "Boys, if you ever pray, pray for me now. I don't know whether you fellows ever had a load of hay fall on you, but when they told me yesterday what had happened, I felt like the moon, the stars, and all the planets had fallen on me."

Only eighteen days into Truman's presidency, Adolf Hitler killed himself in a bunker in bomb-ravaged Berlin. On May 8 Germany surrendered.

As the great powers jockeyed for influence after Germany's surrender, neither the spirit nor the letter of Yalta held firm. The crumbling of the Grand Alliance became evident at the Potsdam Conference, which began in mid-July. Truman—a novice at international diplomacy—was less patient with the Soviets than Roosevelt had been. Truman also was emboldened by learning during the conference that a test of the new atomic weapon had been successful; the United States, possessing such a weapon, no longer needed or even wanted the Soviet Union in the Pacific war. The Allies did agree that Japan must surrender unconditionally. But with the defeat of Hitler and the end of the European war, the wartime bonds between the Allies were strained to breaking.

With Hitler defeated, the Pacific war continued. Since halting the Japanese advance in the Battle of Midway in

WAR IN THE PACIFIC

June 1942, American strategy had been to "island-hop" toward Japan, skipping the most strongly fortified islands whenever possible and taking the weaker ones, aiming to strand the Japanese armies on their island outposts. To cut off the supply of raw materials being shipped from Japan's home islands, Americans also set out to sink the Japanese merchant marine.

■ On Okinawa, a wounded G.I. prays while awaiting evacuation to a field hospital. Medical advances, such as the discovery of penicillin and the use of glucose saline solution to replace lost blood, greatly improved the survival rate for those wounded in combat. But where combat was especially horrific, as it was on Okinawa, psychiatric casualties might outnumber combat deaths three to one. (W. Eugene Smith/Timepix/ Getty Images)

Allied and Japanese forces fought savagely for control of tiny specks of land scattered throughout the Pacific. By 1944 Allied troops—from the United States, Britain, Australia, and New Zealand—had secured the Solomon, Gilbert, Marshall, and Mariana Islands. General Douglas MacArthur landed at Leyte to retake the Philippines for the United States in October 1944.

In February 1945, while the Big Three were meeting at Yalta, U.S. and Japanese troops battled for Iwo Jima, an island less than 5 miles long, located about 700 miles south of Tokyo. Twenty-one thousand Japanese defenders occupied the island's high ground. Hidden in a network of caves, trenches, and underground tunnels, they were protected from the aerial bombardment U.S. forces used to clear the way for an amphibious landing. The stark volcanic island offered no cover, and marines were slaughtered as they came ashore. For twenty days, U.S. forces fought their way, yard by yard, up Mount Suribachi, the highest and most heavily fortified point on Iwo Jima. The struggle for Iwo Jima cost the lives of 6,821 Americans and more than 20,000 Japanese—some of whom committed suicide rather than surrender. Only 200 Japanese survived.

A month later, American troops landed on Okinawa, an island in the Ryukyus chain at the southern tip of Japan, from which Allied forces planned to mount an invasion of the main Japanese islands. Fighting raged for two months; death was everywhere. The monsoon rains began in May, turning battlefields into seas of mud filled with decaying corpses. The supporting fleet endured waves of mass *kamikaze* (suicide) attacks, in which Japanese pilots intentionally crashed bomb-laden planes into American ships. Almost 5,000 seamen perished in these attacks. On Okinawa, 7,374 American soldiers and marines died in battle. Almost the entire Japanese garrison of 100,000 was killed. More than one-quarter of Okinawa's people, or approximately 80,000 civilians, perished as the two powers struggled over their island.

With American forces entrenched just 350 miles from Japan's main islands, Japanese leaders still refused to admit defeat. A powerful military faction was determined to avoid the humiliation of an unconditional surrender and to preserve the emperor's sovereignty. They hung on even while American bombers leveled their cities. On the night of March 9, 1945, 333 American B-29 Superfortresses dropped a mixture of explosives and incendiary devices on a 4-by-3-mile area of Tokyo. Attempting to demonstrate the strategic value of airpower, they created a firestorm, a blaze so fierce that it sucked all the oxygen from the air, creating hurricane-force winds and growing so hot it could melt concrete and steel. Almost 100,000 people were incinerated, suffocated, or boiled to death in canals where they had taken refuge from the fire. Over the following five months, American bombers attacked sixty-six Japanese cities, leaving 8 million people homeless, killing almost 900,000.

BOMBING OF JAPAN

Japan, at the same time, was attempting to bomb the U.S. mainland. Thousands of bomb-bearing high-altitude balloons, constructed by schoolgirls of rice paper and flour-potato paste, were launched into the jetstream. Those that did reach the United States fell on unpopulated areas, occasionally starting forest fires. The only mainland U.S. casualties in the war were five children and an adult on a Sunday school picnic in Oregon who accidentally detonated a balloon bomb they found in the underbrush. As General Yamamoto had realized at the war's beginning, American resources would far outlast Japan's.

Early in the summer of 1945, Japan began to send out peace feelers through the Soviets. Japan was not, however, willing to accept the "unconditional surrender" terms upon which the Allied leaders had agreed at Potsdam, and Truman and his advisers chose not to pursue a negotiated peace. By this time, U.S. troops were mobilizing for an invasion of the Japanese home islands. The experiences of Iwo Jima and Okinawa weighed heavily in the planning; Japanese troops had fought on, well past any hope of victory, and death tolls for Japanese and American troops alike had been enormous. News of the success of the Manhattan Project offered another option, and President Truman took it. Using atomic bombs on Japan, Truman believed, would end the war quickly and save American lives.

Historians still debate Truman's decision to use the atomic bomb. Why would he not negotiate surrender terms? Was Japan on the verge of an unconditional surrender, as some argue? Or was the antisurrender faction of Japanese military leaders strong enough to prevail? Truman knew the bomb could give the United States both real and psychological power in negotiating the peace; how much did his desire to demonstrate the bomb's power to the Soviet Union influence his decision? Did racism or a desire for retaliation play any role? How large were the projected casualty figures for invasion on which Truman based his decision, and were they accurate? No matter the answers to these ongoing debates, bombing (whether conventional or atomic) fit the established U.S. strategy of using machines rather than men whenever possible.

■ This scorched watch, found in the rubble at Hiroshima, stopped at the time of the blast—8:16. The shock waves and fires caused by the atomic bomb leveled great expanses of the city. Radiation released by the bomb caused lingering deaths for thousands who survived the explosion. The photo of Hiroshima shown above was taken eight months after the attack. (Watch: John Launois/Black Star; Hiroshima: U.S. Air Force)

The decision to use the bomb did not seem as momentous to Truman as it does in retrospect. The moral line had already been crossed, as wholesale bombing of civilian populations continued throughout the war: The Japanese had bombed the Chinese city of Shanghai in 1937. Germans had "terror-bombed" Warsaw, Rotterdam, and London. British and American bombers had purposely created firestorms in German cities; on a single night in February 1945, 225,000 people perished in the bombing of Dresden. The American bombing of Japanese cities—accomplished with conventional weapons—had already killed close to a million people and destroyed 56 square miles of Tokyo alone. What distinguished the atomic bombs from conventional bombs was their power and their efficiency—not that they killed huge numbers of innocent civilians in unspeakably awful ways.

On July 26, 1945, the Allies delivered an ultimatum to Japan: promising that the Japanese people would not be "enslaved," the Potsdam Declaration called for the Japanese to surrender unconditionally or face "prompt and utter destruction." Tokyo radio announced that the government would respond with *mokusatsu* (literally, "kill with silence," or ignore the ultimatum). On August 6, 1945, a B-29 bomber named after the pilot's mother, the *Enola Gay*, dropped an atomic bomb above the city of Hiroshima. A flash of dazzling light shot across the sky; then a huge purplish mushroom cloud boiled forty thousand feet into the atmosphere. Much of the city was leveled by the blast. The bomb ignited a firestorm, and thousands who survived the initial blast burned to death. Approximately 130,000 people were killed. Tens of thousands more would suffer the effects of radiation poisoning.

American planes continued their devastating conventional bombing. On August 8, the Soviet Union declared war on Japan. On August 9, a second American atomic bomb fell on Nagasaki, killing at least 60,000 people. Five days later, on August 14, Japan surrendered. The Allies promised that the Japanese emperor could remain as the nation's titular head. Formal surrender ceremonies were held September 2 aboard the battleship *Missouri* in Tokyo Bay. The Second World War was over.

Summary

*H*itler once prophesied, "We may be destroyed, but if we are, we shall drag a world with us—a world in flames." In that, at least, Hitler was right. World War II devastated much of the globe. In Asia and in Europe, ghostlike people wandered through rubble, searching desperately for food. One out of nine people in the Soviet Union had perished: a total of at least 21 million civilian and military war dead. The Chinese calculated their war losses at 10 million; the Germans and Austrians at 6 million; the Japanese at 2.5 million. Up to 1 million died of famine in Japanese-controlled Indochina. Almost 11 million people had been systematically murdered in Nazi death camps. Across the globe, the Second World War killed at least 55 million people.

Waging war required the cooperation of Allied nations with very different goals and interests. Tensions remained high throughout the war, as Stalin unsuccessfully pushed the United States and Britain to open a second front to draw German soldiers away from the Soviet Union. The United States, meanwhile, was fighting a brutal war in the Pacific, pushing Japanese forces back toward their home islands. By the time Japan surrendered in August 1945, the strains between the Soviet Union and its English-speaking Allies made postwar peace and stability unlikely.

American men and machines were a critical part of the Allied war effort. American servicemen covered the globe, from the Arctic to the tropics. And on the home front, Americans worked around the clock to make the weapons that would win the war. Though they made sacrifices during the war—including almost 300,000 who gave their lives—many Americans found that the war had changed their lives for the better. Mobilization for war ended the Great Depression, reducing unemployment practically to zero. War jobs demanded workers, and Americans moved in huge numbers to war-production centers. The influx of workers strained the resources of existing communities and sometimes led to social friction and even violence. But many Americans—African Americans, Mexican Americans, women, poor whites from the South—found new opportunities for employment in well-paid war jobs.

The federal government, in order to manage the nation's war efforts, became a stronger presence in the lives of individual Americans—regulating business and employment; overseeing military conscription, training, and deployment; and even controlling what people could buy to eat or to wear. The Second World War was a powerful engine of social change.

Americans emerged from World War II fully confident that theirs was the greatest country in the world. It was certainly the most powerful: at war's end, only the United States had the capital and economic resources to spur international recovery; only the United States was more prosperous and more secure than when war began. In the coming struggle to fashion a new world out of the ashes of the old, soon to be called the Cold War, the United States held a commanding position. For better or worse—and clearly there were elements of each—the Second World War was a turning point in the nation's history.

LEGACY FOR A PEOPLE AND A NATION
Atomic Waste

Although victory in the Second World War tasted sweet to the American people, the war's environmental legacy proved noxious, not to mention toxic and deadly. New industries brought with them hazardous pollutants. The production of synthetic rubber spewed forth sulfur dioxide, carbon monoxide, and other dangerous gases. War industries fouled the water and the soil with both solid and petrochemical wastes. Air pollution—smog—was first detected in Los Angeles in 1943, the result of that city's rapid wartime industrialization combined with widespread dependence on the automobile. Although these were ominous signs, few people at the time worried about human-made threats to America's seemingly endless supplies of fresh air, water, and soil.

No wartime or postwar weapons program became more threatening to the natural environment than the project to develop the atomic bomb. Many of the bomb's ingredients—notably plutonium, beryllium, and mercury—are highly toxic and contaminate the environment. The storing of radioactive waste began during the war at Oak Ridge, Tennessee, and Hanford, Washington, where plutonium was produced. During the postwar nuclear arms race with the Soviet Union, the United States opened other production facilities—for example, at Rocky Flats in Colorado and on the Savannah River in South Carolina. At these sites, radioactive waste seeped from leaky barrels into the soil and water, threatening human life and killing fish, birds, and other wildlife. Moreover, during 1945–1963, nuclear testing, which was done above ground, killed an estimated 800,000 Americans from cancers attributable to radioactive fallout.

The environmental legacy of the atomic bomb continues to threaten the American people. The biggest problem of the new millennium remains the oldest problem: how to dispose of radioactive materials. In 1999, when the federal government opened the nation's first nuclear storage facility in New Mexico, the initial shipment came from Los Alamos National Laboratory, New Mexico, birthplace of the atomic bomb. Scientists are skeptical that current technology is up to the task of cleaning soil and water at the nuclear weapons sites. "The technology . . . used to remediate contaminated sites," said the chairman of a National Resource Council task force that studied the problem, "is simply ineffective and unable to accomplish the massive job that needs to be done."

The **history companion** *powered by Eduspace*®
Your primary source for interactive quizzes, exercises, and more to help you learn efficiently.
http://history.college.hmco.com/students

THE COLD WAR AND AMERICAN GLOBALISM 1945–1961

*O*n July 16, 1945, the "Deer" Team leader parachuted into northern Vietnam, near Kimlung, a village in a valley of rice paddies. Colonel Allison Thomas could not know that the end of the Second World War was just weeks away, but he and the other five members of his Office of Strategic Services (OSS) unit knew their mission: to work with the Vietminh, a nationalist Vietnamese organization, to sabotage Japanese forces that in March had seized Vietnam from France. After disentangling himself from the banyan tree into which his parachute had slammed him, Thomas spoke a "few flowery sentences" to two hundred Vietminh soldiers assembled near a banner proclaiming "Welcome to Our American Friends." Ho Chi Minh, head of the Vietminh, ill but speaking in good English, cordially greeted the OSS team and offered supper. The next day Ho denounced the French but remarked that "we welcome 10 million Americans." "Forget the Communist Bogy," Thomas radioed OSS headquarters in China.

A communist who had worked for decades to win his nation's independence from France, Ho joined the French Communist Party after World War I to use it as a vehicle for Vietnamese independence. For the next two decades, living in China, the Soviet Union, and elsewhere, Ho patiently planned and fought to free his nation from French colonialism. During World War II, Ho's Vietminh warriors harassed both French and Japanese forces and rescued downed American pilots. In March 1945 Ho met with U.S. officials in China, where he read the *Encyclopaedia Britannica* and *Time* magazine at an Office of War Information facility. Receiving no aid from his ideological allies in the Soviet Union, Ho hoped that the United States would favor his nation's long quest for liberation from colonialism.

Other OSS personnel soon parachuted into Kimlung, including a male nurse who diagnosed Ho's ailments as malaria and dysentery; quinine and sulfa drugs

◄ The Vietnamese nationalist Ho Chi Minh (1890–1969) meets with OSS "Deer" team members in 1945. On the far left is Ho's military aide Vo Nguyen Giap. (Private Collection)

CHRONOLOGY

1945 • Roosevelt dies and Truman becomes president
     • Atomic bombings of Japan

1946 • Kennan's "long telegram" criticizes USSR
     • Vietnamese war against France erupts

1947 • Truman Doctrine seeks aid for Greece and Turkey
     • Marshall offers Europe economic assistance
     • National Security Act reorganizes government

1948 • Communists take power in Czechoslovakia
     • Truman recognizes Israel
     • U.S. organizes Berlin airlift

1949 • NATO founded as anti-Soviet alliance
     • Soviet Union explodes atomic bomb
     • Mao's communists win power in China

1950 • NSC-68 recommends major military buildup
     • Korean War starts in June; China enters in fall

1951 • U.S. signs Mutual Security Treaty with Japan

1953 • Eisenhower becomes president
     • Stalin dies
     • U.S. helps restore shah to power in Iran
     • Korean War ends

1954 • Geneva accords partition Vietnam
     • CIA-led coup overthrows Arbenz in Guatemala

1955 • Soviets create Warsaw Pact

1956 • Soviets crush uprising in Hungary
     • Suez crisis sparks war in Middle East

1957 • Soviets fire first ICBM and launch *Sputnik*

1958 • U.S. troops land in Lebanon
     • Berlin crisis

1959 • Castro ousts Batista in Cuba

1960 • Eighteen African colonies become independent
     • Vietcong organized in South Vietnam

restored his health, but Ho remained frail. As a sign of friendship, the Americans in Vietnam named Ho "OSS Agent 19." Everywhere the Americans went, impoverished villagers thanked them with gifts of food and clothing, despite the devastating famine of 1944–1945 in which at least a million Vietnamese died. The villagers interpreted the foreigners' presence as a sign of U.S. anti-colonial and anti-Japanese sentiments. In early August the Deer Team began to give Vietminh soldiers weapons training. During many conversations with the OSS members, Ho said he hoped young Vietnamese could study in the United States and that American technicians could help build an independent Vietnam. Citing history, Ho remarked that "your statesmen make eloquent speeches about . . . self-determination. We are self-determined. Why not help us? Am I any different from . . . your George Washington?"

A second OSS unit, the "Mercy" Team, headed by Captain Archimedes Patti, arrived in the city of Hanoi on August 22. When Patti met Ho—"this wisp of a man," as Patti put it—the Vietminh leader applauded America's assistance and called for future "collaboration." But, unbeknownst to these OSS members, who believed that President Franklin D. Roosevelt's general sympathy for eventual Vietnamese independence remained U.S. policy, the new Truman administration in Washington had decided to let France decide the fate of Vietnam. That change in policy explains why Ho never received answers to the several letters and telegrams he sent to Washington—the first dated August 30, 1945.

On September 2, 1945, amid great fanfare in Hanoi, with OSS personnel present, an emotional Ho Chi Minh read his declaration of independence for the Democratic Republic of Vietnam: "All men are created equal; they are endowed by their Creator with certain unalienable Rights; among these are Life, Liberty, and the pursuit of Happiness." Having borrowed from the internationally renowned 1776 American document, Ho then itemized Vietnamese grievances against France. At one point in the ceremonies, two American P-38 aircraft swooped down over the crowded square. The Vietnamese cheered, interpreting the flyby as U.S. endorsement of their independence. Actually, the pilots had no orders to make a political statement; they just wanted to see what was happening.

By late September both OSS teams had departed Vietnam. In a last meeting with Captain Patti, Ho expressed his sadness that the United States had armed the French to reestablish their colonial rule in Vietnam. Sure, Ho said, U.S. officials in Washington judged him a "Moscow puppet" because he was a communist. But Ho claimed that he drew inspiration from the American struggle for independence and that he was foremost "a free agent," a nationalist. If necessary, Ho insisted, the Vietnamese would go it alone, with or without American or Soviet help. And they did—first against the French and eventually against more than half a million U.S. troops in what became America's longest war. How different world history would have been had President Harry S Truman responded favorably to Ho Chi Minh's last letter to Washington, dated February 16, 1946, which asked the United States "as guardians and champions of World Justice to take a decisive step in support of our independence."

Because Ho Chi Minh and many of his nationalist followers had declared themselves communists, U.S. leaders rejected their appeal. Endorsing the containment doctrine to draw the line against communism everywhere, American presidents from Truman to George H. W. Bush believed that a ruthless Soviet Union was directing a worldwide communist conspiracy against peace, free-market capitalism, and political democracy. Soviet leaders from Joseph Stalin to Mikhail Gorbachev protested that a militarized, economically aggressive United States sought nothing less than world domination. This protracted contest between the United States and the Soviet Union acquired the name Cold War.

The primary feature of world affairs for more than four decades, the Cold War was fundamentally a bipolar contest between the United States and the Soviet Union over spheres of influence, over world power. Decisions made in Washington and Moscow dominated world politics as the capitalist "West" squared off with the communist "East." The contest dominated international relations and eventually took the lives of millions, cost trillions of dollars, spawned fears of doomsday, and destabilized one nation after another. On occasion the two superpowers negotiated at summit conferences and signed agreements to temper their dangerous arms race; at other times they went to the brink of war and armed allies to fight vicious Third World conflicts. Sometimes, these allies had their own ideas and ambitions, and they often proved adept at resisting pressure applied on them by one or both of the superpowers. Over time, American and Soviet leaders came to realize that, notwithstanding the immense military might at their disposal, their power to affect change was in key respects limited.

Vietnam was part of the Third World, a general term for those nations that during the Cold War era wore neither the "West" (the "First World") nor the "East" (the "Second World") label. Sometimes called "developing countries," Third World nations on the whole were nonwhite, nonindustrialized, and located in the southern half of the globe—in Asia, Africa, the Middle East, and Latin America. Many had been colonies of European nations or Japan, and they were vulnerable to the Cold War rivalry that intruded on them. U.S. leaders often interpreted their anticolonialism, political instability, and restrictions on foreign-owned property as Soviet or communist inspired or capable of being exploited by Moscow—in short, as Cold War matters rather than as expressions of profound indigenous nationalism. As an example, Vietnam became one among many sites where Cold War fears and Third World aspirations intersected, prompting American intervention. Such intervention bespoke a globalist foreign policy, meaning U.S. officials now regarded the entire world as the appropriate sphere for America's influence.

Critics in the United States challenged the architects of the Cold War, questioning their exaggerations of threats from abroad, meddlesome interventions in the Third World, and the expensive militarization of foreign policy. But when leaders such as Truman described the Cold War in extremist terms as a life-and-death struggle against a monstrous enemy, legitimate criticism became suspect and dissenters were discredited. Critics' searching questions about America's global, interventionist foreign policy and its reliance on nuclear weapons were drowned out by charges that dissenters were "soft on communism," if not un-American. Decision makers in the United States successfully cultivated a Cold War consensus that stifled debate and shaped the mindset of generations of Americans. ■

From Allies to Adversaries

*T*he Second World War had a deeply unsettling effect on the international system. At its end, Germany was in ruins. Great Britain was badly overstrained and exhausted; France, having endured five years of Nazi occupation, was rent by internal division. Italy also emerged drastically weakened, while in Asia Japan was decimated and under occupation and China was headed toward a renewed civil war. Throughout Europe and Asia, factories and transportation and communications links had been reduced to rubble. Agricultural production plummeted, and displaced persons wandered around in search of food and family. How would the devastated economic world be pieced back together? The United States and the Soviet Union, though they had been allies in the war, offered very different answers and models. The collapse of Germany and Japan, moreover, had created power vacuums that drew the two major powers into collision as they sought influence in countries where the Axis aggressors once had held sway. And the political turmoil that many nations experienced after the war also spurred Soviet-American competition. For example, in Greece and China, where civil wars raged between leftists and conservative regimes, the two powers supported different sides.

The international system also became unstable because empires were disintegrating, creating the new Third World. Financial constraints and *DECOLONIZATION* nationalist rebellions forced the imperial states to set their colonies free. Britain exited India (and Pakistan) in 1947 and Burma and Sri Lanka (Ceylon) in 1948. The Philippines gained independence from the United States in 1946. After four years of battling nationalists in Indonesia, the Dutch left in 1949. In the Middle East, Lebanon (1943), Syria (1946), and Jordan (1946) gained independence, while in Palestine British officials faced growing pressure from Zionists intent on creating a Jewish homeland and from Arab leaders opposed to the prospect. In Iraq, too, nationalist agitation increased against the British-installed government. Washington and Moscow paid close attention to this anticolonial ferment, seeing these new or emerging Third World states as potential allies that might provide military bases, resources, and markets. Not all new nations were willing to play along; some chose nonalignment in the Cold War. "We do not intend to be the playthings of others," declared India's leader, Jawaharlal Nehru.

Driven by different ideologies and different economic and strategic needs in this volatile international *STALIN'S AIMS* climate, the United States and the Soviet Union assessed their most pressing tasks in very different terms. The Soviets, though committed to seeking ultimate victory over the capitalist countries, were most concerned about preventing another invasion of their homeland. It was a homeland much less secure than the United States, for reasons both geographical and historical. Its land mass was huge—three times as large as that of the United States—but it had only 10,000 miles of seacoast, much of which was under ice for a large part of the year. Russian leaders both before and after the revolution had made increased maritime access a chief foreign policy aim.

What is more, the geographical frontiers of the USSR were hard to defend. Siberia, vital for its mineral resources, lay 6,000 miles east of Moscow, and was vulnerable to encroachment by Japan and China. In the west, the border with Poland had generated violent clashes ever since World War I, and eastern Europe had been the launching pad for Hitler's invasion in 1941: the resulting war cost the lives of at least 20 million Russians and caused massive physical destruction. Henceforth, Soviet leaders determined, they could have no dangers along their western borders.

Overall, however, Soviet territorial objectives were limited. Though many Americans were quick to compare Stalin to Hitler, Stalin did not have the Nazi leader's grandiose plans for world hegemony (predominance). In general, his aims resembled those of czars before him: he wanted to push the USSR's borders to include the Baltic states of Estonia, Latvia, and Lithuania, as well as the eastern part of prewar Poland. Fearful of a revived Germany, he sought pro-Soviet governments in eastern Europe. To the south, Stalin wanted to have a presence in northern Iran, and he pressed the Turks to grant him naval bases and free access out of the Black Sea. Economically, the Soviet government promoted economic independence more than trade with other countries; suspicious of their European neighbors, they did not promote rapid rebuilding of the war-ravaged economies of the region or, more generally, expanded world trade.

The leadership in the United States, by contrast, came out of the war extremely confident in the immediate security of the country's borders. Separated *U.S. ECONOMIC* from the other world powers by *AND STRATEGIC* two vast oceans, the American home *NEEDS* base had been virtually immune from attack during the fighting—only an occasional shell from a submarine or hostile balloon reached the shores of the continental United States. American casualties were fewer than any of the other major combatants—in comparison with the Soviet Union, hugely so. With its fixed capital intact, its resources more plentiful than ever, and in lone possession of the atomic bomb, the United States was the strongest power in the world at war's end.

Yet this was no time for complacency, Washington officials reminded one another. Some other power—almost certainly the USSR—could take advantage of the political and economic instability in war-torn Europe and Asia and eventually seize control of these areas, with dire implications for America's physical and economic security. To prevent this eventuality, officials in Washington sought forward bases overseas, in order to keep an airborne enemy at bay. To further enhance U.S. security, American planners, in direct contrast to their Soviet counterparts, sought the quick reconstruction of nations—including the former enemies Germany and Japan—and a world economy based on free trade. Such a system, they reasoned, was essential to preserve America's economic well-being.

The Soviets, on the other hand, refused to join the new World Bank and International Monetary Fund (IMF), created at the July 1944 Bretton Woods Conference by forty-four nations to stabilize trade and finance. They held that the United States dominated both institutions and used them to promote private investment and open international commerce, which Moscow saw as capitalist tools of exploitation. With the United States as its largest donor, the World Bank opened its doors in 1945 and began to make loans to help members finance reconstruction projects; the IMF, also heavily backed by the United States, helped members meet their balance-of-payments problems through currency loans.

The personalities of the two countries' leaders also mattered. Joseph Stalin, though hostile to the Western

STALIN AND TRUMAN

powers and capable of utter ruthlessness against his own people (his periodic purges since the 1930s had taken the lives of millions), had no wish for an immediate war. With the huge Russian losses in World War II, he was all too aware of his country's weakness vis-à-vis the United States. For a time, at least, he appears to have believed he could achieve his aspirations peacefully, through continued cooperation with the Americans and the British. Over the long term, though, he envisaged more conflict. Stalin believed that Germany and Japan would rise again to threaten the USSR, probably by the 1960s, and his suspicion of the other capitalist powers knew no bounds. Many have concluded Stalin was clinically paranoid: the first to do so, a leading Russian neuropathologist in 1927, died a few days later! As historian

■ The wartime Grand Alliance of the United States, Britain, and the Soviet Union was never without tension, but it succeeded in producing a victory over the Axis powers. This cover of *Time* magazine from May 14, 1945, celebrates the defeat of Nazi Germany. It was a high point in Soviet-American relations, but it would not last. (Time Life Pictures/Time Life Picture Collection/Getty Images)

David Reynolds has noted, this paranoia, coupled with Stalin's xenophobia (fear of anything foreign) and his Marxist-Leninist ideology, created in the Soviet leader a mental map of "them" versus "us" that decisively influenced his approach to world affairs.

Harry Truman had none of Stalin's capacity for deception or ruthlessness, but to a lesser degree he, too, was prone to a "them" versus "us" worldview. Truman often glossed over nuances, ambiguities, and counterevidence; he preferred the simple answer stated in either/or terms. As Winston Churchill, who admired Truman's decisiveness, once observed, the president "takes no notice of delicate ground, he just plants his foot firmly on it." Truman constantly exaggerated, as when he declared in his undelivered farewell address that he had "knocked the socks off the communists" in Korea. Shortly after Roosevelt's death in early 1945, Truman met the Soviet commissar of foreign affairs, V. M. Molotov, at the White House. When the president sharply protested that the Soviets were not fulfilling the Yalta agreement on Poland, Molotov stormed out. Truman had self-consciously developed what he called his "tough method," and he bragged after the encounter that "I gave it to him straight 'one-two to the jaw.'" Truman's display of toughness became a trademark of American Cold War diplomacy.

At what point did the Cold War actually begin? No precise start date can be given. The origins must be thought of as a process, one that arguably began in 1917 with the Bolshevik Revolution and the Western powers' hostile response, but which in a more meaningful sense began in mid-1945 as World War II drew to a close. By the spring of 1947, certainly, the struggle had begun.

THE BEGINNING OF THE COLD WAR

One of the first Soviet-American clashes came in Poland in 1945, when the Soviets refused to allow the Polish government-in-exile in London to be a part of the communist government Moscow sponsored. The Soviets also snuffed out civil liberties in the former Nazi satellite of Romania, justifying their actions by pointing to what they claimed was an equivalent U.S. manipulation of Italy. Moscow initially allowed free elections in Hungary and Czechoslovakia, but as the Cold War accelerated and U.S. influence in Europe expanded, the Soviets encouraged communist coups in Hungary (1947) and Czechoslovakia (1948). Yugoslavia stood as a unique case: its independent communist government, led by Josip Broz Tito, successfully broke with Stalin in 1948.

To defend their actions, Moscow officials pointed out that the United States was reviving their traditional enemy, Germany. Twice in the lifetime of Soviet leaders Germany had wrought enormous suffering on Russia, and Stalin and his associates were determined to prevent a third occurrence. The Soviets also protested that the United States was meddling in eastern Europe. They cited clandestine American meetings with anti-Soviet groups, repeated calls for elections likely to produce anti-Soviet regimes, and the use of loans to gain political influence (financial diplomacy). Moscow charged that the United States was pursuing a double standard—intervening in the affairs of eastern Europe but demanding that the Soviet Union stay out of Latin America and Asia. Americans called for free elections in the Soviet sphere, Moscow

noted, but not in the U.S. sphere in Latin America, where several military dictatorships ruled.

The atomic bomb also divided the two major powers. The Soviets believed that the United States was practicing "atomic diplomacy"—maintaining a nuclear monopoly to scare the Soviets into diplomatic concessions. Secretary of State James F. Byrnes thought that the atomic bomb gave the United States bargaining power and could serve as a deterrent to Soviet expansion, but Secretary of War Henry L. Stimson thought otherwise in 1945. If Americans continued to have "this weapon rather ostentatiously on our hip," he warned Truman, the Soviets' "suspicions and their distrust of our purposes and motives will increase."

ATOMIC DIPLOMACY

In this atmosphere of suspicion and distrust, Truman refused to turn over the weapon to an international control authority. In 1946 he backed the Baruch Plan, named after its author, financier Bernard Baruch. Largely a propaganda ploy, this proposal provided for U.S. abandonment of its atomic monopoly only after the world's fissionable materials were brought under the authority of an international agency. The Soviets retorted that this plan would require them to shut down their atomic-bomb development project while the United States continued its own. Washington and Moscow soon became locked into an expensive and frightening nuclear arms race.

By the middle of 1946, the wartime Grand Alliance was but a fading memory; that year, Soviets and Americans clashed on every front. When the United States turned down a Soviet request for a reconstruction loan but gave a loan to Britain, Moscow upbraided Washington for using its dollars to manipulate foreign governments. The two Cold War powers also backed different groups in Iran, where the United States helped bring the pro-West shah to the throne. Unable to agree on the unification of Germany, the former allies built up their zones independently.

After Stalin gave a speech in February 1946 that depicted the world as threatened by capitalist acquisitiveness, the American chargé d'affaires in Moscow, George F. Kennan, sent a pessimistic "long telegram" to Washington. Kennan asserted that Soviet fanaticism made even a temporary understanding impossible. His widely circulated report fed a growing belief among American officials that only toughness would work with the Soviets. The following month, Winston Churchill delivered a stirring speech in Fulton, Missouri. The former British prime minister warned that a Soviet-erected "iron curtain" had cut off eastern Euro-

WARNINGS FROM KENNAN AND CHURCHILL

pean countries from the West. With an approving Truman sitting on the stage, Churchill called for Anglo-American partnership to resist the new menace.

The growing Soviet-American tensions had major implications for the functioning of the United Nations. The delegates who gathered in San Francisco in April 1945 to sign the U.N. charter had agreed on an organization that would include a General Assembly of all member states as well as a smaller Security Council that would take the lead on issues of peace and security. Five great powers were given permanent seats on the council—the United States, the Soviet Union, Great Britain, China, and France. These permanent members could not prohibit discussion of any issue, but they could exercise a veto against any proposed action. To be effective on the major issues of war and peace, therefore, the U.N. needed great-power cooperation of the type that had existed in wartime but was a distant memory by mid-1946. Of the fifty-one founding states, twenty-two came from the Americas and another fifteen from Europe, which in effect gave the United States a large majority in the assembly. In retaliation, Moscow began to exercise its veto in the Security Council.

Some high-level U.S. officials were dismayed by the administration's harsh anti-Soviet posture. Secretary of Commerce Henry A. Wallace, who had been Roosevelt's vice president before Truman, charged that Truman's get-tough policy was substituting atomic and economic coercion for diplomacy. Wallace told a Madison Square Garden audience in September 1946 that " 'getting tough' never brought anything real and lasting—whether for schoolyard bullies or businessmen or world powers. The tougher we get, the tougher the Russians will get." Truman soon fired Wallace from the cabinet, blasting him privately as "a real Commy and a dangerous man" and boasting that he, Truman, had now "run the crackpots out of the Democratic Party."

East-West tensions escalated further in early 1947, when the British requested American help in Greece

TRUMAN DOCTRINE

to defend their conservative client-government (a government that is dependent on the economic or military support of a more powerful country) in a civil war against leftists. In his March 12, 1947, speech to Congress, Truman requested $400 million in aid to Greece and Turkey. He had a selling job to do. The Republican Eightieth Congress wanted less, not more, spending; many of its members had little respect for the Democratic president whose administration the voters had repudiated in the 1946 elections by giving the GOP ("Grand Old Party," the Republican Party) majorities in

both houses of Congress. Republican senator Arthur Vandenberg of Michigan, a bipartisan leader who backed Truman's request, bluntly told the president that he would have to "scare hell out of the American people" to gain congressional approval.

With that advice in mind, the president delivered a speech laced with alarmist language intended to stake out the American role in the postwar world. Truman claimed that communism, feeding on economic dislocations, imperiled the world. "If Greece should fall under the control of an armed minority," he gravely concluded in an early version of the domino theory (see page 784), "the effect upon its neighbor, Turkey, would be immediate and serious. Confusion and disorder might well spread throughout the entire Middle East." Truman articulated what became known as the Truman Doctrine: "I believe that it must be the policy of the United States to support free peoples who are resisting attempted subjugation by armed minorities or by outside pressures."

Critics correctly pointed out that the Soviet Union was little involved in the Greek civil war, that the communists in Greece were more pro-Tito than pro-Stalin, and that the resistance movement had noncommunist as well as communist members. Nor was the Soviet Union threatening Turkey at the time. Others suggested that such aid should be channeled through the United Nations. Truman countered that should communists gain control of Greece, they might open the door to Soviet power in the Mediterranean. After much debate, the Senate approved Truman's request by 67 to 23 votes. Using U.S. dollars and military advisers, the Greek government defeated the insurgents in 1949, and Turkey became a staunch U.S. ally on the Soviets' border.

In the months after Truman's speech, the term Cold War slipped into the lexicon as a description of the Soviet-

INEVITABLE COLD WAR?

American relationship. Less than two years had passed since the glorious victory over the Axis powers, and the two Grand Alliance members now found themselves locked in a tense struggle for world dominance. It would last almost half a century. Could the confrontation have been avoided? Not altogether, it seems clear. Even before World War II had ended, perceptive observers anticipated that the United States and the USSR would seek to fill the power vacuum that would exist after the armistice, and that friction would result. The two countries had a history of hostility and tension, and both were militarily powerful. Most of all, the two nations were divided by sharply differing political economies with widely divergent needs, and a deep ideological chasm. Some kind of confrontation was destined to occur.

■ On March 5, 1946, former British prime minister Winston S. Churchill (1874–1965) delivered a speech, which he intended for a worldwide audience, at Westminster College in Fulton, Missouri. President Harry S Truman *(right)* had encouraged Churchill *(seated)* to speak on two themes: the need to block Soviet expansion and the need to form an Anglo-American partnership. Always eloquent and provocative, Churchill denounced the Soviets for drawing an "iron curtain" across eastern Europe. This speech became one of the landmark statements of the Cold War.   (Harry S Truman Library)

It is far less clear that the conflict had to result in a Cold War. The "cold peace" that had prevailed from the revolution in 1917 through World War II could conceivably have been maintained into the postwar years as well. Neither side's leadership wanted war. Both hoped—at least in the initial months—that a spirit of cooperation could be maintained. The Cold War resulted from decisions by individual human beings who might well have chosen differently, who might have done more, for example, to maintain diplomatic dialogue, to seek negotiated solutions to complex international problems. For decades, many Americans would wonder if the high price they were paying for victory in the superpower confrontation was necessary.

Containment in Action

*H*aving committed themselves to countering Soviet and communist expansion, the Truman team had to figure out just how to fight the Cold War. The policy they chose, containment, was in place before the term was coined. George Kennan, having moved from the U.S. embassy in Moscow to the State Department in Washington, published an influential statement of the containment doctrine. Writing as "Mr. X" in the July 1947 issue of the magazine *Foreign Affairs*, Kennan advocated a "policy of firm containment, designed to confront the Russians with unalterable counterforce at every point where they show signs of encroaching upon the interests of a peaceful and stable world." Such counterforce, Kennan argued, would check Soviet expansion and eventually foster a "mellowing" of Soviet behavior. Along with the Truman Doctrine, Kennan's "X" article became a key manifesto of Cold War policy.

The veteran journalist Walter Lippmann took issue with the containment doctrine in his slim but powerful book *The Cold War* (1947), calling it a "strategic monstrosity" that failed to distinguish between areas vital and peripheral to U.S. security. If American leaders defined every place on earth as strategically important, Lippmann reasoned, the nation's patience and resources soon would be drained. Nor did Lippmann share Truman's conviction that the Soviet Union was plotting to take over the world. The president, he asserted, put too little emphasis on diplomacy. Ironically, Kennan himself agreed with much of Lippmann's critique, and he soon began to distance himself from the doctrine he had helped to create.

LIPPMANN'S CRITIQUE

Invoking the containment doctrine, the United States in 1947 and 1948 began to build an international economic and defensive network to protect American prosperity and security and to advance U.S. hegemony. In western Europe, the region of primary concern, American diplomats pursued a range of objectives, including economic reconstruction and fostering a political environment friendly to the United States. They sought the ouster of communists from governments, as occurred in 1947 in France and Italy, and blockage of "third force" or neutralist tendencies. To maintain political stability in key capitals, U.S. officials worked to keep the decolonization of European empires orderly. In Germany, they advocated the unification of the western zones. At the same time, American culture—consumer goods, music, consumption ethic, and production techniques—permeated

European societies. Some Europeans resisted Americanization, but transatlantic ties strengthened.

The first instrument designed to achieve U.S. goals in western Europe was the Marshall Plan. European

MARSHALL PLAN nations, still reeling economically and unstable politically, lacked the dollars to buy vital American-made goods. Americans, who already had spent billions of dollars on European relief and recovery by 1947, remembered all too well the troubles of the 1930s: global depression, political extremism, and war born of economic discontent. Such cataclysms could not be allowed to happen again; communism must not replace fascism. Western Europe, said one State Department diplomat, was "the keystone in the arch which supports the kind of a world which we have to have in order to conduct our lives."

In June 1947 Secretary of State George C. Marshall announced that the United States would finance a massive European recovery program. Launched in 1948, the Marshall Plan sent $12.4 billion to western Europe be-

fore the program ended in 1951 (see Map 28.1). To stimulate business at home, the legislation required that Europeans spend the foreign-aid dollars in the United States on American-made products. The Marshall Plan proved a mixed success; some scholars today even argue that Europe could have revived without it. The program caused inflation, failed to solve a balance-of-payments problem, took only tentative steps toward economic integration, and further divided Europe between "East" and "West." But the program spurred impressive western European industrial production and investment and started the region toward self-sustaining economic growth. From the American perspective, moreover, the plan succeeded because it helped contain communism.

To streamline the administration of U.S. defense, Truman worked with Congress on the National Security

NATIONAL SECURITY ACT Act of July 1947. The act created the Office of Secretary of Defense (which became the Department of Defense two years later) to oversee all branches of

■ Under official postwar relief and recovery programs, including the Marshall Plan, the United States shipped billions of dollars' worth of food and equipment to western European nations struggling to overcome the destruction of the Second World War. Private efforts also succeeded, such as this one in 1950. The people of Jersey City, New Jersey, sent this snowplow to the mountainous village of Capracotta, Italy.   (Corbis-Bettmann)

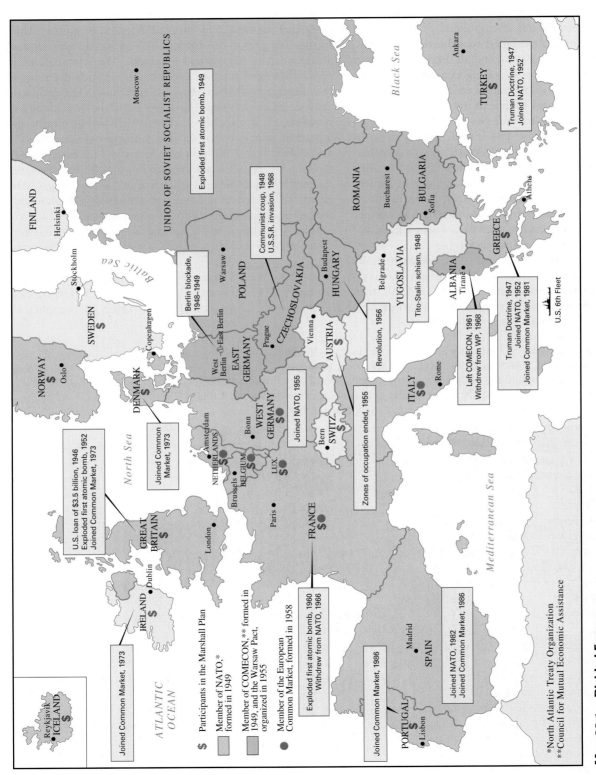

Map 28.1   Divided Europe

After the Second World War, Europe broke into two competing camps. When the United States launched the Marshall Plan in 1948, the Soviet Union countered with its own economic plan the following year. When the United States created NATO in 1949, the Soviet Union answered with the Warsaw Pact in 1955. On the whole, these two camps held firm until the late 1980s.

the armed services, the National Security Council (NSC) of high-level officials to advise the president, and the Central Intelligence Agency (CIA) to conduct spy operations and information gathering overseas. By the early 1950s the CIA had become a significant member of the national security state and had expanded its functions to include covert (secret) operations aimed at overthrowing unfriendly foreign leaders and, as a high-ranking American official put it, a "Department of Dirty Tricks" to stir up economic trouble in "the camp of the enemy." Taken together, the components of the National Security Act gave the president increased powers with which to conduct foreign policy.

In the wake of the Marshall Plan and the National Security Act, Stalin hardened his Cold War posture. He forbade communist satellite governments in eastern Europe to accept Marshall Plan aid and ordered communist parties in western Europe to work to thwart the plan. He also created the Cominform, an organization designed to coordinate communist activities around the world. It was a classic example of what the historian Herbert Butterfield called the "security dilemma": whereas American planners saw the Marshall Plan as helping their European friends achieve security against a potential Soviet threat, in Stalin's mind it raised anew the specter of capitalist penetration. He responded by tightening his grip on eastern Europe—most notably, he engineered a coup in Czechoslovakia in February 1948 that ensured full Soviet control of the country—which in turn created more anxiety in the United States. In this way the U.S.-Soviet relationship became a downward spiral that seemed to gain in velocity with each passing month.

The German problem remained especially intractable. In June 1948, the Americans, French, and British agreed to fuse their German zones, including their three sectors of Berlin. They sought to integrate West Germany (the Federal Republic of Germany) into the western European economy, complete with a reformed German currency. Fearing a resurgent Germany tied to the American Cold War camp, the Soviets cut off Western land access to the jointly occupied city of Berlin, located well inside the Soviet zone. In response to this bold move, President Truman ordered a massive airlift of food, fuel, and other supplies to Berlin. Their spoiling effort blunted, the Soviets finally lifted the blockade in May 1949 and founded the German Democratic Republic, or East Germany.

BERLIN BLOCKADE AND AIRLIFT

The successful airlift was a big victory for Harry Truman, and it may have saved his political career: he surprised pundits by narrowly defeating Republican Thomas E. Dewey in the presidential election that occurred in the middle of the crisis in November 1948. Safely elected, Truman took the major step of formalizing what was already in essence a military alliance among the United States, Canada, and the nations of western Europe. In April 1949, twelve nations signed a mutual defense treaty, agreeing that an attack on any one of them would be considered an attack on all, and establishing the North Atlantic Treaty Organization (NATO) (see Map 28.1).

The treaty aroused considerable domestic debate, for not since 1778 had the United States entered a formal European military alliance, and some critics, such as Senator Robert A. Taft, Republican of Ohio, claimed that NATO would provoke rather than deter war. Other critics argued that the Soviet threat was political, not military. Administration officials themselves did not anticipate a Soviet military thrust against western Europe, but they responded that, should the Soviets ever probe westward, NATO would function as a "tripwire," bringing the full force of the United States to bear on the Soviet Union. Truman officials also hoped that NATO would keep western Europeans from embracing communism or even neutralism in the Cold War. The Senate ratified the treaty by 82 votes to 13, and the United States soon began to spend billions of dollars under the Mutual Defense Assistance Act.

By the summer of 1949, Truman and his advisers were basking in the successes of their foreign policy. Containment was working splendidly, they and many outside observers had concluded. West Germany was on the road to recovery. The Berlin blockade had been defeated, and NATO had been formed. In western Europe, the threat posed by communist parties seemed lessened. True, there was trouble in China, where the communists under Mao Zedong were winning that country's civil war. But that struggle would likely wax and wane for years or even decades to come, and besides, Truman could not be held responsible for events there. Just possibly, some dared to think, Harry Truman was on his way to winning the Cold War.

Then, suddenly, in late September, came the "twin shocks," two momentous developments that made Americans feel in even greater danger than ever before—two decades later, they were still dealing with the reverberations. First, an American reconnaissance aircraft detected unusually high radioactivity in the atmosphere. The news stunned U.S. officials: the Soviets had exploded an atomic bomb. With the American nuclear monopoly erased, western Europe seemed more vulnerable. At the

TWIN SHOCKS

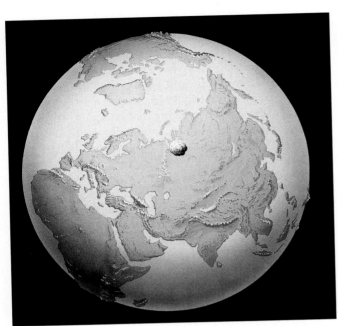

■ Richard Edes Harrison's illustration of the Soviet Union's detonation of an atomic bomb appeared in the October 1949 issue of *Life* magazine. A leading journalist-cartographer of the mid-20th century, Harrison was known for incorporating a global perspective in his work. Here he uses a single cloud of smoke to suggest the potentially far-reaching effects of an isolated bomb explosion. (Library of Congress)

same time, the communists in China completed their conquest—the end came more quickly than many expected. Now the world's largest and most populous countries were ruled by communists, and one of them had the atomic weapon. The bipartisan foreign policy of 1945–1948 broke down as Republicans, bitter over Truman's reelection, declared that traitors in America must have given Stalin the bomb and allowed China to be "lost."

Rejecting calls by Kennan and others for high-level negotiations, Truman in early 1950 gave the go-ahead to begin production of a hydrogen bomb, the "Super," and ordered his national security team to undertake a thorough review of policy. Kennan bemoaned the militarization of the Cold War and was replaced at the State Department by Paul Nitze. The National Security Council delivered to the president in April 1950 a significant top-secret document tagged NSC-68. Predicting continued tension with expansionistic communists all over the world and describing "a shrinking world of polarized power," the report, whose primary author was Nitze, appealed for a much enlarged military budget and the mobilization of public opinion to support such an increase. The Cold War was about to become a vastly more expensive, more far-reaching affair.

The Cold War in Asia

Though Europe was the principal battleground in the early Cold War, Asia gradually became ensnared in the conflict as well. Indeed, it was in Asia that the consequences of an expansive containment doctrine would exact its heaviest price on the United States, in the form of large-scale and bloody wars in Korea and Vietnam. Though always less important to both superpowers than Europe, Asia would be the continent where the Cold War most often turned hot.

From the start, Washington officials saw Japan as a key element in its Asian strategy. Much to Stalin's dismay, the United States monopolized Japan's reconstruction through a military occupation directed by General Douglas MacArthur, who envisioned turning the Pacific Ocean into "an Anglo-Saxon lake." Truman did not like "Mr. Prima Donna, Brass Hat" MacArthur, but the general initiated "a democratic revolution from above," as the Japanese called it, that reflected Washington's wishes. MacArthur wrote a democratic constitution, gave women voting rights, revitalized the economy, and destroyed the nation's weapons. U.S. authorities also helped Americanize Japan through censorship; films that hinted at criticism of the United States (for the destruction of Hiroshima, for example) or that depicted traditional Japanese customs such as suicide, arranged marriages, and swordplay were banned. In 1951, against Soviet protests, the United States and Japan signed a separate peace that restored Japan's sovereignty and ended the occupation. A Mutual Security Treaty that year provided for the stationing of U.S. forces on Japanese soil, including a base on Okinawa.

The administration had less success in China. The United States had long backed the Nationalists of Jiang Jieshi (Chiang Kai-shek) against Mao Zedong's communists. But after the Second World War, Generalissimo Jiang became an unreliable partner who rejected U.S. advice. His government had become corrupt, inefficient, and out of touch with discontented peasants, whom the communists enlisted with promises of land reform. Jiang also subverted American efforts to negotiate a cease-fire and a coalition government. "We picked a bad horse," Truman admitted, privately denouncing the Nationalists as "grafters and crooks." Still, seeing Jiang

CHINESE CIVIL WAR

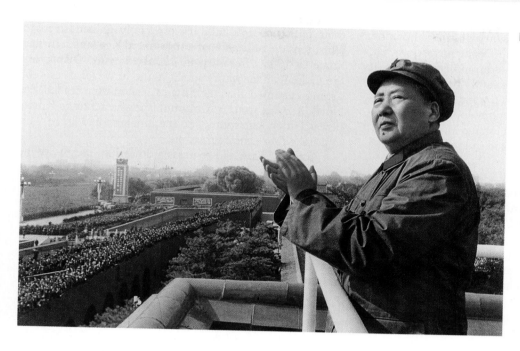

■ Mao Zedong was a military theoretician who also involved himself in day-to-day military decision making. He was responsible for, or at least approved, all of the major strategic moves the communists made on their way to power. This image shows him applauding soldiers and other supporters on Tiananmen Square in Beijing.   (Sovfoto/Eastfoto)

as the only alternative to Mao, Truman backed him to the end.

American officials divided on the question of whether Mao was a puppet of the Soviet Union. Some considered him an Asian Tito—communist but independent—but most believed him to be part of an international communist movement that might give the Soviets a springboard into Asia. Thus when the Chinese communists made secret overtures to the United States to begin diplomatic talks in 1945 and again in 1949, American officials rebuffed them. Mao decided to "lean" to the Soviet side in the Cold War. Because China always maintained a fierce independence that rankled the Soviets, before long a Sino-Soviet schism opened. Indeed, Mao deeply resented the Soviets' refusal to aid the communists during the civil war; Stalin offered no help, "not even a fart," Mao once growled.

Then came Mao's victory in September 1949. Jiang fled to the island of Formosa (Taiwan), and in Beijing (formerly Peking) Mao proclaimed the People's Republic of China (PRC). Truman hesitated to extend diplomatic recognition to the new government, even after the British prime minister asked him: "Are we to cut ourselves off from all contact with one-sixth of the inhabitants of the world?" U.S. officials became alarmed by the 1950 Sino-Soviet treaty of friendship and by the harassment of Americans and their property in China. Truman also chose nonrecognition because a vocal group of Republican critics, the so-called China lobby, was winning head-

lines by asking the question, "Who lost China?" The publisher Henry Luce, Senator William Knowland of California, and Representative Walter Judd of Minnesota pinned Jiang's defeat on Truman. The president stoutly answered that the self-defeating Jiang, despite billions of dollars in American aid, had proven a poor instrument of the containment doctrine. The administration nonetheless took the politically safe route and rejected recognition. (Not until 1979 did official Sino-American relations resume.)

Mao's victory in China drew urgent American attention to Indochina, the southeast Asian peninsula that had

VIETNAM'S QUEST FOR INDEPENDENCE

been held by France for the better part of a century. The Japanese had wrested control over Indochina during World War II, but even then Vietnamese nationalists dedicated to independence grew in strength. Their leader Ho Chi Minh hoped to use Japan's defeat to assert Vietnamese independence, and he asked for U.S. support. American officials had few kind things to say about French colonial policy, and many were pessimistic that France could achieve a military solution to the conflict. Nevertheless, they rejected Ho's appeals in favor of a restoration of French rule, mostly to ensure France's cooperation in the Cold War. Paris warned that American support of the Vietnamese independence movement would alienate French public opinion and strengthen the French Communist Party, perhaps even drive France into the arms of the USSR. In addition, the Truman administration was wary of Ho Chi Minh's communist politics. Ho, the State Department declared, was an "agent of international communism," who, it was assumed, would assist Soviet and, after 1949, Chinese expansionism. Overlooking the native roots of the nationalist rebellion against French colonialism, and the tenacious Vietnamese resistance to foreign intruders, Washington officials interpreted events in Indochina through a Cold War lens.

Even so, when war between the Vietminh and France broke out in 1946, the United States initially took a hands-off approach. But when Jiang's regime collapsed in China three years later, the Truman administration made two crucial decisions—both in early 1950, before the Korean War. First, in February, Washington recognized the French puppet government of Bao Dai, a playboy and former emperor who had collaborated with the French and Japanese. In the eyes of many Vietnamese, the United States thus became in essence a colonial power, an ally of the hated French. Second, in May, the administration agreed to send weapons, and ultimately military advisers, to sustain the French in Indochina. From 1945 to 1954, the United States gave $2 billion of the $5 billion that France spent to keep Vietnam within its empire—to no avail, as we shall see (in Chapters 30 and 31). How Vietnam ultimately became the site of America's longest war, and how the world's most powerful nation failed to subdue a peasant people who suffered enormous losses, is one of the most remarkable and tragic stories of modern history.

The Korean War

Before Vietnam, however, the United States would fight another large-scale military conflict, in Korea. In the early morning of June 25, 1950, a large military force of the Democratic People's Republic of Korea (North Korea) moved across the 38th parallel into the Republic of Korea (South Korea). Colonized by Japan since 1910, Korea had been divided in two by the victorious powers after Japan's defeat in 1945. Although the Soviets had armed the North and the Americans had armed the South (U.S. aid had reached $100 million a year), the Korean War began as a civil war. Virtually from the moment of the division, the two parts had been skirmishing along their supposedly temporary border while antigovernment (and anti-U.S.) guerrilla fighting flared in the South.

Both the North's communist leader Kim Il Sung and the South's president Syngman Rhee sought to reunify their nation. Kim's military especially gained strength when tens of thousands of battle-tested Koreans returned home in 1949 after serving in Mao's army. Displaying the Cold War mentality of the time, however, President Truman claimed that the Soviets had masterminded the North Korean attack. "Communism was acting in Korea just as Hitler, Mussolini, and the Japanese had acted," he said, recalling Axis aggression.

Actually, Kim had to press a doubting Joseph Stalin, who only reluctantly approved the attack after Kim predicted an easy, early victory and after Mao backed Kim. Whatever Stalin's reasoning, his support for Kim's venture remained lukewarm. When the U.N. Security Council voted to defend South Korea against the invasion from the north, the Soviet representative was not even present to veto the resolution because the Soviets were boycotting the United Nations to protest its refusal to grant membership to the People's Republic of China. During the war, Moscow gave limited aid to North Korea and China, which grew angry at Stalin for reneging on promised Soviet airpower. Stalin, all too aware of his strategic inferiority vis-à-vis the United States, did not want to be dragged into a costly war.

STALIN'S DOUBTS

The president first ordered General Douglas MacArthur to send arms and troops to South Korea. He did not seek congressional approval for the decision—he and his aides feared that lawmakers would initiate a lengthy and perhaps divisive debate—and thereby set the precedent of waging war on executive authority alone. Worried that Mao might use the occasion to take Formosa, Truman also directed the Seventh Fleet to patrol the waters between the Chinese mainland and Jiang's sanctuary on Formosa, thus inserting the United States again into Chinese politics. After the Security Council voted to assist South Korea, MacArthur became commander of U.N. forces in Korea. Sixteen nations contributed troops to the U.N. command, but 40 percent were South Korean and about 50 percent American. In the war's early weeks, North Korean tanks and superior firepower sent the South Korean army into chaotic retreat. The first American soldiers, taking heavy casualties, could not stop the North Korean advance. Within weeks, the South Koreans and Americans had been pushed into the tiny Pusan perimeter at the tip of South Korea (see Map 28.2).

U.S. FORCES INTERVENE

General MacArthur planned a daring operation: an amphibious landing at heavily fortified Inchon, several hundred miles behind North Korean lines. After U.S. guns and bombs pounded Inchon, marines sprinted ashore on September 15, 1950. The operation was a brilliant success, and the troops soon liberated the South Korean capital of Seoul and pushed the North Koreans back to the 38th parallel. Even before Inchon, Truman had redefined the U.S. war goal, changing it from the containment of North Korea to the reunification of Korea by force. Communism not only would be stopped; it would be rolled back.

In September Truman authorized U.N. forces to cross the 38th parallel. These troops drove deep into North Korea, and American aircraft began strikes against bridges on the Yalu River, the border between North Korea and China. The Chinese watched warily, fearing that the Americans would next stab at the People's Republic. Mao publicly warned that China could not permit the bombing of its transportation links with Korea and would not accept the annihilation of North Korea itself. MacArthur shrugged off the warnings, and Washington officials agreed with the strong-willed general, drawing further confidence from the fact that, as MacArthur had predicted, the Soviets were not preparing for war.

CHINESE ENTRY INTO THE WAR

MacArthur was right about the Soviets, but wrong about the Chinese. Mao, concluding that the "Americans would run more rampant" unless stopped, on October 25 sent Chinese soldiers into the war near the Yalu. Perhaps to lure American forces into a trap or to signal willingness to begin negotiations, they pulled back after a brief and successful offensive against South Korean troops. Then, after MacArthur sent the U.S. Eighth Army northward, tens of thousands of Chinese troops counterattacked on November 26, surprising American forces and driving them pell-mell southward. One U.S. officer termed it "a sight that hasn't been seen for hundreds of years: the men of a whole United States Army fleeing from a battlefield, abandoning their wounded, running for their lives."

By early 1951 the front had stabilized around the 38th parallel. A stalemate set in. Both Washington and Moscow welcomed negotiations, but MacArthur had other ideas. The theatrical general recklessly called for an attack on China and for Jiang's return to the mainland. Now was the time, he insisted, to smash communism by destroying its Asian flank. Denouncing the concept of limited war (war without nuclear weapons, confined to one place), MacArthur hinted that the president was practicing appeasement. In April, backed by the Joint Chiefs of Staff (the heads of the various armed services), Truman fired MacArthur.

TRUMAN'S FIRING OF MACARTHUR

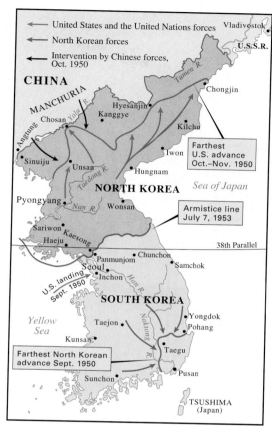

Map 28.2   The Korean War, 1950–1953

Beginning as a civil war between North and South, this war became international when the United States, under the auspices of the United Nations, and the People's Republic of China intervened with their military forces.   (Source: Adapted from Thomas G. Paterson, J. Garry Clifford, and Kenneth J. Hagan, *American Foreign Relations: A History,* vol. 2, 5th ed. Copyright © 2000 by Houghton Mifflin Company.)

The general, who had not set foot in the United States for more than a decade, returned home a hero, with ticker-tape parades and cheers on the lecture circuit. Truman's popularity sagged, but he weathered scattered demands for his impeachment.

Armistice talks began in July 1951, but the fighting and dying went on for two more years. The most contentious point in the negotiations was the fate of prisoners of war (POWs). Defying the Geneva Prisoners of War Convention (1949), U.S. officials announced that only those North Korean and Chinese POWs who wished to go home would be returned. Responding to the American statement that there would be no forced repatriation,

■ Chinese soldiers guard marching American prisoners of the Korean War during the cold winter of 1950. (Xinhua, New China News Agency)

the North Koreans denounced forced retention. Both sides undertook "reeducation" or "brainwashing" programs to persuade POWs to resist repatriation.

As the POW issue stalled negotiations, U.S. officials made deliberately vague public statements about using atomic weapons in Korea. American bombers obliterated dams (whose rushing waters then destroyed rice fields), factories, airfields, and bridges in North Korea. Casualties on all sides mounted. Not until July 1953 was an armistice signed. Stalin's death in March and the coming to power of a more conciliatory Soviet government helped ease the way to a settlement that the Chinese especially welcomed. The combatants agreed to hand over the POW question to a special panel of neutral nations, which later gave prisoners their choice of staying or leaving. (In the end, 70,000 of about 100,000 North Korean and 5,600 of 20,700 Chinese POWs elected to return home; 21 American and 325 South Korean POWs of some 11,000 decided to stay in North Korea.) The North Korean–South Korean borderline was set near the 38th parallel, the prewar boundary, and a demilitarized zone was created between the two Koreas.

PEACE AGREEMENT

American casualties totaled 54,246 dead and 103,284 wounded. Close to 5 million Asians died in the war: 2 million North Korean civilians and 500,000 soldiers; 1 million South Korean civilians and 100,000 soldiers; and at least 1 million Chinese soldiers—ranking Korea as one of the costliest wars of the twentieth century.

The Korean War carried major domestic political consequences. The failure to achieve victory and the public's impatience with a stalemated war undoubtedly helped to elect Republican Dwight Eisenhower to the presidency in 1952, as the former general promised to "go to Korea" to end the war. The powers of the presidency grew as Congress repeatedly deferred to Truman. The president had never asked Congress for a declaration of war, believing that as commander-in-chief he had the authority to send troops wherever he wished. A few dissenters such as Senator Taft disagreed, but Truman saw no need to consult Congress—except when he wanted the $69.5 billion Korean War bill paid. In addition, the war, which occurred in the midst of the "Who Lost China?" debate, inflamed antileftist politics in the United States. Republican lawmakers, including Wis-

CONSEQUENCES OF THE WAR

consin senator Joseph McCarthy, accused Truman and Acheson of being "soft on communism" in failing first to prevent, and then to go all-out to win, the war; their verbal attacks strengthened the administration's determination to take an uncompromising position in the negotiations.

The impact on foreign policy was even greater. The Sino-American hostility generated by the war ensured that there would be no U.S. reconciliation with the Beijing government, and that South Korea and Formosa would become major recipients of American foreign aid. The alliance with Japan strengthened as the island's economy boomed after filling large procurement orders from the United States. Australia and New Zealand joined the United States in a mutual defense agreement, the ANZUS Treaty (1951). The U.S. Army sent four divisions to Europe, and the administration initiated plans to rearm West Germany. The Korean War, Acheson cheerfully noted, removed "the recommendations of NSC-68 from the realm of theory and made them immediate budget issues." Indeed, the military budget shot up from $14 billion in 1949 to $44 billion in 1953; it remained between $35 billion and $44 billion a year throughout the 1950s. The Soviet Union sought to match this military buildup, and the result was a major arms race between the two nations. In sum, Truman's legacy was a highly militarized U.S. foreign policy active on a global scale.

Unrelenting Cold War

The new foreign policy team of President Eisenhower and Secretary of State John Foster Dulles largely sustained Truman's Cold War policies. Both brought abundant experience in foreign affairs to their posts. Eisenhower had lived and traveled in Europe, Asia, and Latin America and, as a general during the Second World War, had negotiated with world leaders. After the war, he had served as army chief of staff and NATO supreme commander. Dulles had been closely involved with U.S. diplomacy since the first decade of the century. "Foster has been studying to be secretary of state since he was five years old," Eisenhower observed. He relied heavily on Dulles to be his emissary abroad. The secretary of state spent so much time traveling to world capitals that critics exclaimed, "Don't do something, Foster, just stand there!"

Eisenhower and Dulles accepted the Cold War consensus about the threat of communism and the need for global vigilance. Though Democrats promoted an

EISENHOWER AND DULLES

image of Eisenhower as a bumbling, passive, aging hero, deferring most foreign policy matters to Dulles, the president in fact commanded the policymaking process and on occasion tamed the more hawkish proposals of Dulles and Vice President Richard Nixon. Even so, the secretary of state's influence was considerable. Few Cold Warriors rivaled Dulles's impassioned anticommunism, often expressed in biblical terms. A graduate of Princeton and George Washington Universities, Dulles had assisted Woodrow Wilson at Versailles and later became a senior partner in a prestigious Wall Street law firm and an officer of the Federal Council of Churches. Though polished and articulate, Dulles impressed people as arrogant, stubborn, and hectoring—and averse to compromise, an essential ingredient in successful diplomacy. Behind closed doors Dulles could show a different side, one considerably more flexible and pragmatic, but there is little evidence that he saw much utility in negotiations, at least where communists were involved. His assertion that neutrality was an "immoral and short-sighted conception" did not sit well with Third World leaders, who resented being told they had to choose between East and West.

Like the president, Dulles conceded much to the anticommunist McCarthyites, who claimed that the State Department was infested with communists (see page 807). The State Department's chief security officer, a McCarthy follower, targeted homosexuals and other "incompatibles" and made few distinctions between New Dealers and communists. Dulles thus forced many talented officers out of the Foreign Service with unsubstantiated charges that they were disloyal. Among them were Asia specialists whose expertise was thus denied to the American leaders who were steadily expanding the U.S. presence on that continent. "The wrong done," the journalist Theodore A. White wrote, "was to poke out the eyes and ears of the State Department on Asian affairs, to blind American foreign policy."

Dulles said he considered containment too defensive a stance toward communism. He called instead for "liberation," although he never explained precisely how the countries of eastern Europe could be freed from Soviet control. "Massive retaliation" was the administration's plan for the nuclear obliteration of the Soviet state or its assumed client, the People's Republic of China, if either one took aggressive actions. Eisenhower said it "simply means the ability to blow hell out of them in a hurry if they start anything." The ability of the United States to make such a threat was thought to

"MASSIVE RETALIATION"

provide "deterrence," the prevention of hostile Soviet behavior.

In their "New Look" for the American military, Eisenhower and Dulles emphasized airpower and nuclear weaponry. The president's preference for heavy weapons stemmed in part from his desire to trim the federal budget ("more bang for the buck," as the saying went). Galvanized by the successful test of the world's first hydrogen bomb in November 1952, Eisenhower oversaw a massive stockpiling of nuclear weapons—from 1,200 at the start of his presidency to 22,229 at the end. Backed by its huge military arsenal, the United States could practice "brinkmanship": not backing down in a crisis, even if it meant taking the nation to the brink of war. Eisenhower also popularized the "domino theory": that small, weak, neighboring nations would fall to communism like a row of dominoes if they were not propped up by the United States.

CIA AS FOREIGN POLICY INSTRUMENT

Eisenhower increasingly utilized the Central Intelligence Agency as an instrument of foreign policy. Headed by Allen Dulles, brother of the secretary of state, the CIA put foreign leaders (such as King Hussein of Jordan) on its payroll; subsidized foreign labor unions, newspapers, and political parties (such as the conservative Liberal Democratic Party of Japan); planted false stories in newspapers through its "disinformation" projects; and trained foreign military officers in counterrevolutionary methods. It hired American journalists and professors; secretly funded the National Student Association to spur contacts with foreign student leaders; used business executives as "fronts"; and conducted experiments on unsuspecting Americans to determine the effects of "mind control" drugs (the MKULTRA program). The CIA also launched covert operations (including assassination schemes) to subvert or destroy governments in the Third World. The CIA helped overthrow the governments of Iran (1953) and Guatemala (1954) but failed in attempts to topple regimes in Indonesia (1958) and Cuba (1961).

The CIA and other components of the American intelligence community followed the principle of plausible deniability: covert operations should be conducted in such a way, and the decisions that launched them concealed so well, that the president could deny any knowledge of them. Thus President Eisenhower disavowed any U.S. role in Guatemala, even though he had ordered the operation. He and his successor Kennedy also denied that they had instructed the CIA to assassinate Cuba's Fidel Castro, whose regime after 1959 became stridently anti-American.

NUCLEAR BUILDUP

It did not take leaders in Moscow long to become aware of Eisenhower's expanded use of covert action, as well as his stockpiling of nuclear weapons. They increased their own intelligence activity, and tested their first H-bomb in 1953. Four years later, they shocked Americans by firing the world's first intercontinental ballistic missile (ICBM) and then propelling the satellite *Sputnik* into orbit in outer space. Americans felt more vulnerable to air attack and inferior in rocket technology, even though in 1957 the United States had 2,460 strategic weapons and a nuclear stockpile of 5,543, compared with the Soviet Union's 102 and 650. As President Eisenhower said, "If we were to release our nuclear stockpile on the Soviet Union, the main danger would arise not from retaliation but from fallout in the earth's atmosphere." The administration enlarged its fleet of long-range bombers (B-52s) and deployed intermediate-range missiles in Europe, targeted against the Soviet Union. At the end of 1960 the United States began adding Polaris missile–bearing submarines to its navy. To foster future technological advancement, the National Aeronautics and Space Administration (NASA) was created in 1958.

Overall, though, Eisenhower sought to avoid any kind of military confrontation with the Soviet Union and China; notwithstanding Dulles's tough talk of "liberation" and "massive retaliation," the administration was content to follow Truman's lead and emphasize the *containment* of communism. Eisenhower declined opportunities to use nuclear weapons, and he proved more reluctant than many other Cold War presidents to send American soldiers into battle. He preferred to fight the Soviets at the level of propaganda. Convinced that the struggle against Moscow would in large measure be decided in the arena of international public opinion, he wanted to win the "hearts and minds" of people overseas. The "People-to-People" campaign, launched in 1956, sought to use ordinary Americans and nongovernmental organizations to enhance the international image of the United States and its people.

Likewise, American cultural exchanges and participation in trade fairs in the Eisenhower years were used to create a favorable atmosphere abroad for U.S. political, economic, and military policies. Sometimes, the propaganda war was waged on the Soviets' own turf. In 1959, Vice President Richard Nixon traveled to Moscow to open an American products fair. In the display of a modern American kitchen, part of a model six-room ranch-style house, Nixon extolled capitalist consumerism, while Soviet premier Nikita Khrushchev, Stalin's successor,

The People-to-People Campaign

Not long after the start of the Cold War, U.S. officials determined that the Soviet-American confrontation was as much psychological and ideological as military and economic. One result was the People-to-People campaign, a state-private venture initiated by the United States Information Agency (USIA) in 1956 that aimed to win the "hearts and minds" of people around the world. In this program American propaganda experts sought to channel the energies of ordinary Americans, businesses, civic organizations, labor groups, and women's clubs to promote confidence abroad in the basic goodness of the American people and, by extension, their government. In addition, the campaign was designed to raise morale at home by giving Americans a sense of personal participation in the Cold War struggle. The People-to-People campaign, one USIA pamphlet said, made "every man an ambassador."

Campaign activities resembled the home-front mobilization efforts of World War II. If during the war Americans were exhorted by the Office of War Information to purchase war bonds, now they were told that thirty dollars could send a ninety-nine-volume portable library of American books to schools and libraries overseas. Publishers donated magazines and books for free distribution to foreign countries—*Woman's Day,* for example, volunteered six thousand copies of the magazine per month. People-to-People committees organized sister-city affiliations and "pen-pal" letter exchanges, hosted exchange students, and organized traveling "People-to-People delegations" representing their various communities. The travelers were urged to behave like goodwill ambassadors when abroad and to "help overcome any feeling that America is a land that thinks money can buy everything." They were to "appreciate [foreigners'] manners and customs, not to insist on imitations of the American way of doing things."

To extol everyday life in the United States, Camp Fire Girls in more than three thousand communities took photographs on the theme "This is our home. This is how we live. These are my People." The photographs, assembled in albums, were sent to girls in Latin America, Africa, Asia, and the Middle East. The Hobbies Committee, meanwhile, connected people with interests in radio, photography, coins, stamps, and horticulture. One group represented dog owners in the belief that "dogs make good ambassadors and are capable of hurdling the barriers of language and ideologies in the quest for peace."

Just what effect the People-to-People campaign had on foreign images of the United States is hard to say. The persistence to this day of the widespread impression that Americans are a provincial, materialistic people suggests that skepticism is in order. But alongside this negative image is a more positive one that sees Americans as admirably open, friendly, optimistic, and pragmatic; if the campaign did not erase the former impression, it may have helped foster the latter. Whatever role the People-to-People campaign played in the larger Cold War struggle, it certainly achieved one of its chief objectives: to link ordinary Americans more closely to people in other parts of the world.

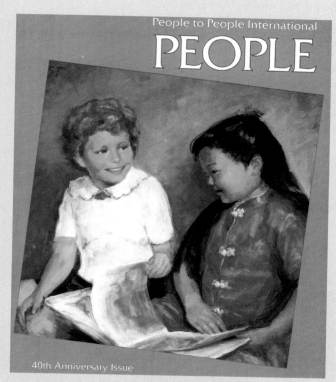

This Alice Nast painting of two girls—one from the United States and one from Taiwan—was commissioned by the Kansas City chapter of People to People and the Kansas City/Tainan Sister City Committee. The painting was presented to the mayor of Tainan in September 1994, prior to the 11th Worldwide Conference of the People-to-People International.   (People to People)

touted the merits of communism. The encounter became famous as the "kitchen debate."

Eisenhower showed his restraint in 1956 when turmoil rocked parts of eastern Europe. In February, Khrushchev called for "peaceful coexistence"

REBELLION IN HUNGARY between capitalists and communists, denounced Stalin, and suggested that Moscow would tolerate different brands of communism. Revolts against Soviet power promptly erupted in Poland and Hungary, testing Khrushchev's new permissiveness. After a new Hungarian government in 1956 announced its withdrawal from the Warsaw Pact (the Soviet military alliance formed in 1955 with communist countries of eastern Europe), Soviet troops and tanks battled students and workers in the streets of Budapest and crushed the rebellion.

Although the Eisenhower administration's propaganda had been encouraging liberation efforts, U.S. officials found themselves unable to aid the rebels without igniting a world war. They stood by, promising only to welcome Hungarian immigrants in greater numbers than American quota laws allowed. Even so, the West could have reaped some propaganda advantage from this display of Soviet brute force had not British, French, and Israeli troops—U.S. allies—invaded Egypt during the Suez crisis just before the Soviets smashed the Hungarian uprising (see page 792).

Hardly had the turmoil subsided in eastern Europe when the divided city of Berlin once again became a Cold War flash point. The Soviets railed against the placement in West Germany of American bombers capable of carrying nuclear warheads, and they complained that West Berlin had become an escape route for disaffected East Germans. In 1958 Khrushchev announced that the Soviet Union would recognize East German control of all of Berlin unless the United States and its allies began talks on German reunification and rearmament. The United States refused to give up its hold on West Berlin or to break West German ties with NATO. Khrushchev backed away from his ultimatum but promised to press the issue again.

Khrushchev hoped to do just that at a summit meeting planned for Paris in mid-1960. But two weeks before the conference, on May 1, a U-2 spy

U-2 INCIDENT plane carrying high-powered cameras crashed 1,200 miles inside the Soviet Union. Moscow claimed credit for shooting down the plane, which the Soviets put on display along with Francis Gary Powers, the captured CIA pilot, and the pictures he had been snapping of Soviet military sites. Khrushchev demanded an apology for the U.S. violation of Soviet airspace. When Washington refused, the Soviets walked out of the Paris summit—"a graveyard of lost opportunities," as a Soviet official put it.

While sparring over Europe, both sides kept a wary eye on the People's Republic of China, which denounced the Soviet call for peaceful coexistence. Despite evidence of a widening Sino-Soviet split, most American offi-

■ President Eisenhower *(left)* confers with Secretary of State John Foster Dulles (1888–1959), known for his strong anticommunism and his often self-righteous, lecturing style. Dulles once remarked that the United States "is almost the only country strong enough and powerful enough to be moral." (© Bettmann/Corbis)

cials still treated communism as a monolithic world movement. The isolation separating Beijing and Washington stymied communication and made continued conflict between China and the United States likely. In 1954, in a dispute over Jinmen (Quemoy) and Mazu (Matsu), two tiny islands off the Chinese coast, the United States and the People's Republic of China lurched toward the brink. Taiwan's Jiang Jieshi used these islands as bases from which to raid the mainland. Communist China's guns bombarded the islands in 1954. Thinking that U.S. credibility was at stake, Eisenhower decided to defend the outposts; he even hinted that he might use nuclear weapons. Why massive retaliation over such an insignificant issue? "Let's keep the Reds guessing," advised John Foster Dulles. "But what if they guessed wrong?" critics replied.

In early 1955, Congress passed the Formosa Resolution, authorizing the president to deploy American forces

FORMOSA RESOLUTION

to defend Formosa and adjoining islands. In so doing, Congress formally surrendered to the president what it had informally given up at the time of the Korea decision in 1950: the constitutional power to declare war. Although the crisis passed in April 1955, war loomed again in 1958 over Jinmen and Mazu. But this time, after Washington strongly cautioned him not to use force against the mainland, Jiang withdrew some troops from the islands. China then relaxed its bombardments. One consequence accelerated the arms race: Eisenhower's nuclear threats persuaded the Chinese that they, too, needed nuclear arms. In 1964 China exploded its first nuclear bomb.

The Struggle for the Third World

*L*ike Truman before him and all Cold War presidents after him, Eisenhower worried most about the fate of western Europe. Over time, however, his administration focused more and more attention on the threat of communist expansion in Africa, Asia, Latin America, and the Middle East. In much of the Third World, the process of decolonization that began during the First World War accelerated after the Second World War, when the economically wracked imperial countries proved incapable of resisting their colonies' demands for freedom. A cavalcade of new nations cast off their colonial bonds (see Map 28.3). In 1960 alone, eighteen new African nations did so. From 1943 to 1994 a total of 125 countries became independent (the figure includes the former Soviet republics that departed the USSR in 1991).

The emergence of so many new states in the 1940s and after, and the instability associated with the transfer of authority, shook the foundations of the international system. Power was redistributed, creating "near chaos," said one U.S. government report. In the traditional U.S. sphere of influence, Latin America, nationalists once again challenged Washington's dominance.

By the late 1940s, when Cold War lines were drawn fairly tightly in Europe, Soviet-American rivalry shifted

INTERESTS IN THE THIRD WORLD

increasingly to the Third World. Much was at stake. The new nations could buy American goods and technology, supply strategic raw materials, and invite investments (more than one-third of America's private foreign investments were in Third World countries in 1959). And they could build cultural ties with the United States. Both great powers, moreover, looked to these new states for votes in the United Nations and sought sites within their borders for military and intelligence bases. But, often poor and unstable—and rife with tribal, ethnic, and class rivalries—many new nations sought to end the economic, military, and cultural hegemony of the West. Many learned to play off the two superpowers against each other to garner more aid and arms. U.S. interventions—military and otherwise—in the Third World, American leaders believed, became necessary to impress Moscow with Washington's might and resolve and to counter nationalism and radical anticapitalist social change that threatened American strategic and economic interests.

To thwart nationalist, radical, and communist challenges, the United States directed massive resources—foreign aid, propaganda, development projects—toward the Third World. By 1961 more than 90 percent of U.S. foreign aid was going to developing nations. Washington also allied with native elites and with undemocratic but anticommunist regimes, meddled in civil wars, and unleashed CIA covert operations. These American interventions often generated resentment among the local populace. When some of the larger Third World states—notably India, Ghana, Egypt, and Indonesia—refused to take sides in the Cold War, Secretary of State Dulles declared that neutralism was a step on the road to communism. Both he and Eisenhower insisted that every nation should take a side in the life-and-death Cold War struggle.

American leaders argued that technologically "backward" Third World countries needed Western-induced capitalist development and modernization in order to enjoy economic growth, social harmony, and political moderation. Often these U.S. officials also ascribed stereotyped

Map 28.3 The Rise of the Third World: Newly Independent Nations Since 1943
Accelerated by the Second World War, decolonization liberated many peoples from imperial rule. New nations emerged in the postwar international system dominated by the Cold War rivalry of the United States and the Soviet Union. Many newly independent states became targets of great-power intrigue but chose nonalignment in the Cold War.

race-, age-, and gender-based characteristics to Third World peoples, seeing them as dependent, emotional, and irrational, and therefore dependent on the fatherly tutelage of the United States. Cubans, CIA director Allen Dulles told the National Security Council in early 1959, "had to be treated more or less like children. They had to be led rather than rebuffed. If they were rebuffed, like children, they were capable of almost anything."

At other times American officials used gendered language, suggesting that Third World countries were weak women—passive and servile, unable to resist the menacing appeals of communists and neutralists. In speaking of India, for example—a neutralist nation that Americans deemed effeminate and submissive—Eisenhower condescendingly described it as a place where "emotion rather than reason seems to dictate policy."

Race attitudes and segregation practices in the United States especially influenced U.S. relations with Third

RACISM AND SEGREGATION AS U.S. HANDICAPS

World countries. In 1955 G. L. Mehta, the Indian ambassador to the United States, was refused service in the whites-only section of a restaurant at Houston International Airport. The insult stung deeply, as did many similar indignities experienced by other Third World diplomats. Fearing damaged relations with India, a large nation whose allegiance the United States sought in the Cold War, John Foster Dulles apologized to Mehta. The secretary thought racial segregation in the United States a "major international hazard," spoiling American efforts to win friends in Third World countries and giving the Soviets a propaganda advantage. American practices and ideals did not align.

Thus when the U.S. attorney general appealed to the Supreme Court to strike down segregation in public schools, he underlined that the humiliation of dark-skinned diplomats "furnished grist for the Communist propaganda mills." When the Court announced its *Brown* decision in 1954 (see page 810), the government quickly broadcast news of the desegregation order around the world in thirty-five languages on its Voice of America overseas radio network. But the problem did not go away. For example, after the 1957 Little Rock crisis (see page 810), Dulles remarked that racial bigotry was "ruining our foreign policy. The effect of this in Asia and Africa will be worse for us than Hungary was for the Russians." Still, when an office of the Department of State decided to counter Soviet propaganda by creating for the 1958 World's Fair in Brussels an exhibit titled "The Unfinished Work"—on race relations in the United States and strides taken toward desegregation—southern

conservatives kicked up such a furor that the Eisenhower administration closed the display.

The hostility of the United States toward revolution also obstructed its quest for influence in the Third World. In the twentieth century, the United States openly opposed revolutions in Mexico, China, Russia, Cuba, Vietnam, Nicaragua, and Iran, among other nations. Americans celebrated the Spirit of '76 but grew intolerant of revolutionary disorder because many Third World revolutions arose against America's Cold War allies and threatened American investments, markets, and military bases. Indeed, by midcentury the United States stood as an established power in world affairs, eager for stability and order to protect American prosperity and security. Like most other great powers throughout history, it generally preferred to maintain the status quo. During revolutionary crises, therefore, the United States usually supported its European allies or the conservative, propertied classes in the Third World. In 1960, for example, when forty-three African and Asian states sponsored a U.N. resolution endorsing decolonization, the United States abstained from the vote.

Yet the American approach also had its element of idealism. Believing that Third World peoples craved

DEVELOPMENT AND MODERNIZATION

modernization and that the American economic model of private enterprise and cooperation among business, labor, and government was best for them, American policymakers launched various "development" projects. Such projects held out the promise of sustained economic growth, prosperity, and stability, which the benefactors hoped would undermine radicalism. In the 1950s the Carnegie, Ford, and Rockefeller Foundations worked with the U.S. Agency for International Development (AID) to sponsor a Green Revolution, a dramatic increase in agricultural production—for example, by the use of hybrid seeds. The Rockefeller Foundation supported foreign universities' efforts to train national leaders committed to nonradical development; in Nigeria from 1958 to 1969 the philanthropic agency spent $25 million. Before Dean Rusk became secretary of state in 1961, he served as president of the Rockefeller Foundation.

To persuade Third World peoples to abandon radical doctrines and neutralism, American leaders, often in cooperation with the business-sponsored Advertising Council, directed propaganda at developing nations. The U.S. Information Agency (USIA), founded in 1953, used films, radio broadcasts, the magazine *Free World*, exhibitions, exchange programs, and libraries (in 162

In the 1950s, these specially outfitted jeeps (equipped with projectors, screens, and films) served America's overseas information program in what the State Department called "isolated areas." Believing that social modernization and economic progress would counter leftist and communist ideas, U.S. propaganda officials dispatched these "mobile motion picture units" to such places as rural Mexico, seeking to reach people with films on U.S. sports, music, health, and agriculture. (National Archives)

cities worldwide by 1961) to trumpet the theme of "People's Capitalism." Citing America's economic success—contrasted with "slave-labor" conditions in the Soviet Union—the message showcased well-paid American workers, political democracy, and religious freedom. To counter ugly pictures of segregation and white attacks on African Americans and civil rights activists in the South, the United States Information Agency applauded success stories of individual African Americans, such as the boxers Floyd Patterson and Sugar Ray Robinson. In 1960 alone some 13.8 million people visited U.S. pavilions abroad, including 1 million at the consumer-products exhibit "Tradeways to Peace and Prosperity" in Damascus, Syria.

Undoubtedly, the American way of life had appeal for some Third World peoples. They, too, wanted to enjoy American consumer goods, rock music, economic status, and educational opportunities. Hollywood movies offered enticing glimpses of middle-class materialism, and American films dominated many overseas markets. Blue jeans, advertising billboards, and soft drinks flooded foreign societies. But if foreigners often envied Americans, they also resented them for having so much and wasting so much while poorer peoples went without. The popular American novel *The Ugly American* (1958) spotlighted the "golden ghettoes" where American diplomats lived in compounds separated from their poorer surroundings by high walls. The people of many countries, moreover, resented the ample profits that U.S. corporations extracted from them. Americans often received

blame for the persistent poverty of the developing world, even though the leaders of those nations made decisions that hindered their own progress, such as pouring millions of dollars into their militaries while their people needed food. Nonetheless, anti-American resentments could be measured in the late 1950s in attacks on USIA libraries in Calcutta, India; Beirut, Lebanon; and Bogotá, Colombia.

When the more benign techniques of containment—aid, trade, cultural relations—proved insufficient to get Third World nations to line up on the American side in the Cold War, the Eisenhower administration often showed a willingness to press harder, by covert or overt means. In Latin America, the president deemed Guatemala an early test case. In 1951 the leftist Jacobo Arbenz Guzmán was elected president of Guatemala, a poor country whose largest landowner was the American-owned United Fruit Company. United Fruit was an economic power throughout Latin America, where it owned 3 million acres of land and operated railroads, ports, ships, and telecommunications facilities. To fulfill his promise of land reform, Arbenz expropriated UF's uncultivated land and offered compensation. The company dismissed the offer and charged that Arbenz posed a communist threat—a charge that CIA officials had already floated because Arbenz employed some communists in his government. The CIA began a secret plot to overthrow Arbenz. He turned to Moscow for military

INTERVENTION IN GUATEMALA

aid, thus reinforcing American suspicions. The CIA airlifted arms into Guatemala, dropping them at United Fruit facilities, and in mid-1954 CIA-supported Guatemalans struck from Honduras. U.S. planes bombed the capital city, and the invaders drove Arbenz from power. The new pro-American regime returned United Fruit's land, but an ensuing civil war staggered the Central American nation for decades thereafter.

Eisenhower also watched with apprehension as turmoil gripped Cuba in the late 1950s. In early 1959

THE CUBAN
REVOLUTION
AND FIDEL
CASTRO

Fidel Castro's rebels, or *barbudos* ("bearded ones"), driven by profound anti-American nationalism, had ousted Fulgencio Batista, a longtime U.S. ally who had welcomed North American investors, U.S. military advisers, and tourists to the Caribbean island. Batista's corrupt, dictatorial regime had helped turn Havana into a haven for gambling and prostitution run by organized crime. Cubans had resented U.S. domination ever since the early twentieth century, when the Platt Amendment had compromised their independence. Curbing U.S. influence became a rallying cry of the Cuban revolution, all the more so after the CIA conspired secretly but futilely to block Castro's rise to power in 1958. From the start Castro sought to roll back the influence of American business, which had invested some $1 billion on the island, and to break the U.S. grasp on Cuban trade.

Castro's increasing authoritarianism, anti-Yankee declarations, and growing popularity in the hemisphere alarmed Washington. In early 1960, after Cuba signed a trade treaty with the Soviet Union, Eisenhower ordered the CIA to organize an invasion force of Cuban exiles to overthrow the Castro government. The agency also began to plot an assassination of the Cuban leader. When the president drastically cut U.S. purchases of Cuban sugar, Castro seized all North American–owned companies that had not yet been nationalized. Threatened by U.S. decisions designed to bring him and his revolution down, Castro appealed to the Soviet Union, which offered loans and expanded trade. Just before leaving office in early 1961, Eisenhower broke diplomatic relations with Cuba and advised president-elect John F. Kennedy to advance plans for the invasion, which came—and failed—in early 1961 (see page 831).

In the Middle East, meanwhile, the Eisenhower administration confronted challenges posed by ongoing tensions

ARAB-ISRAELI
CONFLICT

between Arabs and Jews and by nationalist leaders in Iran and Egypt (see Map 33.2). Prior to the end of World War II, only France and Britain among

the great powers had been much concerned with this region of the world; they had effectively dominated the area during the prior three decades. But the dissolution of empires and the rise of Cold War tensions drew Washington into the region, as did the deepening tensions in British-held Palestine. From 1945 to 1947, Britain tried to enlist U.S. officials in the effort to find a solution to the vexing question of how to split Palestine between the Arabs and Jews who lived there. The Truman administration rejected London's solicitations, and the British, despairing at the violence between Arabs and Jews and the rising number of British deaths, in 1947 turned the issue over to the United Nations, which voted to partition Palestine into separate Arab and Jewish states. Arab leaders opposed the decision, but in May 1948 Jewish leaders announced the creation of Israel.

The United States, which had lobbied hard to secure the U.N. vote, extended recognition to the new state mere minutes after the act of foundation. A moral conviction that Jews deserved a homeland after the suffering of the Holocaust, and that Zionism was a worthy movement that would create a democratic Israel, influenced Truman's decision, as did the belief that Jewish votes might swing some states to the Democrats in the 1948 election. These beliefs trumped concerns on the part of some senior officials that Arab oil producers might turn against the United States, and that close Soviet-Israeli ties could turn Israel into a pro-Soviet bastion in the Middle East. The Soviet Union did promptly recognize the new nation, but Israeli leaders kept Moscow at arm's length, in part because they had more pressing concerns. Palestinian Arabs, displaced from land they considered theirs, joined with Israel's Arab neighbors to make immediate war on the new state. The Israelis stopped the offensive in bloody fighting over the next six months until a U.N.-backed truce was called.

In the years thereafter, American policy in the Middle East centered on ensuring Israel's survival and cementing ties with Arab oil producers. U.S. oil holdings were extensive: American companies produced about half of the region's petroleum in the 1950s. Oil-rich Iran became a special friend. Its ruling shah had granted American oil companies a 40 percent interest in a new petroleum consortium in return for CIA help in the successful overthrow, in 1953, of his rival, Mohammed Mossadegh, who had attempted to nationalize foreign oil interests.

American officials faced a more formidable foe in Egypt, in the form of Gamal Abdul Nasser, a towering figure in a pan-Arabic movement to reduce Western interests in the Middle East. Nasser vowed to expel the

■ In the years 1948–1950, hundreds of thousands of Jewish refugees arrived in the state of Israel. Legendary war photographer Robert Capa snapped this picture of refugees arriving on a boat in Haifa in 1949. A few years later, while on assignment for *Life* magazine, Capa would be killed by a land mine in Indochina. (Robert Capa/ Magnum Photos, Inc.)

British from the Suez Canal and the Israelis from Palestine. The United States wished neither to anger the Arabs, for fear of losing valuable oil supplies, nor to alienate its ally Israel, which was supported at home by politically active American Jews. But when Nasser declared neutrality in the Cold War, Dulles lost patience.

In 1956 the United States abruptly reneged on its offer to Egypt to help finance the Aswan Dam, a project to provide inexpensive electricity and water for thirsty Nile valley farmland. Secretary Dulles's blunt economic pressure backfired, for Nasser responded by nationalizing the British-owned Suez Canal, intending to use its profits to build the dam. At a mass rally in Alexandria, Nasser expressed the profound nationalism typical of Third World peoples shedding an imperial past: "Tonight our Egyptian canal will be run by Egyptians. Egyptians!" Fully 75 percent of western Europe's oil came from the Middle East, most of it transported through the Suez Canal. Fearing an interruption in this vital trade, the British and French conspired with Israel to bring down Nasser. On October 29, 1956, the Israelis invaded Suez, joined two days later by British and French forces.

SUEZ CRISIS

Eisenhower fumed. America's allies had not consulted him, and the attack had shifted attention from Soviet intervention in Hungary. The president also feared that the invasion would cause Nasser to seek help from the Soviets, inviting them into the Middle East. Eisenhower sternly demanded that London, Paris, and Tel Aviv pull their troops out, and they did. Egypt took possession of the canal, the Soviets built the Aswan Dam,

and Nasser became a hero to Third World peoples. To counter Nasser, the United States determined to "build up" as an "Arab rival" the conservative King Ibn Saud of Saudi Arabia. Although the monarch renewed America's lease of an air base, few Arabs respected the notoriously corrupt Saud.

Washington officials worried that a "vacuum" existed in the Middle East—and that the Soviets might fill it. Nasserites insisted that there was no vacuum but rather a growing Arab nationalism that provided the best defense against communism. In an effort to improve the deteriorating Western position in the Middle East and to protect American interests there, the president proclaimed the Eisenhower Doctrine in 1957. The United States would intervene in the Middle East, he declared, if any government threatened by a communist takeover asked for help. In 1958 fourteen thousand American troops scrambled ashore in Lebanon to quell an internal political dispute that Washington feared might be exploited by pro-Nasser groups or communists.

EISENHOWER DOCTRINE

Cold War concerns also drove Eisenhower's policy toward Vietnam, where nationalists battled the French for independence. Despite a substantial U.S. aid program initiated under Truman, the French lost steadily to the Vietminh. Finally, in early 1954, Ho's forces surrounded the French fortress at Dienbienphu in northwest Vietnam (see Map 30.2). Although some of Eisenhower's advisers recommended a massive American air strike against Vietminh positions,

NATIONALIST VICTORY IN VIETNAM

perhaps even using tactical atomic weapons, the president moved cautiously. The United States had been advising and bankrolling the French, but it had not committed its own forces to the war. If American airpower did not save the French, would ground troops be required next, and in hostile terrain? As one high-level doubter remarked, "One cannot go over Niagara Falls in a barrel only slightly."

Worrying aloud about a communist victory, Eisenhower pressed the British to help form a coalition to address the Indochinese crisis, but they refused. At home, influential members of Congress—including Lyndon Baines Johnson of Texas, who as president would wage large-scale war in Vietnam—told Eisenhower they wanted "no more Koreas" and warned him against any U.S. military commitment, especially in the absence of cooperation from America's allies. Some felt very uneasy about supporting colonialism. The issue became moot on May 7, when the weary French defenders at Dienbienphu surrendered.

Peace talks, already under way in Geneva, brought Cold War and nationalist contenders together—the United

GENEVA ACCORDS

States, the Soviet Union, Britain, the People's Republic of China, Laos, Cambodia, and the competing Vietnamese regimes of Bao Dai and Ho Chi Minh. John Foster Dulles, a reluctant participant, feared the communists would get the better of any agreement, yet in the end the Vietminh received less than their dominant military position suggested they should. The 1954 Geneva accords, signed by France and Ho's Democratic Republic of Vietnam, temporarily divided Vietnam at the 17th parallel; Ho's government was confined to the North, Bao Dai's to the South. Only after pressure from the Chinese and the Soviets, who feared U.S. intervention in Vietnam without an agreement, did Ho's government agree to this compromise. The 17th parallel was meant to serve as a military truce line, not a national boundary; the country was scheduled to be reunified after national elections in 1956. In the meantime, neither North nor South was to join a military alliance or permit foreign military bases on its soil.

Confident that the Geneva agreements ultimately would mean communist victory, the United States from an early point set about trying to undermine them. Soon after the conference, a CIA team entered Vietnam and undertook secret operations against the North, including commando raids across the 17th parallel. In the South, the United States helped Ngo Dinh Diem push Bao Dai aside and inaugurate the Republic of Vietnam. A Catholic in a Buddhist nation, Diem was a dedicated nationalist and anticommunist, but he had little mass support. He staged a fraudulent election in South Vietnam that gave him 99 percent of the vote (in Saigon he received 200,000 more votes than there were registered voters). When Ho and some in the world community pressed for national elections in keeping with the Geneva agreements, Diem and Eisenhower refused, fearing that the popular

■ French soldiers assemble one of the eight tanks that were flown into Dienbienphu in parts. In the background are the airstrip and fortifications of the garrison. The tanks proved largely ineffectual in the fighting that followed.
(Everette Dixie Reece/George Eastman House)

Vietminh leader would win. From 1955 to 1961, the Diem government received more than $1 billion in American aid, most of it military. American advisers organized and trained Diem's army, and American agriculturalists worked to improve crops. Diem's Saigon regime became dependent on the United States for its very existence, and the culture of South Vietnam became increasingly Americanized.

Diem proved a difficult ally. He acted dictatorially, abolishing village elections and appointing to public office people beholden to him. He threw dissenters in jail and shut down newspapers that criticized his regime. When U.S. officials periodically urged him to implement meaningful land reform, he blithely ignored them. Noncommunists and communists alike began to strike back at Diem's repressive government. In Hanoi, Ho's government initially focused on solidifying its control on the North, but in the late 1950s it began to send aid to southern insurgents, who embarked on a program of terror, assassinating hundreds of Diem's village officials. In late 1960 southern communists, acting at the direction of Hanoi, organized the National Liberation Front (NLF), known as the Vietcong. The Vietcong in turn attracted other anti-Diem groups in the South. And the Eisenhower administration, all too aware of Diem's shortcomings and his unwillingness to follow American advice, continued to affirm its commitment to the preservation of an independent, noncommunist South Vietnam.

NATIONAL
LIBERATION
FRONT

Summary

The United States emerged from the Second World War as the preeminent world power. Confident in the nation's immediate physical security, Washington officials nevertheless worried that the unstable international system, an unfriendly Soviet Union, and the decolonizing Third World could upset American plans for the postwar peace. Locked with the Soviet Union in a "Cold War," U.S. leaders marshaled their nation's superior resources to influence and cajole other countries. Foreign economic aid, atomic diplomacy, military alliances, client states, covert operations, interventions, propaganda, cultural infiltration—these and more became the instruments to wage the Cold War, a war that began as a conflict over the future of Europe but soon spread to encompass the globe.

America's claim to international leadership was welcomed by many in western Europe and elsewhere who feared Stalin's intentions and those of his successors in the Soviet Union. The reconstruction of former enemies Japan and (West) Germany helped those nations recover swiftly and become staunch members of the Western alliance. But U.S. policy also sparked resistance. Communist countries condemned financial and atomic diplomacy, while Third World nations, many of them newly independent, sought to undermine America's European allies and sometimes identified the United States as an imperial co-conspirator. On occasion even America's allies bristled at a United States that boldly proclaimed itself economic master and global policeman and haughtily touted its hegemonic status.

At home, liberal and radical critics protested that Presidents Truman and Eisenhower exaggerated the communist threat, wasting U.S. assets on immoral foreign ventures; crippled legitimate nationalist aspirations; and displayed racial bias. Still, these presidents and their successors held firm to the mission of creating a nonradical, capitalist, free-trade international order in the mold of domestic America. Determined to contain Soviet expansion, fearful of domestic charges of being in "soft on communism," they worked to enlarge the U.S. sphere of influence and shape the world. In their years of nurturing allies and applying the containment doctrine worldwide, Truman and Eisenhower held the line—against the Soviet Union and the People's Republic of China, and against nonalignment, communism, nationalism, and revolution everywhere. One consequence was a dramatic increase in presidential power in the realm of foreign affairs—what the historian Arthur M. Schlesinger Jr. called "the Imperial Presidency"—as Congress ceded constitutional power.

Putting itself at odds with many in the Third World, the United States usually stood with its European allies to slow decolonization and to preach evolution rather than revolution. The globalist perspective of the United States prompted Americans to interpret many troubles in the developing world as Cold War conflicts, inspired if not directed by Soviet-backed communists. The intensity of the Cold War obscured for Americans the indigenous roots of most Third World troubles, as the wars in Korea and Vietnam attested. Nor could the United States abide developing nations' drive for economic independence—for gaining control of their own raw materials and economies. Deeply intertwined in the global economy as importer, exporter, and investor, the United States read challenges from this "periphery" as threats to the American standard of living and a way of life characterized by private enterprise. The Third World, in short, challenged U.S. strategic power by forming a third force in the Cold War, and it challenged American economic power by seeking a new economic order of shared interests. Overall, the rise of the Third World introduced new actors to the world stage, challenging the bipolarity of the international system and diffusing power.

All the while, the threat of nuclear war unsettled Americans and foreigners alike. In the film *Godzilla* (1956), a prehistoric monster, revived by atomic bomb tests, rampages through Tokyo. Stanley Kramer's popular but disturbing movie *On the Beach* (1959), based on Nevil Shute's bestselling 1957 novel, depicts a nuclear holocaust in which the last humans on earth choose to swallow government-issued poison tablets so that they can die before H-bomb radiation sickness kills them. Such doomsday or Armageddon attitudes contrasted sharply with official U.S. government assurances that Americans would survive a nuclear war. In *On the Beach*, a dying wife asks her husband, "Couldn't anyone have stopped it?" His answer: "Some kinds of silliness you just can't stop." Eisenhower did not halt it, even though he told Khrushchev in 1959 that "we really should come to some sort of agreement in order to stop this fruitless, really wasteful rivalry."

LEGACY FOR A PEOPLE AND A NATION
The National Security State

To build a cathedral, someone has observed, you first need a religion, and a religion needs inspiring texts that command authority. For decades, America's Cold War religion has been national security; its texts the Truman Doctrine, the "X" article, and NSC-68; and its cathedral the national security state. The word *state* in this case means "civil government." During the Cold War, embracing preparedness for total war, the U.S. government essentially transformed itself into a huge military headquarters that interlocked with corporations and universities. Preaching the doctrine of national security, moreover, members of Congress strove to gain lucrative defense contracts for their districts.

Overseen by the president and his advisory body, the National Security Council, the national security state has had as its core what the National Security Act of 1947 called the National Military Establishment; in 1949 it became the Department of Defense. This department ranks as a leading employer; its payroll by 2000 included 1.3 million people on active duty and almost 600,000 civilian personnel, giving it more em-

ployees than ExxonMobil, Ford, General Motors, and GE combined. Almost a quarter of a million of these troops and civilians served overseas, in 130 countries covering every time zone. Though spending for national defense declined in the years after the end of the Cold War, it never fell below $290 billion. In the aftermath of the terrorist attacks of September 11, 2001, the military budget rose again, reaching $400 billion in 2003. That figure represents the size of the entire economy of Australia or the Netherlands, and it is larger than the economy of Cold War adversary Russia. It equals the combined military spending of the twenty-five countries with the next-largest defense budgets.

Joining the Department of Defense as instruments of national security policy were the Joint Chiefs of Staff, Central Intelligence Agency, and dozens more government bodies. The focus of all of these entities was on finding the best means to combat real and potential threats from foreign governments. But what about threats from within? The terrorist attacks of September 2001 made starkly clear that enemies existed who, while perhaps beholden to a foreign entity—it need not be a government—launched their attacks from inside the nation's borders. Accordingly, in 2002 President George W. Bush proposed the creation of a Department of Homeland Security, which would have 170,000 employees and would include all or part of twenty-two agencies, including the Coast Guard, the Customs Service, the Federal Emergency Management Administration, and the Internal Revenue Service. It would involve the biggest overhaul of the federal bureaucracy since the Department of Defense was created, and it signified a more expansive notion of national security.

In 1961 President Eisenhower warned against a "military-industrial complex," while others feared a "garrison state" or "warfare state." Despite the warnings, by the start of the twenty-first century, the national security state remained vigorous, a lasting legacy of the early Cold War period for a people and a nation.

The *history companion* powered by Eduspace®

Your primary source for interactive quizzes, exercises, and more to help you learn efficiently.

http://history.college.hmco.com/students

*A*MERICA AT MIDCENTURY 1945–1960

*E*venings after supper, when the hot sticky heat of the Georgia summer days had started to ebb, most of the families on Nancy Circle went out for a walk. The parents stood chatting, watching the children play swing-the-statue or hide-and-seek.

In 1959, the twenty houses on Nancy Circle were just a couple of years old. Some lots still looked raw, but in that climate grass grew quickly and the few remaining vacant lots were covered over with kudzu. The small houses stood on land that had once belonged to the Cherokees, in a development carved from the old Campbell plantation, which stood along the route General William Tecumseh Sherman had taken in his march to the sea during the Civil War. Slaves had picked cotton there a century before, but no African Americans lived in the suburban homes. Sometimes an elderly black man came by on a mule cart, selling vegetables.

Nancy Circle was part of a new suburban development in Smyrna, Georgia, just northwest of Atlanta, but few of the people who lived there worked in the city. Most, instead, traveled the other direction, to the massive Lockheed Georgia airplane plant that had been created, in large part, by Cold War defense spending. This suburb was born of the union of Cold War and baby boom: families with small children lived there. With three small bedrooms, two baths, a kitchen, a combined living-dining room, and a garage for about $17,000, the houses on Nancy Circle were ones young families could afford.

On Nancy Circle, children ran in and out of each other's houses and women gathered to drink coffee and gossip in the mornings. The men left early for work. There were several aerospace engineers, three career military men (one of whom was rumored to be in military intelligence), an auto mechanic, and a musician. Only two women held paid jobs. One had almost-grown children and taught second grade; the other was divorced and worked as a secretary. She dyed her hair blonde and drove a convertible. People were suspicious of her but liked her sister, born with dwarfism, who had left her job in a North Carolina textile

◀ A 4-year-old boy stares at military aircraft, the real version of the toy he holds in his hand. The Cold War growth of defense industry plants, such as Lockheed-Georgia near Atlanta, meant that many children grew up in suburbs shaken by sonic booms from military aircraft being tested overhead.   (© Bettmann/Corbis)

CHRONOLOGY

1945 • World War II ends

1946 • Marriage and birth rates skyrocket, creating baby boom
• More than 1 million veterans enroll in colleges under GI Bill
• More than 5 million U.S. workers go on strike

1947 • Taft-Hartley Act limits power of unions
• Truman orders loyalty investigation of 3 million government employees
• Mass-production techniques used to build Levittown houses

1948 • Truman issues executive order desegregating armed forces and federal government
• Truman elected president

1949 • Soviet Union explodes atomic bomb
• National Housing Act promises decent housing for all Americans

1950 • Korean War begins
• McCarthy alleges communists in government
• "Treaty of Detroit" creates model for new labor-management relations

1951 • Race riots in Cicero, Illinois, as white residents oppose residential integration

1952 • Eisenhower elected president

1953 • Korean War ends
• Congress adopts termination policy for Native American tribes
• Rosenbergs executed as atomic spies

1954 • *Brown v. Board of Education* decision reverses "separate but equal" doctrine
• Senate condemns McCarthy

1955 • Montgomery bus boycott begins

1956 • Highway Act launches interstate highway system
• Eisenhower reelected
• Elvis Presley appears on *Ed Sullivan Show*

1957 • King elected first president of Southern Christian Leadership Conference
• School desegregation crisis in Little Rock, Arkansas
• Congress passes Civil Rights Act
• Soviet Union launches *Sputnik*

1958 • Congress passes National Defense Education Act

mill to move to Nancy Circle and help care for her nephew. Two war brides—one Japanese and one German—lived in the neighborhood. The Japanese woman spoke little English, and people worried that she was unhappy. The German woman taught the girls in the neighborhood to do Swedish embroidery and to crochet.

The people who lived on Nancy Circle read national magazines that criticized the homogeneity and conformity of suburban life, but it didn't feel that way to them. On this single street, people from deep Appalachia or the small farms of south Georgia lived side by side with people who grew up in city tenement apartments; a Pennsylvania Dutch family brought Southern Baptist neighbors to join the new Lutheran church they'd helped found; and women who'd done graduate work baked Christmas cookies with women who had not finished high school. These new suburbanites were creating for themselves a new world and a new middle-class culture. They had grown up with the Great Depression and world war; now, on this suburban street, they believed they had found good lives.

Of all the major nations in the world, only the United States emerged from World War II stronger and more prosperous than when war began. Europe and Asia had been devastated, but America's farms and cities and factories were intact. U.S. production capacity had increased during the war and, despite social tensions and inequalities, the fight against fascism gave Americans a unity of purpose. Victory seemed to confirm their struggles. But sixteen years of depression and war shadowed the U.S. victory, and memories of these experiences would continue to shape the choices Americans made in their private lives, their domestic policies, and their relations with the world.

In the postwar era, the actions of the federal government and the choices made by individual Americans began a profound reconfiguration of American society. Postwar social policies that sent millions of veterans to college on the GI Bill, linked the nation with high-speed interstate highways, fostered the growth of suburbs and the Sunbelt, and disrupted regional isolation helped to create a national middle-class culture that encompassed an unprecedented majority of the nation's citizens. Countless individual decisions—to go to college, to marry young, to have a large family, to move to the suburbs, to start a business—were made possible by these federal initiatives. The cumulative weight of these individual decisions would change the meanings of class and ethnicity in American society. Americans in the postwar era defined a new American Dream: one that centered on the family, on a new level of material comfort and consumption, and on a shared sense of belonging to a common culture. Elite cultural critics roundly denounced this ideal of suburban comfort as "conformism," but many Americans found satisfaction in this new way of life.

Almost a quarter of the American people did not share in the postwar prosperity—but they were ever less visible to the middle-class majority. Rural poverty continued, and inner cities became increasingly impoverished as more-affluent Americans moved to the suburbs and new migrants—poor black and white southerners, new immigrants from Mexico and Puerto Rico, Native Americans resettled by the federal government from tribal lands—arrived.

As class and ethnicity became less important in the suburban landscape, race continued to divide the American people. African Americans faced racism and discrimination throughout the nation, but the war had been a turning point in the struggle for equal rights. The 1950s saw some important federal actions to protect the civil rights of African Americans, including the climax of the NAACP's ongoing legal challenges, the Supreme Court's school desegregation decision in *Brown v. Board of Education*. During this period, African Americans increasingly took direct action, and in 1955, the year-long Montgomery bus boycott launched the modern civil rights movement.

After the dramatic accomplishments of the New Deal, the national politics of the postwar era were circumscribed. Truman pledged to expand the New Deal but was stymied by a conservative Congress. General Dwight D. Eisenhower, elected in 1952 as the first Republican president in twenty years, offered a solid Republican platform, seeking—though rarely attaining—a balanced budget, reduced taxes, and lower levels of government spending. Both men focused primarily on the foreign policy challenges of the Cold War. The most significant domestic political ferment, in fact, was a byprod-

uct of the Cold War: a ferocious anticommunism that narrowed the boundaries of acceptable dissent.

The economic boom that began with the end of the war lasted twenty-five years, bringing new prosperity to the American people. Though fears—of nuclear war, of returning hard times—lingered, by the late 1950s that prosperity had bred complacency. At the close of the decade, people sought satisfaction in their families and in the consumer pleasures newly available to so many. ■

Shaping Postwar America

*a*s Americans celebrated the end of World War II and mourned those who would never return, many feared the challenges that lay ahead. It seemed almost inevitable that the economy would plunge back into depression—and in the immediate aftermath of the war, unemployment rose and a wave of strikes rocked the nation. But economists who made dire predictions were wrong. In the postwar years the American economy flourished and Americans' standard of living improved. And the GI Bill and other new federal programs created new opportunities for Americans that changed the nation in fundamental ways.

As the end of the war approached and the American war machine slowed, factories began to lay off workers.

POSTWAR ECONOMIC UNCERTAINTY

At Ford Motor Company's massive Willow Run plant outside Detroit, where nine thousand Liberator bombers had been produced, most workers were let go in the spring of 1945. Ten days after the victory over Japan, 1.8 million people nationwide received pink slips, and 640,000 filed for unemployment compensation. More than 15 million GIs awaited demobilization; how were they to be absorbed into the shrinking job base?

Anticipating a postwar crisis, the federal government planned for demobilization even while some of the war's most difficult battles lay ahead. In the spring of 1944—a year before V-E Day—Congress unanimously passed the Servicemen's Readjustment Act, known as the GI Bill of Rights. The GI Bill showed the nation's gratitude to the men who fought. But it also attempted to keep the flood of demobilized veterans from swamping the U.S. economy: year-long unemployment benefits allowed veterans to be absorbed into civilian employment gradually, and higher-education benefits were designed to keep men in college and out of the job market. In winter 1945, congressional Democrats introduced a national Full Employment Act guaranteeing work to all who were able and willing, through public sector employment if necessary. By the time conservatives in Congress finished with the bill and Truman signed it into law in early 1946, key provisions regarding guaranteed work had virtually disappeared. But the act did reaffirm the federal government's responsibility for managing the economy and created a Council of Economic Advisors to assist the president in preventing economic downturns.

The nation's conversion to a peacetime economy hit workers hard, especially as the end of wartime price
POSTWAR STRIKES AND THE TAFT-HARTLEY ACT controls sent the inflation rate skyrocketing. Though workers had accepted wartime limits on wages, they would not stand by as unemployment threatened and their paychecks were eaten away. More than 5 million workers walked off the job in the year following Japan's surrender. Unions shut down the coal, automobile, steel, and electric industries and halted railroad and maritime transportation. So disruptive were the strikes that Americans began to hoard food and gasoline.

By the spring of 1946, Americans were losing patience with the strikes and with the Democratic administration they saw as partly responsible. When unions threatened a national railway strike, President Truman made a dramatic appearance before a joint session of Congress. If strikers in an industry deemed vital to national security refused to honor a presidential order to return to work, he announced, he would ask Congress to immediately draft into the armed forces "all workers who are on strike against their government." The Democratic Party, Truman made clear, would not offer unlimited support to organized labor.

Making the most of public anger at the strikes, in 1947 a group of pro-business Republicans and their conservative Democratic allies worked to restrict the power of labor unions. The Taft-Hartley Act permitted states to enact right-to-work laws that outlawed "closed shops," in which all workers were required to join the union if a majority of their number voted in favor of a union shop. The law also mandated an eighty-day cooling-off period before unions initiated strikes that imperiled the national security. These restrictions limited unions' ability to expand their membership, especially in the South and West, where states passed right-to-work laws. Though Truman had used the power of the presidency to avert a national railroad strike, he did not want to see union power so limited. But Congress passed the Taft-Hartley Act over Truman's veto.

Despite the fears of workers, employers, and politicians, economic depression did not return. The first year
ECONOMIC GROWTH of adjustment to a peacetime economy was difficult, but the economy recovered quickly, fueled by consumer spending. During the war, although Americans had brought home steady paychecks, they had little on which to spend them. No new cars, for example, had been built since 1942. Americans had saved their money for four years—and when new cars and appliances appeared at war's end, they were ready to buy. Companies like General Motors, which flouted conventional wisdom about a coming depression and expanded its operations by close to 50 percent just after the war, found millions of eager buyers. And because most other factories around the world were in ruins, U.S. corporations expanded their global dominance. America's leading corporations rode this postwar boom, increasing dramatically in size. Many created huge conglomerates. International Telegraph and Telephone (IT&T), for instance, bought up companies in several fields, including suburban development, insurance, and hotels. In keeping with the thrust of America's postwar boom, the country's ten largest corporations were in automobiles (GM, Ford, Chrysler); oil (Standard Oil of New Jersey, Mobil, Texaco); and electronics and communications (GE, IBM, IT&T, AT&T).

The agricultural sector contributed to postwar economic growth as well. New machines, such as mechanical cotton-, tobacco-, and grape-pickers and crop-dusting planes, revolutionized farming methods, and the increased use of fertilizers and pesticides raised the total value of farm output from $24.6 billion in 1945 to $38.4 billion in 1961. At the same time, the productivity of farm labor tripled. Large investors were drawn to agriculture by its increased profitability, and the average size of farms increased from 195 to 306 acres during this period.

Economic growth was also fueled by government programs, such as the GI Bill, that pumped money into the economy. By 1949, veterans had received close to $4 billion dollars in unemployment compensation. But the GI Bill did more than help forestall economic collapse. It offered veterans low-interest loans to buy a house or start a business, and—perhaps most significantly—stipends to cover college or technical school tuition and living expenses. As individuals grasped these opportunities, they changed their own lives and the shape of American society.

Before the war, higher education was for the affluent; about 7.5 percent of young Americans went to college. With GI benefits, almost half of America's returning veterans sought some form of higher education. The resulting increase in the number of well-educated or technically trained workers benefited the American economy. And though University of Chicago president Robert Maynard Hutchins protested that the GI Bill would turn universities into "educational hobo jungles," the flood of students and federal dollars into the nation's colleges and universities created a golden age for higher education.

Education obtained through the GI Bill created social mobility: children of barely literate menial laborers became white-collar professionals. And postwar universities, like the military, brought together people from vastly different backgrounds. The GI Bill fostered the emergence of a national middle-class culture, for as colleges exposed people to new ideas and to new experiences, their students tended to become less provincial, less rooted in ethnic or regional cultures.

During the Great Depression, young people had delayed marriage, and the nation's birth rate had plummeted. As war brought economic recovery, both marriage and birth rates began to rise. But the end of the war brought a boom. In 1946, the U.S. marriage rate was higher than that of any record-keeping nation (except Hungary) in the history of the twentieth century. The birth rate soared as Americans reversed the downward trend of the past 150 years. "Take the 3,548,000 babies born in 1950," wrote Sylvia F. Porter in her syndicated newspaper column. "Bundle them into a batch, bounce them all over the bountiful land that is America. What do you get?" Porter's answer: "Boom. The biggest, boomiest boom ever known in history. Just imagine how much these extra people, these new markets, will absorb—in food, clothing, in gadgets, in housing, in services. Our factories must expand just to keep pace." Though the baby boom peaked in 1957, more than 4 million babies were born every year until 1965 (see Figure 29.1). The baby-boom generation was the largest by far in the nation's history. As this vast cohort grew older, it had successive impacts on housing, nursery schools, grade schools, and high schools, fads and popular music, colleges and universities, the job market, and retirement funds, including Social Security.

Where were all these baby-boom families to live? Scarcely any new housing had been built since the 1920s. Almost 2 million families were doubled up with relatives in 1948; 50,000 people were living in Quonset huts, and in Chicago housing was so tight that 250 used trolley cars were sold as homes.

A combination of market forces, government actions, and individual decisions solved the housing crisis

BABY BOOM

SUBURBANIZATION and, in so doing, changed the way most Americans lived. In the postwar years, white Americans moved to the suburbs. Their reasons varied. Some moved to escape the crowds and noise of the city. People from rural areas moved closer to city jobs. Some white families moved out of urban neighborhoods because African American families were moving in. Many new suburbanites wanted more political influence and more control over their children's education. Most who moved to the suburbs, however, simply wanted to own their own homes—and suburban developments were where the affordable housing was. While suburban development predated World War II, the massive migration of 18 million Americans to the suburbs from cities, small towns, and farms between 1950 and 1960 was on a wholly different scale (see Table 29.1).

In the years following World War II, suburban developers applied techniques of mass production to create acres of modest suburban houses in what had recently been pastures and fields. In 1947 builder William Levitt adapted Henry Ford's assembly-line methods to revolutionize the process of home building.

Figure 29.1   Birth Rate, 1945–1964

The birth rate began to rise in 1942 and 1943, but it skyrocketed during the postwar years beginning in 1946, reaching its peak in 1957. From 1954 to 1964, the United States recorded more than 4 million births every year.
(Source: Adapted from U.S. Bureau of the Census, *Historical Statistics of the United States, Colonial Times to 1970,* Bicentennial Edition [Washington, D.C., U.S. Government Printing Office, 1975], p. 49.)

■ Housing was so tight in the years following World War II that many young couples had to move in with one set of their parents—or accept some unusual housing options. Former marine lieutenant Willard Pedrick and his family made their home in a Quonset hut on the campus of Northwestern University in Evanston, Illinois, where Pedrick was an associate professor in the Economics department.   (© Bettmann/Corbis)

TABLE 29.1

Geographic Distribution of the U.S. Population, 1930–1970 (in Percentages)

Year	Central Cities	Suburbs	Rural Areas and Small Towns
1930	31.8%	18.0%	50.2%
1940	31.6	19.5	48.9
1950	32.3	23.8	43.9
1960	32.6	30.7	36.7
1970	31.4	37.6	31.0

Source: Adapted from U.S. Bureau of the Census, *Decennial Censuses, 1930–1970* (Washington, D.C., U.S. Government Printing Office).

Suburban development could never have happened on such a large scale, however, without federal policies that encouraged it. Low-interest GI mortgages and loans made possible by Federal Housing Administration (FHA) mortgage insurance helped families purchase houses in the new suburbs. New highways also promoted suburban development. Congress authorized construction of a 37,000-mile chain of highways in 1947, and in 1956 passed the Highway Act to create a 42,500-mile interstate highway system. Intended to facilitate commerce and rapid mobilization of the military in case of a threat to national security, these highways also allowed workers to live farther and farther from their jobs in central cities.

Postwar federal programs did not benefit all Americans equally. First, federal policies often assisted men at the expense of women. The federal Selective Service Act guaranteed veterans (overwhelmingly men) priority in postwar employment over the war workers who had replaced them. As industry laid off civilian workers to make room for veterans, women lost their jobs at a rate 75 percent higher than men. Many women stayed in the work force but were pushed into less well paying jobs. Universities made room for veterans on the GI Bill by excluding qualified women students; a much smaller percentage of college degrees went to women after the war than before.

INEQUALITY IN BENEFITS

Inequities were also based on race. African American, Native American, Mexican American, and Asian American veterans, like European American veterans, received educational benefits and hiring preference in civil service jobs following the war. But war workers from

By 1949, instead of 4 or 5 custom homes per year, Levitt's company could build 180 houses a week. They were very basic—four and a half rooms on a 60-by-100-foot lot, all with identical floorplans—the Model T of houses. But the same floorplan could be disguised by four different exteriors, and by rotating seven paint colors Levitt guaranteed that only one in every twenty-eight houses would be identical. In the Levittown on Long Island, a tree was planted every 28 feet (two and a half trees per house). The basic house, appliances included, sold for $7,990. Other homebuilders quickly adopted Levitt's techniques.

these groups found themselves among the first laid off as factories made room for white, male veterans. Federal housing policies also exacerbated racial inequality. Federal loan officers and bankers often labeled African American or racially mixed neighborhoods "high risk" for lending, denying mortgages to members of racial minorities regardless of individual credit-worthiness. This practice, called "redlining" because such neighborhoods were outlined in red on lenders' maps, kept African Americans and many Hispanics from buying into the great economic explosion of the postwar era. White families who bought homes with mortgages guaranteed by the federal government saw their small investments increase in worth dramatically over the years. Discriminatory policies denied most African Americans and other people of color that opportunity.

Domestic Politics in the Cold War Era

Though the major social and economic transformations of the postwar era were due in great part to federal policies and programs, domestic politics were not at the forefront of American life during these years. Foreign affairs were usually paramount, as Democratic president Harry Truman and Republican president Dwight D. Eisenhower both faced significant challenges in the expanding Cold War. Domestically, Truman attempted to build on the New Deal's liberal agenda, while Eisenhower called for balanced budgets and business-friendly policies. But neither administration ever approached the level of political and legislative activism seen earlier in the 1930s New Deal.

HARRY S TRUMAN AND POSTWAR LIBERALISM

Harry Truman, the plain-spoken former haberdasher from Missouri, had never expected to be president. In 1944, when Franklin Roosevelt asked him to join the Democratic ticket as the vice-presidential candidate, he almost refused. Roosevelt, the master politician, played hardball. "If he wants to break up the Democratic Party in the middle of the war, that's his responsibility," the president said flatly. "Oh shit," said Truman, "if that's the situation, I'll have to say yes." But the president, with his hands full as America entered its fourth year of war, had little time for his new vice president and left Truman in the dark about everything from the Manhattan Project to plans for postwar domestic policy. When Roosevelt died, suddenly, in April 1945, Truman was unprepared to take his place.

Truman stepped forward, however, placing a sign on his desk that proclaimed: "The Buck Stops Here." Most of Truman's presidency focused on the challenges of foreign relations, as he led the nation through the last months of World War II and into the new Cold War with the Soviet Union. Domestically, he oversaw the process of reconversion from war to peace and attempted to keep a liberal agenda—the legacy of Roosevelt's New Deal—alive.

In his 1944 State of the Union address, President Roosevelt had offered Americans a "Second Bill of Rights": the right to employment, healthcare, education, food, and housing. This declaration that the government would take responsibility for the welfare of the nation and its citizens was the cornerstone of postwar liberalism, and Truman's legislative program was designed to maintain the federal government's active role in guaranteeing social welfare, promoting social justice, managing the economy, and regulating the power of business corporations. Truman proposed an increase in the minimum wage and national housing legislation offering loans for mortgages, and he supported the Full Employment Act. To pay for his proposed social welfare programs, Truman gambled that full employment would generate sufficient tax revenue and that consumer spending would fuel economic growth.

The gamble on economic growth paid off, but Truman quickly learned the limits of his political influence. The conservative coalition of Republicans and southern Democrats that had stalled Roosevelt's New Deal legislation in the late 1930s was even less inclined to support Truman. Congress gutted the Full Employment Act, refused to raise the minimum wage, and passed the anti-union Taft-Hartley Act over Truman's veto. With powerful congressional opposition, Truman had little chance of major legislative accomplishments. But his inexperience contributed to the political impasse. "To err is Truman," people began to joke. As Truman presided over the rocky transition from a wartime to a peacetime economy, he had to deal with massive inflation (briefly hitting 35 percent), shortages of consumer goods, and a wave of postwar strikes that slowed production of eagerly awaited consumer goods and drove prices up further. Truman's approval rating plunged from 87 percent in late 1945 to 32 percent in 1946.

1948 ELECTION

By 1948 it seemed that Republicans would win the White House in November. A confident Republican Party nominated Thomas Dewey, the man Roosevelt had defeated in 1944, as its presidential candidate. The Republicans were counting on schisms in the Democratic Party to give them victory. Two years before, Henry A.

■ Crowds on Harlem's 125th Street cheer President Truman during a campaign appearance in 1948. African American voters were an increasingly important political force in the postwar era, and Truman was the first presidential candidate to go to Harlem seeking support.
(© Bettmann/Corbis)

Wallace, the only remaining New Dealer in the cabinet, had been fired by Truman for publicly criticizing U.S. foreign policy. In 1948 Wallace ran for president on the Progressive Party ticket, which advocated friendly relations with the Soviet Union, racial desegregation, and nationalization of basic industries. A fourth party, the Dixiecrats (States' Rights Democratic Party), was organized by white southerners who walked out of the 1948 Democratic convention when it adopted a pro–civil rights plank; they nominated the fiercely segregationist governor Strom Thurmond of South Carolina. If Wallace's candidacy did not destroy Truman's chances, experts said, the Dixiecrats certainly would.

Truman, however, refused to give up. He resorted to red-baiting, denouncing "Henry Wallace and his communists" at every opportunity. Most important, he directly appealed to the burgeoning population of African American voters in northern cities, becoming the first presidential candidate to campaign in Harlem. In the end, Truman prevailed. The Progressive and Dixiecrat Parties attracted far fewer voters than had been predicted; most Democrats saw Truman—in contrast to Thurmond or Wallace—as an appealing moderate. African American voters made the difference, giving Truman the electoral votes of key northern states. Roosevelt's New Deal coalition—African Americans, union members, northern urban voters, and most southern whites—had endured.

Truman began his new term brimming with confidence. It was time, he believed, for government to fulfill its responsibility to provide economic security for the poor and the elderly. As he worked on his 1949 State of the Union message, he penciled in his intentions: "I expect to give every segment of our population a fair deal." Truman, unlike Roosevelt, pushed forward legislation to support the civil rights of African Americans, including the antilynching law Roosevelt had given only lukewarm support. He proposed a national health insurance program and federal aid for education. Once again, however, little of Truman's legislative agenda came to fruition. A filibuster by southern conservatives in Congress destroyed his civil rights legislation; the American Medical Association denounced his health insurance plan as "socialized medicine"; and the Roman Catholic Church opposed aid to education because it would not include parochial schools.

When the postwar peace proved short-lived and Truman ordered troops to Korea in June 1950 (see Chapter 28), there was much grumbling among Americans as the

TRUMAN'S FAIR DEAL

nation again mobilized for war. People remembered the shortages of the last war and stocked up on sugar, coffee, and canned goods. Fueled by panic buying, inflation began to rise again. Many reservists and national guardsmen resented being called to active duty. An unpopular war and charges of influence peddling by some of Truman's cronies pushed the president's public approval rating to an all-time low of 23 percent in 1951, where it stayed for a year. Once again it appeared that the Republican Party would win the presidency.

"It's Time for a Change" was the Republican campaign slogan, and voters agreed, especially when the Republican candidate was General Dwight

EISENHOWER'S DYNAMIC CONSERVATISM

D. Eisenhower. Americans hoped that the immensely popular World War II hero could end the Korean War. And Eisenhower appealed to moderates in both parties (in fact, the Democrats had tried to recruit him as their presidential candidate).

Smiling Ike, with his folksy style, garbled syntax, and frequent escapes to the golf course, provoked Democrats to charge that he failed to lead. But Dwight D. Eisenhower was not that simple. He was no stranger to hard work. His low-key, "hidden-hand" style was a way of playing down his role as politician and highlighting his role as chief of state. Eisenhower relied heavily on staff work, delegating authority to cabinet members. Sometimes he gave the impression that he was out of touch with his own government. In fact, he was not, and he remained a very popular president.

With a Republican in the White House for the first time in twenty years, conservatives hoped to roll back New Deal liberal programs such as the mandatory Social Security system. But Eisenhower had no such intention. The president and his appointees realized that dismantling New Deal and Fair Deal programs was politically impossible. Instead, Eisenhower adopted an approach he called "dynamic conservatism": being "conservative when it comes to money and liberal when it comes to human beings." On the liberal side, in 1954 Eisenhower signed into law amendments to the Social Security Act that raised benefits and added 7.5 million workers, mostly self-employed farmers, to the Social Security rolls. The Eisenhower administration also increased government funding for education—though increases were motivated by Cold War fears, not liberal principles. When the Soviet Union launched *Sputnik*, the first earth-orbiting satellite, in 1957 (and America's first launch exploded seconds after liftoff), education became an issue of national security. Congress responded in 1958 with the National Defense Education Act (NDEA), which

funded enrichment of elementary and high-school programs in mathematics, foreign languages, and the sciences and offered fellowships and loans to college students. This attempt to win the "battle of brainpower" increased the educational opportunities available to young Americans.

Overall, however, Eisenhower's was unabashedly "an Administration representing business and industry,"

GROWTH OF THE MILITARY-INDUSTRIAL COMPLEX

as Interior Secretary Douglas McKay acknowledged. The Eisenhower administration's tax reform bill raised business depreciation allowances, and the Atomic Energy Act of 1954 granted private companies the right to own reactors and nuclear materials for the production of electricity. Eisenhower also attempted to reduce the federal budget but did not always succeed. In fact, he balanced only three of his eight budgets, turning to deficit spending to cushion the impact of three recessions (in 1953–1954, 1957–1958, and 1960–1961) and to fund the tremendous cost of America's global activities. In 1959 federal expenditures climbed to $92 billion, about half of which went to the military, much of that for developing new weapons.

Just before leaving office in early 1961, at the end of his second term, Eisenhower went on national radio and television to deliver his farewell address to the nation. Because of the Cold War, he observed, the United States had begun to maintain a large standing army—3.5 million men. And ever greater percentages of the nation's budget went to developing and building weapons of war. Condemning the new "conjunction of an immense military establishment and a large arms industry," Eisenhower warned: "The total influence—economic, political, even spiritual—is felt in every city, every statehouse, every office of the federal government" and threatened the nation's democratic process. Eisenhower, the former five-star general and war hero, urged Americans to "guard against . . . the military-industrial complex."

During Eisenhower's presidency both liberal Democrats and moderate Republicans seemed satisfied to be occupying what the historian Arthur M. Schlesinger Jr. called "the vital center." And with the Cold War between the United States and the Soviet Union portrayed as a battle between good and evil, a struggle for the future of the world, criticism of American society seemed suspect—even unpatriotic. British journalist Godfrey Hodgson described this time as an era of "consensus," when Americans were "confident to the verge of complacency about the perfectibility of American society, anxious to the point of paranoia about the threat of communism."

Cold War Fears and Anticommunism

International relations had a profound influence on America's domestic politics in the years following World War II. Americans were frightened by the Cold War tensions between the United States and the Soviet Union—and there were legitimate reasons for fear. Reasonable fears, however, spilled over into anticommunist demagoguery and witch hunts. Fear allowed the trampling of civil liberties, the suppression of dissent, and the persecution of thousands of innocent Americans.

Anticommunism was not new in American society. A "red scare" had swept the nation following the Russian Revolution of 1917, and opponents of America's labor movement had used charges of communism to block unionization through the 1930s. In the immediate aftermath of World War II, Soviet aggression heightened American anticommunism. Many saw the Soviet Union's virtual takeover of eastern Europe in the late 1940s as an alarming parallel to Nazi Germany's takeover of neighboring states. People remembered the failure of "appeasement" at Munich and worried that the United States was "too soft" in its policy toward the Soviet Union.

■ Cold War fears reached deep into American life during the 1950s. Here, the Jensen family of Fort Myer, Virginia, model Federal Civil Defense Administration gas masks. The daughter, Susan, wears a "Mickey Mouse Protective Mask." (National Archives)

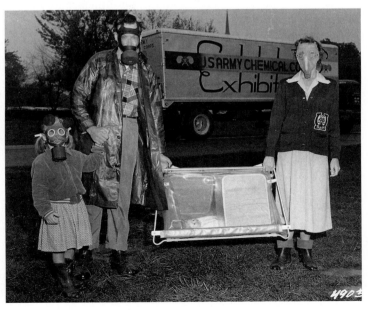

In addition, the Soviet Union was spying on the United States in an attempt to gain nuclear secrets. (The United States also had spies within the Soviet Union.) American intelligence officers in a top-secret project code-named "Venona" decrypted almost three thousand Soviet telegraphic cables that proved Soviet spies had infiltrated U.S. government agencies and nuclear programs. To prevent the Soviets from realizing that their codes were compromised, intelligence officials kept this evidence from the American public. But the U.S. government was determined to combat Soviet espionage in the United States.

ESPIONAGE AND NUCLEAR FEARS

Fear of nuclear war also contributed to American anticommunism. For four years, the United States alone possessed what seemed the ultimate weapon, but in 1949, the Soviet Union exploded its own atomic bomb. President Truman, initiating a national atomic civil defense program shortly thereafter, told Americans: "I cannot tell you when or where the attack will come or that it will come at all. I can only remind you that we must be ready when it does come." Children practiced "duck-and-cover" positions in their school classrooms, learning how to shield their faces from the atomic flash and flying debris in the event of an attack. *Life* magazine featured backyard fallout shelters. Americans worried that the United States was newly vulnerable to attack on its own soil and feared anything that might give the USSR an advantage in the global struggle.

At the height of the Cold War, American leaders, including Presidents Truman and Eisenhower, did not always draw a sufficient line between prudent attempts to prevent Soviet spies from infiltrating important government agencies and anticommunist scare-mongering for political gain. Truman consciously employed alarmist language about the communist threat to gain support for aid to Greece and Turkey in 1947. Republican politicians used red-baiting tactics effectively against Democratic opponents, eventually targeting the Truman administration as a whole. In 1947, President Truman ordered investigations into the loyalty of more than 3 million employees of the U.S. government. As anticommunist hysteria grew, the government began discharging people deemed "security risks," among them alcoholics, homosexuals, and debtors thought susceptible to blackmail. In most cases there was no evidence of disloyalty.

THE POLITICS OF ANTICOMMUNISM

Taking the lead in the anticommunist crusade was the House Un-American Activities Committee (popularly known as HUAC). Created in 1938 to investigate "subversive and un-American propaganda," the viciously anti–New Deal committee had lost credibility during the 1930s by charging that film stars—including eight-year-old Shirley Temple—were dupes of the Communist Party. By 1947, in a shameless publicity-grabbing tactic, HUAC was back in Hollywood. Using Federal Bureau of Investigation (FBI) files and testimony of people such as Screen Actors Guild president Ronald Reagan (who was also a secret informant for the FBI, complete with code name), the committee went on the attack. Members of a group of screenwriters and directors known as the "Hollywood Ten" were sent to prison for contempt of Congress when they refused to "name names" of suspected communists for HUAC. At least a dozen others committed suicide. Studios panicked and blacklisted hundreds of actors, screenwriters, directors, even makeup artists, who were suspected of communist affiliations. With no evidence of wrongdoing, these men and women had careers—and sometimes lives—ruined.

University professors were also targets of the growing "witch hunt." In 1949 HUAC demanded lists of the

MCCARTHYISM AND THE GROWING "WITCH HUNT"

textbooks used in courses at eighty-one universities. When the board of regents at the University of California, Berkeley, instituted a loyalty oath for faculty, firing twenty-six who resisted on principle, protests from faculty members across the nation forced the regents to back down. But many professors, afraid of the reach of HUAC, began to downplay controversial material in their courses. The labor movement also was powerfully affected. The CIO expelled eleven unions, with a combined membership of over 900,000, for alleged communist domination. The red panic reached its nadir in February 1950, when a relatively obscure U.S. senator came before an audience in Wheeling, West Virginia, to charge that the U.S. State Department was "thoroughly infested with Communists." Republican senator Joseph R. McCarthy of Wisconsin was not an especially credible source. He made charges and then retracted them, claiming first that there were 205 communists in the State Department, then 57, then 81. He had a severe drinking problem; downing a water glass full of Scotch in a single gulp, he would follow it with a quarter-pound stick of butter, hoping to counteract the effects of the liquor. He had a record of dishonesty as a lawyer and judge in his hometown of Appleton, Wisconsin. But McCarthy crystallized the anxieties many felt as they faced a new and difficult era in American life, and the anticommunist excesses of this era came to be known as McCarthyism.

In 1954 Senator Joseph R. McCarthy, surrounded by his own newspaper headlines, adorns the cover of *Time* magazine. His downfall came later that year, during the televised Army-McCarthy hearings. McCarthy's wild accusations and abusive treatment of witnesses disgusted millions of viewers. (© 1954 Time Inc.)

With HUAC and McCarthy on the attack, Americans began pointing accusing fingers at one another. The anticommunist crusade was embraced by labor union officials, religious leaders, and the media, as well as by politicians. A bootblack at the Pentagon was questioned by the FBI seventy times because he had given $10 during the 1930s to a defense fund for the Scottsboro Boys (see page 706), who had been represented by an attorney from the Communist Party. Women in New York who lobbied for the continuation of wartime daycare programs were denounced as communists by the *New York World Telegram*. "Reds, phonies, and 'parlor pinks,'" in Truman's words, seemed to lurk everywhere.

In such a climate, most public figures found it too risky to stand up against McCarthyist tactics. And most Democrats did support the domestic Cold War and its

ANTICOMMUNISM IN CONGRESS anticommunist actions. In 1950, with bipartisan support, Congress passed the Internal Security (McCarran) Act, which required members of "Communist-front" organizations to register with the government and prohibited them from holding government jobs or traveling abroad. In 1954, the Senate unanimously passed the Communist Control Act (there were two dissenting votes in the House), which effectively made membership in the Communist Party illegal. Its chief sponsor, Democratic senator Hubert H. Humphrey of Minnesota, told his colleagues just before he cast his vote: "We have closed all of the doors. The rats will not get out of the trap."

The anticommunist fervor was fueled by spectacular and controversial trials of Americans accused of passing secrets to the Soviet Union. In 1948, Congressman Richard Nixon of California, a member of HUAC, was propelled onto the national stage when he accused former State Department official Alger Hiss of espionage. In 1950, Hiss was convicted of lying about his contacts with Soviet agents. That same year, Ethel and Julius Rosenberg were arrested for passing atomic secrets to the Soviets; they were found guilty of treason and executed in 1953. For decades, many historians believed that the Rosenbergs were primarily victims of a witch hunt. In fact, there was strong evidence of Julius Rosenberg's guilt in cables decrypted by the Venona Project (as well as evidence that Ethel Rosenberg was less involved than charged), but this evidence was not presented at their trial for reasons of national security. The cables remained top secret until 1995, when a Clinton administration initiative opened the files to historians.

Some of the worst excesses of Cold War anticommunism waned when Senator McCarthy was discredited on national television in 1954. McCarthy was himself a master at using the press, making sensational accusations—front-page material—just before reporters' deadlines. When the evidence didn't pan out or McCarthy's charges proved untrue, retractions appeared in the back pages of the newspapers. Even journalists who knew McCarthy was unreliable continued to report his charges. Sensational stories sell papers, and McCarthy became a celebrity.

THE WANING OF THE RED SCARE

But McCarthy badly misunderstood the power of television. His crucial mistake was taking on the U.S. Army in front of millions of television viewers. At issue was the senator's wild accusation that the army was shielding and promoting communists; he cited the case of one army dentist. The so-called Army-McCarthy hearings, held by a Senate subcommittee in 1954, became a showcase for the senator's abusive treatment of witnesses. McCarthy, apparently drunk, alternately ranted and slurred his words. Finally, after he maligned a young lawyer who was not even involved in the hearings, army counsel Joseph Welch protested, "Have you no sense of decency, sir?" The gallery erupted in applause, and McCarthy's career as a witch-hunter was over. In December 1954 the Senate voted to "condemn" McCarthy for sullying the dignity of the Senate. He remained a senator, but exhaustion and alcohol took their toll, and he died in 1957 at the age of forty-eight. With McCarthy discredited, the most virulent strand of anticommunism had run its course. However, the use of fear tactics for political gain and the narrowing of American freedoms and liberties were chilling legacies of the domestic Cold War.

The Struggle for Civil Rights

The Cold War—at home and abroad—also shaped African American struggles for social justice and the nation's responses to them. As the Soviet Union was quick to point out, the United States could hardly pose as the leader of the free world or condemn the denial of human rights in eastern Europe and the Soviet Union if it practiced segregation at home. Nor could the United States convince new African and Asian nations of its dedication to human rights if African Americans were subjected to segregation, discrimination, disfranchisement, and racial violence. Some African American leaders, in fact, understood their struggle for equal rights in the United States as part of a larger, international movement. To win the support of nonaligned nations, the United States would have to live up to its own ideals. At the same time, many Americans viewed social criticism of any kind as a Soviet-inspired attempt to weaken the United States in the ongoing Cold War. The Federal Bureau of Investigation and local law enforcement agencies commonly used such anticommunist fears to justify attacks on civil rights activists. In this heated environment, African Americans struggled to seize the political initiative.

Americans had seen the Second World War as a struggle for democracy and against hatred. African Americans who had helped win the war were determined that their lives in postwar America would be better because of their sacrifices. Moreover, politicians such as Harry Truman were beginning to pay attention to black aspirations, especially as black voters in some urban-industrial states began to control the political balance of power.

GROWING BLACK POLITICAL POWER

President Truman had compelling political reasons for supporting African American civil rights. But he also felt a moral obligation to do something, for he genuinely believed it was only fair that every American, regardless of race, should enjoy the full rights of citizenship. Truman was disturbed by a resurgence of racial terrorism, as a revived Ku Klux Klan was burning crosses and murdering blacks who sought civil rights and racial justice in the aftermath of World War II. But what really horrified Truman was the report that police in Aiken, South Carolina, had gouged out the eyes of a black sergeant just three hours after he had been discharged from the army. Several weeks after this atrocity, in December 1946, Truman signed an executive order establishing the President's Committee on Civil Rights. The Committee's Report, *To Secure These Rights,* would become the agenda for the civil rights movement for the next twenty years. It called for antilynching and antisegregation legislation and for laws guaranteeing voting rights and equal employment opportunity. For the first time since Reconstruction, a president had acknowledged the federal government's responsibility to protect blacks and strive for racial equality.

Truman took this responsibility seriously, and in 1948 he issued two executive orders declaring an end to racial discrimination in the federal government. One proclaimed a policy of "fair employment throughout the federal establishment" and created the Employment Board of the Civil Service Commission to hear charges of discrimination. The other ordered the racial desegregation of the armed forces and appointed the Committee on Equality of Treatment and Opportunity in the Armed Services to oversee this process. Despite strong, even fierce, opposition to desegregation within the military, segregated units were being phased out by the time the Korean War broke out.

At the same time, African Americans were successfully challenging racial discrimination in the courts. In 1939, the NAACP had established its Legal Defense and Education Fund under Charles Hamilton Houston and Thurgood Marshall. By the 1940s, Marshall (who in 1967 would become the first African American Supreme Court justice) and his colleagues were working to destroy the separate-but-equal doctrine established in *Plessy v. Ferguson* (1896) by insisting on its literal interpretation. In higher education, the NAACP calculated, the cost of true equality in racially separate schools would be prohibitive. "You can't build a cyclotron for one student," as the president of the University of Oklahoma acknowledged. As a result of NAACP lawsuits, African American students won admission to

SCHOOL DESEGREGATION AND SUPREME COURT VICTORIES

professional and graduate schools at a number of formerly segregated state universities. The NAACP also won major victories through the Supreme Court in *Smith v. Allwright* (1944), which outlawed the whites-only primaries held by the Democratic Party in some southern states; *Morgan v. Virginia* (1946), which struck down segregation in interstate bus transportation, and *Shelley v. Kraemer* (1948), in which the Court held that racially restrictive covenants (private agreements among white homeowners not to sell to blacks) could not legally be enforced.

A change in social attitudes accompanied these gains in black political and legal power. Gunnar Myrdal's social science study *An American Dilemma* (1944) and Richard Wright's novel *Native Son* (1940) and his autobiography *Black Boy* (1945) had increased white awareness of the social injustices that plagued African Americans. A new and visible black middle class was emerging, composed of college-educated activists, war veterans, and union workers. Blacks and whites also worked together in CIO unions and service organizations such as the National Council of Churches. In 1947 a black baseball player, Jackie Robinson, broke the major league color barrier and electrified Brooklyn Dodgers fans with his spectacular hitting and base running.

■ Jackie Robinson cracked the color line in major league baseball when he joined the Brooklyn Dodgers for the 1947 season. Sliding safely into third base, Robinson displays the aggressive style that won him rookie-of-the-year honors. He was later elected to the Baseball Hall of Fame. (Hy Peskin, *Life* Magazine © Time Inc.)

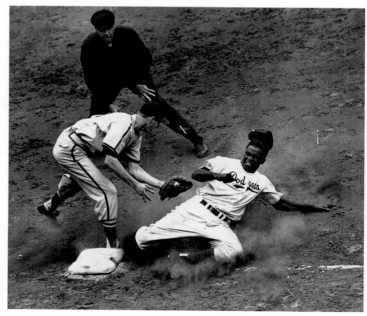

Even so, segregation was still standard practice in the 1950s, and blacks continued to suffer disfranchisement, job discrimination, and violence, including the bombing murder in 1951 of the Florida state director of the NAACP and his wife. But in 1954 the NAACP won a historic victory that stunned the white South and energized African Americans to challenge segregation on several fronts. *Brown v. Board of Education of Topeka,* which Thurgood Marshall argued before the high court, incorporated school desegregation cases from several states. The Court's unanimous decision was written by Chief Justice Earl Warren, who, as California's attorney general, had pushed for the internment of Japanese Americans during World War II. The Court concluded that "in the field of public education the doctrine of 'separate but equal' has no place. Separate educational facilities are inherently unequal." But the ruling that overturned *Plessy v. Ferguson* (see Chapter 20) did not demand immediate compliance. A year later the Court finally ordered school desegregation, but only "with all deliberate speed." The lack of a timetable encouraged the southern states to resist.

Some communities in border states like Kansas and Maryland quietly implemented the school desegregation order, and many southern moderates advocated a gradual rollback of segregation. But the forces of white resistance soon came to dominate, urging southern communities to defy the Court. The Klan experienced another resurgence, and white violence against blacks increased. In 1955, Emmett Till, a fourteen-year-old from Chicago, was murdered by white men in Mississippi who took offense at the way he spoke to a white woman. Business and professional people created White Citizens' Councils for the express purpose of resisting the school desegregation order. Known familiarly as "uptown Ku Klux Klans," the councils brought their economic power to bear against black civil rights activists. They also pushed through state laws that provided private-school tuition for white children who left public schools to avoid integration. When FBI director J. Edgar Hoover briefed President Eisenhower on southern racial tensions in 1956, he warned of communist influences among the civil rights activists, and even suggested that if the Citizens' Councils did not worsen the racial situation, they might "control the rising tension."

WHITE RESISTANCE

White resistance to civil rights also gained strength in large northern cities, such as Chicago and Detroit. African Americans had moved to Chicago in large numbers between 1940 and 1960; the city's black population increased from 275,000 to 800,000. The newcomers found good jobs in industry, while their increased numbers gave them political power. At the same time, they faced housing segregation. In 1951 in Cicero, a town adjoining Chicago, several thousand whites who were determined to keep blacks out of their neighborhood provoked a race riot. So racially divided was Chicago that the U.S. Commission on Civil Rights in 1959 described it as "the most residentially segregated city in the nation." Detroit and other northern cities were not far behind. And because children attended neighborhood schools, education was segregated as well.

Unlike Truman, President Eisenhower wanted to avoid dealing with civil rights, preferring gradual and voluntary change in race relations over executive orders and court mandates. Although the president disapproved of racial segregation, he objected to "compulsory federal law," believing instead that race relations would improve "only if [desegregation] starts locally." He also feared that the ugly public confrontations likely to follow rapid desegregation would jeopardize Republican inroads in the South. Thus Eisenhower did not state forthrightly that the federal government would enforce the *Brown* decision as the nation's law. In short, instead of leading, he spoke ambiguously and thereby tacitly encouraged white resistance.

FEDERAL AUTHORITY AND STATES' RIGHTS

Events in Little Rock, Arkansas, forced the president to stop sidestepping the issue. In September 1957 Arkansas governor Orval E. Faubus defied a court-ordered desegregation plan for Little Rock's Central High School. Faubus went on television the night before school began and told Arkansans that "blood would run in the streets" if black students tried to enter the high school the next day, and he deployed 250 Arkansas National Guard troops to block their entrance. Eight black teenagers tried to enter Central High on the second day of school but were turned away by the National Guard. The ninth, separated from the others, was surrounded by jeering whites and narrowly escaped the mob with the help of a sympathetic white woman.

The "Little Rock Nine" entered Central High for the first time more than two weeks after school began, after a federal judge intervened. An angry crowd surrounded the school, and television broadcast the scene to the nation and the world. Eisenhower, fearing violence and angry at what he saw as Faubus's attempt to provoke a crisis, nationalized the Arkansas National Guard (placing it under federal, not state, control) and dispatched one thousand army paratroopers to Little Rock. Troops guarded the students for the rest of the year. Eisenhower's use of federal power in Little Rock was a critical

In 1957 white teenagers in Little Rock, Arkansas, angrily confront African American students who, under federal court order, are attempting to enter, and thus desegregate, Central High School. The Supreme Court's *Brown* decision of 1954 was resisted by whites throughout the South.   (Wide World Photos, Inc.)

step in America's struggle over racial equality, for he directly confronted the conflict between federal authority and states' rights. However, state power triumphed the following year when Faubus closed all public high schools in Little Rock rather than desegregate them.

By the mid-1950s, a growing number of African Americans were no longer waiting for action from the Supreme Court or the White House; they were directly engaged in a grass-roots struggle for civil rights. In 1955 Rosa Parks, a department store seamstress and long-time NAACP activist, was arrested when she refused to give up her seat to a white man on a public bus in Montgomery, Alabama. Her arrest gave local black women's organizations and civil rights groups a cause around which to organize a boycott of the city's bus system. They selected Martin Luther King Jr., a recently ordained minister who had just arrived in Montgomery, as their leader. King launched the boycott with a moving speech in which he declared: "If we are wrong, the Constitution is wrong. If we are wrong, God Almighty is wrong. If we are wrong, Jesus of Nazareth was merely a utopian dreamer. . . . If we are wrong, justice is a lie."

Martin Luther King Jr. was a twenty-six-year-old Baptist minister who recently had earned a Ph.D. degree

MONTGOMERY BUS BOYCOTT

at Boston University. Committed to the transforming potential of Christian love, and schooled in the teachings of India's leader Mohandas K. Gandhi, King believed in nonviolent protest and civil disobedience. King hoped, by refusing to obey unjust and racist laws, to focus the nation's attention on the immorality of Jim Crow. Although he was jailed for "conspiring" to boycott and a bomb blew out the front of his house, King persisted.

During the year-long Montgomery bus boycott, blacks young and old rallied in their churches, sang hymns, and prayed that the nation would awaken to the evils of segregation and racial discrimination. They maintained their boycott through heavy rains and the steamy heat of summer, often walking miles a day. One elderly black woman, offered a ride to work by a white reporter, told him, "No, my feets is tired, but my soul is rested." With the bus company near bankruptcy and downtown merchants hurt by declining sales, city officials adopted harassment tactics to bring an end to the boycott. But the black people of Montgomery persevered. Thirteen months after the boycott began the Supreme Court declared Alabama's bus segregation laws unconstitutional.

The boycott propelled King to the forefront of a new, grassroots civil rights activism in which black churches played a major role. In 1957 King became the

■ For leading the movement to gain equality for blacks riding city buses in Montgomery, Alabama, Martin Luther King Jr. (1929–1968) and other African Americans, including twenty-three other ministers, were indicted by an all-white jury for violating an old law banning boycotts. In late March 1956 King was convicted and fined $500. A crowd of well-wishers cheered a smiling King (here with his wife, Coretta) outside the courthouse, where King proudly declared, "The protest goes on!" King's arrest and conviction made the bus boycott front-page news across America.   (© Bettmann/Corbis)

first president of the Southern Christian Leadership Conference (SCLC), organized to coordinate civil rights activities. That same year, Congress passed the first Civil Rights Act since Reconstruction. It created the United States Commission on Civil Rights to investigate systematic discrimination, such as in voting. This measure, like a voting rights act passed three years later, proved ineffective, and critics charged that the Eisenhower administration was interested more in suppressing the civil rights question than in addressing it. However, with the success in Montgomery and the gains won through the Supreme Court and the Truman administration, African Americans were poised to launch a major movement for civil rights in the decade to come.

Creating a Middle-Class Nation

Even as African Americans encountered massive resistance in their struggles for civil rights during the 1950s, in other ways the United States was becoming a more inclusive society. More Americans than ever before participated in a broad, middle-class and suburban culture, and divisions among Americans based on class, ethnicity, religion, and regional identity became less important. National prosperity offered ever greater numbers of Americans material comfort and economic security—entrance into an economic middle class. Old European ethnic identities were fading, as an ever smaller percentage of America's people were first- or second-generation immigrants.

In the new suburbs, people from different backgrounds worked together to create communities and build institutions such as schools and churches. Middle-class Americans, like those on Nancy Circle, increasingly looked to powerful national media rather than to regional or ethnic traditions for advice on matters ranging from how to celebrate Thanksgiving to what car to buy to how to raise children. New opportunities for consumption—whether the fads of a powerful teenage culture or the suburban ranch-style house—also tied Americans from different backgrounds together. In the postwar years, a new middle-class way of life was transforming the United States.

During the 1950s, sustained economic growth created unprecedented levels of prosperity and economic

PROSPERITY
FOR MORE
AMERICANS security for a broad range of America's people (see Figure 29.2). Several factors contributed to the economic boom. In great part, it was driven by consumer spending. Americans eagerly bought consumer goods that had not been available during the war, and industries expanded production to meet consumer demand. Government spending also played an important role. As the Cold War deepened, the government poured money into defense industries, creating jobs and stimulating the economy.

A new era of labor relations helped bring economic prosperity to more Americans. By 1950, labor and management created a new, more stable, relationship. In peaceful negotiations, the United Auto Workers (UAW) and General Motors led the way for other corporations in providing workers with health insurance, pension plans, and guaranteed cost-of-living adjustments, or COLAs, to protect wages against inflation. The 1950 agreement *Fortune* magazine called "The Treaty of Detroit" gave GM's workers a five-year contract, with regular wage increases tied to corporate productivity. This was a turning point for the labor movement. In exchange for wages and benefits, organized labor gave up its demands for greater control in corporate affairs. And with wage increases tied to corporate productivity, labor cast its lot with management: workplace stability and efficiency, not strikes, would bring higher wages. During the 1950s, wages and benefits often rivaled those of college-educated professionals and propelled union families into the ranks of the economic middle class.

Just as labor agreements helped create prosperity for union members and their families, government policies helped bring the nation's poorest region into the American economic mainstream. In the 1930s, Roosevelt had called the South "the nation's No. 1 economic problem." During World War II, new defense industry plants and military training camps channeled federal money to the region, stimulating economic growth. In the postwar era, huge levels of defense spending, especially for the nation's aerospace industry, continued to shift economic development from the Northeast and Midwest to the South and Southwest—the Sunbelt (see Map 29.1). Government actions—including generous tax breaks for oil companies, siting of military bases, and awarding of defense and aerospace contracts—were crucial to the new prosperity of this region.

The spectacular growth of the Sunbelt also was due to agribusiness, the oil industry, real-estate development, and recreation. Sunbelt states aggressively—and

Figure 29.2   Gross National Product and Per Capita Income, 1946–1962

Both gross national product and per capita income soared during the economic boom from 1946 to 1962.   (Source: Adapted from U.S. Bureau of the Census, *Historical Statistics of the United States, Colonial Times to 1970,* Bicentennial Edition [Washington, D.C., U.S. Government Printing Office, 1975], p. 224.)

successfully—sought foreign investment. Industry was drawn to the South by right-to-work laws, which outlawed closed shops, and by low taxes and low heating bills. The development of air conditioning for offices, houses, and cars was also crucial, for it made bearable even the hottest summer days. Houston, Phoenix, Los Angeles, San Diego, Dallas, and Miami all boomed; the population of Houston, a center of the aerospace industry and also of oil and petrochemical production, more than tripled between 1940 and 1960. California absorbed no less than one-fifth of the nation's entire population increase in the 1950s—enough by 1963 to make it the most populous state in the Union.

Cold War military and aerospace spending, unintentionally, also broadened America's middle class. The government's weapons development and space programs created a need for highly educated scientists, engineers, and other white-collar professionals. By the early 1960s, universities and academic researchers had received several billion dollars in space program research funding alone. Their research, in turn, transformed American industry and society. The transistor, invented during the 1950s, made possible both the computer revolution and everyday consumer goods like the transistor radio.

THE SUNBELT
AND ECONOMIC
GROWTH

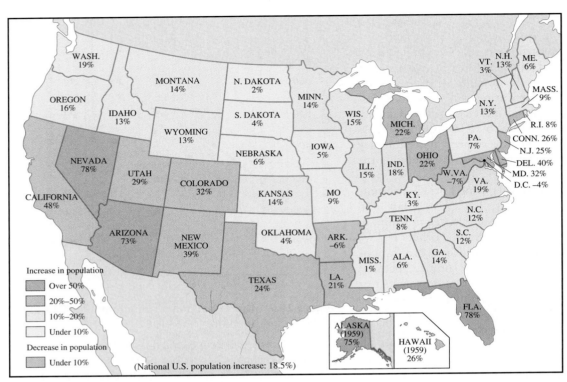

Map 29.1   Rise of the Sunbelt, 1950–1960

The years after the Second World War saw a continuation of the migration of Americans
to the Sunbelt states of the Southwest and the West Coast.

By the 1950s, it seemed that America was becoming a middle-class nation. Unionized blue-collar workers gained middle-class incomes, and veterans with GI Bill college educations swelled the growing managerial and professional class. In 1956, for the first time, the United States had more white-collar workers than blue-collar workers, and in 1957 there were 61 percent more salaried middle-class workers than just a decade earlier. Also for the first time, a majority of families—60 percent—had incomes in the middle-class range (approximately $3,000 to $9,000 a year in the mid-1950s).

A New Middle-Class Culture

However, middle-class identity was not simply a matter of economics. Even half of teenagers whose fathers did unskilled menial labor or whose mothers had only a sixth-grade education, a major 1952 survey discovered, believed their families were "middle class" (not working class or lower class). Paradoxically, the strength of unions in the postwar era contributed to a decline in working-class identity: as large numbers of blue-collar workers participated fully in the suburban middle-class culture, the lines separating working class and middle class seemed less important. Increasingly, a family's standard of living mattered more than what sort of work made the standard of living possible. People of color did not share equally in America's postwar prosperity, and were usually invisible in American representations of "the good life." However, many middle-income African Americans, Latinos, and Asian Americans did participate in the broad middle-class culture.

The emergence of a national middle-class culture was possible, in part, because America's population was more homogeneous in the 1950s than before or since. In the nineteenth and early twentieth centuries, the United States had restricted or prohibited immigration from Asia, Africa, and Latin America while accepting millions of Europeans to America's shores. This large-scale European immigration had been shut off in the 1920s, so that by 1960, only 5.7 percent of Americans were foreign born (compared with approximately 15 percent in 1910 and 10 percent in 2000). In 1950, 88 percent of Americans were of European an-

Whiteness and National Culture

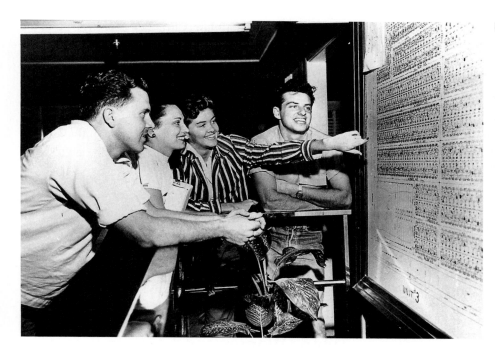

■ Eager buyers select house sites in a new development carved out of a former sugar beet field ten miles southeast of Los Angeles. Lakewood Park, with 17,500 homes, was the largest housing development in the nation's history. Houses included a "garbage pulverizer" and one tree per lot.   (National Archives)

cestry (compared with 69 percent in 2000); 10 percent of the population was African American; 2 percent was Hispanic; and Native Americans and Asian Americans each accounted for about one-fifth of 1 percent. But almost all European-Americans were at least a generation removed from immigration. Instead of "Italians" or "Russians" or "Jews," they were increasingly likely to describe themselves as "white."

Although the new suburbs were peopled mostly by white families, these suburbs were usually more diverse than the communities from which their residents had come. America's small towns and urban ethnic enclaves were quite homogeneous and usually intolerant of difference and of challenges to traditional ways. In the suburbs, people from different backgrounds came together: migrants from the city and the country; from different regions of the nation, different ethnic cultures, and different religious backgrounds. It was in the suburbs, paradoxically, that many people encountered different customs and beliefs. But as they joined with neighbors to forge new communities, the new suburbanites frequently adopted the norms of the developing national middle class. They traded the provincial homogeneity of specific ethnic or regional cultures for a new sort of homogeneity: a national, middle-class culture.

Because many white Americans were new to the middle class, they were uncertain about what behaviors were proper and expected of them. They found instruction, in

TELEVISION part, in the national mass media. Women's magazines helped housewives replace the ethnic and regional dishes they had grown up with with "American" recipes created from national brandname products—such as casseroles made with Campbell's cream of mushroom soup. Television also fostered America's shared national culture and taught Americans how to be middle class. Though televisions cost about $300—the equivalent of $2,000 today— almost half of American homes had TVs by 1953. Television ownership rose to 90 percent by 1960, when more American households had a television than a washing machine or an electric iron.

On television, suburban families such as the Andersons (*Father Knows Best*) or the Cleavers (*Leave It to Beaver*) ate dinner at a properly set dining room table. The mothers were always well groomed; June Cleaver did housework in carefully ironed dresses. When children faced moral dilemmas, parents gently but firmly guided them toward correct decisions. Every crisis was resolved through paternal wisdom—and a little humor. In these families, no one ever yelled or hit. These popular family situation comedies portrayed and reinforced the suburban middle-class ideal so many American families sought.

The "middle-classness" of television programming was due in part to the economics of the television industry. Advertising paid for television programming, and the corporations that bought advertising did not want to offend potential consumers. Thus, while African American musician Nat King Cole drew millions of viewers to his NBC television show, it never found a sponsor. National corporations were afraid that being linked to a black performer like Cole would hurt their sales among whites—especially in the South. Since African Americans made up only about 10 percent of the population and many had little disposable income, they had little power in this economics-driven system. The *Nat King Cole Show* was canceled within a year; it was a decade before the networks again tried to anchor a show around a black performer.

Television's reach extended beyond the suburbs. People from the inner cities and from isolated rural areas also watched family sitcoms or laughed at the antics of Milton Berle and Lucille Ball. With only three TV networks available—ABC, CBS, and NBC—at any one time 70 percent or more of all viewers might be watching the same popular program. (In the early twenty-first century, the most popular shows might attract 12 percent of the viewing audience.) Television gave Americans a shared set of experiences; it also helped to create a more homogeneous, white-focused, middle-class culture.

Linked by a shared national culture, Americans also found common ground in a new abundance of consumer

CONSUMER CULTURE

goods. After decades of scarcity, Americans had what seemed a dazzling array of consumer goods from which to choose, and they embraced them with unmatched exuberance. Even the most utilitarian objects got two-tone paint jobs or rocket-ship details; there was an optimism and vulgar joy in the popularity of turquoise refrigerators, furniture shaped like boomerangs, and cars designed to resemble fighter jets. In this consumer society, people used consumer choices to express their personal identities and to claim status within the broad boundaries of the middle class. Cars, more than anything else, embodied the consumer fantasies and exuberance of newly prosperous Americans. Expensive Cadillacs were the first to develop tailfins, and soon fins soared from midrange Chevys, Fords, and Plymouths. Americans spent $65 billion on automobiles in 1955—a figure equivalent to almost 20 percent of the gross national product. To pay for all those cars—and for suburban houses with modern appliances—America's consumer debt rose from $5.7 billion in 1945 to $58 billion in 1961.

In the same years, Americans turned in unprecedented numbers to organized religion. Membership (primarily in

RELIGION

mainline Christian churches) doubled between the end of World War II and the beginning of the 1960s. The uncertainties of the nuclear age likely contributed to the resurgence of religion, and some Americans may have sought spiritual consolation in the wake of the immensely destructive world war. The increasingly important national mass media played a role, as preachers such as Billy Graham created national congregations from television audiences, preaching a message that combined the promise of salvation with Cold War patriotism. But along with religious teachings, local churches and synagogues offered new suburbanites a sense of community. They welcomed newcomers, celebrated life's rituals, and supported the sick and the bereaved who were often far from their extended families and old communities. It is difficult to measure the depth of religious belief in postwar America, but church fellowship halls were near the center of the new postwar middle-class culture.

Men, Women, and Youth at Midcentury

Most of all, Americans pursued "the good life" and sought refuge from the tensions of the Cold War world through their homes and families. Having survived the Great Depression and a world war, many sought fulfillment in private life rather than public engagement; they saw their commitment to home and family as an expression of faith in the future. However, despite the real satisfactions many Americans found in family life, both men and women found their life choices limited by powerful social pressures to conform to narrowly defined gender roles.

During the 1950s, few Americans remained single, and most people married very young. By 1959, almost

MARRIAGE AND FAMILIES

half of American brides had yet to reach their nineteenth birthdays; their husbands were usually only a year or so older. This trend toward early marriage was endorsed by experts and approved by most parents, in part as a way to prevent premarital sex. As Americans accepted psychotherapeutic insights in the years following the war, they worried not only that premarital sex might leave the young woman pregnant or ruin her "reputation," but that the experience could so damage her psychologically that she could never adjust to "normal" marital relations. One popular women's magazine argued: "When two people are ready for sexual intercourse at the fully human level they are ready for marriage. . . . Not to do so is moral cowardice. And society has no right to stand in their way."

Many young couples—still teenagers—found autonomy and freedom from parental authority by marrying and setting up their own households. Most newlyweds quickly had babies—an average of three—completing their families while still in their twenties. Birth control (condoms and diaphragms) was widely available and widely used, for most couples planned the size of their families. But almost all married couples, regardless of race or class, wanted large families. Two children were the American ideal in 1940; by 1960, most couples wanted four children. And while many families looked nothing like television's June, Ward, Wally, and Beaver Cleaver, 88 percent of children under eighteen lived with two parents (in 2000, the figure was 69 percent). Fewer children were born outside marriage; only 3.9 percent of births were to unmarried women in 1950 (compared with more than one-third of births in 2000). Divorce rates were also lower. As late as 1960, there were only 9 divorces per 1,000 married couples.

In these fifties families, men and women usually took distinct and different roles, with male breadwinners and female homemakers. This division of labor, contemporary commentators insisted, was based on the timeless and essential differences between the sexes. In fact, the economic and social structure and the cultural values of postwar American society largely determined what choices were available to American men and women.

GENDER ROLES IN FIFTIES FAMILIES

During the 1950s, it was possible for many families to live in modest middle-class comfort on one (male) salary. There were strong incentives for women to stay at home, especially while children were young. Good childcare was rarely available, and fewer families lived close to the grandparents or other relatives who had traditionally helped with the children. A new cohort of childcare experts, including Dr. Spock, whose 1946 *Baby and Child Care* sold millions of copies, insisted that a mother's full-time attention was necessary to her child's well-being. Because of discrimination in hiring, women who could afford to stay home often didn't find the jobs available to them attractive enough to justify doing a double shift of cooking and housework at the end of the day. Many women thus chose to devote their considerable energies to family life. America's schools and religious institutions also benefited immensely from their volunteer labor.

■ New appliances promised "push-button technology" to take the work out of housework. "All you do is press the button," promised an ad for a Hotpoint dishwasher. "It does the rest." The time saved by washing machines, dryers, dishwashers, and electric ranges meant that women had more time for child-raising, volunteer work, or even paid employment. (Picture Research Consultants & Archives)

A great number of women, however, found that their lives didn't completely match the ideal of 1950s family life. Suburban domesticity left many women feeling isolated, cut off from the larger world of experiences their husbands still inhabited. The popular belief that one should find complete emotional satisfaction in private life put unrealistic pressures on marriages and family relationships. And finally, despite near-universal celebration of women's domestic roles, many women found themselves managing both job and family responsibilities (see Figure 29.3). Twice as many women were employed in 1960 as in 1940, including

WOMEN AND WORK

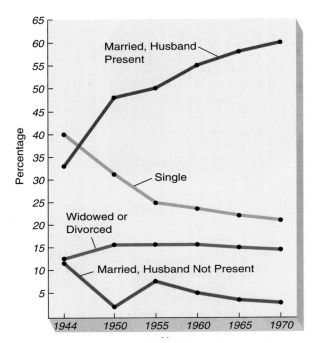

Figure 29.3   Marital Distribution of the Female Labor Force, 1944–1970

The composition of the female labor force changed dramatically from 1944 to 1970. In 1944, 41 percent of women in the labor force were single; in 1970, only 22 percent were single. During the same years, the percentage of the female labor force who had a husband in the home jumped from 34 to 59. The percentage who were widowed or divorced remained about the same from 1944 to 1970.   (Source: Adapted from U.S. Bureau of the Census, *Historical Statistics of the United States, Colonial Times to 1970*, Bicentennial Edition [Washington, D.C., U.S. Government Printing Office, 1975], p. 133.)

39 percent of women with children between the ages of six and seventeen. A majority of these women worked part-time for some specific family goal: a new car; college tuition for the children. They did not see these jobs as violating their primary roles as housewives; these jobs were in service to the family, not a means to independence from it.

Whether she worked to supplement a middle-class income, to feed her children, or to support herself, however, a woman faced discrimination in the world of work. Want ads were divided into "Help Wanted—Male" and "Help Wanted—Female" categories. Female full-time workers earned, on average, just 60 percent of what male full-time workers were paid and were restricted to less well-paid "female" fields: women were maids, secre-

taries, teachers, and nurses. Women with exceptional talent or ambition often found their aspirations blocked. A popular book, *Modern Woman: The Lost Sex*, explained that ambitious women and "feminists" suffered from "penis envy." Textbooks for college psychology and sociology courses warned women not to "compete" with men, while magazine articles described "career women" as a "third sex." Medical schools commonly limited the admission of women to 5 percent of each class. In 1960, less than 4 percent of lawyers and judges were female. When future Supreme Court Justice Ruth Bader Ginsburg graduated at the top of her Columbia Law School class in 1959, she could not find a job.

While academics and mass media critics alike stressed the importance of "proper" female roles, they devoted equal attention to the plight of the American male. American men faced a "crisis of masculinity," proclaimed the nation's mass-circulation magazines, quoting an array of psychological experts. In a bestselling book, sociologist William H. Whyte explained that postwar corporate employees had become "organization men," succeeding through cooperation and conformity, not through individual initiative and risk. Women, too, were blamed for men's crisis: women's "natural" desire for security and comfort, experts insisted, was stifling men's natural instincts for adventure. Some even linked concerns about masculinity to the Cold War, arguing that unless America's men recovered masculinity diminished by white-collar work or a suburban, family-centered existence, the nation's future was at risk. At the same time, however, men who did not conform to current standards of male responsibility—husband, father, breadwinner—were forcefully condemned, sometimes in the same magazines that preached the crisis of masculinity. One influential book advocated mandatory psychotherapy for men who reached thirty without having married; such single men were open to charges of "emotional immaturity" or "latent homosexuality."

"THE CRISIS OF MASCULINITY"

Sexuality was complicated terrain in postwar America. Only heterosexual intercourse within marriage was deemed socially acceptable, and consequences for sexual misconduct could be severe. Women who became pregnant outside marriage were often ostracized by friends and family and expelled from schools or colleges. Homosexuality was grounds for dismissal from a job, expulsion from college, even jail. At the same time, a great many Americans were breaking the sexual rules of the era. In his major works on human sexuality, *Sexual Behavior in the Human Male* (1948) and *Sexual Behavior*

SEXUALITY

in the Human Female (1953), Dr. Alfred Kinsey, director of the Institute for Sex Research at Indiana University, informed Americans that, while more than 80 percent of his female sample disapproved of premarital sex on "moral grounds," half of these women had had premarital sex. He also reported that at least 37 percent of American men had had "some homosexual experience." Americans made bestsellers of Kinsey's dry, quantitative studies—as many rushed to condemn him. One congressman charged Kinsey with "hurling the insult of the century against our mothers, wives, daughters and sisters"; the *Chicago Tribune* called him a "menace to society." While Kinsey's population samples did not provide a completely accurate picture of American sexual behavior, his findings made many Americans aware that they were not alone in breaking certain rules.

Another challenge to the sexual rules of 1950s America came from Hugh Hefner, who launched *Playboy* magazine in 1953. Within three years, the magazine had a circulation of 1 million. Hefner saw *Playboy* as an attack on America's "ferocious anti-sexuality [and] dark antieroticism," and his nude "playmates" as a means for men to combat what he considered the increasingly "blurred distinctions between the sexes" in a family-centered suburban culture.

As children grew up in relative stability and prosperity, a distinctive "youth culture" developed. Youth culture was really a set of subcultures; the culture of white, middle-class suburban youth was not the same as that of black, urban teens or even of the white working class. Youth culture was, however, distinct from the culture of adults. Its customs and rituals were created within peer groups and were shaped by national media—teen magazines, movies, radio, advertising, music—targeted toward this huge potential audience.

YOUTH CULTURE

The sheer numbers of "baby boom" youth made them a force in American society. People sometimes described the baby-boom generation as "a pig in a python," and as this group moved from childhood to youth, communities successively built elementary schools, junior high schools, and high schools. America's corporations quickly learned the power of youth, as children's fads launched multimillion-dollar industries. Slinky, selling for a dollar, began loping down people's stairs in 1947; Mr. Potato Head—probably the first toy advertised on television—had $4 million in sales in 1952. In the mid-1950s, when Walt Disney's television show *Disneyland* featured Davy Crockett, "King of the Wild Frontier," every child in America (and more than a few adults) just *had* to have a coonskin cap. The price of raccoon fur sky-

rocketed from 25 cents to $8 a pound, and many children made do with a Davy Crockett lunchbox or toothbrush instead. As these baby-boom children grew up, their buying power shaped American popular culture.

By 1960, America's 18 million teenagers were spending $10 billion a year. Seventy-two percent of movie tickets in the 1950s were sold to teenagers, and Hollywood catered to this audience with a flood of teen films, ranging from forgettable B-movies like *The Cool and the Crazy* or *Senior Prom* to controversial and influential movies such as James Dean's *Rebel Without a Cause.* Adults worried that teens would be drawn to romantic images of delinquency in *Rebel Without a Cause,* and teenage boys did copy Dean's rebellious look. The film, however, blamed parents for teenage confusion, drawing heavily on popular psychological theories about sexuality and the "crisis of masculinity": "What can you do when you have to be a man?" James Dean's character implored his father.

Movies helped shape teen fads and fashions, but nothing defined youth culture so much as its music. Young Americans were electrified by the driving energy and beat of Bill Haley and the Comets, Chuck Berry, Little Richard, and Buddy Holly. Elvis Presley's 1956 appearance on TV's *Ed Sullivan Show* touched off a frenzy of teen adulation—and a flood of letters from parents scandalized by his "gyrations." As one reviewer noted, "When Presley executes his bumps and grinds, it must be remembered that even the 12-year-old's curiosity may be overstimulated." Though few white musicians acknowledged the debt, the roots of rock 'n' roll lay in African American rhythm and blues. The raw energy and sometimes sexually suggestive lyrics of early rock music faded as the music industry sought white performers, such as Pat Boone, to do blander, more acceptable "cover" versions of music by black artists.

The distinct youth culture that developed in the 1950s made many adults uneasy. Parents worried that the common practice of "going steady" made it more likely that teens would "go too far" sexually. Juvenile delinquency was a major concern. Crime rates for young people had, in fact, risen dramatically in the years following World War II, but that was partly because there were so many young people, and they were under greater scrutiny than before. Much juvenile delinquency was "status" crimes—curfew violations, sexual experimentation, underage drinking—activities that were criminal because of the person's age, not because of the action itself. Congress held extensive hearings on juvenile delinquency, with experts testifying to the corrupting power of youth-oriented popular culture, comic books in particular. In

Barbie

Barbie, the "All-American Doll," is—like many Americans—an immigrant. Though Barbie was introduced in 1959 by the American toy company Mattel, her origins lie in Germany, where she went by the name Lilli.

As many mothers at the time suspected, noting the new doll's figure (equivalent to 39-21-31 in human proportions), Barbie's background was not completely respectable. The German Lilli doll was a toy for adult men, not little girls. She was based on a character cartoonist Reinhard Beuthien drew to fill some empty space in the June 24, 1952, edition of the German tabloid *Das Bild*. The cartoon was meant to appear just once, but Lilli was so popular that she became a regular feature. Soon Lilli appeared in three-dimensional form as *Bild* Lilli, an eleven-and-a-half-inch-tall blonde doll—with the figure Barbie would make famous. Dressed in a variety of sexy outfits, Lilli was sold in tobacco shops and bars as a "novelty gift" for men.

Lilli came to America with Ruth Handler, one of the founders and codirectors of the Mattel toy corporation. In a time when girls were given baby dolls, Handler imagined a grown-up doll that girls could dress as they did their paper dolls. When she glimpsed Lilli while on vacation in Europe, Handler bought three—and gave one to her daughter Barbara, after whom Lilli would be renamed. Mattel bought the rights to Lilli (the doll and the cartoon, which Mattel quietly retired) and unveiled "Barbie" in March 1959. Despite mothers' hesitations about buying a doll that looked like Barbie, within the year Mattel had sold 351,000 Barbies at $3 each (or about $17 in 2000 dollars). The billionth Barbie was sold in 1997.

In 2002, international labor-rights groups called for a boycott of Barbie. They cited studies showing that half of all Barbies are made by exploited young women workers in mainland China: of the $10 retail cost of an average Barbie, Chinese factories receive only 35 cents per doll to pay for all their costs, including labor. But the eleven-and-a-half-inch doll is popular throughout the world, sold in more than 150 countries. Today, the average American girl has ten Barbies—and the typical German girl owns five. Over the years, Barbie has continued to link the United States and the rest of the world.

Before Barbie became an American child's toy, she was "Lilli," a German sex symbol. Mattel transformed the doll into a wholesome American teenager with a new wardrobe to match.   (Spielzeug Museum, Munich)

1955, *Life* magazine reported: "Some American parents, without quite knowing what it is their kids are up to, are worried that it's something they shouldn't be." Most youthful behavior, however—from going steady to fads in music and dress—fit squarely into the consumer culture that youth shared with their parents. "Rebellious youth" rarely questioned the logic of postwar American culture.

The Limits of the Middle-Class Nation

During the 1950s, America's popular culture and mass media celebrated the opportunities available to the nation's people. At the same time, a host of influential critics rushed to condemn the new middle-class culture as a wasteland of conformity, homogeneity, and ugly consumerism.

These critics were not lone figures crying out in the wilderness. Americans, obsessed with self-criticism even

CRITICS OF
CONFORMITY

as most participated wholeheartedly in the celebratory culture of their age, rushed to buy books like John Keats's *The Crack in the Picture Window* (1957), which portrayed three families—the "Drones," the "Amiables," and the "Fecunds"—who lived in identical suburban tract houses "vomited" up by developers and sacrificed their remaining individuality in the quest for consumer goods. Some of the most popular fiction of the postwar era, such as J. D. Salinger's *The Catcher in the Rye* and Norman Mailer's *The Naked and the Dead*, was profoundly critical of American society. Americans even made bestsellers of difficult academic works such as David Riesman's *The Lonely Crowd* (1950) and William H. Whyte's *The Organization Man* (1955), both of which criticized the rise of conformity in American life. Versions of these critiques also appeared in mass-circulation magazines like *The Ladies' Home Journal* and *Reader's Digest*. Steeped in such cultural criticism, many Americans even understood *Invasion of the Body Snatchers*—a 1956 film in which zombielike aliens grown in huge pods gradually replace a town's human inhabitants—as criticism of suburban conformity and the bland homogeneity of postwar culture.

Most of these critics were attempting to understand large-scale and significant changes in American society. Americans were contending with some loss of autonomy in work as large corporations replaced smaller businesses; they experienced the homogenizing force of mass production and a national consumer culture; they saw distinctions among ethnic groups and even among socioeconomic classes decline in importance. Many wanted to understand these social dislocations better. Critics of the new culture, however, were often elitist and antidemocratic. Many saw only bland conformity and sterility in the emerging middle-class suburban culture, and so missed something important. Identical houses did not produce identical souls; instead, inexpensive suburban housing gave healthier, and perhaps happier, lives to millions who had grown up in dank, dark tenements or ramshackle farmhouses without indoor plumbing. In retrospect, however, other criticisms are obvious.

■ During the Second World War, DDT was used to protect American troops against bug-borne diseases and was hailed as a miracle insecticide. The use of DDT spread in postwar America, but little attention was paid to its often fatal consequences for birds, mammals, and fish. In 1945, even as children ran alongside, this truck sprayed DDT as part of a mosquito-control program at New York's Jones Beach State Park.   (© Bettmann/Corbis)

First, the new consumer culture encouraged wasteful habits and harmed the environment. *Business Week* noted

ENVIRONMENTAL DEGRADATION

during the 1950s that corporations need not rely on "planned obsolescence," purposely designing a product to wear out so that consumers would have to replace it. Americans replaced products because they were "out of date," not because they didn't work,

Map 29.2 Racial Composition of the United States, 1950 and 2000

Compared with present-day America, most states were fairly racially homogeneous in 1950. The exception was the Deep South, where most African Americans still lived. (Source: Adapted from "Demographic Trends in the Twentieth Century," U.S. Census Bureau; www.census.gov/population/www/censusdata/hiscendata.html.)

1950

2000

Percent Races Other Than White

30 or more
20—29
10—19
Less than 10
Not applicable

and automakers, encouraging the trend, revamped designs every year. New and inexpensive plastic products and detergents made consumers' lives easier—but were not biodegradable. And America's new consumer society used an ever larger share of the world's resources. By the 1960s the United States, with only 5 percent of the world's population, consumed more than one-third of the world's goods and services.

The rapid economic growth that made the middle-class consumer culture possible exacted environmental costs. Steel mills, coal-powered generators, and internal-combustion car engines burning lead-based gasoline polluted the atmosphere and imperiled people's health. As suburbs spread farther out from jobs in urban centers and neighborhoods were built without public transportation or shopping within walking distance of people's homes, Americans relied on private automobiles, consuming the nonrenewable resources of oil and gasoline and filling cities and suburbs with smog. Vast quantities of water were diverted from lakes and rivers to meet the needs of America's burgeoning Sunbelt cities, including the swimming pools and golf courses that dotted parched Arizona and southern California.

Defense contractors and farmers were among the country's worst polluters. Refuse from nuclear weapons facilities at Hanford, Washington, and at Colorado's Rocky Flats arsenal poisoned soil and water resources for years. Agriculture began employing massive amounts of pesticides and other chemicals. DDT, a chemical used on Pacific islands during the war to kill mosquitoes and lice, was used widely in the United States from 1945 until after 1962, when wildlife biologist Rachel Carson specifically indicted DDT for the deaths of mammals, birds, and fish in her bestselling book *Silent Spring*.

In the midst of prosperity, few understood the consequences of the economic transformation taking place. The nation was moving toward a postindustrial economy in which providing goods and services to consumers was more important than producing goods. Therefore, though union members prospered during the 1950s, union membership grew slowly—because most new jobs were being created not in heavy industries that hired blue-collar workers but in the union-resistant white-collar service trades. Technological advances increased productivity, as automated electronic processes replaced slower mechanical ones—but they pushed people out of relatively well paid blue-collar jobs into the growing and less well paid service sector.

Largely oblivious to the environmental degradation and work-sector shifts that accompanied economic growth and consumerism, the new middle-class culture also

CONTINUING
RACISM

largely ignored those who did not belong to its ranks. Race remained a major dividing line in American society, even as fewer Americans were excluded because of ethnic identities. Racial discrimination stood unchallenged in most of 1950s America. Suburbs, both north and south, were almost always racially segregated. Many white Americans had little or no contact in their daily lives with people of different races—not only because of residential segregation but also because the relatively small populations of nonwhite Americans were not dispersed equally throughout the nation: in 1960, there were 68 people of Chinese descent and 519 African Americans living in Vermont; 181 Native Americans lived in West Virginia; Mississippi had just 178 Japanese American residents. Most white Americans in the 1950s—especially those outside the South, where there was a large African American population—gave little thought to race. They did not think of the emerging middle-class culture as "white," but as "American," marginalizing people of color in image as in reality (see Map 29.2).

The new middle-class culture also was indifferent to the plight of the poor. In an age of abundance, more than one in five Americans lived in poverty. One-fifth of the poor were people of color, including almost half of the nation's African American population and more than half of all Native Americans. Two-thirds of the poor lived in households headed by a person with an eighth-grade education or less, one-fourth in households headed by a single woman. More than one-third were under eighteen. One-fourth of the poor were over age sixty-five; Social Security payments helped the elderly, but many retirees were not yet covered and, in the years before Medicare, medical costs drove many older Americans into poverty. Few of these people had much reason for hope.

Poverty was becoming increasingly urban. As millions of Americans (most of them white) were settling in the suburbs, the poor were ever more concentrated in the inner cities. African American migrants from the South were joined by poor whites from the southern Appalachians, many of whom moved to Chicago, Cincinnati, Baltimore, and Detroit. Meanwhile, Latin Americans were arriving in growing numbers from Mexico, the Dominican Republic, Colombia, Ecuador, and Cuba. According to the 1960 census, over a half-million Mexican Americans had migrated to the barrios of the Los Angeles–Long Beach area since 1940. And New York City's Puerto Rican population exploded from 70,000 in 1940 to 613,000 in 1960.

POVERTY IN
AN AGE OF
ABUNDANCE

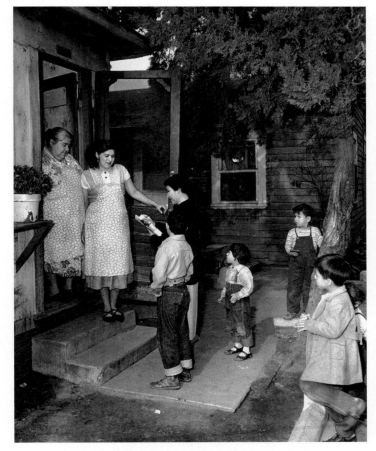

■ A volunteer from the Community Service Organization (CSO) registers a Mexican American mother and daughter as part of a massive voter registration drive in postwar Los Angeles. Women played a critical role in the CSO, which was founded in 1947 to address Mexican American civil rights issues, including education and labor, in East Los Angeles.   (Los Angeles Daily News Collection, Department of Special Collections, University Research Library, UCLA)

All of these newcomers to the cities came seeking better lives and greater opportunities. Because of the strong economy and low unemployment rate, many did gain a higher standard of living. But discrimination limited their advances, and they endured crowded and decrepit housing and poor schools. In addition, the federal programs that helped middle-class Americans sometimes made the lives of the poor worse. For example, the National Housing Act of 1949, passed to make available "a decent home . . . for every American family," provided for "urban redevelopment." Redevelopment meant slum

■ After the war, American Indians lost sacred land to both big corporations and the federal government. In 1948 George Gillette *(left)*, chairman of the Fort Berthold, North Dakota, Indian Tribal Council, covers his face and weeps as Secretary of the Interior J. A. Krug signs a contract buying 155,000 acres of tribal land for a reservoir. (Wide World Photos, Inc.)

clearance. Many poor people lost what housing they had as entire neighborhoods were leveled and replaced with luxury high-rise buildings, parking lots, or even highways.

Rural poverty was a long-standing problem in America, but the growth of large "agribusinesses" pushed more tenant farmers and owners of small farms off the land. From 1945 to 1961 the nation's farm population declined from 24.4 million to 14.8 million. When the harvesting of cotton in the South was mechanized in the 1940s and 1950s, more than 4 million people were displaced. Southern tobacco growers dismissed their tenant farmers, bought tractors to plow the land, and hired migratory workers to harvest the crops. Many of these displaced farmers traded southern rural poverty for northern urban poverty. And in the West and Southwest, Mexican citizens continued to serve as cheap migrant labor under the *bracero* program. Almost 1 million Mexi-

can workers came legally to the United States in 1959; many more were undocumented workers. Entire families labored, enduring conditions little better than in the Great Depression of the 1930s.

Native Americans were America's poorest people, with an average annual income barely half that of the poverty level. Conditions for Native peoples were made worse by a federal policy implemented during the Eisenhower administration: termination. "Termination" reversed the Indian Reorganization Act of 1934 (see page 700), allowing Indians to terminate their tribal status and so remove reservation lands from federal protection that prohibited their sale. Sixty-one tribes were terminated between 1954 and 1960. Termination could only take place with a tribe's agreement, but pressure was sometimes intense—especially when reservation land was rich in natural resources. The Klamaths of Oregon, for example, lived on a reservation rich in ponderosa pine, which lumber interests coveted. Enticed by cash payments, almost four-fifths of the Klamaths accepted termination and voted to sell their shares of the forest land. With termination, their way of life collapsed. Many Indians left reservation land for the city, joining the influx of other poor Americans seeking jobs and new lives. By the time termination was halted in the 1960s, observers compared the situation of Native Americans to the devastation their forbears had endured in the nineteenth century. Like most of the poor, these Americans were invisible to the growing middle class in the suburbs.

Overall, Americans who had lived through the devastation of the Great Depression and World War II enjoyed the relative prosperity and economic security of the postwar era. But those who had made it to the comfortable middle class often ignored the plight of those left behind. It would be their children—the generation of the baby boom, many reared in suburban comfort—who would see racism, poverty, and the self-satisfaction of postwar suburban culture as a failure of American ideals.

Summary

*a*s the experiences of economic depression and world war receded, Americans worked to create good lives for themselves and their families. People married and had children in record numbers. Millions of veterans used the GI Bill to attend college, buy homes, and start businesses. Though American leaders feared that the nation would lapse back into economic depression after wartime government spending ended, consumer spending brought economic growth. The sustained economic growth of the postwar era lifted a majority of Americans into an expanding middle class.

During the Cold War presidencies of Truman and Eisenhower, the country was engaged in a mortal struggle with communism. Both presidents were more focused on international relations than on domestic politics. Within the United States, Cold War fears provoked an extreme anticommunism that stifled political dissent and diminished Americans' civil liberties and freedoms.

The continuing African American struggle for civil rights drew national attention during the Montgomery bus boycott, reminding whites that not all Americans enjoyed equality. African Americans won important victories in the Supreme Court, including the landmark decision in *Brown v. Board of Education,* and both Truman and Eisenhower used federal power to guarantee the rights of black Americans. With these victories, a national civil rights movement began to coalesce, and racial tensions within the nation increased.

Despite continued racial divisions, the United States became in many ways a more inclusive nation in the 1950s as a majority of Americans participated in a national, consumer-oriented, middle-class culture. This culture largely ignored the poverty that remained in the nation's cities and rural areas, and contributed to rapidly increasing economic degradation. But for the growing number of middle-class Americans who, for the first time, lived in modest material comfort, the American dream seemed a reality.

LEGACY FOR A PEOPLE AND A NATION
The Pledge of Allegiance

The Pledge of Allegiance that Americans recite in school classrooms and sports stadiums throughout the nation today was shaped by America's Cold War struggle against the Soviet Union. Congress added the phrase "under God" to the existing pledge in 1954, as part of an attempt to emphasize the difference between the god-fearing United States and the "godless communists" of the Soviet Union.

The Pledge of Allegiance was not always an important part of American public life. The original version was written in 1892 by Francis Bellamy, editor of *The Youth's Companion,* to commemorate the four hundredth anniversary of Columbus's arrival in North America. On October 11, 1892, more than 11 million schoolchildren recited the words "I pledge allegiance to my flag and the Republic for which it stands; one nation indivisible, with liberty and justice for all." In 1942, Congress officially adopted a revised version of this pledge as an act of wartime patriotism. The Supreme Court ruled in 1943, however, that schoolchildren could not be forced to say the "Pledge to the Flag."

During the Cold War years, the pledge became more and more important as a way to demonstrate loyalty to the United States. Cold War fears lent force to a campaign by the Knights of Columbus, a Catholic men's service organization, to include "under God" in the pledge. Supporting the bill, President Eisenhower proclaimed that

> in this way we are reaffirming the transcendence of religious faith in America's heritage and future; in this way we shall constantly strengthen those spiritual weapons which forever will be our country's most powerful resource in peace and war. From this day forward, the millions of our schoolchildren will daily proclaim in every city and town, every village and every rural schoolhouse, the dedication of our nation and our people to the Almighty.

Some Americans, citing the doctrine of separation of church and state, have protested the inclusion of "under God" in the nation's pledge. In June 2002, the Ninth District Court (covering California and eight other western states) touched off a major controversy by ruling that the 1954 version of the pledge was unconstitutional because it conveyed a "state endorsement" of a religious belief. Questions about the proper role of religion in American life are sure to remain controversial, a legacy for a people and a nation, as America's people become even more diverse in the twenty-first century.

The **history companion** *powered by Eduspace®*
Your primary source for interactive quizzes, exercises, and more to help you learn efficiently.
http://history.college.hmco.com/students

THE TUMULTUOUS SIXTIES 1960-1968

*I*t was late at night, and Ezell Blair had a big exam the next day. But there he was with his friends in the dormitory, talking—as they so often did—about injustice, and discrimination, and about living in a nation that proclaimed equality for all but denied full citizenship to some of its people because of the color of their skins. They were complaining about all the do-nothing adults, condemning pretty much the entire black community of Greensboro—and not for the first time—when Franklin McCain said, as if he meant it, "It's time to fish or cut bait." And Joe McNeil said, "Yes, we're a bunch of hypocrites. Come on, let's do it. Let's do it tomorrow." McCain's roommate, David Richmond, agreed. Blair hesitated. "I was thinking about my grades," he said later, just "trying to deal with that architecture and engineering course I was taking."

But Blair was outvoted. The next day, February 1, 1960, after their classes at North Carolina Agricultural and Technical College were over, the four freshmen walked into town. At the F. W. Woolworth's on South Elm Street, one of the most profitable stores in the national chain, each bought a few small things, mostly school supplies. Then, nervously, they sat down on the vinyl-covered stools at the lunch counter and tried to order coffee. These young men—seventeen and eighteen years old—were prepared to be arrested, even physically attacked. But nothing happened. The counter help ignored them as long as possible; they never got their coffee. When one worker finally reminded them, "We don't serve colored here," the four made their point: they had already been served just a few feet away when they made their purchases. Why not at the lunch counter? An elderly white woman came up to the boys and told them how proud she was of them. "We got so much courage and so much pride" from that "little old lady," McCain said later. But still nothing happened. The store closed; the manager turned out the lights. After sitting in near darkness for

CHAPTER OUTLINE

Kennedy and the Cold War

Marching for Freedom

Liberalism and the Great Society

Johnson and Vietnam

A Nation Divided

LINKS TO THE WORLD
The British Invasion

1968

Summary

LEGACY FOR A PEOPLE AND A NATION
The Immigration Act of 1965

◀ When four freshmen from North Carolina Agricultural and Technical College sat down and tried to order coffee at the whites-only Woolworth's lunch counter in Greensboro, North Carolina, they did not know if they would be met with arrest or even violence. This photograph is from the second day of the sit-in, when the young men were joined by classmates. Two of the original four, Joseph McNeil and Franklin McCain, are on the left. (© Corbis-Bettmann)

CHRONOLOGY

1960 • Sit-ins begin in Greensboro
• Birth-control pill approved for contraceptive use
• John F. Kennedy elected president
• Young Americans for Freedom write Sharon Statement
• Freedom Rides protest segregation in transportation

1962 • Students for a Democratic Society issues Port Huron Statement

1963 • Civil rights March on Washington for Jobs and Freedom draws more than 250,000
• John F. Kennedy assassinated; Lyndon B. Johnson becomes president

1964 • Civil Rights Act outlaws discrimination in hiring and public accommodation
• Race riots break out in first of the "long, hot summers"
• Free Speech Movement begins at UC Berkeley
• Lyndon B. Johnson elected president

1965 • Lyndon Johnson launches Great Society programs
• Voting Rights Act outlaws practices that prevent most African Americans from voting in southern states
• Immigration and Nationality Act lowers barriers to immigration from Asia and Latin America
• Malcolm X assassinated
• Watts riot leaves thirty-four dead

1966 • National Organization for Women founded

1967 • Summer of Love in San Francisco's Haight-Ashbury district
• Race riots erupt in Newark, Detroit, and other cities

1968 • Tet Offensive causes fear of losing war in Vietnam
• Martin Luther King Jr. assassinated
• Robert Kennedy assassinated
• Antiwar protests escalate
• Violence erupts at Democratic National Convention
• Richard Nixon elected president

about forty-five minutes, the four men who had begun the sit-in movement got up and walked from the store.

The next day they returned, but they weren't alone. Twenty fellow students joined the sit-in. By February 3, sixty-three of the sixty-five seats were taken. On February 4, students from other colleges arrived, and the sit-in spread to the S. H. Kress store across the street. By February 7, there were sit-ins in Winston-Salem; by February 8, in Charlotte; on February 9, sit-ins began in Raleigh. By the third week in February students were picketing Woolworth's stores in the North, and at lunch counters throughout the South, well-dressed young men and women sat, politely asking to be served. On July 26, 1960, they won. F. W. Woolworth's ended segregation, not only in Greensboro but in all its stores.

When these four college freshmen sat down at the Woolworth's lunch counter in Greensboro, they signaled the beginning of a decade of public activism rarely matched in American history. During the 1960s millions of Americans—many of them young people—took to the streets. Some marched for civil rights or against the war in Vietnam; others lashed out in anger over the circumstances of their lives. Passion over the events of the day revitalized democracy—and threatened to tear the nation apart.

John F. Kennedy, the nation's youngest president, told Americans as he took office in 1961: "The torch has been passed to a new generation." Despite his inspirational language, Kennedy had only modest success implementing his domestic agenda. As he began his third year as president, pushed by the bravery of civil rights activists and the intransigence of their white opponents, Kennedy began to offer more active support for civil rights and to propose more ambitious domestic policies. But Kennedy was assassinated in November 1963. His death seemed, to many, the end of an era of hope.

Lyndon Johnson, Kennedy's successor, called upon the memory of the martyred president to launch an ambitious program of civil rights and other liberal legislation. Johnson meant to use the power of the federal government to eliminate poverty and to guarantee equal rights to all America's people. He called his vision the Great Society.

Despite liberal triumphs in Washington, D.C., and real gains by the African American civil rights movement, social tensions escalated during the mid-1960s. A revitalized conservative movement emerged, and Franklin Roosevelt's old New Deal coalition fractured as white southerners abandoned the Democratic Party. Many African Americans, especially in the North, were angry that poverty and racial discrimination persisted despite the passage of landmark civil rights laws, and their discontent exploded during the "long, hot summers" of the mid-1960s. White youth culture, which seemed intent on rejecting everything an older generation had worked for, created a division Americans came to call "the generation gap."

Developments overseas also contributed to a growing national instability. After the Cuban missile crisis of 1962 brought the Soviet Union and the United States close to nuclear disaster, Kennedy and Khrushchev moved to deescalate bilateral tensions in 1963, with the result that Cold War pressures in Europe lessened appreciably. In the rest of the world, however, the superpowers continued their frantic competition. Throughout the 1960s the United States used a variety of approaches—including foreign aid, CIA covert actions, military assaults, cultural penetration, economic sanctions, and diplomacy—in its attempts to win the Cold War, draw unaligned nations into its orbit, and defuse revolutionary nationalism. In Vietnam, Kennedy chose to expand U.S. involvement significantly. Johnson "Americanized" the war, increasing U.S. troops to more than half a million in 1968.

By 1968, the war in Vietnam had divided the American people and undermined Johnson's Great Society. With the assassinations of Martin Luther King Jr. and Robert Kennedy—two of America's brightest leaders—that spring, with cities in flames, and with tanks in the streets of Chicago in August, the fate of the nation seemed to hang in the balance. ■

Kennedy and the Cold War

President John F. Kennedy was, as the writer Norman Mailer observed, "our leading man." Young, handsome, and vigorous, the new chief executive was the first president born in the twentieth century. Kennedy had a genuinely inquiring mind, and as a patron of the arts he brought wit and sophistication to the White House. He was born to wealth and politics: his Irish American grandfather had been mayor of Boston,

and his millionaire father, Joseph P. Kennedy, had served as ambassador to Great Britain. In 1946 the young Kennedy, having returned from the Second World War a naval hero (the boat he commanded had been rammed and sunk by a Japanese destroyer in 1943, and Kennedy had saved his crew), continued the family tradition by campaigning to represent Boston in the U.S. House of Representatives. He won easily, served three terms in the House, and in 1952 was elected to the Senate.

As a Democrat, Kennedy inherited the New Deal commitment to America's social welfare system. He generally

JOHN FITZGERALD KENNEDY

cast liberal votes in line with the pro-labor sentiments of his low-income, blue-collar constituents. But he avoided controversial issues such as civil rights and the censure of Joseph McCarthy. Kennedy won a Pulitzer Prize for his *Profiles in Courage* (1956), a study of politicians who had acted on principle, but he shaded the truth when he claimed sole authorship of the book, which had been written largely by aide Theodore Sorensen (though based on more than a hundred pages of notes dictated by Kennedy). In foreign policy, Senator Kennedy endorsed the Cold War policy of containment, and his interest in world affairs deepened as the 1950s progressed. His record as a legislator was not impressive, but he enjoyed an enthusiastic following, especially after his landslide reelection to the Senate in 1958.

Kennedy and his handlers worked hard to cultivate an image of him as a happy and healthy family man. To some extent, it was a ruse. He was a chronic womanizer, and his liaisons continued even after he married Jacqueline Bouvier in 1953. Nor was he the picture of physical vitality that his war-hero status and youthful handsomeness seemed to project. As a child he had almost died of scarlet fever, and he spent large portions of his early years in bed, suffering from one ailment after another. He developed severe back problems, and these were made worse by his fighting experience in World War II. After the war Kennedy was diagnosed with Addison's disease, an adrenalin deficiency that required daily injections of cortisone in order to be contained. At the time the disease was thought to be terminal; though Kennedy survived, he was often in acute pain. As president he would require plenty of bed rest and frequent therapeutic swims in the White House pool.

Kennedy's rhetoric and style captured the imagination of many Americans. Yet his election victory over

ELECTION OF 1960

Republican Richard Nixon in 1960 was extraordinarily narrow—118,000 votes out of nearly 69 million cast.

President John F. Kennedy, his wife Jacqueline, and their two young children, John Jr. and Caroline, symbolized youthful energy and idealism. This photograph was taken at their vacation home at Hyannisport on Cape Cod in July 1963.   (John F. Kennedy Library)

Kennedy achieved only mixed success in the South, but he ran well in the Northeast and Midwest. His Roman Catholic faith hurt him in some states, where voters feared he would take direction from the pope, but helped in states with large Catholic populations. As the sitting vice president, Nixon was saddled with the handicaps of incumbency; he had to answer for sagging economic figures and the Soviet downing of a U-2 spy plane (see page 786). Nixon also looked disagreeable on TV; in televised debates against the telegenic Kennedy, he looked alternately nervous and surly, and the camera made him appear unshaven. Perhaps worse, Eisenhower gave Nixon only a tepid endorsement. Asked to list Nixon's significant decisions as vice president, Eisenhower replied, "If you give me a week, I might think of one."

In a departure from the Eisenhower administration's staid, conservative image, the new president surrounded himself with mostly young advisers of intellectual verve who proclaimed that they had fresh ideas for invigorating the nation; the writer David Halberstam called them "the best and the brightest." Secretary of Defense Robert McNamara (age forty-four) had been an assistant professor at Harvard at twenty-four and later the whiz-kid president of the Ford Motor Company. Kennedy's special

assistant for national security affairs, McGeorge Bundy (age forty-one) had become a Harvard dean at thirty-four with only a bachelor's degree. Secretary of State Dean Rusk, the old man in the group at fifty-two, had been a Rhodes scholar in his youth. Kennedy himself was only forty-three, and his brother Robert, the attorney general, was thirty-five.

It was no accident that most of these "best and brightest" operated in the realm of foreign policy. From the start, Kennedy gave top priority to waging the Cold War. In the campaign he had criticized Eisenhower's foreign policy as unimaginative, accusing him of missing chances to reduce the threat of nuclear war with the Soviet Union and of weakening America's standing in the Third World. Kennedy and his advisers exuded confidence that they would change things. As national security adviser McGeorge Bundy put it, "The United States is the engine of mankind, and the rest of the world is the caboose." Kennedy's inaugural address suggested no halfway measures: "Let every nation know that we shall pay any price, bear any burden, meet any hardship, support any friend, oppose any foe to assure the survival and the success of liberty."

In reality, Kennedy in office would not be prepared to pay any price or bear any burden in the struggle against communism. He came to understand, sooner than many of his advisers, that there were limits to American power abroad; overall he showed himself to be cautious and pragmatic in foreign policy. More than his predecessor, he proved willing to initiate dialogue with the Soviets, sometimes using his brother Robert as a secret back channel to Moscow. Yet Kennedy also sought victory in the Cold War. After Soviet leader Nikita Khrushchev endorsed "wars of national liberation" such as the one in Vietnam, Kennedy called for "peaceful revolution" based on the concept of nation building. The administration set out to help developing nations through the early stages of nationhood with aid programs aimed at improving agriculture, transportation, and communications. Kennedy thus oversaw the creation of the multibillion-dollar Alliance for Progress in 1961 to spur economic development in Latin America. In the same year he also created the Peace Corps, dispatching thousands of American teachers, agricultural specialists, and health workers, many of them right out of college, to assist authorities in developing nations.

Cynics then and later dismissed the Alliance and the Peace Corps as Cold War tools by which Kennedy sought to counter anti-Americanism and defeat communism in

NATION BUILDING AND COUNTERINSURGENCY

the developing world. The programs did have those aims, but both also were born of genuine humanitarianism. The Peace Corps, in particular, embodied both the idealistic can-do spirit of the 1960s and Americans' long pursuit of moral leadership in the world. "More than any other entity," the historian Elizabeth Cobbs Hoffman has written, "the Peace Corps broached an age-old dilemma of U.S. foreign policy: how to reconcile the imperatives and temptations of power politics with the ideals of freedom and self-determination for all nations."

It was one thing to broach the dilemma, and quite another to resolve it. Kennedy and his aides considered themselves to be supportive of social revolution in the Third World, but they could not imagine the legitimacy of communist involvement in any such uprising, or that developing countries might wish to be neutral in the East-West struggle. In addition to largely benevolent programs such as the Peace Corps, therefore, the administration also relied on the more insidious concept of counterinsurgency to defeat revolutionaries who challenged pro-American Third World governments. American military and technical advisers trained native troops and police forces to quell unrest.

Nation building and counterinsurgency encountered numerous problems. The Alliance for Progress was only partly successful; infant mortality rates improved, but Latin American economies registered unimpressive growth rates, and class divisions continued to widen, exacerbating political unrest. Americans assumed that the U.S. model of capitalism and representative government could be transferred successfully to foreign cultures. But although many foreign peoples welcomed U.S. economic assistance and craved American material culture, they resented meddling by outsiders. And because aid was usually funneled through a self-interested elite, it often failed to reach the very poor. To people who preferred the relatively quick solutions of a managed economy, moreover, the American emphasis on private enterprise seemed inappropriate.

Nor did the new president have success in relations with the Soviet Union. A summit meeting with Soviet leader Nikita Khrushchev in Vienna in June 1961 went poorly, with the two leaders disagreeing over the preconditions for peace and stability in the world. Consequently, the administration's first year witnessed little movement on controlling the nuclear arms race or even on getting a superpower ban on testing nuclear weapons in the atmosphere or underground. The latter objective mattered a great deal to Kennedy, who saw a test ban as a prerequisite to pre-

SOVIET-AMERICAN TENSIONS

venting additional nations from getting the terrifying weapon. Instead, both superpowers continued testing and accelerated their arms production. In 1961 the U.S. military budget shot up 15 percent; by mid-1964, U.S. nuclear weapons had increased by 150 percent. Government advice to citizens to build fallout shelters in their backyards intensified public fear of devastating war.

If war occurred, many believed it would be over the persistent problem of Berlin. In mid-1961 Khrushchev ratcheted up the tension by demanding an end to Western occupation of West Berlin and a reunification of East and West Germany. Kennedy replied that the United States would stand by its commitment to West Berlin and West Germany. In August the Soviets, at the urging of the East German regime, erected a concrete and barbed-wire barricade to halt the exodus of East Germans into the more prosperous and politically free West Berlin. The Berlin Wall inspired protests throughout the noncommunist world, but Kennedy privately sighed that "a wall is a hell of a lot better than a war." The ugly barrier shut off the flow of refugees, and the crisis passed.

Yet Kennedy knew that Khrushchev would continue to press for advantage in various parts of the globe. The president was particularly rankled by the growing Soviet assistance to the Cuban government of Fidel Castro. Kennedy once acknowledged that most American allies thought the United States had a "fixation" with Cuba; whether true of the country as a whole, he himself certainly did. The Eisenhower administration had contested the Cuban revolution and bequeathed to the Kennedy administration a partially developed CIA plan to overthrow Fidel Castro (see page 791): CIA-trained Cuban exiles would land and secure a beachhead; the Cuban people would rise up against Castro and welcome a new government brought in from the United States.

BAY OF PIGS INVASION

Kennedy approved the plan, and the attack took place on April 17, 1961, as twelve hundred exiles landed at the swampy Bay of Pigs in Cuba. But no discontented Cubans were there to greet them, only troops loyal to the Castro government. The invaders were quickly surrounded and captured. Kennedy had tried to keep the U.S. participation in the operation hidden (for this reason he refused to provide air cover for the attackers), but the CIA's role swiftly became public. Anti-American sentiments shot up throughout the region. Castro, concluding that the United States would not take defeat well and might launch another invasion, looked even more toward the Soviet Union for a military and economic lifeline.

Embarrassed by the Bay of Pigs fiasco, Kennedy vowed to bring Castro down. The CIA soon hatched a project called Operation Mongoose to disrupt the island's trade, support raids on Cuba from Miami, and plot to kill Castro. The agency's assassination schemes included providing Castro with cigars laced with explosives and deadly poison and an attempt to harpoon him while he was snorkeling at a Caribbean resort. The United States also tightened its economic blockade and undertook military maneuvers in the Caribbean. The Joint Chiefs of Staff sketched plans to spark a rebellion in Cuba that would be followed by an invasion of U.S. troops. "If I had been in Moscow or Havana at that time," Defense Secretary Robert McNamara later remarked, "I would have believed the Americans were preparing for an invasion."

McNamara knew whereof he spoke: we now know that both Castro and Khrushchev believed an invasion was coming. This was one reason for the Soviet leader's risky decision in 1962 to secretly deploy nuclear missiles in Cuba: he hoped the presence of such weapons on the island would deter any attack. But Khrushchev also had other motives. Installing atomic weaponry in Cuba would instantly improve the Soviet

CUBAN MISSILE CRISIS

position in the nuclear balance of power, he believed, and might also force Kennedy to resolve the German problem once and for all. Khrushchev still wanted to oust the West from Berlin, and he also worried that Washington might provide West Germany with nuclear weapons. What better way to prevent such a move than to put Soviet missiles just 90 miles off the coast of Florida? With Castro's support, Khrushchev moved to install the weapons. The world soon faced brinkmanship at its most frightening.

In mid-October 1962 a U-2 plane flying over Cuba photographed the missile sites. The president immediately organized a special Executive Committee (ExComm) of advisers to find a way to force the missiles and their nuclear warheads out of Cuba. Options the ExComm considered ranged from full-scale invasion to limited bombing to quiet diplomacy. McNamara proposed the formula that the president ultimately accepted: a naval quarantine of Cuba.

Kennedy addressed the nation on television on October 22 to demand that the Soviets retreat. U.S. warships began crisscrossing the Caribbean, while B-52s with nuclear bombs took to the skies. Khrushchev replied that

■ The October 29 meeting of the "ExComm," or Executive Committee (the only meeting photographed). To President Kennedy's immediate right is Secretary of State Dean Rusk; to his left (in front of the Presidential Seal on the wall) is Secretary of Defense Robert McNamara. Presidential adviser Theodore Sorensen (on near side, third from right) later wrote: "I saw first-hand how brutally physical and mental fatigue can numb the good sense as well as the senses of normally articulate men." (John F. Kennedy Library)

the missiles would be withdrawn if the United States pledged never to attack Cuba. And he added that American Jupiter missiles aimed at the Soviet Union must be removed from Turkey. Edgy advisers predicted war, and for several days the world teetered on the brink of disaster. Then, on October 28, came a compromise. The United States promised not to invade Cuba, secretly pledging to withdraw the Jupiters from Turkey in exchange for the withdrawal of Soviet offensive forces from Cuba. Fearing accidents or some provocative action by Castro that might start a "real fire," Khrushchev decided to settle without consulting the Cubans. The missiles were removed from the island.

Many observers then and later called it Kennedy's finest hour. The recently released Kennedy White House tapes (Kennedy had a taping system installed in the Oval Office in mid-1962, and most of the ExComm meetings during the crisis were recorded) reveal a deeply engaged, calmly authoritative commander-in-chief, committed to removing the missiles peacefully if possible. Critics claim that Kennedy helped cause the crisis in the first place with his anti-Cuban projects; some contend that quiet diplomacy could have achieved the same result, without the extraordinary tension. Other skeptics assert that Kennedy rejected a diplomatic solution because he feared the Republicans would ride the missiles to victory in the upcoming midterm elections. Still, it cannot be denied that the president handled the crisis skillfully, exercising both restraint and flexibility. At this most tense moment of the Cold War, Kennedy had proven equal to the task.

The Cuban missile crisis was a watershed in the Soviet-American relationship. Both Kennedy and Khrushchev acted with greater prudence in its aftermath, taking determined steps toward improved bilateral relations. Much of the hostility drained out of the relationship. In June 1963 Kennedy spoke at American University in conciliatory terms, urging cautious Soviet-American steps toward disarmament. In August the adversaries signed a treaty banning nuclear tests in the atmosphere, the oceans, and outer space. They also installed a coded wire-telegraph "hot line" staffed around the clock by translators and technicians, to allow near-instant communication between the capitals. Both sides refrained from further confrontation in Berlin.

Individually these steps were small, but together they reversed the trend of the previous years and began to build much-needed mutual trust. One could even argue that, by the autumn of 1963, the Cold War in Europe was drawing to a close. Both sides, it seemed, were prepared to accept the status quo of a divided continent and a fortified border. At the same time, though, the arms race continued and in some respects accelerated, and the superpower competition in the Third World showed little sign of cooling down.

Marching for Freedom

President Kennedy believed that the Cold War was the most important issue facing the American people. But many African Americans believed that civil rights must finally become a national priority. In the early 1960s, young civil rights activists seized the national stage and demanded that the force of the federal government be mobilized behind them.

The sit-in at the Woolworth's lunch counter begun by the four freshmen from North Carolina A&T marked

STUDENTS AND THE MOVEMENT

a turning point in the African American struggle for civil rights. In 1960, six years after the *Brown* decision declared "separate but equal" unconstitutional, little had changed for African Americans in the South. Fewer than 7 percent of black students in the seventeen southern states attended integrated schools. Water fountains in public places were still labeled "White Only" and "Colored Only." One year after the young men had sat down at the all-white lunch counter in Greensboro, more than seventy thousand Americans—most of them college students—had participated in the sit-in movement. City by city, they challenged Jim Crow segregation in the South and protested at the northern branches of national chains that practiced segregation in their southern stores.

Like Martin Luther King Jr., who had led the African American citizens of Montgomery to triumph in their bus boycott, the young people who created the Student Nonviolent Coordinating Committee (SNCC) in the spring of 1960 to help orchestrate the growing sit-in movement were committed to nonviolence. In the years to come, SNCC stalwarts—including lifelong activist Diane Nash; future NAACP chair Julian Bond; future Washington, D.C., mayor Marion Barry; and future member of the U.S. House of Representatives John Lewis—would risk their lives in the struggle for social justice.

On May 4, 1961, thirteen members of the Congress of Racial Equality (CORE), a nonviolent civil rights

FREEDOM RIDES

organization formed during World War II (see Chapter 27), purchased bus tickets in Washington, D.C., for a 1,500-mile trip through the South to New Orleans. This racially integrated group, calling themselves Freedom Riders, meant to demonstrate that despite Supreme

Court rulings ordering the desegregation of interstate buses and bus stations, Jim Crow still ruled in the South. These men and women knew they were risking their lives, and some suffered injuries from which they never recovered. One bus was firebombed outside Anniston, Alabama. Riders were badly beaten in Birmingham. In Montgomery, after reinforcements replaced the injured, a mob of more than a thousand whites attacked riders on another bus with baseball bats and steel bars. Police were nowhere to be seen; Montgomery's police commissioner declared: "We have no intention of standing guard for a bunch of troublemakers coming into our city."

News of the violent attacks made headlines around the world. In the Soviet Union, commentators pointed out the "savage nature of American freedom and democracy." One southern business leader learned firsthand about the peripheral costs of racial violence: in Tokyo to promote Birmingham as a site for international business development, he discovered that photographs of the Birmingham attacks carried by Tokyo newspapers had destroyed the interest of his Japanese hosts.

In America, the violence—reported by the national news media—forced many to confront the reality of racial discrimination and hatred in their nation. Middle- and upper-class white southerners had participated in the "massive resistance" to integration following the *Brown* decision, and many white southerners, even racial moderates, remained highly suspicious of interference by the "Yankee" federal government almost a century after the Civil War. The Freedom Rides made some think differently. Even the *Atlanta Journal* editorialized: "[I]t is time for the decent people . . . to muzzle the jackals." The national and international outcry pushed a reluctant President Kennedy to act. In a direct challenge to southern doctrines of states' rights, Kennedy sent federal marshals to Alabama to safeguard the Freedom Riders and their supporters. At the same time, bowing to white southern pressure, he allowed the Freedom Riders to be arrested in Mississippi.

While some activists pursued these "direct action" tactics, others worked to build black political power in the South. Beginning in 1961, thousands of SNCC volunteers, many of them high school and college students, risked their lives walking the dusty back roads of Mississippi and Georgia, encouraging African Americans to resist segregation and register to vote. They formed Freedom Schools, teaching literacy and constitutional rights. Some SNCC volunteers were white, and some were from the North, but many were black southerners, and many were from low-income families. These volunteers understood from experience how racism, powerlessness, and poverty intersected in the lives of African Americans.

These efforts achieved national attention during the Freedom Summer of 1964, when over a thousand young people joined the struggle in Mississippi. Because Mississippi laws made it almost impossible for blacks to participate in the electoral process, the Freedom Summer volunteers created a racially integrated grassroots political party, the Mississippi Freedom Democratic Party. Not all went smoothly: local black activists were sometimes frustrated when well-educated and often affluent white volunteers stepped into decision-making roles, and tensions over interracial sexual relationships complicated an already difficult situation. Far worse, project workers were arrested over a thousand times and were shot at, bombed, and beaten. Local black activist James Cheney and two white volunteers, Michael Schwerner and Andrew Goodman, were murdered by a Klan mob. That summer, black and white activists risked their lives together, challenging the racial caste system of the Deep South.

FREEDOM SUMMER

The Freedom Riders had captured the attention of the nation and the larger Cold War world, and had forced the hand of the president. Martin Luther King Jr., having risen through the Montgomery bus boycott to leadership in the movement, understood the implications of these events. He and his allies, still committed to principles of nonviolence, concluded that the only way to move to the next stage of the struggle for civil rights was to provoke a crisis. King and the SCLC began to plan a 1963 campaign in the most violently racist city in America: Birmingham, Alabama. Fully aware that their nonviolent protests would draw violent response, they called their plan "Project C"—for "confrontation." King wanted all Americans to see the racist hate and violence that marred their nation.

BIRMINGHAM AND THE CHILDREN'S CRUSADE

Nonviolent protest marches led to hundreds of arrests. Then, in a controversial action, King and the parents of Birmingham put children on the front lines of protest. As about a thousand black children, some as young as six, marched for civil rights, police commissioner Eugene "Bull" Connor ordered his police to train "monitor" water guns—powerful enough to strip bark from a tree at 100 feet—on them. The water guns mowed down the children, and then police loosed attack dogs. It was all captured on television, as the nation watched in horror. President Kennedy, once again, was pushed into action. He demanded that Birmingham's white business and political elite negotiate a settlement. Under pressure, they agreed. The Birmingham movement had won a concrete victory. Even more, activists had pushed civil rights to the fore of President Kennedy's political agenda.

Kennedy was generally sympathetic to—though not terribly committed to—the civil rights movement, and he realized that racial oppression hurt the United States in the Cold War struggle for international opinion. However, he also understood that if he alienated conservative southern Democrats in Congress, his legislative programs would founder. Thus he appointed five die-hard segregationists to the federal bench in the Deep South and delayed issuing an executive order forbidding segregation in federally subsidized housing (a pledge made in the 1960 campaign) until late 1962. Furthermore, he allowed FBI director J. Edgar Hoover to harass Martin Luther King and other civil rights leaders, using wiretaps and surveillance to gather personal information and circulating rumors of communist connections and of personal improprieties in efforts to discredit their leadership.

KENNEDY AND CIVIL RIGHTS

But grassroots civil rights activism—and the violence of white mobs—relentlessly forced Kennedy's hand. In September 1962, the president ordered 500 U.S. marshals to protect James Meredith, the first African American student to attend the University of Mississippi. In response, thousands of whites attacked the marshals with guns, gasoline bombs, bricks, and pipes. The mob killed two men and seriously wounded 160 federal marshals. The marshals did not back down, nor did James Meredith. He broke the color line at "Ole Miss."

The following spring, the Kennedy administration confronted the defiant governor of Alabama, George C. Wallace, who promised to "bar the schoolhouse door" himself to prevent the desegregation of the University of Alabama. With Wallace vowing, "Segregation now, segregation tomorrow, segregation forever!" and with the nation rocked by protests and the violence of white mobs, Kennedy committed the power of the federal government to guarantee racial justice—even over the opposition of individual states. In a televised address Kennedy told the American people: "Now the time has come for this nation to fulfill its promise." That same night, civil rights leader Medgar Evers was murdered—in front of his children—in his driveway in Jackson, Mississippi. A week later, the president asked Congress to pass a comprehensive civil rights bill that would end legal discrimination on the basis of race in the entire United States.

On August 28, 1963, a quarter of a million Americans gathered in the steamy heat on the Washington Mall. They came from all over America to show Congress their support for Kennedy's civil rights bill; many also wanted federal action to guarantee work opportunities for oppressed African Americans. Behind the scenes, organizers from the major civil rights groups—SCLC, CORE, SNCC, the NAACP, the Urban

MARCH ON WASHINGTON

■ A historic moment for the civil rights movement was the March on Washington of August 28, 1963. The Reverend Martin Luther King Jr. *(center)* joined a quarter of a million black people and white people in their march for racial equality. Addressing civil rights supporters, and the nation, from the steps of the Lincoln Memorial, King delivered his "I Have a Dream" speech.   (R. W. Kelley, *Life* magazine © Time, Inc.)

League, and A. Philip Randolph's Brotherhood of Sleeping Car Porters—grappled with growing tensions within the movement. SNCC activists saw Kennedy's proposed legislation as too little, too late, and wanted radical action. King and other older leaders counseled the virtues of moderation. The movement was beginning to splinter.

What Americans saw, however, was a celebration of unity. Black and white celebrities joined hands; folk singers sang songs of freedom. Television networks cut away from afternoon soap operas as Martin Luther King Jr., in southern-preacher cadences, prophesied a day when "all God's children, black men and white men, Jews and Gentiles, Protestants and Catholics, will be able to join hands and sing in the words of the old Negro spiritual, 'Free at last! Free at last! Thank God Almighty, we are free at last!'" The 1963 March on Washington for Jobs and Freedom was a moment of triumph, powerfully demonstrating to the nation the determination of its African American citizens to secure equality and justice. But the struggle was far from over. Just days later, white supremacists bombed the Sixteenth Street Baptist Church in Birmingham, killing four black girls.

Liberalism and the Great Society

By 1963, with civil rights at the top of his domestic agenda, Kennedy seemed to be taking a new path. Campaigning for the presidency in 1960, he had promised to lead Americans into a "New Frontier," a society in which the federal government would work to eradicate poverty, restore the nation's cities, guarantee healthcare to the elderly, and make sure there were decent schools for all America's children. But few of Kennedy's domestic initiatives were passed into law, in part because Kennedy did not use his political capital to support them. Lacking a popular mandate in the 1960 election, fearful of alienating southern Democrats in Congress, and without a strong vision of domestic reform, Kennedy let his administration's social policy agenda languish.

Instead, Kennedy focused on less controversial attempts to fine-tune the American economy, believing that continued economic growth and prosperity would solve America's social problems. Kennedy's vision was perhaps best realized in America's space program. As the Russians drew ahead in the Cold War space race, Kennedy vowed in 1961 that America would put a man on the moon before the decade's end. With billions in new funding, the National Aeronautics and Space Administration (NASA) began the Apollo program. And in February 1962, astronaut John Glenn orbited the earth in the space capsule *Friendship Seven*.

The nation would not learn what sort of president John Kennedy might have become. On November 22, 1963, Kennedy visited the home state of his vice president, Lyndon Johnson. Riding with his wife, Jackie, in an open-top limousine, Kennedy was cheered by thousands of people lining the motorcade's route. Suddenly gunshots rang out. The president crumpled, shot in the head. Tears ran down the cheeks of CBS anchorman Walter Cronkite as he told the nation their president was dead. The word spread quickly, in whispered messages to classroom teachers, by somber announcements in factories and offices, through the stunned faces of people on the street.

THE KENNEDY ASSASSINATION

That same day police captured a suspect: Lee Harvey Oswald, a former U.S. marine (dishonorably discharged) who had once attempted to gain Soviet citizenship. Just two days later, in full view of millions of TV viewers, Oswald himself was shot dead by shady nightclub owner Jack Ruby. Americans, already in shock, were baffled. What was Ruby's motive? Was he silencing Oswald to prevent him from implicating others? The seven-member Warren Commission, headed by U.S. Supreme Court Chief Justice Earl Warren, concluded that Oswald had acted alone. But debates still rage over whether Oswald was a lone assassin or part of a larger conspiracy.

For four days, the tragedy played uninterrupted on American television. Millions of Americans watched their president's funeral: the brave young widow behind a black veil; a riderless horse; three-year-old "John-John" saluting his father's casket. In one awful moment in Dallas, the reality of the Kennedy presidency had been transformed into myth, the man into martyr. People would remember Kennedy less for any specific accomplishment than for his youthful enthusiasm, his inspirational rhetoric, and the romance he brought to American political life. In a peculiar way, he accomplished more in death than in life. In the postassassination atmosphere of grief and remorse, Lyndon Johnson, sworn in as president aboard *Air Force One,* called upon the memory of the fallen president to push through the most ambitious program of legislation since the New Deal.

The new president was a big and passionate man, different from his predecessor in almost every respect. While Kennedy had been raised to wealth and privilege and was educated at Harvard, Johnson had grown up in modest circumstances in the Texas hill country and was graduated from South-

JOHNSON AND THE GREAT SOCIETY

west Texas State Teachers' College. He was as earthy as Kennedy was elegant, prone to colorful curses and willing to use his physical size to his advantage. Advisers and aides reported that he expected them to follow him into the bathroom and conduct business while he showered or used the toilet. But Johnson had been in national politics most of his adult life. He filled an empty congressional seat from Texas in 1937, and as Senate majority leader from 1954 to 1960, he had learned how to manipulate people and wield power to achieve his ends. Now, as president, he used these political skills in an attempt to unite and reassure the nation. "Let us here highly resolve," he told a joint session of Congress five days after the assassination, "that John Fitzgerald Kennedy did not live—or die—in vain."

Johnson, a liberal in the style of Franklin D. Roosevelt, believed the federal government must work actively to improve the lives of Americans. In a 1964 commencement address at the University of Michigan, he described his vision of a nation built upon "abundance and liberty for all . . . demand[ing] an end to poverty and racial injustice . . . a place where every child can find knowledge to enrich his mind and to enlarge his talents . . . where every man can renew contact with nature . . . where men are more concerned with the quality of their goals than the quantity of their goods." Johnson called this vision "The Great Society."

Johnson made civil rights his top legislative priority, and in July he signed into law the Civil Rights Act of 1964. This legislation ended *legal* discrimination on the basis of race, color, religion, national origin, and sex in federal programs, voting, employment, and public accommodation. The original bill did not include discrimination on the basis of sex; that provision was added by a southern congressman who hoped it would torpedo the bill. When a bipartisan group of women members of the House of Representatives took up the cause, however, the bill was passed—with sex as a protected category. Significantly, the Civil Rights Act of 1964 created mechanisms for enforcement, giving the government authority to withhold federal funds from public agencies or federal contractors that discriminated and establishing the Equal Employment Opportunity Commission (EEOC) to investigate and judge claims of job discrimination.

CIVIL RIGHTS ACT

Many Americans did not share Johnson's belief that it was the job of the federal government to end racial discrimination or to fight poverty. Many white southerners, especially, resented federal intervention in what they considered to be local customs. And throughout the nation,

■ Surrounded by an illustrious group of civil rights leaders and members of Congress, President Lyndon B. Johnson signs the Civil Rights Act of 1964. Standing behind the president is the Reverend Martin Luther King Jr. (Corbis-Bettmann)

millions of conservative Americans believed that since the New Deal the federal government had been overstepping its constitutional boundaries. They sought a return to local control and states' rights in the face of growing federal power. In the 1964 election, this conservative vision was championed by the Republican candidate, Arizona senator Barry Goldwater.

Goldwater had not only voted against the 1964 Civil Rights Act; he also opposed the national Social Security system. Like many conservatives, he believed that individual *liberty,* not equality, was the most important American value. Goldwater also believed that the United States needed a more powerful national military to wage the fight against communism; in campaign speeches he suggested that the United States should use tactical nuclear weapons against its enemies. "Extremism in the defense of liberty is no vice," he told the assembled delegates at the Republic National Convention during the summer of 1964.

THE ELECTION OF 1964

Goldwater's campaign slogan, "In your heart you know he's right," was turned against him by Lyndon Johnson supporters: "In your heart you know he's right . . . far right," one punned. Another version warned of Goldwater's willingness to use nuclear weapons: "In your heart you know he might." Johnson campaigned on his record, with an unemployment rate under 4 percent and economic growth at better than 6 percent. But he knew that his support of civil rights had broken apart the New Deal coalition. Shortly after signing the Civil Rights Act of 1964, he told an aide, "I think we just delivered the south to the Republican Party for my lifetime and yours."

The tension between Johnson's support of civil rights and his need of support from southern Democrats came to a head at the 1964 Democratic National Convention. Two delegations had arrived from Mississippi, each demanding to be seated. The Democratic Party's official delegation was exclusively white; the Mississippi Freedom Democratic Party (MFDP) sent a racially mixed delegation to represent a state in which discriminatory literacy tests and fearsome violence disenfranchised its black citizens. White delegates from all the southern states threatened to walk out if the MFDP delegates were seated. In powerful testimony to the convention's credentials committee, MFDP delegate Fannie Lou Hamer told of the

threats and violence she'd faced when she tried to register to vote. "[If] the Freedom Party is not seated now, I question America," Hamer said. Johnson tried to engineer a compromise, but the MFDP had no interest in political deals. "We didn't come all this way for no two seats," Hamer said, and the delegation walked out.

Despite his maneuvering, Johnson could not hold the white South. Though he won the election by a landslide, he lost the Deep South—the first Democrat since the Civil War to do so. Yet American voters also gave him the most liberal Congress in American history. With the mandate provided by a record 61.1 percent of the popular vote, Johnson launched his Great Society. Congress responded in 1965 and 1966 with the most sweeping reform legislation since 1935.

Soon after his inauguration, following a massive demonstration for voting rights in Selma, Alabama, Johnson signed a second monumental civil rights bill, the 1965 Voting Rights Act, which outlawed practices that had prevented most black citizens in the Deep South

Map 30.1   African American Voting Rights, 1960–1971

After passage of the 1965 Voting Rights Act, African American registration skyrocketed in Mississippi and Alabama and rose substantially in other southern states.   (Source: Harold W. Stanley, *Voter Mobilization and the Politics of Race: The South and Universal Suffrage, 1952–1984* [Praeger Publishers, an imprint of Greenwood Publishing Group, Westport, CT, 1987], p. 97. Copyright © 1987 by Greenwood Publishing Group. Reproduced with permission of Greenwood Publishing Group, Inc., Westport, CT.)

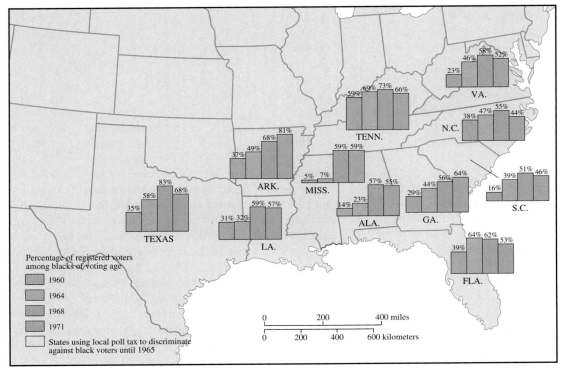

from voting and provided for federal oversight of elections in districts where there was evidence of past discrimination (see Map 30.1). Within two years the percentage of African Americans registered to vote in Mississippi jumped from 7 percent to more than 60 percent. With more black voters, black elected officials became increasingly common in southern states over the following decade.

Seeking to improve the quality of American life, the Johnson administration moved on several additional fronts, establishing new student loan and grant programs to help low- and moderate-income Americans attend college and creating the National Endowment for the Arts and the National Endowment for the Humanities. The Immigration Act of 1965 ended the racially based quotas that had shaped American immigration policy for decades. And Johnson supported important consumer protection legislation, including the 1966 National Traffic and Motor Vehicle Safety Act, which was motivated by Ralph Nader's exposé of the automobile industry, *Unsafe at Any Speed* (1965).

IMPROVING AMERICAN LIFE

Environmentalists found an ally in the Johnson administration, as well. First Lady Claudia Alta Taylor Johnson (known to all as "Lady Bird") successfully pushed for legislation to restrict the billboards and junkyards that had sprung up along the nation's new interstate highway system. Johnson signed "preservation" legislation aiming to protect America's remaining wilderness and also supported legislation addressing environmental pollution.

At the heart of Johnson's Great Society was the War on Poverty. Johnson and other liberals believed that, in a time of great economic affluence, the nation had the resources for programs that could end "poverty, ignorance and hunger as intractable, permanent features of American society." Beginning in 1964, the Johnson administration passed more than a score of major legislative acts meant to do so (see Table 30.1).

WAR ON POVERTY

Johnson's goal, in his words, was "to offer the forgotten fifth of our people opportunity, not doles." Thus many new laws focused on increasing opportunity.

TABLE 30.1

Great Society Achievements, 1964–1966

	1964	1965	1966
Civil Rights	Civil Rights Act Equal Employment Opportunity Commission Twenty-fourth Amendment	Voting Rights Act	
War on Poverty	Economic Opportunity Act Office of Economic Opportunity Job Corps Legal Services for the Poor VISTA		Model Cities
Education		Elementary and Secondary Education Act Head Start Upward Bound	
Environment		Water Quality Act Air Quality Act	Clean Water Restoration Act
New Government Agencies		Department of Housing and Urban Development National Endowments for the Arts and Humanities	Department of Transportation
Miscellaneous		Medicare and Medicaid Immigration and Nationality Act	

The Great Society of the mid-1960s saw the biggest burst of reform legislation since the New Deal of the 1930s.

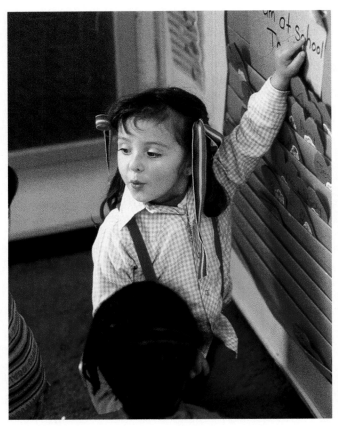

This three-year-old Hispanic girl learns to read in a Head Start program. One of several programs established by the 1964 Economic Opportunity Act, Head Start prepared preschoolers from low-income families for grade school.
(E. Crews/The Image Works)

Billions of federal dollars were channeled to municipalities and school districts to improve opportunities for the poverty-stricken, from preschoolers (Head Start) to high schoolers (Upward Bound) to young adults (Job Corps). The Model Cities program offered federal funds to upgrade employment, housing, education, and health in targeted urban neighborhoods, and Community Action Programs involved the poor in creating local grassroots antipoverty programs for their own communities.

The Johnson administration also tried to ensure basic economic safeguards for all Americans, expanding the existing Food Stamp program and earmarking billions of dollars for constructing public housing and subsidizing rents. Two massive federal programs guaranteed healthcare for specific groups of Americans: Medicare for those sixty-five and older, and Medicaid for the poor. Finally, Aid to Families with Dependent Children

(AFDC), the basic welfare program created during the New Deal, was greatly expanded to increase benefits and the number of people eligible to receive them.

The War on Poverty was controversial from its beginnings. Leftists believed that the government was doing too little to change fundamental structural inequality. Conservatives argued that Great Society programs created dependency among America's poor. Policy analysts noted that specific programs were ill conceived and badly implemented. Even supporters acknowledged that programs were vastly underfunded and marred by political compromises. Responding to criticisms, Joseph Califano, one of the "generals" in the War on Poverty, claimed: "Whatever historians of the Great Society say twenty years later, they must admit we tried, and I believe they will conclude that America is a better place because we did."

Decades later, most historians judge the War on Poverty a mixed success. It did alleviate the effects of poverty, directly addressing the debilitating housing, health, and nutritional deficiencies from which the poor had long suffered. Between 1965 and 1970, federal spending for Social Security, healthcare, welfare, and education more than doubled, and the trend continued into the next decade. By 1975, for instance, the number of Americans receiving food stamps had increased from 600,000 (in 1965) to 17 million. Poverty among the elderly fell from about 40 percent in 1960 to 16 percent in 1974, due largely to increased Social Security benefits and to Medicare. The War on Poverty improved the quality of life for many low-income Americans (see Figure 30.1).

But War on Poverty programs less successfully addressed the root causes of poverty. Neither the Job Corps nor Community Action Programs showed significant results. Economic growth, not Johnson administration policies, was primarily responsible for the dramatic decrease in government-measured poverty during the 1960s—from 22.4 percent of the population in 1959 to 11 percent in 1973. And one structural determinant of poverty remained unchanged: 11 million Americans in female-headed households remained poor at the end of the decade—the same number as in 1963.

Political compromises that shaped Great Society programs also created long-term problems. For example, Congress accommodated the interests of doctors and hospitals in its Medicare legislation by allowing federal reimbursements of hospitals' "reasonable costs" and doctors' "reasonable charges" in treating elderly patients. With no incentives for doctors or hospitals to hold prices down, the cost of healthcare rose dramatically. National healthcare expenditures as a percentage of the gross national product rose by almost 44 percent from 1960 to

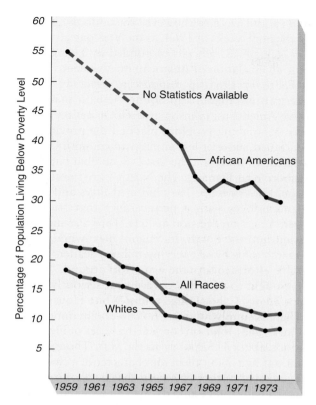

Figure 30.1   Poverty in America for Whites, African Americans, and All Races, 1959–1974

Because of rising levels of economic prosperity, combined with the impact of Great Society programs, the percentage of Americans living in poverty in 1974 was half as high as in 1959. African Americans still were far more likely than white Americans to be poor. In 1959 more than half of all blacks (55.1 percent) were poor; in 1974 the figure remained high (30.3 percent). The government did not record data on African American poverty for the years 1960 through 1965.

1971. Johnson's Great Society was not an unqualified success, but it was a moment in which many Americans believed they could solve the problems of poverty and disease and discrimination—and that it was necessary to try.

Johnson and Vietnam

J ohnson's domestic ambitions were threatened from an early point by turmoil overseas. In foreign policy, Johnson held firmly to ideas about U.S. superiority and the menace of communism. He saw the world in simple, bipolar terms—them against us—

and he saw a lot of "them." But mostly, he preferred not to see the world beyond America's shores at all. International affairs had never much interested him, and he had little appreciation for foreign cultures. Once, on a visit to Thailand while vice president, he flew into a rage when an aide gently advised him that the Thai people recoil from physical contact with strangers. Dammit, Johnson exploded, he shook hands with people everywhere, and they loved it. At the Taj Mahal in India, Johnson tested the monument's echo with a Texas cowboy yell. And on a trip to Senegal he ordered that an American bed, a special showerhead, and cases of Cutty Sark be sent along with him. "Foreigners," Johnson quipped early in his administration, only half-jokingly, "are not like the folks I am used to."

Yet Johnson knew from the start that foreign policy, especially regarding Vietnam, would demand a good deal of his attention. Since the late 1950s, hostilities in Vietnam had increased, as Ho Chi Minh's North assisted the Vietcong guerrillas in the South to advance the reunification of the country under a communist government. President Kennedy had stepped up aid dollars to the Diem regime in Saigon, increased the airdropping of raiding teams into North Vietnam, and launched crop destruction by herbicides to starve the Vietcong and expose their hiding places. Kennedy also strengthened the U.S. military presence in South Vietnam, to the point that by 1963 more than sixteen thousand military advisers were in the country, some authorized to take part in combat alongside the U.S.-equipped Army of the Republic of Vietnam (ARVN).

KENNEDY'S LEGACY IN VIETNAM

Meanwhile, opposition to Diem's repressive regime increased, and not just by communists. Peasants objected to programs that removed them from their villages for their own safety, and Buddhist monks, protesting the Roman Catholic Diem's religious persecution, poured gasoline over their robes and ignited themselves in the streets of Saigon. Though Diem was personally honest, he countenanced corruption in his government and concentrated power in the hands of family and friends. He jailed critics to silence them. Eventually U.S. officials, with Kennedy's approval, encouraged ambitious South Vietnamese generals to remove Diem. On November 1, 1963, the generals struck, murdering Diem. Just a few weeks later Kennedy himself was assassinated.

The timing of Kennedy's murder ensured that Vietnam would be the most controversial aspect of his legacy. Just what would have happened in Southeast Asia had Kennedy returned from Texas alive can never be known, of course, and the speculation is made more difficult by his contradictory record on the conflict. He expanded U.S. involvement and approved a coup against Diem, but despite the urgings of top advisers he refused to commit American ground forces to the struggle. Over time he became increasingly skeptical about South Vietnam's prospects and hinted that he would end the American commitment after winning reelection in 1964. Some authors have gone further and argued that he was ending U.S. involvement even at the time of his death, but the evidence for this claim is thin. More likely, Kennedy arrived in Dallas that fateful day still uncertain about how to solve the Vietnam problem, postponing the truly difficult choices until later.

Lyndon Johnson viewed his Vietnam options through the lens of the impending 1964 election. He wanted to do nothing that could complicate his aim of winning the presidency in his own right, and that meant keeping Vietnam on the back burner. Yet Johnson also sought victory, or at least that he would not lose the war, which in practice amounted to the same thing. As a result, throughout 1964 the administration secretly considered expanding the war to North Vietnam and never seriously considered negotiating a settlement.

TONKIN GULF INCIDENT AND RESOLUTION

In early August 1964, an incident in the Gulf of Tonkin, off the coast of North Vietnam, drew Johnson's involvement (see Map 30.2). Twice in three days, U.S. destroyers reported coming under attack from North Vietnamese patrol boats. Despite conflicting evidence as to whether the second attack occurred, Johnson ordered retaliatory air strikes against selected North Vietnamese patrol boat bases and an oil depot. He also directed aides to rework a long-existing congressional resolution on the use of force. By a vote of 416 to 0 in the House and 88 to 2 in the Senate, Congress quickly passed the Gulf of Tonkin Resolution, which gave the president the authority to "take all necessary measures to repel any armed attack against the forces of the United States and to prevent further aggression." In so doing, Congress essentially surrendered its warmaking powers to the executive branch. The resolution, Secretary of Defense McNamara later noted, served "to open the floodgates."

President Johnson, delighted with the broad authority the resolution gave him, used a different metaphor. "Like grandma's nightshirt," he quipped, "it covered everything." He also appreciated what the Gulf of Tonkin affair did for his political standing—his public approval ratings went up dramatically, and his show of force effectively removed Vietnam as a campaign issue for GOP presidential nominee Barry Goldwater. On the

DECISION FOR ESCALATION

ground in South Vietnam, however, the outlook remained grim in the final weeks of 1964, as the Vietcong continued to make gains. U.S. officials responded by laying secret plans for an escalation of American involvement.

In February 1965, in response to Vietcong attacks on American installations in South Vietnam that killed thirty-two Americans, Johnson ordered Operation Rolling Thunder, a bombing program planned the previous fall that continued, more or less uninterrupted, until October 1968. Then, on March 8, the first U.S. combat battalions came ashore near Danang. The North Vietnamese, however, would not give up. They hid in shelters and rebuilt roads and bridges with a perseverance that frustrated and awed American decision makers. They also increased infiltration into the South. In Saigon, meanwhile, coups and countercoups by self-serving military leaders undermined U.S. efforts to turn the war effort around. "I don't think we ought to take this government seriously," Ambassador Henry Cabot Lodge told a White House meeting. "There is simply no one who can do anything."

In July 1965, Johnson convened a series of high-level discussions about U.S. policy in the war. Though these deliberations had about them the character of a charade—Johnson wanted history to record that he agonized over a choice he had in fact already made—they did confirm that the American commitment would be more or less open-ended. On July 28, Johnson publicly announced a significant troop increase, disclosing that others would follow. By the end of 1965, more than 180,000 U.S. ground troops were in South Vietnam. In 1966 the figure climbed to 385,000. In 1967 alone U.S. warplanes flew 108,000 sorties and dropped 226,000 tons of bombs on North Vietnam. In 1968 U.S. troop strength reached 536,100 (see Figure 30.2). Each American escalation brought not victory, but a new North Vietnamese escalation. The Soviet Union and China responded to the stepped-up U.S. involvement by increasing their material assistance to the Hanoi government.

The initiation of Rolling Thunder and the U.S. troop commitment "Americanized" the war. What could have been seen as a civil war between North and South, or a war of national reunification, was now clearly an American war against the communist Hanoi government. This "Americanization" of the war in Vietnam came despite deep misgivings on the part of influential and informed voices at home and abroad. In the key months of decision, Democratic leaders in the Senate, major newspapers such as the *New York Times* and the *Wall Street Journal,* and prominent columnists like Walter Lippmann warned against deepening involvement.

OPPOSITION TO AMERICANIZATION

CHINA

Red R.

MYANMAR
(BURMA)

Black R.

• Dienbienphu

Hanoi •

Haiphong •

Harbor mined, 1972

Gulf of Tonkin

U.S. bombing begins, 1964
Communist–Pathet Lao victory, 1975

PLAIN OF JARS

Maddox
incident, 1964

NORTH VIETNAM

• Vinh
• Mù Gia Pass

Ca R.

L A O S

Vientiane •

Mekong R.

Udon Thani ■ • Nakhon Phanom ■

U.S. Seventh Fleet
operations during the war

Demilitarized Zone

17°

Demarcation Line, 1954

• Khon Kaen

Khe Sanh ■ Quang Tri
Sépone • • A Chau
Kang Vei • Hue

*South
China Sea*

T H A I L A N D

• Ta Khli

Kham Duc • Da Nang
• My Lai

Ubon Ratchathani ■
• Rachasima

Chu Lai
• Dak To   ■ *Quang Ngai*

• Don Muang

Kontum
• Pleiku   *An Khe*

• Bangkok

Duc Co • ■ • Qui Nhon

Mekong R.

CENTRAL
HIGHLANDS • Tuy Hoa

• Sattahip

C A M B O D I A
(KAMPUCHEA)

• Ban Me Thuot

U.S. bombing
begins, 1969

• Nha Trang

U.S. invasion, 1970

Communist–Khmer Rouge victory, 1975

Bu Dop •

• Dalat   *Can Ranh Bay*

Phnom Penh •

Vietnamese invasion, 1978

SOUTH VIETNAM

Gulf of Siam

Cholon • Bien Hoa
Tan Son Nhut ■ • Long Binh
Chau Duc • Saigon ■
My Tho • ■ Vung Tau

Vietcong–North Vietnamese
victory and U.S. withdrawal,
1975

Mayaguez incident, 1975

Vinh Long •
• Ben Tre

Can Tho • *Mekong Delta*

→ Ho Chi Minh Trail

Ca Mau •

⇨ Boat-people refugees after 1975

CA MAU PENINSULA

☆ Major battles of the Tet Offensive,
January 1968

0   100   200 miles
0   100   200   300 kilometers

■ Major U.S. bases during the war

Map 30.2   Southeast Asia and the Vietnam War

To prevent communists from coming to power in Vietnam, Cambodia, and Laos in the 1960s, the
United States intervened massively in Southeast Asia. The interventions failed, and the remaining
American troops made a hasty exit from Vietnam in 1975, when the victorious Vietcong and North
Vietnamese took Saigon and renamed it Ho Chi Minh City.

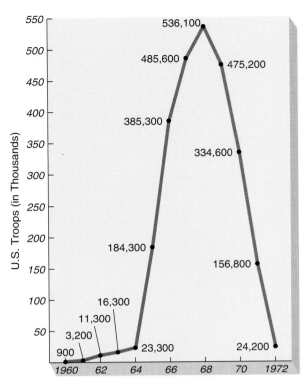

Figure 30.2   U.S. Troops in Vietnam, 1960–1972

These numbers show the Americanization of the Vietnam War under President Johnson, who ordered vast increases in troop levels. President Nixon reversed the escalation, so that by the time of the cease-fire in early 1973 fewer than 25,000 American troops remained in Vietnam. Data are for December 31 of each year.
(Source: U.S. Department of Defense.)

ible. The Soviets and Chinese would be emboldened to challenge U.S. interests elsewhere in the world, and allied governments might conclude they could not depend on Washington. For at least some key players too, including the president himself, domestic political credibility and personal credibility were also on the line. Johnson worried that failure in Vietnam would harm his domestic agenda; even more, he feared the personal humiliation he imagined would inevitably accompany a defeat—and for him, a negotiated withdrawal constituted defeat. As for the stated objective of helping a South Vietnamese ally repulse external aggression, that too figured into the equation, but not as much as it would have had the Saigon government—racked with infighting among senior leaders and possessing little popular support—done more to assist in its own defense.

Even as Johnson Americanized the Vietnam War, he sought to keep the publicity surrounding the action as low as possible. Thus he rejected the Joint Chiefs' view that U.S. reserve forces should be mobilized and a national emergency declared. This decision not to call up reserve units had a momentous impact on the makeup of the American fighting force sent to Vietnam. It forced the military establishment to rely more heavily on the draft, which in turn meant that Vietnam became a young man's war— the average age of soldiers was twenty-two, as compared with twenty-six in World War II. It also became a war of the poor and the working class. Through the years of heavy escalation (1965–1968), college students could get deferments, as could teachers and engineers. (In 1969 the draft was changed so that some students were called up through a lottery system.) The poorest and least educated young men were less likely to be able to avoid the draft, and also more likely to volunteer. The armed services recruited hard in poor communities, many of them heavily African American and Latino, advertising the military as an avenue of training and advancement; very often, the pitch worked. Once in uniform, those with fewer skills were far more likely to see combat, and hence to die.

AMERICAN SOLDIERS IN VIETNAM

Infantrymen on maneuvers carried heavy rucksacks into thick jungle growth, where every step was precarious. Booby traps and land mines were a constant threat. Insects swarmed, and leeches sucked at weary bodies. Boots and human skin rotted from the rains, which alternated with withering suns. "It was as if the sun and the land itself were in league with the Vietcong," recalled marine officer Philip Caputo in *A Rumor of War* (1977), "wearing us down, driving us mad, killing us." The en-

So did some within the administration, including Vice President Hubert H. Humphrey and Undersecretary of State George W. Ball. Abroad, virtually all of America's allies—including France, Britain, Canada, and Japan— cautioned against escalation and urged a political settlement, on the grounds that no military solution favorable to the United States was possible. Remarkably, top U.S. officials themselves shared this deep pessimism. Most of them knew that the odds of success were small. They certainly hoped that the new measures would cause Hanoi to end the insurgency in the South, but it cannot be said they were confident.

Why, then, did America's leaders choose war? At stake was "credibility." They feared that, if the United States failed to prevail in Vietnam, friends and foes around the world would find American power less credemy, meanwhile, was hard to find, often burrowed into elaborate underground tunnels or melded into the population, where any Vietnamese might be a Vietcong.

The American forces fought well, and their entry into the conflict in 1965 helped stave off a South Vietnamese defeat. In that sense, Americanization achieved its most immediate and basic objective. But if the stepped-up fighting that year demonstrated to Hanoi leaders that the war would not swiftly be won, it also showed the same thing to their counterparts in Washington. As the North Vietnamese matched each American escalation with one of their own, the war became a stalemate. The U.S. commander, General William Westmoreland, proved mistaken in his belief that a strategy of attrition represented the key to victory—the enemy had a seemingly endless supply of recruits to throw into battle. Under Westmoreland's strategy, the measure of success became the "body count"—that is, the number of North Vietnamese and Vietcong corpses found after battle. From the start, the counts were subject to manipulation by officers eager to convince superiors of the success of an operation. Worse, the American reliance on massive military and other technology—including carpet bomb-

ing, napalm (jellied gasoline), and crop defoliants that destroyed entire forests—alienated many South Vietnamese and brought new recruits to the Vietcong.

Increasingly, Americans divided into those who supported the war and those who did not. As television coverage brought the war—its body counts and body bags, its burned villages and weeping refugees—into homes every night, the number of opponents grew. On college campuses professors and students organized debates and lectures on American policy. Sometimes going around the clock, these intense public discussions became a form of protest, called "teach-ins" after the sit-ins of the civil rights movement. The big campus and street demonstrations were still to come, but pacifist groups such as the American Friends Service Committee and the Women's International League for Peace and Freedom organized early protests.

In early 1966 Senator Fulbright held televised public hearings on whether the national interest was being served by pursuing the war. What exactly was the threat? senators asked. To the surprise of some, George F. Kennan testified that his containment doctrine was meant for

DIVISIONS AT HOME

Europe, not the volatile environment of Southeast Asia. America's "preoccupation" with Vietnam, Kennan asserted, was undermining its global obligations. Whether many minds were changed by the Fulbright hearings is hard to say, but they constituted the first in-depth national discussion of the U.S. commitment in Vietnam. They provoked Americans to think about the conflict and the nation's role in it. No longer could anyone doubt that there were deep divisions on Vietnam among public officials, or that two of them, Lyndon Johnson and William Fulbright, had broken completely over the war.

Defense Secretary Robert McNamara, who despite private misgivings championed the Americanization of the war in 1965, became increasingly troubled by the killing and destructiveness of the bombing. Already in November 1965 he expressed skepticism that victory could ever be achieved, and in the months thereafter he agonized over how the United States looked in the eyes of the world. American credibility, far from being protected by the staunch commitment to the war, was suffering grievous damage, McNamara feared. "The picture of the world's greatest superpower killing or seriously injuring 1,000 noncombatants a week, while trying to pound a tiny backward nation into submission on an issue whose merits are hotly disputed, is not a pretty one," he told Johnson in mid-1967.

But Johnson was in no mood to listen or reconsider. Determined to prevail in Vietnam, he dug in, snapping at "those little shits on the campuses." Though on occasion he halted the bombing to encourage Ho Chi Minh to negotiate, and to disarm critics, such pauses often were accompanied by increases in American troop strength. And the United States sometimes resumed or accelerated the bombing just when a diplomatic breakthrough seemed possible. The North demanded a complete suspension of bombing raids before sitting down at the conference table. And Ho could not accept American terms, which amounted to abandonment of his lifelong dream of an independent, unified Vietnam.

A Nation Divided

*a*s Johnson struggled to overcome an implacable foe in Vietnam, his liberal vision of a Great Society faced challenges at home. The divisions among Americans over policy in Vietnam were only one fissure in a society that was fracturing along many different lines: black and white, youth and age, radical and conservative.

Even as the civil rights movement was winning important victories in the mid-1960s, many African Americans had given up on the promise of liberal reform. Beginning in 1964, shortly after President Johnson signed into law the landmark Civil Rights Act, racial violence erupted in northern cities. Angry residents of Harlem took to the streets after a white police officer shot a black teenager in July 1964. The following summer, in the predominantly black Watts section of Los Angeles, crowds burned, looted, and battled police for five days and nights. The riot, which began when a white police officer attempted to arrest a black resident on suspicion of drunken driving, left thirty-four dead and more than one thousand injured. In July 1967 twenty-six people were killed in street battles between African Americans and police and army troops in Newark, New Jersey. A week later, in Detroit, forty-three died as 3 square miles of the city went up in flames. In 1967 alone, there were 167 violent outbreaks in 128 cities (see Map 30.3).

URBAN UNREST

The "long, hot summers" of urban unrest in the 1960s differed from almost all previous race riots. Typically, in the past, white mobs had begun the violence. Here, black residents exploded in anger and frustration over the lack of opportunity in their lives. They looted and burned stores, most of them white-owned. But in the process they devastated their own neighborhoods.

In 1968 the National Advisory Commission on Civil Disorders, chaired by Governor Otto Kerner of Illinois, warned that America was "moving towards two societies, one white, one black—separate and unequal," and blamed white racism for the riots. "What white Americans have never fully understood—but what the Negro can never forget—is that white society is deeply implicated in the ghetto. White institutions created it, white institutions maintain it, and white society condones it," concluded the Kerner Commission. Some white Americans rejected this interpretation. Others, shocked at what appeared to be senseless violence, wondered why African Americans were venting their frustration so destructively just when they were making real progress in the civil rights struggle.

The answer stemmed, in part, from regional differences. The civil rights movement had focused mostly on fighting *legal* disenfranchisement and discrimination in the South. But northern African Americans also suffered racial discrimination. Increasingly concentrated in the deteriorating ghettos of inner cities, most northern African Americans lived in societies as segregated as any in the Deep South. They faced discrimination in housing,

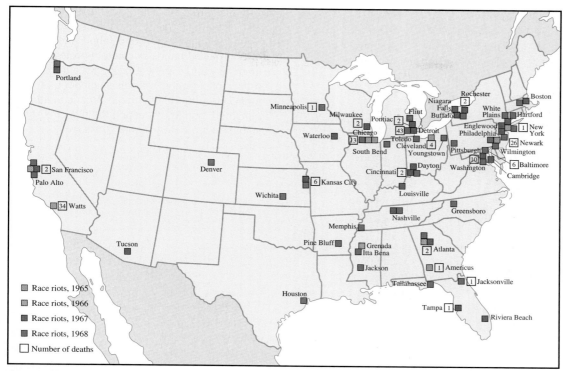

Map 30.3   Race Riots, 1965–1968

The first major race riot of the 1960s exploded in the Los Angeles neighborhood of Watts in 1965. The bloodiest riots of 1967 were in Newark, New Jersey, and Detroit. Scores of riots erupted in the aftermath of Martin Luther King Jr.'s assassination in 1968.

in the availability of credit and mortgages, and in employment. The median income of northern blacks was little more than half that of northern whites, and their unemployment rate was twice as high. Many northern blacks had given up on the civil rights movement, and few believed that Great Society liberalism would solve their plight.

In this climate, a new voice emerged, one that urged blacks to seize their freedom "by any means necessary."

BLACK POWER   It was the voice of Malcolm X, a one-time pimp and street hustler who had converted while in prison to the Nation of Islam faith. Members of the Nation of Islam, commonly known as Black Muslims, espoused black pride and separatism from white society. Their faith, combining elements of traditional Islam with a belief that whites were subhuman "devils" whose race would soon be destroyed, also emphasized the importance of sobriety, thrift, and social responsibility. By the early 1960s Mal-

colm X had become the Black Muslims' chief spokesperson, and his advice was straightforward: "If someone puts a hand on you, send him to the cemetery." But Malcolm X was murdered in early 1965 by members of the Nation of Islam who believed he had betrayed their cause by breaking with the Black Muslims to start his own, more racially tolerant organization. In death, Malcolm X became a powerful symbol of black defiance and self-respect.

A year after Malcolm X's death, Stokely Carmichael, SNCC chairman, denounced "the betrayal of black dreams by white America." To be truly free from white oppression, Carmichael proclaimed, blacks had to "stand up and take over"—to elect black candidates, to organize their own schools, to control their own institutions. "Black Power," his listeners chanted. That year, SNCC expelled its white members and repudiated both nonviolence and integration. CORE followed suit in 1967.

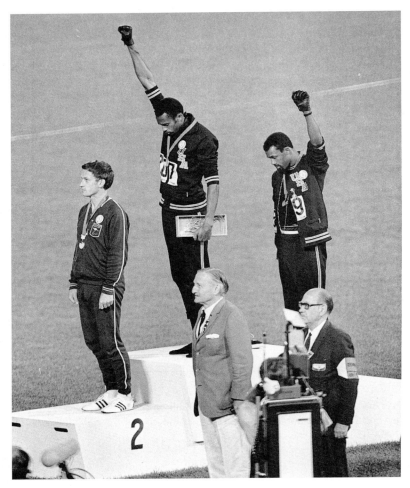

■ During award ceremonies at the 1968 Olympic Games in Mexico City, American sprinters Tommie Smith *(center)* and John Carlos *(right)* extend gloved hands skyward to protest racial inequality and express Black Power. In retaliation, Olympic officials suspended Smith and Carlos, but other African American athletes emulated them by repeating the clenched-fist salute on the victory stand.   (Wide World Photos, Inc.)

The best known black radicals of the era were the Black Panthers, an organization formed in Oakland, California, in 1966. Blending black separatism and revolutionary communism, the Panthers dedicated themselves to destroying both capitalism and "the military arm of our oppressors," the police in the ghettos. In direct contrast to earlier, nonviolent civil rights protesters, who had worn suits and ties or dresses to demonstrate their respectability, male Panthers dressed in commando gear, carried weapons, and talked about killing "pigs"—and did kill eleven officers by 1970. Police responded in kind; most infamously, Chicago police murdered local Panther leader Fred Hampton in his bed. However, the group—led by its women members—also worked to improve life in their neighborhoods by instituting free breakfast and healthcare programs for ghetto children, offering courses in African American history, and demanding jobs and decent housing for the poor. The Panthers' platform attracted many young African Americans, and as calls for Black Power spread, many white Americans reacted with fear. Radicalism, however, was not limited to black nationalist groups. Before the end of the decade, a vocal minority of America's young would join in calls for revolution.

By the mid-1960s, 41 percent of the American population was under the age of twenty. These young people

YOUTH AND POLITICS

spent more time in the world of peer culture than any previous generation, as three-quarters of them graduated from high school (up from one-fifth in the 1920s) and almost half of them went to college (up from 16 percent in 1940). As this large baby-boom generation came of age, many young people took seriously the idea that they must provide democratic leadership for their nation. Black college students had begun the sit-in movement, infusing new life into the struggle for African American civil rights. Some white college students—from both the political left and right—also committed themselves to changing the system.

In the fall of 1960, a group of conservative college students came together at the family estate of William F. Buckley in Sharon, Connecticut, to create Young Americans for Freedom (YAF). Their manifesto, the "Sharon Statement," endorsed Cold War anticommunism and a vision of limited government power directly opposed to New Deal liberalism and its heritage. "In this time of moral and political crises," they wrote, "it is the responsibility of the youth of America to affirm certain eternal truths. . . . [F]oremost among the transcendent values is the individual's use of his God-given free will." The YAF planned to capture the Republican Party and move it to the political right; Goldwater's selection as the Republican candidate for president in 1964 demonstrated their early success.

At the other end of the political spectrum, an emerging "New Left" soon joined conservative youth in rejecting liberalism. While conservatives believed liberalism's activist government encroached on individual liberty, these young Americans believed liberalism was not enough, that it could never offer true democracy and equality to all America's people. At a meeting in Port Huron, Michigan, in 1962, founding members of Students for a Democratic Society (SDS) proclaimed: "We are people of this generation, bred in at least modest comfort, housed now in the universities, looking uncomfortably to the world we inherit." Their "Port Huron Statement" condemned racism, poverty in the midst of plenty, and the Cold War. Calling for "participatory democracy," SDS sought to wrest power from the corporations, the military, and the politicians and return it to "the people."

The first indication of the new power of activist white youth came at the University of California, Berkeley. In

FREE SPEECH MOVEMENT

the fall of 1964 the university administration banned political activity—including recruiting volunteers for civil rights work in Mississippi—from its traditional place along a university-owned sidewalk bordering the campus. When the administration called police to arrest a CORE worker who defied the order, some four thousand students surrounded the police car. Berkeley graduate student and Mississippi Freedom Summer veteran Mario Savio ignited the movement, telling students: "You've got to put your bodies upon the levers . . .

[and] you've got to indicate to the people who run it, to the people who own it, that unless you're free, the machine will be prevented from working at all."

Student political groups, left and right, came together to create the Free Speech Movement (FSM). The FSM did win back the right to political speech, but not before state police had arrested almost eight hundred student protesters. Berkeley students took two lessons from the Free Speech Movement. Many saw the administration's actions as a failure of America's democratic promises, and they were radicalized by the experience. But the victory of the FSM also demonstrated to students their potential power. By the end of the decade, the activism born at Berkeley would spread to hundreds of college and university campuses (see Map 30.4).

Many student protesters in the 1960s sought greater control over their lives as students, demanding more

STUDENT ACTIVISM

relevant class offerings, more freedom in selecting their courses of study, and a greater voice in the running of universities. A major target of protest was the doctrine of in loco parentis, which until the late 1960s put universities legally "in the place of parents" to their students, allowing control over student behavior that went well beyond the laws of the land. The impact of in loco parentis fell heaviest on women, who were subject to strict curfew regulations called *parietals,* while men had no such rules. Protesters demanded an end to discrimination on the basis of sex, but rejected in loco parentis for other reasons as well. A group at the University of Kansas demanded the administration explain how its statement that "college students are assumed to have maturity of judgment necessary for adult responsibility" squared with the minute regulation of students' nonacademic lives. One young man complained that "a high school dropout selling cabbage in a supermarket" had more rights and freedoms than successful university students. Increasingly, students insisted they should be allowed the full rights and responsibilities of citizens in a democratic society.

It was the war in Vietnam, however, that mobilized a nationwide student movement. Believing that it was the

YOUTH AND THE WAR IN VIETNAM

democratic responsibility of citizens to learn about and speak out on issues of vital national importance, university students and faculty held "teach-ins" about U.S. involvement in Vietnam as the war escalated in 1965. Students for a Democratic Society sponsored the first major antiwar march that year, drawing twenty thousand protesters to Washington, D.C. Local SDS

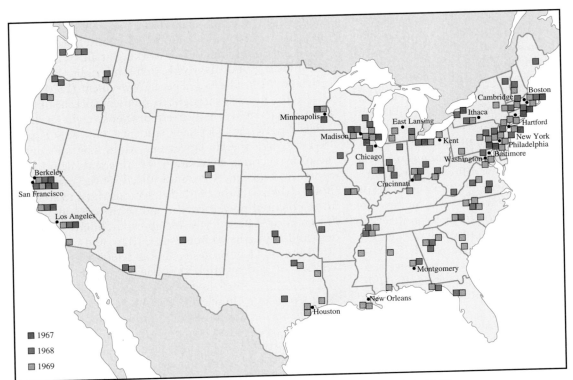

Map 30.4   Disturbances on College and University Campuses, 1967–1969
Students on campuses from coast to coast protested against the Vietnam War. Some protests were peaceful; others erupted into violent confrontations between protesters and police and army troops.

chapters grew steadily as opposition to the war increased. On campuses throughout the nation, students adopted tactics developed in the civil rights movement, picketing ROTC buildings and protesting military research and recruiting done on their campuses. However, despite the visibility of campus antiwar protests, most students did not yet oppose the war: in 1967, only 30 percent of male college students declared themselves "doves" on Vietnam, while 67 percent proclaimed themselves "hawks." And many young men were, in fact, in Vietnam fighting the war. But as the war continued to escalate, an increasing number of America's youth came to distrust the government that turned a deaf ear to their protests, as well as the university administrations that seemed more a source of arbitrary authority than of democratic education.

During the 1960s, the large baby-boom generation would change the nation's culture more than its politics. Though many young people protested the war and marched for social justice, most did not. And Sixties "youth culture" was never homogeneous. Fraternity and

YOUTH CULTURE
AND THE
COUNTERCULTURE

sorority life stayed strong on most campuses, even as radicalism flourished. And while there was some crossover, black, white, and Latino youth had different cultural styles: different music, different clothes, even different versions of a youth dialect often incomprehensible to adults. Nonetheless, as potential consumers, young people as a group exercised tremendous cultural authority. Their music and their styles drove American popular culture in the late 1960s.

The most unifying element of youth culture was the importance of music. The Beatles had electrified American teenagers—73 million viewers watched their first television appearance on the *Ed Sullivan Show* in 1964. Bob Dylan promised revolutionary answers in "Blowin' in the Wind"; Janis Joplin brought the sexual power of the blues to white youth; James Brown and Aretha Franklin proclaimed black pride; and the psychedelic rock of the Jefferson Airplane and the Grateful Dead— along with hallucinogenic drugs—redefined reality. That new reality took brief form in the Woodstock Festival in upstate New York in 1969, as more than 400,000 people reveled in the music and in a world of their own making, living in rain and mud for four days without shelter and without violence.

Some young people hoped to turn youth rebellion into something more than a consumer-based lifestyle, rejecting what they saw as hypocritical middle-class values. They attempted to craft an alternative way of life, or "counterculture," liberated from competitive materialism and celebrating the legitimacy of pleasure. "Sex, Drugs, and Rock 'n' Roll" became a mantra of sorts, offering these "hippies," or "freaks," a path to a new consciousness. Many did the hard work of creating communes and intentional communities, whether in cities or in hidden stretches of rural America. Though the New Left criticized the counterculture as apolitical, many freaks did envision revolutionary change. As John Sinclair, manager of the rock band MC-5, explained, mindblowing experiences with sex, drugs, or music were far more likely to

change the young people's minds than earnest speeches: "Rather than go up there and make some speech about our moral commitment in Vietnam, you just make 'em so freaky they'd never want to go into the army in the first place."

The nascent counterculture had first burst on the national consciousness during the summer of 1967, when tens of thousands of young people poured into the Haight-Ashbury district of San Francisco, the heart of America's psychedelic culture, for the "Summer of Love." As an older generation of "straight" (or Establishment) Americans watched with horror, white youth came to look—and act—more and more like the counterculture. Coats and ties disappeared, as did stockings—and bras. Young men grew long hair, and parents throughout the nation complained, "You can't tell the boys from the girls." Millions experimented with marijuana or hallucinogenic drugs, read underground newspapers, and thought of themselves as alienated from

■ In a protest on San Francisco's Market Street in 1967, Americans call for an end to U.S. involvement in the Vietnam War. There were more than 485,000 American troops in Vietnam in 1967.   (Lisa Law/Image Works)

The British Invasion

The British invasion began in earnest on February 7, 1964. London and Paris had already fallen, reported *Life* magazine, and New York was soon to follow. Three thousand screaming American teenagers were waiting when Pan Am's Yankee Clipper touched down at Kennedy Airport with four British "moptops" aboard. "I Want to Hold Your Hand" was already at the top of the U.S. charts, and the Beatles' conquest of America was quick. Seventy-three million people—the largest television audience in history— watched them on the *Ed Sullivan Show* the following Sunday night.

Though the Beatles led the invasion, they did not conquer America alone. The Rolling Stones' first U.S. hit single also came in 1964. The Dave Clark Five appeared on *Ed Sullivan* eighteen times. And there was a whole list of others, some now forgotten, some not: Freddie and the Dreamers; Herman's Hermits; The Animals; the Yardbirds; the Hollies; the Kinks; Gerry and the Pacemakers; Chad and Jeremy; Petula Clark.

The British invasion was, at least in part, the triumphal return of American music, part of a transatlantic exchange that reinvigorated both nations. American rock 'n' roll had lost much of its early energy by the early 1960s, and in England, the London-centered popular music industry was pumping out a highly produced, saccharine version of American pop. But other forms of American music had made their way across the Atlantic, often carried by travelers through port cities such as Liverpool, where the Beatles were born. By the late 1950s, young musicians in England's provincial cities were listening to the music of African American bluesmen Muddy Waters and Howlin' Wolf; they were playing cover versions of the early rock 'n' roll of Buddy Holly and Chuck Berry; and they were experimenting with skiffle, a sort of jazz- and blues-influenced folk music played mostly with improvised instruments. None of this music had a large popular audience in the United States, where *Billboard* magazine's number one hit for 1960 was Percy Faith's "Theme from *A Summer Place*" (a movie starring Sandra Dee and Troy Donahue), and the Singing Nun was at the top of the charts just before the Beatles arrived.

Young British musicians, including John Lennon, Eric Clapton, and Mick Jagger, recreated American musical forms and reinvented rock 'n' roll. By the mid-1960s, the Beatles and the other bands of the British invasion were at the heart of a youth culture that transcended the boundaries of nations. This music not only connected Britain and America but reached across the Atlantic and the Pacific to link America's youth with young people throughout the world.

The Beatles perform on the *Ed Sullivan Show* in February 1964. Though Britain's Queen Mother thought the Beatles "young, fresh, and vital," American parents were appalled when the "long" Beatles haircut swept the nation. (AP/Wide World Photos, Inc.)

"straight" culture even though they were attending high school or college, not completely "dropping out" of the Establishment.

Some of the most lasting cultural changes involved attitudes about sex. The mass media were fascinated with "Free Love," and some people did embrace a truly promiscuous sexuality. More important, however, was that premarital sex no longer destroyed a woman's "reputation." The birth-control pill, distributed since 1960 and widely available to single women by the late 1960s, greatly lessened the risk of unplanned pregnancy, and venereal diseases were easily cured by a basic course of antibiotics. The number of couples living together—"without benefit of matrimony," as the phrase went at the time—increased 900 percent from 1960 to 1970; many young people no longer tried to hide the fact that they were sexually active. Still, 68 percent of American adults disapproved of premarital sex in 1969.

Adults were baffled and often angered by the behavior of youth. A generation that had grown up in the hard decades of depression and war, many of whom saw middle-class respectability as crucial to success and stability, just did not understand. How could young people put such promising futures at risk by having sex without marriage, taking drugs, or opposing the American government over the war in Vietnam?

1968

By the beginning of 1968, it seemed that the nation was coming apart. Divided over the war in Vietnam, frustrated by the slow pace of social change or angry over the racial violence that wracked America's cities, Americans looked for solutions as the nation faced the most serious domestic crisis of the postwar era.

The year opened with a major attack in Vietnam. On January 31, 1968, the first day of the Vietnamese New Year (Tet), Vietcong and North Vietnamese forces struck all across South Vietnam, capturing provincial capitals (see Map 30.2). During the carefully planned offensive, the Saigon airport, the presidential palace, and the ARVN headquarters came under attack. Even the American embassy compound in the city was penetrated by Vietcong soldiers, who occupied its courtyard for six hours. U.S. and South Vietnamese units eventually regained much of the ground they had lost, inflicting heavy casualties and devastating numerous villages.

THE TET OFFENSIVE

Although the Tet Offensive ultimately counted as a U.S. military victory, the heavy fighting called into question American military leaders' confident predictions in earlier months that the war would soon be won. Had not the Vietcong and North Vietnamese demonstrated that they could strike when and where they wished? If America's airpower, dollars, and half a million troops could not now defeat the Vietcong, could they ever do so? Had the American public been deceived? In February, the highly respected CBS television anchorman Walter Cronkite went to Vietnam to find out. The military brass in Saigon assured him that "we had the enemy just where we wanted him." The newsman recalled, "Tell that to the Marines, I thought—the Marines in the body bags on that helicopter."

Top presidential advisers sounded notes of despair. Clark Clifford, the new secretary of defense, told Johnson that the war—"a sinkhole"—could not be won, even with the 206,000 additional soldiers requested by Westmoreland. Aware that the nation was suffering a financial crisis prompted by rampant deficit spending to sustain the war and other global commitments, they knew that taking the initiative in Vietnam would cost billions more, further derail the budget, panic foreign owners of dollars, and wreck the economy. Clifford heard from his associates in the business community: "These men now feel we are in a hopeless bog," he told the president. To "maintain public support for the war without the support of these men" was impossible.

Controversy over the war split the Democratic Party, just as a presidential election loomed in November. Senator Eugene McCarthy of Minnesota and Robert F. Kennedy (now a senator from New York), both strong opponents of Johnson's war policies, forcefully challenged the president in early primaries. Strained by exhausting sessions with skeptical advisers, troubled by the economic implications of escalation, and sensing that more resources would not bring victory, Johnson changed course. During a March 31 television address he announced a halt to most of the bombing, asked Hanoi to begin negotiations, and stunned his listeners by withdrawing from the presidential race. He had become a casualty of the war, his presidency doomed by a seemingly interminable struggle 10,000 miles from Washington. Peace talks began in May in Paris, but the war ground on.

JOHNSON'S EXIT

Less than a week after Johnson's shocking announcement, Martin Luther King Jr. was murdered in Memphis. It is still not clear why James Earl Ray, a white forty-year-old drifter and petty criminal who was born in Illinois, shot King—or whether he acted alone or as part of a conspiracy. By 1968 King, the senior statesman of

ASSASSINATIONS

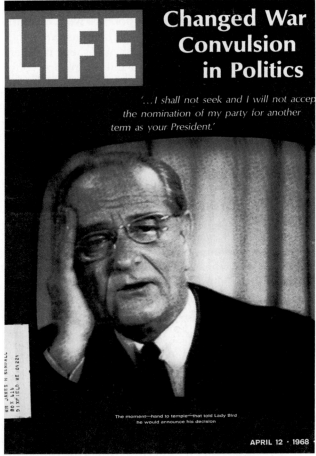

LIFE

Changed War
Convulsion
in Politics

'...I shall not seek and I will not accept
the nomination of my party for another
term as your President.'

The moment—hand to temple—that told Lady Bird
he would announce his decision

APRIL 12 · 1968

■ *Life* magazine captures the moment that President Lyndon Johnson, in a televised address, told the nation he would not seek another term as president of the United States. Johnson's face shows the toll taken by his years in the White House, as the war in Vietnam gradually destroyed his presidency and divided the nation. (Time Life Pictures / Time Life Picture Collection / Getty Images)

the civil rights movement, had become an outspoken critic of the Vietnam War and of American capitalism. He had many detractors, but he was also widely honored. Most Americans mourned his death, even as black rage and grief exploded into riots in 130 cities throughout the nation. Once again, ghetto neighborhoods burned; thirty-four blacks and five whites died. The violence provoked a backlash from whites, primarily urban, working-class people who were tired of violence and quickly losing whatever sympathy they might have had for black Americans' increasingly radical demands. In

Chicago, Mayor Richard Daley ordered police to shoot rioters.

An already shaken nation watched in disbelief as another leader fell to violence only two months later. Antiwar Democratic candidate for president Robert Kennedy was shot and killed as he celebrated his victory in the California primary. His assassin, Sirhan Sirhan, an Arab nationalist, targeted Kennedy because of his support for Israel.

Violence erupted again in August at the Democratic National Convention in Chicago. Thousands of protesters converged on the city: students who'd gone "Clean for Gene," cutting long hair and donning "respectable" clothes to campaign for antiwar candidate Eugene McCarthy; members of America's counterculture drawn by the anarchist Yippies' promise of a "Festival of Life" to counter the "Convention of Death"; members of antiwar groups that ranged from radical to mainstream. Chicago's mayor, resolved that no one would disrupt "his" convention, assigned twelve thousand police to twelve-hour shifts and had twelve thousand army troops with bazookas, rifles, and flamethrowers on call as backup. Police attacked peaceful antiwar protesters and journalists. "The Whole World is Watching," chanted the protesters, as club-swinging police indiscriminately beat people to the ground and Americans gathered around their television sets, despairing over the future of their nation.

CHICAGO
DEMOCRATIC
NATIONAL
CONVENTION

Though American eyes were focused on the clashes in Chicago, upheavals spread around the world that spring and summer. In France, university students protested both rigid academic policies and the Vietnam War. They received support from French workers, who occupied their factories and paralyzed public transport; the turmoil contributed to the collapse of Charles de Gaulle's government the following year. In Italy, Germany, England, Ireland, Sweden, Canada, Mexico, Chile, Japan, and South Korea, students also protested—sometimes violently—against universities, governments, and the Vietnam War. In Czechoslovakia, hundreds of thousands of demonstrators flooded the streets of Prague, demanding democracy and an end to repression by the Soviet-controlled government. This so-called "Prague Spring" developed into a full-scale national rebellion before being crushed by Soviet tanks.

GLOBAL
PROTEST

Why so many uprisings occurred in so many places simultaneously is not altogether clear. Sheer numbers had an impact. The postwar baby boom experienced by

■ A military truck with civilians waving Czech flags drives past a Soviet truck in Prague on August 21, 1968, shortly after Warsaw Pact troops invaded Czechoslovakia. More than one hundred people were killed in the clashes, and several "Prague Spring" leaders, including Alexander Dubček, were arrested and taken to Moscow. Dubček's attempts to create "socialism with a human face" are often seen as historical and ideological forerunners to Mikhail Gorbachev's reform policies in the 1980s in the Soviet Union.   (Hulton Archive/Getty Images)

many nations produced by the late 1960s a huge mass of teenagers and young adults, many of whom had grown up in relative prosperity with high expectations for the future. The expanded reach of global media also mattered. Technological advances allowed the nearly instantaneous transmittal of televised images around the world, so protests in one country could readily inspire similar actions in others. Although the worldwide demonstrations might have occurred even without the Vietnam War, television news footage showing the wealthiest and most industrialized nation carpet-bombing a poor and developing one—whose leader was the charismatic revolutionary Ho Chi Minh—surely helped fuel the agitation.

The presidential election of 1968, coming at the end of such a difficult year, did little to heal the nation. Democratic nominee Hubert Humphrey, Johnson's vice president, seemed a continuation of the old politics. Republican candidate Richard Nixon, no newcomer to the

NIXON'S ELECTION

political scene, appealed to a nation tired of violence and unrest with calls for "law and order" and a promise to "bring us together." He reached out to those he called "the great, quite forgotten majority—the nonshouters and the nondemonstrators, the millions who ask principally to go their own way in decency and dignity." On Vietnam, Nixon vowed he would "end the war and win the peace." Governor George Wallace of Alabama, who only five years before had vowed "segregation forever!" and who proposed using nuclear weapons on Vietnam, ran as a third-party candidate. Wallace carried five southern states, drawing almost 14 percent of the popular vote, and Nixon was elected president with the slimmest of margins (see Map 30.5). Divisions among Americans deepened.

Yet on Christmas Eve, 1968—in a step toward fulfilling the pledge John Kennedy had made at the opening of a tumultuous decade—*Apollo 8* entered lunar orbit. Looking down on a troubled world, the astronauts

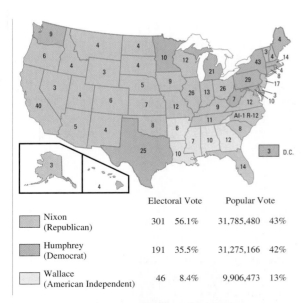

	Electoral Vote	Popular Vote
Nixon (Republican)	301 56.1%	31,785,480 43%
Humphrey (Democrat)	191 35.5%	31,275,166 42%
Wallace (American Independent)	46 8.4%	9,906,473 13%

Map 30.5   Presidential Election, 1968

The popular vote was almost evenly split between Richard M. Nixon and Hubert Humphrey, but Nixon won 31 states to Humphrey's 14 and triumphed easily in electoral votes. George Wallace, the American Independent Party candidate, won 5 states in the Deep South.

broadcast photographs of the earth seen from space, a fragile blue orb floating in darkness. As people around the world listened, the astronauts read aloud the opening passages of Genesis: "In the beginning, God created the heaven and the earth . . . and God saw that it was good," and many listeners found themselves moved to tears.

Summary

The 1960s began with high hopes for a more democratic America. Civil rights volunteers, often risking their lives, carried the quest for racial equality to all parts of the nation. Gradually, the nation's leaders put their support behind the movement, and the passage of the Civil Rights Act of 1964 and the Voting Rights Act of 1965 were major landmarks in the quest for a more just society. America was shaken by the assassination of President John Kennedy in 1963, but under President Johnson, the liberal vision of government power used to create a better life for the nation's citizens reached new heights, as a flood of legislation was enacted in hopes of creating a Great Society.

But throughout this period, the nation was troubled by threats to its stability. The Cold War between the United States and the USSR grew in size and scope during the 1960s. The world came close to nuclear war in the 1962 Cuban missile crisis. Cold War geopolitics led the United States to become more and more involved in the ongoing war in Vietnam. Determined not to let Vietnam "fall" to communists, the United States sent military forces to prevent the victory of communist Vietnamese nationalists led by Ho Chi Minh in that nation's civil war. By 1968 there were more than half a million American ground troops in Vietnam. America's war in Vietnam divided the country, undermined Great Society domestic programs, and destroyed the presidency of Lyndon Johnson.

Despite real gains in civil rights and in attempts to promote justice and end poverty, divisions among Americans deepened. Many African Americans turned away from the civil rights movement, seeking more immediate change in their lives. Poor African American neighborhoods burned as riots spread through the nation. Integrationists and civil rights advocates fought both separatist Black Power militants and white segregationists. Vocal young people—and some of their elders—questioned whether democracy truly existed in the United States. Large numbers of the nation's white youth embraced another form of rebellion, claiming membership in a "counterculture" that rejected white middle-class respectability. With great passion, Americans struggled over the future of their nation.

1968 was a year of crisis, of assassinations and violence in the streets. The decade that had started with such promise was moving toward its end in fierce political polarization.

LEGACY FOR A PEOPLE AND A NATION
The Immigration Act of 1965

When President Johnson signed the 1965 Immigration Act in a ceremony at the foot of the Statue of Liberty, he stated, "This bill that we sign today is not a revolutionary bill. It does not affect the lives of millions. It will not reshape the structure of our daily lives, or really add importantly to our wealth and power." Though Johnson believed that the act was important because it "repair[ed] a very deep and painful flaw in the fabric of American justice" by ending national-origins quotas that all but excluded "Polynesians, orientals, and Negroes" (as Hawai'i's senator Hiram Fong pointed out in 1963), the president and his advisers saw it as primarily symbolic. They were wrong. This relatively obscure act may have greater long-term impact on Americans' lives than any other piece of Great Society legislation.

The architects of the Immigration Act did not expect the scale or the sources of immigration to change. Attorney General Robert Kennedy argued that abolishing immigration restrictions for Asia and the Pacific would probably produce about five thousand new immigrants, after which such immigration would subside. But world events decreed otherwise. Rapidly growing population in many of the world's poorer nations created a large pool of potential immigrants.

Immigration rates skyrocketed, and by the 1990s immigration accounted for almost 60 percent of America's population growth. By 2000, more Americans were foreign-born than at any time since the 1930s—and their numbers continued to grow. No longer were most immigrants from western Europe. The majorities came from Mexico, the Philippines, Vietnam, China, the Dominican Republic, Korea, India, the USSR, Jamaica, and Iran.

More than two-thirds of the new immigrants settled in six states—New York, California, Florida, New Jersey, Illinois, and Texas—but many found their way to parts of America that had previously been much more homogeneous. By the late twentieth century, Spanish-language signs appeared in South Carolina, and Hmong farmers from the mountains of Southeast Asia offered their produce at the farmers' market in Missoula, Montana. The legacy of the 1965 Immigration Act was unintended, but profound: the United States is a much more diverse nation today than it otherwise would have been.

CONTINUING DIVISIONS AND NEW LIMITS 1969–1980

*I*n 1969 Daniel Ellsberg was a thirty-eight-year-old former aide to Assistant Secretary of Defense John McNaughton. At the Pentagon Ellsberg had worked on a top-secret study of U.S. decision making in Vietnam requested by Secretary of Defense Robert S. McNamara. When he left office following the election of Richard Nixon, Ellsberg gained access to a copy of the study being stored at the Rand Corporation, where he intended to resume his pregovernment career as a researcher. He spent the next six months poring over the forty-seven volumes and seven thousand pages that made up what would come to be called the Pentagon Papers.

Initially supportive of U.S. military intervention in Vietnam, Ellsberg had in the last years of his government career grown deeply disillusioned. A Harvard-trained Ph.D., a former marine officer, and a Cold Warrior with a moral fervor to preserve America's nuclear deterrence, he had spent nearly two years in South Vietnam, from 1965 to 1967, assessing the war's progress for his superiors in Washington. Several times he had gone on combat patrols and come under enemy fire, and he had interviewed military officials, U.S. diplomats, and Vietnamese leaders. The war, he concluded, was in multiple respects—military, political, moral—a lost enterprise.

Ellsberg was at first reluctant to act on that conviction and disassociate himself from the policy. "Like so many," he later recalled, "I put personal loyalty to the president . . . above all else." But when in 1969 it became clear that the incoming Nixon administration had no intention of ending the war, he decided on a bold course of action: he would make the Pentagon Papers public, even though doing so might land him in prison. The study, he believed, showed incontrovertibly

◀ Daniel Ellsberg talks to reporters on January 17, 1973, after the opening session of his trial. Behind him is co-defendant Anthony Russo, Ellsberg's colleague at the Rand Corporation who had assisted in the secret photocopying of the Pentagon Papers. The government indicted Ellsberg and Russo on charges of espionage, theft, and conspiracy, but in May 1973 a federal court judge dismissed all charges against them because of improper government conduct. (© Corbis-Bettmann)

CHRONOLOGY

1969 • Stonewall Inn uprising begins gay liberation movement
  • *Apollo 11* Astronaut Neil Armstrong becomes first person to walk on moon's surface
  • National Chicano Liberation Youth Conference held in Denver
  • "Indians of All Tribes" occupy Alcatraz Island
  • Nixon administration begins affirmative-action plan

1970 • United States invades Cambodia
  • Students at Kent State and Jackson State Universities shot by National Guard troops
  • First Earth Day celebrated
  • Environmental Protection Agency created

1971 • Pentagon Papers published

1972 • Nixon visits China and Soviet Union
  • CREEP stages Watergate break-in
  • Congress approves ERA and passes Title IX, which creates growth in women's athletics

1973 • Peace agreement in Paris ends U.S. involvement in Vietnam
  • OPEC increases oil prices, creating U.S. "energy crisis"
  • *Roe v. Wade* legalizes abortion
  • Agnew resigns; Ford named vice president

1974 • Nixon resigns under threat of impeachment; Ford becomes president

1975 • In deepening economic recession, unemployment hits 8.5 percent
  • New York City saved from bankruptcy by federal loan guarantees
  • Congress passes Indian Self-Determination and Education Assistance Act in response to Native American activists

1976 • Carter elected president

1978 • *Regents of the University of California v. Bakke* outlaws quotas but upholds affirmative action
  • California voters approve Proposition 13

1979 • Three Mile Island nuclear accident raises fears
  • Camp David accords signed by Israel and Egypt
  • American hostages seized in Iran
  • Soviet Union invades Afghanistan
  • Consumer debt doubles from 1975 to hit $315 billion

that presidents had repeatedly escalated the American commitment in Vietnam despite uniformly pessimistic estimates from their advisers—and that they had repeatedly lied to the public about what they were doing and the results achieved. Perhaps, Ellsberg thought, disclosure of this information would generate sufficient uproar to force a dramatic change in policy.

With the assistance of a Rand colleague, Ellsberg surreptitiously photocopied the entire study, then spent months pleading with antiwar senators and representatives to release it. When they refused, he went to the press. On June 13, 1971, the world first learned of the Pentagon Papers through a front-page article in the *New York Times*. Numerous other newspapers soon began publishing excerpts as well.

Ellsberg's act of leaking a top-secret study became intensely controversial, particularly with Nixon's decision to try to stop the papers' publication—the first such effort to muzzle the press since the American Revolution—and to discredit Ellsberg and deter other leakers through the illegal actions of a group of petty operatives. To many Americans, Ellsberg was a hero whose defiant act might at least indirectly shorten an illegitimate war. To many others, he was a publicity-seeking traitor. These divergent views reflected the deep schisms in American society during the latter stages of the Vietnam era.

The 1970s would be, for Americans, a decade of division and an age of limits. The violence and chaos of 1968 continued in Richard Nixon's first years as president. Opposition to the war in Vietnam became more radical. As government deceptions were exposed, the American people were ever more polarized over U.S. policy in Vietnam. The movements for racial equality and social justice that had flowered in the 1960s also became more radical by the early 1970s. While some continued to work for racial integration, many activists embraced cultural nationalism, which emphasized the differences among Americans and sought separatist cultures and societies. Even the women's movement, which was the strongest social movement of the 1970s and won great victories against sex discrimination, had a polarizing effect. Opponents, many of them women, understood feminism as an attack on their chosen way of life, and mobilized a conservative grassroots movement that had great political importance over the subsequent decades.

This divided America faced great challenges abroad and at home. To some of these challenges, leaders responded boldly and imaginatively. Richard Nixon and his national security adviser, Henry Kissinger, understood that in foreign affairs America's capacity to effect change was limited. They grasped that the United States and the Soviet Union, weakened by the huge costs of their competition and challenged by other nations, faced an international system in which power had become diffused. Accordingly, even as they stubbornly and futilely pursued victory in Vietnam, Nixon and Kissinger worked to improve relations with the People's Republic of China and the Soviet Union. In an increasingly multipolar system, they reasoned, the maintenance of world order depended on stable relations among the great powers. Through the opening to China and through improved relations with the USSR, the two men helped reduce the threat of great-power war.

Ultimately, however, exposure of Richard Nixon's illegal acts in the political scandal known as "Watergate" shook the faith of Americans not already disillusioned by presidential deception over the war in Vietnam. By the time Nixon, under threat of impeachment, submitted his resignation, the American people were cynical about politics and skeptical of military and executive leaders. Neither of Nixon's successors, Gerald Ford or Jimmy Carter, though both honorable men, was able to regain the faith of the American people. Despite some domestic successes, Carter's presidency was undermined by international events beyond his control. In the Middle East—a region of increasing importance in U.S. foreign policy—Carter helped broker a peace deal between Egypt and Israel but proved powerless to end a lengthy crisis in Iran involving American hostages. The Soviet invasion of Afghanistan in 1979, meanwhile, ended the era of détente and revived Cold War tensions.

Adding to Carter's woes was a deepening economic crisis that defied traditional remedies. Suddenly in the 1970s, middle-class Americans saw their savings disappearing to double-digit inflation and their seemingly secure jobs vanishing overnight. The economic crisis was caused in large part by changes in the global economy and international trade, made worse by the oil embargo launched by Arab members of the Organization of Petroleum Exporting Countries in 1973. Americans realized anew that they were vulnerable to decisions made in far-off lands—decisions the United States could not control. ■

The New Politics of Identity

By the end of the 1960s, as divisions continued to deepen among the American people, movements for social justice and racial equality had become stronger, louder, and often more radical. The civil rights movement, begun in a quest for equal rights and integration, splintered as many young African Americans turned away from the tactics of nonviolence, rejected integration for separatism, and embraced a distinct African American culture. Mexican Americans and Native Americans, inspired by the civil rights movement to struggle against their own marginalization in American society, had created powerful "Brown Power" and "Red Power" movements by the early 1970s. Like young African Americans, they demanded not only equal rights but recognition of their distinct cultures. These movements fueled the development of a new "identity politics." Advocates of identity politics believed that differences among American racial and ethnic groups were critically important. Group identity, these Americans argued, must be the basis for political action. And government and social leaders must stop imagining the American public as individuals and instead address the needs of different identity-based groups.

By 1970, most African American activists no longer sought political power and racial justice through the universalist claim of the civil rights movement: "We are all the same but for the color of our skins." Instead, they emphasized the distinctiveness of black culture and society. These ideas attracted a large following, even among older, less radical people. Many black Americans had been powerfully disillusioned by the racism that outlasted the end of legal segregation. Many had come to believe that integration would mean subordination in a white-dominated society that had no respect for their history and cultural traditions.

AFRICAN AMERICAN CULTURAL NATIONALISM

In the early 1970s, though mainstream groups such as the NAACP continued to seek political and social equality through the nation's courts and ballot boxes, many African Americans (like the white youth of the counterculture) looked to culture rather than to narrow political action for social change. Rejecting current European American standards of beauty, young people let their hair grow into "naturals" and "Afros"; they claimed the power of black "soul." Seeking strength in their own histories and cultural heritages, black college students and young faculty members fought successfully to create black studies departments in American universities. African traditions were reclaimed—or sometimes created. The new holiday Kwanzaa, created in 1966 by Maulana Karenga, professor of black studies at California State University, Long Beach, brought African Americans together to celebrate their culture and shared African heritage. Many African Americans found a new pride in their history and culture; the most radical activists gave up on the notion of a larger "American" culture altogether.

■ In 1976, folk singer Joan Baez and César Chávez, leader of the United Farm Workers (UFW), marched with other mourners through vineyards near Delano, California, at the funeral of Juan de la Cruz, a farm worker. De la Cruz had been murdered in a drive-by shotgun attack on a UFW picket line.   (© 1976 Bob Fitch/Take Stock)

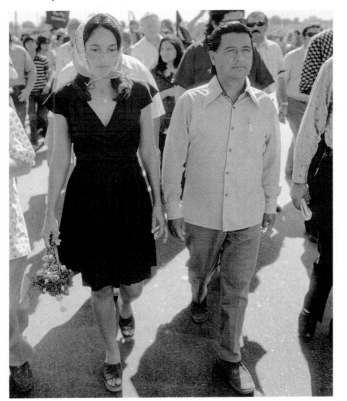

In 1970, the nation's 9 million Mexican Americans (4.3 percent of America's total population) were heavily concentrated in the Southwest and California. Though these Americans were officially classified as white by the federal government—all Hispanics were counted as white in the federal census—discrimination against Mexican Americans in hiring, pay, housing, schools, and the courts was commonplace. In cities, poor Mexican Americans lived in rundown barrios. In rural areas, poverty was widespread. Almost half of Mexican Americans were functionally illiterate, and even among the young, high school drop-out rates were astronomical. By the 1970s, though growing numbers of Mexican Americans were middle class, almost one-quarter of Mexican American families remained below the poverty level. Especially dire was the plight of migrant farm workers.

MEXICAN AMERICAN ACTIVISM

The national Mexican American movement for social justice began with these migrant workers. From 1965 through 1970, labor organizers César Chávez and Dolores Huerta led migrant workers, the majority of whom were of Mexican ancestry, in a strike (*huelga*) against large grape growers in California's San Joaquin valley. Chávez and the AFL-CIO-affiliated United Farm Workers (UFW) drew national attention to the working conditions of migrant laborers, who were paid as little as 10 cents an hour (the minimum wage in 1965 was $1.25) and often housed by their employers in squalid conditions without running water or indoor toilets. A national consumer boycott of table grapes brought the growers to the bargaining table, and in 1970 the UFW won their fight for better wages and working conditions. The UFW's roots in the Mexican and Mexican American communities were critical to its success. The union resembled nineteenth-century Mexican *mutualistas*, or cooperative associations, as much as it did a traditional American labor union. Its members founded cooperative groceries, a Spanish-language newspaper, and a theater group; they called upon the Virgin de Guadalupe for assistance in their struggle.

During the same period, more radical struggles were also beginning. In northern New Mexico, Reies Tijerina created the Alianza Federal de Mercedes (Federal Alliance of Grants) to fight for the return of land the organization claimed belonged to local *hispano* villagers, whose ancestors had occupied the territory before it was claimed by the United States, under the 1848 Treaty of Guadalupe Hidalgo. In Denver, former boxer Rudolfo "Corky" Gonzáles drew Mexican American youth to his "Crusade for Justice"; more than one

CHICANO MOVEMENT

thousand young people gathered there for the National Chicano Liberation Youth Conference in 1969. They adopted a manifesto, *El Plan Espiritual de Aztlán,* which condemned the "brutal 'Gringo' invasion of our territories" and declared "the Independence of our . . . Nation."

These young activists called for the liberation of "La Raza" (from "La Raza de Bronze," the brown people) from the oppressive force of American society and culture, not for equal rights through integration. They also rejected a hyphenated "Mexican-American" identity. The "Mexican American," they explained in *El Plan Espiritual de Aztlán,* "lacks respect for his culture and ethnic heritage . . . [and] seeks assimilation as a way out of his 'degraded' social status." These young people called themselves "Chicanos" or "Chicanas"—a term drawn from barrio slang and associated with *pachucos* (see page 750), the hip, rebellious, and sometimes criminal young men who symbolized much of what "respectable" Mexican Americans despised.

Many middle-class Mexican Americans and members of the older generations never embraced the term "Chicano" or the separatist, cultural nationalist agenda of *el movimiento.* Throughout the 1970s, however, younger activists continued to seek "Brown Power" based on a separate and distinct Chicano/a culture. They succeeded in introducing Chicano studies into local high school and college curricula and in creating a strong and unifying sense of cultural identity for Mexican American youth. Some activists made clear political gains, as well, founding La Raza Unida (RUP), a Southwest-based political party that registered tens of thousands of voters and won several local elections. The Chicano movement was never as influential nationally as the African American civil rights movement or the Black Power movement. However, it did effectively challenge discrimination on the local level and created a basis for political action as the Mexican American (and broader Latino) population of the United States grew dramatically over the following decades.

Between 1968 and 1975, Native American activists forced American society to hear their demands and to

NATIVE AMERICAN ACTIVISM reform U.S. government policies toward native peoples. Like African Americans and Mexican Americans, young Native American activists were greatly influenced by cultural nationalist beliefs. Many young activists, seeking a return to the "old ways," joined with "traditionalists" among their elders to challenge tribal leaders who advocated assimilation and cooperation with federal agencies.

In November 1969 a small group of activists, calling themselves "Indians of All Tribes," occupied Alcatraz Is-

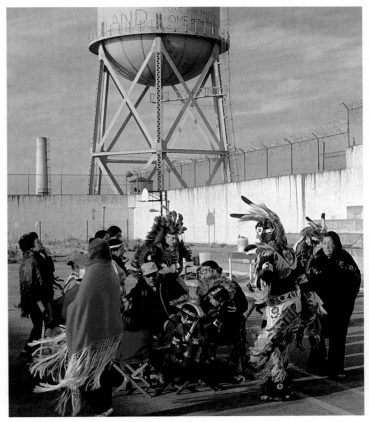

■ Calling their movement "Red Power," these American Indian activists dance in 1969 while "reclaiming" Alcatraz Island in San Francisco Bay. Arguing that an 1868 Sioux treaty entitled them to possession of unused federal lands, the group occupied the island until mid-1971. (Ralph Crane, *Life* magazine © Time, Inc.)

land in San Francisco Bay and demanded that the land be returned to native peoples for an Indian cultural center. The protest, which lasted nineteen months and eventually involved more than four hundred people from fifty different tribes, marked the consolidation of a "pan-Indian" approach to activism. Before Alcatraz, protests tended to be reservation based and concerned with specific local issues. Many of the Alcatraz activists were urban Indians, products in part of government policies that led Native Americans to leave reservations and seek jobs in the nation's cities. They were interested in claiming a shared "Indian" identity that transcended tribal differences. Although the protesters did not succeed in reclaiming Alcatraz Island, they drew national attention to their struggle and inspired the growing "Red Power" movement. In 1972, members of the radical American Indian Movement occupied a Bureau of Indian Affairs office in Washington, D.C., and then in 1973 a trading post at Wounded Knee, South Dakota, where U.S. Army troops had massacred three hundred Sioux men, women, and children in 1890.

At the same time, more moderate activists, working through pan-tribal organizations such as the National Congress of American Indians and the Native American Rights Fund, lobbied Congress for greater rights and resources to govern themselves and to strengthen their tribal cultures. In response to those demands, Congress and the federal courts returned millions of acres of land to tribal ownership, and in 1975 Congress passed the Indian Self-Determination and Education Assistance Act. Despite these successes, conditions for most Native Americans remained grim during the 1970s and 1980s: American Indians had a higher rate of tuberculosis, alcoholism, and suicide than any other group. Nine of ten lived in substandard housing, and unemployment rates for Indians were almost 40 percent.

As activists from various groups made all Americans increasingly aware of discrimination and inequality, policymakers struggled to frame reme-

AFFIRMATIVE ACTION

dies. As early as 1965, President Johnson had acknowledged the limits of civil rights legislation. "You do not take a person who, for years, has been hobbled by chains and liberate him, bring him up to the starting line of a race and then say, 'you are free to compete with all the others,'" Johnson told an audience at Howard University, "and still justly believe that you have been completely fair." In this speech, Johnson called for "not just legal equality . . . but equality as a fact and equality as a result." Here Johnson joined his belief that the federal government must help *individuals* attain the skills necessary to compete in American society to a new concept: equality could be measured by *group* outcomes or results.

Practical issues also contributed to the shift in emphasis from individual opportunity to group outcomes. The 1964 Civil Rights Act had outlawed discrimination but seemingly had stipulated that action could be taken only when an employer "intentionally engaged" in discrimination against an individual. This individual, case-by-case approach to equal rights created a nightmare for the Equal Employment Opportunity Commission (EEOC). The tens of thousands of cases filed suggested a pervasive pattern of racial and sexual discrimination in American education and employment, but each required proof of "intentional" actions against an individual. Some people were beginning to argue that it was possible, instead, to prove discrimination by "results"—by the relative number of African Americans or women, for example, an employer had hired or promoted.

In 1969, the Nixon administration implemented the first major government affirmative-action program to promote "equality of results." The Philadelphia Plan (so called because it targeted government contracts in that city) required businesses contracting with the federal government to show (in the words of President Nixon) "affirmative action to meet the goals of increasing minority employment" and set specific numerical "goals," or quotas, for employers. Affirmative action for women and members of racial and ethnic minorities was soon required by all major government contracts, and many large corporations and educational institutions began their own programs.

Supporters saw affirmative action as a way to address the lasting effects of past discrimination. Critics (some of whom were supporters of racial and sexual equality) argued that attempts to create proportional representation for women and minorities meant discrimination against other individuals who had not created past discrimination, and that group-based remedies violated the principle that individuals should be judged on their own merits. As affirmative-action programs began to have an impact in hiring and university admissions, bringing members of underrepresented groups into college classrooms, law firms, schoolrooms, construction companies, police stations, and firehouses nationwide, a deepening recession made jobs scarce. Thus, increasing the number of minorities and women hired often meant reducing the number of white men. White working-class men, who were most adversely affected by the policy, often reacted with anger and resentment.

The Women's Movement and Gay Liberation

During the 1950s, even as more and more women joined the paid work force and participated in the political life of the nation, American society and culture emphasized women's private roles as wives and mothers. The women's movement that had won American women the vote in the 1920s had all but disappeared. But during the 1960s, a "second wave" of the American women's movement emerged, and by the 1970s mainstream and radical activists had joined to wage a multifront battle for "women's liberation."

The key event that marked the reemergence of the women's movement in the postwar era was the surprise popularity of Betty Friedan's 1963 book *The Feminine Mystique*. Writing as a housewife and mother (though she had a long history of political activism, as well), Friedan described "the problem with no name," the dissatisfaction of educated, middle-class wives and mothers like herself, who—looking at their nice homes and families—wondered guiltily if that was all there was to life. This "problem" was not new; the vague sense of dissatisfaction plaguing housewives was a staple topic for women's magazines in the 1950s. But Friedan, instead of blaming individual women for failing to adapt to women's proper role, blamed the role itself and the society that created it.

The organized, liberal wing of the women's movement emerged in 1966, with the founding of the National Organization for Women (NOW).

LIBERAL AND RADICAL FEMINISM

NOW, made up primarily of educated, professional women, was a traditional lobbying group; its goal was to pressure the EEOC to enforce the 1964 Civil Rights Act (see page 837). Racial discrimination was the EEOC's focus, and discrimination on the basis of sex was such a low priority that the topic could be treated as a joke. When a reporter asked EEOC chair Franklin Roosevelt Jr., "What about sex?" Roosevelt laughed: "Don't get me started. I'm all for it." Women who faced workplace discrimination were not amused by such comments, and by 1970, NOW had one hundred chapters with more than three thousand members nationwide.

Another strand of the women's movement developed from the nation's increasingly radical movements for social justice. In 1968, a group of women gathered outside the Miss America Pageant in Atlantic City to protest the "degrading mindless-boob girlie symbol" represented by the beauty pageant. Though nothing was burned, the pejorative 1970s term for feminists, "bra-burners," came from this event, in which women threw items of "enslavement" (girdles, high heels, curlers, and bras) into a "Freedom Trashcan." Many of these young women, as well as others who helped create a radical feminist movement, had been active in the movements for civil rights or against the war in Vietnam. But even in groups dedicated to social change, they found themselves treated as second-class citizens. Too often, they made coffee, not policy. As they analyzed America's social and political structure, these young women began to discuss their own oppression, and the oppression of all women, in American society.

The feminism embraced by these young activists was never a single, coherent set of beliefs. Some argued that the world should be governed by peaceful, noncompetitive values they believed were intrinsically female; others claimed that society imposed gender roles and that there were no innate differences between men and women. Most radical feminists, however, practiced what they called "personal politics." They believed, as feminist au-

thor Charlotte Bunch explained, that "there is no private domain of a person's life that is not political, and there is no political issue that is not ultimately personal." Some of these young women began to meet in "consciousness-raising" groups to discuss how, in their everyday lives, women were subordinated by men and by a patriarchal society. In the early 1970s, women throughout the nation came together in suburban kitchens, college dorm rooms, and churches or synagogues to create their own consciousness-raising groups, exploring topics such as power relationships in romance and marriage, sexuality, abortion, healthcare, work, and family.

During the 1970s, the diverse groups that made up the women's movement claimed significant achievements.

ACCOMPLISHMENTS OF THE WOMEN'S MOVEMENT

On March 22, 1972, after massive lobbying by women's organizations, Congress approved the Equal Rights Amendment (ERA) to the Constitution. The amendment stated simply that "equality of rights under the law shall not be denied or abridged by the United States or by any State on account of sex." By the end of the year twenty-two states (of the thirty-eight necessary to amend the Constitution) had ratified the ERA. Also in 1972, Congress passed Title IX of the Higher Education Act, which prevented federal funds from going to any college or university that discriminated against women. As a result, universities began to channel money to women's athletics, and women's participation in sports boomed.

Feminists worked for reforms that touched all aspects of American life. At the state and local level, women challenged understandings of rape such as the one voiced by a psychiatrist at the University of Kansas student health center in 1970: "A woman sometimes plays a big part in provoking her attacker by . . . her overall attitude and appearance." By the end of the decade, activists working on the state and local level had established rape crisis centers, educated local police and hospital officials about procedures to protect survivors of rape, and even succeeded in changing laws.

Feminists also questioned the ways women were treated by the medical establishment. *Our Bodies, Ourselves* was created by the Boston Women's Health Collective in 1971 to help women understand—and take control over—their own sexual and reproductive health. Women who sought the right to safe and legal abortions won a major victory in 1973 when the Supreme Court, in a 7-2 decision on *Roe v. Wade*, ruled that privacy rights protected a woman's choice to end a pregnancy.

Women greatly increased their roles in religious organizations, including the Church of Christ, the Unitarian and Episcopalian churches, and Reform and

■ In 1970, young women marched down Fifth Avenue in New York City, celebrating the fiftieth anniversary of women's suffrage in the United States and demanding "women's liberation." Throughout the decade, Americans would struggle over the meaning of equality and the proper roles for men and for women in American society. (John Olsen)

Conservative Judaism, and more religious denominations accepted the ordination of women. Finally, women made enormous gains in the workplace and in education during the decade. In 1970, only 8.4 percent of medical school graduates and 5.4 percent of law school graduates were women. In 1979, those percentages had climbed to 23 percent and 28.5 percent, respectively; they would continue to grow. Colleges and universities also established women's studies departments, and by 1980 more than thirty thousand college courses focused on the study of women or gender relations.

The women's movement encompassed a broad range of women, but it also was met by powerful opposition, much of it from women. Many women believed that middle-class feminists did not understand the realities of their world. They had no desire to be "equal" if that meant giving up traditional gender roles in marriage or going out to work at low-wage, physically exhausting jobs. African American women and Chicanas, many of whom had been active in movements for the liberation of their peoples and some of whom had helped create second-wave feminism, often came to regard feminism as a "white" movement that ignored their cultural traditions and needs; some believed that the women's movement diverted time and energy away from the fight for racial equality.

OPPOSITION TO THE WOMEN'S MOVEMENT

Organized opposition to feminism came primarily from conservative, often religiously motivated men and women. As one conservative Christian writer claimed, "The Bible clearly states that the wife is to submit to her husband's leadership . . . just as she would to Christ her Lord." Such religious beliefs, along with fears about changing gender roles and expectations, fueled a movement to stop ratification of the Equal Rights Amendment. The STOP-ERA movement was led by Phyllis Schlafly, a lawyer and prominent conservative political activist. Schlafly argued that ERA supporters were "a bunch of bitter women seeking a constitutional cure for their personal problems." She attacked the women's movement as "a total assault on the role of the American woman as wife and mother, and on the family as the basic unit of society." Schlafly and her supporters argued that the ERA would decriminalize rape, force Americans to use unisex toilets, and make women subject to the military draft.

Many women saw feminism as an attack on the choices they had made and felt that by opposing the ERA they were defending their traditional roles. In the fight against the ERA, tens of thousands of women became politically experienced; they fed a growing grassroots conservative movement that would come into its own in the 1980s. And by the mid-1970s, the STOP-ERA movement had stalled the Equal Rights Amendment. Despite a congressional extension of the ratification deadline, the amendment would fall three states short of ratification and expire in 1982.

At the beginning of the 1970s, gay men and lesbians faced widespread discrimination. Consensual sexual
_____ intercourse between people of the same
GAY LIBERATION sex was illegal in almost every state, and until 1973 homosexuality was labeled a mental disorder by the American Psychiatric Association. Homosexual couples did not receive partnership benefits such as health insurance; they could not marry or adopt children. The issue of gay and lesbian rights divided even progressive organizations: in 1970 the New York City chapter of NOW expelled its lesbian officers. As open racism declined, gay men and women remained targets of discrimination in hiring and endured public ridicule, harassment, and physical attacks.

Gay men and lesbians, unlike most members of racial minorities, could conceal the identity that made them vulnerable to discrimination and harassment. Remaining "in the closet" offered individuals some protection, but that option also made it very difficult to organize a political movement. There were small "homophile" organizations, such as the Mattachine Society (named for the Société Mattachine, a medieval musical organization whose members performed in masks, to evoke the "masked" lives of gay Americans) and the Daughters of Bilitis (after a work of love poems between women), that had worked for gay rights since the 1950s. But the symbolic beginning of the gay liberation movement came on June 28, 1969, when New York City police raided the Stonewall Inn, a gay bar in Greenwich Village. (New York City law made it illegal for more than three homosexual patrons to occupy a bar at the same time.) That night, for the first time, patrons stood up to the police. As word spread through New York's gay community, hundreds more joined the confrontation. The next morning, New Yorkers found a new slogan spray-painted on neighborhood walls: Gay Power.

Inspired by the Stonewall riot, some men and women decided the time had come to work openly and militantly for gay rights. They focused on a dual agenda: legal equality and the promotion of Gay Pride. In a version of the identity politics adopted by racial and ethnic communities, some rejected the notion of fitting into straight (heterosexual) culture and helped create distinctive gay communities and lifestyles. "Look out, straights," wrote gay liberation activist Martha Shelley in 1970. "We're gonna make our own revolution." By 1973, there were about eight hundred gay organizations in the United States. Centered in big cities and on college campuses,

most organizations tried to create supportive environments for gay men and lesbians to come "out of the closet." Once "out," they could use their numbers ("We are everywhere" was a popular slogan) to push for political reform, such as nondiscrimination statutes similar to those that protected women and racial minority groups. By the end of the decade, gay men and lesbians had become a public political force in several cities, especially New York, Miami, and San Francisco, and played an increasingly visible role in the social and political life of the nation.

The End in Vietnam

Of all the divisions in American politics and society at the end of the 1960s, none was so pervasive as that over the war in Vietnam. "I'm not going to end up like LBJ," Richard Nixon vowed after winning the 1968 presidential election, recalling that the war had destroyed Johnson's political career. "I'm going to stop that war. Fast." But he did not. He understood that the conflict was generating deep divisions at home and hurting the nation's image abroad, yet—like officials in the Johnson administration—he feared that a precipitous withdrawal would harm American credibility on the world stage. Anxious to get American troops out of Vietnam, Nixon was at the same time no less committed than his predecessors to preserving an independent, noncommunist South Vietnam. To accomplish these aims, he set upon a policy that at once contracted and expanded the war.

A centerpiece of Nixon's policy was "Vietnamization"—the building up of South Vietnamese forces to
_____ replace U.S. forces. Nixon hoped such
INVASION OF a policy would quiet domestic opposi-
CAMBODIA tion and also advance the peace talks under way in Paris since May 1968. Accordingly, the president began to withdraw American troops from Vietnam, decreasing their number from 543,000 in the spring of 1969 to 156,800 by the end of 1971, and to 60,000 by the fall of 1972. Vietnamization did help limit domestic dissent—as did the replacement of the military draft with a lottery system, by which only those nineteen-year-olds with low lottery numbers would be subject to conscription—but it did nothing to end the stalemate in the Paris negotiations. Even as he embarked on this troop withdrawal, therefore, Nixon intensified the bombing of North Vietnam and enemy supply depots in neighboring Cambodia, hoping to pound Hanoi into concessions (see Map 30.2 on page 843).

The bombing of neutral Cambodia commenced in March 1969. Over the next fourteen months, B-52 pilots flew 3,600 missions and dropped over 100,000 tons of bombs on that country. At first the administration went to great lengths to keep the bombing campaign secret. When the North Vietnamese refused to buckle, Nixon turned up the heat: in April 1970 South Vietnamese and U.S. forces invaded Cambodia in search of arms depots and North Vietnamese army sanctuaries. The president announced publicly that he would not allow "the world's most powerful nation" to act "like a pitiful, helpless giant."

Instantly, the antiwar movement rose up as students on about 450 college campuses went out on strike and hundreds of thousands of demonstra-

PROTESTS AND COUNTER-DEMONSTRATIONS

tors gathered in various cities to protest the administration's policies. The crisis atmosphere intensified further on May 4 when National Guardsmen in Ohio fired into a crowd of fleeing students at Kent State University, killing four young people. Ten days later, police and state highway patrolmen armed with automatic weapons blasted a women's dormitory at Jackson State, a historically black university in Mississippi, killing two students and wounding nine others. The police claimed they had been shot at, but no evidence of sniping could be found. In Congress, where opposition to the war had been building over the previous months, Nixon's widening of the war sparked outrage, and in June the Senate terminated the Tonkin Gulf Resolution of 1964. After two months, U.S. troops withdrew from Cambodia, having accomplished little.

Americans still, however, remained divided on the war. Although a majority told pollsters they thought the original American troop commitment to Vietnam to have been a mistake, 50 percent said they believed Nixon's claim that the Cambodia invasion would shorten the war. Angered by the sight of demonstrating college students, many voiced support for the president and the war effort. In New York City, construction workers—much to the satisfaction of White House officials—organized counterdemonstrations against the antiwar protests. Nevertheless, though Nixon welcomed these expressions of support, the tumult over the invasion served to reduce his options on the war. Henceforth, solid majorities could be expected to oppose any new missions for U.S. ground troops in Southeast Asia.

Nixon's troubles at home mounted in June 1971 when, as we have seen, the *New York Times* began to publish the Pentagon Papers, the top-secret official study of U.S. decisions in the Vietnam War. Nixon secured an injunc-tion to prevent publication, but the Supreme Court over-turned the order. Americans learned from this study that political and military leaders frequently had lied to the public about their aims and strategies in Southeast Asia.

Equally troubling, to both opponents and supporters of the war, was the growing evidence of decay within the armed forces. Morale and discipline

MORALE PROBLEMS IN MILITARY

among troops had been on the decline even before Nixon took office, and there were growing reports of drug addiction, desertion, racial discord, even the murder of unpopular officers by enlisted men (a practice called "fragging"). Stories of atrocities committed by U.S. troops also began to make their way home. The court-martial and conviction in 1971 of Lieutenant William Calley, who was charged with overseeing the killing of more than three hundred unarmed South Vietnamese civilians in the hamlet of My Lai in 1968, got particular attention. An army photographer captured the horror in graphic pictures. For many, the massacre signified the dehumanizing impact of the war on those who fought it.

The Nixon administration, meanwhile, stepped up its efforts to pressure Hanoi into a settlement. Johnson had lacked the will to "go to the

CEASE-FIRE AGREEMENT

brink," Nixon told Kissinger; "I have the will in spades." When the North Vietnamese launched a major offensive across the border into South Vietnam in March 1972, Nixon responded with a massive aerial onslaught against North Vietnam. In December 1972, after an apparent peace agreement collapsed when the South Vietnamese refused to moderate their position, the United States launched a massive air strike on the North—the so-called "Christmas bombing."

A diplomatic agreement was, however, close. Months earlier, Kissinger and his North Vietnamese counterpart in the negotiations, Le Duc Tho, had resolved many of the outstanding issues. Most notably, Kissinger agreed that North Vietnamese troops could remain in the South after the settlement, while Tho abandoned Hanoi's insistence that the Saigon government of Nguyen Van Thieu be removed. Nixon had instructed Kissinger to make concessions because the president was eager to improve relations with the Soviet Union and China, to win back the allegiance of America's allies, and to restore stability at home. On January 27, 1973, Kissinger and Le Duc Tho signed a cease-fire agreement, and Nixon compelled a reluctant Thieu to accept it by threatening to cut off U.S. aid while at the same time promising to defend the South if the North violated the agreement. In the accord, the United States promised to withdraw all of its troops within sixty days. North Vietnamese troops would be allowed to stay in South Vietnam, and a coalition government that included the Vietcong eventually would be formed in the South.

The United States pulled its troops out of Vietnam, leaving behind some military advisers. Soon, both North and South violated the cease-fire, and full-scale war erupted once more. The feeble South Vietnamese government could not hold out. Just before its surrender, hundreds of Americans and Vietnamese who had worked for them were hastily evacuated from Saigon. On April 29, 1975, the South Vietnamese government collapsed, and Vietnam was reunified under a communist government based in Hanoi. Shortly thereafter Saigon was renamed Ho Chi Minh City for the persevering patriot, who had died in 1969.

The overall costs of the war were immense. More than 58,000 Americans and between 1.5 and 3 million Vietnamese had died. Civilian deaths in Cambodia and Laos numbered in the hundreds of thousands. The war cost the United States at least $170 billion, and billions more would be paid out in veterans' benefits. The vast sums spent on the war became unavailable for investment in domestic programs. Instead, the nation

COSTS OF THE VIETNAM WAR

suffered inflation and retreat from reform, as well as political schism and abuses of executive power. The war also delayed accommodation with the Soviet Union and the People's Republic of China, fueled friction with allies, and alienated Third World nations.

In 1975 communists assumed control and formed repressive governments in Vietnam, Cambodia, and Laos, but beyond Indochina the domino effect once predicted by U.S. officials never occurred. Acute hunger afflicted the people of those devastated lands. Soon refugees—"boat people"—crowded aboard unsafe vessels in an attempt to escape their battered homelands. Many emigrated to the United States, where they were received with mixed feelings by Americans reluctant to be reminded of defeat in Asia. But many Americans faced the fact that the United States, which had relentlessly bombed, burned, and defoliated once-rich agricultural lands, bore considerable responsibility for the plight of the southeast Asian peoples.

Americans seemed both angry and confused about the nation's war experience. As historian William Appleman Williams observed, for the first time Americans had had their overseas sphere of influence pushed back, violently, and they were suffering from a serious case of "empire shock." Hawkish

DEBATE OVER THE LESSONS OF VIETNAM

observers claimed that America's failure in Vietnam undermined the nation's credibility and tempted enemies to exploit opportunities at the expense of U.S. interests. They pointed to a "Vietnam syndrome"—a resulting American suspicion of foreign entanglements—that they feared would inhibit the future exercise of U.S. power. America lost in Vietnam, they asserted, because Americans lost their guts at home.

Dovish analysts drew different conclusions, denying that the military had suffered undue restrictions. Some blamed the war on an imperial presidency that had permitted strong-willed men to act without restraint, and on a weak Congress that had conceded too much power to the executive branch. Make the president adhere to the checks-and-balances system—make him go to Congress for a declaration of war—these critics counseled, and America would become less interventionist. This view found expression in the War Powers Act of 1973, which sought to limit the president's warmaking freedom. Henceforth, Congress would have to approve any commitment of U.S. forces to combat action lasting more than sixty days.

Vietnam Veterans   Public discussion of the lessons of the Vietnam War also was stimulated by veterans' calls for help in dealing with posttraumatic stress disorder, which afflicted thousands of the 2.8 million Vietnam veterans. Once home, they suffered nightmares and extreme nervousness. Doctors reported that the disorder stemmed primarily from the soldiers' having seen so many children, women, and elderly people killed. Some GIs inadvertently killed these people; some killed them vengefully and later felt guilt. Other veterans heightened public awareness of the war by publicizing their deteriorating health from the effects of the defoliant Agent Orange and other herbicides they had handled or were accidentally sprayed with in Vietnam. The Vietnam Veterans Memorial, erected in Washington, D.C., in 1982, has kept the issue alive, as have many oral history projects of veterans conducted by school and college students in classes to this day.

■ Dedicated in 1993 in Washington, D.C., the Vietnam Women's Memorial honors the several thousand military women who served in Vietnam, many of them as nurses who volunteered for duty. One nurse, Judy Marron, remembered treating wounded soldiers round the clock: "There were days when the stress and strain and blood and guts almost had to equal the frontlines." This bronze sculpture, by Glenna Goodacre, stands near the long wall on which are etched the names of Americans who died in Vietnam. (Brad Markel/Liaison Agency)

Nixon, Kissinger, and the World

Even as Nixon and Kissinger tried to achieve victory in Vietnam, they understood that the United States had overreached in the 1960s with a military commitment that had caused massive bloodshed, deep domestic divisions, and economic dislocation. The difficulties of the war signified to them that American power was limited and, in relative terms, in decline. This reality necessitated a new approach to the Cold War, and both moved quickly to reorient American policy. In particular, they believed the United States had to adapt to a new multipolar international system; no longer could that system be defined simply by the Soviet-American rivalry. Western Europe was becoming a major player in its own right, as was Japan. The Middle East loomed increasingly large. Above all, Americans had to come to grips with the reality of China by rethinking the policy of hostile isolation.

They were an unlikely duo—the reclusive, ambitious Californian, born of Quaker parents, and the sociable, dynamic Jewish intellectual who had fled Nazi Germany as a child. Nixon, ten years older, was more or less a career politician, while Kissinger had made his name as a Harvard professor and foreign policy consultant. Whereas Nixon was a staunch Republican, Kissinger would have been quite prepared to join Hubert Humphrey's administration had the Democrat prevailed in the election. What the two men had in common was a tendency toward paranoia about rivals and a capacity to think in large conceptual terms about America's place in the world.

In July 1969 Nixon and Kissinger acknowledged the limits of American power and resources when they announced the Nixon Doctrine. The

NIXON DOCTRINE

United States, they said, would continue to provide economic aid to allies in Asia and elsewhere, but these allies should no longer count on American troops. It was an admission that Washington could no longer afford to sustain its many overseas commitments and therefore would have to rely more on regional allies—including, it turned out, many authoritarian regimes—to maintain an anticommunist world order. Although Nixon did not say so, his doctrine amounted to a partial retreat from the 1947 Truman Doctrine, with its promise to support noncommunist governments facing internal or external threats to their existence.

If the Nixon Doctrine was one pillar of the new foreign policy, the other was détente: measured cooperation with the Soviets through negotiations

DÉTENTE

within a general environment of rivalry. Détente's primary purpose, like that of the containment doctrine it resembled, was to check Soviet expansion and limit the Soviet arms buildup, though now that goal would be accomplished through diplomacy and mutual concessions. The second part of the strategy sought to curb revolution and radicalism in the Third World so as to quash threats to American interests. More specifically, the Cold War and limited wars such as in Vietnam were costing too much; expanded trade with friendlier Soviets and Chinese might reduce the huge U.S. balance-of-payments deficit. And improving relations with both communist giants, at a time when Sino-Soviet tensions were increasing, might exacerbate feuding between the two, weakening communism.

The Soviet Union's leadership had its own reasons for wanting détente. The Cold War was a drain on its resources, too, and by the late 1960s defense needs and

■ Henry A. Kissinger (b. 1923) *(right)* walks with President Nixon. An ambitious, knowledgeable, and self-flattering German-born political scientist from Harvard University, Kissinger served as assistant for national security affairs and secretary of state. Although he and the president shared basic assumptions about U.S. foreign relations, especially the need to promote détente and curb revolution, Kissinger judged Nixon an "egomaniac." Critics on the left compared Kissinger to Dr. Strangelove, the fictional Germanic adviser—played by Peter Sellers in the movie of the same name—who was so deranged that he welcomed a nuclear holocaust. Critics on the right thought Kissinger too conciliatory to the communists. (Dennis Brack/Black Star)

consumer demands were increasingly at odds. Improved relations with Washington would also allow the USSR to focus its energies on the threat from China, and might generate serious progress on outstanding European issues, including the status of Germany and Berlin. Some ideologues in the Moscow leadership remained deeply suspicious of cozying up to the American capitalists, but they did not prevail over advocates of change. Thus in May 1972 the United States and the USSR agreed to slow the costly arms race by limiting the construction and deployment of intercontinental ballistic missiles and antiballistic missile defenses.

While cultivating détente with the Soviet Union, the United States took dramatic steps to end more than two decades of Sino-American hostility. The Chinese welcomed the change because they wanted to spur trade and hoped that friendlier Sino-American relations would make their onetime ally and now enemy, the Soviet Union, more cautious. Nixon reasoned the same way: "We're using the Chinese thaw to get the Russians shook." In early 1972 Nixon made a historic trip to "Red China," where he and the venerable Chinese leaders Mao Zedong and Zhou Enlai agreed to disagree on a number of issues, except one: the Soviet Union should not be permitted to make gains in Asia. Sino-American relations improved slightly, and official diplomatic recognition and the exchange of ambassadors came in 1979.

OPENING TO CHINA

The opening to communist China and the policy of détente with the Soviet Union reflected Nixon's and Kissinger's belief in the importance of maintaining stability among the great powers. In the Third World, too, they sought stability, though there they hoped to get it not by change but by maintaining the status quo. As it happened, events in the Third World would provide the Nixon-Kissinger approach with its greatest test, and not merely because of Vietnam.

In the Middle East the situation had grown more volatile in the aftermath of the Arab-Israeli Six-Day War in 1967. In that conflict Israel had scored victories against Egypt and Syria, seizing the Sinai Peninsula and the Gaza Strip from Egypt, the West Bank and East Jerusalem from Jordan, and the Golan Heights from Syria (see Map 33.2). Instantly, Israel's regional position was transformed as it gained 28,000 square miles and could henceforth defend itself more easily against invading military forces. But the victory came at a price. Gaza and the West Bank were the ancestral home of hundreds of thousands of Palestinians and the more recent home of additional hundreds of thousands of Palestinian refugees from the 1948 Arab-Israeli conflict (see Chapter 28). Suddenly Israel found itself governing large numbers of people who wanted nothing more than to see Israel destroyed. When the Israelis began to establish Jewish settlements in their newly won areas, Arab resentment grew even stronger. Terrorists associated with the Palestinian Liberation Organization (PLO) made hit-and-run raids on Jewish settlements, hijacked jetliners, and murdered Israeli athletes at the 1972 Olympic Games in Munich,

WARS IN THE MIDDLE EAST

West Germany. The Israelis retaliated by assassinating PLO leaders.

In October 1973, on the Jewish High Holy Day of Yom Kippur, Egypt and Syria attacked Israel. Their motives were complex, but primarily they sought revenge for the 1967 defeat. Caught by surprise, Israel reeled before launching an effective counteroffensive against Soviet-armed Egyptian forces in the Sinai. In an attempt to punish Americans for their pro-Israel stance, the Organization of Petroleum Exporting Countries (OPEC), a group of mostly Arab nations that had joined together to raise the price of oil, embargoed shipments of oil to the United States and other supporters of Israel. An energy crisis and dramatically higher oil prices rocked the nation. Soon Kissinger arranged a cease-fire in the war, but not until March 1974 did OPEC lift the oil embargo. The next year Kissinger persuaded Egypt and Israel to accept a U.N. peacekeeping force in the Sinai. But peace did not come to the region, for Palestinians and other Arabs still vowed to destroy Israel, and Israelis insisted on building more Jewish settlements in occupied lands.

In Latin America, meanwhile, the Nixon administration sought to preserve stability and to thwart radical leftist challenges to authoritarian rule. In Chile, after voters in 1970 elected a Marxist president, Salvador Allende, the CIA began secret operations to disrupt Chile and encouraged military officers to stage a coup. In 1973 a military junta ousted Allende and installed an authoritarian regime under General Augusto Pinochet. (Allende was subsequently murdered.) Washington publicly denied any role in the affair that implanted iron-fisted tyranny in Chile for two decades.

ANTIRADICALISM IN LATIN AMERICA AND AFRICA

In Africa, as well, Washington preferred the status quo. Nixon backed the white-minority regime in Rhodesia (now Zimbabwe) and activated the CIA in a failed effort to defeat a Soviet- and Cuban-backed faction in newly independent Angola's civil war. In South Africa, Nixon tolerated the white rulers who imposed the segregationist policy of apartheid on blacks and mixed-race "coloureds" (85 percent of the population), keeping them poor, disfranchised, and ghettoized in prisonlike townships. After the leftist government came to power in Angola, however, Washington took a keener interest in the rest of Africa, building economic ties and sending arms to friendly black nations such as Kenya and the Congo. The administration also began to distance the United States from the white governments of Rhodesia and South Africa. America had to "prevent the radicalization of Africa," said Kissinger.

OPEC and the 1973 Oil Embargo

If one date can be said to have marked the relative decline of American power in the Cold War era and the arrival of the Arab nations of the Middle East as important players on the world stage, it would be October 20, 1973. That day, the Arab members of the Organization of Petroleum Exporting Countries (OPEC)—Saudi Arabia, Iraq, Kuwait, Libya, and Algeria—imposed a total embargo on oil shipments to the United States and to other allies of Israel. The move was in retaliation against U.S. support of Israel in the two-week-old Yom Kippur War. The embargo followed a decision by the members three days earlier to unilaterally raise oil prices, from $3.01 to $5.12 per barrel. In December, the five Arab countries, joined by Iran, raised prices again, to $11.65 per barrel, close to a fourfold increase from early October. "This decision," said National Security Adviser Henry Kissinger of the price hike, "was one of the pivotal events in the history of this century."

If Kissinger exaggerated, it was not by much. Gasoline prices surged across America, and some dealers ran low on supplies. Frustrated Americans endured endless lines at the pumps and shivered in underheated homes. Letters to newspaper editors expressed anger not merely at the Arab governments but also at the major oil companies, whose profits soared. When the embargo was lifted after five months, in April 1974, oil prices stayed high, and the aftereffects of the embargo would linger through the decade. Like no other event could, it confirmed the extent to which Americans no longer exercised full control over their own economic destiny.

Just twenty years before, in the early 1950s, Americans had produced at home all the oil they needed. Detroit automakers had no difficulty selling ever larger gas-guzzlers with ever more outrageous tailfins. By the early 1960s the picture had begun to change, as American factories and automobiles now were dependent on foreign sources for one out of every six barrels of oil they used. By 1972, the figure had gone up to about two out of six, or more than 30 percent. Although in absolute terms the amount was massive—U.S. motorists consumed one of every seven barrels used in the world each day—few Americans worried. Hence the shock of the embargo. As author Daniel Yergin has put it, "The shortfall struck at fundamental beliefs in the endless abundance of resources, convictions so deeply rooted in the American character and experience that a large part of the public did not even know, up until October 1973, that the United States imported any oil at all."

Though after the embargo ended Americans resumed their wasteful ways, an important change had occurred, whether people understood it or not. The United States had become a dependent nation, its economic future linked to decisions by Arab sheiks half a world away.

In 1976, OPEC sharply raised the price of oil a second time, prompting this editorial cartoon by Don Wright of the *Miami News.* (Don Wright in the *Miami News,* 1976, Tribune Media Services)

874 Chapter 31 Continuing Divisions and New Limits

Presidential Politics and the Crisis of Leadership

Richard Nixon took pride in his foreign policy accomplishments, but they were overshadowed by his failures at home. He betrayed the public trust and broke laws, large and small. His misconduct, combined with Americans' growing belief that their leaders had lied to them repeatedly about the war in Vietnam, shook Americans' faith in government. This new mistrust joined with conservatives' traditional suspicion of big, activist government to create a crisis of leadership and undermine liberal policies that had governed the nation since the New Deal. Nixon's successors, Gerald Ford and James Earl Carter, found their accomplishments limited by the American public's profound suspicion of presidential leadership and government action.

Richard Nixon was one of America's most complex presidents. Brilliant, driven, politically cunning, able to address changing global realities with creativity—Nixon was also crude, prejudiced against Jews and African Americans, happy to use dirty tricks and the power of the presidency against those he considered his enemies, and driven by a sense of resentment that bordered on paranoia. Nixon was the son of a grocer from an agricultural region of southern California who, despite his tenacity and intelligence, was never accepted by the sophisticated northeastern liberal elite. (After Nixon's election, *Washingtonian* magazine joked that "cottage cheese with ketchup" had replaced elegant desserts at White House dinners.) Nixon loathed the liberal establishment, which loathed him back, and his presidency was driven by that hatred as much as by any strong philosophical commitment to conservative principles.

NIXON'S DOMESTIC AGENDA

Nixon's domestic policy initiatives have long confused historians. Much of his agenda was liberal, even progressive. The Nixon administration pioneered affirmative action. It doubled the budgets of the new National Endowment for the Humanities (NEH) and National Endowment for the Arts (NEA). Nixon supported the ERA, signed major environmental legislation, created the Occupational Safety and Health Administration, actively attempted to manage the economy using deficit spending, and even proposed a guaranteed minimum income for all Americans.

At the same time, Nixon pursued a conservative agenda. One of his major legislative goals was "devolution," or shifting federal government authority to states and localities. He promoted revenue-sharing programs that distributed federal funds back to the states to use as they saw fit, thus appealing to those who were angry about, as they saw it, paying high taxes to support liberal "giveaway" programs for poor and minority Americans. As president, Nixon worked to equate the Republican Party with law and order and the Democrats with permissiveness, crime, drugs, radicalism, and the "hippie lifestyle." He used his outspoken vice president, Spiro Agnew, to attack protesters and critics as "naughty children," "effete . . . snobs," and "ideological eunuchs." He appointed four conservative justices to the Supreme Court (Chief Justice Warren Burger, Harry Blackmun, Lewis Powell Jr., and William Rehnquist); ironically, however, Nixon's appointees did not always vote as he would have wished.

With such a confusing record, was Nixon liberal, conservative, or simply pragmatic? Most of his "liberal" agenda was not so much liberal as it was tricky—a term commonly applied to Nixon at the time. Instead of attacking liberal programs and the entrenched government bureaucracies that administered them, Nixon attempted to undermine them while appearing to offer support. For example, when the Nixon administration proposed a guaranteed minimum income for all Americans, including the working poor, his larger goal was to dismantle the federal welfare system and destroy its liberal bureaucracy of social workers (no longer necessary under Nixon's model). And though Nixon doubled funding for the NEA, his expansion took funding away from the northeastern art establishment, with its commitment to "elite," avant-garde art, awarding grants instead to local and regional art groups that sponsored more popular art forms, such as representational painting or folk music.

In addition, recognizing the possibility of attracting white southerners to the Republican Party, Nixon pursued a "southern strategy." He nominated two southerners for positions on the Supreme Court—one of whom had a segregationist record—and when Congress declined to confirm either nominee, Nixon protested angrily, saying, "I understand the bitter feelings of millions of Americans who live in the South." After the Supreme Court upheld a school desegregation plan that required a North Carolina school system—still highly segregated fifteen years after the *Brown* decision—to achieve racial integration by removing both black and white children from their neighborhood schools and busing them to schools elsewhere in the county (*Swann v. Charlotte-Mecklenburg*, 1971), Nixon denounced busing as a reckless and extreme remedy.

As the presidential election of 1972 approached, Nixon was almost sure of a second victory. His Democratic

ENEMIES AND DIRTY TRICKS

opponent was George McGovern, a progressive senator from South Dakota and strong opponent of the Vietnam War. McGovern appealed to the left and essentially wrote off the middle, declaring, "I am not a centrist candidate." Alabama governor George Wallace, running on a third-party ticket, withdrew from the race after he was paralyzed during an assassination attempt in a campaign appearance at a Maryland shopping center. The Nixon campaign, however, was taking no chances. On June 17, four months before the election, five men were caught breaking into the Democratic National Committee's offices at the Watergate apartment and office complex in Washington, D.C. The men were associated with the Committee to Re-elect the President, known as CREEP. The break-in got little attention at the time, and Nixon was swept into office in November with 60 percent of the popular vote. McGovern, his opponent, carried only Massachusetts and the District of Columbia. But even as Nixon triumphed, events had already been set in motion that would lead to his downfall.

From the beginning of his presidency, Nixon was obsessed with the belief that, in a time of national turmoil, he was surrounded by enemies. He made "enemies lists," hundreds of names long, that included all black members of Congress and the presidents of most Ivy League universities. The Nixon administration worked, in their words, to "use the available federal machinery to screw our political enemies." On Nixon's order, his aide Charles Colson (best known for his maxim "When you've got them by the balls, their hearts and minds will follow") formed a secret group called the Plumbers. Their first job was to break into the office of the psychiatrist treating Daniel Ellsberg, the former Pentagon employee who had gone public with the Pentagon Papers, looking for material to discredit him. The Plumbers expanded their "dirty tricks" operations during the 1972 presidential primaries and campaign, bugging phones, infiltrating campaign staffs, even writing and distributing anonymous letters falsely accusing Democratic candidates of sexual misconduct. They had already bugged the Democratic National Committee offices and were going back to plant more surveillance when they were caught by the D.C. police at the Watergate complex.

Nixon was not directly implicated in the Watergate affair. But instead of distancing himself and firing the people directly involved, he chose to cover up their connection to the break-ins. He had the CIA stop the FBI's investigation, citing reasons of national security. At this

WATERGATE COVER-UP AND INVESTIGATION

point, Nixon had obstructed justice—a felony, and under the Constitution, an impeachable crime—but he had also, it seemed, succeeded in halting the investigation. However, two young, relatively unknown reporters for the *Washington Post*, Carl Bernstein and Bob Woodward, would not give up on the story. Aided secretly by an anonymous, highly placed government official they code-named Deep Throat (the title of a notorious 1972 X-rated film), they began to follow a money trail that led straight to the White House.

The Watergate cover-up continued to unravel under the scrutiny of both the courts and Congress. From May to August 1973, the Senate held televised public hearings on the Watergate affair. White House Counsel John Dean, fearful that he was being made the fall guy for the entire Watergate fiasco, gave damning testimony. Then, on July 13, a White House aide told the Senate Committee that Nixon regularly recorded his conversations in the Oval Office. These tape recordings were the "smoking gun" that could prove Nixon's direct involvement in the cover-up—but Nixon refused to turn the tapes over to Congress.

As Nixon and Congress fought over the tapes, Nixon faced scandals on other fronts. In October 1973,

IMPEACHMENT AND RESIGNATION

Vice President Spiro Agnew resigned following charges that he had accepted bribes while governor of Maryland. Following constitutional procedures, Nixon appointed and Congress approved Michigan's Gerald Ford, the House Minority Leader, as Agnew's replacement. Meanwhile, Nixon's own staff members were becoming increasingly concerned about his excessive drinking and seeming mental instability. Then, on October 24, 1973, the House of Representatives began impeachment proceedings against the President.

Under court order, Nixon began to release edited portions of the Oval Office tapes to Congress. Though the first tapes revealed no criminal activity, the public was shocked by Nixon's constant obscenities and racist slurs. Finally, in July 1974, the Supreme Court ruled that Nixon must release all the tapes. Despite "mysterious" erasures on two key tapes, the House Judiciary Committee found evidence to impeach Nixon on three grounds: obstruction of justice, abuse of power, and contempt of Congress. On August 9, 1974, facing certain impeachment and conviction, Richard Nixon became the first president of the United States to resign his office.

The Watergate scandal shook the confidence of American citizens in their government. It also prompted

■ Resigning in disgrace as impeachment for his role in the Watergate cover-up became a certainty, Richard Nixon flashes the "V for victory" sign as he leaves the White House for the last time.   (Nixon Presidential Materials Project, National Archives and Record Administration)

Congress to reevaluate the balance of power between the executive and legislative branches. Beginning in 1973, Congress passed several major bills aimed at restricting presidential power. They included not only the War Powers Act, but also the 1974 Budget and Impoundment Control Act, which made it impossible for the president to disregard congressional spending mandates.

Gerald Ford, the nation's first unelected president, faced a nation awash in cynicism. He had inherited a discredited presidency. The nation's economy was in decline. Its people were divided. Ford was a decent and honorable man who did his best to end what he called "the long national nightmare." But when, in one of his first official acts as president, he issued a full pardon to Richard Nixon, his approval ratings plummeted from 71 to 41 percent. Some suggested, with no evidence, that he had struck some sort of sordid deal with Nixon.

FORD'S PRESIDENCY

Ford accomplished little domestically during his two and a half years in office. The Democrats gained a large margin in the 1974 congressional elections and, after Watergate, Congress was willing to exercise its power. Ford almost routinely vetoed its bills—39 in one year—but Congress often overrode his veto. In addition Ford, during the course of his brief presidency, was the object of constant mockery. In political cartoons, comedy monologues, and especially on the new hit television show *Saturday Night Live*, he was portrayed as a buffoon and a klutz. When he slipped on the steps exiting *Air Force One*, footage appeared on major newscasts. The irony of portraying Ford—who had turned down a chance to play in the National Football League in order to attend Yale Law School—as physically inept was extraordinary. But as Ford understood, these portrayals began to give the impression that he was a "stumbler," in danger of making blunders of all kinds. Ford caught the fallout of disrespect Nixon's actions had unleashed. No longer would respect for the office of the presidency prevent the mass media from reporting presidential slips, stumbles, frailties, or misconduct. Ford was the first president to discover how much the rules had changed.

Jimmy Carter, who was elected in 1976 by a slim margin, benefited at first from Americans' suspicion of political leadership. Carter was a one-term governor of Georgia, one of the new southern leaders who were committed to racial equality and integration. He had grown up in the rural Georgia town of Plains, where his family owned a peanut farm, graduated from the Naval Academy, then served as an engineer in the navy's nuclear submarine program. Carter, a deeply religious born-again Christian, made a virtue of his lack of political experience. Promising the American people, "I will never lie to you," he emphasized his distance from Washington and the political corruption of recent times.

CARTER AS "OUTSIDER" PRESIDENT

From his inauguration, when he broke with the convention of a motorcade and walked down Pennsylvania Avenue holding hands with his wife and close adviser, Rosalynn, and their young daughter Amy, Carter rejected the trappings of the imperial presidency and emphasized his populist, outsider appeal. But the outsider status that gained him the presidency would be one of Carter's major problems as president. Though an astute policymaker, he scorned the deal making that was necessary to pass legislation in Congress.

Carter faced problems that would have challenged any leader: the economy continued to decline; energy shortages had not abated; the American people distrusted their government. More than any other American leader of the postwar era, Carter was willing to tell the American people things they did not want to hear. As shortages of natural gas forced schools and businesses to close down during the bitterly cold winter of 1977, Carter—wearing a cardigan sweater—spoke to the American people about the new era of limits and called for "sacrifice." Carter put energy conservation measures into effect at the White House and government buildings, and proposed to Congress a detailed energy plan that emphasized conservation. In the defining speech of his presidency, as the nation struggled with a sense of uncertainty and unease, Carter told Americans that the nation suffered from a crisis of the spirit. He talked about the false lures of "self-indulgence and consumption," about "paralysis and stagnation and drift." And he called for a "new commitment to the path of common purpose." But he was unable to offer practical solutions for the national malaise.

Carter did score some noteworthy domestic accomplishments. He worked to ease burdensome government regulations without destroying consumer and worker safeguards, and created the Departments of Energy and Education. He also created environmental protections, establishing a $1.6 billion "superfund" to clean up abandoned chemical-waste sites and placing more than 100 million acres of Alaskan land under the federal government's protection as national parks, national forests, and wildlife refuges.

Economic Crisis

*a*mericans' loss of confidence in their political leaders was intensified by a growing economic crisis. Since World War II, except for a few brief downturns, prosperity had been a fundamental condition of American life. A steadily rising gross national product, based largely on growing rates of productivity, had propelled large numbers of Americans into the economically comfortable middle class. Prosperity had made possible the great liberal initiatives of the 1960s and improved the lives of America's poor and elderly citizens. But in the early 1970s, that long period of economic expansion and prosperity came to an end. Almost every economic indicator drove home bad news. In 1974 alone, the gross national product dropped two full percentage points. Industrial production fell 9 percent. Inflation—the increase in costs of goods and services—skyrocketed, and unemployment grew.

STAGFLATION AND ITS CAUSES

Throughout most of the 1970s, the U.S. economy floundered in a condition that economists dubbed "stagflation": a stagnant economy characterized by high unemployment combined with out-of-control inflation (see Figure 31.1). Stagflation was almost impossible to manage with traditional economic remedies. When the federal government increased spending to stimulate the economy, and so reduce unemployment, inflation grew. When the federal government tried to rein in inflation by cutting government spending or tightening the money supply, the recession deepened and unemployment rates skyrocketed.

Figure 31.1   "Discomfort Index" (Unemployment Plus Inflation), 1974–1989

Americans' economic discomfort directly determined their political behavior. When the "discomfort index" was high in 1976 and 1980, Americans voted for a change in presidents. When economic discomfort declined in 1984 and 1988, Ronald Reagan and George Bush were the political beneficiaries.
(Source: Adapted from *Economic Report of the President,* 1992 [Washington, D.C., 1992], pp. 340, 365.)

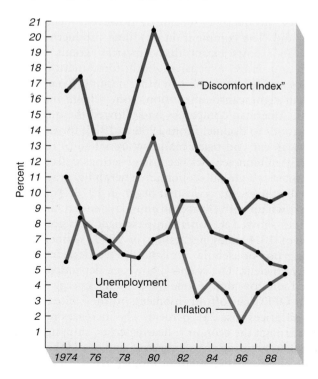

The causes of the economic crisis were complex. Federal management of the economy was in part to blame: President Johnson had reversed conventional economic wisdom and created inflationary pressure by insisting that the United States could have both "guns and butter" as he waged a very expensive war in Vietnam while greatly expanding domestic spending in his Great Society programs. But fundamental problems also came from America's changing role in the global economy. After World War II, with most leading industrial nations in ruins, the United States had stood alone at the pinnacle of the global economy. But the war-ravaged nations—often with major economic assistance from the United States—rebuilt their productive capacities with new, technologically advanced industrial plants. By the early 1970s both of America's major wartime adversaries, Japan and Germany, had become major economic powers—and major competitors in global trade. In 1971, for the first time since the end of the nineteenth century, the United States imported more goods than it exported, beginning an era of American trade deficits.

American corporate actions also contributed to the growing trade imbalance. During the years of global dominance, few American companies had reinvested in upgrading and improving production techniques and in educating their workers. In part because of these practices, American productivity—that is, the average output of goods per hour of labor—had begun to decline. As workers' productivity declined, however, their wages rarely did. The combination of falling productivity and high labor costs meant that American goods became more and more expensive—both for American consumers and for consumers in other nations. Even worse, without significant competition from foreign manufacturers, American companies had allowed the quality of their goods to decline. From 1966 to 1973, for example, American car and truck manufacturers had to recall almost 30 million vehicles because of serious defects.

America's global economic vulnerability was driven home by the energy crisis that began in 1973. Americans had grown up with cheap and abundant energy, and their lifestyles showed it. American passenger cars got an average of 13.4 miles per gallon in 1973; neither home heating nor household appliances were designed to be energy-efficient. The country, however, depended on imported oil for almost one-third of its energy supply. When OPEC cut off oil shipments to the United States, U.S. oil prices rose 350 percent. The increases reverberated through the economy: heating costs, shipping costs, and manufacturing costs increased, and so did the cost of goods and services. Inflation jumped from 3 percent in

early 1973 to 11 percent in 1974. Sales of gas-guzzling American cars plummeted as people rushed to buy energy-efficient subcompacts from Japan and Europe. American car manufacturers, stuck with machinery for producing large cars, were hit hard. GM laid off 6 percent of its domestic work force and put an even larger number on rolling unpaid leaves. As the ailing automobile industries quit buying steel, glass, and rubber, manufacturers of these goods laid off their workers as well.

American political leaders tried desperately to manage economic problems, but their actions often exacerbated them instead. As America's rising trade deficit undermined international confidence in the dollar, the Nixon administration ended the dollar's link to the gold standard; free-floating exchange rates increased the price of foreign goods in the United States and stimulated inflation. President Ford created a voluntary program, Whip Inflation Now (complete with red and white "WIN" buttons) in 1974 to encourage grassroots anti-inflation efforts. Following the tenets of monetary theory, which held that with less money available to "chase" the supply of goods, price increases would gradually slow down, ending the inflationary spiral, Ford curbed federal spending and encouraged the Federal Reserve Board to tighten credit—and prompted the worst recession in forty years. In 1975, unemployment climbed to 8.5 percent.

ATTEMPTS TO FIX THE ECONOMY

Carter first attempted to bring unemployment rates down by stimulating the economy, but inflation careened out of control; he then tried to slow the economy down—and prompted a major recession during the election year of 1980. In fact, Carter's larger economic policies, including his 1978 deregulation of airline, trucking, banking, and communications industries, would eventually foster economic growth—but not soon enough. After almost a decade of decline, Americans were losing faith in the American economy and in the ability of their political leaders to manage it.

IMPACTS OF THE ECONOMIC CRISIS

The economic crisis of the 1970s affected many realms of American life. First, it accelerated the transition from an industrial to a service economy. During the 1970s, the American economy "deindustrialized." Automobile companies laid off workers. Massive steel plants shut down, leaving entire communities devastated. Other manufacturing concerns moved overseas, seeking lower labor costs and fewer government regulations. New jobs were created—27 million of them—but they were overwhelmingly in what economists called the "service sector": retail sales,

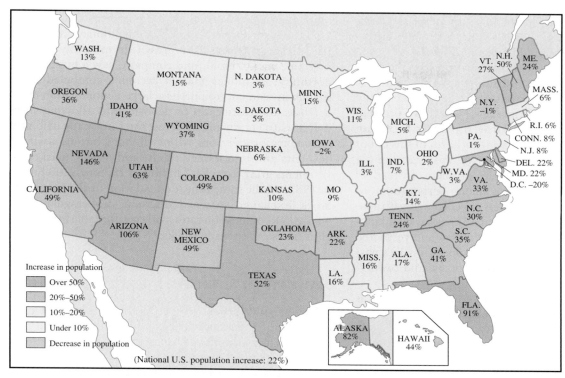

Map 31.1   The Continued Shift to the Sunbelt in the 1970s and 1980s

Throughout the 1970s and 1980s, Americans continued to leave economically declining areas of the North and East in pursuit of opportunity in the Sunbelt. States in the Sunbelt and in the West had the largest population increases.   (Source: "Shift to the Sunbelt," *Newsweek,* September 10, 1990.)

restaurants, and other service providers. As heavy industries collapsed, formerly highly paid, unionized workers took jobs in the growing but not unionized service sector. These jobs—such as warehouse work or retail sales, for example—paid much lower wages and often lacked benefits such as healthcare.

Formerly successful blue-collar workers saw their middle-class standards of life slipping away from them. More married women joined the work force because they had to—though some were drawn by new opportunities. Even in the best of times the economy would have been hard pressed to produce jobs for the millions of baby boomers who joined the labor market in the 1970s. Young people graduating from high school or college in the 1970s, raised with high expectations, suddenly found very limited possibilities—if they found jobs at all.

The economic crisis also helped to shift the economic and population centers of the nation. As the old industrial regions of the North and Midwest went into decline, people fled the "snow belt" or the "rust belt," speeding

up the "sunbelt" boom already in progress (see Map 31.1). The Sunbelt was where the jobs were. The federal government had invested heavily in the South and West during the postwar era, especially in military and defense industries and in the infrastructures necessary for them. Never a major center for heavy manufactures, the Sunbelt was primed for the rapid growth of modern industries and services—aerospace, defense, electronics, transportation, research, banking and finance, and leisure. City and state governments competed to lure businesses and investment dollars, in part by preventing the growth of unions. Atlanta and Houston and other southern cities marketed themselves as cosmopolitan, sophisticated, and racially tolerant; they bought sports teams and built museums.

This population shift south and west, combined with the flight of middle-class taxpayers to the suburbs, created disaster in northern and midwestern cities. New York City, close to financial collapse by late 1975, was saved only when the House and Senate Banking

Committees approved federal loan guarantees. Cleveland defaulted on its debts in 1978, the first major city to do so since Detroit declared bankruptcy in 1933.

American politics was also transformed by the combined effects of stagflation and Sunbelt growth as a "tax

TAX REVOLTS

revolt" movement began in the rapidly growing American West. In California, inflation had driven property taxes up rapidly, hitting middle-class taxpayers hard. In this era of economic decline and post-Watergate suspicion, angry taxpayers saw government as the problem. Instead of calling for wealthy citizens and major corporations to pay a larger share of taxes, voters rebelled against taxation itself. California's Proposition 13, passed by a landslide in 1978, rolled back property taxes and restricted future increases. Within months of Proposition 13's passage, thirty-seven states cut property taxes, and twenty-eight lowered their state income-tax rates.

The impact of Proposition 13 and similar initiatives was cushioned at first by state budget surpluses, but as those surpluses turned to deficits states cut services—closing fire stations and public libraries, ending or limiting mental health services and programs for the disabled. Public schools were hit especially hard. The tax revolt movement signaled the growth of a new conservatism; voters who wanted lower taxes and smaller government would help bring Ronald Reagan to the White House in the election of 1980.

The runaway inflation of the 1970s also changed how Americans managed their money. Before this era, home

CREDIT AND INVESTMENT

mortgages and auto loans were the only kind of major debt most Americans would venture. National credit cards had only become common in the late 1960s, and few Americans—especially those who remembered the Great Depression—were willing to spend money they did not have. In the 1970s, however, thriftiness stopped making sense. Double-digit inflation rates meant double-digit declines in the purchasing power of a dollar. It was economically smarter to buy goods before their prices went up—even if it meant borrowing the money. Since debt was paid off later with devalued dollars, the consumer came out ahead. In 1975, consumer debt hit a high of $167 billion; it almost doubled, to $315 billion, by 1979.

The 1970s were also the decade in which average Americans became investors rather than savers. Throughout the 1970s, because of regulations created during the Great Depression, the interest rates banks could pay on individual savings accounts were capped. An average savings account bearing 5 percent interest actually *lost*

more than 20 percent of its value from 1970 through 1980 because of inflation. That same money, invested at market rates, would have grown dramatically. Fidelity Investments, a mutual fund company, saw a business opportunity: its money market accounts combined many smaller investments to purchase large-denomination treasury bills and certificates of deposit, thus allowing small investors to get the high interest rates normally available only to major investors. Money flooded out of passbook accounts and into money funds, and money market investments grew from $1.7 billion in 1974 to $200 billion in 1982. At the same time, deregulation of the New York Stock Exchange spawned discount brokerage houses, whose low commission rates made it affordable for middle-class investors to trade stocks.

An Era of Cultural Transformation

The 1970s have been dismissed as a cultural wasteland, an era in which the nation confronted new limits without much passion or creativity. But it was during the 1970s, as Americans struggled with economic recession, governmental betrayal, and social division, that major strands of late-twentieth-century culture were developed or consolidated. The current environmental movement, a "therapeutic culture" and the growth of born-again Christianity, contemporary forms of sexuality and the family, and America's emphasis on diversity all have roots in this odd decade sandwiched between the political vibrancy of the 1960s and the conservatism of the 1980s.

Just as Americans were forced to confront the end of postwar prosperity, a series of ecological crises drove

ENVIRONMENTALISM

home the limits on natural resources and the fragility of the environment. In 1969 a major oil spill took place off the coast of Santa Barbara, California; that same year the polluted Cuyahoga River, flowing through Cleveland, caught fire. Though the energy crisis of the 1970s was due to an oil embargo, not a scarcity of oil, it drove home the real limits of the world's supplies of oil and natural gas. In 1979 human error contributed to a nuclear accident at the Three Mile Island nuclear power plant near Harrisburg, Pennsylvania, and in 1980 President Carter declared a federal emergency at New York State's Love Canal, which had served as a dump site for a local chemical manufacturer, after it was discovered that 30 percent of local residents had suffered chromosome damage. Public activism during the 1970s produced major environmental regulations and initiatives, from the Environmental Protection Agency (EPA), created (under strong public pressure) in 1970 by the Nixon administration, to eighteen major environmental laws enacted by Congress during the decade.

When almost 20 million Americans—half of them schoolchildren—gathered in local communities to celebrate the first Earth Day on April 22, 1970, they signaled the triumph of a relatively new understanding of environmentalism. Traditional concerns about preserving "unspoiled" wilderness had joined with a new focus on "ecology," which stressed the connections between the earth and all living organisms, including humans. Central to this movement was a recognition that earth's resources were finite and must be both conserved and protected from the consequences of human action, such as pollution. In 1971, biologist Barry Commoner insisted: "The present course of environmental degradation . . . is so serious, that, if continued, it will destroy the capability of the environment to support a reasonably civilized human society." Many of those concerned about the strain on earth's resources also identified rapid global population growth as a problem, and state public health offices frequently dispensed contraceptives as a way to stem this new "epidemic."

During these years, Americans became increasingly uneasy about the science and technology that had been one source of America's might. In a triumph of technology, American astronaut Neil Armstrong stepped onto the lunar surface on July 20, 1969, as people worldwide watched the grainy television transmission and heard, indistinctly, his first words—"One small step for man, one giant step for mankind." But the advances that could take a man to the moon seemed unable to cope with earthbound problems of poverty, crime, pollution, and urban decay; and the failure of technological warfare to deliver victory in Vietnam came at the same time antiwar protesters were questioning the morality of using such technology. Some Americans joined a movement for "appropriate technology" and human-scale development, but the nation was profoundly dependent on complex technological systems. And it was during the 1970s that the foundation was laid for America's computer revolution. The integrated circuit was created in 1970, and by 1975 the MITS Altair 8800—operated by toggle switches that entered individual binary numbers, boasting 256 bytes of memory, and requiring about thirty hours to assemble—could be mail-ordered from Albuquerque, New Mexico.

TECHNOLOGY

As Americans confronted material limits, they increasingly sought spiritual fulfillment and well-being. Some turned to religion, though not to traditional main-

■ Celebrants of the first Earth Day, on April 22, 1970, gather in an urban park. More than 20 million Americans across the nation participated in local teach-ins, celebrations, and protests to draw attention to environmental issues. By 1990 Earth Day was celebrated globally, drawing 200 million participants from 141 countries.   (Ken Regan)

RELIGION AND THE THERAPEUTIC CULTURE

stream Protestantism. Methodist, Presbyterian, and Episcopalian churches all lost members during this era, while membership in evangelical and fundamentalist Christian churches grew dramatically. Protestant evangelicals, professing a personal relationship with their savior, described themselves as "born again" and emphasized the immediate, daily presence of God in their lives. Even some Catholics, such as the Mexican Americans who embraced the *cursillo* movement (a "little course" in faith), sought a more personal relationship with God. Other Americans looked to the variety of beliefs and practices described as "New Age." The New Age movement drew from and often combined versions of nonwestern spiritual and religious practices, including Zen Buddhism, yoga, and shamanism, along with insights from western psychology and a form of spiritually oriented environmentalism.

Also in the 1970s, America saw the full emergence of a "therapeutic" culture. Though some Americans were disgusted with the self-centeredness of the "Me-Decade," bestselling books by therapists and self-help gurus insisted that individual feelings offered the ultimate measure of truth; emotional honesty and self-awareness were social goods surpassing the bonds of community, friendship, or family. Self-help books with titles such as *I Ain't Much Baby—But I'm All I've Got,* or *I'm OK—You're OK* (first published in 1967, it became a bestseller in the mid-1970s) made up 15 percent of all bestselling books during the decade.

One such self-help book was *The Joy of Sex* (1972), which sold 3.8 million copies in two years. Sex became

SEXUALITY AND THE FAMILY

much more visible in America's public culture during the 1970s as network television loosened its regulation of sexual content. At the beginning of the 1960s, married couples in television shows were required to occupy twin beds; in the 1970s, hit television shows included *Three's Company,* a situation comedy based on the then-scandalous premise that a single man shared an apartment with two beautiful female roommates—and got away with it only by pretending to their suspicious landlord that he was gay. *Charlie's Angels,* another major television hit, capitalized on what people called the "jiggle factor," and displayed (for the time) lots of bare female flesh. The major youth fad of the era was "streaking," running naked through public places. Donna Summers's 1975 disco hit, "Love to Love You Baby," contained sixteen minutes of sexual moaning. And though very few Americans participated in heterosexual orgies at New York City's Plato's Retreat, many knew about them through a *Time* magazine feature story.

Sexual behaviors had also changed. The seventies were the era of singles bars and gay bathhouses, and some Americans led sexual lives virtually unrestrained by the old rules. For most Americans, however, the major changes brought about by the "sexual revolution" were a broader public acceptance of premarital sex and a limited acceptance of homosexuality, especially among more educated Americans. More and more heterosexual young people "lived together" without marriage during the 1970s; the census bureau even coined the term "POSSLQ" (persons of opposite sex sharing living quarters) to describe the relationship. When First Lady Betty Ford said on *60 Minutes* that she wouldn't be surprised if her then-seventeen-year-old daughter Susan began a sexual relationship, it was clear that much had changed in the course of a decade.

Changes in sexual mores and in the roles possible for women helped to alter the shape of the American family as well. Both men and women married later than in recent decades, and American women had fewer children. The birth rate had dropped almost 40 percent from its 1957 peak by the end of the 1970s. Almost a quarter of young single women in 1980 said they did not plan to have children. And a steadily rising percentage of babies were born to unmarried women, as the number of families headed by never-married women rose 400 percent during the 1970s. The divorce rate also rose, in part because states implemented "no fault" divorce, which did not require evidence of adultery, physical cruelty, abandonment, or other wrongdoing. While families seemed less stable in the 1970s than in the previous postwar decades, Americans also developed a greater acceptance of various family forms (the blended family of television's *Brady Bunch,* for example), and many young couples sought greater equality between the sexes in romantic relationships or marriages.

The racial-justice and identity movements of the late 1960s and 1970s made all Americans more aware of

DIVERSITY

differences among the nation's peoples—an awareness made stronger by the great influx of new immigrants, not from Europe but from Latin America and Asia following changes in immigration law during the mid-1960s. It was a challenge, however, to figure out how to acknowledge the new importance of "difference" in public policy. The solution developed in the 1970s was the idea of "diversity." Difference was not a problem but a strength; the nation should not seek policies to diminish differences among its peoples but should instead seek to foster the "diversity" of its schools, workplaces, and public culture.

One major move in this direction came in the 1978 Supreme Court decision *Regents of the University of California v. Bakke.* Allan Bakke, a thirty-three-year-old white man with a strong academic record, had been denied admission to the medical school of the University of California at Davis. Bakke sued, charging that he had been denied "equal protection" of the law because the medical school's affirmative-action program reserved 16 percent of its slots for racial-minority candidates, who were held to lower standards than other applicants. The case set off furious debates nationwide over the legitimacy of affirmative action. In 1978 the Supreme Court, in a split decision, decided in favor of Bakke. Four justices argued that any race-based decision violated the

Civil Rights Act of 1964; four saw affirmative-action programs as constitutionally acceptable remedies for past discrimination. The deciding vote, though for Bakke, contained an important qualification. A "diverse student body," Justice Lewis Powell wrote, is "a constitutionally permissible goal for an institution of higher education." To achieve the positive quality of "diversity," educational institutions could take race into account when making decisions about admissions.

Renewed Cold War and Middle East Crisis

*W*hen Jimmy Carter took office in 1977, he asked Americans to put their "inordinate fear of Communism" behind them. With reformist zeal, Carter vowed to reduce the U.S. military presence overseas, to cut back arms sales (which had reached the unprecedented height of $10 billion per year under Nixon), and to slow the nuclear arms race. At the time, more than 400,000 American military personnel were stationed abroad, the United States had military links with ninety-two nations, and the CIA was active on every continent. Carter promised to avoid new Vietnams through an activist preventive diplomacy in the Third World and to give more attention to environmental issues as well as relations between rich and poor nations. He especially determined to improve human rights abroad—the freedom to vote, worship, travel, speak out, and get a fair trial. Like his predecessors, however, Carter identified revolutionary nationalism as a threat to America's prominent global position.

Carter spoke and acted inconsistently, in part because in the post-Vietnam years no consensus existed in

CARTER'S DIVIDED ADMINISTRATION

foreign policy and in part because his advisers squabbled among themselves. One source of the problem was the stern-faced Zbigniew Brzezinski, a Polish-born political scientist who became Carter's national security adviser. An old-fashioned Cold Warrior, Brzezinski blamed foreign crises on Soviet expansionism. Carter gradually listened more to Brzezinski than to Secretary of State Cyrus Vance, an experienced public servant who advocated quiet diplomacy. Vocal neoconservative intellectuals such as Norman Podhoretz, editor of *Commentary* magazine, and the Committee on the Present Danger, founded in 1976 by Cold War hawks such as Paul Nitze, who had composed NSC-68 in 1950, criticized Carter for any relaxation of the Cold War and demanded that he jettison détente.

Nitze got his wish. Under Carter, détente deteriorated, and the Cold War deepened. But it did not happen right away. Initially, Carter maintained fairly good relations with Moscow and was able to score some foreign policy successes around the world. In Panama, where citizens longed for control over the Canal Zone, which they believed had been wrongfully taken from them in 1903 (see Chapter 22), Carter reenergized negotiations that had begun after anti-American riots in Panama in 1964. The United States signed two treaties with Panama in 1977. One provided for the return of the Canal Zone to Panama in 2000, and the other guaranteed the United States the right to defend the canal after that time. With conservatives denouncing a retreat from greatness, the Senate narrowly endorsed both agreements in 1978. The majority agreed with Carter's argument that relinquishing the canal was the best way to improve U.S. relations with Latin America.

Important though it was, the Panama agreement paled next to what must be considered the crowning accomplishment of Carter's presidency: the Camp

CAMP DAVID ACCORDS

David accords, the first mediated peace treaty between Israel and an Arab nation. Through tenacious personal diplomacy at a Camp David, Maryland, meeting in September 1978 with Egyptian and Israeli leaders, the president persuaded Israel and Egypt to agree to a peace treaty, gained Israel's promise to withdraw from the Sinai Peninsula, and forged an agreement that provided for continued negotiations on the future status of the Palestinian people living in the occupied territories of Jordan's West Bank and Egypt's Gaza Strip (see Map 33.2). Other Arab states denounced the agreement for not requiring Israel to relinquish all occupied territories and for not guaranteeing a Palestinian homeland. But the treaty at least ended warfare along one frontier in that troubled area of the world. On March 26, 1979, Israeli prime minister Menachem Begin and Egyptian president Anwar al-Sadat signed the formal treaty at the White House, with a beaming Carter looking on.

Carter's moment of diplomatic triumph did not last long, for soon other foreign policy problems pressed in.

SOVIET INVASION OF AFGHANISTAN

Relations with Moscow had deteriorated, with U.S. and Soviet officials sparring over the Kremlin's reluctance to lift restrictions on Jewish emigration from the USSR, and over the Soviet decision to deploy new intermediate-range ballistic missiles aimed at western Europe. Then, in December 1979, the Soviets invaded Afghanistan. A remote, mountainous country, Afghanistan had been a source of great-power conflict because of its

On March 26, 1979, Egypt's president Anwar el-Sadat (1918–1981) on the left, Israel's prime minister Menachem Begin (1913–1992) on the right, and U.S. president Jimmy Carter (b. 1924) signed a peace treaty known as the Camp David accords. Studiously negotiated by Carter, the Egyptian-Israeli peace has held to this day—despite conflict in much of the rest of the Middle East. (Jimmy Carter Presidential Library)

strategic position. In the nineteenth century it was the fulcrum of the Great Game, the contest between Britain and Russia for control of Central Asia and India. Following World War II, Afghanistan settled into a pattern of ethnic and factional squabbling; few in the West paid attention until the country spiraled into anarchy in the 1970s. In late 1979 the Red Army bludgeoned its way into Afghanistan to shore up a faltering communist government under siege by Muslim rebels. Moscow officials calculated they could be in and out of the country before anyone really noticed, including the Americans.

To their dismay, Carter not only noticed but reacted forcefully. He suspended shipments of grain and high-technology equipment to the Soviet Union, withdrew a major new arms control treaty from Senate consideration, and initiated an international boycott of the 1980 Summer Olympics in Moscow. He also secretly authorized the CIA to distribute aid, including arms and military support, to the Mujahidin (Islamic guerillas) fighting the communist government and sanctioned military aid to their backer, Pakistan. Announcing the Carter Doctrine, the president asserted that the United States would intervene, unilaterally and militarily if necessary, should Soviet aggression threaten the petroleum-rich Persian Gulf. This string of measures represented a victory of the hawkish Brzezinski over the pro-détente Vance. Indeed,

Carter seemed more ardent than Brzezinski in his denunciations of the Kremlin. He warned aides that the Soviets, unless checked, would likely attack elsewhere in the Middle East, but declassified documents confirm what critics at the time said: that the Soviet invasion was largely defensive in orientation and did not presage a push southwest to the Persian Gulf.

Carter's overheated rhetoric on Afghanistan may be partly explained by the fact that he simultaneously faced a tough foreign policy test in neighboring Iran. The shah, long the recipient of American favor, had been driven from his throne by a broad coalition of Iranians, many of whom resented that their traditional ways had been dislocated by the shah's attempts at modernization. American analysts failed to perceive the volatility this dislocation generated and were caught off guard when riots led by anti-American Muslim clerics erupted in late 1978. The shah went into exile, and in April 1979 Islamic revolutionaries, led by the Ayatollah Khomeini, an elderly cleric who denounced the United States as the stronghold of capitalism and western materialism, proclaimed a Shi'ite Islamic Republic. In November, with the exiled shah in the United States for medical treatment, mobs stormed the U.S. embassy in Teheran. They took American personnel as hostages, demanding the re-

IRANIAN HOSTAGE CRISIS

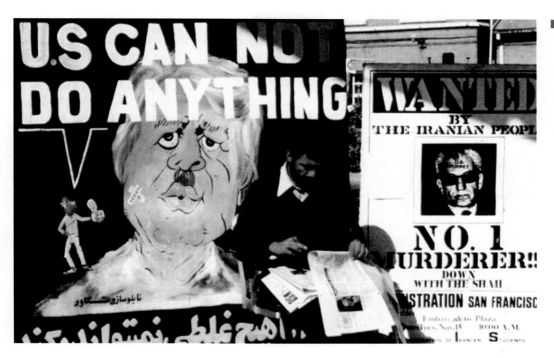

An Iranian is pictured reading a newspaper not long before mobs in Teheran stormed the American embassy and took more than fifty Americans hostage. Behind him are posters mocking U.S. President Carter and denouncing the shah.   (Picture Research Consultants & Archives)

turn of the shah to stand trial. The Iranians eventually released a few American prisoners, but fifty-two others languished under Iranian guard. They suffered solitary confinement, beatings, and terrifying mock executions.

Unable to gain the hostages' freedom through diplomatic intermediaries, Carter said that he felt "the same kind of impotence that a powerful person feels when his child is kidnapped." He took steps to isolate Iran economically, freezing Iranian assets in the United States. When the hostage takers paraded their blindfolded captives before television cameras, Americans felt taunted and humiliated. In April 1980, frustrated and at a low ebb in public opinion polls, Carter broke diplomatic relations with Iran and ordered a daring rescue mission. But the rescue effort miscarried after equipment failure in the sandy Iranian desert, and during the hasty withdrawal two aircraft collided, killing eight American soldiers. The hostages were not freed until January 1981, after Carter left office and the United States unfroze Iranian assets and promised not to intervene again in Iran's internal affairs.

The Iranian revolution, together with the rise of the Mujahidin in Afghanistan, signified the emergence of Islamic fundamentalism as a force in world affairs. Socialism and capitalism, the great answers that the two superpowers offered to the problems of modernization, had failed to solve the problems in Central Asia and the Middle East, let alone satisfy the passions and expecta-

tions they had aroused. Nor had they assuaged deeply held feelings of humiliation generated by centuries of western domination. As a result, Islamic orthodoxy found growing support for its message: that secular leaders such as Nasser in Egypt and the shah in Iran had taken their peoples down the wrong path, necessitating a return to conservative Islamic values and Islamic law. The Iranian revolution, in particular, expressed a deep and complex mixture of discontents within many Islamic societies.

U.S. officials took some consolation from the fact that Iran faced growing friction from the avowedly secular government in neighboring Iraq. Ruled by the Ba'athist Party, Iraq had already won favor in Washington for its ruthless pursuit and execution of Iraqi communists. When a Ba'athist leader named Saddam Hussein took over as president of Iraq in 1979 and began threatening the Teheran government, U.S. officials were not displeased; to them, Saddam seemed likely to offset the Iranian danger in the Persian Gulf region. As border clashes between Iraqi and Iranian forces escalated in 1980, culminating in the outbreak of large-scale war in September, Washington policymakers took an officially neutral position but soon tilted toward Iraq.

RISE OF SADDAM HUSSEIN

Jimmy Carter's record in foreign affairs sparked considerable criticism from both left and right. He had earned some diplomatic successes in the Middle East, Africa, and Latin America, but the revived Cold War and the prolonged Iranian hostage crisis had hurt the administration politically. Contrary to Carter's goals, more American military personnel were stationed overseas in 1980 than in 1976; the defense budget climbed and sales of arms abroad grew to $15.3 billion in 1980. On human rights, the president proved inconsistent. He practiced a double standard by applying the human-rights test to some nations (the Soviet Union, Argentina, and Chile) but not to U.S. allies (South Korea, the shah's Iran, and the Philippines). Still, if inconsistent, Carter's human-rights policy was not unimportant: he gained the release and saved the lives of some political prisoners, and he popularized and institutionalized concern for human rights around the world. But Carter did not satisfy Americans who wanted a post-Vietnam restoration of the economic dominance and military edge the United States once enjoyed. He lost the 1980 election to the hawkish Ronald Reagan, former Hollywood actor and governor of California.

Summary

The 1970s were a difficult decade for Americans. From the crisis year of 1968 on, it seemed that Americans were ever more polarized—over the war in Vietnam, over the best path to racial equality and equal rights for all Americans, over the meaning of equality, and over the meaning of America itself. As many activists for social justice turned to "cultural nationalism," or group-identity politics, notions of American unity seemed a relic of the past. And while a new women's movement won great victories against sex discrimination, a powerful opposition movement arose in response.

During this era, Americans became increasingly disillusioned with politics and presidential leadership. Richard Nixon's abuses of power in the Watergate scandal and cover-up, combined with growing awareness that the administration had lied to its citizens repeatedly about America's role in Vietnam, produced a profound suspicion of government. A major economic crisis ended the post–World War II expansion that had fueled the growth of the middle class and social reform programs alike, and Americans struggled with the psychological impact of a new age of limits and with the effects of stagflation: rising unemployment rates coupled with high rates of inflation.

Overseas, a string of setbacks—defeat in Vietnam, the oil embargo, and the Iranian hostage crisis—signified the waning of American power during the 1970s. The nation seemed increasingly unable to have its own way on the world stage. Détente with the Soviet Union had flourished for a time, as both superpowers sought to adjust to the new geopolitical realities; however, by 1980 Cold War tensions were again on the rise. But if the nation's most important bilateral relationship remained that with the USSR, an important change, not always perceptible at the time, was under way: more and more, the focus of U.S. foreign policy was on the Middle East.

Plagued by political, economic, and foreign policy crises, America ended the 1970s bruised, battered, and frustrated. The age of liberalism was long over; the elements for a conservative resurgence were in place.

LEGACY FOR A PEOPLE AND A NATION
Human Rights

Human rights—basically the notion that all people everywhere are entitled to life, liberty, and the pursuit of happiness—is not a recent proposition. A distinctly western idea, it had been expressed most famously in declarations on the "Rights of Man" in the American and French Revolutions.

It was not until the twentieth century, however, that the concept emerged as a consistent theme in U.S. foreign policy, and only in the 1970s did it become a central tenet of American diplomacy. In the wake of the Vietnam War, many Americans yearned for some means to restore America's international moral position. Congress took the lead in mid-decade by restricting economic or military aid to nations that engaged "in a consistent pattern of gross violations of internationally recognized human rights."

Jimmy Carter picked up the theme, declaring that human rights would be a centerpiece of his administration's foreign policy. "Because we are free we can never be indifferent to the fate of freedom elsewhere," he declared in his inaugural address. "Our commitment to human rights must be absolute." Under Carter, the State Department gained a Bureau of Human Rights that would monitor the behavior of governments worldwide.

The campaign encountered problems, threatening arms control negotiations, alliances, and trade. There were inconsistencies, as Carter sometimes embraced authoritarian leaders and the United States denounced abuses in nations where it had minimal economic or strategic interests and was almost silent where the interests were greater. Many found the "holier than thou" attitude of Washington's human rights bureaucrats offputting.

Still, the human rights emphasis of the Carter years altered the international landscape. It emboldened men and women around the world to challenge repressive governments and brought the release of political prisoners in many countries. It improved America's image overseas and helped restore a domestic consensus behind foreign policy. Though human rights concerns became less central in the foreign policies of Carter's successors, they remained on the agenda, both in the United States and elsewhere. In June 1993, delegates from 180 countries met in Vienna for the first World Conference on Human Rights. Controversies abounded, but the conference—and others like it in the decade—indicated that human rights had been placed firmly on the international map. It proved to be the Carter administration's greatest legacy, a fact duly noted by the committee that awarded the former president the 2002 Nobel Peace Prize.

The *history companion* powered by Eduspace®

Your primary source for interactive quizzes, exercises, and more to help you learn efficiently.
http://history.college.hmco.com/students

CONSERVATISM REVIVED 1980–1992

*N*guyet Thu Ha was twenty-two years old in 1975 when South Vietnam capitulated to North Vietnamese and Vietcong forces. As the fighting drew close to her home, Ha—who had never spent a night away from her parents—fled with her four teenage brothers and sisters and her six-year-old nephew, entrusted to her by his distraught parents. She found them passage out of Vietnam on a fishing ship dangerously overcrowded with refugees. The ship made it to the U.S. territory of Guam, a small Pacific island more than 2,000 miles from Vietnam. From there, they were sent to a refugee camp in Arkansas. Eventually, Nguyet Ha and the children settled in Kansas City, Missouri, where they would live throughout the 1980s.

In Kansas City, with five children to support, Nguyet Ha worked seven days a week as a hotel housekeeper, and then as a waitress. She saved every possible penny toward buying a house. "I'm very tough about my budget," Ha explained, "even if I know something I really like to buy. I tell myself, 'Hold it, hold it until you can do it. For now, just forget it.'" Ha soon had the down payment for a $16,000 house; continuing her grueling work schedule, she paid off the mortgage in three years. She also married and had two daughters of her own. In 1989 the thirty-six-year-old Ha bought a laundromat, five adjoining lots, and a vacant building she hoped would eventually house the family members she'd left behind in Vietnam fourteen years earlier. Now able to pursue her ambition to become a teacher, Ha earned two associate of arts degrees and was hired as a paraprofessional at Kansas City's Northeast High School, a magnet school for law and public service.

Through the years of hard work and hardship, Nguyet Thu Ha was sustained by her dream of reuniting her family. Soon after she and the children fled Vietnam, Ha's father died, perhaps of sadness, she thought. Ha often dreamed about her mother, who remained in Vietnam, and sometimes her sobbing woke her daughters. "They wake me up and they wipe my tears and they say,

◀ New immigrants were often eager to become new citizens. In 1996, in a naturalization ceremony held in San Jose, California, a woman from Southeast Asia proudly held an American flag as she took the oath to become a citizen of the United States. (© David Butow/Saba)

CHRONOLOGY

1980 • Reagan elected president

1981 • AIDS first observed in United States
   • Economic problems continue; prime interest rate reaches 21.5 percent
   • Reagan breaks air traffic controllers strike
   • "Reaganomics" plan of budget and tax cuts approved by Congress

1982 • Unemployment reaches 10.8 percent, highest rate since Great Depression
   • ERA dies after Stop-ERA campaign prevents ratification in key states

1983 • Reagan introduces SDI
   • Terrorists kill U.S. Marines in Lebanon
   • U.S. invasion of Grenada

1984 • Reagan aids contras despite congressional ban
   • Economic recovery; unemployment rate drops and economy grows without inflation
   • Reagan reelected
   • Gorbachev promotes reforms in the USSR

1986 • Iran-contra scandal erupts

1987 • Stock market drops 508 points in one day
   • Palestinian *intifada* begins

1988 • George H. W. Bush elected president

1989 • Tiananmen Square massacre in China
   • Berlin Wall torn down
   • U.S. troops invade Panama
   • Gulf between rich and poor at highest point since 1920s

1990 • Americans with Disabilities Act passed
   • Communist regimes in eastern Europe collapse
   • Iraq invades Kuwait
   • South Africa begins to dismantle apartheid

1991 • Persian Gulf War
   • USSR dissolves into independent states
   • United States enters recession

1992 • Annual federal budget deficit reaches high of $300 billion at end of Bush presidency

'Mommy, it's OK.'" For ten years, Ha filled out U.S. government forms and telephoned and visited the offices of the Immigration and Naturalization Service (INS). Finally she received a call from the INS: Ha's mother, two brothers, a sister-in-law, and a niece would be arriving in a couple of days at Kansas City International Airport. Her mother, the last to leave the airplane, was engulfed by hugs. By 1997, not only Ha's mother but all eight of her siblings, most with their children, were living in the United States.

Nguyet Thu Ha and her family were part of the "new immigration" that began in the early 1970s and grew throughout the 1980s as record numbers of immigrants came to the United States from Asia, Mexico, Central and South America, and the Caribbean. These immigrants came to America under a wide range of circumstances, and they had different experiences once in the United States. Ha's is a story of hardship overcome, but not all immigrants—or all Americans—fared so well in the 1980s. The decade saw increasing divisions between rich and poor in America. A host of social problems—drugs, violence, homelessness, the growing AIDS epidemic—made life even more difficult for the urban poor. But for those on the other side of the economic divide, the 1980s were an era of luxury and ostentation. One of the most

■ On a snowy November day, a homeless man makes his bed on park benches in Lafayette Square, across the street from the White House. This 1987 photograph symbolized the stark contrasts between dire poverty and great wealth in 1980s America.   (© Corbis-Bettmann)

poignant images from the 1980s was of a homeless man huddled just outside the Reagan White House—the two Americas, divided by a widening gulf.

The election of Ronald Reagan in 1980 began a twelve-year period of Republican rule, as Reagan was succeeded by his vice president, George Bush, in 1988. Reagan was a popular president who seemed to restore the confidence and optimism that had been shaken by the social, economic, and political crises of the 1970s. Throughout the 1980s, Reagan drew support from a wide variety of Americans: wealthy people who liked his pro-business economic policies; the religious New Right who sought the creation of "God's America"; white middle- and working-class Americans attracted by Reagan's charisma and his embrace of "old-fashioned" values.

Reagan supported social issues that were important to the New Right: he was anti-abortion; he embraced causes such as prayer in schools; he reversed the GOP's position in support of the ERA. Most importantly, Reagan appointed judges to the Supreme Court and to the federal bench whose judicial rulings strengthened social-conservative agendas. Nonetheless, the Reagan administration focused primarily on the agendas of political and economic conservatives: reducing the size and power of the federal government and creating favorable conditions for business and industry. The U.S. economy recovered from the stagflation that had plagued the nation in the 1970s and boomed through much of the 1980s. But corruption flourished in financial institutions freed from government oversight, and taxpayers too often paid the bill for bailouts. By the end of the Reagan-Bush era, a combination of tax cuts and massive increases in defense spending left a budget deficit five times larger than when Reagan took office.

Some of the major developments of the Reagan-Bush presidencies were not domestic, but international. In the span of a decade, the Cold War intensified drastically and then ended. The key figure in the first development was Reagan, who entered office promising to reassert America's military might and stand up to the Soviet Union, and he delivered on both counts. The central player in ending the conflict was Soviet leader Mikhail Gorbachev, who came to power in 1985 determined to address the USSR's long-term economic decline and needed a more

amicable superpower relationship to do so. Gorbachev, though no revolutionary—he hoped to reform the Soviet system, not eradicate it—lost control of events as a wave of revolutions in eastern Europe toppled one communist regime after another. In 1991, the Soviet Union itself disappeared, and the United States found itself the world's lone superpower. The Persian Gulf War of that same year demonstrated America's unrivaled world power, and also the unprecedented importance of the Middle East in U.S. foreign policy. ■

Reagan and the Conservative Resurgence

The 1970s had been a hard decade for Americans: defeat in Vietnam; the resignation of a president in disgrace; the energy crisis; economic "stagflation" that combined rampant inflation with high unemployment; and finally, the humiliation of American hostages held in Iran. In the election year of 1980, President Carter's public approval rating stood at 21 percent, lower even than Richard Nixon's during the depths of the Watergate crisis. The nation was divided and dispirited as people who had grown accustomed to seemingly endless economic growth and unquestioned world power confronted new limits at home and abroad. The time was ripe for a challenge to Carter's presidential leadership, to the Democratic Party, and to the liberal approaches that had, in the main, governed the United States since Franklin Roosevelt's New Deal.

In 1980 several conservative Republican politicians ran for the White House. Foremost among them was Ronald Reagan, former movie star and

RONALD REAGAN two-term governor of California. In the 1940s, as president of the Screen Actors Guild in Hollywood, Reagan had been a New Deal Democrat. But in the 1950s, as a corporate spokesman for General Electric, he became increasingly conservative. In 1964 Reagan's televised speech in support of Republican presidential candidate Barry Goldwater catapulted him to the forefront of conservative politics. America, Reagan said, had come to "a time for choosing" between free enterprise and big government, between individual liberty and "the ant heap of totalitarianism."

Elected governor of California just two years later, Reagan became well known for his right-wing rhetoric: America should "level Vietnam, pave it, paint stripes on it, and make a parking lot out of it," Reagan claimed.

And when student protestors occupied "People's Park" near the University of California in Berkeley, he threatened a "bloodbath" and dispatched National Guard troops in full riot gear. Reagan was often pragmatic, however, about policy decisions. He denounced welfare but presided over reform of the state's social welfare bureaucracy. And he signed one of the nation's most liberal abortion laws.

In the election of 1980 Reagan, in stark contrast to incumbent Jimmy Carter, offered an optimistic vision for

THE NEW CONSERVATIVE COALITION

America's future. With his Hollywood charm and strong conservative credentials, he succeeded in forging very different sorts of American conservatives into a new political coalition. Reagan built on a natural constituency of political conservatives. These strong anticommunists wanted to strengthen national defense; they also believed the federal government should play a more limited role in the nation's domestic life and wished to roll back the liberal programs begun under the New Deal in the 1930s and the Great Society in the 1960s. Reagan also reached out to less ideologically oriented economic conservatives, gaining their support by promising economic deregulation and tax policies that would benefit corporations, wealthy investors, and entrepreneurs.

In a major accomplishment, Reagan managed to unite these political and economic conservatives with two new constituencies. He tapped into the sentiments that fueled the tax revolt movement of the 1970s, even attracting voters from traditionally Democratic constituencies such as labor unions and urban ethnic groups. Many middle- and working-class whites resented their hard-earned money going to what they saw as tax-funded welfare for people who didn't work. Many also thought Reagan's joke that there was nothing more frightening than finding a government official on the doorstep saying, "I'm from the government and I'm here to help," rang true. These "Reagan Democrats" found the Republican critique of tax-funded social programs and "big government" appealing, even though Reagan's proposed economic policies would benefit the wealthy at their expense.

Finally, in the largest leap, Reagan united these groups with the religiously based New Right, an increasingly powerful movement of social conservatives. "When political conservative leaders began to . . . strike an alliance with social conservatives—the pro-life people, the anti-ERA people, the evangelical and born-again Christians, the people concerned about gay rights, prayer in the schools, sex in the movies or whatever"—explained conservative fundraiser Richard Viguerie, "that's when this whole movement began to come alive."

On election day, Reagan and his running mate, George Bush, claimed victory with 51 percent of the popular

REAGAN'S CONSERVATIVE AGENDA

vote. Jimmy Carter carried only six states. Reagan's victory in 1980 began more than a decade of Republican power in Washington: Reagan served two terms as president, followed by his vice president, George Bush, who was elected as Reagan's successor in 1988. Reagan, as much as any president since Franklin Roosevelt, defined the era over which he presided.

Reagan, as president, was not especially focused on the details of governing or the specifics of policies and programs. When outgoing president Jimmy Carter briefed him on urgent issues of foreign and domestic policy, Reagan listened politely but took not a single note and didn't ask questions. Critics argued that his lack of knowledge could prove dangerous—as when he insisted that intercontinental ballistic missiles carrying nuclear warheads could be called back once launched, or said that "approximately 80 percent of our air pollution stems from hydrocarbons released by vegetation."

But supporters insisted that Reagan was a great president in large part because he focused on the big picture. When he spoke to the American people, he offered what seemed to be simple truths—and he did it with the straightforwardness of a true believer and the warmth and humor of an experienced actor. While many—even among Reagan supporters—winced at his willingness to reduce complex policy issues to simple (and often misleading) stories, Reagan was to most Americans the "Great Communicator." He won admiration for his courage after he was seriously wounded in an assassination attempt just sixty-nine days into his presidency. Reagan quipped to doctors preparing to remove the bullet lodged near his heart: "I hope you're all Republicans."

Most important, Reagan had a clear vision for America's future. He and his advisers wanted nothing less than to roll back the liberalism of the past fifty years that had made government responsible for the health of the nation's economy and for the social welfare of its citizens. In the words of David Stockman, a Reagan appointee who headed the Office of Management and Budget, the administration meant to "create a minimalist government" and sever "the umbilical cords of dependency that run from Washington to every nook and cranny of the nation."

Reagan, like traditional conservatives, believed that America's social problems could not be solved by the

ATTACKS ON
SOCIAL WELFARE
PROGRAMS

federal government. But he also tapped into a broader, and less coherent, backlash against the social policies and programs of the Great Society. Many Americans who struggled to make ends meet during the economic crises of the 1970s and early 1980s resented paying taxes that, they believed, went to fund government "handouts" to people who did not work. Lasting racial tensions also fueled public resentment: Reagan fed a stereotype of welfare recipients as unwed, black, teenage mothers who kept having babies to collect larger checks. Even before he became president, Reagan played to these resentments with fabricated tales of a Chicago "welfare queen" who collected government checks under eighty different false names.

In 1981, the administration succeeded in cutting funding for social welfare programs by $25 billion. But "welfare" (Aid to Families with Dependent Children and food stamp programs) was a small part of the budget compared with Social Security and Medicare—social welfare programs that benefited Americans of all income levels, not just the poor. Major budget cuts for these popular, broadly based programs proved impossible. The Reagan administration did shrink the *proportion* of the federal budget devoted to social welfare programs (including Social Security and Medicare) from 28 to 22 percent by the late 1980s—but a $1.2 trillion increase in defense spending, rather than budget cuts, was responsible for the shift.

Reagan also attacked federal environmental, health, and safety regulations that, he believed, reduced business profits and discouraged economic growth. Administration officials claimed that removing the stifling hand of government regulation would restore the energy and creativity of America's free-market system. However, they did not so much end government's role as deploy government power to aid corporate America. The president went so far as to appoint opponents of federal regulations to head agencies charged with enforcing them—letting foxes guard the chicken coop, critics charged.

PRO-BUSINESS
POLICIES
AND THE
ENVIRONMENT

Environmentalists were appalled when Reagan appointed James Watt, a well-known antienvironmentalist, as secretary of the interior. Watt was a leader in the "Sagebrush Rebellion," which sought the return of publicly owned lands in the West, such as national forests, from federal to state control. Land control issues were complicated: the federal government controlled more than half of western lands—including 83 percent of the land in Nevada, 66 percent in Utah, and 50 percent in

■ Ronald Reagan, the Republican presidential candidate in 1980, campaigned for "family values," an aggressive anti-Soviet foreign and military policy, and tax cuts. He also exuded optimism and appealed to Americans' patriotism. This poster issued by the Republican National Committee included Reagan's favorite campaign slogan, "Let's make America great again."   (Collection of David J. and Janice L. Frent)

Wyoming—and many westerners believed that eastern policymakers did not understand the realities of western life. But states' ability to control land within their borders was not the sole issue; Watt and his group wanted to open western public lands to private businesses for logging, mining, and ranching.

Watt also dismissed the need to protect national resources and public wilderness lands for future generations, telling members of Congress during his 1981 Senate confirmation hearing, "I don't know how many generations we can count on until the Lord returns." As interior secretary, Watt allowed private corporations to acquire oil, mineral, and timber rights to federal lands for minuscule payments. He was forced to resign in 1983 after he dismissively referred to a federal advisory panel as "a black . . . a woman, two Jews, and a cripple." Even before Watt's resignation, his appointment had backfired as his actions reenergized the nation's environmental movement and even provoked opposition from business leaders who understood that uncontrolled strip-mining and clear-cut logging of western lands could destroy lucrative tourism and recreation industries in western states.

As part of its pro-business agenda, the Reagan administration undercut organized labor's ability to negotiate wages and working conditions. Union power was already waning; labor union membership declined in the 1970s as jobs in heavy industry disappeared, and efforts to unionize the high-growth electronics and service sectors of the economy had not succeeded. Reagan's policies made hard times for unions worse. Setting the tone for his administration, Reagan intervened in a strike by the Professional Air Traffic Controllers Organization (PATCO) in August 1981. The air traffic controllers—federal employees, for whom striking was illegal—had walked out in protest over working conditions they believed compromised the safety of American air travel. Only forty-eight hours into the strike, Reagan fired the 11,350 strikers and stipulated that they could never be rehired by the Federal Aviation Administration.

ATTACKS ON ORGANIZED LABOR

With the support of an anti-union secretary of labor and appointees to the National Labor Relations Board who consistently voted for management and against labor, businesses took an increasingly hard line with labor during the 1980s, and unions failed to mount an effective opposition. Yet an estimated 44 percent of union families had voted for Reagan in 1980, and despite his treatment of organized labor many were still drawn to his geniality, espousal of old-fashioned values, and vigorous anticommunist rhetoric.

Though much of Reagan's domestic agenda focused on traditional conservative political and economic goals, the New Right and its agenda played an increasingly important role in Reagan-era social policy. It is surprising that the strongly religious New Right was drawn to Reagan, a divorced man without strong ties to religion or, seemingly, his own children. But the non-church-going Reagan lent his support to New Right social issues important to many of his supporters: he endorsed the anti-abortion cause, and his White House issued a report supporting prayer in public schools.

THE NEW RIGHT

Reagan's judicial nominations also pleased the religious New Right. The Senate, in a bipartisan vote, refused to confirm Supreme Court nominee Robert Bork

after eighty-seven hours of antagonistic hearings in which Senator Ted Kennedy proclaimed: "Robert Bork's America is a land in which women would be forced into back-alley abortions, blacks would sit at segregated lunch counters, and school children could not be taught about evolution." But Reagan added Anton Scalia and Sandra Day O'Connor (the first woman) to the Court and elevated Nixon appointee William Rehnquist to chief justice.

All these appointments made the Court more conservative. In 1986, for example, the Supreme Court upheld a Georgia law that punished consensual anal or oral sex between men with up to twenty years in jail (*Bowers v. Hardwick*); in 1989 justices ruled that a Missouri law restricting the right to an abortion was constitutional (*Webster v. Reproductive Health Services*), thus encouraging further challenges to *Roe v. Wade*. In federal courts, Justice Department lawyers argued New Right positions on such social issues, and Reagan's 378 appointees to the federal bench usually ruled accordingly. Overall, however, the Reagan administration did not push a conservative social agenda as strongly as some members of the new Republican coalition had hoped.

"Reaganomics"

The centerpiece of Reagan's domestic agenda was the economic program that took his name: Reaganomics. The U.S. economy was in bad shape at the beginning of the 1980s. Stagflation had proved resistant to traditional economic remedies: when the government increased spending to stimulate a stagnant economy, inflation skyrocketed; when it cut spending or tightened the money supply to reduce inflation, the economy plunged deeper into recession and unemployment rates jumped. Everyone agreed that something had to be done to break the cycle. Even some Democrats, such as Colorado senator Gary Hart, voiced a "nonideological skepticism about the old, Rooseveltian solutions to social problems."

Reagan offered the American people a simple answer to economic woes. Instead of focusing on the complexities of global competition, deindustrialization, and OPEC's control of oil, Reagan argued that U.S. economic problems were caused by government intrusion in the free-market system. At fault were intrusive government regulation of business and industry, expensive government social programs that offered "handouts" to nonproductive citizens, high taxes, and deficit spending—in short, government itself. The Reagan administration's economic agenda was closely tied to its larger conservative ideology of limited government: it sought to "un-shackle" the free-enterprise system from government regulation and control, to slash spending on social programs, to limit government's use of taxes to redistribute income among the American people, and to balance the budget by reducing the role of the federal government.

Reagan's economic policy was based largely on "supply-side economics," the theory that tax cuts (rather than government spending) will create economic growth. Economist Arthur Laffer had proposed one key concept for supply-siders, sketching his soon-to-be famous "Laffer curve" onto a cocktail napkin for a *Wall Street Journal* writer and President Ford's chief of staff (and the future vice president) Richard Cheney in 1974. According to Laffer's theory, at some point rising tax rates discourage people from engaging in taxable activities (such as investing their money): if profits from investments simply disappear to taxes, what is the incentive to invest? As people invest less, the economy slows. Even though tax rates remain high, the government collects less in tax revenue because the economy stalls. Cutting taxes, on the other hand, reverses the cycle and increases tax revenues.

"SUPPLY-SIDE ECONOMICS"

Though economists at the time accepted the larger principle behind Laffer's curve, almost none believed that U.S. tax rates approached the point of disincentive. Even conservative economists were highly suspicious of supply-side principles. Reagan and his staff, however—on the basis of the unproven assumption that both corporate and personal tax rates in the United States had reached a level that discouraged investment—sought a massive tax cut. They argued that American corporations and individuals would invest funds freed up by lower tax rates, producing new plants, new jobs, and new products. Economic growth would more than make up for the tax revenues lost. And as prosperity returned, the profits at the top would "trickle down" to the middle classes and even to the poor.

Reagan's economic program was most fully developed by David Stockman, head of the Office of Management and Budget. Stockman proposed a five-year plan to balance the federal budget through economic growth (created by tax cuts) and deep cuts, primarily in social programs. Congress cooperated with a three-year, $750 billion tax cut, the largest ever in American history. Cutting the federal budget, however, proved more difficult. Stockman's plan for balancing the budget assumed $100 billion in cuts from government programs, including Social Security and Medicare—and Congress was not about to cut Social Security and Medicare benefits. Rea-

■ The "Ronnie Voo-Doo Doll" might have appealed to Democrats frustrated by Ronald Reagan's continuing popularity. The doll was inspired by the term "voo-doo economics," used in the 1980 election Republican primaries by Reagan's rival (and later vice president) George Bush to describe Reagan's proposed economic policies. (Smithsonian Institution, Washington, D.C.)

gan, meanwhile, canceled out domestic spending cuts by dramatically increasing annual defense spending.

Major tax cuts; big increases in defense spending; small cuts in social programs: the numbers did not add up. The annual federal budget deficit exploded—from $59 billion in 1980, to more than $100 billion in 1982, to almost $300 billion by the end of George Bush's presidency in 1992. The federal government borrowed money to make up the difference, transforming the United States from the world's largest creditor nation to its largest debtor (see Figure 32.1). The national debt grew to almost $3 trillion. Because an ever greater share of the federal budget went to pay the interest on this ballooning debt, less was available for federal programs, foreign or domestic.

Reaganomics attempted to stimulate the economy—but economic growth would not solve the persistent problem of inflation. Here the Federal Reserve Bank, an autonomous federal agency, stepped in. In 1981, the Federal Reserve Bank raised interest rates

HARSH MEDICINE FOR INFLATION

Figure 32.1   America's Rising National Debt, 1974–1989

America's national debt, which rose sporadically throughout the 1970s, soared to record heights during the 1980s. Under President Reagan, large defense expenditures and tax cuts caused the national debt to grow by $1.5 trillion.   (Source: Adapted from U.S. Bureau of the Census, *Statistical Abstract of the United States* [Washington, D.C., 1992], p. 315.)

for bank loans to a unprecedented 21.5 percent, battling inflation by tightening the money supply and slowing the economy down. The nation plunged into recession. During the last three months of the year, the gross national product (GNP) fell 5 percent, and sales of cars and houses dropped sharply. With declining economic activity, unemployment soared to 8 percent, the highest level in almost six years.

By late 1982, unemployment had reached 10.8 percent, the highest rate since 1940. Many of the unemployed were blue-collar workers in ailing "smokestack industries" such as steel and automobiles. African Americans suffered a jobless rate of 20 percent. Reagan and his advisers promised that consumers would lift the economy out of the recession by spending their tax cuts. But as late as April 1983, unemployment still stood at 10 percent and people were angry. Jobless steelworkers paraded through McKeesport, Pennsylvania, carrying a coffin that bore the epitaph "American Dream." Agriculture, too, was faltering and near collapse. Farmers suffered not only from falling crop prices due to overproduction, but also from floods and droughts and from burdensome debts they had incurred at high interest rates. Many lost their property through mortgage fore-

closures and farm auctions. Others filed for bankruptcy. As the recession deepened, poverty rose to its highest level since 1965.

It was harsh medicine, but the Federal Reserve Bank's plan to end stagflation worked. High interest rates helped drop inflation from 12 percent in 1980 to less than 7 percent in 1982. The economy also benefited from OPEC's 1981 decision, after eight years of engineering an artificial scarcity of oil, to increase oil production, thus lowering prices. In 1984 the GNP rose 7 percent, the sharpest increase since 1951, and midyear unemployment fell to a four-year low of 7 percent. The economy was booming, but without sparking inflation.

By the presidential election of 1984, the recession was only a memory. Reagan got credit for the recovery, though it had little to do with his supply-side policies. In fact, the Democratic candidate, former vice president Walter Mondale, repeatedly hammered at Reagan's economic policies. Insisting that the rapidly growing budget deficit would have dire consequences for the American economy, he said (honestly, but probably not very astutely) that he would raise taxes. And he focused on themes of fairness and compassion; not all

"MORNING IN AMERICA"

Americans, Mondale told the American public, were prospering in Reagan's America. Reagan, in contrast, proclaimed: "It's morning again in America." Television ads showed heartwarming images of American life, as an off-screen narrator told viewers: "Life is better. America is back. And people have a sense of pride they never felt they'd feel again." Reagan won in a landslide, with 59 percent of the vote. Mondale (with running mate Geraldine Ferraro, the first woman vice-presidential candidate) carried only his home state of Minnesota.

Supply-side economics was not the only policy that transformed America's economy in the 1980s. Deregula-

_____ tion, begun under Jimmy Carter and
DEREGULATION expanded vastly under Reagan (the *Federal Register*, which contains all federal regulations, shrank from 87,012 pages in 1980 to 47,418 pages in 1986), also created new opportunities for American business and industry. The 1978 deregulation of the airline industry lowered ticket prices both short-term and long-term; airline tickets cost almost 45 percent less in the early twenty-first century (in constant dollars) than in 1978. Deregulation of telecommunications industries created serious competition for the giant AT&T, and long-distance calling became inexpensive.

As part of its deregulation agenda, the Reagan administration loosened regulation of American banking and finance industries and purposely cut the enforcement ability of the Securities and Exchange Commission (SEC), which oversees Wall Street. In the early 1980s, Congress deregulated the nation's savings-and-loan institutions (S&Ls), organizations previously required to [in]vest depositors' savings in thirty-year, fixed-rate mortgages secured by property within a 50-mile radius of the main office. The stagflation of the 1970s had already [left] many S&Ls insolvent, but the 1980s legislation [create]d conditions for a larger collapse. By ending [federal?] oversight of investment practices, while [allowing S&Ls] to cover losses from bad investments [with] depositors' savings, Congress left no penal[ty as] S&Ls increasingly put depositors' money [in in]vestments and engaged in shady—even [illegal—investments].

[As such inves]tments carried the day on Wall Street, [Michael] Milken, a reclusive bond trader for [the] firm Drexel Firestone, pioneered [the "]junk bond" industry and created [new] lucrative investment possibilities. [Milken] offered financing to debt-ridden [or other]wise weak corporations that [used lo]w-interest bank loans to fund [venture]s that paid investors high

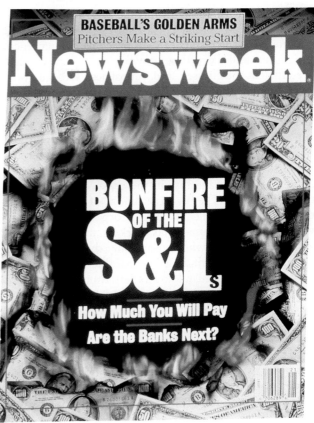

The 1980s savings and loan crisis led to the greatest collapse of U.S. financial institutions since the Great Depression. The federal bailout of S&Ls would cost American taxpayers at least $124 billion. (© 1990 Newsweek, Inc. All rights reserved. Reprinted by permission.)

interest rates because they were high-risk (thus "junk" bonds). Many of these corporations, Milken realized, were attractive targets for takeover by other corporations or investors—who, in turn, could finance takeovers with junk bonds. Such "predators" could use the first corporation's existing debt as a tax write-off, sell off unprofitable units, and lay off employees to create a more efficient—thus more profitable—corporation. Investors in the original junk bonds could make huge profits by selling their shares to the corporate raiders.

By the mid-1980s, it was no longer only weak corporations that were targeted for these "hostile takeovers"; hundreds of major corporations—including giants Walt Disney and Conoco—fell prey to "merger mania." Profits for investors were staggering, and by 1987 Milken, the guru of junk bonds, was earning $550 million a year—about $1,046 a minute—in salary; counting investment returns, Milken's income was about $1 billion a year.

What were the results of such practices? Heightened competition and corporate downsizing often created more-efficient businesses and industries. Deregulation helped smaller and often innovative corporations challenge the virtual monopolies of giant corporations in fields like telecommunications. And through much of the 1980s, the American economy boomed. Though the stock market plunged 508 points on a single day in October 1987—losing 22.6 percent of its value, or almost double the percentage loss in the crash of 1929—it rebounded quickly. The high-risk boom of the 1980s did, however, have significant costs. Corporate downsizing meant layoffs for white-collar workers and management personnel, many of whom (especially those past middle age) had difficulty finding comparable positions. The wave of mergers and takeovers left American corporations as a whole more burdened by debt than before. It also helped to consolidate sectors of the economy—such as media—under the control of an ever smaller number of players.

The high-risk, deregulated boom of the 1980s, furthermore, was rotten with corruption. By the late 1980s, insider trading scandals—in which people used "inside" information about corporations not available to the

THE RICH GET RICHER general public to make huge profits trading stocks—rocked financial markets and sent some of the most prominent figures on Wall Street to jail (albeit "country club" jails). Savings and loans made billions of dollars' worth of bad investments, sometimes turning to fraud to cover them up. Scandal reached all the way to the White House when it was revealed that Vice President Bush's son Neil was involved in shady S&L deals. The Reagan-Bush administration's bailout of the S&L industry cost taxpayers half a trillion dollars.

Finally, during the 1980s, the rich got richer and the poor got poorer (see Figure 32.2). Merger mania and the financial market bonanza contributed: the number of Americans reporting an annual income of $500,000 increased tenfold between 1980 and 1989, and the salary and benefits of corporate chief executive officers increased from approximately 30 times that of the average factory worker in 1980 to 130 times the worker's average by 1989. In 1987, the United States had forty-nine billionaires—up from one in 1978. While the number of very wealthy Americans grew, middle-class incomes were stagnant.

Most of the new inequality was due to Reagan's economic policies, which benefited the wealthy at the expense of middle- and lower-income Americans. Re

Figure 32.2 While the Rich Got Richer in the 1980s, the Poor Got Poorer

Between 1977 and 1989, the richest 1 percent of American families reaped most of the gains from economic growth. In fact, the average pretax income of families in the top percentage rose 77 percent. At the same time, the typical family saw its income edge up only 4 percent. And the bottom 40 percent of families had actual declines in income. (Source: Data from the *New York Times*, March 5, 1992.)

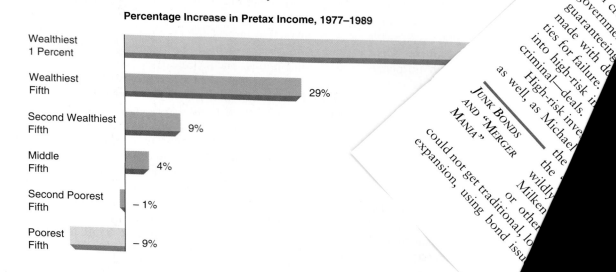

CNN

When Ted Turner launched CNN, his Cable News Network, on June 1, 1980, few people took it seriously. CNN, with a staff of three hundred—mostly young, mostly inexperienced—operated out of the basement of a converted country club in Atlanta. Dismissed by critics as the Chicken Noodle Network, CNN was at first best known for its on-air errors, as when a cleaning woman walked onto the set and emptied anchor Bernard Shaw's trash during his live newscast. But by 1992, against all expectations, CNN was seen in more than 150 nations worldwide, and *Time* magazine named Ted Turner its "Man of the Year" for realizing media theorist Marshall McLuhan's vision of the world as a "global village" united by mass media.

Throughout the 1980s, CNN steadily built relations with local news outlets in nations throughout the world. As critical—and sometimes unanticipated—events reshaped the world, CNN reported live from Tiananmen Square and from the Berlin Wall in 1989. Millions watched as CNN reporters broadcast live from Baghdad in the early hours of the Gulf War in 1991. CNN changed not only viewers' experience of these events but diplomacy itself. When the Soviet Union wanted to denounce the 1989 U.S. invasion of Panama, officials called CNN's Moscow bureau instead of the U.S. embassy. During the Gulf War, Saddam Hussein reportedly kept televisions in his bunker tuned to CNN, and U.S. generals relied on its broadcasts to judge the effectiveness of missile attacks. In 1992, President George H. W. Bush noted, "I learn more from CNN than I do from the CIA."

While Turner's twenty-four-hour news network had a global mission, its American origins were often apparent. During the U.S. invasion of Panama, CNN cautioned correspondents not to refer to the American military forces as "our" troops. Turner himself once sent his staff a memo insisting that anyone who used the word *foreign* instead of *international* would be fined $100. What CNN offered was not so much international news, but a global experience: people throughout the world joined in watching the major moments in contemporary history as they unfolded. America's CNN created new links among the world's people. But, as *Time* magazine noted (while praising Turner as the "Prince of the Global Village"), such connections "did not produce instantaneous brotherhood, just a slowly dawning awareness of the implications of a world transfixed by a single TV image."

The "Boys of Baghdad"—CNN reporters Bernard Shaw, John Holliman, and Peter Arnett—broadcast live by satellite from Suite 906 of the Al Rashid Hotel as Allied bombs fell on Baghdad throughout the night of January 16, 1991. Despite their dramatic reporting on the first night of the war, critics charged that continuing network coverage of Operation Desert Storm, with distant shots of cruise missiles seeking targets and heavy use of animation, graphics, and even theme music, made the war appear more like a video game than a bloody conflict. (CNN)

tax policies decreased the "total effective tax rates"—income taxes plus Social Security taxes—for the top 1 percent of American families by 14.4 percent. But they increased tax rates for the poorest 20 percent of families by 16 percent. By 1990, the richest 1 percent of Americans controlled 40 percent of the nation's wealth; fully 80 percent of wealth was controlled by the top 20 percent. Not since the 1920s had America seen such economic inequality.

Reagan and the World

a key element in Reagan's winning strategy in the 1980 election was his forthright call for the United States to assert itself on the world stage. Though lacking a firm grasp of world issues, history, and geography—friends and associates often marveled at his ability to get even elementary facts wrong—Reagan adhered to a few core principles. One was a deep and abiding anticommunism that had dictated his world-view for decades and that formed the foundation of his presidential campaign. A second was an underlying optimism about the ability of American power and values to bring positive change in the world. Reagan liked to quote Tom Paine of the American Revolution: "We have it in our power to begin the world over again." Yet Reagan was also a political pragmatist, particularly as time went on and his administration became mired in scandal. Together, these elements of the president's personality help explain both his aggressive anticommunist foreign policy and his willingness to respond positively in his second term to Soviet leader Mikhail Gorbachev's call for "new thinking" in world affairs.

Initially, toughness vis-à-vis Moscow was the watchword. Embracing the strident anticommunism that characterized U.S. foreign policy in the early Cold War, Reagan and his advisers rejected both the détente of the Nixon years and the Carter administration's focus on extending human rights abroad. Where Nixon and Carter perceived an increasingly multipolar international system, the Reagan team reverted to a bipolar perspective defined by the Soviet-American relationship. In his first presidential press conference Reagan described a malevolent Soviet Union, whose leaders thought they had "the right to commit any crime, to lie, to cheat." When Poland's pro-Soviet leaders in 1981 cracked down on an independent labor organization, Solidarity, Washington responded by restricting Soviet-American trade and hurled angry words at Mos-

SOVIET-AMERICAN TENSION

cow. In March 1983, Reagan told an audience of evangelical Christians in Florida that the Soviets were "the focus of evil in the modern world . . . an evil empire." That same year Reagan restricted commercial flights to the Soviet Union after a Soviet fighter pilot mistakenly shot down a South Korean commercial jet that had strayed some 300 miles off course into Soviet airspace. The world was shocked by the death of 269 passengers, and Reagan exploited the tragedy to score Cold War points.

A key Reagan tenet held that a substantial military buildup would thwart the Soviet threat and intimidate Moscow. Accordingly, the administration launched the largest peacetime arms buildup in American history, driving up the federal debt. In 1985, when the military budget hit $294.7 billion (a doubling since 1980), the Pentagon was spending an average of $28 million an hour. Assigning low priority to arms control talks, Reagan announced in 1983 his desire for a space-based defense shield against incoming ballistic missiles: the Strategic Defense Initiative (SDI). His critics tagged it "Star Wars" and said such a system could never be made to work scientifically—some enemy missiles would always get through the shield. Moreover, the critics warned, SDI would have the effect of elevating the arms race to dangerous new levels. But Reagan was undaunted, and in the years that followed, SDI research and development consumed tens of billions of dollars.

Because he attributed Third World disorders to Soviet intrigue, the president declared the Reagan Doctrine:

REAGAN DOCTRINE

the United States would openly support anticommunist movements—"freedom fighters"—wherever they were battling the Soviets or Soviet-backed governments. In Afghanistan, the president continued Jimmy Carter's policy of providing covert assistance, through Pakistan, to the Mujahidin rebels in their war against the Soviet occupation. CIA director William J. Casey made numerous trips to Pakistan to coordinate the flow of arms and other assistance. When the Soviets stepped up the war in 1985, the Reagan administration responded by sending more high-tech weapons. Particularly important were the anti-aircraft Stinger missiles. Easily transportable and fired by a single soldier, the Stingers turned the tide in the Afghan war by making Soviet jets and helicopters vulnerable below fifteen thousand feet.

The administration also applied the Reagan Doctrine aggressively in the Caribbean and Central America. Senior officials believed that the Soviets and Castro's Cuba were fomenting disorder in the region (see Map 32.1). Accordingly, in October 1983 the president sent U.S. troops into the tiny Caribbean island of Grenada to

Map 32.1 The United States in the Caribbean and Central America

The United States often has intervened in the Caribbean and Central America. Geographical proximity, economic stakes, political disputes, security links, trade in illicit drugs, and Cuba's alliance with the Soviet Union and defiance of the United States have kept North American eyes fixed on events in the region.

oust a pro-Marxist government that appeared to be forging ties with Moscow and Havana. In El Salvador, he provided military and economic assistance to a military-dominated government engaged in a struggle with left-wing revolutionaries. The regime used (or could not control) right-wing death squads, which by the end of the decade had killed forty thousand dissidents and other citizens as well as several American missionaries who had been working with landless peasants. By the end of the decade the United States had spent more than $6 billion there in a counterinsurgency war. In January 1992 the Salvadoran combatants finally negotiated a U.N.-sponsored peace.

The Reagan administration also meddled in the Nicaraguan civil war. In 1979 leftist insurgents in

CONTRA WAR IN NICARAGUA

Nicaragua overthrew Anastasio Somoza, a long-time ally of the United States and member of the dictatorial family that had ruled the Central American nation since the mid-1930s. The revolutionaries called themselves Sandinistas in honor of César Augusto Sandino—who had headed the nationalistic, anti-imperialist Nicaraguan opposition against U.S. occupation in the 1930s, battled U.S. Marines, and was finally assassinated by Somoza henchmen—and they denounced the tradition of U.S. imperialism in their country. When the Sandinistas aided rebels in El Salvador, bought Soviet weapons, and invited Cubans to work in Nicaragua's hospitals and schools and to help reorganize the Nicaraguan army, Reagan officials charged that Nicaragua was becoming a Soviet client. In 1981 the CIA began to train, arm, and direct more than ten thousand counterrevolutionaries, known as contras, to overthrow the Nicaraguan government.

The U.S. interventions in El Salvador and Nicaragua sparked a debate much like the earlier one over Vietnam. Many Americans, including Democratic leaders in Congress, were skeptical about the communist threat to the region and warned that Nicaragua could become another Vietnam. Congress in 1984 voted to stop U.S. military aid to the contras. Secretly, the Reagan administration lined up other countries, including Saudi Arabia, Panama, and South Korea, to funnel money and weapons to the contras, and in 1985 Reagan imposed an economic embargo against Nicaragua. The president might have opted for a diplomatic solution, but he rejected a plan proposed by Costa Rica's president Oscar Arias Sánchez in 1987 to obtain a cease-fire in Central America through negotiations and cutbacks in military aid to all rebel forces. (Arias won the 1987 Nobel Peace Prize.) Three years later, after Reagan had left office, all of the Central American presidents at last brokered a settle-

ment; in the national election that followed, the Sandinistas lost to a U.S.-funded party. After nearly a decade of civil war, thirty thousand Nicaraguans had died, and the ravaged economy had dwindled to one of the poorest in the hemisphere.

Reagan's obsession with defeating the Sandinistas almost caused his political undoing. In November 1986 it

IRAN-CONTRA SCANDAL

became known that the president's national security adviser, John M. Poindexter, and an aide, marine lieutenant colonel Oliver North, in collusion with CIA director Casey, had covertly sold weapons to Iran as part of a largely unsuccessful attempt to win the release of several Americans being held hostage by Islamic fundamentalist groups in the Middle East. During the same period, Washington had been condemning Iran as a terrorist nation and demanding that America's allies not trade with the Islamic state. Still more damaging was the revelation that money from the Iran arms deal had been illegally diverted to a fund to aid the contras—this after Congress had unambiguously rejected providing such aid. North later admitted that he illegally had destroyed government documents and lied to Congress to keep the operation clandestine.

Though Reagan survived the scandal—it remained unclear just what he did and did not know about the operation—his presidency suffered a major blow. His personal popularity declined, and an emboldened Congress began to reassert its authority over foreign affairs. In late 1992 outgoing president George Bush pardoned several former government officials who had been convicted of lying to Congress. Critics smelled a cover-up, for Bush himself, as vice president, had participated in high-level meetings on Iran-contra deals. As for North, his conviction was overturned on a technicality. In view of its deliberate thwarting of congressional authority, the Iran-contra secret network, the scholar William LeoGrande has argued, "posed a greater threat to democracy in the United States than Nicaragua ever did."

The Iran-contra scandal also pointed to the increased importance in U.S. foreign policy of the Middle

U.S. INTERESTS IN THE MIDDLE EAST

East and terrorism (see Map 33.2). As before, the United States had as its main goals in the Middle East to preserve access to oil and to support its ally Israel, while at the same time checking Soviet influence in the region. In the 1980s, though, American leaders faced new pressures, in the form of a deepened Israeli-Palestinian conflict and an anti-American and anti-Israeli Islamic fundamentalist movement that began to spread after the ouster of the shah of Iran in 1979.

The 1979 Camp David accords between Israel and Egypt (see page 883) had raised hopes of a lasting settlement involving self-government for the Palestinian Arabs living in the Israeli-occupied Gaza Strip and West Bank. It did not happen, as Israel and the Palestinian Liberation Organization (PLO) remained at odds. In 1982, in retaliation for Palestinian shelling of Israel from Lebanon, Israeli troops invaded Lebanon, reaching the capital, Beirut, and inflicting massive damage. The beleaguered PLO and various Lebanese factions called on Syria to contain the Israelis. Thousands of civilians died in the multifaceted conflict, and a million people became refugees. Soon after Reagan sent U.S. Marines to Lebanon to join a peacekeeping force, the American troops became embroiled in a war between Lebanese factions. In October 1983 terrorist bombs demolished a barracks, killing 241 American servicemen. Four months later, Reagan recognized failure and pulled the remaining marines out.

The attack on the marine barracks showed the growing danger of terrorism to the United States and other

TERRORISM

Western countries. In the 1980s, numerous otherwise powerless groups, many of them associated with the Palestinian cause or with Islamic fundamentalism, relied on terrorist acts to further their political aims. Often they targeted American citizens and property, on account of Washington's support of Israel and U.S. involvement in the Lebanese civil war. Of the 690 hijackings, kidnappings, bombings, and shootings around the world in 1985, for example, 217 were against Americans. Most of these actions originated in Iran, Libya, Lebanon, and the Gaza Strip. In June 1985, for example, Shi'ite Muslim terrorists from Lebanon hijacked an American jetliner, killed one passenger, and held thirty-nine Americans hostage for seventeen days. Three years later, a Pan American passenger plane was destroyed over Scotland, probably by pro-Iranian terrorists who concealed the bomb in a cassette player.

Washington, firmly allied with Israel, continued to propose peace plans designed to persuade the Israelis to

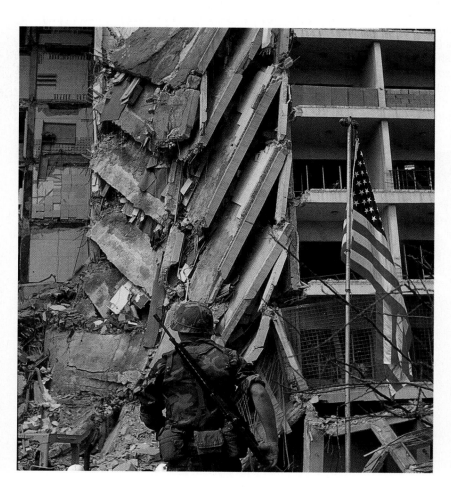

■ On April 18, 1983, a car bomb placed by terrorists demolished the U.S. embassy in Beirut, Lebanon, killing 63 people, 17 of them Americans. An American soldier stands guard near the destroyed building. Then in October of the same year, terrorist bombs leveled a military barracks, killing 241 American personnel. A few months later, President Reagan withdrew U.S. Marines from a multinational peacekeeping force that had been dispatched to Lebanon to calm a war waged there by Israel against PLO and Syrian forces.   (Bill Pierce/Sygma)

give back occupied territories and the Arabs to give up attempts to push the Jews out of the Middle East (the "land-for-peace" formula). As the peace process stalled in 1987, Palestinians living in the West Bank began an *intifada* (Arabic for "uprising") against Israeli forces. Israel refused to negotiate, but the United States decided to talk with PLO chief Yasir Arafat after he renounced terrorism and accepted Israel's right to live in peace and security. For the PLO to recognize Israel and, in effect, for the United States to recognize the PLO were major developments in the Arab-Israeli conflict, even as a lasting settlement remained elusive.

In South Africa, too, American diplomacy became more aggressive as the decade progressed. At first, the Reagan administration followed a policy of "constructive engagement"—asking the increasingly isolated government to reform its apartheid system, designed to

In one of several summit meetings, top Soviet leader Mikhail Gorbachev (b. 1932) and President Ronald Reagan (b. 1911) met in Moscow in May 1988 in hopes of signing a Strategic Arms Reduction Talks (START) agreement. The "chemistry" of warm friendship that Reagan later claimed characterized his personal relationship with Gorbachev fell short of producing cuts in dangerous strategic weapons. But their cordial interaction encouraged the diplomatic dialogue that helped end the Cold War.   (Ronald Reagan Presidential Library)

SOUTH AFRICA preserve white supremacy. But many Americans demanded economic sanctions: cutting off imports from South Africa and pressuring some 350 American companies—top among them Texaco, General Motors, Ford, and Goodyear—to cease operations there. Some American cities and states passed divestment laws, withdrawing dollars (such as pension funds used to buy stock) from American companies active in South Africa. Public protest and congressional legislation forced the Reagan administration in 1986 to impose economic restrictions against South Africa. Within two years, about half of the American companies in South Africa had pulled out.

American conservatives were not happy with the South Africa sanctions policy, and the more extreme among them soon found another reason to be disenchanted with Reagan. A new Soviet leader, Mikhail S. Gorbachev, had come to power, and Reagan, his own popularity declining, showed a newfound willingness to enter negotiations with the "evil empire." Gorbachev called for a friendlier superpower relationship and a new, more cooperative world system. At a 1985 Geneva summit meeting between the two men, Reagan agreed in principle with Gorbachev's contention that strategic weapons should be substantially reduced, and at a 1986 Reykjavik, Iceland, meeting they came very close to a major reduction agreement. SDI, however, stood in the way: Gorbachev insisted that the initiative be shelved, and Reagan refused to part with it despite continuing scientific objections that the plan would cost billions of dollars and never work.

ENTER GORBACHEV

But Reagan and Gorbachev got on well, despite the language barrier and their differing personalities. Reagan's penchant for telling stories rather than discussing the intricacies of policy did not trouble the detail-oriented Gorbachev. As General Colin Powell commented, while the Soviet leader was far superior to Reagan in mastery of specifics, he never exhibited even a trace of condescension. He understood that Reagan was, as Powell put it, "the embodiment of his people's down-to-earth character, practicality, and optimism." And Reagan toned down his strident anti-Soviet rhetoric, particularly as his more hawkish advisers left the administration in the late 1980s.

The turnaround in Soviet-American relations stemmed more from changes abroad than from Reagan's decisions. As Reagan said near the end of his presidency, he had been "dropped into a grand historical moment." Under the dynamic Gorbachev, a younger

PERESTROIKA AND GLASNOST

generation of Soviet leaders came to power in 1985. They began to modernize the highly bureaucratized, decaying economy through a reform program known as *perestroika* ("restructuring") and to liberalize the authoritarian political system through *glasnost* ("openness"). For these reforms to work, however, Soviet military expenditures had to be reduced and foreign aid decreased.

In 1987 Gorbachev and Reagan signed the Intermediate-Range Nuclear Forces (INF) Treaty banning all land-based intermediate-range nuclear missiles in Europe. Soon began the destruction of 2,800 missiles, including Soviet missiles targeted at western Europe and NATO missiles aimed at the Soviet Union. Gorbachev also unilaterally reduced his nation's armed forces, helped settle regional conflicts, and began the withdrawal of Soviet troops from Afghanistan. After more than forty chilling years, the Cold War was coming to an end.

A Polarized People: American Society in the 1980s

*A*s the Cold War waned, so too did the power of the belief in an America united by a set of shared, middle-class values. Though the ideal of shared values was never a reality, it had exercised a powerful hold in the nation's public culture from World War II well into the 1960s. By the 1980s, after years of social struggle and division, few Americans believed in the reality of that vision; many rejected it as undesirable. And though the 1980s were never so contentious and violent as the era of social protest in the 1960s and early 1970s, deep social and cultural divides existed among Americans. A newly powerful group of Christian conservatives challenged the secular culture of the American majority. A growing class of affluent, well-educated Americans seemed a society apart from the urban poor that sociologists and journalists began calling "the underclass." At the same time, the composition of the American population was changing dramatically, as people immigrated to the United States from more different nations than ever before.

As late as 1980, many Americans believed that the 1925 Scopes Trial (see page 668–669), in which biology teacher John Scopes was convicted of violating Tennessee law by teaching evolution, had been the last gasp of fundamentalist Christianity in the United States. They were wrong. Since the 1960s, America's mainline liberal Protestant churches—Episcopalian, Presbyterian, Methodist—had been losing

GROWTH OF THE RELIGIOUS RIGHT

members while Southern Baptists and other denominations that offered the spiritual experience of being "born again" through belief in Jesus Christ and accepted the literal truth of the Bible (fundamentalism) had grown rapidly. Fundamentalist preachers reached out to vast audiences through television: by the late 1970s, televangelist Oral Roberts was drawing an audience of 3.9 million. Close to 20 percent of Americans identified themselves as fundamentalist Christians in 1980.

Most fundamentalist Christian churches stayed out of the social and political conflicts of the 1960s and early 1970s, arguing that preaching the "pure saving gospel of Jesus Christ" was more important. But in the late 1970s—motivated by what they saw as the betrayal of God's will in an increasingly permissive American society—some influential preachers began to mobilize their flocks for political struggle. In a "Washington for Jesus" rally in 1980, fundamentalist leader Pat Robertson told crowds: "We have enough votes to run the country.... And when the people say, 'We've had enough,' we are going to take over." The Moral Majority, founded in 1979 by Jerry Falwell, sought to create a "Christian America," in part by supporting political candidates on the local and national levels. Falwell's defense of socially conservative "family values" and his condemnation of feminism (he called NOW the "National Order of Witches"), homosexuality, pornography, and abortion resonated with many Americans.

Throughout the 1980s, the coalition of conservative Christians known as the New Right waged campaigns against America's secular culture. Rejecting the idea—associated with multiculturalism that different cultures and lifestyle choices were equally valid—the New Right worked to establish what they believed to be "God's law" as the basis for American society. Concerned Women for America, founded by Beverly LaHayes in 1979, attempted to have elementary school readers containing "unacceptable" religious beliefs (including excerpts from *The Diary of Anne Frank* and *The Wizard of Oz*) removed from school classrooms. In 1989, the American Family Association protested network television shows such as *Cheers* and *Nightline*. Fundamentalist Christian groups once again began to challenge the teaching of evolutionary theory in public schools. The Reagan administration frequently turned to James Dobson, founder of the conservative Focus on the Family organization, for policy advice. Conservative Christians also joined with Roman Catholics, Mormons, and other religious opponents of abortion in the anti-abortion or "prolife" movement, which had sprung up in the wake of the Supreme Court's 1973 decision in *Roe v. Wade*.

■ The Reverend Jerry Falwell, an evangelical preacher whose "Old Time Gospel Hour" program reached 15 million Americans, founded the Moral Majority in 1979. This conservative political action group drew support from fundamentalist Christians and played a major role in the political elections of the 1980s.   (Dennis Brack/Black Star)

Though the New Right often found an ally in the Reagan White House, many other Americans vigorously opposed a movement they saw as preaching a doctrine of intolerance and threatening basic freedoms—including the freedom of religion for those whose beliefs did not accord with the conservative Christianity of the New Right. In 1982, the politically progressive television producer Norman Lear, influential former congresswoman Barbara Jordan, and other prominent figures from the fields of business, religion, politics, and entertainment founded People for the American Way to support American civil liberties and freedoms, the separation of church and state, and the values of tolerance and diversity. The struggle between the religious right and their opponents for the future of the nation came to be known as the "culture wars."

"CULTURE WARS"

It was not only organized groups, however, that opposed the agenda of the religious right. Many beliefs of Christian fundamentalists ran counter to the ways most Americans lived—especially when it came to women's roles. The women's movement, like the civil rights movement, had brought about significant changes in American society. By the 1980s, a generation of girls had grown up expecting freedoms and opportunities their mothers never had. Legislation such as the Civil Rights Act of 1964 and Title IX (see pages 837 and 865) had opened both academic and athletic programs to girls and women. In 1960, there were thirty-eight male lawyers for every female lawyer in the United States; by 1983, the ratio was 5.5 to 1. By 1985, more than half of married women with children under three worked outside the home. The religious right's insistence that women's place was in the home, subordinated to her husband, contradicted not only the gains made toward sexual equality in American society but also the reality of many women's lives.

As Americans fought the "culture wars" of the 1980s, another major social divide threatened the nation. A 1988 national report on race relations looked back to the 1968 Kerner Commission report to claim: "America is again becoming two separate societies," white and black. It argued that African Americans endured poverty, segregation, and crime in inner-city ghettos while most whites lived comfortably in suburban enclaves. In fact, America's separate societies of comfort and hardship were not wholly determined by race. The majority of America's poor were white, and the black middle class was strong and expanding. But people of color made up a disproportionate share of America's poor. In 1980, 33 percent of blacks and 26 percent of Latinos lived in poverty, compared with 10 percent of whites (see Figure 32.3).

THE NEW INEQUALITY

Reasons for poverty varied. For people of color, the legacies of racism played a role. The changing job structure was partly responsible, as the overall number of well-paid jobs for unskilled workers decreased, replaced by lower-paid service jobs. New York alone had 234,000 fewer blue-collar workers in 1980 than at the beginning of the 1970s. In addition, families headed by a single mother were more likely to be poor—five times more likely than families of the same race maintained by a married couple. By 1990, a high rate of unwed pregnancy and a rising divorce rate meant that about a quarter of all children lived in households without fathers. Racial differences were significant: by 1992, 59 percent of African American children and 17 percent of white children lived in female-headed households, and almost half of black children lived in poverty.

As inequality increased, so too did social pathology. In impoverished and often hopeless inner-city neighborhoods, violent crime—particularly homicides and gang warfare—grew alarmingly, as did school dropout rates,

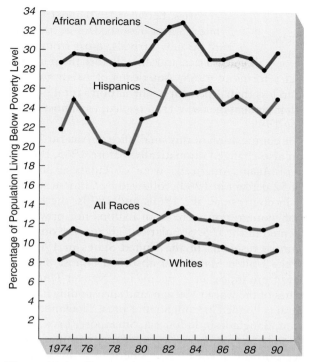

Figure 32.3   Poverty in America by Race, 1974–1990

Poverty in America rose in the early 1980s but subsided afterward. Many people of color, however, experienced little relief during the decade. Notice that the percentage of African Americans living below the poverty level was three times higher than that for whites. It also was much higher for Hispanics.   (Source: Adapted from U.S. Bureau of the Census, *Statistical Abstract of the United States* [Washington, D.C., 1992], p. 461.)

numbers. By 2000, young black men were more likely to have been arrested than to have graduated from a four-year college.

Rates of homelessness also grew during the 1980s. Some of the homeless were impoverished families; many of the people living on the streets had problems with drugs or alcohol. About a third of the homeless were former psychiatric patients discharged from psychiatric wards in a burst of enthusiasm for "deinstitutionalization." By 1985, 80 percent of the total number of beds in state mental hospitals had been eliminated on the premise that small neighborhood programs would be more responsive to people's needs than large state hospitals. Such local programs failed to materialize. Without adequate medical supervision and medication, many of America's mentally ill citizens wandered the streets.

Another social crisis confronting Americans in the 1980s was the global spread of autoimmune deficiency

THE AIDS EPIDEMIC

syndrome, or AIDS. Caused by the human immunodeficiency virus (HIV), which attacks cells in the immune system, AIDS leaves its victims susceptible to deadly infections and cancers. The human immunodeficiency virus itself is spread through the exchange of blood or body fluids, often through sexual intercourse or needle sharing by intravenous drug users.

■ In the 1980s there was an alarming spread of sexually transmitted diseases, especially acquired immune deficiency syndrome (AIDS). Campaigns for "Safe Sex," such as this New York City subway ad, urged people to use condoms.   (Reprinted with permission of Saatchi & Saatchi)

SOCIAL CRISES IN AMERICAN CITIES

crime rates, and child abuse. Some poverty-stricken men and women tried to find escape in hard drugs, especially crack, a derivative of cocaine, which first struck New York City's poorest neighborhoods in 1985. Crack's legacy included destroyed families, abused children, and heavily armed teenage drug dealers. Gang shootouts over drugs were deadly: the toll in Los Angeles in 1987 was 387 deaths; more than half of the victims were innocent bystanders. Shocked by the violence, many states instituted mandatory prison sentences for possessing small amounts of crack, making penalties for a gram of crack equivalent to those for 100 grams of cocaine, the drug of choice for more-affluent, white Americans during the 1980s. Owing in large part to drug-sentencing policies, America's prison population grew almost fourfold from 1980 to the mid-1990s, with black and Latino youth arrested in disproportionate

First observed in the United States in 1981, AIDS initially struck male homosexuals, then spread more widely. Between 1981 and 1988, of the fifty-seven thousand AIDS cases reported, nearly thirty-two thousand resulted in death. Politicians were slow to devote resources to combating AIDS, in part because it was perceived initially as a "gay man's disease" that didn't threaten other Americans. "A man reaps what he sows," declared the Reverend Jerry Falwell of the Moral Majority. AIDS, along with other sexually transmitted diseases such as genital herpes and chlamydia, ended an era defined by penicillin and "the pill," in which sex was freed from the threat of serious disease or unwanted pregnancy.

As America confronted the spreading AIDS epidemic, as well as what seemed to be epidemics of drug addiction, violence, and urban despair,

AN ERA OF OSTENTATION

some Americans were living extraordinarily well. "Greed is all right," Wall Street financier Ivan Boesky told students at U.C. Berkeley, the center of 1960s campus protest, and he was met with cheers and laughter. For the rich, the 1980s were an era of ostentation. New York entrepreneur Donald Trump's $29 million yacht had gold-plated bathroom fixtures. Publisher Malcolm Forbes flew eight hundred guests to Morocco for his seventieth birthday; with an honor guard of three hundred Berber horsemen and six hundred acrobats, jugglers, and belly dancers to entertain the guests, the party cost $2 million.

With Wall Street booming, just-graduated M.B.A.'s were offered starting salaries of eighty thousand dollars, new graduates from top law schools the same. Nineteen eighty-four was the "Year of the Yuppie"—Young Urban Professional—proclaimed *Newsweek* magazine. *Yuppie* was a derogatory term from the beginning (as was *Buppie*, for Black Urban Professional), but it described the lives of many ambitious and successful young Americans who worked hard in demanding careers and who created an identifiable lifestyle defined by consumer goods: BMWs, Sub-Zero refrigerators, Armani suits, Häagen-Dazs ice cream. Americans in the 1980s seemed fascinated with tales of the super-rich (making *Dallas* a top-rated television show) and with Yuppie lifestyles (chronicled on the popular show *thirtysomething*). But Yuppies also represented those who got ahead without caring about those left behind. As Yuppies led the way in gentrifying urban neighborhoods, displacing poorer residents, graffiti began to appear in New York: "Die, Yuppie Scum."

The polarizing forces affecting American society in the 1980s were complicated by the arrival of large numbers of new immigrants who did not fit cleanly into old racial

NEW IMMIGRANTS FROM ASIA

categories. Between 1970 and 1990 the United States absorbed more than 13 million new arrivals, most from Latin America and Asia. Before the immigration act reforms of 1965, Americans of Asian ancestry made up less than 1 percent of the nation's total population; that percentage more than tripled, to almost 3 percent, by 1990.

The composition of this small slice of America's population also changed dramatically. Before 1965, the majority of Asian Americans were of Japanese ancestry (about 52 percent in 1960), followed by Chinese and Filipino. In contrast, in the 1960s and 1970s, the highest rates of immigration were from nations not previously represented in the U.S. population. There were only 603 Vietnamese residents of the United States in 1964. By 1990, the United States had absorbed almost 800,000 refugees from Indochina—people like Nguyet Thu Ha—casualties of the war in Vietnam and surrounding nations. Immigrants flooded in from South Korea, Thailand, India, Pakistan, Bangladesh, Indonesia, Singapore, Laos, Cambodia, and Vietnam. Japanese Americans became a much smaller portion of the Asian American population, at 15 percent surpassed by Chinese and Filipino Americans and rivaled by the Vietnamese.

Immigrants from Asia tended to be either highly skilled or unskilled. Unsettled conditions in the Philippines in the 1970s and 1980s created an exodus of well-educated Filipino men and women to the United States. India's economy was not able to support its abundance of well-trained physicians and healthcare workers, who increasingly found employment in the United States and elsewhere. Korea, Taiwan, and China also lost skilled and educated workers to the United States. Other immigrants from China, however, had few job skills and spoke little or no English. Large numbers of new immigrants crowded into neighborhoods like New York's Chinatown, where women worked long hours under terrible conditions in the city's nonunion garment industry. Immigrants from Southeast Asia were the most likely to be unskilled and to live in poverty in the United States, though some, like Nguyet Thu Ha, found opportunities for success.

But even highly educated immigrants often found their options limited. A 1983 study found that Korean immigrants or Korean Americans owned three-quarters of the approximately twelve hundred greengroceries in New York City. Though often cited as a great immigrant success story, Korean greengrocers usually had descended the professional ladder: 78 percent of them had college or professional degrees.

Applicants for visas wait in line at the U.S. embassy in New Delhi, India. In 1985, 140,000 people were on the waiting list for one of 20,000 annual immigrant visas. Many poorer nations, such as India, experienced a "brain drain" of highly educated people to the United States and western Europe. (Tucci/Gamma Liaison)

Though immigration from Asia was high, unprecedented rates of immigration coupled with a high birth rate made Latinos the fastest-growing group of Americans. New immigrants from Mexico joined Mexican Americans and other Spanish-surnamed Americans, many of whose families had lived in the United States for generations. In 1970, Latinos comprised 4.5 percent of the nation's population; that percentage jumped to 9 percent by 1990, when one out of three Los Angelenos and Miamians were Hispanic, as were 48 percent of the population of San Antonio and 70 percent of El Paso. Mexican Americans, concentrated in California and the Southwest, made up the majority of this population, but Puerto Ricans, Cubans, Dominicans, and other immigrants from the Caribbean also lived in the United States, clustered principally in East Coast cities.

THE GROWING LATINO POPULATION

During the 1980s, people from Guatemala and El Salvador fled civil war and government violence, and many found their way to the United States. Though the U.S. government commonly refused to grant them political asylum (about 113,000 Cubans received political refugee status during the 1980s, compared with fewer than 1,400 El Salvadorans), a national "sanctuary movement" of Christian churches defied the law to protect refugees from deportation back to places where they risked violence or death. Economic troubles in Mexico and throughout Central and South America also produced a flood of a different sort of refugee, undocumented

workers who crossed the poorly guarded 2,000-mile border between the United States and Mexico, seeking economic opportunities. Some were sojourners, who moved back and forth across the border. A majority meant to stay. These new Americans created a new hybrid culture that became an important part of the American mosaic. "We want to be here," explained Daniel Villanueva, a TV executive in Los Angeles, "but without losing our language and our culture. They are a richness, a treasure that we don't care to lose."

The incorporation of so many newcomers into American society was not always easy, especially during economic hard times. Many Americans believed new arrivals threatened their jobs and economic security, and nativist violence and simple bigotry increased during the 1980s. In 1982, twenty-seven-year-old Vincent Chin was beaten to death in Detroit by an unemployed auto worker and his uncle. American auto plants were losing in competition with Japanese imports, and the two men seemingly mistook the Chinese-American Chin for Japanese, reportedly shouting at him: "It's because of you little [expletive deleted] that we're out of work." In New York, Philadelphia, and Los Angeles, inner-city African Americans boycotted Korean groceries. Riots broke out in Los Angeles schools between black students and newly arrived Mexicans. In Dade County, Florida, voters passed an "antibilingual" measure that led to the removal of Spanish-language signs on public transportation, while at the state and national level people debated initiatives declaring English the "official" language of the United

States. Public school classrooms, however, struggled with practical issues: in 1992, more than one thousand school districts in the United States enrolled students from at least eight different language groups.

Concerned about the flow of illegal aliens into the United States, Congress passed Immigration Reform and Control (Simpson-Rodino) Act in 1986. The act's purpose was to discourage illegal immigration by imposing sanctions on employers who hired undocumented workers, but it also provided amnesty to millions who had immigrated illegally before 1982. As immigration continued at a high rate into the 1990s, however, it would further transform the face of America, offering the richness of diverse cultures and the potential for continued social conflict.

The End of the Cold War and Global Disorder

The departure of Ronald Reagan from the presidency coincided with a set of changes in world affairs that would lead in short order to the end of the Cold War and the dawn of a new international system. The U.S. chief executive during these years was the man who had been Reagan's vice president, George Herbert Walker Bush. The scion of a Wall Street banker who had been a U.S. senator from Connecticut, Bush had attended an exclusive boarding school and then gone on to Yale. An upper-class, Eastern "Establishment" figure of the type that was becoming increasingly rare in the Republican Party, he had the advantage over his rivals for the presidential nomination in that he had been a loyal vice president. And he possessed a formidable résumé—he had been ambassador to the United Nations, chairman of the Republican Party, special envoy to China, and director of the CIA. He also had been a war hero, flying fifty-eight combat missions in the Pacific in World War II and receiving the Distinguished Flying Cross.

Bush entered the 1988 presidential campaign trailing his Democratic opponent, Massachusetts governor *1988 PRESIDENTIAL CAMPAIGN* Michael Dukakis, by a wide margin. Republican operatives turned that around by waging one of the most negative campaigns in American history. Most notoriously, the Bush camp aired a television commercial featuring a black convicted murderer, Willie Horton, who had terrorized a Maryland couple, raping the woman, while on weekend furlough—a temporary release program begun under Dukakis's Republican predecessor. The Republicans also falsely suggested that Dukakis had a history of psychiatric prob-

lems. His patriotism was questioned, as was that of his wife, who was wrongly accused of having burned an American flag while protesting the Vietnam War. These personal attacks generally did not come from Bush himself, but neither did he disavow them. Dukakis, meanwhile, did not engage in personal attacks on Bush but ran an uninspired campaign. On election day, Bush won by eight percentage points in the popular vote and received 426 electoral votes to Dukakis's 112. The Democrats, however, retained control of both houses of Congress.

From the start, Bush focused most of his attention on foreign policy. By nature cautious and reactive in world affairs, Bush seemed to set few long-range goals except to envision the United States as the supreme power in a unipolar world. Yet he also knew that the Cold War was drawing to a close. Mikhail Gorbachev's cascading changes in the Soviet Union were now taking on a life of their own, stimulating reforms in eastern Europe that ultimately led to revolution. In 1989, many thousands of people in East Germany, Poland, Hungary, Czechoslovakia, and Romania, motivated by a longing for personal freedom, startled the world by repudiating their communist governments and staging mass protests against a despised ideology. In November 1989, Germans scaled the Berlin Wall and then tore it down; the following October, the two Germanys reunited after forty-five years of separation. By then, the other communist governments in the region had either fallen or were about to do so.

Other challenges to communist rule met with less success. In June 1989 Chinese armed forces stormed into *TIANANMEN SQUARE* Beijing's Tiananmen Square, slaughtering hundreds—perhaps thousands—of unarmed students and other citizens who for weeks had been holding peaceful pro-democracy rallies. With this action the Chinese government, whose successful economic reforms had won much admiration in the 1980s, emphatically rejected political liberalization; henceforth, the "Chinese solution" came to mean the choice of repression in response to popular calls for freedom.

Yet China was an exception. Elsewhere, even in places far removed from the Soviet empire, the forces of democratization proved too powerful to resist. In South Africa, a new government under F. W. De Klerk, responding to increased domestic and international pressure, began a cautious retreat from the apartheid system. In February 1990 De Klerk legalized all political parties in South Africa, including the African National Congress, the chief black party, and ordered the release of Nelson Mandela, a hero to black South Africans, after a twenty-seven-year imprisonment. Then, in a staged

■ In May 1994, after three centuries of white rule, South Africa held its first multiracial election. Turnout was much higher than expected, with millions of black voters elated to be casting their first ballots. Nelson Mandela's African National Congress (ANC) party won 252 of the 400 seats, and Mandela, only four years removed from prison, became president.   (TomasMuscionico/Contact)

process lasting several years, the government repealed its apartheid laws and opened up the vote to all citizens regardless of color. Mandela, who became South Africa's first black president in 1994, called the transformation of his country "a small miracle."

Some observers used that same phrase to describe what happened in 1991 in the cradle of communist power, the Soviet Union itself. In 1990,

COLLAPSE OF SOVIET POWER

the Baltic states of Lithuania, Latvia, and Estonia declared independence from Moscow's rule; the following year, the Soviet Union ceased to exist, disintegrating into independent successor states—Russia, Ukraine, Tajikistan, and many others (see Map 32.2). Muscled aside by Russian reformers who thought he was moving too slowly toward democracy and free-market economics, Gorbachev himself lost power. The breakup of the Soviet empire, the dismantling of the Warsaw Pact (the Soviet military alliance formed in 1955 with communist countries of eastern Europe), the repudiation of communism by its own leaders, German reunification, and a significantly reduced risk of nuclear war signaled the end of the Cold War. The Soviet-American rivalry that for half a century

had dominated international politics—and circumscribed domestic prospects in both countries—was over.

The United States and its allies had won. The containment policy followed by nine presidents—from Truman through Bush—had had many critics over the years, on both the left and the right, but it had succeeded on a most basic level: it had contained communism for four-plus decades without blowing up the world and without obliterating freedom at home. Two systems competed in this East-West confrontation, and that of the West had clearly triumphed—as anyone who experienced life in both a NATO country and a Warsaw Pact nation quickly realized. Next to the glitz and bustle and well-stocked store shelves of the former were the drab housing projects, polluted skies, and scarce consumer goods of the latter. Over time, the Soviet socialist economy proved less and less able to compete with the American free-market one, less and less able to cope with the demands of the Soviet and eastern European citizenry.

Yet the Soviet empire might have survived for years more had it not been for Gorbachev, one of the most influential figures of the twentieth century. His ascension to the top of the Soviet leadership was the single most important event in the final phase of the Cold War, and it is hard to imagine the far-reaching changes of the 1985–1990 period without his influence. Through a series of unexpected overtures and decisions, Gorbachev fundamentally transformed the nature of the superpower relationship, in a way that could scarcely have been anticipated a few years before. Ronald Reagan's role was less central but still vitally important, not so much because of his hard-line policies in his first term as because of his later willingness to enter into serious negotiations and treat Gorbachev more as a partner than as an adversary. George H. W. Bush, too, followed this general approach. In this way, just as personalities mattered in starting the Cold War, so they mattered in ending it.

The victory in the Cold War elicited little celebration among Americans. The struggle had exacted a heavy price in money and lives. The confronta-

COSTS OF VICTORY

tion may never have become a hot war on a global level, but the period after 1945 nevertheless witnessed numerous bloody Cold War–related conflicts claiming millions of lives. In the Vietnam War alone, at least 1.5 million people died, more than 58,000 of them Americans. Military budgets, meanwhile, had eaten up billions upon billions of dollars, thereby shortchanging myriad domestic programs. Some Americans wondered whether the steep price had been necessary, whether the communist threat had ever been as grave as officials, from the late 1940s on, claimed.

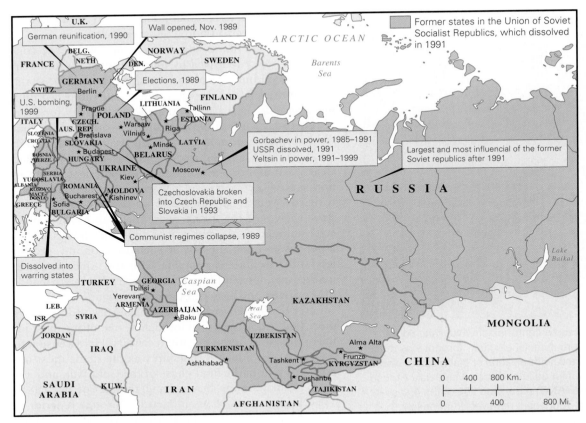

Map 32.2   The End of the Cold War in Europe

When Mikhail Gorbachev came to power in the Soviet Union in 1985, he initiated reforms that ultimately undermined the communist regimes in eastern Europe and East Germany and led to the breakup of the Soviet Union itself, ensuring an end to the Cold War.

Bush proclaimed a "new world order," but for him and his advisers, the question was, What happens next? As the Cold War closed, they struggled futilely to describe the dimensions of an international system they said would be based on democracy, free trade, and the rule of law. The administration signed important arms reduction treaties with the Soviet Union in 1991, and with the postbreakup Russia in 1993, leading to major reductions in nuclear weapons on both sides, but the United States sustained a large defense budget and continued to station large numbers of military forces overseas. As a result, Americans were denied the "peace dividend" they hoped would reduce taxes and free up funds to address domestic problems.

In Central America, the Bush administration cooled the zeal with which Reagan had meddled, because the interventions had largely failed, and, with the Cold War over, anticommunism seemed irrelevant. Still, like so many presidents before him, Bush showed no reluctance

to intervene forcefully and unilaterally in the region to further U.S. aims. In December 1989, American troops invaded Panama to oust the military leader Manuel Noriega. A long-time drug trafficker, Noriega had stayed in Washington's favor in the mid-1980s by providing logistical support for the contras in nearby Nicaragua. When exposés of Noriega's sordid record provoked protests in Panama, however, Bush decided to dump the dictator. Noriega was captured in the invasion and taken to Miami, where, in 1992, he was convicted of drug trafficking and imprisoned. Devastated Panama, meanwhile, became all the more dependent on the United States, which offered little reconstruction aid.

The strongest test of Bush's foreign policy came in the Middle East. The Iran-Iraq War had ended inconclusively in August 1988, after eight years of fighting and almost 400,000 dead. The Reagan administration had assisted the Iraqi war effort with weapons and in-

SADDAM HUSSEIN'S GAMBLE

■ In the Persian Gulf War of early 1991, Operation Desert Storm forced Iraqi troops out of Kuwait. Much of that nation's oil industry was destroyed by bombs and the retreating Iraqis, who torched oil facilities as they left. Oil wells burned for months, darkening the sky over these American forces and causing environmental damage. (Bruno Barbey/Magnum Photos, Inc.)

telligence, as had many other NATO countries. In mid-1990 Iraqi president Saddam Hussein, facing massive war debts and growing domestic discontent, invaded neighboring Kuwait, hoping thereby to enhance his regional power and his oil revenues and also shore up domestic support. He counted on Washington to look the other way. Instead, George Bush condemned the invasion and vowed to defend Kuwait. He was outraged by Hussein's act of aggression and also feared that Iraq might threaten U.S. oil supplies, not merely in Kuwait but in petroleum-rich Saudi Arabia next door.

Within weeks, Bush had convinced virtually every important government, including most of the Arab and Islamic states, to sign on to an economic boycott of Iraq. Then, in Operation Desert Shield, Bush dispatched more than 500,000 U.S. forces to the region, where they were joined by more than 200,000 from the allies. Likening Saddam to Hitler and declaring the moment the first post–Cold War "test of our mettle," Bush rallied a deeply divided Congress to authorize "all necessary means" to oust Iraq from Kuwait (a vote of 250 to 183 in the House and 52 to 47 in the Senate). Though Bush did not invoke the 1973 War Powers Act, numerous observers saw his seeking a congressional resolution of approval as reinforcing the intent of the act. Many Americans believed that economic sanctions imposed on Iraq should be given more time to work, but Bush would not wait. "This will not be another Vietnam," the president said, by which he meant it would not be a drawn-out and frustrating affair. Victory would come swiftly and cleanly.

Operation Desert Storm began on January 16, 1991, with the greatest air armada in history pummeling Iraqi targets. American missiles reinforced round-the-clock bombing raids on Baghdad, Iraq's capital. It was a television war, in which CNN reporters broadcast live from a Baghdad hotel while bombs were falling in the city, and millions of Americans sat transfixed in their living rooms, eyes glued to the TV. In late February, coalition forces launched a ground war that quickly routed the Iraqis from Kuwait. When the war ended on March 1, at least 40,000 Iraqis had been killed, while the death toll for allied troops stood at 240 (148 of them Americans). Almost a quarter of the American dead were killed by "friendly fire"—by weapons fired by U.S. or allied troops.

OPERATION DESERT STORM

Bush rejected a call from some of his advisers to take Baghdad and topple Hussein's regime. Coalition members would not have agreed to such a plan—it would go beyond the original objective of forcing Iraq out of Kuwait—and anyway it was not clear who in Iraq would replace the dictator. So Saddam Hussein survived in power, though with his power curtailed. The U.N. maintained an arms and economic embargo, and the Security Council issued Resolution 687, demanding that Iraq provide full disclosure of all aspects of its program to develop weapons of mass destruction and ballistic missiles with a range greater than 150 kilometers. In Resolution 688, the Security Council condemned a brutal crackdown by the Iraqi regime against Kurds in northern Iraq and Shia Muslims in the south and demanded access for humanitarian groups. The United States, Britain, and France seized on Resolution 688 to create a northern "no-fly zone" prohibiting Iraqi aircraft flights. A similar no-fly zone was set up in southern Iraq in 1992 and expanded in 1996.

Though in time many would question President Bush's decision to stop short of Baghdad, initially there were few objections. In the wake of Desert Storm the president's popularity in the polls soared to 91 percent, beating the previous high of 89 percent set by Harry Truman in June 1945 after the surrender of Germany. Cocky White House advisers thought Bush could ride his popularity right through the 1992 election and beyond. In the afterglow of military victory it seemed a good bet, particularly as Bush could also claim achievements on the domestic front that seemed to affirm his inauguration-day pledge to lead a "kinder, gentler nation."

DOMESTIC PROBLEMS

In 1990, for example, Bush had signed the Americans with Disabilities Act, which banned job discrimination, in companies with twenty-five or more employees, against the blind, deaf, mentally retarded, and physically impaired, as well as against those who are HIV-positive or have cancer. The act, which covered 87 percent of all wage earners, also required that "reasonable accommodations," such as wheelchair ramps, be made available to people with disabilities. Also in 1990, the president, much to the disappointment of conservatives, signed the Clean Air Act, which sought to reduce acid rain by limiting emissions from factories and automobiles. And in 1991, after many months of contentious debate, Bush and Congress agreed on a civil rights bill to protect against job discrimination.

Yet not long after reaching their historic highs, Bush's poll numbers started falling and kept falling, largely because of the president's ineffectual response to the weakening American economy. He was slow to grasp the implications of the heavy burden of national debt and massive federal deficit that had been out of control for nearly a decade. When the nation entered into a full-fledged recession in the months after the Gulf War, Bush did not respond, beyond proclaiming that things were not really *that* bad. Echoed his treasury secretary Nicholas Brady: "I don't think it's the end of the world even if we have a recession. We'll pull out of it again. It's no big deal."

For millions of ordinary Americans, it was a big deal. Business shrank, despite low interest rates that theoretically should have encouraged investment. Real estate prices plummeted. American products faced steadily tougher competition from products made overseas, especially in Japan and elsewhere in Asia. As unemployment climbed to 8 percent, consumer confidence sank. By late 1991, fewer than 40 percent of the American people felt comfortable with the way the country was going. Many demanded that the federal government address neglected problems such as the rising cost of healthcare.

Bush's credibility was diminished further by confirmation hearings for Clarence Thomas, whom Bush nominated to the Supreme Court in the fall of 1991. The Bush administration hoped that those who opposed the nomination of yet another conservative to the high court might nonetheless support the addition of an African American justice. But in October, Anita Hill, an African American law professor at the University of Oklahoma, charged that Thomas had sexually harassed her when she worked for him during the early 1980s. The Judiciary Committee hearings, carried live on television, turned ugly, and some Republican members suggested that Hill was either lying or mentally ill. Thomas described himself as the "victim" of a "high-tech lynching," and African American groups were passionately divided over the Hill-Thomas testimony. However, Hill's testimony focused the nation's attention on issues of power, gender, sex, and the workplace. And the Senate's confirmation of Thomas, along with the attacks on Hill, angered many, further increasing the gender gap in American politics.

CLARENCE THOMAS NOMINATION

As George H. W. Bush and the Republicans entered the election year 1992, the glow of military victory in the Gulf War had faded completely.

Summary

When Ronald Reagan left the White House in 1988, succeeded by his vice president, George Bush, the *New York Times* summed up his presidency: "Ronald Reagan leaves no Vietnam War, no Watergate, no hostage crisis. But he leaves huge question marks—and much to do." George H. W. Bush fulfilled the foreign policy promises of the 1980s, as the Soviet Union collapsed and America achieved victory in the decades-long Cold War. He also led the United States into war with Iraq—a war that ended in swift and decisive victory but left Saddam Hussein in power.

During the 1980s, the United States moved from deep recession to economic prosperity. However, deep tax cuts and massive increases in defense spending created huge budget deficits, increasing the national debt from $994 billion to more than $2.9 trillion. This enormous debt would limit the options of subsequent presidential administrations. Pro-business policies, such as deregulation, created opportunities for the development of new technologies and prompted economic growth, but also opened the door to corruption and fraud. Policies that benefited the wealthy at the expense of middle-class or poor Americans widened the gulf between the rich and everyone else. The social pathologies of drug addiction, crime, and violence grew, especially in the nation's most impoverished areas. The legacies of the 1980s included thousands of children born addicted to crack, who would live the rest of their lives with mental and physical impairments, and prisons that overflowed with young men.

The 1980s also saw the beginning of the "culture wars" between fundamentalist Christians who sought to "restore" America to God and opponents who championed separation of church and state and embraced liberal values. The nation shifted to the right politically, though the coalitions of economic and social conservatives that supported Reagan were fragile and did not guarantee continued Republican dominance.

Finally, during the 1980s, the face of America changed. A society that many had thought of as white and black became ever more diverse. The nation's Latino population grew in size and visibility. New immigrants from Asia arrived in large numbers; though still a small part of the population, they would play an increasingly important role in American society. During the Reagan-Bush years, America had become both more polarized and more diverse. In the years to come, Americans and their leaders would struggle with the legacies of the "Reagan Era."

LEGACY FOR A PEOPLE AND A NATION
The Americans with Disabilities Act

The Americans with Disabilities Act (ADA), passed by large bipartisan majorities in Congress and signed into law by President George Bush on July 26, 1990, built on the legacy of America's civil rights movement: President Bush called it "the world's first comprehensive declaration of equality for people with disabilities." But the ADA did more than prohibit discrimination against people with physical and mental disabilities. It mandated that public and private entities—including schools, stores, restaurants and hotels, libraries and other government buildings, and public transportation authorities—provide "reasonable accommodations" to allow people with disabilities to participate fully in the life of their communities and their nation.

In less than two decades, the equal-access provisions of the ADA have changed the landscape of America. Steep curbs and stairs once blocked access to wheelchair users; now ramps and lifts are common. Buses "kneel" for passengers with limited mobility; crosswalks and elevators use audible signals for the sight-impaired; schools and universities offer qualified students a wide range of assistance. People with a whole spectrum of disabilities have traveled into the Grand Canyon or Glacier National Park, thanks to active "accessibility" programs of the National Park Service. Lee Page, a wheelchair user and sports fan from Virginia, described the impact of ADA standards for sports stadiums: "We were able to see over the standing spectators as the anthem was sung. I could see the flag and everything that was happening down on the field. . . . I finally felt like a part of the crowd."

At the same time that the ADA has offered greater opportunity to many Americans, regulations covering employment have generated some difficult legal questions. Which conditions are covered by the ADA? (The Supreme Court has ruled that asymptomatic HIV infection is a covered disability and carpal tunnel syndrome is not.) Employers may not discriminate against qualified people who can, with "reasonable" accommodation, perform the "essential" tasks of a job—but what is "reasonable" and what is "essential"? The specific provisions of the ADA will likely continue to be contested and redefined in the courts. But as Attorney General Janet Reno noted as she celebrated the tenth anniversary of the ADA with a ceremony at Warm Springs, Georgia, where President Franklin Roosevelt had sought therapy for the effects of polio, the true legacy of the ADA is the determination "to find the best in everyone and to give everyone equal opportunity."

The **history companion** powered by Eduspace®
Your primary source for interactive quizzes, exercises, and more to help you learn efficiently.
http://history.college.hmco.com/students

GLOBAL BRIDGES IN THE NEW MILLENNIUM
America Since 1992

*a*t 8:46 A.M. on that fateful Tuesday morning, Jan Demczur, a window washer, stepped into an elevator in the North Tower of the World Trade Center in New York City. The elevator started to climb, but before it reached its next landing, one of the six occupants recalled, "We felt a muted thud. The whole building shook. And the elevator swung from side to side like a pendulum." None of the occupants knew it, but American Airlines Flight 175 had just crashed into the building, at a speed of 440 miles per hour.

The elevator started plunging. Someone pushed the emergency stop button, and the descent stopped. For several minutes, nothing happened. Then a voice came over the intercom to deliver a blunt message: there had been an explosion. The line went dead, as smoke began to seep through the elevator's doors. Using the wooden handle of Demczur's squeegee, several of the men forced open the doors, but discovered they were on the fiftieth floor, five hundred feet above the ground, where this elevator did not stop. In front of them was a wall.

Demczur, a Polish immigrant who once worked as a builder, saw that the wall was made of Sheetrock, a plasterboard he knew could be cut. Using the squeegee, he started to scrape the metal edge against the wall, back and forth, over and over again. When the blade broke and fell down the shaft, he used a short metal handle he had in his bucket. It took more than an hour, but the six men took turns scraping and poking, and finally burst through to a men's bathroom. Startled firefighters guided them to a stairwell. After an agonizingly slow descent through the heavy smoke, they finally burst onto the street at 10:23 A.M. Five minutes later the tower collapsed.

It was September 11, 2001.

Only later that day did Demczur learn what had happened: terrorists had hijacked four airliners and turned them into missiles. Two had been flown into the

◀ "The Tribute of Light," dedicated to the memory of the victims of the World Trade Center terrorist attacks, lights up the sky above Lower Manhattan on March 11, 2002, the six-month anniversary of the attacks. The Brooklyn Bridge is seen in the foreground. (Daniel P. Derella/AP/Wide World Photos, Inc.)

CHRONOLOGY

1992 • Violence erupts in Los Angeles over Rodney King verdict
   • Major economic recession
   • Clinton elected president
   • U.S. sends troops to Somalia

1993 • Congress approves North American Free Trade Agreement (NAFTA)
   • U.S. withdraws from Somalia

1994 • Contract with America helps Republicans win majorities in House and Senate
   • Genocide in Rwanda
   • U.S. intervention in Haiti

1995 • Domestic terrorist bombs Oklahoma City federal building
   • U.S. diplomats broker peace for Bosnia

1996 • Welfare reform bill places time limits on welfare payments
   • Clinton reelected

1998 • House votes to impeach Clinton

1999 • Senate acquits Clinton of impeachment charges
   • NATO bombs Serbia over Kosovo crisis
   • Antiglobalization demonstrators disrupt World Trade Organization (WTO) meeting in Seattle

2000 • Nation records longest economic expansion in its history
   • Supreme Court settles contested presidential election in favor of Bush

2001 • Economy dips into recession; begins period of low growth and high unemployment
   • Bush becomes president
   • Al Qaeda terrorists attack World Trade Center and Pentagon
   • PATRIOT Act passed by Congress
   • Enron business scandal results in Justice Department investigation
   • U.S. attacks Al Qaeda positions in Afghanistan, topples ruling Taliban regime

2003 • U.S. invades Iraq, ousts Saddam Hussein regime

World Trade Center, one had slammed into the Pentagon in Washington, D.C., and one had crashed in a field in rural Pennsylvania after passengers tried to wrest control of the plane from the hijackers. Both World Trade Center towers had collapsed, killing close to three thousand people, including Demczur's close friend Roko Camaj, a window washer from Albania.

It was the deadliest attack the United States had ever suffered on its soil, and it would lead to far-ranging changes in American life. But the events of day sent shock waves well beyond the country's shores, indeed around the globe, and made starkly clear just how interconnected the world had become at the dawn of the twenty-first century. At the World Trade Center alone, nearly five hundred foreigners from more than eighty countries lost their lives. Sixty-seven Britons died, twenty-one Jamaicans, and twenty-seven Japanese. Mexico lost seventeen of its citizens; India lost thirty-four. Sixteen Canadians perished, as did fifteen Australians and seven Haitians. The tiny Caribbean nation of Trinidad and Tobago counted fifteen deaths.

The list of victims revealed the extraordinary diversity of people who inhabited New York, showing the city once again to be a melting pot of world cultures. According to a chaplain at "ground zero," the victims' families communicated their grief in well over a hundred languages. Many of the victims were, like Demczur and Camaj, immigrants who had come to New York to seek a better life for themselves and their families; others were there on temporary work visas. But all helped to make the World Trade Center a kind of global city within a city, where some 50,000 people worked and another 140,000 visited on any given day.

A symbol of U.S. financial power, the World Trade Center towers were also—as their very name suggested—a symbol of the globalization of world trade that had been a central phenomenon in the 1980s and 1990s. The towers housed the offices and Wall Street infrastructure of more than 400 businesses, including some of the world's leading financial institutions—the Bank of America, Switzerland's Credit Suisse Group, Germany's Deutsche Bank, and Japan's Dai-Ichi Kangyo Bank.

Globalization had become one of the buzzwords of the 1990s, and by most definitions went beyond trade and investment to include the web of connections—in commerce, communications, and culture—that increasingly bound the world together. The terrorists, who were tied to a radical Islamic group called Al Qaeda, sought to strike a blow at that globalization, yet their attack was also an expression of it. That is, Al Qaeda depended on the same international technological, economic, and travel infrastructure that had fueled the global integration. Cell phones, computers, intercontinental air travel—the plotters made full use of these instruments of globalization in preparing to carry out their attack, then turned four modern jetliners into lethal weapons.

Islamic militants had actually struck at the World Trade Center before, in 1993, detonating a massive bomb in the center's underground parking garage that caused significant damage. But Americans at the time paid only fleeting attention. With the demise of Soviet communism and the end of the Cold War, most were intent on focusing inward. President Bill Clinton had come into office in 1993 determined to concentrate less on foreign policy and more on domestic issues such as healthcare and deficit reduction. Convinced that advances in digital technology would change fundamentally how Americans did business at home and abroad, Clinton sought to harness the forces of globalization to America's benefit.

For a broad majority of the American people, the last decade of the century offered good times. The stock market soared, unemployment dropped, and more Americans than ever before owned their own homes. But the 1990s were also marked by violence and cultural conflict—the first multiethnic uprising in Los Angeles; domestic terrorism in Oklahoma City; shootings by students at their schools; hate crimes that shocked the nation.

These were also years of political volatility and divisions. From the first days of Clinton's presidency, conservative Republicans blocked the Democrats' legislative programs. With a conservative agenda of limited government and "family values"—spelled out in his "Contract with America"—House minority whip Newt Gingrich led a "Republican Revolution" that routed Democrats in the 1994 midterm elections. But Republicans overestimated their power, alienating many voters by forcing the federal government to shut down during the winter of 1995–1996 in a standoff over the federal budget, and Clinton was reelected in 1996. However, scandal plagued the Clinton White House, and in 1999 Clinton was impeached by the House of Representatives, which alleged that he had committed perjury and obstructed justice. Clinton survived the crisis; the Senate failed to convict him, and his popularity figures remained high. But his ability to lead the nation was compromised, and his presidency tarnished.

Clinton's successor, George W. Bush, successful in an extremely close and controversial election, struggled to find his footing in the early months. But the 9/11 attacks galvanized him as he declared a "war on terrorism." In so doing, he committed his administration and the nation to a complex and dangerous campaign of undefined scope and duration. Twice within eighteen months, Bush ordered U.S. forces into large-scale military action, first in Afghanistan where Al Qaeda had its headquarters at the blessing of the ruling Taliban regime, then in Iraq to oust the government of Saddam Hussein. Both operations went well, militarily, as the Taliban and the Iraqi government were quickly beaten. Al Qaeda, however, did not cease being a threat, and Iraq endured postwar instability. At home, Bush enjoyed high approval ratings, despite weak economic figures and a ballooning budget deficit. Bush had declared his a "war presidency," and Americans, following the pattern of many previous wars, rallied around the flag and around the president. ■

Social Strains and New Political Directions

Though the 1990s would be remembered as an era of relative peace and prosperity, the decade did not start that way. Stories on the evening news portrayed a divided and troubled nation. Scourges of drugs, homelessness, and crime plagued America's cities. Racial tensions had worsened; the gulf between rich and poor grown more pronounced. The economy, slowing since 1989, had tipped into recession. Public disillusion with political leaders ran strong, but members of an otherwise ineffective and scandal-ridden Congress had voted themselves a pay raise. As the 1992 presidential election year began, Americans were frustrated and looking for a change.

The racial tensions that troubled the nation erupted in Los Angeles in the spring of 1992. Some people called

VIOLENCE IN LOS ANGELES

the violence that began on April 29 in South Central L.A. a riot; others labeled it a rebellion. Like most such outbreaks of violence, there was an immediate cause. A jury (with no African American members) had acquitted four white police officers charged with beating a black man, Rodney King, who had fled a pursuing police car at speeds exceeding 110 miles per hour. A bystander captured the beating on videotape, and CNN, the new twenty-four-hour news network, replayed it so frequently that CNN's vice president referred to the footage as "wallpaper." Thus the local event became a national story, the beating a symbol of continuing racism in American society. Within hours of the verdict, fires were burning in South Central.

The roots of this violence, however, went deeper. Well-paid jobs had disappeared from the area in the deindustrialization of the 1970s and 1980s, as Firestone, Goodyear, and Bethlehem Steel—along with more than a hundred other manufacturing and industrial plants—shut their doors. By the early 1990s, almost a third of South Central residents lived below the poverty line—a rate 75 percent higher than for the city as a whole.

Tensions increased as new immigrants sought a foothold in the area—Latino immigrants from Mexico and Central America who competed with African American residents for scarce jobs; Korean immigrants trying to establish small businesses such as grocery stores. Outside the legitimate economy, the 40 Crips (an African American gang) and the 18th Street gang (Latino) struggled over control of territory in South Central as the crack epidemic further decimated the neighborhood and the homicide rate soared. The police did not succeed in controlling gang violence, but the tactics they used in that attempt alienated neighborhood residents. Relations between African Americans and Korean immigrants were especially strained. Many African American and Latino residents saw high prices in Korean-owned shops as exploitation and claimed that shopkeepers treated them disrespectfully, while Korean shopkeepers complained of frequent shoplifting, robberies, even beatings.

The violence in Los Angeles (what the Korean community called Sa-I-Gu, or 4-29, for the date it began) left at least fifty-three people dead, some victims of random violence, some targeted because of their race or ethnicity, some killed by law enforcement, a few victims of accidents in the overwhelming chaos. Almost a billion dollars in property was destroyed, including twenty-three hundred stores owned by Koreans or Korean Americans.

More than sixteen thousand people were arrested, half of them Latinos, many of them recent immigrants.

Americans were shocked by the events in L.A. They were also increasingly worried about the economy. During

ECONOMIC TROUBLES AND THE 1992 ELECTION

the Bush administration, the economy had grown slowly or not at all, the worst showing since the Great Depression of the 1930s. Some city and state governments faced bankruptcy. In 1978, California's Proposition 13—the first in a series of "tax revolts" across the nation—had cut property taxes while the population boomed, and the state government, out of money in mid-1992, paid its workers and bills in IOUs. California was not alone; thirty states were in financial trouble in the early 1990s. Many businesses, deeply burdened with debt, closed down or cut back. By 1992 several million Americans had joined the unemployment rolls. Factory employment was at its lowest level since the recession of 1982, and corporate downsizing meant that well-educated white-collar workers were losing jobs as well. In 1991 median household incomes hit the most severe decline since the 1973 recession; in 1992, the number of poor people in America reached the highest level since 1964. "The recession that won't go away," *Newsweek* reported in November 1991, "has average Americans spooked and politicians running scared."

As economic woes continued, President Bush's approval rating fell—down to half its high point of 91 percent after the Persian Gulf War. Americans seized on a news story about the president's amazed reaction to a grocery store price scanner—even though Bush was admiring the prototype for a new scanning mechanism at a trade fair and not encountering a supermarket scanner for the first time—as evidence that the president was out of touch with the everyday lives and problems of American citizens. Despite the credit Bush gained for foreign policy—the end of the Cold War and the quick victory in the Gulf War—economic woes and a lack of what he once called the "vision thing" left him vulnerable in the 1992 presidential election.

Democratic nominee Bill Clinton, the governor of Arkansas, offered a profound contrast to George Bush. Clinton's campaign headquarters bore signs with the four-word reminder: "It's the economy, stupid." In a town-hall-format presidential debate, a woman asked how the economic troubles had affected each candidate, and Clinton moved from behind the podium to ask her, "Tell me how it's affected you again? You know people who've lost their jobs and lost their homes?" George Bush was caught on camera looking at his watch.

During a 1992 debate, Republican candidate and current president George Bush checked his watch while Democratic candidate Bill Clinton empathized with an audience member about economic hard times. The Democratic National Convention had used the refrain, "They just don't get it!" to attack the Republican administration; George Bush seemed to play into their hands. Reform Party candidate Ross Perot sits in the background.   (Wide World Photos, Inc.)

Third-party candidate Ross Perot, a Texas billionaire, was certainly insulated by his vast fortune from the everyday problems of most Americans. However, his appeals to common sense and his folksy populism (he announced on a TV call-in show that he would run for president if voters in all fifty states put his name on the ballot) attracted many who were fed up with politics-as-usual in Washington.

On election day, Americans denied George Bush a second term. Ross Perot claimed almost 20 percent of the popular vote—the highest percentage for a third-party candidate in eighty years—but did not carry a single state. Clinton and his running mate, Al Gore, with 43 percent of the popular vote, nevertheless swept all of New England, the West Coast, and much of the industrial Midwest, even making inroads into the South and drawing "Reagan Democrats" back to the fold. The American people were voting for a change, and discontent with the status quo carried over to congressional elections. Though the Democrats remained in control of both houses, incumbents did not fare well. The 103rd Congress had 110 new representatives and 11 new senators. Many of the first-term members of Congress were—like Clinton—baby boomers in their forties.

Bill Clinton was one of the most paradoxical presidents in American history. A journalist described him in a 1996 story for the *New York Times* as "one of the biggest, most talented, articulate, intelligent, open, colorful characters ever to inhabit the White House," while noting that Clinton "can also be an undisciplined, fumbling, obtuse, defensive, self-justifying rogue. . . . He is breathtakingly bright while capable of doing really dumb things." Clinton was a larger-than-life figure, a born politician from a small town called Hope who had wanted to be president most of his life. In college at Georgetown University in Washington, D.C., during the 1960s he'd protested the Vietnam War and (like many of his generation) had maneuvered to keep himself from being sent to Vietnam. Clinton had won a Rhodes scholarship to Oxford, earned his law degree from Yale, and returned to his home state of Arkansas, where he was elected governor in 1978 at the age of thirty-two.

WILLIAM JEFFERSON CLINTON

In 1975, Clinton had married Hillary Rodham, whom he met when they were both law students at Yale. Rodham Clinton, who made Law Review at Yale (an honor not shared by her husband), was the first First Lady to have a significant career of her own during her married life, and she spoke of balancing her commitments to her professional life with those to her husband and their daughter, Chelsea. Though Clinton boasted during the campaign that his slogan might be "Buy one, get one free," Rodham Clinton was quickly attacked by conservatives and anti-feminists. After she told a hostile interviewer, "I suppose I could have stayed home and baked cookies and had teas. But what I decided to do was pursue my profession, which I entered before my husband was in public life," the *New York Post* called her "a buffoon, an insult to most women."

Politically, Bill Clinton was a "new Democrat." He, along with other members of the new Democratic Leadership Council, advocated a more centrist—though still socially progressive—position for the Democratic

A NEW DEMOCRAT'S PROMISE AND PITFALLS

Party. Clinton and his colleagues asked whether large government bureaucracies were still appropriate tools for addressing social problems in modern America. They emphasized private-sector economic development rather than public jobs programs, focusing on job training and other policies they believed would promote opportunity, not dependency. They championed a global outlook in both foreign policy and economic development. Finally, they emphasized an ethic of "mutual responsibility" and "inclusiveness." Some Democrats found Clinton's policies too conservative. However, the political right attacked Clinton with vehemence unmatched since the attacks on Franklin Roosevelt's New Deal, and the political struggles of the 1990s were exceptionally partisan and rancorous.

Clinton began his presidency with a great sense of promise. "Profound and powerful forces are shaking and remaking our world," he proclaimed in his inaugural address. "Well, my fellow citizens, this is our time. Let us embrace it." Clinton plunged into an ambitious program of reform and revitalization, beginning with his goal of appointing a cabinet that "looks like America" in all its diversity. But almost immediately he ran into trouble. Republicans, determined not to allow Clinton the traditional "honeymoon" period, maneuvered him into fulfilling a campaign pledge to end the ban on gays in the military before he had secured congressional or widespread military support. Amidst great public controversy, Clinton finally accepted a "don't ask, don't tell" compromise that alienated liberals and conservatives, the gay community and the military.

Clinton's major goal upon taking office was to make healthcare affordable and accessible for all Americans, including the millions who had no insurance coverage. But special interests mobilized to oppose the reforms: the insurance industry worried about lost profits; the business community feared higher taxes to support the uninsured; the medical community worried about more regulation, lower government reimbursement rates, and reduced healthcare quality. The administration's healthcare task force, co-chaired by Hillary Rodham Clinton, could not create a political coalition strong enough to defeat these forces. Within a year, the centerpiece of Clinton's fledgling presidency had failed.

Early defeats were exacerbated by persistent scandal. Rumors of Clinton's past marital infidelities continued to circulate. The suicide of Vincent Foster, deputy White House counsel and close friend of the Clintons, spurred wild theories of murder and conspiracy. By December

1993, Republicans were calling for a special prosecutor to investigate the Clintons' involvement in Whitewater, a private Arkansas land deal that figured in one of the savings-and-loan scandals of the 1980s. In January 1994, under strong political pressure, Attorney General Janet Reno named a special prosecutor to investigate these allegations.

With Clinton beleaguered, new-style Republicans seized the chance to challenge the new Democrat. Standing on the steps of the U.S. Capitol in September 1994, shortly before the midterm congressional elections, more than three hundred Republican candidates for the House of Representatives proclaimed their endorsement of the "Contract with America," a list of ten policy proposals the Republicans pledged themselves to pass. Developed under the leadership of the conservative representative from Georgia, Newt Gingrich, the "Contract" promised "the end of government that is too big, too intrusive, and too easy with the public's money [and] the beginning of a Congress that respects the values and shares the faith of the American family." It included calls for a balanced-budget amendment to the Constitution, reduction of the capital gains tax, a two-year limit on welfare payments (with payments prohibited for unmarried mothers under eighteen), and increased defense spending.

THE "REPUBLICAN REVOLUTION"

In the midterm elections, the Republican Party mobilized socially conservative voters to score one of the most smashing victories in American political history. Republicans took control of both houses of Congress for the first time since 1954 and made huge gains in state legislatures and governorships. Gingrich was rewarded by being made Speaker of the House, and Bob Dole of Kansas became majority leader of the Senate. Ideological passions ran high, and the Republicans launched a counterrevolution to reverse more than sixty years of federal dominance and to dismantle the welfare state.

The Republicans of the 104th Congress, however, miscalculated. Though many Americans applauded the idea of cutting government spending, they opposed cuts to most specific programs, including Medicare and Medicaid, education and college loans, highway construction, farm subsidies, veterans' benefits, and Social Security. Republicans made a bigger mistake when they issued President Clinton an ultimatum on the federal budget. Clinton refused to accept their terms; Republicans refused to pass a continuing resolution to provide interim funding; and the government was forced to suspend all nonessential action during the winter of 1995–1996. An angry public blamed the Republicans.

Such struggles showed Clinton's resolve, but they also led him to make compromises that moved American politics to the right. For example, Clinton signed the 1996 Personal Responsibility and Work Opportunity Act, a welfare reform act that eliminated the provision in the 1935 Social Security Act guaranteeing cash assistance for poor children (Aid to Families with Dependent Children). Instead, each state received a lump sum of federal money to design and run its own "welfare-to-work" programs. The law mandated that heads of families on welfare must find work within two years—though states could exempt up to 20 percent of recipients—and limited welfare benefits to five years over an individual's lifetime. It also made many legal immigrants ineligible for welfare. The Telecommunications Act of 1996, signed by Clinton, reduced diversity in America's media by permitting companies to own more television and radio stations.

POLITICAL COMPROMISE AND THE ELECTION OF 1996

Clinton and Gore were reelected in 1996 (defeating Republican Bob Dole and Reform Party candidate Ross Perot), in part because Clinton stole some of the conservatives' thunder. He declared that "the era of big government is over" and invoked family values, a centerpiece of the Republican campaign. Sometimes Clinton's actions were true compromises with conservative interests; other times he attempted to reclaim issues from the conservatives, as when he redefined family values as "fighting for the family-leave law or the assault-weapons ban or . . . trying to keep tobacco out of the hands of kids." In this election, however, the Democrats had two other major advantages. First was the gender gap: women, concerned about issues such as health insurance, daycare for children, and education, were much more likely than men to vote Democratic. And the American economy was strong. Despite scandal and gridlock and ideological chasms that divided politicians and the American people alike, Clinton's election-year promise to "build a bridge to the future" seemed plausible in a time of increasing prosperity.

"The New Economy" and Globalization

*J*ust how much credit Clinton deserved for the improved economic figures in mid-decade is a matter of debate. Presidents typically get too much blame when the economy struggles and too much credit when times are good. The roots of the 1990s boom were in the 1970s, when American corporations began investing in new technologies, retooling plants to become more energy-efficient, and cutting labor costs. Specifically,

■ President Bill Clinton suffered political repudiation in the Republican sweep of Congress in 1994. But two years later his popularity was on the upswing. Here he and Hillary Clinton and Vice President Al Gore (with wife Tipper) celebrate their renomination at the 1996 Democratic National Convention in Chicago. (Wide World Photos, Inc.)

companies reduced the influence of organized labor by moving operations, some to the South and West, where unions were weak, and some out of the United States entirely, to countries such as China and Mexico, where labor was cheap and pollution controls were lax.

Even more important than the restructuring of existing corporations was the emergence of a powerful new sector of the economy associated with digital technology. The rapid development of what came to be called "information technology"—computers, fax machines, cellular phones, and the Internet—had a huge economic impact beginning in the 1980s and accelerating in the 1990s. New companies and industries sprang up, seemingly overnight, many headquartered in the "Silicon Valley" near San Francisco. By the second half of the 1990s, the Forbes list of the Four Hundred Richest People in America was replete with founders of high-tech companies, among them Bill Gates of Microsoft, Michael Dell of Dell Computer, and Larry Ellison of Oracle. Gates became the wealthiest person in the world, his worth approaching $100 billion, as his company produced the software for operating most personal computers. The high-tech industries, which together employed hundreds of thousands of people, had considerable spillover effects on the broader economy, generating improved productivity, new jobs, and sustained economic growth.

DIGITAL REVOLUTION

At the heart of this technological revolution was the microprocessor. First introduced in 1970 by Intel, the microprocessor miniaturized the central processing unit of a computer, meaning small machines could now perform calculations that hitherto only large machines could do. In the next decades the power of these integrated circuits increased by a factor of seven thousand. Computing chores that took a week in the early 1970s by 2000 took one minute, while the cost of storing one megabyte of information, or enough for a 320-page book, fell from more than $5,000 in 1975 to 17 cents in 1999. The implications for business were enormous.

Analysts dubbed this technology-driven sector "The New Economy," and it would have emerged whether or not Bill Clinton had won the White House. Yet Clinton and his advisers had some responsibility for the dramatic upturn that occurred on their watch. Taking office as the U.S. budget deficit reached more than $500 billion, they made deficit reduction a top priority. It was a risky move, politically, as it meant delaying or abandoning programs Clinton had promised during the campaign—most notably a middle-class tax cut—but White House officials concluded the risk was worth taking: if the deficit could be brought under control, interest rates would be re-

duced and the economy would rebound. And that's what happened. The budget deficit started to come down (by 1997 it had been erased), a development that lowered interest rates, which in turn helped boost investment. Stock prices soared to unprecedented levels and the gross national product rose by an average of 3.5 to 4 percent per year.

Clinton perceived early on that the technology revolution would shrink the world and make it more interconnected. He was convinced that, with the demise of Soviet communism, capitalism was spreading around the globe—if not full-blown capitalism, at least the introduction of market forces, freer trade, and widespread deregulation. The triumph of capitalism amounted to a globalization of business, and Clinton and his economic advisers were certain that international trade and investment would play a much larger role in America's economic life than ever before.

GLOBALIZATION OF BUSINESS

Globalization was not a new phenomenon—arguably, it had been under way for a century—but now it had unprecedented momentum. The journalist Thomas L. Friedman asserted that the post–Cold War world was "the age of globalization," characterized by the integration of markets, finance, and technologies. U.S. officials agreed, and they strove to lower trade and investment barriers, completing the North American Free Trade Agreement (NAFTA) with Canada and Mexico in 1993, and in 1994 concluding the Uruguay Round of the General Agreement on Tariffs and Trade (GATT), which lowered tariffs significantly for the seventy member nations that accounted for about 80 percent of world trade. The administration also endorsed the creation, in 1995, of the World Trade Organization (WTO), to administer and enforce agreements made at the Uruguay Round. In a sign of how important trade had become to the administration's foreign agenda, the president formed a National Economic Council to complement the National Security Council and established a "war room" in the Commerce Department to promote trade missions around the world.

Multinational corporations were the hallmark of this global economy. By 2000 there were 63,000 parent companies worldwide and 690,000 foreign affiliates, as well as a large number of interfirm arrangements. Many corporations were truly international, with offices around the world and production in several countries. The Nike Corporation, for example, subcontracted production of its sports shoes to whichever developing countries had the lowest labor costs; the Gap did the same for its clothing and accessories. Such arrangements created a "new international division of labor" and generated a boom in

■ Protesting that the World Trade Organization (WTO) possessed the dangerous power to
challenge any nation's environmental laws if the WTO deemed them barriers to trade,
chanting demonstrators marched in the streets of Seattle on November 30, 1999. Critics of
the WTO have claimed that sea turtles and dolphins have already been victimized by the
WTO. Demonstrators identified the WTO as an example of globalization gone wrong. The
WTO meeting went on, but the results proved meager because nations could not agree on
rules governing dumping, subsidies for farm goods, genetically altered foods, and lower
tariffs on high-tech goods.   (Paul Joseph Brown/*Seattle Post-Intelligencer*)

world exports, which, at $5.4 trillion in 1998, had doubled in two decades. U.S. exports climbed steadily, reaching $680 billion in 1998, but imports rose even higher, to $907 billion in the same year (for a trade deficit of $227 billion). Sometimes the multinationals directly impacted foreign policy, as when Clinton in 1995 extended full diplomatic recognition to Vietnam partly in response to pressure from corporations such as Coca-Cola, Citigroup, General Motors, and United Airlines that wanted to enter the emerging market in the former U.S. adversary.

While the administration promoted open markets, critics became more numerous and vocal as the decade progressed. Labor unions argued that free-trade agreements exacerbated the trade deficit and often harmed workers by exporting jobs from the advanced to the less developed nations. Average real wages

CRITICS OF GLOBALIZATION

for American workers declined steadily after 1973, from $320 per week to $260 by the mid-1990s, a drop labor leaders blamed on the inability of laid-off workers in import-competing industries to find jobs at their previous pay. Other critics extended this argument to the global level, maintaining that globalization was widening the gap between rich and poor countries, creating a mass of "slave laborers" in poor countries who endured working conditions that would never be tolerated in the West. Environmentalists charged that globalization exported not merely jobs but also pollution and toxic wastes into countries unprepared to deal with them, and warned of increased loss of biodiversity and the depletion of natural resources the world over. Still other critics warned that the power of multinational corporations and the global financial markets threatened both national sovereignty and traditional cultures.

Antiglobalization fervor reached a peak in the fall of 1999, when WTO ministers met in Seattle to plan a new set of world trade negotiations called the Millennium Round. Tens of thousands of protesters took to the streets and effectively shut down the meeting. Hundreds were arrested. In the months that followed, there were smaller but sizable protests at meetings of the International Monetary Fund (IMF), which controls international credit and exchange rates, and the World Bank, which issues funds for development projects in numerous countries. In July 2001, some fifty thousand demonstrators descended on Genoa, Italy, to protest a meeting of the IMF and World Bank. Clashes with police resulted in one death and hundreds of injuries. That same month, twenty-five thousand marched and shouted antiglobalization slogans during a European Union leadership gathering in Göteborg, Sweden.

Activists also targeted individual corporations such as the Gap, Starbucks, Nike, and, especially, McDonald's,

■ McDonald's restaurants circled the globe by the early twenty-first century, exemplifying the globalization of American culture. This Ukrainian woman in Kiev seems to enjoy both her hamburger and a conversation with the human symbol of the fast-food chain, Ronald McDonald. (Wide World Photos, Inc.)

TARGET: McDONALD'S

which by 1995 was serving 30 million customers a day in some twenty thousand franchises in over one hundred countries. Critics assailed the company's slaughterhouse techniques, its alleged exploitation of low-skilled workers, and its high-fat menu, as well as its role in a global culture they denounced as increasingly homogeneous and sterile, a so-called McWorld. Starting in 1996 and continuing for the next six years, McDonald's endured hundreds of often-violent protests, including bombings in Rome, Prague, London, Macao, Rio de Janeiro, and Jakarta. At the 2001 World Economic Forum in Davos, Switzerland, two thousand anti-free-trade demonstrators broke store windows and smashed car windshields at a local McDonald's.

Others decried both the violence and the underlying arguments of the antiglobalization campaigners. True, some economists noted, statistics showed that global inequality had grown in recent years. But if one included quality-of-life measurements such as literacy and health, global inequality had actually declined. Even in countries where increasing inequality did coincide with a period of globalization, they added, it could not be concluded that open markets were to blame. In the United States, some studies found, wage and job losses for workers were caused not primarily by globalization factors such as imports, production outsourcing, and immigration, but by technological change that made production processes more efficient and reduced the need for unskilled labor. Other researchers saw no evidence that governments' sovereignty had been seriously compromised as a result of globalization or that there was a "race to the bottom" in environmental standards. For them, the essential point was incontrovertible: poor countries that increased their economic openness enjoyed higher growth rates, while no country had prospered by turning its back on the world economy.

The notion of a homogeneous global culture also found its share of critics. McDonald's, they said, supposedly a prime mover of "McWorld," tailored its menu and operating practices to local tastes. And although American movies, TV programs, music, computer software, and other "intellectual property" often dominated world markets in the 1990s—the TV soap opera *The Young and the Restless* became popular in New Delhi, for example, while people in Warsaw watched *Dr. Quinn, Medicine Woman*—foreign competition also made itself felt in America. Millions of American children were gripped by the Japanese fad game Pokemon, and if satellite television established a worldwide following for Michael Jordan and the Chicago Bulls, it did the same for soccer's David Beckham and Manchester United. An influx of foreign players added to the international appeal of both the National Basketball Association and major league baseball, while in the National Hockey League some 20 percent of players by the late 1990s hailed from Europe.

Yet if it was erroneous to glibly equate globalization with Americanization, it remained true that the United States occupied a uniquely powerful position on the world stage. This was true in the global economy and in popular culture, and it was true in international diplomacy. The demise of the Soviet Union had created a one-superpower world, in which the United States stood far above other powers in terms of political and military might. The "unipolar moment" was the phrase one commentator used in urging an aggressive U.S. posture. Yet in his first term Clinton was far more wary in handling the traditional aspects of foreign policy—great-power diplomacy, arms control, regional disputes—than in facilitating American cultural and trade expansion. He was deeply suspicious of foreign military involvements. The Vietnam debacle had taught him that the American public had limited patience for wars lacking clear-cut national interest, a lesson he found confirmed by George Bush's failure to gain lasting political strength from the Gulf War victory.

CLINTON'S DIPLOMACY

This mistrust of foreign interventions was cemented for Clinton by the difficulties he inherited from Bush in Somalia. In 1992, Bush had sent U.S. Marines to the East African nation as part of a U.N. effort to ensure that humanitarian supplies reached starving Somalis. But in the summer of 1993, when Americans came under deadly attack from forces loyal to a local warlord, Clinton withdrew U.S. troops. Stung by the Somalia experience, Clinton chose not to intervene in Rwanda, where in 1994 the majority Hutus butchered 800,000 of the minority Tutsis in a brutal civil war.

That Somalia and Rwanda were on the policy agenda at all testified to the growing importance of humanitarian concerns in post–Cold War U.S. policy. Many high-level administration officials argued for using America's unmatched power to contain ethnic hatreds, support human rights, and promote democracy around the world. Clinton in principle agreed, but he insisted on moving cautiously, as when instability threatened in nearby Haiti. In 1991 a military coup had overthrown the democratically elected president, Jean-Bertrand Aristide. After the succeeding rulers imposed a harsh new system, tens of thousands of

CRISIS IN HAITI

Haitians fled in boats for U.S. territory, spawning an immigration crisis. After swinging between tough talk and indecision, Clinton sent former president Jimmy Carter to Haiti to negotiate an arrangement that would facilitate Aristide's return to power.

The program of humanitarian intervention faced its most severe test in the Balkans, which erupted in a series of ethnic wars. Bosnian Muslims, Serbs, and Croats were soon killing one another by the hundreds of thousands. Clinton, critical of Europe's reluctance to act in its own backyard, talked tough against Serbian aggression and atrocities in Bosnia-Herzegovina, especially the Serbs' cruel "ethnic cleansing" of Muslims through massacres and rape camps. On occasion he ordered U.S. airpower to strike Serb positions, but he put primary emphasis on diplomacy. In late 1995, after American diplomats brokered an agreement among the belligerents for a new multiethnic state in Bosnia-Herzegovina, a fragile peace took hold.

But Yugoslav president Slobodan Milosevic did not stop the anti-Muslim and anti-Croat fervor. When Serb forces moved to violently rid Serbia's southern province of Kosovo of its majority ethnic Albanians, Clinton was pressed to intervene on a large scale. Initially, he was reluctant; the ghosts of Vietnam were ever present in the Oval Office deliberations. But reports of Serbian atrocities against the Muslim Kosovars and a major refugee crisis generated by the Yugoslavian military action stirred world opinion and finally caused Clinton to act. In 1999, NATO forces led by the United States launched a massive aerial bombardment of Serbia. Milosevic withdrew his brutal military from Kosovo, where U.S. troops joined a U.N. peacekeeping force. That same year, the International War Crimes Tribunal indicted Milosevic and his top aides for atrocities.

KOSOVO WAR

In the Middle East, Clinton took an active role in trying to bring the PLO and Israel together to settle their differences. In September 1993 the PLO's Yasir Arafat and Israel's prime minister Yitzhak Rabin signed an agreement at the White House for Palestinian self-rule in the Gaza Strip and the West Bank's Jericho. The following year Israel signed a peace accord with Jordan, further reducing the chances of another full-scale Arab-Israeli war. Radical anti-Arafat Palestinians, however, continued to stage bloody terrorist attacks on Israelis, while extremist Israelis killed Palestinians and, in November 1995, Rabin himself. Only after American-conducted negotiations and renewed violence in the West Bank did Israel agree in early 1997 to withdraw its forces from the

■ In spring 1999, as NATO bombing raids pounded Serbia (Yugoslavia) and Serb military positions in Kosovo to punish Serbia for killing and displacing ethnic Albanians, the number of Kosovar refugees dramatically increased. Desperate and hungry, they fled to neighboring nations. Here, in a NATO-run refugee camp outside Skopje, Macedonia, U.S. Marines distribute food to some of the 850,000 forced to leave their Kosovo homes.   (Wide World Photos, Inc.)

Palestinian city of Hebron. Thereafter the peace process alternately sagged and spurted.

The same could be said of international efforts to protect the environment, which gathered pace in the 1990s. The Bush administration had opposed many of the provisions of the 1992 Rio de Janeiro Treaty protecting the diversity of plant and animal species and had blocked efforts to draft stricter rules to reduce global warming. Clinton, urged on by Vice President Al Gore, an ardent environmentalist, took a more proactive posture. Most notably, his administration signed the 1997 Kyoto protocol, which aimed to combat emissions of carbon dioxide and other gases that most scientists believe trap heat in the atmosphere. The treaty required the United States to reduce its emissions by 2012 to 7 percent below its 1990 levels. But Clinton faced strong congressional opposition to the protocol, and he never submitted it for ratification to the Republican-controlled Senate.

ENVIRONMENTAL DIPLOMACY

Far less publicized than the Israeli-Palestinian conflict or the debate over Kyoto was the growing administration

BIN LADEN AND AL QAEDA

concern about the threat to U.S. interests posed by Islamic fundamentalism.

In particular, senior officials worried about the rise of Al Qaeda (Arabic for "the base"), an international terrorist network led by Osama bin Laden that was dedicated to purging Muslim countries of what it saw as the profane influence of the West and installing fundamentalist Islamic regimes.

The son of a Yemen-born construction tycoon in Saudi Arabia, bin Laden had supported the Afghan Mujahidin in their struggle against Soviet occupation. He then founded Al Qaeda and began financing terrorist projects with the fortune he received on his father's death. U.S. officials grew steadily more concerned, particularly as it became clear that bin Laden intended to go after American targets. In 1995, a car bomb in Riyadh killed 7 people, 5 of them Americans. In 1998, simultaneous bombings at the American embassies in Kenya and Tanzania killed 224 people, including 12 Americans. In Yemen in 2000, a small boat laden with explosives hit the destroyer U.S.S. *Cole*, killing 17 American sailors.

Though bin Laden was understood to have masterminded and financed these attacks, he eluded U.S. attempts to apprehend him. In 1998, Clinton approved a plan to assassinate bin Laden at an Al Qaeda camp in Afghanistan, but the attempt failed.

Paradoxes of Prosperity

*D*espite conflicts abroad and partisan struggles in Washington, the majority of Americans experienced the late 1990s as a time of unprecedented peace and prosperity. Fueling Americans' sense of prosperity was the dizzying rise of the stock market. The Dow Jones Industrial Average increased almost twelvefold in the last two decades of the twentieth century. Between 1991 and 1999 alone, it climbed from 3,169 to a high of 11,497 (see Figure 33.1). The booming market benefited the middle class as well as the wealthy, for the mutual

funds created during the 1970s and other new investment vehicles such as 401(k) retirement plans had drawn a majority of Americans into the stock market. In 1952, only 4 percent of American households owned stocks. That percentage soared to almost 60 percent by the year 2000.

As investors watched their investments grow, working Americans also benefited from the economic boom. At the end of the 1990s, the unemployment rate stood at 4.3 percent—the lowest peacetime rate since 1957. Plentiful jobs made it easier for states to implement welfare reform, and welfare rolls were cut almost in half. The standard of living rose for all income groups: both the richest 5 percent and the least well-off 20 percent of American households saw their incomes rise almost 25 percent. But as that meant an average gain of $50,000 for the top 5 percent and only $2,880 for the bottom 20 percent, the gap between rich and poor continued to grow. However, by the end of the decade, more than two-thirds of Americans were homeowners—the highest

Figure 33.1 The American Stock Market

This graph of the Dow Jones Industrial Average, climbing steadily in the bull market of the 1990s, illustrates the great economic expansion of the decade.   (Source: Adapted from Dow Jones & Company.)

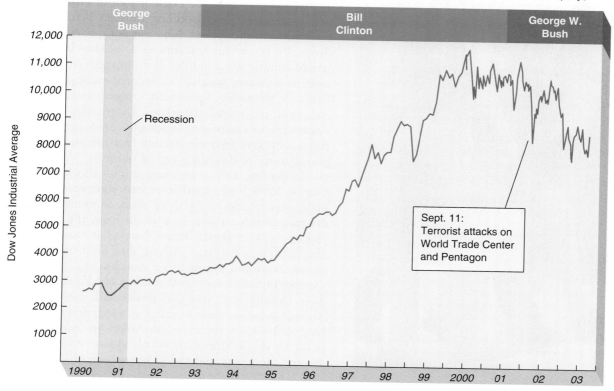

percentage in history. Differences among groups were significant but declining: 52 percent of families earning less than the median income were homeowners in 2000, as were 48 percent of people of color. Other statistics indicated improvements in the nation's health and safety. Teen pregnancy rates began to decline. Infant mortality dropped to the lowest rate in American history. Violent crime decreased; murder rates hit a thirty-year low.

While some of the problems that had plagued the United States began to recede, unexpected new crises shook the nation. On April 19, 1995, 168 children, women, and men were killed in a powerful bomb blast that destroyed the nine-story Alfred P. Murrah Federal Building in downtown Oklahoma City. At first, many thought the bomb had come from abroad, perhaps

OKLAHOMA CITY BOMBING

■ On April 20, 1999, students evacuated Columbine High School in Littleton, Colorado, after two schoolmates went on a shooting rampage, killing twelve students and a teacher before killing themselves. (Wide World Photos, Inc.)

set off by Middle Eastern terrorists. But a charred piece of truck axle located two blocks from the explosion, with the vehicle identification number still legible, proved otherwise. The bomber was Timothy McVeigh, a native-born white American and a veteran of the Persian Gulf War. He sought revenge for the deaths of members of the Branch Davidian religious sect, whom he believed the FBI had deliberately slaughtered in a standoff over firearms charges on that date two years before in Waco, Texas.

In the months that followed, reporters and government investigators discovered networks of militias, tax resisters, and various white-supremacist groups throughout the nation. These groups were united by distrust of the federal government. Many saw federal gun control laws such as the Brady Bill, signed into law in 1993, as a dangerous usurpation of citizens' right to bear arms. Members of these groups believed that the federal government was controlled by "sinister forces," including Zionists, corrupt politicians, cultural elitists, Queen Elizabeth, the Russians, and the United Nations. After McVeigh's act of domestic terrorism these groups lost members but also turned to the new Internet to spread their beliefs.

Other forms of violence also haunted America. On April 20, 1999, eighteen-year-old Eric Harris and seventeen-year-old Dylan Klebold opened fire on classmates and teachers at Columbine High School in Littleton, Colorado, killing thirteen before turning their guns on themselves. No clear reason why two academically successful students in a middle-class suburb would commit mass murder ever emerged. And the Columbine massacre was not an isolated event: students in Paducah, Kentucky; Springfield, Oregon; and Jonesboro, Arkansas, massacred classmates. Disgruntled employees opened fire on coworkers; shootings by U.S. Postal Service employees were frequent enough that the phrase "going postal" came to describe a violent outburst.

VIOLENCE AND HATE CRIMES

In the late 1990s, two hate crimes shocked the nation. In 1998 James Byrd Jr., a forty-nine-year-old black man, was murdered by three white supremacists who dragged him for miles by a chain from the back of a pickup truck in Jasper, Texas. Later that year, Matthew Shepherd, a gay college student, died after being beaten unconscious and left tied to a wooden fence in freezing weather outside Laramie, Wyoming. His killers said they were "humiliated" when he flirted with them at a bar. Though some see these murders as a sign that racism and homophobia remain strong in American society, others point to the horror with which almost all Americans greeted these acts and the growing support for federal legislation against hate crimes as a demonstration of positive change.

Throughout the Clinton years, scandals plagued the White House. Bill Clinton's character was often the issue, and jokes about Clinton's sexual infi-

SCANDAL IN THE CLINTON WHITE HOUSE

delities were a staple of late-night television. But as one reporter noted, "If Ronald Reagan was the Teflon President, then Bill Clinton is the Timex President. He takes his lickings and keeps on ticking."

The independent counsel's office would eventually spend $72 million investigating allegations of wrongdoing by Hillary and Bill Clinton. Independent counsel Kenneth Starr, a conservative Republican and former judge, was originally charged with investigating Whitewater, the Arkansas real estate deal in which the Clintons had invested during the 1970s. He never found any evidence that the Clintons had engaged in illegal activities. However, Starr did find evidence that the president had committed perjury.

Early in Clinton's presidency, former Arkansas state employee Paula Jones had brought charges of sexual harassment against the president. Clinton denied the charges, which were eventually dropped. But when asked during questioning before a grand jury whether he had engaged in sexual relations with a twenty-two-year-old White House intern, Monica Lewinsky, Clinton denied that allegation as well. Kenneth Starr discovered evidence proving that the president had lied.

When confronted with these charges, Clinton angrily declared: "I want to say one thing to the American people. I want you to listen to me. I'm going to say this again. I did not have sexual relations with that woman, Miss Lewinsky." In fact, Clinton had at least ten sexual encounters, as well as fifteen "phone sex" conversations, with Lewinsky. Starr produced evidence of the sexual relationship, including phone conversations recorded without Lewinsky's knowledge by her supposed friend Linda Tripp. Most infamously, Starr obtained DNA evidence against the president: a navy blue dress of Lewinsky's, stained with Clinton's semen.

In a 445-page report to Congress, Starr outlined eleven possible grounds for impeachment of the president,

IMPEACHMENT

accusing Clinton of lying under oath, obstruction of justice, witness tampering, and abuse of power. On December 19, 1998, the House voted on four articles of impeachment against Clinton; largely along party lines, the House passed two of the articles, one alleging that the president had committed perjury in his grand jury testimony, the other that he had obstructed justice. With the

House vote, Clinton became only the second president—and the first in 130 years—to face a trial in the Senate, which has the constitutional responsibility to decide (by two-thirds vote) whether to remove a president from office.

Despite such evidence against Clinton, the American people did not want him removed from office. Polls showed large majorities approved of the president's job performance, even as many condemned his personal behavior. And many did not believe the president's wrongdoing rose to the level of "high crimes and misdemeanors" (normally acts such as treason) required by the Constitution as grounds for impeachment. In the 1998 congressional election, voters expressed their opposition to the partisan drive for impeachment by reducing the Republican majority in the House to just ten seats. The Republican-controlled Senate, responding at least in part to popular opinion, voted against the charge of perjury 55-45, and voted 50-50 to clear Clinton of obstructing justice. The vote, while close, did not approach the two-thirds majority required for conviction. For his part, Clinton appeared contrite, saying that he was "profoundly sorry . . . for what I did and said to trigger these events and the great burden they have imposed on the Congress and the American people."

Clinton, of course, bears responsibility for his own actions. However, how those actions became grounds for

POLITICAL PARTISANSHIP, THE MEDIA, AND CELEBRITY CULTURE

impeachment, with the explicit sexual details contained in the Starr Report circulated by Internet around the world, is part of a larger story. Clinton was not the first president to engage in illicit sex. President Kennedy had numerous and well-known sexual affairs, including one with a nineteen-year-old intern. But after the Watergate scandals of the early 1970s, the mass media were no longer willing to turn a blind eye to presidential misconduct. The fiercely competitive twenty-four-hour news networks that began with CNN in 1980 relied on scandal, spectacle, and crisis to lure viewers. Public officials also contributed to the blurring of lines between public and private, celebrity and statesman. Clinton, for example, had appeared on MTV during his first campaign and answered a question about his preference in underwear (boxers).

The partisan political wars of the 1990s created a take-no-prisoners climate in which no politician's missteps would be overlooked. As fallout from the Clinton impeachment, both Republican Speaker of the House Newt Gingrich and his successor, Robert Livingston, resigned when faced with evidence of their own extramarital affairs. Finally, as former Clinton aide Sidney Blumenthal writes, the impeachment struggle was about more than presidential perjury and sexual infidelity. It was part of the "culture wars" that divided the American people: "a monumental battle over very large political questions about the Constitution, about cultural mores and the position of women in American society, and about the character of the American people. It was, ultimately, a struggle about the identity of the country."

Clinton's specific legislative accomplishments during his two terms in office were modest but included programs that made life easier for American families. The Family and Medical Leave Act guaranteed 91 million workers the right to take time off to care for ailing relatives or their newborn children. The Health Insurance Portability and Accountability Act ensured that when Americans changed jobs, they would not lose health insurance because of preexisting medical conditions. Government became more efficient: the federal government operated with 365,000 fewer employees by the end of Clinton's term, and Vice President Gore led an initiative that eliminated sixteen thousand pages of federal regulations. Clinton created national parks and monuments that protected 3.2 million acres of American land and made unprecedented progress cleaning up toxic waste dumps throughout the nation.

CLINTON'S LEGISLATIVE RECORD

Going into the 2000 presidential election, Vice President Al Gore seemed to be the favorite. The son of a prominent senator from Tennessee, Gore had grown up

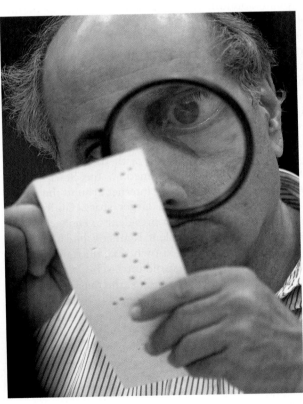

■ A ballot from the 2000 presidential election is examined in Florida. Though Democratic candidate Al Gore won the U.S. popular vote, electoral college victory depended on the outcome in Florida, where approximately 180,000 ballots (many of them cast on old punch-card voting machines) were decertified as not indicating a clear choice of presidential candidate. (Alan Diaz/AP/Wide World Photos, Inc.)

Map 33.1   Presidential Election, 2000

Democratic candidate Al Gore won the popular vote, but George W. Bush succeeded in gaining electoral victory by four votes. Among white males, Bush ran extremely well, while Gore won a majority of minority and women voters. Ralph Nader's Green Party won less than 3 percent of the national vote, but his votes in Florida may have detracted from the Gore tally, helping Bush win the critical electoral votes. (Source: Carol Berkin, et al., *Making America,* Third Edition. Used by permission of Houghton Mifflin Company.)

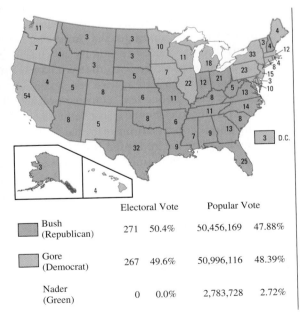

	Electoral Vote		Popular Vote	
Bush (Republican)	271	50.4%	50,456,169	47.88%
Gore (Democrat)	267	49.6%	50,996,116	48.39%
Nader (Green)	0	0.0%	2,783,728	2.72%

THE BUSH-GORE RACE

with politics. After graduating cum laude from Harvard in 1969, he enlisted in the army despite his reservations about the war, and served in Vietnam. Gore was elected to the House and to the Senate, serving six terms, and wrote a well-received book on global environmental issues. In the Clinton administration, Gore had played a greater role than any vice president in history, and after eight years of prosperity and relative peace, he had a strong platform on which to run. Gore, however, failed to inspire voters. Earnest and highly intelligent, he appeared to many as a well-informed policy wonk rather than a charismatic leader.

Gore's Republican opponent was best known nationally as the son of George H. W. Bush, the forty-first president of the United States. An indifferent student, George W. Bush had graduated from Yale in 1968 and pulled strings to jump ahead of a one-and-a-half-year waiting list for the Texas Air National Guard, thus avoiding service in Vietnam. After a difficult period, which included a rocky career in the oil business, at the age of forty Bush gave up alcohol and embraced Christianity. His fortunes improved while his father was pres-

ident, and in 1994 he was elected to the first of two terms as governor of Texas.

As a presidential candidate, Bush made up for his limited foreign policy knowledge, often garbled syntax, and lack of interest in the intricacies of public policy with a direct, confident style that connected with many Americans. Unlike Gore, who peppered his stump speeches with statistics and programmatic initiatives, Bush spoke of his relationship with God and his commitment to conservative social values, styling himself a "compassionate conservative." Supported heavily by prominent Republicans and business leaders, Bush amassed the largest campaign war chest in history ($67 million, compared with Gore's $28 million).

Finally, in 2000, consumer rights activist Ralph Nader ran on the Green Party ticket. Condemning globalization and environmental despoilation, he attacked both Bush and Gore, calling them "Tweedledee and Tweedledum." However, Nader drew support from left-liberal voters who would have been more likely to vote for Gore and so helped tip some districts to Bush.

On election day 2000, Al Gore narrowly won the popular vote (see Map 33.1). But he did not win the presidency.

Figure 33.2 The Gender Gap in American Presidential Elections

The gender gap, or the difference in voting patterns between men and women, was first identified in 1980 by National Organization for Women president Eleanor Smeal, and has been recognized as an important force in American politics ever since. In every presidential election, greater percentages of women than men voted for the Democratic candidate. More women than men—no matter their race or ethnicity, income, level of education, or marital status—voted for Gore than for Bush in the 2000 presidential election.   (Source: Based on data from the Center for American Women and Politics.)

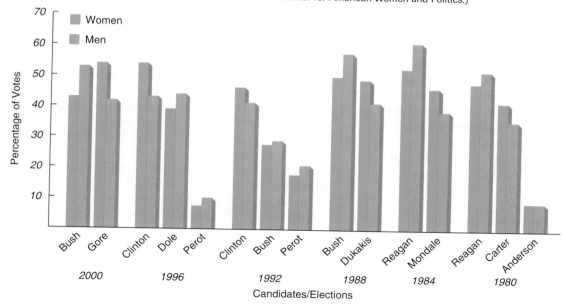

THE CONTESTED ELECTION OF 2000
It all came down to Florida (where Bush's brother Jeb was governor) and its twenty-five electoral votes. At first, television election coverage declared that Gore had won the state. Florida's electoral votes would have given Gore the presidency. But by the early hours of the morning, it was clear that this election would not soon be decided. When the Florida votes were first tallied, Bush narrowly edged out Gore, but by so close a margin that an automatic recount was legally required. Charges and countercharges flew. In several heavily African American counties, tens of thousands of votes were not counted because voters failed to fully dislodge the "chads," or small perforated squares, when punching the old-fashioned paper ballots. Lawyers struggled over whether "hanging chads" (partially detached) and "pregnant chads" (punched but not detached) were sufficient signs of voter intent. In Palm Beach County, many elderly Jewish residents were confused by a poorly designed ballot. Thinking they were selecting Gore, they voted instead for a minor Reform Party candidate, the allegedly anti-Semitic Pat Buchanan. After thirty-six days of confusion, with court cases at the state and federal levels, the Supreme Court voted 5 to 4 along narrowly partisan lines to end the recount process. Florida's electoral votes—and the presidency—went to George Bush.

In the 2000 election, Gore won the West Coast, Northeast, and industrial Midwest. The South, Rocky Mountain West (except New Mexico), and heartland went to Bush. More than 90 percent of black voters selected Gore, as did 63 percent of Latinos and 55 percent of Asian Americans. Bush won 60 percent of the white vote, and, overall, 95 percent of his supporters were white. The gender gap was 12 points: 54 percent of women voted for Gore, as opposed to 42 percent of men (see Figure 33.2). With such divisions, Bush faced a difficult challenge. He had no popular mandate, and the election struggles had further polarized the nation. As Bush waited for the January inaugural, critics and comics began referring to him as the "president-select."

September 11 and the War on Terrorism

In view of the close election and bitter Florida controversy, many believed that Bush would govern from the center. Some also thought he was philosophically centrist, as his father had been, and that he had moved to the right only to ensure turnout among conservative evangelical Christians, who made up an increasingly large part of the Republican base. From the administration's first days, however, Bush governed from the right, arguably farther to the right than any administration of modern times. As the head of the Heritage Foundation, a conservative Washington think tank, enthused, the new team was "more Reaganite than the Reagan administration."

The centerpiece of the Bush agenda was a massive tax cut, to be financed by the predicted budget surplus.

BUSH'S TAX PLAN
"A surplus in tax revenue, after all, means that taxpayers have been overcharged," the president said. "And usually when you've been overcharged, you expect to get something back." Critics replied that a massive cut would wipe out the surplus and that the Bush plan favored the wealthy, but Bush persisted, using his party's control of Congress to push through the largest tax cut in U.S. history—$1.3 trillion. To the dismay of environmentalists, he also reiterated his campaign proposal to drill for oil in America's last wilderness, the Arctic National Wildlife Refuge, and chose a secretary of the interior with close ties to the energy industry and who favored scaling back regulations protecting the environment.

In international affairs, the administration moved swiftly to chart a more unilateralist course. Given America's preponderant power, senior Bush officials reasoned, it did not need the help of others in the international system; accordingly they attached less importance to consultation and cooperation than had the Clinton administration. Soon after taking office, Bush announced that the United States would exit the 1972 Anti-Ballistic Missile Treaty with Russia to develop a National Missile Defense system (forbidden under the treaty) broadly similar to Reagan's "Star Wars" plan. Such a system, Bush said, would protect the United States from missile threats by potentially hostile nations such as North Korea, Iraq, and Iran. The White House also renounced the 1997 Kyoto protocol on controlling global warming and registered opposition to a carefully negotiated protocol to strengthen the 1972 Biological and Toxin Weapons Convention. All three decisions caused consternation in Europe, as did administration's hands-off policy toward the Israeli-Palestinian peace process.

Bush suffered a major setback in May 2001 when Senator James Jeffords of Vermont, a moderate Republican disaffected by the conservative tenor of both the White House and congressional leadership, declared himself an independent. The move shifted control of the Senate to the Democrats, thereby complicating Bush's ability to secure his domestic and foreign agenda. By early September, the press described an administration adrift, a president who did not seem to be enjoying his job. Late-night comedians mercilessly ribbed Bush's bumbling syntax and alleged lack of intelligence, and his public approval rating fell to 51 percent.

Then came September 11. On that sunny Tuesday morning, nineteen hijackers seized control of four commercial jets that had taken off from East Coast airports. At 8:46 A.M. one plane crashed into the 110-story North Tower of the World Trade Center in New York City, causing a huge explosion and a fire. At 9:03 A.M., a second plane flew into the South Tower. In less than two hours, both buildings collapsed, killing thousands of office workers, firefighters, and police officers. At 9:43, the third plane crashed into the Pentagon, leaving a huge hole in its west side. The fourth plane was also headed toward Washington, but several passengers—learning of the World Trade Center attacks through cell-phone conversations—stormed the cockpit; in the scuffle that followed, the plane crashed in Somerset County, Pennsylvania, killing all aboard.

9/11

All told, more than three thousand people died, making this the deadliest act of terrorism in history. Not since the Japanese assault on Pearl Harbor in 1941 had the United States experienced such a devastating attack on its soil. The hijackers—fifteen Saudi Arabians, two Emiratis, one Lebanese, and, leading them, an Egyptian—had ties to Al Qaeda, Osama bin Laden's radical Islamic organization. Some officials in the Clinton and Bush administrations had warned that an attack by Al Qaeda was inevitable: when Clinton's national security adviser met with his successor, Condoleezza Rice, shortly before Bush's inauguration, he told her, "You're going to spend more time during your four years on terrorism generally and Al Qaeda specifically than any issue." Broadly speaking, however, neither administration made counterterrorism a top foreign policy priority.

In an instant, counterterrorism was priority number one. President Bush decided immediately, indeed before 9/11 had become 9/12, to respond with large-scale military force. Al Qaeda operated out of Afghanistan with the blessing of the ruling Taliban, a repressive Islamic fundamentalist group that had gained power in 1996 in the turmoil following the defeat of the Soviet-backed government in 1989. In early October, the United States launched a sustained bombing campaign against Taliban and Al Qaeda positions and sent special operations forces to help a resistance organization based in northern Afghanistan. Within two months, the Taliban

AFGHANISTAN WAR

had been driven from power, though bin Laden as well as top Taliban leaders eluded capture.

As administration officials were quick to acknowledge, the swift military victory did not end the terrorist threat. Bush spoke of a long and difficult struggle that he called a war against evil forces, in which the nations of the world were either with the United States or against it. Some questioned whether a "war on terrorism" could ever be won in a meaningful sense, given that the foe was a nonstate actor weak in the traditional measures of power—territory and governmental power—and with little to lose. A war against such an adversary could have no definable end, observers noted, and they questioned whether Bush, by speaking in such unambiguous terms, was setting himself and the nation up for eventual failure. Most Americans, however, were ready to believe. Stunned by September 11, they experienced a renewed sense of national unity and pride. Flag sales soared, and Bush's approval ratings skyrocketed. Citizenship applications from immigrants rose dramatically.

But the new patriotism had a dark side. White House spokesman Ari Fleischer told Americans that they should "watch what they say, watch what they do." Congress passed the USA PATRIOT Act (Uniting and Strengthening America by Providing Appropriate Tools Required to Intercept and Obstruct Terrorism), making it easier for law enforcement to conduct searches, wiretap telephones, and obtain electronic records on individuals. Attorney General John Ashcroft approved giving FBI agents new powers to monitor the Internet, mosques, and rallies. Civil libertarians charged that the Justice Department had overstepped sensible boundaries, and some judges ruled against the tactics. Yet, according to a June 2002 Gallup poll, 80 percent of Americans were willing to give up some freedoms for security. But polls also showed that Americans did not support restrictions on Muslims. Acts of violence against Muslims and others of Middle Eastern appearance did occur in the aftermath of 9/11, but fewer than many had anticipated and feared.

PATRIOT ACT

In other respects, too, early predictions for the post-9/11 era were not borne out. Despite assertions that the attacks had "forever changed America," the nature and extent of the changes were unclear. Certainly, Americans' complacency about the nation's physical security was shattered. It *could* happen here, not just in military or diplomatic installations overseas. U.S. military superiority might be overwhelming, but the nation was still vulnerable to attacks from people willing to die for their cause.

These were sobering realizations for Americans. In surveys weeks after the attacks, 71 percent of respondents said they felt depressed, and a third said they had trouble sleeping. The figures dropped thereafter, but anxiety remained. The discovery of anthrax-laden letters in several East Coast cities heightened the fears, particularly after post offices and government buildings were closed and five people died. Investigators found no evidence to connect the letters to the 9/11 hijackings, but also no good clues as to who the perpetrator might be, despite conducting more than 5,000 interviews and pursuing hundreds of leads.

Yet continuity was as evident as change. People continued shopping in malls, visiting amusement parks, purchasing cars and homes. Employees still showed up for work, even in skyscrapers, and still gossiped around the lunch table. Though airline bookings dropped significantly in the early weeks (causing severe economic problems for many airlines), people still took to the skies. Some even complained about the new security measures at airports. In Washington, the partisanship that had all but disappeared after 9/11 returned, as Democrats and Republicans sparred over judicial appointments, energy policy, and the proposed new Department of Homeland Security. Approved by Congress in November 2002, the department was designed to coordinate intelligence and consolidate defenses against terrorism. Incorporating parts of eight cabinet departments and twenty-two agencies, it was the first new department since the Department of Veterans Affairs in 1989.

On the economy, too, the two parties disagreed sharply. The months before September 11 had witnessed a collapse of the so-called dot-coms, the Internet companies that had been the darlings of Wall Street in the 1990s. In the course of 2001 some five hundred dot-coms declared bankruptcy or closed, and analysts warned of worse to come. There were other economic warning signs as well, most notably a meager 0.2 percent growth rate in the nation's goods and services for the second quarter of 2001—the slowest growth in eight years. Corporate revenues were down as well.

Economic concerns deepened after 9/11 with a four-day closing of Wall Street and a subsequent sharp drop in stock prices. The week after the markets reopened, the Dow Jones Industrial Average plunged 14.26 percent—the fourth largest weekly drop in percentage terms since 1900. The markets eventually rebounded, but then a major scandal hit the headlines. Enron Corporation, a Houston-based energy company that was one of the largest commodity trading firms in

ENRON COLLAPSE

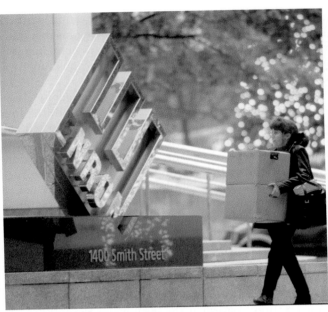

A worker carts away some remains of Enron's once mighty headquarters in downtown Houston. The trademark "tilted-E" sign in the background subsequently fetched $44,000 at an auction held to raise money for creditors. "The reason we bought this was to preserve this business icon," declared the winning bidder, representing a Houston computer store. "It also signifies a lot of sweat, greed, and fraud in business." Among the other items up for bid: stress balls, coffee mugs, and an air hockey table. (Steve Ueckert—Houston *Chronicle*)

the world, filed for bankruptcy. Enron's twenty thousand employees lost billions of dollars in their pension plans while many executives—who had advised the White House on energy policies—allegedly raked in profits, selling their shares before the steep fall in prices. In one year, the price of Enron stock dropped from $85 to less than $1 a share.

The Enron collapse marked the biggest corporate failure in U.S. history, and it generated a Justice Department criminal investigation into its business practices. But although Bush's relationship with Enron was close, going back to his days as Texas governor, the president seemed largely unscathed by the scandal, underscoring just how much his political position had been strengthened by 9/11 and his early responses to it. Despite growing signs of economic weakness, the general absence of a White House domestic agenda, and the failure to capture Osama bin Laden and top Taliban leaders, Bush's approval ratings remained high.

Just how powerful Bush remained became clear in the midterm congressional elections. The GOP retook

GOP MIDTERM GAINS

control of the Senate and added to its majority in the House, a most unusual achievement for a party holding the White House. The Republicans' core message—that a country at war should unite behind the president—resonated with voters. Now the Republicans not only controlled Congress and the White House but held a majority of governorships and could claim to have appointed a majority of Supreme Court justices.

Overseas, the president's standing was not nearly so high. Immediately after September 11, there was an

INTERNATIONAL RESPONSES

outpouring of support from people everywhere. "We are all Americans now," said the French newspaper *Le Monde* the day after the attacks. Moments of silence in honor of the victims were held in many countries, and governments all over the world announced they would cooperate with Washington in the struggle against terrorism. But a year later, attitudes had changed dramatically. Bush's bellicose stance and good-versus-evil terminology had put off many foreign observers from the start, but they initially swallowed their objections. When, however, the president started hinting that America might unilaterally strike Saddam Hussein's Iraq or deal forcefully with North Korea or Iran—the three countries of Bush's "axis of evil"—many allied governments registered strong objections.

At issue was not merely the prospect of a U.S. attack on one of these countries but the underlying rationale that would accompany it. Bush and other top officials were in effect saying that the strategy of containment and deterrence that had guided U.S. foreign policy for more than fifty years was outmoded. In an age of terrorism, they maintained, the United States would not wait for a potential security threat to become real; henceforth, it would strike first. "In the world we have entered, the only path to safety is the path of action and this nation will act," Bush declared. Americans had to be "ready for preemptive action when necessary to defend our liberty and to defend our lives." Critics of the strategy, among them many world leaders, called it recklessly aggressive and contrary to international law, and they wondered what would happen if dictators around the world began claiming the same right of preemption.

But Bush was determined, particularly on Iraq. Several of his top advisers, including Secretary of Defense

REGIME CHANGE IN IRAQ

Donald Rumsfeld and Vice President Dick Cheney, had wanted to oust Saddam Hussein for years, indeed since the

end of the Gulf War in 1991; they now saw an opportunity to fold that objective into the larger war on terrorism. While they argued that a Saddam-free Iraq was essential to U.S. long-term interests in the Middle East, cynics wondered whether the focus on Hussein was intended to deflect attention from the poor economy and the failure to track down bin Laden. In September 2002, Bush challenged the United Nations to immediately enforce its resolutions against Iraq (see pages 913–914) or the United States would be compelled to act on its own. In the weeks that followed, he and his aides offered sometimes-shifting reasons for getting tough with Iraq, if necessary through military action. They said Hussein was a major threat to the United States and its allies, a leader who possessed and would use banned biological and chemical "weapons of mass destruction" and who actively sought to acquire nuclear weapons. They claimed he had ties to Al Qaeda and could be linked to the 9/11 attacks. They said he brutalized his own people and generated regional instability with his tyrannous rule.

Like his father in 1991, Bush claimed he did not need congressional authorization to launch military action against Iraq; and like his father, he nevertheless sought such backing. In early October, the House of Representatives voted 296-133 and the Senate 77-23 to authorize the use of force against Iraq. The lopsided vote was misleading; many who voted yes were unwilling to defy a president so close to a midterm election, even though they opposed military action without U.N. sanction. Both inside and outside Congress, critics complained that the president had not presented evidence that Saddam Hussein constituted an imminent threat or was connected to the 9/11 attacks. Bush switched to a less hawkish and unilateral stance and in so doing gained U.N. backing: in early November, the U.N. Security Council unanimously approved Resolution 1441, imposing rigorous new arms inspections on Iraq.

Behind the scenes, though, the Security Council was deeply divided over what should happen next. In late January 2003 the weapons inspector's report castigated Iraq for failing to carry out "the disarmament that was demanded of it" but also said it was too soon to tell whether the inspections would succeed. While U.S. and British officials emphasized the first point and said the time for diplomacy was up, France, Russia, and China emphasized the second point and called for more inspections. As the U.N. debate continued, and as massive antiwar demonstrations took place around the world, Bush sent about 250,000 soldiers to the region. Britain sent about 45,000 troops.

In late February the United States floated a draft resolution to the U.N. that proposed issuing an ultimatum to Iraq, but only three of the fifteen Security Council members affirmed support. Faced with an embarrassing political defeat, Bush abandoned the resolution and all further diplomatic efforts on March 17 when he ordered Saddam Hussein to leave Iraq within forty-eight hours or face an attack. Saddam ignored the ultimatum, and on March 19 the United States and Britain launched an aerial bombardment of Baghdad and other areas. A ground invasion followed a few days later (see Map 33.2). The Iraqis initially offered stiff resistance, but soon the advancing forces gained momentum. On April 9, Baghdad fell to American troops.

FALL OF BAGHDAD

The military victory was swift and decisive, but stability was slow to return to Iraq, raising concerns that Washington might win the war and lose the peace. U.S. occupying forces faced frequent ambushes and hit-and-run attacks by disaffected Iraqis, leading Deputy Secretary of Defense Paul Wolfowitz, an architect of the Iraq campaign, to warn that a "guerrilla war" had begun. In December 2003 elite U.S. forces captured Saddam Hussein, raising hopes that the insurgency could be brought under control. But concerns existed about the potential costs of the postwar occupation, particularly given the uncertain economic climate at home. Would the United States have the money to pay for its far-flung commitments, given domestic needs and a huge budget deficit? That question loomed large, even among backers of the Iraq war.

Nor was it simply the federal budget that was in the red; state and local governments across the nation faced severe budget shortfalls. The two largest areas of state spending, education and Medicaid, took the brunt of the cuts, but many states also raised taxes. Some tried more creative measures. The governor of Missouri, for example, ordered

STATE ECONOMIC WOES

■ Capture of Saddam in Iraq. Acting on a tip from a senior figure in the Iraqi Special Security Organization, U.S. Troops captured Saddam Hussein in December 2003. The former dictator of Iraq was discovered in a small underground "spider hole" about 10 miles southeast of the city of Tikrit, close to his birthplace. (© 2003 The New York Times Company. Reprinted with permission)

"All the News That's Fit to Print"

The New York Times

New England Edition
Boston: Windy, some clearing late. High 37. Mainly clear, brisk. Low 28. Tomorrow, partly sunny and not as cold, much lighter winds. High 42. Weather map appears on Page D12.

VOL. CLIII .... No. 52,698   Copyright © 2003 The New York Times   MONDAY, DECEMBER 15, 2003   ONE DOLLAR

HUSSEIN CAUGHT IN MAKESHIFT HIDE-OUT; BUSH SAYS 'DARK ERA' FOR IRAQIS IS OVER

BETRAYED BY CLAN

Breakthrough Capped a Renewed Effort to Ferret Out Leads

By ERIC SCHMITT

BAGHDAD, Iraq, Dec. 14 — The hunt for Saddam Hussein ended late Saturday with information from a member of his tribal clan.

Seizing Mr. Hussein, a man who one senior general said had 20 to 30 hide-outs and moved as often as every three to four hours, had become a maddening challenge. Eleven previous times in the last several months, a brigade combat team from the Army's Fourth Infantry Division thought it had a bead on Mr. Hussein and began raids to kill or capture him, only to come up empty, sometimes missing its man by only a matter of hours, military officials here said.

But at 8:26 p.m. Saturday, less than 11 hours after receiving the decisive tip, 600 American soldiers and Special Operations forces backed by tanks, artillery and Apache helicopter gunships surrounded two farmhouses, and near one of them found Mr. Hussein hiding alone at the bottom of an eight-foot hole.

He surrendered without a shot. "He was just caught like a rat," Maj. Gen. Raymond T. Odierno, the commander of the Fourth Infantry Division, told reporters at his headquarters in Tikrit on Sunday. "He could have been hiding in a hundred different places, a thousand different places like this all around Iraq. It just takes finding the right person who will give you a good idea where he might be."

In recent weeks, American officials had started a new effort to draw

Arrest by U.S. Soldiers — President Still Cautious

By SUSAN SACHS

BAGHDAD, Iraq, Dec. 14 — Saddam Hussein, once the all-powerful leader of Iraq, was arrested without a fight on Saturday night by American soldiers who found him crouching in an eight-foot hole at an isolated farm near Tikrit, haggard, dirty and disoriented after eluding capture for nearly nine months.

News of Mr. Hussein's arrest, announced Sunday after being kept secret for 18 hours, electrified Iraq and much of the world, sending joyous Iraqis into the streets with the first real catharsis of liberation since the invasion toppled him in April.

For the Bush administration, which has been struggling to stabilize Iraq, the capture of Mr. Hussein was the most triumphal moment since American forces ousted him.

"In the history of Iraq, a dark and painful era is over," President Bush said in a televised noontime address from Washington. "A hopeful day has arrived. All Iraqis can now come together and reject violence and build a new Iraq." But Mr. Bush was careful to couch his message with caution that Iraq remains violent and dangerous.

American officials said Mr. Hussein was being held in Iraq, but they would not disclose the exact location. They said he had been unresistant in medical tests and other procedures but was not cooperating with interrogators on substantive matters.

American-appointed Iraqi leaders said he would eventually face a war crimes trial, but it was unclear when.

Reuters Television
President Bush, in a brief televised speech yesterday. Page A16.

Maj. Gen. Raymond T. Odierno, commander of the Fourth Infantry Division, which captured Mr. Hussein with a force of 600 soldiers, said he was armed with only a pistol and had surrendered without firing a shot. Two AK-47 rifles and $750,000 in American cash were found nearby.

It was an ignominious ending for Mr. Hussein, 66, who survived American attempts to kill him during the invasion and had eluded capture apparently by moving from one dingy hide-out to another.

Whether his arrest will undermine the insurgency against the American-led forces in Iraq is unclear. Hours after his capture but before it was announced publicly, a car bomb killed at least 17 people in a town west of Baghdad. [Page A12.]

Even in hiding, Mr. Hussein had

Continued on Page A12

In the Streets, a Shadow Lifts

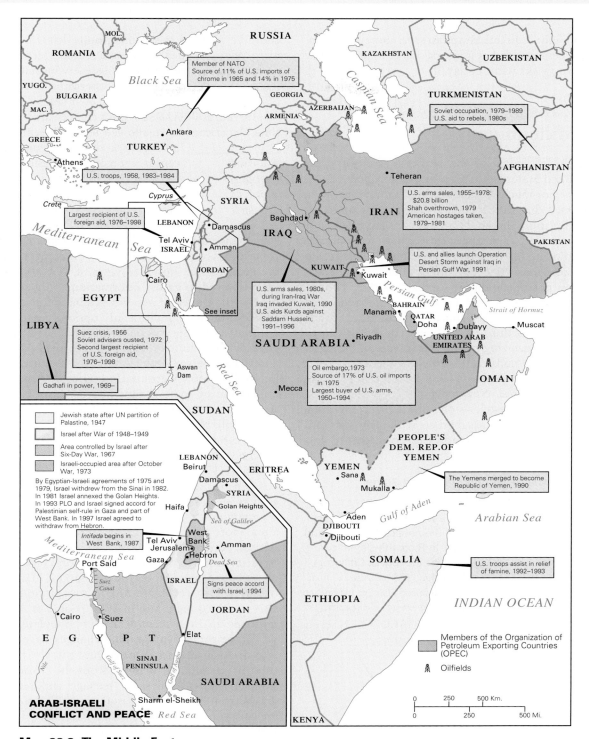

Map 33.2 The Middle East

Extremely volatile and often at war, the nations of the Middle East maintained precarious relations with the United States. To protect its interests, the United States extended large amounts of economic and military aid and sold huge quantities of weapons to the area. At times, Washington ordered U.S. troops to the region. The Arab-Israeli dispute particularly upended order, although the peace process moved forward intermittently.

every third light bulb unscrewed to save money. In Oklahoma, teachers doubled as janitors, while in Oregon they worked two weeks without pay.

Americans in the New Millennium

*a*t the beginning of the twenty-first century, the United States is a nation of extraordinary diversity. For much of the twentieth century, however, it had seemed that the United States was moving in the opposite direction. Immigration quotas had been very low from the 1920s through 1965. New technologies such as radio and television had a homogenizing effect at first, for these mass media were dependent on reaching the broadest possible audience—a mass market. Though local and ethnic traditions persisted, more and more Americans participated in a shared mass culture.

During the last third of the twentieth century, however, those homogenizing trends were reversed. Immigration reform in the mid-1960s opened American borders to large numbers of people from a wider variety of nations than ever before. New technologies—the Internet, and cable and satellite television with their proliferation of channels—replaced mass markets with niche markets. Everything from television shows to cosmetics to cars

Figure 33.3   The Growth of the United States' Hispanic Population

"Hispanic" combines people from a wide variety of national origins or ancestries—including all the nations of Central and South America, Mexico, Cuba, Puerto Rico, the Dominican Republic, Spain—as well as those who identify as Californio, Tejano, Nuevo Mexicano, and Mestizo.   (Source: Adapted from the U.S. Department of Commerce, Economics and Statistics Information, Bureau of the Census, 1993 report "We, the American . . . Hispanics"; also recent census bureau figures for the Hispanic population.)

could be targeted at specific groups defined by age, ethnicity, class, gender, or lifestyle choices. These changes did not simply make American society more fragmented. Instead, they helped to make Americans' understandings of identity more fluid and more complex.

In the 2000 U.S. government census, for the first time, Americans were allowed to identify themselves as belonging to more than one race. New census categories recognized that notions of biological "race" were problematic. Why could a white woman bear a "black" child when a black woman could not bear a white child? The change also acknowledged the growing number of Americans born to parents of different racial backgrounds. Critics, however, worried that because census data are used to gather information about social conditions in the United States and as a basis for allocating resources, the new "multiracial" option would reduce the visibility and clout of minority groups. Thus the federal government counted those who identified both as white and as members of a racial or ethnic minority as belonging to the minority group. Under this system, the official population of some groups increased: more Americans than ever before, for example, identified themselves as at least partly Native American. Others rejected racial and ethnic categories altogether: 20 million people identified themselves simply as "American," up more than 50 percent since 1990.

RACE AND ETHNICITY IN RECENT AMERICA

During the 1990s, the population of people of color grew twelve times as fast as the white population, fueled by immigration and birth rates. The Latino population alone more than doubled. By 2003, Latinos moved past African Americans to become the second largest ethnic or racial group in the nation (after non-Hispanic whites), making the United States the fifth largest "Latino" country in world (see Figure 33.3). Immigration from Asia also remained high, and in 2000 people of Asian ancestry made up 3.6 percent of the U.S. population.

These rapid demographic changes have altered the face of America. At a Dairy Queen in the far southern suburbs of Atlanta, 6 miles from the "Gone with the Wind Historical District," teenage children of immigrants from India and Pakistan serve Blizzards and Mister Mistys. In the small town of Ligonier, Indiana, the formerly empty main street now boasts three Mexican restaurants and a Mexican western-wear shop; Mexican immigrants drawn by plentiful industrial jobs in the 1990s cross paths with the newest immigrants, Yemenis, some in traditional dress, and with Amish families riding horse-drawn buggies. Still, more than half of American counties were still at least 85 percent white in 2000—and more than half of all Latinos lived in just eight metropolitan areas (see Map 33.3).

American popular culture embraced the influences of this new multiethnic population. Economics were

*A MORE
DIVERSE
CULTURE*

important: the buying power of the growing Latino population exceeded $561 billion in 2000, and average income for Asian American households topped all other groups. But American audiences also crossed racial and ethnic lines. Superstar Jennifer Lopez (of Puerto Rican descent) was the most

Map 33.3 Mapping America's Diversity

Aggregate figures (more than 12 percent of the U.S. population is African American and about 4 percent is Asian American, for example) convey America's ethnic and racial diversity. However, as this map shows, members of racial and ethnic groups are not distributed evenly throughout the nation.   (Source: Adapted from the *New York Times* National Edition, April 1, 2001, "Portrait of a Nation," p. 18. Copyright © 2001 by The New York Times Co. Reprinted with permission.)

This 21st-century American family shows the increasing complexity of racial and ethnic identities. The father is Chinese, Irish, French, German, and Swedish; the mother Italian, Irish, and Japanese. (Terrence Mielse/*Newsweek*)

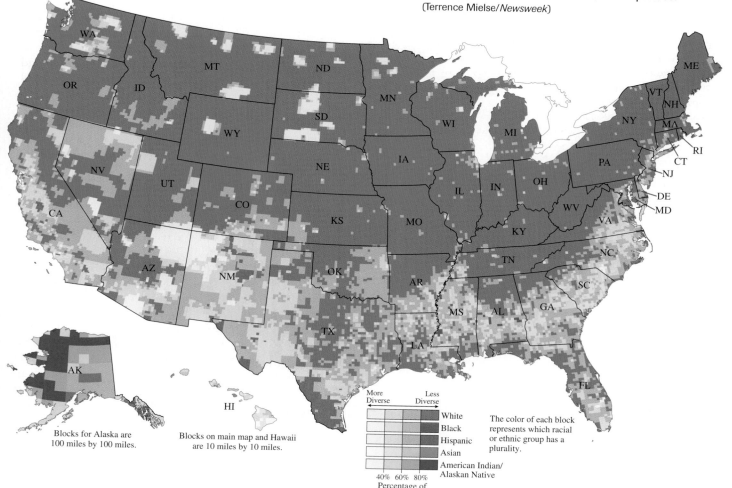

Blocks for Alaska are 100 miles by 100 miles.

Blocks on main map and Hawaii are 10 miles by 10 miles.

More Diverse — Less Diverse

White
Black
Hispanic
Asian
American Indian/ Alaskan Native

40% 60% 80%
Percentage of total population

The color of each block represents which racial or ethnic group has a plurality.

"bankable" musician/actress in the nation; black basketball great Michael Jordan had more commercial endorsements than any other celebrity in America's history. Latin dancing styles swept the club scene; white teens in the nation's suburbs took up urban rap and hip-hop culture. Golfer Tiger Woods became a symbol of this new, hybrid, multiethnic nation: of African, European, Native American, Thai, and Chinese descent, he calls himself "Cablinasian" (CAucasian-BLack-INdian-ASIAN).

Americans were divided over the meaning of other changes, as well—especially the changing shape of American families (see Figure 33.4). The number of people liv-

THE CHANGING AMERICAN FAMILY

ing together without marriage jumped 72 percent during the 1990s, to 5.5 million. Of those, at least 600,000 were same-sex couples—perhaps 1 percent of households nationwide. A third of female-partner households and one-fifth of male-partner households had children, and in 2002 the American Academy of Pediatrics endorsed adoption by gay couples. A vocal antigay movement coexisted with rising support for the legal equality of gay, lesbian, transgendered, and bisexual Americans. While many states and private corporations extended domestic-partner benefits to gay couples, the federal Defense of Mar-

Figure 33.4   The Changing American Family

American households became smaller in the latter part of the twentieth century, as more people lived alone and women had, on average, fewer children. (Source: Adapted from U.S. Bureau of the Census: http://www.census.gov/prod/2002pubs/censr-4.pdf and http://www.census.gov/population/pop-profile/2000/chap04.pdf)

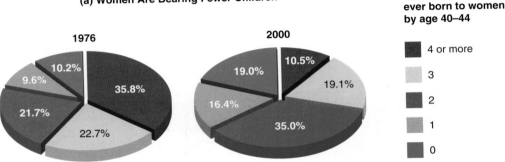

(a) Women Are Bearing Fewer Children

Number of children ever born to women by age 40–44

- 4 or more
- 3
- 2
- 1
- 0

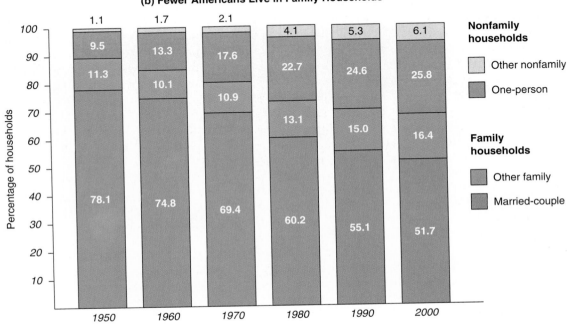

(b) Fewer Americans Live in Family Households

Nonfamily households
- Other nonfamily
- One-person

Family households
- Other family
- Married-couple

riage Act, passed by Congress in 1996, defined marriage as "only" a union between one man and one woman.

More children were born outside marriage than ever before—almost a third of all children, and more than two-thirds of those born to African American women. Mothers of small children commonly worked outside the home, and in the majority of married-couple families with children under eighteen, both parents held jobs. The divorce rate stayed high; statistically, a couple that married in the late 1990s had about a 50-50 chance of divorce. While almost a third of families with children had only one parent present—usually the mother—children also lived in blended families created by second marriages, or moved back and forth between households of parents who had joint custody.

Increasingly, new reproductive technologies allowed infertile women or couples to conceive and bear children.

NEW TECHNOLOGIES AND NEW CHALLENGES In 2000, more than 100,000 attempted in vitro fertilizations—in which sperm and egg combine in a sterile dish or test tube and the fertilized egg or eggs are then transferred to the uterus—resulted in the birth of more than 35,000 babies. From the beginning, such techniques have raised legal and ethical questions. What are the comparable rights and responsibilities of sperm and egg donors, the woman who carries the fetus, and male and female prospective parents? At the same time, the children these new technologies made possible have brought joy to many families.

This rapidly developing field of biogenetics offers even more possibilities for good, and also even knottier philosophical and ethical conundrums. The five- or six-cell blastocytes formed by the initial division of fertilized eggs during in vitro procedures contain stem cells, unspecialized cells that can be induced to become cells with specialized functions. For example, stem cells might become insulin-producing cells of the pancreas—and thus a cure for diabetes; or they might become dopamine-producing neurons, offering therapy for Parkinson's disease, a progressive disorder of the nervous system affecting over 1 million Americans. President Bush, in 2001, acknowledged the "tremendous hope" promised by this research but called embryonic stem cell research "the leading edge of a series of moral hazards," including the possibility of cloning humans for spare body parts. In a highly controversial decision, Bush limited federally funded research to the existing seventy-eight stem cell lines, not all of which are viable for research.

For middle-aged and older Americans, the stem cell debate was another indicator of the rapid pace of scientific

CENTURY OF CHANGE advancement during their lifetime. The twentieth century had seen more momentous change than any previous century: change for better; change for worse; change that brought enormous benefits to human beings; change that threatened the very existence of the human species. Research in the physical and biological sciences had greatly broadened horizons and had provided deep insight into the structure of matter and of the universe. Technology—the application of science—had made startling advances that benefited tens of millions of Americans in nearly every aspect of life: better health, more wealth, more mobility, less drudgery, greater access to information.

As a result, Americans at the start of the new century were more connected to the rest of humankind. This interconnectivity of people was perhaps the most powerful product of globalization. A commodities trader in Chicago in March 2003 could send an e-mail to his fiancée in Tokyo while he spoke on the phone to a trader in Frankfurt and kept one eye on CNN's real-time coverage of the air war over Baghdad; within a minute or two he could receive a reply from his fiancée saying she missed him too. If he felt sufficiently lovesick, he could board an airplane and be in Japan the following day.

The world had shrunk to the size of an airplane ticket. In 1955, 51 million people a year traveled by plane. By the turn of the century 1.6 billion were airborne every year, and 530 million crossed international borders—or about 1.5 million each day. For our Chicago trader and for millions of other Americans, this permeability of national boundaries brought many benefits, as did the integration of markets and the global spread of information that occurred alongside it.

But there was a flip side to this growing connectivity that even many advocates of globalization perceived. For one thing, whereas people still needed passports and sometimes visas to travel from one country to another, infectious diseases did not. The rapid increase in international air travel was a particularly potent force for global disease dissemination, as flying made it possible for people to reach the other side of the world in far less time than the incubation period for many ailments. Thus in early 2003, a respiratory illness known as severe acute respiratory syndrome (SARS) spread from Guangdong Province of China to Hong Kong to various other countries in the world, chiefly via air passengers who unwittingly carried the disease in their lungs. Public health officials also warned that increased human mobility promised more trade in illegal products and contaminated

The Global AIDS Epidemic

AIDS, first reported in the United States in 1981, has become a global epidemic. Researchers now believe that the first infection with HIV, the human immunodeficiency virus that causes AIDS, may have appeared in West Africa around 1930. HIV/AIDS began spreading rapidly in the late 1970s, in part as a byproduct of globalization. In-

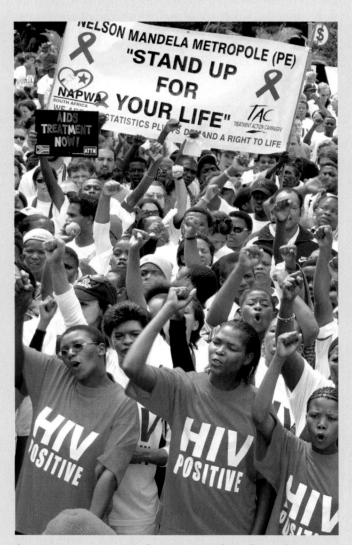

Activists protest outside Parliament in Cape Town, South Africa, calling upon South Africa president Thabo Mbeki to make the struggle against AIDS a national priority. An estimated 20 percent of South Africans between the ages of fifteen and forty-nine are HIV-positive.   (AP/Wide World Photos, Inc.)

creasingly commonplace international travel allowed for sexual transmission of HIV between populations; the international heroin trade that grew in the 1970s stimulated intravenous drug use—another means of transmission; and the international circulation of blood for transfusions in medical procedures also contributed to the virus's spread. In 2003, the World Health Organization estimated that 58 million people worldwide were living with HIV/AIDS and that 23 million had died from the disease.

Globally, AIDS claims 350 lives per hour, and while altered behavior and new drug therapies have slowed the progress of the disease in North America and western Europe, infection and death rates continue to grow rapidly in sub-Saharan Africa, eastern Europe and the former Soviet Union, and Latin America, especially the Caribbean. In the African nation of Malawi, one in six adults is HIV-positive, and the nation expects to lose almost a quarter of its work force to AIDS in the next decade. Half of current teenagers in the hardest-hit African nations will eventually die of AIDS; more than 14 million children across the globe have been orphaned by the disease.

The human suffering is staggering. However, U.S. worries about the global spread of AIDS are not based solely on humanitarian concerns. In 2000, the U.S. National Intelligence Council concluded that AIDS and other new and reemerging infectious diseases must be treated as threats to the health of U.S. citizens and to global security, stating: "These diseases will endanger U.S. citizens at home and abroad, threaten U.S. armed forces deployed overseas, and exacerbate social and political instability in key countries and regions in which the United States has significant interests." In nations already facing shortages of food and clean water and riven by war and ethnic conflict, AIDS has further undermined both individual and governmental ability to cope with crisis; political instability and social disorder result.

In 2002, U.N. secretary general Kofi Annan estimated that between $7 billion and $10 billion are needed each year to combat the spread of AIDS—and of tuberculosis and malaria, both of which have reemerged as major threats to world health. President Bush called for major increases in U.S. spending to combat AIDS internationally, but many believe the United States must take more responsibility for combating the epidemic. In the era of globalization, diseases do not stop at borders or respect wealth and power. The links between Americans and the rest of the world's peoples cannot be denied.

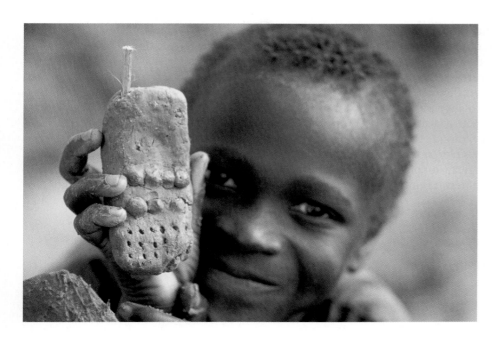

■ At the dawn of the twenty-first century, information technology brought hope and excitement—as well as anger and resentment—to young people in parts of the world that seemed to have missed the information revolution. In this photo from 2003, a Cameroonian boy shows off his clay phone. (Reinout Van Den Bergh–Hollandse Hoogte)

foodstuffs, with negative implications for the world's population.

Environmental degradation was another powerful contributor to pressing global health threats. In 2003, the World Health Organization (WHO) estimated that nearly a quarter of the global burden of disease and injury was related to environmental disruption and decline. For example, some 90 percent of diarrheal diseases (such as cholera), which were killing 3 million people a year, resulted from contaminated water. WHO also pointed to globalization and environmental disruption as contributing to the fact that, in the final two decades of the twentieth century, more than thirty infectious diseases were identified in humans for the first time—including AIDS, Ebola virus, hantavirus, and hepatitis C and E. Environmentalists, meanwhile, continued to insist that the growing interaction of national economies was having a deleterious impact on the ecosystem through climate change, ozone depletion, hazardous waste, and damage to fisheries.

But if the interaction between national economies and the rapid increase in person-to-person contacts were responsible for many health and other problems, they also were essential in mobilizing the world to find solutions. Whereas it took centuries to identify the cause of cholera and two years to identify the virus that caused AIDS, in the case of SARS, thirteen labs in ten countries put everything else aside

INTERNATIONAL RESPONSE TO DISEASE

and in a matter of weeks determined that the coronavirus was responsible. Within a month, laboratories from Vancouver to Atlanta to Singapore had mapped the genome, whereupon efforts to devise a diagnostic test for the virus began. Thus although the disease spread internationally with unprecedented speed, so did the response. Speed of communication allowed for a coordinated international effort at finding the cause of SARS and also allowed individual countries, including the United States, to adopt measures that succeeded, in the early months at least, in keeping the epidemic out.

Even in the interconnected world of the new millennium, then, national borders still mattered. There were limits to their permeability. In the wake of 9/11, indeed, the process of integration was to some degree reversed. To prevent future terrorist attacks, the United States and other countries imposed tighter security measures on air travelers, imported goods, immigration, and information flows. Some economists predicted these measures would stall the global movement toward integration of markets; in the short term they certainly did, but the long-term outlook was less clear. Trade and investment shrank in 2001, but they were falling before September 11 as a result of economic slowdowns in the world's biggest economies, including the United States, Europe, and Japan. Moreover, the falloff in international economic activity in the months after the attacks was not massive.

In military and diplomatic terms, though, 9/11 made a deep and lasting impression. The attacks that day

CONFRONTING TERRORISM brought home what Americans had only dimly perceived before then: that globalization had shrunk the natural buffers that distance and two oceans provided the United States. Al Qaeda, it was clear, had used the increasingly open, integrated, globalized world to give themselves new power and reach. They had shown that small cells of terrorists could become true transnational threats—thriving around the world without any single state sponsor or home base. According to American intelligence, Al Qaeda operated in more than ninety countries—including the United States.

How would one go about vanquishing such a foe? Was a decisive victory even possible? These remained open questions two years after the World Trade Center collapsed. Unchallenged militarily and seeing no rival great power, the United States no longer felt constrained from intervening in sensitive areas like the Middle East or Central Asia should national security interests demand it. Yet the nation took little comfort from this superiority. It continued to spend vast sums on its military, more indeed than the next twenty-five nations combined. (In 2003, the Pentagon spent about $400 billion, or roughly $50 million dollars per hour.) America had

---

TABLE 33.1

U.S. Military Personnel on Active Duty in Foreign Countries, 2001[1]

Region/Country[2]	Personnel	Region/Country	Personnel
United States and Territories		Singapore	160
Continental U.S.	947,955	Thailand	114
Alaska	15,926	**North Africa, Near East, and South Asia**	
Hawaii	33,191	Bahrain	1,280
Guam	3,398	Diego Garcia	537
Puerto Rico	2,525	Egypt	665
Europe		Israel	38
Belgium*	1,554	Kuwait	4,300
Bosnia and Herzegovina	3,109	Oman	560
France*	70	Qatar	72
Germany*	71,434	Saudi Arabia	4,802
Greece*	526	United Arab Emirates	207
Greenland*	153	**Sub-Saharan Africa**	
Iceland*	1,713	Kenya	50
Italy*	11,854	South Africa	30
Macedonia	346	**Western Hemisphere**	
Netherlands*	696	Brazil	40
Norway*	187	Canada	165
Portugal*	992	Chile	30
Russia	88	Colombia	59
Serbia (includes Kosovo)	5,200	Cuba (Guantanamo)	461
Spain*	1,778	Honduras	426
Turkey*	2,170	Peru	40
United Kingdom*	11,361	Venezuela	30
East Asia and Pacific		**Total foreign countries[2]**	**255,065**
Australia	188	**Ashore**	**212,262**
China (includes Hong Kong)	54	**Afloat**	**42,803**
Indonesia (includes Timor)	48	**Total worldwide [2]**	**1,384,812**
Japan	39,691	**Ashore**	**1,242,524**
Korea, Rep. of	37,972	**Afloat**	**142,288**
Philippines	31		

*NATO countries
[1] Only countries with 30 or more U.S. military personnel are listed.
[2] Includes all regions/countries, not simply those listed.
Source: U.S. Department of Defense, *Selected Manpower Statistics,* Annual

taken on military commitments all over the globe, from the Balkans and Iraq to Afghanistan and Korea (see Table 33.1). Its armed forces looked colossal, but its obligations looked even larger.

Summary

The 1990s were, for most Americans, good times. A digitized revolution in communications and information—as fundamental as the revolution brought about by electricity and the combustion engine a century earlier, or the steam engine a century before that—was generating prosperity and transforming life in America and around the globe. The longest economic expansion in American history—from 1991 to 2001—meant that most Americans who wanted jobs had them, that the stock market boomed, that the nation had a budget surplus instead of a deficit, and that more Americans than ever before owned their own homes. And America was not only prosperous; it was powerful. With the Soviet Union gone and no other formidable rival on the horizon, the United States stood as the world's lone superpower, its economic and military power daunting to friend and foe alike.

Yet although America seemed at the apex of power and prosperity, unsettling events troubled the nation. The Cold War continued to complicate the shaping of the new world order. Localized and ethnic conflicts in the Balkans, the Middle East, and Africa crowded the international agenda, as did human rights and the natural environment. At home, high-profile acts of violence—the domestic terrorist attack in Oklahoma City in 1995; a rash of school shootings—captured headlines, even as the crime rate dropped. And scandal further undermined the faith of Americans in their government, as President Bill Clinton was impeached by the House of Representatives.

Just minutes before midnight on December 31, 1999, President Clinton called on the American people not to fear the future, but to "welcome it, create it, and embrace it." The challenges of the future would be greater than Americans imagined as they welcomed the new millennium that night. In 2000, the contested presidential election was decided by the Supreme Court in a partisan 5-4 vote; in 2001, the ten-year economic expansion came to an end.

Then, on September 11 of that year, radical Islamic terrorists attacked the World Trade Center and the Pentagon, killing thousands and altering many aspects of American life. The new president, George W. Bush, declared a "war on terrorism," one with both foreign and domestic components. While U.S. air and ground forces went after targets in Afghanistan, Congress moved to create the Department of Homeland Security and passed the PATRIOT Act, expanding the federal government's powers of surveillance. To counter a troubled economy, Bush pressed for tax cuts each of his first three years in office, something no wartime president had ever done. Congress went along, but the economic impact was uncertain, and the lost revenues added to a ballooning budget deficit.

The world Americans found in the first years of the 21st century was much different than the one they'd looked forward to with confidence and high hopes as they celebrated the coming of the new millennium on New Year's Eve, 1999. The horror of the terror attacks of September 11, 2001, shook America to its core. Throughout the nation, people declared that life would never be the same. And it wasn't, not for those who'd lost loved ones that day, or for a people now forcibly aware of the powerful and inescapable links that bind their nation to the rest of the world's nations and peoples. But as Americans attempted to cope with the aftermath of 9/11, crafting new foreign and domestic policies, the resilience of the American people was clear. For Americans continued to struggle over these plans and policies, over the direction of their nation, with the passion and commitment that keeps democracy alive.

LEGACY FOR A PEOPLE AND A NATION
The Internet

"Google it." The phrase, essentially unknown before the new century, had within its first years become a household expression, like "Xerox it" or "FedEx it." Google was the hugely popular Internet search engine that had gone from obscurity in the mid-1990s to a point where it responded, more or less instantly, to 200 million queries per day from around the world—almost 40 percent of all Internet search requests.

Google's phenomenal rise was one sign among many of how the Internet had become, by the early years of the twenty-first century, an ordinary, expected part of many Americans' daily lives. For younger people, in particular, the Internet was something to be taken for granted, like refrigerators and microwaves and stereos and televisions.

Yet the widespread use of the Internet was a recent phenomenon, even though its history went back some four decades. In the mid-1960s, the U.S. military's Advanced Research Projects Agency (ARPA) hoped to create a communications network for government and university researchers spread out across the nation. In 1969, the first portions of the experimental system, called ARPANET, went online at UCLA, U.C. Santa Barbara, Stanford Research Institute, and the University of Utah. By 1971, twenty-three computers were connected, and gradually the numbers grew, reaching close to a thousand by 1984. This system, which by the late 1980s had been renamed the Internet, transmitted only words, but in 1990 computer scientists developed the World Wide Web, which used the Internet to send also graphic and multimedia information. Then in 1993 the first commercial "browser" to aid navigation through the Web hit the market. It was followed in 1994 and 1995 by two superior browsers: Netscape and Internet Explorer. The prospect of millions of computers connected worldwide had become a reality.

By 2003, there were close to half a billion Internet users worldwide, including 140 million Americans. Thanks to technological advances, and to the new forms of "broadband" access that provided high-speed connections, these users could do an astonishing array of things online. They could send and receive e-mail, join online discussion groups, read newspapers, book vacations, download movies and music, purchase everything from books to private jets, even do their banking—all through a small computer in their home. For the American people in the new globally connected millennium, there could be no more fitting legacy of the twentieth century than the Internet.

The **history companion** powered by Eduspace®

Your primary source for interactive quizzes, exercises, and more to help you learn efficiently.

http://history.college.hmco.com/students

APPENDIX

Suggestions for Further Reading

Chapter 1

General

Noble D. Cook, *Born to Die: Disease and New World Conquest, 1492–1650* (1998); Alfred W. Crosby, *The Columbian Exchange: Biological and Cultural Consequences of 1492* (1972); Alfred W. Crosby, *Ecological Imperialism: The Biological Expansion of Europe, 800–1900* (1986); John R. Elliott, *The Old World and the New* (1970); Bernard Lewis, *Cultures in Conflict: Christians, Muslims, and Jews in the Age of Discovery* (1995); D. W. Meinig, *Atlantic America, 1492–1800* (1986); Herman Viola and Carolyn Margolis, eds., *Seeds of Change: Five Hundred Years Since Columbus* (1991); Eric Wolf, *Europe and the People Without History* (1982).

Mesoamerican Civilizations

Inga Clendinnen, *Aztecs: An Interpretation* (1991); Michael Coe, *Mexico from the Olmecs to the Aztecs* (1994); Brian Fagan, *Kingdoms of Gold, Kingdoms of Jade: The Americas Before Columbus* (1991); John S. Henderson, *The World of the Ancient Maya* (1997); Eduardo Matos Moctezuma and David Carrasco, *Moctezuma's Mexico: Visions of the Aztec World* (1992); Linda Schele and David Friedel, *A Forest of Kings* [on the Mayas] (1990).

North American Indians

Kathleen Bragdon, *The Columbia Guide to American Indians of the Northeast* (2002); Kathleen Bragdon, *Native People of Southern New England, 1500–1650* (1996); Sally A. Kitt Chappell, *Cahokia: Mirror of the Cosmos* (2002); Linda S. Cordell, *Ancient Pueblo Peoples* (1994); Brian Fagan, *Ancient North America: The Archaeology of a Continent* (1991); Brian Fagan, *The Great Journey: The Peopling of Ancient America* (1987); Francis Jennings, *The Founders of America: From the Earliest Migrations to the Present* (1993); Alvin Josephy, Jr., ed., *America in 1492* (1992); Theda Perdue and Michael Green, *The Columbia Guide to American Indians of the Southeast* (2001); Elsa Redmond, ed., *Chiefdoms and Chieftaincy in the Americas* (1999); Lynda N. Shaffer, *Native Americans Before 1492: The Moundbuilding Centers of the Eastern Woodlands* (1992); Colin F. Taylor, ed., *The Native Americans: The Indigenous People of North America* (1992); Bruce Trigger and Wilcomb Washburn, eds., *The Cambridge History of the Native Peoples of the Americas*, vol. 1: *North America* (1996); Be-

loine W. Young and Melvin L. Fowler, *Cahokia: The Great Native American Metropolis* (2000).

Africa

Jacob Ade Ajayi and Michael Crowder, *History of West Africa* (1985); Basil Davidson, *Africa in History*, rev. ed. (1991); Philip Curtin et al., eds., *African History: From Earliest Times to Independence*, rev. ed. (1995); John Iliffe, *Africans: The History of a Continent* (1996); Robert July, *A History of the African People* (1992); Paul Lovejoy, *Transformations in Slavery: A History of Slavery in Africa* (1983); Roland Oliver and J. D. Fage, *A Short History of Africa* (1988); John Thornton, *Africa and Africans in the Making of the Atlantic World, 1400–1680* (1992).

Europe in the Age of Discovery

Christopher Allmand, *The Hundred Years' War: England and France at War, ca. 1300–ca. 1450* (1988); Fernand Braudel, *The Mediterranean and the Mediterranean World in the Age of Philip II*, 2 vols., 2d ed. (1977); Roger Chartier, ed., *A History of Private Life*, vol. 3: *Passions of the Renaissance* (1989); G. R. Elton, ed., *The Reformation* (1990); Anthony Grafton, *New Worlds, Ancient Texts: The Power of Tradition and the Shock of Discovery* (1992); Denys Hay, *Europe in the Fourteenth and Fifteenth Centuries*, 2d ed. (1989); H. G. Koenigsberger et al., *Europe in the Sixteenth Century*, 2d ed. (1989); Robert McGhee, *The Arctic Voyages of Martin Frobisher: An Elizabethan Adventure* (2002); Anthony Pagden, *Lords of All the World: Ideologies of Empire in Spain, Britain and France, 1500–1800* (1995); J. R. S. Phillips, *The Medieval Expansion of Europe* (1988); Philip Ziegler, *The Black Death* (1982).

Exploration and Discovery

Emerson Baker et al., eds., *American Beginnings: Exploration, Culture, and Cartography in the Land of Norumbega* (1994); Fredi Chiappelli et al., eds., *First Images of America: The Impact of the New World on the Old*, 2 vols. (1976); Kathleen Deagan and José María Cruxent, *Columbus's Outpost among the Taínos: Spain and America at La Isabela, 1493–1498* (2002); Felipe Fernández-Armesto, *Before Columbus: Exploration and Colonization from the Mediterranean to the Atlantic, 1229–1492* (1987); Felipe Fernández-Armesto, *Columbus* (1991); Charles Hudson, *Knights of Spain, Warriors of the Sun: Hernando de Soto and the South's Ancient Chiefdoms* (1997);

Jerald T. Milanich, *Florida Indians and the Invasion from Europe* (1995); Jerald T. Milanich and Susan Milbrath, eds., *First Encounters: Spanish Explorations in the Caribbean and the United States, 1492–1570* (1989); Samuel Eliot Morison, *The European Discovery of America: The Northern Voyages*, A.D. 1500–1600 (1971); Samuel Eliot Morison, *The European Discovery of America: The Southern Voyages*, A.D. 1492–1616 (1974); J. H. Parry, *The Age of Reconnaissance* (1963); J. H. Parry, *The Discovery of the Sea* (1974); William and Carla Phillips, *The Worlds of Christopher Columbus* (1992); David B. Quinn, *North America from Earliest Discovery to First Settlements* (1977); Irving Rouse, *The Tainos: Rise and Decline of the People Who Greeted Columbus* (1992); P. E. Russell, *Portugal, Spain, and the African Atlantic* (1995); P. E. Russell, *Prince Henry "The Navigator": A Life* (2000); Kirsten Seaver, *The Frozen Echo: Greenland and the Exploration of North America, ca.* A.D. *1000–1500* (1995); Roger C. Smith, *Vanguard of Empire: Ships of Exploration in the Age of Columbus* (1993).

Early European Conquest and Settlements

Kenneth Andrews, *Trade, Plunder and Settlement: Maritime Enterprise and the Genesis of the British Empire, 1480–1630* (1984); Nancy Farriss, *Maya Society Under Colonial Rule* (1984); Charles Gibson, *Spain in America* (1966); Ross Hassig, *Mexico and the Spanish Conquest* (1994); Paul E. Hoffman, *A New Andalucia and a Way to the Orient: The American Southeast during the Sixteenth Century* (1990); Karen O. Kupperman, *Roanoke, the Abandoned Colony* (1984); Miguel León-Portilla, ed., *The Broken Spears: The Aztec Account of the Conquest of Mexico* (1992); James Lockhart, ed. and trans., *We People Here: Nahuatl Accounts of the Conquest of Mexico* (1993); James Lockhart, *The Nahuas after the Conquest: A Social and Cultural History of the Indians of Central Mexico, Sixteenth Through Eighteenth Centuries* (1992); A. J. R. Russell-Wood, *A World on the Move: The Portuguese in Africa, Asia, and America, 1415–1808* (1993); Hugh Thomas, Conquest: *Montezuma, Cortés, and the Fall of Old Mexico* (1993).

Chapter 2

General

Christine Daniels and Michael Kennedy, eds., *Negotiated Empires: Centers and Peripheries in the Americas, 1500–1820* (2002); David Hackett Fischer, *Albion's Seed: Four British Folkways in America* (1989); Alison Games, *Migration and the Origins of the English Atlantic World* (1999); Karen O. Kupperman, ed., *America in European Consciousness, 1493–1750* (1995); D. W. Meinig, *Atlantic America, 1492–1800* (1986); Gary B. Nash, *Red, White, and Black: The Peoples of Early America*, 4th ed. (2000); Mary Beth Norton, *Founding Mothers & Fathers: Gendered Power and the Forming of American Society* (1996); John E. Pomfret, *Founding the American Colonies, 1583–1660* (1970); Alan Taylor, *American Colonies* (2001); Paula Treckel, *To Comfort the Heart: Women in Seventeenth-Century America* (1996); Alden T. Vaughan, *Roots of American Racism* (1994).

New Spain, New Netherland, New France, and the Caribbean

Karen Anderson, *Chain Her by One Foot: The Subjugation of Native Women in Seventeenth-Century New France* (1991); Charles R. Boxer, *The Dutch Seaborne Empire, 1600–1800* (1965); Denys Delâge, *Bitter Feast: Amerindians and Europeans in Northeastern North America, 1600–64* (1993); Richard S. Dunn, *Sugar and Slaves: The Rise of the Planter Class in the English West Indies, 1624–1713* (1972); William J. Eccles, *France in America*, rev. ed. (1990); Carol Hoffecker et al., eds., *New Sweden in America* (1995); Jonathan Israel, *Dutch Primacy in World Trade, 1585–1740* (1989); Robert Kapitzke, *Religion, Power, and Politics in Colonial St. Augustine* (2001); Karen O. Kupperman, *Providence Island, 1630–1641: The Other Puritan Colony* (1993); Donna Merwick, *Possessing Albany, 1630–1710* (1990); Sidney Mintz, *Sweetness and Power: The Place of Sugar in Modern History* (1985); Peter N. Moogk, *La Nouvelle France: The Making of French Canada, A Cultural History* (2000); Carroll Riley, *The Kachina and the Cross: Indians and Spaniards in the Early Southwest* (2000); Marc Simmons, *The Last Conquistador: Juan de Oñate and the Settling of the Far Southwest* (1991); David J. Weber, *The Spanish Frontier in North America* (1992).

England

Susan Dwyer Amussen, *An Ordered Society: Gender and Class in Early Modern England* (1988); Carl Bridenbaugh, *Vexed and Troubled Englishmen, 1590–1642*, rev. ed. (1976); Patrick Collinson, *The Religion of Protestants: The Church in English Society, 1559–1625* (1982); A. G. Dickens, *The English Reformation*, 2d ed. (1989); Ralph Houlbrooke, *The English Family, 1450–1700* (1984); Peter Laslett, *The World We Have Lost*, 3d ed. (1984); J. P. Sommerville, *Politics and Ideology in England, 1603–1640* (1986); Keith Wrightson, *English Society, 1580–1680* (1982).

Early Contact Between Europeans and Indians

James Axtell, *The Invasion Within: The Contest of Cultures in Colonial North America* (1985); Russell Bourne, *Gods of War, Gods of Peace: How the Meeting of Native and Colonial Religion Shaped Early America* (2002); Alfred Cave, *The Pequot War* (1997); William Cronon, *Changes in the Land: Indians, Colonists, and the Ecology of New England* (1983); Frederic W. Gleach, *Powhatan's World and Colonial Virginia: A Conflict of Cultures* (1997); Francis Jennings, *The Invasion of America: Indians, Colonialism, and the Cant of Conquest* (1975); Karen O. Kupperman, *Indians and English: Facing Off in Early America* (2000); Patrick Malone, *The Skulking Way of War: Technology and Tactics Among the Indians of New England* (1991); Kenneth Morrison, *The Embattled Northeast: The Elusive Ideal of Alliance in Abnaki-Euroamerican Relations* (1984); Daniel Richter, *Facing East from Indian Country: A Native History of Early America* (2001); Daniel Richter, *The Ordeal of the Longhouse: The Peoples of the Iroquois League in the Era of European Colonization* (1992); Helen C. Rountree, *Pocahontas's People: The Powhatan Indians of Virginia Through Four Centuries* (1990); Neal Salisbury, *Manitou and Providence: Indians, Europeans, and the Making of New England, 1500–1643* (1982); Bernard Sheehan, *Savagism and Civility: Indians and Englishmen in Colonial Virginia* (1980); Timothy Silver, *A New Face on the Countryside: Indians, Colonists, and Slaves in South Atlantic Forests, 1500–1800* (1990); Alden T. Vaughan, *The New England Frontier: Puritans and Indians, 1620–1675*, rev. ed. (1979); Peter Wood et al., eds., *Powhatan's Mantle: Indians in the Colonial Southeast* (1989).

Chesapeake Society and Politics

Lois Green Carr et al., *Robert Cole's World: Agriculture and Society in Early Maryland* (1991); David Galenson, *White Servitude in Colonial America: An Economic Analysis* (1981); James Horn, *Adapting to a New World: English Society in the Seventeenth-Century Chesapeake* (1994); Ivor Noel Hume, *The Virginia Adventure: Roanoke to James Towne* (1994); A. J. Leo Lemay, *The American Dream of Captain John Smith* (1991); Gloria L. Main, *Tobacco Colony: Life in Early Maryland, 1650–1720* (1983); Edmund S. Morgan, *American Slavery, American Freedom: The Ordeal of Colonial Virginia* (1975); James Perry, *The Formation of a Society on Virginia's Eastern Shore, 1615–1655* (1990); Darrett Rutman and Anita Rutman, *A Place in Time: Middlesex County, Virginia, 1650–1750* (1984); Alden T. Vaughan, *American Genesis: Captain John Smith and the Founding of Virginia* (1975).

New England Communities, Politics, and Religion

David Grayson Allen, *In English Ways: The Movement of Societies and the Transferral of English Law and Custom to Massachusetts Bay in the 17th Century* (1981); Virginia DeJohn Anderson, *New England's Generation: The Great Migration and the Formation of Society and Culture in the 17th Century* (1991); Richard Archer, *Fissures in the Rock: New England in the Seventeenth Century* (2001); Charles Cohen, *God's Caress: The Psychology of Puritan Religious Experience* (1986); Philip Gura, *A Glimpse of Sion's Glory: Puritan Radicalism in New England, 1620–1660* (1984); David D. Hall, *Worlds of Wonder, Days of Judgment: Popular Religious Belief in Early New England* (1989); Stephen Innes, *Creating the Commonwealth: The Economic Culture of Puritan New England* (1995); Stephen Innes, *Labor in a New Land: Economy and Society in 17th-Century Springfield* (1983); Sydney V. James, *Colonial Rhode Island* (1975); George Langdon, *Pilgrim Colony: A History of New Plymouth, 1620–1691* (1966); Kenneth A. Lockridge, *A New England Town: The First Hundred Years (Dedham, Massachusetts, 1636–1736)* (1970); John Frederick Martin, *Profits in the Wilderness: Entrepreneurship and the Founding of New England Towns in the 17th Century* (1991); Edmund S. Morgan, *The Puritan Dilemma: The Story of John Winthrop* (1958); Darrett Rutman, *Winthrop's Boston* (1965); Roger Thompson, *Divided We Stand: Watertown, Massachusetts, 1630–1680* (2001).

New England Women and Family Life

David Cressy, *Coming Over: Migration and Communication Between England and New England in the Seventeenth Century* (1987); James Deetz and Patricia Deetz, *The Times of Their Lives: Life, Love, and Death in Plymouth Colony* (2000); John P. Demos, *A Little Commonwealth: Family Life in Plymouth Colony* (1970); Lyle Koehler, *A Search for Power: The "Weaker Sex" in Seventeenth-Century New England* (1980); Edmund S. Morgan, *The Puritan Family*, rev. ed. (1966); Amanda Porterfield, *Female Piety in Puritan New England* (1992); Roger Thompson, *Sex in Middlesex: Popular Mores in a Massachusetts County, 1649–1699* (1986); Laurel Thatcher Ulrich, *Good Wives: Image and Reality in the Lives of Women in Northern New England, 1650–1750* (1982).

Chapter 3

General

Colin Calloway, *New Worlds for All: Indians, Europeans, and the Remaking of Early America* (1997); Wesley Frank Craven, *The Colonies in Transition, 1660–1713* (1968); W. J. Eccles, *France in America*, rev. ed. (1990); Jack P. Greene and J. R. Pole, eds., *Colonial British America* (1984); Peter Linebaugh and Marcus Rediker, *The Many-Headed Hydra: Sailors, Slaves, Commoners, and the Hidden History of the Revolutionary Atlantic* (2000); John J. McCusker and Russell R. Menard, *The Economy of British America, 1607–1789* (1985); John J. McCusker and Kenneth Morgan, eds., *The Early Modern Atlantic Economy* (2000).

New Netherland and the Restoration Colonies

Edwin Bronner, *William Penn's "Holy Experiment": The Founding of Pennsylvania, 1681–1701* (1962); Wesley Frank Craven, *New Jersey and the English Colonization of North America* (1964); Joyce Goodfriend, *Before the Melting Pot: Society and Culture in Colonial New York City, 1664–1730* (1992); Donna Merwick, *Death of a Notary: Conquest and Change in Colonial New York* (1999); Donna Merwick, *Possessing Albany, 1630–1710: The Dutch and English Experiences* (1990); Oliver Rink, *Holland on the Hudson: An Economic and Social History of Dutch New York* (1986); Robert C. Ritchie, *The Duke's Province: A Study of Politics and Society in Colonial New York, 1660–1691* (1977); Robert M. Weir, *Colonial South Carolina: A History* (1983).

Imperial Trade and Administration

David Armitage, *The Ideological Origins of the British Empire* (2000); Robert M. Bliss, *Revolution and Empire: English Politics and the American Colonies in the Seventeenth Century* (1991); Lawrence W. Harper, *The English Navigation Laws: A Seventeenth-Century Experiment in Social Engineering* (1939); Marcus Rediker, *Between the Devil and the Deep Blue Sea: Merchant Seamen, Pirates, and the Anglo-American Maritime*

World, 1700–1750 (1987); Robert C. Ritchie, *Captain Kidd and the War Against the Pirates* (1986); I. K. Steele, *Politics of Colonial Policy: The Board of Trade in Colonial Administration* (1968); Stephen Saunders Webb, *Lord Churchill's Coup: The Anglo-American Empire and the Glorious Revolution Reconsidered* (1995); Stephen Saunders Webb, *1676: The End of American Independence* (1984); Stephen Saunders Webb, *The Governors-General: The English Army and the Definition of the Empire, 1569–1681* (1979).

Africa and the Slave Trade

Robin Blackburn, *The Making of New World Slavery: From the Baroque to the Modern, 1492–1800* (1997); Jay Coughtry, *The Notorious Triangle: Rhode Island and the African Slave Trade, 1700–1807* (1981); Philip D. Curtin, *The Atlantic Slave Trade: A Census* (1969); David Eltis, *The Rise of African Slavery in the Americas* (1998); Joseph Inikori and Stanley Engerman, eds., *The Atlantic Slave Trade* (1992); Herbert Klein, *The Middle Passage* (1978); Robin Law, *The Slave Coast of West Africa, 1550–1750: The Impact of the Atlantic Slave Trade on an African Society* (1991); Daniel C. Littlefield, *Rice and Slaves: Ethnicity and the Slave Trade in Colonial South Carolina* (1981); James Rawley, *The Transatlantic Slave Trade: A History* (1981); Barbara Solow, ed., *Slavery and the Rise of the Atlantic System* (1991).

Africans in America

Ira Berlin, *Many Thousands Gone: The First Two Centuries of Slavery in North America* (1998); T. H. Breen and Stephen Innes, *"Myne Owne Ground": Race and Freedom on Virginia's Eastern Shore, 1640–1676* (1980); Judith Carney, *Black Rice: The African Origins of Rice Cultivation in the Americas* (2001); Douglas Deal, *Race and Class in Colonial Virginia: Indians, Englishmen, and Africans on the Eastern Shore During the Seventeenth Century* (1993); Michael A. Gomez, *Exchanging Our Country Marks: The Transformation of African Identities in the Colonial and Antebellum South* (1998); Graham R. Hodges, *Root & Branch: African Americans in New York and East Jersey, 1613–1863* (1999); Allan Kulikoff, *Tobacco and Slaves: The Development of Southern Cultures in the Chesapeake, 1680–1800* (1986); Jane Landers, *Black Society in Spanish Florida* (1999); Edgar J. McManus, *Black Bondage in the North* (1973); Edmund S. Morgan, *American Slavery, American Freedom: The Ordeal of Colonial Virginia* (1975); Lorena S. Walsh, *From Calabar to Carter's Grove: The History of a Virginia Slave Community* (1997); Betty Wood, *The Origins of American Slavery* (1997); Peter H. Wood, *Black Majority: Negroes in Colonial South Carolina from 1670 Through the Stono Rebellion* (1974).

European–Native American Relations in the North

Russell Bourne, *The Red King's Rebellion: Racial Politics in New England, 1675–1678* (1991); John Demos, *The Unredeemed Captive: A Family Story from Early America* (1994);

Matthew Dennis, *Cultivating a Landscape of Peace: Iroquois-European Encounter in Seventeenth-Century America* (1993); James D. Drake, *King Philip's War: Civil War in New England, 1675–1676* (2000); Francis Jennings, *The Ambiguous Iroquois Empire* (1984); Jill Lepore, *The Name of War: King Philip's War and the Origins of American Identity* (1998); Peter Mancall, *Deadly Medicine: Indians and Alcohol in Early America* (1995); Michael Puglisi, *Puritans Beseiged: The Legacies of King Philip's War in the Massachusetts Bay Colony* (1991); Daniel Richter, *Facing East from Indian Country: A Native History of Early America* (2001); Daniel Richter, *The Ordeal of the Longhouse: The Peoples of the Iroquois League in the Era of European Colonization* (1992); Daniel Richter and James Merrell, eds., *Beyond the Covenant Chain: The Iroquois and Their Neighbors in Indian America, 1600–1800* (1987); Richard White, *The Middle Ground: Indians, Empires, and Republics in the Great Lakes Region, 1650–1815* (1991).

European–Native American Relations in the South and West

David H. Corkran, *The Creek Frontier, 1540–1783* (1967); Verner W. Crane, *The Southern Frontier, 1660–1732* (1929); Carl Ekberg, *French Roots in the Illinois Country: The Mississippi Frontier in Colonial Times* (1998); Alan Gallay, *The Indian Slave Trade: The Rise of the English Empire in the American South, 1670–1717* (2002); Ramón Gutiérrez, *When Jesus Came, the Corn Mothers Went Away: Marriage, Sexuality, and Power in New Mexico, 1500–1846* (1991); Elizabeth A. H. John, *Storms Brewed in Other Men's Worlds: The Confrontation of Indians, Spanish, and French in the Southwest, 1540–1795* (1975); Andrew Knaut, *The Pueblo Revolt of 1680* (1995); James Merrell, *The Indians' New World: Catawbas and Their Neighbors from European Contact through the Era of Removal* (1989); Jim Norris, *After the Year Eighty: The Demise of Franciscan Power in Spanish New Mexico* (2000); Daniel H. Usner, Jr., *Indians, Settlers, and Slaves in a Frontier Exchange Economy: The Lower Mississippi Valley before 1783* (1992).

Colonial Politics

Patricia U. Bonomi, *The Lord Cornbury Scandal: The Politics of Reputation in British America* (1998); Lois Green Carr and David W. Jordan, *Maryland's Revolution of Government, 1689–1692* (1974); Richard P. Johnson, *Adjustment to Empire: The New England Colonies, 1675–1715* (1981); David S. Lovejoy, *The Glorious Revolution in America* (1972); Jack M. Sosin, *English America and Imperial Inconstancy: The Rise of Provincial Autonomy, 1696–1715* (1985); Jack M. Sosin, *English America and the Restoration Monarchy of Charles II* (1980); Jack M. Sosin, *English America and the Revolution of 1688* (1982).

New England

Bernard Bailyn, *The New England Merchants in the Seventeenth Century* (1955); Richard Bushman, *From Puritan to Yankee: Character and the Social Order in Connecticut,*

1690–1765 (1967); Christine Heyrman, *Commerce and Culture: The Maritime Communities of Colonial Massachusetts, 1690–1750* (1984); Richard Melvoin, *New England Outpost: War and Society in Colonial Deerfield* (1990); Amanda Porterfield, *Female Piety in Puritan New England* (1991); Laurel Thatcher Ulrich, *Good Wives: Image and Reality in the Lives of Women in Northern New England, 1650–1750* (1982).

New England Witchcraft

Paul Boyer and Stephen Nissenbaum, *Salem Possessed: The Social Origins of Witchcraft* (1974); Elaine Breslaw, *Tituba, Reluctant Witch of Salem: Devilish Indians and Puritan Fantasies* (1996); John Demos, *Entertaining Satan: Witchcraft and the Culture of Early New England* (1982); Richard Godbeer, *The Devil's Dominion: Magic and Religion in Early New England* (1992); Peter Hoffer, *The Devil's Disciples: Makers of the Salem Witchcraft Trials* (1996); Carol Karlsen, *The Devil in the Shape of a Woman: Witchcraft in Early New England* (1987); Mary Beth Norton, *In the Devil's Snare: The Salem Witchcraft Crisis of 1692* (2002); Bernard Rosenthal, *Salem Story: Reading the Witch Trials of 1692* (1993); Richard Weisman, *Witchcraft, Magic, and Religion in 17th-Century Massachusetts* (1984).

Chapter 4

General

Jack P. Greene, *Pursuits of Happiness: The Social Development of the Early Modern British Colonies and the Formation of American Culture* (1988); Richard Hofstadter, *America at 1750: A Social Portrait* (1971); Allan Kullikoff, *From British Peasants to Colonial American Farmers* (2000); D. W. Meinig, *Atlantic America, 1492–1800* (1986); Stephanie G. Wolf, *As Various as Their Land: The Everyday Lives of 18th-Century Americans* (1992).

New France and New Spain

Ramón Gutiérrez, *When Jesus Came, the Corn Mothers Went Away: Marriage, Sexuality, and Power in New Mexico, 1500–1846* (1991); Gwendolyn Midlo Hall, *Africans in Colonial Louisiana: The Development of Afro-Creole Culture in the Eighteenth Century* (1992); Dale Miquelon, *New France, 1701–1744* (1987); G. F. G. Stanley, *New France, 1744–1760* (1968); David J. Weber, *The Spanish Frontier in North America* (1992).

European–Native American Relations

James F. Brooks, *Captives & Cousins: Slavery, Kinship, and Community in the Southwest Borderlands* (2002); Peter C. Mancall, *Deadly Medicine: Indians and Alcohol in Early America* (1995); James H. Merrell, *Into the American Woods: Negotiators on the Pennsylvania Frontier* (1999); Daniel H. Usner, Jr., *Indians, Settlers, and Slaves in a Frontier Exchange Economy: The Lower Mississippi Valley Before 1783* (1992); Richard White, *The Middle Ground: Indians, Empires, and Republics in the Great Lakes Region, 1650–1815* (1991).

Anglo-American Society

T. H. Breen, *Tobacco Culture* (1985); Carl Bridenbaugh, *Cities in Revolt: Urban Life in America, 1743–1776* (1955); Trevor Burnard, *Creole Gentlemen: The Maryland Elite 1691–1776* (2002); Lois Green Carr et al., eds., *Colonial Chesapeake Society* (1988); David Conroy, *In Public Houses: Drink and the Revolution of Authority in Colonial Massachusetts* (1995); Rhys Isaac, *The Transformation of Virginia, 1740–1790* (1982); Christopher Jedrey, *The World of John Cleaveland: Family and Community in Eighteenth-Century New England* (1979); Sung Bok Kim, *Landlord and Tenant in Colonial New York: Manorial Society, 1664–1775* (1978); Peter C. Mancall, *Valley of Opportunity: Economic Culture Along the Upper Susquehanna, 1700–1800* (1991); Gary B. Nash, *The Urban Crucible: Social Change, Political Consciousness, and the Origins of the American Revolution* (1979); Michael Rozbicki, *The Complete Colonial Gentleman: Cultural Legitimacy in Plantation America* (1998); Sharon Salinger, *Taverns and Drinking in Early America* (2002); David S. Shields, *Civil Tongues and Polite Letters in British America* (1997); Peter Thompson, *Rum Punch & Revolution: Taverngoing & Public Life in Eighteenth-Century Philadelphia* (1999).

American Economic Development

Richard Bushman, *The Refinement of America: Persons, Houses, Cities* (1992); Cary Carson et al., eds., *Of Consuming Interests: The Style of Life in the Eighteenth Century* (1994); Marc Egnal, *New World Economies: The Growth of the Thirteen Colonies and Early Canada* (1999); David Hancock, *Citizens of the World: London Merchants and the Integration of the British Atlantic Community, 1735–1785* (1995); Phyllis W. Hunter, *Purchasing Identity in the Atlantic World: Massachusetts Merchants, 1670–1780* (2001); Stephen Innes, ed., *Work and Labor in Early America* (1988); Alice Hanson Jones, *Wealth of a Nation to Be: The American Colonies on the Eve of the Revolution* (1980); Cathy Matson, *Merchants and Empire: Trading in Colonial New York* (1998); John J. McCusker and Russell R. Menard, *The Economy of British America, 1607–1789* (1985); Margaret E. Newell, *From Dependency to Independence: Economic Revolution in Colonial New England* (1998); Gary M. Walton and James F. Shepherd, *The Economic Rise of Early America* (1979).

Anglo-American Politics

Bernard Bailyn, *The Origins of American Politics* (1968); Patricia U. Bonomi, *A Factious People: Politics and Society in Colonial New York* (1971); Richard Bushman, *King and People in Provincial Massachusetts* (1985); Edward M. Cook, Jr., *The Fathers of the Towns: Leadership and Community Structure in Eighteenth-Century New England* (1976); Jack P. Greene, *The Quest for*

Power: The Lower Houses of Assembly in the Southern Royal Colonies, 1689–1776 (1963); Marjoleine Kars, *Breaking Loose Together: The Regulator Rebellion in Pre-Revolutionary North Carolina* (2002); John Gilman Kolp, *Gentleman and Freeholders: Electoral Politics in Colonial Virginia* (1998).

Immigration to British America

Bernard Bailyn, *The Peopling of British North America* (1986); Bernard Bailyn, *Voyagers to the West* (1986); Bernard Bailyn and Philip Morgan, eds., *Strangers Within the Realm* (1991); Marilyn Baseler, *"Asylum for Mankind": America 1607–1800* (1998); Jon Butler, *The Huguenots in America* (1983); R. J. Dickson, *Ulster Immigration to Colonial America, 1718–1775* (1966); David Dobson, *Scottish Immigration to Colonial America, 1607–1785* (1994); A. Roger Ekirch, *Bound for America: The Transportation of British Convicts to the Colonies, 1718–1775* (1987); Aaron Fogleman, *Hopeful Journeys: German Immigration, Settlement, and Political Culture in Colonial America, 1717–1775* (1996); Patrick Griffin, *The People with No Name: Ireland's Ulster Scots, America's Scots Irish, and the Creation of a British Atlantic World, 1689–1764* (2001); Colin Kidd, *British Identities before Nationalism: Ethnicity and Nationhood in the British Atlantic World, 1600–1800* (1999); Ned Landsman, ed., *Nation and Province in the First British Empire: Scotland and the Americas, 1600–1800* (2001); Ned Landsman, *Scotland and Its First American Colony* (1985); A. G. Roeber, *Palatines, Liberty, and Property: German Lutherans in Colonial British America* (1993); Marianne Wokeck, *Trade in Strangers: The Beginnings of Mass Migration to North America* (1999).

African Americans

Ira Berlin, *Many Thousands Gone: The First Two Centuries of Slavery in North America* (1998); Ira Berlin and Philip Morgan, eds., *Cultivation and Culture: Labor and the Shaping of Slave Life in the Americas* (1993); Thomas J. Davis, *A Rumor of Revolt: The "Great Negro Plot" in Colonial New York* (1985); Michael A. Gomez, *Exchanging Our Country Marks: The Transformation of African Identities in the Colonial and Antebellum South* (1998); Graham R. Hodges, *Root & Branch: African Americans in New York and East Jersey, 1613–1863* (1999); Marvin L. Michael Kay and Lorin Lee Cary, *Slavery in North Carolina, 1748–1775* (1995); Allan Kulikoff, *Tobacco and Slaves: The Development of Southern Cultures in the Chesapeake, 1680–1800* (1986); Philip D. Morgan, *Slave Counterpoint: Black Culture in the Eighteenth-Century Chesapeake and Low Country* (1998); Gerald [Michael] Mullin, *Flight and Rebellion: Slave Resistance in Eighteenth-Century Virginia* (1972); Michael Mullin, *Africa in America: Slave Acculturation and Resistance in the American South and the British Caribbean, 1736–1834* (1992); Robert Olwell, *Masters, Slaves, and Subjects: The Culture of Power in the South Carolina Low Country 1740–1790* (1998); William Pierson, *Black Yankees: The Development of an Afro-American Subculture*

in Eighteenth-Century New England (1988); Mechal Sobel, *The World They Made Together: Black and White Values in Eighteenth-Century Virginia* (1987); Betty Wood, *Women's Work, Men's Work: The Informal Slave Economies of Low Country Georgia* (1995); Anne Yentsch, *A Chesapeake Family and Their Slaves* (1994).

American Women, Men, and Families

Carol R. Berkin, *First Generations: Women in Colonial America* (1996); Kathleen M. Brown, *Good Wives, Nasty Wenches, and Anxious Patriarchs: Gender, Race, and Power in Colonial Virginia* (1996); Cornelia Hughes Dayton, *Women Before the Bar: Gender, Law, and Society in Connecticut, 1639–1789* (1995); Kirsten Fischer, *Suspect Relations: Sex, Race, and Resistance in Colonial North Carolina* (2002); Philip J. Greven, *The Protestant Temperament: Patterns of Child-Rearing, Religious Experience, and the Self in Early America* (1977); Joan Gundersen, *To Be Useful to the World: Women in Eighteenth-Century America* (1996); Barry J. Levy, *Quakers and the American Family* (1988); June Namias, *White Captives: Gender and Ethnicity on the American Frontier* (1993); Ann Marie Plane, *Colonial Intimacies: Indian Marriage in Early New England* (2000); Marylynn Salmon, *Women and the Law of Property in Early America* (1986); Daniel Blake Smith, *Inside the Great House: Planter Family Life in Eighteenth-Century Chesapeake Society* (1980); Merril D. Smith, *Breaking the Bonds: Marital Discord in Pennsylvania, 1730–1830* (1992); Linda Sturtz, *Within Her Power: Propertied Women in Colonial Virginia* (2002); Lisa Wilson, *Ye Heart of a Man: The Domestic Life of Men in Colonial New England* (1999).

Anglo-American Education, Science, and the Enlightenment

Patricia Cline Cohen, *A Calculating People: The Spread of Numeracy in Early America* (1982); Lawrence A. Cremin, *American Education: The Colonial Experience, 1607–1783* (1970); Richard Beale Davis, *Intellectual Life in the Colonial South, 1585–1763* (1978); Brooke Hindle, *The Pursuit of Science in Revolutionary America* (1956); J. David Hoeveler, *Creating the American Mind: Intellect and Politics in the Colonial Colleges* (2002); Kenneth Lockridge, *Literacy in Colonial New England* (1974); Henry F. May, *The Enlightenment in America* (1976); Amy R. W. Meyers and Margaret Beck Pritchard, eds., *Nature's Empire: Mark Catesby's New World Vision* (1998); Thomas P. Slaughter, *The Natures of John and William Bartram* (1996); William Sloan and Julie Williams, *The Early American Press, 1690–1783* (1994); Raymond P. Stearns, *Science in the British Colonies of America* (1970).

Religion and the Great Awakening

Robert W. Brockway, *A Wonderful Work of God: Puritanism and the Great Awakening* (2003); Catherine Brekus, *Strangers and Pilgrims: Female Preaching in America, 1740–1845* (1998); Patricia U. Bonomi, *Under the Cope of Heaven: Reli-*

gion, Society, and Politics in Colonial America (1986); J. M. Bumstead and John E. Van de Wetering, *What Must I Do to Be Saved? The Great Awakening in Colonial America* (1976); Jon Butler, *Awash in a Sea of Faith: Christianizing the American People* (1990); Michael Crawford, *Seasons of Grace: Colonial New England's Revival Tradition in Its British Context* (1991); Alan E. Heimert, *Religion and the American Mind: From the Great Awakening to the Revolution* (1966); Frank Lambert, *Inventing the "Great Awakening"* (1999); Rebecca Larson, *Daughters of Light: Quaker Women Preaching and Prophesying in the Colonies and Abroad, 1700–1775* (1999); David S. Lovejoy, *Religious Enthusiasm in the New World* (1985); John K. Nelson, *A Blessed Company: Parishes, Parsons, and Parishioners in Anglican Virginia, 1690–1776* (2001); Harry S. Stout, *The Divine Dramatist: George Whitefield and the Rise of Modern Evangelicalism* (1991); Patricia Tracy, *Jonathan Edwards, Pastor* (1980).

Chapter 5

General

Ian R. Christie and Benjamin W. Labaree, *Empire or Independence, 1760–1776: A British-American Dialogue on the Coming of the American Revolution* (1976); Barbara DeWolfe, ed., *Discoveries of America: Personal Accounts of British Emigrants to North America during the Revolutionary Era* (1997); Marc Egnal, *A Mighty Empire: The Origins of the American Revolution* (1988); Ronald Hoffman et al., eds., *The Economy of Early America: The Revolutionary Period, 1763–1790* (1988); Merrill Jensen, *The Founding of a Nation: A History of the American Revolution, 1763–1776* (1968); John Phillip Reid, *The Constitutional History of the American Revolution* (1995); Robert W. Tucker and David C. Hendrickson, *The Fall of the First British Empire: Origins of the War of American Independence* (1982).

Colonial Warfare and the British Empire

Fred Anderson, *Crucible of War: The Seven Years' War and the Fate of Empire in British North America* (2000); Fred Anderson, *A People's Army: Massachusetts Soldiers and Society in the Seven Years' War* (1984); Frank W. Brecher, *Losing a Continent: France's North American Policy, 1753–1763* (1998); Stephen Brumwell, *Redcoats: The British Soldier and War in the Americas, 1755–1763* (2002); Lawrence Henry Gipson, *The British Empire Before the American Revolution* (1736–1770); Douglas Leach, *Roots of Conflict: British Armed Forces and Colonial Americans, 1677–1763* (1986); William Pencak, *War, Politics, and Revolution in Provincial Massachusetts* (1981); Geoffrey Plank, *An Unsettled Conquest: The British Campaign Against the Peoples of Acadia* (2001); Alan Rogers, *Empire and Liberty: American Resistance to British Authority, 1755–1763* (1974); John Shy, *Toward Lexington: The Role of the British Army in the Coming of the American Revolution*

(1965); David C. Skaggs and Larry Nelson, eds., *The Sixty Years' War for the Great Lakes, 1754–1814* (2001); Ian K. Steele, *Warpaths: Invasions of North America* (1994); James Titus, *The Old Dominion at War: Society, Politics, and Warfare in Late Colonial Virginia* (1991).

British Politics and Policy

Colin Bonwick, *English Radicals and the American Revolution* (1977); James E. Bradley, *Popular Politics and the American Revolution in England* (1986); John Brewer, *Party Ideology and Popular Politics at the Accession of George III* (1976); John Brooke, *King George III* (1972); John L. Bullion, *A Great and Necessary Measure: George Grenville and the Genesis of the Stamp Act, 1763–1765* (1981); Eliga Gould, *The Persistence of Empire: British Political Culture in the Age of the American Revolution* (2000); Michael Kammen, *A Rope of Sand: The Colonial Agents, British Politics, and the American Revolution* (1968); Nancy F. Koehn, *The Power of Commerce: Economy and Governance in the First British Empire* (1994); Colin Nicolson, *The "Infamas Governer": Francis Bernard and the Origins of the American Revolution* (2000); P. D. G. Thomas, *Tea Party to Independence* (1991); P. D. G. Thomas, *The Townshend Duties Crisis* (1987); P. D. G. Thomas, *British Politics and the Stamp Act Crisis* (1975).

Native Americans and the West

Richard Aquila, *The Iroquois Restoration: Iroquois Diplomacy on the Colonial Frontier, 1701–1754* (1983); Andrew Cayton and Fredrika Teute, eds., *Contact Points: American Frontiers from the Mohawk Valley to the Mississippi, 1750–1830* (1998); David H. Corkran, *The Cherokee Frontier: Conflict and Survival, 1740–1762* (1962); Gregory Dowd, *A Spirited Resistance: The North American Indian Struggle for Unity, 1745–1815* (1992); Gregory Dowd, *War Under Heaven: Pontiac, the Indian Nation, and the British Empire* (2002); Tom Hatley, *The Dividing Paths: Cherokees and South Carolinians through the Revolutionary Era* (1995); Eric Hinderaker, *Elusive Empires: Confronting Colonialism in the Ohio Valley 1673–1800* (1997); Eric Hinderaker and Peter C. Mancall, *At the Edge of Empire: The Backcountry in British North America* (2003); Francis Jennings, *Empire of Fortune: Crowns, Colonies and Tribes in the Seven Years' War in America* (1988); James H. Merrell, *Into the American Woods: Negotiators on the Pennsylvania Frontier* (1999); Howard H. Peckham, *Pontiac and the Indian Uprising* (1947); Timothy Shannon, *Indians and Colonists at the Crossroads of Empire: The Albany Congress of 1754* (1999); Jack M. Sosin, *Whitehall and the Wilderness: The Middle West in British Colonial Policy, 1760–1775* (1961); Richard White, *The Middle Ground: Indians, Empires and Republics in the Great Lakes Region, 1650–1815* (1991).

Political and Economic Thought

Bernard Bailyn, *The Ideological Origins of the American Revolution* (1967); J. C. D. Clark, *The Language of Liberty,*

1660–1832: Political Discourse and Social Dynamics in the Anglo-American World (1994); J. E. Crowley, *This Sheba, Self: The Conceptualization of Economic Life in Eighteenth-Century America* (1974); Jay Fliegelman, *Prodigals and Pilgrims: The American Revolution Against Patriarchal Authority, 1750–1800* (1982).

American Resistance

T. H. Breen, *Tobacco Culture: The Mentality of the Great Tidewater Planters on the Eve of the Revolution* (1985); Joseph Albert Ernst, *Money and Politics in America, 1755–1775: A Study in the Currency Act of 1764 and the Political Economy of Revolution* (1973); David Conroy, *Drink and the Revolution of Authority in Colonial Massachusetts* (1995); Dirk Hoerder, *Crowd Action in Revolutionary Massachusetts, 1765–1780* (1977); Woody Holton, *Forced Founders: Indians, Debtors, Slaves, and the Making of the American Revolution in Virginia* (1999); Benjamin W. Labaree, *The Boston Tea Party* (1964); Pauline R. Maier, *The Old Revolutionaries: Political Lives in the Age of Samuel Adams* (1980); Pauline R. Maier, *From Resistance to Revolution: Colonial Radicals and the Development of American Opposition to Britain, 1765–1776* (1972); Edmund S. Morgan and Helen M. Morgan, *The Stamp Act Crisis: Prologue to Revolution* (1953); Gary B. Nash, *The Urban Crucible: Social Change, Political Consciousness, and the Origins of the American Revolution* (1979); Bruce A. Ragsdale, *A Planters' Republic: The Search for Economic Independence in Revolutionary Virginia* (1996); Richard Ryerson, *The Revolution Has Now Begun: The Radical Committees of Philadelphia, 1765–1776* (1978); Peter Shaw, *American Patriots and the Rituals of Revolution* (1981); Peter Thompson, *Rum Punch & Revolution: Taverngoing & Public Life in Eighteenth-Century Philadelphia* (1999); Joseph Tiedemann, *Reluctant Revolutionaries: New York City and the Road to Independence, 1763–1776* (1997); John W. Tyler, *Smugglers and Patriots: Boston Merchants and the Advent of the American Revolution* (1986); Richard Walsh, *Charleston's Sons of Liberty: A Study of the Artisans, 1763–1789* (1959); Hiller B. Zobel, *The Boston Massacre* (1970).

Chapter 6

General

Colin Bonwick, *The American Revolution* (1991); Edward Countryman, *The American Revolution*, rev. ed. (2002); Theodore Draper, *A Struggle for Power: The American Revolution* (1996); John Ferling, *A Leap in the Dark: The Struggle to Create the American Republic* (2003); Ronald Hoffman and Peter J. Albert, eds., *The Transforming Hand of Revolution: Reconsidering the American Revolution as a Social Movement* (1995); Robert Middlekauff, *The Glorious Cause: The American Revolution, 1763–1783* (1982); Andrew J. O'Shaughnessy, *An Empire Divided: The American Revolution and the British Caribbean* (2000); Harry M. Ward, *The American Revolution:*

Nationhood Achieved, 1763–1788 (1995); Gordon S. Wood, *The American Revolution* (2002); Alfred F. Young, ed., *Beyond the American Revolution* (1993); Alfred F. Young, ed., *The American Revolution: Explorations in the History of American Radicalism* (1976).

Continental Congress, Committees, and the Declaration of Independence

David Ammerman, *In the Common Cause: American Response to the Coercive Acts of 1774* (1974); Richard D. Brown, *Revolutionary Politics in Massachusetts: The Boston Committee of Correspondence and the Towns, 1772–1774* (1970); Jay Fliegelman, *Declaring Independence: Jefferson, Natural Language, & the Culture of Performance* (1993); Pauline Maier, *American Scripture: Making the Declaration of Independence* (1997); Jerrilyn Marston, *King and Congress: The Transfer of Political Legitimacy, 1774–1776* (1987); Garry Wills, *Inventing America: Jefferson's Declaration of Independence* (1978); Ann Withington, *Toward a More Perfect Union: Virtue and the Formation of American Republics* (1992).

Military Affairs

Jeremy Black, *War for America: The Fight for Independence, 1775–1783* (1991); Wayne Bodle, *The Valley Forge Winter: Civilians and Soldiers in War* (2002); Richard Buel, *In Irons: Britain's Naval Supremacy and the American Revolutionary Economy* (1999); E. Wayne Carp, *To Starve the Army at Pleasure: Continental Army Administration and American Political Culture, 1775–1783* (1984); Stephen Conway, *The War of American Independence, 1775–1783* (1995); Elizabeth Fenn, *Pox Americana: The Great Smallpox Epidemic of 1775–82* (2001); Don Higginbotham, *The War of American Independence: Military Attitudes, Policies, and Practice, 1763–1789* (1971); Ronald Hoffman and Peter Albert, eds., *Arms and Independence: The Military Character of the American Revolution* (1984); Richard Ketchum, *Saratoga: Turning Point of America's Revolutionary War* (1997); Piers Mackesy, *The War for America, 1775–1783* (1964); James K. Martin, *Benedict Arnold, Revolutionary Hero* (1997); James K. Martin and Mark Lender, *"A Respectable Army": The Military Origins of the Republic, 1763–1789* (1982); Charles Niemeyer, *America Goes to War: A Social History of the Continental Army* (1997); Charles Royster, *A Revolutionary People at War: The Continental Army and American Character, 1775–1783* (1980); John Shy, *A People Numerous and Armed: Reflections on the Military Struggle for American Independence*, rev. ed. (1990).

Local and Regional Studies

Michael Bellesiles, *Revolutionary Outlaws: Ethan Allen and the Struggle for Independence on the Early American Frontier* (1993); Richard Buel, *Dear Liberty: Connecticut's Mobilization for the Revolutionary War* (1980); Edward Countryman, *A People in Revolution: The American Revolution and Political Society in New York, 1760–1790* (1981); Elaine Crane, *A*

Dependent People: Newport, Rhode Island, in the Revolutionary Era (1985); Jeffrey Crow and Larry Tise, eds., *The Southern Experience in the American Revolution* (1978); Thomas Doerflinger, *A Vigorous Spirit of Enterprise: Merchants and Economic Development in Revolutionary Philadelphia* (1986); John Mack Faragher, *Daniel Boone* (1992); David Hackett Fischer, *Paul Revere's Ride* (1994); Craig T. Friend, ed., *The Buzzel about Kentucky: Settling the Promised Land* (1999); Francis S. Fox, *Sweet Land of Liberty: The Ordeal of the American Revolution in Northampton County, Pennsylvania* (2002); Robert A. Gross, *The Minutemen and Their World* (1976); Eric Hinderaker, *Elusive Empires: Constructing Colonialism in the Ohio Valley, 1673–1800* (1997); Ronald Hoffman, *A Spirit of Dissension: Economics, Politics, and the Revolution in Maryland* (1973); Ronald Hoffman, Thad W. Tate, and Peter Albert, eds., *An Uncivil War: The Southern Backcountry During the American Revolution* (1985); Woody Holton, *Forced Founders: Indians, Debtors, Slaves, and the Making of the American Revolution in Virginia* (1999); Jean B. Lee, *The Price of Nationhood: The American Revolution in Charles County* (1994); Wayne E. Lee, *Crowds of Soldiers in Revolutionary North Carolina: The Culture of Violence in Riot and War* (2001); Stephen Rosswurm, *Arms, Country, and Class: The Philadelphia Militia and the "Lower Sort" During the American Revolution* (1988); John Selby, *The Revolution in Virginia, 1775–1783* (1988).

Indians and African Americans

Colin Calloway, *The American Revolution in Indian Country* (1995); Sylvia Frey, *Water from the Rock: Black Resistance in a Revolutionary Age* (1991); Barbara Graymont, *The Iroquois in the American Revolution* (1972); Isabel T. Kelsey, *Joseph Brant, 1743–1807: Man of Two Worlds* (1984); James H. O'Donnell III, *Southern Indians in the American Revolution* (1973); Anthony F. C. Wallace, *The Death and Rebirth of the Seneca* (1969).

Loyalists

Bernard Bailyn, *The Ordeal of Thomas Hutchinson* (1974); Robert McCluer Calhoon, *The Loyalists in Revolutionary America, 1760–1781* (1973); Mary Beth Norton, *The British-Americans: The Loyalist Exiles in England, 1774–1789* (1972); Janice Potter, *The Liberty We Seek: Loyalist Ideology in Colonial New York and Massachusetts* (1983); Paul H. Smith, *Loyalists and Redcoats: A Study in British Revolutionary Policy* (1964); James W. St. G. Walker, *The Black Loyalists: The Search for a Promised Land in Nova Scotia and Sierra Leone, 1783–1870* (1976).

Women

Richard Buel and Joy Buel, *The Way of Duty: A Woman and Her Family in Revolutionary America* (1984); Patricia Cleary, *Elizabeth Murray: A Woman's Pursuit of Independence in Eighteenth-Century America* (2000); Edith Gelles, *Portia: The World of Abigail Adams* (1992); Ronald Hoffman and Peter J. Albert, eds., *Women in the Age of the American Revolution* (1989); Linda K. Kerber, *Women of the Republic: Intellect and Ideology in Revolutionary America* (1980); Holly Mayer, *Belonging to the Army: Camp Followers and Community during the American Revolution* (1996); Mary Beth Norton, *Liberty's Daughters: The Revolutionary Experience of American Women, 1750–1800* (1980); Rosemary Zagarri, *A Woman's Dilemma: Mercy Otis Warren and the American Revolution* (1995).

Foreign Policy

Jonathan Dull, *A Diplomatic History of the American Revolution* (1985); Ronald Hoffman and Peter Albert, eds., *Peace and the Peacemakers: The Treaty of 1783* (1986); Ronald Hoffman and Peter Albert, eds., *Diplomacy and Revolution: The Franco-American Alliance of 1778* (1981); Lawrence Kaplan, ed., *The American Revolution and a "Candid World"* (1977); Jan Willem Schulte Nordholt, *The Dutch Republic and American Independence* (1982); Richard W. Van Alstyne, *Empire and Independence: The International History of the American Revolution* (1965).

Patriot Leaders

John K. Alexander, *Samuel Adams: America's Revolutionary Politician* (2002); Joyce O. Appleby, *Thomas Jefferson* (2003); Fawn M. Brodie, *Thomas Jefferson: An Intimate History* (1974); Joseph J. Ellis, *American Sphinx: The Character of Thomas Jefferson* (1997); John E. Ferling, *The First of Men: A Life of George Washington* (1988); Eric Foner, *Tom Paine and Revolutionary America* (1976); Don Higginbotham, *George Washington: Uniting a Nation* (2002); Ronald Hoffman, *Princes of Ireland, Planters of Maryland: A Carroll Saga, 1500–1782* (2000); David McCullough, *John Adams* (2001); Edmund S. Morgan, *Benjamin Franklin* (2002); John Rhodehamel, *The Great Experiment: George Washington and the American Republic* (1998); Charles Royster, *Light-Horse Harry Lee and the Legacy of the American Revolution* (1981); Sheila Skemp, *Benjamin and William Franklin: Father and Son, Patriot and Loyalist* (1994); Esmond Wright, *Franklin of Philadelphia* (1986).

Chapter 7

General

Joyce Appleby, *Inheriting the Revolution: The First Generation of Americans* (2000); Richard Beeman et al., eds., *Beyond Confederation: Origins of the Constitution and American National Identity* (1987); Andrew Burstein, *Sentimental Democracy: The Evolution of America's Romantic Self-Image* (1999); John E. Crowley, *The Privileges of Independence: Neomercantilism and the American Revolution* (1993); Francis Jennings, *The Creation of America: From Revolution to Empire* (2000); Mark E. Kann, *A Republic of Men: The American Founders, Gendered Language, and Patriarchal Politics* (1998); Cathy

Matson and Peter S. Onuf, *A Union of Interests: Political and Economic Thought in Revolutionary America* (1990); Forrest McDonald, *Novus Ordo Seclorum: The Intellectual Origins of the Constitution* (1985); Edmund S. Morgan, *Inventing the People: The Rise of Popular Sovereignty in England and America* (1988); W. M. Verhoeven, ed., *Revolutionary Histories: Transatlantic Cultural Nationalism, 1775–1815* (2002); David Waldstreicher, *In the Midst of Perpetual Fetes: The Making of American Nationalism, 1776–1820* (1997); Gordon S. Wood, *The Radicalism of the American Revolution* (1992); Gordon S. Wood, *The Creation of the American Republic, 1776–1787* (1969); Robert E. Wright, *The Origins of Commercial Banking in America, 1750–1800* (2001); Alfred F. Young et al., eds., *We the People: Voices and Images of the New Nation* (1993); Rosemary Zagarri, *The Politics of Size: Representation in the United States, 1776–1850* (1988).

Continental Congress and Articles of Confederation

E. James Ferguson, *The Power of the Purse: A History of American Public Finance, 1776–1790* (1961); H. James Henderson, *Party Politics in the Continental Congress* (1974); Merrill Jensen, *The New Nation: A History of the United States During the Confederation, 1781–1789* (1950); Richard B. Morris, *The Forging of the Union, 1781–1789* (1987); Peter S. Onuf, *Statehood and Union: A History of the Northwest Ordinance* (1987); Jack N. Rakove, *The Beginnings of National Politics: An Interpretive History of the Continental Congress* (1979).

State Politics

Willi Paul Adams, *The First American Constitutions: Republican Ideology and the Making of the State Constitutions in the Revolutionary Era* (1980); Robert Gross, ed., *In Debt to Shays* (1992); Ronald Hoffman and Peter Albert, eds., *Sovereign States in an Age of Uncertainty* (1981); Donald Lutz, *Popular Consent and Popular Control: Whig Political Theory in the Early State Constitutions* (1980); Jackson Turner Main, *Political Parties Before the Constitution* (1973); Jackson Turner Main, *The Sovereign States, 1775–1783* (1973); David P. Szatmary, *Shays' Rebellion: The Making of an Agrarian Insurrection* (1980).

The Constitution

Thornton Anderson, *Creating the Constitution: The Convention of 1787 and the First Congress* (1993); Lance Banning, *The Sacred Fire of Liberty: James Madison and the Founding of the Federal Republic* (1995); Carol Berkin, *A Brilliant Solution: Inventing the American Constitution* (2002); Roger H. Brown, *Redeeming the Republic: Federalists, Taxation, and the Origins of the Constitution* (1993); Saul Cornell, *The Other Founders: Anti-Federalism & the Dissenting Tradition in America, 1788–1828* (1999); Christopher Duncan, *The Anti-Federalists and Early American Political Thought* (1995); Jackson Turner Main, *The Anti-Federalists: Critics of the Constitution, 1781–1788* (1961); Frederick W. Marks III, *Independence on Trial: Foreign Affairs and the Making of the Constitution* (1973); Jack N. Rakove, *Original Meanings: Politics and Ideas in the Making of the Constitution* (1996); Jack N. Rakove, *James Madison and the Creation of the American Republic* (1990); Robert A. Rutland, *The Ordeal of the Constitution: The Antifederalists and the Ratification Struggle of 1787–88* (1966); Abraham Sofaer, *War, Foreign Affairs, and Constitutional Power*, vol. 1: *The Origins* (1976).

Religion, Education, and Culture

Dee Andrews, *The Methodists and Revolutionary America, 1760–1800* (2000); Cathy N. Davidson, *Revolution and the Word: The Rise of the Novel in America* (1987); Joseph M. Ellis, *After the Revolution: Profiles of Early American Culture* (1979); Charles P. Hanson, *Necessary Virtue: The Pragmatic Origins of Religious Liberty in New England* (1998); Ronald Hoffman and Peter J. Albert, eds., *Religion in a Revolutionary Age* (1994); Carl F. Kaestle, *Pillars of the Republic: Common Schools and American Society, 1780–1860* (1983); Mechal Sobel, *Teach Me Dreams: The Search for Self in the Revolutionary Era* (2000); Russel B. Nye, *The Cultural Life of the New Nation, 1776–1803* (1960); Kenneth Silverman, *A Cultural History of the American Revolution* (1976).

Women

Susan Branson, *These Fiery Frenchified Dames: Women and Political Culture in Early National Philadelphia* (2001); Edith Gelles, *Portia: The World of Abigail Adams* (1992); Ronald Hoffman and Peter Albert, eds., *Women in the Age of the American Revolution* (1989); Susan Juster, *Disorderly Women: Sexual Politics and Evangelicalism in Revolutionary New England* (1994); Linda K. Kerber, *Women of the Republic: Intellect and Ideology in Revolutionary America* (1980); Mary Beth Norton, *Liberty's Daughters: The Revolutionary Experience of American Women, 1750–1800* (1980); Sheila Skemp, *Judith Sargent Murray* (1998).

African Americans and Slavery

Ira Berlin, *Many Thousands Gone: The First Two Centuries of Slavery in North America* (1998); Ira Berlin and Ronald Hoffman, eds., *Slavery and Freedom in the Age of the American Revolution* (1983); Patricia Bradley, *Slavery, Propaganda, and the American Revolution* (1998); David Brion Davis, *The Problem of Slavery in the Age of Revolution, 1770–1823* (1975); Paul Finkelman, *Slavery and the Founders: Race and Liberty in the Age of Jefferson* (1996); Carol V. R. George, *Segregated Sabbaths: Richard Allen and the Emergence of Independent Black Churches, 1760–1840* (1973); Michael A. Gomez, *Exchanging Our Country Marks: The Transformation of African Identities in the Colonial and Antebellum South* (1998); Graham R. Hodges, *Root & Branch: African Americans in New York and East Jersey, 1613–1863* (1999); Winthrop Jordan, *White over Black: American Attitudes Toward the Negro, 1550–1812* (1968); Duncan J. Macleod, *Slavery, Race, and the American Revolution (1974); Joanne Pope Melish, *Disowning Slavery: Gradual Emancipation and "Race" in New England, 1780–1860* (1998); Gary Nash, *Forging Freedom: The Formation of Philadelphia's Black Community, 1720–1840* (1988); Donald L. Robinson, *Slavery in the Structure of American Politics, 1765–1820* (1971); Shane White, *Somewhat More Independent: The End of Slavery in New York City, 1770–1810* (1991); T. Stephen Whitman, *The Price of Freedom: Slavery and Manumission in Baltimore and Early National Maryland* (2000); Arthur Zilversmit, *The First Emancipation: The Abolition of Slavery in the North* (1967).

Indians

Harvey L. Carter, *The Life and Times of Little Turtle* (1987); Gregory E. Dowd, *A Spirited Resistance: The North American Indian Struggle for Unity, 1745–1815* (1992); Frederick Hoxie, et al., eds, *Native Americans and the Early Republic* (1999); Dorothy Jones, *License for Empire: Colonialism by Treaty in Early America* (1982); Wiley Sword, *President Washington's Indian War: The Struggle for the Old Northwest, 1790–1795* (1985); Anthony F. C. Wallace, *The Death and Rebirth of the Seneca* (1969); Richard White, *The Middle Ground: Indians, Empires, and Republics in the Great Lakes Region, 1650–1815* (1991).

Chapter 8

National Government and Administration

Charlene Bickford and Kenneth Bowling, *Birth of the Nation: The Federal Congress, 1789–1791* (2002); Kenneth Bowling, *The Creation of Washington, D.C.* (1991); Richard Brookhiser, *Alexander Hamilton, American* (1999); Ralph Adams Brown, *The Presidency of John Adams* (1975); William Casto, *The Supreme Court in the Early Republic: The Chief Justiceships of John Jay and Oliver Ellsworth* (1995); Stanley Elkins and Eric McKitrick, *The Age of Federalism, 1788–1800* (1993); Joseph J. Ellis, *Founding Brothers: The Revolutionary Generation* (2000); Morton Frisch, *Alexander Hamilton and the Political Order* (1991); Ronald Hoffman and Peter J. Albert, eds., *Launching the "Extended Republic": The Federalist Era* (1998); James H. Hutson, ed., *Religion and the New Republic: Faith in the Founding of America* (1999); Richard Kohn, *Eagle and Sword: The Federalists and the Creation of the Military Establishment in America, 1783–1802* (1975); Tadahisa Kuroda, *The Origins of the Twelfth Amendment: The Electoral College in the Early Republic, 1787–1804* (1994); Stuart Leiberger, *Founding Friendship: George Washington, James Madison, and the Creation of the American Republic* (1999); Forrest McDonald, *Alexander Hamilton* (1979); Forrest McDonald, *The Presidency of George Washington* (1974); John R. Nelson, Jr., *Liberty and Property: Political Economy and Policymaking in the New Nation, 1789–1812* (1987); Mark D. Rozell, et al., eds., *George Washington and the Origins of the American Presidency* (2000); James R. Sharp, *American Politics in the Early Republic: The*

New Nation in Crisis (1993); Garry Wills, *Cincinnatus: George Washington and the Enlightenment* (1984).

Partisan Politics

Lance Banning, *The Jeffersonian Persuasion: Evolution of a Party Ideology* (1978); Richard Buel, *Securing the Revolution: Ideology in American Politics, 1789–1815* (1972); Joseph Charles, *The Origins of the American Party System* (1956); Noble E. Cunningham, *The Jeffersonian Republicans: The Formation of Party Organization, 1789–1801* (1957); Manning J. Dauer, *The Adams Federalists* (1953); Richard Hofstadter, *The Idea of a Party System: The Rise of Legitimate Opposition in the United States, 1780–1840* (1970); Thomas Slaughter, *The Whiskey Rebellion* (1986); John Zvesper, *Political Philosophy and Rhetoric: A Study of the Origins of American Party Politics* (1977).

Economics in Thought and Practice

Joyce Appleby, *Capitalism and a New Social Order: The Republican Vision of the 1790s* (1984); Christopher Clark, *The Roots of Rural Capitalism: Western Massachusetts, 1780–1860* (1990); Paul Gilje, ed., *Wages of Independence: Capitalism in the Early American Republic* (1997); James A. Henretta, *The Origins of American Capitalism* (1991); Allan Kulikoff, *The Agrarian Origins of American Capitalism* (1992); Curtis Nettels, *The Emergence of a National Economy, 1775–1815* (1962); Winifred Rothenberg, *From Market-Places to Market Economy: The Transformation of Rural Massachusetts, 1750–1850* (1992).

Foreign Relations

Harry Ammon, *The Genet Mission* (1973); Samuel F. Bemis, *Jay's Treaty* (1962); Samuel F. Bemis, *Pinckney's Treaty* (1960); Jerald A. Combs, *The Jay Treaty* (1970); Alexander DeConde, *The Quasi-War: Politics and Diplomacy of the Undeclared War with France, 1797–1801* (1966); Alexander DeConde, *Entangling Alliance: Politics and Diplomacy Under George Washington* (1958); Felix Gilbert, *To the Farewell Address: Ideas of Early American Foreign Policy* (1961); Reginald Horsman, *The Diplomacy of the New Republic, 1776–1815* (1985); Lawrence Kaplan, *"Entangling Alliances with None": American Foreign Policy in the Age of Jefferson* (1987); Conor Cruise O'Brien, *The Long Affair: Thomas Jefferson and the French Revolution, 1785–1800* (1996); Bradford Perkins, *The First Rapprochement: England and the United States, 1795–1805* (1967); Matthew Spalding and Patrick J. Garrity, *A Sacred Union of Citizens: George Washington's Farewell Address and American Character* (1996); William Stinchcombe, *The XYZ Affair* (1981); William E. Weeks, *Building the Continental Empire: American Expansion from the Revolution to the Civil War* (1996).

Civil Liberties

Ronald Hoffman and Peter Albert, eds., *The Bill of Rights: Government Proscribed* (1997); Leonard W. Levy, *Emergence* of a Free Press (1985); Leonard W. Levy, *Origins of the Fifth Amendment* (1968); Robert A. Rutland, *The Birth of the Bill of Rights, 1776–1791* (1983); James Morton Smith, *Freedom's Fetters: The Alien and Sedition Laws and American Civil Liberties* (1956).

Indians and African Americans

Douglas Egerton, *Gabriel's Rebellion: The Virginia Slave Conspiracies of 1800 and 1802* (1993); Dorothy Jones, *License for Empire: Colonization by Treaty in Early America* (1982); Michael A. Morrison and James B. Stewart, eds., *Race and the Early Republic: Racial Consciousness and Nation-Building in the Early Republic* (2002); Theda Perdue, *Cherokee Women: Gender and Culture Change, 1700–1835* (1998); Theda Perdue, *"Mixed Blood" Indians: Racial Construction in the Early South* (2003); Francis Paul Prucha, *American Indian Policy in the Formative Years: The Indian Trade and Intercourse Acts, 1790–1834* (1962); James Sidbury, *Ploughshares into Swords: Race, Rebellion, and Identity in Gabriel's Virginia, 1730–1810* (1997); Mechal Sobel, *The World They Made Together: Black and White Values in Eighteenth-Century Virginia* (1987); Anthony F. C. Wallace, *The Death and Rebirth of the Seneca* (1969).

Chapter 9

General

Henry Adams, *History of the United States of America During the Administration of Thomas Jefferson and of James Madison,* 9 vols. (1889–1891); Noble E. Cunningham, Jr., *The United States in 1800: Henry Adams Revisited* (1988); Jean V. Matthews, *Toward a New Society: American Thought and Culture, 1800–1830* (1991); John Mayfield, *The New Nation, 1800–1845* (1981); Marshall Smelser, *The Democratic Republic, 1801–1815* (1968).

Political Culture

Catherine Allgor, *Parlor Politics: In Which the Ladies of Washington Help Build a City and a Government* (2000); James M. Banner, *To the Hartford Convention: The Federalists and the Origins of Party Politics in the Early Republic, 1789–1815* (1967); Noble E. Cunningham, Jr., *The Jeffersonian Republicans in Power: Party Operations, 1801–1809* (1963); David Hackett Fischer, *The Revolution of American Conservatism: The Federalist Party in the Era of Jeffersonian Democracy* (1965); Joanne B. Freeman, *Affairs of Honor: National Politics in the New Republic* (2001); Carol Sue Humphrey, *The Press of the Young Republic, 1783–1833* (1994); Roger G. Kennedy, *Burr, Hamilton, and Jefferson: A Study in Character* (1999); Linda K. Kerber, *Federalists in Dissent* (1970); Richard P. McCormick, *The Presidential Game: The Origins of American Presidential Politics* (1982); Drew McCoy, *The Elusive Republic* (1980); Samuel Eliot Morison, *Harrison Gray Otis, 1765–1848: The Urbane Federalist* (1969); David Paul Nord, *Communities of Journalism: A History of American Newspapers and Their Readers* (2001); Peter S. Onuf, *Jefferson's Empire: The Language of American Nationhood* (2000); Jeffrey L. Pasley, *"The Tyranny of Printers": Newspaper Politics in the Early American Republic* (2001); Arnold A. Rogow, *A Fatal Friendship: Alexander Hamilton and Aaron Burr* (1998); James Roger Sharp, *American Politics in the Early Republic: The New Nation in Crisis* (1993); James Sterling Young, *The Washington Community, 1800–1828* (1966).

Jefferson and Madison

Noble E. Cunningham, Jr., *In Pursuit of Reason: The Life of Thomas Jefferson* (1987); Noble E. Cunningham, Jr., *The Process of Government Under Jefferson* (1978); Joseph J. Ellis, *American Sphinx: The Character of Thomas Jefferson* (1996); Annette Gordon-Reed, *Thomas Jefferson and Sally Hemings: An American Controversy* (1997); Ralph Ketcham, *Presidents Above Party: The First American Presidency, 1789–1829* (1984); Drew R. McCoy, *The Last of the Fathers: James Madison and the Republican Legacy* (1989); Peter S. Onuf, ed., *Jeffersonian Legacies* (1993); Merrill D. Peterson, *Thomas Jefferson and the New Nation* (1970); Norman K. Risjord, *Thomas Jefferson* (1994); Robert Allen Rutland, *The Presidency of James Madison* (1990); Robert W. Tucker and David C. Hendrickson, *Empire of Liberty: The Statecraft of Thomas Jefferson* (1990).

The Supreme Court and the Law

Leonard Baker, *John Marshall: A Life in Law* (1974); Robert Lowry Clinton, *Marbury v. Madison and Judicial Review* (1989); Richard E. Ellis, *The Jeffersonian Crisis: Courts and Politics in the Young Republic* (1971); Morton J. Horowitz, *The Transformation of American Law, 1780–1860* (1977); Herbert A. Johnson, *The Chief Justiceship of John Marshall, 1801–1835* (1997); R. Kent Newmyer, *The Supreme Court Under Marshall and Taney* (1968); Thomas C. Shevory, *John Marshall's Law: Interpretation, Ideology, and Interest* (1994); Francis N. Stites, *John Marshall: Defender of the Constitution* (1981).

Louisiana and Lewis and Clark

Stephen E. Ambrose, *Undaunted Courage: Meriwether Lewis, Thomas Jefferson, and the Opening of the American West* (1996); Alexander De Conde, *This Affair of Louisiana* (1976); Albert Furtwangler, *Acts of Discovery: Visions of America in the Lewis and Clark Journals* (1993); Donna J. Kessler, *The Making of Sacagawea: A Euro-American Legend* (1996); James P. Ronda, *Lewis and Clark Among the Indians* (1984); James P. Ronda, ed., *Thomas Jefferson and the Changing West* (1997); James P. Ronda, ed., *Voyage of Discovery: Essays on the Lewis and Clark Expedition* (1998).

Indian Resistance

Gregory Evans Dowd, *A Spiritual Resistance: The North American Indian Struggle for Unity, 1745–1815* (1992); R. David Edmunds, *Tecumseh and the Quest for Indian Leadership* (1984); R. David Edmunds, *The Shawnee Prophet* (1983); John Sugden, *Tecumseh: A Life* (1998); Anthony F. C. Wallace, *Jeffeson and the Indians: The Tragic Fate of the First Americans* (1999); James Wilson, *The Earth Shall Weep: A History of Native America* (1998).

Expansionism, the War of 1812, and Foreign Relations

Robert J. Allison, *The Crescent Obscured: The United States and the Muslim World, 1776–1815* (1995); Paul Baepler, ed., *White Slaves, African Masters: An Anthology of American Barbary Captivity Narratives* (1999); Roger H. Brown, *The Republic in Peril* (1964); Clifford L. Egan, *Neither Peace nor War: Franco-American Relations, 1803–1812* (1983); Kenneth J. Hagan, *This People's Navy* (1991); Donald R. Hickey, *The War of 1812: A Short History* (1995); Frank Lawrence Owsley, Jr., and Gene A. Smith, *Filibusters and Expansionists: Jeffersonian Manifest Destiny, 1800–1821* (1997); Bradford Perkins, *The Creation of a Republican Empire, 1776–1865* (1993); Julius W. Pratt, *Expansionists of 1812* (1925); Robert V. Remini, *The Battle of New Orleans: Andrew Jackson and America's First Military Victory* (1999); David Curtis Skaggs and Gerard T. Atloff, *A Signal Victory: The Lake Erie Campaign 1812–1813* (1997); J. C. A. Stagg, *Mr. Madison's War: Politics, Diplomacy, and Warfare in the Early Republic, 1783–1830* (1983); Anders Stephanson, *Manifest Destiny: American Expansionism and the Empire of Right* (1995); Steve Watts, *The Republic Reborn: War and the Making of a Liberal America, 1790–1820* (1987); David J. Weber, *The Spanish Frontier in North America* (1992); J. Leitch Wright, Jr., *Creeks and Seminoles: The Destruction and Regeneration of the Muscogulge People* (1986).

Commerce and Industry

Robert F. Dalzell, Jr., *Enterprising Elite: The Boston Associates and the World They Made* (1987); David A. Hounshell, *From the American System to Mass Production, 1800–1932: The Development of Manufacturing Technology in the United States* (1984); David J. Jeremy, *Transatlantic Industrial Revolution: The Diffusion of Textile Technologies Between Britain and America, 1790s–1830s* (1981): Walter Licht, *Industrializing America: The Nineteenth Century* (1995); Peter Temin (ed.), *Engines of Enterprise: An Economic History of New England* (2000).

Chapter 10

General

Stanley L. Engerman and Robert E. Gallman (eds.), *The Cambridge Economic History of the United States, vol. II, The Long Nineteenth Century* (2000); Jack Larkin, *The Reshaping of Everyday Life, 1790–1840* (1988); D. W. Meinig, *The Shaping of America: A Geographical Perspective on 500 Years of History*, vol. 2: *Contininental America, 1800–1867* (1993); Charles G. Sellers, Jr., *The Market Revolution: Jacksonian America, 1815–1840* (1991); Melvyn Stokes and Stephen Conway, eds., *The Market Revolution in America: Social, Political, and Religious Expressions, 1800–1860* (1996).

Postwar Nationalism

Harry Ammon, *James Monroe: The Quest for National Identity* (1971); Noble E. Cunningham, *The Presidency of James Monroe* (1996); Mary W. M. Hargreaves, *The Presidency of John Quincy Adams* (1985); Morton J. Horowitz, *The Transformation of American Law, 1780–1860* (1977); Ralph Ketcham, *Presidents Above Party: The First American Presidency, 1789–1829* (1984); Walter LaFeber, ed., *John Quincy Adams and American Continental Empire* (1965); Ernest R. May, *The Making of the Monroe Doctrine* (1976); Paul C. Nagel, *John Quincy Adams: A Public Life, a Private Life* (1997); R. Kent Newmyer, *The Supreme Court Under Marshall and Taney* (1968); Dexter Perkins, *Hands Off: A History of the Monroe Doctrine* (1941); Robert V. Remini, *Henry Clay: Statesman for the Union* (1991); Thomas C. Shevory, *John Marshall's Law: Interpretation, Ideology, and Interest* (1994); William Earl Weeks, *John Quincy Adams and American Global Empire* (1992).

The Market Economy, Manufacturing, and Commerce

Stuart Bruchey, *Enterprise: The Dynamic Economy of a Free People* (1990); Alfred D. Chandler, Jr., *The Visible Hand: Managerial Revolution in American Business* (1977); William Cronon, *Nature's Metropolis: Chicago and the Great West* (1991); Paul A. Gilje, ed., *Wages of Independence: Capitalism in the Early American Republic* (1997); Louis Hartz, *Economic Policy and Democratic Thought: Pennsylvania, 1776–1860* (1954); David A. Hounshell, *From the American System to Mass Production, 1800–1932: The Development of Manufacturing Technology in the United States* (1984); David J. Jeremy, *Transatlantic Industrial Revolution: The Diffusion of Textile Technologies Between Britain and America, 1790s–1830s* (1981); Herbert A. Johnson, *The Chief Justiceship of John Marshall, 1801–1835* (1997); David Klingaman and Richard Vedder, eds., *Essays in Nineteenth-Century History* (1975); Stanley I. Kutler, *Privilege and Creative Destruction: The Charles River Bridge Case* (1971); Walter Licht, *Industrializing America: The Nineteenth Century* (1995); Otto Mayr and Robert C. Post, eds., *Yankee Enterprise: The Rise of the American System of Manufacturers* (1981); Douglass C. North, *Economic Growth of the United States, 1790–1860* (1966); Theodore Steinberg, *Nature Incorporated: Industrialization and the Waters of New England* (1991); Peter Temin (ed.), *Engines of Enterprise: An Economic History of New England* (2000).

Transportation

Albert Fishlow, *American Railroads and the Transformation of the Ante-Bellum Economy* (1965); Carter Goodrich, *Government Promotion of American Canals and Railroads, 1800–1890* (1960); Louis C. Hunter, *Steamboats on the Western Rivers* (1949); Richard R. John, *Spreading the News: The American Postal System from Franklin to Morse* (1995); John Laurite Larson, *Internal Improvement: National Public Works and the Promise of Popular Government in the Early United States* (2001); Harry N. Scheiber, *Ohio Canal Era: A Case Study of Government and the Economy, 1820–1861* (1969); Ronald E. Shaw, *Canals for a Nation: The Canal Era in the United States, 1790–1860* (1990); Carol Sheriff, *The Artificial River: The Erie Canal and the Paradox of Progress, 1817–1862* (1996); George R. Taylor, *The Transportation Revolution, 1815–1860* (1951); James A. Ward, *Railroads and the Character of America, 1820–1887* (1986).

Commercial Farming

"American Agriculture, 1790–1840, A Symposium," *Agricultural History* 46 (January 1972); Jeremy Atack and Fred Bateman, *To Their Own Soil: Agriculture in the Antebellum North* (1987); Allen G. Bogue, *From Prairie to Corn Belt: Farming on the Illinois and Iowa Prairies in the Nineteenth Century* (1963); Christopher Clark, *The Roots of Rural Capitalism: Western Massachusetts, 1780–1860* (1990); Clarence Danhof, *Change in Agriculture: The Northern United States, 1820–1870* (1969); Paul W. Gates, *The Farmer's Age: Agriculture, 1815–1860* (1962); Benjamin H. Hibbard, *A History of Public Land Policies* (1939); Joan M. Jensen, *Loosening the Bonds: Mid-Atlantic Farm Women, 1750–1850* (1986); Robert Leslie Jones, *History of Agriculture in Ohio to 1880* (1983); Peter D. McClelland, *Sowing Modernity: America's First Agricultural Revolution* (1999); Sally McMurry, *Transforming Rural Life: Dairying Families and Agricultural Change, 1820–1885* (1995); Gavin Wright, *The Political Economy of the Cotton South* (1978).

Workers

Mary H. Blewett, *Men, Women, and Work: Class, Gender, and Protest in the New England Shoe Industry, 1780–1910* (1988); Jeanne Boydston, *Home and Work: Housework, Wages, and the Ideology of Labor in the Early Republic* (1990); Thomas Dublin, *Transforming Women's Work: New England Lives in the Industrial Revolution* (1994); Thomas Dublin, *Women at Work: The Transformation of Work and Community in Lowell, Massachusetts, 1826–1860* (1979); Bruce Laurie, *Artisans into Workers: Labor in Nineteenth-Century America* (1989); Howard B. Rock, Paul A. Gilje, and Robert Asher, eds., *American Artisans: Crafting Social Identity, 1750–1850* (1995); Sean Wilentz, *Chants Democratic: New York City and the Rise of the American Working Class, 1788–1850* (1984); David A. Zonderman, *Aspirations and Anxieties: New England Workers and the Mechanized Factory System, 1815–1850* (1992).

Americans on the Move

Joan Cashin, *A Family Venture: Men and Women on the Southern Frontier* (1991); James E. Davis, *Frontier America 1800–1840: A Comparative Demographic Analysis of the Frontier Process* (1977); Stewart Holbrook, *The Yankee Exodus: An Account of Migration from New England* (1950); Julie Roy Jeffrey, *Frontier Women: The Trans-Mississippi West, 1840–1880* (1979); Peter D. McClelland and Richard J. Zeckhauser, eds., *Demographic Dimensions of the New Republic* (1982); Virginia E. and Robert W. McCormick, *New Englanders on the Ohio Frontier* (1998); Gerald McFarland, *A Scattered People: An American Family Moves West* (1985); James Hebron Moore, *The Emergence of the Cotton Kingdom in the Old Southwest: Mississippi, 1770–1860* (1987); James Oakes, *The Ruling Race: A History of American Slaveholders* (1982); Malcom J. Rohrbough, *The Trans-Appalachian Frontier: People, Societies, and Institutions, 1775–1850* (1978); Russell Thornton, *American Indian Holocaust and Survival: A Population History Since 1492* (1987); David J. Weber, *The Spanish Frontier in North America* (1992); Richard White, *"It's Your Misfortune and None of My Own": A History of the American West* (1991).

Native American Resistance and Removal

Linda Barrington (ed.), *The Other Side of the Frontier: Economic Explorations into Native American History* (1999); Robert F. Berkhofer, Jr., *The White Man's Indian* (1978); Paul H. Carlson, *The Plains Indians* (1998); James W. Covington, *The Seminoles of Florida* (1993); Carol Devens, *Countering Colonization: Native American Women and Great Lakes Missions, 1630–1900* (1992); Michael D. Green, *The Politics of Indian Removal: Creek Government and Society in Crisis* (1982); Joseph B. Herring, *The Enduring Indians of Kansas: A Century and a Half of Acculturation* (1990); Stanley W. Hoig, *The Cherokees and Their Chiefs in the Wake of Empire* (1998); William G. McLoughlin, *Cherokee Renascence in the New Republic* (1986); Theda Perdue, *Slavery and the Evolution of Cherokee Society, 1540–1866* (1979); Ronald N. Satz, *American Indian Policy in the Jacksonian Era* (1975); Daniel H. Usner, Jr., *American Indians in the Lower Mississippi Valley* (1998); Anthony F. C. Wallace, *The Long, Bitter Trail: Andrew Jackson and the Indians* (1993); Richard White, *The Roots of Dependency: Subsistence, Environment, and Social Change Among the Choctaws, Pawnees, and Navajos* (1983); James Wilson, *The Earth Shall Weep: A History of Native America* (1998); J. Leitch Wright, Jr., *Creeks and Seminoles: The Destruction and Regeneration of the Muscogulge People* (1986).

Chapter 11

General

George Dangerfield, *The Awakening of American Nationalism, 1815–1828* (1965); Daniel Feller, *The Jacksonian Promise:*

America, 1815–1840 (1995); Isabelle Lehru, *Carnival on the Page: Popular Print Media in Antebellum America* (2000); Jean V. Matthews, *Toward a New Society: American Thought and Culture, 1800–1830* (1991); John Mayfield, *The New Nation, 1800–1845* (1981); Charles Sellers, *The Market Revolution: Jacksonian America, 1815–1846* (1991).

Religion, Revivalism, and Reform

Robert H. Abzug, *Cosmos Crumbling: American Reform and the Religious Imagination* (1994); Michael Barkun, *Crucible of the Millennium: The Burned-over District of New York in the 1840s* (1986); Terry Bilhartz, *Urban Religion and the Second Great Awakening: Church and Society in Early National Baltimore* (1986); Paul K. Conkin, *The Uneasy Center: Reformed Christianity in Antebellum America* (1995); Clifford S. Griffen, *Their Brothers' Keepers: Moral Stewardship in the United States, 1800–1865* (1960); Keith J. Hardman, *Charles Grandison Finney, 1792–1875: Revivalist and Reformer* (1987); Nathan O. Hatch, *The Democratization of American Christianity* (1989); Christine Leigh Heyrman, *Southern Cross: The Beginnings of the Bible Belt* (1997); Winthrop S. Hudson and John Corrigan, *Religion in America*, 6th ed. (1999); Curtis D. Johnson, *Islands of Holiness: Rural Religion in Upstate New York, 1790–1860* (1989); Paul E. Johnson, *A Shopkeeper's Millennium: Society and Revivals in Rochester, New York, 1815–1837* (1978); Steven Mintz, *Moralists and Modernizers: America's Pre-Civil War Reformers* (1995); Timothy L. Smith, *Revivalism and Social Reform in Mid-Nineteenth Century America* (1957); Alice Felt Tyler, *Freedom's Ferment* (1944); Ronald G. Walters, *American Reformers, 1815–1860*, rev. ed. (1997).

Temperance, Asylums, and Antimasonry

Thomas J. Brown, *Dorothea Dix: New England Reformer* (1998); Steven C. Bullock, *Revolutionary Brotherhood: Freemasonry and the Transformation of the American Social Order, 1730–1840* (1996); David Gollaher, *Voice for the Mad: The Life of Dorothea Dix* (1995); Paul Goodman, *Towards a Christian Republic: Antimasonry and the Great Transition in New England, 1826–1836* (1988); Gerald N. Grob, *Mental Institutions in America: Social Policy to 1875* (1973); Kathleen Smith Kutolowski, "Antimasonry Reexamined: Social Bases of the Grass-Roots Party," *Journal of American History* 71 (September 1984): 269–293; W. J. Rorabaugh, *The Alcoholic Republic: An American Tradition* (1979); David J. Rothman, *The Discovery of the Asylum: Social Order and Disorder in the New Republic* (1971); Ian R. Tyrrell, *Sobering Up: From Temperance to Prohibition in Antebellum America, 1800–1860* (1979); William Preston Vaughn, *The Antimasonic Party in the United States, 1826–1843* (1983).

Women and Reform

Barbara J. Berg, *The Remembered Gate: Origins of American Feminism: The Woman and the City, 1800–1860* (1977); Ellen C. Du Bois, *Feminism and Suffrage: The Emergence of an Independent Woman's Movement in America, 1848–1869* (1978); Barbara Leslie Epstein, *The Politics of Domesticity: Women, Evangelism, and Temperance in Nineteenth-Century America* (1981); Lori D. Ginzberg, *Women and the Work of Benevolence: Morality, Politics, and Class in the Nineteenth-Century United States* (1990); Debra Gold Hansen, *Strained Sisterhood: Gender and Class in the Boston Female Anti-Slavery Society* (1993); Nancy A. Hewitt, *Women's Activism and Social Change: Rochester, New York, 1822–1872* (1984); Sylvia D. Hoffert, *When Hens Crow: The Woman's Rights Movement in Antebellum America* (1995); Nancy Isenberg, *Sex and Citizenship in Antebellum America* (1998); Gerda Lerner, *The Grimké Sisters of South Carolina* (1967); Jean V. Matthews, *Women's Struggle for Equality: The First Phase, 1828–1876* (1997); Amanda Porterfield, *Mary Lyon and the Mount Holyoke Missionaries* (1997); Carla L. Peterson, "*Doers of the Word*": African-American Women Speakers and Writers in the North, 1830–1880* (1995); Mary P. Ryan, *Cradle of the Middle Class: The Family in Oneida County, New York, 1790–1865* (1981); Mary P. Ryan, *Women in Public: Between Banners and Ballots, 1825–1880* (1990); Jean Fagan Yellin, *Women & Sisters: The Antislavery Feminists in American Culture* (1989).

Antislavery and Abolitionism

James Brewer Stewart, *Holy Warriors: The Abolitionists and American Slavery*, rev. ed. (1996); David Brion Davis, *Slavery and Human Progress* (1984); Frederick Douglass, *Life and Times of Frederick Douglass* (1881); Audrey Fisch, *American Slaves in Victorian England: Aboolitionist Politics in Popular Literature and Culture* (2000); George M. Fredrickson, *The Black Image in the White Mind: The Debate on Afro-American Character and Destiny, 1817–1914* (1971); Paul Goodman, *Of One Blood: Abolitionism and the Origins of Racial Equality* (1998); David Grimsted, *American Mobbing, 1828–1861* (1998); Julie Roy Jeffrey, *The Great Silent Army of Abolitionism: Ordinary Women in the AntiSlavery Movement* (1998); Aileen S. Kraditor, *Means and Ends in American Abolitionism: Garrison and His Critics on Strategy and Tactics* (1967); Henry Mayer, *All on Fire: William Lloyd Garrison and the Abolition of Slavery* (1998); William Lee Miller, *Arguing About Slavery: The Great Battle in the United States Congress* (1995); Richard J. Newman, *The Transformation of American Abolitionism: Fighting Slavery in the Early Republic* (2002); William H. Pease and Jane H. Pease, *They Who Would Be Free: Blacks' Search for Freedom, 1830–1861* (1974); Benjamin Quarles, *Black Abolitionists* (1969); Peter C. Ripley, (ed.), *The Black Abolitionist Papers, vol. I, The British Isles, 1830–1865* (1985); John Stauffer, *The Black Hearts of Men: Radical Abolitionists and the Transformation of Race* (2002); John L. Thomas, *The Liberator: William Lloyd*

Garrison (1963); Ronald G. Walters, *The Antislavery Appeal: American Abolitionism After 1830* (1976); Shirley J. Yee, *Black Women Abolitionists: A Study in Activism, 1828–1860* (1992).

Politics and Diplomacy, 1816–1828

Harry Ammon, *James Monroe: The Quest for National Identity* (1971); Noble E. Cunningham, *The Presidency of James Monroe* (1996); Mary W. M. Hargreaves, *The Presidency of John Quincy Adams* (1985); Morton J. Horowitz, *The Transformation of American Law, 1780–1860* (1977); Ralph Ketcham, *Presidents Above Party: The First American Presidency, 1789–1829* (1984); Walter LaFeber, ed., *John Quincy Adams and American Continental Empire* (1965); Ernest R. May, *The Making of the Monroe Doctrine* (1976); Paul C. Nagel, *John Quincy Adams: A Public Life, a Private Life* (1997); R. Kent Newmyer, *The Supreme Court Under Marshall and Taney* (1968); Dexter Perkins, *Hands Off: A History of the Monroe Doctrine* (1941); Robert V. Remini, *Henry Clay: Statesman for the Union* (1991); Thomas C. Shevory, *John Marshall's Law: Interpretation, Ideology, and Interest* (1994); William Earl Weeks, *John Quincy Adams and American Global Empire* (1992).

Andrew Jackson and the Jacksonians

Donald B. Cole, *Martin Van Buren and the American Political System* (1984); Michael F. Holt, *Political Parties and American Political Development from the Age of Jackson to the Age of Lincoln* (1992); Richard B. Latner, *The Presidency of Andrew Jackson* (1979); John F. Marszalek, *The Petticoat Affair: Manners, Mutiny, and Sex in Andrew Jackson's White House* (1997); Marvin Meyers, *The Jacksonian Persuasion* (1960); John Niven, *Martin Van Buren* (1983); Edward Pessen, *Jacksonian America: Society, Personality, and Politics*, rev. ed. (1979); Robert V. Remini, *The Legacy of Andrew Jackson: Essays on Democracy, Indian Removal, and Slavery* (1988); Robert V. Remini, *The Life of Andrew Jackson* (1988); Harry L. Watson, *Liberty and Power: The Politics of Jacksonian America* (1990).

Democrats and Whigs

William J. Cooper, *The South and the Politics of Slavery, 1828–1856* (1978); Ronald P. Formisano, *The Transformation of Political Culture: Massachusetts Parties, 1790s–1840s* (1983); William W. Freehling, *Prelude to Civil War: The Nullification Controversy in South Carolina* (1966); Michael F. Holt, *The Rise and Fall of the American Whig Party* (1999); Daniel Walker Howe, *The Political Culture of the American Whigs* (1979); Lawrence Frederick Kohl, *The Politics of Individualism: Parties and the American Character in the Jacksonian Era* (1989); Richard P. McCormick, *The Second American Party System: Party Formation in the Jacksonian Era* (1966); Merrill D. Peterson, *The Great Triumvirate: Webster, Clay, and Calhoun* (1987); Norma Lois Peterson, *The Presidencies of William Henry Harrison and John Tyler* (1989); James Roger Sharp, *The Jacksonians Versus the Banks: Politics in the States After the Panic of 1837* (1970).

Manifest Destiny and Foreign Policy

John M. Belohlavek, *Let the Eagle Soar! The Foreign Policy of Andrew Jackson* (1985); T. R. Fehrenbach, *Lone Star: A History of Texas and the Texans* (1968); Norman B. Graebner, ed., *Manifest Destiny* (1968); Thomas R. Hietala, *Manifest Destiny: Anxious Aggrandizement in Late Jacksonian America* (1985); Reginald Horsman, *Race and Manifest Destiny* (1981); Michael Hunt, *Ideology and U.S. Foreign Policy* (1987); Bradford Perkins, *The Creation of a Republican Empire, 1776–1865* (1993); David M. Pletcher, *The Diplomacy of Annexation: Texas, Oregon, and the Mexican War* (1973); Charles G. Sellers, Jr., *James K. Polk: Continentalist, 1843–1846* (1966); Anders Stephanson, *Manifest Destiny: American Expansionism and the Empire of Right* (1995); Paul A. Varg, *United States Foreign Relations, 1820–1860* (1979); David J. Weber, *The Spanish Frontier in North America* (1992); Albert K. Weinberg, *Manifest Destiny* (1935).

The Supreme Court and the Law

Leonard Baker, *John Marshall: A Life in Law* (1974); Francis N. Stites, *John Marshall: Defender of the Constitution* (1981).

Chapter 12

Rural and Utopian Communities

Leonard J. Arrington and Davis Bitton, *The Mormon Experience: A History of the Latterday Saints* (1979); Priscilla J. Brewer, *Shaker Communities, Shaker Lives* (1986); David B. Danbom, *Born in the Country: A History of Rural America* (1995); John Mack Faragher, *Sugar Creek: Life on the Illinois Prairie* (1986); Laurence Foster, *Religion and Sexuality: Three American Communal Experiments of the Nineteenth Century* (1981); Steven Hahn and Jonathan Prude, eds., *The Countryside in the Age of Capitalist Transformation* (1985); Joan M. Jensen, *Loosening the Bonds: Mid-Atlantic Farm Women, 1750–1850* (1986); Sally McMurry, *Families and Farmhouses in Nineteenth Century America: Vernacular Design and Social Change* (1988); Anthony F. C. Wallace, *Rockdale: The Growth of an American Village in the Early Industrial Revolution* (1978); Kenneth H. Winn, *Exiles in a Land of Liberty: Mormons in America, 1830–1846* (1989).

The West

William Benemann (ed.), *A Year of Mud and Gold: San Francisco in Letters and Diaries, 1819–1850* (1999); John Mack Faragher, *Women and Men on the Overland Trail* (1979); Ramón A. Gutiérrez and Richard J. Orsi, eds., *Contested Eden: California Before the Gold Rush* (1998); Julie Roy Jeffrey, *Frontier Women: The Trans-Mississippi West, 1840–1880* (1979); Rudolph M. Lapp, *Blacks in Gold Rush California* (1977); Kenneth N. Owens (ed.), *Riches for All: The California Gold Rush and the World* (2002); Malcolm J. Rohrbough, *Days of Gold: The California Gold Rush and the American Nation* (1997); Quintard Taylor, *In Search of the Racial Fron-*

tier: *African Americans in the American West, 1528–1990* (1998); John D. Unruh, Jr., *The Overland Emigrants and the Trans-Mississippi West, 1840–1860* (1979); David J. Weber, *The Spanish Frontier in North America* (1992); Richard White, *"It's Your Misfortune and None of My Own": A History of the American West* (1991).

Urban Communities

Melvin A. Adelman, *A Sporting Time: New York City and the Rise of Modern Athletics, 1820–1870* (1986); Tyler Anbinder, *Five Points* (2001); Stuart M. Blumin, *The Emergence of the Middle Class: Social Experience in the American City, 1760–1900* (1989); Edwin G. Burrows and Mike Wallace, *Gotham: A History of New York City to 1898* (1999); Susan G. Davis, *Parades and Power: Street Theater in Nineteenth-Century Philadelphia* (1986); Timothy J. E. Gilfoyle, *City of Eros: New York City, Prostitution, and the Commercialization of Sex, 1790–1920* (1992); Karen V. Hansen, *A Very Social Time: Crafting Community in Antebellum New England* (1994); Carl Kaestle, *Pillars of the Republic: Common Schools and American Society, 1780–1860* (1982); Jack Larkin, *The Reshaping of Everyday Life, 1790–1840* (1988); Timothy R. Mahoney, *Provincial Lives: Middle-Class Experience in the Antebellum Middle West* (1999); Edward Pessen, *Riches, Class and Power Before the Civil War* (1973); Christine Stansell, *City of Women: Sex and Class in New York, 1789–1860* (1986); Richard B. Stott, *Workers in the Metropolis: Class, Ethnicity, and Youth in Antebellum New York City* (1990); Alexis de Tocqueville, *Democracy in America*, 2 vols. (1835, 1840).

Family Life

Virginia K. Bartlett, *Keeping House: Women's Lives in Western Pennsylvania, 1790–1850* (1994); Janet Farrell Brodie, *Contraception and Abortion in Nineteenth-Century America* (1994); Lee Virginia Chambers-Schiller, *Liberty, A Better Husband: Single Women in America: The Generations of 1780–1840* (1984); Clifford Edward Clark, Jr., *The American Family Home, 1800–1960* (1986); Nancy F. Cott, *The Bonds of Womanhood: Woman's Sphere in New England, 1780–1835* (1977); Linda Gordon, *Woman's Body, Woman's Rights: A Social History of Birth Control in America* (1976); Joan Hoff, *Law, Gender and Injustice: A Legal History of U.S. Women* (1991); Suzanne Lebsock, *The Free Women of Petersburg: Status and Culture in a Southern Town, 1784–1860* (1984); Glenda Riley, *Divorce: An American Tradition* (1991); Mary P. Ryan, *Cradle of the Middle Class: The Family in Oneida County, New York, 1790–1865* (1981); Kathryn Kish Sklar, *Catharine Beecher: A Study in American Domesticity* (1973); Maris A. Vinovskis, *Fertility in Massachusetts from the Revolution to the Civil War* (1981); Robert V. Wells, *Revolutions in Americans' Lives* (1982); Barbara Welter, "The Cult of True Womanhood, 1820–1860," *American Quarterly* 18 (Summer 1966): 151–174.

Immigrants and Hispanics

Thomás Almaguer, *Racial Fault Lines: The Historical Origins of White Supremacy in California* (1994); Gunther Barth, *Bitter Strength: A History of Chinese in the United States, 1850–1870* (1964); Ronald H. Bayor and Timothy J. Meagher (eds.), *The New York Irish* (1996); Kathleen Neils Conzen, *Immigrant Milwaukee: 1836–1860* (1976); Arnoldo De León, *The Tejano Community, 1836–1900* (1982); Hasia R. Diner, *Erin's Daughters in America: Irish Immigrant Women in the Nineteenth Century* (1983); David A. Gerber, *The Making of an American Pluralism: Buffalo, New York, 1825–60* (1989); David T. Gleeson, *The Irish in the South, 1815–1877* (2001); Victor R. Greene, *American immigrant Leaders 1800–1910* (1987); Noel Ignatiev, *How the Irish Became White* (1995); Matthew Frye Jacobson, *Whiteness of a Different Color: European Immigrants and the Alchemy of Race* (1998); Walter D. Kamphoefner, *The Westfalians: From Germany to Missouri* (1987); Dale T. Knobel, *Paddy and the Republic: Ethnicity and Nationality in Antebellum America* (1986); Sallie A. Marston, "Public rituals and community power: St. Patrick's Day parades in Lowell, Massachusetts, 1841–1874," *Political Geography Quarterly* 8 (July, 1989), 255–269; Timothy M. Matovina, *Tejano Religion and Ethnicity: San Antonio, 1821–1860* (1995); Kerby A. Miller, *Emigrants and Exiles: Ireland and the Irish Exodus to North America* (1985); Brian Mitchell, *The Paddy Camps: The Irish of Lowell, 1821–61* (1988); Stanley Nadel, *Little Germany: Ethnicity, Religion, and Class in New York City, 1845–80* (1990); David Roediger, *The Wages of Whiteness: Race and the Making of the Working Class* (1991); David J. Weber, *The Spanish Frontier in North America* (1992); Mark Wyman, *Immigrants in the Valley: Irish, Germans, and Americans in the Upper Mississippi, 1830–1860* (1984).

Free People of Color and Race

Ira Berlin, *Slaves Without Masters: The Free Negro in the Antebellum South* (1974); Elizabeth Rauh Bethel, *The Roots of African-American Identity: Memory and History in Antebellum Free Communities* (1997); Dale Cockrell, *Demons of Disorder: Early Blackface Minstrels and Their World* (1997); Leonard P. Curry, *The Free Black in Urban America, 1800–1850* (1981); Thomas F. Gossett, *Race: The History of an Idea in America* (1963); James O. Horton and Lois E. Horton, *In Hope of Liberty: Culture, Community and Protest Among Northern Free Blacks, 1700–1860* (1996); Luther Porter Jackson, *Free Negro Labor and Property Holding in Virginia, 1830–1860* (1942); David M. Katzman, *Before the Ghetto: Black Detroit in the Nineteenth Century* (1973); W. T. Lhamon, Jr., *Raising Cain: Blackface Performance from Jim Crow to Hip Hop* (1998); Leon Litwack, *North of Slavery: The Negro in the Free States, 1790–1860* (1961); Eric Lott, *Love and Theft: Blackface Minstrelsy and the American Working Class* (1995); Joanne Pope Melish, *Disowning Slavery: Gradual Emancipation and Race in New England, 1780–1860* (1998); Floyd J. Miller, *The Search for a Black Nationality:*

Black Colonization and Emigration, 1787–1863 (1975); Gary B. Nash, *Forging Freedom: The Formation of Philadelphia's Black Community, 1720–1840* (1988); Benjamin Quarles, *Black Abolitionists* (1969); Patrick Rael, *Black Identity & Black Protest in the Antebellum North* (2002); Quintard Taylor, *In Search of the Racial Frontier: African Americans in the American West, 1528–1990* (1998); Shane White and Graham White, *Stylin': African American Expressive Culture from its Beginnings to the Zoot Suit* (1998); Julie Winch, *A Gentleman of Color: The Life of James Forten* (2002); Arthur Zilversmit, *The First Emancipation: The Abolition of Slavery in the North* (1967).

Chapter 13

The Peculiar South

Wilbur J. Cash, *The Mind of the South* (1939); Carl N. Degler, *Place Over Time* (1977); David Goldfield, *Still Fighting the Civil War: The American South and Southern History* (2002); Drew G. Faust, "The Peculiar South Revisited," in John B. Boles and Evelyn T. Nolen, eds., *Interpreting Southern History* (1987), 78–119; James Oakes, *Slavery and Freedom* (1990); C. Vann Woodward, *The Burden of Southern History* (1960).

Southern Society

Edward L. Ayers, *Vengeance and Justice* (1984); Bradley G. Bond, *Political Culture in the Nineteenth-Century South* (1995); Randolph B. Campbell, "Planters and Plain Folks," in Boles and Nolen, eds., *Interpreting Southern History* (1987); William J. Cooper, *The South and the Politics of Slavery, 1828–1856* (1978); William W. Freehling, *Prelude to Civil War* (1965); Eugene D. Genovese, *The Political Economy of Slavery* (1965); Peter Kolchin, *Unfree Labor: American Slavery and Russian Serfdom* (1987); Donald G. Mathews, *Religion in the Old South* (1977); Christine L. Heyrman, *Southern Cross* (1997); James Hebron Moore, *The Emergence of the Cotton Kingdom in the Old Southwest: Mississippi, 1770–1860* (1987); Frederick Law Olmsted, *The Slave States*, ed. Harvey Wish (1959); Manisha Sinha, *The Counter-Revolution of Slavery* (2000); Charles S. Sydnor, *The Development of Southern Sectionalism, 1819–1848* (1948); Larry E. Tise, *Proslavery* (1987); Ralph A. Wooster, *Politicians, Planters, and Plain Folk* (1975); Gavin Wright, *The Political Economy of the Cotton South* (1978); Bertram Wyatt-Brown, *Southern Honor* (1982).

Slaveholders and Nonslaveholders

Edward L. Ayers and John C. Willis, eds., *The Edge of the South* (1991); Bennet H. Barrow, *Plantation Life in the Florida Parishes of Louisiana*, ed. Edwin Adams Davis (1943); Ira Berlin, *Slaves Without Masters* (1974); Joan E. Cashin, *A Family Venture* (1991); Bill Cecil-Fronsman, *The Common Whites* (1992); Charles B. Dew, *Bond of Iron* (1995); Stanley Engerman, Seymour Drescher, and Robert Paquette, eds., *Slavery* (2001); Paul D. Escott, ed., *North Carolina Yeoman* (1996);

Drew Faust, *James Henry Hammond and the Old South* (1982); Drew Faust, *A Sacred Circle: The Dilemma of the Intellectual in the Old South* (1977); Drew Faust, ed., *The Ideology of Slavery* (1981); J. Wayne Flynt, *Dixie's Forgotten People* (1979); John Hope Franklin, *The Militant South, 1800–1861* (1956); John Inscoe, *Mountain Masters* (1989); Michael P. Johnson and James L. Roark, *Black Masters* (1984); Kenneth S. Greenberg, *Masters and Statesmen* (1985); Stephanie McCurry, *Masters of Small Worlds* (1995); Robert Manson Myers, ed., *The Children of Pride* (1972); James Oakes, *The Ruling Race* (1982); Frank L. Owsley, *Plain Folk of the Old South* (1949); Loren Schweninger, *Black Property Owners in the South, 1790–1915* (1990); J. Mills Thornton III, *Politics and Power in a Slave Society: Alabama, 1800–1860* (1978).

Southern Women

Carol Bleser, *In Joy and in Sorrow* (1990); Carol Bleser, ed., *Tokens of Affection* (1995); Victoria Bynum, *Unruly Women* (1992); Jane Turner Censer, *North Carolina Planters and Their Children, 1800–1860* (1984); Catherine Clinton, *The Plantation Mistress* (1982); Elizabeth Fox-Genovese, *Within the Plantation Household* (1988); Jean E. Friedman, *The Enclosed Garden* (1985); Harriet Jacobs, *Incidents in the Life of a Slave Girl*, ed. Jean Fagan Yellin (1987); Jacqueline Jones, *Labor of Love, Labor of Sorrow* (1985); Frances Anne Kemble, *Journal of a Residence on a Georgia Plantation in 1838–1839* (1863); Suzanne Lebsock, *Free Women of Petersburg* (1984); Ann Patton Malone, *Sweet Chariot: Slave Family and Household Structure in Nineteenth Century Louisiana* (1992); Sally McMillen, *Motherhood in the Old South* (1990); Patricia Morton, ed., *Discovering the Women in Slavery* (1995); Elisabeth Muhlenfeld, *Mary Boykin Chesnut* (1981); Deborah G. White, *Ar'n't I a Woman?* (1985); Virginia Ingraham Burr, ed., *The Secret Eye* (1990).

Conditions of Slavery

Larry E. Hudson, Jr., *To Have and to Hold* (1997); Kenneth F. Kiple and Virginia H. Kiple, "Black Tongue and Black Men," *Journal of Southern History* 43 (August 1977): 411–428; Wilma King, *Stolen Childhood* (1995); Peter Kolchin, *American Slavery, 1619–1877* (1993); Walter Johnson, *Soul by Soul: Life Inside the Antebellum Slave Market* (1999); Randall M. Miller and John David Smith, eds., *Dictionary of Afro-American Slavery* (1997); Randall M. Miller, ed., *The Afro-American Slaves: Community or Chaos* (1981); Orlando Patterson, *Rituals of Blood* (1998); Todd L. Savitt, *Medicine and Slavery* (1978); Mark M. Smith, *Mastered by the Clock* (1997); Kenneth M. Stampp, *The Peculiar Institution* (1956); Robert S. Starobin, *Industrial Slavery in the Old South* (1970); Brenda E. Stevenson, *Life in Black and White: Family and Community in the Slave South* (1996); Michael Tadman, *Speculators and Slaves* (1989).

Slave Culture and Resistance

Herbert Aptheker, *American Negro Slave Revolts* (1943); William F. Allen, Charles P. Ware, and Lucy McKim, *Slave Songs of the United States* (1867); John W. Blassingame, *The Slave Community* (1979); John Blassingame, ed., *Slave Testimony* (1977); Ira Berlin et al., eds., *Remembering Slavery* (1998); Frederick Douglass, *Narrative of the Life of Frederick Douglass*, David W. Blight, ed. (1993); Douglas R. Egerton, *He Shall Go Out Free: The Lives of Denmark Vesey* (1999); Paul D. Escott, *Slavery Remembered: A Record of Twentieth-Century Slave Narratives* (1979); Thomas Wentworth Higginson, "Negro Spirituals," *Atlantic Monthly* 19 (June, 1867); John Hope Franklin and Loren Schweninger, *Runaway Slaves* (1999); Eugene D. Genovese, *From Rebellion to Revolution* (1979); Eugene D. Genovese, *Roll, Jordan, Roll* (1974); Michael A. Gomez, *Exchanging Our Country Marks* (1998); Kenneth Greenberg, ed., *The Confessions of Nat Turner and Related Documents* (1996); Herbert G. Gutman, *The Black Family in Slavery and Freedom, 1750–1925* (1976); Vincent Harding, *There Is a River* (1981); Michael P. Johnson, "Denmark Vesey and His Co-Conspirators," *William and Mary Quarterly* LVIII (October 2001); Charles Joyner, *Down by the Riverside* (1984); Lawrence W. Levine, *Black Culture and Black Consciousness* (1977); Albert J. Raboteau, *Slave Religion* (1978); David Robertson, *Denmark Vesey* (1999); James Sidbury, *Plowshares into Swords: Gabriel's Virginia* (1997); Sterling Stuckey, *Slave Culture* (1987).

Chapter 14

Politics: General

Tyler Anbinder, *Nativism and Slavery* (1992); Maurice G. Baxter, *One and Inseparable: Daniel Webster and the Union* (1984); Paul Bergeron, *The Presidency of James K. Polk* (1987); Frederick J. Blue, *The Free Soilers: Third Party Politics, 1848–1854* (1973); Gabor S. Boritt, ed., *Why the Civil War Came* (1996); Richard J. Carwardine, *Evangelicals and Politics in Antebellum America* (1997); Don E. Fehrenbacher, *The Dred Scott Case* (1978); Don E. Fehrenbacher, *The Slaveholding Republic* (2001); George M. Fredrickson, *The Black Image in the White Mind* (1971); William W. Freehling and Craig M. Simpson, eds., *Secession Debated* (1992); William W. Freehling, *The Road to Disunion* (1990); Holman Hamilton, *Prologue to Conflict: The Crisis and Compromise of 1850* (1964); Michael F. Holt, *Political Parties and American Political Development* (1992); Michael F. Holt, *The Political Crisis of the 1850s* (1978); Daniel Walker Howe, *The Political Culture of the American Whigs* (1979); Stephen E. Maizlish and John J. Kushma, eds., *Essays on American Antebellum Politics, 1840–1860* (1982); William Lee Miller, *Arguing About Slavery* (1996); Chaplain W. Morrison, *Democratic Politics and Sectionalism: The Wilmot Proviso Controversy* (1967); Merrill D. Peterson, *The Great Triumvirate: Webster, Clay, and Calhoun* (1987); David M. Potter, *The Impending Crisis, 1848–1861* (1976); James A. Rawley, *Race and Politics* (1969); Robert V. Remini,

Henry Clay: Statesman for the Union (1991); Richard H. Sewell, *A House Divided: Sectionalism and the Civil War, 1848–1865* (1988); Joel H. Silbey, *The Transformation of American Politics, 1840–1960* (1967); Joel H. Silbey, ed., *The American Party Battle*, 2 vols. (1999); Elbert B. Smith, *The Presidency of James Buchanan* (1975); Kenneth M. Stampp, *America in 1857* (1991); Kenneth M. Stampp, *And the War Came* (1950); Richard White, *"It's Your Misfortune and None of My Own": A History of the American West* (1991); Gerald W. Wolff, *The Kansas-Nebraska Bill* (1977).

The South and Slavery

William L. Barney, *The Secessionist Impulse* (1974); Malcolm Bell, Jr., *Major Butler's Legacy: Five Generations of a Slaveholding Family* (1987); Steven A. Channing, *A Crisis of Fear: Secession in South Carolina* (1970); William J. Cooper, Jr., *The South and the Politics of Slavery, 1828–1856* (1978); Avery O. Craven, *The Growth of Southern Nationalism, 1848–1861* (1953); Daniel W. Crofts, *Reluctant Confederates: Upper South Unionists in the Secession Crisis* (1989); Charles B. Dew, *Apostles of Disunion: Southern Secession Commissioners and the Causes of the Civil War* (2001); Merton L. Dillon, *Slavery Attacked* (1991); Drew G. Faust, *The Ideology of Slavery* (1981); Drew G. Faust, *A Sacred Circle: The Dilemma of the Intellectual in the Old South* (1978); Lacy K. Ford, Jr., *Origins of Southern Radicalism* (1988); Eugene D. Genovese, *The World the Slaveholders Made* (1969); Michael P. Johnson, *Toward a Patriarchal Republic: The Secession of Georgia* (1977); John Niven, *John C. Calhoun and the Price of Union* (1988); James Oakes, *Slavery and Freedom* (1991); David M. Potter, *The South and the Sectional Conflict* (1968); Thomas E. Schott, *Alexander H. Stephens of Georgia* (1988); William R. Stanton, *The Leopard's Spots* (1960); J. Mills Thornton III, *Politics and Power in a Slave Society* (1978); Larry E. Tise, *Proslavery* (1987); Ralph Wooster, *The Secession Conventions of the South* (1962).

The North and Antislavery

Eugene H. Berwanger, *The Frontier Against Slavery* (1967); Gary Collison, *Shadrach Minkins: From Fugitive Slave to Citizen* (1997); David Donald, *Charles Sumner and the Coming of the Civil War* (1960); Paul Finkelman, ed., *His Soul Goes Marching On: Responses to John Brown and the Harpers Ferry Raid* (1995); Eric Foner, *Free Soil, Free Labor, Free Men* (1970); Louis S. Gerteis, *Morality and Utility in American Antislavery Reform* (1987); William E. Gienapp, *The Origins of the Republican Party, 1852–1856* (1986); Joan D. Hedrick, *Harriet Beecher Stowe* (1994); James O. and Lois E. Horton, *In Hope of Liberty* (1997); James O. Horton, *Free People of Color* (1993); Henry V. Jaffa, *Crisis of the House Divided* (1959); Robert W. Johannsen, *Lincoln, the South, and Slavery* (1991); Robert W. Johannsen, *Stephen A. Douglas* (1973); Stephen B. Oates, *To Purge This Land with Blood*, 2d ed. (1984); Lewis Perry and Michael Fellman, eds., *Antislavery Reconsidered* (1979); Benjamin Quarles, *Black Abolitionists*

(1969); Patrick Rael, *Black Identity and Black Protest in the Antebellum North* (2002); Leonard Richards, *The Slave Power: The Free North and Southern Domination, 1780–1860* (2000); C. Peter Ripley, et al., ed., *Witness for Freedom: African American Voices on Race, Slavery and Freedom* (1993); Jeffrey Rossbach, *Ambivalent Conspirators* (1982); Richard Sewell, *Ballots for Freedom: Antislavery Politics in the United States, 1837–1860* (1976); Jason H. Silverman, *Unwelcome Guests: Canada West's Response to American Fugitive Slaves* (1985); Thomas P. Slaughter, *Bloody Dawn: The Cristiana Riot and Racial Violence* (1991); John Stauffer, *The Black Hearts of Men: Radical Abolitionists and the Transformation of Race* (2002); James B. Stewart, *Holy Warriors: The Abolitionists and American Slavery*, 2d ed. (1996); Albert J. Von Frank, *The Trials of Anthony Burns* (1998).

The Mexican War and Foreign Policy

K. Jack Bauer, *Zachary Taylor* (1985); Gene M. Brack, *Mexico Views Manifest Destiny, 1821–1846* (1976); Richard Griswold del Castillo, *The Treaty of Guadalupe Hidalgo* (1990); Neal Harlow, *California Conquered* (1982); Reginald Horsman, *Race and Manifest Destiny* (1981); Robert W. Johannsen, *To the Halls of the Montezumas: The Mexican War and the American Imagination* (1985); Ernest M. Lander, Jr., *Reluctant Imperialists: Calhoun, the South Carolinians, and the Mexican War* (1980); Robert E. May, *The Southern Dream of a Caribbean Empire, 1854–1861* (1973); Frederick Merk, *Manifest Destiny and Mission in American History* (1963); David M. Pletcher, *The Diplomacy of Annexation: Texas, Oregon, and the Mexican War* (1973); Dirk Raat, *Mexico and the United States* (1992); John H. Schroeder, *Mr. Polk's War: American Opposition and Dissent* (1973); Otis A. Singletary, *The Mexican War* (1960); Anders Stephanson, *Manifest Destiny* (1995); David J. Weber, *The Mexican Frontier, 1821–1846* (1982).

Chapter 15

The War and the South

Thomas B. Alexander and Richard E. Beringer, *The Anatomy of the Confederate Congress* (1972); Stephen Ash, *When the Yankees Came* (1995); Edward L. Ayers, *In the Presence of Mine Enemies: War in the Heart of America, 1859–1863* (2002); Richard E. Beringer et al., *Why the South Lost the Civil War* (1986); William A. Blair, *Virginia's Private War: Feeding Body and Soul in the Confederacy* (1998); Gabor S. Boritt, ed., *Why the Confederacy Lost* (1992); Richard N. Current, *Lincoln's Loyalists* (1992); William C. Davis, *Jefferson Davis* (1991); Robert F. Durden, *The Gray and the Black: The Confederate Debate on Emancipation* (1972); Paul D. Escott, *Many Excellent People* (1985); Paul D. Escott, *After Secession: Jefferson Davis and the Failure of Confederate Nationalism* (1978); Eli N. Evans, *Judah P. Benjamin* (1987); Drew Gilpin Faust, *The Creation of Confederate Nationalism* (1988); William

W. Freehling, *The South vs. the South* (2001); Mark Grimsley, *The Hard Hand of War* (1995); J. B. Jones, *A Rebel War Clerk's Diary*, 2 vols., ed. Howard Swiggett (1935); Mary Elizabeth Massey, *Refugee Life in the Confederacy* (1964); Larry E. Nelson, *Bullets, Ballots, and Rhetoric: Confederate Policy for the United States Presidential Contest of 1864* (1980); Alan T. Nolan, *Lee Considered* (1991); James L. Roark, *Masters Without Slaves* (1977); Daniel Sutherland, *Seasons of War* (1995); Emory M. Thomas, *The Confederate Nation* (1979); Emory M. Thomas, *The Confederacy as a Revolutionary Experience* (1971); William A. Tidwell, *April '65* (1995); Bell Irvin Wiley, *The Life of Johnny Reb* (1943); Bell Irvin Wiley, *The Plain People of the Confederacy* (1943).

The War and the North

Ralph Andreano, ed., *The Economic Impact of the American Civil War* (1962); Iver Bernstein, *The New York City Draft Riots* (1990); David Donald, ed., *Why the North Won the Civil War* (1960); J. Matthew Gallman, *The North Fights the Civil War* (1994); James W. Geary, *We Need Men* (1991); Susan-Mary Grant and Peter J. Parish, eds., *Legacy of Disunion: The Enduring Significance of the American Civil War* (2003); Wood Gray, *The Hidden Civil War* (1942); Randall C. Jimerson, *The Private Civil War* (1988); Frank L. Klement, *The Copperheads in the Middle West* (1960); Melinda Lawson, *Patriot Fires: Forging a New American Nationalism in the Civil War North* (2002); James M. McPherson, *Battle Cry of Freedom* (1988); James H. Moorhead, *American Apocalypse* (1978); Mark E. Neely, Jr., *The Union Divided: Party Conflict in the Civil War North* (2002); Phillip S. Paludan, *"A People's Contest": The Union and the Civil War, 1861–1865* (1989); Robert Hunt Rhodes, ed., *All for the Union: The Civil War Diary and Letters of Elisha Hunt Rhodes* (1991); Anne C. Rose, *Victorian America and the Civil War* (1992); George Winston Smith and Charles Burnet Judah, *Life in the North During the Civil War* (1966); George Templeton Strong, *Diary*, 4 vols., ed. Allan Nevins and Milton Hasley Thomas (1952); Maris A. Vinovskis, ed., *Toward a Social History of the American Civil War* (1990); Michael Vorenberg, *Final Freedom: The Civil War, the Abolition of Slavery, and the Thirteenth Amendment* (2001); Bell Irvin Wiley, *The Life of Billy Yank* (1952).

Women

John Q. Anderson, ed., *Brokenburn: The Journal of Kate Stone* (1955); John R. Brumgardt, ed., *Civil War Nurse: The Diary and Letters of Hannah Ropes* (1980); Catherine Clinton and Nina Silber, eds., *Divided Houses: Gender and the Civil War* (1992); Beth Gilbert Crabtree and James W. Patton, eds., *"Journal of a Secesh Lady": The Diary of Catherine Ann Devereux Edmondston, 1860–1866* (1979); Alice Fahs, *The Imagined Civil War: Popular Literature of the North and South* (2001); Drew Gilpin Faust, *Mothers of Invention* (1996); Jacqueline Jones, *Labor of Love, Labor of Sorrow* (1985); George C. Rable, *Civil Wars: Women and the Crisis of South-*

ern Nationalism (1989); Mary D. Robertson, ed., Lucy Breck-inridge of Grove Hill: The Journal of a Virginia Girl, 1862–1864 (1979); Lyde Cullen Sizer, The Political Work of Northern Women Writers and the Civil War (2000); Lee Ann Whites, The Civil War as a Crisis in Gender (1995); C. Vann Woodward and Elisabeth Muhlenfeld, eds., Mary Chesnut's Civil War (1981).

African Americans

Virginia M. Adams, ed., On the Altar of Freedom: A Black Soldier's Civil War Letters from the Front (1991); Ira Berlin, ed., Freedom: A Documentary History of Emancipation, 1861–1867, Series I, The Destruction of Slavery (1979), and Series II, The Black Military Experience (1982); Richard M. Blackett, ed., Thomas Morris Chester: Black Civil War Correspondent (1989); David W. Blight, Frederick Douglass' Civil War (1989); Dudley Cornish, The Sable Arm (1956); Barbara Jeanne Fields, Slavery and Freedom on the Middle Ground (1985); Joseph T. Glatthaar, Forged in Battle (1990); James G. Hollandsworth, The Louisiana Native Guards (1995); Leon Litwack, Been in the Storm So Long (1979); James M. McPherson, The Negro's Civil War (1965); James M. McPherson, The Struggle for Equality (1964); Clarence L. Mohr, On the Threshold of Freedom (1986); Lynda J. Morgan, Emancipation in Virginia's Tobacco Belt, 1850–1870 (1992); Benjamin Quarles, The Negro in the Civil War (1953); Edwin S. Redkey, ed., A Grand Army of Black Men (1992); John David Smith, ed., Black Soldiers in Blue (2002).

Military History

Nancy Scott Anderson and Dwight Anderson, The Generals: Ulysses S. Grant and Robert E. Lee (1987); David W. Blight, ed., When This Cruel War Is Over: The Civil War Letters of Charles Harvey Brewster (1992); Albert Castel, Decision in the West (1992); Bruce Catton, Grant Takes Command (1969); Bruce Catton, A Stillness at Appomattox (1953); Peter Cozzens, This Terrible Sound (1992); Michael Fellman, Citizen Sherman (1995); Shelby Foote, The Civil War, a Narrative, 3 vols. (1958–1974); Douglas Southall Freeman, Lee's Lieutenants, 3 vols. (1942–1944); Douglas Southall Freeman, R. E. Lee, 4 vols. (1934–1935); Gary W. Gallagher, The Confederate War (1997); Gary W. Gallagher, Lee and His Generals in War and Memory (1998); Joseph T. Glatthaar, The March to the Sea and Beyond (1985); Herman Hattaway and Archer Jones, How the North Won (1983); Laurence M. Hauptman, Between Two Fires: American Indians in the Civil War (1995); Robert V. Hine and John Mack Faragher, The American West: A New Interpretive History (2000); Archer Jones, Civil War Command and Strategy (1992); Alvin M. Josephy, Jr., The Civil War in the American West (1991); Gerald F. Linderman, Embattled Courage (1989); Thomas L. Livermore, Numbers and Losses in the Civil War in America (1957); Grady McWhiney and Perry D. Jamieson, Attack and Die (1982); Reid Mitchell, Civil War Soldiers (1988); Reid Mitchell, The Vacant Chair (1993); Roy

Morris, Jr., Sheridan (1992); George C. Rable, Fredericksburg! Fredericksburg! (2002); Charles Royster, The Destructive War (1991); Stephen W. Sears, To the Gates of Richmond (1992); Stephen W. Sears, George B. McClellan (1988); Emory M. Thomas, Robert E. Lee (1995); Emory M. Thomas, Bold Dragoon: The Life of J. E. B. Stuart (1987); Noah Andre Trudeau, The Last Citadel (1991); Steven E. Woodworth, Jefferson Davis and His Generals (1990).

Foreign Relations

Stuart L. Bernath, Squall Across the Atlantic: American Civil War Prize Cases and Diplomacy (1970); R. J. M. Blackett, Divided Hearts: Britain and the American Civil War (2001); David P. Crook, The North, the South, and the Powers, 1861–1865 (1974); Charles P. Cullop, Confederate Propaganda in Europe (1969); Norman B. Ferris, The Trent Affair (1977); Howard Jones, Union in Peril (1992); Frank J. Merli, Great Britain and the Confederate Navy (1970); Frank L. Owsley and Harriet Owsley, King Cotton Diplomacy (1959); Gordon H. Warren, Fountain of Discontent: The Trent Affair and Freedom of the Seas (1981).

Abraham Lincoln and the Union Government

Allan G. Bogue, The Earnest Men: Republicans of the Civil War Senate (1981); Gabor S. Borit, ed., The Historian's Lincoln (1989); Fawn Brodie, Thaddeus Stevens (1959); Richard N. Current, The Lincoln Nobody Knows (1958); Leonard P. Curry, Blueprint for Modern America: Non-Military Legislation of the First Civil War Congress (1968); David Donald, Charles Sumner and the Rights of Man (1970); David Donald, Lincoln (1995); William E. Gienapp, Abraham Lincoln and Civil War America (2002); Allen Guelzo, Abraham Lincoln: Redeemer President (1999); Peyton McCrary, Abraham Lincoln and Reconstruction: The Louisiana Experiment (1978); James M. McPherson, Abraham Lincoln and the Second American Revolution (1990); Mark Neely, The Fate of Liberty (1991); Stephen B. Oates, With Malice Toward None (1977); Philip S. Paludan, The Presidency of Abraham Lincoln (1994); Heather Cox Richardson, The Greatest Nation of the Earth: Republican Economic Policies During the Civil War (1997); Joel Silbey, A Respectable Minority: The Democratic Party in the Civil War Era (1977); Benjamin P. Thomas, Abraham Lincoln (1952); Hans L. Trefousse, The Radical Republicans (1969); Glyndon G. Van Deusen, William Henry Seward (1967); T. Harry Williams, Lincoln and His Generals (1952); T. Harry Williams, Lincoln and the Radicals (1941).

Chapter 16

National Policy, Politics, and Constitutional Law

Richard H. Abbott, *The Republican Party and the South, 1855–1877* (1986); Herman Belz, *Emancipation and Equal Rights* (1978); Herman Belz, *A New Birth of Freedom* (1976); Michael Les Benedict, *A Compromise of Principle: Congressional Republicans and Reconstruction, 1863–1869* (1974); Michael Les Benedict, *The Impeachment and Trial of Andrew Johnson* (1973); Charles S. Campbell, *The Transformation of American Foreign Relations, 1865–1900* (1976); Adrian Cook, *The Alabama Claims* (1975); Michael Kent Curtis, *No State Shall Abridge* (1987); David Donald, *Charles Sumner and the Rights of Man* (1970); Harold M. Hyman, *A More Perfect Union* (1973); William S. McFeely, *Grant* (1981); William S. McFeely, *Yankee Stepfather: General O. O. Howard and the Freedmen* (1968); Eric L. McKitrick, *Andrew Johnson and Reconstruction* (1966); James M. McPherson, *The Abolitionist Legacy* (1975); Joel Silbey, *A Respectable Minority: The Democratic Party in the Civil War Era* (1977); Brooks D. Simpson, *Let Us Have Peace* (1991); Brooks D. Simpson, *The Reconstruction Presidents* (1998); Kenneth M. Stampp, *The Era of Reconstruction* (1965); Hans L. Trefousse, *Andrew Johnson* (1989).

The Freed Slaves

Roberta Sue Alexander, *North Carolina Faces the Freedmen* (1985); Ira Berlin, ed., *Freedom: A Documentary History of Emancipation, 1861–1867* (1984); Elizabeth R. Bethel, *Promiseland* (1981); Orville Vernon Burton, *In My Father's House Are Many Mansions* (1985); Edmund L. Drago, *Black Politicians and Reconstruction in Georgia* (1982); Paul D. Escott, *Slavery Remembered* (1979); Eric Foner, "Reconstruction and the Crisis of Free Labor," in *Politics and Ideology in the Age of the Civil War*, ed. Eric Foner (1980); Gerald Jaynes, *Branches Without Roots: The Genesis of the Black Working Class in the American South, 1862–1882* (1986); Leon Litwack, *Been in the Storm So Long* (1979); Edward Magdol, *A Right to the Land* (1977); Robert Morris, *Reading, 'Riting and Reconstruction* (1981); Howard Rabinowitz, ed., *Southern Black Leaders in Reconstruction* (1982); Emma Lou Thornbrough, ed., *Black Reconstructionists* (1972); Clarence Walker, *A Rock in a Weary Land* (1982); Elliot West, "Reconstructing Race," *Western Historical Quarterly* (Spring, 2003).

Politics and Reconstruction in the South

James A. Baggett, *The Scalawags: Southern Dissenters in the Civil War and Reconstruction* (2003); Robert W. Coakley, *The Role of Federal Military Forces in Domestic Disorders, 1789–1878* (1988); Richard N. Current, *Those Terrible Carpetbaggers* (1988); W. E. B. Du Bois, *Black Reconstruction* (1935); Paul D. Escott, *Many Excellent People: Power and Privilege in North Carolina, 1850–1900* (1985); Michael W. Fitzgerald, *The Union League Movement in the Deep South* (1989); Eric Foner, *Reconstruction: America's Unfinished Revolution, 1863–1877* (1988); Eric Foner, *Nothing but Freedom* (1983); Steven Hahn, *A Nation Under Our Feet: Black Political Struggles in the Rural South from Slavery to the Great Migration* (2003); William C. Harris, *The Day of the Carpetbagger* (1979); Thomas Holt, *Black over White: Negro Political Leadership in South Carolina During Reconstruction* (1977); J. Morgan Kousser and James M. McPherson, eds., *Region, Race and Reconstruction* (1982); Elizabeth Studley Nathans, *Losing the Peace* (1968); Michael Perman, *The Road to Redemption* (1984); Michael Perman, *Reunion Without Compromise* (1973); Lawrence N. Powell, *New Masters* (1980); George C. Rable, *But There Was No Peace* (1984); James Roark, *Masters Without Slaves* (1977); James Sefton, *The United States Army and Reconstruction, 1865–1877* (1967); Mark W. Summers, *Railroads, Reconstruction, and the Gospel of Prosperity* (1984); Allen Trelease, *White Terror* (1967); Ted Tunnell, *Carpetbagger from Vermont* (1989); Ted Tunnell, *Crucible of Reconstruction* (1984); Michael Wayne, *The Reshaping of Plantation Society* (1983); Sarah Woolfolk Wiggins, *The Scalawag in Alabama Politics, 1865–1881* (1977).

Women, Family, and Social History

Virginia I. Burr, ed., *The Secret Eye* (1990); Ellen Carol Dubois, *Feminism and Suffrage* (1978); Herbert G. Gutman, *The Black Family in Slavery and Freedom, 1750–1925* (1976); Elizabeth Jacoway, *Yankee Missionaries in the South* (1979); Jacqueline Jones, *Labor of Love, Labor of Sorrow* (1985); Jacqueline Jones, *Soldiers of Light and Love* (1980); Robert C. Kenzer, *Kinship and Neighborhood in a Southern Community* (1987); Mary P. Ryan, *Women in Public* (1990); Rebecca Scott, "The Battle over the Child," *Prologue* 10 (Summer 1978): 101–113.

The End of Reconstruction

Michael Les Benedict, "Southern Democrats in the Crisis of 1876–1877," *Journal of Southern History* 66 (November 1980): 489–524; William Gillette, *Retreat from Reconstruction, 1869–1879* (1980); William Gillette, *The Right to Vote* (1969); Keith Ian Polakoff, *The Politics of Inertia* (1973); Heather Richardson, *The Death of Reconstruction* (2001); John G. Sproat, *"The Best Men": Liberal Reformers in the Gilded Age* (1968); C. Vann Woodward, *Reunion and Reaction* (1951).

Reconstruction's Legacy for the South and the Nation

Robert G. Athearn, *In Search of Canaan* (1978); Edward L. Ayers, *The Promise of the New South* (1992); David W. Blight, *Race and Reunion: The Civil War in American Memory* (2001); Norman L. Crockett, *The Black Towns* (1979); Steven Hahn, *The Roots of Southern Populism* (1983); Leon Litwack, *Trouble in Mind: Black Southerners in the Age of Jim Crow* (1998); Jay R. Mandle, *The Roots of Black Poverty* (1978); Nell Irvin Painter, *Exodusters* (1976); Howard Rabinowitz, *Race Relations in the Urban South, 1865–1890* (1978); Roger L. Ransom and Richard Sutch, *One Kind of Freedom* (1977); Laurence Shore, *Southern Capitalists* (1986); Peter Wallenstein, *From Slave South to New South* (1987); Jonathan M. Wiener, *Social Origins of the New South* (1978); C. Vann Woodward, *Origins of the New South* (1951).

Chapter 17

Native Americans

Leonard A. Carlson, *Indians, Bureaucrats, and Land: The Dawes Act and the Decline of Indian Farming* (1981); David Courtwright, *Violent Land* (1996); Sterling Evans, ed., *American Indians in American History, 1870–2001* (2002); Frederick E. Hoxie, *A Final Promise: The Campaign to Assimilate the Indians, 1880–1920* (1984); Janet A. McDonnell, *The Dispossession of the American Indian* (1991); Francis Paul Prucha, *The Great Father: The United States Government and the American Indians* (1984); Robert M. Utley, *The Lance and the Shield: The Life and Times of Sitting Bull* (1993); Robert M. Utley, *The Indian Frontier of the American West, 1846–1890* (1984); Philip Weeks, *Farewell, My Nation: The American Indian and the United States* (1990); Richard White, *The Roots of Dependency* (1983).

The Western Frontier

Ray A. Billington and Martin Ridge, *Westward Expansion*, 5th ed. (1982); Sara Deutsch, *No Separate Refuge: Culture, Class, and Gender on an Anglo-Hispanic Frontier in the American Southwest* (1987); James R. Grossman, ed., *The Frontier in American Culture* (1994); Robert V. Hine and John Mack Faragher, *The American West* (2000); Julie Roy Jeffrey, *Frontier Women* (1979); Patricia Limerick, *The Legacy of Conquest: The Unbroken Past of the American West* (1987); Timothy R. Mahoney, *River Towns in the Great West* (1990); Peggy Pascoe, *Relations of Rescue: The Search for Female Moral Authority in the American West* (1990); Rodman W. Paul, *The Far West and the Great Plains in Transition, 1859–1900* (1988); Robert J. Rosenbaum, *Mexican Resistance in the Southwest* (1981); Richard White, *"It's Your Misfortune and None of My Own": A New History of the American West* (1991).

Water and the Environment

Karl Jacoby, *Crimes Against Nature* (2001); Roderick Nash, *American Environmentalism*, 3d ed. (1990); Thurman Wilkins, *John Muir: Apostle of Nature* (1995); Donald Worster, *Rivers of Empire: Water, Aridity, and the Growth of the American West* (1985); Donald Worster, *An Unsettled Country: Changing Landscapes of the American West* (1994).

Railroads

Alfred D. Chandler, ed., *Railroads* (1965); Edward C. Kirkland, *Men, Cities, and Transportation* (1948); George R. Taylor and Irene Neu, *The American Railroad Network* (1956); Alan Trachtenberg, *The Incorporation of America* (1982); O. O. Winther, *The Transportation Frontier* (1964).

Ranching and Settlement of the Plains

William Cronon, *Nature's Metropolis: Chicago and the Great West* (1991); Gilbert C. Fite, *The Farmer's Frontier* (1963); Robert V. Hine, *Community on the American Frontier* (1980); David Igler, *Industrial Cowboys* (2001); Richard W. Slatta, *Cowboys of the Americas* (1990).

Chapter 18

General

Daniel J. Boorstin, *The Americans: The Democratic Experience* (1973); Alan Dawley, *Struggle for Justice: Social Responsibility and the Liberal State* (1991); Stephen Diner, *A Very Different Age* (1998); Samuel P. Hays, *The Response to Industrialism* (1975); Thomas J. Schlereth, *Victorian America: Transformations in Everyday Life* (1991).

Technology and Invention

Robert W. Bruce, *Bell: Alexander Graham Bell and the Conquest of Solitude* (1973); Gary Cross and Rich Szostak, *Technology and American Society* (1995); David Hounshell, *From the American System to Mass Production* (1984); Thomas Parke Hughes, *American Genesis: A Century of Technological Enthusiasm* (1989); John P. Kasson, *Civilizing the Machine: Technology and Republican Values in America* (1976); Andre Millard, *Edison and the Business of Innovation* (1990); David E. Nye, *Electrifying America* (1990).

Industrialism, Industrialists, and Corporate Growth

W. Eliot Brownlee, *Dynamics of Ascent: A History of the American Economy*, 2d ed. (1979); Vincent P. Carosso, *The Morgans* (1987); Alfred D. Chandler, *The Visible Hand: The Managerial Revolution in American Business* (1977); Thomas C. Cochran, *Business in American Life* (1972); David F. Hawkes, *John D.: The Founding Father of the Rockefellers* (1980); Robert Higgs, *The Transformation of the American Economy, 1865–1914* (1971); Harold C. Livesay, *Andrew Carnegie and the Rise of Big Business* (1975); Roland Marchand, *Creating the Corporate Soul* (1998); Glen Porter, *The Rise of Big Business* (1973); Richard Tedlow, *The Rise of the American Business Corporation* (1991); Joseph Wall, *Alfred I. du Pont: The Man and His Family* (1990).

Work and Labor Organization

Alan Derickson, *Workers' Health, Workers' Democracy: The Western Miners' Struggle, 1891–1925* (1988); Melvin Dubofsky, *We Shall Be All: A History of the Industrial Workers of the World* (1969); Sarah Eisenstein, *Give Us Bread, Give Us Roses: Working Women's Consciousness in the United States* (1983); Leon Fink, *Workingmen's Democracy: The Knights of Labor and American Politics* (1982); Philip S. Foner, *The Great Labor*

Uprising of 1877 (1977); Herbert G. Gutman, *Work, Culture and Society in Industrializing America* (1976); Alice Kessler-Harris, *Out to Work: A History of Wage Earning Women in the United States* (1982); Susan Lehrer, *Origins of Protective Labor Legislation for Women* (1987); Harold Livesay, *Samuel Gompers and Organized Labor in America* (1978); Milton Meltzer, *Bread and Roses: The Struggle of American Labor, 1865–1915* (1967); Ruth Milkman, ed., *Women, Work, and Protest* (1985); David Montgomery, *The Fall of the House of Labor: The Workplace, the State, and American Labor Activism, 1865–1925* (1987); Stephen H. Norwood, *Labor's Flaming Youth: Telephone Operators and Worker Militancy* (1990); Elizabeth Ann Payne, *Reform, Labor, and Feminism: Margaret Dreier Robins and the Women's Trade Union League* (1988); Leon J. Wolff, *Lockout: The Story of the Homestead Strike of 1892* (1965).

Living Standards and New Conveniences

Susan Porter Benson, *Counter Cultures: Saleswomen, Managers, and Customers in American Department Stores, 1890–1940* (1986); T. J. Jackson Lears and Richard W. Fox, eds., *The Culture of Consumption* (1983); Harvey A. Levenstein, *Revolution at the Table: The Transformation of the American Diet* (1988); Kathy Peiss, *Hope in a Jar: The Making of America's Beauty Culture* (1998); Daniel Pope, *The Making of Modern Advertising* (1983); Peter R. Shergold, *Working Class Life* (1982); Susan Strasser, *Satisfaction Guaranteed: The Making of the American Mass Market* (1989); Gwendolyn Wright, *Building the Dream: A Social History of Housing in America* (1983).

Attitudes Toward Industrialism

Louis Galambos and Barbara Barron Spence, *The Public Image of Big Business in America* (1975); Richard Hofstadter, *Social Darwinism in American Thought*, rev. ed. (1955); T. J. Jackson Lears, *No Place of Grace: Antimodernism and the Transformation of American Culture* (1981); John L. Thomas, *Alternative America: Henry George, Edward Bellamy, Henry Demarest Lloyd, and the Adversary Tradition* (1983).

Southern Industrialism

Edward Ayers, *The Promise of the New South* (1992); James C. Cobb, *Industrialization and Southern Society, 1877–1984* (1984); Paul M. Gaston, *The New South Creed* (1970); C. Vann Woodward, *Origins of the New South* (1951); Gavin Wright, *Old South, New South* (1986).

Chapter 19

Urban Growth

Howard P. Chudacoff and Judith E. Smith, *The Evolution of American Urban Society*, 5th ed. (1999); Robert M. Fogelson, *Downtown: Its Rise and Fall* (2001); David Goldfield, *Cotton Fields and Skyscrapers: Southern City and Region* (1982); Kenneth T. Jackson, *The Crabgrass Frontier: The Suburbanization of the United States* (1985); Harold Platt, *City Building in the New South* (1983); Jon Teaford, *The Unheralded Triumph: City Government in America, 1870–1900* (1984).

Immigration, Ethnicity, and Religion

Aaron I. Abell, *American Catholicism and Social Action* (1960); John Bodnar, *The Transplanted* (1985); John Bodnar, Roger Simon, and Michael P. Weber, *Lives of Their Own: Blacks, Italians, and Poles in Pittsburgh, 1900–1960* (1982); Sucheng Chan, ed., *Entry Denied: Exclusion and the Chinese Community in America, 1882–1943* (1990); Elizabeth Ewen, *Immigrant Women in the Land of Dollars* (1985); Donna R. Gabaccia, *From the Other Side: Women, Gender, and Immigrant Life in the United States* (1994); Mario T. Garcia, *Desert Immigrants: The Mexicans of El Paso, 1880–1920* (1981); Oscar Handlin, *The Uprooted*, 2d ed. (1973); John Higham, *Strangers in the Land: Patterns of American Nativism* (1955); Yusi Ichioka, *The Issei: The World of the First Japanese Immigrants, 1885–1924* (1988); Matthew Frye Jacobson, *Whiteness of a Different Color: European Immigrants and the Alchemy of Race* (1998); Matt S. Maier and Felciano Rivera, *The Chicanos* (1972); Werner Sollors, *Beyond Ethnicity* (1986); Ron Takaki, *Iron Cages: Race and Culture in Nineteenth-Century America* (1979); Stephan Thernstrom, ed., *Harvard Encyclopedia of American Ethnic Groups* (1980).

Urban Services

Christine Boyer, *Dreaming the Rational City: The Myth of American City Planning* (1983); Charles W. Cheape, *Moving the Masses* (1980); Lawrence A. Cremin, *American Education: The Metropolitan Experience* (1988); David R. Johnson, *American Law Enforcement* (1981); Martin V. Melosi, *Garbage in the Cities* (1981); Eric Monkkonen, *America Becomes Urban* (1988); Mark Rose, *Cities of Light and Heat* (1995); David Stradling, *Smokestacks and Progressive Environmentalists* (1999); Stanley K. Schultz, *Constructing Urban Culture: American Cities and City Planning* (1989).

Family and Individual Life Cycles

George Chauncey, *Gay New York* (1995); Howard P. Chudacoff, *The Age of the Bachelor* (1999); Howard P. Chudacoff, *How Old Are You? Age in American Culture* (1989); Nancy F. Cott, *Public Vows: A History of Marriage and the Nation* (2000); Sarah Deutsch, *Women and the City* (2000); John D'Emilio and Estelle B. Freedman, *Intimate Matters: A History of Sexuality in America* (1988); Carole Haber, *Beyond Sixty-five: Dilemmas of Old Age in America's Past* (1983); Joseph Kett, *Rites of Passage: Adolescence in America* (1979); Kathleen W. Jones, *Taming the Troublesome Child* (1999); Elizabeth Pleck, *Celebrating the Family* (2000); E. Anthony Rotundo, *American Manhood* (1994).

Mass Entertainment and Leisure

Jessica H. Foy and Thomas J. Schlereth, eds., *American Home Life, 1880–1930* (1992); Donna R. Gabaccia, *We Are What We Eat: Ethnic Food and the Making of Americans* (1998); Allen Guttmann, *A Whole New Ball Game: An Interpretation of American Sports* (1988); Katrina Hazzard-Gordon, *Lookin': The Rise of Social Dance Formulations in African-American Culture* (1990); George Juergens, *Joseph Pulitzer and the New York World* (1966); John F. Kasson, *Amusing the Million: Coney Island at the Turn of the Century* (1978); David Nasaw, *The Chief: The Life of William Randolph Hearst* (2000); David Nasaw, *Going Out: The Rise and Fall of Popular Amusements* (1993); Kathy Peiss, *Cheap Amusements: Working Women and Leisure in Turn-of-the-Century New York* (1986); Benjamin G. Rader, *American Sports*, 4th ed. (1999); Steven A. Riess, *City Games* (1989); Roy Rosenzweig, *Eight Hours for What We Will! Workers and Leisure in an Industrial City, 1870–1920* (1983); Robert Sklar, *Movie-Made America* (1976); Ronald A. Smith, *Sports and Freedom: The Rise of Big-Time College Athletics* (1988); Robert V. Snyder, *The Voice of the City: Vaudeville and Popular Culture in New York City, 1880–1920* (1990); Robert C. Toll, *On with the Show: The First Century of Show Business in America* (1976).

Mobility and Race Relations

James Borchert, *Alley Life in Washington* (1980); Clyde Griffen and Sally Griffen, *Natives and Newcomers* (1977); Jacqueline Jones, *Labor of Love, Labor of Sorrow: Black Women, Work and the Family from Slavery to the Present* (1985); Kenneth L. Kusmer, *A Ghetto Takes Shape* (1976); Gilbert Osofsky, *Harlem: The Making of a Ghetto* (1966); Elizabeth H. Pleck, *Black Migration and Poverty: Boston, 1865–1900* (1979); Howard N. Rabinowitz, *Race Relations in the Urban South* (1978); Allan H. Spear, *Black Chicago* (1967); Stephan Thernstrom, *The Other Bostonians: Poverty and Progress in the American Metropolis* (1973); Olivier Zunz, *The Changing Face of Inequality* (1982).

Boss Politics

Alexander B. Callow, Jr., ed., *The City Boss in America* (1976); Lyle Dorsett, *The Pendergast Machine* (1968); Leo Hershkowitz, *Tweed's New York: Another Look* (1977); Terrence J. McDonald, *The Parameters of Urban Fiscal Policy* (1986); Zane L. Miller, *Boss Cox's Cincinnati* (1968); Bruce M. Stave and Sondra Stave, eds., *Urban Bosses, Machines, and Progressive Reformers* (1984).

Urban Reform

John D. Buenker, *Urban Liberalism and Progressive Reform* (1973); Doris Groshen Daniels, *Always a Sister: The Feminism of Lillian D. Wald* (1989); Allen F. Davis, *Spearheads for Reform* (1967); Lori Ginzberg, *Women and the Work of Benevolence* (1991); Rivka Shpak Lissack, *Pluralism and Progressives: Hull House and the New Immigrants, 1890–1919* (1989); Roy M. Lubove, *The Progressives and the Slums* (1962); Clay McShane, *Technology and Reform* (1974); Robyn Muncy, *Creating a Female Dominion in American Reform* (1991); Martin J. Schiesl, *The Politics of Efficiency* (1977); Kathryn Kish Sklar, *Florence Kelley and the Nation's Work* (1995).

Chapter 20

General

Charles W. Calhoun, ed., *The Gilded Age: Essays on the Origins of Modern America* (1995); Sean Denis Cashman, *America in the Gilded Age* (1984); Steven J. Diner, *A Very Different Age* (1998); Nell Irvin Painter, *Standing at Armageddon* (1987).

Parties and Political Issues

John M. Dobson, *Politics in the Gilded Age* (1972); Ari A. Hoogenboom, *Outlawing the Spoils: The Civil Service Movement* (1961); Morton Keller, *Affairs of State* (1977); Paul Kleppner, *The Third Electoral System, 1853–1892* (1979); Michael E. McGerr, *The Decline of Popular Politics* (1986); A. M. Paul, *Conservative Crisis and the Rule of Law: Attitudes of Bar and Bench, 1887–1895* (1969); John G. Sproat, *The Best Men: Liberal Reformers in the Gilded Age* (1968); Hal R. Williams, *Years of Decision: American Politics in the 1890s* (1978).

The Presidency

Kenneth E. Davison, *The Presidency of Rutherford B. Hayes* (1972); Justus D. Doenecke, *The Presidencies of James A. Garfield and Chester A. Arthur* (1981); Lewis L. Gould, *The Presidency of William McKinley* (1981); Homer E. Socolotsky and Allen B. Spetter, *The Presidency of Benjamin Harrison* (1987); Richard G. Welch, *The Presidency of Grover Cleveland* (1988).

Women's Rights and Disfranchisement of African Americans

Edward L. Ayers, *The Promise of the New South* (1992); Paula Baker, *The Moral Framework of Public Life* (1991); Beverly Beeton, *Women Vote in the West: The Suffrage Movement, 1869–1896* (1986); Fitzhugh Brundage, *Lynching in the New South* (1993); Margaret Mary Finnegan, *Selling Suffrage: Consumer Culture and Votes for Women* (1999); Glenda Elizabeth Gilmore, *Gender & Jim Crow* (1996); Elisabeth Griffith, *In Her Own Right: The Life of Elizabeth Cady Stanton* (1984); Leon Litwak, *Trouble in Mind: Black Southerners in the Age of Jim Crow* (1998); Michael Perman, *Struggle for Mastery: Disfranchisement in the South* (2001); Sandra F. VanBurkleo, *"Belonging to the World": Women's Rights and American Constitutional Culture* (2001).

Protest and Socialism

William M. Dick, *Labor and Socialism in America* (1972); Elliott Gorn, *Mother Jones: The Most Dangerous Woman in America* (2001); J. Anthony Lukas, *Big Trouble* (1997); Nick

Salvatore, *Eugene V. Debs: Citizen and Socialist* (1982); Carlos A. Schwantes, *Coxey's Army* (1985); David Shannon, *The Socialist Party of America* (1955).

Populism and the Election of 1896

Donna A. Barnes, *Farmers in Rebellion: The Rise and Fall of the Southern Farmers Alliance and People's Party in Texas* (1984); Lawrence Goodwyn, *Democratic Promise: The Populist Movement in America* (1976); Steven Hahn, *The Roots of Southern Populism* (1983); J. Morgan Kousser, *The Shaping of Southern Politics* (1974); Robert C. McMath, Jr., *American Populism* (1993); Walter T. K. Nugent, *The Tolerant Populists* (1963); Jeffrey Ostler, *Prairie Populism* (1993); Barton C. Shaw, *The Wool-Hat Boys: Georgia's Populist Party* (1984); Allan Weinstein, *Prelude to Populism: Origins of the Silver Issue* (1970).

Chapter 21

General

Paul M. Boyer, *Urban Masses and Moral Order in America, 1820–1920* (1978); Walter M. Brasch, *Forerunners of Revolution: Muckrakers and the American Social Conscience* (1990); John M. Cooper, Jr., *The Pivotal Decades* (1990); Steven J. Diner, *A Very Different Age: Americans of the Progressive Era* (1998); Richard Hofstadter, *The Age of Reform* (1955); William R. Hutchinson, *The Modernist Impulse in American Protestantism* (1976); Morton Keller, *Regulating a New Economy* (1990); Gabriel Kolko, *The Triumph of Conservatism* (1963); Sidney M. Milkis and Jerome M. Mileur, eds., *Progressivism and the New Democracy* (1999); Daniel T. Rodgers, *Atlantic Crossings: Social Politics in a Progressive Age* (1998); Robert Wiebe, *The Search for Order* (1968).

Regional Studies

Dewey Grantham, *Southern Progressivism* (1983); William A. Link, *The Paradox of Southern Progressivism* (1992); David P. Thelen, *Robert La Follette and the Insurgent Spirit* (1976); Richard White, *"It's Your Misfortune and None of My Own": A History of the American West* (1991); C. Vann Woodward, *Origins of the New South* (1951).

Legislative Issues and Reform Groups

Ruth H. Crocker, *Social Work and Social Order* (1992); Robert M. Crunden, *Ministers of Reform: The Progressives' Achievement in American Civilization* (1982); Allen F. Davis, *Spearheads for Reform: The Social Settlements and the Progressive Movement, 1890–1914* (1967); Ruth Rosen, *The Lost Sisterhood: Prostitution in America, 1900–1918* (1982); W. J. Rorabaugh, *The Alcoholic Republic* (1979); Kathryn Kish Sklar, *Florence Kelley and the Nation's Work* (1995); Walter I. Trattner, *Crusade for the Children* (1970); James Harvey Young, *Pure Food* (1989). (For works on socialism, see the listings under "Protest and Socialism, Chapter 20.)

Education, Law, and the Social Sciences

Jerold S. Auerback, *Unequal Justice: Lawyers and Social Change in Modern America* (1976); Paula S. Fass, *Outside In: Minorities and the Transformation of American Education* (1989); Ellen Fitzpatrick, *Endless Crusade: Women Social Scientists and Progressive Reform* (1990); Lynn D. Gordon, *Gender and Higher Education in the Progressive Era* (1990); Thomas L. Haskell, *The Emergence of Professional Social Science* (1977); Helen Horowitz, *Alma Mater: Design and Experience in Women's Colleges* (1984); David W. Marcell, *Progress and Pragmatism: James, Dewey, Beard, and the American Idea of Progress* (1974); Edward A. Purcell, Jr., *Brandeis and the Progressive Constitution* (2000); Lawrence Veysey, *The Emergence of the American University* (1970).

Women

Ruth Borden, *Women and Temperance* (1980); Ellen Chesler, *Woman of Valor: The Life of Margaret Sanger* (1992); Nancy F. Cott, *The Grounding of American Feminism* (1987); Carl N. Degler, *At Odds: Women and the Family in America* (1980); Linda Gordon, *Woman's Body, Woman's Right: A Social History of Birth Control in America* (1976); Evelyn Higginbotham, *Righteous Discontent: The Women's Movement in the Black Baptist Church, 1880–1920* (1993); Alice Kessler-Harris, *Out to Work: A History of Wage-Earning Women in the United States* (1982); Robyn Muncy, *Creating a Female Dominion in American Reform* (1991); Rosalind Rosenberg, *Beyond Separate Spheres: Intellectual Roots of Modern Feminism* (1982); Sheila M. Rothman, *Woman's Proper Place* (1978).

African Americans

John Dittmer, *Black Georgia in the Progressive Era* (1977); George Frederickson, *The Black Image in the White Mind* (1971); Glenda Elizabeth Gilmore, *Gender & Jim Crow* (1996); Louis R. Harlan, *Booker T. Washington*, 2 vols. (1972 and 1983); Jacqueline Jones, *Labor of Love, Labor of Sorrow: Black Women, Work and the Family from Slavery to the Present* (1985); David Levering Lewis, *W. E. B. Du Bois* (1993); Patricia A. Schroeder, *Ida B. Wells-Barnett and American Reform* (2001).

Roosevelt, Taft, and Wilson

Francis L. Broderick, *Progressivism at Risk: Electing a President in 1912* (1989); Paolo E. Coletta, *The Presidency of William Howard Taft* (1973); John M. Cooper, Jr., *The Warrior and the Priest: Woodrow Wilson and Theodore Roosevelt* (1983); Lewis Gould, *The Presidency of Theodore Roosevelt* (1991); August Hecksher, *Woodrow Wilson* (1991); Edmund Morris, *The Rise of Theodore Roosevelt* (1979); James Pednick, Jr., *Progressive Politics and Conservation: The Ballinger-Pinchot Affair* (1968).

Chapter 22

General

Robert L. Beisner, *From the Old Diplomacy to the New, 1865–1900*, 2d ed. (1986); Manfred F. Boemeke et al., eds., *Anticipating Total War: The German and American Experiences, 1871–1914* (1999); Daniel R. Headrick, *The Invisible Weapon: Telecommunications and International Politics, 1851–1945* (1991); Paul Kennedy, *The Rise and Fall of the Great Powers* (1987); Paul A. C. Koistinen, *Mobilizing for Modern War: The Political Economy of American Warfare, 1865–1919* (1997); Walter LaFeber, *The American Search for Opportunity, 1865–1913* (1993); Walter LaFeber, *The New Empire*, anniv. ed. (1998); Ernest R. May, *American Imperialism* (1968); Emily Rosenberg, *Spreading the American Dream: American Economic and Cultural Expansion, 1890–1945* (1982); William Appleman Williams, *The Tragedy of American Diplomacy*, new ed. (1988); Fareed Zakaria, *From Wealth to Power: The Unusual Origins of America's World Role* (1998); Warren Zimmermann, *First Great Triumph: How Five Americans Made Their Country a World Power* (2002).

Imperial Promoters

Howard K. Beale, *Theodore Roosevelt and the Rise of America to World Power* (1956); H. W. Brands, *T.R.: The Last Romantic* (1997); John M. Cooper, Jr., *The Warrior and the Priest: Woodrow Wilson and Theodore Roosevelt* (1983); Edward P. Crapol, *James G. Blaine* (1999); Lewis L. Gould, *The Presidency of Theodore Roosevelt* (1991); Lewis L. Gould, *The Presidency of William McKinley* (1981); Frederick Marks III, *Velvet on Iron: The Diplomacy of Theodore Roosevelt* (1979); Edmund Morris, *Theodore Rex* (2001); Ernest N. Paolino, *The Foundations of the American Empire: William Henry Seward and U.S. Foreign Policy* (1973); William N. Tilchin, *Theodore Roosevelt and the British Empire* (1997); William C. Widenor, *Henry Cabot Lodge and the Search for an American Foreign Policy* (1980).

Economic and Financial Expansion

William H. Becker, *The Dynamics of Business-Government Relations* (1982); Robert B. Davies, *Peacefully Working to Conquer the World: Singer Sewing Machines in Foreign Markets, 1854–1920* (1976); David Pletcher, *The Diplomacy of Trade and Investment* (1998); Emily Rosenberg, *Financial Missionaries to the World: The Politics and Culture of Dollar Diplomacy, 1900–1930* (1999); Tom Terrill, *The Tariff, Politics, and American Foreign Policy, 1874–1901* (1973); Mira Wilkins, *The Emergence of the Multinational Enterprise* (1970).

Ideology and Culture

Gail Bederman, *Manliness & Civilization* (1995); Alexander DeConde, *Ethnicity, Race, and American Foreign Policy* (1992); Thomas G. Dyer, *Theodore Roosevelt and the Idea of Race* (1980); Willard B. Gatewood, Jr., *Black Americans and the White Man's Burden* (1975); Michael H. Hunt, *Ideology and U.S. Foreign Policy* (1987); Amy Kaplan and Donald E. Pease, eds., *Cultures of United States Imperialism* (1993); Robert Rydell, *All the World's a Fair* (1985).

Religious Missionaries

Nancy Boyd, *Emissaries: The Overseas Work of the American YWCA, 1895–1970* (1986); Wayne Flynt and Gerald W. Berkley, *Taking Christianity to China* (1997); Gael Graham, *Gender, Culture, and Christianity: American Protestant Mission Schools in China, 1880–1930* (1995); Patricia R. Hill, *The World Their Household* (1985); Jane Hunter, *The Gospel of Gentility: American Missionaries in Turn-of-the-Century China* (1984); Ian Tyrrell, *Woman's World, Woman's Empire: The Woman's Christian Temperance Union in International Perspective, 1880–1930* (1991).

Navalism and the Navy

Benjamin F. Cooling, *Gray Steel and Blue Water Navy* (1979); Frederick C. Drake, *The Empire of the Seas: A Biography of Rear Admiral Robert W. Shufelt* (1984); Kenneth J. Hagan, *This People's Navy* (1991); Mark R. Shulman, *Navalism and the Emergence of American Sea Power* (1995); Robert Seager II, *Alfred Thayer Mahan* (1977); Ronald Spector, *Admiral of the New Empire: The Life and Career of George Dewey* (1974).

The Spanish-American-Cuban-Filipino War

Kristin L. Hoganson, *Fighting for American Manhood: How Gender Politics Provoked the Spanish-American and Philippine-American Wars* (1998); Gerald F. Linderman, The Mirror of War (1974); Ivan Musicant, *Empire by Default: The Spanish-American War and the Dawn of the American Century* (1998); John Offner, *An Unwanted War: The Diplomacy of the United States and Spain over Cuba, 1895–1898* (1992); Louis A. Perez, Jr., *The War of 1898: The United States and Cuba in History and Historiography* (1998); David F. Trask, *The War with Spain in 1898* (1981).

Anti-imperialism and the Peace Movement

Robert L. Beisner, *Twelve Against Empire* (1968); Kendrick A. Clements, *William Jennings Bryan* (1983); Charles DeBenedetti, *Peace Reform in American History* (1980); C. Roland Marchand, *The American Peace Movement and Social Reform, 1898–1918* (1973); Thomas J. Osborne, *"Empire Can Wait": American Opposition to Hawaiian Annexation* (1981).

Cuba, Mexico, Panama, and Latin America

Richard H. Collin, *Theodore Roosevelt's Caribbean* (1990); David Healy, *Drive to Hegemony: The United States in the Caribbean, 1898–1917* (1989); Walter LaFeber, *Inevitable Revolutions: The United States in Central America*, 2d rev. ed. (1993); Walter LaFeber, *The Panama Canal*, updated ed. (1990); Lester D. Langley, *The United States and the Caribbean, 1900–1970* (1980); John Major, *Prize Possession: The United States and the Panama Canal, 1903–1979* (1993); David

McCullough, *The Path Between the Seas: The Creation of the Panama Canal, 1870–1914* (1977); A. Pérez, Jr., *Cuba Under the Platt Amendment, 1902–1934* (1986); Fredrick B. Pike, *The United States and Latin America* (1992); Brenda G. Plummer, *Haiti and the Great Powers, 1902–1915* (1988); Mary A. Renda, *Taking Haiti: Military Occupation and the Culture of U.S. Imperialism* (2001); Ramón E. Ruíz, *The People of Sonora and Yankee Capitalists* (1988); Lars Schoultz, *Beneath the United States* (1998); Josefina Vázquez and Lorenzo Meyer, *The United States and Mexico* (1985).

Hawai'i, China, Japan, and the Pacific

Warren I. Cohen, *America's Response to China*, 4th ed. (2000); Michael H. Hunt, *The Making of a Special Relationship* (1983); Akira Iriye, *Pacific Estrangement* (1972); Paul M. Kennedy, *The Samoan Tangle* (1974); Walter LaFeber, *The Clash: A History of U.S. Japanese Relations* (1997); Brian M. Linn, *Guardians of Empire: The U.S. Army and the Pacific, 1902–1940* (1997); Charles J. McClain, *In Search of Equality: The Chinese Struggle Against Discrimination in Nineteenth-Century America* (1994); Thomas J. McCormick, *China Market* (1967); Eileen Scully, *Bargaining with the State from Afar* (2001); Craig Storti, *Incident at Bitter Creek: The Story of the Rock Springs Chinese Massacre* (1991); Marilyn Blatt Young, *The Rhetoric of Empire* (1968).

The Philippines and the Insurrection

Stanley Karnow, *In Our Image: America's Empire in the Philippines* (1989); Brian M. Linn, *The Philippine War, 1899–1902* (2000); Brian M. Linn, *The U.S. Army and Counterinsurgency in the Philippine War* (1989); Glenn A. May, *Battle for Batangas: A Philippine Province at War* (1991); Glenn A. May, *Social Engineering in the Philippines: The Aims, Execution, and Impact of American Colonial Policy, 1900–1913* (1980); Stuart C. Miller, *"Benevolent Assimilation"* (1982); Richard E. Welch, *Response to Imperialism: American Resistance to the Philippine War* (1972).

Chapter 23

General

Steven J. Diner, *A Very Different Age: Americans and the Progressive Era* (1998); Paul Fussell, *The Great War and Modern Memory* (1975); Otis L. Graham, Jr., *The Great Campaigns* (1971); Ellis W. Hawley, *The Great War and the Search for a Modern Order*, 2d ed. (1999); Clayton D. James and Anne S. Wells, *America and the Great War* (1998); Stuart I. Rochester, *American Liberal Disillusionment in the Wake of World War I* (1977); Daniel T. Rodgers, *Atlantic Crossings: Social Politics in a Progressive Age* (1998); John A. Thompson, *Reformers and War* (1987); Robert H. Zieger, *America's Great War: World War I and the American Experience* (2000).

Wilson, Wilsonianism, and World War I

Lloyd E. Ambrosius, *Wilsonian Statecraft: Theory and Practice of Liberal Internationalism* (1991); Lloyd E. Ambrosius, *Wilsonianism: Woodrow Wilson and His Legacy in American Foreign Relations* (2002); H. W. Brands, *Woodrow Wilson* (2003); John W. Coogan, *The End of Neutrality* (1981); Robert H. Ferrell, *Woodrow Wilson and World War I* (1985); Manfred Jonas, *The United States and Germany* (1984); Thomas J. Knock, *To End All Wars: Woodrow Wilson and the Quest for a New World Order* (1992); N. Gordon Levin, Jr., *Woodrow Wilson and World Politics* (1968); Arthur S. Link, *Woodrow Wilson: Revolution, War and Peace* (1979); Ernest R. May, *The World War and American Isolation* (1959); Frank Ninkovich, *The Wilsonian Century: U.S. Foreign Policy Since 1900* (1999); J. W. Schulte Nordholt, *Woodrow Wilson* (1991); Diana Preston, *Lusitania: An Epic Tragedy* (2002); Tony Smith, *America's Mission: The United States and the Worldwide Struggle for Democracy in the Twentieth Century* (1994); Edwin A. Weinstein, *Woodrow Wilson: A Medical and Psychological Biography* (1981).

Fighting and Remembering the Great War in Europe

Allan M. Brandt, *No Magic Bullet: A Social History of Venereal Disease in the United States Since 1880* (1985); John W. Chambers, *To Raise an Army* (1987); James J. Cooke, *The U.S. Air Service in the Great War: 1917–1919* (1996); Byron Farwell, *Over There: The United States in the Great War, 1917–1918* (1999); Martin Gilbert, *The First World War* (1994); John Keegan, *The First World War* (1999); Jennifer D. Keene, *Doughboys, the Great War, and the Remaking of America* (2001); G. Kurt Piehler, *Remembering War the American Way* (1995); Donald Smythe, *Pershing: General of the Armies* (1986); Stephen R. Ward, ed., *The War Generation: Veterans of the First World War* (1975); Russell F. Weigley, *The American Way of War* (1973).

The Home Front

William J. Breen, *Labor Market Politics and the Great War* (1997); Nancy Bristow, *Making Men Moral: Social Engineering During the Great War* (1996); Valerie Jean Conner, *The National War Labor Board* (1983); Alfred W. Crosby, *America's Forgotten Pandemic: The Influenza of 1918* (1989); Leslie M. DeBauche, *Reel Patriotism: The Movies and World War I* (1997); David M. Kennedy, *Over Here: The Home Front in the First World War* (1980); Gina Kolata, *Flu: The Story of the Great Influenza Pandemic of 1918 and the Search for the Virus That Caused It* (1999); Seward W. Livermore, *Politics Is Adjourned: Woodrow Wilson and the War Congress, 1917–1918* (1966); Frederick C. Luebke, *Bonds of Loyalty: German Americans and World War I* (1974); Joseph A. McCartin, *Labor's Great War* (1997); George H. Nash, *The Life of Herbert Hoover*, vol. 3 (1996); Ronald Schaffer, *America in the Great War: The Rise of the War Welfare State* (1991); Stephen L. Vaughn, *Holding Fast the Inner Lines: Democracy, Nationalism, and the Committee on Public Infor-

mation (1979); Neil A. Wynn, *From Progressivism to Prosperity* (1986).

Women and the War

Frances H. Early, *A World Without War: How U.S. Feminists and Pacifists Resisted World War I* (1997); Lettie Gavin, *American Women in World War I* (1997); Kathleen Kennedy, *Disloyal Mothers and Scurrilous Citizens: Women and Subversion During World War I* (1999); Erika A. Kuhlman, *Petticoats and White Feathers* (1997); Dorothy Schneider and Carl J. Schneider, *Into the Breach: American Women Overseas in World War I* (1991); Barbara J. Steinson, *American Women's Activism in World War I* (1982).

African Americans and Migration

Arthur E. Barbeau and Florette Henri, *The Unknown Soldiers* (1974); Marvin E. Fletcher, *The Black Soldier and Officer in the United States Army, 1891–1917* (1974); James B. Grossman, *Land of Hope: Chicago, Black Southerners, and the Great Migration* (1989); Robert V. Haynes, *A Night of Violence: The Houston Riot of 1917* (1976); Carole Marks, *Farewell—We're Good and Gone: The Great Black Migration* (1989); Joe William Trotter, Jr., ed., *The Great Migration in Historical Perspective* (1991); William M. Tuttle, Jr., *Race Riot: Chicago in the Red Summer of 1919*, rev. ed. (1996).

Dissenters, Wartime Civil Liberties, and the Red Scare

David Brody, *Labor in Crisis: The Steel Strike of 1919* (1965); Charles Chatfield, *The American Peace Movement* (1992); Charles DeBenedetti, *Origins of the Modern Peace Movement* (1978); C. Roland Marchand, *The American Peace Movement and Social Reform* (1973); Charles H. McCormick, *Seeing Reds: Federal Surveillance of Radicals in the Pittsburgh Mill District, 1917–1921* (1997); Elizabeth McKillen, *Chicago Labor and the Quest for a Democratic Diplomacy* (1995); Paul L. Murphy, *World War I and the Origin of Civil Liberties* (1979); Robert K. Murray, *Red Scare* (1955); William Pencak, *For God and Country: The American Legion, 1919–1941* (1989); Richard Polenberg, *Fighting Faiths: The Abrams Case, the Supreme Court, and Free Speech* (1987); William Preston, *Aliens and Dissenters: Federal Suppression of Radicals, 1903–1933* (1995); Francis Russell, *A City in Terror: 1919, the Boston Police Strike* (1975).

The United States and the Bolshevik Revolution

Peter G. Filene, *Americans and the Soviet Experiment, 1917–1933* (1967); David S. Foglesong, *America's Secret War Against Bolshevism* (1995); John Lewis Gaddis, *Russia, the Soviet Union, and the United States*, 2d ed. (1990); Christopher Lasch, *The American Liberals and the Russian Revolution* (1962); David McFadden, *Alternative Paths: Soviets and Americans, 1917–1920* (1993); Betty M. Unterberger, *The United States, Revolutionary Russia, and the Rise of Czechoslovakia* (1989).

Paris Peace Conference, Treaty of Versailles, and League Fight

Lloyd Ambrosius, *Woodrow Wilson and the American Diplomatic Tradition* (1987); Manfred F. Boemeke et al., eds., *The Treaty of Versailles* (1998); John Milton Cooper Jr., *Breaking the Heart of the World: Woodrow Wilson and the Fight for the League of Nations* (2001); Inga Floto, *Colonel House in Paris* (1973); Arno Mayer, *Politics and Diplomacy of Peacemaking* (1967); Margaret Macmillan, *Paris 1919: Six Months That Changed the World* (2002); Arthur Walworth, *Wilson and the Peacemakers* (1986); William C. Widenor, *Henry Cabot Lodge and the Search for an American Foreign Policy* (1980).

Chapter 24

Overviews of the 1920s

William E. Akin, *Technocracy and the American Dream* (1977); Paul A. Carter, *Another Part of the Twenties* (1977); Lynn Dumenil, *Modern Temper* (1995); David J. Goldberg, *Discontented America: The United States in the 1920s* (1999); William E. Leuchtenburg, *The Perils of Prosperity* (1958); Robert Lynd and Helen Lynd, *Middletown* (1929); Geoffrey Perrett, *America in the Twenties* (1982).

Business and the Economy

William W. Barber, *Herbert Hoover, the Economists, and American Economic Policy, 1921–1933* (1986); Irving L. Bernstein, *The Lean Years: A History of the American Worker, 1920–1933* (1960); Morton Keller, *Regulating a New Economy* (1990); David Montgomery, *The Fall of the House of Labor* (1987); Allan Nevins, *Ford*, 2 vols. (1954–1957); Emily Rosenberg, *Spreading the American Dream* (1982).

Politics and Law

Christine Bolt, *American Indian Policy and American Reform* (1987); Paula Eldot, *Governor Alfred E. Smith: The Politician as Reformer* (1983); Allan J. Lichtman, *Prejudice and the Old Politics: The Presidential Election of 1928* (1979); Alpheus Mason, *The Supreme Court from Taft to Warren* (1958); Donald R. McCoy, *Calvin Coolidge* (1967); Robert K. Murray, *The Politics of Normalcy* (1973); George Tindall, *The Emergence of the New South* (1967); James Weinstein, *The Decline of Socialism in America, 1912–1925* (1967); Joan Hoff Wilson, *Herbert Hoover: The Forgotten Progressive* (1975).

African Americans, Asians, and Hispanics

Rodolfo Acuna, *Occupied America: A History of Chicanos* (1980); Yong Chen, *Chinese San Francisco, 1850–1943* (2000); James R. Grossman, *Land of Hope* (1989); Jacquelyn Jones, *Labor of Love, Labor of Sorrow* (1985); Gilbert Osofsky, *Harlem: The Making of a Ghetto* (1965); Ricardo Romo, *East Los Angeles: History of a Barrio* (1983); George Sanchez,

Becoming Mexican American (1993); Judith Stein, *The World of Marcus Garvey* (1986); Ronald Takaki, *Strangers from a Different Shore* (1989).

Women, Family, and Lifestyles

W. Andrew Achenbaum, *Shades of Gray: Old Age, American Values, and Federal Policies Since 1920* (1983); Beth Bailey, *From Front Porch to Back Seat: Courtship in Twentieth-Century America* (1988); Dorothy M. Brown, *Setting a Course: American Women in the 1920s* (1987); George Chauncey, *Gay New York* (1995); Howard P. Chudacoff, *How Old Are You? Age in American Culture* (1989); Nancy F. Cott, *The Grounding of Modern Feminism* (1987); John D'Emilio and Estelle B. Freedman, *Intimate Matters: A History of Sexuality in America* (1988); Elizabeth Ewen, *Immigrant Women in the Land of Dollars* (1985); Lillian Faderman, *Odd Girls and Twilight Lovers* (1991); Linda Gordon, *Woman's Body, Woman's Right: A Social History of Birth Control in America* (1976); J. Stanley Lemons, *The Woman Citizen: Social Feminism in the 1920s* (1973); Lois Scharf, *To Work and to Wed* (1980); Susan Strasser, *Never Done: A History of American Housework* (1982); Winifred D. Wandersee, *Women's Work and Family Values, 1920–1940* (1981).

Lines of Defense

Paul Avrich, *Sacco and Vanzetti* (1991); Edith L. Blumhofer, *Aimee Semple McPherson* (1993); Roger A. Burns, *Preacher: Billy Sunday and Big-Time American Evangelism* (1992); Norman H. Clark, *Deliver Us From Evil: An Interpretation of American Prohibition* (1976); John Higham, *Strangers in the Land: Patterns of American Nativism* (1955); Kenneth T. Jackson, *The Ku Klux Klan and the City* (1967); Edward J. Larson, *Summer for the Gods* (1997); Nancy Maclean, *Behind the Mask of Chivalry: The Making of the Second Ku Klux Klan* (1994); George M. Marsden, *Fundamentalism and American Culture* (1980).

Mass Culture

Stanley Coben, *Rebellion Against Victorianism* (1991); Robert Creamer, *Babe* (1974); Kenneth S. Davis, *The Hero, Charles A. Lindbergh* (1959); Susan J. Douglas, *Inventing American Broadcasting* (1987); Paula Fass, *The Damned and the Beautiful: American Youth in the 1920s* (1977); James J. Flink, *The Car Culture* (1975); Richard Wightman Fox and T. Jackson Lears, eds., *The Culture of Consumption* (1983); William R. Leach, *Land of Desire* (1993); Harvey J. Levenstein, *Revolution at the Table: The Transformation of the American Diet* (1988); Roland Marchand, *Advertising the American Dream* (1985); Randy Roberts, *Jack Dempsey, the Manassa Mauler* (1979); Virgnina Scharff, *Taking the Wheel: Women and the Coming of the Motor Age* (1991); Robert Sklar, *Movie-made America* (1976); Ronald A. Smith, *Sports and Freedom: The Rise of Big-Time College Athletics* (1988); Susan Smulyan, *Selling Radio* (1994).

Literature and Thought

Mary Campbell, *Harlem Renaissance: Art of Black America* (1987); Robert Crunden, *From Self to Society: Transition in American Thought, 1919–1941* (1972); Nathan I. Huggins, *Harlem Renaissance* (1971); David L. Lewis, *When Harlem Was in Vogue* (1981); Cary D. Mintz, *Black Culture and the Harlem Renaissance* (1988); Roderick Nash, *The Nervous Generation: American Thought, 1917–1930* (1969); Kenneth M. Wheller and Virginia L. Lussier, eds., *Women and the Arts and the 1920s in Paris and New York* (1982).

Boom and Bust: The Crash

Peter Fearon, *War, Prosperity, and Depression* (1987); John Kenneth Galbraith, *The Great Crash: 1929* (1989); and Robert T. Patterson, *The Great Boom and Panic, 1921–1929* (1965).

Chapter 25

Hoover and the Worsening Depression

William J. Barber, *Herbert Hoover, the Economists, and American Economic Policy, 1921–1933* (1986); Michael A. Bernstein, *The Great Depression: Delayed Recovery and Economic Change in America, 1929–1939* (1988); John A. Garraty, *The Great Depression* (1986); Joan Hoff, *Herbert Hoover: Forgotten Progressive* (1992); Maury Klein, *Rainbow's End: The Crash of 1929* (2001); Jordan A. Schwarz, *Interregnum of Despair* (1970).

The New Deal

Anthony J. Badger, *The New Deal: The Depression Years, 1933–1940* (1989); William J. Barber, *Designs Within Disorder: Franklin D. Roosevelt, the Economists, and the Shaping of American Economic Policy, 1933–1945* (1996); Alan Brinkley, *Liberalism and Its Discontents* (1998); Alan Brinkley, *The End of Reform: New Deal Liberalism in Recession and War* (1995); Ronald Edsforth, *The New Deal: America's Response to the Great Depression* (2000); Steve Fraser and Gary Gerstle, eds., *The Rise and Fall of the New Deal Order, 1930–1980* (1989); David M. Kennedy, *Freedom from Fear: The American People in Depression and War, 1929–1945* (1999); Suzanne Mettler, *Divided Citizens: Gender and Federalism in New Deal Public Policy* (1998); Richard White, *"It's Your Misfortune and None of My Own": A New History of the American West* (1991).

Franklin and Eleanor Roosevelt

Blanche Wiesen Cook, *Eleanor Roosevelt: Volume One, 1884–1933* (1992), and *Volume Two, 1933–1938* (1999); Kenneth S. Davis, *FDR: Into the Storm, 1937–1940* (1993); Kenneth S. Davis, *FDR: The New Deal Years, 1933–1937* (1986); Frank Freidel, *Franklin D. Roosevelt: A Rendezvous with Destiny* (1990); George McJimsey, *The Presidency of Franklin Delano Roosevelt* (2000); Arthur M. Schlesinger, Jr., *The Age of Roosevelt*, 3 vols. (1957–1960).

Voices from the Depression

James Agee, *Let Us Now Praise Famous Men* (1941); Federal Writers' Project, *These Are Our Lives* (1939); Robert Cohen, *Dear Mrs. Roosevelt: Letters from Children of the Great Depression* (2002); Robert S. McElvaine, ed., *Down and Out in the Great Depression* (1983); Studs Terkel, *Hard Times: An Oral History of the Great Depression* (1970); Tom E. Terrill and Jerrold Hirsch, eds., *Such as Us: Southern Voices of the Thirties* (1978).

Alternatives to the New Deal

Alan Brinkley, *Voices of Protest: Huey Long, Father Coughlin, and the Great Depression* (1982); William Ivy Hair, *The Kingfish and His Realm: The Life and Times of Huey P. Long* (1992); Robin D. G. Kelley, *Hammer and Hoe: Alabama Communists During the Great Depression* (1991); Fraser M. Ottanelli, *The Communist Party of the United States from the Depression to World War II* (1991); Leo Ribuffo, *The Old Christian Right: The Protestant Far Right from the Great Depression to the Cold War* (1983); Donald Warren, *Radio Priest: Charles Coughlin, the Father of Hate Radio* (1996); Clyde P. Weed, *The Nemesis of Reform: The Republican Party During the New Deal* (1994).

Workers, Organized Labor and Business

Irving Bernstein, *Turbulent Years: A History of the American Worker, 1933–1941* (1969); Lizabeth Cohen, *Making a New Deal: Industrial Workers in Chicago, 1919–1939* (1991); Melvin Dubofsky and Warren Van Tine, *John L. Lewis* (1977); David Farber, *Sloan Rules: Alfred P. Sloan and the Triumph of General Motors* (2002); Sidney Fine, *Sit-Down: The General Motors Strike of 1936–1937* (1969); Gary Gerstle, *Working-Class Americanism: The Politics of Labor in a Textile City, 1914–1960* (1989); Colin Gordon, *New Deals: Business, Labor, and Politics in America, 1920–1935* (1994); Roger Horowitz, *Negro and White, Unite and Fight: A Social History of Unionism in Meatpacking, 1930–1990* (1997); Nelson Lichtenstein, *The Most Dangerous Man in Detroit: Walter Reuther and the Fate of American Labor* (1995); Robert H. Zieger, *The CIO, 1935–1955* (1995).

Agriculture and the Environment

William U. Chandler, *The Myth of TVA: Conservation and Development in the Tennessee Valley, 1933–1983* (1984); David E. Conrad, *The Forgotten Farmers: The Story of Sharecroppers in the New Deal* (1965); James N. Gregory, *American Exodus: The Dust Bowl Migration and Okie Culture in California* (1989); David E. Hamilton, *From New Day to New Deal: American Farm Policy from Hoover to Roosevelt, 1928–1933* (1991); Pamela Riney-Kehrberg, *Rooted in Dust* (1994); Theodore M. Saloutos, *The American Farmer and the New Deal* (1982); John L. Shover, *Cornbelt Rebellion: The Farmers' Holiday Association* (1965); Donald Worster, *Dust Bowl: The Southern Plains in the 1930s* (1979).

African Americans, Mexican Americans, and Native Americans

Sarah Deutsch, *No Separate Refuge: Culture, Class, and Gender on an Anglo-Hispanic Frontier in the American Southwest, 1880–1940* (1987); James Goodman, *Stories of Scottsboro* (1994); Camille Guerin-Gonzales, *Mexican Workers and American Dreams: Immigration, Repatriation, and California Farm Labor, 1900–1939* (1994); Laurence C. Kelly, *The Assault on Assimilation: John Collier and the Origins of Indian Policy Reform* (1983); George Lipsitz, *The Possessive Investment in Whiteness: How White People Profit from Identity Politics* (1998); Kenneth R. Philip, *Termination Revisited: American Indians on the Trail to Self-Determination, 1933–1953* (1999); George J. Sanchez, *Becoming Mexican American: Ethnicity, Culture and Identity in Chicano Los Angeles, 1900–1945* (1993); Harvard Sitkoff, *A New Deal for Blacks* (1978); Patricia Sullivan, *Days of Hope: Race and Democracy in the New Deal Era* (1996); Mark V. Tushnet, *The NAACP's Legal Strategy against Segregated Education, 1925–1950* (1987); Nancy J. Weiss, *Farewell to the Party of Lincoln: Black Politics in the Age of FDR* (1983).

Women, Men, and Children

Julia Kirk Blackwelder, *Women of the Depression: Caste and Culture in San Antonio, 1929–1939* (1984); Glen H. Elder, Jr., *Children of the Great Depression: Social Change in Life Experience* (1974); Linda Gordon, *Pitied but Not Entitled: Single Mothers and the History of Welfare, 1890–1935* (1994); Robert Griswold, *Fatherhood in America: A History* (1993); Alice Kessler-Harris, "Providers: Gender Ideology in the 1930s," in Linda Kerber and Jane Sherron De Hart, eds., *Women's America*, 5th ed. (2000); Lois Scharf, *To Work and to Wed: Female Employment, Feminism, and the Great Depression* (1980); Errol Lincoln Uys, *Riding the Rails: Teenagers on the Move During the Great Depression* (1999); Susan Ware, *Holding Their Own: American Women in the 1930s* (1982); Susan Ware, *Beyond Suffrage: Women in the New Deal* (1981); Judy Yung, "Coping with the Great Depression in San Francisco's Chinatown," in Kerber and De Hart, eds., *Women's America*, 5th ed. (2000).

Cultural and Intellectual History

Michael Denning, *The Cultural Front: The Laboring of American Culture in the Twentieth Century* (1997); Jerre Mangione, *The Dream and the Deal: The Federal Writers' Project, 1935–1943* (1972); Sean McCann, *Gumshoe America: Hardboiled Crime Fiction and the Rise and Fall of New Deal Liberalism* (2000); Barbara Melosh, *Engendering Culture: Manhood and Womanhood in New Deal Public Art and Theater* (1991); Bill Mullen, *Popular Fronts: Chicago and African-American Cultural Politics, 1935–1946* (1999); Tey Marianna Nunn, *Sin Nombre: Hispana and Hispano Artists of the New Deal Era* (2001); Richard H. Pells, *Radical Visions and American Dreams: Culture and Social Thought in the Depression Years* (1973); Warren I. Susman, "The Culture of the Thirties," in Warren I. Susman, ed., *Culture as History* (1984).

Chapter 26

General

Warren I. Cohen, *Empire Without Tears* (1987); Justus D. Doenecke and John E. Wilz, *From Isolation to War*, 2d ed. (1991); David M. Kennedy, *Freedom from Fear: The American People in Depression and War, 1929–1945* (1999); Karen A. J. Miller, *Populist Nationalism: Republican Insurgency and American Foreign Policy, 1918–1925* (1999); Brenda G. Plummer, *Rising Wind: Black Americans and U.S. Foreign Affairs, 1935–1960* (1996); Emily S. Rosenberg, *Spreading the American Dream: American Economic and Cultural Expansion, 1890–1945* (1982); David F. Schmitz, *Thank God They're on Our Side: The United States and Right-Wing Dictatorships, 1921–1945* (1999); Joan Hoff Wilson, *Herbert Hoover* (1975).

Arms Control and the Military

Thomas H. Buckley, *The United States and the Washington Conference, 1921–1922* (1970); Emily O. Goldman, *Sunken Treaties* (1994); Paul A. C. Koistinen, *Planning War, Pursuing Peace: The Political Economy of American Warfare, 1920–1939* (1998); Brian M. Linn, *Guardians of Empire: The U.S. Army and the Pacific, 1902–1940* (1997); Michael S. Sherry, *The Rise of American Airpower* (1987); Mark A. Stoler, *George Marshall* (1989).

Peace Groups and Leaders

Harriet H. Alonso, *The Women's Peace Union and the Outlawry of War* (1989); Charles Chatfield, *For Peace and Justice* (1971); Charles DeBenedetti, *The Peace Reform in American History* (1980); Charles DeBenedetti, *Origins of the Modern American Peace Movement, 1915–1929* (1978); Carrie A. Foster, *The Women and the Warriors* (1995); Robert D. Johnson, *The Peace Progressives and American Foreign Relations* (1995); Warren F. Kuehl and Lynne K. Dunn, *Keeping the Covenant* (1997); Linda A. Schott, *Reconstructing Women's Thoughts: The Women's International League for Peace and Freedom Before World War II* (1997); Lawrence Wittner, *Rebels Against War* (1984).

Economic and Financial Relations

Frederick Adams, *Economic Diplomacy* (1976); Derek H. Aldcroft, *From Versailles to Wall Street, 1919–1929* (1977); Michael Butler, *Cautious Visionary: Cordell Hull and Trade Reform, 1933–1937* (1998); Michael J. Hogan, *Informal Entente: The Private Structure of Cooperation in Anglo-American Economic Diplomacy* (1977); Charles Kindleberger, *The World in Depression* (1973); Stephen J. Randall, *United States Foreign Oil Policy, 1919–1948* (1986); Emily S. Rosenberg, *Financial Missionaries: The Politics and Culture of Dollar Diplomacy, 1900–1930* (1999); Mira Wilkins, *The Maturing of Multinational Enterprise* (1974); Joan Hoff Wilson, *American Business and Foreign Policy, 1920–1933* (1971).

Cultural Expansion and Philanthropy

Frank Costigliola, *Awkward Dominion* (1984); Marcos Cueto, ed., *Missionaries of Science: The Rockefeller Foundation and Latin America* (1994); Mary Nolan, *Visions of Modernity: American Business and the Modernization of Germany* (1994); Thomas J. Saunders, *Hollywood in Berlin* (1994).

Latin America and the Good Neighbor Policy

G. Pope Atkins and Larman C. Wilson, *The Dominican Republic and the United States* (1998); John A. Britton, *Revolution and Ideology: Images of the Mexican Revolution in the United States* (1995); Bruce J. Calder, *The Impact of Intervention: The Dominican Republic During the U.S. Occupation of 1916–1924* (1984); Arturo Morales Carrión, *Puerto Rico* (1983); Paul J. Dosal, *Doing Business with the Dictators* (1993); Paul W. Drake, *The Money Doctors in the Andes* (1989); Alton Frye, *Nazi Germany and the American Hemisphere, 1933–1941* (1967); Irwin F. Gellman, *Good Neighbor Diplomacy* (1979); Linda B. Hall, *Oil, Banks, and Politics: The United States and Postrevolutionary Mexico, 1917–1924* (1995); Walter LaFeber, *Inevitable Revolutions: The United States in Central America*, 2d and extended ed. (1993); Lester D. Langley, *The United States and the Caribbean, 1900–1970* (1980); Abraham F. Lowenthal, ed., *Exporting Democracy* (1991); John Major, *Prize Possession: The United States and the Panama Canal, 1903–1979* (1993); Louis A. Pérez, *Cuba and the United States*, 2d ed. (1997); Louis A. Pérez, *Cuba Under the Platt Amendment* (1986); Fredrick B. Pike, *FDR's Good Neighbor Policy* (1995); Brenda G. Plummer, *Haiti and the United States* (1992); W. Dirk Raat, *Mexico and the United States* (1997); Mary A. Renda, *Taking Haiti: Military Occupation and the Culture of U.S. Imperialism, 1915–1940* (2001); Friedrich E. Schuler, *Mexico Between Hitler and Roosevelt* (1998); Bryce Wood, *The Making of the Good Neighbor Policy* (1961).

Isolationists and Isolationism

Wayne S. Cole, *Roosevelt and the Isolationists, 1932–1945* (1983); Manfred Jonas, *Isolationism in America, 1935–1941* (1966); Thomas C. Kennedy, *Charles A. Beard and American Foreign Policy* (1975); Richard C. Lower, *A Bloc of One: The Political Career of Hiram W. Johnson* (1993); Richard Lowitt, *George W. Norris* (1963–1978); John Wiltz, *In Search of Peace: The Senate Munitions Inquiry* (1963).

Europe, Roosevelt's Policies, and the Coming of World War II

J. Garry Clifford and Samuel R. Spencer, Jr., *The First Peacetime Draft* (1986); David H. Culbert, *News for Everyman* (1976) (on radio); Robert Dallek, *Franklin D. Roosevelt and American Foreign Policy* (1995); Robert A. Divine, *Roosevelt and World War II* (1969); Justus D. Doenecke, *Storm on the Horizon: The Challenge to American Intervention, 1939–1941* (2000); Barbara R. Farnham, *Roosevelt and the Munich Crisis* (1997); Frank Freidel, *Franklin D. Roosevelt* (1990); Manfred Jonas, *The United States and Germany* (1984); Warren F. Kimball, *The Juggler* (1991); Warren F. Kimball, *The Most Unsordid Act: Lend-Lease, 1939–1941* (1969); Melvyn P. Leffler, *The Elusive Quest: America's Pursuit of European Stability and French Security, 1919–1933* (1979); Douglas Little, *Malevolent Neutrality: The United States, Great Britain, and the Origins of the Spanish Civil War* (1985); Thomas R. Maddux, *Years of Estrangement: American Relations with the Soviet Union, 1933–1941* (1980); Arnold A. Offner, *American Appeasement* (1969); David Reynolds, *The Creation of the Anglo-American Alliance* (1982); David F. Schmitz, *The United States and Fascist Italy* (1988); James C. Schneider, *Should America Go to War?* (1989); Richard Steele, *Propaganda in an Open Society* (1985); Donald C. Watt, *How War Came* (1989); Theodore A. Wilson, *The First Summit* (1991).

China, Japan, and the Coming of War in Asia

Dorothy Borg and Shumpei Okomoto, eds., *Pearl Harbor as History* (1973); R. J. C. Butow, *Tojo and the Coming of War* (1961); Warren I. Cohen, *America's Response to China*, 3d ed. (1990); Peter Conn, *Pearl S. Buck* (1996); Hilary Conroy and Harry Wray, eds., *Pearl Harbor Reexamined* (1990); Herbert Feis, *The Road to Pearl Harbor* (1950); Marc S. Gallicchio, *The African American Encounter With Japan and China: Black Internationalism in Asia, 1895–1945* (2000); Waldo H. Heinrichs, Jr., *Threshold of War* (1988); Akira Iriye, *The Origins of the Second World War in Asia and the Pacific* (1987); Akira Iriye, *Across the Pacific* (1967); Akira Iriye, *After Imperialism* (1965); T. Christopher Jespersen, *American Images of China* (1996); Walter LaFeber, *The Clash: A History of U.S.-Japan Relations* (1997); James Morley, ed., *The Final Confrontation* (1994); Jonathan Utley, *Going to War with Japan* (1985).

Attack on Pearl Harbor

Akira Iriye, *Pearl Harbor and the Coming of the Pacific War* (1999); David Kahn, *The Codebreakers* (1967); Robert W. Love, Jr., ed., *Pearl Harbor Revisited* (1995); Martin V. Melosi, *The Shadow of Pearl Harbor* (1977); Gordon W. Prange, *Pearl Harbor* (1986); Gordon W. Prange, *At Dawn We Slept* (1981); John Toland, *Infamy* (1982); Roberta Wohlstetter, *Pearl Harbor* (1962).

Chapter 27

The Second World War

Michael C. C. Adams, *The Best War Ever: America and World War II* (1994); John Keegan, *The Second World War* (1989); David M. Kennedy, *Freedom from Fear: The American People in Depression and War, 1929–1945* (1999); Eric Larabee, *Commander in Chief* (1987); Ronald Schaffer, *Wings of Judgment: American Bombing in World War II* (1985); Michael Sherry, *The Rise of American Air Power: the Creation of Armageddon* (1987); Michael Sherry, *In the Shadow of War: the United States since the 1930s* (1995); Ronald H. Spector, *Eagle Against the Sun: The American War with Japan* (1984); Ger-

hard L. Weinberg, *A World at Arms: A Global History of World War II* (1994).

Fighting the War: Americans in Combat

Robert H. Abzug, *Inside the Vicious Heart: Americans and the Liberation of Nazi Concentration Camps* (1985); Stephen E. Ambrose, *The Victors* (1998); Stephen E. Ambrose, *Citizen Soldiers* (1997); Stephen E. Ambrose, *D-Day, June 6, 1944* (1994); Allan Bérubé, *Coming Out Under Fire: The History of Gay Men and Women in World War II* (1990); Craig Cameron, *American Samurai: Myth, Imagination, and the Conduct of Battle in the First Marine Division, 1941–1951* (1994); Michael D. Doubler, *Closing with the Enemy: How GIs Fought the War in Europe, 1944–1945* (1994); Paul Fussell, *Wartime* (1989); Gerald F. Linderman, *The World Within the War: America's Combat Experience in World War II* (1997); David Reynolds, *Rich Relations: The American Occupation of Britain, 1942–1945* (1995); E. B. Sledge, *With the Old Breed at Peleliu and Okinawa* (1990).

Wartime Diplomacy

Michael Beschloss, *The Conquerors: Roosevelt, Truman and the Destruction of Hitler's Germany, 1941–1945* (2002); Russell Buhite, *Decisions at Yalta* (1986); Robert Dallek, *Franklin D. Roosevelt and American Foreign Policy, 1932–1945* (1979); Henry L. Feingold, *Bearing Witness: How America and Its Jews Responded to the Holocaust* (1995); George C. Herring, *Aid to Russia, 1941–1946* (1973); Gary R. Hess, *The United States at War, 1941–1945* (1986); Robert C. Hilderbrand, *Dumbarton Oaks* (1990); Townsend Hoopes and Douglas Brinkley, *Franklin D. Roosevelt and the Creation of the United Nations* (1997); Akira Iriye, *Power and Culture: The Japanese-American War, 1941–1945* (1981); Warren Kimball, *Forged in War: Roosevelt, Churchill, and the Second World War* (1997); Gabriel Kolko, *The Politics of War: The World and United States Foreign Policy, 1943–1945*, rev. ed. (1990); Walter LaFeber, *The Clash: A History of U.S.-Japan Relations* (1997); Verne W. Newton, ed., *FDR and the Holocaust* (1996); Keith Sainsbury, *Churchill and Roosevelt at War* (1994); Mark Stoler, *The Politics of the Second Front* (1977); David S. Wyman, *The Abandonment of the Jews* (1984).

Mobilizing for War

Amy Bentley, *Eating for Victory: Food Rationing and the Politics of Domesticity* (1998); George Q. Flynn, *The Draft, 1940–1973* (1993); Gregory Hooks, *Forging the Military-Industrial Complex: World War II's Battle of the Potomac* (1991); Clayton R. Koppes and Gregory D. Black, *Hollywood Goes to War* (1987); Nelson Lichtenstein, *Labor's War at Home: The CIO in World War II* (1983); George H. Roeder, Jr., *The Censored War: American Visual Experience During World War II* (1993); Lawrence R. Samuel, *Pledging Allegiance: American Identity and the Bond Drive of World War II* (1997); Bartholomew H.

Sparrow, *From the Outside In: World War II and the American State* (1996); Richard W. Steele, *Free Speech in America's Good War* (1999); Harold G. Vatter, *The U.S. Economy in World War II* (1985); Allen M. Winkler, *The Politics of Propaganda: The Office of War Information, 1942–1945* (1978).

The Home Front

Beth Bailey, *Sex in the Heartland* (1999); John Morton Blum, *V Was for Victory: Politics and American Culture During World War II* (1976); John D'Emilio, *Sexual Politics, Sexual Communities: The Making of a Homosexual Minority in the United States, 1940–1970* (1983); Lewis A. Erenberg and Susan E. Hirsch, eds., *The War in American Culture* (1996); Doris Kearns Goodwin, *No Ordinary Time: Franklin and Eleanor Roosevelt: The Home Front in World War II* (1994); Gerald D. Nash, *The American West Transformed* (1985); William L. O'Neill, *A Democracy at War: America's Fight at Home and Abroad in World War II* (1993); Studs Terkel, ed., *"The Good War": An Oral History of World War Two* (1984); William M. Tuttle, Jr., *"Daddy's Gone to War": The Second World War in the Lives of America's Children* (1993).

The Internment of Japanese Americans and Enemy Aliens

Roger Daniels, *Prisoners Without Trial* (1993); Stephen Fox, *The Unknown Internment: An Oral History of the Relocation of Italian Americans During World War II* (1990); Peter Irons, *Justice at War* (1983); Arnold Krammer, *Undue Process: The Untold Story of America's German Alien Internees* (1997); Gary Okihiro, *Cane Fires: The Anti-Japanese Movement in Hawaii, 1865–1945* (1991); Page Smith, *Democracy on Trial: The Japanese American Evacuation and Relocation in World War II* (1995).

Race, Ethnicity, and War

Beth Bailey and David Farber, *The First Strange Place: Race and Sex in World War II Hawaii* (1992); Nat Brandt, *Harlem at War* (1996); Dominic J. Capeci, Jr., and Martha Wilkerson, *Layered Violence: The Detroit Rioters of 1943* (1991); John W. Dower, *War Without Mercy: Race and Power in the Pacific War* (1986); Edward J. Escobar, *Race, Police, and the Making of a Political Identity: Mexican Americans and the Los Angeles Police Department, 1900–1945* (1999); Gary Gerstle, *American Crucible: Race and Nation in the Twentieth Century* (2001); Daniel Kryder, *Divided Arsenal: Race and the American State During World War II* (2000); Mauricio Mazón, *The Zoot-Suit Riots* (1989); Barbara Diane Savage, *Broadcasting Freedom: Radio, War, and the Politics of Race, 1938–1948* (1999); Ronald T. Takaki, *Double Victory: A Multicultural History of America in World War II* (2000).

Women at War

Karen T. Anderson, *Wartime Women* (1981); D'Ann Campbell, *Women at War with America* (1984); Claudia Goldin, *Understanding the Gender Gap: An Economic History of American Women* (1990); Susan M. Hartmann, *The Home Front and Beyond* (1982); Leslie Haynsworth and David Toomey, *Amelia Earhart's Daughters* (1998) (about American women aviators in the war); Judy Barrett Litoff and David C. Smith, eds., *We're in This War, Too: World War II Letters from American Women in Uniform* (1994); Leisa D. Meyer, *Creating GI Jane: Sexuality and Power in the Women's Army Corps During World War II* (1996); Ruth Milkman, *Gender at Work: The Dynamics of Job Discrimination by Sex During World War II* (1987); Leila J. Rupp, *Mobilizing Women for War: German and American Propaganda, 1939–1945* (1978).

The Atomic Bomb and Japan's Surrender

Gar Alperovitz, *The Decision to Use the Atomic Bomb and the Architecture of an American Myth*, 2d ed. (1995); Sadao Asada, "The Shock of the Atomic Bomb and Japan's Decision to Surrender—A Reconsideration," *Pacific Historical Review* 67 #4 (1998); Michael Hogan, ed., *Hiroshima in History and Memory* (1995); Robert Jay Lifton and Greg Mitchell, *Hiroshima in America: Fifty Years of Denial* (1995); Richard Rhodes, *The Making of the Atomic Bomb* (1987); Stephen I. Schwartz, ed., *Atomic Audit: The Costs and Consequences of U.S. Nuclear Weapons since 1940* (1998); Martin J. Sherwin, *A World Destroyed: The Atomic Bomb and the Grand Alliance* (rev. ed., 2003); Leon V. Sigal, *Fighting to a Finish* (1994); Ferenc Szasz, *The Day the Sun Rose Twice: The Story of the Trinity Site Nuclear Explosion* (1984); Ronald Takaki, *Hiroshima: Why America Dropped the Atomic Bomb* (1995); J. Samuel Walker, *Prompt and Utter Destruction: Truman and the Use of the Atomic Bombs Against Japan* (1997).

Chapter 28

The Cold War: Overviews

H. W. Brands, *The Devil We Knew* (1993); Warren Cohen, *America in the Age of Soviet Power, 1945–1991* (1993); Gordon A. Craig and Francis L. Loewenheim, eds., *The Diplomats, 1939–1979* (1994); John Lewis Gaddis, *We Now Know: Rethinking Cold War History* (1997); John Lewis Gaddis, *The Long Peace* (1987); John Lewis Gaddis, *Strategies of Containment* (1982); Walter Isaacson and Evan Thomas, *The Wise Men* (1986); Robert H. Johnson, *Improbable Dangers: U.S. Perceptions of Threat in the Cold War and After* (1994); Paul Kennedy, *The Rise and Fall of the Great Powers* (1987); Walter LaFeber, *America, Russia, and the Cold War, 1945–1996*, 8th ed. (1996); Ralph Levering, *The Cold War*, 2d ed. (1994); Thomas McCormick, *America's Half-Century*, 2d ed. (1994); Robert J. McMahon, *The Cold War: A Very Short Introduction* (2003); David S. Painter, *The Cold War: An International History* (1999); Thomas G. Paterson, *On Every Front: The Making and Unmaking of the Cold War*, rev. ed. (1992); Thomas G. Paterson, *Meeting the Communist Threat* (1988); Michael S. Sherry, *In the Shadow of War* (1995).

Relations with the Third World: Overviews

Richard J. Barnet, *Intervention and Revolution* (1972); Edward H. Berman, *The Influence of the Carnegie, Ford, and Rockefeller Foundations on American Foreign Policy* (1983); Scott L. Bills, *Empire and Cold War* (1990); H. W. Brands, *The Specter of Neutralism* (1989); Gabriel Kolko, *Confronting the Third World* (1988); Michael L. Krenn, *Black Diplomacy: African Americans and the State Department, 1945–1969* (1998); Michael L. Krenn, ed., *Race and U.S. Foreign Policy During the Cold War* (1998); James H. Meriwether, *Proudly We Can Be Africans: Black Americans and Africa, 1953–1961* (2002); Brenda G. Plummer, *Rising Wind: Black Americans and U.S. Foreign Affairs, 1935–1960* (1996); David F. Schmitz, *Thank God They're on Our Side: The U.S. and Right-Wing Dictatorships, 1921–1965* (1999); Penny M. von Eschen, *Race Against Empire: Black Americans and Anticolonialism, 1937–1957* (1996).

Truman and the Early Cold War

James Chace, *Acheson* (1998); Carolyn W. Eisenberg, *Drawing the Line: The American Decision to Divide Germany, 1944–1949* (1996); Richard M. Fried, *The Russians Are Coming! The Russians Are Coming!* (1998); Lloyd C. Gardner, *Architects of Illusion: Men and Ideas in American Foreign Policy 1941–1949* (1970); Walter Hixson, *George F. Kennan* (1990); Michael J. Hogan, *A Cross of Iron: Harry S. Truman and the Origins of the National Security State* (1998); Michael J. Hogan, *The Marshall Plan* (1987); Lawrence S. Kaplan, *The United States and NATO* (1984); Gabriel Kolko and Joyce Kolko, *The Limits of Power* (1972); Bruce R. Kuniholm, *The Origins of the Cold War in the Near East* (1980); Melvyn Leffler, *The Specter of Communism* (1994); Melvyn Leffler, *A Preponderance of Power: National Security, the Truman Administration, and the Cold War* (1992); Alan Milward, *The Reconstruction of Western Europe* (1984); Wilson D. Miscamble, *George F. Kennan and the Making of American Foreign Policy, 1947–1950* (1992); Arnold Offner, *Another Such Victory: President Truman and the Cold War, 1945–1953* (2002); Chester J. Pach, *Arming the Free World* (1981); David Reynolds, ed., *The Origins of the Cold War in Europe* (1994); Thomas A. Schwartz, *America's Germany* (1991); Anders Stephanson, *Kennan and the Art of Foreign Policy* (1989); Mark A. Stoler, *George C. Marshall* (1989); Marc Trachtenberg, *A Constructed Peace: The Making of the European Settlement, 1945–1963* (1999); Lawrence S. Wittner, *American Intervention in Greece, 1943–1949* (1982); Vladislav Zubok and Constantine Pleshakov, *Inside the Kremlin's Cold War* (1996); Randall B. Woods, *A Changing of the Guard: Anglo-American Relations, 1941–1946* (1990).

Eisenhower-Dulles Foreign Policy

Stephen E. Ambrose, *Eisenhower*, 2 vols. (1982, 1984); Michael Beschloss, *MAYDAY: Eisenhower, Khrushchev, and the U-2 Affair* (1986); Robert R. Bowie and Richard Immerman, *Waging Peace: How Eisenhower Shaped an Enduring Cold War Strategy* (1997); Jeff Broadwater, *Eisenhower and the Anti-Communist Crusade* (1992); Robert A. Divine, *Eisenhower and the Cold War* (1981); Fred Greenstein, *The Hidden-Hand Presidency* (1982); Townsend Hoopes, *The Devil and John Foster Dulles* (1973); Richard Immerman, *John Foster Dulles* (1998); Burton I. Kaufman, *Trade and Aid* (1982); Frederick W. Marks, *Power and Peace* (1993); Chester J. Pach, *The Presidency of Dwight D. Eisenhower* (1991).

The CIA and Counterinsurgency

Douglas S. Blaufarb, *The Counterinsurgency Era* (1977); Peter Grose, *Gentleman Spy: The Life of Allen Dulles* (1994); Rhodi Jeffreys-Jones, *The CIA and American Democracy* (1989); Loch K. Johnson, *America's Secret Power* (1989); Mark Lowenthal, *U.S. Intelligence* (1984); John Prados, *Presidents' Secret Wars* (1995); John Ranelagh, *The Agency* (1986); Jeffrey T. Richelson, *A Century of Spies* (1995); Jeffrey T. Richelson, *The U.S. Intelligence Community* (1999); Evan Thomas, *The Very Best Men* (1995).

Atomic Diplomacy, Nuclear Arms Race, and Public Attitudes

Howard Ball, *Justice Downwind: America's Atomic Testing Program in the 1950s* (1986); Paul Boyer, *By the Bomb's Early Light* (1986); McGeorge Bundy, *Danger and Survival* (1988); Campbell Craig, *Destroying the Village: Eisenhower and Thermonuclear War* (1998); Robert A. Divine, *The Sputnik Challenge* (1993); Robert A. Divine, *Blowing on the Wind: The Nuclear Test Ban Debate, 1954–1960* (1978); Margot Henriksen, *Dr. Strangelove's America* (1997); Gregg Herken, *Counsels of War* (1985); Gregg Herken, *The Winning Weapon* (1981); James G. Hershberg, *James B. Conant* (1993); Richard G. Hewlett and Jack M. Hall, *Atoms for Peace and War, 1953–1961* (1989); David Holloway, *Stalin and the Bomb* (1994); Robert Jervis, *The Meaning of the Nuclear Revolution* (1989); Fred Kaplan, *The Wizards of Armageddon* (1983); Milton Katz, *Ban the Bomb* (1986); Stuart W. Leslie, *The Cold War and American Science* (1994); John Newhouse, *War and Peace in the Nuclear Age* (1989); Richard Rhodes, *Dark Sun: The Making of the Hydrogen Bomb* (1995); Martin Sherwin, *A World Destroyed* (1975); Allan M. Winkler, *Life Under a Cloud* (1993); Lawrence S. Wittner, *The Struggle Against the Bomb* (1993, 1998).

Cultural Relations and Expansion

Thomas Borstelmann, *The Cold War and the Color Line: American Race Relations in the Global Arena* (2001); Mary L. Dudziak, *Cold War Civil Rights: Race and the Image of American Democracy* (2000); Jessica Gienow-Hecht, *Transmission Impossible: American Journalism as Cultural Diplomacy in Postwar Germany, 1945–1955* (1999); Robert H. Haddow, *Pavilions of Plenty* (1997); Walter L. Hixson, *Parting the Curtain: Propaganda, Culture, and the Cold War* (1997); Frank A.

Ninkovich, *The Diplomacy of Ideas* (1981); Richard Pells, *Not Like Us: How Europeans Have Loved, Hated, and Transformed American Culture Since World War II* (1997); Reinhold Wagnleitner, *Coca-Colonization and the Cold War* (1994).

Japan, China, and Asian Issues

Kenton J. Clymer, *Quest for Freedom: The United States and India's Independence* (1995); Gordon Chang, *Friends and Enemies* (1990); Thomas J. Christensen, *Useful Adversaries* (1996); Warren I. Cohen, *America's Response to China*, 3d ed. (1990); Nick Cullather, *Illusions of Influence: The Political Economy of United States–Philippines Relations, 1942–1960* (1994); Richard B. Finn, *Winners in Peace* (1995); Marc S. Gallicchio, *The Cold War Begins in Asia* (1988); Chen Jian, *Mao's China and the Cold War* (2001); E. J. Kahn, Jr., *The China Hands* (1975); Walter LaFeber, *The Clash: A History of U.S.-Japan Relations* (1997); Paul G. Lauren, ed., *The "China Hands" Legacy* (1987); Robert J. McMahon, *The Limits of Empire: The United States and Southeast Asia Since World War II* (1999); Robert J. McMahon, *Colonialism and Cold War: The United States and the Struggle for Indonesian Independence, 1945–49* (1981); Dennis Merrill, *Bread and the Ballot: The United States and India's Economic Development, 1947–1963* (1990); Robert P. Newman, *Owen Lattimore and the "Loss" of China* (1992); Andrew J. Rotter, *Comrades at Odds: The United States and India, 1947–1964* (2000); Michael Schaller, *Douglas MacArthur* (1989); Michael Schaller, *The American Occupation of Japan* (1985); Nancy B. Tucker, *Patterns in the Dust: Chinese-American Relations and the Recognition Controversy, 1945–1950* (1983); William O. Walker III, *Opium and Foreign Policy* (1991); Philip West et al., eds., *America's Wars in Asia* (1998).

The Korean War

Roy E. Appleman, *Disaster in Korea* (1992); Roy E. Appleman, *Escaping the Trap* (1990); Roy E. Appleman, *Ridgeway Duels for Korea* (1990); Conrad C. Crane, *American Airpower Strategy in Korea* (2000); Bruce Cumings, *Korea's Place in the Sun* (1997); Bruce Cumings, *The Origins of the Korean War* (1980, 1991); Rosemary Foot, *A Substitute for Victory* (1990); Rosemary Foot, *The Wrong War* (1985); Sergei Goncharov et al., *Uncertain Partners: Stalin, Mao, and the Korean War* (1993); Chen Jian, *China's Road to the Korean War* (1995); Burton I. Kaufman, *The Korean War*, 2d ed. (1997); Callum A. MacDonald, *Korea* (1987); James Matray, *The Reluctant Crusade* (1985); William Stueck, *The Korean War* (1995); William Stueck, *Rethinking the Korean War* (2002); Shu Guang Zhang, *Mao's Military Romanticism* (1996).

Vietnam

David L. Anderson, *Trapped by Success* (1991); Melanie Billings-Yun, *Decision Against War: Eisenhower and Dien Bien Phu, 1954* (1988); Mark Philip Bradley, *Imagining Vietnam and America: The Making of Postcolonial Vietnam 1919–1950*

(2000); William J. Duiker, *Ho Chi Minh* (2000); Lloyd C. Gardner, *Approaching Vietnam* (1988); George C. Herring, *America's Longest War*, 4th ed. (2001); Gary Hess, *The United States' Emergence as a Southeast Asian Power* (1987); Lawrence S. Kaplan et al., eds., *Dien Bien Phu and the Crisis of Franco-American Relations* (1990); Gabriel Kolko, *Anatomy of a War* (1986); Fredrik Logevall, *The Origins of the Vietnam War* (2001); David G. Marr, *Vietnam 1945* (1995); Joseph G. Morgan, *The Vietnam Lobby: The American Friends of Vietnam, 1955–1975* (1997); Andrew Rotter, *The Path to Vietnam* (1987); Robert D. Schulzinger, *A Time for War* (1997); Stein Tonnesson, *The Vietnamese Revolution of 1945* (1991); Marilyn B. Young, *The Vietnam Wars* (1991).

Latin America

Cole Blasier, *Hovering Giant* (1974); John Coatsworth, *Central America and the United States* (1994); Michael Conniff, *Panama and the United States* (1992); Nick Cullather, *Secret History: The CIA's Classified Account of Its Operations in Guatemala, 1952–1954* (1999); Mark T. Gilderhus, *The Second Century* (2000); Piero Gleijeses, *Shattered Hope: The Guatemalan Revolution and the United States, 1944–1954* (1991); Richard Immerman, *The CIA in Guatemala* (1982); Walter LaFeber, *Inevitable Revolutions: The United States in Central America*, 2d and expanded ed. (1993); Walter LaFeber, *The Panama Canal*, updated ed. (1990); Lester Langley, *America and the Americas* (1989); Abraham F. Lowenthal, ed., *Exporting Democracy* (1991); A. W. Maldonado, *Teodoro Moscoso and Puerto Rico's Operation Bootstrap* (1997); Thomas G. Paterson, *Contesting Castro* (1994); Louis A. Pérez, Jr., *Cuba and the United States*, 2d ed. (1997); W. Dirk Raat, *Mexico and the United States*, 2d ed. (1997); Stephen G. Rabe, *Eisenhower and Latin America* (1988); Stephen G. Rabe, *The Road to OPEC: United States Relations with Venezuela* (1982); Lars Schoultz, *Beneath the United States* (1998); Gaddis Smith, *The Last Years of the Monroe Doctrine* (1994); Peter H. Smith, *Talons of the Eagle* (1996).

Middle East and Africa

Nigel J. Ashton, *Eisenhower, Macmillan, and the Problem of Nasser* (1996); James A. Bill, *The Eagle and the Lion: The Tragedy of American-Iranian Relations* (1988); Thomas Borstelmann, *Apartheid's Reluctant Uncle: The United States and Southern Africa in the Early Cold War* (1993); Michael J. Cohen, *Truman and Israel* (1990); Michael J. Cohen, *Palestine and the Great Powers, 1945–1948* (1983); Mark Gasiorowski, *U.S. Foreign Policy and the Shah* (1991); Peter L. Hahn, *The United States, Great Britain, and Egypt, 1945–1956* (1991); Mary Ann Heiss, *Empire and Nationhood: The United States, Great Britain, and Iranian Oil, 1950–1954* (1997); Burton I. Kaufman, *The Arab Middle East and the United States* (1996); Diane Kunz, *The Economic Diplomacy of the Suez Crisis* (1991); Zach Levy, *Israel and the Great Powers* (1998); Douglas Little, *American Orientalism: The United States and the Middle East Since 1945* (2002); Donald Neff, *Warriors at Suez* (1981); Thomas J. Noer,

Cold War and Black Liberation (1985); David Schoenbaum, *The United States and the State of Israel* (1993); Robert W. Stookey, *America and the Arab States* (1975); Daniel Yergin, *The Prize: The Epic Quest for Oil, Money, and Power* (1991).

Chapter 29

Postwar America

John Patrick Diggins, *The Proud Decades: America in War and Peace, 1941–1960* (1988); David Halberstam, *The Fifties* (1993); Marty Jezer, *The Dark Ages: Life in the United States, 1945–1960* (1982); William L. O'Neill, *American High: The Years of Confidence, 1945–1960* (1986); James T. Patterson, *Grand Expectations: The United States, 1945–1974* (1996).

Cold War Culture

Paul Boyer, *By the Bomb's Early Light: American Thought and Culture at the Dawn of the Atomic Age* (1985); Tom Engelhardt, *The End of Victory Culture: Cold War America and the Disillusioning of a Generation* (1995); William S. Graebner, *The Age of Doubt: American Thought and Culture in the 1940s* (1991); Margot A. Henriksen, *Dr. Strangelove's America: Society and Culture in the Atomic Age* (1997); Lary May, ed., *Recasting America: Culture and Politics in the Age of Cold War* (1989); Richard H. Pells, *The Liberal Mind in a Conservative Age* (1985); Lisle A. Rose, *The Cold War Comes to Main Street: America in 1950* (1999); Stephen J. Whitfield, *The Culture of the Cold War*, rev. ed. (1996).

The Presidencies of Truman and Eisenhower

Stephen E. Ambrose, *Eisenhower: The President* (1984); Robert F. Burk, *Dwight D. Eisenhower* (1986); Robert J. Donovan, *Tumultuous Years: The Presidency of Harry S. Truman, 1949–1953* (1982); Robert J. Donovan, *Conflict and Crisis: The Presidency of Harry S. Truman, 1945–1948* (1977); Fred I. Greenstein, *The Hidden-Hand Presidency* (1982); Alonzo L. Hamby, *Man of the People: The Life of Harry S. Truman* (1995); Michael J. Hogan, *A Cross of Iron: Harry S. Truman and the Origins of the National Security State* (1998); David McCullough, *Truman* (1992); Chester J. Pach, Jr., and Elmo Richardson, *The Presidency of Dwight D. Eisenhower*, rev. ed. (1991); Geoffrey Perret, *Eisenhower* (1999).

McCarthyism

Richard M. Fried, *Nightmare in Red* (1990); Robert Griffith, *The Politics of Fear: Joseph R. McCarthy and the Senate*, rev. ed. (1987); John Earl Haynes and Harvey Klehr, *Venona: Decoding Soviet Espionage in America* (1999); Harvey Klehr et al., *The Soviet World of American Communism* (1998); David M. Oshinsky, *A Conspiracy So Immense: The World of Joe McCarthy* (1983); Richard Gid Powers, *Not Without Honor: The History of American Anticommunism* (1995); Ellen W. Schrecker, *Many Are the Crimes: McCarthyism in America* (1998); Ellen W. Schrecker, *No Ivory Tower: McCarthyism in the Universities* (1986).

Race Relations and the Civil Rights Movement

Taylor Branch, *Parting the Waters: America in the King Years, 1954–1963* (1988); Robert F. Burk, *The Eisenhower Administration and Black Civil Rights* (1984); William H. Chafe, *Civilities and Civil Rights: Greensboro, North Carolina, and the Black Struggle for Freedom* (1980); Mary Dudziak, *Cold War Civil Rights: Race and the Image of American Democracy* (2000); David J. Garrow, *Bearing the Cross: Martin Luther King, Jr., and the Southern Christian Leadership Conference* (1986); Juan Gomez-Quinones, *Chicano Politics: Reality and Promise, 1940–1990* (1990); Arnold R. Hirsch, *Making the Second Ghetto: Race and Housing in Chicago, 1940–1960* (1983); Richard Kluger, *Simple Justice: The History of Brown v. Board of Education and Black America's Struggle for Equality* (1975); Gail Williams O'Brien, *The Color of Law: Race, Violence, and Justice in the Post–World War II South* (1999); James T. Patterson, *Brown v. Board of Education: A Civil Rights Milestone and Its Troubled Legacy* (2001); Thomas J. Sugrue, *The Origins of the Urban Crisis: Race and Inequality in Postwar Detroit* (1996); Jules Tygiel, *Baseball's Great Experiment: Jackie Robinson and His Legacy*, rev. ed. (1997); Juan Williams, *Thurgood Marshall: American Revolutionary* (1998).

The Baby Boom, Youth Culture, Gender, and Cold War Families

Beth Bailey, *From Front Porch to Back Seat: Courtship in 20th Century America* (1988); Wini Breines, *Young, White, and Miserable: Growing Up Female in the Fifties* (1992); Susan J. Douglas, *Where the Girls Are: Growing Up Female with the Mass Media* (1994); Barbara Ehrenreich, *The Hearts of Men: American Dreams and the Flight from Commitment* (1983); Ruth Feldstein, *Motherhood in Black and White: Race and Sex in American Liberalism, 1930–1965* (2000); James Gilbert, *A Cycle of Outrage: America's Reaction to the Juvenile Delinquent* (1986); William Graebner, *Coming of Age in Buffalo: Youth and Authority in the Postwar Era* (1990); Landon Y. Jones, *Great Expectations: America and the Baby Boom Generation* (1980); James H. Jones, *Alfred C. Kinsey* (1997); Elaine Tyler May, *Homeward Bound: American Families in the Cold War Era*, rev. ed. (1999); Joanne J. Meyerowitz, ed., *Not June Cleaver: Women and Gender in Postwar America, 1945–1960* (1994); John Modell, *Into One's Own: From Youth to Adulthood in the United States, 1920–1975* (1989); Grace Palladino, *Teenagers* (1996); Lori Rotskoff, *Love on the Rocks: Men, Women, and Alcohol in Post-World War II America* (2002).

Suburbia and the Spread of Education

Paula Fass, *Outside In: Minorities and the Transformation of American Education* (1989); Robert Fishman, *Bourgeois*

Utopias (1987); Mark I. Gelfand, *A Nation of Cities* (1975); Dolores Hayden, *Redesigning the American Dream* (1984); Kenneth T. Jackson, *Crabgrass Frontier: The Suburbanization of the United States* (1985); Zane L. Miller, *Suburb* (1982); Diane Ravitch, *The Troubled Crusade: American Education, 1945–1980* (1983); Joel Spring, *The Sorting Machine: National Educational Policy Since 1945* (1976).

Women's Rights

Myra Dinnerstein, *Women Between Two Worlds* (1992); Cynthia Harrison, *On Account of Sex: The Politics of Women's Issues, 1945–1968* (1988); Susan Lynn, *Progressive Women in Conservative Times* (1992); Glenna Matthews, *"Just a Housewife"* (1987); Leila J. Rupp and Verta Taylor, *Survival in the Doldrums: The American Women's Rights Movement, 1945 to the 1960s* (1987).

The Affluent Society and Social Transformation

Loren Baritz, *The Good Life: The Meaning of Success for the American Middle Class* (1982); Lizabeth Cohen, *A Consumer's Republic: The Politics of Mass Consumption in Postwar America* (2003); Pete Daniel, *Lost Revolutions: The South in the 1950s* (2000); Kevin Fernlund, ed., *The Cold War American West* (1998); John Kenneth Galbraith, *The Affluent Society* (1958); Thomas Hine, *Populuxe* (1986); Ann Markusen et al., *Rise of the Gunbelt: The Military Remapping of Industrial America* (1991); Kirkpatrick Sale, *Power Shift: The Rise of the Southern Rim and Its Challenge to the Eastern Establishment* (1975); Bruce J. Schulman, *From Cotton Belt to Sunbelt: Federal Policy, Economic Development, and the Transformation of the South, 1938–1980* (1991).

Farmers and Laborers

Richard B. Craig, *The Bracero Program* (1971); Gilbert C. Fite, *American Farmers* (1981); James R. Green, *The World of the Worker* (1980); Nelson Lichtenstein, *The Most Dangerous Man in Detroit: Walter Reuther and the Fate of American Labor* (1995); George Lipsitz, *Rainbow at Midnight: Labor and Culture in the 1940s* (1994); John L. Shover, *First Majority—Last Minority: The Transforming of Rural Life in America* (1976).

The Other America

Donald L. Fixico, *Termination and Relocation: Federal Indian Policy, 1945–1960* (1986); J. Wayne Flint, *Dixie's Forgotten People: The South's Poor Whites* (1979); Michael Harrington, *The Other America*, rev. ed. (1981); James T. Patterson, *America's Struggle Against Poverty, 1900–1994*, rev. ed. (1994).

Chapter 30

The 1960s

David Burner, *Making Peace with the 60s* (1996); Dominick Cavallo, *A Fiction of the Past: The Sixties in American History* (1999); David Chalmers, *And the Crooked Places Made Straight: The Struggle for Social Change in the 1960s* (1991); David Farber, *The Age of Great Dreams* (1994); David Farber, ed., *The Sixties* (1994); James J. Farrell, *The Spirit of the Sixties* (1997); Godfrey Hodgson, *America in Our Time* (1976); Michael Kazin and Maurice Isserman, *America Divided: The Civil War of the 1960s* (2000); Arthur Marwick, *The Sixties* (1998); Allen J. Matusow, *The Unraveling of America: A History of Liberalism in the 1960s* (1984); James T. Patterson, *Grand Expectations: The United States, 1945–1974* (1996).

Foreign Policy in th 1960s: Kennedy and Johnson

Michael Beschloss, *The Crisis Years: Kennedy and Khrushchev, 1960–1963* (1991); Kai Bird, *The Color of Truth: McGeorge Bundy and William Bundy: Brothers in Arms* (1998); H. W. Brands, ed., *The Foreign Policies of Lyndon Johnson: Beyond Vietnam* (1999); H. W. Brands, *The Wages of Globalism: Lyndon Johnson and the Limits of American Power* (1995); Warren I. Cohen and Nancy B. Tucker, eds., *Lyndon Johnson Confronts the World* (1995); Robert Dallek, *Flawed Giant: Lyndon Johnson and His Times, 1961–1973* (1998); Lawrence Freedman, *Kennedy's Wars: Berlin, Cuba, Laos, and Vietnam* (2000); David Halberstam, *The Best and the Brightest* (1972); Elizabeth Cobbs Hoffman, *All You Need Is Love: The Peace Corps and the Spirit of the 1960s* (1998); Robert D. Johnson, *Ernest Gruening and the American Dissenting Tradition* (1998); Doris Kearns, *Lyndon Johnson and the American Dream* (1976); Herbert S. Parmet, *JFK: The Presidency of John F. Kennedy* (1983); Thomas G. Paterson, ed., *Kennedy's Quest for Victory: American Foreign Policy, 1961–1963* (1989); Arthur M. Schlesinger, Jr., *Robert Kennedy and His Times* (1978); Thomas A. Schwartz, *Lyndon Johnson and Europe: In the Shadow of Vietnam* (2003); Mark J. White, ed., *Kennedy: The New Frontier Revisited* (1998); Randall Woods, *Fulbright: A Biography* (1995).

The Kennedy Presidency

Irving Bernstein, *Promises Kept: John F. Kennedy's New Frontier* (1991); James Giglio, *The Presidency of John F. Kennedy* (1991); Robert Dallek, *An Unfinished Life: John F. Kennedy, 1917–1963* (2003); Posner, *Case Closed: Lee Harvey Oswald and the Assassination of JFK* (1993); Thomas C. Reeves, *A Question of Character* (1991); W. J. Rorabaugh, *Kennedy and the Promise of the Sixties* (2002); Arthur M. Schlesinger, Jr., *A Thousand Days: John F. Kennedy in the White House* (1965); Ronald Steel, *In Love with Night: The American Romance with Robert Kennedy* (1999).

Cuba and the Missile Crisis

Graham Allison and Philip Zelikow, *Essence of Decision: Explaining the Cuban Missile Crisis*, 2d ed. (1999); James G. Blight and Peter Kornbluh, eds., *Politics of Illusion: The Bay of Pigs Invasion Reexamined* (1998); Aleksandr Fursenko and Timothy Naftali, *"One Hell of a Gamble": Khrushchev, Castro, and Kennedy, 1958–1964* (1997); Trumbull Higgins, *The Perfect Failure: Kennedy, Eisenhower, and the CIA at the Bay of Pigs* (1987); Richard Ned Lebow and Janice Gross Stein, *We All Lost the Cold War* (1993); Ernest R. May and Philip Zelikow, eds., *The Kennedy Tapes: Inside the White House During the Cuban Missile Crisis* (1997); Thomas G. Paterson, *Contesting Castro: The United States and the Triumph of the Cuban Revolution* (1994); Louis A. Perez, Jr., *Cuba and the United States*, 2d ed. (1997); Robert, Weisbrot, *Maximum Danger: Kennedy, the Missiles, and the Crisis of American Confidence* (2001); Mark J. White, *Missiles in Cuba: Kennedy, Khrushchev, Castro and the 1962 Crisis* (1998).

Lyndon B. Johnson and the Great Society

Irving Bernstein, *Guns or Butter: The Presidency of Lyndon Johnson* (1996); Robert Dallek, *Flawed Giant: Lyndon Johnson and His Times, 1961–1973* (1998); Steve Fraser and Gary Gerstle, eds., *The Rise and Fall of the New Deal Order, 1930–1980* (1989); Doris Kearns, *Lyndon Johnson and the American Dream* (1976); Charles Murray, *Losing Ground: American Social Policy, 1950–1980* (1983); James T. Patterson, *America's Struggle Against Poverty, 1900–1994*, rev. ed. (1994); Bruce J. Schulman, *Lyndon Johnson and American Liberalism* (2001); Irwin Unger, *The Best of Intentions: The Triumph and Failure of the Great Society Under Kennedy, Johnson, and Nixon* (1996).

The Rise of a Conservative Movement

John A. Andrew III, *The Other Side of the Sixties: Young Americans for Freedom and the Rise of Conservative Politics* (1997); Mary C. Brennan, *Turning Right in the Sixties* (1995); Dan T. Carter, *The Politics of Rage: George Wallace, the Origins of the New Conservatism, and the Transformation of American Politics* (1995); Robert Alan Goldberg, *Barry Goldwater* (1995); Rebecca E. Klatch, *Generation Divided: The New Left, the New Right, and the 1960s* (1999); Lisa McGirr, *Suburban Warriors: The Origins of the New American Right* (2001); Rick Perlstein, *Before the Storm: Barry Goldwater and the Unmaking of the American Consensus* (2001); Jonathan Schoenwald, *A Time for Choosing: The Rise of Modern American Conservatism* (2001).

The Vietnam War

See Duiker, Herring, Schulzinger, and Young listed under Chapter 28 and Christian J. Appy, *Working-Class War: American Combat Soldiers and Vietnam* (1993); Robert K. Brigham, *Guerilla Diplomacy: The NFL's Foreign Relations and the Viet Nam War* (1999); Robert Buzzanco, *Vietnam and the Transformation of American Life* (1999); Charles DeBenedetti and Charles Chatfield, *An American Ordeal: The Antiwar Movement of the Vietnam War* (1990); David L. DiLeo, *George Ball, Vietnam, and the Rethinking of Containment* (1991); Frances FitzGerald, *Fire in the Lake: The Vietnamese and the Americans in Vietnam* (1972); Lloyd C. Gardner, *Pay Any Price: Lyndon Johnson and the Wars for Vietnam* (1995); Marc J. Gilbert, ed. *Why the North Won the Vietnam War* (2002); George C. Herring, *LBJ and Vietnam: A Different Kind of War* (1994); Neil L. Jamieson, *Understanding Vietnam* (1993); Howard Jones, *Death of a Generation: How the Assassinations of Diem and Kennedy Prolonged the Vietnam War* (2003); David Kaiser, *American Tragedy: Kennedy, Johnson, and the Origins of the Vietnam War* (2000); Fredrik Logevall, *Choosing War: The Lost Chance for Peace and the Escalation of War in Vietnam* (1999); George McT. Kahin, *Intervention: How America Became Involved in Vietnam* (1986); Robert S. McNamara, *In Retrospect: The Tragedy and Lessons of Vietnam* (1995); Edwin E. Moise, *Tonkin Gulf and the Escalation of the Vietnam War* (1996); Ronald H. Spector, *After Tet: The Bloodiest Year in Vietnam* (1992).

The Civil Rights Movement, Black Power, and Urban Riots

Taylor Branch, *Pillar of Fire: America in the King Years, 1963–1965* (1998); Taylor Branch, *Parting the Waters: America in the King Years, 1954–1963* (1988); Clayborne Carson, *In Struggle: SNCC and the Black Awakening of the 1960s* (1981); John Dittmer, *Local People: The Struggle for Civil Rights in Mississippi* (1994); David J. Garrow, *Bearing the Cross: Martin Luther King, Jr., and the Southern Christian Leadership Conference* (1986); Gary Gerstle, *American Crucible* (2001); David Halberstam, *The Children* (1998); Gerald Horne, *Fire This Time: The Watts Uprising and the 1960s* (1996); Chana Kai Lee, *For Freedom's Sake: The Life of Fannie Lou Hamer* (1999); Malcolm X and Alex Haley, *The Autobiography of Malcolm X* (1965); August Meier and Elliott Rudwick, *CORE* (1973); Charles M. Payne, *I've Got the Light of Freedom: The Organizing Tradition and the Mississippi Freedom Struggle* (1995); David Remmick, *King of the World: Muhammad Ali and the Rise of An American Hero* (1999); Belinda Robnett, *How Long? How Long? African-American Women in the Struggle for Civil Rights* (1997); William Van Deburg, *New Day in Babylon: The Black Power Movement and American Culture, 1965–1975* (1992).

The Warren Court

Gerald Dunne, *Hugo Black and the Judicial Revolution* (1977); Morton J. Horwitz, *The Warren Court and the Pursuit of Justice* (1998); Bernard Schwartz, *Super Chief: Earl Warren and His Supreme Court* (1983); G. Edward White, *Earl Warren* (1982).

The New Left and Social Protest

Terry H. Anderson, *The Movement and the Sixties* (1995); Wini Breines, *Community and Organization in the New Left, 1962–1968*, rev. ed. (1989); Charles DeBenedetti, *An American Ordeal: The Antiwar Movement of the Vietnam Era* (1990); Sara Evans, *Personal Politics* (1978); Todd Gitlin, *The Sixties* (1987); James Miller, *"Democracy Is in the Streets": From Port Huron to the Siege of Chicago* (1987); Doug Rossinow, *The Politics of Authenticity: Liberalism, Christianity, and the New Left in America* (1998); Tom Wells, *The War Within: America's Battle over Vietnam* (1994).

The Counterculture

Peter Braunstein and Michael Doyle, eds., *Imagine Nation: The American Counterculture of the 1960s and '70s* (2001); James Miller, *Flowers in the Dustbin: The Rise of Rock and Roll, 1947–1977* (1999); Tim Miller, *The Hippies and American Values* (1991); Charles Perry, *The Haight-Ashbury* (1984); Jay Stevens, *Storming Heaven: LSD and the American Dream* (1987); Jon Weiner, *Come Together: John Lennon in His Time* (1984); Tom Wolfe, *The Electric Kool-Aid Acid Test* (1968).

Society and Culture

Beth Bailey, *Sex in the Heartland* (1999); Robert S. Ellwood, *The Sixties Spiritual Awakening* (1994); Alice Cobb Hoffman, *All You Need is Love: The Peace Corps and American Culture* (1998); John Howard, *Men Like That: A Southern Queer History* (1999); Thomas Frank, *The Conquest of Cool: Business Culture, Counterculture, and the Rise of Hip Consumerism* (1997); Daniel Horowitz, *Betty Friedan and the Making of the "Feminine Mystique"* (1999); John A. Jackson, *American Bandstand* (1997); Hal Rothman, *The Greening of a Nation: Environmentalism in the United States Since 1945* (1997); Suzanne E. Smith, *Dancing in the Street: Motown and the Cultural Politics of Detroit* (1999); Rickie Solinger, *Wake Up Little Susie: Single Pregnancy and Race before Roe v. Wade* (1992); Lynn Spigel and Michael Curtin, eds., *The Revolution Wasn't Televised: Sixties Television and Social Conflict* (1997); Reed Ueda, *Postwar Immigrant America: A Social History* (1994).

Year of Shocks: 1968

David Farber, *Chicago '68* (1988); Carole Fink et al., eds., *1968: The World Transformed* (1998); Charles Kaiser, *1968 in America* (1988); Jeremi Suri, *Power and Protest: Global Revolution and the Rise of Détente* (2003); Jules Witcover, *The Year the Dream Died: Revisiting 1968 in America* (1997).

Chapter 31

Overviews

Bruce J. Schulman, *The Seventies: The Great Shift in American Culture, Society, and Politics* (2001).

Cultural Nationalism and the Politics of Identity

Ernesto Chávez, *"¡Mi Raza Primero!": Nationalism, Identity, and Insurgency in the Chicano Movement in Los Angeles, 1966–1978* (2002); Harold Cruse, *Plural but Equal* (1987); Ronald P. Formisano, *Boston Against Busing: Race, Class, and Ethnicity in the 1960s and 1970s* (1991); Ian F. Haney Lopéz, *Racism on Trial: The Chicano Fight for Justice* (2003); Joanne Nagel, *American Indian Ethnic Revival: Red Power and the Resurgence of Identity and Culture* (1996); Francisco A. Rosales, *Chicano!: The History of the Mexican American Civil Rights Movement* (1996); Vicki L. Ruíz, *From Out of the Shadows: Mexican Women in Twentieth-Century America* (1998); Peter Skerry, *Mexican Americans: The Ambivalent Minority* (1993); Paul Chaat Smith and Robert Allen Warrior, *Like a Hurricane: The Indian Movement from Alcatraz to Wounded Knee* (1996); Ronald Takaki, *Strangers from a Different Shore* (1989); James Treat, *Around the Sacred Fire: Native Religious Activism in the Red Power Era* (2003); William Van Deburg, *New Day in Babylon: The Black Power Movement and American Culture, 1965–1975* (1992).

Movements for Gender and Sexual Liberation

David Allyn, *Make Love, Not War* (2000); Beth Bailey, *Sex in the Heartland* (1999); Nancy Caraway, *Segregated Sisterhood: Racism and the Politics of American Feminism* (1986); Flora Davis, *Moving the Mountain: The Women's Movement in America Since 1960* (1991); Dudley Clendinen and Adam Nagourney, *Out for Good: The Struggle to Build a Gay Rights Movement in America* (1998); Martin Duberman, *Stonewall* (1993); Alice Echols, *Daring to Be Bad: Radical Feminism in America, 1965–1975* (1989); David J. Garrow, *Liberty and Sexuality: The Right to Privacy and the Making of Roe v. Wade* (1994); Alice Kessler-Harris, *In Pursuit of Equity: Women, Men and the Pursuit of Economic Citizenship in 20th-Century America* (2001); Rebecca Klatch, *Women of the New Right* (1987); Ruth Rosen, *The World Split Open: How the Modern Women's Movement Changed America* (2000); Winifred D. Wandersee, *On the Move: American Women in the 1970s* (1988); Joan Hoff-Wilson, ed., *Rights of Passage: The Past and Future of the ERA* (1986).

Nixon and Vietnam, and the War's Legacy

See Herring, Schulzinger, and Young listed under Chapter 29 and Christian Appy, *Patriots: The Vietnam War Remembered from All Sides* (2003); Michal Belknap, *The Vietnam War on Trial: The My Lai Massacre and Court-Martial of Lieutenant*

Calley (2002); Larry Berman, *No Peace, No Honor: Nixon, Kissinger, and Betrayal in Vietnam* (2001); Eric T. Dean, Jr., *Shook Over Hell: Post-Traumatic Stress, Vietnam, and the Civil War* (1998); Daniel Ellsberg, *Secrets: A Memoir of Vietnam and the Pentagon Papers* (2002); John Hellman, *American Myth and the Legacy of Vietnam* (1986); Rhodri Jeffreys-Jones, *Peace Now! American Society and the Ending of the Vietnam War* (1999); Jeffrey Kimball, *Nixon's Vietnam War* (1998); David Levy, *The Debate over Vietnam* (1991); Robert Mann, *A Grand Delusion: America's Descent into Vietnam* (2001); Robert McMahon, *The Limits of Empire: The United States and Southeast Asia Since World War II* (1999); Norman Podhoretz, *Why We Were in Vietnam* (1982); William Shawcross, *Sideshow: Kissinger, Nixon, and the Destruction of Cambodia* (1979); Lewis Sorley, *A Better War: The Unexamined Victories and Final Tragedy of America's Last Years in Vietnam* (1999); Harry G. Summers, Jr., *On Strategy* (1982).

Nixon, Kissinger, and the World

Stephen E. Ambrose, *Nixon*, 3 vols. (1987–1991); William P. Bundy, *A Tangled Web: The Making of Foreign Policy in the Nixon Presidency* (1998); Christopher Coker, *The United States and South Africa, 1968–1985* (1986); Raymond L. Garthoff, *Détente and Confrontation: American-Soviet Relations from Nixon to Reagan* (1985); Seymour Hersh, *The Price of Power: Kissinger in the Nixon White House* (1983); Joan Hoff, *Nixon Reconsidered* (1994); William G. Hyland, *Mortal Rivals: Superpower Relations from Nixon to Reagan* (1987); Walter Isaacson, *Kissinger: A Biography* (1992); James Mann, *About Face: A History of America's Curious Relationship with China, From Nixon to Clinton* (1999); Robert K. Massie, *Loosing the Bonds: The United States and South Africa in the Apartheid Years* (1997); Keith L. Nelson, *The Making of Détente: Soviet-American Relations in the Shadow of Vietnam* (1995); Herbert S. Parmet, *Richard Nixon and His America* (1990); Robert D. Schulzinger, *Henry Kissinger: Doctor of Diplomacy* (1989); Melvin Small, *The Presidency of Richard Nixon* (1999).

The Nixon Presidency and Watergate

Stephen E. Ambrose, *Nixon*, 3 vols. (1987–1991); William C. Berman, *Right Turn: From Nixon to Bush* (1994); Stanley I. Kutler, ed., *Abuse of Power: The New Nixon Tapes* (1997); Stanley I. Kutler, *The Wars of Watergate* (1990); Kim McQuaid, *The Anxious Years: America in the Vietnam-Watergate Era* (1989); Allen J. Matusow, *Nixon's Economy: Booms, Busts, Dollars, and Votes* (1998); Herbert S. Parmet, *Richard Nixon and His America* (1990); James A. Reichley, *Conservatives in an Era of Change: The Nixon and Ford Administrations* (1981); Richard Reeves, *President Nixon: Alone in the White House* (2001); Michael Schudson, *Watergate in American Memory* (1992); Melvin Small, *The Presidency of Richard Nixon* (1999); Tom Wicker, *One of Us*

(1991); Garry Wills, *Nixon Agonistes* (1970); Bob Woodward and Carl Bernstein, *All the President's Men* (1974).

The Ford and Carter Administrations

W. Carl Biven, *Jimmy Carter's Economy: Policy in an Age of Limits* (2002); Gary M. Fink and Hugh Davis Graham, eds., *The Carter Presidency* (1998); John Robert Greene, *The Presidency of Gerald R. Ford* (1995); Erwin C. Hargrove, *Jimmy Carter as President* (1989); Burton I. Kaufman, *The Presidency of James Earl Carter, Jr.* (1993).

Economic Woes and Transformations

Barry Bluestone and Bennett Harrison, *The Deindustrialization of America* (1982); Richard Feldman and Michael Betzold, *End of the Line: Autoworkers and the American Dream* (1988); Robert Heilbroner and Peter Bernstein, *The Debt and the Deficit* (1989); John P. Hoerr, *And the Wolf Finally Came: The Decline of the American Steel Industry* (1988); Gregory Pappas, *The Magic City: Unemployment in a Working-Class Community* (1989); Bruce J. Schulman, *From Cotton Belt to Sunbelt* (1991); Richard White, *"It's Your Misfortune and None of My Own": A New History of the American West* (1991).

Society and Culture in 1970s America

Howard Ball, *The Bakke Case: Race, Education, and Affirmative Action* (2000); Eva S. Moskowitz, *In Therapy We Trust: America's Obsession With Self-Fulfillment* (2001); Hal Rothman, *The Greening of a Nation: Environmentalism in the United States Since 1945* (1997); David Szatmary, *Rockin' in Time* (1991); Robert Wuthnow, *After Heaven: Spirituality in America Since the 1950s* (1998).

Carter Foreign Policy and Human Rights

Anne H. Cahn, *Killing Détente: The Right Attacks the CIA* (1998); Gary M. Fink and Hugh Davis Graham, eds., *The Carter Presidency* (1998); Erwin C. Hargrove, *Jimmy Carter as President* (1988); Burton I. Kaufman, *The Presidency of James Earl Carter, Jr.* (1993); David S. McLellan, *Cyrus Vance* (1985); Richard A. Melanson, *Reconstructing Consensus* (1990); A. Glenn Mower, Jr., *Human Rights and American Foreign Policy* (1987); Gaddis Smith, *Morality, Reason, and Power: American Diplomacy in the Carter Years* (1986); Cyrus Vance, *Hard Choices: Critical Years in America's Foreign Policy* (1983); Sandy Vogelsang, *American Dream, Global Nightmare* (1980); Odd Arne Westad, ed., *The Fall of Détente* (1997).

The Middle East and Iranian Hostage Crisis

James A. Bill, *The Eagle and the Lion: The Tragedy of American-Iranian Relations* (1988); William J. Burns and Richard W. Cottam, *Iran and the United States* (1988); Mark Gasiorowski, *U.S. Foreign Policy and the Shah* (1991); James E. Goode, *The*

United States and Iran (1997); Burton I. Kaufman, *The Arab Middle East and the United States* (1996); Douglas Little, *American Orientalism: The United States and the Middle East Since 1945* (2002); William B. Quandt, *Camp David: Peacemaking and Politics* (1986); Cheryl A. Rubenberg, *Israel and the American National Interest* (1986); David Schoenbaum, *The United States and the State of Israel* (1993); Gary Sick, *All Fall Down: America's Fateful Encounter with Iran* (1985); Steven L. Spiegel, *The Other Arab-Israeli Conflict* (1985); Daniel Yergin, *The Prize: The Epic Quest for Oil, Money, and Power* (1991).

Chapter 32

The New Conservatism

William C. Berman, *America's Right Turn* (1994); Sara Diamond, *Not by Politics Alone: The Enduring Influence of the Christian Right* (1998); Thomas Byrne Edsall, *The New Politics of Inequality* (1984); Lee Edwards, *The Conservative Revolution* (1999); Godfrey Hodgson, *The World Turned Right Side Up: A History of the Conservative Ascendancy in America* (1996).

Ronald Reagan and His Presidency

Lou Cannon, *President Reagan* (1991); Thomas Byrne Edsall and Mary D. Edsall, *Chain Reaction: The Impact of Race, Rights, and Taxes on American Politics* (1991); Paul D. Erickson, *Reagan Speaks: The Making of an American Myth* (1985); Mark Hertsgaard, *On Bended Knee: The Press and the Reagan Presidency* (1988); Haynes Johnson, *Sleepwalking Through History: America in the Reagan Years* (1991); B. B. Kymlicka and Jean V. Matthews, eds., *The Reagan Revolution?* (1988); Nicholas Laham, *The Reagan Presidency and the Politics of Race* (1998); Jane Mayer and Doyle McManus, *Landslide: The Unmaking of the President, 1984–1988* (1988); William A. Niskanen, *Reaganomics* (1988); Charles Noble, *Liberalism at Work: The Rise and Fall of OSHA* (1986); William E. Pemberton, *Exit with Honor: The Life and Presidency of Ronald Reagan* (1997); Kevin Phillips, *The Politics of Rich and Poor* (1990); Michael Schaller, *Reckoning with Reagan: America and Its President in the 1980s* (1992); John W. Sloan, *The Reagan Effect: Economics and Presidential Leadership* (1999); Garry Wills, *Reagan's America* (1987).

Reagan's Foreign Policy

Dana H. Allin, *Cold War Illusions: America, Europe, and Soviet Power, 1969–1989* (1995); Theodore Draper, *A Very Thin Line: The Iran-Contra Affairs* (1991); John Ehrman, *The Rise of Neoconservatism* (1995); Frances FitzGerald, *Way Out There in the Blue: Reagan, Star Wars, and the End of the Cold War* (2000); Seymour Hersh, *"The Target Is Destroyed": What Really Happened to Flight 007 and What America Knew About It* (1986); Walter LaFeber, *Inevitable Revolutions: The United States in Central America*, 2d ed. (1993); William LeoGrande,

Our Own Backyard: The United States in Central America, 1977–1992 (1999); Peter Kornbluh and Malcolm Byrne, eds., *The Iran-Contra Scandal* (1993); Michael McCgwire, *Perestroika and Soviet National Security* (1991); Robert A. Pastor, *Condemned to Repetition: The United States and Nicaragua* (1987); Michael Schaller, *Reckoning with Reagan* (1992); Strobe Talbott, *The Master of the Game: Paul Nitze and the Nuclear Peace* (1988).

A Polarized Society in the 1980s

Jim Baumohl, *Homelessness In America* (1996); Dale D. Chitwood, et al., *The American Pipe Dream: Crack, Cocaine, and the Inner City* (1995); Chandler Davidson, *Race and Class in Texas Politics* (1990); E. J. Dionne, Jr., *Why Americans Hate Politics* (1991); David T. Ellwood, *Poor Support: Poverty in the American Family* (1988); Michael Harrington, *The New American Poverty* (1984); Susan Faludi, *Backlash: The Undeclared War Against American Women* (1991); Reynolds Farley and Walter R. Allen, *The Color Line and the Quality of Life in America* (1987); Jonathan Kozol, *Rachel and Her Children: Homeless Families in America* (1988); William Martin, *With God on Our Side: The Rise of the Religious Right in America* (1996); Martin E. Marty and R. Scott Appleby, *The Glory and the Power: The Fundamentalist Challenge to the Modern World* (1992); Nicolaus Mills, ed., *Culture in an Age of Money: The Legacy of the 1980s in America* (1990); Katherine S. Newman, *Declining Fortunes: The Withering of the American Dream* (1993); Benjamin Shepard, *White Nights and Ascending Shadows: A History of the San Francisco AIDS Epidemic* (1997); Randy Shilts, *And the Band Played On: Politics, People and the AIDS Epidemic* (1987); Studs Terkel, *The Great Divide* (1988); William Julius Wilson, *The Truly Disadvantaged: The Inner City, the Underclass, and Public Policy* (1987); Edward N. Wolff, *Top Heavy: A Study of Increasing Inequality in America* (1995).

New Immigrants

Nancy Foner, ed., *New Immigrants in New York* (1987); Alejandro Portes and Rubén G. Rumbaut, *Immigrant America: A Portrait* (rev. ed., 1996); David M. Reimers, *Still the Golden Door: The Third World Comes to America* (1985); Sanford J. Ungar, *Fresh Blood: The New Immigrants* (1995); Helen Zia, *Asian American Dreams: The Emergence of an American People* (2000).

The Bush Administration

Donald L. Bartlett and James B. Steele, *America: What Went Wrong?* (1992); Michael Duffy and Don Goodgame, *Marching in Place: The Status Quo Presidency of George Bush* (1992); John Robert Greene, *The Presidency of George Bush* (2000); Dilys M. Hill and Phil Williams, eds., *The Bush Presidency* (1994); Herbert S. Parmet, *George Bush: The Life of a Lone Star Yankee* (1998).

The End of the Cold War

Michael R. Beschloss and Strobe Talbott, *At the Highest Levels: The Inside Story of the End of the Cold War* (1993); Robert D. English, *Russia and the Idea of the West: Gorbachev, Intellectuals, and the End of the Cold War* (2000); Matthew Evangelista, *Unarmed Forces: The Transnational Movement to End the Cold War* (1999); Beth A. Fischer, *The Reagan Reversal: Foreign Policy and the End of the Cold War* (1997); John Lewis Gaddis, *The United States and the End of the Cold War: Implications, Reconsiderations, Provocations* (1995); Raymond L. Garthoff, *The Great Transition: American-Russian Relations and the End of the Cold War* (1994); Michael J. Hogan, ed., *The End of the Cold War: Its Meanings and Implications* (1992); Robert G. Kaiser, *Why Gorbachev Happened* (1991); Stephen Kotkin, *Armageddon Averted: The Soviet Collapse, 1977–2000* (2002); Don Oberdorfer, *From the Cold War to a New Era: The United States and the Soviet Union, 1983–1991* (1998); David Remnick, *Lenin's Tomb: The Last Days of the Soviet Empire* (1993); Philip Zelikow and Condoleezza Rice, *Germany Unified and Europe Transformed: A Study in Statecraft* (1995).

Bush and the Gulf War

Rick Atkinson, *Crusade: The Untold Story of the Persian Gulf War* (1994); A. J. Bacevich et al., *The Gulf War of 1991 Reconsidered* (2003); Lawrence Freedman and Efraim Karsh, *The Gulf Conflict 1990–1991: Diplomacy and War in the New World Order* (1993); Dilip Hiro, *Desert Shield to Desert Storm: The Second Gulf War* (1992); Bruce Jentleson, *With Friends Like These: Reagan, Bush, and Saddam* (1994); Sandra Mackey, *The Reckoning: Iraq and the Legacy of Saddam Hussein* (2002); Jean Edward Smith, *George Bush's War* (1992).

Chapter 33

Politics in the 1990s

Dan Balz and Ronald Brownstein, *Storming the Gates: Protest Politics and the Republican Revival* (1996); Sara Diamond, *Not by Politics Alone: The Enduring Influence of the Christian Right* (1998); E. J. Dionne, Jr., *Why Americans Hate Politics* (1991); Elizabeth Drew, *Showdown: The Struggle Between the Gingrich Congress and the Clinton White House* (1996); Alan Ehrenhalt, *The United States of Ambition: Politicians, Power, and the Pursuit of Office* (1991); David Frum, *Dead Right* (1994); William Greider, *Who Will Tell the People: The Betrayal of American Democracy* (1992); Howard Gillman, *The Votes That Counted: How the Court Decided the 2000 Presidential Election* (2001); Kevin Phillips, *The Politics of Rich and Poor* (1990); Gerald Posner, *Citizen Perot* (1996).

Antigovernment Movements and Culture Wars

James Fallows, *Breaking the News: How the Media Undermine American Democracy* (1996); Daniel Levitas, *The Terrorist Next Door: The Militia Movement and the Radical Right* (2002); Edward Linenthal, *The Unfinished Bombing: Oklahoma City in American Memory* (2001); Larry J. Sabato and Glenn R. Simpson, *Dirty Little Secrets: The Persistence of Corruption in American Politics* (1996); Neil J. Smelser and Jeffrey C. Alexander, eds., *Diversity and Its Discontents: Cultural Conflict and Common Ground in Contemporary American Society* (1999); Kenneth S. Stern, *A Force upon the Plain: The American Militia Movement and the Politics of Hate* (1996).

Clinton's Presidency, Impeachment, and Survival

Sidney Blumenthal, *The Clinton Wars* (2003); Hillary Clinton, *Living History* (2003); Joe Klein, *The Natural: The Misunderstood Presidency of Bill Clinton* (2002); Roger Morris, *Partners in Power: The Clintons and Their America* (1996); Richard A. Posner, *Affair of State: The Investigation, Impeachment, and Trial of President Clinton* (1999); James B. Stewart, *Blood Sport: The President and His Adversaries* (1996); Jeffrey Toobin, *A Vast Conspiracy: The Real Story of the Sex Scandal That Nearly Brought Down a President* (2000); DeWayne Wickham, *Bill Clinton and Black America* (2002); Bob Woodward, *The Agenda: Inside the Clinton White House* (1994).

Globalization: Economic and Cultural

Roger Alcaly, *The New Economy: What It Is, How It Happened, and Why It Is Likely to Stay* (2003); Benjamin R. Barber, *Jihad vs. McWorld: How the Planet Is Both Falling Apart and Coming Together and What This Means for Democracy* (1995); Richard J. Barnet and John Cavangh, *Global Dreams: Imperial Corporations and the New World Order* (1994); Thomas L. Friedman, *The Lexus and the Olive Tree: Understanding Globalization* (1999); Laurie Garrett, *Microbes Versus Mankind: The Coming Plague* (1997); Anthony Giddens, *Runaway World: How Globalization Is Reshaping Our World* (2000); George W. Grayson, *The North American Free Trade Agreement* (1995); William Greider, *One World, Ready or Not: The Manic Logic of Global Capitalism* (1997); Richard Kuisel, *Seducing the French: The Dilemma of Americanization* (1993); Robert Kuttner, *Everything for Sale: The Virtues and Limits of Markets* (1996); Richard Pells, *Not Like Us: How Europeans Have Loved, Hated, and Transformed American Culture Since World War II* (1997); Peter Singer, *One World: The Ethics of Globalization* (2002); Robert Soloman, *Money on the Move: The Revolution in International Finance Since 1980* (1999); Paul B. Stares, *Global Habit: The Drug Problem in a Borderless World* (1996); Joseph E. Stiglitz, *Globalization and Its Discontents* (2002); Reinhold Wagnleitner and Elaine Tyler May, eds., *"Here, There, and Everywhere": The Foreign Politics of American Popular Culture* (2000); James L. Watson, ed., *Golden Arches East: McDonald's in East Asia* (1997).

Clinton's Foreign Policy

Andrew J. Bacevich and Eliot Cohen, eds., *War Over Kosovo: Politics and Strategy in a Global Age* (2002); Lester H. Brune, *The United States and Post–Cold War Interventions: Bush and Clinton in Somalia, Haiti, and Bosnia, 1992–1998*; Wesley K. Clark, *Waging Modern War: Bosnia, Kosovo, and the Future of Combat* (2001); Ivo H. Daalder, *Getting to Dayton: The Making of America's Bosnia Policy* (2000); David Halberstam, *War in a Time of Peace: Bush, Clinton, and the Generals* (2001); Richard N. Haass, *Intervention: The Use of American Military Force in the Post–Cold War World* (1999); Thomas H. Henriksen, *Clinton's Foreign Policy in Somalia, Bosnia, Haiti, and North Korea* (1996); John L. Hirsch and Robert B. Oakley, *Somalia and Operation Restore Hope* (1995); Richard Holbrooke, *To End a War* (1998); Richard A. Melanson, *American Foreign Policy Since the Vietnam War: The Search for Consensus from Nixon to Clinton* (2001).

The Bush Presidency and the War on Terrorism

Daniel Benjamin and Steven Simon, *The Sacred Age of Terror* (2002); Peter L. Bergen, *Holy War, Inc: Inside the Secret World of Osama bin Laden* (2001); Frank Bruni, *Ambling Into History: The Unlikely Odyssey of George W. Bush* (2002); John L. Esposito, *Unholy War: Terror in the Name of Islam* (2002); Thomas L. Friedman, *Longitudes and Attitudes: Exploring the World After September 11* (2002); David Frum, *The Right Man: The Surprise Presidency of George W. Bush* (2003); Avigdor Haselkorn, *The Continuing Storm: Iraq, Poisonous Weapons, and Deterrence* (1999); Robert Kagan, *Of Paradise and Power: America and Europe in the New World Order* (2003); Sandra Mackey, *The Reckoning: Iraq and the Legacy of Saddam Hussein* (2002); Joseph S. Nye Jr., *The Paradox of American Power: Why the World's Only Superpower Can't Go It Alone* (2002); Paul R. Pillar and Michael H. Armacost, *Terrorism and U.S. Foreign Policy* (2001); Kenneth M. Pollack, *The Threatening Storm: The Case for Invading Iraq* (2002); Ahmed Rashid, *Taliban: Militant Islam, Oil, and Fundamentalism in Central Asia* (2000); Bob Woodward, *Bush at War* (2002); Robin Wright, *Sacred Rage: The Wrath of Militant Islam* (2001); Fareed Zakaria, *The Future of Freedom: Illiberal Democracy at Home and Abroad* (2003).

American Society and Culture

Lou Cannon, *Official Negligence: How Rodney King and the Riots Changed Los Angeles and the LAPD* (1997); Adam Cohen, *The Perfect Store: Inside eBay* (2002); Sheldon Danziger and Peter Gottschalk, *American Unequal* (1996); Robert H. Frank and Philip J. Cook, *The Winner-Take-All Society* (1995); Herbert J. Gans, *The War Against the Poor* (1995); Barry Glassner, *The Culture of Fear* (1999); David M. Gordon, *Fat and Mean: The Corporate Squeeze of Working Americans and the Myth of Managerial "Downsizing"* (1996); John De Graaf, David Wann, and Thomas H. Naylor, *Affluenza: The All-Consuming Epidemic* (2001); Katie Hafner, *Where Wizards Stay Up Late: The Origins of The Internet* (1996); Haynes Johnson, *The Best of Times: America in the Clinton Years* (2001); Eric Klinenberg, *Heat Wave: A Social Autopsy of Disaster in Chicago* (2002); Robert D. Putnam, *Bowling Alone: the Collapse and Revival of American Community* (2000); Robert J. Samuelson, *The Good Life and Its Discontents: The American Dream in an Age of Entitlements* (1995); Eric Schlosser, *Fast Food Nation: The Dark Side of the All-American Meal* (2001); Benjamin Shepard and Ronald Hayduk, eds., *From ACT UP to the WTO: Urban Protest and Community Building in the Era of Globalization* (2002); Arlene Stein, *The Stranger Next Door: The Story of a Small Community's Battle over Sex, Faith, and Civil Rights* (2001).

Race and Ethnicity in American Life

Geoffrey Fox, *Hispanic Nation: Culture, Politics, and the Constructing of Identity* (1996); Hugh Davis Graham, *Collision Course: The Strange Convergence of Affirmative Action and Immigration Policy in America* (2002); Jennifer L. Hochschild, *Facing Up to the American Dream: Race, Class, and the Soul of the Nation* (1995); Marcelo M. Suárez-Orozco and Mariela M. Páez, eds., *Latinos: Remaking America* (2002); Roberto Suro, *Strangers Among Us: How Latino Immigration Is Transforming America* (1998); Stephan Thernstrom and Abigail Thernstrom, *America in Black and White: One Nation, Indivisible* (1997); Frank H. Wu, *Yellow: Race in America Beyond Black and White* (2002); Helen Zia, *Asian American Dreams: The Emergence of an American People* (2002).

Documents

DECLARATION OF INDEPENDENCE IN CONGRESS, JULY 4, 1776

When, in the course of human events, it becomes necessary for one people to dissolve the political bonds which have connected them with another, and to assume, among the powers of the earth, the separate and equal station to which the laws of nature and of nature's God entitle them, a decent respect to the opinions of mankind requires that they should declare the causes which impel them to the separation.

We hold these truths to be self-evident: That all men are created equal; that they are endowed by their Creator with certain unalienable rights; that among these are life, liberty, and the pursuit of happiness; that, to secure these rights, governments are instituted among men, deriving their just powers from the consent of the governed; that whenever any form of government becomes destructive of these ends, it is the right of the people to alter or to abolish it, and to institute new government, laying its foundation on such principles, and organizing its powers in such form, as to them shall seem most likely to effect their safety and happiness. Prudence, indeed, will dictate that governments long established should not be changed for light and transient causes; and accordingly all experience hath shown that mankind are more disposed to suffer, while evils are sufferable, than to right themselves by abolishing the forms to which they are accustomed. But when a long train of abuses and usurpations, pursuing invariably the same object, evinces a design to reduce them under absolute despotism, it is their right, it is their duty, to throw off such government, and to provide new guards for their future security. Such has been the patient sufferance of these colonies; and such is now the necessity which constrains them to alter their former systems of government. The history of the present King of Great Britain is a history of repeated injuries and usurpations, all having in direct object the establishment of an absolute tyranny over these states. To prove this, let facts be submitted to a candid world.

He has refused his assent to laws, the most wholesome and necessary for the public good.

He has forbidden his governors to pass laws of immediate and pressing importance, unless suspended in their operation till his assent should be obtained; and, when so suspended, he has utterly neglected to attend to them.

He has refused to pass other laws for the accommodation of large districts of people, unless those people would relinquish the right of representation in the legislature, a right inestimable to them, and formidable to tyrants only.

He has called together legislative bodies at places unusual, uncomfortable, and distant from the depository of their public records, for the sole purpose of fatiguing them into compliance with his measures.

He has dissolved representative houses repeatedly, for opposing, with manly firmness, his invasions on the rights of the people.

He has refused for a long time, after such dissolutions, to cause others to be elected; whereby the legislative powers, incapable of annihilation, have returned to the people at large for their exercise; the state remaining, in the mean time, exposed to all the dangers of invasions from without and convulsions within.

He has endeavored to prevent the population of these states; for that purpose obstructing the laws for naturalization of foreigners; refusing to pass others to encourage their migration hither, and raising the conditions of new appropriations of lands.

He has obstructed the administration of justice, by refusing his assent to laws for establishing judiciary powers.

He has made judges dependent on his will alone, for the tenure of their offices, and the amount and payment of their salaries.

He has erected a multitude of new offices, and sent hither swarms of officers to harass our people and eat out their substance.

He has kept among us, in times of peace, standing armies, without the consent of our legislatures.

He has affected to render the military independent of, and superior to, the civil power.

He has combined with others to subject us to a jurisdiction foreign to our constitution, and unacknowledged by our laws, giving his assent to their acts of pretended legislation:

For quartering large bodies of armed troops among us;

For protecting them, by a mock trial, from punishment for any murders which they should commit on the inhabitants of these states;

For cutting off our trade with all parts of the world;

For imposing taxes on us without our consent;

For depriving us, in many cases, of the benefits of trial by jury;

For transporting us beyond seas, to be tried for pretended offenses;

For abolishing the free system of English laws in a neighboring province, establishing therein an arbitrary government, and enlarging its boundaries, so as to render it at once an example and fit instrument for introducing the same absolute rule into these colonies;

For taking away our charters, abolishing our most valuable laws, and altering fundamentally the forms of our governments;

For suspending our own legislatures, and declaring themselves invested with power to legislate for us in all cases whatsoever.

He has abdicated government here, by declaring us out of his protection and waging war against us.

He has plundered our seas, ravaged our coasts, burned our towns, and destroyed the lives of our people.

He is at this time transporting large armies of foreign mercenaries to complete the works of death, desolation, and tyranny already begun with circumstances of cruelty and perfidy scarcely paralleled in the most barbarous ages, and totally unworthy the head of a civilized nation.

He has constrained our fellow-citizens, taken captive on the high seas, to bear arms against their country, to become the executioners of their friends and brethren, or to fall themselves by their hands.

He has excited domestic insurrection among us, and has endeavored to bring on the inhabitants of our frontiers the merciless Indian savages, whose known rule of warfare is an undistinguished destruction of all ages, sexes, and conditions.

In every stage of these oppressions we have petitioned for redress in the most humble terms; our repeated petitions have been answered only by repeated injury. A prince, whose character is thus marked by every act which may define a tyrant, is unfit to be the ruler of a free people.

Nor have we been wanting in our attentions to our British brethren. We have warned them, from time to time, of attempts by their legislature to extend an unwarrantable jurisdiction over us. We have reminded them of the circumstances of our emigration and settlement here. We have appealed to their native justice and magnanimity; and we have conjured them, by the ties of our common kindred, to disavow these usurpations, which would inevitably interrupt our connections and correspondence. They, too, have been deaf to the voice of justice and of consanguinity. We must, therefore, acquiesce in the necessity which denounces our separation, and hold them, as we hold the rest of mankind, enemies in war, in peace friends.

We, therefore, the representatives of the United States of America, in General Congress assembled, appealing to the Supreme Judge of the world for the rectitude of our intentions, do, in the name and by the authority of the good people of these colonies, solemnly publish and declare, that these United Colonies are, and of right ought to be, FREE AND INDEPENDENT STATES; that they are absolved from all allegiance to the British crown, and that all political connection between them and the state of Great Britain is, and ought to be, totally dissolved; and that, as free and independent states, they have full power to levy war, conclude peace, contract alliances, establish commerce, and do all other acts and things which independent states may of right do. And for the support of this declaration, with a firm reliance on the protection of Divine Providence, we mutually pledge to each other our lives, our fortunes, and our sacred honor.

ARTICLES OF CONFEDERATION

Whereas the Delegates of the United States of America in Congress assembled did on the fifteenth day of November in the Year of our Lord One Thousand Seven Hundred and Seventy seven, and in the Second Year of the Independence of America agree to certain articles of Confederation and perpetual Union between the States of Newhampshire, Massachusetts-bay, Rhode-island and Providence Plantations, Connecticut, New-York, New-Jersey, Pennsylvania, Delaware, Maryland, Virginia, North-Carolina, South-Carolina and Georgia in the Words following, viz. "Articles of Confederation and perpetual Union between the states of Newhampshire, Massachusetts-bay, Rhodeisland and Providence Plantations, Connecticut, New-York, New-Jersey, Pennsylvania, Delaware, Maryland, Virginia, North-Carolina, South-Carolina and Georgia.

Article I   The Stile of this confederacy shall be "The United States of America."

Article II   Each state retains its sovereignty, freedom and independence, and every Power, Jurisdiction and right, which is not by this confederation expressly delegated to the United States, in Congress assembled.

Article III   The said states hereby severally enter into a firm league of friendship with each other, for their common defence, the security of their Liberties, and their mutual and general welfare, binding themselves to assist each other, against all force offered to, or attacks made upon them, or any of them, on account of religion, sovereignty, trade, or any other pretence whatever.

Article IV   The better to secure and perpetuate mutual friendship and intercourse among the people of the different states in this union, the free inhabitants of each of these states, paupers, vagabonds and fugitives from Justice excepted, shall be entitled to all privileges and immunities of free citizens in the several states; and the people of each state shall have free ingress and regress to and from any other state, and shall enjoy therein all the privileges of trade and commerce, subject to the same duties, impositions and restrictions as the inhabitants thereof respectively, provided that such restriction shall not extend so far as to prevent the removal of property imported into any state, to any other state of which the Owner is an inhabitant; provided also that no imposition, duties or restriction shall be laid by any state, on the property of the united states, or either of them.

If any Person guilty of, or charged with treason, felony, or other high misdemeanor in any state, shall flee from Justice, and be found in any of the united states, he shall upon demand of the Governor or executive power, of the state from which he fled, be delivered up and removed to the state having jurisdiction of his offence.

Full faith and credit shall be given in each of these states to the records, acts and judicial proceedings of the courts and magistrates of every other state.

Article V   For the more convenient management of the general interests of the united states, delegates shall be annually appointed in such manner as the legislature of each state shall direct, to meet in Congress on the first Monday in November, in every year, with a power reserved to each state, to recall its delegates, or any of them, at any time within the year, and to send others in their stead, for the remainder of the Year.

No state shall be represented in Congress by less than two, nor by more than seven Members; and no person shall be capable of being a delegate for more than three years in any term of six years; nor shall any person, being a delegate, be capable of holding any office under the united states, for which he, or another for his benefit receives any salary, fees or emolument of any kind.

Each state shall maintain its own delegates in a meeting of the states, and while they act as members of the committee of the states.

In determining questions in the united states, in Congress assembled, each state shall have one vote.

Freedom of speech and debate in Congress shall not be impeached or questioned in any Court, or place out of Congress, and the members of congress shall be protected in their persons from arrests and imprisonments, during the time of their going to and from, and attendance on congress, except for treason, felony, or breach of the peace.

Article VI   No state without the Consent of the united states in congress assembled, shall send any embassy to, or receive any embassy from, or enter into any conference, agreement, or alliance or treaty with any King, prince or state; nor shall any person holding any office of profit or trust under the united states, or any of them, accept of any present, emolument, office or title of any kind whatever from any king, prince or foreign state; nor shall the united states in congress assembled, or any of them, grant any title of nobility.

No two or more states shall enter into any treaty, confederation or alliance whatever between them, without the consent of the united states in congress assembled, specifying accurately the purposes for which the same is to be entered into, and how long it shall continue.

No state shall lay any imposts or duties, which may interfere with any stipulations in treaties, entered into by the united states in congress assembled, with any king, prince or state, in pursuance of any treaties already proposed by congress, to the courts of France and Spain.

No vessels of war shall be kept up in time of peace by any state, except such number only, as shall be deemed necessary by the united states in congress assembled, for the defence of such state, or its trade; nor shall any body of forces be kept up by any state, in time of peace, except such number only, as in the judgment of the united states, in congress assembled, shall be deemed requisite to garrison the forts necessary for the defence of such state; but every state shall always keep up a well regulated and disciplined militia, sufficiently armed and accoutred, and shall provide and constantly have ready for use, in public stores, a due number of field pieces and tents, and a proper quantity of arms, ammunition and camp equipage.

No state shall engage in any war without the consent of the united states in congress assembled, unless such state be actually invaded by enemies, or shall have received certain advice of a resolution being formed by some nation of Indians to invade such state, and the danger is so imminent as not to admit of a delay, till the united states in congress assembled can be consulted: nor shall any state grant commissions to any ships or vessels of war, nor letters of marque or reprisal, except it be after a declaration of war by the united states in congress assembled, and then only against the kingdom or state and the subjects thereof, against which war has been so declared, and under such regulations as shall be established by the united states in congress assembled, unless such state be infested by pirates, in which case vessels of war may be fitted out for that occasion, and kept so long as the danger shall continue, or until the united states in congress assembled shall determine otherwise.

Article VII   When land-forces are raised by any state for the common defence, all officers of or under the rank of colonel, shall be appointed by the legislature of each state respectively by whom such forces shall be raised, or in such manner as such state shall direct, and all vacancies shall be filled up by the state which first made the appointment.

Article VIII   All charges of war, and all other expences that shall be incurred for the common defence or general welfare, and allowed by the united states in congress assembled, shall be defrayed out of a common treasury, which shall be supplied by the several states, in proportion to the value of all land within each state, granted to or surveyed for any Person, as such land and the buildings and improvements thereon shall be estimated according to such mode as the united states in congress assembled, shall from time to time direct and appoint. The taxes for paying that proportion shall be laid and levied by the authority and direction of the legislatures of the several states within the time agreed upon by the united states in congress assembled.

Article IX   The united states in congress assembled, shall have the sole and exclusive right and power of determining on peace and war, except in the cases mentioned in the sixth article—of sending and receiving ambassadors—entering into treaties and alliances, provided that no treaty of commerce shall be made whereby the legislative power of the respective states shall be restrained from imposing such imposts and duties on foreigners, as their own people are subjected to, or from prohibiting the exportation or importation of any species of goods or commodities whatsoever—of establishing rules for deciding in all cases, what captures on land or water shall be legal, and in what manner prizes taken by land or naval forces in the service of the united states shall be divided or appropriated.—of granting letters of marque and reprisal in times of peace—appointing courts for the trial of piracies and felonies committed on the high seas and establishing courts for receiving and determining final appeals in all cases of captures, provided that no member of congress shall be appointed a judge of any of the said courts.

The united states in congress assembled shall also be the last resort on appeal in all disputes and differences now subsisting or that hereafter may arise between two or more states concerning boundary, jurisdiction or any other cause whatever; which authority shall always be exercised in the manner following. Whenever the legislative or executive authority or lawful agent of any state in controversy with another shall present a petition to congress, stating the matter in question and praying for a hearing, notice thereof shall be given by order of congress to the legislative or executive authority of the other state in controversy, and a day assigned for the appearance of the parties by their lawful agents, who shall then be directed to appoint by joint consent, commissioners or judges to constitute a court for hearing and determining the matter in question: but if they cannot agree, congress shall name three persons out of each of the united states, and from the list of such persons each party shall alternately strike out one, the petitioners beginning, until the number shall be reduced to thirteen; and from that number not less than seven, nor more than nine names as congress shall direct, shall in the presence of congress be drawn out by lot, and the persons whose names shall be so drawn or any five of them, shall be commissioners or judges, to hear and finally determine the controversy, so always as a major part of the judges who shall hear the cause shall agree in the determination: and if either party shall neglect to attend at the day appointed, without shewing reasons, which congress shall judge sufficient, or being present shall refuse to strike, the congress shall proceed to nominate three persons out of each state, and the secretary of congress shall strike in behalf of such party absent or refusing; and the judgment and sentence of the court to be appointed, in the manner before prescribed, shall be final and conclusive; and if any of the parties shall refuse to submit to the authority of such court, or to appear to defend their claim or cause, the court shall nevertheless proceed to pronounce sentence, or judgment, which shall in like manner be final and decisive, the judgment or sentence and other proceedings being in either case transmitted to congress, and lodged among the acts of congress for the security of the parties concerned: provided that every commissioner, before he sits in judgment, shall take an oath to be administered by one of the judges of the supreme or superior court of the state, where the cause shall be tried, "well and truly to hear and determine the matter in question, according to the best of his judgment, without favour, affection or hope of reward:" provided also that no state shall be deprived of territory for the benefit of the united states.

All controversies concerning the private right of soil claimed under different grants of two or more states, whose jurisdictions as they may respect such lands, and the states which passed such grants are adjusted, the said grants or either of them being at the same time claimed to have originated antecedent to such settlement of jurisdiction, shall on the petition of either party to the congress of the united states, be finally determined as near as may be in the same manner as is before prescribed for deciding disputes respecting territorial jurisdiction between different states.

The united states in congress assembled shall also have the sole and exclusive right and power of regulating the alloy and value of coin struck by their own authority, or by that of the respective states—fixing the standard of weights and measures throughout the united states.—regulating the trade and managing all affairs with the Indians, not members of any of the states, provided that the legislative right of any state within its own limits be not infringed or violated—establishing and regulating post-offices from one state to another, throughout all the united states, and exacting such postage on the papers passing thro' the same as may be requisite to defray the expences of the said office—appointing all officers of the land forces, in the service of the united states, excepting regimental officers.—appointing all the officers of the naval forces, and commissioning all officers whatever in the service of the united states—making rules for the government and regulation of the said land and naval forces, and directing their operations.

The united states in congress assembled shall have authority to appoint a committee, to sit in the recess of congress, to be denominated "A Committee of the States," and to consist of one delegate from each state; and to appoint such other committees and civil officers as may be necessary for managing the general affairs of the united states under their direction—to appoint one of their number to preside, provided that no person be allowed to serve in the office of president more than one year in any term of three years; to ascertain the necessary sums of Money to be raised for the service of the united states, and to appropriate and apply the same for defraying the public expences—to borrow money, or emit bills on the credit of the united states, transmitting every half year to the respective states an account of the sums of money so borrowed or emitted,—to build and equip a navy—to agree upon the number of land forces, and to make requisitions from each state for its quota, in proportion to the number of white inhabitants in such state; which requisition shall be binding, and thereupon the legislature of each state shall appoint the regimental officers, raise the men and cloath, arm and equip them in a soldier like manner, at the expence of the united states, and the officers and men so cloathed, armed and equipped shall march to the place appointed, and within the time agreed on by the united states in congress assembled: But if the united states in congress assembled shall, on consideration of circumstances judge proper that any state should not raise men, or should raise a smaller number than its quota, and that any other state should raise a greater number of men than the quota thereof, such extra number shall be raised, officered, cloathed, armed and equipped in the same manner as the quota of such state, unless the legislature of such state shall judge that such extra number cannot be safely spared out of the same, in which case they shall raise, officer, cloath, arm and equip as many of such extra number as they judge can be safely spared. And the officers and men so cloathed, armed and equipped, shall march to the place appointed, and within the time agreed on by the united states in congress assembled.

The united states in congress assembled shall never engage in a war, nor grant letters of marque and reprisal in time of peace, nor enter into any treaties or alliances, nor coin money, nor regulate the value thereof, nor ascertain the sums and expences necessary for the defence and welfare of the united states, or any of them, nor emit bills, nor borrow money on the credit of the united states, nor appropriate money, nor agree upon the number of vessels of war, to be built or purchased, or the number of land or sea forces to be raised, nor appoint a commander in chief of the army or navy, unless nine states assent to the same: nor shall a question on any other point, except for adjourning from day to day be determined, unless by the votes of a majority of the united states in congress assembled.

The congress of the united states shall have power to adjourn to any time within the year, and to any place within the united states, so that no period of adjournment be for a longer duration than the space of six Months, and shall publish the Journal of their proceedings monthly, except such parts thereof relating to treaties, alliances or military operations as in their judgment require secresy; and the yeas and nays of the delegates of each state on any question shall be entered on the Journal, when it is desired by any delegate; and the delegates of a state, or any of them, as his or their request shall be furnished with a transcript of the said Journal, except such parts as are above excepted, to lay before the legislatures of the several states.

Article X   The committee of the states, or any nine of them, shall be authorised to execute, in the recess of congress, such of the powers of congress as the united states in congress assembled, by the consent of nine states, shall from time to time think expedient to vest them with; provided that no power be delegated to the said committee, for the exercise of which, by the articles of confederation, the voice of nine states in the congress of the united states assembled is requisite.

Article XI   Canada acceding to this confederation, and joining in the measures of the united states, shall be admitted into, and entitled to all the advantages of this union: but no other colony shall be admitted into the same, unless such admission be agreed to by nine states.

Article XII   All bills of credit emitted, monies borrowed and debts contracted by, or under the authority of congress, before the assembling of the united states, in pursuance of the present confederation, shall be deemed and considered as a charge against the united states, for payment and satisfaction whereof the said united states, and the public faith are hereby solemnly pledged.

Article XIII   Every state shall abide by the determinations of the united states in congress assembled, on all questions which by this confederation are submitted to them. And the Articles of this confederation shall be inviolably observed by every

state, and the union shall be perpetual; nor shall any alteration at any time hereafter be made in any of them; unless such alteration be agreed to in a congress of the united states, and be afterwards confirmed by the legislatures of every state.

AND WHEREAS it hath pleased the Great Governor of the World to incline the hearts of the legislatures we respectively represent in congress, to approve of, and to authorize us to ratify the said articles of confederation and perpetual union. Know Ye that we the under-signed delegates, by virtue of the power and authority to us given for that purpose, do by these presents, in the name and in behalf of our respective constituents, fully and entirely ratify and confirm each and every of the said articles of confederation and perpetual union, and all and singular the matters and things therein contained: And we do further solemnly plight and engage the faith of our respective constituents, that they shall abide by the determinations of the united states in congress assembled, on all questions, which by the said confederation are submitted to them. And that the articles thereof shall be inviolably observed by the states we respectively represent, and that the union shall be perpetual. In Witness whereof we have hereunto set our hands in Congress. Done at Philadelphia in the state of Pennsylvania the ninth Day of July in the Year of our Lord one Thousand seven Hundred and Seventy-eight, and in the third year of the independence of America.

CONSTITUTION OF THE UNITED STATES OF AMERICA AND AMENDMENTS*

Preamble

We the people of the United States, in order to form a more perfect union, establish justice, insure domestic tranquillity, provide for the common defense, promote the general welfare, and secure the blessings of liberty to ourselves and our posterity, do ordain and establish this Constitution for the United States of America.

Article I

Section 1   All legislative powers herein granted shall be vested in a Congress of the United States, which shall consist of a Senate and a House of Representatives.

Section 2   The House of Representatives shall be composed of members chosen every second year by the people of the several States, and the electors in each State shall have the qualifications requisite for electors of the most numerous branch of the State Legislature.

No person shall be a Representative who shall not have attained to the age of twenty-five years, and been seven years a citizen of the United States, and who shall not, when elected, be an inhabitant of that State in which he shall be chosen.

Representatives and direct taxes shall be apportioned among the several States which may be included within this

*Passages no longer in effect are printed in italic type.

Union, according to their respective numbers, *which shall be determined by adding to the whole number of free persons, including those bound to service for a term of years and excluding Indians not taxed, three-fifths of all other persons.* The actual enumeration shall be made within three years after the first meeting of the Congress of the United States, and within every subsequent term of ten years, in such manner as they shall by law direct. The number of Representatives shall not exceed one for every thirty thousand, but each State shall have at least one Representative; *and until such enumeration shall be made, the State of New Hampshire shall be entitled to choose three, Massachusetts eight, Rhode Island and Providence Plantations one, Connecticut five, New York six, New Jersey four, Pennsylvania eight, Delaware one, Maryland six, Virginia ten, North Carolina five, South Carolina five, and Georgia three.*

When vacancies happen in the representation from any State, the Executive authority thereof shall issue writs of election to fill such vacancies.

The House of Representatives shall choose their Speaker and other officers; and shall have the sole power of impeachment.

Section 3   The Senate of the United States shall be composed of two Senators from each State, *chosen by the legislature thereof,* for six years; and each Senator shall have one vote.

Immediately after they shall be assembled in consequence of the first election, they shall be divided as equally as may be into three classes. The seats of the Senators of the first class shall be vacated at the expiration of the second year, of the second class at the expiration of the fourth year, and of the third class at the expiration of the sixth year, so that one-third may be chosen every second year; *and if vacancies happen by resignation or otherwise, during the recess of the legislature of any State, the Executive thereof may make temporary appointments until the next meeting of the legislature, which shall then fill such vacancies.*

No person shall be a Senator who shall not have attained to the age of thirty years, and been nine years a citizen of the United States, and who shall not, when elected, be an inhabitant of that State for which he shall be chosen.

The Vice-President of the United States shall be President of the Senate, but shall have no vote, unless they be equally divided.

The Senate shall choose their other officers, and also a President *pro tempore,* in the absence of the Vice-President, or when he shall exercise the office of President of the United States.

The Senate shall have the sole power to try all impeachments. When sitting for that purpose, they shall be on oath or affirmation. When the President of the United States is tried, the Chief Justice shall preside: and no person shall be convicted without the concurrence of two-thirds of the members present.

Judgment in cases of impeachment shall not extend further than to removal from the office, and disqualification to hold and enjoy any office of honor, trust or profit under the United States: but the party convicted shall nevertheless be liable and subject to indictment, trial, judgment and punishment, according to law.

Section 4   The times, places and manner of holding elections for Senators and Representatives shall be prescribed in each State by the legislature thereof; but the Congress may at any time by law make or alter such regulations, except as to the places of choosing Senators.

The Congress shall assemble at least once in every year, and such meeting *shall be on the first Monday in December, unless they shall by law appoint a different day.*

Section 5   Each house shall be the judge of the elections, returns and qualifications of its own members, and a majority of each shall constitute a quorum to do business; but a smaller number may adjourn from day to day, and may be authorized to compel the attendance of absent members, in such manner, and under such penalties, as each house may provide.

Each house may determine the rules of its proceedings, punish its members for disorderly behavior, and with the concurrence of two-thirds, expel a member.

Each house shall keep a journal of its proceedings, and from time to time publish the same, excepting such parts as may in their judgment require secrecy; and the yeas and nays of the members of either house on any question shall, at the desire of one-fifth of those present, be entered on the journal.

Neither house, during the session of Congress, shall, without the consent of the other, adjourn for more than three days, nor to any other place than that in which the two houses shall be sitting.

Section 6   The Senators and Representatives shall receive a compensation for their services, to be ascertained by law and paid out of the treasury of the United States. They shall in all cases except treason, felony and breach of the peace, be privileged from arrest during their attendance at the session of their respective houses, and in going to and returning from the same; and for any speech or debate in either house, they shall not be questioned in any other place.

No Senator or Representative shall, during the time for which he was elected, be appointed to any civil office under the authority of the United States, which shall have been created, or the emoluments whereof shall have been increased, during such time; and no person holding any office under the United States shall be a member of either house during his continuance in office.

Section 7   All bills for raising revenue shall originate in the House of Representatives; but the Senate may propose or concur with amendments as on other bills.

Every bill which shall have passed the House of Representatives and the Senate, shall, before it become a law, be presented to the President of the United States; if he approve he shall sign it, but if not he shall return it with objections to that house in which it originated, who shall enter the objections at large on their journal, and proceed to reconsider it. If after such reconsideration two-thirds of that house shall agree to pass the bill, it shall be sent, together with the objections, to the other house, by which it shall likewise be reconsidered, and, if approved by two-thirds of that house, it shall become a law. But in all such cases the votes of both houses shall be determined by yeas and nays, and the names of the persons voting for and against the bill shall be entered on the journal of each house respectively. If any bill shall not be returned by the President within ten days (Sundays excepted) after it shall have been presented to him, the same shall be a law, in like manner as if he had signed it, unless the Congress by their adjournment prevent its return, in which case it shall not be a law.

Every order, resolution, or vote to which the concurrence of the Senate and House of Representatives may be necessary (except on a question of adjournment) shall be presented to the President of the United States; and before the same shall take effect, shall be approved by him, or being disapproved by him, shall be repassed by two-thirds of the Senate and House of Representatives, according to the rules and limitations prescribed in the case of a bill.

Section 8   The Congress shall have power

To lay and collect taxes, duties, imposts, and excises, to pay the debts and provide for the common defense and general welfare of the United States; but all duties, imposts and excises shall be uniform throughout the United States;

To borrow money on the credit of the United States;

To regulate commerce with foreign nations, and among the several States, and with the Indian tribes;

To establish an uniform rule of naturalization, and uniform laws on the subject of bankruptcies throughout the United States;

To coin money, regulate the value thereof, and of foreign coin, and fix the standard of weights and measures;

To provide for the punishment of counterfeiting the securities and current coin of the United States;

To establish post offices and post roads;

To promote the progress of science and useful arts by securing for limited times to authors and inventors the exclusive right to their respective writings and discoveries;

To constitute tribunals inferior to the Supreme Court;

To define and punish piracies and felonies committed on the high seas and offenses against the law of nations;

To declare war, grant letters of marque and reprisal, and make rules concerning captures on land and water;

To raise and support armies, but no appropriation of money to that use shall be for a longer term than two years;

To provide and maintain a navy;

To make rules for the government and regulation of the land and naval forces;

To provide for calling forth the militia to execute the laws of the Union, suppress insurrections, and repel invasions;

To provide for organizing, arming, and disciplining the militia, and for governing such part of them as may be employed in the service of the United States, reserving to the States respectively the appointment of the officers, and the authority of training the militia according to the discipline prescribed by Congress;

To exercise exclusive legislation in all cases whatsoever, over such district (not exceeding ten miles square) as may, by cession of particular States, and the acceptance of Congress, become the seat of government of the United States, and to exercise like authority over all places purchased by the consent of the legislature of the State, in which the same shall be, for erection of forts, magazines, arsenals, dockyards, and other needful buildings; —and

To make all laws which shall be necessary and proper for carrying into execution the foregoing powers, and all other powers vested by this Constitution in the government of the United States, or in any department or officer thereof.

Section 9   *The migration or importation of such persons as any of the States now existing shall think proper to admit shall not be prohibited by the Congress prior to the year 1808; but a tax or duty may be imposed on such importation, not exceeding $10 for each person.*

The privilege of the writ of habeas corpus shall not be suspended, unless when in cases of rebellion or invasion the public safety may require it.

No bill of attainder or ex post facto law shall be passed.

No capitation, or other direct, tax shall be laid, unless in proportion to the census or enumeration herein before directed to be taken.

No tax or duty shall be laid on articles exported from any State.

No preference shall be given by any regulation of commerce or revenue to the ports of one State over those of another; nor shall vessels bound to, or from, one State, be obliged to enter, clear, or pay duties in another.

No money shall be drawn from the treasury, but in consequence of appropriations made by law; and a regular statement and account of the receipts and expenditures of all public money shall be published from time to time.

No title of nobility shall be granted by the United States: and no person holding any office of profit or trust under them, shall, without the consent of the Congress, accept of any present, emolument, office, or title, of any kind whatever, from any king, prince, or foreign state.

Section 10   No State shall enter into any treaty, alliance, or confederation; grant letters of marque and reprisal; coin money; emit bills of credit; make anything but gold and silver coin a tender in payment of debts; pass any bill of attainder, ex post facto law, or law impairing the obligation of contracts, or grant any title of nobility.

No State shall, without the consent of Congress, lay any imposts or duties on imports or exports, except what may be absolutely necessary for executing its inspection laws: and the net produce of all duties and imposts, laid by any State on imports or exports, shall be for the use of the treasury of the United States; and all such laws shall be subject to the revision and control of the Congress.

No State shall, without the consent of Congress, lay any duty of tonnage, keep troops or ships of war in time of peace, enter into any agreement or compact with another State, or with a foreign power, or engage in war, unless actually invaded, or in such imminent danger as will not admit of delay.

Article II

Section 1 The executive power shall be vested in a President of the United States of America. He shall hold his office during the term of four years, and, together with the Vice-President, chosen for the same term, be elected as follows:

Each State shall appoint, in such manner as the legislature thereof may direct, a number of electors, equal to the whole number of Senators and Representatives to which the State may be entitled in the Congress; but no Senator or Representative, or person holding an office of trust or profit under the United States, shall be appointed an elector.

The electors shall meet in their respective States, and vote by ballot for two persons, of whom one at least shall not be an inhabitant of the same State with themselves. And they shall make a list of all the persons voted for, and of the number of votes for each; which list they shall sign and certify, and transmit sealed to the seat of government of the United States, directed to the President of the Senate. The President of the Senate shall, in the presence of the Senate and House of Representatives, open all the certificates, and the votes shall then be counted. The person having the greatest number of votes shall be the President, if such number be a majority of the whole number of electors appointed; and if there be more than one who have such majority, and have an equal number of votes, then the House of Representatives shall immediately choose by ballot one of them for President; and if no person have a majority, then from the five highest on the list said house shall in like manner choose the President. But in choosing the President the votes shall be taken by States, the representation from each State having one vote; a quorum for this purpose shall consist of a member or members from two-thirds of the States, and a majority of all the States shall be necessary to a choice. In every case, after the choice of the President, the person having the greatest number of votes of the electors shall be the Vice-President. But if there should remain two or more who have equal votes, the Senate shall choose from them by ballot the Vice-President.

The Congress may determine the time of choosing the electors and the day on which they shall give their votes; which day shall be the same throughout the United States.

No person except a natural-born citizen, *or a citizen of the United States at the time of the adoption of this Constitution,* shall be eligible to the office of President; neither shall any person be eligible to that office who shall not have attained to the age of thirty-five years, and been fourteen years a resident within the United States.

In cases of the removal of the President from office or of his death, resignation, or inability to discharge the powers and duties of the said office, the same shall devolve on the Vice-President, and the Congress may by law provide for the case of removal, death, resignation, or inability, both of the President and Vice-President, declaring what officer shall then act as President, and such officer shall act accordingly, until the disability be removed, or a President shall be elected.

The President shall, at stated times, receive for his services a compensation, which shall neither be increased nor diminished during the period for which he shall have been elected, and he shall not receive within that period any other emolument from the United States, or any of them.

Before he enter on the execution of his office, he shall take the following oath or affirmation:—"I do solemnly swear (or affirm) that I will faithfully execute the office of the President of the United States, and will to the best of my ability preserve, protect and defend the Constitution of the United States."

Section 2 The President shall be commander in chief of the army and navy of the United States, and of the militia of the several States, when called into the actual service of the United States; he may require the opinion, in writing, of the principal officer in each of the executive departments, upon any subject relating to the duties of their respective offices, and he shall have power to grant reprieves and pardons for offenses against the United States, except in cases of impeachment.

He shall have power, by and with the advice and consent of the Senate, to make treaties, provided two-thirds of the Senators present concur; and he shall nominate, and by and with the advice and consent of the Senate, shall appoint ambassadors, other public ministers and consuls, judges of the Supreme Court, and all other officers of the United States, whose appointments are not herein otherwise provided for, and which shall be established by law: but Congress may by law vest the appointment of such inferior officers, as they think proper, in the President alone, in the courts of law, or in the heads of departments.

The President shall have power to fill up all vacancies that may happen during the recess of the Senate, by granting commissions which shall expire at the end of their next session.

Section 3 He shall from time to time give to the Congress information of the state of the Union, and recommend to their consideration such measures as he shall judge necessary and expedient; he may, on extraordinary occasions, convene both houses, or either of them, and in case of disagreement between them, with respect to the time of adjournment, he may adjourn them to such time as he shall think proper; he shall receive ambassadors and other public ministers; he shall take care that the laws be faithfully executed, and shall commission all the officers of the United States.

Section 4 The President, Vice-President and all civil officers of the United States shall be removed from office on impeachment for, and on conviction of, treason, bribery, or other high crimes and misdemeanors.

Article III

Section 1 The judicial power of the United States shall be vested in one Supreme Court, and in such inferior courts as the Congress may from time to time ordain and establish. The judges, both of the Supreme and inferior courts, shall hold their offices during good behavior, and shall, at stated times, receive for their services a compensation which shall not be diminished during their continuance in office.

Section 2 The judicial power shall extend to all cases, in law and equity, arising under this Constitution, the laws of the United States, and treaties made, or which shall be made, under their authority;—to all cases affecting ambassadors, other public ministers and consuls;—to all cases of admiralty and maritime jurisdiction;—to controversies to which the United States shall be a party;—to controversies between two or more States;—*between a State and citizens of another State;*—between citizens of different States;—between citizens of the same State claiming lands under grants of different States, and between a State, or the citizens thereof, and foreign states, citizens or subjects.

In all cases affecting ambassadors, other public ministers and consuls, and those in which a State shall be party, the Supreme Court shall have original jurisdiction. In all the other cases before mentioned, the Supreme Court shall have appellate jurisdiction, both as to law and fact, with such exceptions, and under such regulations, as the Congress shall make.

The trial of all crimes, except in cases of impeachment, shall be by jury; and such trial shall be held in the State where said crimes shall have been committed; but when not committed within any State, the trial shall be at such place or places as the Congress may by law have directed.

Section 3 Treason against the United States shall consist only in levying war against them, or in adhering to their enemies, giving them aid and comfort. No person shall be convicted of treason unless on the testimony of two witnesses to the same overt act, or on confession in open court.

The Congress shall have power to declare the punishment of treason, but no attainder of treason shall work corruption of blood, or forfeiture except during the life of the person attainted.

Article IV

Section 1 Full faith and credit shall be given in each State to the public acts, records, and judicial proceedings of every other State. And the Congress may by general laws prescribe the manner in which such acts, records, and proceedings shall be proved, and the effect thereof.

Section 2 The citizens of each State shall be entitled to all privileges and immunities of citizens in the several States.

A person charged in any State with treason, felony, or other crime, who shall flee from justice, and be found in another State, shall on demand of the executive authority of the State from which he fled, be delivered up, to be removed to the State having jurisdiction of the crime.

No person held to service or labor in one State, under the laws thereof, escaping into another, shall, in consequence of any law or regulation therein, be discharged from such service or labor, but shall be delivered up on claim of the party to whom such service or labor may be due.

Section 3 New States may be admitted by the Congress into this Union; but no new State shall be formed or erected within the jurisdiction of any other State; nor any State be formed by the junction of two or more States, or parts of States, without the consent of the legislatures of the States concerned as well as of the Congress.

The Congress shall have power to dispose of and make all needful rules and regulations respecting the territory or other property belonging to the United States; and nothing in this Constitution shall be so construed as to prejudice any claims of the United States, or of any particular State.

Section 4 The United States shall guarantee to every State in this Union a republican form of government, and shall protect each of them against invasion; and on application of the legislature, or of the executive (when the legislature cannot be convened), against domestic violence.

Article V

The Congress, whenever two-thirds of both houses shall deem it necessary, shall propose amendments to this Constitution, or, on the application of the legislatures of two-thirds of the several States, shall call a convention for proposing amendments, which, in either case, shall be valid to all intents and purposes, as part of this Constitution, when ratified by the legislatures of three-fourths of the several States, or by conventions in three-fourths thereof, as the one or the other mode of ratification may be proposed by the Congress; provided *that no amendments which may be made prior to the year one thousand eight hundred and eight shall in any manner affect the first and fourth clauses in the ninth section of the first article;* and that no State, without its consent, shall be deprived of its equal suffrage in the Senate.

Article VI

All debts contracted and engagements entered into, before the adoption of this Constitution, shall be as valid against the United States under this Constitution, as under the Confederation.

This Constitution, and the laws of the United States which shall be made in pursuance thereof; and all treaties made, or which shall be made, under the authority of the United States, shall be the supreme law of the land; and the judges in every State shall be bound thereby, anything in the Constitution or laws of any State to the contrary notwithstanding.

The Senators and Representatives before mentioned, and the members of the several State legislatures, and all executive and judicial officers, both of the United States and of the several States, shall be bound by oath or affirmation to support this Constitution; but no religious test shall ever be required as a qualification to any office or public trust under the United States.

Article VII

The ratification of the conventions of nine States shall be sufficient for the establishment of this Constitution between the States so ratifying the same.

Done in Convention by the unanimous consent of the States present, the seventeenth day of September in the year of our Lord one thousand seven hundred and eighty-seven and of the

Independence of the United States of America the twelfth. In witness whereof we have hereunto subscribed our names.

Amendments to the Constitution*

Amendment I

Congress shall make no law respecting an establishment of religion, or prohibiting the free exercise thereof; or abridging the freedom of speech, or of the press; or the right of the people peaceably to assemble, and to petition the government for a redress of grievances.

Amendment II

A well-regulated militia being necessary to the security of a free State, the right of the people to keep and bear arms shall not be infringed.

Amendment III

No soldier shall, in time of peace, be quartered in any house without the consent of the owner, nor in time of war, but in a manner to be prescribed by law.

Amendment IV

The right of the people to be secure in their persons, houses, papers, and effects, against unreasonable searches and seizures, shall not be violated, and no warrants shall issue but upon probable cause, supported by oath or affirmation, and particularly describing the place to be searched, and the persons or things to be seized.

Amendment V

No person shall be held to answer for a capital, or otherwise infamous crime, unless on a presentment or indictment of a grand jury, except in cases arising in the land or naval forces, or in the militia, when in actual service in time of war or public danger; nor shall any person be subject for the same offense to be twice put in jeopardy of life or limb; nor shall be compelled in any criminal case to be a witness against himself, nor be deprived of life, liberty, or property, without due process of law; nor shall private property be taken for public use without just compensation.

Amendment VI

In all criminal prosecutions, the accused shall enjoy the right to a speedy and public trial, by an impartial jury of the State and district wherein the crime shall have been committed, which district shall have been previously ascertained by law, and to be informed of the nature and cause of the accusation; to be confronted with the witnesses against him; to have compulsory process for obtaining witnesses in his favor, and to have the assistance of counsel for his defense.

*The first ten Amendments (the Bill of Rights) were adopted in 1791.

Amendment VII

In suits at common law, where the value in controversy shall exceed twenty dollars, the right of trial by jury shall be preserved, and no fact tried by a jury shall be otherwise reexamined in any court of the United States, than according to the rules of the common law.

Amendment VIII

Excessive bail shall not be required, nor excessive fines imposed, nor cruel and unusual punishments inflicted.

Amendment IX

The enumeration in the Constitution, of certain rights, shall not be construed to deny or disparage others retained by the people.

Amendment X

The powers not delegated to the United States by the Constitution, nor prohibited by it to the States, are reserved to the States respectively, or to the people.

Amendment XI

[Adopted 1798]
The judicial power of the United States shall not be construed to extend to any suit in law or equity, commenced or prosecuted against one of the United States by citizens of another State, or by citizens or subjects of any foreign state.

Amendment XII

[Adopted 1804]
The electors shall meet in their respective States, and vote by ballot for President and Vice-President, one of whom, at least, shall not be an inhabitant of the same State with themselves; they shall name in their ballots the person voted for as President, and in distinct ballots the person voted for as Vice-President, and they shall make distinct lists of all persons voted for as President, and of all persons voted for as Vice-President, and of the number of votes for each, which lists they shall sign and certify, and transmit sealed to the seat of government of the United States, directed to the President of the Senate;—the President of the Senate shall, in the presence of the Senate and House of Representatives, open all the certificates and the votes shall then be counted;—the person having the greatest number of votes for President shall be the President, if such number be a majority of the whole number of electors appointed; and if no person have such majority, then from the persons having the highest numbers not exceeding three on the list of those voted for as President, the House of Representatives shall choose immediately, by ballot, the President. But in choosing the President, the votes shall be taken by States, the representation from each State having one vote; a quorum for this purpose shall consist of a member or members from two-thirds of the States, and a majority of all the States shall be necessary to a choice. And if the House of Representatives shall not choose a President

whenever the right of choice shall devolve upon them, before *the fourth day of March* next following, then the Vice-President shall act as President, as in the case of the death or other constitutional disability of the President.

The person having the greatest number of votes as Vice-President shall be the Vice-President, if such number be a majority of the whole number of electors appointed; and if no person have a majority, then from the two highest numbers on the list the Senate shall choose the Vice-President; a quorum for the purpose shall consist of two-thirds of the whole number of Senators, and a majority of the whole number shall be necessary to a choice. But no person constitutionally ineligible to the office of President shall be eligible to that of Vice-President of the United States.

Amendment XIII

[Adopted 1865]

Section 1 Neither slavery nor involuntary servitude, except as a punishment for crime whereof the party shall have been duly convicted, shall exist within the United States, or any place subject to their jurisdiction.

Section 2 Congress shall have power to enforce this article by appropriate legislation.

Amendment XIV

[Adopted 1868]

Section 1 All persons born or naturalized in the United States, and subject to the jurisdiction thereof, are citizens of the United States and of the State wherein they reside. No State shall make or enforce any law which shall abridge the privileges or immunities of citizens of the United States; nor shall any State deprive any person of life, liberty, or property, without due process of law; nor deny to any person within its jurisdiction the equal protection of the laws.

Section 2 Representatives shall be apportioned among the several States according to their respective numbers, counting the whole number of persons in each State, excluding Indians not taxed. But when the right to vote at any election for the choice of Electors for President and Vice-President of the United States, Representatives in Congress, the executive and judicial officers of a State, or the members of the legislature thereof, is denied to any of the male inhabitants of such State, being twenty-one years of age and citizens of the United States, or in any way abridged, except for participation in rebellion, or other crime, the basis of representation therein shall be reduced in the proportion which the number of such male citizens shall bear to the whole number of male citizens twenty-one years of age in such State.

Section 3 No person shall be a Senator or Representative in Congress, or Elector of President and Vice-President, or hold any office, civil or military, under the United States, or under any State, who, having previously taken an oath, as a member of Congress, or as an officer of the United States, or as a member of any State legislature, or as an executive or judicial officer of any State, to support the Constitution of the United States, shall have engaged in insurrection or rebellion against the same, or given aid or comfort to the enemies thereof. Congress may, by a vote of two-thirds of each house, remove such disability.

Section 4 The validity of the public debt of the United States, authorized by law, including debts incurred for payment of pensions and bounties for services in suppressing insurrection or rebellion, shall not be questioned. But neither the United States nor any State shall assume or pay any debt or obligation incurred in aid of insurrection or rebellion against the United States, or any claim for the loss of emancipation of any slave; but all such debts, obligations, and claims shall be held illegal and void.

Section 5 The Congress shall have power to enforce, by appropriate legislation, the provisions of this article.

Amendment XV

[Adopted 1870]

Section 1 The right of citizens of the United States to vote shall not be denied or abridged by the United States or by any State on account of race, color, or previous condition of servitude.

Section 2 The Congress shall have power to enforce this article by appropriate legislation.

Amendment XVI

[Adopted 1913]

The Congress shall have power to lay and collect taxes on incomes, from whatever source derived, without apportionment among the several States, and without regard to any census or enumeration.

Amendment XVII

[Adopted 1913]

Section 1 The Senate of the United States shall be composed of two Senators from each State, elected by the people thereof, for six years; and each Senator shall have one vote. The electors in each State shall have the qualifications requisite for electors of [voters for] the most numerous branch of the State legislatures.

Section 2 When vacancies happen in the representation of any State in the Senate, the executive authority of such State shall issue writs of election to fill such vacancies: Provided, that the Legislature of any State may empower the executive thereof to make temporary appointments until the people fill the vacancies by election as the Legislature may direct.

Section 3 This amendment shall not be so construed as to affect the election or term of any Senator chosen before it becomes valid as part of the Constitution.

Amendment XVIII

[Adopted 1919; Repealed 1933]

Section 1 After one year from the ratification of this article the manufacture, sale, or transportation of intoxicating liquors within, the importation thereof into, or the exportation thereof from the United States and all territory subject to the jurisdiction thereof, for beverage purposes, is hereby prohibited.

Section 2 The Congress and the several States shall have concurrent power to enforce this article by appropriate legislation.

Section 3 This article shall be inoperative unless it shall have been ratified as an amendment to the Constitution by the legislatures of the several States, as provided by the Constitution, within seven years from the date of the submission thereof to the States by the Congress.

Amendment XIX

[Adopted 1920]

Section 1 The right of citizens of the United States to vote shall not be denied or abridged by the United States or by any State on account of sex.

Section 2 The Congress shall have power to enforce this article by appropriate legislation.

Amendment XX

[Adopted 1933]

Section 1 The terms of the President and Vice-President shall end at noon on the 20th day of January, and the terms of Senators and Representatives at noon on the 3rd day of January, of the years in which such terms would have ended if this article had not been ratified; and the terms of their successors shall then begin.

Section 2 The Congress shall assemble at least once in every year, and such meeting shall begin at noon on the 3d day of January, unless they shall by law appoint a different day.

Section 3 If, at the time fixed for the beginning of the term of the President, the President-elect shall have died, the Vice-President–elect shall become President. If a President shall not have been chosen before the time fixed for the beginning of his term, or if the President-elect shall have failed to qualify, then the Vice-President–elect shall act as President until a President shall have qualified; and the Congress may by law provide for the case wherein neither a President-elect nor a Vice-President–elect

shall have qualified, declaring who shall then act as President, or the manner in which one who is to act shall be selected, and such persons shall act accordingly until a President or Vice-President shall have qualified.

Section 4 The Congress may by law provide for the case of the death of any of the persons from whom the House of Representatives may choose a President whenever the right of choice shall have devolved upon them, and for the case of the death of any of the persons from whom the Senate may choose a Vice-President whenever the right of choice shall have devolved upon them.

Section 5 Sections 1 and 2 shall take effect on the 15th day of October following the ratification of this article.

Section 6 This article shall be inoperative unless it shall have been ratified as an amendment to the Constitution by the Legislatures of three-fourths of the several States within seven years from the date of its submission.

Amendment XXI

[Adopted 1933]

Section 1 The eighteenth article of amendment to the Constitution of the United States is hereby repealed.

Section 2 The transportation or importation into any State, Territory, or Possession of the United States for delivery or use therein of intoxicating liquors, in violation of the laws thereof, is hereby prohibited.

Section 3 This article shall be inoperative unless it shall have been ratified as an amendment to the Constitution by conventions in the several States, as provided in the Constitution, within seven years from the date of submission thereof to the States by the Congress.

Amendment XXII

[Adopted 1951]

Section 1 No person shall be elected to the office of President more than twice, and no person who has held the office of President, or acted as President, for more than two years of a term to which some other person was elected President shall be elected to the office of President more than once. But this article shall not apply to any person holding the office of President when this article was proposed by the Congress, and shall not prevent any person who may be holding the office of President, or acting as President, during the term within which this article becomes operative from holding the office of President or acting as President during the remainder of such term.

Section 2 This article shall be inoperative unless it shall have been ratified as an amendment to the Constitution by the legislatures of three-fourths of the several States within seven years from the date of its submission to the States by the Congress.

Amendment XXIII

[Adopted 1961]

Section 1   The District constituting the seat of Government of the United States shall appoint in such manner as the Congress may direct:

A number of electors of President and Vice-President equal to the whole number of Senators and Representatives in Congress to which the District would be entitled if it were a State, but in no event more than the least populous State; they shall be in addition to those appointed by the States, but they shall be considered for the purposes of the election of President and Vice-President, to be electors appointed by a State; and they shall meet in the District and perform such duties as provided by the twelfth article of amendment.

Section 2   The Congress shall have the power to enforce this article by appropriate legislation.

Amendment XXIV

[Adopted 1964]

Section 1   The right of citizens of the United States to vote in any primary or other election for President or Vice-President, for electors for President or Vice-President, or for Senator or Representative in Congress, shall not be denied or abridged by the United States or any State by reason of failure to pay any poll tax or other tax.

Section 2   The Congress shall have the power to enforce this article by appropriate legislation.

Amendment XXV

[Adopted 1967]

Section 1   In case of the removal of the President from office or of his death or resignation, the Vice-President shall become President.

Section 2   Whenever there is a vacancy in the office of the Vice-President, the President shall nominate a Vice-President who shall take office upon confirmation by a majority vote of both Houses of Congress.

Section 3   Whenever the President transmits to the President pro tempore of the Senate and the Speaker of the House of Rep-

resentatives his written declaration that he is unable to discharge the powers and duties of his office, and until he transmits to them a written declaration to the contrary, such powers and duties shall be discharged by the Vice-President as Acting President.

Section 4   Whenever the Vice-President and a majority of either the principal officers of the executive departments or of such other body as Congress may by law provide, transmit to the President pro tempore of the Senate and the Speaker of the House of Representatives their written declaration that the President is unable to discharge the powers and duties of his office, the Vice-President shall immediately assume the powers and duties of the office as Acting President.

Thereafter, when the President transmits to the President pro tempore of the Senate and the Speaker of the House of Representatives his written declaration that no inability exists, he shall resume the powers and duties of his office unless the Vice-President and a majority of either the principal officers of the executive department[s] or of such other body as Congress may by law provide, transmit within four days to the President pro tempore of the Senate and the Speaker of the House of Representatives their written declaration that the President is unable to discharge the powers and duties of his office. Thereupon Congress shall decide the issue, assembling within forty-eight hours for that purpose if not in session. If the Congress, within twenty-one days after receipt of the latter written declaration, or, if Congress is not in session, within twenty-one days after Congress is required to assemble, determines by two-thirds vote of both Houses that the President is unable to discharge the powers and duties of his office, the Vice-President shall continue to discharge the same as Acting President; otherwise, the President shall resume the powers and duties of his office.

Amendment XXVI

[Adopted 1971]

Section 1   The right of citizens of the United States, who are eighteen years of age or older, to vote shall not be denied or abridged by the United States or by any State on account of age.

Section 2   The Congress shall have power to enforce this article by appropriate legislation.

Amendment XXVII

[Adopted 1992]

No law, varying the compensation for the services of the Senators and Representatives, shall take effect, until an election of Representatives shall have intervened.

The American People and Nation: A Statistical Profile

Population of the United States

Year	Number of States	Population	Percent Increase	Population Per Square Mile	Percent Urban/ Rural	Percent Male/ Female	Percent White/ Non-white	Persons Per House-hold	Median Age
1790	13	3,929,214		4.5	5.1/94.9	NA/NA	80.7/19.3	5.79	NA
1800	16	5,308,483	35.1	6.1	6.1/93.9	NA/NA	81.1/18.9	NA	NA
1810	17	7,239,881	36.4	4.3	7.3/92.7	NA/NA	81.0/19.0	NA	NA
1820	23	9,638,453	33.1	5.5	7.2/92.8	50.8/49.2	81.6/18.4	NA	16.7
1830	24	12,866,020	33.5	7.4	8.8/91.2	50.8/49.2	81.9/18.1	NA	17.2
1840	26	17,069,453	32.7	9.8	10.8/89.2	50.9/49.1	83.2/16.8	NA	17.8
1850	31	23,191,876	35.9	7.9	15.3/84.7	51.0/49.0	84.3/15.7	5.55	18.9
1860	33	31,443,321	35.6	10.6	19.8/80.2	51.2/48.8	85.6/14.4	5.28	19.4
1870	37	39,818,449	26.6	13.4	25.7/74.3	50.6/49.4	86.2/13.8	5.09	20.2
1880	38	50,155,783	26.0	16.9	28.2/71.8	50.9/49.1	86.5/13.5	5.04	20.9
1890	44	62,947,714	25.5	21.2	35.1/64.9	51.2/48.8	87.5/12.5	4.93	22.0
1900	45	75,994,575	20.7	25.6	39.6/60.4	51.1/48.9	87.9/12.1	4.76	22.9
1910	46	91,972,266	21.0	31.0	45.6/54.4	51.5/48.5	88.9/11.1	4.54	24.1
1920	48	105,710,620	14.9	35.6	51.2/48.8	51.0/49.0	89.7/10.3	4.34	25.3
1930	48	122,775,046	16.1	41.2	56.1/43.9	50.6/49.4	89.8/10.2	4.11	26.4
1940	48	131,669,275	7.2	44.2	56.5/43.5	50.2/49.8	89.8/10.2	3.67	29.0
1950	48	150,697,361	14.5	50.7	64.0/36.0	49.7/50.3	89.5/10.5	3.37	30.2
1960	50	179,323,175	18.5	50.6	69.9/30.1	49.3/50.7	88.6/11.4	3.33	29.5
1970	50	203,302,031	13.4	57.4	73.6/26.4	48.7/51.3	87.6/12.4	3.14	28.0
1980	50	226,542,199	11.4	64.1	73.7/26.3	48.6/51.4	85.9/14.1	2.75	30.0
1990	50	248,718,301	9.8	70.3	75.2/24.8	48.7/51.3	83.9/16.1	2.63	32.8
1998	50	270,299,000	8.0	76.4	NA	48.9/51.1	82.5/17.5	2.62	35.2
2000	50	281,421,906	1.09	74.0	79.0/21.0	49.1/50.9	75.1/24.9	2.59	35.3

NA = Not available.

Vital Statistics

| Year | Birth Rate* | Death Rate* | Life Expectancy in Years | | | | | Marriage Rate | Divorce Rate |
			Total Population	White Females	Nonwhite Females	White Males	Nonwhite Males		
1790	NA	NA	NA	NA	NA	NA	NA	NA	NA
1800	55.0	NA	NA	NA	NA	NA	NA	NA	NA
1810	54.3	NA	NA	NA	NA	NA	NA	NA	NA
1820	55.2	NA	NA	NA	NA	NA	NA	NA	NA
1830	51.4	NA	NA	NA	NA	NA	NA	NA	NA
1840	51.8	NA	NA	NA	NA	NA	NA	NA	NA
1850	43.3	NA	NA	NA	NA	NA	NA	NA	NA
1860	44.3	NA	NA	NA	NA	NA	NA	NA	NA
1870	38.3	NA	NA	NA	NA	NA	NA	NA	NA
1880	39.8	NA	NA	NA	NA	NA	NA	NA	NA
1890	31.5	NA	NA	NA	NA	NA	NA	NA	NA
1900	32.3	17.2	47.3	48.7	33.5	46.6	32.5	NA	NA
1910	30.1	14.7	50.0	52.0	37.5	48.6	33.8	NA	NA
1920	27.7	13.0	54.1	55.6	45.2	54.4	45.5	12.0	1.6
1930	21.3	11.3	59.7	63.5	49.2	59.7	47.3	9.2	1.6
1940	19.4	10.8	62.9	66.6	54.9	62.1	51.5	12.1	2.0
1950	24.1	9.6	68.2	72.2	62.9	66.5	59.1	11.1	2.6
1960	23.7	9.5	69.7	74.1	66.3	67.4	61.1	8.5	2.2
1970	18.4	9.5	70.8	75.6	69.4	68.0	61.3	10.6	3.5
1980	15.9	8.8	73.7	78.1	73.6	70.7	65.3	10.6	5.2
1990	16.6	8.6	75.4	79.4	75.2	72.7	67.0	9.8	4.7
1998	14.4	8.5	76.5†	73.9†	76.1°	74.3†	68.9°	8.9†	4.3
2000	14.7	8.7	76.9	80.0	74.9	74.8	68.2	8.5	4.1

Note: Data per one thousand for Birth, Death, Marriage, and Divorce Rates.

NA = Not available. *Data for 1800, 1810, 1830, 1850, 1870, and 1890 for whites only. †Data for 1997. °Data for 1996.

Immigrants to the United States

| Immigration Totals by Decade | | | |
Years	Number	Years	Number
1820–1830	151,824	1921–1930	4,107,209
1831–1840	599,125	1931–1940	528,431
1841–1850	1,713,251	1941–1950	1,035,039
1851–1860	2,598,214	1951–1960	2,515,479
1861–1870	2,314,824	1961–1970	3,321,677
1871–1880	2,812,191	1971–1980	4,493,314
1881–1890	5,246,613	1981–1990	7,338,062
1891–1900	3,687,546	1991–1997	6,944,591
1901–1910	8,795,386	1991–2000	9,095,417
1911–1920	5,735,811	Total	66,089,431

Major Sources of Immigrants by Country or Region (in thousands)

Period	Asia[a]	Germany	Mexico	Italy	Great Britain (UK)[b]	Ireland	Canada	Austria and Hungary	Soviet Union (Russia)	Caribbean	Central America and South America	Norway and Sweden
1820–1830	–	8	5	–	27	54	2	–	–	4	–	–
1831–1840	–	152	7	2	76	207	14	–	–	12	–	1
1841–1850	–	435	3	2	267	781	42	–	–	14	4	14
1851–1860	42	952	3	9	424	914	59	–	–	11	2	21
1861–1870	65	787	2	12	607	436	154	8	3	9	1	109
1871–1880	124	718	5	56	548	437	384	73	39	14	1	211
1881–1890	70	1,453	2[c]	307	807	655	393	354	213	29	3	568
1891–1900	75	505	1[c]	652	272	388	3	593	505	33	2	321
1901–1910	324	341	50	2,046	526	339	179	2,145	1,597	108	25	440
1911–1920	247	144	219	1,110	341	146	742	896	921	123	59	161
1921–1930	112	412	459	455	340	211	925	64	62	75	58	166
1931–1940	17	114	22	68	32	11	109	11	1	16	14	9
1941–1950	37	227	61	58	139	20	172	28	–	50	43	21
1951–1960	153	478	300	185	203	48	378	104	–	123	136	45
1961–1970	428	191	454	214	214	33	413	26	2	470	359	33
1971–1980	1,588	74	640	129	137	11	170	16	39	741	430	10
1981–1990	2,738	92	2,336	67	160	32	157	25	58	872	930	15
1991–2000	2,796	93	2,249	63	152	57	192	25	463	979	1,067	18
Total	8,816	7,176	6,818	5,435	5,272	4,780	4,488	4,368	3,903	3,683	3,134	2,163

Notes: Numbers for periods are rounded. Dash indicates less than 1,000. [a]Includes Middle East. [b]Since 1925, includes England, Scotland, Wales, and Northern Ireland data. [c]No data available for 1886–1894.

The American Worker

Year	Total Number of Workers	Males as Percent of Total Workers	Females as Percent of Total Workers	Married Women as Percent of Female Workers	Female Workers as Percent of Female Population	Percent of Labor Force Unemployed	Percent of Workers in Labor Unions
1870	12,506,000	85	15	NA	NA	NA	NA
1880	17,392,000	85	15	NA	NA	NA	NA
1890	23,318,000	83	17	14	19	4 (1894 = 18)	NA
1900	29,073,000	82	18	15	21	5	3
1910	38,167,000	79	21	25	25	6	6
1920	41,614,000	79	21	23	24	5 (1921 = 12)	12
1930	48,830,000	78	22	29	25	9 (1933 = 25)	11.6
1940	53,011,000	76	24	36	27	15 (1944 = 1)	26.9
1950	62,208,000	72	28	52	31	5.3	31.5
1960	69,628,000	67	33	55	38	5.5	31.4
1970	82,771,000	62	38	59	43	4.9	27.3
1980	106,940,000	58	42	55	52	7.1	21.9
1990	125,840,000	55	45	54	58	5.6	16.1
2000	138,820,935	54	46	53	57.5	3.7	13.9

NA = Not available.

The American Economy

Year	Gross National Product (GNP) and Gross Domestic Product (GDP)[a] (in $ billions)	Steel Production (in tons)	Corn Production (millions of bushels)	Automobiles Registered	New Housing Starts	Foreign Trade (in $ millions) Exports	Foreign Trade (in $ millions) Imports
1790	NA	NA	NA	NA	NA	20	23
1800	NA	NA	NA	NA	NA	71	91
1810	NA	NA	NA	NA	NA	67	85
1820	NA	NA	NA	NA	NA	70	74
1830	NA	NA	NA	NA	NA	74	71
1840	NA	NA	NA	NA	NA	132	107
1850	NA	NA	592[d]	NA	NA	152	178
1860	NA	13,000	839[e]	NA	NA	400	362
1870	7.4[b]	77,000	1,125	NA	NA	451	462
1880	11.2[c]	1,397,000	1,707	NA	NA	853	761
1890	13.1	4,779,000	1,650	NA	NA	910	823
1900	18.7	11,227,000	2,662	8,000	328,000	1,499	930
1910	35.3	28,330,000	2,853	458,300	189,000	1,919	1,646
1920	91.5	46,183,000	3,071	8,131,500	387,000 (1918 = 118,000)	8,664	5,784
1930	90.7	44,591,000	2,080	23,034,700	247,000 (1925 = 937,000)	4,013	3,500
1940	100.0	66,983,000	2,457	27,465,800	330,000 (1933 = 93,000)	4,030	7,433
1950	286.5	96,836,000	3,075	40,339,000	603,000 (1944 = 142,000)	9,997	8,954
1960	506.5	99,282,000	4,314	61,682,300	1,952,000	19,659	15,093
1970	1,016.0	131,514,000	4,200	89,279,800	1,434,000	42,681	40,356
1980	2,819.5	111,835,000	6,600	121,601,000	1,292,000	220,626	244,871
1990	5,764.9	98,906,000	7,933	143,550,000	1,193,000	394,030	485,453
1998	8,511.0	107,600,000	9,761	129,749,000[f]	1,617,000	682,100	911,900
2000	9,256.1	108,800,000[g]	9,968	131,839,000[g]	1,535,000	695,000	1,025,000

[a]In December 1991 the Bureau of Economic Analysis of the U.S. government began featuring Gross Domestic Product rather than Gross National Product as the primary measure of U.S. production.

[b]Figure is average for 1869–1878.

[c]Figure is average for 1879–1888.

[d]Figure for 1849.

[e]Figure for 1859.

[f]Figure for 1997.

[g]Figure for 1998.

NA = Not available.

Federal Budget Outlays and Debt

Year	Defense[a]	Veterans Benefits[a]	Income Security[a]	Social Security[a]	Health and Medicare[a]	Education[a,d]	Net Interest Payments[a]	Federal Debt (dollars)
1790	14.9	4.1[b]	NA	NA	NA	NA	55.0	75,463,000[c]
1800	55.7	.6	NA	NA	NA	NA	31.3	82,976,000
1810	48.4 (1814: 79.7)	1.0	NA	NA	NA	NA	34.9	53,173,000
1820	38.4	17.6	NA	NA	NA	NA	28.1	91,016,000
1830	52.9	9.0	NA	NA	NA	NA	12.6	48,565,000
1840	54.3 (1847: 80.7)	10.7	NA	NA	NA	NA	.7	3,573,000
1850	43.8	4.7	NA	NA	NA	NA	1.0	63,453,000
1860	44.2 (1865: 88.9)	1.7	NA	NA	NA	NA	5.0	64,844,000
1870	25.7	9.2	NA	NA	NA	NA	41.7	2,436,453,000
1880	19.3	21.2	NA	NA	NA	NA	35.8	2,090,909,000
1890	20.9 (1899: 48.6)	33.6	NA	NA	NA	NA	11.4	1,222,397,000
1900	36.6	27.0	NA	NA	NA	NA	7.7	1,263,417,000
1910	45.1 (1919: 59.5)	23.2	NA	NA	NA	NA	3.1	1,146,940,000
1920	37.1	3.4	NA	NA	NA	NA	16.0	24,299,321,000
1930	25.3	6.6	NA	NA	NA	NA	19.9	16,185,310,000
1940	17.5 (1945: 89.4)	6.0	16.0	.3	.5	20.8	9.4	42,967,531,000
1950	32.2	20.3	9.6	1.8	.6	.6	11.3	256,853,000,000
1960	52.2	5.9	8.0	12.6	.9	1.0	7.5	290,525,000,000
1970	41.8	4.4	8.0	15.5	6.2	4.4	7.3	308,921,000,000
1980	22.7	3.6	14.6	20.1	9.4	5.4	8.9	909,050,000,000
1990	23.9	2.3	11.7	19.8	12.4	3.1	14.7	3,266,073,000,000
1998	16.2	2.5	14.1	22.9	19.6	3.3	14.7	5,555,565,000,000
2000	16.2	2.6	14.0	22.7	19.9	3.5	12.3	5,685,181,000,000

[a]Figures represent percentage of total federal spending for each category. Not included are transportation, commerce, housing, and various other categories.

[b]1789–1791 figure.

[c]1791 figure.

[d]Includes training, employment, and social services.

NA = Not available.

Presidential Elections

Year	Number of States	Candidates	Parties	Popular Vote	% of Popular Vote	Electoral Vote	% Voter Participation[a]
1789	10	**George Washington**	No party designations			69	
		John Adams				34	
		Other candidates				35	
1792	15	**George Washington**	No party designations			132	
		John Adams				77	
		George Clinton				50	
		Other candidates				5	
1796	16	**John Adams**	Federalist			71	
		Thomas Jefferson	Democratic-Republican			68	
		Thomas Pinckney	Federalist			59	
		Aaron Burr	Democratic-Republican			30	
		Other candidates				48	
1800	16	**Thomas Jefferson**	Democratic-Republican			73	
		Aaron Burr	Democratic-Republican			73	
		John Adams	Federalist			65	
		Charles C. Pinckney	Federalist			64	
		John Jay	Federalist			1	
1804	17	**Thomas Jefferson**	Democratic-Republican			162	
		Charles C. Pinckney	Federalist			14	
1808	17	**James Madison**	Democratic-Republican			122	
		Charles C. Pinckney	Federalist			47	
		George Clinton	Democratic-Republican			6	
1812	18	**James Madison**	Democratic-Republican			128	
		DeWitt Clinton	Federalist			89	
1816	19	**James Monroe**	Democratic-Republican			183	
		Rufus King	Federalist			34	
1820	24	**James Monroe**	Democratic-Republican			231	
		John Quincy Adams	Independent Republican			1	

Presidential Elections (continued)

Year	Number of States	Candidates	Parties	Popular Vote	% of Popular Vote	Electoral Vote	% Voter Participation[a]
1824	24	**John Quincy Adams**	Democratic-Republican	108,740	30.5	84	26.9
		Andrew Jackson	Democratic-Republican	153,544	43.1	99	
		Henry Clay	Democratic-Republican	47,136	13.2	37	
		William H. Crawford	Democratic-Republican	46,618	13.1	41	
1828	24	**Andrew Jackson**	Democratic	647,286	56.0	178	57.6
		John Quincy Adams	National Republican	508,064	44.0	83	
1832	24	**Andrew Jackson**	Democratic	701,780	54.2	219	55.4
		Henry Clay	National Republican	484,205	37.4	49	
		Other candidates		107,988	8.0	18	
1836	26	**Martin Van Buren**	Democratic	764,176	50.8	170	57.8
		William H. Harrison	Whig	550,816	36.6	73	
		Hugh L. White	Whig	146,107	9.7	26	
1840	26	**William H. Harrison**	Whig	1,274,624	53.1	234	80.2
		Martin Van Buren	Democratic	1,127,781	46.9	60	
1844	26	**James K. Polk**	Democratic	1,338,464	49.6	170	78.9
		Henry Clay	Whig	1,300,097	48.1	105	
		James G. Birney	Liberty	62,300	2.3		
1848	30	**Zachary Taylor**	Whig	1,360,967	47.4	163	72.7
		Lewis Cass	Democratic	1,222,342	42.5	127	
		Martin Van Buren	Free Soil	291,263	10.1		
1852	31	**Franklin Pierce**	Democratic	1,601,117	50.9	254	69.6
		Winfield Scott	Whig	1,385,453	44.1	42	
		John P. Hale	Free Soil	155,825	5.0		
1856	31	**James Buchanan**	Democratic	1,832,955	45.3	174	78.9
		John C. Frémont	Republican	1,339,932	33.1	114	
		Millard Fillmore	American	871,731	21.6	8	
1860	33	**Abraham Lincoln**	Republican	1,865,593	39.8	180	81.2
		Stephen A. Douglas	Democratic	1,382,713	29.5	12	
		John C. Breckinridge	Democratic	848,356	18.1	72	
		John Bell	Constitutional Union	592,906	12.6	39	
1864	36	**Abraham Lincoln**	Republican	2,206,938	55.0	212	73.8
		George B. McClellan	Democratic	1,803,787	45.0	21	
1868	37	**Ulysses S. Grant**	Republican	3,013,421	52.7	214	78.1
		Horatio Seymour	Democratic	2,706,829	47.3	80	

Presidential Elections (continued)

Year	Number of States	Candidates	Parties	Popular Vote	% of Popular Vote	Electoral Vote	% Voter Participation[a]
1872	37	**Ulysses S. Grant**	Republican	3,596,745	55.6	286	71.3
		Horace Greeley	Democratic	2,843,446	43.9	[b]	
1876	38	**Rutherford B. Hayes**	Republican	4,036,572	48.0	185	81.8
		Samuel J. Tilden	Democratic	4,284,020	51.0	184	
1880	38	**James A. Garfield**	Republican	4,453,295	48.5	214	79.4
		Winfield S. Hancock	Democratic	4,414,082	48.1	155	
		James B. Weaver	Greenback-Labor	308,578	3.4		
1884	38	**Grover Cleveland**	Democratic	4,879,507	48.5	219	77.5
		James G. Blaine	Republican	4,850,293	48.2	182	
		Benjamin F. Butler	Greenback-Labor	175,370	1.8		
		John P. St. John	Prohibition	150,369	1.5		
1888	38	**Benjamin Harrison**	Republican	5,447,129	47.9	233	79.3
		Grover Cleveland	Democratic	5,537,857	48.6	168	
		Clinton B. Fisk	Prohibition	249,506	2.2		
		Anson J. Streeter	Union Labor	146,935	1.3		
1892	44	**Grover Cleveland**	Democratic	5,555,426	46.1	277	74.7
		Benjamin Harrison	Republican	5,182,690	43.0	145	
		James B. Weaver	People's	1,029,846	8.5	22	
		John Bidwell	Prohibition	264,133	2.2		
1896	45	**William McKinley**	Republican	7,102,246	51.1	271	79.3
		William J. Bryan	Democratic	6,492,559	47.7	176	
1900	45	**William McKinley**	Republican	7,218,491	51.7	292	73.2
		William J. Bryan	Democratic; Populist	6,356,734	45.5	155	
		John C. Wooley	Prohibition	208,914	1.5		
1904	45	**Theodore Roosevelt**	Republican	7,628,461	57.4	336	65.2
		Alton B. Parker	Democratic	5,084,223	37.6	140	
		Eugene V. Debs	Socialist	402,283	3.0		
		Silas C. Swallow	Prohibition	258,536	1.9		
1908	46	**William H. Taft**	Republican	7,675,320	51.6	321	65.4
		William J. Bryan	Democratic	6,412,294	43.1	162	
		Eugene V. Debs	Socialist	420,793	2.8		
		Eugene W. Chafin	Prohibition	253,840	1.7		
1912	48	**Woodrow Wilson**	Democratic	6,296,547	41.9	435	58.8
		Theodore Roosevelt	Progressive	4,118,571	27.4	88	
		William H. Taft	Republican	3,486,720	23.2	8	
		Eugene V. Debs	Socialist	900,672	6.0		
		Eugene W. Chafin	Prohibition	206,275	1.4		
1916	48	**Woodrow Wilson**	Democratic	9,127,695	49.4	277	61.6
		Charles E. Hughes	Republican	8,533,507	46.2	254	

Presidential Elections (continued)

Year	Number of States	Candidates	Parties	Popular Vote	% of Popular Vote	Electoral Vote	% Voter Participation[a]
		A. L. Benson	Socialist	585,113	3.2		
		J. Frank Hanly	Prohibition	220,506	1.2		
1920	48	**Warren G. Harding**	Republican	16,143,407	60.4	404	49.2
		James M. Cox	Democratic	9,130,328	34.2	127	
		Eugene V. Debs	Socialist	919,799	3.4		
		P. P. Christensen	Farmer-Labor	265,411	1.0		
1924	48	**Calvin Coolidge**	Republican	15,718,211	54.0	382	48.9
		John W. Davis	Democratic	8,385,283	28.8	136	
		Robert M. La Follette	Progressive	4,831,289	16.6	13	
1928	48	**Herbert C. Hoover**	Republican	21,391,993	58.2	444	56.9
		Alfred E. Smith	Democratic	15,016,169	40.9	87	
1932	48	**Franklin D. Roosevelt**	Democratic	22,809,638	57.4	472	56.9
		Herbert C. Hoover	Republican	15,758,901	39.7	59	
		Norman Thomas	Socialist	881,951	2.2		
1936	48	**Franklin D. Roosevelt**	Democratic	27,752,869	60.8	523	61.0
		Alfred M. Landon	Republican	16,674,665	36.5	8	
		William Lemke	Union	882,479	1.9		
1940	48	**Franklin D. Roosevelt**	Democratic	27,307,819	54.8	449	62.5
		Wendell L. Wilkie	Republican	22,321,018	44.8	82	
1944	48	**Franklin D. Roosevelt**	Democratic	25,606,585	53.5	432	55.9
		Thomas E. Dewey	Republican	22,014,745	46.0	99	
1948	48	**Harry S Truman**	Democratic	24,179,345	49.6	303	53.0
		Thomas E. Dewey	Republican	21,991,291	45.1	189	
		J. Strom Thurmond	States' Rights	1,176,125	2.4	39	
		Henry A. Wallace	Progressive	1,157,326	2.4		
1952	48	**Dwight D. Eisenhower**	Republican	33,936,234	55.1	442	63.3
		Adlai E. Stevenson	Democratic	27,314,992	44.4	89	
1956	48	**Dwight D. Eisenhower**	Republican	35,590,472	57.6	457	60.6
		Adlai E. Stevenson	Democratic	26,022,752	42.1	73	
1960	50	**John F. Kennedy**	Democratic	34,226,731	49.7	303	62.8
		Richard M. Nixon	Republican	34,108,157	49.5	219	
1964	50	**Lyndon B. Johnson**	Democratic	43,129,566	61.1	486	61.7
		Barry M. Goldwater	Republican	27,178,188	38.5	52	
1968	50	**Richard M. Nixon**	Republican	31,785,480	43.4	301	60.6
		Hubert H. Humphrey	Democratic	31,275,166	42.7	191	
		George C. Wallace	American Independent	9,906,473	13.5	46	
1972	50	**Richard M. Nixon**	Republican	47,169,911	60.7	520	55.2

Presidential Elections (continued)

Year	Number of States	Candidates	Parties	Popular Vote	% of Popular Vote	Electoral Vote	% Voter Participation[a]
		George S. McGovern	Democratic	29,170,383	37.5	17	
		John G. Schmitz	American	1,099,482	1.4		
1976	50	**James E. Carter**	Democratic	40,830,763	50.1	297	53.5
		Gerald R. Ford	Republican	39,147,793	48.0	240	
1980	50	**Ronald W. Reagan**	Republican	43,904,153	50.7	489	52.6
		James E. Carter	Democratic	35,483,883	41.0	49	
		John B. Anderson	Independent	5,720,060	6.6	0	
		Ed Clark	Libertarian	921,299	1.1	0	
1984	50	**Ronald W. Reagan**	Republican	54,455,075	58.8	525	53.3
		Walter F. Mondale	Democratic	37,577,185	40.6	13	
1988	50	**George H. W. Bush**	Republican	48,886,097	53.4	426	50.1
		Michael S. Dukakis	Democratic	41,809,074	45.6	111[c]	
1992	50	**William J. Clinton**	Democratic	44,909,326	43.0	370	55.2
		George H. W. Bush	Republican	39,103,882	37.4	168	
		H. Ross Perot	Independent	19,741,048	18.9	0	
1996	50	**William J. Clinton**	Democratic	47,402,357	49.2	379	49.1
		Robert J. Dole	Republican	39,196,755	40.7	159	
		H. Ross Perot	Reform	8,085,402	8.4	0	
		Ralph Nader	Green	684,902	0.7	0	
2000	50	**George W. Bush**	Republican	50,456,002	47.87	271	51.21
		Al Gore	Democrat	50,999,897	48.38	266	
		Ralph Nader	Green	2,882,955	2.74	0	
		Patrick J. Buchanan	Reform/ Independent	448,895	.42	0	

Candidates receiving less than 1 percent of the popular vote have been omitted. Thus the percentage of popular vote given for any election year may not total 100 percent.

Before the passage of the Twelfth Amendment in 1804, the Electoral College voted for two presidential candidates; the runner-up became vice president.

Before 1824, most presidential electors were chosen by state legislatures, not by popular vote.

[a]Percent of voting-age population casting ballots.

[b]Greeley died shortly after the election; the electors supporting him then divided their votes among minor candidates.

[c]One elector from West Virginia cast her Electoral College presidential ballot for Lloyd Bentsen, the Democratic Party's vice-presidential candidate.

Presidents and Vice Presidents

1. President	**George Washington**	1789–1797	
Vice President	John Adams	1789–1797	
2. President	**John Adams**	1797–1801	
Vice President	Thomas Jefferson	1797–1801	
3. President	**Thomas Jefferson**	1801–1809	
Vice President	Aaron Burr	1801–1805	
Vice President	George Clinton	1805–1809	
4. President	**James Madison**	1809–1817	
Vice President	George Clinton	1809–1813	
Vice President	Elbridge Gerry	1813–1817	
5. President	**James Monroe**	1817–1825	
Vice President	Daniel Tompkins	1817–1825	
6. President	**John Quincy Adams**	1825–1829	
Vice President	John C. Calhoun	1825–1829	
7. President	**Andrew Jackson**	1829–1837	
Vice President	John C. Calhoun	1829–1833	
Vice President	Martin Van Buren	1833–1837	
8. President	**Martin Van Buren**	1837–1841	
Vice President	Richard M. Johnson	1837–1841	
9. President	**William H. Harrison**	1841	
Vice President	John Tyler	1841	
10. President	**John Tyler**	1841–1845	
Vice President	None		
11. President	**James K. Polk**	1845–1849	
Vice President	George M. Dallas	1845–1849	
12. President	**Zachary Taylor**	1849–1850	
Vice President	Millard Fillmore	1849–1850	
13. President	**Millard Fillmore**	1850–1853	
Vice President	None		
14. President	**Franklin Pierce**	1853–1857	
Vice President	William R. King	1853–1857	
15. President	**James Buchanan**	1857–1861	
Vice President	John C. Breckinridge	1857–1861	
16. President	**Abraham Lincoln**	1861–1865	
Vice President	Hannibal Hamlin	1861–1865	
Vice President	Andrew Johnson	1865	
17. President	**Andrew Johnson**	1865–1869	
Vice President	None		
18. President	**Ulysses S. Grant**	1869–1877	
Vice President	Schuyler Colfax	1869–1873	
Vice President	Henry Wilson	1873–1877	
19. President	**Rutherford B. Hayes**	1877–1881	
Vice President	William A. Wheeler	1877–1881	
20. President	**James A. Garfield**	1881	
Vice President	Chester A. Arthur	1881	
21. President	**Chester A. Arthur**	1881–1885	
Vice President	None		
22. President	**Grover Cleveland**	1885–1889	
Vice President	Thomas A. Hendricks	1885–1889	
23. President	**Benjamin Harrison**	1889–1893	
Vice President	Levi P. Morton	1889–1893	
24. President	**Grover Cleveland**	1893–1897	
Vice President	Adlai E. Stevenson	1893–1897	
25. President	**William McKinley**	1897–1901	
Vice President	Garret A. Hobart	1897–1901	
Vice President	Theodore Roosevelt	1901	
26. President	**Theodore Roosevelt**	1901–1909	
Vice President	Charles Fairbanks	1905–1909	
27. President	**William H. Taft**	1909–1913	
Vice President	James S. Sherman	1909–1913	
28. President	**Woodrow Wilson**	1913–1921	
Vice President	Thomas R. Marshall	1913–1921	
29. President	**Warren G. Harding**	1921–1923	
Vice President	Calvin Coolidge	1921–1923	
30. President	**Calvin Coolidge**	1923–1929	
Vice President	Charles G. Dawes	1925–1929	
31. President	**Herbert C. Hoover**	1929–1933	
Vice President	Charles Curtis	1929–1933	
32. President	**Franklin D. Roosevelt**	1933–1945	
Vice President	John N. Garner	1933–1941	
Vice President	Henry A. Wallace	1941–1945	
Vice President	Harry S Truman	1945	
33. President	**Harry S Truman**	1945–1953	
Vice President	Alben W. Barkley	1949–1953	
34. President	**Dwight D. Eisenhower**	1953–1961	
Vice President	Richard M. Nixon	1953–1961	
35. President	**John F. Kennedy**	1961–1963	
Vice President	Lyndon B. Johnson	1961–1963	
36. President	**Lyndon B. Johnson**	1963–1969	
Vice President	Hubert H. Humphrey	1965–1969	

Presidents and Vice Presidents (continued)

37. President	**Richard M. Nixon**	1969–1974
Vice President	Spiro T. Agnew	1969–1973
Vice President	Gerald R. Ford	1973–1974
38. President	**Gerald R. Ford**	1974–1977
Vice President	Nelson A. Rockefeller	1974–1977
39. President	**James E. Carter**	1977–1981
Vice President	Walter F. Mondale	1977–1981
40. President	**Ronald W. Reagan**	1981–1989
Vice President	George H. W. Bush	1981–1989
41. President	**George H. W. Bush**	1989–1993
Vice President	J. Danforth Quayle	1989–1993
42. President	**William J. Clinton**	1993–2001
Vice President	Albert Gore	1993–2001
43. President	**George W. Bush**	2001–2005
Vice President	Richard B. Cheney	2001-2005

For a complete list of Presidents, Vice Presidents, and Cabinet Members, go to http://college.hmco.com.

Party Strength in Congress

Period	Congress	House Majority Party		House Minority Party		House Others	Senate Majority Party		Senate Minority Party		Senate Others	Party of President	
1789–91	1st	Ad	38	Op	26		Ad	17	Op	9		F	Washington
1791–93	2nd	F	37	DR	33		F	16	DR	13		F	Washington
1793–95	3rd	DR	57	F	48		F	17	DR	13		F	Washington
1795–97	4th	F	54	DR	52		F	19	DR	13		F	Washington
1797–99	5th	F	58	DR	48		F	20	DR	12		F	J. Adams
1799–1801	6th	F	64	DR	42		F	19	DR	13		F	J. Adams
1801–03	7th	DR	69	F	36		DR	18	F	13		DR	Jefferson
1803–05	8th	DR	102	F	39		DR	25	F	9		DR	Jefferson
1805–07	9th	DR	116	F	25		DR	27	F	7		DR	Jefferson
1807–09	10th	DR	118	F	24		DR	28	F	6		DR	Jefferson
1809–11	11th	DR	94	F	48		DR	28	F	6		DR	Madison
1811–13	12th	DR	108	F	36		DR	30	F	6		DR	Madison
1813–15	13th	DR	112	F	68		DR	27	F	9		DR	Madison
1815–17	14th	DR	117	F	65		DR	25	F	11		DR	Madison
1817–19	15th	DR	141	F	42		DR	34	F	10		DR	Monroe
1819–21	16th	DR	156	F	27		DR	35	F	7		DR	Monroe
1821–23	17th	DR	158	F	25		DR	44	F	4		DR	Monroe
1823–25	18th	DR	187	F	26		DR	44	F	4		DR	Monroe
1825–27	19th	Ad	105	J	97		Ad	26	J	20		C	J. Q. Adams
1827–29	20th	J	119	Ad	94		J	28	Ad	20		C	J. Q. Adams
1829–31	21st	D	139	NR	74		D	26	NR	22		D	Jackson
1831–33	22nd	D	141	NR	58	14	D	25	NR	21	2	D	Jackson
1833–35	23rd	D	147	AM	53	60	D	20	NR	20	8	D	Jackson
1835–37	24th	D	145	W	98		D	27	W	25		D	Jackson
1837–39	25th	D	108	W	107	24	D	30	W	18	4	D	Van Buren
1839–41	26th	D	124	W	118		D	28	W	22		D	Van Buren
1841–43	27th	W	133	D	102	6	W	28	D	22	2	W	W. Harrison W Tyler
1843–45	28th	D	142	W	79	1	W	28	D	25	1	W	Tyler
1845–47	29th	D	143	W	77	6	D	31	W	25		D	Polk
1847–49	30th	W	115	D	108	4	D	36	W	21	1	D	Polk
1849–51	31st	D	112	W	109	9	D	35	W	25	2	W	Taylor W Fillmore
1851–53	32nd	D	140	W	88	5	D	35	W	24	3	W	Fillmore
1853–55	33rd	D	159	W	71	4	D	38	W	22	2	D	Pierce
1855–57	34th	R	108	D	83	43	D	40	R	15	5	D	Pierce
1857–59	35th	D	118	R	92	26	D	36	R	20	8	D	Buchanan
1859–61	36th	R	114	D	92	31	D	36	R	26	4	D	Buchanan
1861–63	37th	R	105	D	43	30	R	31	D	10	8	R	Lincoln
1863–65	38th	R	102	D	75	9	R	36	D	9	5	R	Lincoln
1865–67	39th	U	149	D	42		U	42	D	10		R	Lincoln R A. Johnson

Party Strength in Congress (continued)

Period	Congress	House Majority Party	House Minority Party	House Others	Senate Majority Party	Senate Minority Party	Senate Others	Party of President
1867–69	40th	R 143	D 49		R 42	D 11		R A. Johnson
1869–71	41st	R 149	D 63		R 56	D 11		R Grant
1871–73	42nd	R 134	D 104	5	R 52	D 17	5	R Grant
1873–75	43rd	R 194	D 92	14	R 49	D 19	5	R Grant
1875–77	44th	D 169	R 109	14	R 45	D 29	2	R Grant
1877–79	45th	D 153	R 140		R 39	D 36	1	R Hayes
1879–81	46th	D 149	R 130	14	D 42	R 33	1	R Hayes
1881–83	47th	D 147	R 135	11	R 37	D 37	1	R Garfield / R Arthur
1883–85	48th	D 197	R 118	10	R 38	D 36	2	R Arthur
1885–87	49th	D 183	R 140	2	R 43	D 34		D Cleveland
1887–89	50th	D 169	R 152	4	R 39	D 37		D Cleveland
1889–91	51st	R 166	D 159		R 39	D 37		R B. Harrison
1891–93	52nd	D 235	R 88	9	R 47	D 39	2	R B. Harrison
1893–95	53rd	D 218	R 127	11	D 44	R 38	3	D Cleveland
1895–97	54th	R 244	D 105	7	R 43	D 39	6	D Cleveland
1897–99	55th	R 204	D 113	40	R 47	D 34	7	R McKinley
1899–1901	56th	R 185	D 163	9	R 53	D 26	8	R McKinley
1901–03	57th	R 197	D 151	9	R 55	D 31	4	R McKinley / R T. Roosevelt
1903–05	58th	R 208	D 178		R 57	D 33		R T. Roosevelt
1905–07	59th	R 250	D 136		R 57	D 33		R T. Roosevelt
1907–09	60th	R 222	D 164		R 61	D 31		R T. Roosevelt
1909–11	61st	R 219	D 172		R 61	D 32		R Taft
1911–13	62nd	D 228	R 161	1	R 51	D 41		R Taft
1913–15	63rd	D 291	R 127	17	D 51	R 44	1	D Wilson
1915–17	64th	D 230	R 196	9	D 56	R 40		D Wilson
1917–19	65th	D 216	R 210	6	D 53	R 42		D Wilson
1919–21	66th	R 240	D 190	3	R 49	D 47		D Wilson
1921–23	67th	R 301	D 131	1	R 59	D 37		R Harding
1923–25	68th	R 225	D 205	5	R 51	D 43	2	R Coolidge
1925–27	69th	R 247	D 183	4	R 56	D 39	1	R Coolidge
1927–29	70th	R 237	D 195	3	R 49	D 46	1	R Coolidge
1929–31	71st	R 267	D 167	1	R 56	D 39	1	R Hoover
1931–33	72nd	D 220	R 214	1	R 48	D 47	1	R Hoover
1933–35	73rd	D 310	R 117	5	D 60	R 35	1	D F. Roosevelt
1935–37	74th	D 319	R 103	10	D 69	R 25	2	D F. Roosevelt
1937–39	75th	D 331	R 89	13	D 76	R 16	4	D F. Roosevelt
1939–41	76th	D 261	R 164	4	D 69	R 23	4	D F. Roosevelt
1941–43	77th	D 268	R 162	5	D 66	R 28	2	D F. Roosevelt
1943–45	78th	D 218	R 208	4	D 58	R 37	1	D F. Roosevelt
1945–47	79th	D 242	R 190	2	D 56	R 38	1	D Truman
1947–49	80th	R 245	D 188	1	R 51	D 45		D Truman
1949–51	81st	D 263	R 171	1	D 54	R 42		D Truman

Party Strength in Congress (continued)

Period	Congress	House Majority Party		House Minority Party		Others	Senate Majority Party		Senate Minority Party		Others	Party of President	
1951–53	82nd	D	234	R	199	1	D	49	R	47		D	Truman
1953–55	83rd	R	221	D	211	1	R	48	D	47	1	R	Eisenhower
1955–57	84th	D	232	R	203		D	48	R	47	1	R	Eisenhower
1957–59	85th	D	233	R	200		D	49	R	47		R	Eisenhower
1959–61	86th	D	284	R	153		D	65	R	35		R	Eisenhower
1961–63	87th	D	263	R	174		D	65	R	35		D	Kennedy
1963–65	88th	D	258	R	117		D	67	R	33		D	Kennedy
												D	L. Johnson
1965–67	89th	D	295	R	140		D	68	R	32		D	L. Johnson
1967–69	90th	D	246	R	187		D	64	R	36		D	L. Johnson
1969–71	91st	D	245	R	189		D	57	R	43		R	Nixon
1971–73	92nd	D	254	R	180		D	54	R	44	2	R	Nixon
1973–75	93rd	D	239	R	192	1	D	56	R	42	2	R	Nixon
1975–77	94th	D	291	R	144		D	60	R	37	3	R	Ford
1977–79	95th	D	292	R	143		D	61	R	38	1	D	Carter
1979–81	96th	D	276	R	157		D	58	R	41	1	D	Carter
1981–83	97th	D	243	R	192		R	53	D	46	1	R	Reagan
1983–85	98th	D	269	R	166		R	54	D	46		R	Reagan
1985–87	99th	D	253	R	182		R	53	D	47		R	Reagan
1987–89	100th	D	258	R	177		D	55	R	45		R	Reagan
1989–91	101st	D	259	R	174		D	55	R	45		R	Bush
1991–93	102nd	D	267	R	167	1	D	56	R	44		R	Bush
1993–95	103rd	D	258	R	176	1	D	57	R	43		D	Clinton
1995–97	104th	R	230	D	204	1	R	52	D	48		D	Clinton
1997–99	105th	R	227	D	207	1	R	55	D	45		D	Clinton
1999–2001	106th	R	223	D	211	1	R	55	D	45		D	Clinton
2001–03	107th	R	221	D	212	2	D	50*	R	49	1	R	G. W. Bush
2003–05	108th	R	229	D	205	1	R	51	D	48	1	R	G. W. Bush

AD = Administration; AM = Anti-Masonic; C = Coalition; D = Democratic; DR = Democratic-Republican; F = Federalist; J = Jacksonian; NR = National Republican; Op = Opposition; R = Republican; U = Unionist; W = Whig. Figures are for the beginning of the first session of each Congress, except the 93rd, which are for the beginning of the second session.

*Note: From January 3 to January 20, 2001, with the Senate divided evenly between the two parties, the Democrats held the majority due to the deciding vote of outgoing Democratic Vice President Al Gore. Senator Thomas A. Daschle served as majority leader at that time. Beginning on January 20, 2001, Republican Vice President Richard Cheney held the deciding vote, giving the majority to the Republicans. Senator Trent Lott resumed his position as majority leader on that date. On May 24, 2001, Senator James Jeffords of Vermont announced his switch from Republican to Independent status, effective June 6, 2001. Jeffords announced that he would caucus with the Democrats, giving the Democrats a one-seat advantage, changing control of the Senate from the Republicans back to the Democrats. Senator Thomas A. Daschle again became majority leader on June 6, 2001. Senator Paul D. Wellstone (D-MN) died on October 25, 2002, and Independent Dean Barkley was appointed to fill the vacancy. The November 5, 2002 election brought to office elected Senator James Talent (R-MO), replacing appointed Senator Jean Carnahan (D-MO), shifting balance once again to the Republicans—but no reorganization was completed at that time since the Senate was out of session. (Source: "Party Division in the Senate, 1789–Present" on http://www.senate.gov)

Justices of the Supreme Court

	Term of Service	Years of Service	Life Span		Term of Service	Years of Service	Life Span
John Jay	1789–1795	5	1745–1829	William B. Woods	1880–1887	7	1824–1887
John Rutledge	1789–1791	1	1739–1800	Stanley Mathews	1881–1889	7	1824–1889
William Cushing	1789–1810	20	1732–1810	Horace Gray	1882–1902	20	1828–1902
James Wilson	1789–1798	8	1742–1798	Samuel Blatchford	1882–1893	11	1820–1893
John Blair	1789–1796	6	1732–1800	Lucius Q. C. Lamar	1888–1893	5	1825–1893
Robert H. Harrison	1789–1790	—	1745–1790	*Melville W. Fuller*	1888–1910	21	1833–1910
James Iredell	1790–1799	9	1951–1799	David J. Brewer	1890–1910	20	1837–1910
Thomas Johnson	1791–1793	1	1732–1819	Henry B. Brown	1890–1906	16	1836–1913
William Paterson	1793–1806	13	1745–1806	George Shiras, Jr.	1892–1903	10	1832–1924
*John Rutledge**	1795	—	1739–1800	Howell E. Jackson	1893–1895	2	1832–1895
Samuel Chase	1796–1811	15	1741–1811	dward D. White	1894–1910	16	1845–1921
Oliver Ellsworth	1796–1800	4	1745–1807	Rufus W. Peckham	1895–1909	14	1838–1909
Bushrod Washington	1798–1829	31	1762–1829	Joseph McKenna	1898–1925	26	1843–1926
Alfred Moore	1799–1804	4	1755–1810	Oliver W. Holmes	1902–1932	30	1841–1935
John Marshall	1801–1835	34	1755–1835	William D. Day	1903–1922	19	1849–1923
William Johnson	1804–1834	30	1771–1834	William H. Moody	1906–1910	3	1853–1917
H. Brockholst Livingston	1806–1823	16	1757–1823	Horace H. Lurton	1910–1914	4	1844–1914
Thomas Todd	1807–1826	18	1765–1826	Charles E. Hughes	1910–1916	5	1862–1948
Joseph Story	1811–1845	33	1779–1845	Willis Van Devanter	1911–1937	26	1859–1941
Gabriel Duval	1811–1835	24	1752–1844	Joseph R. Lamar	1911–1916	5	1857–1916
Smith Thompson	1823–1843	20	1768–1843	*Edward D. White*	1910–1921	11	1845–1921
Robert Trimble	1826–1828	2	1777–1828	Mahlon Pitney	1912–1922	10	1858–1924
John McLean	1829–1861	32	1785–1861	James C. McReynolds	1914–1941	26	1862–1946
Henry Baldwin	1830–1844	14	1780–1844	Louis D. Brandeis	1916–1939	22	1856–1941
James M. Wayne	1835–1867	32	1790–1867	John H. Clarke	1916–1922	6	1857–1945
Roger B. Taney	1836–1864	28	1777–1864	*William H. Taft*	1921–1930	8	1857–1930
Philip P. Barbour	1836–1841	4	1783–1841	George Sutherland	1922–1938	15	1862–1942
John Catron	1837–1865	28	1786–1865	Pierce Butler	1922–1939	16	1866–1939
John McKinley	1837–1852	15	1780–1852	Edward T. Sanford	1923–1930	7	1865–1930
Peter V. Daniel	1841–1860	19	1784–1860	Harlan F. Stone	1925–1941	16	1872–1946
Samuel Nelson	1845–1872	27	1792–1873	*Charles E. Hughes*	1930–1941	11	1862–1948
Levi Woodbury	1845–1851	5	1789–1851	Owen J. Roberts	1930–1945	15	1875–1955
Robert C. Grier	1846–1870	23	1794–1870	Benjamin N. Cardozo	1932–1938	6	1870–1938
Benjamin R. Curtis	1851–1857	6	1809–1874	Hugo L. Black	1937–1971	34	1886–1971
John A. Campbell	1853–1861	8	1811–1889	Stanley F. Reed	1938–1957	19	1884–1980
Nathan Clifford	1858–1881	23	1803–1881	Felix Frankfurter	1939–1962	23	1882–1965
Noah H. Swayne	1862–1881	18	1804–1884	William O. Douglas	1939–1975	36	1898–1980
Samuel F. Miller	1862–1890	28	1816–1890	Frank Murphy	1940–1949	9	1890–1949
David Davis	1862–1877	14	1815–1886	*Harlan F. Stone*	1941–1946	5	1872–1946
Stephen J. Field	1863–1897	34	1816–1899	James F. Byrnes	1941–1942	1	1879–1972
Salmon P. Chase	1864–1873	8	1808–1873	Robert H. Jackson	1941–1954	13	1892–1954
William Strong	1870–1880	10	1808–1895	Wiley B. Rutledge	1943–1949	6	1894–1949
Joseph P. Bradley	1870–1892	22	1813–1892	Harold H. Burton	1945–1958	13	1888–1964
Ward Hunt	1873–1882	9	1810–1886	*Fred M. Vinson*	1946–1953	7	1890–1953
Morrison R. Waite	1874–1888	14	1816–1888	Tom C. Clark	1949–1967	18	1899–1977
John M. Harlan	1877–1911	34	1833–1911	Sherman Minton	1949–1956	7	1890–1965

Justices of the Supreme Court (continued)

	Term of Service	Years of Service	Life Span		Term of Service	Years of Service	Life Span
Earl Warren	1953–1969	16	1891–1974	Lewis F. Powell, Jr.	1972–1987	15	1907–1998
John Marshall Harlan	1955–1971	16	1899–1971	*William H. Rehnquist*	1972–	—	1924–
William J. Brennan, Jr.	1956–1990	34	1906–1977	John P. Stevens III	1975–	—	1920–
Charles E. Whittaker	1957–1962	5	1901–1973	Sandra Day O'Connor	1981–	—	1930–
Potter Stewart	1958–1981	23	1915–1985	Antonin Scalia	1986–	—	1936–
Byron R. White	1962–1993	31	1917–	Anthony M. Kennedy	1988–	—	1936–
Arthur J. Goldberg	1962–1965	3	1908–1990	David H. Souter	1990–	—	1939–
Abe Fortas	1965–1969	4	1910–1982	Clarence Thomas	1991–	—	1948–
Thurgood Marshall	1967–1991	24	1908–1993	Ruth Bader Ginsburg	1993–	—	1933–
Warren C. Burger	1969–1986	17	1907–1995	Stephen Breyer	1994–	—	1938–
Harry A. Blackmun	1970–1994	24	1908–1998				

Note: Chief justices are in italics.

*Appointed and served one term, but not confirmed by the Senate.

INDEX

AAA, *see* Agricultural Adjustment Act (AAA)
A&P stores, 500
Abd al-Rahman (slave), 91
Abenaki Indians, 28, 70, 83
Abendroth Bros. company, 598(illus.)
Abolition and abolitionism, 277–281, 395; northern emancipation and, 172; in Old Northwest, 180; Quakers and, 196; women and, 278(illus.), 280–281, 339; international antislavery movement and, 279; factions in, 280; 1844 election and, 294; failures of, 322; southern slavery and, 330; non-slaveholding westerners on, 349; Slave Power and, 359; violence and, 363; Kansas-Nebraska Act and, 367; John Brown and, 370, 374; *Dred Scott* decision and, 371–372, 373
Abolition of Negro Slavery (Dew), 330
Aborigines (Australia), 466
Abortion and abortion rights, 314, 530, 593, 865, 892, 894
Abraham Lincoln Battalion, 724
Absalom, Absalom! (Faulkner), 337
Academies: women's education in, 170
Acadia, *see* Nova Scotia (Acadia)
Acadians: as Louisiana Cajuns, 121
Accommodation: by Indians, 264
Accommodation policy: of Booker T. Washington, 580–581
Acheson, Dean, 783
Acid rain, 701
ACLU, *see* American Civil Liberties Union (ACLU)
Acoma pueblo, 35, 35(illus.)
Activism: Townshend Act protests and, 133; African American, 321, 552–553, 861; in West, 700; in civil rights movement, 828; Mexican American and Chicano, 862–863; Indian, 863–864, 863(illus.); environmental, 880–881. *See also* specific groups and issues
Act of Religious Toleration (Maryland, 1649), 46
Act of Union (1800, Britain), 297
Adams, Abigail, 159, 170–171, 206
Adams, Charles Francis, 411
Adams, Henry, 559, 599
Adams, John, 116, 131, 205(illus.); Boston Massacre and, 134; on Boston Tea Party, 137; at First Continental Congress, 143; Continental Army and, 152; Declaration of Independence and, 153–154; Treaty of Paris and, 162; as vice president, 196; 1796 election and, 205; political dissent and, 206–208, 213; Jefferson and, 217; 1800 election and, 224(map)
Adams, John Quincy, 241, 242 (illus.); War of 1812 and, 235; Monroe Doctrine and, 243; on gag rule, 280; 1824 election and, 282–283, 282(map); U.S. boundaries under, 293; on Mexican War, 358; on Cuba, 366

Adams, Samuel, 134–135, 170; Tea Act and, 136; at First Continental Congress, 143; as Antifederalist, 188
Adamson Act (1916), 591
Adams-Onís (Transcontinental) Treaty, 243
Addams, Jane, 529, 568, 623; woman suffrage and, 582; anti-imperialism of, 609; as antiwar advocate, 627, 639, 714; ACLU and, 649
Adding machines, 486, 489
Adkins v. Children's Hospital, 653
Administration: colonial, 81–82, 84, 108
Adolescence, 532. *See also* Teenagers; Youth
Adoptions: by gay couples, 942
Advanced Research Projects Agency (ARPA), 948
Advertising, 500–502, 500(illus.); of consumption rituals, 104(illus.); in 1920s, 652, 658; on radio, 658; guilt in, 663, 664(illus.); in Second World War, 748; on television, 815–816
Advertising Council: propaganda from, 789
Aerospace industry: in Cold War, 813
AFDC, *see* Aid to Families with Dependent Children (AFDC)
Affirmative action, 864; Bakke decision and, 882–883
Affluence: industrialization and, 496–497. *See also* Prosperity; Wealth and wealthy
Afghanistan: Soviets and, 861, 883–884, 900; U.S. and, 900; military intervention in, 919; bombing of Taliban and Al Qaeda in, 935
AFL, *see* American Federation of Labor (AFL)
Africa: human origins in, 5; in 1400, 11(map); agriculture in, 12; Portuguese in, 17–18; navigation around, 18, 21(illus.); slave origins in, 89, 90(map); black emigration to, 322, 580; cultural influences of, 342; American missionaries in, 544; imperialism in, 597; Second World War in, 742; new nations in, 787; Nixon and, 872; AIDS in, 944. *See also* African Americans; Slaves and slavery; West Africa
African Americans, 72, 85; task system and, 79–80; in North, 81; families of, 106, 344–345; resistance by, 107; as Baptists, 112; in Revolution, 148, 157, 158(illus.); Sierra Leone and, 149; redcoats joined by, 160; voting by, 171, 321; by end of 18th century, 208, 211–212, 211(map); at Battle of New Orleans, 234(illus.); after War of 1812, 236; unions and, 261, 492, 494; movement of free people, 263; Seminoles and, 268; at revivals, 273; as abolitionists, 279; in California gold rush, 304; stereotypes of, 307, 308(illus.); free, 319–322; population of, 319–322, 815; in

middle class, 321, 809; newspapers of, 321; culture of, 321–322, 520; U.S.-born population of, 342; citizenship of, 354; *Dred Scott* decision and, 371–372, 373; in Civil War, 382, 395, 399, 400, 402–403, 402(illus.); emancipation of slaves and, 397; draft riots and, 408, 408(illus.); Decoration Day and, 420; leaders after Civil War, 425; Fifteenth Amendment and, 436; southern Republican Party and, 436–438; officeholding by, 437, 439; "Negro Rule" myth and, 439; Klan and, 440–441; 1876 election and, 446–447; as exodusters, 462; in West, 462; in tobacco production, 485(illus.); migration by, 513–515, 623, 638, 746; occupational mobility and, 519; segregation and, 520, 551–552, 578; in urban borderlands, 520; urban violence against, 525; women and, 529, 552–553, 582–583, 637, 665, 866; vaudeville and, 537; as missionaries, 544; violence against, 550, 551(illus.); disfranchisement of, 550–551; Jim Crow and, 552; Farmers' Alliance movement and, 556, 557; organizations of, 570; southern Progressive politics and, 573; all-black colleges for, 578; Booker T. Washington, 580–581; in Progressive era, 580–582; Niagara movement and, 581; Du Bois, 581–582; in Spanish-American War, 609; First World War and, 629–630, 642–643; Red Summer (1919) and, 642; militancy of, 642–643; Great Migration of, 659; Marcus Garvey and, 659–661; nationalist movements of, 659–661; Harlem Renaissance and, 673; jazz and, 673; in Great Depression, 682, 690; in government positions, 694; radio and, 702; 1936 Olympic Games and, 703; Eleanor Roosevelt and, 706, 707; Scottsboro Boys and, 706, 707(illus.); Second World War and, 741, 745–746, 754–755, 755(illus.), 756–757; as Tuskegee Airmen, 755, 755(illus.); after Second World War, 799, 802–803; 1948 election and, 804; civil rights movement and, 808–812, 833–836; on Supreme Court, 809; in Chicago and Detroit, 810; television and, 816; lunch counter sit-ins and, 826(illus.), 827–828; poverty among, 841(illus.); in Vietnam, 844; protest by, 846; Afro-American culture of, 861; employment of, 896; in 1980s, 906; Korean groceries and, 909; in Los Angeles, 921; 2000 election and, 934; children born outside marriage, 943. *See also* Abolition and abolitionism; Free blacks; Freedpeople (Civil War); Indentured servants; People of color; Race and racism; Slaves and slavery
African Methodist Episcopal (AME) Church, 173, 320, 320(illus.), 425, 520, 583; free blacks in, 335

181–182; exclusion from representation, 186; "civilizing" of, 208–210, 265–266; at end of 18th century, 208–211; removal of, 220, 263–264; resistance by, 225–226; War of 1812 and, 232, 233, 235–236; in Battle of the Thames, 234; suppression of, 263; assimilation and, 264–265, 458, 460; conflicts among migrating groups, 268; Jackson and, 283–284; reparations to, 351; in Civil War, 385–386, 408–409; wars against, 408–409; Sand Creek Massacre of, 409, 457; on Plains, 452; subsistence cultures of, 453–454; salmon and, 454, 455; buffalo and, 454–455; organizations of, 455–456, 570; territorial treaties and, 456; reservation policy and, 456–457; clothing of, 456(illus.); Indian wars and resistance of, 457; Indian policy and, 457–458, 700; art of, 457(illus.); Dawes Severalty Act and, 458, 459–460; sexual division of labor, 458; Ghost Dance and, 458–459; Wounded Knee massacre of, 459; landholdings of, 459–460; occupational mobility and, 519; in Progressive era, 582; in First World War, 629(illus.); in 1920s, 656; New Deal and, 700, 701(illus.); after Second World War, 802–803, 824(illus.); population of, 815; poverty among, 823; termination program for, 824; activism of, 863–864; Red Power movement and, 863(illus.), see specific groups
Americanization, 717; of Philippines, 610–611; of British culture, 617–618. *See also* Assimilation
American League, 534
American Legion, 641–642, 729
American Library Association, 631
American Medical Association: on national health insurance, 804
American Missionary Association, 425
American Museum, 308
American Olympic Committee (AOC), 703
American Party, *see* Know-Nothing (American) Party
American Peace Commission, 644
American Peace Society, 274
American Protestant Magazine: on alcohol use, 276
American Psychiatric Association: on homosexuality, 867
American Railway Union, 494, 560, 572
American Relief Administration, 713
American Renaissance, 302
American Revolution, 141(illus.), 150–154; British and Americans in, 142–143; backcountry migration and, 145; Indians and, 146; patriots and loyalists in, 147; neutral citizens in, 148; nations created through, 149; in North, 154–157, 154(map); Campaign of 1777 in, 155(map); army and home life in, 157–159; disease in, 158–159, 159(illus.); in South, 159–162, 160(map); control of seas in, 160; costs of, 162; Treaty of Paris after, 162; use of term and legacy of, 163; slave manumission after, 172

American Samoa, 597
"American Scholar, The" (Emerson), 302
American Society for the Promotion of Temperance, 275
American Sugar Refining Company, 504, 545
American Sunday School Union, 274
Americans with Disabilities Act (ADA, 1990), 914, 915
American System: of Clay, 283, 285
American system of manufacturing, 255, 256
American Tin Plate Company, 504
American Tobacco Company, 485, 502
American Union Against Militarism, 627
American University (Beirut), 544
American Woman Suffrage Association (AWSA), 553
Amity and Commerce, Treaty of, 157
Amnesty Act (1872), 443
Amusement parks, 533(illus.)
Anaconda Copper Company, 460
Anaconda plan, 384, 404(map)
Anacostia Flats: Bonus Army at, 686
Anarchism, 641; Haymarket Riot and, 493; UNIA and, 661; Sacco and Vanzetti case and, 668
Anasazi people, 6
Anderson, Marian, 706
Anderson, Mary, 496, 746
Andes Mountains, 5
Randolph, John: War of 1812 and, 231
Andros, Edmund, 82, 82(illus.)
Anglican Church, *see* Church of England
Anglo-African, 397
Anglo-American colonies, 62(map), 70. *See also* Colonies and colonization; England (Britain); specific colonies
Anglo-American relations, 203, 617–618; in 1830s and 1840s, 290; U.S. neutrality and, 625
Anglo-Americans: religious conflicts in settlements of, 33; stratification of, 88; assimilation into culture of, 93; families of, 105; politics and, 108–110
Anglo-Dutch wars: of 1672, 61
Anglos: in Texas, 262–263; Tejanos and, 318; White Hats and, 555–556
Angola, 76, 872
Animals: in Columbian Exchange, 24, 28
Annan, Kofi, 944
Annapolis Convention, 184, 197
Annexation: of Texas, 290, 291; Hawai'i and, 365, 604–605, 605(illus.), 609; of Cuba, 366; by cities, 512–513; of Virgin Islands, 602; Samoa and, 609; of Wake Island, 609; suburbs and, 662
Antebellum period, 327–332; free southerners in, 332–339; slavery in, 339–350; slaveholder-nonslaveholder conflict in, 349–350
Anthony, Susan B., 422, 431, 553
Anti-abortion movement, 891, 905
Anti-Ballistic Missile Treaty (1972), 934
Anti-Bolshevism: of Wilson, 643–644
Anti-Bookerites, 581
Anti-Catholicism, 318, 675
Anti-Comintern Pact, 724

Anticommunism: in 1950s, 799; in Cold War, 806–808; Reagan Doctrine and, 900; in U.S. foreign policy, 900
Antietam, Battle of, 388, 388(illus.), 398
Antifederalists, 165, 187–188, 204
Anti-German attitudes: in First World War, 625; vigilantism and, 639–640
Antiglobalization, 925–926, 925(illus.)
Antigua: anti-Stamp Act protests in, 129
Anti-imperialism, 602, 609–610
Anti-Imperialist League, 610
Anti-Klan law (1871), 441, 443
Antilynching legislation, 654, 706, 804, 809
Anti Masonic Almanac, 276
Antimasonry, 273, 276–277, 277(illus.); 1832 election and, 286
Antiradicalism: of Red Scare (1919), 641–642
Anti-Saloon League, 576
Antisegregation legislation, 809
Anti-Semitism: Brandeis and, 591; of Father Coughlin, 693; 1936 Berlin Olympics and, 703; of Hitler, 723–724, 724(illus.); U.S. immigration restrictions and, 725–726. *See also* Jews and Judaism
Anti-Slavery Convention (1835), 280
Antislavery movement, 278–281; international, 279; riots and, 309; Republican Party and, 368. *See also* Abolition and abolitionism; Slaves and slavery
Antitrust laws, 505–506, 586, 635, 648, 717
Antiwar coalition: First World War and, 627
Antiwar protests: in Civil War, 407–408; First World War and, 622, 627, 628, 628(illus.), 639, 640; in Vietnam War, 849–850, 868; 1968 Democratic National Convention and, 854; Iraq and, 937
ANZUS Treaty, 783
Apache Indians, 105, 409
Apartheid, 872, 910–911
Apollo 8: lunar orbit of, 855–856
Appalachian Mountains region: land in, 109–110; settlements in, 119(map); settlement west of, 261; migrants from, 749, 823
Appeal courts, 195
Appeal . . . to the Colored Citizens (Walker), 278
Appeasement policy: toward Nazi Germany, 724, 725
Appleton, Nathan, 229
Appliances: electric, 653; in 1950s, 816; housework and, 817(illus.)
Appomattox Court House: Lee's surrender at, 414
Apportionment: in Congress, 185–186
Appropriation bills: originating body for, 185
Appropriation rights, 465, 467
Arabic (ship), 626–627
Arab-Israeli conflicts, 791; in 1948, 872; Six-Day War (1967), 872; Yom Kippur War (1973) and, 872. *See also* Israeli-Palestinian conflict

Arab world: Israel and, 791; OPEC members from, 873. *See also* Arab-Israeli conflicts
Arafat, Yasir, 904, 927
Aragon, Rafael, 319(illus.)
Arapaho Indians, 408, 452
Arbella (ship), 51
Arbenz Guzmán, Jacobo, 790–791
Arbuckle, Fatty, 670
Archer, Jim, 346
Archipelago, 612
Architecture: Jefferson on, 170; moral standards in, 170; skyscrapers, 673
Arctic National Wildlife Refuge: oil drilling proposals for, 934
Arctic Ocean: Barents' expedition to, 18(illus.)
Argentina (ship), 752
Argonne Forest, *see* Meuse-Argonne offensive
Arias Sánchez, Oscar: Nobel Peace Prize for, 902
Aristide, Jean-Bertrand, 927
Aristocracy: of wealth, 310–311; American, 311; of planters, 337; southern values and, 348
Arizona (ship), 734
Arizona (state), 358, 699
Arizona Territory: American Indians in, 409
Arkansas, 261, 377, 377(map), 384, 421
Armada, *see* Spanish Armada
Armed forces, 742; Continental Army as, 152; African Americans in, 157, 382, 395, 399, 400, 402–403, 402(illus.), 609; quartering troops and, 195; in War of 1812, 231, 232, 233–234; after War of 1812, 236; in Mexican War, 357; desertions from Confederate, 406–407; after Civil War, 436; women in, 629; in Russian civil war, 643–644; Franklin Roosevelt and, 726; in Second World War, 751(illus.); Operation War Bride and, 752, 752(illus.). *See also* Federal troops; Military; Soldiers; specific wars
Armed neutrality, 628
"Armed Slave, The" (Sprang), 423(illus.)
Armistice: Spanish-American War and, 606, 607, 609; in First World War, 633; in Korean War, 781
Armour Foods, 684(illus.)
Arms and armaments: Constitution on, 195; Neutrality Act (1935) and, 725; Second World War and, 725, 729, 735(illus.); to Britain, 731–732; wartime production of, 745. *See also* Disarmament; Weapons
Arms control: appeals for, 647; summit meetings on, 904; INF Treaty and, 905; treaties (1991, 1993), 912
Arms inspections: in Iraq, 937
Arms race, 783, 871–872; Eisenhower and, 795; Kennedy and, 831; Cuban missile crisis and, 833; Carter and, 883; SDI and, 900
Armstrong, Louis, 673
Armstrong, Neil, 881
Army Industrial College, 647

Army-McCarthy hearing, 808
Army of Northern Virginia, 407
Army of the Potomac, 381, 389, 403
Army of the Republic of Vietnam (ARVN), 841
Arnett, Peter, 899(illus.)
Arnold, Benedict, 158
Around the World with General Grant (Young), 442
ARPANET, 948
Arrowsmith (Lewis), 672
"Arsenal of democracy": U.S. as, 744, 744(illus.)
Art(s): in New England, 54(illus.); moral standards in, 168–169; slave, 341–342; of Plains Indians, 457(illus.). *See also* specific arts
Arthur, Chester, 545, 548
Arthur, Timothy Shay, 275
Articles of Confederation, 175; government under, 175–177; taxation under, 177, 178(illus.); problems under, 177–178; deficiencies in, 182
Articles of Constitution, 195–196
Article 10: of League of Nations, 646, 647
Artisans: vs. merchants, 132–133; in South, 350; resistance of, 487–488
Arts projects: of WPA, 695–696
Asante peoples, 12(illus.), 76
Ashcan School, 569(illus.), 674(illus.)
Asia: Muslim trade with, 10; oceanic route to, 17–18; immigration from, 315, 667, 882, 890, 908; imperialism in, 597, 611(map); Second World War and, 742, 764; Cold War in, 778–780. *See also* specific countries and groups
Asian Americans: occupational mobility and, 519; in urban borderlands, 520; after Second World War, 802–803; ancestries of, 908; 2000 election and, 934; population growth of, 940. *See also* People of color
Asians: African American intermarriage with, 85; in West, 462; discrimination and isolation in cities, 520–521, 521(illus.)
Assassinations: of Lincoln, 414; of James Garfield, 483, 545, 548; of McKinley, 585, 613; of Franz Ferdinand, 623; of Huey Long, 829, 847(map); of King, 853–854; of John Kennedy, 836; of Diem, 841; of Malcolm X, 847; of Robert Kennedy, 854; Reagan attempt and, 892; of Sandino, 902; of Rabin, 927
Assemblies: House of Burgesses as, 45, 46; in Plymouth, 50; in New York colony, 63; in Jerseys, 64; parliamentary dissolution of, 82; powers of, 108
Assembly lines, 482–484, 484(illus.), 487, 533, 802
Assimilation: of ethnic groups, 93; of Indians, 264–265, 458, 460, 582; of Cherokee, 266–267; immigrants and, 518(illus.), 519; religion and, 522; public recreation, holidays, and, 538; by African Americans, 580
Associated Press (AP), 718

Associationalism: Hoover and, 684
Associations: leisure, 308; in black communities, 320
Astor, John Jacob, 310, 311
Astrolabe, 15
Astronomy, 6, 101
Aswan Dam, 792
Asylums: reform of, 276
AT&T, 897
Athletics, 578; intercollegiate, 677; for women, 865. *See also* Sports; Title IX
Atkins, Josiah, 171
Atlanta, 412, 525, 601
Atlanta Exposition (1895): Booker T. Washington at, 581
Atlanta University, 425, 552
Atlantic Charter, 732–733, 733(illus.)
Atlantic colonies, 62(map)
Atlantic creoles, 72
Atlantic region: exploration of, 16; winds and currents in, 16; French settlement in, 36; trade in, 73–78, 74(map); Civil War in, 404(map); in Second World War, 742
Atomic bomb: Manhattan project and, 745; at Hiroshima and Nagasaki, 762–764, 763(illus.); damage from, 765; after Second World War, 772; Soviet, 777–778, 778(illus.), 806
Atomic diplomacy, 772
Atomic Energy Act (1954), 805
Attorney general, 195
Auburn prison, 276
Auction in Chatham Street (Didier), 246(illus.)
Auctions, *see* Slave auctions
Audio tapes: in Kennedy White House, 833; in Nixon office, 875
Augusta, Georgia, 160
Austin, Moses and Stephen, 291
Australia: American Revolution and, 149; California gold rush and, 303; frontier of, 466; in Second World War, 762; ANZUS Treaty and, 783
Austria, 633, 644; German annexation of, 724; in Second World War, 764
Austro-Hungarian Empire (Austria-Hungary), 635; immigrants from, 515; in First World War, 623–624, 624(map), 628; after First World War, 644, 645(map)
Authoritarianism: in Germany and Japan, 735
Authority: limitations on state governments, 175
Autobiographies, 307
Autobiography (Franklin), 113
Autoimmune deficiency syndrome, *see* AIDS epidemic
Automobile and automobile industry, 482–484, 658(illus.); emissions and, 507; in 1920s, 653; effects of, 657–658; for working class, 659; suburban growth and, 662; housewives and, 663; in Great Depression, 682; NIRA and, 689; strikes in, 698–699, 698(illus.); in Second World War, 744, 745; after Second World War, 800; interstate highways and, 802; in 1950s, 816; energy crisis and, 878

Avery, William Waightstill: duel by, 348
Axis powers, 724, 734, 757–758
Aycock, Charles B., 573
Ayer, N. W., & Son (advertising agency), 501
Azores, 16
Aztecs: Cortés and, 23; smallpox and, 26–27

Ba'athist Party (Iraq), 885
Babbitt (Lewis), 672
Baby and Child Care (Spock), 817
Baby boom: Social Security and, 709; after Second World War, 801; youth culture and, 819, 848–849; uprisings by, 854–855; labor market and, 879
Backcountry, 93, 121, 145–146, 148
Back to Africa movement, 322
Bacon's Rebellion, 71
Bacteriology research: life expectancy and, 663
Baez, Joan, 862(illus.)
Baffin Island, 20
Baghdad: U.S. bombing of, 938
Bahamas: Columbus in, 19
Bailey, Thomas A., 737
Bailey v. Drexel Furniture Company, 653
Baker, Josephine, 673
Baker, Newton, 632
Bakke decision, 882–883
Balanced budget: Franklin Roosevelt and, 705
Balance of payments, 599
Balance of power, 616, 617, 623, 876
Balance of trade: favorable, 599, 599(illus.)
Balboa, Vasco Nuñez de, 23
Balch, Emily Greene, 640, 714
Baldwin, Matthew, 254
Baldwin, Roger: ACLU and, 648–649
Balfour Declaration, 644
Balkan region, 623, 624(map), 927
Ball, George W., 844
Ballinger, Richard A., 588
Ballou's Pictorial Drawing-Room Companion, 234(illus.)
Baltic region: Soviets and, 726–727, 770
Baltimore, 246, 304, 306
Baltimore, Lords, *see* Calvert family
Bangladesh: immigrants from, 908
Bank(s) and banking, 258; Jackson and, 286–287; in 1837, 288; Panic of 1857 and, 374; national, 394; investments and, 504; robberies of, 525; 1890s depression and, 558; regulation of, 590; in First World War, 625; corporate debt and, 675; in Great Depression, 682; crisis in (1932), 688; in Germany, 723
Bank holiday, 688
Bank notes, 286; in Civil War, 394
Bank of America, 918
Bank of the United States, 199; Second, 241–242, 245, 258, 286
Bankruptcy: in 1980s, 896; of city and state governments, 921; of dot-coms, 936; of Enron, 936
Banks, Nathaniel, 411
Banneker, Benjamin, 174
Bantu-speaking peoples, 12

Bao Dai (Vietnam), 780, 793
Baptists, 520; in Virginia, 11–112; African American, 211; revivalism and, 274; regional split in, 295; slavery defended by, 350
Barbados, 38, 40–41, 65, 79
Barbary Coast: piracy and, 214(illus.), 215–216
Barbed wire, 475, 475(illus.), 504
Barbie dolls, 820(illus.), 821
Barbudos (Cuba), 791
Barents, William, 18(illus.)
Barnum, P. T., 308
Barone, Michael, 699
Barren Ground (Glasgow), 673
Barrios: of Mexican Americans, 521; of Puerto Ricans, 662; in Los Angeles-Long Beach, 823
Barrow, Bennet, 335
Barry, Marion, 833
Barter: in New England, 74
Barton, Clara, 395
Bartram, John and William, 101
Baruch, Bernard, 636
Baruch Plan, 772
Baseball, 308, 534; Japanese, 535, 535(illus.); in 1920s, 670; on radio, 702; integration of, 809, 809(illus.); foreign players in, 927
Basin and Range province, 453
Basketball, 534
Bataan Death March: in Second World War, 742
Batangas, 610
Batista, Fulgencio, 722, 791
Battle, William, 348
"Battle Hymn" (Howe), 415
Battles: in Revolutionary War, 150. *See also* specific battles and wars
Baum, L. Frank, 565
Bayard, Thomas F., 600
Bay of Pigs invasion, 831
B.C.E. (Before the Common Era), 5
Beach, Moses Yale, 310–311
Beals, Jessie Tarbox, 601(illus.)
Beard, Charles A., 579, 640
Beatles, 850, 852, 852(illus.)
Beaufort, South Carolina: French and, 2(illus.)
Beauregard, P. G. T., 383
Beaver pelts, *see* Fur trade
Beaver Wars, 68
Beckham, David, 927
Bedrock Tom, 465
Beecher family: Catherine and Mary, 313
Begin, Menachem, 883, 884(illus.)
Beijing: Tiananmen Square slaughter in, 910
Beirut, Lebanon: U.S. embassy bombing in, 903(illus.)
Belgium: in First World War, 624, 624(map); Nazi invasion of, 731; Second World War Allies in, 759
Bell, John, 375
Bellamy, Edward, 505
Bellamy, Francis, 825
Belleau Wood, battle at, 633, 633(map)
Bemis, Charlie, 463(illus.)

Bemis, Edward, 505
Bemis, Polly, 463(illus.)
Benefits: for Second World War workers, 747; for veterans, 802; for workers, 813; for gay partners, 867
Benet, Stephen Vincent, 379
Benin, 76(illus.)
Bennitt, James and Nancy, 334
Berenson, Senda, 534
Bergen-Belsen, 756(illus.)
Berger, Victor, 572
Beringia, 5
Bering Strait: land bridge at, 5
Berkeley: Free Speech Movement in, 849
Berkeley, John Lord, 63, 63(illus.), 64
Berkeley, William, 71
Berlin: airlift to, 777; Soviet occupation of, 777; zones in, 777; crisis in 1956, 786; Khrushchev and, 831; Nixon and, 871
Berlin, Ira, 72, 245
Berlin Wall, 831, 899, 910
Bermuda: military base in, 732
Bernard, Francis, 131
Bernstein, Carl, 875
Bethlehem Steel, 637
Bethune, Mary McLeod, 694, 694(illus.)
Beuthien, Reinhard, 820
Beverages: exotic, 103, 104
Beveridge, Albert, 610
Biardot, Alphonse, 539
Bibb, Henry, 322
Bible: Reformation and, 41–42
Bible belt, 273, 294–295
Bicameral legislatures, 175, 185
Bickerdyke, Mary Ann, 395
Bicycle, 534
"Big Bill," *see* Emergency Relief Appropriation Act
Big business, 542, 559, 574; in Reconstruction South, 438; ranching as, 475–476; and property rights, 542; Theodore Roosevelt and, 588; First World War and, 635–636; in 1920s, 653–654
Big Four: after First World War, 644
Bight of Benin: slaves from, 89
Bight of Biafra, 76, 77; slaves from, 89
Big Three (Second World War): on Germany, 760–761
Bilingualism: education in Los Angeles and, 306; antibilingual measures, 909
"Billion-Dollar Congress," 550
Bill of Rights (U.S.), 187, 195; constitutional ratification and, 188; discrimination and, 321; Second, 803
Bills of rights: in states, 175
Billy the Kid, 466
Bin Laden, Osama, 928–929, 935, 936
Biodiversity: globalization and, 925
Biogenetics, 943
Biological and Toxin Weapons Convention (1972), 934
Bipolar world: after Second World War, 769
Birmingham, Alabama: steel industry in, 438, 438(illus.); civil rights issues and, 834–835, 836
Birney, James G., 280, 294

Board of Education of Topeka; Civil rights movement
Desertions: during Civil War, 406–407
Deserts: in Africa, 10
Détente policy, 871, 883
Detroit, 304; Fort, 123, 124, 146(illus.), 233; in War of 1812, 234; in Second World War, 749; race riot in, 750; segregation in, 810; bankruptcy of (1933), 880
Detroit Unemployment Councils, 685
Developing nations, 769; United States as, 250. *See also* Third World
Dew, Thomas R., 330–331
Dewey, Alice, 577
Dewey, George, 609
Dewey, John, 577
Dewey, Thomas E., 777, 803–804
DeWitt, John L., 754
Dia de la Raza, 31
Dialect: Gullah as, 79
Dial magazine, 302
Diamond Match Company, 504
Diaphragms (birth control device), 530
Diary of Anne Frank, The, 905
Dias, Bartholomew, 18, 21(illus.)
Díaz, Porfirio, 616
Dickens, Charles, 322
Dickinson, John, 131, 143, 167, 185, 283
Dickson, Jephta, 554
Dictatorship: in Nazi Germany, 723
Didier, E., 246(illus.)
Diem, Ngo Dinh, 793–794, 841
Dienbienphu, 792–793, 793(illus.)
Diet (food), 96; of North American Indians, 7; beef in, 475; food refrigeration and, 486; processed and preserved foods in, 498–499; reform in, 499; cultural adaptation and, 522; ethnic foods and, 539; life expectancy and, 663. *See also* Food
Digital technology, 924
Dingley Tariff, 546, 564
Dinwiddie, Robert, 118
Diplomacy: independence and, 142; after Revolution, 166; by private citizens, 193–194; John Quincy Adams and, 242; in Civil War, 409–411; *Alabama* claims and, 445, 603–604; racism and, 601; status of U.S. in, 603; before Spanish-American War, 606–607; Open Door policy, 611–613, 611(map); dollar, 617; Wilson's Fourteen Points and, 632; with Japan, 734; atomic, 772; Dulles and, 783; of Clinton, 927
Diplomatic code: Japanese, 734
Direct election: of senators, 543, 574, 588
Direct investments: American, 599
Direct primaries, 571, 572, 574
"Dirty tricks": Nixon and, 875
Disabled people: Americans with Disabilities Act and, 914, 915
Disarmament: through Rush-Bagot Treaty, 242; Washington Naval Conference and, 714–715
"Discomfort index" (1974–1989), 877(illus.)
Disco music, 882
Discount rate, 590

Discrimination: by race, 85; against African Americans, 173, 321, 403, 580, 810; in cities, 520–521; in voting, 550–551; and segregation, 551–552; against women, 578, 818; against female workers, 682–683; in New Deal, 706; during Second World War, 746; after Second World War, 803; Civil Rights Act (1964) and, 837; urban violence and, 846–847; affirmative action and, 864; racial, 864; against disabled people, 914, 915
Disease: Black Death as, 14–15; indigenous populations and, 17; in Columbian Exchange, 24–28; in Chesapeake region, 47; among slaves, 71(illus.), 339; inoculation and, 101; imported, 108; among soldiers in Revolution, 158–159, 159(illus.); Indians and, 225, 700; in Civil War, 382, 400; buffalo and, 455; among western Indians, 455; in early 20th century, 498; germ theory of, 498, 524, 525; coal smoke and, 506; in cities, 524; water pollution and, 525; in Spanish-American War, 608–609; in First World War, 633; in 1920s, 663; globalization and, 943–945; environmental disruption and, 945; international response to, 945
Disfranchisement: of blacks, 550–551, 810. *See also* Voting and voting rights
Disinformation projects: of CIA, 784
Disney, Walt, 819; company of, 897
Dissent: John Adams and, 206–208; in wartime, 213; in Civil War, 383
Dissenters, 33; move to America by, 43; Roger Williams as, 55–56; Anne Hutchinson as, 56
Distribution of goods, 257
Distribution of wealth: in North and South, 327; in Great Depression, 681; in 1980s, 898–899, 898(illus.); globalization and, 925; in 1990s, 929
District banks, 590
District courts, 195
District of Columbia: slave trade abolished in, 361. *See also* Washington, D.C.
Districts: in cities, 512
Diversification of crops, 98
Diversity: in New York colony, 61–63; in colonies, 88; religious, 93; in suburbs, 815; after Immigration Act (1965), 857; in 1970s, 882–883; in New York City, 918; in media, 923; cultural in 2000s, 941–942
Divine, Father (George Baker), 669
Divine right of kings: in England, 43
Division of labor: in Europe, 13; globalization and, 924
Divorce, 312, 532; Indian, 9, 105; in Reconstruction South, 437; in 1920s, 663; in Second World War, 750; in postwar period, 817; increase in, 882; children and, 906; in 2000s, 943
Dix, Dorothea, 270(illus.), 271–272, 395
Dixie: South as, 331
Dixiecrats (States' Rights Democratic Party): in 1948, 803
Dixon, Archibald, 365

Dobson, James, 905
Doctors, *see* Physicians
Doctrine of the covenant, 51–52
Dodd, Samuel, 503
Doeg Indians, 71
Dole, Bob, 922, 923
Dole, Sanford B., 605, 605(illus.)
Dollar (U.S.): abandonment of gold standard and, 878
Dollar-a-year executives, 635
Dollar diplomacy, 617
Dolls: Barbie as, 820, 820(illus.)
Domesticity: in postwar period, 817–818
Domestic policy, *see* specific presidents
Domestic politics: in Cold War, 803–805
Domestic service, 488–489, 550, 683
Domestic terrorism, 919, 930
Dominican missionaries, 24
Dominican Republic, 445, 602, 616; Columbus in, 23; intervention in, 625; U.S. troops in, 720; immigrants from, 909
Dominion of New England, 81–82, 82(illus.)
Donegal county (Pennsylvania), 93
Donelson, Fort, battle at, 386
Donnell, Ed, 471
Donnelly, Ignatius, 558
"Don't ask, don't tell" policy, 922
Doolittle raid, 742
Dos Passos, John, 673
Dot-coms: collapse of, 936
"Double V" campaign: in Second World War, 754
Doughboys, 630
"Doughnut Girl," 638(illus.)
Douglas, Aaron, 673
Douglas, Frederick, 279
Douglas, Stephen A., 360, 361, 365; *Dred Scott* decision and, 373; 1860 election and, 375
Douglas, William O., 705
Douglass, Frederick, 276, 278(illus.), 280, 307, 319, 320, 355, 397, 398, 446–447; women's rights movement and, 281; magic and, 342; on fugitive slave law, 363; after *Dred Scott* decision, 373; on John Brown, 379; on black soldier, 399; on assimilation, 580
Doves: in Vietnam War, 850, 870
Dow Jones Industrial Average: in 1990s, 929, 929(illus.); after September 11, 936
Down, John, 316
Dowry: in New England, 55
Dr. Strangelove (movie), 871(illus.)
Draft (military): in Confederacy, 389, 392, 405, 406; in Union, 408; in First World War, 629, 630; exemptions in First World War, 639; in Second World War, 742, 756; in Vietnam War, 867
Draft riots: in Civil War, 408, 408(illus.)
Dragging Canoe (Cherokees), 145–146
Drake, Francis, 29, 75
Drama, 536
Dred Scott v. Sanford, 371–372, 373, 445
Drexel Firestone, 897
Drinking, *see* Alcohol and alcoholism; Temperance

Ludlow, Louis, 714(illus.)
Ludlow amendment, 726
Lukens, Rebecca, 313(illus.)
Lumber industry, 460–462, 461(map), 486
Luna Park, 533(illus.)
Lusitania (ship), 621–622, 621(illus.), 626
Luther, Martin, 41–42
Lutherans, 93
Luxuries, 96
Lynch, James, 437
"Lynchburg Negro Dance" (Miller), 343(illus.)
Lynchings, 550, 551(illus.), 642, 643, 685
Lyon, Mary, 190
Lyon, Matthew, 207–208

MacArthur, Douglas: Bonus Army and, 686; in Philippines, 742, 762; in postwar Asia, 778; in Korean War, 780–781
Machine Age, *see* Industrialization; Industry
Machine guns, 597
Machinery, 254; for spinning, 256; productivity and, 480
Machines (political), *see* Political machines
Machine-tool industry, 247, 255, 484, 486
MacIntosh, Ebenezer, 128
MacKenzie, Alexander, 221
Mackinac Island, 233
Macon's Bill Number 2, 230
Macune, Charles W., 558
Macy's, 500
Madeira, 16; plantation economy in, 17
Madison, Dolley, 231, 234
Madison, James, 184(illus.), 234; as constitutional delegate, 184; *Federalist* and, 188; in First Congress, 195; on Bank of the United States, 199; state debts and, 199; as Democratic-Republican, 201; Alien and Sedition Acts and, 208; 1808 election and, 230; War of 1812 and, 230–235; 1812 election and, 236; armed forces and, 236; nationalism and, 241
Madison Square Gardens, 622
Magazines, 538; muckraking articles in, 571; social criticisms in, 821. *See also* specific publications
Magee, Christopher, 527
Maghreb, *see* Barbary Coast
MAGIC, *see* Operation MAGIC
Mahan, Alfred Thayer, 604
Mahone, William, 543
Mail, 538; Latin American air service, 660. *See also* Postal service
Mailer, Norman, 821
Mail-order companies, 472
Maine, 52; English in, 43; Indian attacks in, 70; Abenaki–Anglo-American disputes over, 83; Massachusetts witchcraft accusations and, 84; statehood for, 261; prohibition in, 276; border dispute in, 290
Maine (battleship), 606, 607
Maize, 5, 25, 25(illus.), 35
Malaria, 47, 614, 944; drugs for, 597
Malawi: HIV in, 944
Malaya, 742

Malcolm X, 847
Male suffrage, 288. *See also* Voting and voting rights
Malinche (Doña Marina), 23
Mammoth Oil Company, 654
Management: of cities, 525–529; labor and, 698
Manassas Junction, Virginia, *see* Bull Run
Manchester United (soccer team), 927
Manchuria: Japan and, 617, 727–728
Mandan, Fort, 221
Mandate system: after First World War, 644
Mandela, Nelson, 910, 911, 911(illus.)
Manhattan Island, 38, 61; battle at, 155
Manhattan Project, 745
Manifest destiny, 273, 290–294; Mexican War and, 356
Manila, 121; Dewey in, 609
Man in the Street, The (Bailey), 737
Mann, Horace, 306, 313
Mann Act (1910), 576
Mann-Elkins Act (1910), 588
Manufacturing, 228–230; mercantilism and, 77; colonial, 95; home, 132; Hamilton on, 199–200; Embargo Act and, 228; machine-tool industry and, 247; South and, 254; rise of, 254–257; American system of, 255; 255(map); employment in, 255(map); in factories, 260; in West, 263; women in, 489; depression of 1890s and, 558; production, 600, 600(illus.); First World War and, 636; in Second World War, 745; movement overseas, 878
Manumission, 112, 172. *See also* Emancipation
Manypenny, George, 458
Mao Zedong, 727, 777, 779(illus.), 872; Soviets and, 779; North Korea and, 780; Korean War and, 781
Maple Floor Association v. U.S., 653
Marbury v. Madison, 219
Marcellus, Henricus: map of, 21(illus.)
March on Washington: in 1941, 745; of 1963, 835–836, 835(illus.)
March to the sea: Sherman's, 412–413, 412(map)
Mariana Islands, 762
Marietta, Ohio, 181
Marijuana, 851
Marin, John, 673
Marines: in Tripoli, 216; in Latin America, 720; Navajo "code talkers" and, 738(illus.), 739–740; in Lebanon, 903, 903(illus.)
Market(s): economic growth and, 94–95; farmers and, 599; foreign, 599, 647
Market economy, 240–241, 299; government and, 245–249, 269; Indians in, 264; farm life and, 300; immigrant workers for, 315–316; in North, 326, 329; in South, 329; reservation policy and, 456
Marketing: in electrical industry, 482; of cigarettes, 485
Marne: Second Battle of, 633, 633(map)
Marquette, Jacques, 67
Marriage: Indian, 9; of French and Indians, 36; in Chesapeake region, 47; in New

England, 55; interracial French-Indian, 69; Abigail Adams on, 170–171; women's rights in, 312; single people and, 314; planter-class women and, 338; African American, 345; Boston marriage, 532; in 1920s, 663; in Second World War, 751; in 1950s, 816–817; age at, 882; living together and, 882; in 2000s, 942
Married-couple families, 943
Married Women's Property Act (Mississippi, 1839), 339
Marryat, Frank, 303(illus.)
Marshall, George C., 755, 775
Marshall, James, 302, 303
Marshall, John: as chief justice, 218–219, 219(illus.); Burr's treason trial and, 224; Supreme Court under, 241–242; on interstate commerce, 247; business competition and, 247–248; on Indian status, 267
Marshall, Thurgood, 448, 755, 809; *Brown* decision and, 810
Marshall Field's, 500
Marshall Plan, 775, 775(illus.), 776(map)
Martha's Vineyard: Wampanoags on, 70
Martha Washington societies, 275
Martí, José, 606
Martial law: Lincoln and, 395
Martin, John B., 219
Martin, Luther, 185
Martinique, 38, 121
Marx, Karl, 358, 560
Mary I (England), 82
Maryland, 46, 61, 384; House of Delegates in, 48; English Civil War and, 65; slavery in, 78, 172, 335; charter of, 81; Glorious Revolution and, 82; immigrants in, 93; Articles of Confederation and, 175; Civil War in, 377, 377(map), 388
Masculinity: Cold War and, 818. *See also* Men
Mashantucket Pequot Museum: Foxwoods Casino and, 57
Mashpee Indians, 57
Mason, George, 186
Mason, James, 361, 411
Masons: Antimasonry attitudes and, 273, 276–277; leisure and, 308; black, 320
Massachusett Indians, 28
Massachusetts: General Court in, 52; Indians and, 52–53; as royal colony, 81, 83; witchcraft charges in, 83; taxation in, 97; Boston State House in, 109(illus.); circular letter in, 131; Coercive Acts and, 137; provincial congress in, 152; free public elementary education, 170; abolition of slavery in, 172; constitution of, 174; textile mills in, 229; public education in, 306
Massachusetts Bay Colony, 55, 81, 82(illus.)
Massachusetts Bay Company, 51
Massachusetts Government Act (1774), 137
Massachusetts Institute of Technology (MIT), 745
Massacres: at Mystic River, 53, 57; of Conestoga Indians, 145; at Wounded Knee, 864; at Columbine High School, 930, 930(illus.). *See also* Boston Massacre

and, 893–894; judicial nominations by, 894; New Right and, 894; organized labor and, 894; 1984 election and, 897; deregulation and, 897; Soviet Union and, 900, 904–905, 904(illus.); Iran-contra scandal and, 902; Gorbachev and, 904–905, 904(illus.); religious fundamentalists and, 905; end of Cold War and, 911
"Reagan Democrats," 892, 921
Reaganomics, 894–900
Real-estate development, 512
Real Whigs, 125; newspaper essays and, 134; constitutional ratification and, 188
Reapers, 393; McCormick, 253, 254(illus.)
Reapportionment: census and, 138–139
Rebellions, see Revolts and rebellions
Rebel Without a Cause (movie), 819
Recall, 571, 574
Recessions: of 1937–1939, 705; Eisenhower and, 805; in 1981, 896; in early 1990s, 921
Reciprocal Trade Agreements Act (1934), 716(illus.), 719
Reconcentration policy: in Cuba, 606, 607; of U.S. in Philippines, 610
Reconstruction, 420–421; Lincoln's 10 percent plan, 421–422; wartime, 421–423; Wade-Davis bill and, 422; presidential, 428–429; congressional plan for, 429–436, 438; Fourteenth Amendment and, 431–432; Radical, 432(map), 433, 433(illus.), 435(illus.), 441; comparison of plans for, 433; Grant and, 436; politics in South, 436–441; myth of "Negro Rule" and, 439; failure of, 441; reversal of, 441–447; West, race, and, 444; judicial retreat from, 445; 1876 election and, 446, 446(map); Compromise of 1877 and, 446, 446(map)
Reconstruction Acts, 434, 435; First (1867), 432(map), 433, 433(illus.); Second, Third, and Fourth (1867–1868), 433
Reconstruction era amendments, see Fifteenth Amendment; Fourteenth Amendment; Thirteenth Amendment
Reconstruction Finance Corporation (RFC), 685
Reconstruction governments, 437–438, 443; taxation and, 439–440; corruption in, 440
Recovery programs: after Second World War, 775–777, 775(illus.)
Recreation, see Leisure
"Red China," see China
Redcoats (Britain), 133–134, 150, 152(illus.). See also American Revolution
Red Cross, 631, 638; plasma segregated by, 754
Redeemer Democrats, 441
Red Power movement, 861, 863; American Indian activists and, 863(illus.)
Red Record, A (Welles), 550
Red Scare: after First World War, 623, 641–643, 647, 806; labor strikes and, 653; immigrant radicalism and, 668; in 1950s, 806–808

"Red Summer" (1919), 642
Reed, John, 641
Reed, Walter, 615
Referendum, 571, 574
Reforestation, 588
Reform and reform movements, 274; in English colonies, 81–84; in banking, 258; labor, 260, 491; mental illness and, 270(illus.), 271–272; Jacksonian, 273, 284; social, 273, 529; evangelical women and, 274–275; networks in, 276; prison, 276; politics and, 282; impact on politics, 288; South and, 330; for yeoman farmers, 349; Indian policy, 457–458; dietary, 499; housing, 523, 529; civic, 528; settlement-house movement, 529; Civil Service, 545; African American female reformers, 552–553; agrarian, 555–557; foreign models of, 570; bread and butter reforms, 571; Social Gospel and, 579; in 1920s, 656; college sports and, 677; by women's movement, 865. See also Populist Party; Progressive era
Reformation: in England, 41–42
Reform Judaism: sermons in, 274
Reform Party, 934; 1992 election and, 921(illus.); 1996 election and, 923
Refrigeration, 486, 499
Refugees: from Haiti, 209; Jewish, 725, 792(illus.); in Second World War, 755–756; Indochinese, 869
Region(s): middle colonies trade and, 96(illus.); wealth and poverty in, 97; Chesapeake trade and, 97(illus.); Lower South trade and, 98(illus.); foreign dominance in international, 719–720. See also specific regions
Regionalism: partisan divisions in Congress and, 204; Democratic-Republican campaigning and, 223–224; in Civil War, 384; in Farmers' Alliance movement, 557
Regressive tax: Social Security as, 697
Regulation: of meatpacking, 586; of trusts, 586; of food and drugs, 586–587; of banking, 590; of economy, 591; Reagan and, 893–894
Regulator movement: in Carolinas, 110
Regulators, 436
Regulatory agencies, 592, 653
Rehnquist, William, 874, 894
Relief programs, 524; in Confederacy, 392; Hoover and, 684–685; in Great Depression, 689, 690–692, 708; Social Security and, 708; after Second World War, 775(illus.)
Religion: Native American, 9; women as Indian leaders, 9; in Upper Guinea, 13; in Europe, 13–14; in Anglo-American settlements, 33–34; in England, 41–43; in Chesapeake region, 49; in New England, 49–50, 55; in New York colony, 63; in Pennsylvania, 64–65; of Pueblo Indians, 69; of African Americans, 91, 107, 342–343; church attendance and, 101; revivalism and, 110–112, 273–274; freedoms of, 175; the Prophet and, 225; political party affiliation by, 288; in Bible

belt, 295; southern evangelicals and, 295; of Irish immigrants, 297; Mormons and, 301; education and, 306; clubs and, 308; ethnic riots and, 309–310; of Hispanics, 319; of yeoman farmers, 334; Union cause and, 395; Ghost Dance, 458–459; immigrants and, 519–520; influx of immigrants and diversity of, 522; in postwar period, 816; women's roles in, 865–866; in 1970s, 881; New Age movement and, 881–882; Islamic orthodoxy and, 884–885. See also Great Awakening; Religious freedom; Revivalism; specific groups and religions
Religious freedom: in Maryland, 46; in Rhode Island, 56; for non-Congregationalists, 81–82; for Quebec Catholics, 137. See also Freedom(s)
Religious fundamentalism: in 1920s, 668; Scopes trial and, 668–669; in 1980s, 905–906. See also New Right
Religious persecution: immigration and, 515
Religious right, see New Right; Religious fundamentalism
Relocation centers: for Japanese Americans, 753–754, 753(illus.)
Removal: of Indians, 263–264, 266(map), 267–268, 409; Jackson and, 283–284; expansion and, 290
Removal Act (1830), 267
Renaissance: American, 302; in Harlem, 673, 673(illus.)
Reno, Janet, 915, 922
Rensselaerswyck, 38
Reparations: for slavery, 350–351; to Indians, 351; German, 644, 648, 676, 724; moratorium on, 685
Report on Manufactures (Hamilton), 199, 200(illus.), 228–229
Report on Public Credit (Hamilton): first and second, 199
Representation: in Chesapeake region, 48; in New York colony, 63; in Jerseys, 64; by colonial assemblies, 108; taxation and, 124–125; census and, 138–139; in Congress, 185; emancipation and, 431. See also Assemblies; Legislature
Reproductive technologies, 943
Republic: creation of, 167–171; as white male society, 174
Republican governments, 174–177
Republicanism, 167–171; in France, 202; Jefferson on, 217; market economy and, 247
Republican Party, 360(illus.); first nominating convention of, 353–354; formation of, 367–368; ideology of, 368–369; 1856 election and, 371; on slavery, 373; in Civil War, 394, 395, 397; 1864 election and, 409; Reconstruction and, 421, 437–438, 439; Klan violence against, 440–441; Liberal Republican revolt and, 443; 1876 election and, 446, 446(map); factions in, 543; groups in, 543; 1896 election and, 562–564, 564(map); in Progressive era, 588; split of, 589;

U.S. Commission on Civil Rights, 810

U.S. embassy: bombing of in Lebanon, 903(illus.)

U.S. Employment Service, 637, 637(illus.)

U.S. First Division, 633

U.S. Forest Service, 587

United States Fuel Administration, 636(illus.)

U.S. Housing Corporation, 637

U.S. Information Agency (USIA), 785, 789–790

United States Magazine and Domestic Review, 290

U.S. National Intelligence Council: on infectious diseases, 944

United States Ordnance Department, 255

U.S. Rubber Company, 504

United States Sanitary Commission, 395

U.S. Steel, 504, 588, 653; in Great Depression, 682, 683

U.S. v. Cruikshank, 445

U.S. v. E. C. Knight Co., 506

U.S. v. Reese, 550–551

Universal Negro Improvement Association (UNIA), 659–661

Universities and colleges, 100; women in, 190, 578, 802, 865; Morrill Land Grant Act and, 394; for freedpeople, 425; state universities, 473, 577(illus.), 578; engineering programs in, 486; football in, 534, 670; for African Americans, 552, 552(illus.), 578; land-grant colleges, 577, 578; growth of, 577–578; curriculum expansion at, 578; scandals and reforms in college sports, 677; in Second World War, 745, 751; after Second World War, 801; HUAC investigations and, 807; Free Speech Movement in, 849; protests in, 849–850, 850(map); black studies departments in, 862; affirmative action and, 864; ARPANET at, 948

University of California (Berkeley), 892; Free Speech Movement and, 849

University of California v. Bakke, 882–883

University of Chicago: Laboratory School at, 577; Manhattan Project and, 745; GI Bill and, 801

University of Illinois: Red Grange at, 671

University of Michigan, 577(illus.)

University of Mississippi: James Meredith in, 835

University of Wisconsin, 578, 579

Unmarried people, 531–532

Unsafe at Any Speed (Nader), 839

Unskilled labor: in West, 463; African Americans and, 515; Hispanics and, 515; migration of, 519; in 1980s, 906

Unwed mothers, 751, 906

Upper Canada, *see* Ontario

Upper class: in Progressive era, 571; in suburbs, 662. *See also* Classes; Elites

Upper Guinea, 12, 13; slave trade and, 76

Upper South: recession and, 377, 377(map); in Confederacy, 384

"Uprising of the 20,000," 495

Uprisings, *see* Revolts and rebellions

Upward Bound, 839(illus.), 840

Urban areas: Mayan, 5–6; in 18th century, 88; social activities in, 299; growth of, 304–310; mass transit in, 306; leisure in, 306–307; riots in, 309–310; wealth in, 310–311; capitalists in, 311; slums in, 311; poverty in, 312(illus.); in South, 329–330; mass transportation and, 512; redevelopment in, 823–824; racial violence in, 846; violence after King assassination, 854. *See also* Cities and towns

Urban borderlands, 520

Urban engineers, 526

Urbanization, 542, 568; railroads and western, 468; industrialization, technology, and, 510; 1870–1920, 512–519, 514(map); family life and, 530–532; in 1920, 659. *See also* Suburbs

Urban League, 682, 835–836

Urban neighborhoods, *see* Neighborhoods

Urban outlaws, 525

Urban reform, 528–529

Ursuline convent (New Orleans), 100(illus.)

Uruguay Round: of the General Agreement on Tariffs and Trade, 924

USA PATRIOT Act (2001), 935

Utah, 464, 464(map), 465; Hispanic movement into, 263; Mormons in, 301; acquisition of, 358; territory of, 361; Mormon War in, 373

Utes, 457

Utilities, 524; private, 306; public ownership of, 574

Utopian communities, 299, 300–302

Utrecht, Peace of, 117

U-2: spy plane incident, 786; Cuban missile crisis and, 832

Valentino, Rudolph, 671–672, 671(illus.)

Vallandigham, Clement L., 407–408, 409, 445

Valley Forge: officers' wives at, 158

Valley of Mexico, 5, 7. *See also* Mexico

Values: of Jackson, 284; women's literature and, 307; of North and South, 327; of southern aristocracy, 348–349; family, 919, 923

Van Buren, Martin, 285; Cherokee removal and, 268; 1832 election and, 286; 1836 election and, 288; 1840 election and, 289; 1844 election and, 293–294; 1848 election and, 360

Vance, Cyrus, 883, 884

Vance, Zebulon, 391, 407

Vandenberg, Arthur, 727, 773

Van Rensselaer family, 311

Vanzetti, Bartolomeo, 668

Vaqueros, 473

Vardamann, James K., 573

Vare, "Duke," 528

Vassa, Gustavus, *see* Equiano, Olaudah

Vaudeville, 536–537

Vaughan, Victor, 634

V-E Day (1945), 758(map)

Veiller, Lawrence, 523

Venereal diseases, *see* Sexually transmitted diseases (STDs)

Venezuela, 616; boundary dispute of, 605–606; investment in, 717; U.S. economic intervention in, 720

Venona Project, 806; Rosenbergs and, 808

Veracruz, 356, 616; in Mexican War, 357; yellow fever in, 711–712

Verdun, battle at, 631

Verennes, France, battle at, 630(illus.)

Vermont: constitution of, 174

Verrazzano, Giovanni da, 22

Versailles: Treaty of, 623, 645(map), 646–647, 724. *See also* Paris Peace Conference

Vertical integration, 503

Vesey, Denmark, 347

Vespucci, Amerigo, 20, 21(illus.)

Veterans: land grants to, 263; Civil War pensions for, 545, 549–550; Bonus Army and, 685–686, 686(illus.); of Second World War, 800–801; of Vietnam War, 870

Veterans Affairs, Department of, 936

Veterans Bureau, 654

Vetoes: judicial, 186; presidential, 186; Jackson and, 287; by Arthur, 548; by Benjamin Harrison, 549; by Cleveland, 549; by Coolidge, 655

Vice-admiralty courts, 78, 125, 131, 133

Vice president: election of, 205–206; Jefferson as, 206; Senate selection of, 288; Ferraro as candidate for, 897; Gore as, 933

"Vices of the Political System of the United States" (Madison), 184

Vicksburg: siege and fall of, 403, 404(map), 406

Victory gardens, 636; in Second World War, 748

"Victory Plan" (Second World War), 742

Victrola Talking Machine Company, 659(illus.)

Vieques island, 617

Vietcong, 795, 841, 842, 843(map)

Vietminh, 767, 768, 780, 793

Vietnam, 793(illus.); Ho Chi Minh and independence of, 766(illus.), 767–769; independence of, 779; revolution in, 789; Eisenhower and, 792–793; division of, 793; Geneva Accords (1954) and, 793; Kennedy and, 841–842; reunification of, 869; immigrants from, 908; diplomatic recognition of, 925. *See also* Vietnam War

Vietnam War, 628(illus.), 829, 843(map), 911; dissent during, 213; Johnson and, 841–846, 853–854; U.S. troops in, 842, 844–845, 844(illus.), 845(illus.), 851(illus.), 867; Americanization of, 842–844, 846; youth protests against, 849–850; in 1968, 853; Pentagon Papers and, 859–860; Vietnamization policy in, 867–868; end of, 867–869; cease-fire agreement in, 868–869; costs and casualties of, 869; veterans of, 870

Vietnam Women's Memorial, 870(illus.)

Vigilantism: in First World War, 639–640; after First World War, 642; of Klan, 667; in Great Depression, 685

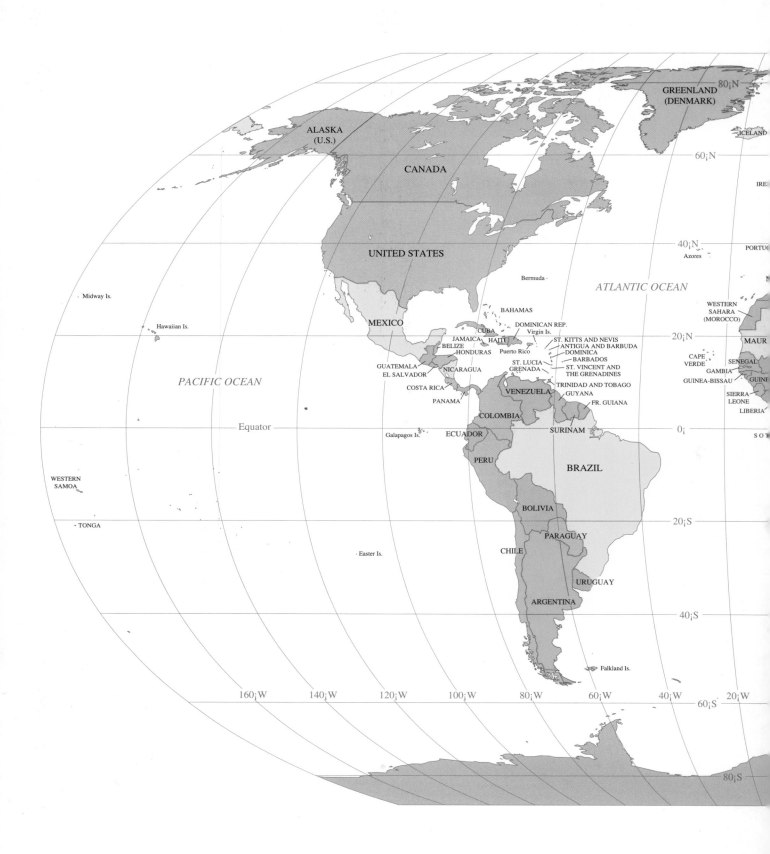